Everyman's

DICTIONARY OF DATES

A volume in

EVERYMAN'S REFERENCE LIBRARY

Everyman's Reference Library

Everyman's

DICTIONARY
OF DATES

Seventh edition revised by
A U D R E Y B U T L E R

J. M. DENT & SONS LTD
LONDON AND MELBOURNE

This book is set in 9½/10½ Linotron Trump Medieval
by The Word Factory, Rossendale

Printed in Great Britain for
J. M. Dent & Sons Ltd
Aldine House, 33 Welbeck Street, London W1M 8LX

FIRST PUBLISHED 1911
Reprinted 1912, 1918, 1924, 1928, 1931
SECOND EDITION 1940
Reprinted 1941, 1942
THIRD EDITION 1954
FOURTH EDITION 1964
FIFTH EDITION 1967
SIXTH EDITION 1971
Reprinted 1972, 1974
Reprinted with revisions 1980
SEVENTH EDITION 1986

British Library Cataloguing in Publication Data

Everyman's dictionary of dates.——7th ed.——
   (Everyman's reference library)
   1. World history——Dictionaries
   I. Butler, Audrey
   903'.21   D20

ISBN 0–460–03033–7

PREFACE

The basic purpose of this work is to make useful dates accessible to the general reader, but even this seemingly simple objective involves a number of problems. It was necessary to include most of the 'obvious' events lest the compiler be accused of 'not even putting in the *Battle of Hastings*,' and yet it was clearly desirable to add many matters—such as the *Shoguns*—which are hard to find quickly elsewhere.

To solve the resulting difficulties of selection, the compiler was guided by a number of principles. Considerable prominence was given to countries, institutions and dynasties of universal influence. Then room was found for notices (however short) on other countries, cities, provinces, institutions, and families of independent status or historical repute. Thirdly, considerable space was devoted to arts, sciences, philosophy, religion, and invention. And, lastly, a large number of miscellaneous facts have been included on grounds of interest or notoriety.

Broadly speaking there are three types of headings: short entries relating to particular matters, e.g. *coach*; narratives, e.g. *United States of America*; and classified entries, e.g. *Sieges*. Logic and exclusiveness have been sacrificed to convenience wherever it was thought desirable, and I have not hesitated to repeat myself if necessary.

Generally the classified entries are the longest, then the narratives, so that if the subject sought by the user is not to be found under its own name he should scan likely general headings in that order. The List of Longer Entries (of all types) given overleaf may be helpful in this respect. It should be borne in mind that this is *not* a biographical dictionary, so that in order to look up 'the dates of George V' one must first know whether the individual in question was the King of England or the last ruler of Hanover of that name, and so on.

Everyman's Dictionary of Dates was first planned over seventy years ago, and has since been extensively revised several times. This seventh edition, while retaining, in its main section, the basic character of its predecessors, is considerably more comprehensive, and there have been extensive changes in content to meet the demands of the fast-changing world of today. The lists of classical emperors, etc., remain; in addition, there are now many newer entries such as *European Economic Community*; *Rockets* and *Space Flights*; *Drug Addiction*; *Social Democratic Party* and *Press Council*. There is also a completely new Chronological section of 'timebanding', from c. 30,000 B.C. to the present day, which is intended to complement the dictionary section, as well as to be used as a 'ready reckoner' of dating in its own right. It is the publishers' belief that this completely revised and enlarged edition of a well-tried, favourite reference book will prove a worthy successor to those of the past half-century.

AUDREY BUTLER

1985

Blank pages have been included so that readers may
make their own notes and additions as required.

LONGER ENTRIES

Calendars.

Abdications; Academies; Admiralty; Algeria; American Literature in English; Arctic and Antarctic Regions; Argentina; Arts, Plastic; Assassinations; Assyrians; Australia; Austria.

Ballet; Battles; Bavaria; Belgium; Bessarabia; Bohemia; Bolivia; Brazil; Bulgaria; Burma; Byzantine Authors.

Caliphs; Cambridge University; Canada; Canterbury, Archbishops of; Castile and Leon; Cathedrals; Chancellor, Lord High; Chile; China; Chinese Literature; Cinematography; Colonies (British); Crusades; Cuba; Czechoslovakia, Czechoslovak Language and Literature.

Danish Literature; Denmark; Dublin; Dutch and Flemish Literature.

Earthquakes; European Economic Community; Egypt; England, Church of; English History; English Literature; English Sovereigns; Essex; Estonia; Ethiopia; Exchequer.

Falkland Islands; Fathers of the Church; Finland; Finnish Literature; Foreign Legions; France; French Literature.

Gauls; Genoa; German Literature; Germany; Germany, Democratic Republic of; Germany, Federal Republic of; Ghana; Graeco-Turkish Wars; Great Britain; Greece, Ancient; Greece, Modern; Greek Authors.

Haiti; Hall Marks; Heretics; Holy Roman Emperors; Holy Roman Empire; Home Office; Hungary.

Icelandic Language and Literature; India; Indonesia; Iraq; Iran; Ireland; Ireland, Northern; Israel; Italy, Italian Literature.

Jacobites; Japan; Jordan.

Kashmir; Kent, Kingdom of; Kenya; Knighthood, Orders of; Korea.

Latin Literature, post-classical; Latvia; Lebanon; Libraries; Libya; Lithuania; Livery Companies; London Diocese; London University.

Macedonia; Malaya; Malta; Mercia; Mexico; Morocco; Mountains, First Ascents of; Musical Composers.

N.A.T.O.; Nepal; Newspapers; New Zealand; Netherlands; Northumbria; Norway; Norwegian Literature.

Ottoman Empire; Oxford University.

Pakistan; Palestine; Papacy; Paraguay; Peruvian Republic; Poland; Portugal; Prime Ministers (British); Provençal and Catalan Writers; Prussia.

Reformation; Regency Acts; Regiments (British); Roman Emperors; Roman Empire, Eastern; Romantic Movement; Rumania; Russia; Russian Literature.

Saudi Arabia; Scotland; Serbia; Serbo-Croatian Language; Seven Years War; Sieges; Singapore; Soldiers and Sailors; Soldiers, Sailors, and Airmen of this Century; Somalia; South Africa; Space Flights; Spain; Spanish Literature; Statesmen and Politicians; Sudan; Suez Canal; Sweden; Swedish Literature; Syria.

Thailand; Tibet; Treaties; Trials; Trieste; Tunisia; Turkish Republic.

United States of America; United States of America, Presidents of; Universities; Uruguay; U.S.S.R.

Venice; Vietnam; Viking Age; Visigoths.
Waldenses; Wales; Wales, Princes of; Welsh Literature; Wessex; World Wars I and II.
York, Archbishopric of; Yugoslavia.
Zimbabwe.

CALENDARS

1 The Old Style and New Style Calendars

The present system of Christian dating originated as follows:

(a) The Roman Era began with the foundation of Rome in 753 B.C. By 46 B.C., owing to various imperfections the Roman Calendar had fallen into confusion and Julius Caesar then reformed it.

(b) The year 46 B.C. was therefore made to consist of 445 days, and is called the 'Year of Confusion'. Thereafter each year consisted of 365 days except that *every* fourth year was a leap year. This Julian or Old Style Calendar remained in general use in Europe until 1582.

(c) By 1582 there was a difference of ten days between the Julian and the tropical year. In that year Pope Gregory XIII ordered that 5 Oct. should be called 15 Oct., and that of the end-century (00) years only the fourth should be a leap year. This Gregorian or New Style Calendar is still in use. It was adopted in:

1582 *Italy, France, Spain, Portugal*

1583 *Prussia, Switzerland, Holland, Flanders,*
     German Catholic States

1586 *Poland*

1587 *Hungary*

1700 *German Protestant States, Denmark*

1872 *Japan*

1912 *China*

1915 *Bulgaria*

1917 *Turkey, USSR*

1919 *Yugoslavia, Rumania*

1923 *Greece*

In Sweden the change was made between 1700 and 1740 by the omission of 11 leap-year days.

In Britain (including N. America and the Colonies) the change was made in 1752 (3 Sept. being called 14), and the beginning of the official year was altered from 25 Mar. (which was the date of the vernal equinox when the Julian Calendar was introduced) to 1 Jan. at the same time.

Calendars

2 Jewish Calendar

A system by which the beginning, length, and sub-division of the year is fixed. Nothing is certain concerning the calendar in use during biblical times. Later the beginning of a month was ascertained by observation of the new moon, but about the middle of the fourth century a constant calendar was introduced, based on earlier practice.

The day is the period between two successive sunsets although, for calendar purposes, it is computed to commence at the beginning of the seventh hour after noon, i.e. at 6 p.m. The week consists of seven days, ending with the Sabbath, the other days having no special name, but being designated as the first day, the second day of the week, etc. A month is the period between two revolutions of the moon. Ordinarily, twelve months containing alternately 30 and 29 days, make a year, which should therefore contain 354 days. But since the Bible ordains that Passover must be celebrated in the month of *Abib* (the fresh ears of grain) and since vegetable growth is dependent on the sun, it is necessary to adjust this lunar year to the solar one of 365¼ days. This is done by intercalating a month of 30 days before the last month of the religious year seven times during every nineteen years (the Metonic cycle), viz. in the third, sixth, eighth, eleventh, fourteenth, seventeenth, and nineteenth years of each cycle. These intercalary or leap years therefore ordinarily contain 384 days. But there are certain factors which make it necessary to lengthen or shorten the regular year of 354 days and the leap year of 384 days by one day.

The Day of Atonement must not fall on the first or sixth day of the week, nor the seventh day of Tabernacles on Sabbath. Consequently the New Year festival must not fall on the first, fourth, or sixth day. Again, the New Year festival must be celebrated on the day on which the new moon becomes visible; consequently if the lunar conjunction occurs at noon or later the festival is postponed to the next day, since the new moon will be seen only at 6 p.m. or later, which period belongs to the following day. For these and other reasons, the eighth month, *Cheshvan*, sometimes has 30 instead of 29 days (when the year is described as 'redundant') and the ninth month, *Kislev*, 29 instead of 30 days (a 'defective' year). Thus the ordinary year may contain 353, 354, or 355 days and the leap year 383, 384, or 385.

The character of a Jewish year is therefore definitely known by the determination of its first day, that which is to be celebrated as its New Year Festival, and by its length, dependent on whether it is an ordinary or leap year and regular, redundant, or defective (i.e. whether any variation is required in the lengths of *Cheshvan* and *Kislev*). Each of the possible fourteen types of year, seven for ordinary and seven for leap years, is described by a 'characteristic' consisting of three Hebrew letters, the first of which intimates the day of the week on which the New Year festival falls, the second whether the year is regular, redundant, or defective, and the third the day of the week on which the first day of Passover falls. The last is not really necessary and is included in the 'characteristic' only because when the incidence of Passover is known the days of the week on which the principal festivals of the following year fall may easily be ascertained. To these three letters is, of course, added the Hebrew word for 'ordinary' or 'leap' as may be required.

The times when the solstices and equinoxes (*Tekufah*) fall must also be computed, since the petition for rain has to be interpolated in the *Amidah* prayer on and after the sixtieth day from the autumnal equinox. Each *Tekufah* is 91 days 7½ hours distant from another, being a quarter of the 365¼ days which, according to Samuel Yarchinai, make up the solar year. Each *Tekufah* returns to the same day of the week and to the same hour every 28 years, which period is termed a 'greater cycle' or a 'solar cycle'. The calculation of the civil date with which any particular Jewish date corresponds and vice versa, is of a complicated character. There is, however, a mathematical formula (that of Gauss), which gives the date of the Passover in any year; from this that of the next New Year festival may easily be calculated, since the number of days between these two festivals is constant. If the characteristic of the year is ascertained any particular date may then be calculated, as in the following table.

TABLE TO RECONCILE JEWISH AND GREGORIAN CALENDARS
Civil date on which the 1st day of each month falls

Jew. Year		Tishri		Cheshvan		Kislev			Tebet
	Civil Year							*Civil Year*	
5681	1920	M. 13 Sept.	W.	13 Oct.	F.	12 Nov.			Sn. 12 Dec.
5682	1921	M. 3 Oct.	W.	2 Nov.	F.	2 Dec.		1922	Sn. 1 Jan.
5683	1922	St. 23 Sept.	M.	23 Oct.	Tu.	21 Nov.			W. 20 Dec.
5684	1923	Tu. 11 Sept.	Th.	11 Oct.	F.	9 Nov.			Sn. 9 Dec.
5685	1924	M. 29 Sept	W.	29 Oct.	F.	28 Nov.			Sn. 28 Dec.
5686	1925	St. 19 Sept.	M.	19 Oct.	W.	18 Nov.			F. 18 Dec.
5687	1926	Th. 9 Sept.	St.	9 Oct.	Sn.	7 Nov.			M. 6 Dec.
5688	1927	Tu. 27 Sept.	Th.	27 Oct.	F.	25 Nov.			Sn. 25 Dec.
5689	1928	St. 15 Sept.	M.	15 Oct.	W.	14 Nov.			F. 14 Dec.
5690	1929	St. 5 Oct.	M.	4 Nov.	Tu.	3 Dec.		1930	W. 1 Jan.
5691	1930	Tu. 23 Sept.	Th.	23 Oct.	F.	21 Nov.			Sn. 21 Dec.
5692	1931	St. 12 Sept.	M.	12 Oct.	W.	11 Nov.			F. 11 Dec.
5693	1932	St. 1 Oct.	M.	31 Oct.	W.	30 Nov.			F. 30 Dec.
5694	1933	Th. 21 Sept.	St.	21 Oct.	Sn.	19 Nov.			Tu. 19 Dec.
5695	1934	M. 10 Sept.	W.	10 Oct.	Th.	8 Nov.			F. 7 Dec.
5696	1935	St. 28 Sept.	M.	28 Oct.	W.	27 Nov.			F. 27 Dec.
5697	1936	Th. 17 Sept.	St.	17 Oct.	Sn.	15 Nov.			Tu. 15 Dec.
5698	1937	M. 6 Sept.	W.	6 Oct.	F.	5 Nov.			Sn. 5 Dec.
5699	1938	M. 26 Sept.	W.	26 Oct.	Th.	24 Nov.			F. 23 Dec.
5700	1939	Th. 14 Sept.	St.	14 Oct.	M.	13 Nov.			W. 13 Dec.
5701	1940	Th. 3 Oct.	St.	2 Nov.	Sn.	1 Dec.			Tu. 31 Dec.
5702	1941	M. 22 Sept.	W.	22 Oct.	F.	21 Nov.			Sn. 21 Dec.
5703	1942	St. 12 Sept.	M.	12 Oct.	Tu.	10 Nov.			W. 9 Dec.
5704	1943	Th. 30 Sept.	St.	30 Oct.	Sn.	28 Nov.			Tu. 28 Dec.
5705	1944	M. 18 Sept.	W.	18 Oct.	F.	17 Nov.			Sn. 17 Dec.
5706	1945	St. 8 Sept.	M.	8 Oct.	Tu.	6 Nov.			W. 5 Dec.
5707	1946	Th. 26 Sept.	St.	26 Oct.	Sn.	24 Nov.			Tu. 24 Dec.
5708	1947	M. 15 Sept.	W.	15 Oct.	F.	14 Nov.			Sn. 14 Dec.
5709	1948	M. 4 Oct.	W.	3 Nov.	F.	3 Dec.		1949	Sn. 2 Jan.
5710	1949	St. 24 Sept.	M.	24 Oct.	Tu.	22 Nov.			W. 21 Dec.
5711	1950	Tu. 12 Sept.	Th.	12 Oct.	F.	10 Nov.			Sn. 10 Dec.
5712	1951	M. 1 Oct.	W.	31 Oct.	F.	30 Nov.			Sn. 30 Dec.
5713	1952	St. 20 Sept.	M.	20 Oct.	W.	19 Nov.			F. 19 Dec.
5714	1953	Th. 10 Sept.	St.	10 Oct.	Sn.	8 Nov.			M. 7 Dec.
5715	1954	Tu. 28 Sept.	Th.	28 Oct.	F.	26 Nov.			Sn. 26 Dec.
5716	1955	St. 17 Sept.	M.	17 Oct.	W.	16 Nov.			F. 16 Dec.
5717	1956	Th. 6 Sept.	St.	6 Oct.	M.	5 Nov.			W. 5 Dec.
5718	1957	Th. 26 Sept.	St.	26 Oct.	Sn.	24 Nov.			Tu. 24 Dec.
5719	1958	M. 15 Sept.	W.	15 Oct.	Th.	13 Nov.			F. 12 Dec.
5720	1959	St. 3 Oct.	M.	2 Nov.	W.	2 Dec.		1960	F. 1 Jan.
5721	1960	Th. 22 Sept.	St.	22 Oct.	Sn.	20 Nov.			Tu. 20 Dec.
5722	1961	M. 11 Sept.	W.	11 Oct.	Th.	9 Nov.			F. 8 Dec.
5723	1962	St. 29 Sept.	M.	29 Oct.	W.	28 Nov.			F. 28 Dec.
5724	1963	Th. 19 Sept.	St.	19 Oct.	Sn.	17 Nov.			Tu. 17 Dec.
5725	1964	M. 7 Sept.	W.	7 Oct.	F.	6 Nov.			Sn. 6 Dec.
5726	1965	M. 27 Sept.	W.	27 Oct.	Th.	25 Nov.			F. 24 Dec.
5727	1966	Th. 15 Sept.	St.	15 Oct.	M.	14 Nov.			W. 14 Dec.
5728	1967	Th. 5 Oct.	St.	4 Nov.	Sn.	3 Dec.		1968	Tu. 2 Jan.
5729	1968	M. 23 Sept.	W.	23 Oct.	F.	22 Nov.			Sn. 22 Dec.
5730	1969	St. 13 Sept.	M.	13 Oct.	Tu.	11 Nov.			W. 10 Dec.

TABLE TO RECONCILE JEWISH AND GREGORIAN CALENDARS
Civil date on which the 1st day of each month falls

Jew. Year	Civil Year	Shebat		Adar		Ve-Adar		Nisan
5681	1921	M. 10 Jan.	W.	9 Feb.	F.	11 Mar.	St.	9 Apr.
5682		M. 30 Jan.	W.	1 Mar.		—	Th.	30 Mar.
5683	1923	Th. 18 Jan.	St.	17 Feb.		—	Sn.	18 Mar.
5684	1924	M. 7 Jan.	W.	6 Feb.	F.	7 Mar.	St.	5 Apr.
5685	1925	M. 26 Jan.	W.	25 Feb.		—	Th.	26 Mar.
5686	1926	St. 16 Jan.	M.	15 Feb.		—	Tu.	16 Mar.
5687	1927	Tu. 4 Jan.	Th.	3 Feb.	St.	5 Mar.	Sn.	3 Apr.
5688	1928	M. 23 Jan.	W.	22 Feb.		—	Th.	22 Mar.
5689	1929	St. 12 Jan.	M.	11 Feb.	W.	13 Mar.	Th.	11 Apr.
5690		Th. 30 Jan.	St.	1 Mar.		—	Sn.	30 Mar.
5691	1931	M. 19 Jan.	W.	18 Feb.		—	Th.	19 Mar.
5692	1932	St. 9 Jan.	M.	8 Feb.	W.	9 Mar.	Th.	7 Apr.
5693	1933	St. 28 Jan.	M.	27 Feb.		—	Tu.	28 Mar.
5694	1934	W. 17 Jan.	F.	16 Feb.		—	St.	17 Mar.
5695	1935	St. 5 Jan.	M.	4 Feb.	W.	6 Mar.	Th.	4 Apr.
5696	1936	St. 25 Jan.	M.	24 Feb.		—	Tu.	24 Mar.
5697	1937	W. 13 Jan.	F.	12 Feb.		—	St.	13 Mar.
5698	1938	M. 3 Jan.	W.	2 Feb.	F.	4 Mar.	St.	2 Apr.
5699	1939	St. 21 Jan.	M.	20 Feb.		—	Tu.	21 Mar.
5700	1940	Th. 11 Jan.	St.	10 Feb.	M.	11 Mar.	Tu.	9 Apr.
5701	1941	W. 29 Jan.	F.	28 Feb.		—	St.	29 Mar.
5702	1942	M. 19 Jan.	W.	18 Feb.		—	Th.	19 Mar.
5703	1943	Th. 7 Jan.	St.	6 Feb.	M.	8 Mar.	Tu.	6 Apr.
5704	1944	W. 26 Jan.	F.	25 Feb.		—	St.	25 Mar.
5705	1945	M. 15 Jan.	W.	14 Feb.		—	Th.	15 Mar.
5706	1946	Th. 3 Jan.	St.	2 Feb.	M.	4 Mar.	Tu.	2 Apr.
5707	1947	W. 22 Jan.	F.	21 Feb.		—	St.	22 Mar.
5708	1948	M. 12 Jan.	W.	11 Feb.	F.	12 Mar.	St.	10 Apr.
5709		M. 31 Jan.	W.	2 Mar.		—	Th.	31 Mar.
5710	1950	Th. 19 Jan.	St.	18 Feb.		—	Sn.	19 Mar.
5711	1951	M. 8 Jan.	W.	7 Feb.	F.	9 Mar.	St.	7 Apr.
5712	1952	M. 28 Jan.	W.	27 Feb.		—	Th.	27 Mar.
5713	1953	St. 17 Jan.	M.	16 Feb.		—	Tu.	17 Mar.
5714	1954	Tu. 5 Jan.	Th.	4 Feb.	St.	6 Mar.	Sn.	4 Apr.
5715	1955	M. 24 Jan.	W.	23 Feb.		—	Th.	24 Mar.
5716	1956	St. 14 Jan.	M.	13 Feb.		—	Tu.	13 Mar.
5717	1957	Th. 3 Jan.	St.	2 Feb.	M.	4 Mar.	Tu.	2 Apr.
5718	1958	W. 22 Jan.	F.	21 Feb.		—	St.	22 Mar.
5719	1959	St. 10 Jan.	M.	9 Feb.	W.	11 Mar.	Th.	9 Apr.
5720		St. 30 Jan.	M.	29 Feb.		—	Tu.	29 Mar.
5721	1961	W. 18 Jan.	F.	17 Feb.		—	St.	18 Mar.
5722	1962	St. 6 Jan.	M.	5 Feb.	W.	7 Mar.	Th.	5 Apr.
5723	1963	St. 26 Jan.	M.	25 Feb.		—	Tu.	26 Mar.
5724	1964	W. 15 Jan.	F.	14 Feb.		—	St.	14 Mar.
5725	1965	M. 4 Jan.	W.	3 Feb.	F.	5 Mar.	St.	3 Apr.
5726	1966	St. 22 Jan.	M.	21 Feb.		—	Tu.	22 Mar.
5727	1967	Th. 12 Jan.	St.	11 Feb.	M.	13 Mar.	Tu.	11 Apr.
5728		W. 31 Jan.	F.	1 Mar.		—	St.	30 Mar.
5729	1969	M. 20 Jan.	W.	19 Feb.		—	Th.	20 Mar.
5730	1970	Th. 8 Jan.	St.	7 Feb.	M.	9 Mar.	Tu.	7 Apr.

TABLE TO RECONCILE JEWISH AND GREGORIAN CALENDARS
Civil date on which the 1st day of each month falls

Jew. Year		Iyar		Sivan		Tammuz		Ab		Elul
5681	M.	9 May	Tu.	7 June	Th.	7 July	F.	5 Aug.	Sn.	4 Sept.
5682	St.	29 Apr.	Sn.	28 May.	Tu.	27 June	W.	26 July	F.	25 Aug.
5683	Tu.	17 Apr.	W.	16 May	F.	15 June	St.	14 July	M.	13 Aug.
5684	M.	5 May	Tu.	3 June	Th.	3 July	F.	1 Aug.	Sn.	31 Aug.
5685	St.	25 Apr.	Sn.	24 May	Tu.	23 June	W.	22 July	F.	21 Aug.
5686	Th.	15 Apr.	F.	14 May	Sn.	13 June	M.	12 July	W.	11 Aug.
5687	Tu.	3 May	W.	1 June	F.	1 July	St.	30 July	M.	29 Aug.
5688	St.	21 Apr.	Sn.	20 May	Tu.	19 June	W.	18 July	F.	17 Aug.
5689	St.	11 May	Sn.	9 June	Tu.	9 July	W.	7 Aug.	F.	6 Sept.
5690	Tu.	29 Apr.	W.	28 May	F.	27 June	St.	26 July	M.	25 Aug.
5691	St.	18 Apr.	Sn.	17 May	Tu.	16 June	W.	15 July	F.	14 Aug.
5692	St.	7 May	Sn.	5 June	Tu.	5 July	W.	3 Aug.	F.	2 Sept.
5693	Th.	27 Apr.	F.	26 May	Sn.	25 June	M.	24 July	W.	23 Aug.
5694	M.	16 Apr.	Tu.	15 May	Th.	14 June	F.	13 July	Sn.	12 Aug.
5695	St.	4 May	Sn.	2 June	Tu.	2 July	W.	31 July	F.	30 Aug.
5696	Th.	23 Apr.	F.	22 May	Sn.	21 June	M.	20 July	W.	19 Aug.
5697	M.	12 Apr.	Tu.	11 May	Th.	10 June	F.	9 July	Sn.	8 Aug.
5698	M.	2 May	Tu.	31 May	Th.	30 June	F.	29 July	Sn.	28 Aug.
5699	Th.	20 Apr.	F.	19 May	Sn.	18 June	M.	17 July	W.	16 Aug.
5700	Th.	9 May	F.	7 June	Sn.	7 July	M.	5 Aug.	W.	4 Sept.
5701	M.	28 Apr.	Tu.	27 May	Th.	26 June	F.	25 July	Sn.	24 Aug.
5702	St.	18 Apr.	Sn.	17 May	Tu.	16 June	W.	15 July	F.	14 Aug.
5703	Th.	6 May	F.	4 June	Sn.	4 July	M.	2 Aug.	W.	1 Sept.
5704	M.	24 Apr.	Tu.	23 May	Th.	22 June	F.	21 July	Sn.	20 Aug.
5705	St.	14 Apr.	Sn.	13 May	Tu.	12 June	W.	11 July	F.	10 Aug.
5706	Th.	2 May	F.	31 May	Sn.	30 June	M.	29 July	W.	28 Aug.
5707	M.	21 Apr.	Tu.	20 May	Th.	19 June	F.	18 July	S.	17 Aug.
5708	M.	10 May	Tu.	8 June	Th.	8 July	F.	6 Aug.	S.	5 Sept.
5709	St.	30 Apr.	Sn.	29 May	Tu.	28 June	W.	27 July	F.	26 Aug.
5710	Tu.	18 Apr.	W.	17 May	F.	16 June	St.	15 July	M.	14 Aug.
5711	M.	7 May	Tu.	5 June	Th.	5 July	F.	3 Aug.	Sn.	2 Sept.
5712	St.	26 Apr.	Sn.	25 May	Tu.	24 June	W.	23 July	F.	22 Aug.
5713	Th.	16 Apr.	F.	15 May	Sn.	14 June	M.	13 July	W.	12 Aug.
5714	Tu.	4 May	W.	2 June	F.	2 July	St.	31 July	M.	30 Aug.
5715	St.	23 Apr.	Sn.	22 May	Tu.	21 June	W.	20 July	F.	19 Aug.
5716	Th.	12 Apr.	F.	11 May	Sn.	10 June	M.	9 July	W.	8 Aug.
5717	Th.	2 May	F.	31 May	Sn.	30 June	M.	29 July	W.	28 Aug.
5718	M.	21 Apr.	Tu.	20 May	Th.	19 June	F.	18 July	Sn.	17 Aug.
5719	St.	9 May	Sn.	7 June	Tu.	7 July	W.	5 Aug.	F.	4 Sept.
5720	Th.	28 Apr.	F.	27 May	Sn.	26 June	M.	25 July	W.	24 Aug.
5721	M.	17 Apr.	Tu.	16 May	Th.	15 June	F.	14 July	Sn.	13 Aug.
5722	St.	5 May	Sn.	3 June	Tu.	3 July	W.	1 Aug.	F.	31 Aug.
5723	Th.	25 Apr.	F.	24 May	Sn.	23 June	M.	22 July	W.	21 Aug.
5724	M.	13 Apr.	Tu.	12 May	Th.	11 June	F.	10 July	Sn.	9 Aug.
5725	M.	3 May	Tu.	1 June	Th.	1 July	F.	30 July	Sn.	29 Aug.
5726	Th.	21 Apr.	F.	20 May	Sn.	19 June	M.	18 July	W.	17 Aug.
5727	Th.	11 May	F.	9 June	Sn.	9 July	M.	7 Aug.	W.	17 Sept.
5728	M.	29 Apr.	Tu.	28 May	Th.	27 June	F.	26 July	Sn.	25 Aug.
5729	St.	19 Apr.	Sn.	18 May	Tu.	17 June	W.	16 July	F.	15 Aug.
5730	Th.	7 May	F.	5 June	Sn.	5 July	M.	3 Aug.	W.	2 Sept.

Calendars

3 Roman Calendar

The ecclesiastical or liturgical year begins on the first Sunday of Advent, which is the first Sunday next, whether before or after the feast of St. Andrew the Apostle (30 Nov.). There follow the four weeks of Advent and the Christmas festivals ending with the Epiphany. The ensuing Sundays are the First, Second, etc. 'of the year'. They can never be more than six, and the series is generally interrupted by Septuagesima, the ninth Sunday before Easter, which is followed by Sexagesima and Quinquagesima, which is the next before Ash Wednesday, on which latter day Lent begins. Lent has six Sundays, the last of which are known as Passion and Palm Sunday. The week beginning with Palm Sunday is called the Great or Holy Week. Easter Sunday, the feast of the Resurrection, upon the date of which the foregoing festivals depend, falls on the Sunday next following the full moon first occurring after 20 Mar.

The weeks between Easter and Pentecost (7th Sunday or 50th day after Easter) are Paschal time, and the Sundays are 'Second, Third etc. 'of Eastertide.' Forty days after Easter (always on a Thursday) is the feast of our Lord's Ascension. Trinity Sunday follows, on the Thursday after which the Church celebrates the feast of Corpus Christi, and after its Octave day the feast of the Sacred Heart of Jesus. Other moveable feasts are those of the Holy Name (Sunday between 1 and 6 Jan., otherwise 2 Jan.); Holy Family (Sunday within the Octave of the Epiphany); Seven Dolours of our Lady (Friday after Passion Sunday); Patronage of St. Joseph (Wednesday after the Second Sunday after Easter).

The remaining Sundays of the year, which cannot number more than twenty-eight nor less than twenty-three, are now known as Tenth, Eleventh etc. 'of the year.'

Concurrently with the above series of celebrations there runs the calendar of festivals fixed to particular days of the month. This varies considerably from country to country, from diocese to diocese, and even between the calendars of certain religious orders. The calendar printed in this volume shows major festivals of universal (excepting certain religious orders) observance. There are rules governing the order of celebration when two feasts of different rank coincide.

Saints and festivals marked with an asterisk occur in the Calendar prefixed to the Anglican *Book of Common Prayer*. Those in square brackets were officially removed from the list of saints by *motu proprio* of Paul VI on 1st January 1970.

Abbreviations

Ab.	Abbot.	K.	King.
Ap.	Apostle.	M.	Martyr.
B.	Bishop.	P.	Pope.
C.	Confessor.	V.	Virgin.
D.	Doctor of the Church.	W.	Widow.

JANUARY

1 Octave of Christmas.—Solemnity of Mary, the Mother of God.—*The Circumcision.

2

3

4

5 St. Telesphorus, P.M.

6 *The Epiphany.

7

8

9 *St. Lucian.

10

11 St. Hyginus, P.M.

12

13 *St. Hilary.

14 St. Hilary, B.C.D.—St. Felix, M.

15 St, Paul, 1st hermit—St. Maurus, Ab.

16 St. Marcellus, P.M.

17 St. Anthony, Ab.

18 St. Peter's Chair at Rome—*St. Prisca, V.M.

19 St. Marius and Companions, MM.—St. Canute, K.M.

20 SS. Fabian* and Sebastian, MM.

21 *St. Agnes, V.M.

22 SS. Vincent* and Anastasius, MM.

23 S. Raymund of Peñfort, C. [St. Emerentiana, V.M.]

24 St. Timothy, B.M.

25 Conversion of St. Paul.

26 St. Polycarp, B.M.

27 St. John Chrysostom, B.C.D.

28 St. Thomas Aquinas, D.

29 St. Francis de Sales, B.C.D.

30 [St. Martina, V.M.]

31 St. John Bosco, C.—St. Peter Nolasco, C.

FEBRUARY

1 St. Ignatius, B.M.

2 *Purification of our Lady.

3 *St. Blaise, B.M.

4 St. Andrew Corsini, B.C.

5 *St. Agatha, V.M.

6 St. Titus, B.C.—St. Dorothy, V.M.

7 St. Romuald, Ab.

8 St. John of Matha, C.

9 St. Cyril of Alexandria, B.C.D.—St. Apolionia, V.M.

10 St. Scholastica, V.

11 Our Lady of Lourdes.

12 The Seven Founders of the Servite Order.

13

14 *St Valentine, M.

15 SS. Faustinus and Jovita, MM.

16

17

18 St. Simeon, B.M.

19

20

21

22 St. Peter's Chair at Antioch.

23 St. Peter Damian, B.C.D.

24 *St. Mathias, Ap.

25

26

27

28

Note. In leap year the feast of St. Mathias is kept on 25 Feb.

MARCH

1 *St. David.

2 *St. Chad.

3

4 St. Casimir, C.—St. Lucius, P.M.

5

6 SS. Perpetua and Felicity, MM.

7 St. Thomas Aquinas, C.D.—*St. Perpetua.

8 St. John of God, C.

9 St. Frances of Rome, W.

10 The Forty Martyrs.

11

12 *St. Gregory the Great, P.C.D.

13

14

15

16

17. St. Patrick, B.C.—*St. Edward, King of the West Saxons.

18 St. Cyril of Jerusalem, B.C.D.

19 St. Joseph.

20

21 *St. Benedict, Ab.

22

23

24 St. Gabriel the Archangel.

25 *The Annunciation.

26

27 St. John Damascene, C.D.

28 St. John Capistran, C.

29

30

31

APRIL
1
2 St. Francis of Paula, C.
3 *St. Richard.
4 St. Isidore, B.C.D.—St. Ambrose.
5 St. Vincent Ferrer, C.
6
7
8
9
10
11 St. Leo the Great, P.C.D.
12
13 St. Hermengild, M.
14 St. Justin, M.—SS. Tiburtius and Valerian, MM.
15
16
17 St. Anicetus, P.M.
18
19 *St. Alphege.
20
21 St. Anselm, B.C.D.·
22 SS. Soter and Caius, PP. MM.
23 *St. George, M.
24 St. Fidelis of Sigmaringen, M.
25 *St. Mark the Evangelist.
26 SS. Cletus and Marcellinus, PP., MM.
27 St. Peter Canisius, C.D.
28 St. Paul of the Cross, C.—St. Vitalis, M.
29 St. Peter, M.
30 St. Catharine of Siena, V.

MAY
1 *SS. Philip and James, App.
2 St. Athanasius, B.C.D.
3 *Finding of the Holy Cross—SS. Alexander, P., and others.
4 St. Monica, W.
5 St. Pius V, P.C.
6 *St. John before the Latin gate.
7 St. Stanislaus, B.M.
8 Apparition of St. Michael the Archangel.
9 St. Gregory Nazianzenus, B.C.D.
10 St. Antoninus, B.C.—SS. Gordian and Epimachus, MM.
11
12 SS. Nereus and others, MM.
13 St. Robert Bellarmine, B.C.D.
14 St. Boniface, M.
15 St. John Baptist de la Salle, C.
16 St. Ubald, Bp. C.

17 St. Pascal Baylon, C.
18 [St. Venantius, M.]
19 *St. Peter Celestine, P.C.—[St. Pudentiana.]—*St. Dunstan.
20 St. Bernardine of Siena, C.
21
22
23
24
25 St. Gregory VII, P.C.—St. Urban, P.M.
26 St. Philip Neri, C.—St. Eleutherius, P.M.—*St. Augustine of Canterbury.
27 *St. Bede, C.D.—St. John, P.M.
28 St. Augustine of Canterbury, B.C.·
29 St. Mary Magdalen dei Pazzi, V.
30 St. Felix, P.M.
31 St. Angela, V.—St. Petronilla, V.

JUNE
1 *St. Nicomede.
2 SS. Peter and Marcellinus, MM.
3
4 St. Francis Carraciolo, C.
5 *St. Boniface, B.M.
6 St. Norbert, B.C.
7
8
9 SS. Primus and Felician.
10 St. Margaret, Queen, W.
11 *St. Barnabas, Ap.
12 St. John of St. Facundo, C.—SS. Basilides and others, MM.
13 St. Antony of Padua, C.
14 St. Basil the Great, B.C.D.
15 St. Vitus and others, MM.
16
17 *St. Alban.
18 St. Ephrem, C.D.—SS. Mark and Marcellianus, MM.
19 St. Juliana, V.—SS. Gervase and Protase, MM.
20 St. Silverius, P.M.—Translation of St. Edward.
21 St. Aloysius, C.
22 St. Paulinus, B.C.
23 Vigil of St. John the Baptist.
24 Nativity of *St. John the Baptist.
25 St. William, Ab.
26 SS. John and Paul, MM.
27
28 St. Irenaeus, B.M.
29 SS. Peter and Paul, App.—*St. Peter.
30 Commemoration of St. Paul.

JULY

1 The Most Precious Blood—Octave of St. John the Baptist.
2 *The Visitation of our Lady—SS. Processus and Martinian, MM.
3 St. Leo II, P.C.
4 *Translation of St. Martin.
5 St. Antony Zaccaria, C.
6 Octave of SS. Peter and Paul—St. Maria Goretti, V.M.
7 SS. Cyril and Methodius, BB., MM.
8 St. Elizabeth, Queen, W.
9 *St. Thomas More.
10 The Seven Brethren, MM.
11 St. Pius, P.M.
12 St. John Gualbert, Ab.—SS. Nabor and Felix, MM.
13 St. Anacletus, P.M.
14 St. Bonaventure, B.C.D.
15 St. Henry, C.
16 Our Lady of Mount Carmel.
17 [St. Alexius, C.]
18 St. Camillus of Lellis—St. Symphorosa and her Sons, MM.
19 St. Vincent de Paul, C.
20 St. Jerome Emilian, C.—[St. Margaret, V.M.]
21 St. Praxedes, V.
22 *St. Mary Magdalene.
23 St. Apollinaris, B.M.—St. Liberius, B.C.
24 Vigil of St. James—St. Christina, V.M.
25 *St. James the Apostle—[St. Christopher, M.]
26 *St. Anne, Mother of our Lady.
27 St. Pantaleon, M.
28 St. Nazarius and others, MM.
29 St. Martha, V.—SS. Felix and others, MM.
30 SS. Abdon and Sennen.
31 St. Ignatius, C.

AUGUST

1 St. Peter's chains.
2 St. Alphonsus, B.C.D.
3 Finding of St. Stephen, 1st martyr.
4 St. Dominic, C.
5 Dedication of our Lady of the Snow.
6 *The Transfiguration of our Lord—SS. Xystus and others, MM.
7 St. Cajetan, C.—St. Donatus, B.M.—Name of Jesus.
8 SS. Cyriacus and others, MM.
9 Vigil of St. Laurence—St. Romanus, M.
10 *St. Laurence, M.
11 SS. Tiburtius and Susanna, MM.
12 S. Clare, V.
13 SS. Hippolytus and Cassian, MM.
14 Vigil of the Assumption—St. Eusebius, C.
15 The Assumption of our Lady.
16 St. Joachim, Father of our Lady.
17 St. Hyacinth, C.—Octave of St. Laurence.
18 St. Agapitus, M.
19 St. John Eudes, C.
20 St. Bernard, Ab. D.
21 St. Jane Frances de Chantal, W.
22 Octave of the Assumption—St. Timothy and others, MM.
23 St. Philip Benizi, C.—St. Rose of Lima, V.
24 *St. Bartholomew, Ap.
25 St. Louis, K.C.
26 St. Zephyrinus, P.M.
27 St. Joseph Calasanctius, C.
28 *St. Augustine, B.C.D.—St. Hermes, M.
29 *Beheading of St. John the Baptist—St. Sabina, M.
30 St. Rose of Lima, V.—SS. Felix and Adauctus, MM.
31 St. Raymund Nonnatus, C.

SEPTEMBER

1 St. Giles, Ab.—The Twelve Brethren, MM.
2 St. Stephen, K.C.
3
4
5 St. Lawrence Justinian.
6
7 *St. Evurtius.
8 *Nativity of our Lady—St. Hadrian, M.
9 St. Gorgonius.
10 St. Nicholas of Tolentino.
11 SS. Protus and Hyacinth, MM.
12 Holy Name of Mary.
13
14 Exaltation of the Holy Cross—*Holy Cross Day.
15 Seven Dolours of our Lady—St. Nicomedes, M.
16 SS. Cornelius and Cyprian, BB., MM.—SS. Euphemia and others, MM.

17 Stigmata of St. Francis—*St. Lambert.
18 St. Joseph of Cupertino, C.
19 St. Januarius and others, MM.
20 [St. Eustace and others, MM.]
21 *St. Matthew, Ap.
22 St. Thomas of Villanova, B.C.—SS. Maurice and others, MM.
23 St. Linus, P.M.
24 Our Lady of Ransom.
25
26 SS. Cyprian* and Justina, MM.
27 SS. Cosmas and Damian.
28 St. Wenceslaus.
29 Dedication of St. Michael—*St. Michael and All Angels.
30 *St. Jerome, C.D.

OCTOBER
1 *St. Remigius, B.C.
2 The Holy Guardian Angels.
3 St. Thérèse of the Child Jesus.
4 St. Francis of Assisi, C.
5 St. Placid and others, MM.
6 St. Bruno, C.—*St. Faith.
7 The Holy Rosary—St. Mark, P.C.—St. Sergius and others, MM.
8 St. Bridget, W.
9 *St. Denys and others, MM.
10 St. Francis Borgia, C.
11
12
13 St. Edward, K.C.—*Translation of St. Edward.
14 St. Callistus, P.M.
15 St. Teresa, V.
16 St. Hedwige, W.
17 St. Margaret Mary Alacoque, V.—*St. Etheldreda.
18 *St. Luke the Evangelist.
19 St. Peter of Alcantara, C.
20 St. John Cantius.
21 St. Hilarion, Ab.—St. Ursula and others, VV., MM.
22
23
24 St. Raphael, Archangel.
25 Forty English Martyrs.—SS. Chrysanthus and Darias, MM—*St. Crispin.
26 St. Evaristus, P.M.
27 Vigil of SS. Simon and Jude.
28 *SS. Simon and Jude, App.
29
30
31 Vigil of All Saints.

NOVEMBER
1 *All Saints.
2 All Souls.
3
4 St. Charles Borromeo, B.C.—SS. Vitalis and Agricola, MM.
5
6 *St. Leonard.
7
8 Octave of All Saints—The Holy Crowned Martyrs.
9 Dedication of St. John Lateran—St. Theodore, M.
10 St. Andrew Avellino, C.—SS. Tryphon and others, MM.
11 *St. Martin, B.C.
12 St. Martin I, P.M.—St. Mennas, M.
13 St. Didacus, C.—*St. Britius.
14 St. Josaphat, B.M.
15 St. Gertrude, V.—*St. Machutus.
16
17 St. Gregory Thaumaturgus, B.C.—*St. Hugh of Lincoln.
18 Dedication of the Basilicas of St. Peter and St. Paul.
19 St. Elizabeth, Queen, W.—St. Pontianus, P.M.
20 St. Felix of Valois, C.—*St. Edmund, K.M.
21 Presentation of our Lady.
22 *St. Cecilia, V.M.
23. *St. Clement, P.M.—St. Felicitas, M.
24 St. John of the Cross, C.D.—St. Chrysogonus, M.
25 *[St. Catherine, V.M.]
26 St. Sylvester, Ab.—St. Peter, M.
27
28
29 Vigil of St. Andrew—St. Saturninus, M.
30 *St. Andrew the Apostle.

DECEMBER
1
2 [St. Bibiana, V.M.]
3 S. Francis Xavier, C.
4 St. Peter Chrysologus, B.C.D.—[St. Barbara, V.M.]
5 St. Sabbas, Ab.
6 *St. Nicholas, B.C.
7 St. Ambrose, B.C.D.
8 The Immaculate Conception of our Lady—*Conception of the B.V.M.
9

10 St. Melchiades, P.M.
11 St. Damasus, P.C.
12
13 *St. Lucy, V.M.
14
15 Octave of the Immaculate Conception.
16 St. Eusebius, B.M.—*O. Sapentia.
17
18
19
20 Vigil of St. Thomas.

21 *St. Thomas the Apostle.
22
23
24 Christmas Eve.
25 *The Nativity of our Lord.
26 *St. Stephen, 1st martyr.
27 *St. John the Evangelist, Ap.
28 *Holy Innocents, MM.
29 St. Thomas of Canterbury, B.M.
30
31 *St. Sylvester, P.C.

4 Orthodox Calendar

The ecclesiastical year of the Orthodox Church begins on 1st September and it is called 'Indiction'. (See 9 below.) On 14th November fasting before Christmas starts. Christmas Festivals end with Epiphany. Then, one to four Sundays follow (it depends on the date of Easter Sunday) and 'Triodion' and the movable feasts begin, which consist of two parts: (a) a period of four Sundays, which is as an introduction to the Lent before Easter, and (b) the whole period of seven weeks of the Lent. The most important Sundays of the second period are: the first, in which the reintroduction of the Holy Ikons is celebrated. The third in which the Holy Cross is worshipped for spiritual strengthening of those who fast. And Palm Sunday, after which the Great and Holy Week begins. Special services, called the 'Akathist Hymn,' are held in honour of Holy Virgin in the afternoons of the first five Fridays of Lent. Easter falls on the first Sunday after the full moon of the Spring Equinox, but if it happens to coincide with the Jewish Passover it is postponed to the next Sunday. This is one reason for the differences in the dating of Easter Sunday between Eastern and Western Churches. The weeks between Easter and Pentecost are Paschal time. The Ascension of Our Lord is forty days after Easter and always on Thursday. On the fiftieth day after Easter the feast of Pentecost is celebrated and it is followed by Trinity Monday. The Sunday next is the day of All Saints. The first fortnight in Ausut is dedicated to the Holy Mother of God, when special services are held and it is kept as a fasting period.

With the above runs the Calendar of Festivals—given below in abridged form owing to lack of space—fixed to particular days of the months.

CALENDAR OF FESTIVALS

(Proper names transliterated from modern Greek orthography)

JANUARY
1 Circumcision. St. Basil the Great.
2
3
4
5
6 The Epiphany.
7 St. John the Baptist.
8
9
10 St. Gregory, Bishop of Nyssis.
11 St. Theodosius.
12
13
14
15
16
17 St. Antonius the Great.
18 St. Athanasius and St. Cyril, Patriarchs of Alexandria.
19
20 St. Efthymios the Great.
21 St. Maximus the Confessor.
22
23
24
25 St. Gregory the Theologian.
26
27 Removal of the Holy remains of St. John Chrysostom.
28
29

30 St. Basil the Great, St. Gregory the
Theologian, and St. John Chrysostom.

31

FEBRUARY

1
2 Purification of Our Lady.
3 SS. Symeon and Anna.
4
5
6 St. Photius the Great, the Confessor.
7
8
9
10 St. Charalambos.
11
12
13
14
15
16
17
18
19
20
21
22
23 St. Polycarpos Bishop of Smyrna.
24
25
26
27
28
29 St. Cassianos.

MARCH

1 St. Evdokia and others.
2
3
4
5
6
7
8
9 Forty Martyrs.
10
11
12
13
14
15
16
17

18 St. Cyril, Archbishop of Jerusalem.
19 SS. Chrysanthos, Daria, Claudius.
20
21
22
23
24
25 The Annunciation.
26
27
28
29
30
31

MAY

1
2 Removal of the Holy remains of
Athanasius the Great.
3
4
5 St. Irene.
6
7
8 St. John the Theologian.
9
10
11
12 St. Epiphanius, Bishop of Cyprus and
St. Germanos, Archbishop of Constantinople.
13
14
15
16
17
18
19
20
21 St. Constantine the Great and St.
Helena.
22
23
24
25
26
27
28
29
30
31

APRIL

1

2	21
3	22
4	23
5	24 Nativity of St. John the Baptist.
6 St. Eftychius, Patriarch of Constanti-	25
nople.	26
7	27
8	28
9	29 St. Peter and Paul.
10 St. Gregory, Patriarch of Constanti-	30 The Twelve Apostles Day.
nople.	
11	JULY
12	1 St. Kosmas and Damianus, the Anar-
13 St. Martinos, Bishop of Rome.	gyroi.
14	2
15	3
16	4
17	5
18	6
19	7 St. Kyriaki.
20 St. Theodorus of Trihina.	8
21	9
22	10
23 St. George's Day.	11 St. Effimia.
24 St. Elisabeth.	12
25 St. Mark the Apostle and Evangelist.	13
26	14
27	15
28	16
29	17 St. Marina.
30	18
	19 St. Makrina.
JUNE	20 St. Elias the Prophet.
1 St. Justin the Apologist and Philo-	21
sopher.	22
2	23
3	24 St. Christine.
4	25 Assumption of St. Anna.
5 St. Dorotheos, Bishop of Tyros.	26 St. Paraskevi.
6	27 St. Panteleimon.
7	28
8 St. Theodoros the Stratilat.	29
9	30
10	31
11	
12	SEPTEMBER
13	1 Indiction. St. Symeon the Stylite.
14	2
15	3
16	4
17	5 St. Zacharias the Prophet.
18	6
19	7
20	8 Nativity of Our Lady.

9 St. Joachim and Anna.
10
11
12
13
14 The Exaltation of the Holy Cross.
15
16 St. Effimia.
17
18
19
20 St. Efstathius.
21
22
23 St. Thecla the Martyr.
24
25
26 Assumption of St. John the Evangelist.
27
28
29
30

AUGUST
1
2 Removal of the Holy remains of St. Stephanos the Protomartyr.
3
4
5
6 The Transfiguration of Our Lord.
7
8 St. Emilianus, Bishop of Kyzikos.
9 St. Mathias the Apostle.
10
11
12
13
14
15 The Assumption of Our Lady.
16
17
18
19
20
21
22
23
24
25
26
27
28

29 Beheading of St. John the Baptist.
30
31

OCTOBER
1
2 St. Cyprianus.
3 St. Dionysios the Areopagite.
4 St. Herotheos Bishop of Athens.
5
6
7
8
9
10
11
12
13
14
15
16
17
18 St. Luke the Apostle and Evangelist.
19
20 St. Artemios.
21
22
23 St. Jacobus the Brother of Our Lord.
24
25
26 St. Demetrius.
27 St. Nestorius.
28
29
30
31 St. Stachios the Apostle, first Bishop of Byzantium.

NOVEMBER
1
2
3
4
5
6
7
8 SS. Michael and Gabriel the Archangels.
9
10
11
12
13 St. John Chrysostom, Archbishop of Constantinople.

14 St. Phillipos the Apostle.
15
16 St. Matthew the Apostle and Evangel-
       ist.
17
18
19
20
21 Presentation of Our Lady.
22 St. Phillimon the Apostle.
23 St. Amphilochius, Bishop of Iko-
       nium.
24
25
26
27
28
29
30 St. Andrew the Protoklite.

DECEMBER
 1
 2
 3
 4 St. Barbara. St. John of Damascus.
 5 St. Savva.
 6 St. Nicholas, Bishop of Myra.

 7 St. Ambrosius, Bishop of Mediolana.
 8
 9 Conception of St. Anna.
10
11
12 St. Spyridon, Bishop of Trimythoun-
       dos.
13
14
15 St. Elefterios.
16
17 St. Dionysios, Archbishop of Aegina.
18
19
20 St. Ignatius.
21
22 St. Anastasia.
23
24
25 The Nativity of Our Lord.
26
27 St. Stephen, First Martyr.
28
29
30
31

(5) *The Moslem Era* begins in A.D. 16 July 622 (The Hegira). The year consists of twelve lunar months.

(6) *The Coptic Era* begins A.D. 29 Aug. 284.

(7) *The Parsee Era* begins A.D. 16 June 632.

(8) *The Japanese Era* begins 11 Feb. 660 B.C.

(9) *The Roman Indiction* was a cyle of fifteen years introduced by Constantine for purposes of taxation. The indictions began on A.D. 1 Sept. 312.

(10) *The Olympiad* was a four-year period used for dating by the Greeks. The first year of the first Olympiad was 776 B.C.

(11) *The French Republican Era* lasted from 22 Sept. 1792 until 31 Dec. 1805. The first days of the months of the French Revolutionary Calendar as they occurred in the year I of the Era are shown in the preceding secular Calendar; in calculating Gregorian dates from Republican dates the following must be borne in mind:

(a) The Republican Calendar was only in actual use from 26 Nov. 1793 till 31 Dec. 1805.

(b) The Republican Year begins with the first Vendémiaire.

(c) In leap years a sixth Sansculottide was added in Sept. Therefore between 28 Feb. and 22 Sept. 1796 it is necessary to *subtract* one day from each date according to the Gregorian Calendar.

(d) On the other hand the year VIII was a leap year, whereas the Gregorian year 1800 was not. Therefore from 23 Sept. 1800 until 31 Dec. 1805 it is necessary to *add* one day to each Gregorian date except in the period 28 Feb.–23 Sept. 1804 (XII), when the clash between the Gregorian and Republican leap years cancels it out.

THE DICTIONARY

A

Aachen or **Aix-la-Chapelle,** Germany. Founded by Romans, A.D. 125. Charlemagne made it his capital, 795. He *d.* and was buried here, 814. For treaties signed here *see* Aix-la-Chapelle, Treaties of.

Aarau, Treaty of 11 Aug. 1712, ended the Second Villmergen War. Helvetic republic proclaimed at, 1798.

Aargau. Swiss canton in the basin of the River Aare, which had been conquered by the Franks under Clovis (*c.* 465–511), is first mentioned, as a county, 763. Ceded some south-western territory to Berne in the fourteenth century. The canton was subject to the Swiss Confederacy, from 1415. Joined, 1798, the Helvetic Confederation, and from then until 1803 was divided into two cantons of Baden and A. Joined the Sonderbund (separate Catholic confederation), 1845.

Abadan, Iran. First oil refinery at, 1909.

Abbaye Prison (Paris), France. Built 1631–5. Massacre at, 2–3 Sept. 1792.

Abbeville, France. Treaties of A. (1) between Henry III of England and Louis IX of France renouncing continental Normandy was made at Paris, 28 May 1258, and confirmed in London, 1259. (2) Between Henry VIII and Francis I, 1527.

Abdications of Sovereigns (including forced abdications and 'desertions'):
Diocletian, Roman emperor A.D. 305
Stephen II of Hungary 1131
Albert the Bear of Brandenburg 1142
Wladislaw III of Poland 1206
Pope Celestine V 13 Dec. 1294
John Balliol of Scotland 1296
Otho (of Bavaria) of Hungary 1309
Edward II of England 1327
Richard II of England 29 Sept. 1399
Eric VII of Denmark 1439
Pope Felix V 1449
Charles V, as Emperor of Germany 25 October 1555
Charles V, as King of Spain 16 Jan. 1556
Mary, Queen of Scots 24 July 1567
Christina of Sweden 16 June 1654
John Casimir of Poland 1668
James II of England (fled) 11 Dec. 1688
Frederick Augustus II of Poland 1704
Philip V of Spain (resumed) 1724
Victor Amadeus of Sardinia 1730
Charles of Naples 1759
Stanislaw II of Poland 1795
Charles Emmanuel IV of Sardinia 4 June 1802
Francis II of Germany, who became Emperor of Austria 11 Aug. 1804
Charles IV of Spain, in favour of his son 19 Mar. 1808
Charles IV of Spain, in favour of Bonaparte (*see* SPAIN) 1 May 1808
Joseph Bonaparte of Naples (for Spain) 1 June 1808
Gustavus IV of Sweden 29 Mar. 1809
Louis Bonaparte of Holland 1 July 1810
Jerome of Westphalia, Bonaparte 20 Oct. 1813
Napoleon I of France 5 Apr. 1814
Victor Emmanuel of Sardinia 13 Mar. 1821
Pedro IV of Portugal 2 May 1826
Charles X of France 2 Aug. 1830
Pedro I of Brazil 7 Apr. 1831
Dom Miguel of Portugal 26 May 1834
William I of Holland 8 Oct. 1840
Louis Philippe of France 24 Feb. 1848
Louis Charles of Bavaria 21 Mar. 1848
Ferdinand of Austria 2 Dec. 1848
Charles Albert of Sardinia 23 Mar. 1849
Leopold II of Tuscany 21 July 1859
Bernhard of Saxe-Meiningen 20 Sept. 1866
Isabella II of Spain 25 June 1870

Amadeus I of Spain 11 Feb. 1873
Prince Alexander of Bulgaria 7 Sept. 1886
Milan, King of Serbia 3 Mar. 1889
Pedro II of Brazil 15 Nov. 1889
Oscar, of Norway and Sweden, recognized Norwegian independence; Norway as separate state 27 Oct. 1905
Abdul Hamid II, Sultan of Turkey 27 Apr. 1909
Manoel of Portugal 4 Oct. 1910
P'u-yi of China 12 Feb. 1912
Nicholas of Montenegro
    Left his country 1916
    Dethroned Apr. 1918
Nicholas II of Russia Mar. 1917
Constantine of Greece 12 June 1917
    Restored Dec. 1920
    Abdicated again 27 Sept. 1922
Ferdinand I of Bulgaria 4 Oct. 1918
Wilhelm II of Germany 9 Oct. 1918
Karl of Austria 11 Nov. 1918
Mohammed VI of Turkey 17 Nov. 1922
George II of Greece 25 Mar. 1924
Hussein, King of the Hedjaz 5 Oct. 1924
Ali, King of the Hedjaz 19 Dec. 1925
Amanullah, Khan of Afghanistan twice in 1929
Alfonso XIII of Spain 11 Apr. 1932
Prajadhipok of Siam 2 Mar. 1935
Haile Selassie of Ethiopia
    Fled 1 May 1936
    Restored 5 Apr. 1941
Edward VIII of Great Britain 11 Dec. 1936
Zog of Albania 8 Apr. 1939
Carol II of Rumania Sept. 1940
Regent Miklós Horthy of Hungary 15 Oct. 1944
Peter II of Yugoslavia Nov. 1945
Victor Emmanuel of Italy 9 May 1946
Umberto of Italy 12 June 1946
Simeon of Bulgaria Sept. 1946
Michael of Rumania 30 Dec. 1947
Wilhelmina of Holland Sept. 1948
Leopold III of Belgium July 1951
Farouk of Egypt 26 July 1952
Talal I of Jordan Aug. 1952
Ahmed Fuad II of Egypt June 1953
Grand Duchess Charlotte of Luxembourg 1964
Idris of Libya Sept. 1969
Zahir of Afghanistan, 24 Aug. 1973
Constantine II of Greece 1974
Haile Selassie of Ethiopia 12 Sept. 1974 (again)
Shah of Iran Jan. 1979
Juliana of Holland Apr. 1980

Abduction, defined and punishable in the U.K. under the Criminal Law Consolidation Act, 1861; Illegal Practices Act, 1883; Criminal Law Amendment Act, 1885; Sexual Offences Act, 1956.

Aberdeen, Scotland, built *c.* 893, made a royal burgh by William the Lion, 1179. Chartered by Robert the Bruce, 1319. Burned by English, 1336. St. Machars Cathedral, 1357–1527. King's College founded by Bishop Elphinstone, 1494. Marischal College, 1593. The two colleges united, 1860. Base for N. Sea oil industry since 1970s.

Aberfan, mining vil. near Merthyr Tydfil, Wales, where on 21 Oct. 1966 a coal tip subsided on the vil., burying the school and killing over 140 people, mainly children.

Aberystwyth, Wales. Castle founded by Gilbert Strongbow, 1109. Town incorporated by Edward I. Castle used by Charles I as a mint during civil war, and demolished, 1647. College opened, 1872. Welsh National Library, 1911. *See* WALES, UNIVERSITY OF.

Abingdon, England. Monastery founded *c.* 675 by Cissa. Burned by Danes *c.* 871. Grammar school founded, 1563. Held by Essex against Charles I, 1645. Defenders put prisoners to death without trial, hence term 'A. Law.'

Abjuration, Oath of, was required to be sworn by all entering on certain public offices after 1688 (but especially up to 1702), denying the claims of the house of Stuart. Regulated by the Promissory Oaths Act, 1868. *See* Nonjurors.

Abjuration of the Realm, a self-imposed sentence of exile following confession of a crime on account of which the criminal had taken sanctuary. Whole procedure of sanctuary and A. was abolished in the reign of James I (1603–25).

Abo, Treaty of, 18 Aug. 1743. Sweden ceded part of Finland to Russia.

Abolitionists (U.S.A.). Party opposed to slavery. First congress, 1774, but party only became active from 1832 onwards. Merged with the Republican Party, 1868.

Abominable Snowman or **Yeti.** Footprints described by Col. Howard-Bury, leader of Everest Expedition, 1921, found at 21,000 feet. A special expedition set out in search of the A. S., 1954, but its findings were inconclusive. Continued alleged sightings of footprints in 1970s and 1980s.

Abortion Act, 27 Oct. 1967. Came into operation 27 April 1968 and considerably liberalized law governing abortion in England, Wales and Scotland. Sept. 1983, referendum voted amendment outlawing abortion into the Irish Constitution.

Abrantes, Treaty of, 29 Nov. 1807, ratified at Madrid after which it is sometimes named. *See* PORTUGAL.

Abruzzi National Park, nature reserve around the Gran Sasso d'Italia, founded, 1922.

Abu Dhabi, *See* UNITED ARAB EMIRATES.

Abuja, official cap. of Nigeria (*q.v.*) since Sept. 1982.

Abydos, Asia Minor, was the eastern end of the pontoon bridge thrown across the Dardanelles by the Persian Army of Xerxes, 480 B.C.

Abydos, Upper Egypt, contains a ruined temple of Seti I, where, in 1817, was found the Table of A., key to the genealogy of early Pharaohs.

Abyssinia. *See* ETHIOPIA.

Academies, From Academia, a grove outside Athens (sacred to the hero Academus). Plato first taught philosophy here, *c.* 387 B.C. Ptolemy Soter founded an academy at Alexandria, 314 B.C. First philosophical academy in France founded by Père Mersenne at Paris, 1635. The following are the principal A. with the dates when they were founded. The A. of Great Britain are also under their various titles.

Ancona, Caliginosi, 1642.

Berlin, Akademie der Wissenschaften, 1700; Architecture, 1799.

Bologna, Ecclesiastical, 1687; Mathematics, 1690; Sciences and Arts, 1712.

Boston, Arts and Sciences, 1780.

Brescia, Erranti, 1626. Brescia Academy, 1801.

Brest and Toulon, Military, 1682.

Brussels, Académie Royale, 1773.

Bucharest, Rumanian Academy, 1866.

Caen, Belles-Lettres, 1705.

Chicago, Sciences, 1865.

Connecticut, Arts and Sciences, 1799.

Copenhagen, Sciences, 1742.

Cortona, Antiquities, 1726.

Dublin, Royal Irish Academy, 1782.

Erfurt, Saxony, Sciences, 1754.

Faenza, Philoponi, 1612.

Florence, Fine Arts, 1270; Platonica, 1474 (dissolved, 1521); Accademia della Crusca, 1582; del Cimento, 1657; Georgofili, 1752 (agricultural); Antiquities, 1807.

Geneva, Medical, 1715.

Genoa, Painting, etc., 1751; Sciences, 1783.

Göttingen, Gesellschaft der Wissenschaften, 1752.

Haarlem, The Sciences, 1760.

Helsinki, Societas Scientiarum.

Istanbul (formerly Constantinople), Academy of, 1851.

Leipzig, Academy of, 1768.

Leningrad, Academy of the U.S.S.R. (formerly the Imperial Academy), 1728.

Lisbon, Portuguese Academy, 1779.

London, Royal Society, 1662 (charter granted); Royal Academy of Arts, 1768; Royal Academy of Music, 1822.

Lyons, Sciences, 1700.

Madrid, Royal Spanish, 1713; History, 1730; Painting and the Arts, 1753.

Mannheim, Sculpture, 1775.

Mantua, Vigilanti (Sciences), 1704.

Marseilles, Belles-Lettres, 1726.

Massachusetts, Arts and Sciences, 1780.

Milan, Sciences, 1719; Academy of, 1838; Architecture, 1880.

Munich, Arts and Sciences, 1759.

Naples, Rossana, 1540; Secretorum Naturae, 1560; Sciences, 1695; Herculaneum, 1755.

Newhaven, U.S.A., Connecticut Academy of Arts and Sciences, 1799.

New York, Literature and Philosophy,

1814; Sciences, 1818; National
Academy, 1863.

Nîmes, Royal Academy, 1682.

Oslo, Academy, 1837.

Padua, Poetry, 1610; Academy of, 1779;
Sciences, 1792.

Palermo, Fine Arts, 1300; Medical,
1645.

Paris, Académie Française, 1637;
Académie Royale de Peinture et de
Sculpture, 1648; Académie de
Peinture, 1648; Académie des
Inscriptions, 1663; Académie Royale
des Sciences, 1666; Académie Royale
d'Architecture, 1671. All these A. at
Paris were suppressed, 1793, and in
1795 one large one, the Institut
National, was founded. This in 1816
was split up in four classes by Louis
XVIII: (a) Académie Française; (b)
Académie des Inscriptions et Belles
Lettres; (c) Académie des Sciences;
(d) Académie des Beaux-Arts, and in
1832 Académie des Sciences Morales
et Politiques.

Parma, Innominati, 1550.

Peking, Academia Sinica (refounded
1949).

Pennsylvania, Academy of Fine Arts,
1805.

Perugia, Insensati, 1561.

Philadelphia, Arts and Sciences,
1749; Natural Sciences, 1812.

Rome, Lincei, 1609; Umoristi, 1611;
Fantastici, 1625; Infecondi, 1653;
Painting, 1656; Arcadi, 1656;
English, 1752; Nuovi Lincei, 1847.

Stockholm, Sciences, 1741; Belles-
Lettres, 1753; Agriculture, 1781.

Toulon, Military, 1682.

Trondhjem, Academy, 1760.

Turin, Sciences, 1757; Fine Arts, 1778.

Uppsala, Royal Society, 1720.

Venice, Medical, 1701; Academy, 1760.

Verona, Music, 1543; Sciences, 1780.

Vienna, Kaiserliche Akademie, 1487;
Sculpture and Arts, 1705; Surgery,
1783; Oriental, 1810; Sciences, 1847.

Warsaw, Languages and History, 1753.

Washington, D. C., Smithsonian
Institute, 1846; National Geographical Society, 1888; International Academy of Sciences, Arts
and Letters, 1910.

Acadia (Acadie). Name changed to Nova
Scotia (*q.v.*), 1713.

Acarnania, Greece. People of A. engaged
in Peloponnesian War, 429 B.C. against
Ambracians, conquered by Spartans,
390 B.C.; by Macedonians, 225 B.C. Defeated by Romans, 197 B.C. Subjugated,
145 B.C., and was included in the province of Achaea.

Accountants. Chartered Institute of England and Wales founded, 1880. Chartered Institute of Scotland founded,
1854. Society of Incorporated A. and
Auditors founded, 1885. Association of
Certified A., 1904.

Accra. Capital of Ghana (*q.v.*), since
1876. Founded 17th cent. as trading
post by Brit. and Dutch.

Achaeans. Hellenic tribe (or group of
tribes) which played a leading part in
the wars and migrations of the Heroic
Age (second millennium B.C.) and
eventually settled on the N. coast of
the Peloponnese, where the **Achaean
League** of twelve city-states, renewed
in 281 B.C., undertook the liberation of
its members from Macedonian hegemony. In 251 it was joined by Sicyon,
then by Corinth, Sparta, and other cities not strictly belonging to Achaea,
defeated the Macedonians and dominated the peninsula until its defeat by
the Romans in 146 B.C., after which
the Greek mainland became the
Roman province (and later the Byzantine theme) of Achaea.

Acoustics. Explained by Pythagoras *c.*
500 B.C. Galileo's important discoveries, A.D. 1600. Speed of sound discovered by Newton, 1698. Brook
Taylor's practical demonstrations of
Galileo's theory, 1714. Mersenne's discovery of 1636 explained by Hel-
mholtz, 1862.

Acre, Saint Jean d' (O.T. *Acco*; N.T.
Ptolemais; Mod. *Akka*). Captured by
Arabs, 638. By Crusaders, 1104. By
Saladin, 1187. By Richard I after two
years' siege, 1191. By Egyptians, 1291.
After its capture by the Turks in 1517
it fell into decay. Successfully defen-
ded against Napoleon by Sir Sydney
Smith, 1799. Captured by Ibrahim,
son of Mehemet Ali Pasha of Egypt,

1832. Stormed by Sir Robert Stopford, 4 Nov. 1840, and returned to Turkey, 1841. Occupied by British, 23 Sept. 1918. Awarded to Arabs by U.N., but taken by the Israelis, 17 May 1948, and became part of Israel. *See* CRUSADES.

Acropolis, at Athens, consisted in the second millennium B.C. of fortifications, which together with most of the other buildings on the site were destroyed in the Persian invasion of 480. An early temple to Athene was replaced by the Erechtheum (completed 409 B.C.). The Parthenon (*q.v.*) built, 447–432, and Propylaea, built 437–433. The theatre of Dionysus on the southern slope was converted to a stone structure between 338 and 326 B.C.

Actinometer. Invented by Sir John Herschel *c.* 1825.

Acton Burnell, Statute of, legislating for the recovery of debt, passed, 1283.

Acts of Parliament or **Statutes.** Earliest mentioned Provisions of Merton, 1236. Earliest existing statute roll 6 Edward I (Statute of Gloucester).

Actuary. Institute of As. founded, 1848. International Congress, 1898. Scottish Faculty of As. established, Edinburgh, 1856. A. Society of America assembled, 24 Apr. 1890.

Addis Ababa. Founded, 1885. Made capital of Ethiopia by Emperor Menelek, 1892. Treaty with Italy signed at, 1896. Occupation by Italians, 1936. Pillage of by Italians, 19–22 Feb. 1937. Liberated by British, 5 Apr. 1941. New opera house completed, 1955. The National Univ., Ethiopia's first univ., founded 1961.

Addled Parliament, 5 Apr.–7 June 1614.

Adelaide. Capital of state of S. Australia. Founded by Col. Light, who arrived 27 July 1837. University founded 1874.

Aden. Taken by Portuguese, 1513, but captured by Turks, 1538. Independent after 1730 till occupied by the E. India Co., 19 Jan. 1839. Control transferred from Indian to British Government, 1927. Crown colony, 1 Apr. 1937. 1962–1967 Nationalist uprising against Britain. On 30 Nov. 1967 A,

and the former federation of S. Arabia became an independent state subsequently known as the **People's Democratic Republic of Yemen** (*q.v.*).

Administrations, British (since the beginning of the modern cabinet system by Sir Robert Walpole, 1721). For list of Prime Ministers, see under PRIME MINISTER

Admiral. Word derived from the Arabic *amir* or *emir* (*lord* or *commander*: cf. *amir-al-bahr*, commander of the sea) and was first used in England in the fourteenth century under Edward III, though the office it denotes is much older. In the U.S.A. the A. was declared the 'ranking officer' in the navy, 2 Mar. 1867; rank abolished, 24 Jan. 1873, but revived in 1899, when Admiral Dewey was appointed. *See* famous A.s listed under SOLDIERS AND SAILORS; and SOLDIERS, SAILORS, AND AIRMEN OF THIS CENTURY.

Admiralty. A commission for discharging the duties of the Lord High Admiral whose office certainly dates from 1405, and probably earlier; it was first placed in commission, 1628. Administrative work of the A., whether in commission or not, was done by the Navy Board instituted in 1546; it performed the duties originally performed by the Keepers of the King's Ships the first of whom was appointed in 1214; the Navy Board was abolished in 1832. The last Lord High Admiral (1827–8) was the Duke of Clarence, later William IV. In 1964, when the A. was absorbed by the Ministry of Defence, the Queen again assumed the title, but not the functions, of Lord High Admiral.

Admiralty Arch erected, as a memorial to Queen Victoria, 1910.

Admiralty Court ceased to have jurisdiction in naval disciplinary affairs under the terms of the Naval Discipline Act, 1866, its only connection with naval matters being its capacity as a Prize Court as defined by the Judicature Acts of 1873 and 1875. (*See also* PROBATE COURT.) Criminal cases were transferred from it to the Central Criminal Court in 1836.

Admiralty Islands. Discovered by Dutch, 1616. Occupied by Germany, 1885. Seized by Australian troops, 1914, and after 1919 administered by Australia as a mandated territory. Taken by Japanese, 1942; retaken by Americans, 1944. Self governing part of Papua New Guinea since 1975.

'Admonition to the Parliament'. Puritan demand for the abolition of episcopacy presented to the House of Commons, 1572. A second pamphlet drawn up and suppressed, 11 June 1573.

Adowa or **Adua,** capital of Tigré, Ethiopia. Ethiopians inflicted crushing defeat on Italians, 1 Mar. 1896. Taken by Italians, 6 Oct. 1935. Recaptured by British and Ethiopian troops, Apr. 1941.

Adrianople (Turk. **Edirne**). Old town enlarged by Emperor Hadrian (*d.* A.D. 138). Constantine I defeated Licinius near, 3 July 323; Valens defeated and slain by Goths, 378; seized by Turks under Murad I, 1361; their capital until 1453; captured by Russians, 20 Aug. 1829; restored, 14 Sept. 1829; occupied by Russians, 20 Jan. 1878. During Balkan Wars, Oct. 1912–Aug. 1913, surrendered to Bulgarians after five months' siege, 26 Mar. 1913; recaptured by Turks, 18 July 1913.

Adrianople, Peace of. Ended Russo-Turkish War, 14 Sept. 1829.

Adulite Monument, an inscription on a marble seat found at Adulis (now Zula or Thulla on the coast of Eritrea near Massawa) referring in Greek to Ptolemy Euergetes, King of Egypt, 246–221 B.C., by Cosmas of Alexandria in the first half of the sixth century A.D.

Advertisements, Book of. A book of ecclesiastical discipline put in force by Archbishop Parker, 1565. It caused great controversy, and is generally taken as marking the beginning of the persecution of Puritans by the Church of England.

Advocate, The Lord, also **King's** or **Queen's** (Scotland). Office created *c.* 1480 by James III. First mentioned as 'Lord' A., 1598.

Advocate General or **King's Advocate** (England). Office vacant since 1872.

Advocates' Library (Edinburgh). Established 1682 by Sir George MacKenzie of Rosehaugh. Non-legal books presented to Scottish nation, 1925.

Aediles. Minor Roman magistrates to superintend finance, sanitation, police, etc. First appointed, 494 B.C. A higher rank of A., Curule A., first appointed, 367 B.C. *See* ROMAN REPUBLIC.

Aegina. Ancient island republic in the Saronic Gulf. Independent till *c.* 456 B.C., when it was subjugated by Athens.

Aemilian Way, giving its name to the region of Emilia, was named after its builder, the consul M. Aemilius Lepidus, at whose orders it was begun in 187 B.C.

Aerial Warfare. *See* Aviation.

Aerodynamics. Chair instituted at Imperial College, London, 1920.

Aeronautical Society of Great Britain. Established, 12 Jan. 1866.

Aeroplanes. *See* AVIATION.

Aether, a putative fine substance first so named by Leibnitz in 1671; a thesis of Kant, 1755, presupposed A., while Thomas Young in 1801 regarded it as the vehicle of light. Michelson and Morley, in 1881 and 1887, tried and failed to find evidence of an A.-drift at the earth's surface.

Affiliation. Process in England governed by the Bastardy Acts, 1845, 1873, and 1923, the Affiliation Order Act, 1914, the Affiliation Proceedings Act, 1957, and the Maintenance Orders Act, 1968.

Afforestation. Forestry Act, 1919, provides for acquisition and A. of land in U.K. Amplified by Forestry Act, 1927. Crown forests transferred to Forestry Commission, 1924.

Afghanistan. Invaded by Alexander the Great, 330 B.C. Unsuccessful Roman attempts to subjugate, 305–255 B.C. Tatar dynasty, A.D. 907. Part of Moghul Empire, 1525. Conquered by Persia, 1737. Became independent under Durrani dynasty, 1747. First Afghan War, 1838–42. Massacre of British at, and disastrous retreat from Kabul, 1841–2. Kabul captured by British, Sept. 1842. Britain helps Afghans by naval support against Persia, 1854.

Second Afghan War, Sept. 1878–Nov. 1890. Relief of Kandahar, Aug. 1880. Amir Habibullah murdered, Feb. 1919. His son Amanullah invades India, May–Aug. 1919 (Third Afghan War). Treaty, Nov. 1921.

Military coup overthrew monarchy, 1973. President killed in left-wing coup, Apr. 1978 which led to estab. of a pro-Soviet gov. Opposition to Russia led to further unrest and in Dec. 1979 Soviet troops invaded A. and replaced the President. Civil war between pro- and anti-Soviet factions in A. since 1979.

Africa Company, Royal, or Guinea Company of Merchants, founded under Charles II, 27 Sept. 1672. Abolished 7 May 1821, when the Crown took possession of all its settlements, forts, and trading posts, etc. Other companies for exploiting the African trade had previously been formed under royal protection in 1588, and in the reigns of Charles I and James I.

Africa, German East, *See* TANGANYIKA.

Africa, North. *See* ALGIERS; TUNISIA; MOROCCO; LIBYA; CARTHAGE.

Africa, South. *See* SOUTH AFRICA, REPUBLIC OF.

African Coast, Early Settlements, etc.
Portuguese: Ceuta, 1415. Guinea voyages begun, 1426. Senegal River, 1445. Sierra Leone, 1460. Gold Coast, 1469. Fernando Po, 1481. Elmina, 1482. Congo, 1484. Dias discovers Cape of Good Hope, 1486. Vasco da Gama explores S.E. coast on way to India, 1497–9. Sofata occupied, 1505. Mozambique, 1507.
French: St. Louis, 1626.
English: Cormantine, 1618. Fort James, 1663. Cape Coast Castle, 1672.
Dutch: St. Thomé, 1637–48. Cape Town, 1652.
Prussia: Fredericksburg, 1682.

African Exploration (Interior). Bruce, 1768–73, to discover sources of Nile. Mungo Park: (1) 1795; (2) 1805, to discover the course of the Niger. Livingstone, 1840–73, Great African Lakes area. Stanley, 1868–95, in Central Africa, Nigeria, and Congo. Niger Expedi-

tion subsidized by Parliament, 1840–1. Richardson explores Sahara, 1845–6 and 1849.

Afrikander Bond. Association of Dutch-speaking S. Africans, formed 1880. Took an active part in the abortive rebellion of 1914.

Agadir, Morocco. Importance as a port declined after revolution of 1773. Destroyed by earthquake, 29 Feb. 1960.

Agadir Crisis. Germans sent the gun-boat *Panther* to A., Aug. 1911, in support of claims in Morocco in order to test the strength of the Anglo-French Entente (*see* ENTENTE CORDIALE). Britain and France united to compel a withdrawal in 1912.

Aga Khan. Hereditary head of the Ismaili Moslems. First A.K. fled from Persia to Bombay in 1836. The third A. K. (1877–1957) was given the status of a First Class Indian Prince, 1916, for political services in World War I. Succeeded by his grandson Karim (*b.* 1936).

Age in law at which a marriage in England is valid was raised to sixteen by an Act of 1929. Age of majority lowered from 21 to 18, 1970, under Family Law Reform Act, 1969.

Agincourt. *See* BATTLES.

Agra, Uttar Pradesh State, India. Captured by Baber, 1526, when Koh-i-Noor was among the booty. Seat of Mogul Government, 1566–1658. Taj Mahal built, 1632. Stormed by Lord Lake, 17 Oct. 1803. Withstood a long siege in Indian Mutiny during which many important buildings were destroyed, 1857. *See* INDIAN MUTINY.

Agricultural Holdings Acts (Great Britain), granted greater certainty of tenure and compensation for improvements to agricultural tenants in Scotland; passed, 1883; amended, 1900, 1908, and 1913. Act applicable to England and Wales passed, 1922. Consolidating Act for England and Wales, 1948; for Scotland, 1949. Modified by the Agricultural (Miscellaneous Provisions Act), 1976.

Agriculture, Fisheries and Food, Ministries of. Board of Agriculture set up, 1793. Dissolved, 1822. Reconstituted,

1889. Became the Board of Agriculture and Fisheries, 1903. Raised to ministry status, 1919. Amalgamated with Ministry of Food, 1955.

Agrigento, Sicily, lies slightly to the W. of the Greek town of Acragas (Lat. Agrigentum), which *fl.* 560–406 B.C., having been founded in 582 as a colony of Gela. Captured and sacked by the Carthaginians, 405, and again in 255; and twice by the Romans, 261 and 210. During the days of its independence as a Greek city it was famous for its architecture. In A.D. 828 A. was captured from the Greeks by the Saracens, and from them by the Norman Roger I, 1086. The name 'Girgenti' was adopted during the Middle Ages, but the present form came into use, 1928.

Ahmedabad, Bombay State, India. Founded, 1411. Subjugated by Akbar, 1572, it became the capital of the Moslem Kingdom of Gujarat. Stormed by British, 1780. Restored to Mahrattas same year. Reverted to British, 6 Nov. 1818. Earthquakes, 1819, 1868. Serious riots at, 11 Apr. 1919.

Ahmednagar, Maharashta State, India. Founded, A.D. 1494. Emperor Aurungzeb *d.* here, 1707. Seized by the Peishwa, 1759. Ceded to Scindiah, 1797. Taken by Wellington, 12 Aug. 1803. Finally annexed to British possessions, 13 June 1817 under Treaty of Poona.

Ahvenanmaa or **Aland Islands.** Swedish till 1809, when they were ceded to Russia at the Peace of Frederikshavn. Finnish from July 1919. Demilitarization convention, 1921, signed by Great Britain, France, Italy, and all Baltic powers except Russia.

Aigues Mortes, France. First Tour de Constance built twelfth century by Raymond V of Toulouse. Port created by St. Louis (IX), who built the present Tour de Constance, and sailed from here for the Crusades of 1248 and 1270. Walls built by Philippe le Hardi, 1272–5. Meeting of Charles V and Francis I, 1538.

Air. Discovered not to be an element by Priestley, who isolated oxygen in 1774. First vacuum by Torricelli *c.* 1646.

First A. pump by O. von Guericke *c.* 1650. First liquefied by Cailletet, 1877. *See also* OXYGEN.

Air Council. Formed, 1918, on model of Army Council to administer Royal Air Force.

Aircraft Carrier. First ship fitted to carry seaplanes, *Hermes,* took part in British naval manœuvres, 1913. But the *Ark Royal* (sunk 1941) was the first A.C. to be effectively used in action. Phased out of Royal Navy, 1968 onwards.

Air Force Regiment, Royal, raised, Feb. 1942.

Air Force, Royal, formed in 1918 by amalgamation of the Royal Flying Corps and Royal Naval Air Service *(see under* FLEET AIR ARM).

Airmen of this Century. *See* SOLDIERS, SAILORS, AND AIRMEN OF THIS CENTURY.

Air Laws. Aerial Navigation Act, 1911, regulated civil air transport in Britain. Extended to naval and military areas. 1913. Present A.L. in Britain based on the Civil Aviation Act, 1949.

Air Mail. *See* AVIATION.

Air Ministry. Instituted, 1922. Absorbed by Ministry of Defence, 1964.

Air Pollution. Extensive powers to prevent this available under the Clean Air Acts, 1946, 1956, and 1968.

Air-Raid Precautions Act, 22 Dec. 1937.

Air Raids. First offensive use of aircraft by Italians in Libya, 1911, and by Greeks against Turks at Dardanelles, Feb. 1913. First raid on a town by German Zeppelin on Lunéville, 9 Aug. 1914. First on Britain by German aeroplanes, Dec. 1914. First British air raid on German hangars at Düsseldorf, 22 Sept. 1914. In World War II daily German A.R. on Britain began 18 June 1940. Flying bomb attacks started June 1944. Heavy allied raids on Germany from Jan. 1943 onwards. American planes dropped first atom bomb on Hiroshima (*q.v.*), 6 Aug. 1945. A.R. played major part in Korean War (from 1950) and in Vietnam 1964–75. Also important in Arab-Israeli conflict, since 1967; in Afghanistan since 1979 and during Falkland Is. campaign 1982. *See* AVIATION and WORLD WARS I and II.

Airships. Invented, 1783. Giffard's steam-driven airship first ascended, 24 Sept. 1852. Gas engine introduced, 1872. Santos Dumont's gasoline-driven airship, 1898. First Zeppelin completed, 1900. Britain abandoned development of A. after the 'R.101' disaster at Beauvais, 5 Oct. 1930; U.S.A. after the 'Akron,' 4 Apr. 1933, and 'Macon' disasters, 12 Feb. 1935. The German airship 'Hindenburg' was burnt out, May 1937, but the 'Graf Zeppelin' remained in service until 1938. Limited revival in Britain in 1980s.

Aix-en-Provence (Lat. **Aquae Sextiae**). Founded by Romans, 120 B.C. Destroyed by Moors and rebuilt, A.D. 796. University founded, 1409. Captured by Charles V, 1535. Church councils at, 1112, 1374, 1409, 1416, 1585, 1612.

Aix-la-Chapelle (city). *See* AACHEN.

Aix-la-Chapelle, Congress of, To regulate European affairs, 29 Sept.–21 Nov. 1818.

Aix-la-Chapelle, Treaties of:
1. Between France and Spain, 2 May 1668.
2. At end of War of Austrian Succession, 1748.

Ajaccio, Corsica. Bishopric since seventh century. Napoleon *b.* at, 15 Aug. 1769.

Akkerman. *See* BELGOROD-DNESTROVSKIY.

Alabama, Explored by De Soto, 1540. Settled by French, 1702. Ceded to Great Britain by Treaty of Paris, 1763. Part occupied by Spain but retaken by U.S.A., 1813. Admitted to the Union as a state, 1819.

'Alabama' Dispute. A Confederate warship equipped, 1862, in England did great damage to U.S. shipping till sunk by U.S.S. *Kearsarge*, 19 June 1864. Treaty of Washington set up a Court of Arbitration, which decided that Britain must pay compensation for damage to U.S.A., Dec. 1871.

Aláis. *See* ALÈS.

Alaska. Discovered by Bering, 1741. Under control of Russian-American company, 1799. Called Russian America till purchased by U.S.A., 1867. Boundary dispute with Britain settled by arbitration, 1903. Became an incorporated territory, 1912. Admitted to the Union as the forty-ninth state, 3 Jan. 1959. Earthquake at Anchorage killed 180 people, 27 March 1964. Commercial oil production began, 1959. Transalaska Pipeline completed, 1978.

Albania. Area in dispute between Bulgars and Byzantines till Michael Comnenus founded Despotate of Epirus, in which A. was included, 1204. Passed to the Orsini family, 1318–58. Conquered by Stephen Dushan, 1358. Scanderbeg's defence of A. against Turks, 1444–66. Venetian attempt to prevent conquest, 1466; fails, 1479–81. Finally became a Turkish province, 1748. Rebellion achieves independence, 1912. Overrun by Austrians and Allies in World War I. Mandated to Italy, 1920. Republic proclaimed with Ahmed Zog as president, 22 Jan. 1925. Zog becomes king, 1928. Italian conquest, Apr. 1939. Invaded by Greeks in Italo-Greek War, Dec. 1940. Tirana recaptured from Italians by Albanian partisans, Nov. 1944. Proclaimed a People's Republic 11 Jan. 1946. British cruisers fired at in Corfu Straits, 15 June 1946. British destroyers mined in Corfu Straits, Nov. 1946. Hague Court of International Justice ordered A. to pay compensation 1951, but A. failed to do so. Since 1960 has been engaged in ideological quarrel with U.S.S.R. Russia broke off diplomatic relations with A., Dec. 1961. 1967: gov. declared A. the first atheist state in the world. 1968: A. withdrew from Warsaw Pact (*q.v.*) and strengthened ties with China, but broke with China 1977 and subsequently completely isolated.

Albany, New York. First European settlement, Fort Nassau, planted by Dutch, 1614; occupied and renamed by English, 1664. Became state capital, 1797.

Albany, Dukes of. Title first created, 1398, for cadets of the Scottish royal house, and so used until 1536; borne by Darnley (*b.* 1545), consort of Mary Stuart, 1565–7; held by James I, Charles I, and James II (*see* ENGLISH SOVEREIGNS AND THEIR CONSORTS); by Ernst August, Bishop of Osnabrück, youngest brother of George I and other Hanoverian princes, intermittently from 1716 to 1827; lastly by Leopold George Duncan Albert, youngest son of Queen Victoria (*b.* 1853), 1881–4, and by his posthumous son, Arthur Charles Edward, who became the last reigning Duke of Saxe-Coburg (abdicated, 22 Oct. 1920).

Albert Canal (Belgium). Antwerp to Liège, opened June 1939.

Albert Memorials. Albert Hall, London, opened by Queen Victoria, 29 Mar. 1871. Memorial in Hyde Park, London, opened, 3 July 1872. Albert Memorial Chapel, Windsor, opened, 1 Dec. 1875. Albert Bridge, Chelsea, opened, 28 Aug. 1873.

Alberta, Canada. Constituted a province, 1905. University opened at Edmonton, 1908. Crude oil pipeline, 1,150 miles long, from Edmonton oilfields to Superior, Wisconsin, U.S.A., completed, 1951. Extended to Sarnia, Ontario, in 1953 (643 miles), making it the longest pipeline then existing in the world. The Trans-Canada natural gas pipeline in A. was longest in world in 1979 (over 5,700 miles).

Albigenses. Neo-Manichean sect, whose beginnings in France were discernible before 1022, and whose doctrines were denounced by councils of Arras (1025), Charroux (*c.* 1028), and Rheims (1049). Name A. first appeared *c.* 1181, derived from Albi, where they were specially numerous. Peter of Castelnau, papal legate sent to extirpate the heresy in the domains of Count Raymond VI of Toulouse, was murdered therein, 1208. Innocent III proclaimed the 'Albigensian Crusade,' 1209. Slaughtered included 20,000 inhabitants of Béziers, many having no connection with A. Raymond VII continued the struggle against the crusaders and Louis VIII; but made peace in 1229, and the persecution of A. was resumed. They disappear from history after the capture of their last stronghold, Mont Ségur, 1245.

Alcantara, Spain. Famous Roman bridge built, A.D. 105; restored, 1860. *See* KNIGHTHOOD, ORDERS OF.

Aldeburgh, Suffolk, was the first corporation in England to have a woman mayor—Mrs. Garrett-Anderson, 1908.

Aldersgate (London). Described as 'Ealdredesgate' *c.* 1000. Gate rebuilt, 1616. Pulled down, 1761.

Aldershot Camp (Hants). Formed, Apr. 1854.

Aldgate (London). Gate rebuilt, 1608. Pulled down, 1761. Pump renovated, 1908.

Aldine Press. Instituted by Aldo Manuzio (Aldus Manutius), at Venice, 1490. Italics first used, 1501. Aldus *d.* 1515. Press continued till 1597, and printed 908 different works.

Aldwych (London). Modern thoroughfare opened by Edward VII, 18 Oct. 1905.

Alençon, France. Castle built, 1026; Seized by William the Conqueror, 1048; by Henry II, 1135; restored to France, 1219. Captured by English, 1424, who were expelled, 1450.

Aleppo, Syria. Founded earlier than 2000 B.C. Taken by the Egyptians, 1460 B.C. Fell to the Crusaders under Baldwin II, A.D. 1124, and to the Tatars under Tamberlaine, 1400. Became Turkish, 1517. Destroyed by earthquake, 1822. *See* SYRIA.

Alès, in the Cevennes, was an important centre of the Huguenots, captured by Richelieu in 1629, who signed with them the Treaty of A., or *Edict of Grace*, depriving them of political privilege but guaranteeing their liberty of conscience. *See also* CAMISARDS.

Alessandria, Italy. Founded, 1168, and named after Pope Alexander III. Academy founded, 1562. French, 1800–1814. Cathedral built, 1823. Headquarters of Piedmontese during Lombardo-Venetian rebellion, 1848–9.

Aleutian Isles. Explored by Bering, 1768; Cook, 1778. Japanese got a foothold on Attu and Kiska islands, 1942, but were driven off by Americans, 1943.

Alexandra Land. *See* NORTHERN TERRITORY.

Alexandria, Egypt. Founded by Alexander the Great, 332 B.C. Capital of Egypt under Ptolemaic dynasty, 323–9 B.C. Captured by Caesar, 47 B.C. By Augustus, 29 B.C. Rebuilt by Hadrian, A.D. 122. Captured by Persians, 616; by Arabs, 640. Recovered and retaken, 644. Plundered by Crusaders, 1365. Taken by Turks, 1517. Captured by French, 1798. Taken by British under Abercromby and retaken by French, 1801. Taken by British under Frazer, 1807. Bombarded by British fleet, 1882. British naval base in World War II. Finally evacuated by British, 1947.

Alexandrian Library. Said to have been commenced by Ptolemy Soter *c.* 284 B.C. Badly damaged by fire, 47 B.C., and again in A.D. 391. Remains finally disappeared at or immediately after Omar's conquest of Alexandria in A.D.642.

Alexandrinus, Codex, or **Alexandrian Codex.** Probably a fifth-century scriptural MS in Greek presented by Patriarch of Alexandria and Constantinople to Charles I of England, 1628. Transferred to British Museum, 1757.

Algebra. First Greek textbook on this subject by Diophantus of Alexandria *c.* A.D. 350. Name originates in title of an Arabic textbook *c.* A.D. 820, '*Al-jebr wa'l-muquábala,*' by Al-Khwarizmi, which was translated into Latin by Robert of Chester *c.* 1146. Study of A. reintroduced to Europe by Leonardo of Pisa, 1202. Cubic equation first solved by Tartaglia, 1555. Descartes linked A. with geometry in 1637.

Algeciras, Spain. Taken by Moors, 711; by Spaniards under Alphonso XI, 1344. Naval engagements: 1. English and Spanish fleets defeated by French, 6 July 1801; 2. Result reversed, 12 July 1801. Conference at, concerning Moroccan affairs, Jan.–Apr. 1906.

Algiers and **Algeria,** Africa. City captured from Turks by Ferdinand of Spain, 1509, but lost again, 1530. The seaboard towns of the province remained the headquarters of the Barbary pirates for three centuries thereafer. The city was bombarded by an Anglo-Dutch fleet in 1816, but the pirates were only finally suppressed

when the French invaded and conquered the province in 1830. Annexed to France, Feb. 1842. Kabyle rising, 1871. From 1881 departments of Algiers, Oran, and Constantine an integral part of metropolitan France. Allies land during World War II at A., 8 Nov. 1942. Immense deposits of oil discovered at Hassi Messaoud, near Ouazgla, 1952 – two large oilfields in production by 1957 and by 1980 a major oil and natural gas producer. 1 Nov. 1954: Nationalist war against France begun in A., 1958: 'Free Algerian gov.' formed in Cairo: Algerian war resulted in fall of Fourth Republic in France and return to power of de Gaulle. 1962: peace signed between A. and France: Algerian independence proclaimed 3 July 1962: Fr. property taken over. Ben Bella became president of the Democratic People's Republic of A. in 1963. Govt. overthrown by military junta under Boumédienne in 1965. Return to civilian govt., 1977.

Algoa Bay, S. Africa. So named by Bartholomew Diaz, 1486. First British colonists landed at, 1820.

Alhambra (Arab. *alhamrah,* the red [castle]) at Granada (*q.v.*), built by the Nasride emirs, beginning A.D. 1213, and enlarged during a period extending into the fourteenth century. Part of the building dates from after the Christian reconquest, and was added in the reign of Charles V (1516–55), being started in 1526, but never finished.

Alicante, Spain. Besieged by Moors, 1331; by French, 1709. Bombarded by Cartagenan insurgents, 1 Oct. 1873. Bombed by Franco's aircraft in Spanish Civil War, 25 May 1938.

Alice Springs. Capital of Cental Australia territory from 1927 to 1931, when Central Australia once again became part of the Northern Territory (*q.v.*).

Aliens Acts (Great Britain). Jan. 1793. Act to register A., 1795. A. Act, 1905, came into force, 1 Jan. 1906. British Nationality and Status of A. Act, 1918, prohibited naturalization of Germans for ten years after official termination of World War I. New provisions, 1933. All Germans naturalized after 31 Dec.

1932 liable to internment under Regulation 18B in World War II. British Nationality Act, 1948, defined an alien as a person who was not a British subject, a British protected person, or a citizen of the Irish Republic. Modified by the requirements of the Commonwealth Immigrants Acts of 1962 and 1968 and by the British Nationality Act of 1981 (amended, 1983).

Alkmaar, Holland. Besieged by Spaniards under Alva, 1573. Town hall built, 1582. Captured by Duke of York's Dutch expedition, 2 Oct. 1799.

Allahabad, Uttar Pradesh State, India. Very anciently a holy place. Great mosque demolished, 1157. Fort built by Akbar, 1583. Occupied by British, 1765. Finally annexed, 1801. Massacre at, during Indian Mutiny, 1857. Univ. founded, 1887. First Indian National Congress held here, 1885.

Allegiance, Oath of. Statutes requiring: Elizabeth, 1559; William and Mary, 1689; Anne, 1701; combined with Oaths of Supremacy (*q.v.*) and Abjuration (*q.v.*); Victoria, 23 July 1858. Power to modify the oath to enable Jews to sit in Parliament, 23 July 1858; amended, 6 Aug. 1860. Form of affirmation in lieu of oath, 8 Apr. 1859.

All Souls' College (Oxford), founded, 1438 by Archbishop Henry Chichele in memory of those killed in action in the French wars of the period.

Almanacs. Earliest known published by Soloman Jarchus, 1150. First printed A. by Purbach, 1450. Bore a stamp duty in Britain, 1710–1834. British almanac first published, 1828. Almanach de Gotha first published, 1763.

Almeida, Portuagal. Taken and lost by Spaniards, 1762. Captured from British by French under Soult, 17 Aug. 1810. Recovered by Wellington, 11 May 1811.

Almeria, Spain, anciently **Urci**, became a Roman town, 19 B.C. Was a petty kingdom from 1288 to 1489. The cathedral dates from 1524.

Almohades. Moslem sect and dynasty founded in twelfth century in N. Africa (Berber). Founded by Mohammed Ibn Tumart. He and his successor,

Abd-el-Mumin, conquered much of N. Africa and Morocco between 1128 and 1149, and invaded Spain. Christian reconquest of Spain checked by them at Allarcos, 1185, but their decline was rapid after their defeat at Navas de Tolosa, 1212. By 1254 they were pinned into Granada, and the last of the line was murdered in 1269. *See* ALMORAVIDES and SPAIN.

Almoravides. Moslem sect and dynasty founded eleventh century. They conquered Morocco (*q.v.*), and founded Marrakesh *c.* 1080. In 1086 their leader Yusuf-ibn-Tashfin invaded Spain, and after uniting the various Moslem emirates there defeated the Christian Alfonso VI at Zalaca, 1086. After this a decline set in until they were superseded by the Almohades (*q.v.*), who captured Marrakesh in 1147.

Alnwick, Northumb., England. Besieged by Scots, 13 Nov. 1093; taken, 1136; burnt by King John of England, 1215; by Scots, 1448. Castle ceased to be residence of Dukes of Northumberland, 1945.

Alps. Crossed by Hannibal, 217 B.C.; by Romans, 154 B.C.; highest mountain (Mount Blanc) climbed by Paccard and Balmat, 1786; crossed by Napoleon, May 1800. Mont Cenis tunnel through A. completed, 25 Dec. 1870. St. Gotthard tunnel completed, 29 Feb. 1880. Simplon tunnel completed, 24 Feb. 1905. First flight by airman over A., Sept. 1910. Susten Pass post-road opened, 1946. Mont Blanc road tunnel opened, 1965.

Alsace. Came under French occupation by Peace of Westphalia, 1648. Annexed by Germany, 1871. Returned to France, 1919. Re-annexed to Germany, 1940. Retaken by France, 1945.

Alsatia. Nickname of district around Whitefriars, London, which had certain privileges of sanctuary and consequently became the resort of criminals. Privileges abolished, 1697.

Althing. *See* ICELAND.

Altona, in Schleswig-Holstein, became Danish in 1640. Burnt down during the Dano-Swedish War, 1713. Fiscal and other privileges granted by the Swedish crown withdrawn, 1853. Occupied by troops of the German Confederation, 1864, and became Prussian territory, 1866.

Altranstadt, Peace of.
1. 24 Sept. 1706, between Charles XII of Sweden and Augustus II of Poland.
2. 7 Mar. 1714, between Louis XIV and the Emperor Charles VI.

Aluminium. Discovered by Sir H. Davy, 1807. Woehler produced A. powder, 1827. First bar made by Deville, 1855.

'Amadis of Gaul'. Romance of uncertain origin, possibly fourteenth century, or possibly written in its present form by Garcia de Montalvo (late fifteenth century). Enlarged, 1492. First printed, 1508, in Spanish. Translated into French by Herberay des Essarts, 1540. Published in English in an abridged form by R. Southey, 1803.

Amalfi, Italy. Important naval power from seventh century. Fleet repulsed a Saracen invasion of Italy, 848. Independence suppressed by King Roger of Sicily, 1131. Town devasted by flood, 1343. Its Code of Sea Laws (*Tavole Amalfitane*) recognized throughout the Mediterranean till 1570.

Amarapura, Burma. Founded, 1783. Capital of Burma till 1823, and from 1837 to 1860.

Amatongaland (Tongaland), part of Natal Province, S. Africa, annexed to Natal, 1897.

Amazon River, S. America, first seen by Europeans under Vicente Yañez Pinzon, 1500. First descended (by Orellana), 1541, from which time the present European name appears to date. First ascended from its mouth as a route to Quito in Bolivia by Pedro Texeira, 1638.

Amboina, Amboyna, or **Ambon,** Moluccas, Indonesia. Trading station in native kingdom of Tidor. Occupied by Portuguese, 1562; seized by Dutch, 1605, who massacred the English merchants there in 1623. It was in British hands, 1790–1801 and 1810–16, when it was returned to the Dutch. Became part of Moluccas government, 1927. Captured by Japanese, Feb. 1942. Sur-

rendered by Japanese, 1945. Cap. of Moluccas Province since establishment of the Republic of Indonesia (*q.v.*) in 1950.

Amboise, Edict of, 19 Mar. 1563. Conceded freedom of worship to Huguenots.

Amboise, Tumult of, Jan. 1560. Huguenot conspiracy against the Guises suppressed by Catherine de' Medici.

Ambrosian Library (Milan). Founded by Cardinal Borromeo, 1602. Opened, 1609.

America, Discovery of. Named in honour of Amerigo Vespucci, a Florentine, who visited land, 1499. Norse colonies established in tenth and eleventh centuries in N. America. Columbus first discovered Cuba, Oct. 1492. Cabot discovered Labrador, 1497. Portuguese under Cabral discovered Brazil, 1500.

American Federation of Labor, founded 1881 by Samuel Gompers. Since 1955 merged with the Congress of Industrial Organizations.

American Literature in English. The following is a list of prominent American authors:

Adams, Henry Brooks (historian), 1838–1918.

Adeler, Max. *See* CLARK.

Alcott, Louisa May (novelist), 1832–88.

Allen, William Hervey (novelist), 1889–1949.

Allston, Washington (poet and novelist), 1779–1843.

Babbitt, Irving (critic), 1865–1933.

Bellow, Saul (novelist), 1905–.

Bemelmans, Ludwig (Austrian-born humorist and cartoonist), 1898–1962.

Benchley, Robert (humorist), 1889–1945.

Bromfield, Louis (novelist), 1896–1956.

Browne, Charles Farrar ('Artemus Ward') (humorist), 1834–67.

Bryant, William Cullen (poet), 1794–1878.

Cabell, James Branch (humorist), 1879–1958.

Cable, George Washington (novelist), 1844–1925.

Cather, Willa Sibert (novelist), 1876–1947.

Clark, Charles Heber ('Max Adeler') (humorist), 1841–1915.

Clemens, Samuel Langhorne ('Mark Twain') (humorist), 1835–1910.

Coolidge, Susan (Sarah Chauncy Woolsey) (children's writer), 1835–1905.

Cooper, James Fenimore (novelist), 1789–1851.

Crane, Stephen (novelist and poet), 1871–1900.

Crawford, Francis Marion (novelist), 1854–1909.

Dana, Richard Henry, jun. (miscellaneous writer), 1815–82.

Davis, Richard Harding (novelist), 1864–1916.

Dickinson, Emily (poetess), 1830–86.

Dos Passos, John Roderigo (novelist), 1896–1970.

Dreiser, Theodore (novelist), 1871–1945.

Dunbar, P. L. (poet), 1872–1916.

Eddy, Mary Baker Glover (Christian Scientist), 1821–1910.

Edwards, Jonathan (theologian), 1703–58.

Emerson, Ralph Waldo (poet and essayist), 1803–82.

Faulkner, William Harrison (novelist), 1897–1962.

Fiske, John (philosopher and historian), 1842–1901.

Fitzgerald, Francis Scott Key (novelist), 1896–1940.

Frost, Robert (poet), 1875–1963.

Franklin, Benjamin (statesman and journalist), 1706–90.

Galbraith, John Kenneth (economist), 1908–.

Gardner, Erle Stanley (detective-storywriter), 1889–1970.

George, Henry (economist), 1839–97.

Greeley, Horace (journalist), 1811–72.

Grey, Zane ('Western' novelist), 1872–1939.

Habberton, John (author of *Helen's Babies*), 1842–1921.

Harris, Joel Chandler (miscellaneous writer), 1848–1908.

Harte, Francis Bret (poet and storywriter), 1839–1902.

Hawthorne, Nathaniel (novelist), 1804–1863.

Hearn, Lafcadio (miscellaneous writer), 1850–1904.

Heller, Joseph (novelist), 1923–.

Hellmann, Lilian (dramatic writer) d. 1984.

Hemingway, Ernest Miller (novelist), 1899–1961.

'Henry, O.' *See* PORTER.

Holmes, Oliver Wendell (poet and miscellaneous writer), 1809–94.

Howe, Julia Ward (poetess), 1819–1910.

Irving, Washington (miscellaneous writer), 1783–1859.

James, Henry (novelist), 1843–1916.

James, William (philosopher), 1842–1910.

Johnson, James Weldon (poet), 1871–1938.

Lardner, Ringgold (Ring) Wilmer (journalist and short story writer), 1885–1933.

Lewis, Sinclair (novelist), 1885–1951.

Lindsay, Nicholas Vachel (poet), 1879–1931.

London, Jack (novelist), 1876–1916.

Longfellow, Henry Wadsworth (poet), 1807–82.

Lowell, Amy Lawrence (critic and poetess), 1874–1925.

Lowell, James Russell (poet and essayist), 1819–91.

Lowell, Robert (poet), 1917–77.

McCarthy, Mary (novelist and critic), 1912–.

Mahan, Alfred Thayer, Admiral (naval historian), 1840–1914.

Mailer, Norman (novelist), 1923–.

Marquis, Donald Robert Perry (humorist), 1878–1937.

Mather, Cotton (divine), 1663–1728.

Mather, Increase (divine), 1639–1723.

Melville, Herman (novelist), 1819–91.

Mencken, Henry Louis (critic), 1880–1956.

Miller, Arthur (dramatist), 1915–.

Miller, Henry (novelist), 1891–1980.

Mitchell, Margaret Munnerlyn (novelist), 1900–1949.

Morley, Christopher Darlington (novelist, poet, and essayist), 1890–1957.

Motley, John Lothrop (historian), 1814–1877.

Nash, Ogden (humorous poet), 1902–71.

Nathan, George Jean (critic), 1882–1958.

Norris, Frank (novelist), 1870–1902.

O'Neill, Eugene Gladstone (playwright), 1888–1953.

Parker, Dorothy (humorist), 1893–1967.

Parkman, Francis (historian), 1823–93.

Poe, Edgar Allan (poet and story-writer), 1809–49.

Porter, William Sydney ('O. Henry') (story-writer), 1867–1910.

Prescott, William Hickling (historian), 1796–1859.

Robinson, Edwin Arlington (poet), 1869–1935.

Roosevelt, Eleanor (diarist), 1884–1962.

Roth, Philip (novelist), 1933–.

Runyon, Alfred Damon (humorist), 1884–1944.

Salinger, J. D. (novelist), 1919–.

Santayana, George (philosopher), 1863–1952.

Sinclair, Upton Beall (novelist), 1878–1968.

Steinbeck, John Ernst (novelist and short-story writer), 1902–68.

Stockton, Frank Richard (story-writer), 1834–1902.

Stowe, Mrs. Harriet Elizabeth Beecher (novelist), 1812–96.

Stratton-Porter, Mrs. Gene (novelist and naturalist), 1868–1924.

Thompson, Dorothy (journalist), 1894–1961.

Thoreau, Henry David (naturalist and author), 1817–62.

Thurber, James Grover (humorist), 1894–1960.

Twain, Mark. *See* CLEMENS.

Updike, John (novelist and short story-writer), 1932–.

Van Doren, Charles Clinton (critic and biographer), 1885–1950.

Van Druten, John William (dramatist and novelist), 1901–57.

Vidal, Gore (novelist), 1925–.

Wallace, Lewis (religious novelist), 1827–1905.

Ward, Artemus. *See* BROWNE.

Warren, Robert Penn (novelist), 1905–.

Webster, Noah (lexicographer), 1758–1843.

Wharton, Edith Newbold (novelist), 1862–1935.

Whitman, Walt (poet), 1819–92.

Whittier, John Greenleaf (poet), 1807–92.

Wiggin, Kate Douglas (Mrs. Riggs) (novelist), 1856–1923.

Williams, Tennessee (dramatist), 1914–1983.

Wilson, Thomas Woodrow (historian and essayist), 1856–1923.

Woolman, John (Quaker essayist), 1720–1772.

Woolsey, Sarah Chauncy, *See* COOLIDGE.

Wouk, Herman (novelist and dramatist), 1915–.

American Republics. Haiti declared its independence, 1804; Chile, 1810; Colombia, 1811 (from this Venezuela and Ecuador seceded, 1830); Argentine, 1816; Paraguay, 1821; Peru, 1821; Mexico, 1821; Central American Confederation, 1828 (from which secession took place as follows: Guatemala, 1839; Costa Rica, 1839; Honduras, 1839; Nicaragua, 1839; Salvador, 1848. All had formed part of Mexico between 1821 and 1823); Bolivia, 1825; Uruguay, 1828 (after successive occupation by Brazilian and Argentine forces); Dominican Republic, 1844; Brazil, 1889; Cuba, 1897; Panama, 1903.

'America's' Cup, The. Cup originally called the Queen's cup, presented by the Royal Yacht Squadron in 1851 and won in that year by the American schooner *America*. Presented to New York Yacht Club by the owner in 1887; it has been called the A.C. ever since, and won by the U.S.A. until 1983, when Australia won it and the A.C. was taken to Australia.

Amiens, France. Cathedral built, 1220–88. Treaty of A. between Henry VIII, represented by Cardinal Wolsey, and Francis I, signed here, 18 Aug. 1527. Taken by Spanish, 11 Mar. 1597;

retaken by French, 25 Sept, 1597. Peace treaty signed, 25 Mar. 1802, between England, France, Spain, and Holland. Germans entered A., 28 Nov. 1870, during Franco-Prussian War. Threatened by Germans, 24 Apr. 1918. Occupied by Germans, 21 May 1940. Liberated by British, Aug. 1944.

Amiens, Mise of. The award pronounced by Louis XI of France, 23 Jan. 1264, in the dispute between Henry III of England and his barons. *See also* OXFORD, PROVISIONS OF.

Amman, Jordan (Biblical *Rabath-Ammon*. Gr. *Philadelphia*). Became capital of Transjordan, 1921. *See* JORDAN.

Amoy or **Hsiamen,** China. Trading with A. permitted, 1676. The fort destroyed by British, July 1840. Town captured, 26 Aug. 1841. Port opened by treaty for trade, 26 Aug. 1842. Occupied by Japanese, 1938. Returned to China, 1945. A. linked to mainland by two stone embankments, 1956.

Amritsar became the headquarters of the Sikh religious movement, 1574. Golden Temple destroyed, 1761; rebuilt, 1764, and roofed with copper gilt by Ranjit Singh, 1802. The 'A. Massacre' took place, 13 Apr. 1919. Indian army stormed Golden Temple, June 1984.

Amsterdam, Holland. Founded, 1204. Charter granted, and Old Church built, 1300. New Church, 1408. Dutch E. India Co. established at, 1602. University founded, 1632. Surrendered to Prussians, 1787. To French, 1795. N. Holland Canal built, 1819–25. N. Sea Canal, 1865–95. Occupied by Germans, 14 May 1940. Liberated, 12 May 1945. Canal linking A. with River Waal opened, 1952.

Anabaptists. Said to have been founded by Thomas Münzer *c.* 1520. A. state established under John of Leyden at Münster, 1533–5. Laws against, 1525–1534. *See* BAPTISTS.

'Anabasis'.
1. *See* TEN THOUSAND.
2. Arrian's account (A.D. 166–8) of Alexander the Great's campaigns.

Anaesthetics. Laughing gas first used as anaesthetic by Sir H. Davy, 1800. Ether by Morton, 1846. Chloroform by Sir J. Y. Simpson, 1847. Local A. first used, 1884.

Analyst, Public. A professional association founded in 1874 adopted the designation 'of Public and other As.' in 1907. Appointment of Public As. is now governed by provisions of the Food and Drugs Act, 1955.

Anarchism. First formulated as a modern political theory by Godwin, 1793. Elaborated by Proudhon, 1840. Four anarchists hanged at Chicago, 1886. Prominent in Sp. Civil War 1936–9. Anarchism blamed for much international terrorism since 1960s, notably in Germany, France and Italy.

Anatolia or **Asia Minor.** Conquered by Cyrus, 546 B.C. By Alexander the Great, 334. Roman province of 'Asia' established, 133. Roman conquest complete, 63 B.C. Invaded by Chosroes II of Persia, 616–26. By Arabs, 668. Central A. subdued by Seljuk Turks, 1071–80. Destruction of Seljuk power by Mongols, 1243. Ottoman power established at Brusa, 1307. Final Ottoman conquest, 1481. (For later history *see* OTTOMAN EMPIRE and TURKISH REPUBLIC.)

Anatomical Society of Great Britain. Founded, 1887.

Ancient Buildings, Society for Protection of. Established, 1877.

Ancient Lights. Law passed, 1 Aug. 1832.

Ancona, Italy. Founded by refugees from Syracuse *c.* 390 B.C. Rebuilt by Trajan, A.D. 107. Besieged: 1. by Frederick Barbarossa, 1167. 2. by Christian, Archbishop of Mainz, 1173. Annexed to Papal States, 1532. Captured by French, 1797; by Austrians, 1799; by French, 1801. Restored to Papal States, 1802. Occupied by French, 1832; evacuated, 1838. Bombarded by Austrians, 18 June 1849. A. (with other towns) rebelled against Papacy, Sept. 1860, and has been since part of Italian state. Severely damaged by bombardment, 1943.

Andaman and **Nicobar Islands,** in the Bay of Bengal. A British settlement was made on North Andamans, 1789.

Used as penal settlement, 1858–1942. Nicobar Is. ceded to Britain by Netherlands, 1869. The Japanese occupied the A.I. 1942–45. Part of India since 1947.

Anderida. *See* SUSSEX.

Andorra (officially **Las Valls d'Andorra**). Small semi-independent republic in the Pyrenees. Counts of Foix and Spanish Bishop of Urgel became co-princes of A., 1278. French office of Co-Prince descended through the French monarchy to the President of the French Republic in modern times, and A. is therefore under French protection. Mild revolution occurred in 1933 when franchise was broadened.

Angers, France. Taken from Romans, A.D. 464; fortified *c.* 859–60. Castle completed by Louis IX. Town burnt by King John of England, 1206; taken by Huguenots, 1585; attacked by Vendéan army, 1793. Church of Saint-Serge built, 1050.

Angevins. *See* ENGLISH SOVEREIGNS.

Angkor, Cambodia. Famous Khmer temple at, built *c.* ninth-twelfth centuries.

Anglesey, Wales. Conquered by Romans under Agricola, A.D. 78. Hugh of Chester's attempt to conquer A. frustrated with Viking assistance, 1098. Subdued and organized by Edward I, 1295–8.

Anglia, East, kingdom founded *c.* A.D. 500. Submitted to Egbert of Wessex, 826. Subsequently invaded by the Danes, who held it until forced to submit to Edward the Elder, 918. One of the four great earldoms under Canute.

Anglia, East, University of, estab. at Norwich, 1963.

Anglo-Saxon Chronicle, or more correctly **Chronicles**. Of the six different texts which survive all appear to have been begun in the reign of Alfred the Great, probably after 880, though they incorporate matter taken from much earlier chronicles which were kept up in Northumbrian religious houses from the middle of the seventh to the end of the eighth century. Between them they record events in Britain from A.D. 449 to 1154.

Angola. Discovered, 1486, and colonized by Portuguese. Occupied by Dutch, 1641. Restored to Portugal, 1648. Anticolonial revolution in A. from 1961, led to a People's Republic of A. being proclaimed, Nov. 1975.

Angoulême, France. Became English possession by marriage of Henry II with Eleanor of Aquitaine, 1152; annexed to France, 1303; restored to England, 1360; reconquered by French, 1373.

Anguilla, W. Indies, discovered and colonized by the British, 1650. Anguillan resentment of gov. from St. Kitts led to Brit. troops being landed there to maintain order, 19 March 1969: reverted to direct Brit. rule 1971. Anguilla Act, 1981, confirmed independence from St. Kitts.

Anhalt, Germany. Separated from Saxony, thirteenth century. Continual subdivision between various petty princes continued till 1800. The remaining duchies of A.-Bernburg and A.-Dessau united, 1863, under Leopold of A.-Dessau. Assisted Prussia in war of 1866. Joined German Empire, 1871. Now mainly in the district of Halle.

Aniline Dyes. Discovered by Unverdorben, 1826.

Anjou, France. Conquered by Henry II of England, 1156; by Philip II of France from King John, 1204; retaken by Edward III and afterwards given up, 1360. Finally annexed to French crown, 1480. Battle of A. (or Beaugé), English defeated by French, 22 Mar. 1421.

Ankara or **Angora** (anciently **Ancyra**). Ottoman capital in fourteenth century. Became capital of Turkey, 1923.

Annam. Under Chinese rule till A.D. 968, when local monarchy established. Independent, 1428. First French expedition to, 1787. French protectorate, 1884. Part of Vietnam since 1945. *See* INDO-CHINA and VIETNAM.

Annapolis, Maryland., U.S.A. U.S. Naval Academy founded, 1845.

Annapolis Royal, Nova Scotia. Settled by French (as Fort Royal), 1605. Taken by English, 1614 and 1710. Ceded to Britain, 1713. Capital of Nova Scotia till 1879. *See* ACADIA and NOVA SCOTIA.

Annapurna. Mountain in Himalayas, N.

Nepal. Height 26,493 ft. Was first peak of over 26,000 ft. to be climbed (by Herzog and Lachenal of the French Himalayan Expedition, 3 June, 1950).

Annates, or **First Fruits.** First year's profits of a living claimed by the bishop. Suppressed in France by edicts, 1406, 1417, 1418, 1463, and 1464. Prohibited in England by Henry IV. Parliament granted them to the crown in 1534, but in 1704 Queen Anne applied them to the augmentation of poor livings. *See also* QUEEN ANNE'S BOUNTY.

Annobon Island, *See* PAGALU.

Annual Register. A yearly record of public events first published in London, 1759 (for the year 1758). For thirty years Edmund Burke (1729–97) wrote the survey of events.

Ansbach, or **Anspach**, Bavaria. Grew up round the monastery founded by St. Humbert in the eighth century. Acquired by Burgraves of Nürnberg, 1331; combined with Bayreuth to form a margravate, 1398. Monastery dissolved, 1560. United with Prussia, 1791; but awarded to Bavaria by Napoleon, 1806.

Anschluss. Political union of Austria and Germany, 12 Mar. 1938.

Antarctica. *See* ARCTIC AND ANTARCTIC REGIONS and QUEEN MAUD LAND.

Antarctic Ocean. *See* ARCTIC AND ANTARCTIC REGIONS.

Anti-Aircraft Command. Established, 1939. Disbanded, 1955.

Anti-Comintern Pact. Between Germany and Japan, 25 Nov. 1936. Joined by Italy, 6 Nov. 1937. By Hungary and Spain, 1939. By Slovakia, Rumania, and Bulgaria, 1941.

Anti-Corn Law League. Founded Manchester, 18 Sept. 1838. Deputies assembled London, 8 Feb. 1842. Corn Laws repealed, 6 June 1846. League dissolved, 2 July 1846.

Antigua. Discovered by Columbus, 1493. First English settlement, 1632. Formally ceded to Britain by Treaty of Breda, 1667. Became part of Leeward Islands Federation, 1871. Crown colony, 1956: independent, Nov. 1981.

Antioch, now **Antakya,** Turkey. Founded 300 B.C. by Seleucus Nicator. Christ-

ians first so-called here, A.D. 42. Destroyed by Persians, A.D. 540. Rebuilt by Justinian, 542–5. Conquered by Arabs, 637. Captured by Crusaders, 1098, and became a Christian principality till 1268, when it was taken by Bibars, Sultan of Egypt. Made part of Syria, 1920, but restored to Turkey, 1939.

Antipopes. *See* PAPACY.

Antiquaries, Society of. Founded, 1572. Dissolved by James I, 1604. Reconstituted, 1707. Charter, 2 Nov. 1751. George III granted the society apartments in Somerset House, 1780.

Anti-Saloon League of America. Founded 1893, in Ohio. Succeeded in 1948 by the Temperance League of America, which merged with the National Temperance Movement in 1950 to form the National Temperance League.

Anti-Slavery Association. *See* SLAVE TRADE.

Antonine Wall, Scotland. Built *c.* A.D. 140–1.

Antwerp, Belgium. Probably founded by Frankish tribes *c.* eighth century. Citadel burnt by Spaniards, 4 Nov. 1576 ('The Spanish Fury'). Besieged and captured by Parma, 1584–5; Marlborough captured, 6 June 1706; Marshal Saxe captured, 9 May 1746; captured by French, 29 Nov. 1792. Part of Netherland kingdom, 1815–30; cession to Belgium confirmed, 1839; besieged by Germans, 4–6 Oct., surrendered, 9 Oct. 1914. Albert Canal linking A. to Liège opened, June 1939. Occupied by Germans, May 1940. Captured by British, Sept. 1944. Bombarded by German V-weapons, Nov. 1944–May 1945.

Anur or **Tarracina,** town of the Volsci (*q.v.*) under Roman supremacy, 509 B.C. Stormed by Volsci, 397. Retaken by Romans, 312. Sacked by Goths, A.D. 409, and again, 595. Temple of Jupiter A. built first century B.C.

Anzac. Landing of As. (i.e. Australia and New Zealand Army Corps) in Gallipoli in World War I, 25 Apr. 1915.

Anzio, anciently **Antium**, conquered by Romans, 468 B.C. Revolted and subdued, 338. The beach-head (known to the Germans as the Nettuno beachhead) established here by Allied Forces, 22 Jan. 1944, was maintained until 25 May, when contact by land was made with Fifth Army.

Anzus. Defence treaty modelled on treaty setting up N.A.T.O. (*q.v.*), signed San Francisco 1951, ratified 1952, dealing with security in the Pacific. Members are Australia, New Zealand, U.S.A. Further strengthened 1954 by the South East Asia Collective Defence Treaty (the Manila Treaty).

Aosta, Valle d', came into possession of Counts of Savoy, 1032. Gran Paradiso area, set aside as a game reserve by the Crown Prince of Piedmont in 1836, became a National Park in 1920. Minor adjustment of Franco-Italian frontier, 1945; confirmed by treaty, 1947.

Apartheid, *See* COLOUR BAR.

Apollo Belvedere. Found at Porto d'Anzio early in the sixteenth century. Bought by Pope Julius II, 1511. Taken to Paris by French, 1797. Restored to Vatican, 1815.

Apollo of Rhodes. 'The Colossus', wonder of the world, sculpture of Chares of Lindus 292–280 B.C. Overthrown by earthquake, 224 B.C. Broken up, A.D. 653.

Apostles' Creed. *See* CREEDS.

Apothecaries. First apothecary in England traditionally John Falcourt of Lucca 1362. Licensed by Bishop of London, 1511. Society chartered, 1606 (with Grocers); separately, 1617. House of Lords pronounced that A. could prescribe for a sick patient without the advice of a physician, 1704. 1774: Society of A. limited its membership to those who were practising A. (i.e. medical practitioners). 1815: Act of Parliament gave society power to examine all A. in England and Wales and grant them licences to practise.

Appeal of Felony. *See* BATTLE, WAGER OF.

Appellants or **Lords Appellant.** The nobles who protested against certain ministers of Richard II in 1387. They caused the death of two of these ministers. In 1388 the L.A. convened the Merciless Parliament.

Appenzell, Swiss canton, settled by Alle-manni before A.D. 600. Joined the Confederation, 1513.

Appian Way (Via Appia) Italy. A famous roadway from Rome to Capua via Albano, begun by Appius Claudius Caecus, 312 B.C. and extended to Brindisi via Benevento. Excavations were instituted by the papal court, 1850–3, and part of the road was reopened. Now Strada Nazionale 6.

Apprentices, Statute of, 1562 (England). No person allowed to work at a trade without previously serving seven years' apprenticeship. Repealed, 1814.

Approved Schools, i.e. approved by the Home Office. Term came into use with the passing of the Children and Young Persons' Act, 1933. Discontinued 1969.

Apsley House (London). Built 1771–8 for Baron Apsley, 2nd Earl Bathurst. Bought by the Duke of Wellington, 1820. Presented by the 7th Duke to the nation, 1947. Opened as a museum 1952.

Apulia or **Puglie,** Italy. Conquered by Rome, 317 B.C. Devastated in Social War, 90–88 B.C. Became part of the Kingdom of the Two Sicilies, 1134; and of Italy, 1861.

Aquileia, Italy. Founded 181 B.C. Strategically important at head of Adriatic. Destroyed by Attila, A.D. 452. Cathedral dates from 11th century. Part of Holy Roman Empire (*q.v.*) then of Austria, until acquired by Italy in 1918.

Aquitaine, E. France. Conquered by Franks, A.D. 507; separate state, 700; united to France, 1137; became part of English crown by marriage of Henry II and Eleanor of A., 1152; province finally lost under Henry VI, 1453.

Arab League. Founded Mar. 1945 and in 1985 consisted of 22 members, including Palestine which was termed an independent state, though Egypt's membership was suspended Mar. 1979, when Tunis was made the A.L's temporary headquarters.

Arabia. Minaean Kingdom in Jauf, 1200–650 B.C. Sabaean (Sheba) Kingdom from 1500 B.C. Rise of the Himyarite Kingdom, 115 B.C. Ethiopian rule in Yemen, A.D. 525–75. (For later

history down to 1917, *see* CA-
LIPHATE; OTTOMAN EMPIRE, etc.) Con-
quered by Ibn Saud, 1924, and renamed
Saudi Arabia (*q.v.*).

Aragon. , N-E Spain. Recovered from the
Moors, 1131. Continuous southward
expansion at the expense of the Moors
checked at battle of Alarcos, 1185. Catalonia united with it, 1137. In alliance
with Castile to win great victory at
Navas de Tolosa, 1212. Valencia united with it, 1238. Moors practically
subdued by Jaime I (1213–76). King
Ferdinand II of A. married Isabella,
Queen of Castile, 1469.

Aragon, Sovereigns of:
Ramiro I 1035–1063
Sancho I 1063–1094
Pedro I 1094–1104
Alfonso I. the Battler 1104–1134
Ramiro II 1134–1137
Petronilla 1137–1162
Alfonso II 1162–1196
Pedro II 1196–1213
Jaime I, the Conqueror 1213–1276
Pedro III 1276–1285
Alfonso III, the Magnificent
  1285–1291
Jaime II 1291–1327
Alfonso IV, the Fair 1327–1336
Pedro IV 1336–1387
Juan I 1387–1395
Martin I 1395–1410
Ferdinand I 1410–1416
Alfonso V, the Magnanimous
  1416–1458
Juan II 1458–1479
Ferdinand II, the Catholic 1479–1516
  (from 1474 Ferdinand V of Castile)
See further under SPAIN, SOVEREIGNS
OF.

Arbitration, Industrial. Purely voluntary
in England until 1896, when legislation placed it on a legal footing, based
on the Conciliation Act, 1896, and
Industrial Courts Act, 1919. Present
practice based on legislation passed in
1970s.

Arbitration, International Court of. Established at The Hague, 1900. Italo-
Greek dispute settled by A., 1923. Bul-
garo-Greek dispute settled by permanent court of International Justice
(*q.v.*), 1924. Ditto Sino-Belgian dis-

pute, 1924, and Franco-Turkish *Lotus*
case, 1926. A re-estab. under U.N.,
1945. 1951: Court of International Justice awarded Britain compensation
against Albania (*q.v.*) for mined destroyers, but Albania ignored the order.
Britain suggested referring Gibraltar
(*q.v.*, dispute between Britain and
Spain to international arbitration,
1966, but Spain rejected the offer. 46
cases referred to A., 1945–82.

Arc de Triomphe de l'Étoile,   Paris.
Begun, 1506. Finished, 1836.

**Archaeological Association and Insti-
tute** (London). Established, 1843.

Archangel (Arkhangel'sk),   Russia.
Founded, 1584. Blockaded by British
fleet, 1854. Allied landing against Bolsheviks, 1918: evacuation, 1919. One
of the ports of destination on the con-
voy route to Russia in World War II.

Archbishop. Title first used in the
Eastern Church 320; in Rome, 420.

Arches, Court of. Sat in St. Mary-le-Bow
from *c.* 1085 till removed to Doctor's
Commons, 1567. In Lambeth Palace
since 1876.

Architectural Societies (London). Institute of British Architects, 1834. Incorporated and made royal by charter, 11
Jan. 1837. Society of Architects
founded, 1884: amalgamated with
Royal Institute of British Architects,
1925. A. Association founded, 1847.
American Institute of Architects,
1857.

Arcot. Former capital of the Carnatic. Its
successful defence by Clive in 1751 was
the decisive event in the Anglo-French
struggle for India. Taken by Hyder Ali,
1780. Ceded to E. India Co., 1801.

Arctic and Antarctic Regions, principal
expeditions before 1912.

Arctic Regions:

Date	Explorer
1496	Sebastian Cabot
1498	John Cabot
1553	Sir Hugh Willoughby and Richard Chancellor
1576 1577 1578	Frobisher
1584 1595	William Barents

1585 ⎫		1853–5	Kane
1586 ⎬ John Davis		1857–9	McClintock
1587 ⎭		1859–60	Hayes
1602	George Waymouth	1870–2	Hall
1607–11	Hudson	1871–2	Merriman
1612–13	Bylot and Button	1872–3	Green
1614	Bylot and Gibbons	1875–6	Nares and Stephenson
1615–16	Baffin	1879	G.W. DeLong
1631	James	1880	Leigh Smith
1676	Capt. Wood	1887	Col. Gilder
1728 ⎫		1893–6	Dr. Nansen
1729 ⎬ Bering		1893	Peary
1741 ⎭		1895	Jackson
1735	Chelyuskin	1897	Andrée
1773	Phipps and Lutwidge	1899	Wellman

1585 ⎫
1586 ⎬ John Davis
1587 ⎭
1602   George Waymouth
1607–11 Hudson
1612–13 Bylot and Button
1614   Bylot and Gibbons
1615–16 Baffin
1631   James
1676   Capt. Wood
1728 ⎫
1729 ⎬ Bering
1741 ⎭
1735   Chelyuskin
1773   Phipps and Lutwidge
        (Horatio Nelson in this
        expedition)
1778   Cook and Clerke
1806 ⎫ Scoresby
1822 ⎭
1818   John Ross
1818   Buchan and Franklin
1819–22 Franklin
1819–20 ⎫
1821–3 ⎬ Parry
1824–5 ⎭
1824   Lyon
1819   ⎫ Parry
1824–5 ⎭
1825–7   Franklin
1826–8   Buchan
1829–33 John Ross
1833–5 ⎫ Back
1836–7 ⎭
1836–9   Dean and Simpson
1845–6   Franklin
1846–7   Rae
1848–9 ⎰ John Ross
        ⎱ Richardson
1848–52 Moore
1849–50 ⎰ Hooper
        ⎱ Saunders
1849–51 Pullen
        ⎧ John Ross
1850–1 ⎨ Penny
        ⎩ De Haven and Kane
1850–4   M'Clure
1850–5   Collinson
1851–2   Kennedy
1851–4   Rae
        ⎧ Maguire
1852–4 ⎨ Belcher
        ⎪ Kellett
        ⎩ Pullen

1853–5   Kane
1857–9   McClintock
1859–60 Hayes
1870–2   Hall
1871–2   Merriman
1872–3   Green
1875–6   Nares and Stephenson
1879   G.W. DeLong
1880   Leigh Smith
1887   Col. Gilder
1893–6   Dr. Nansen
1893   Peary
1895   Jackson
1897   Andrée
1899   Wellman
1902   ⎰ Peary
       ⎱ Sverdrup
1909   Peary (discovery of N. Pole,
        6 Apr.)
        ⎧ Mikkelsen
1909–12 ⎨ Amundsen
        ⎩ Stefansson

Capt. Sedoff's Russian expedition started for Franz Josef Land, 1912; returned, 1915, without Sedoff, who, having set out for N. Pole, had perished. Vilkitsky's expedition, 1915. Stefansson's *Karluk*, on Alaskan expedition on behalf of Canadian Government, sank 40 miles from Wrangel Islands, Jan. 1914; in 1915 he discovered new land N. of Prince Patrick Islands; in 1916 more new land W. of Axel Heiberg Islands, and in 1918 he explored Beaufort Sea, disproving existence of Keenan Land. Amundsen's aeroplane voyage toward N. Pole from Spitzbergen, 21 May–15 June 1925. Byrd flew over N. Pole, 1926. In 1928 Sir Hubert Wilkins flew from Alaska to Dead Man's Land, Spitzbergen; in the same year Gen. Nobile made three flights in his dirigible *Italia*, but was wrecked off N.E. Land. He was rescued, but Amundsen, who had joined in the relief expeditions, perished. Gino Watkins on the Greenland ice-cap, 1931. Ushakov expedition N. of Cape Chelyuskin, 1931–2. Soviet exploration of Nordenskjold Island, 1936; French Polar research ship *Pourquoi Pas* sank off Iceland, Sept. 1936; Otto Schmidt's meteorological survey of N. Polar regions, 1937.

Antarctic Regions.

Visited by Cook in 1773 and 1774. Land discovered by Bellingshausen (Peter I and Alexander I Lands), 1821; by Capt. Biscoe, Feb. 1831; by Capt. D'Urville, 1838. Ross discovered and explored Victoria Land, 1839–1843; Nares in the *Challenger* first crossed the Antarctic Circle, 1874. Principal expeditions to: Christensen first to set foot on Antarctic continent, 1894; C. E. Borchgrevink landed at Cape Adare, 23 Feb. 1895; second expedition, equipped by Sir George Newnes, reached Cape Adare, 17 Feb. 1899; de Gerlache expedition, 16 Aug. 1897–28 Mar. 1899; German expedition, under Capt. H. Ruser, 11 Aug. 1901; British expedition, under Capt. Scott, 24 Dec. 1901–10 Sept. 1904; Dr. Bruce's Scottish expedition, Jan. 1903–July 1904; Dr. Jean Charcot, French expedition, 1904–5 and 1908–10; Lieut. (later Sir Ernest) Shackleton's expedition, 1907–9; Dr. David, with Mr. D. Mawson and Dr. Mackay, found the S. magnetic pole to be at 72° 25′ S., 155° 16′ E. on 16 Jan. 1909; Capt. Amundsen's expedition, 1910, S. Pole reached, 16 Dec. 1911; Capt. Scott, British expedition, 1910–13, reached S. Pole, 17 Jan. 1912 (Capt. Scott was found dead by a search party, 12 Nov. 1913); Sir Ernest Shackleton's *Endurance* left on 'Farther South' expedition, 1 Aug. 1914; returned, 1916; Shackleton, with *Quest*, started, 1921; reached S. Georgia, where Shackleton *d.*, 5 Jan. 1922; in 1928 Wilkins flew over Graham Land and proved that it was not part of the main mass of the Antarctic continent; the British Colonial Office, through the 'Discovery Committee', sent out *Discovery I* on whaling research expedition; *Discovery II* was sent out in 1930 and 1931, and between 1935 and 1937 circumnavigated Antarctic continent; Norwegian expeditions, 1935 and 1937; Byrd expeditions (U.S. Navy), 1928–9; 1933–8; 1939–40; 1946; 1947–50: Fuchs organized the Falkland Islands Dependencies Survey in the Antarctic; 1957–8: Expeditions from various countries co-operated in Antarctic exploration to mark the International Geophysical Year; 1957–8: Fuchs and Hillary led British Transantarctic Expedition: Fuchs left Shackleton Base on Weddell Sea, 24 Nov. 1957; reached S. Pole, 19 Jan. 1958; Scott Base on McMurdo Sound, 2 Mar. 1958. Fuchs thus became first man to traverse the Antarctic, completing 2,200 miles in ninety-nine days. Antarctic Treaty, 1 Dec. 1959 signed between major powers regulating status of ter. claims in Antarctica. Considerable scientific research carried out since then, notably by U.S.A. *See also* QUEEN MAUD LAND.

Arezzo, anciently **Arretium,** an Etruscan city, made a treaty with Rome, 308 B.C. Beseiged by Gauls, 283. Defeated in a war with Florence, A.D. 1289, and became a Florentine possession, 1348. Church of St. Francis built, 1322.

Argentaeus, Codex, discovered in the abbey library of Werden, Westphalia, by the topographer Mercator (alias Gerhard Kraemer, 1512–94), and brought to Prague for the collection of the Emperor Rudolf II (reigned 1576–1611); on the storming of the city by the Protestant faction in 1648, the looted MS. was taken to Stockholm by Count Königsmark. It was presented by Marshal de la Gardie to Upsala University, 1669. It was first reproduced in print, 1665.

Argentina. Rio de la Plata visited by Spaniards, 1515. Buenos Aires (*q.v.*) founded 1536 by Pedro de Mendoza, and made part of the Viceroyalty of Peru. Buenos Aires captured by British expedition from Cape Town, 1806, but British surrendered shortly after. Viceroy deposed, 25 May 1810. Independence proclaimed at Congress of Tucuman, 9 July 1816. Independence recognized by Britain and U.S.A., 1823. By Spain, 1842. Republic extended to Rio Negro, 1878–80. Patagonia divided with Chile (*q.v.*) by treaty, 1881. Peron became president, June 1946 and carried through sweeping radical changes involving considerable nationalization. Revolution by dissident factions resulted in Peron's deposition (22 Sept. 1955) and exile. Peronists in power again 1973–76, but unstable economic and political situation led to a series of military coups. Argentine forces invaded the Falkland Is. (*q.v.*) 2 Apr. 1982: defeated by the British and surrendered 14 June. Galtieri resigned as president, succeeded by Bignone. Democratic elections, 1983 and radical Alfonsin elected. Trials of junta leaders followed.

Heads of the State (Presidents) from the Establishment of the Republic, 1853:

Urquiza 1853–1860
Derqui 1860–1862
Mitre 1862–1868
Sarmiento 1868–1874
Avellaneda 1874–1880
Roca 1880–1886
Celman 1886–1890
Pellegrini 1890–1892
Pena 1892–1898
Roca 1898–1904
Quintana 1904–1906
Alcorta 1906–1910
Pena 1910–1914
De la Plaza 1914–1916
Irigoyen 1916–1922
Alvear 1922–1928
Irigoyen 1928–1930
Uriburu 1930–1932
Justo 1932–1938
Ortiz 1938–1942
Castillo 1942–1943
Rawson (two days)June 1943
Ramirez June 1943–1944
Farrell 1944–1946
Peron 1946–1955
Lonardi (3 weeks) 1955
Arambru 1955–1958
Frondizi 1958–1962
Guido 1962–1963
Illia 1963–1966
Ongania 1966–1970
Levingston 1970–71
Lanusse 1971–73
Cámpora 1973
Peron 1973–74
Maria Peron 1974–76
Videla 1976–81
Galtieri 1981–82
Bignone 1982–83
Alfonsin 1983–

Arianism. Propounded by Arius (256–336) *c.* 321. Synod of Bithynia upheld him against St. Athanasius, who was banished, 323. Condemned by Council of Nicaea, 325. His doctrines have since been condemned by numerous councils, but were the basis of 'State' churches in the Gothic and Vandal kingdoms (*q.v.*). As an organized creed A. died out before 600.

Arizona. Discovered by Marcos de Niza, 1539; first settled by Spanish missionaries *c.* 1772. Largely ceded as a result of the Mexican War, 1848; the remaining territory, comprising modern A., was acquired by the Gadsden Purchase of 1853, and its present boundaries were fixed in 1863: admitted to the Union, 14 Feb. 1912.

Arkansas, explored by De Soto, 1541, and settled by French, 1686. Purchased by U.S. Government, 1803; organized as a territory, 1819; admitted to the Union, 1836.

Arles, France. Greek colony refounded by the Romans *c.* 47 B.C. Roman theatre and amphitheatre built, second century A.D. Became capital of Gaul and an archbishopric in fourth century, and became capital of the kingdom of Provence or Arelate at end of ninth century. First Synod of A., 314. Cathedral built, eleventh century, and rebuilt twelfth and fourteenth centuries. Amphitheatre converted into a fortress, twelfth century. Archbishopric abolished, 1790.

Armada, The Spanish. Left Lisbon, 29 May 1588; arrived off Lizard, 19 July; Howard met A., 21 July, and kept up running fight until 25 July; A. anchored in Calais Roads, 26 July; met there by Howard and pursued until 22 Aug., though organized fighting ended 30 July.

Armagnacs or **Orléanists.** The anti-Burgundian (and therefore patriotic) party formed in 1396, first under the leadership of the Duke of Orleans. They played a decisive part in driving the British from France. Their objects being achieved by the Treaty of Arras, 1435, the faction ceased to exist.

'Armed Neutrality'. Confederacy of northern powers against maritime policy of England, commenced by Russia, 1780: its objects defeated, 1781; renewed, 16 Dec. 1800; dissolved after Nelson's victory at Copenhagen, 16 Dec. 1801.

Armenia (Hayastan), Asia. Subject in turn to Assyrians, Medes, and Persians. Conquered by Alexander, 325 B.C. Under Roman influence in early part of Christian era. Christianity introduced by St. Gregory the Illuminator in third century. Conquered by Mongols, 1242. Reigning dynasty overthrown by Saracens, 1375. Continually persecuted by Turks. Massacres, 1895–7. In 1918, during the Russian Revolution, an independent 'Republic of Transcaucasia' was formed by union of A. with Azerbaijan and Georgia. Occupied by Red Army, 1920, and transformed into a Soviet republic, which in 1922 was included in the Transcaucasian Federal Republic of the U.S.S.R. When this was abolished, 1936, A. itself became a constituent republic of the U.S.S.R.

Arminianism. A doctrine of free will propounded by Jacobus Arminius, who was professor at Leyden University from 1603 till his death in 1609. A. savagely persecuted by Calvinists after the Synod of Dort (*q.v.*), 1618–19.

Armistice between Germany and Allies signed at Compiègne, 11 Nov. 1918. Between France and Germany at Compiègne, 22 June 1940. Between France and Italy, near Rome, 24 June 1940. Between N. Korea and the U.N. forces, 27 July 1953.

Army, British. Oldest English corps, the Yeomen of the Guard (*q.v.*), founded, 1485. Gentlemen-at-Arms (*q.v.*) 1509. Honourable Artillery Company, chartered 1537. 1st Foot (Royal Scots), 1633. Household troops established, 1661. Standing armies declared illegal in First Mutiny Act, 1689; Second Act, 1803. E. India Co.'s army absorbed, 1858. Flogging abolished in peacetime, 1868. A. Act, 1881. Short Service Act, 1870, and abolition of commission by purchase, 1871—part of the Cardwell (Secretary of War, 1868–74) reforms. Haldane's new A. scheme,

1906. Territorial and Reserve forces Act, July 1907. Kitchener's A., 1915. Derby Scheme, 1915. Conscription introduced, 1916; ended, 1918. Territorial A. formed, 1920. Southern Irish regiments disbanded and cavalry regiments reduced, 1922. Field Punishment No. 1 abolished, 1923. Mechanization, 1935. Conscription into militia (*q.v.*) introduced, 9 May 1939; ended, 1960. Army reorganization, complete by the end of 1962, included reducing the number of line cavalry and infantry regiments by amalgamation. *See also* REGIMENTS OF THE BRITISH ARMY and VOLUNTEERS.

Army Council. When office of C.-in-C. abolished A.C. was set up under the Secretary of State for War, 1904.

Army Plot, a rumoured attempt by the Royal A. to coerce parliament to obey Charles I, 1641.

Arnhem, Holland. Sir Philip Sidney *d.* at 1586. Fortified by Cohoorn, 1702. Taken by French, 1795; by Prussians, 1813. Scene of the famous and unsuccessful landing of the British Airborne Divisions and Polish Parachute Brigade, 17–26 Sept. 1944.

Aroostook Dispute. Boundary dispute, 1839–42 between New Brunswick and Maine, so named on account of the Aroostook River.

Arras, Treaties of. Armagnacs and Burgundians, 1414; France and Burgundy, 20 Sept. 1435; Louis XI and Flemings, 1482. Catholic union between Hainault, Douai, and Artois signed at A., 5 Jan. 1579.

Arrest, Freedom from, a privilege enjoyed by members of Parliament from very early times, confirmed by Edward I, 1290. Recognized by Act of Parliament 1433. *See also* PARLIAMENT.

Arromanches, Harbour of. Artificial prefabricated harbour used during Anglo-American invasion of Normandy, 1944. Prototype constructed in Scotland, 1943. Equipment dispatched across Channel, 6 June 1944, and harbour functioning fully by the end of June.

Arrondissements or sub-prefectures, territorial divisions of French departments, under the administrative system introduced in 1799.

Arson remained a capital crime in England until the passing of the Malicious Damage Act, 1861.

Articles, The Six, statute passed, 1539; repealed, 1547.

Articles, The Thirty-nine, as now printed in the Prayer Book, are based on the Forty-Two Articles of 1553 (see next article), which were revised by Archbishop Parker and submitted to Convocation in 1562, and finally authorized by Parliament, 1571, the Declaration preceding them being drawn up by Archbishop Laud and added in 1628. Subscription thereto ceased to be obligatory on proceeding to a degree at Oxford or Cambridge, 1871.

Articles of Religion (Anglican), other than those mentioned above, were drawn up as follows:

Ten A., 1536.

Institution of a Christian Man (Bishop's Book), 1537.

Thirteen A., 1538.

Necessary Doctrine, etc. (King's Book), 1543.

Forty-two A., 1553.

Articles of War continued to form the legal basis for the discipline of the British Army until the Mutiny Act (*q.v.*) of 1789.

Artificial Silk or **Rayon.** Idea of imitating silk expressed by Réaumur, 1754; thread obtained from nitro-cellulose and called A.S. by Audemars in 1855. Process developed by de Chardonnet, 1886.

Artois, northern French province, conquered by Franks in the fifth century, but ruled by the Counts of Flanders until they ceded it to the Kings of France, 1180, who made it into a county, 1237, but in the fourteenth century ceded it to Burgundy, whence it passed to Austria, but returned to France under the Treaty of the Pyrenees, 1659. In 1789 it became the department of Pas-de-Calais. First artesian well in Europe sunk in A., 1126 (hence the name).

Arts, The Plastic. *See* ENGRAVING and PAINTING for history. The names of prominent performers in these departments are:

American:

Allston, Washington (painter), 1779–1843.

Audubon, John James (painter), 1785–1851.

Cassatt, Mary (painter), 1855–1925.

Copley, John Singleton (painter), 1738–1815.

French, Daniel Chester (sculptor), 1850–1931.

Homer, Winslow (painter), 1836–1910.

Moses, Mrs. Anna Mary Robertson (painter), 1860–1961.

Saint-Gaudens, Augustus (sculptor), 1848–1907.

Sargent, John Singer (painter), 1856–1925.

West, Benjamin (painter), 1738–1820.

Whistler, James Abbott McNeill (painter and etcher), 1834–1903.

Wright, Frank Lloyd (architect), 1869–1959.

Chinese:

Chao Mêng-fu (painter), 1254–1322.

Chien Lung (painter and architect), 1722–96.

Han Kan (painter), *fl.* 600–50.

Hsieh-Ho (painter), *fl.* 450–500.

Ki K'ai-chih (painter), *fl.* 350–400.

Kuo Hsi (painter), *fl.* 1100–50.

Wu Tao-Tzu (painter), *fl.* 700–50.

Wu Wei (painter), 1458–1508.

Dutch:

Bosch, Jerome (Hieronymus van Acken) (painter), active 1480–1 *d.* 1516.

Brouwer, Adrian (painter), 1605–38.

Cuyp, Aalbert (painter), 1620–91.

Gogh, Vincent Willem van (painter), 1853–90.

Hals, Frans (painter), 1580–1666.

Heem, Jan Davidsz van (painter), 1606–1684.

Hobbema, Meindert (painter), 1638–1709.

Hooch, Pieter de (painter), 1630–*c.* 1681.

Israels, Josef (painter), 1824–1911.

Jongkind, Johann Barthold (painter and engraver), 1819–91.

Mauve, Anton (painter), 1838–88.

Metsu, Gabriel (painter), 1630–67.

Mondrian, Piet (abstract painter), 1872–1944.

Ostade, Adriaan van (painter and etcher), 1610–85.

Ostade, Isaack van (painter), 1621–49.

Rembrandt van Rijn (painter), 1606–69.

Ruisdael, Jakob Isaac van (painter), *c.* 1628–82.

Terborch, Gerard (painter), 1617–81.

Vandevelde, Adrian (painter and etcher), 1636–72.

Vandevelde, Jan (engraver), 1593–after 1641.

Vandevelde, Willem (I), 1611–93; and (II) (draughtsman), 1633–1707.

Vermeer van Delft, Jan (painter), 1632–75.

English, Scottish, Irish, and Welsh:

Abercrombie, Sir Patrick (architect). 1879–1957.

Adam, Robert (architect),1728–92.

Alma-Tadema, Sir Lawrence (painter), 1836–1912.

Beardsley, Aubrey (illustrator), 1872–98.

Bewick, Thomas (engraver), 1753–1828.

Blake, William (engraver), 1757–1827.

Bonington, Richard Parkes (painter), 1802–28.

Brown, Ford Madox (painter), 1821–93.

Browne, Hablôt Knight ('Phiz') (caricaturist), 1815–82.

Burne-Jones, Sir Edward (painter), 1833–1898.

Clausen, Sir George (painter), 1852–1944.

Constable, John (painter), 1776–1837.

Cooper, Samuel (miniaturist), 1609–1702.

Cooper, Thomas Sidney (painter), 1803–1902.

Cotman, John Sell (painter), 1782–1842.

Cox David (painter), 1793–1859.

Cozens, John Robert (painter), 1752–99.

Crome, John (painter), 1769–1821.

Cruikshank, George (caricaturist and illustrator), 1792–1878.

Dobson, Frank (sculptor), 1889–1963.

Epstein, Sir Jacob (sculptor), 1880–1959.

Etty, William (painter), 1787–1849.

Flaxman, John (sculptor), 1755–1826.

Forbes, Stanhope Alexander (painter), 1857–1947.

Frampton, Sir George (sculptor), 1860–1928.

Gainsborough, Thomas (painter), 1727–88.

Gibbons, Grinling (sculptor and woodcarver), 1648–1721.

Gibbs, James (architect), 1674–1754.

Gilbert, Sir Alfred (sculptor), 1854–1934.

Gill, Eric Rowland (sculptor, engraver, and typographer), 1882–1940.

Gillray, James (caricaturist), 1757–1815.

Girtin, Thomas (painter), 1775–1802.

Guthrie, Sir James (painter), 1859–1930.

Hawksmoor, Nicholas (architect), 1661–1736.

Hepworth, Dame Barbara (sculptor), 1903–75.

Hockney, David (painter), 1937–.

Hogarth, William (painter and engraver), 1697–1764.

Hoppner, John (painter), 1758–1810.

Hunt, William Holman (painter), 1827–1910.

John, Augustus Edwin (painter), 1879–1961.

Jones, Inigo (architect), *c.* 1573–*c.* 1652.

Keene, Charles Samuel (illustrator), 1823–91.

Kneller, Sir Godfrey (painter), 1646–73.

Knight, Dame Laura (painter), 1877–1970.

Landseer, Sir Edwin (painter), 1802–73.

Lavery, Sir John (painter), 1857–1941.

Lawrence, Sir Thomas (painter), 1769–1830.

Leighton, Frederick Leighton, Baron (painter and sculptor), 1830–96.

Lely, Sir Peter (painter), 1618–80.

Lewis, Percy Wyndham (painter), 1884–1957.

Low, David (cartoonist), 1891–1963.

Lutyens, Sir Edwin Landseer (architect), 1869–1944.

Mackintosh, Charles Rennie (architect), 1869–1928.

May, Philip William (illustrator), 1864–1903.

Millais, Sir John Everett (painter), 1829–96.

Moore, Henry (sculptor), 1898–.

Morland, George (painter), 1763–1804.

Moser, Mary (painter), 1744–1819.

Munnings, Sir Alfred (painter), 1878–1959.

Nash, John (architect), 1752–1835.

Nash, Paul (painter and theatrical designer), 1889–1946.

Nevinson, Christopher Richard Wynne (painter), 1889–1946.

Nicholson, Ben (painter), 1894–1982.

Opie, John (painter), 1761–1807.

Orchardson, Sir William Quiller (painter), 1835–1910.

Orpen, Sir William (painter), 1878–1931.

Rackham, Arthur (painter and illustrator), 1867–1939.

Raeburn, Sir Henry (painter), 1756–1823.

Rennie, John (architect), 1761–1821.

Reynolds, Sir Joshua (painter), 1723–92.

Richardson, Sir Albert (architect), 1880–1965.

Romney, George (painter), 1734–1802.

Rossetti, Dante Gabriel (painter) 1828–1882.

Rothenstein, Sir William (painter and etcher), 1872–1945.

Rowlandson, Thomas (caricaturist), 1756–1827.

Scott, Sir George Gilbert (architect), 1811–78.

Scott, Sir Giles Gilbert (architect), 1880–1960.

Sickert, Walter Richard (painter), 1860–1942.

Sisley, Alfred (painter), 1840–99.

Spence, Sir Basil (architect), 1907–76.

Spencer, Sir Stanley (painter), 1892–1959.

Steer, Philip Wilson (painter), 1860–1942.

Stevens, Alfred (sculptor), 1818–75.

Stone, Marcus (painter), 1840–1921.

Stone, Nicholas (sculptor), 1586–1647.

Stubbs, George (painter), 1724–1806.

Sutherland, Graham (painter), 1903–1980.

Tenniel, Sir John (cartoonist and illustrator), 1820–1914.

Turner, Joseph Mallord William (painter), 1775–1851.

Vanbrugh, Sir John (architect), 1664–1726.

Varley, John (painter), 1778–1842.

Watts, George Frederick (painter and sculptor), 1817–1904.

Wilkie, Sir David (painter), 1785–1841.

Wilson, Richard (painter), 1714–82.

Wint, Peter de (painter), 1784–1849.

Wren, Sir Christopher (archietect), 1632–1723.

Yeats, Jack Butler (painter), 1871–1957.

Flemish:

Breughel, Jan (painter), 1508–1625.

Breughel, Pieter the Elder (painter), 1520–69.

Breughel, Pieter the Younger (painter), 1564–1637.

Eyck, Hubert van (painter), c. 1379–1426.

Eyck, Jan van (painter), c. 1390–1441.

Hoorenbault, Gerard (painter), 1480–1540.

Mabuse, Jan van (painter), c. 1475–1536.

Matsys, Quintin (painter), 1466–1530.

Memlinc, Hans (painter), c. 1430–94.

Rubens, Peter Paul (painter and etcher), 1577–1640.

Teniers the Younger, David (painter), 1610–94.

Van der Weyden, Rogier (painter), c. 1400–64.

Van Dyck, Sir Anthony (painter and etcher), 1599–1641.

French:

Blanche, Jacques Émile (painter), 1861–1942.

Boucher, François (painter), 1703–70.

Bourdelle, Émile Antoine (sculptor), 1861–1929.

Braque, Georges (painter), 1881–1963.

Cézanne, Paul (painter), 1839–1906.

Chagall, Marc (Russian b. painter) 1887–1985.

Chardin, Jean Baptiste Siméon (painter), 1699–1779.

Claude de Lorraine (painter), 1600–82.

Clouet, or Janet, François (painter), c. 1510–72.

Corot, Jean Baptiste Camille (painter), 1796–1875.

Courbet, Gustave (painter), 1819–77.

Dalon, Jules (sculptor), 1838–1902.
Daubigny, Charles François (painter), 1817–78.
Daumier, Honoré (caricaturist and painter), 1808–79.
David, Jacques Louis (painter), 1748–1825.
Degas, Edgar Hilaire Germaine (painter and engraver), 1834–1917.
Delacroix, Eugène (painter), 1798–1863.
Diaz de la Peña, Narcisse Virgile (painter), 1808–76.
Duvet, Jean (engraver), c. 1485–1561.
Fantin-Latour, Ignace Henri Jean Théodore (painter), 1836–1894.
Fragonard, Jean Honoré (painter), 1732–1806.
Gauguin, Paul (painter and sculptor), 1848–1903.
Greuze, Jean Baptiste (painter), 1725–1805.
Houdon, Jean Antoine (sculptor), 1741–1828.
Ingres, Jean Auguste Dominique (painter), 1780–1867.
Le Brun, Charles (painter), 1619–90.
Lebrun, Elisabeth Vigée (painter), 1755–1842.
Le Nain, Antoine (painter), 1588–1648.
Le Nain, Louis (painter), 1593–1648.
Le Nain, Mathieu (painter), 1607–77.
Maillol, Aristide (sculptor), 1861–1944.
Manet, Édouard (painter), 1832–83.
Matisse, Henri (painter), 1869–1954.
Méryon, Charles (engraver), 1821–68.
Millet, Jean François (painter), 1814–75.
Monet, Claude Oscar (painter), 1840–1926.
Pissarro, Camille (painter), 1830–1903.
Poussin, Nicolas (painter), 1594–1665.
Renoir, Pierre Auguste (painter), 1841–1919.
Rodin, François Auguste (sculptor and etcher, 1840–1917.
Rouault, Georges (painter), 1871–1954.
Rousseau, Henri Julien (painter), 1844–1910.
Rousseau, Pierre Étinee Théodore (painter), 1812–67.
Seurat, Georges Pierre (painter), 1859–91.

Signac, Paul (painter), 1863–1935.
Toulouse-Lautrec, Henry de (painter), 1864–91.
Troyon, Constant (painter), 1810–65.
Utrillo, Maurice (painter), 1883–1955.
Viollet-le-Duc, Eugène Emmanuel (architect), 1814–79.
Watteau, Antoine (painter), 1684–1721.

German:
Altdorfer, Albrecht (painter and engraver), c. 1480–1538.
Carstens, Asmus Jakob (Danish-born painter), 1754–98.
Corinth, Lovis (painter), 1858–1925.
Cornelius, Peter von (painter), 1783–1867.
Cranach, Lucas (painter), 1472–1553.
Dürer, Albrecht (painter, engraver, and etcher), 1471–1528.
Elsheimer, Adam (sculptor), 1578–1610.
Friedrich, Caspar David (painter), 1774–1840.
Gropius, Walter (architect: became naturalized U.S. citizen), 1883–1969.
Grünewald, Matthias (painter), c. 1470–1529.
Holbein the Elder, Hans (painter), c. 1460–1524.
Holbein the Younger, Hans (painter), 1497–1543.
Kampf, Arthur von, 1864–1950.
Kaulbach, Wilhelm von (painter), 1805–1874.
Liebermann, Max (painter), 1847–1935.
Marc, Franz (painter), 1880–1916.
Mengs, Anton Raphael (painter), 1728–79.
Schadow, Johann Gottfried (sculptor), 1764–1850.
Schongauer, Martin (painter and engraver), c. 1445–c. 1499.
Schwind, Moritz von (painter), 1805–71.
Strigel, Bernhardin (painter), 1460–1528.
Wilhelm of Cologne (painter), *fl.* 1358, d. c. 1378.

Greek, Ancient:
Apelles (painter), *fl.* 350 B.C.
Lysippus (sculptor), c. 336–270 B.C.

Myron (sculptor), fifth century, B.C.
Pheidias (sculptor), *c.* 500–432 B.C.
Polyclitus of Argos (sculptor), *c.*
  452–412 B.C.
Polygnotus (painter), *fl.* 500–425 B.C.
Praxiteles (sculptor), *fl.* 364–330 B.C.
Scopas (sculptor), *fl.* 395–350 B.C.

Italian:

Alberti, Leon Battista (architect),
  1404–1472.
Andrea del Castagno (painter), *c.*
  1423–1457.
Andrea del Sarto (painter), 1488–1530.
Angelico, Fra Giovanni da Fiesole
  (painter), 1387–1455.
Annigoni, Pietro (painter), 1910–.
Bartolommeo, Fra, of S. Marco
  (painter), 1475–1517.
Bellini, Giovanni (painter), 1422–1516.
Bernini, Giovanni Lorenzo (sculptor,
  painter, and architect), 1598–1680.
Borromini, Francesco (architect),
  1599–1677.
Botticelli, Sandro (painter), 1445–1510.
Bramante da Urbino (architect),
  1444–1514.
Brunelleschi, Filippo (sculptor and
  architect), 1379–1446.
Canaletto, or Antonio Canale (painter),
  1697–1768.
Canova, Antonio (sculptor and
  painter), 1757–1822.
Caravaggio, Michelangelo Amerighi da
  (painter), 1573–1610.
Cellini Benvenuto (sculptor and
  jeweller), 1500–71.
Cimabue, Giovanni (painter),
  1240–1302.
Correggio, Antonio da (painter),
  1494–1534.
Donatello (Donato di Betto Bardi)
  (sculptor), 1386–1466.
Duccio di Buoninsegna (painter), *c.*
  1260–1319.
Ghiberti, Lorenzo (sculptor),
  1378–1455.
Ghirlandaio, Domenico (painter),
  1449–94.
Giorgione da Castelfranco (painter),
  1477–1511.
Giotto (painter, sculptor, and
  architect), 1266–1337.
Gozzoli, Benozzo (painter), 1421–97.
Guardi, Francesco (painter), 1712–93.

Lippi, Filippino (painter), *c.* 1457–
  1504.
Lippi, Fra Filippo (painter), 1406–69.
Luca della Robbia (sculptor),
  1399–1482.
Mantegna, Andrea (painter),
  1431–1506.
Masaccio di S. Giovanni (painter),
  1401–1428.
Michelangelo Buonarotti (painter,
  sculptor, and architect), 1475–1564.
Modigliani, Amadeo (painter),
  1884–1920.
Moroni, Giambattista (painter),
  1510–78.
Palladio, Andrea (architect), 1508–80.
Perugino, Pietro (painter), 1446–1523.
Piero della Francesca (painter),
  1416–92.
Piranesi, Giovanni Battista (engraver),
  1720–78.
Pollaiuolo, Antonio (painter), 1432–98.
Raphael of Urbino (painter and
  architect), 1483–1520.
Sansovino, Andrea (sculptor and
  architect), 1460–1529.
Sansovino, Jacopo (sculptor and
  architect), 1486–1570.
Segantini, Giovanni (painter), 1858–99.
Tiepolo, Giovanni Battista (painter),
  1696–1770.
Tintoretto (Jacop Robusti) (painter),
  1518–94.
Titian, or Tiziano Vecellio (painter),
  1477–1576.
Uccello, Paolo (painter), 1397–1475.
Veronese, Paolo (painter), 1528–88.
Verrocchio, Andrea del (sculptor and
  painter), 1435–88.
Vinci, Leonardo da (painter and
  sculptor), 1452–1519.

Japanese:

Cho Denshu (painter), 1351–1427.
Doncho (Korean painter), *fl.* sixth
  century.
Hidari Jingaró (sculptor), *d.* 1634.
Hishigawa Moronobu (painter of
  engravings), 1618–94.
Hokusai (painter of engravings),
  1760–1849.
Jositsu (painter, *fl.* fifteenth century.
Kosé-no-Kanaoka (painter), *fl.* 850.
Utamora (painter of engravings),
  1754–1806.

Russian:

Bakst, Leon (painter and costume designer), 1866–1924.

Fabergé, Peter Carl (goldsmith and lapidary), 1846–1920.

Kandinsky, Vasily (painter), 1866–1944.

Repin, Ilya Yefimovich (painter), 1844–1918.

Rublyov, Andrea (painter of icons), *c.* 1370–1430.

Scandinavian:

Burgesson, John (Icelandic sculptor), *d.* 1910.

Jensen, Georg (Danish silversmith), 1866–1935.

Milles, Carl (Swedish sculptor), 1875–1955.

Munch, Edvard (Norwegian painter), 1863–1944.

Thorwaldsen, Bertel (Danish sculptor), 1770–1844.

Vigeland, Gustaf (Norwegian sculptor), 1869–1943.

Zorn, Anders Leonard (Swedish etcher and engraver), 1860–1920.

Spanish:

Cano, Alonso (painter, sculptor, and architect), 1601–67.

Dali, Salvador (painter), 1904–.

Fortuny y Carbo, Mariano José Bernardo (painter), 1839–74.

Goya y Lucientes, Francisco José de (painter and etcher), 1746–1828.

Greco, El, or Domenico Theotocopuli (Greek-Spanish painter), 1541–1614.

Miro, Joan (surrealist painter), 1893–1984.

Murillo, Bartolomé Estéban (painter), 1617–82.

Picasso, Pablo (painter), 1881–1973.

Pradilla, Francisco (painter), 1847–1921.

Ribera, Jusepe de (painter), 1588–1656.

Velázquez, Diego de Silva y (painter), 1599–1660.

Zurbaran, Francisco (painter), 1598–1662.

Various:

Brancusi, Constantin (Rumanian sculptor), 1876–1957.

Ensor, James (Belgian painter), 1860–1947.

Giacometti, Alberto (Swiss sculptor), 1901–66.

Kauffmann, Angelica (Swiss painter), 1741–1807.

Klee, Paul (Swiss painter), 1879–1940.

Le Corbusier (Charles Édouard Jeanneret) (Swiss-French architect), 1887–1965.

Meunier, Constantin (Belgian sculptor), 1831–1905.

Mylsbeč, Joseph Wenceslas (Czech sculptor), 1848–1922.

Arts Council of Great Britain, name adopted on 9 Aug. 1946 by the former C.E.M.A. (*q.v.*).

Arts, Society of, London, established, 1754; incorporated, 1847. Edinburgh, established, 1821; incorporated, 1841.

Arya Samja. Reformist Hindu society founded about 1866 by Dayananda Sarasvati (1825?–82).

Ascalon (modern **Ashkelon**), Israel. Biblical Philistine city. Captured by Saladin, 1187, and by Bibars, Sultan of Egypt, who demolished its fortifications, 1270. *See* CRUSADES.

Ascension Island, discovered on A. Day, 1501, by João da Nova. First occupied by British, 1815, and administered by the Admiralty until 1922, when it was made a dependency of St. Helena. Fuelling post for Falklands Campaign, 1982.

Ascot, Berks., first race meeting held at, 11 Aug. 1711: Gold Cup first awarded, 1807.

Ashanti, Ghana. First British expedition to, 1807. Wars with Great Britain: (1) 1863–4; (2) 1873–4; (3) 1895–1900 (relief of Kumasi). Protectorate, 1896; annexed, 1901.

Asean (Association of South East Asian Nations), estab. Aug. 1967 at Bangkok to further economic progress and cooperation in S.E. Asia. First summit held Bali, 1976. Members (1985): Indonesia, Malaysia, Philippines, Singapore, Thailand.

Asburton Treaty, 1842, settled the frontiers between U.S.A. and Canada.

Ashes, The, non-existent cricket trophy, competed for between England and Australia, first mentioned 29 Aug. 1882.

Ashmolean Museum, Oxford. Founded, 1683, by Elias Ashmole (1617–92). Its contents separated, 1860, 1886, and 1894, and the bulk of them placed in the present building.

Asiento, The. Contract originally between France and Spain for supplying Negro slaves to Spanish colonies, 1702. Transferred by Spain to Britain, 1713. Twice lost, it was finally restored for remaining period of two years, 1748.

Assam, State of India since 1947. Conquered by British, 1826. Tea planting inaugurated, 1835. Separate province, 1919. Immigration from Bangladesh after 1972 led to rioting and murders, 1983.

Assassinations. The most famous victims of assassination include:

Hipparchus of Athens, by Harmodius and Aristogiton, 514 B.C.

Artaxerxes III of Persia, by Bagoas, B.C. 338.

Philip II of Macedon, by Pausanias, 336 B.C.

Darius III of Persia, by Bessus, 330 B.C.

Julius Caesar, by Brutus and others, 15 Mar. 44 B.C.

Caius Caligula, by a tribune, A.D. 41.

Claudius I, poisoned by his wife, Agrippina, A.D. 54.

Edmund, St., King of E. Anglia, 870.

Edmund the Elder of England, 26 May 946.

Edward the Martyr of England, 18 Mar. 978.

Albert I of Germany, by his nephew John, 1 May 1308.

Edward II of England, 27 Sept. 1327.

St. Thomas Becket, Archbishop of Canterbury, 29 Dec. 1170.

James I of Scotland, by nobles, 21 Feb. 1437.

Edward V of England, July 1483.

James III of Scotland, by nobles, 11 June 1488.

David Rizzio, Mary Stuart's secretary, by Darnley's followers, 9 Mar. 1566.

Lord Henry Darnley, Mary Stuart's husband, by persons unknown, 10 Feb. 1567.

William the Silent, of Orange, by Balthazar Gérard, 12 July 1584.

Henry III of France, by Jacques Clément, 1 Aug. 1589.

Henry IV of France, by Ravaillac, 14 May 1610.

George Villiers, Duke of Buckingham, by John Felton, 23 Aug. 1628.

Gustavus III of Sweden, by Ankarström, 29 Mar. 1792.

Marat, by Charlotte Corday, 13 July 1793.

Paul, Tsar of Russia, by nobles, 24 Mar. 1801.

Spencer Perceval, British Prime Minister, by John Bellingham, 11 May 1812.

Abraham Lincoln, President of U.S.A., by Wilkes Booth, 14 Apr. 1865.

Michael, Prince of Serbia, 10 June 1868.

Abdul Aziz, Sultan of Turkey, alleged suicide, 4 June 1876.

Mehemet Ali Pasha, by Albanians, 7 Sept. 1878.

Alexander II of Russia, 13 Mar. 1881.

General Garfield, President of U.S.A., by Charles Jules Guiteau, *d.* 19 Sept., 2 July 1881.

Chief Secretary for Ireland, Lord Frederick Cavendish, by Fenians, 6 May 1882.

Sadi Carnot, President of France, by Santo Caserio, 24 June 1894.

Nasr-ed-Deen, Shah of Iran, by Mullah Reza a Sayyid, 1 May 1896.

Elizabeth, Empress of Austria, by Luccheni, 10 Sept. 1898.

Humbert I of Italy, by Gaetano Bresci, 29 July 1900.

William McKinley, President of U.S.A., by Leon Czolgosz, *d.* 14 Sept., 5 Sept. 1901.

Alexander I of Serbia and wife, Draga, 10 June 1903.

King Carlos and Crown Prince of Portugal, by Buica and Da Costa, 1 Feb. 1908.

Peter Stolypin, Russian premier, 14 Sept. 1911.

Francisco I. Madero, President of Mexico, and Vice-President José Pino Saurez, 23 Feb. 1913.

George I of Greece, 18 Mar. 1913.

Archduke Francis Ferdinand of Austria-Hungary and wife, by

Gabriel Princip, 28 June 1914.

Jean L. Jaurès, French Socialist leader, 31 July 1914.

Tsar Nicholas of Russia and family, at Ekaterinburg, by the Bolsheviks, 16 July 1918.

General Venustiano Carranza, President of Mexico, 20 May 1920.

Field-Marshal Sir Henry H. Wilson, in London, 22 June 1922.

Dr. Walter Rathenau, German Foreign Minister, 24 June 1922.

Michael Collins, by rebels, near Bandon, County Cork, 22 Aug. 1922.

Gabriel Narutowicz, first President of Polish Republic, by Capt. Niewadowski, 16 Dec. 1922.

Giacomo Matteoti, Italian Socialist leader, kidnapped by Fascists, body found 15 Aug., 10 June 1924.

Kevin O'Higgins, Vice-President of Irish Free State, 10 July 1927.

Paul Doumer, President of France, by Paul Gargolov, 6 May 1932.

Luis M. Sanchez Cerro, President of Peru, by Abelardo Hurtado de Mendoza, 30 Apr. 1933.

Nadir Shah, King of Afghanistan, by Abdul Khallig, student, 8 Nov. 1933.

Ernst Roehm, General Schleicher, his wife, and others, by Nazi Party, 30 June 1934.

Engelbert Dollfuss, Austrian Chancellor, by Otto Planetta, 25 July 1934.

Alexander, King of Yugoslavia, and French Foreign Minister Louis Barthou, at Marseilles, by Georgief, 9 Oct. 1934.

Senator Huey Long of Louisiana, by Carl Weiss, 8 Sept. 1935.

Ernst von Rath, German diplomat, by Herschel Grynszpan, in Paris, 7 Nov. 1938.

Leon Trotsky, exiled Russian leader, at Coycacán, Mexico, by Jacques Mornard, 21 Aug. 1940.

Darlan, Jean François, French admiral, at Algiers, 24 Dec. 1942.

Benito Mussolini, dictator of Italy, and his mistress, by Italian partisans, 28 April 1945.

Ananda Mahidol, King of Thailand, 9 July 1946.

Mohandas Karamchand Gandhi, by Natheram Jodre, 30 Jan. 1948.

Imam Yahya of the Yemen, 17 Feb. 1948.

Count Folke Bernadotte, United Nations mediator, by Israeli terrorists, at Jerusalem, 17 Sept. 1948.

President Chalbaud of Venezuela, 13 Nov. 1950.

King Abdullah of Jordan, 20 July 1951.

Liaquat Ali Khan, Prime Minister of Pakistan, by Said Akbar, 16 Oct. 1951.

President Somoza of Nicaragua, 29 Sept. 1956.

King Feisal II of Iraq, his family and Prime Minister, by revolutionary nationalists, 14 July 1958.

Mr. Bandaranaike, Prime Minister of Sri Lanka, by Buddhist extremists, 25 Sept. 1959.

General Rafael Trujillo, dictator of the Dominican Republic, 30 May 1961.

President Sylvanus Olympio of Togo, 13 Jan. 1963.

President Ngo Dinh Diem of S. Vietnam, 1 Nov. 1963.

John F. Kennedy, President of U.S.A., at Dallas, Texas, 22 Nov. 1963.

Pierre Ngendandumwe, Premier of Burundi, 15 Jan. 1965.

Mr. Mansur, Premier of Iran, 21 Jan. 1965.

'Malcolm X', leader of the Black Muslims, 21 Feb. 1965.

Sir Abubakar Balewa, Premier of Nigeria, *c.* 15 Jan. 1966.

Hendrik Verwoerd, Premier of S. Africa, 6 Sept. 1966.

Dr. Martin Luther King, Amer. Negro leader, at Memphis, Tennessee, 4 April 1968.

Senator Robert Kennedy, brother of President John F. Kennedy, at Los Angeles, 5 June 1968: he *d.* 6 June.

Tom Mboya, leading Kenyan politician, in Nairobi, 5 July 1969.

President Allende of Chile, 11 Sept. 1973.

King Feisal of Saudi Arabia, 25 Mar. 1975.

Mujibar Rahman, President of Bangladesh, 15 Aug. 1975.

President Daoud of Afghanistan, Apr. 1978.

Airey Neave, M.P., by I.R.A., 30 Mar. 1979.

Lord Mountbatten of Burma, by I.R.A., 27 Aug. 1979.

President Park of S. Korea, 1979.

President Tolbert of Liberia, 12 Apr. 1980.

Archbishop Romero, in San Salvador cathedral, May 1980.

President Ziaur Rahman of Bangladesh, 30 May 1981.

President Sadat of Egypt, 6 Oct. 1981.

President Bashir Gemayel of Lebanon, 14 Sept. 1982.

Benigno Aquino, Philippine opposition leader, 21 Aug. 1983.

4 S. Korean cabinet ministers, at Rangoon, 10 Oct. 1983.

Maurice Bishop, Premier of Grenada, and 3 of his ministers, 20 Oct. 1983.

Indira Gandhi, Indian Premier, 31 Oct., 1984.

Father Jerzy Popieluszko, Oct. 1984.

Assassins, powerful Moslem secret society founded in Syria by Hassan ibn Sabbah (*fl.* 1080), the original 'Old Man of the Mountain' (*Sheikh-el-Jebel*). Massacre of 1255 virtually exterminated the sect.

Assent, Royal, last refused to a parliamentary bill, 1707.

Assignats and **Mandats.** French revolutionary paper currency, first issued, 1790, secured originally on confiscated church and *émigré* property. Withdrawn 1797.

Assiniboia. Name previously applied to two districts in Canada. First formed, 1835, by the Hudson's Bay Co. and ceased to exist, 1870, on the transference of Rupert's Land to Canada. Second created, 1882, as a provisional district within the North-West Territories, and became part of Saskatchewan in 1905.

Assize Courts. *See* COURTS, ENGLISH.

Assize of Clarendon, 1166, first legislative direction to employ the jury (*q.v.*).

Assize of Northampton, 1176.

Assumption of the Virgin Mary established as an article of the Roman Catholic faith by a papal pronouncement *ex cathedra*, 1950.

Assyria became independent of Babylon (*q.v.*), seventeenth century B.C.; rose into prominence under Tiglath-Pileser I *c.* 1120 B.C., who conquered Babylon. Nineveh became capital under Tiglath-Pileser III (745–727 B.C.), whose empire was maintained by Sargon II, 722–705, and Sennacherib, 705–681 (*see* Bible). Essarhaddon, 681–668, conquered Egypt, but on his death the empire was divided and an alliance of Medes and Babylonians stormed and destroyed Nineveh and overthrew the Assyrian Empire, 612 B.C.

Assyrians (Modern). About A.D. 1400 the Chaldaean Christians of N. Iraq, who had survived the reign of Timur-i-Leng the Mongol, fled to the Hakkiari mountains N. of Mosul. Their tradition stated that they were the descendants of the ancient A., converted to Christianity in the first century A.D. by Thaddaeus. They were affected to some extent by the Nestorian heresy *c.* 400. Between 1550 and 1750 various sections submitted to Rome as 'Chaldaean Uniates'. The remainder in the face of Moslem pressure and Kurdish massacres appealed for help to the Archbishop of Canterbury, 1843. An Anglican mission came out in 1876. On 10 May 1915 the Mar Shimun (Patriarch Benjamin of the A. declared war on Turkey, and after fighting Turkish troops and Kurdish irregulars retired into Persian territory. Until the spring of 1917 the A. fought as Russian auxiliaries. Driven out of the Urmiya area they retired to Hamadan, Aug.–Sept. 1918. In the autumn of 1920 the Agha Petros attempted to set up an Assyrian state in the upper valley of the Great Zab River, but failed. Settled in N. Iraq, 1921–30, employed against Kurdish guerrillas. In July 1933 the Malik Yacu attempted to lead a dissident faction of A. into Syria. Turned back by French frontier officials he came into conflict with Iraqi forces on the Tigris. In Aug. 1933, while Assyrian villages were being looted and their inhabitants massacred by the Kurds, followers of Yacu who gave themselves up were shot at the instigation or with the connivance of the Iraqi generals Beqir Sidqi, Nuri es Said, and Rashid Ali.

Asteroids, designation given to minor planets, 1802, by Sir William Herschel (1738–1822). First and largest asteroid, Ceres, discovered by Piazzi at Palermo on 1 Jan. 1801.

Aston University, Birmingham, estab. 1966.

Astronomer Royal. Office established, 1675.

Astronomical Association, British. First meeting, 24 Oct. 1890.

Astronomical Society, Royal. Founded, 1820. Incorporated, 1831.

Astronomy. Copernicus (founder of present system), *b.* 1473, *d.* 1543; Kepler discovered planetary motions, 1609, 1619; Galileo discovered Jupiter's moons, sunspots, 1610; Newton's discoveries, 1666, etc.; Greenwich Observatory, 1675; Halley's observations, 1705, etc.; Herschel's observations, 1781, etc.; Lord Rosse completed famous telescope, 1845; Lick telescope erected at Mt. Hamilton, California, 1887; Professor Perrine discovered new satellites of Jupiter, 1904–5, 1908. The work of stellar spectroscopy begun in America in 1872 by Henry Draper (1837–82). Spectra interpreted, 1913; Michelson measured angular diameter of a star, 1920, at the Mt. Wilson Observatory. Solar telescopy developed specifically since *c.* 1900; notably since 1930s. Jodrell Bank Radio Telescope, then largest in the world, completed, 1958. Kitt Peak National Observatory Telescope, U.S.A., 1970; Anglo-Australian Telescope installed at Siding Spring, N.S.W., 1974.

Asuncion, Paraguay. Founded, 1537.

Aswan or **Assuan,** Egypt. Dam built, 1902. Raised, 1912.Raised again, 1929–1931. High Dam commenced, 1955: stored water from 1964: operational, 1970.

Asylum, Right of. Exercised by embassies in Europe, 1862 (Greece) and 1875 (Spain). In twentieth century exercised intermittently in S. America, more recently in Europe. Nov. 1956: Nagy, the Hungarian Prime Minister, sought asylum in the Yugoslav Embassy, and Cardinal Mindszenty, Hungarian primate, in the U.S. embassy in Budapest. Pentecostal Russians sought A. in U.S. embassy in Moscow, 1978: allowed to emigrate to Israel, 1983.

Athanasian Creed. *See* CREEDS.

Athelney, Somerset. King Alfred fled here in 878–9. The Alfred Jewel found, 1693.

'Athenaeum' The. Literary weekly founded, 2 Jan. 1828. Absorbed into the *Nation,* Feb. 1921; amalgamated with *New Statesman,* 1931.

Athenaeum Club (London). Founded, 1824.

Athens.

History: Dracon's legal code, 621 B.C. Reforms of Solon, 594. Tyranny of the Peisistratids, 560–510. Reforms of Cleisthenes, 508. Persian Wars, 490; 480–479; 468; 450–449. First Delian League, 478–404; second, 377–338. Age of Pericles, 443–429. Peloponnesian War, 431–421; 416–413; 412–404, when A. surrendered to Lysander. Government of the Thirty, 404–403, when the democracy was restored. A. again at war with Sparta, 378–371. Social War, 357–355. Athenian and allied forces defeated by Philip II of Macedon at Chaeronea, 338. Lamian War, 323–322, when A. was occupied by Antipater and compelled to modify her constitution. The democracy restored by Demetrius Poliorcetes, 307. A. included in the Roman province of Achaia, 146. Captured by Sulla, 86 B.C. Philosophical schools closed by Justinian, A.D. 529. A. captured by Latins, 1205, and remained a Latin duchy till 1261. Captured by Turks, 1454; by Venetians, 1466; recaptured by Turks, 1479. Venetians attack and explode the Parthenon, which had been made a powder magazine, 1687; retaken by Turks, 1690. Captured by Greeks, 1822; retaken by Turks, 1827. Became capital of Greece, 1834. Occupied by French and English, 1854–6; by Allies, Dec. 1916. Germans occupied A., 27 Apr. 1941. British liberated A., 14 October 1944. Fighting between Communists and Allied forces, 5–30 Dec. 1944.

Ancient Buildings: A. sacked and destroyed by Persians, 480 B.C. City wall, built by Themistocles soon after 479 B.C.; reconstructed by Conon in 393 and by Lycurgus *c.* 333; enlarged by Hadrian. Erechtheum: building started between 431 and 421; completed, 409; repaired after fire, early fourth century; west front reconstructed, first century A.D. Long Walls: North and Phaleric completed *c.* 457 B.C., Middle or South *c.* 445; all destroyed, 404. North and Middle restored, 393; both finally destroyed by Sulla, 86 B.C. Monument of Lysicrates, 335–334. Odeum of Herodes Alticus, *c.* A.D. 162. Parthenon: begun, 447 B.C.; dedicated, 438; sculptures completed, 432. Propylaea, 437–433. Stadium, *c.* 330 B.C.; rebuilt *c.* A.D. 143; restored, late nineteenth century. Stoa of Attalus *c.* 158 B.C.; restored, A.D. 1955. Temple of Hephaestus, fifth century B.C. Temple of Olympian Zeus: Begun by Hippias *c.* 520 B.C.; continued, 175–164; completed, A.D. 132. Theatre of Dionysus: site first used for temporary wooden structure, 490 B.C.; permanent stone structure, between 338 and 326; alterations to stage and orchestra under Nero and Hadrian. Tower of the Winds, second or third century.

Atlantic Charter. Declaration of the Four Freedoms issued by Franklin Roosevelt and Winston Churchill from a warship in the Atlantic, 11 Aug. 1941.

Atlantic Flights. *See* AVIATION.

Atlantic Passage Record since the first crossing by a steamer, *Sirius*, in 1838, was held by the *Queen Mary*, 1938, until broken by the *United States*, 7 July 1952, with a time of 3 days, 10 hours, 40 minutes. Bid by Brit. *Virgin Challenger* failed when boat sank, Aug. 1985

Atlantic Telegraph Cable, begun Aug. 1857. First message, 5 Aug. 1858. Relaid 1866.

Atlantic Telephone Cable. First one

successfully laid and opened to traffic, 1956.

Atom. First split by Lord Rutherford, 1919.

Atomic Bomb. First detonated experimentally, 16 July 1945; first used operationally at Hiroshima, 6 Aug., and at Nagasaki 9 Aug. 1945.

Atomic Energy Research Establishment. Established at Harwell, Berks., 1945.

Atomic Power. Radioactivity discovered by Becquerel, 1896. Einstein's equation, 1905.

A.T.S. (Auxillary Territorial Service). *See* WOMAN'S ROYAL ARMY CORPS.

Attainder, Act of. First Bill of A. recorded against Despenser family, 1321. Most famous against Strafford after his impeachment had failed, 1641. Last against Lord E. Fitzgerald for participation in the Irish Rebellion, 1797.

Atterbury's Plot. Abortive Jacobite plot led by Francis Atterbury, Bishop of Rochester (1662–1732) in 1721. Atterbury was banished.

Attorney-General. William de Giselham, first recorded A.-G., 1278. A.-G. has sat in House of Commons since 1673. Ceased to practise at the Bar privately in return for increased salary, 1945.

Auckland. Founded, 1840. Was capital of New Zealand till 1865.

Augmentation, Court of, set up, 1536, under Act of Dissolution. Dissolved, 1553.

Augsburg. Founded by Romans *c.* 15 B.C. (as **Augusta Vindelicorum**). Free city, 1276. Confession of A. drawn up by Luther and Melanchthon and presented to Charles V at Diet of A., 25 June 1530. Interim of A., 15 May 1548. Religious peace of A., 1555. League of A. against France, 9 July 1686. Annexed by Bavaria, 1806.

Augustales, games, sacred to the memory of the Emperor Augustus, held on his birthday, beginning in 11 B.C.

Augusteo, Roman concert hall on the site of the Mausoleum of Augustus, opened in 1908.

Augustinian Canons. Order established consequent on the Lateran synod of 1059.

Auk, Great. Last known specimen killed, 4 June 1844, on the Stack of Eldey, off S.W. Iceland.

Aulic Council. Established by Emperor Maximilian I, 1497, to assist in governing the Holy Roman Empire (*q.v.*).

Auschwitz. *See* OSWIECIM.

Ausgleich (compromise). A treaty governing the joint affairs of the Dual Monarchy, concluded between its several partners, Austria and Hungary, in 1867, and renewed in 1878, 1887, 1902, and 1907.

Australia. N. coast sighted by various Dutch voyagers, seventeenth century. Explored by Capt. Dampier, 1688; by Capt. Cook, 1769–70; Bass and Flinders, 1798. Colonized by English convicts, 1788. Last convicts landed, 1840. Divided into provinces, 1829, 1834, 1850, 1859. New South Wales Constitution, 1842. Australian Colonies Act passed, 1850; granted power to various provinces to draw up own constitution. Goldrush began, 1851. S. Australian Constitution, 27 Oct. 1856. Victoria Parliament opened at Melbourne, 17 Jan. 1867. Commonwealth Bill of A. Constitution, 9 July 1900. First governor-general appointed, 14 July 1900. Australians played major role in World War I campaigns, notably at Gallipoli. Australian Federal Parliament was opened at Canberra (*q.v.*) by Duke of York, 9 May 1927. Increased urbanization and growth of unions increased power of Labour movement between World Wars 1919–39. Unsuccessful attempt by W.A. to secede from Commonwealth, 1933–5. A. played major role in World War II, notably in N. Africa and Far E. Troops sent to Vietnam, 1965. Increased non-British immigration after 1945 and constitutional crisis, 1975, led to growth of republican movement, 1975 onwards, emphasized by election of Labour gov. under Hawke, 1983. Hawke re-elected, 1984.

Governor-Generals since 1901:
Earl of Hopetoun 1901–1902
Lord Tennyson 1902–1904
Lord Northcote 1904–1908
Earl of Dudley 1908–1911

Lord Denman 1911–1914
Visc. Novar 1914–1920
Lord Forster 1920–1925
Lord Stonehaven 1925–1930
Lord Somers (acting) 1930–1931
Sir Isaac Alfred Isaacs 1931–1936
Lord Gowrie 1936–1944
Sir Winston Dugan (acting) 1944–1945
H.R.H. the Duke of Gloucester 1945–1947
Sir Winston Dugan (acting) 1947
Sir William John McKell 1947–1952
Sir William Slim 1953–1960
Lord Dunrossil 1960–1961
Viscount De L'Isle 1961–1965
Lord Casey 1965–1969
Sir Paul Hasluck 1969–1974
Sir John Kerr 1974–1977
Sir Zelman Cowen 1977–1982
Sir Ninian Stephen 1982–

Heads of Administrations (Prime Ministers) from 1901:
Barton 1901–1903
Deakin 1903–1904
Watson (Apr.–Aug.) 1904
Reid 1904–1905
Deakin 1905–1908
Fisher 1908–1909
Deakin 1909–1910
Fisher 1910–1913
Cook 1913–1914
Fisher 1914–1915
Hughes 1915–1923
Bruce 1923–1929
Scullin 1929–1931
Lyons 1931–1939
Menzies 1939–1941
Fadden (Aug.–Oct. 1941
Curtin 1941–1945
Chifley 1945–1949
Menzies 1949–1966
Holt 1966–68
McEwen (acting) 1968
Gorton 1968–1971
McMahon 1971–1972
Whitlam 1972–1975
Fraser 1975–1983
Hawke 1983–

Austria (Ger. **Oesterreich**). Roman provinces of Rhaetia, Noricum, and Pannonia *c.* 33 B.C. Organized as a march (*Ostmark*) of the Holy Roman Empire (*q.v.*) by Charlemagne. 791–6. Created a duchy, 1156. Given by Emperor Rudolf I of Hapsburg to his son Rudolf, 1282. Carinthia annexed, 1335. Defeated twice by Swiss at Zürich, 1358. Annexation of Tyrol, 1363. Leopold III killed by Swiss at battle of Sempach, 1386. Albert V becomes King of Bohemia and Hungary, 1437–40. Created archduchy, 6 Jan. 1453. Recognizes Swiss independence, 1474. Vienna captured by Matthias of Hungary, 1485. A. given to Ferdinand, brother of Emperor Charles V, 1521. Annexation of Bohemia and Silesia, 1526. First Turkish siege of Vienna, 1529. 'Imperial' Hungary ceded to A., 1541. Truce of Adrianople with Turks, 1545. Zapolya renounces Hungary to A., 1570. Thirty Years War (*q.v.*), 1618–48. Peace of Westphalia (*q.v.*), 1648. Hungary conquered from Turks, 1688; acquisition confirmed by Treaty of Carlowitz, 1699. War of Austrian Succession, 1741–8.Seven Years War (*q.v.*), 1756–63. French Revolutionary Wars begun 1792. Lombardy and the Netherlands secured by France, 1797. Defeat at battle of Hohenlinden, Dec. 1800. Pact of Lunéville, Feb. 1801. Defeat at battle of Ulm, 1805. At Austerlitz, Dec. 1805. Pact of Pressburg, Dec. 1805. Battle of Wagram, 1809. Battle of Leipzig, 1813. Treaty of Paris, May 1814. Congress of Vienna, 1814–15. The Karlsbad Decrees, 1819. Revolution and resignation of Metternich, Mar. 1848. Czech revolt suppressed, June 1848. Hungarian rebellion under Kossuth, Sept. 1848. Windischgrätz suppressed Vienna insurrection, Oct. 1848. Hungarians capitulate to Russians at Vilagos, Aug. 1849. Convention of Olmütz (Olomouc), 1850. Occupation of Rumania, 1854. Austro-Prussian invasion of Denmark, 1864. War with Prussia, 1866. Battle of Sadowa, 3 July 1866. Sardinia annexed Venetia, 1866. The '*Ausgleich*' ('compromise') with Hungary, 1867. Alliance with Russia and Germany (*Dreikaiserbund*), 1873. Renewed, 1881, 1884. Annexation of Bosnia-Herzegovina, 1908. Archduke Franz Ferdinand assassinated at Sarajevo, 28 June 1914. World War I (*q.v.*),

1914–18. *Bundesrepublik* (Federal Republic) declared secession from Dual Monarchy, 12 Nov. 1918. New boundaries settled by Treaty of St. Germain, 10 Sept. 1919. Federal Constitution, Nov. 1920. Dollfuss suppresses Socialists in Vienna by military force, Feb. 1934. Assassinated by Nazis, 25 July 1934. A. annexed by Germany, 12–14 Mar. 1938. Russian armies invaded A., 1945, and captured Vienna, 13 Apr. Karl Renner (1870–1950) elected president, 1945, of revived *Bundesrepublik*. Agreement with Italy on S. Tyrol, 6 Sept. 1946. Austrian peace treaty signed, 15 May 1955. Last occupation forces left A., Sept. 1955.

Austria, Emperors of:

The rulers of the house of Hapsburg (Grand Dukes of Austria) took the title of Emperor of A. on 11 Aug. 1804, and Francis II renounced the crown of the Holy Roman Empire (*q.v.*), 6 Aug. 1806. The following were the Emperors of A.:

Franz II and I 1804–1835
Ferdinand I 1835–1848
Franz Josef 1848–1916
Karl (abdicated) 1916–1918

Effective Heads of Administration:

The government of the Austrian Empire cannot be compared with the system of responsible government existing in England at the same time. Its heads relied in the last resort upon the emperor, and his personal policy could decide which member of the administration was to be the effective head, regardless of their actual titles of office. The following is a list of the most influential figures in Austrian government. It does not purport to be a list of the holders of one particular office.

Stadion 1806–1809
Von Metternich 1809–1848
Kolowrat 1848
Ficquelmont 1848
Von Pillersdorf 1848
Wessenberg 1848
Schwarzenberg 1848–1852
Bach 1852–1859
Goluchowski 1859–1860
Von Schmerling 1861–1865

Belcredi 1865–1867
Beust 1867–1870
Taaffe 1870–1871
Hohenwart 1871
Von Auersperg 1871–1878
Stremayr 1878–1879
Taaffe 1879–1893
Windischgrätz 1893–1895
Badeni 1895–1897
Gautsch 1897–1898
Von Thun 1898–1899
Clary-Aldringen 1899
Von Körber 1900–1904
Gautsch 1905–1906
Von Hohenlohe 1906
Beck 1906–1908
Biernerth 1908–1911
Gautsch 1911
Stürgkh 1912–1916
Von Körber 1916
Clam-Martinic 1917
Von Seidler 1917–1918
Hussarek 1918
Lammasch 1918
Presidents, since 1920:
Hainisch 1920–1928
Miklas 1928–1938
(13 Mar.)
Renner 1945–1950
Koerner 1951–1957
Schärf 1957–1965
Jonas 1965–1974
Kirchsläger 1974–
Heads of Administration since 1919 (Chancellors):
Renner Mar. 1919–Oct. 1919
Mayr Oct. 1919–July 1920
'Proporz' Cabinet July 1920–Nov. 1920
Mayr Nov. 1920–May 1921
Schober July 1921–May 1922
Seipel May 1922–Nov. 1924
Ramek Nov. 1924–Oct. 1926
Seipel Oct. 1926–Apr. 1929
Steeruwitz May 1929–Sept. 1929
Schober Sept. 1929–Sept. 1930
Vaugoin Sept. 1930–Nov. 1930
Ender Dec. 1930–June 1931
Seipel 18 June 1931–20 June 1931
Buresch June 1931–May 1932
Dollfuss May 1932–July 1934
Von Schuschnigg July 1934–12 Mar. 1938
Seyss-Inquart was nominally chancellor from 12–14 Mar. 1938. After 'inviting' Hitler to annex Austria, he became first governor of *Ostmark*.
Renner Apr. 1945–Oct. 1945 (provisional)
Figl Nov. 1945–1953
Raab 1953–1959
Gorbach 1959–1964
Klaus 1964–1970
Kreisky 1970–1983
Sinowatz 1983–

Austrian Succession, War of the Broke out, 1741. Ended by Treaty of Aix-la-Chapelle, 1748.

Authorized Version of the Bible, rendered into English by a commission of 47 translators working, 1607–10, and first published, 1611.

Auto-da-fé, or ceremonial burning of heretics by the Inquisition, last performed in Mexico, 1815.

Automobile Association. Founded, 1905.

Autun, France Ancient Augustodunum, founded by Augustus, who removed thither the population of nearby Gallic Bibracte. Destroyed, A.D. 240; but rebuilt 340; sacked by Vandals, 406; Burgundians, 414; Huns, 451; Franks, 534; Arabs, 739; Normans, 895; English, 1379.

Auxiliary Territorial Service. *See* WOMEN'S ROYAL ARMY CORPS.

Aviation. Borelli's artificial wings, 1670; Sir George Cayley's machine, 1796; Henson's aerostat, 1843; Wenham's aeroplane, 1866; Dr. Pettigrew's elastic screws demonstrated, 1867; Moy's aerial steamer, 1874; Langley's steam-driven model, 1893; Sir H. Maxim's experiments, 1880–1890, 1893–4; Lilienthal killed on gliding machine, 1896; W. and O. Wright's experiments begun, 1900; they first flew, 1903; S. Dumont's aeroplane, 1906; Farman biplane, 1907; Blériot flew across Channel, 25 July 1909; Paulhan's altitude record, Jan. 1910. First air mail service between Hendon and Windsor, 1911. Single-seater planes used solely for fighting first used by British, Dec. 1914. First airship and aeroplane crossing of Atlantic, 1919. First solo transatlantic flight, New York-Paris, by Lindbergh, in just over thirty-three hrs, reaching Paris, 21 May 1927. First jet-propelled plane in service (German), 1944. First pilotless plane to cross Atlantic, Oct. 1947 Maiden flights of both Fr. and Brit. models of the Anglo-Fr. supersonic *Concorde*, 1969.First 'Jumbo-jet' flew Atlantic on commercial flight, 1970. Worst single A. accident Aug. 1985 (Boeing 747 in Japan: 520 died).

Avignon. Popes went into residence at, 1309. Purchase from France, 1348. Papal Palace built, 1342–60. Popes left for rome, 1377. French antipopes at A., 1378–1408. Became an archbishopric, 1475. Annexed by France, 1797.

Avlona. *See* VLÖNE.

Avoirdupois Weight. First Act directing use of, 1532. *See* WEIGHTS AND MEASURES.

Avon, non-metropolitan county estab. 1974 under the Local Government Act of 1972 and based in Bristol (*q.v.*).

Avranches, Concordat of, whereby Henry II of England withdrew all his demands concerning jurisdiction over 'criminous clerks', and other causes of his disputes with Becket, and in return was absolved of all complicity in the archbishop's murder, 1172.

'Axis', The. Italo-German alliance of 1936.

Aylesbury Election Case, 1704, or **Ashby** *v.* **White.** Decided that the courts would protect any one whose right to vote was wrongfully denied.

Aynthia, Siam. Founded, 1351. Capital till 1782, when it was sacked by Burmese.

Azerbaijan(Iranian). Russian attempt to subvert frustrated, 1946.

Azerbaijan(Russian). Soviet republic, 1920. Included in the Transcaucasian Republic, 1922. Since 1936 a constituent republic of the U.S.S.R.

Azores. Discovered by Portuguese under Cabral, 1431–2. First settled, 1444. British allowed temporary naval and air bases under agreement with Portuguese, 12 Oct. 1943.

Azov, Russia. Founded, twelfth century. Taken by Tamerlane, 1395; by Russians, 1696; restored to Turks, 1711. Fortifications demolished, 1739. Ceded to Russia, 1774. Occupied by Germans, 1941; retaken, 1943.

Aztecs. Settled in Mexico (*q.v.*) c. A.D. 1200. Overthrown by Cortes, 1519.

B

Baal, major figure in several Syriac-Palestinian cults, co-existent with the Old Testament, in which B. is specifically mentioned.

Baalbek, or Heliopolis, Syria. Captured by Assyrians, 738 B.C. Became a Roman colony under Augustus (31 B.C.–A.D. 14). Sanctuary built, 150–210. Converted into church c. 330. Captured by Arabs, 635. Dome removed to the 'Dome of the Rock' in Jerusalem c. 710. Walls demolished, 745. Sacked by Mongols, 1400. Earthquake, 1759. Laid waste, 1760–70, by Turks.

Babi. *See* BAHA'I.

Babington's Conspiracy. Anthony B. (1561–86) and others plotted to kill Queen Elizabeth and liberate Mary, Queen of Scots. Leaders of plot executed, Sept. 1586.

Babylon (town). Settled about 4000 B.C. by the Sumerians; first mentioned in a cuneiform tablet c. 2700 B.C. Capital c. 2200 B.C. After 1100 B. became subject to or dependent on Assyria until the New Babylonian Empire (620–539) was founded by Nebuchadnezzar. 'New Palace' built, 604. The town was destroyed by Sennacherib the Assyrian, 696 B.C., and rebuilt by Essarhaddon, 680–670. Captured by Cyrus, 538. The most important excavations of the city took place, A.D. 1899–1917.

Babylonia. First mentioned as an independent state c. 2200 B.C. Elamites driven out by Hammurapi (the biblical Amraphel) c. 2037. Kassite conquest of B. c. 1743. Rise of Assyria, 1900–1400. Assyrians became supreme under Shalmanezer I, 1300. First Assyrian Empire reaches its climax under Tiglath-Pileser I c 1110. Civil war, 824–746, leads to establishment of Second Assyrian Empire by Pul (Tiglath-Pileser III),

745. Pul crowned at Babylon, 729. Merodachbaladan leads rebellion against Assyria, 722–710. Assyrian power destroyed by the Babylonians and Medes c. 610, and end of B.'s independence, 538, by Persian conquest.

Babylonian Captivity. Jewish historical term to describe the period between the capture or destruction of Jerusalem by Nebuchadnezzar, 599 or 586, and the deportation of its inhabitants, to the edict of Cyrus, 538, allowing the tribes of Judah, Benjamin, and Levi to return home.

'Babylonish Captivity'. Name applied by critical contemporaries to the Papacy's residence at Avignon (*q.v.*), 1309–77.

Bachelor of Arts. Degree first conferred in various universities in the thirteenth century.

Bachelor Tax. Imposed in England, 1695 and 1785.

Bacteria. Discovered by van Leeuwenhoek, 1680. F. J. Cohn (1828–98) founder of modern bacteriology.

Bactria. Old Persian province now part of Afghanistan (*q.v.*). Conquered by Cyrus c. 540 B.C., by Alexander, 325. After 323 ruled by Seleucids until the beginning of the independent Graeco-Bactrian kingdom (255–140) founded by Diodotos which was conquered by the Scythians, who ruled until A.D. 560.

Badajoz (Rom. **Pax Augusta**), Spain. Originally a Celtic settlement, then a town in Roman times. Capital of a Moorish kingdom, 1031. Besieged very frequently, the most recent being the sieges by the Portuguese, 1385, 1396, 1542, and 1705; the French, 1808–9, and Feb. 1811; the British, May and June 1811. It was finally stormed by

British, 6 Apr. 1812. During Spanish Civil War taken by insurgents, Aug. 1936.

Badakhshan visited by Marco Polo, 1272–3, was part of the Graeco-Bactrian kingdom (*See* BACTRIA). From the thirteenth century until the time of Nadir Shah of Persia (1688–1747), ruled by a local dynasty claiming descent from Alexander the Great. Conquered by the Uzbeks *c*. 1800; Afghan supremacy was restored, 1859. Gorno.-B. has been an autonomous region of Tajikstan (*q.v.*) since 1929.

Baden, Grand Duchy and Republic of, split between several rulers of the Zähringen family till 1771, when it was united under one margrave. Became a Grand Duchy and substantially enlarged, 1806. Constitution granted, 1818. Hecker and Struve established a republic, 1848; grand duke reinstated, 1849. Joined Austria against Prussia, 1866. Joined German Empire, 1871. Republic declared, 1918. Suppressed by Hitler 1934. *Land* of Baden-Württemberg, since 1952.

Baden-Baden, Germany. Founded as **Aurelia Aquensis** by Hadrian, in the second century A.D. The ruins on Castle Hill (Schlossberg) are of a castle destroyed by the French in 1689, as was the original 'new castle' built in the sixteenth century, of which the extant building is a facsimile. Famous nineteenth-century spa and gambling resort.

Badminton. Seat of the Dukes of Beaufort in Gloucestershire, came into the hands of the Somerset family, 1608; the present building was erected by Henry Somerset (1629–99), first Duke of Beaufort in 1682, one of the finest surviving examples of the Palladian style. The game of B. was invented at B. House *c*. 1870. B. Horse Trials estab. after Second World War.

Baffin Bay. Discovered by William Baffin, 1616.

Bagdad, Iraq. Founded, A.D. 763, by the Abbasid Caliph Al-Mansur, it reached its highest splendour in the reign of Haroun-al-Rashid (786–809). Besieged and stormed by Persians under Tahir

(812–13). Seljuk Sultan Toghrul Beg acclaimed here, 1055. Seljuks ousted, 1181. Kwarismian attack, 1216. Sacked by Hulagu, the Mongol emperor, 1258. Captured by Timur, 1393. Turkish from 1638. Captured by British, 11 Mar. 1917. Became capital of Iraq, 1921. Headquarters of the B. Pact (*q.v.*), 1955–8. Revolution overthrowing the monarchy originated in B., July 1958.

Bagdad Pact. Defensive and economic pact, so called because it was first signed at Bagdad between Turkey and Iraq in Feb. 1955. Subsequently Britain (Apr.), Pakistan (Sept.), and Iran (Nov.) signed it. In 1958 Iraq left the organization which was renamed CENTO (Central Treaty Organization) (*q.v.*).

Baha'i or **Babi.** Followers of an originally Persian sect founded *c*. 1844 by Mirza Ali Mohammed (1819–*c*. 1850) of Shiraz. After the martyrdom of its founder at Tabriz in 1850 the sect spread through the Ottoman Empire, and is still extant to-day, about two-thirds of its adherents being converts from Islam or the descendants of such, the remainder mostly W. Europeans and Americans.

Bahamas (formerly **Lucayos**). Discovered by Columbus, 1492. The first island colonized was Eleuthera, 1646; then New Providence, 1666. English expelled by French and Spaniards, 1703; recolonized by English, 1717; reduced by Spain, 1781; restored, 1783, by treaty. Extensive cyclone damage, 1866, 1883, 1945. Duke of Windsor (formerly Edward VIII) appointed governor, 1940–45. Independent within Commonwealth, 1973.

Bahrain. Archipelago in Persian Gulf, B. was occupied by the Portuguese for the whole of the sixteenth century, who were then dispossessed by Arab subjects of the Shah. Britain undertook B's defence and foreign relations under treaties of 1882 and 1892. Oil discovered, 1931. Independent, 1971.

Baia, formerly **Bahia,** Brazil. Visited by Amerigo Vespucci, 1510. Colonized, 1536. Refounded, 1549, and seat of viceroys of Brazil until 1763.

Bailey or **Old Bailey.** The street in London (first extant reference, 1444–5) in which have stood a succession of courts for the trial of criminals. One, built 1773, was destroyed, 1780; rebuilt, 1785–1786; enlarged, 1808. Rebuilt on site of Newgate Prison, 1902–7.

Bailey Bridge, invented by Donald Bailey, 1941, and successfully used during World War II and since.

Baireuth. *See* BAYREUTH.

Bakelite, invented 1908, in U.S.A. First plastic.

Baku, U.S.S.R. Under Persia, 1509–1723. Under Russia, 1723–35. Persia, 1735–1806. Finally annexed by Russia, 1806. Oil refineries severely damaged in civil disturbances, 1904–5, 1914–21, and in World War II. Reported riots since 1945.

Balaklava or **Balaclava,** U.S.S.R, anciently *Portus Cymbolorum,* became a Genoese 'factory' in the fourteenth century, and remained so until the Turkish conquest of the Crimea (*q.v.*). Became a garrison town under Catherine the Great (1762–96). Held by British expeditionary force, 1854–6. *See* BATTLES.

Balasore was the first English settlement in India, 1642, and the last (as distinct from the Portuguese and French possessions) of the other European stations; the Danish 'factory' here was sold to the E. India Co., 1846.

Balearic Islands. Colonized by the Phoenicians *c.* fourth century B.C. Conquered by Romans, 123 B.C. By Vandals *c.* A.D. 426. By Moors, 798. Independent Moorish kingdom, 1009–1232. Independent Christian kingdom of Majorca, 1276–1349, when it became a dependency of Aragon. *See* MAJORCA and MINORCA.

Balfour Declaration. *See* PALESTINE, MODERN.

Bali. During the period of Moslem expansion in the fifteenth century A.D. many Buddhists and Brahmins fled to B. and the religion of the island is a synthesis of these two faiths both in a more archaic form than any extant elsewhere. Trade relations with the Dutch began in 1597, and some coastal areas came under the rule of the Netherlands in 1845; Dutch rule not firmly established until 1908. B. was captured by the Japanese in 1942, and they remained in possession until 3 Mar. 1946. Part of Indonesia since 1946. Volcanic eruption, Mar. 1963, killed over 1,000 people on B.

Balkan Entente. Between Yugoslavia, Rumania, Turkey, and Greece, signed in Athens, 9 Feb. 1934. Bulgaria signed non-aggression pact with B.E., 31 July 1938. Renewed for seven years, 3 Feb. 1940, but a dead letter after 1941.

Balkan Mountains. Became frontier line of Turkish dominions by Treaty of Berlin, 13 July 1878.

Balkan Wars, Oct. 1912 to Aug. 1913, fall into three divisions: 1. First B. War—the war of the B. League against Turkey in which the League conquered Macedonia, Albania, and a large part of Thrace. Armistice, Dec. 1912. 2. Greece continued the war. The armistice denounced, Feb. 1913, and the other allies continued the war. 3. Second B. War. B. League broke up, June 1913, then followed the war of Serbia, Greece, and Montenegro against Bulgaria, assisted by Rumania, which now intervened, and Turkey. The first B. War ended by Treaty of London, 30 May 1913; the second by Treaty of Bucharest, 10 Aug. 1913, and by the treaty between Bulgaria and Turkey, 18 Sept. 1913.

Ballarat goldfield was opened up, 1851. The rebellion of miners at Eureka Stockade, 3 Dec. 1854, is the only battle ever fought on Australian soil.

Ballet. The culmination of a long tradition of European dance technique, difficult to trace historically, but perhaps first reaching a form which would be recognizable to-day at the courts of England, Scotland, and France late in the fifteenth century. To this was added the influence of Italian pantomime; the kind of entertainment devised *c.* 1555 for Catherine de Medici by her Master of Music Baltazarini (who *d. c.* 1587) is the first to be called B. In the classical comedy of seventeenth-century France B. forms an integral part of the entertainment and it did not become finally disengaged from 'legitimate' drama and opera until the mid-nineteenth century. The classical European B. of to-day derives from the Russian school of St. Petersburg, the formative period of which was 1840–80, though the Imperial B. had been founded in 1735, largely under French and Italian tuition. The return impact of Russian dancing on the W. had its greatest force in the years 1910–20, just after the influence of Isadora Duncan (1878–1927) had been felt in St. Petersburg. Nijinsky became Imperial B. Master, 1913. Massine produced his first B., 1917.

Prominent names in the world of modern B. include:

Ashton, Sir Frederick (Brit. dancer and choreographer), 1906–.

Balanchine, George (Russian-b. choreographer), 1904–83.

de Valois, Dame Ninette (Brit. ballerina and choreographer), 1898–1982.

Diaghilev, Sergei (Russian impresario and choreographer), 1872–1929.

Duncan, Isadora (American dancer), 1878–1927.

Fonteyn, Dame Margot (Brit. ballerina), 1919–.

Helpmann, Sir Robert (Australian dancer and choreographer), 1907–.

Markova, Dame Alicia (Brit. ballerina), 1910–.

Massine, Leonid (Russian dancer and choreographer), 1896–1979.

Nijinsky, Vaslav (Russian dancer), 1890–1950.

Nureyev, Rudolf (Rusian-b. dancer), 1939–.

Pavlova, Anna (Russian ballerina), 1885–1931.

Rambert, Dame Marie (Polish-b. ballerina), 1889–.

Balloons. Principal experiments, etc., with: Joseph Montgolfier made first fire balloon, 1782. Brothers Montgolfier successfully made an ascent in a fire balloon, 1783. First ascent in balloon filled with hydrogen at Paris by Professor Charles, Aug. 1783. First ascent in England by Vincent Lunardi,

Sept. 1784. Channel crossed by Blanchard and Jefferies, 7 Jan. 1785. Nassau balloon left London and descended at Nassau, 1836. Nadar's balloon ascended with fourteen persons, 4 Oct. 1863 (the first balloon with steering apparatus). Glaisher and Coxwell rose to a height of seven miles in a balloon, 5 Sept. 1862. Godard's Montgolfier balloon ascended, 28 July and 3 Aug. 1864. Giffard's experiments with dirigible, 1852. Zeppelin, 1900, 1908. Alberto Santos Dumont's experiments with steerable balloon, July–Oct. 1901; Feb. 1902. B. were used for observation purposes by the French, 1794, but Napoleon disbanded the Balloon Corps, 1798. Used as artillery observation posts in Italian war of Liberation, 1860: American Civil War (*q.v.*); in Franco- Prussian War, 1870–1871; and in Spanish-American War, 1898. German Balloon Corps formed, 1884; British Balloon Corps, 1879. B. first used by the Royal Navy at Gallipoli, 1915, and on the western front during World War I; and in mass as a barrage against aircraft, World War II.

Ballot Box. First used in England at election of London aldermen, 1526. Bills authorizing parliamentary voting by ballot thrown out by Lords, 1710; passed, 18 July 1872. First parliamentary election in England by secret ballot at Pontefract, 15 Aug. 1872.

Ballymote, Book of. A MS. in Middle Irish, a miscellany of prose and verse copied in 1391 by the monks of B. in Sligo.

Balmoral Castle. Purchased by Prince Albert, 1852; present building commenced, 1853; completed, 1855.

Baltic and Black Sea Canal. Projected by Peter the Great, said to have been completed 70 years after his death, afterwards fell into disuse.

Baltic and White Sea Canal (length, 142 miles). Begun, Dec. 1931; opened, 1933.

Baltic Entente. Alliance between Estonia, Latvia, Lithuania, and Poland, Mar. 1922.

Baltic Exchange. The Baltic merchants began in Elizabethan times to meet in the Virginia and Baltic inns. In the eighteenth century merchants interested in Baltic trade met in the Baltic Coffee House. The Baltic Club founded, 1823. The association thus formed was united in 1899 with the London Shipping Exchange to form the modern B. E.

Baltic Expeditions.
1. Under Admirals Parker and Nelson, 1801.
2. Under Admiral Gambier and Lord Cathcart, 1807. 3. Under Admiral Napier, 11 Mar. 1854. 4. Under Rear- Admiral Dundas, 4 Apr. 1855.

Baltic Sea. Whole surface frozen over, 1658, 1809. Holstein Canal, connecting River Eider with Baltic, opened, 1785; B. and N. Sea Canal for large vessels, 1891.

Baltic States. Estonia, Lithuania, and Latvia (*see* all these) proclaimed independent republics, 1918. All these states were annexed to the U.S.S.R., July 1940. Occupied by Germany, 1941–4, and incorporated in the Reich Commissariat 'Ostland'. Reconquered by the U.S.S.R., 1944–5. Subsequently reincorporated into the U.S.S.R.

Baltimore, Maryland. Founded, 1729. Named after the first Lord B. Incorporated, 1796. Greater part of business area destroyed by fire, 1904. Subsequent rebuilding and considerable expansion. *See* MARYLAND.

Baluchistan, Asia. Occupied by British successively, 1839, 1840, 1841. British B. incorporated in India, 1887. Became part of Pakistan (*q.v.*), 15 Aug. 1947.

Bamberg, Germany. Prince Bishopric founded, A.D. 1007. University existed between 1648 and 1803. Secular power finally abolished, 1806.

Bamburgh Castle. The stronghold of the Bernician (*q.v.*) kings, built by Ida the Anglian chief, 547; besieged by the Mercian pagan King Penda, 641. Destroyed by Olaf of Dublin, 993. Besieged by William II, 1095. Extensively added to in Norman times, especially under Robert de Mowbray, Earl of Northumberland, 1080–93; and often restored, especially in 1721.

Bought by Lord Armstrong and made into almhouses, 1894.

Bampton Lectures in divinity at Oxford founded by Rev. John B. (1690–1751). Begun, 1780.

Banat, the. Area between Transylvanian Alps and rivers Tisza, Mures and Danube. Originally ruled by Hungary, but under the Austrian crown, 1849–60. Treaty of Trianon, 1920, divided it between Yugoslavia and Rumania.

Banbury, England. Castle erected at by Alexander, Bishop of Lincoln, 1125. Battle of (Wars of Roses), 1469. Surrendered to Charles I, Oct. 1642; besieged, 1643, 1644, and in 1646, when it surrendered to parliamentary forces.

Band of Hope. Temperance association for juveniles, started in Leeds, 1847. Organized into the Band of Hope Union, 1855.

Banda Islands discovered (1512) and settled (1520) by Portuguese; occupied by Dutch, 1814, who had expelled the Portuguese, 1580. Formal cession by Britain to Netherlands, 1816. Joined Indonesia, 1950.

Bandoeng or **Bandung,** Indonesia, on island of Java. The Bandoeng Conference, a meeting of Afro-Asian delegates, held here, 18–27 Apr. 1955.

Banff, Scotland. Granted charter by Malcolm IV, 1163; by Robert Bruce, 1324; and Robert II, 1372. Present castle built, 1750.

Bangkok, Thailand. Became capital of Siam (now Thailand) after Burmese destroyed Aynthia, 1782. The Emerald Buddha chapel built, 1785.

Bangladesh. Independent republic since 1971, formerly E. Pakistan. Original constitution provided for parliamentary democracy but this ceased Jan. 1975 with presidency of Mujibur Rahman (assassinated Aug. 1975). Several subsequent military coups.

Bangor, Wales. Bishopric and cathedral reputed founded by St. Deiniol *c.* 550. Old cathedral destroyed, 1071. Present cathedral dates from 1496 to 1532. N. Wales University College opened, 18 Oct. 1884.

Bank. Chinese said to have had a paper

currency *c.* A.D. 800. In 808 Lombard Jews established a B. in Italy. Private Bs. existed in Venice in 1270. Bank of St. George, Genoa, 1407. The Banco di Rialto was established in Venice, 1584 and 1587—the first public B. in Europe. Banco del Giro, or B. of Venice, established, 1619; B. of Amsterdam, 1609; first B. established in England by Francis Child *c.* 1603; Bank of Hamburg, 1619–1873; Riksbank of Stockholm established, 1656; issued the first banknote, 1658.

Bank Amalgamations (British). Major stage completed, 1918, when 'big five' emerged; Barclays Bank, founded, 1896; Lloyd's Bank, founded, 1865; National Provincial Bank, founded, 1833; Midland Bank, founded, 1836; Westminster Bank, founded, 1836. Gurney & Co., last of the English private provincial Bs., founded, 1809, bought up by Barclays, Feb. 1953. National Provincial took over the District Bank, 1962. In 1968 National Provincial and Westminster Banks merged to form the National Westminster: and in 1969 Barclays absorbed Martin's Bank.

Bank Holidays Act. Introduced by Sir John Lubbock; passed, 25 May 1871.

Bank of England. Founded by William Paterson, who is said to have originated the project in 1691. Incorporated by charter, 27 July 1694. Special privileges: monopoly conferred, 1709; restricted, 1826, 1833. Cash payments suspended, 1797; resumed, 1821. Under Bank Charter is remodelled, 19 July 1844; Bank Charter suspended: 25 Oct. 1847; 12 Nov. 1857; 11 May 1866. Important changes in management, 16 June 1892. Rebuilding begun, 24 Nov. 1924. Nationalized, 1946.

Bank of France. Founded by Napoleon, 1800. Nationalized, 2 Dec. 1945.

Bank of Ireland. Established, 1 June 1783. Irish Banking Act passed, 21 July 1845. Central Bank of Eire established, 1 Feb. 1943.

Bank of Scotland. Set up at Edinburgh by Act of Scottish Parliament, 1695.

Bankruptcy (Great Britain). Court of, established by Act of Parliament, 1831.

Bankruptcy Acts (U.S.A.). Bill passed by Congress, 19 Aug. 1841; repealed, 3 Mar. 1843. National B. A., 1898 forms basis of subsequent bankruptcy laws.

Banks, American. Congress chartered the Bank of N. America, 26 May 1781; opened in Philadelphia, 1782; second bank established at Boston, 1784; Bank of U.S.A. established Philadelphia, 20 Dec. 1790; Bank of New York established, 1790; first Bank of the United States chartered, 1791–1811; second, 1816–36.

Bannockburn. *See* BATTLES.

Baptists (for earlier history of, *see* ANABARTISTS). First English Baptist church founded in Amsterdam by John Smyth and Thomas Helwys, 1609–11. Helwys formed first Baptist church in England, London, 1612 (General Baptist, or Arminian). First Particular Baptist (Calvinist) church formed, Southwark, 1633. Confession of Faith published by the seven Particular Baptist churches in London, 1644. Baptist Missionary Society founded, 1792. Baptist Union formed, 1812–13. Roger Williams formed first regular congregation of B. in America in Rhode Island *c.* Mar. 1639. Baptist World Alliance formed, 1905.

Bar, Confederation of the. An anti-Russian coalition of Polish nobles, formed 1768 and dissolved, 1776.

Bar, Trial at, i.e. a trial in the King's Bench division before a full bench of judges, was the usual procedure up to 1285; the last Trial at B. to date was that of Sir Roger Casement, for treason, 1916.

'Baralong' Case. German prize crew on board American ship killed by crew of British auxiliary 'B.' 19 Aug. 1915. German Government threatened Zeppelin warfare in retaliation, Dec. 1915.

Barbados, W. Indies. First mention, 1518. Thought to have been visited by Portuguese *c.* 1536; formally acquired by English, 1625. Independent state within the Commonwealth, 30 Nov. 1966.

Barbed Wire invented in America, 1873.

B. W. Act, concerning the fencing of land adjoining highways, passed, 1893.

Barbers, as a guild, were incorporated in England, 1461, and separated from surgeons, 1745.

Barbican Arts Centre, London E.C.2., opened 3 Mar. 1982, comprises a theatre, concert hall, cinemas, art gallery, library and restaurants.

Barcelona, Spain (*q.v.*). Said to have been built by Hamilcar Barca, third century B.C. Became a Roman colony; conquered by Visigoths, A.D. 415, and Moors, 713. Independent county, 762; incorporated with Aragon, 1164. Cathedral begun, 1298. University founded, 1450. Treaty of B. between France and Spain, 1493. Captured by the French under Vendôme, 1697; by the English under Peterborough, 1706. Taken by the Duke of Berwick (James FitzJames), for Philip V, 1714; by Napoleon, 1808. Restored to Spain by Treaty of Paris, 1814. Execution of Ferrer for conspiracy at, 13 Oct. 1909. Last capital of the republic, 1937. Surrendered to Gen. Franco, 1939.

Barebones Parliament, or Little Parliament, of members, selected from nominees of the congregations in each county. Met, 4 July 1653; dissolved, 12 Dec. 1653. Named after a certain Praise-God B. or P. Barbon (1596?–1679), who attended as member for London.

Barfleur, France. William, son of Henry I of England, wrecked and drowned, in the 'White Ship', off B., 28 Nov. 1120. Destroyed by English, 1346. French fleet destroyed off B. by Admiral Russell, 19 May, 1692.

Bargain and Sale. An obsolete form of real estate conveyance, facilitated by the Statute of Uses, 1535; fell into desuetude after the passing of the Real Property Act, 1845.

Bari (anct. **Barium**), Apulia, first mentioned, 180 B.C. Captured by Saracens, A.D. 812; retaken by Greeks, 885; by Robert Guiscard, 1071. Annexed to Kingdom of Naples, 1558. After Sept. 1943 was temporary seat of Badoglio's provisional government.

Barking, Essex. Benedictine abbey founded by St. Erconwald, 670, burnt by Vikings, 870. All Hallows, B. by the Tower, belonged to the abbey and was built in the seventh century; burnt down, 1087; rebuilt before 1100; rebuilt again in the thirteenth century and largely destroyed by bombing 29 Dec. 1941; but rebuilt after 1945.

Barnard Castle (County Durham). Built by Guy Baliol B. (1112–32). Taken from the rebel John Baliol by the English, 1296.

Barnardo's Homes, Dr., for orphans, founded 1866 by Thomas John B. (1845–1905).

Barnburners. Political faction in the U.S.A., active 1844–52.

Baroda, India. *See* MAHRATTAS.

Barometer. First made by Torricelli, a Florentine, *c.* 1643. Pascal's experiments, 1646. Aneroid B. said to have been invented by Conté, 1798. The English patent, however, was registered by Vidi for his invention of 1844. Vidi *d.*, 1866.

Baron.
1. Peerage title first used in England after Norman conquest, 1066. First created by patent, 1387. Wensleydale peerage case, 1856, decided that it must be hereditary to carry a seat in the House of Lords (*see* LORDS, HOUSE OF). This principle amended by Appellate Jurisdiction Act, 1876, and Life Peerages Act, 1958. Further modified by Peerages Act, 1963.
2. County Palatine of Chester had its own Bs. till 1679.
3. Ditto of Durham till 1716.
4. The Cinque Ports still have Bs. elected for life.

Baronet. Order of knighthood instituted by James I of England, 22 May 1611, to replenish his exchequer. The first B. was Sir Nicholas Bacon of Redgrave.

Barons' War. Caused by disputes between Henry III of England and the B. First important engagement, the taking of Northampton for the king by Prince Edward, 4 Apr. 1264; king's army defeated at Lewes, 14 May 1264; De Montfort killed and B. defeated at battle at Evesham, 4 Aug. 1265.

Barrier Act passed by the General Assembly of the Church of Scotland, 1697.

Barrier Treaties. By the first B. Treaty, between Great Britain and the States-General (29 Oct. 1709), 'Great Britain undertook to procure for the for the Dutch an adequate *barrier . . .*' to secure Holland against French aggression. The second (29 Jan. 1713) modified the first; by it British undertook to obtain right for Dutch to garrison the frontier fortresses 'from the future sovereign of the Spanish Netherlands.' The third, signed 15 Nov. 1715, was supplemental.

Barrow-in-Furness became industrially important with the discovery of haematite ore locally, 1840. Docks opened, 1867.

Bartholomew, Massacre of St., (of Huguenots), at Paris, 24 Aug. 1572.

Bartholomew, St. Old fair held on festival in London, 1133–1855. Hospital of St. B. (London) founded by Rahere, 1123; refounded, 1547; rebuilt, 1730–66. Medical college founded, 1843.

Baseball, mentioned by Jane Austen, 1798. Form of B. played in England and America before 1839; modern game said to have been evolved by Doubleday (1819–83). First professional team formed in U.S.A., 1871. National league organized, 1876. Rules standardized, 1887. World Series B. Contests began, 1903.

Basel or **Bâle,** Switzerland. Council of, 1431–49. University founded, 1460. Joined Swiss Confederation, 1501. The bishopric abolished, 1529. Treaty between France and Prussia, 22 July 1795. Canton divided into two half-cantons, 1833 (Basel-Stadt and Basel-Land).

Bashkiria. Autonomous republic of R.S.F.S.R., set up, 1919.

Basic English, first word-list of printed, 1929. First dictionary published, 1932. Committee of ministers reported on, 1943, and Government purchased copyright in, 1947.

Basketball invented in the U.S.A., 1891, by James Naismith.

Basques. *See* NAVARRE.

Basra, Iraq. Founded by Caliph Omar, 637.

Bassein, Burma. Founded *c.* 1250.

Bassein, India. Ceded to the Portuguese, 1534. Taken by the Mahrattas, 1739. Taken over by the British, 1818.

Bass Rock, Firth of Forth, Scotland. St. Baldred (*d.* 756) had a hermitage here. It was bought by the English Government, fortified and made into a political prison, 1671, where leading Covenanters were detained. In 1691 four young Jacobites captured the island by a trick and held it against the Williamite forces from June 1691 to Apr. 1694. Fort demolished, 1701.

Bastaards or **Bastards.** *See* GRIQUAS.

Bastard. *See* LEGITIMACY ACT.

Bastille (Paris). Built, 1369–83, destroyed, 14–15 July 1789.

Basutoland. *See* LESOTHO.

Bataan, Philippine Is. Famous stand against Japanese by MacArthur's troops, 9 Dec. 1941–9 Apr. 1942.

Batavia. *See* JAKARTA.

Batavian Republic. Holland was reorganized under this name under French hegemony, May 1795–June 1806.

Bates's Case. Tried before Court of Exchequer, 1606. John Bates, a Levant merchant, refused to pay excess duty not authorized by Parliament, but four Barons of the Exchequer found against him.

Bath, England. (Rom. **Aquae Sulis**). Roman baths begun, A.D. 84. Used until *c.* 400. Cathedral founded, A.D.775. King Edgar crowned at B., A.D. 973. Bishopric amalgamated with Wells, 1139. Present abbey, founded 1405–99, superseded cathedral. Grammar school founded, 1552. Roman baths uncovered, partly, 1788, but not excavated. Rediscovered, 1879, and excavated, 1888–90, 1923 and during 1980s. Pump room built as a result of resolution by the corporation of 1705. Rebuilt, 1751 and 1795. National Hospital for Rheumatic Diseases founded, 1738, largely at the instance of Beau Nash (1674–1761). Univ. estab., 1966.

Battersea first mentioned in a document of 693. The park was opened, 1853. In connection with Festival of Britain, 1951. Pleasure Gardens opened 28 May, later discontinued.

Battle, Wager of, and **Appeal of Felony.** Last waged in Court of Common Pleas, 1571. Court of Chivalry, 1631. Court of Durham, 1638. As a result of an attempted Trial by Combat in 1818 both were formally abolished, 1819.

Battle Abbey. Founded by William the Conqueror on site of battle of Hastings, 1067. Consecrated, 1094. Its abbot sat in the House of Lords until the Dissolution of the Monasteries (*q.v.*), 1539.

Battle Abbey Roll, purporting to be a nominal roll of Norman officers present at the battle of Hastings, is a forgery, probably of the fourteenth century.

Battles. *See also* WORLD WARS I and II and SIEGES. Most famous or important battles are printed in **bold type.** Those described in Creasy's *Fifteen Decisive Battles of the World* are marked ¶.

On Land

B. connected with Napoleon are marked N, with Wellington W, with Marlborough M, and with Frederick the Great F.

Aboukir,
  (1) 25 July 1799 (N)
  (2) 8 Mar. 1801
Abu Klea, 17 Jan. 1885
Acs, 2 and 10 July 1849
Adowa, 1 Mar. 1896
Adrianople,
  (1) 3 July 323
  (2) 9 Aug. 378
  (3) 20 Aug. 1829
Agincourt, 25 Oct. 1415
Agnadello, 14 May 1509
Aisne
  (1) 13–28 Sept. 1914
  (2) 16–20 Apr. 1917
  (3) 27 May–6 June 1918
Ajnadain, 30 July 634
Akhalzikh, 24 Aug. 1828
Alamein, 23 Oct.–7 Nov. 1942
Alamo, 24 Feb.–6 Mar. 1836
Alarcos, 1185
Albans, St.,
  (1) 22 or 23 May 1455
  (2) 17 Feb. 1461

Albuera, 16 May 1811 (W)
Albufera, 4 Jan. 1812 (W)
Alexandria,
  (1) 21 Mar. 1801
  (2) 11–13 July 1882
Alford, 2 July 1645
Aliwal, 28 Jan. 1846
Allia, 16 July 390 B.C.
Alma, 20 Sept. 1854
Almansa, 25 Apr. 1707
Almenara, 28 July 1710
Angora, 28 July 1402
Anjou, 22 Mar. 1421
Antietam, 16–17 Sept. 1862
Antioch, 28 June 1098
Anzio, 22–25 May 1944
¶**Arbela, 1 Oct. 331** B.C.
Arcis-sur-Aube, 20–21 Mar. 1814
Arcole, 14–17 Nov. 1796 (N)
Ardennes, 16–22 Dec. 1944
Argaum, 29 Nov. 1803
Argentario, 378
Arklow, 10 June 1798
Arnhem, 17–26 Sept. 1944
Arques, 13–28 Sept. 1589
Aspern, 21–2 May 1809 (N)
Aspromonte, 29 Aug. 1862
Assandun (Ashingdon), 1016
Assaye, 23 Sept. 1803 (W)
Asunden (Lake), Jan. 1520
Atbara, The, 8 Apr. 1898
Atherton Moor, 30 June 1643
Atlanta, 22 July 1864
Auerstädt, 14 Oct. 1806 (N)
Aughrim, 12 July 1691
Auneau, 24 Nov. 1587
Austerlitz, 2 Dec. 1805 (N)
Ayacucho, 9 Dec. 1824
Aylesford, *c.* 455
Badajoz, 6 Apr. 1812 (W)
Balaklava, 25 Oct. 1854
Bannockburn, 24 June 1314
Bapaume, 2–3 Jan. 1871
Barnet, 14 Apr. 1471
Barrosa, 5 Mar. 1811 (W)
Bassano, 8 Sept. 1796
Bastogne, Dec. 1944
Bautzen, 20–21 May 1813 (N)
Baylen, 20 July 1808 (W)
Beaugé. *See* ANJOU
Belfort (siege), 3 Nov. 1870–8 Feb. 1871
Belgrade (siege), 22 July–4 Sept. 1456
Belmont, 23 Nov. 1899
Benevento, 26 Feb. 1266

Bennington, 16 Aug. 1777
Beresina, 26–28 Nov. 1812 (N)
Berlin, 15 Apr.–2 May 1945
Big Bethel, 10 May 1861
Bir Hakim, 26 May–11 June 1942
Bitonto, 27 May 1734
¶ **Blenheim, 13 Aug. 1704** (M)
Blore Heath, 23 Sept. 1459
Blumenau, 22 July 1866
Borghetto, 30 May 1796 (N)
Borisov, 27 Nov. 1812
Borodino, 7 Sept. 1812 (N)
Bosworth Field, 22 Aug. 1485
Bothwell Bridge, 22 June 1679
Bouvines, 27 July 1214
Boxtel, 17 Sept. 1794
Boyne, 1 July 1690
Braila, 19 June 1773
Brandywine, 11 Sept. 1777
Brechin, 18 May 1452
Brentford, 12 Nov. 1642
Breslau, 22 Nov. 1757 (F)
Briars Creek, 3 May 1779
Brienne, 29 Jan. 1814 (N)
Brunanburh, c. 937
'Bulge, The'. *See* ARDENNES
Bull Run,
  (1) 21 July 1861
  (2) 29–30 Aug. 1862
Bunker Hill, 17 June 1775
Burlington Heights, 6 June 1813
Busaco, 27 Sept. 1810 (W)
Buxar, 1764
Caen, 25 June–8 July 1944
Calatafimi, 15 May 1860
Camden (U.S.A.),
  (1) 16 Aug. 1780
  (2) 25 Apr. 1781
Cannae, 2 Aug. 216 B.C.
Caporetto, 24 Oct.–18 Nov. 1917
Carberry Hill, 15 June 1567
Carrhae, 53 B.C.
Cassano,
  (1) 16 Aug. 1705
  (2) 27–29 Apr. 1799
Cassino, 5 Feb.–8 May 1944
Castalla, 13 Apr. 1813
Castelnuovo, 21 Nov. 1796
Castiglione, 5 Aug. 1796 (N)
Castillion, 17 July 1453
Castlebar, 7 Aug. 1798
Cawnpore,
  (1) 16 July 1857
  (2) 27–28 Nov. 1857

  (3) 6 Dec. 1857
Cedar Creek, 19 Oct. 1864
Cerignola, 28 Apr. 1503
Cerisoles, 14 Apr. 1454
Ceva, 1796 (N)
Chaeronea,
  (1) 7 Aug. 338 B.C.
  (2) 86 B.C.
Chalgrove, 18 June 1643
¶ **Châlons,** A.D. **451**
Champaubert, 10 Feb. 1814 (N)
Chancellorsville, 2–4 May 1863
Chataila, 17–18 Nov. 1912
Châteaudun, 18 Oct. 1870
Château Thierry,
  (1) 13 Feb. 1814 (N)
  (2) 27 June 1918
Chattanooga, 23–25 Nov. 1863
Chebrëiss, 24 July 1798 (N)
Chickahominy, 26 June–1 July 1862
Chickamauga, 19–20 Sept. 1863
Chilianwála, 13 Jan. 1849
Chippewa, 5 July 1814
Citate, 6 Jan. 1854
Clifton Moor, 18 Dec. 1745
Clontarf, 23 Apr. 1014
Cold Harbor, 1 and 3 June 1864
Colenso, 15 Dec. 1899
Corinth, Miss., 3–4 Oct. 1862
Corunna, 16 Jan. 1809 (W)
Courtrai, 1302
Coutras, 20 Oct. 1587
Craonne, 6–7 Mar. 1814 (N)
Crécy or Cressy, 26 Aug. 1346
Crete, 20 May–3 June 1941
Cropredy Bridge, 29 June 1644
Culloden, 16 Apr. 1746
Custozza,
  (1) 23–25 July 1848
  (2) 24 June 1866
Cynoscephalae, 190 B.C.
Czaslau or Chotusitz, 17 May 1742 (F)
Dannevirke,
  (1) 1331
  (2) 23 Apr. 1848
Dego, 14 Apr. 1796 (N)
Delhi,
  (1) 8 Sept. 1803
  (2) 7–16 Oct. 1804
  (3) after siege, 14–20 Sept. 1857
Dennewitz, 6 Sept. 1813
Dettingen, 27 June (N.S.) 1743
Devizes, 13 July 1643
Dien-Bien-Phu, Apr.–May 1954

Dieppe, 14 Aug. 1942
Donnington, Glos, 21 Mar. 1645
Dorylaeum, 1097
Douro, 12 May 1809 (W)
Dresden, 27 Aug. 1813 (N)
Dreux, 19 Dec. 1562
Drumclog, 1 June 1679
Drummossie. *See* CULLODEN
Dunbar,
　(1) 27 Apr. 1296
　(2) 3 Sept. 1650
Dunes, 4 (14 N.S.) June 1658
Dungan Hill, 8 Aug. 1647
Dunkirk,
　(1) *See* DUNES
　(2) **(Evacuation of) 29 May–3 June
　1940**
Eckmühl, 22 Apr. 1809 (N)
Edgehill, 23 Oct. 1642
Edington, summer 878
Elandslaagte, 21 Oct. 1899
Elchingen, 14 Oct. 1805
Enghien, 3 Aug. (N.S.) 1692
Enslin, 25 Nov. 1899
Espierres, 22 May 1794
Essling. *See* ASPERN
Eutaw, 8 Sept. 1781
Evesham, 4 Aug. 1265
Eylau, 7–9 Feb. 1807 (N)
Fair Oaks, 31 May–1 June 1862
Falkirk,
　(1) 22 July 1298
　(2) 17 Jan. 1746
Famars, 23–24 May 1793
Fehrbellin, 1675
Firozshahr, 21–22 Dec. 1845
Fleurus,
　(1) 1622
　(2) 1 July 1690
　(3) 26 June 1794
Flodden Field, 9 Sept. 1513
Flushing, 15 Aug. 1809
Fontenoy, 11 May (N.S.) 1745
Formigny, 1450
Fornovo, 6 July 1495
Fredericksburg,
　(1) 13 Dec. 1862
　(2)*See* CHANCELLORSVILLE
Friedland, 14 June 1807 (N)
Fuentes de Onoro, 3–5 May 1811 (W)
Gaugamela. *See* ARBELA
Gembloux, June 1578
Germantown, 4 Oct. 1777
Gettysburg, 1–3 July 1863

Gitschin, 29 June 1866
Glencoe (S. Africa), 20 Oct. 1899
Goose Green, Falkland Is., 28 May
　1982
Gorey, co. Wexford, 4 June 1798
Gravelotte, 18 Aug. 1870
Great Meadows, July 1754
Grochow, 19–20 Feb. 1831
Gross Beeren, 23 Aug. 1813 (N)
Gross Jaegerndorf, 30 Aug. 1757 (F)
Guadalajara, 1937
Guinegatte, 16 Aug. 1513
Gujerát, 21 Feb. 1849
Halidon Hill, 19 July 1333
Hanau, 30 Oct. 1813
Harlaw, 24 July 1411
Hasbain, 23 or 24 Sept. 1408
¶ **Hastings, 14 Oct. 1066**
Hatfield, 632
Hennersdorf, 23 Nov. 1745 (F)
Herrera, 24 Aug. 1837
Hexham, 8 May 1464
Himera, 408 B.C.
Hochkirch, 14 Oct. 1758 (F)
Hochstädt. *See* BLENHEIM
Hohenfriedberg, 3–4 June 1745
Hohenlinden, 3 Dec. 1800
Homildon, 14 Sept. 1402
Idstädt, 25 July 1850
Imjin River, 23–5 Apr. 1951
Ingogo, 8 Feb. 1881
Ingour, 6 Nov. 1855
Inkerman, 5 Nov. 1854
Ipsus, 301 B.C.
Isandlhwana, 22 Jan. 1879
Ivry, 14 Mar. 1590
Jarnac, 13 Mar. 1569
Jemappes, 6 Nov. 1792
Jena, 14 Oct. 1806 (N)
Kalisz, 1706
Kalka, 1224
Katzbach, 26 Aug. 1813 (N)
Kazan, 1552
Kesselsdorf, 15 Dec. 1745 (F)
Khart, 19 July 1829
Killiecrankie, 27 July 1689
Kilsyth, 15 Aug. 1645
Kirk-Kilisse, 22–24 Oct. 1912
Kissingen, 10 July 1866
Klissow, July 1702
'Knightsbridge' (N. Africa), 28 May–15
　June 1942
Kohima, 10 Apr.–18 May 1942
Kolin, 18 Jan. 1757 (F)

Konieh, 21 Dec. 1832
Königgrätz. *See* SADOWA
Kossovo,
  (1) 1389
  (2) 1448
Krasnoi, 15–17 Nov. 1812
Kulikovo, 1380
Kumanovo, 23–25 Oct. 1912
Kunersdorf, 12 Aug. 1759 (F)
Kurdla, 1795
La Bicocca, 29 Apr. 1522
Laffeldt, 2 July 1747
Laingsnek, 28 Jan. 1881
Landen, 29 (19 O.S.) July 1693
Landshut, Apr. 1809 (N)
Langensalza, 27 June 1866
Langport, 10 July 1645
Langside (Glasgow), 13 May 1568
Lansdown, 5 July 1643
Laon, 9–10 Mar. 1814 (N)
Largs, 1263
Lauffeld, 2 July 1746
Leipzig, 16–19 Oct. 1813 (N)
Lens, 20 Aug. 1648
Leuctra, 371 B.C.
Leuthen, 5 Dec. 1757 (F)
Lewes, 14 May 1264
Lexington,
  (1) 19 Apr. 1775
  (2) 20 Sept. 1861
Liaoyang, Sept. 1904
Libenau, 25 June 1866
Liegnitz, 15 Aug. 1760 (F)
Ligny, 16 June 1815 (N)
Lincelles, 18 Aug. 1793
Lincoln,
  (1) 2 Feb. 1141
  (2) 20 May 1217
Linlithgow Bridge, Sept. 1526
Lioppo, 16 May 1860
Lipau, 1434
Lippstadt, 6 Nov. 1632
Lissa. *See* LEUTHEN (F)
Lodi, 10 May 1796 (N)
Lonato, 3 Aug. 1796 (N)
Lüle Burgas, 28–30 Oct. 1912
Lundy's Lane, 25 July 1814
Lützelberg, 10 Oct. 1758
Lützen,
  (1) 6 (16 N.S.) Nov. 1632
  (2) 2 May 1813 (N)
Magenta, 4 June 1859
Magersfontein, 11 Dec. 1899
Magnano, 5 Apr. 1799

Magnesia, 190 B.C.
Maharajpur, 29 Dec. 1843
Maida, 4 July 1806 (W)
Majuba, 27 Feb. 1881
Malplaquet, 11 Sept. 1709 (M)
Malvalli, 27 Mar. 1799
Mantinea,
  (1) 418 B.C.
  (2) *c.* 367 B.C.
  (3) 295 B.C.
  (4) 242 B.C.
  (5) 207 B.C.
Manzikert, 1071
¶ **Marathon, 28 or 29 Sept. 490** B.C.
Marengo, 14 June 1800 (N)
Margus,
  (1) 285
  (2) 505
Marignano,
  (1) 13–14 Sept. 1515
  (2) *See* PAVIA
  (3) 8 June 1859
Marne, The,
  (1) 6–9 Sept. 1914
  (2) 15 July–31 Aug. 1918
Marston Moor, 2 July 1644
Maserfield, 641
Mechanicsville, or White Oaks, 26
  June 1862
Medina del Rio Seco. *See* RIO SECO
¶ **Metaurus, 207** B.C.
Metz, 31 Aug. 1870
Milazzo, 20 June 1860
Millesimo, 13–14 Apr. 1796 (N)
Milli Duzov, 1–2 June 1829
Milvian Bridge, 312
Mincio,
  (1) 29 May 1796 (N)
  (2) 8 Feb. 1814
Minden, 1 Aug. 1759
Möckern,
  (1) 5 Apr. 1813
  (2) 16 Oct. 1813
Modder River, 28 Nov. 1899
Moeskirch, 5 May 1800
Mohács,
  (1) 29 Aug. 1526
  (2) 12 Aug. 1687
Mohilev, 23 July 1812
Mollwitz, 10 Apr. 1741 (F)
Monastir, 15–18 Nov. 1912
Moncontour, 3 Oct. 1569
Mondovi, 22 Apr. 1796 (N)
Mons, Aug. 1914

Mons Badonicus *c.* **500**
Montebello,
(1) 1796 (N)
(2) 1805
Montebello Casteggio,
(1) 9 June 1800
(2) 20 May 1859
Montenotte, 12 Apr. 1796
Montinirail, 11 Feb. 1814 (N)
Mookerheede, 1574
Morat, 22 June 1476
Morgarten, 15 Nov. 1315
Mortimer's Cross, 2 Feb. 1461
Mount Tabor, 16 Apr. 1799 (N)
Mudki, 18 Dec. 1845
Mukden, 1–9 Mar. 1905
Multan, 7 Nov. 1848
Münchengrätz, 28 June 1866
Munda, 45 B.C.
Muret, 12 Sept. 1213
Murfreesboro,
(1) 31 Dec. 1862
(2) 2 Jan. 1863
Naas, 24 May 1798
Nachod, 27 June 1866
Najara, 3 Apr. 1367
Nantwich, 25–28 Jan. 1644
Narva, 30 Nov. 1700
Narvik, 28 May–10 June 1940
Naseby, 14 June 1645
Navas de Tolosa, 1212
Nedao, 454
Neerwinden, 18 Mar. 1793
Nesbit, 7 May 1402
Neville's Cross, 17 Oct. 1346
Newburn, 28 Aug. 1640
Newbury,
(1) 20 Sept. 1643
(2) 27 Oct. 1644
New Ross, 5 June 1798
Newtownbutler, 30 July 1689
Nicholson's Nek, 30 Oct. 1899
Nive, 9–13 Dec. 1813
Nivelles, 10 Nov. 1813
Nördlingen,
(1) 27 Aug. 1634
(2) 3 Aug. 1645
Northallerton. *See* STANDARD, THE
Northampton, 10 July 1460
Novara, 23 Mar. 1849
Novi,
(1) 15 Aug. 1799
(2) 8 Jan. 1800
Obidos, 17 Aug. 1808

Oltenitza, 4 Nov. 1853
Omdurman, 2 Sept. 1898
Oporto. *See* DOURO
¶ **Orleans,**
(1) **29 Apr. 1429**
(2) 11 Oct. 1870
Ormuz, 1622
Orthez, 27 Feb. 1814
Ortona, Dec. 1943
Ostrolenka, 26 May 1831
Otterburn, 15 Aug. 1388
Oudenarde, 11 July 1708 (M)
Oulart, 27 May 1798
Ourique, 25 July 1139
Paardeberg, 16, 18–27 Feb. 1900
Palestro, 31 May 1859
Palo Alto, 8 May 1846
Panipat,
(1) 1526
(2) 1556
(3) 1761
Parma, 29 June 1734
Passchendaele, 26 Oct.–10 Nov. 1917
Patay, 18 June 1429
Pavia, 24 Feb. 1525
Pelekanon, 1326
Pelusium, 525 B.C.
Pfaffendorf, 15 Aug. 1760
Pharsalia or Pharsalus, summer of 48
    B.C.
Philiphaugh, 13 Sept. 1645
Piacenza, 16 June 1746
Pinkie, 10 Sept. 1547
Pirmasens, 14 Sept. 1793
Plassey, 23 June 1757
Plataea, 479 B.C.
Plevna, July, Sept., and Dec. 1877
Podoll, 26 June 1866
Poitiers, 19 Sept. 1356
Polotzk, 30–31 July 1812
¶ **Poltava, 8 July 1709**
Port Arthur, 21 Nov. 1894
Porto Novo (S. India), 1 July 1781
Prague, 6 May 1757 (F)
Preston,
(1) 17 Aug. 1648
(2) 12–13 Nov. 1715
Prestonpans, 21 Sept. 1745
Pultusk, 26 Dec. 1806
Pusan Perimeter, 1 Sept.–1 Oct. 1950
Pyramids, The, 13, 21 July 1798
Pyrenees, The, 25 July–2 Aug. 1813
Quatre Bras, 16 June 1815 (W)
Ramillies, 23 May 1706 (M)

Rathmines, 2 Aug. 1649
Raucoux, 11 Oct. 1746
Ravenna, 11 Apr. 1512
Redinha, 12 Mar. 1811
Resaca de la Palma, 9 May 1846
Rheinfelden, 3 Mar. 1638
Rietfontein, 24 Oct. 1899
Rieti, 7 Mar. 1821
Rio Seco, 14 July 1808
Rivoli, 14–15 Jan. 1797 (N)
Rocroi, 19 May 1643
Rolica, 17 Aug. 1808
Rorke's Drift, 22 Jan. 1879
Rosebecque or Roosebeke, 26 or 27
   Nov. 1382
Rossbach, 5 Nov. 1757 (F)
Roveredo, 4 Sept. 1796 (N)
Ruremonde, 18 Sept. 1794
Saarbrücken (an undefended assault), 2
   Aug. 1870
Sadowa, 3 July 1866
Sagunto, 25 Oct. 1811
Saint-Antoine, 2 July 1652
Saint-Denis, 10 Nov. 1567
Saint-Dizier, 27 Jan. 1814 (N)
Saintes, 22 July 1242
Saint-Quentin,
   (1) 10 Aug. 1557
   (2) 19 Jan. 1871
Sakaria, The, 23 Aug.–13 Sept. 1921
Salamanca, 22 July 1812 (W)
Salerno, 9 Sept.–1 Oct. 1943
Sangro, 2 Nov.–27 Dec. 1943
Santa Lucia, 6 May 1848
Saragossa,
   (1) 20 Aug. 1710
   (2) 20 Feb. 1809
Sarantoporon, Oct. 1912
¶ **Saratoga, 17 Oct. 1777**
Schwechat, 30 Oct. 1848
Sedan, 29 Aug.–1 Sept. 1870
Sedgemoor, 6 July 1685
Seidlitz, 10 Apr. 1831
Selby, 11 Apr. 1644
Seminara, 21 Apr. 1503
Sempach, 9 July 1386
Seneffe, 11 Aug. 1674
Seringapatam,
   (1) 15 May 1791
   (2) 6 Feb. 1792
Sesia, The, Jan. 1524
Sheriffmuir, 13 Nov. 1715
Shiloh, 6–7 Apr. 1862
Shrewsbury, 21 July 1403

Simancas, 939
Skalitz, 28 June 1866
Smolensk,
   (1) 16–17 Aug. 1812 (N)
   (2) 1941
Sobraon, 10 Feb. 1846
Soissons, 486
Solferino, 24 June 1859
Solway Moss, 24 Nov. 1542
Soor,
   (1) Sept. 1745 (F)
   (2) 28 June 1866
Somme,
   (1) 21 Mar–5 Apr. 1918
   (2) 21 Aug–5 Sept. 1918
Spion Kop, 24–25 Jan. 1900
Spottsylvania, 7–21 May 1864
Spurs, The. *See* GUINEGATTE
Stalingrad, Sept. 1942–Jan. 1943
Standard, The, 22 Aug. 1138
Steenkirk, 23 July (3 Aug. N.S.) 1692
Stoke, 16 June 1487
Stone River. *See* MURFREESBORO
Stow-on-the-Wold. *See* DONNINGTON
Strasburg, 20 Dec. 1888
¶ **Syracuse, 413** B.C.
Szegedin, 4 Aug. 1849
Tagliacozzo, 1268
Talavera, 27–28 July 1809 (W)
Tannenberg,
   (1) 1410
   (2) 26–30 Aug. 1914
Tara, 26 May 1798
Tarbes, 20 Mar. 1814 (W)
Tchernaya, 16 Aug. 1855
Teb, El, 29 Feb. 1884
Tel-el-Kebir, 13 Sept. 1882
¶ **Teutoburger Wald,** A.D. **9**
Tewkesbury, 4 May 1471
Thabor, 16 Apr. 1799
Thapsus, 46 B.C.
Thermopylae, 480 B.C.
Torgau, 3 Nov. 1760 (F)
Toulouse, 10 Apr. 1814 (W)
Tournai, 25 Apr. 1794
¶ **Tours, 10 Oct. 732**
Towton, 29 Mar. 1461
Trautenau, 28 June 1866
Trebbia,
   (1) 218 B.C.
   (2) 17–19 June 1799
Truellas, 22 Sept. 1793
Tudela, 23 Nov. 1808
Ucles, 13 Jan. 1809

Ulm, 20 Oct. 1805 (N)
Vareggio, 25 July 1848
¶ **Valmy, 20 Sept. 1792**
Valteline, 19 Aug. 1812
Valtezza, 27 May 1821
Varna, 10 Nov. 1444
Vilagos, 25 Apr. 1521
Vauchamps, 14 Feb. 1814 (N)
Villafranca, 10 Apr. 1812
Villaviciosa, 10 Dec. 1710
Vilna, 18 June 1831
Vimiero, 21 Aug. 1808 (W)
Vimy Ridge, 9–10 Apr. 1917
Vinegar Hill, 21 June 1798
Vitebsk, 14 Nov. 1812 (N)
Vitoria, 21 June 1813 (W)
Volturno, 1 Oct. 1860
Vouillé, 507
Wagram, 6 July 1809 (N)
Waitzen, 14–17 July 1849
Wakefield, 30 Dec. 1460
Wandiwash, 22 Jan. 1760
Warsaw,
  (1) 28–30 July 1656
  (2) 17 Apr. 1794
  (3) 4–8 Nov. 1794
  (4) 7 Sept. 1831
  (5) 14–27 Sept. 1939
  (6) 19–28 Apr. 1943
  (7) 1 Aug.–3 Oct. 1944
¶ **Waterloo, 18 June 1815 (N.W)**
Wavre, 18, 19 June 1815
Wawz, 31 Mar. 1831
White Mountain, 1620
White Oak Swamp, 30 June 1862
White Oaks. *See* MECHANICSVILLE
White Plains, 28 Oct. 1776
Wilderness, 5–6 May 1864
Williamsburg, 5 May 1862
Winwaed, 654
Worcester,
  (1) 23 Sept. 1642
  (2) 3 Sept. 1651
Wörth, 6 Aug. 1870
Wurschen, 21 May 1813
Würtzburg, 3 Sept. 1796
Ximena, 10 Sept. 1811
Yenidje Vardar, 2, 3, 5 Nov. 1912
Yarmuk, 20 Aug. 636
Ypres,
  (1) **19 Oct.–31 Oct. 1914**
  (2) **22 Apr.–25 May 1915**
  (3) **31 July–10 Nov. 1917**
  (4) **Sept. 1918**

Zallaca, 1086
Zama, 202 B.C.
Zela, 47 B.C.
Zenta, 11 Sept. 1697
Zorndorf, 25–26 Aug. 1758 (F)
Züllichau, 23 July 1759
Zürich, 24–25 Sept. 1799
Naval Battles
  B. connected with Nelson are marked
  N.
Aboukir. *See* NILE, THE
Acre, 3 Nov. 1840
Actium, 2 Sept. 31 B.C.
Aegadean Isles, 241 B.C.
Aegospotami, 404 B.C.
Aix Roads, 11–12 Apr. 1809
Alexandria bombarded, 11–13 July
  1882
Algeciras, 6 and 12 July 1801
Algiers bombarded, 27 Aug. 1816
Altmark (boarding), 15 Feb. 1940
¶ **Armada, 21–30 July 1588**
Basque Roads. *See* AIX ROADS
Beachy Head, 30 June 1690
Bismarck (pursuit and sinking), 22–7
  May 1941
Bismarck Sea, 1–3 Mar. 1943
Cadiz, 1587
Camperdown, 11 Oct. 1797
Cartagena, 1588
Champlain, 1814
Chesapeake Bay, 5 Sept. 1781
Copenhagen,
  (1) 2 Apr. 1801 (N)
  (2) 25 Sept. 1807
Coral Sea, 4–8 May 1942
Coronel, 1 Nov. 1914
Dannoura, 1185
Dogger Bank,
  (1) 5 Aug. 1781
  (2) 24 Jan. 1915
Dominica. *See* SAINTS, THE
Dover,
  (1) 19 May 1652
  (2) 2–3 June 1653
Downs, The, 3 June 1666
Dungeness, 1652
Dunkirk, 1666
Falkland Is., 8 Dec. 1914
Finisterre, Cape,
  (1) 3 May 1747
  (2) 14 Oct. 1747
  (3) 1805
Gibraltar Bay, 13 Sept. 1782

Guadeloupe. *See* SAINTS, THE

Hampton Roads, 8–9 Mar. 1862

Hangö, 27 July 1714

Harwich, 1666

Heligoland, 28 Aug. 1914

Itamarca, 1640

Japan Sea, 14 Aug. 1904

Java, 27–8 Feb. 1942

Jutland, 31 May 1916

Lagos, 18 Aug. 1759

La Hogue, 14–16 May 1692

Lake Champlain, 11 Sept. 1814

Lemnos, 18 Jan. 1913

Lepanto, 7 Oct. 1571

Lissa, 20 July 1866

Macassar Strait, 23–25 Jan. 1942

Malaga, 13 Aug. 1704

Malaya, 10 Dec. 1941

Manila, 1 May 1898

Matapan, 28 Mar. 1941

Messina, 1676

Midway, 3–6 June 1942

Minorca, 1756

Narvik, 10 and 13 Apr. 1940

Navarino, 20 Oct. 1827

Negapatam, 6 July 1782

New Orleans, 25 Apr. 1862

Newport News. *See* HAMPTON ROADS

Nile, The, 1 Aug. 1798 (N)

North Foreland,

(1) 2–3 June 1653

(2) 1 June 1666

(3) 25–6 July 1666

Oran, 3 July 1940

Passaro Cape, 11 Aug. 1718

Pearl Harbor, 7 Dec. 1941

Philippine Sea, 23–25 Oct. 1944

Plate River, 14 Dec. 1939

Portland, 18–20 Feb. 1653

Quiberon, 20 Nov. 1759

Rosas Bay, 1 Nov. 1809

St. Vincent,

(1) 16 June 1693

(2) 16 Jan. 1780

(3) 14 Feb. 1797 (N)

Saints, The, 12 Apr. 1782

Santa Cruz,

(1) 20 Apr. 1657

(2) 1797

Salamis, 480 B.C.

Samos, 16–17 Aug. 1824

Santiago, 3 July 1898

Sevastopol bombarded, 17 Oct. 1854

Sinope, 30 Nov. 1853

Sirte, 22–4 Mar. 1942

Sluys, 24 June 1340

Sole or Southwold Bay, 28 May 1672

Taranto, 11 Nov. 1940

Tchesiné, 7–9 July 1770

Texel, 9 Aug. 1653

Trafalgar, 21 Oct. 1805 (N)

Tsu Shima, 27–8 May 1905

Ushant,

(1) 27 July 1778

(2) 1 June 1794

Yalu, 17 Sept. 1894

Yellow Sea (two battles), 10 Aug. 1904

Zeebrugge, 23 Apr. 1918

Air Battles

Britain, 8 Aug.–29 Oct. 1940

Battleship. First ship with turrets the *Rolf Krake* designed for Danish Navy by British Capt. C. P. Coles, R.N., 1860. First turret ship in action the U.S.S. *Monitor,* 9 Mar. 1862. B. design revolutionized by launching of H.M.S. *Dreadnought,* 1906. German 'pocket B' *Deutschland* launched, May 1931. Bs. obsolescent by 1960.

Bavaria (Ger. **Bayern**). One of the original 'tribal duchies' of Germany. Earliest (probably Celtic) inhabitants subdued by Romans *c.* 10–5 B.C. Ravaged by Odoacer, A.D. 476–86. Settled by Germanic tribes, 488–520. Conquered by Franks, 555, and governed by Frankish dukes till Charlemagne deposed Tassilo III, 788. Wittelsbach family take throne from Henry the Lion, 1180. Duchy divided till accession of the Emperor Louis the Bavarian, 1314. Becomes an electorate, 1623. Annexes the Upper Palatinate, 1648. Alliance with France leads to occupation by British and Austrian troops before battle of Blenheim, 1704. Attempt to dismember Austria with Prussian help, leads to defeat and occupation, 1742. Becomes a kingdom, 1805. Allied to Austria in Austro-Prussian War, 1866. Makes military convention with Prussia, Aug. 1866. Joins in Franco-Prussian War, 1870, against France. Joins German Empire, 1871. Jesuits expelled, 1873. Wittelsbachs deposed and Communist Republic proclaimed by Kurt Eisner, 1918. Eisner murdered, Feb. 1919. Moderate Government re-established by force 1 May 1919. Attempted Munich *putsch* of Hitler and Ludendorff, 8 Nov. 1923. Democratic government abolished by Hitler, 1933. Occupied by American forces, 1945. Separate *Land* government set up 1946. Christian Social Union has since dominated Bavarian politics.

Heads of State.

From the foundation of the electorate, 1623, until the declaration of the republic, 1918.

Electors:

Maximilian I 1597–1651
Ferdinand Maria I 1651–1679
Maximilian II 1679–1726
Karl Albrecht I 1726–1745
Maximilian III 1745–1777
Karl Theodor I 1777–1799
Maximilian IV *(elector)* and I
  (king) 1799–1825

Kings:

Ludwig I 1825–1848
Maximilian II 1848–1864
Ludwig II 1864–1886
Otto I (incurably insane) 1886–1913
Luitpold (Regent) 1886–1912
Ludwig (Regent) 1912–13
Ludwig III 1913–1918

Bay of Pigs, abortive invasion of Cuba by anti-Castro dissidents, with U.S. connivance, 1962.

Bayeux, Normandy, has a cathedral built from the eleventh to the thirteenth century. Bishopric dates from the fourth century. Taken by Rollo, 890. Pillaged by Henry I of England, 1106. It was the first French town to be recaptured by the Allies in June 1944.

Bayeux Tapestry of panoramic scenes embroidered in worsted on a linen ground, and depicting the events of the reign of King Harold II of England, which culminated in the battle of Hastings (*q.v.*), was almost certainly executed shortly after Oct. 1066, probably under the patronage of Odo (*d.* 1097), Bishop of B. and Earl of Kent and half-brother of William the Conqueror. First recorded mention, 1476.

Bayonet. 'Plug B'., supposed to have been invented at Bayonne *c.* 1647, but in use before; external screw allowing the firelock to be fired without unfixing B.,

invented by Gen. Hugh Mackay (1640–1692), after battle of Killiecrankie, 1689.

Bayonne, France. Meeting-place of Catherine de Medici and the Spanish Duke of Alva, 1565. Ferdinand VII of Spain was here induced by his father, the exking Charles IV, to abdicate in favour of Napoleon, 2 May 1808. Invested by British, 1814. Convention of B., signed, 10 May 1808.

Bayonne Decree, 17 Apr. 1808 Napoleon ordered seizure of all American vessels.

Bayreut(h), Bavaria, founded 1194, became in 1248 a dependency of Nürnberg (*q.v.*) and later combined with Ansbach to form a principality ruled by a cadet branch of the Hohenzollerns before becoming Prussian in 1791, finally passing to Bavaria, 1810. The Wagner Theatre was opened in 1876, the Opera House proper, 1748.

B.B.C. *See* BRITISH BROADCASTING CORPORATION.

Bear-baiting in Britain banned by Act of Parliament, 1835.

Beaufort Scale standard for measuring velocity of wind invented, 1805, by Rear-Admiral Sir Francis B., naval hydrographer (1774–1857).

Beauvais, France. Cathedral choir built, 1227–1347. Unsuccessfully besieged by Charles of Burgundy, 1472, owing to valour of Jeanne Lainé (La Hachette). Transepts and tower of cathedral completed, 1547. Tower (the highest in Europe) fell, 1573. Monument to La Hachette, 1850. British airship 'R.101' crashed at B., Oct. 1930.

Bec, Normandy, a Benedictine abbey, founded, 1034, by Herlwin, became famous for the school founded there, 1045, by Lanfranc (1005–89), later Archbishop of Canterbury. Though decline set in during the thirteenth century it survived until 1789, and its last prior was Talleyrand (1754–1838).

Bechuanaland. *See* BOTSWANA.

Bedford, England. Burned by Danes, 1010. B. School refounded, 1552. B. Modern School founded, 1566. Bunyan imprisoned, 1660–72.

Bedford Level, England. The large area of the Fens drained, *c.* 1640, by Cornelius

Vermuyden at expense of the third Duke of B.

Bedlam from Bethlehem Hospital founded in London by Simon Fitzmary, 1247. Became madhouse, 1407. Moved to Moorfields, 1676; to Lambeth, 1815; to Beckenham, Kent, 1931.

Béguines. Order of sisters devoted to education, etc., founded at Liège in the twelfth century by Le Bèghe. Most famous house was at Bruges.

Beirut, capital of the Lebanon. Destroyed by earthquake in the sixth century. Seized by Ibrahim Pasha, 1832; Egyptian Army totally defeated at, Oct. 1840; massacre at, May 1860. Bombarded during Italo-Turkish war, 1912. Occupied by Allenby's army, 8 Oct. 1918. Captured from French by British, July 1941. Became capital of the independent republic of the Lebanon, 26 Nov. 1941. Since 1968 scene of considerable fighting in Arab/Israeli wars. B. airport raided by Israelis 1968: B. temporarily largely occupied by Israelis, 1982, who were superseded by a U.N. peace-keeping force, 1983, which withdrew, 1984. Heavy fighting in B. followed.

Belfast, Ireland. Castle built *c.* 1177; destroyed by Edward Bruce, 1316. B. attacked by Earl of Kildare, 1503, 1512. Town and castle repaired by Hugh O'Neill, who acquired them in 1552. B. granted by James I to Sir Arthur Chichester, 1612, received its charter, 1613. Taken by Gen. Monck, 1648; by Lord Montgomery, 1649. Mayor became Lord Mayor, 1892. University founded as Queen's College, 1845; received royal charter, 1909. Parliament Buildings at Stormont opened, 1932. Queen Elizabeth bridge opened by the Queen, 1966. Scene of several riots and murders caused by Catholic and Protestant extremists since 1968.

Belfort, France. Ceded to France, 1648. Famous for its skilful and resolute defence by Col. Denfert-Rochereau, Nov. 1870–Feb. 1871 against the Prussians. The General Delegation for Occupied France was set up here by Fernand de Brinon, 7 Sept. 1940.

Belgae. A mixed Celtic-Germanic group of tribes in NE. Gaul, part of whom migrated to southern Britain *c.* 75 B.C.

Belgium. Its Celtic inhabitants conquered by Julius Caesar, 51 B.C. Was southern part of Spanish Netherlands, the northern part of which broke away in 1579. A separate kingdom under Spanish ruler, 1598–1621. Ceded to Austria by Peace of Utrecht, 1713. Overrun by the French, 1744–8. Republic, 1787–90. Passed to France by Treaty of Campo Formio, 1797. Restored to Austria, 1814. United with Holland, 1815. Revolution commenced, 25 Aug. 1830. Treaty between Holland and B. regarding latter's independence signed at London, 19 Apr. 1839, and guaranteed by principal European powers; commercial treaty with Great Britain, 22 Aug. 1862. Neutrality violated by German Army, 4 Aug. 1914. 'Pact of Mutual Guarantee' (for security of Belgian independence) signed at London, 1 Dec. 1925. Equality of Flemish and French languages recognized, 1932. Invaded by Germany, 10 May 1940. Leopold III capitulated, 28 May. B. liberated Sept.–Nov. 1944. Minor modifications in B.'s favour on Belgian-German frontier, Apr. 1949. Monarchy crisis, 1944–51. 1950: Referendum pronounced narrowly in favour of recalling Leopold III; his return followed by rioting, and in Aug. he delegated his powers to his son, finally abdicating in his favour, July 1951. Member of the European Economic Community (the Common Market). 1958. Congo (*q.v.*) became independent of B., 30 June 1960. 'Language frontiers' estab. 1962–3.

Kings

Leopold I 1831–1865
Leopold II 1865–1909
Albert I 1909–1934
Leopold III 1934–*1951
Prince Charles, Regent 1944–1950
Leopold III (20 July–10 Aug.) 1950
Baudouin, Prince Royal (since 11 Aug.) 1950
Baudouin I 1951–
*Prisoner of war, May 1940–May 1945. Prince Charles was Regent from Aug. 1944 to July 1950. Leopold

exercised his prerogatives during July and Aug. 1950, but Prince Baudouin took them over in the latter month. Leopold abdicated, 16 July 1951, and Baudouin was enthroned, 17 July 1951.

Belgorod-Dnestrovskiy, Bessarabia, formerly **Akkerman** (Rum. **Cetatea Alba**). Taken by Russians from Turks, 1770; restored, 1774; ceded to Russia, 1806. Russo-Turkish Treaty of, 4 Sept. 1826. Rumanian 1918–40 and 1941–4. Re-named B.-D., 1944.

Belgrade (Serb.. **Beograd**), **Yugoslavia.** Roman town of Singidunum, said to have stood on an earlier Celtic settlement. Destroyed by the Avars in the sixth century. Seized by Hungarians from Greeks, 1124, besieged by Turks unsuccessfully, 1444, 1456; captured by Turks, 1522; imperial forces, 1688; Turks, 1690; Prince Eugene, 1717; restored to Turks, 1739; captured by Austrians, 1789; restored to Turks, 1792; surrendered to Serbia, 1867; independence of Serbia declared at B., 22 Aug. 1878; king and queen murdered by army, 10 June 1903; captured by von Mackensen, 7 Oct. 1915; capital of Yugoslavia (*q.v.*) since 1919; bombed by Germans, 6 Apr. 1941; occupied, 12 Apr. 1941; liberated by partisans and Russians, 20 Oct. 1944. *See also* SERBIA and YUGOSLAVIA.

Belize, Central America, probably discovered by Columbus, 1502. First settled by Brit. woodcutters from Jamaica *c.* 1638 and Spain acknowledged Brit. rights, 1670. Governed as a colony from Jamaica, 1862–84. Independent since Sept. 1981: independence guaranteed by Brit. garrison due to longstanding territorial claims by Guatemala (*q.v.*).

Bell Rock Lighthouse (N. Sea). Built by Robert Stevenson, 1807–11. The rock is famous through Southey's ballad, *The Inchcape Rock.*

Bells. Used in France *c.* 550. In the capitulation of Jerusalem, A.D. 637, the twelfth article stipulated that the Christians 'shall not ring, but only toll their bells'. Prominent among the ritual objects of the Celtic Church, in

the sixth century. First mentioned as used in churches in England in seventh century by the Venerable Bede. Largest B. in the world is the 'Tsar Kolokol' of Moscow, cast in 1773. *See also* CURFEW.

Belorussia, Byelorussia. Independent Belorussian republic proclaimed, 1918. Communists established a more limited Belorussian republic, 1921, which became a constituent republic of the U.S.S.R. in 1922.

Belsen (Hanover). Concentration camp set up in 1933, and taken by British troops, Apr. 1945. Its commandant, Josef Kramer, and eleven of his staff were sentenced to death for torture and murder of prisoners, 17 Nov. 1945.

Belvoir Castle (Leics.). Seat of the dukes of Rutland, built 1808 after a fire had destroyed the previous building.

Benares or **Banaras,** India. Holy City of great antiquity. Sacked by the Moslems, 1194. Annexed by E. India Co., 1775. College opened, 1791. Hindu university opened. 1916.

Benedictine Order. Founded by St. Benedict, 529. Introduced into England, 596. Expelled from France, 1880. Commissioned by Pope Pius X to revise the Vulgate, May 1907.

Benefit of Clergy, by which after Becket's murder (1170) English clerics, and later all who could read, were exempt from punishment by a civil court. After 1489 B. of C. could be claimed only once. Ben Jonson escaped gallows by, 1598. Finally abolished, 1827.

Benelux. Economic union of Belgium, the Netherlands, and Luxemburg, came into force 1 Jan. 1948. Fuller economic union operative from 1 Nov. 1960.

Benevento, Italy. Captured by Romans *c.* 277 B.C.; conquered by Lombards, 571; ceded by Emperor Henry III to Pope Leo IX 1052. Charles of Anjou defeated Manfred of Sicily at B., 26 Feb. 1266. Seized by King of Naples, but restored, 1773; taken by French, 1798; restored to pope, 1815; Napoleon made Talleyrand prince of B., 1806; annexed to Italy, 1866.

Benevolences. Forced loans levied by English monarchs; so called from reign of

Edward IV onwards. Parliament declared them unlawful, 1484, but they continued to be levied. Finally declared illegal by Bill of Rights (*q.v.*), 1689.

Bengal, independent, 1340. Annexed to Mogul Empire, 1576. Under British influence after battle of Plassey, 1757. Ceded to E. India Co., 1765. Made chief presidency of India, 16 June 1773. Warren Hastings governor of, 1772–83. Assam annexed to B., 1826–74. Divided into two parts, 1905. This partition revoked, 1911, and B. reconstituted, 1912, Bihar, Orissa, and Chota Nagpur being made a separate province (*see* BIHAR). E.B. and part of Assam became part of Pakistan, 15 Aug. 1947: part of Bangladesh (*q.v.*) since 1971. Area subject to frequent disastrous flooding, e.g. tidal wave May 1985 causing thousands of deaths.

Benghazi, Libya. Occupied by Italians, 20 Oct. 1911. Captured by Australians, 7 Feb. 1941; lost again, 3 Apr.; recaptured, 24 Dec. 1941; lost, 29 Jan. 1942, and finally recaptured by the British, 20 Nov. 1942. *See* WORLD WAR II.

Benin, formerly **Dahomey**. W. Africa. Fr. protectorate, 1863; annexed, 1894. Independant republic, 1960; name changed from Dahomey to B., 1975.

Ben Nevis observatory built, 1883; abandoned, 1904.

Berar, India. Formerly part of Hyderabad State, leased by British Government, 1853–1947. Now part of Madhya Pradesh State.

Berchtesgaden, Bavaria. Has salt-mines which have been worked since 1140. Priors of B. made princes of the Empire, 1495. Principality secularized, 1803. The Berghof, B., was a country residence of Hitler, and here he interviewed Neville Chamberlain about the Sudeten crisis, 15 Sept. 1938. Bombed by allied air forces, Apr. and May 1945; the living-quarters of German leaders were destroyed but the solid stone mountain pavilion or 'Eagle's Nest' was undamaged until taken by the French First Armoured Division, 5 May 1945.

Berg, a county of Westphalia from early in the twelfth century, became a duchy, 1380, and passed to the electorate of Bavaria, 1799. Made a Grand Duchy, and handed to Joachim Murat by Napoleon, 1806. Awarded to Prussia by Treaty of Vienna, 1815.

Bergen, Norway. Seaport founded by King Olaf the Peaceful, 1070–5. Cathedral founded, 1248: rebuilt, 1537. Germans landed and occupied port, 9 Apr. 1940. German naval command in Norway surrendered to British and Norwegians, 15 May 1945. Museum founded, 1825. University established, 1946, opened 30 Aug. 1948.

Bergen op Zoom. Fortified, 1576, unsuccessfully besieged by Spaniards, 1588, 1605, 1622. Held by the French from 1795 to 1815.

Berlin, Germany. First became important during reign of Frederick William the Great Elector (*d.* 1688). Seized by Russians and Austrians, Oct. 1760; entered by French after battle of Jena, 1806. Capital of German Empire from 1871 to 1918. B. Congress, June–July 1878. Became capital of Third Reich, 1933. Surrendered to Russians, 2 May 1945, after heavy bombing and fighting had destroyed about 75 per cent of the city proper. Subsequently partitioned into Russian, American, French, and British sectors; from 1948 effectively only into Russian and Western sectors. Its blockade by the Russians, 28 June 1948–12 May 1949, failed in the face of allied air supply. W. Berlin a *Land* of the Federal German Republic, and simultaneously a city, under constitution of 1 Sept. 1950. E. Berlin the capital of the German Democratic Republic since 1949. Riots in Soviet sector (E. Berlin) suppressed, 17 June 1953. Scene of four-power Conference, 26 Jan.–17 Feb. 1954. 13 Aug. 1961: E. Germany sealed off the Berlin border, and began constructing a permanent concrete wall along it, subsequently reinforced with anti-tank barriers, etc.

Berlin Decrees, 21 Nov. 1806. *See* CONTINENTAL SYSTEM.

Bermudas or **Somers Islands,** Atlantic Ocean. First recorded on map, dated

1511. Visited and named by Juan Bermudez, 1515; settled, 1609, by Sir George Somers. Administration transferred from B. Company to crown, 1684. Colonized in seventeenth century from Virginia, and during the American Revolution by Loyalists. Air and naval bases leased to U.S.A. for 99 years in 1941. Royal naval dockyard closed, 1951. Self-governing colony since 1968.

Bern or **Berne.** Joined Swiss League, 1353. The town of B. resisted Rudolph of Hapsburg, 1288; surrendered to French, 12 Apr. 1798; capital of Switzerland, 1848. International Geographical Congress, 1891. Bears have been kept in B. at public expense ever since 1513.

Bernicia. The more northerly of the two Anglian kingdoms which later merged into Northumbria (*q.v.* for list of rulers). Its area roughly corresponded to that of the counties of Northumberland and Durham, but it was only a kingdom distinct from Deira (*q.v.*) from 547 to 605 and from 633 to 655. *See also* BAMBURGH.

Berrow's Worcester Journal, the oldest surviving British newspaper, was founded in 1690, but did not acquire the name B. until 1753.

Berwick-on-Tweed. Given up to England by Scotland, 1176; seized by Robert Bruce, 1318; surrendered to English, 1333. Independent of England and Scotland, 1551. Peace of Berwick, between England and Scotland, 1639. Surrendered to Cromwell, 1648; to Gen. Monck, 1659.

Beryllium. Discovered in the form of oxide in the mineral beryl, 1798. Isolated by Wöhler, 1828.

Besançon, France. Became a free city of the empire, 1184. In Spanish hands, 1648–78. Became capital of Franche-Comté. (*q.v.*) when that province was ceded to France, 1678.

Bessarabia (Ukrainian **Budzhak**). Region on the W. coast of the Black Sea between the Danube and the Dniestr, called after the Basarab dynasty or else after the Bessi, a Thracian tribe who lived in the area. Rumania controlled part of B. 1918–1940 and 1941–44 but this subsequently incorporated with the rest of B. in the U.S.S.R., confirmed by the peace treaty of 1947.

Bessel's Functions, in mathematics, indicate certain relationships between two variables. Introduced by F. W. Bessel, 1817.

Bessemer Process, for purifying iron and steel, invented by Sir Henry Bessemer, 1856.

Bethlehem (modern **Beit-Lahm**), Israel. The village dates from before 1000 B.C. Christian pilgrimage began earlier than 132 (*see* NATIVITY, CHURCH OF THE), but the village was devastated in 1244 and again in 1489.

Béthune, France. Founded in the eleventh century. Ceded to France at the Treaty of Nijmegen, 1678.

Betting. B. Acts of 1853 and 1874, and the B. and Lotteries Act of 1934, regulated B. in Britain until the B. and Gaming Act, 1960, provided for the establishment of licensed B. shops. Amending Acts passed in 1968. Ready-money B. on football, as a business, prohibited, 1920. B. Duty imposed, 1926. In 1928 the B. tax was reduced; in 1930 abolished. Tax on dog totalizators and football pools, Nov. 1947. Tax on betting first imposed, 1966. *See also* GAMING AND GAMBLING.

Betting-houses (Great Britain). Suppressed, 1853. Licensed betting shops allowed under the Betting and Gaming Act, 1960.

Beveridge Plan. National insurance scheme signed by Lord Beveridge (1879–1963), chairman of the Interdepartmental Committee on Social Insurance and Allied Services, 1941–2, and published by H.M. Stationery Office, 20 Nov. 1942. It formed the basis of post-war legislation in the fields of social insurance and social security.

Beverley (E. Yorks.). Its principal church, of the twelfth century, is built on the site of that founded by St. John of B. (*c.* 640–721), who is also the reputed founder of B. grammar school. A charter of the town is mentioned as having been granted in 925, but is not extant;

but one granted between 1120 and 1135 is. Weaving became an important industry early in the fourteenth century.

Bhopal. Former Indian princely state, merged into Madhya Pradesh since 1956. Founded by Dost Mohammed Khan, 1723. Over 2000 killed by emission of poison gas from factory, Dec. 1984.

Bhutan (Bhotian, **Druk-Yul**) was invaded by Tibetans in ninth century A.D. and Indian population driven out. Treaty with E. India Co., 1774. Dispute with Britain terminated by treaty, 1865 and further treaty, 1910. British representation in B. succeeded by Indian, Aug. 1947. Treaty of friendship with India, 1949.

Biafra, name given 1967–70 to the Eastern States of Nigeria (*q.v.*) by secessionists who on 30 May 1967 announced their withdrawal from the federal republic of Nigeria, and renamed the region B. The name B. and the act of secession were never recognized by Nigeria, which mounted a full-scale military campaign to reconquer B. B. finally capitulated Jan. 1970 and the area was reunited with Nigeria.

Bible, Translations of. The first translation of the Old Testament into Greek, called the Septuagint, made in stages between 284 B.C. and A.D. 100. Origen's collection of versions, *Hexapla,* commenced, A.D. 231. Psalms believed to have been translated into Old English before Alfred's time. Cædmon's metrical paraphrase of a portion of the B. *c.* A.D. 670. Bede's St. John (735) and Aelfric's partial Old Testament (990). Division into chapters, often ascribed to Lanfranc (eleventh century), was probably a result of the labours of Hugh de Sancto Caro (*c.* 1200–63). Wycliffe's English versions *c.* 1382 and 1388. The whole Bible divided into verses first in the Geneva version of 1557–60. Tyndale's (New Testament) printed, 1525; Coverdale's (first complete English B.) printed, 1535; Cranmer's B. first authorized, 1539; authorized version published, 1611 (*see* HAMPTON COURT CONFER-

ENCE); revised version, New Testament, 1881; Old Testament, 1884. Dr. James Moffat's translations published: New Testament, 1913; Old Testament, 1924. New version of the New Testament in modern English, 1961; Old Testament new version, 1970, the combined new Old and New Testaments being put together as 'The New English Bible'. Several further modern versions since 1970, including *Good News* and abbreviated versions; *New International Bible*, 1973. For Latin B., and translations therefrom, *see* separate article, VULGATE.

Bible Society, British and Foreign. Begun, 1803; organized, 1804. American B.S. organized at Philadelphia, 1808; various American B.Ss. amalgamated to form the American and Foreign B.S., 1839.

Bibliothèque Nationale. The building in Paris which now houses the collection was bought for the purpose by the crown in 1721, having been built in the mid-seventeenth century. The nucleus of the collection is the books owned by Louis XI (*d.* 1483).

Bicycle. *See* CYCLE.

Bigamy in England is punishable under the Offences against the Person Act, 1861; in Scotland it is merely another form of perjury punishable by statute of 1551; in the U.S.A. the law of B. varies from state to state, but in general it is based on an English statute of 1603.

Big Ben (London). First hung, 1858. Clock in use from 1859. Chimes first broadcast, 1923. Named after Sir Benjamin Hall (1802–67), Commissioner of Works at the time: he became Baron Llanover, 1859.

'Big Bertha'. Nickname given to German long-range gun which fired on Paris during 1918.

Bihar, India. Separated from Bengal, 1911. From Orissa, 1935. Serious riots in 1942 and 1946.

Bilbao, Spain. Founded *c.* 1300; taken by French, July 1795, and in 1808; bombarded by Carlists, but relieved, 1874; fell to Nationalist forces, 18 June 1937.

Billiards. Known in England in

Shakespeare's time. It has been ascribed to Henri Devigne, 1571.

Billingsgate, London. Tolls collected there from tenth century. Opened, 1588, as a landing-place for provisions; free market, 1699; extended, 1848; rebuilt, 1852, 1875: site of fish market moved to Isle of Dogs, Jan. 1982.

Bill of Rights. *See* RIGHTS, BILL OF.

Bills of Exchange Act, 1882, codified existing practice concerning B. of E. in the U.K.

Bills of Exchequer first issued, 1696.

Bills of Sale or **Chattel Mortgages** are regulated by the Acts of 1878 and 1882 in England and Wales only.

Bingen, Rhenish Palatinate, was important for the water-borne traffic of the Rhine as the nearest harbour to the dangerous rapids of Bingerloch until these were cleared by blasting in 1834. The conspicuous statue of Germania —'Die Dame ohne Verhältnisse'—was erected, 1877–83.

Binomial Theorem. First published by Isaac Newton, 1676.

Birdcage Walk. Perhaps really Bocage W., but James I (1603–25) built an aviary there, and the nearby cock-pit was not done away with until 1816.

Birkbeck College. Founded as the London Mechanics' Institute by Dr. George Birkbeck, 1823. Became a constituent college of London University, 1920.

Birkenhead, England. Dock opened, Aug. 1847. *See* LIVERPOOL.

Birmingham, England. Appears in Domesday Book, 1086. Market charters granted, 1166, 1189, 1249, 1295. Sacked by Royalists, 1643. Canal opened, 1767. 'Church and king' riots in, 1791. Chartist riot, 15 July 1839. John Bright first elected M.P. for, 1857. Became a city, 1889. Office of lord mayor created, 1896. University chartered, 1900. Became a bishopric, 1904. Univ. of Aston (*q.v.*) estab. in B., 1966.

Birth, Concealment of, in Scotland, was considered to be proof of infanticide, a capital offence, until 1803, when it was made punishable by a maximim of two years' imprisonment, as in England and Wales.

Birth Control. *See* CONTRACEPTION.

Bishoprics (England and Wales). Following are dates of foundation of the Anglican sees (not suffragan sees):

Bangor *c.* 550
Bath and Wells 1139
Birmingham 1904
Blackburn 1927
Bradford 1919
Bristol 1541
Canterbury 597
Carlisle 1133
Chelmsford 1927
Chester 1541
Chichester 1075
Coventry 1919
Derby 1927
Durham 995
Ely 1109
Exeter 1050
Gloucester 1541
Guildford 1927
Hereford 676
Leicester 1919
Lichfield 669
Lincoln 1067
Liverpool 1880
Llandaff *c.* 550
London 605
Manchester 1847
Monmouth 1920
Newcastle 1882
Norwich 1094
Oxford 1542
Peterborough 1541
Portsmouth 1927
Ripon 1877
Rochester 604
St. Albans 1877
St. Asaph *c.* 550
St. Davids *c.* 550
St. Edmundsbury and Ipswich 1914
Salisbury 1075
Sheffield 1914
Sodor and Man *c.*1134
Southwark 1905
Southwell 1884
Swansea and Brecon 1920
Truro 1876
Wakefield 1888
Winchester *c.* 650
Worcester *c.* 680
York 625

Bishops (U.K.). Earliest British B. *c.* 180. For dates of foundation of sees, *see* BISHOPRICS. In Scotland replaced by superintendents, 1561. Restored, 1573. Abolished, 1638. Abolished in England, 1646. Restored in both countries, 1661. Expelled by Scottish convention, 1689.

Bishops (U.S.A.). Samuel Seabury, Bishop of Connecticut, Nov. 1784, first Protestant bishop consecrated for U.S.A. First bishop of New York consecrated in London, 4 Feb. 1787.

Bishops, Seven, committed to the Tower for seditious libel (i.e. opposing the Declaration of Indulgence), but found not guilty at the Bar of the King's Bench, 29 June 1688.

Bisley (Surrey). Scene of National Rifle Association meetings since 1890.

Bismarck Archipelago. Discovered by Dampier, 1699, and named New Britain, but by agreement of 1885 assigned to the German sphere of influence and their name changed to B.A. Occupied by Australian forces, Sept. 1914, and after 1918 attached to the Australian mandated territories in New Guinea. Parts of the independent state of Papua New Guinea since 1975.

Bithynia, Asia Minor. Became part of the kingdom of Lydia, 570 B.C., but absorbed with it by the Persian Empire, 546. After recovery of its independence Nicomedia was founded by 264 B.C. The last king of B. bequeathed his state to Rome, 74 B.C. Conquered by Turks, A.D. 1298.

Bizerta, Tunisia, N. Africa (anciently **Hippo Zarytis**). Occupied by French, 1881. Captured from Germans, 9 May 1943. Fr. maintained base at B. till 1961.

Black Death. Identical with bubonic plague. Supposed to have originated in China. Raged there, 1340–8. In Europe, 1346–9, 1361–2, and 1369.

Blackfriars Bridge (London). Old bridge, 1760–1860; new bridge opened, 6 Nov. 1869; enlarged, 1909.

Black Friday.

    1. 6 Dec. 1745. Young Pretender's entry into Derby announced in London, causing a run on the bank and closing of shops.

    2. 11 May 1866. Overend, Gurney & Co., the bankers, stopped payment, causing commerical panic; partners tried for conspiracy to defraud, but acquitted, Dec. 1869.

Blackheath, England. Wat Tyler's men assembled on, 12 June 1381; Jack Cade, 1 June 1450. Cornish rebels defeated at, 22 June 1497.

Black Hole of Calcutta. Suraj-ud-Dowlah, Nawab of Bengal, imprisoned 146 English people in, on 19 June 1756; only twenty-three survived the night there.

Black Monday. Certain Easter Mondays upon which tradition records disasters to the English: 1. 29 Mar. 1209. 500 settlers massacred by Irish at Collenswood, Dublin; 2. 9 Apr. 1357. Black Prince's army sustained terrible losses through a storm; 3. 13 Apr. 1360. In Edward III's army near Paris many men died of cold.

Black Prince. Eldest son of Edward III; *b.* 15 June 1330; at battle of Poitiers, 1356; *d.* 8 June 1376.

Black Rod. Office instituted, 1349.

Blackwall Tunnel, London, begun, 1892; opened, 1897. Reopened after £1,000,000 improvements, April 1969.

Blanc, Mont, highest mountain in the Alps (15,782 ft.). First climbed by Paccard and Balmat, 1786.

Blandford, England. Whole town almost destroyed by fire, 1731.

Blarney Castle, County Cork, Ireland, gave its name to the phrase for flattery which cannot be traced—in writing— further back than 1819. Castle stands on the site of one founded by Cormac McCarthy in 1446, the date also inscribed on the B. Stone.

Blasket Islands, County Kerry, Gaelic-speaking stronghold, evacuated July 1953.

Blasphemy. Act of 1697 was repealed by the Criminal Law Act, 1967.

Bleaching. Artificial B. invented by Dutch early in eighteenth century; first bleach-field in Scotland established at Salton *c.* 1730; introduced into England, 1768; Berthollet's discoveries with chlorine *c.* 1785; Tennant's patent, 1798; Mather's improvements, 1885.

Blenheim Palace (Woodstock, England). Built by Sir J. Vanbrugh at national expense for the first Duke of Marlborough between 1705 and 1722.

Bloemfontein, capital of the Orange Free State, S. Africa. Founded, 1846.

Blois, France. Sold to Louis, Duke of Orleans, 1391; States-General held at, 1576 and 1588; Henry of Guise assassinated at, 23 Dec. 1588.

Blood, Circulation of the. Principal discoveries regarding, due to William Harvey between 1616 and 1628.

Blood's (Colonel) Conspiracy. Attempt to steal crown jewls, 9 May 1671, by Col. Thomas B., *b. c.* 1628, *d.* 1680.

Blood Transfusion was practised on animals as early as the seventeenth century. Janssky in 1907 discovered the principle of the four human blood groups. A method of B. T. not direct from artery to artery was discovered in 1916, as was refrigeration. Plasma, as opposed to whole blood, first transfused on a large scale, 1940.

'Bloody Assize'. The trials by Judge George Jeffreys (1648–89), in Aug. 1685, after Monmouth's rebellion (*q.v.*).

'Bloody Sunday'. Jan. 1972, when 13 Catholics were shot dead by the Brit. Army in Londonderry.

Blue-Books. Parliamentary and state reports, so called from their blue paper wrappers. These reports first printed in 1681.

Blue-stocking. Term originated *c.* 1750, when a literary circle was established in London, consisting of ladies and gentlemen among whom was Benjamin Stillingfleet, who habitually wore blue stockings.

Board of Trade, founded 1661, but modern form dated from 1786. Became **Department of Trade and Industry**, 1970. Many functions taken over by other departments and renamed **Department of Trade**, 1974.

Boat Race, Oxford and Cambridge. First held in 1829, this did not become an annual event until 1856. A dead-heat was rowed in 1877. Score to date (1985): Cambridge 68, Oxford, 62. 1 dead-heat. Oxford boat sank, 1951; Cambridge, 1977, and in 1984 Cambridge boat sank before race started. Cambridge subsequently lost in a borrowed boat.

Bodleian Library. *See* LIBRARIES, MODERN.

Boeotia, Greece. United under Theban leadership, *c.* 1100 B.C. Victory over Spartans at Leuctra, 371 B.C., gave B. supremacy in Greece till death of Epaminondas at battle of Mantinea, 362 B.C.

Boers. Emigrated from Cape Colony, 1835–7; founded Orange Free State, 1836; Transvaal Republic, 1848. *See* SOUTH AFRICAN WAR; CAPE COLONY; TRANSVAAL, etc.

Boer Wars, First B. War, 1880–1. Virtually ended by the British defeat at Majuba Hill, 27 Feb. 1881. Second B. War, 1899–1902. Concluded by the Peace of Vereeniging (*See under* TREATIES), 31 May 1902.

Bogomils, Old Slavonic for 'God's beloved', were a sect of heretics in the Balkans first mentioned in Greek sources, 1115. Their leader Basil was interrogated by the Emperor Alexius Comnenus, and then burnt by his orders, 1118. Slavonic sources mention the sect earlier, in the mid-tenth century, as of Manichaean (*See* MANICHAEISM) type. Driven out of Serbia *c.* 1200, they took refuge in Bosnia, where they survived until the fifteenth century.

Bogotá, formerly **Santa Fé de Bogotá**, capital of Colombia since 1831, was founded in 1538 and became an episcopal see in 1561, capital of the viceroyalty of New Granada in 1598.

Bohemia. Christianity introduced from Moravia during ninth century. Dukedom, AD. 891. Rulers known as kings soon after. 'Good King Wenceslas' murdered by Boleslav the Cruel, 929. Recognized as a kingdom by emperor, 1088. Reign of Ottokar begins, 1253. Extinction of Przemyslid dynasty, 1306. John of Luxembourg elected king, 1310. Killed at Crécy, 1346. University of Prague founded, 1348. John Hus *b. c.* 1373. Hussites adopt heretical doctrines, 1390 onwards. Hus burned by Council of Constance, 1415. 'The Twelve Years (Hussite) War', 1419–31. Battle of Taus, 1431. Destruction of the Taborites at battle of Lipau, 1434. Religious Pact of Iglau, 1436. George of Podebrad elected king, 1457. Ferdinand of Hapsburg became king, 1526. Ferdinand had himself declared hereditary ruler of B., so that B. became a permanent Hapsburg appanage, 1547. Toleration of Protestantism promised by Emperor Rudolf's *Letter of Majesty*, July 1609. The *Letter* violated by Ferdinand II. Defenestration of Prague, 1619. Battle of the White Mountain, 1620. Thirty Years War, 1618–48. After Treaty of Westphalia, 1648, history of B. became generally coincident with that of Austria, (*q.v.*) until 1918, thereafter with that of Czechoslovakia (*q.v.*). Sudeten territories incorporated in Germany, Oct. 1938. With Moravia became the 'Protectorate of B.-Moravia', and liberties suppressed under Germany, Mar. 1939. Liberated by Russians and Americans, 1945. Sudeten Germans forcibly driven out, 1945–6.

Rulers of, from the beginning of the historical period, *c.* 922, until 1918.

Princes:

Wenceslas I (Saint), the Good *c.* 922–*c.* 929

Boleslav I, the Cruel *c.* 929–967
Boleslav II 967–999
Boleslav III 999–1002
Vladivoj I 1002–1003
Jaromir I 1003–1012
Ulrich I 1012–1037
Bretislav I 1037–1055
Spytihinev II 1055–1061
Vratislav II (King) 1061–1092
Bretislav II 1092–1110
Borivoj II 1110–1120
Vladislav I 1120–1125
Sobeslav I 1125–1140
Vladislav II (as King, I) 1140–1173
Sobeslav II 1173–1189
Conrad Otho I 1189–1191
Wenceslas II 1191–1192

Kings:

Premysl Ottokar I 1198–1230
Wenceslas I 1230–1253
Premysl Ottokar II 1253–1278

Wenceslas II 1278–1305
Wenceslas III 1305–1306
Rudolf I of Hapsburg 1306–1307
Henry of Carinthia 1307–1310
John 1310–1346
Charles I (IV) 1346–1378
Wenceslas IV 1378–1419
Sigismund 1419–1437
Albert of Hapsburg 1437–1439
Ladislas Posthumus 1439–1457
George of Podebrad 1458–1471
Vladislav II 1471–1516
Louis I 1516–1526
Ferdinand I 1526–1564
Maximilian I 1564–1576
Rudolf II 1576–1612
Matthias 1612–1619
Frederick of the Palatinate
  *1619–1620
Ferdinand II *1619–1637
Ferdinand III 1637–1657
Leopold I 1657–1705
Josef I 1705–1711
Karl II (VI) 1711–1740
Maria Theresa *1740–1780
Karl of Bavaria *1740–1743
Josef II 1780–1790
Leopold II 1790–1792
Franz I 1792–1835
Ferdinand IV (I) 1835–1848
Franz Josef 1848–1916
Karl III (I) 1916–1918
*Disputed succession

Bohemian Brethren. *See* MORAVIAN BRETHREN.

Bokhara or **Bukhara,** Asia. Conquered in seventh century by Arabs, under whom it *fl.* until 1220. Seized by Uzbeks *c.* 1500. Emirate abolished and Soviet regime estab. 1921.

Bolivia. Conquered by Spain during the sixteenth century, and formed part of the viceroyalty of Peru. Separated from Peru, 1776, and added to the viceroyalty of Buenos Aires. War of Independence, 1810–24; royalists defeated at battle of Ayacucho, and independence granted, 1825. Boundary dispute with Chile, 1879–83; with Brazil, 1903. War over Gran Chaco with Paraguay 1933–36. Frontier with Paraguay settled by arbitration, 1938. Political instability since 1945 caused by economic problems: frequent military coups.

Bologna, Italy. (Lat. **Bolonia**). Roman colony, 189 B.C. University grew out of schools of liberal arts, which fl. in eleventh century; first statutes, 1252. Pope Julius II took and entered, 11 Nov. 1506. Taken by French, 1796; by Austrians, 1799; by French 1800; restored to pope, 1815; taken by Austrians, 16 May 1849, who evacuated, 12 June 1859, and papal legate left. Became part of kingdom of Italy, 1860.

Bolsheviks. That part of the revolutionary Socialist party which professed Marxist Communism and happened to be in a *majority* (bolshestvo) at the end of the Second Congress of the Russian Social-Democratic Labour Party, in 1903, when several delegates had already left the congress. Independent Bolshevik Party founded (calling itself Social-Democratic Labour Party), 1912. Led by Lenin and Trotsky it seized power in Russia in Nov. 1917. Known by name 'Communist Party' ('Bolsheviks') from 1918; word 'Bolsheviks' dropped, 1952, and term now only used in Russia in an historical sense. *See* OCTOBER REVOLUTION; RUSSIA; MENSHEVIKS; COMMUNISM.

Bolton Abbey (W. Yorkshire.) Founded 1121, at Embsay, and transferred to the site in Wharfedale, 1151. Really a priory, not abbey, of Augustinians. Dissolved, 1540.

Bombay, India. Acquired by Portuguese, 1509; given to Charles II of England as marriage portion of Catherine of Braganza, 1661; granted to E. India Co., 1668. University founded, 1857. Capital of Maharashta state, 1960.

Bomber. The first specialized military aircraft for this purpose was the German Gotha, twin-engined push-bi-plane, taken into service, 1917.

Bomber Command, British, estab. 1936. Saturation bombing of Germany by B. C. under Harris, 1942–45.

Bombs of a type similar to the modern mortar-bomb first mentioned in English, 1588. The word was also used to describe *shells*, an expression not used until the middle of the seventeenth century.

Bonaparte. *See* BUONAPARTE.

Bond Street, New. Built, 1721.

Bond Street, Old. Built 1686, by Sir Thomas Bond, who in 1683 bought and demolished Clarendon House for a building site.

Bonin or **Ogasawara Islands.** Discovered by Quast and Tasman, 1639. British, 1827. Japanese, 1878. Administered by the U.S.A., 1945–1968, then returned to Japan.

Bonn, Germany. Became residence of the electors and archbishops of Cologne during the Middle Ages. Became Prussian after 1815. Academy founded, 1777; made a university, 1786; abolished, 1802; restored and enlarged, 1818. Albert (Prince Consort) educated at, from 1837. Occupied by allied troops after World War I until 31 Jan. 1926. Seat of German Federal Government since 5 May 1949.

Book of Common Prayer. *See* PRAYER, BOOK OF COMMON.

Boomerang, probably existed in Australia by about 4800 B.C.

Bordeaux, France. Taken by Goths, A.D. 412; by Clovis, 508; became subject to England in 1154 by reason of the royal marriage in 1151; surrendered to France, 14 Oct. 1453; entered by British troops, 27 Feb. 1814. Temporary seat of French Government, Sept.–Dec. 1914 and 15–30 June 1940.

Bordeaux Mixture invented by Alexis Millerdet (1838–1902) to combat phylloxera and mildew in vines.

Border, The, between England and Scotland, dates in its present form as to the eastern sector form 1018 when the Scots under Malcolm II recovered Lothian, and as to the western sector from the reconquest of Cumberland by the English in 1157 (*See* STRATHCLYDE). It ceased to be a political frontier in 1603. Following are some battles important in the annals of B. warfare.

Halidon Hill, 1333
Otterburn, 1388
Nisbet, 1402
Homildon, 1402
Hedgeley Moor, 1464
Flodden, 1513
Solway Moss, 1542

Ancrum Moor, 1544

Borneo, Indian Ocean. First European resident in B., Francisco Serrão (Portuguese), 1511–21. Visited by Magellan's comrades in 1522. Dutch established trading posts, 1604. Dutch B. became part of Indonesia (*q.v.*) after World War II. The nucleus of British North B. was territory acquired in 1878 by a syndicate which transferred to the British N. B. Co., chartered, 1881. Sarawak (*q.v.*) became, 1841, the rajahship of Sir James Brooke, and his descendants; enlarged, 1861, 1882, 1884, 1890, 1904. British N. B., Sarawak, and the diminished State of Brunei became British protectorates in 1888. Sarawak and British N.B. annexed by British Government, 15 July 1946, to form British B., which also included Brunei and the is. of Labuan. N.B. joined the federation of Malaysia (*q.v.*) 1 Aug. 1963, and from then on was known as the state of Sabah.

Bornu, Kingdom of. First discovered by Europeans, 1823. Partitioned about 1900 between Nigeria and Fr. W. Africa.

Borough. The Municipal Corporations Act, 1835, defined what was and what was not a municipal B., and reformed their constitutions. It was superseded by the Municipal Corporations Act, 1882, and the Local Government Acts of 1933, 1958 and 1972.

Borough, The. *See* SOUTHWARK.

Borstal. Originally at B., near Chatham, 1902. Made a regular part of prison system, 1908, under heading of B. detention; name changed to B. training, 1948; system revised completely after 1983.

Boscobel, parish in Shropshire. Charles II hid in an oak-tree there after his defeat at Worcester in 1651.

Bosnia. Incorporated with Turkey, 1463; rebellion against Turkish rule, 1849–1851 and 1875; occupied by Austria, 1878, and formally annexed by her, 1908. Became part of Yugoslavia, 1918. *See also* HERZEGOVINA.

Bosnia-Herzegovina. A national committee sat at Sarajevo from Oct. 1918, in close touch with the Yugoslav national council at Zagreb. On formation of the state of Yugoslavia (*q.v.*), B.-H. became part thereof. Became one of the Federated Republics of Yugoslavia, 1945.

Boston (Lincs.). St. Botolph founded a monastery here, 654, which was destroyed by the Danes in 870. In the Guildhall (1450) those subsequently famous as the Pilgrim Fathers were imprisoned, 1607.

Boston, Mass., U.S.A. Founded by John Winthrop, 1630. First American newspaper, *Boston News-Letter*, Apr. 1704 (*See* NEWSPAPERS). Tea chests destroyed in B. Harbour, 16 Dec. 1773, in event known as the B. Tea Party.

Botanic Gardens (Kew). Established, 1759; enlarged, 1841–65. B.Gs. were estab. in Italy in the sixteenth century (Padua and Pisa) and at Oxford in the seventeenth century.

Botanic Society's Gardens, Royal (Regent's Park). Established, 1839.

Botany Bay, Australia. Discovered 28 Apr. 1770, by Capt. Cook. Capt. Arthur Phillip, R.N., commissioned to form penal colony here in 1787, but found locality unsuitable (Jan. 1788), and removed to site on which Sydney now stands. Transportation of convicts ceased, 1840.

Botswana, formerly **Bechuanaland,** independent republic within the Commonwealth. Ravaged by Matabele tribe, 1817. London Missionary Society estab. at Kuruman, 1818. Boer encroachments led to Brit. protectorate being estab., 10 Sept. 1884. Whole country under Brit. protection, 30 Sept. 1885. S. Bechuanaland added to Cape Colony, 1895, but rest of country remained a Brit. protectorate. Caprivi Appendix, formerly part of German SW. Africa, incorporated, 1922. On independence, 30 Sept. 1966, Bechuanaland was renamed Botswana. Seretse Khama became its first President.

Boulder Dam on the Colorado River between Nevada and Arizona completed, 1935–6.

Boulogne, France. Sacked by the Normans, 882. Unsuccessfully besieged by Edward III, 1347. Seized by Duke of Burgundy (?1419), seizure confirmed by Treaty of Arras, 1435; united to France, 1477. Treaty between Henry VIII (of England) and Francis I at B., 28 Oct. 1532. Besieged by English, 1492; taken by English, 14 Sept. 1544; restored, 1550. Napoleon I mustered his forces at B. with the intention of invading England, 1803. British defence of, 22–24 May 1940. Liberated by Canadian First Army, 19 Sept. 1944.

'Bounty' Mutiny. H.M.S. *Bounty* sailed in Dec. 1787 to the Society Islands on a scientific mission under command of Capt. William Bligh (1754–1817). On 28 Apr. 1789, in the Indian Ocean, the crew mutinied and put Bligh and eighteen others in an open boat which he sailed to Timor, reaching that island on 9 June. The mutineers returned to Tahiti, which nine of them left in 1790 for Pitcairn Island, accompanied by Tahitian wives and some Tahitian men. *See also* PITCAIRN ISLAND. Bligh published his narrative of the mutiny and his subsequent voyage, 1792.

Bourbon, House of. First Duke of B., 1327. From this house sprang royal families of France, Naples, Parma, and Spain.

Bourbonnais, ancient province united to the French crown on the confiscation of the Constable of Bourbon's domains by Francis I in 1527. From 1661 to 1789 held by the house of Bourbon Condé. Became the department of Allier, 1794.

Bourges, capital, under the name of Avaricum, of the Gallic Biturigan territory. Avaricum was sacked by Julius Caesar, 52 B.C. The cathedral was built, 1200–60, but not consecrated until 1324. Pragmatic Sanction of B., 1437. For a period *c.* 1440 was capital of France.

Bourse. *See* EXCHANGES, FOREIGN.

Bouvetoya (Bouvet Island). Island in the S. Atlantic, was discovered by the Frenchman Pierre Bouvet, 1739; in 1825 the British flag was hoisted. Britain waived claim to B., 1928, and it was proclaimed Norwegian territory, 27 Feb. 1930.

Bouvines. *See* BATTLES.

Bowling. Played in Germany and the Low Countries, and in England under the name 'skittles', since the fourteenth century. Taken to America in the seventeenth century by Dutch settlers, and played out of doors until 1840. B. alleys opened in Britain, 1959 onwards.

Bowls has been played in England since at least 1299. Word first occurs in Act of 1511.

Bow Street. Magistrates' court first sat, 1735; police court building erected 1881, replacing that of 1749, which was sacked by the Gordon rioters, 1780. The street was first built up in 1637. Covent Garden Theatre built, 1858. B.S. Runners formed the only criminal detection force in London *c.* 1750–1829, after which date their functions were taken over by the police.

Boxers. Chinese secret society founded 1896, encouraged in 1899 by the agents of the Dowager Empress to provoke anti-foreign incidents. For Boxer Rising of 1900, *See* CHINA.

Boxing. First B. booth opened in London, 1719. Became a legal sport in England, 1901.

Boxing Day. Officially recognized as a Bank Holiday, 1874.

Boycott. Term derived from Capt. Charles B. (1832–97), land agent to Lord Erne in County Mayo, Ireland, who was the victim of a B. in 1880, organized by the Land League (*q.v.*) in retaliation for certain evictions.

Boyles' Law. Formulated, 1662, by Robert Boyle (1627–91).

Boys' Brigade. Founded, 1883, by Sir W. Smith (*d.* 1914). Amalgamated with Boys' Life Brigade, 1926.

Boys' Clubs, National Association of. Founded, 1925.

Boys' Club of America. Founded, 1906.

Boy Scouts. Organization began in 1908 in the U.K. Adopted by Chile, 1909, the U.S.A., France, and Scandinavia, 1910, and ultimately over one hundred other countries. First World Jamboree, 1920. First Chief Scout, the founder, Sir Robert Baden-Powell (who became Baron Baden-Powell of Gilwell in 1929), was *b.* 1857 and *d.* 1941. Movement prohibited in Nazi Germany, 1933, and in territories subsequently occupied by Germany. Restarted there after 1945 but not in ters. controlled by Communist regimes.

Brabant, Low Countries. Duchy, 1190, passed through the house of Burgundy to Philip II of Spain. At the division of the Spanish Netherlands, 1579, North B. became part of the United Provinces and was recognized as belonging to them at the Treaty of Westphalia (*q.v.*), 1648. This is the modern Dutch province of N.B. S.B. remained Spanish till 1714, when it was transferred to Austria. When Belgium was annexed by France at Treaty of Campo Formio, 1797, S.B. was further divided into what are now the Belgian provinces of B. (capital Brussels) and Antwerp (capital Antwerp (*q.v.*)).

Bradford, Yorkshire, existed during the reign of Edward the Confessor. Besieged in 1642 and 1643 by royalist forces. First woollen weaving mill opened, 1798. Incorporated, 1847; became city, 1897. Univ. estab. 1966. Considerable Jewish immigration, nineteenth century; Asian immigration, twentieth century. Fire at B. football stadium, May 1985, with over 50 fatalities.

Braganza. Family descended from Alfonso (*d.* 1461), son of King John I (1357–1433), who was made Duke of B., 1442. The family ruled Portugal (*q.v.*), 1640–1910, and Brazil (*q.v.*) 1822–89. Catherine of B. (1638–1705) married King Charles II in 1662.

Brandenburg. Frederick of Hohenzollern became margrave of, 1415. Neumark acquired, 1455. Kottbus, 1462. Züllichen, 1482. Zossen, 1490. Reversion of Prussia secured by agreement, 1569. Ravensberg, Mark and Wesel acquired, 1614. Prussia acquired, 1618. E. Pomerania, 1648–79, from Sweden. Elector of B. takes title of King in Prussia, 1701. Henceforth known as Prussia (*q.v.*), except for a district, corresponding to the Altmark, which became in 1949 a province of the German Democratic Republic.

Electors of B., 1415–1701:
Frederick I 1415–1440
Frederick II the Iron 1440–1470

Albert Achilles 1470–1486
John Cicero 1486–1499
Joachim I 1499–1535
Joachim II 1535–1571
John George 1571–1598
Joachim Frederick III 1598–1608
John Sigismund 1608–1619
George William 1619–1640
Frederick William, 'The Great
  Elector' 1640–1688
Frederick III 1688–1713
(From 1701, Frederick I, King of
  Prussia.)
See further under PRUSSIA, KINGS OF.

Branding, was abolished for civilians in England and Wales, 1822; in France, 1832. In 1858 the British Mutiny Act ordered deserters to be branded below the left arm-pit; this Act was repealed in 1879. Concentration camp prisoners in Nazi Germany were branded 1936–45.

Brasenose College (Oxford). Founded, 1509.

Brasilia, capital of Brazil (*q.v.*). Inaugurated, 21 Apr. 1960.

Bratislava (Hun. **Pozsony;** Ger. **Pressburg**). Founded *c.* A.D. 1000. Became capital of 'imperial' Hungary after capture of Buda by Turks, 1541 until 1784. The Hungarian kings were crowned in the cathedral of St. Martin, 1526–1916, and the Hungarian Parliament met in the Landhaus down to 1848. Incorporated in Czechoslavakia, 1918. Capital of 'independent' Slovakia, 1939–44.

Brawling in church was punishable under statutes of Edward VI, which replaced the pre-Reformation canon laws on the offence. The B. Act of 1860 applies to places of worship of all denominations; hitherto only the Anglican churches had been so protected since the Reformation.

Brazil. Treaty of Tordesilhas, drawing a dividing line between Spanish and Portuguese colonial interest, giving the southern American continent to Portugal, 1494. Pedro Alvares Cabral landed on the coast of B., 22 Apr. 1500, and formally took possession of the country for the crown of Portugal. Treaty of Tordesilhas ratified, 1506. Martin Alfonso de Souza arrived at

Pernambuco, 30 Jan. 1530. Appointed first governor-general, 1531. Colonization started effectively. Traffic in African slaves begun, 1532. Foundation of the city of Bahia, which becomes capital of B., 1549. São Paulo founded, 1554. Rio de Janeiro founded 1567 after driving the French back from their foothold. B. partitioned, ruled by two governors from Bahia and Rio de Janeiro, 1572–81. Spanish domination 1581–1640. Dutch try to colonize parts of B., 1630–61. Portuguese rebellion and Dutch naval victory over the Spaniards at Itamarca result in re-establishment of Portuguese rule, 1640. Dutch expelled during Anglo-Dutch wars of the English Commonwealth, 1654. Gold found in Minas Gerais, 1699. Coffee plant brought to B., 1727. Progress of commercial cultivation only about 100 years later. Bandeirantes found diamonds in Minas Gerais, 1730. The colony became state of viceroyalty. Rio de Janeiro, became capital 1763. Napoleon's invasion of Portugal results in D. João VI moving to B., with the Portuguese royal family, 1808. B. declared kingdom, 1815. D. João VI, returning to Portugal, leaves the regentship to his son, D. Pedro, 1821. D. Pedro declared independence of B. and crowned as first Emperor of B, 7 Sept. 1822. First constitution, 1824. D. Pedro I was forced to abdicate in favour of his five-year-old son, 7 Apr. 1831. Slave trade abolished, 1850. War against Argentina, 1851. War against Paraguay, 1865–70. Complete abolition of slavery, 1888. Proclamation of republic, 15 Nov. 1889. Civil war, 1893–4. Begins great industrial revolution, especially in São Paulo, 1920. Civil war broke 1930. New constitution: Vargas was elected president and ruled for fifteen years on steadily increasing totalitarian principles, 24 Oct. 1930. Military revolution dismissed Vargas, 30 Oct. 1945, but he returned to power, 1951, and *d.* 1954. New constitution, 1969. Period of economic expansion in 1970s ended, 1982, with heavy international debts.

Presidents of the Republic:
Marshal Manuel Deodoro da Fonseca 1890–1891
Marshal Floriano Peixoto 1891–1894
Dr. Prudente José de Moraes Barros 1894–1898
Dr. Manuel Ferraz de Campos Salles 1898–1902
Dr. Francisco da Paula Rodrigues Alves 1902–1906
Dr. Alfonso Augusto Moreira Penna 1906–1909
Dr. Nilo Peçanha 1909–1910
Marshal Hermes Rodrigues da Fonseca 1910–1914
Dr. Wenceslau Braz Pereira Gomes 1914–1918
Dr. Francisco da Paula Rodrigues Alves 1918
Dr. Delfim Moreira da Costa Ribeiro 1918–1919
Dr. Epitácio da Silva Pessoa 1919–1922
Dr. Arturo da Silva Bernardes 1922–1926
Dr. Washington Luiz Pereira de Souza 1926–1930
Dr. Getúlio Dornelles Vargas 1930–1945
Dr. José Linhares 1945–1946
Gen. Eurico Gaspar Dutra 1946–1951
Dr. Getúlio Dornelles Vargas 1951–1954
Carlos Coimbra de Luz (3 days) 1955
Nereu Ramos, 1955–1956
Juscelino Kubitscheck 1956–1961
Dr. Janio Quadros (6 months) 1961
Dr. João Goulart 1961–1964
Gen. Castelo Branco 1964–1966
Marshal Costa e Silva 1967–1969
Garrastazu Medici 1969–1974
Ernesto Geisel 1974–1979
Baptista de Oliveiro Figueiredo 1979–85
Tancredo Neves 1985 (d. before being sworn in).

Brazzaville, Congo. Founded by the French explorer, Count P. P. F. C. S. de Bazza (1852–1905) in 1886.

Breda, Holland. Captured from Spaniards by Prince Maurice of Nassau, 1590; retaken by Spaniards, 1625; by Dutch, Oct. 1637. Compromise of B., 1566. Charles II's Declaration from B., 1660. Peace of B., 1667. Taken by French, 1794; French expelled, 1813.

Brehon Laws. Ancient laws of Ireland, going back to the third century (reign of Cormac MacArt), and prevailing until the middle of the seventeenth century. Penalites against submitting to, 1366.

Bremen, Germany.
1. City. Principal member of Hanseatic League (*q.v.*), fourteenth century. Free city, 1646. Taken by Denmark, 1712. Sold to Hanover, 1715. Independence recognized by George II, 1730. Taken by French 1757. Restored 1758. Annexed by Napoleon, 1810. Independence restored, 1813. Joined German Empire, 1871. Heavily bombed in World War II and fell to the British Second Army, 23–8 Apr. 1945.
2. Archbishopric. Became an ecclesiastical principality early in the thirteenth century. Secularized and acquired by Sweden, 1648. Territory taken by Denmark, 1712, and sold to Hanover, 1715.
3. Verden from 1405 to 1550 was a free city of the empire, on the River Aller some 23 miles SE. of B. At the Peace of Westphalia (1648) it became Swedish; until 1715 it had the same history as B. Purchase confirmed by Treaty of Stockholm, negotiated by George I of England, 1719.

Brenner Pass first traversed by a carriage-way, 1772, and by railway, 1864–7. Motorway completed after World War II.

Breslau, *See* WROCLAW.

Brest. Founded, 1240; in English hands, 1342–97. Last attacked from the sea by English, 1694. The *Scharnhorst, Gneisenau,* and *Prinz Eugen* in the docks attracted R.A.F. bombing, 1941–2. German garrison surrendered, 19 Sept. 1944, after six-week siege.

Brest-Litovsk (Rus. or Pol. **Brzesc Nad Bugiem**). A fortress town since 1017; became Lithuanian, 1319; Polish, 1569; Russian, 1795; Polish 1918. Has been Russian since Sept. 1939, except for German military occupation during World War II. At a synod held here, 1594, the Uniate Church of Ruthenia was brought to the Roman obedience. In 1831 the old town was demolished by the Russians and a fortress built on the site. The Russian and German armies made contact here after the Polish campaign of 1939, 18 Sept.

Brest-Litovsk, Treaty. Imposed on Russia by Germany, 3 Mar. 1918.

Brethren, Church of the, *See* GERMAN BAPTISTS.

Brethren of the Common Lot or **Life.** The name given to a brotherhood founded in the Low Countries by Gerard Groote of Deventer, *c.* 1380. Erasmus was at one of the their schools in 'S Hertogenbosch *c.* 1483. They began to decline in the sixteenth century, and died out in the seventeeth.

Brétigny, Peace of, 8 May 1360 *See* HUNDRED YEARS WAR.

Bretton Woods Agreement. An International Monetary and Financial Conference at B.W., begun 1 July 1944, and signed its Final Act, 22 July. This was ratified first by the U.S. Congress in 1945.

Bribery of voters in the U.K. first punishable under the Corrupt Practices Act, 1854. Now dealt with under the Representation of the People Act, 1949.

Bridewell (London). Saxon palace on site of a Roman fort. Rebuilt by Henry I. King John held council, 1210. Wolsey rebuilt palace, 1522. Edward VI granted manor-house and palace of B. to the city of London as a house of correction for vagrants, 1552. Destroyed in Fire of London, 1666. Women's prison built after 1666. Pulled down, 1864.

Bridgewater Canal. Begun, 1755. Opened, 17 July 1761.

Brighton, England. Originally Brighthelmstone. Pavilion begun, 1784, by Prince of Wales (later George IV) and finished, 1827. W. Pier built, 1866. Palace Pier, 1900. University of Sussex opened at, Oct, 1961.

Brindisi, Italy. Ancient Greek colony founded fifth century, B.C. Taken from the Sallentini by the Romans, 267 B.C. Cathedral founded, 1089. Base of Italian fleet in 1866 and of the Otranto Barrage in World War I. Seat of Badoglio's pro-Allied government, Sept. 1943.

Brisbane, Australia. First occupied as penal settlement by Thomas B, 1824. Became capital of Queensland, 1859.

Bristol, England. Importance as a town began c. 1000. Came by marriage into possession of Earl of Gloucester, 1119. Cathedral founded 1148. First charter, 1171. Recognized as a staple town, 1353. Church of St. Mary Redcliffe built c. end of the fourteenth century. Brothers Cabot sailed for N. America from, 1497. Slave trade *fl.* 1580–1640. Taken by Prince Rupert, 1643; by Fairfax, 1645. Attempt to fire shipping in harbour, 1777. Modern harbour constructed, 1809. Half city burnt in rioting, 1831. University College founded, 1876. University established, 1909; H.Q. of Avon (*q.v.*) since 1974.

Britain. Invaded by Julius Caesar, 55 and 54 B.C., Cunobelin, King of the Catuvellauni c. A.D. 5. Invaded and conquered by Romans under Aulus Plautius, A.D. 43–7. Caractacus defeated by Ostorius and deported to Rome, 50. Romans massacred by Boudicca, 60. Boudicca defeated, 61. Christianity said to have been taught, 64. Agricola reforms government and defeats the Picts, 78–85. Hadrian's Wall begun c. 122. Antonine's Wall built by Lollius Urbicus, 142, on site of Agricola's field fortifications. Hadrian's Wall strengthened by Severus, 208. Constantine proclaimed emperor at York, 25 July 306. Saxon raids on coastal areas, from beginning of third century onwards. British bishops attend Council of Arles, 314. War with Picts and Scots, 360; invasion of southern B., 367. Driven out, 368. Romans finally quit B. some time shortly before 429, and abandon responsibility for the defence, 446. Anglo-Saxon invasions begin on a large scale c. 449. *See* ENGLAND.

Britain, Battle of. Name for the air attack on B. by day, 8 Aug.–29 Oct. 1940, intended to be the first stage of a series of operations culminating in Operation Sealion (*q.v.*), which would have been the seaborne invasion of S.E. England. In the phase 8–18 Aug. the Luftwaffe attacked shipping, ports, and later fighter airfields between Harwich and the Isle of Wight. Aug. 13–'Eagle Day' in the German planning timetable—was the date by which it was hoped that all R.A.F. fighter stations would be out of action. In the second phase up to 5 Sept. similar objectives farther W. and N. along the coast and farther inland to the NW. were attacked by formations relatively stronger in fighters and weaker in bombers. A mass daylight attack on London (7 Sept.) by 350 bombers began the third phase: until 5 Oct. there were thirty-seven more day attacks on London, besides diversionary attacks on other south-eastern targets, The last phase consisted of night attacks on London by fighters and fighter-bombers and lasted until the end of Oct.

'Britannia'. Naval training ship for officer cadets, 1859–1903. The Royal Naval College, Dartmouth, became officially H.M.S. *B.* in 1921. Royal yacht *B.* (4,000 tons) built to replace the *Victoria and Albert*, and completed in Jan. 1954.

British Academy. Incorporated 18 Aug. 1902, after foundation in 1901 to promote 'study of the moral and political sciences'.

British Association for the Advancement of Science. Established, 1831. Kew Observatory presented to, by Queen Victoria, 1842.

British Broadcasting Corporation (B.B.C.). Succeeded B.B.Co., which was formed, 1922, and established, on national footing, 1923; Chelmsford longwave station opened, 1924. B.B.Co's charter expired, 31 Dec. 1926. Daventry stations opened, 1925 and 1927; Chelmsford (short wave), 1927. Chartered Corporation, 1927. Droitwich took over long-wave from Daventry, 1934. Television from Alexandra Palace, 1936. Foreign broadcasts commenced, 1937. Television service reopened, June 1946. First colour-television in Europe started on B.B.C. 2, 1 July 1967.

British Columbia, W. Canada, Discovered by Perez, 1774; visited by Cook, 1778. Made a British colony, Aug.

1858. Vancouver Island incorporated with, 1866. Annexed to Canada, 1871.

British Council. Established, Nov. 1934, and inaugural meeting held, 2 July 1935; Charter granted, 1940.

British Electricity Authority. *See* CENTRAL ELECTRICITY AUTHORITY.

British Guiana. *See* GUYANA.

British Honduras *See* BELIZE.

British Industries Fair first held, 1915. Moved to Olympia, 1930. Closed, 1956.

British Legion. Originally the name of numerous now forgotten military organizations in the service of foreign powers or revolutionary movements (e.g. in the Spanish American wars of Liberation *c.* 1810–25), but now usually referring to the combined ex-service organization which was formed 1 July 1921. Royal charter, Apr. 1925. Now the Royal B.L.

British Library, estab. July 1973 under the British Library Act, 1972. Its reference section embraces the former library depts. of the British Museum (*q.v.*) including the Newspaper Library at Colindale, the India Office Library and Records and the Science Reference Library. The Lending Division is made up of the former National Central Library and the former National Lending Library for Science and Technology. The former Copyright Receipt Office and British National Bibliography Ltd. comprise the Bibliographic Services Division. H.Q. of the B.L. is at 2 Sheraton St., W.1.

British Medical Association. Founded, 1832; took is present name in 1856.

British Museum. Grant made by Parliament, 5 Apr. 1753. Old Royal Library presented to, 1757. Building opened, 16 Jan. 1759. New buildings erected, 1823–1847. Elgin Marbles acquired, 1816; Grenville Library, 1847. Reading-room opened, 18 May 1857. Natural history collection removed to S. Kensington, 1881. Foundation-stone of extension laid by Edward VII, 27 June 1907; the extension opened, 1914. British Museum Act, 1963, separated by National History Museum from the British Museum. British Library (*q.v*)

which includes the library housed in the B.M., estab. July 1973 under British Library Act. 1972. *See also* LIBRARIES and COTTONIAN LIBRARY.

British Standard Time, operated 1968–71. Abolished due to public outcry.

British Standards Institution. Founded as the Engineering Standards Committee, 1901; royal charter, 1929.

British Telecom, public corporation estab. under the Telecommunication Act, 1981, to operate the telecommunications network formerly controlled by the Post Office (*q.v.*). Privatized by Conservative govt., 1984.

British Union of Fascists. Founded by Sir Oswald Mosley, 1932. It disintegrated at the outbreak of World War II, but various bodies resembling it founded after 1945 of which the National Front is (1985) the most prominent.

Brittany. Conquered by Julius Caesar, 57–56 B.C. and called **Armorica** by the Romans. Large influx of Celts from Britain to B. in the fifth and sixth centuries. Independent duchy *c.* 1000. Under Norman suzerainty, 1066. Bestowed as a duchy by Henry II on his brother Geoffrey, 1159. Succession disputed, 1161, 1171, 1186, 1343. By marriage of Charles VIII of France and Anne of Brittany, 1491, united under crown of France. Finally and irrevocably incorporated into France, 1532.

Brixham, Devon, scene of William of Orange's landing, 1688.

Broad Bottom Administration. Formed out of a coalition, 24 Nov. 1744. Dissolved by death of the Premier Henry Pelham 6 Mar. 1754.

Broadmoor Institution. State institution for the criminally insane, in Berkshire. Opened, 1863.

Brooklyn, New York. Settled (as Breuckelen) by Dutch, 1636. Incorporated as a city, 1834. Bridge to New York City opened, 24 May 1883. Borough of New York since 1893.

Bruges (Fr.) or **Brugge** (Flem.), Belgium. Capital of Flanders till 1180. Town hall begun, 1376. Belfry, end of thirteenth century. Order of the Golden Fleece instituted here, 1430. Ceased to be an important port after final silting up of the River Zwyn, 1490. Market hall built, 1561–6. Docks and canal built, 1885–95. Greatly extended, 1930–9.

Brumaire, Coup d'État of. On 18 B. of the year VIII (9 Nov. 1799) Napoleon abolished the Directory. *See* FRENCH REVOLUTION, THE GREAT.

Brunei, N.W. Borneo. Treaty between Britain and Sultan of B., 1847. British protectorate, 1888. Declined to become part of Malaysia, 1962–3. Became fully independent of Britain, 1 Jan. 1984.

Brunel University, Uxbridge, estab. 1966.

Brunswick (Ger. **Braunschweig**), a fragment of the old tribal duchy of Saxony, which in the tenth century was the fief of one Bruno from whom the name derives. When in 1181 Saxony was dismembered Duke Henry the Lion was allowed to keep that part which he had personality inherited; in 1267 the territory was divided into separate duchies of B.-Lüneburg and B.-Wolfenbüttel under two branches of the house of Guelf. Alternate reunification and repartition took place down to 1735, the most significant partition being that of 1596, which led to the rise of the ducal house of Lüneburg-Celle, from which the electoral house of Hanover (*q.v.*) derived. The duchy was merged in the kingdom of Westphalia, 1806–14. The ducal house abdicated, 1918, and the territory constituted a free state under the Weimar Republic (1919–33). The Third Reich (1933–45) reduced B. to the status of a mere administrative province, and since 1945 it has formed part of the Lower Saxon *Land.*

Brussels, Belgium. Mentioned in eighth century as *Bruchsella.* Church of Sainte-Gudule completed, 1273. Capital of Low Countries, 1507. Alva's rule, 1567. Union of B., 1578. Bombarded by Villeroi, Aug. 1956. Taken by French, 1701; by Duke of Marlborough, 1706; by Saxe, 1746; by Dumouriez, 1802. Capital of Belgium, 1831. University founded, 1834. Germans occupied city

from Aug. 1914 to Nov. 1918. Again occupied by Germans, 17 May 1940. Liberated, 3 Sept. 1944. Serious rioting in B. during the crisis over the monarchy, 1950. N.A.T.O. H.Q. since 1967 and H.Q. of several E.E.C. agencies since 1958. Riot in Heysel stadium, 1985, bt. Liverpool and Juventus football fans: over 50 deaths.

Brussels, Treaty of, signed 17 Mar. 1948, an instrument of the Western Union (*q.v.*) policy. Signatories were Great Britain, France, Belgium, Holland, Luxembourg. Federal Germany and Italy acceded to the Treaty, 1954.

Bubastis (Arab. **Tel Basta**), city of Lower Egypt, famous for its temple of Pasht or Basht, the cat (originally lioness) goddess, the ruins of which were excavated in 1887, the city having been in ruins since shortly after its capture by the Persians, 352. B.C..

Buccaneers. Sixteenth-century associations of piratical adventurers, chiefly French and English. In 1630 they captured Tortuga and used it as a stronghold. In 1655 they helped the Commonwealth Navy to capture Jamaica. In 1685 they defied the Spanish fleet in the bay of Panama. Their last great achievement was the capture of Cartagena, 1697.

Buchan's Predictions. Meteorological forecasts of periodic cold snaps by Alexander Buchan (1829–1907), made in 1869.

Bucharest (Bucuresti), Rumania. Became capital, 1859. Held by Germans, Dec. 1916–Nov. 1918. Treaty between Rumania and Central Powers, 7 May 1918, nullified, 11 Nov. 1918.

Buchenwald, near Weimar. Site of a notorious German concentration camp, opened in 1934. Liberated by the Americans, 11 Apr. 1945.

Buckingham Palace. Built, 1703. Property of Queen Charlotte, 1761. New building occupied by Queen Victoria, 13 July 1837, after extensive alterations, started in 1825, had been completed. New façade, 1913. Art gallery opened to the public, 25 July 1962.

Buckingham University, founded as the University College at Buckingham, 1973, independent of govt. assistance. Chartered, 1983.

Budapest, Hungary. Buda, capital of Hungary, 1320–1526. Captured by Turks, 1541. Recovered, 1686. Palaces built, 1770. University, 1784. Buda and Pest united as one city, 1872. Occupied by Rumanians, Aug.–Nov. 1919. Prolonged fighting between Russian and German troops in 1944–5; finally captured by the Russians, 13 Feb. 1945. The city was largely rebuilt after World War II, but again suffered heavy damage during the abortive revolt of Oct.–Nov. 1956.

Buddhism. The Buddha, or Siddhattha Gotama, c .563–480 B.C.

Buenos Aires. Capital of Argentina. City founded, 1535; refounded, 1580. Taken by British, 27 June 1806; retaken by Spaniards, 12 Aug; British attack repulsed 5 July 1807. Independent state, Oct. 1853; reunited to Argentina, Nov. 1859.

Buffalo, New York. Founded, 1803 as New Amsterdam; got its present name, 1810. Burned by British, 1813. President McKinley assassinated at, 5 Sept. 1901.

Buganda, former province of Uganda (*q.v.*), now under the 1967 constitution, divided into two. British officials became the Kabaka's accepted advisers 1890. Kabaka exiled by British Government on grounds of non-co- operation, 1953–55. In 1963 the Kabaka, Mutesa II, became President of Uganda (*q.v.*): he was deposed by the Ugandan premier (1966), who took over his office. The Kabaka fled to Britain, where he *d.* in 1969.

Building Societies. Earliest recorded B.S. founded Birmingham *c.* 1780.

Bukovina, originally part of Moldavia (*q.v.*), inhabited principally by Slavs of the Ruthenian (Ukrainian) linguistic division, was under Turkish sovereignty from 1512 until its occupation by the Russians in 1769, but was taken from them by the Austrians, 1774, to whom it was ceded by Turkey, 1775, becoming part of Galicia until 1849, when it was separated and made a crown land of the Hungarian kingdom. Granted autonomy, 1861. Sèvres treaty of 1920 recognized all B. as Ru-

manian territory. Northern B., together with Bessarabia, was ceded to the U.S.S.R. to comply with an ultimatum of 27 June 1940, but was again Rumanian from 1941 to 1944. It was finally ceded to Russia under the peace treaty of 1947 and forms part of the Ukrainian S.S.R.

Bulgaria. For early history *see* BULGARS. Treaty of Berlin set up the principality of B. and the autonomous province of Eastern Rumelia, 13 July 1878. Prince Alexander of Battenberg elected ruler, 1879; after his abdication, Prince Ferdinand of Saxe-Coburg elected, 7 July 1887. Independence proclaimed, 22 Sept. 1908, and the prince took title of Tsar. B. entered World War I on German side, Oct. 1915, and surrendered to the Allies unconditionally, Oct. 1918. Tsar abdicated, 3 Oct. 1918, in favour of his son, Boris III. By Treaty of Neuilly, 1919, B. ceded territory to Greece, Rumania, and Yugoslavia. Military *coup d'état*, 1934; from 1935 Boris ruled as virtual dictator. Treaty of Craiova, 8 Sept. 1940, ceded S. Dobrudja to B., thus restoring the frontier of 1912. German troops entered B., Mar. 1941. B. invaded Yugoslavia and Greece, Apr. 1941, and occupied Thrace and Macedonia until 26 Aug. 1944. People's Republic (i.e. Communists) since 1946.

The peace treaty with the Allies was signed at Paris, 10 Feb. 1947, and a separate treaty with Yugoslavia, 27 Nov.

Rulers of B., 1879–1946:
Alexander (Prince) 1879–1886
Ferdinand (King 1908) 1887–1918
Boris III 1918–1943
Simeon II 1943–1946
President of the Bulgarian People's Republic:
Neichev 1947–1950
There is now no single Head of State, but (1985) Todor Zhikov is Chairman of the Council of State, and first Secretary of the Communist Party.

Bulgars, originally a Ural-Altaic people from Central Asia, occupied the space between the Urals and the Volga in the fourth century A.D. After splitting

(433) into two main groups, one of them formed a strong state on the northern shore of the Black Sea which was destroyed about 560 by the Avars. The other branch, after a period of subjection, first to the Avars and then to the Turks, recovered its independence, 582, and founded a state on the Volga known as Great Bulgaria (Volgaria), which persisted into the thirteenth century. A faction split off from this state, under pressure from the Khazars, migrated westwards, and crossed the Danube, 679, into Moesia, where they easily conquered the local population compounded of Illyrians and more recent Slavonic immigrants, who had first appeared in the third century. The Slavonic immigration into Moesia, which became the country now known as Bulgaria, was still in progress, and the Slavonic language was adopted by the B., who soon lost all memory of their original non-Aryan tongue. In 811 the Bulgar Khan Krum defeated and slew the Emperor Nicephorus. The Khan Boris (857–88) adopted Orthodox Christianity in 870. After a period of maximum expansion and power under Simeon (893–927) the Tsar Samuel was defeated by the Emperor Basil II Bulgaroktonos—'the slayer of B.'—in 1014. The whole Bulgar territory was subject to the empire from 1018 until 1186, when the northern part became independent under the Asen dynasty, who in the reign of Ivan II (c. 1230) ruled the whole Balkan peninsula as far W. as Albania and Epirus. The dynasty died out, 1280, and the B., weakened by internal dissension and Mongol invasions, were defeated and subjected to Serbian rule, 28 July 1330, at the battle of Kustendil; this lasted until 1356, but only forty years of Bulgar independence remained before conquest by the Turks and the end of the first Bulgarian kingdom in 1396. The B. remained under Turkish rule until 1878; the 'Bulgarian atrocities' of 1876 led to Russia declaring war on Turkey (1877), and this paved the way for Bulgarian independence. *See further under* BULGARIA.

The following is a list of medieval Bulgar rulers:

Khans:
Krum *c.* 802–814
Omurtag 814–*c.* 830
Malomir (Presiam) *c.* 830–852

Princes:
Boris I (Saint) 852–888
Vladimir 888–893

Tsars:
Simeon I, the Great 893–927
Peter 927–969
Boris II 969–971
Samuel *c.* 971–1014
Gabriel Roman 1014–1015
Ivan Vladislav 1015–1018
Bulgaria subject to Byzantium
1018–1186
Ivan Asen I 1185–1194
Peter Asen 1185–1195
Kalojan Asen 1195–1207
Boril 1207–1218
Ivan Asen II 1218–1241
Kaliman I 1241–1246
Michael Asen 1246–1254
Kaliman II 1254–1257
Constantine Asen 1257–1278
Ivail 1278–1279
Ivan Asen III 1279–1280
George Terteri I 1280–1282
Smilec 1282
Choki 1282
Theodore Svetslav 1282–1322
George Terteri II 1322
Michael 1322–1330
Ivan Istvan 1330
Ivan Alexander 1330–1365
Ivan Sracimir 1365
Ivan Sisman 1365–1395

Bull-baiting made illegal in Britain, 1835.

Bullfighting. Prohibited in France, 1894; but prohibition openly ignored since 1932.

Bull Moose. Name of a third party formed in 1912 by the supporters of Theodore Roosevelt, in the U.S.A. It ceased to exist, 1916, when Roosevelt declined to stand for it again.

Bundesrat, Federal Council:
1. The supreme executive of the Swiss confederation, seven men elected for four years by the Bundesversammlung (*q.v.*). The vice-president of

this body is a first magistrate co-equal with the President of the Confederation, according to the constitution of 1874, modifying that of 1848.

2. Body corresponding to the Privy Council or Cabinet of the N. German League, 1866–71, and the Hohenzollern 'Second Reich', 1871–1918.

3. In Austria, a second chamber of provincial representatives, under the federal constitution of 1929; readopted, 1945.

4. Upper house, Federal German Republic, 1949.

Bundestag, German for Federal Diet, was the name (1) of an assembly of representatives of the German League (*Deutscher Bund*), 1815–66 (not a legislative body, more like a Council of Ambassadors); (2) or lower house of the Federal German Republic Parliament from 1949.

Bundesversammlung. German for Federal Assembly, name given to the two legislative houses of the Swiss Confederation, the *Ständerat* and the *Nationalrat*, when sitting jointly, under the constitution of 1874.

Bunhill Fields (London). Used by Dissenters. Burying ground first used, 1665; John Bunyan buried, 1688; Defoe, 1731; Susannah Wesley, 1742; Issac Watts, 1748; William Blake, 1827. Opened as a public garden, 1869.

Buonaparte, House of. Following are the principal members of this family: 1. *Joseph, b.* 1768. King of Naples, 1806–8. King of Spain, 1808–13; *d.* Florence, 1844. 2. *Napoléon I, b.* 1769. First Consul of France, 1800. Consul for life, 1802. Emperor of the French, 18 May 1804. Abdicated, Apr. 1814. At Elba, May 1814–Feb. 1815. Landed at Antibes, Feb. 1815. Abdicated again, June 1815; *d.* St. Helena, 5 May 1821. 3. *Lucien, b.* 1775. President of the Council of Five Hundred, 1799. Prince of Canino; *d.* 1840. 4. *Louis, b.* 1778. King of Holland, 1806–10. Father of Napoléon III below; *d.* 1846. 5. *Jerome, b.* 1784. King of Westphalia, 1806–13. Marshal and President of the French

Senate under Napoléon III; *d.* 1860. 6. *Napoléon III, b.* 1808. President of French Republic, Dec. 1848. Emperor, 1852. Abdicated, 2 Sept. 1870; *d.* 9 Jan. 1873, at Chislehurst, England. 7. *Eugène Napoléon, b.* 1856. Prince Imperial. Killed at battle of Ulundi, 1879.

Burgos, Spain. Burial place of the Cid, *d.* 1099. Cathedral begun, 1221. Attacked by the Duke of Wellington, 18–19 Sept. 1812; another attempt failed, 18 Oct.; French blew up castle and retired, 12 June 1813. Franco's headquarters, 1936–9.

Burgundy, France. Burgundians, Germanic tribe arrived in SE. Gaul *c.* 411. Region around Worms-Mainz became known as B., but the centre of gravity of Burgundian kingdom shifted to Rhône valley, 475. Conquered by Franks, 534. After death of Charlemagne (*q.v.*) partitioned between France and Lotharingia by Treaty of Verdun, 843. There then arose (1) a *kingdom* of B. (888–1032), dependent on Lotharingia, later in the empire; (2) a *county* of B. (Franche-Comté), which first merged with the duchy *c.* 1470, but in 1483 passed to the empire, and ultimately, with the southern Netherlands, to the crown of Spain; (3) a *duchy* of B., independent *c.* 888–1363, then a fief of France, under duke of the French royal house. On the death of Duke Charles the Bold, 1479, B. became an ordinary province of France.

Burial Acts in the U.K. still wholly or partly in force are those of 1852, 1855, 1879, 1880, 1906, and the Cremation Acts, 1902 and 1952.

Burke's Peerage. Started 1826 by John Burke (1787–1848).

Burlingame Treaty, between U.S.A. and China. Negotiated Washington, 1868; confirmed Peking, 23 Nov. 1869. Authorized mutual immigration. Anson B. (1820–70) was the American representative in China.

Burlington House (London). Built for 1st Earl of Burlington, 1665–8; reconstructed by 3rd Earl, 1716; bought by Government, July 1854. Royal, Linnean, and Chemical Societies' quarters at, 1857. Exhibition rooms date from

1866, 3rd Earl's colonnade removed same year. Royal Academy acquired lease of building and garden behind it, 1867. Royal Academy first opened at, 3 May 1869. New building erected, 1869–72.

Burma. Divided in earliest times into a number of principalities of fluctuating size, among which the two dynasties established at Tagaung play a leading part. According to legend these were succeeded by establishment of a kingdom at Tharakhetara, 483 B.C.–A.D. 84. A new dynasty was established at Pagân, 95. B. Calendar era established by Thenga Raja, 639. Most of B. united under King Anoarahta Soa, who established Buddhism permanently (1044?–1077?). Conquest of Arakan by Alaungsithu, 1103. Pagân captured by Mongols, 1287. Collapse of the Pagân monarchy, 1298. B. divided between two Shan monarchies at Panya and at Sagaing, 1298–1364. Ava founded, 1364. B. in state of civil war under Shan monarchy at Ava until rise of the Burmese Taungu dynasty, 1530–1752. Arrival of Portuguese at Martaban, 1519. B. united under Bureng Naung, 1551–81. Again divided into Pegu and B., 1581–99. Taungu dynasty unites B., 1599. Portuguese expelled from Martaban, 1613. Capital moved to Ava, 1629. Chinese freebooting invasion, 1658–61. Chinese refugee emperor surrendered to a Manchu Army, 1662. Taungu dynasty extinguished at capture of Ava by Talaings, 1752. Alaungpaya reconquers Ava, 1753. Founds Rangoon, 1755. Subdues the whole country, 1758. Invades Siam, 1759. Siam conquered, 1767. Chinese invasions, 1767–9. Amarapura made capital, 1783. First war with Britain, 1824–6. British annex Lower B., 1826. British resident appointed, 1830. Second Burmese War, 1852. Lower B. annexed to Britain, 1853. Accession of Thibaw, 1878. Deteriorating situation led to whole of B. becoming part of the British Empire, 1885, though pacification of Upper B. took several years. Province of British India 1923–37. Road to China built, 1936–8. Invaded by Japanese, 8 Feb. 1942. Allies recapture Rangoon, 3 May 1945. Becomes independent republic, 4 Jan. 1948. New constitution, 1973 under which U Ne Win became Head of State of the People's Republic.

Presidents of Burma:
Sao Shwe Thaik 1948–1952
Sir Ba U 1952–1957
U Win Maung 1957–1962
U Ne Win 1862–1981
U San Yu 1981–

Burma Road. Constructed 1936–8 from Lashio to Chungking.

Burschenschaft, was an association of German undergraduates of all universities, started at Jena in 1817 under the patronage of the Grand Duke of Saxe Weimar. Suppressed by the Carlsbad Decrees of 1833, it was revived in 1848. *See also* WARTBURG.

Burundi, Africa. Independent kingdom created by the granting of independence to Ruanda-Urundi (*q.v.*), on 1 July 1962.

Buryat Mongolia, an autonomous Soviet Socialist Republic set up 1 Mar. 1920.

Bury St. Edmunds, England. Named after St. Edmund, King of E. Anglia, martyred 870, whose remains were transferred hither from Hoxne, 903. Grammar school refounded by Edward VI, 1550. Plague, 1636. Diocese of St. Edmundsbury and Ipswich founded, 1914.

Bydgoszcz, (Ger. **Bromberg**). Polish till 1772. Prussian, 1772–1919. Polish, 1919–39. German, 1939–45. Polish since 1945.

Byzantine Authors: Some earlier B. historians wrote in Latin, e.g. Eunapius (*c.* 400), Olympiodorus and Priscus (*c.* 450), Malchus (*c.* 490), and Zosimus (*c.* 500). Some authors writing in Greek are:

Nonnus, *c.* 400, epic poet.
Procopius of Caesaraea, *b. c.* 500, *d.* after 559, historian.
Jordanes, *fl. c.* 500 historian.
George Pisiaes, seventh century, panegyrist.
Agathias, 522–88, historian.
Andreas of Crete, *c.* 650–720, hymnologist.

Theodorus of Studium, 759–812, epigrammatist.
Theophanes Confessor, *fl.* 800–13, chronicler.
George Syncellus, *d. c.* 800, chonicler.
Photius, 820–91, philologist.
Leo of Salonika (*c.* 829–56), encyclopaedist.
Leo the Deacon, *fl.* 995, chronicler.
Constantine VII Porphyrogenitus (905–959), historian.
Cometas Chartularius, *fl.* 950?, epigrammatist.
Theodosius Diaconus, tenth century, panegyrist.
Michael Psellus, 1018–78, historian.
Christopher of Mytilene, eleventh century, lyric poet.
Anna Comnena, 1083–1145, historian.

Nicephorus Bryennius, late eleventh century, historian.
Johannes Cimmanus, *c.* 1143–85, historian.
John Scylitzes, *d.* after 1081.
Constantine Manasses, *fl.* 1143–80, rhyming chronicler.
Theodorus Prodromus, *d.* after 1159, epic poet.
George Cedrenus, early twelfth-century chronicler.
Nicetas Acominates, *c.* 1140–1220, historian.
George Acropolita, *c.* 1250, historian.
Critobulos of Imbros, late fifteenth century.

Byzantium. *See* CONSTANTINOPLE and ROMAN EMPIRE, EASTERN.

C

Cab. Abbreviation for *cabriolet de place,* invented by Nicolas Sauvage *c.* 1660, became current *c.* 1825. C. first licensed in London, 1823. Hansom C. patented, 1834. Cabmen's shelters established, 1875. London C. Act, 1896, and London C. and Stage Carriage Act, 1907, are still in force, as amended by the London Cab Act, 1968. *See also* HACKNEY COACHES.

Cabal. In later Stuart times the term used for the group of politicians who held power. Originally the so-called C. Ministry of 1671. The letters of the word stood for *Clifford, Arlington, Buckingham, Ashley, Lauderdale,* its principal members.

Cabinet. *See* COUNCIL.

Cabinet, Imperial War. First met, 1917.

Cable. First successful submarine C. between S. Foreland and Sangatte, 1851. Atlantic C. laid successfully, 5 Aug. 1858. New pattern C. laid to Holland, Dec. 1947. Pacific C. laid, 1962.

Cade's Insurrection. Mob led by Jack C., May 1450. Entered London, 27 June. C. killed, 11 July.

Cadiz, Spain. Traditionally founded by Phoenicians *c.* 1000 B.C. Captured by Romans *c.* 206 B.C. Remained part of Roman Empire under name of *Gades* till conquest of Spain by Visigoths, A.D. 409–20. Reconquered after Justinian's reconquest of Africa *c.* 535. Taken by Moors, 711. Sacked by Normans, 813, and joined to Castile by Alfonso X, 1262. Spanish fleet destroyed by Drake ('singeing of the King of Spain's beard'), 1587. Sacked by Earl of Essex, 15 Sept. 1596. Bombarded by British, July 1797. Blockaded by Lord St. Vincent, 1797–9. Besieged by French, July 1812. Constitution of 1812 promulgated here.

Cadmium. Discovered by Strohmeyer, 1817.

Caen, France. Old capital of Normandy and burial-place of William the Conqueror (*d.* 1087) and his queen. Taken by English, 1346, 1417. University founded by Duke of Bedford, 1432. Taken by French, 1 July 1450. Heavily bombed and half destroyed by Allies, 5–9 June 1944. Restored university inaugurated, 1957.

Caerleon on Usk. Site of Roman fortress (Isca Silurum), planned by Sextus Julius Frontinus, governor of Britain A.D. 74–8, about A.D. 75. Excavations, 1926 and 1939, showed occupation at least down to 350, possibly later. Excavations in 1954 discovered a large town on an adjacent site.

Caernarvon or **Carnarvon,** Wales. A Roman military station and residence of a Welsh prince till *c.* 893. Castle built by Edward I, 1284. First English Prince of Wales (afterwards Edward II) *b.* at, 25 Apr. 1284. Charles, Prince of Wales, eldest son of Queen Elizabeth II, invested at, 1 July 1969.

Caesaraea (Kaisarieh), Israel. Built by Herod the Great, 25–13 B.C. Jewish rising against Romans, A.D. 66. After A.D. 70 capital of Roman Palestine and residence of the procurators, and the ecclesiastical capital until 451. Occupied by Arabs, 638. Taken by Crusaders, 1101; by Saladin, 1187; by Richard Cœur-de-Lion, 1191. Demolished by Bibars, 1265.

Caesaraea Philippi (Banias), Syria. Founded by Philip the Tetrarch, 3 B.C. Taken by Crusaders, 1129, but lost, 1132. Burnt out, 1157.

Caesarean Section, performed at least as early as A.D. 1500, although one tradition asserts that Julius Caesar was delivered by this method, hence the name.

Caesium. Discovered by Bunsen and Kirchoff, 1860.

Cagliari. Traditionally founded by the Phoenicians. Important in Carthaginian and Roman times. Taken by Vandals, 485; by Byzantines, 533; by Saracens, twelfth century. Aragonese from 1326 until 1714. Cathedral begun *c.* 1257. University founded, 1606. *See* SARDINIA.

Cahors, France. Became a banking centre in thirteenth century. Liberties suppressed by French kings, 1316. University founded by Pope John XXII, 1331. United with University of Toulouse, 1751.

Caicos Island, or **The Keys.** Discovered *c.* 1512. Settled (from Bermuda), 1678. Jurisdiction transferred to Bahamas, 1804; to Jamaica, 1854. Became Jamaican dependency, 1874.

'Ça ira!' Famous French revolutionary song, traditionally by Ladié, first heard, 5 Oct. 1789.

Cairo, Egypt. Founded by Amr. *c.* A.D. 641 as *Masr.* Became independent capital under Ibn Tulun, 868–83. El Azhar University founded, 941. Refounded on new site a mile from old by Jauhar el-Kaid, 968, as El-Kahira, eventually corrupted to C. Citadel built by Saladin, 1176. Captured by Turks, 1517. Great earthquake, 1754. Taken by Napoleon, 23 July 1798. Recaptured with British help, 27 June 1801. Capital of Mehemet Ali's independent kingdom, 1811. British occupation, 1882–1946.

Cairo Declaration, 1 Dec. 1943, by China, Great Britain, and U.S.A. regarding war aims and the future of Korea and Formosa (Taiwan).

Calabar, Nigeria. Came under British influence, 1884; protection, 1889. Ceased to be known as Old C., 1904.

Calabria, Italy. The *Iapygia* of the Greeks conquered by Romans, 266 B.C.; subdued by Odoacer, A.D. 476; part of the Ostrogothic kingdom of Theodoric, 493; recovered for empire by Belisarius, 536. After 873 C. constituted part of the SW. peninsula. Invaded by Otho I, 968, who defeated Greeks, 969; invaded by Peter of Aragon, 1283; invaded by Sicilians, 1296.

Part of kingdom of the Two Sicilies, 1597.

Calais, France. Became important port, tenth century. Taken by Edward III, 4 Aug. 1347; finally taken from the English by the Duke of Guise, 7 Jan. 1558; taken by Spaniards, Apr. 1596; restored, 1598. Captured by Germans 22–7 May 1940. Invested, 20 Sept., and taken, 30 Sept. 1944 by Canadian First Army.

Calcium. First isolated in 1808 by Sir Humphry Davy in his electrolytic researches.

Calculating Machines. Constructed by Napier of Merchiston, 1617; Blaise Pascal, 1642; Sir S. Moreland, 1666; Leibnitz, 1671; Visc. Mahon, 1775; Hahn, 1779; Müller, 1784; C. Babbage, 1822. Colmar's arithmometer *c.* 1850. First cash-adding machine by Burroughs, 1888. First electronic C. M. built 1939–44. In general business use in W. world since 1960s.

Calcutta, India. Founded, 1687, by Job Charnock, an East India merchant. Fort built, 1696. Confinement of prisoners in Black Hole, 19 June 1756, after capture of town by Dowlah; retaken, Jan. 1757; centre of British India, 1773–1912.

Calder Hall. British atomic energy station. Construction began, 1949; formally opened by Queen Elizabeth II, Oct. 1956.

Caldey, island off the Pembrokeshire coast. A Cistercian priory was established here in 1929.

Caledonian Canal (Scotland). Building begun, 1804; opened, 1822, but work not complete until 1847.

California, U.S.A. Discovered by Spaniards, 1542; visited by Drake, 1579; subject to Mexico, 1822; occupied by U.S. Army, 1847; ceded to U.S.A., 1848; admitted to Union as a state, 1850. University of C. opened, 1869.

Caliphate. The spiritual and political headship of Islam in succession to Mohammed. The first three 'Orthodox' caliphs were: Abu Bekr, 632–4; Omar I, 634–44; Othman, 644–56. At the murder of Othman a civil war between Ali, elected at Mecca, and Moawiya of the Ommayad House led eventually to the establishment of the Ommayad C., 661, which was in its turn overthrown by the Abbasids, 750, who reached their greatest prosperity under Haroun al Rashid, 786–809, and were destroyed effectively at the capture of Bagdad by Hulagu Khan the Mongol, 1258. A puppet C. under the domination of the Mamelukes continued, however, in Egypt (*q.v.*), 1261, until its conquest by the Turks, 1517. In 1520 the last of these puppets, Al Motawakkil, surrendered his office to the Turkish Sultan Suleiman the Magnificent, and the title was borne by the Turkish sultans till Nov. 1922, when it was made elective in the Turkish imperial family. On 3 Mar. 1924 the C. was abolished by the Turkish parliament.

Caliphs. Following is a list of C. from the death of Mohammed until the extinction of the genuine caliphate at Bagdad in 1258. Those marked 'O' were of the Ommayad House. Thereafter the remainder were Abbasids. Those marked 'B' were dominated by Buweiyid princes and ministers. Those marked 'S' were virtually vassals of the Seljuk Turks.

Abu Bekr 632–634
Omar I 634–644
Othman 644–656
Ali 656–661
Hasan 661
Moawiya I (O) 661–680
Yezid I (O) 680–683
Moawiya II (O) 683–684
Merwan I (O) 684–685
Abd-el-Melik (O) 685–705
Welid I (O) 705–715
Suleiman (O) 715–717
Omar II (O) 717–720
Yezid II(O) 720–724
Hisham (O) 724–743
Welid II (O) 743–744
Yezid III (O) 744
Ibrahim (O) 744
Merwan II (O) 744–750
Abul Abbas (as Saffah) 750–754
Al Mansur 754–775
Al Mehdi 775–785
Al Hadi 785
Haroun al Rashid 786–809

Al Amin ⎱ 809–813
Al Mamun ⎰
Al Mamun alone 813–833
Al Motassim 833–842
Al Wathik 842–847
Al Mutawakil 847–861
Al Muntasir 861–862
Al Mustain 862–866
Al Motazz 866–869
Al Muhtadi 869–870
Al Motamid 870–892
Al Motadid 892–902
Al Muktafi 902–907
Al Muktadir 907–932
Al Kahir 932–934
Ar-Radi 934–940
Al Muttaki 941–944
Al Mustakfi 944–946
Al Muti (B) 946–974
Al Tai (B) 974–991
Al Kadir (B) 991–1031
Al Kaim (B) 1031–1075
Al Muktadi (S) 1075–1094
Al Mustazhir (S) 1094–1118
Al Mustarshid (S) 1118–1135
Ar Rashid (S) 1135–1136
Al Muktafi (S) 1136–1161
Al Mustanjid (S) 1161–1170
Al Mustadi (S) 1170–1180
An-Nasir (S) 1180–1225
Zahir (S) 1225–1235
Al Mustansir (S) 1235–1242
Al Mustasim 1242–1258

Callao, Peru. Old city destroyed by earthquake, 1746.

Calotype. Photographic method invented by Dr. Fox Talbot, 1841.

Calvinists. Protestant movement named after John Calvin (1509–64).

Cambodia. The Khmer Kingdom was founded in A.D. fifth century. Rose to its zenith in ninth century. Angkor-Thom completed by Yasovarman *c.* 900. Angkor-Vat built, twelfth century. Empire reached its greatest extent under Jayavarman VII early in thirteenth century. Angkor abandoned for Lovek in fifteenth century. Lovek abandoned end of sixteenth century. By seventeenth century the Khmer monarchs were puppets alternately under Thai and Annamese influence. C. became a French protectorate in 1863. Became Associated State of

French Union, 1949. Complete independence from France, Jan. 1955. Communist guerrilla movement existed in C. from 1945 and Prince Sihanouk was deposed, Mar. 1970 and C. renamed the Khmer Republic. Civil war continued with U.S. and Vietnamese intervention, 1970–3. Khmer Rouge estab. brutal regime, 1975, but this was opposed by Vietnam and after fighting 1977–8 Khmer Rouge defeated and country renamed **Kampuchea** (*q.v.*).

Cambrai, France. Church councils at, 1064, 1303, 1383, 1565. League of C., 10 Dec. 1508; Paix des Dames Treaty, 1529. Captured by the Emperor Charles V, 1544; by French, 1667; cathedral destroyed, 1793; French defeated by British under Duke of York, 24 Apr. 1794; taken by Austrians, 10 Sept. 1798; by British under Sir Charles Colville, 1815. *See* BATTLES.

Cambridge, England. Taken by barons, 1215. University charter, 1231. Residence of Henry II, who repaired castle, 1265. Castle possessed by Cromwell, 1643. Observatory, 1820. Fitzwilliam Museum founded at, 1837.

Cambridge, Mass., U.S.A. Harvard College (*q.v.*) founded here, 1638. One of the earliest printing presses was set up at C., which published the *Bay Psalm Book*, the first book printed in British America, in 1640.

Cambridge University. First charter, 1231; formally recognized, 1318. Records burnt by Wat Tyler, 1381. Written examinations introduced, 1772. New statutes, 1856. Religious tests abolished, 1871. Oxford and Cambridge Act, 1882. Present statutes date from 1926. Women admitted as full members, 1947. First women undergraduates admitted to traditional men's colleges, 1972: first women's college admitted men, 1979. The following are the principal colleges and halls, founded for men, but most now (1985) admitting women, with the dates of their foundation and their founders:

Ayerst Hall, opened, 21 Apr. 1884; closed, 1896.

Caius (Gonville and Caius College), founded by Edmund Gonville, 1348.

John Caius, M.D., in 1557 obtained royal charter.

Cavendish College, founded 1876 by County College Association; closed, Dec. 1891.

Christ's College, founded 1505 by Lady Margaret Beaufort, Countess of Richmond and Derby, mother of King Henry VII.

Churchill College, founded 1960.

Clare College, founded by Richard Badew as University Hall, 1326; refounded, 1338, by Lady Elizabeth, sister of Gilbert, Earl of Clare.

Corpus Christi, founded 1352; owes foundation to two tradesmen's guilds in the town, called the Guilds of Corpus Christi and of the Blessed Virgin Mary.

Darwin, founded 1964.

Downing College, founded under will of Sir George Downing, Bt., dated 20 Dec. 1717; received charter, 22 Sept. 1800.

Emmanuel College, founded 1584 by Sir Walter Mildmay, Chancellor of the Exchequer.

Fitzwilliam House (non-collegiate), founded 1869; college, 1966.

Jesus College, founded 1496 by John Alcock, Bishop of Ely.

King's College, founded 1441 by Henry VI.

Magdalene College, founded 1542 by Thomas, Baron Audley, of Walden. Replaced Buckingham College, founded by Henry Stafford, Duke of Buckingham (1455–83).

Pembroke College, founded 1347 under name of Valence-Mary, who was in reality Mary de St. Paul, widow of Aymer de Valence, Earl of Pembroke. Henry VI was a liberal benefactor, and is known as second founder.

Queens' College, founded 1448 by Margaret of Anjou, wife of Henry VI; refounded 1465 by Elizabeth Woodville, wife of Edward IV.

Robinson College, founded 1977.

St. Catherine's College, founded 1473 by Robert Wodelarke, D.D., Chancellor of the University.

College of St. John the Evangelist (St. John's College), founded 1511 by

Lady Margaret Beaufort (founder of Christ's College, *q.v.*).

St. Peter's College (or Peterhouse), founded 1284 by Hugh de Balsham, Bishop of Ely.

Selwyn College, founded 1882, built by public subscription in memory of George Augustus Selwyn, Bishop of Lichfield.

Sidney Sussex College, founded 1596 under will of Lady Frances Sidney, Dowager Countess of Sussex.

Trinity College, founded 1546 by Henry VIII, who combined three other smaller colleges into one, and added to revenues.

Trinity Hall, founded 1350 by William Bateman, Bishop of Norwich.

Wolfson College, founded 1965.

The following were founded as women's colleges:

Girton College, founded at Hitchin, 1869. Removed to Girton, near Cambridge, 1873. Admitted as a college of the university, 1947.

Newnham College, founded 1871. Amalgamated with association for promoting higher education for women, 1880. Royal charter, 1915. Admitted as college of university, 1947.

New Hall. founded Oct. 1954.

Cambridge University Press. Univ. given power to appoint a printer, 1534: began printing, 1584.

Cambuskenneth Abbey. Founded by, David I of Scotland, 1147. First Scottish Parliament assembled at, 1326.

Camera Obscura. Known to Euclid, 300 B.C. and described by Alhazen of Cairo (*d.* A.D. 1038), but popularized by Giovanni Battista della Porta, 1569. First used for photographic purposes by Thomas Wedgwood, 1794.

Cameroons, Africa. Colonized by Germans, 1884. Conquered by French and British, 1914–17. Under British and French mandates, 1922. The French mandate became independent under the name of the Cameroon republic, 1 Jan. 1960. N. part of Brit. mandate joined Nigeria and S. joined Cameroon republic, 1961. Unitary and bilingual state of the United Republic of Cameroon estab. after referendum, 1972.

Camisards. Huguenots of the Cévennes who rebelled after the revocation of the Edict of Nantes (1685). Camisard war, 1702–6, in which the royal forces were commanded successively by Marshals Montrevel, Villars, and Berwick. Jean Cavalier, the chief Camisard leader, *d.* in 1740, having been made a British brigadier-general in 1735.

Camorra. Secret society founded in Naples jail *c.* 1820. Entered political field, 1848. Suppressed 1911.

Camp David Agreement. In Sept. 1978 President Carter of the U.S.A. convened a conference at Camp David at which agreement on a peace formula was reached between Israel and Egypt (*qq.v.*). A resultant peace treaty was signed in Washington, 26 Mar. 1979.

Campaign for Nuclear Disarmament (C.N.D.), first prominent in Britain in the 1950s, Canon Collins being its chairman 1958–64. Subsequently declined, but revived in 1980s, gaining official Labour Party support. Committed to unilateral nuclear disarmament and banning (or removal) of Cruise and Pershing missiles from Britain.

Campbellites (Disciples of Christ). Sect founded in the U.S.A. by Alexander Campbell (1788–1866) in 1812.

Campo Formio, Treaty of, 17 Oct. 1797, between Napoleon and Austria, by which (*inter alia*) the republic of Venice was abolished.

Canada. Probably discovered by Norsemen *c.* 1000. Discovered by John Cabot, 1497. The St. Lawrence discovered by Jacques Cartier, 1535. Quebec founded by Champlain, 1608. C. explored by La Salle, 1669, 1678. Hudson's Bay Co. founded, 1670. C. given up to England by France, 1763, after war of 1759–60 (*See* QUEBEC). C. divided into two provinces, 1791; reunited, 1840; again separated on establishment of the Confederation, 1867. British N. America Act for union of C., Nova Scotia, and New Brunswick, under title of Dominion of C., passed 29 Mar. 1867. Territories of Hudson Bay (Manitoba) added, 1869; of British Columbia, 1871; of Prince Edward Island, 1873; of Alberta and Saskatchewan, 1 Sept. 1905. Canadian

Pacific Railway opened, 8 Nov. 1885. Statute of Westminster (*q.v.*) approved, 30 June 1931. Privy Council judgment upholding abolition of Appeals to Privy Council, 13 Jan. 1947. Newfoundland entered Dominion, 31 Mar. 1949. C. signed North Atlantic Treaty, 4 Apr. 1949. Opening of the St. Lawrence Seaway, 1959. Trans-C. Highway opened, 3 Sept. 1962. Growth of separatism in Fr-speaking C., 1970s onwards. Amended constitution to replace the Brit. North America Act received Royal Assent. Mar. 1982. The following are the Governor-Generals since the union:

Lord Monck 1867–1868
Lord Lisgar 1868–1872
Lord Dufferin 1872–1878
Marquess of Lorne 1878–1883
Lord Lansdowne 1883–1888
Lord Stanley of Preston 1888–1893
Earl of Aberdeen 1893–1898
Earl of Minto 1898–1904
Earl Grey 1904–1911
Duke of Connaught 1911–1916
Duke of Devonshire 1916–1921
Viscount Byng of Vimy 1921–1926
Viscount Willingdon 1926–1931
Earl of Bessborough 1931–1935
Lord Tweedsmuir 1935–1940
Earl of Athlone 1940–1946
Viscount Alexander 1946–1952
Vincent Massey 1952–1959
Georges Philias Vanier 1959–1967
Roland Michener 1967–1974
Jules Leger 1974–1979
Edward Schreyer 1979–84
Mrs Jeanne Sauve 1984–

The following are the Prime Ministers of Canada, from 1867:
Macdonald 1867–1873
Mackenzie 1873–1878
Macdonald 1878–1891
Abbott 1891–1892
Thompson 1892–1894
Bowell 1894–1986
Tupper 1896
Laurier 1896–1911
Borden 1911–1920
Meighen 1920–1921
Mackenzie King 1921–1926
Meighen 1926
Mackenzie King 1926–1930

Bennett 1930–1935
Mackenzie King 1935–1948
St. Laurent 1948–1957
Diefenbaker 1957–1963
Pearson 1963–1968
Trudeau 1968–1979
Clark 1979–1980
Trudeau 1980–1984
Turner 1984
Mulroney 1984–

Canals. For the principal ones in Great Britain and Ireland, *see under* various headings. The following are among the most noted C. outside Great Britain, with the dates of their openings:
Albert (Antwerp to Liège) 1939
American Erie 1817
Amsterdam 1876
Amsterdam and N. Sea 1876
Baltic and N. Sea (Kiel Ship Canal) 1895
Bordeaux and Narbonne 1884
Bourbon 1790
Burgundy 1775
Corinth 1893
Du Midi (Languedoc) 1681
Ganges 1854
Hitler (Upper Silesia to Oder) 1939
Holstein 1785
Kattegat and Baltic 1806
Leningrad and Kronstadt 1884
Michigan-Mississippi 1900
Mittelland (Rhine—Ems to Königsberg) 1938
Moscow-Volga 1937
Orleans 1675
Princess Juliana (Netherlands) 1935
Seine et Loire 1791
Twenthe (Zutphen to Enschede) 1936
Welland (Erie to Ontario) 1932
White Sea and Baltic (Archangel to Leningrad) 1933
See also SUEZ; PANAMA.

Canary or **Fortunate Islands,** NW. Africa. Granted by Pope Clement VI to Juan de la Cerda, 1346; since 1496 under Spanish rule.

Canberra. Officially became capital of Australia, 20 Jan. 1910. Foundation stone laid, 12 Mar. 1923. Parliament opened by Duke of York, 9 May 1927. Centre of Australian federal administration; of increasing international importance since 1945.

Candia. *See* CRETE.

Candia, War of, 1635–94. *See* CRETE and VENICE.

Candlemas. Christian feast of Presentation of Christ in the Temple and Purification of Blessed Virgin Mary, celebrated Feb. 2. Became widespread after Emperor Justinian ordered its observance, 542.

Cannes, France. Popularity as a resort dates from Lord Brougham's visit, 1834. Film festival held annually at since World War II.

Canon. The office of C. appears to have been introduced into the church in the eighth century, and arose from the desire to impose something like a monastic rule on the cathedral clergy.

Canonization was not known before the tenth century, but traditionally the first C. was celebrated by Leo III, A.D. 804. The canonizing of any deceased Christian without the bishop's consent was prohibited in the ninth century. John XV was the first pope who exercised the right, and in A.D. 993 made Udalric, Bishop of Augsburg, a saint. *Douleia* of 'canonized saints' enjoined by Council of Trent (1545–63). Added to calendar in recent times: Joan of Arc, 16 May 1920; Jean Baptiste Vianny, 1925; Theresa of Lisieux, 1925; John Bosco, 1934; Sir Thomas More and Bishop John Fisher, 19 May 1935: Forty Martyrs of England and Wales, 25 Oct. 1970: Maximilian Kolbe, 1982.

Canon Law. *See* DECRETALS.

Canossa. Emperor Henry IV submitted to Pope Gregory VII at, Jan. 1077.

Canterbury, England. Walls of the Roman *Durovernum* were built in the second century A.D. Jutish settlement at, fifth century. St. Augustine arrived from Rome at C., A.D. 596. See founded, 597. Castle taken by Louis of France, 1216. Kentish rebels under Wat Tyler left C. for London, 1381. Cathedral founded by Augustine, 602; pillaged by Roric, 851; entirely rebuilt by Archbishop Lanfranc, 1070; choir completed, 1130. Thomas Becket murdered in choir, 1170. Choir burnt down, 1174: rebuilt, 1174–84. Shrine to Becket erected, 1175; demolished and robbed of its valuable gifts by Henry VIII, 1538. St. Martin's Church, frequented by Queen Bertha before the landing of Augustine, said to be the oldest Saxon church in England. Chequers Inn for pilgrims mentioned by Chaucer, built 1400; mostly burnt down, 1865; bombed and badly damaged, 1 Jan. 1942; rebuilding after 1945 led to discovery of Roman town plan. Univ. of Kent. estab. at, 1965. Pope John Paul II visited C. cathedral, 1982.

Canterbury, Archbishops of. The following is a list since the foundation of the see:

Augustine 597–605
Laurentius 605–619
Mellitus 619–624
Justus 624–627
Honorius 627–653
Deusdedit 655–664
Theodore 668–690
Berhtwald 693–731
Taetwine 731–734
Nothelm 734–740
Cuthbert 740–758
Breogwine 759–762
Jaenberht 763–790
Æthelheard 790–803
Wulfred 803–829
Fleogild 829–830
Ceolnoth 830–870
Æthelred 870–889
Plegemund 891–923
Æthelm 923–925
Wulfelm 928–941
Odo 941–958
Ælsine 958–959
Dunstan 959–988
Æthelgar 988–989
Sigeric 990–994
Ælfric 995–1005
Ælfeah or Alphege 1006–1012
Lyfing 1013–1020
Æthelnoth 1020–1038
Eadsige 1038–1050
Robert of Jumièges 1051–1052
Stigand 1052–1070
Lanfranc 1070–1089
Anselm 1093–1109
Ralph de Turbine 1114–1122
William de Corbeuil 1123–1136
Theobald 1139–1161
Thomas Becket 1162–1170

Richard 1174–1184
Baldwin 1185–1190
Reginald Fitz-Jocelin 1191
Hubert Walter 1193–1205
Stephen Langton 1207–1228
Richard Wethershed 1229–1231
Edmund Rich (of Abingdon)
    1233–1240
Boniface of Savoy 1240–1270
Robert Kilwardby 1273–1278
John Peckham 1279–1292
Robert Winchelsea 1293–1313
Walter Reynolds 1313–1327
Simon de Meopham 1327–1333
John Stratford 1333–1348
John de Ufford 1348–1349
Thomas Bradwardin 1349
Simon Islip 1349–1366
Simon Langham 1366–1368
William Wittlesey 1368–1374
Simon Sudbury 1375–1381
William Courtenay 1381–1396
Thomas Fitzalan 1396–1398
Roger Walden 1398
Thomas Arundel 1399–1414
Henry Chicheley 1414–1443
John Stafford 1443–1452
John Kemp 1452–1454
Thomas Bourchier 1454–1486
John Morton 1486–1500
Henry Deane 1501–1503
William Warham 1503–1532
Thomas Cranmer 1533–1556
Reginald Pole 1556–1558
Matthew Parker 1559–1575
Edmund Grindal 1575–1583
John Whitgift 1583–1604
Richard Bancroft 1604–1610
George Abbot 1611–1633
William Laud 1633–1645
William Juxon 1660–1663
Gilbert Sheldon 1663–1677
William Sancroft 1678–1691
John Tillotson 1691–1694
Thomas Tenison 1694–1715
William Wake 1716–1737
John Potter 1737–1747
Thomas Herring 1747–1757
Matthew Hutton 1757–1758
Thomas Ecker 1758–1768
Frederick Cornwallis 1768–1783
John Moore 1783–1805
Charles Manners-Sutton 1805–1828
William Howley 1828–1848

John Bird Sumner 1848–1868
Charles T. Longley 1862–1868
Archibald Campbell Tait 1868–1882
Edward W. Benson 1882–1896
Frederick Temple 1896–1902
Randall Davidson 1903–1928
Cosmo Gordon Lang 1928–1942
William Temple 1942–1944
Geoffrey Francis Fisher 1945–1961
Arthur Michael Ramsey 1961–1974
Donald Coggan 1974–1979
Robert Runcie 1979–

'Canterbury Tales', by Geoffrey Chaucer (1340?–1400); composed *c.* 1380 and first printed by Caxton, 1477.

Canton, China. King of Portugal obtained right to trade with, 1517. First visited by English, 1634; besieged and taken by Sir Hugh Gough, 31 May 1841; Convention of C., July 1841; captured by Japanese, 21 Oct. 1938. Restored to China, 1945.

Cape Coast, Ghana. Early settlement of Portuguese, 1610, when castle built; taken from them by Dutch, 1642; ceded to England by Peace of Breda, 1667.

Cape Horn. Sighted by Drake, 1578; so named by Dutch sailors, 1616.

Cape Province (formerly **Cape Colony**). Cape of Good Hope discovered by Bartholomew Diaz, 1488. Cape Town founded by Dutch, 1652. Colony of Cape Town captured by English, 16 Sept. 1795; restored, 1802; retaken 8 Jan. 1806. Wars with Kaffirs, 1811–12, 1817–19, 1834–5, 1846–8, 1850–3. Finally ceded to English by Netherlands, 13 Aug. 1814. Boers in large numbers crossed Orange River and left colony ('The Great Trek'), 1835. Natal annexed to C.C., 2 Aug. 1843. Orange River territory annexed to C.C., Mar. 1851. Orange River territory formed into a free state, Mar. 1854. Discovery of diamonds, 1867–70. Transvaal Republic annexed, 12 Apr. 1877. Transvaal independent as S. African Republic, 1880 (*See* TRANSVAAL). Houses of Parliament opened, 1885. Annexation of Orange Free State (*q.v.*), 28 May 1900; of Transvaal, 3 Sept. 1900. Became a province of the Union of South Africa after the passing of the South Africa Act, 1909. *See* SOUTH AFRICA, REPUBLIC OF.

Capet Dynasty. *See* FRANCE.

Cape Town (Kaapstad). Factory established by Dutch E. India Co., 1652. Occupied by British when Holland became French dependency, 1806; restored by Treaty of Amiens, 1810; but reoccupied by British, 1814, to whom the province was finally awarded same year. Castle built, 1666; observatory, 1820; university built, 1873.

Cape Verde. Discovered 1443, by Nuño Tristao.

Cape Verde Islands. Annexed to Portugal, 1441–56. Independent republic, 1975.

Capital Gains Tax, first levied in Britain under Finance Act, 1965. Amended in 1971 and 1976. Capital Gains Tax Act, 1979 amended and consolidated all previous legislation.

Capital Levy. First recorded demand for a C.L. in Britain made by a private member in the House of Commons in 1914. Remained part of Labour Party programme until 1927 and revived several times since. The 'Special Contribution' levied by the Labour Government in 1948 is the closest approach to a C.L. so far.

Capital Punishment, British law relating to, reformed, 1826 (in the light of Beccaria's *Treatise on Crimes and Punishments,* 1764), when varieties of capital crime reduced from over 200 to treason, arson, piracy, murder only. Homicide Act, 21 Mar. 1957, divided murders into capital and non-capital categories. The Murder (Abolition of Death Penalty) Act suspended C.P. in Britain for all murder cases, Nov. 1965 for an experimental 5-year period. In Dec. 1969, on a free vote, Parliament approved the permanent abolition of the death penalty in Britain.

Capitol. See ROME; WASHINGTON.

Capri Island. Residence of Emperor Tiberius, A.D. 27–37. Captured by British 1806; by French, 1808. Restored to Naples and Sicily, 1814.

Capua, Italy. Alliance with Rome, 338 B.C. Went over to Hannibal, 216 B.C.; captured by Romans, 211 B.C.; cap-

tured by Vandals, A.D. 456; destroyed by Saracens, 840; rebuilt, ninth century. Councils at, 391, 1087, 1118. Captured by Caesar Borgia, 24 July 1501; occupied by French, 23 Jan. 1799; surrendered to British, 28 July 1799; capitulated to Sardinian forces, Nov. 1860.

Capuchins. Offshoot of Franciscans, founded by Matteo di Bassi, 1528. Became an independent order, 1619.

Carberry Hill, Midlothian. Mary Stuart and James Bothwell surrendered to the confederate lords of Scotland, 15 June 1756.

Carbolic Acid. Discovered by Runge, 1834.

Carbonari. Secret society, originated in Naples between 1806 and 1814. Spread to the whole of Italy by 1820. Adherence made high treason in Piedmont and Naples, 1821. Active, 1830–1.

Carcassonne, France. Oldest fortifications still existing seventh century. Completed in present form, thirteenth century. Restored late nineteenth century by Viollet-le-Duc. C. occupied by Saracens, 725–c. 750.

Cardiff, S. Wales. Site occupied since first century A.D., when Roman fort established. Besieged by Owen Glendower, 1404. Oldest charter extant, dated 14 Oct. 1338. University College of S. Wales and Monmouthshire established at, 1883. C. made capital of Wales, Dec. 1955.

Cardinals *(see also* CONCLAVE). Term first applied to chief priest of a Roman parish. Pope Stephen III, about A.D. 770, seems to have been the first to select seven bishops out of the Roman see and give them the title of cardinal. The Council of Rome, under Pope Nicholas II, 1059, granted the College of C. the principal voice in the election of a pope. The number in the College of C. was fixed at seventy in 1586. Number increased by Pope John XXIII (1958–63). Style of 'Eminence' conferred by Urban VIII.

Cards, Playing, and Games of Cards. Earliest written allusion quotes a manuscript of 1299 (Italian). Chinese dictionary of seventeenth century claims for China the invention in 1120. They spread rapidly in fifteenth century. Before 1643 C. were manufactured in England, where a duty was first imposed in 1615.

Caribbean Community and Common Market (CARICOM), formed as result of Treaty of Chaguaramas, 1973, and had 12 members in 1981. Function primarily furtherance of economic integration between member states, but played part in re-estab. of law in Grenada (*q.v.*), 1983.

Caribbean Federation. Established by the British Federation Act, 1956, and the W. Indies Order in Council, 1957. Dissolved, Apr. 1962.

Carinthia (Kärnten), duchy of the Holy Roman Empire and Austrian province. Last independent duke, Boruch, accepted Bavarian suzerainty and baptism, 738. Conquered by Franks under Charlemagne, 791–7. Became part of Ostmark, 811. Part of kingdom of Bohemia, 1270. Acquired by Rudolph of Hapsburg, 1276. Pawned to the counts of Gorizia, but recovered, 1335. Occupied by French, 1809–13; partly by Serbs and Slovenes, 1919 and 1945; by British, 1945.

Carlisle, Cumbria, England. *Luguvallium* of Roman Britain, the Celtic *Caer-luel.* Mentioned by Bede under the year 687 as an inhabited 'city'. Sacked by Danes under Halfdan Ragnarsson, 875. Fortified by William Rufus, 1092; diocese of, 1133; charter, 1158; grammar school, 1170; surrendered to Young Pretender, 15 Nov. 1745; submitted to Duke ('Butcher') of Cumberland, 15 Dec. 1745. Public-houses and breweries all acquired by state, 1916; Licensing Act of 1921 transferred the wholesale and retail licensed trade of C. to the Home Secretary.

Carlists (Spain). Supporters of Don Carlos of Bourbon's claim to the Spanish throne. Principally to be found among the Basques, they fought two civil wars, 1834–9 and 1872–6, and there were abortive short-lived Carlist risings in 1846 and 1848. Finally suppressed, 1875.

Carlsbad (Karlovy Vary), Bohemia. Medicinal hot springs patronized by Emperor Charles IV, 1358; baths founded 1364. Congress of Powers, 1819, to repress Liberal press, etc.

Carmelite Order. Founded by Berthold, Count of Limoges, about 1156 on Mt. Carmel; received its first rule from Albert, Patriarch of Jerusalem, 1209; sanctioned by Pope Honorius III, 1226. Driven out of Palestine by the Saracens, 1238. Pope Innocent IV changed the Carmelites from hermits to mendicant friars, 1247. First general chapter held in England, 1247. Nuns affiliated to the order from 1452. Discalced Cs., sixteenth century. Teresa of Avila reformed the Carmelite nuns, 1562.

Carnarvon. *See* CAERNARVON.

Carnatic, India. Taken under direct British rule, 1801.

Carnegie Trust Funds. Administered by a corporation set up, 1911, and also by the Carnegie Foundation for the Advancement of Teaching (instituted 1906), both in U.S.A. Carnegie Trust for universities of Scotland was instituted, 1901, and Carnegie United Kingdom Trust, 1914. Carnegie Endowment for International Peace instituted, 1910.

Caroline Islands, Pacific Ocean. First sighted by Portuguese under Diego da Rocha, 1537. Ruled successively by Portugal and Spain, 1537–1899; sold to Germany, 1899. Mandate entrusted to Japan, 1919. Administered by U.S.A. since 1946 as a U.N. Trusteeship.

Carolingian Dynasty. *See* FRANCE.

Carpet-Bagger, absentee political candidate in U.S.A., especially of the 'Reconstruction' period in the S. *c.* 1865–7.

Cartagena, Spain. Founded by Carthaginian Hasdrubal as capital of Carthaginian Spain *c.* 227 B.C. Captured by Scipio Africanus the Elder, 210 B.C. Sacked by Goths, A.D. 425, and by Drake, 1588. Republican naval base during civil war, 1936–9.

Cartel, term first used in Germany, 1879, to describe a combine of railway material manufacturers. *See also* TRUSTS.

Carthage. Phoenician city founded near site of modern Tunis *c.* 700 B.C. Attempt to conquer Sicily defeated at Himera, 480. N. African Empire reached its height, fourth century B.C. First war with Rome (*q.v.*) (First Punic war), 264–241 B.C. Second Punic War begun, 218, as result of Hannibal's capture of Saguntum in previous year. His victory at Cannae, 216. The destruction of Hannibal's brother Hasdrubal's army at the Metaurus, 207, led to the conquest of Carthaginian Spain by the Romans, and their invasion of Africa resulted in Hannibal's defeat at Zama, 202. C. accepted terms of peace, 201. In the Third Punic War (149–146 B.C.) the Romans destroyed the city after a three-year siege. Rebuilt, 10 B.C.–A.D. 10 and named Colonia Julia Carthago. Captured by Vandals, A.D. 439, who made it their capital till its reconquest by Belisarius, 533. Finally destroyed by the Arabs, 697.

Carthusian Order. Founded by St. Bruno, A.D. 1086; recognized by pope, 1176. In England the Carthusians settled in 1180, and had a famous monastery in London, since called the 'Charterhouse', founded 1371. Female branch instituted at Salette, France, 1229.

Casablanca, Morocco. Founded fifteenth century by Portuguese. Taken by French, 1907. Conference of allied statesmen at which unconditional surrender of Axis powers decided upon 14–24 Jan. 1943.

Cashel, Rock of, Tipperary. Fortress built by Cormack MacCarthy, King of Munster, 1127, and cathedral built. 1169.

Casket Letters. Documents relating to the events of 1567 and the murder of Darnley, produced by the Earl of Morton before Commissions at London and York; the originals were lost after 1584 and never recovered. Authenticity doubted by many historians.

Cassel or **Kassel,** Germany. Fortified, 1526. Refuge for French Protestants after 1685. Taken by French, 1760; besieged by Count Lippe, 1761, and by Prince Ferdinand, who took it, 1 Nov. 1762; fortifications destroyed, 1767;

occupied by French, 1806. Capital of kingdom of Westphalia, 1807–13.

Cassino. *See* MONTECASSINO.

Castel Gandolfo. Papal villa near Lake Albano, in the Castelli area outside Rome built by the architect Carlo Maderno (1556–1629) on estate bought by Clement VIII, 1596. It was used by the popes as a summer residence until 1870, and again since 1929, when C.G. was declared part of the Vatican City.

Castile, Spain. First Count Roderic, A.D. 791. Subject to Leon till 1028, when it was seized by Sancho, King of Navarre, who gave it as a kingdom to his son Ferdinand, first King of C., 1039. Alfonso VI captured Toledo, 1085, but severely defeated by the Almoravides (*q.v.*) at Zallaca, 1086. Alfonso VIII defeated by Almohades (*q.v.*) at Alarcos, 1195, but in alliance with Aragon and Navarre won crushing victory at Navas de Tolosa, 1212. Ferdinand and Isabella sovereigns of, 1474. Moors finally driven out, 1492. United with Aragon under Spanish crown, 1504.

Castile and Leon, Heads of State of (from 1033). Though Ferdinand I ranks as the first King of C. proper, this monarchy traced its history back to the Christian remnant which continued to resist at the height of Mohammedan power in Spain. This early history, however, is obscure, and many of the kings mentioned are known merely as names.

C. and L., although often ruled by the same sovereign, were not finally united until 1230, under (Saint) Ferdinand III.

Sovereign	Leon	Castile
Ferdinand I, the Great	1037–1065	1039–1065
Sancho II		1065–1072
Alfonso VI	1065–1109	1072–1109
Urraca	1109–1126	1109–1126
Alfonso VII	1126–1157	1126–1157
Sancho III		1157–1158
Ferdinand II	1157–1188	
Alfonso VIII, the Good		1158–1214
Alfonso IX, the Slobberer	1188–1230	
Enrique I		1214–1217
Ferdinand III, the Saint	1230–1252	1217–1252

Kings of Castile and Leon:

Alfonso X, the Wise 1252–1284
Sancho IV, the Fierce 1284–1296

Ferdinand IV 1296–1312
Alfonso XI, the Avenger 1312–1350
Pedro I, the Cruel 1350–1368
Enrique II, the Bastard, or the Magnificent 1368–1379
Juan I 1379–1390
Enrique III, the Sickly 1390–1406
Juan II 1406–1454
Enrique IV, the Impotent 1454–1474
{Isabella the Catholic 1474–1504
{Ferdinand V, the Catholic 1474–1504
　(from 1479 Ferdinand II of Aragon)
Joanna and Philip 1504–1506
Ferdinand V (again) 1506–1516
See further under SPAIN.

Catalonia, Spain. (Sp. **Cataluña;** Cat. **Catalunya.**) Conquered by Moors, 712. By Charlemagne, 788. United with Aragon (*q.v.*), 1137. Philip IV of Spain attempted to suppress liberties, 1640. Occupation by French, 1640–59, 1694–7. Liberties and cortes abolished by Philip V, 1714. Civil war, 1823. Divided in four provinces, 1833. Granted local autonomy, 1932–4: then declared a federal republic. Deprived of autonomy, 1939: re-estab., 1980.

Catania, Sicily. Founded by Greeks, 729 B.C. Population removed by Hiero I to Leontini, 467 B.C.; returned, 461 B.C. C. plundered by Dionysius I, 403 B.C. Became subject to Rome, 263 B.C. Cathedral built eleventh–eighteenth centuries; fort, A.D. 1237; university, 1434. Volcanic disasters, 123 B.C., A.D. 1669, 1693.

Câteau Cambrésis, Peace of. Between Philip II of Spain and Elizabeth of England of the one part and Henry II of France of the other, 2–3 Apr. 1559. Calais was finally ceded to France by this treaty.

Catechisms, the earliest written schemes extant are those of Kero of St. Gall (eighth century) and Otfried of Weissenburg (ninth century). For early Protestant C. *see* REFORMATION; these provoked the *Summa Doctrinarum* of Peter Canisius, 1566; that of the Council of Trent (*q.v.*); and other C. of the counter-reformation, e.g. those of Bellarmine, 1603; Bossuet, 1687. A modern Roman catechism is the *Schema de Parvo*, 1870. The Calvinists used

the *Geneva Catechism*, 1536, and, in Scotland, Craig's, 1592. The Church of England produced a catechism contemporaneously with the Prayer Book in 1549, expanded in the reign of James I; that still in use was compiled by the Assembly of Divines, 1648.

Catharists. Heretical Christian sect, which spread to Bulgaria (Bogomils) and in the tenth century to France (Albigensians), where it was brutally eradicated in the fourteenth. *See* ALBIGENSES.

Cathedrals in England. The following are the principal Anglican cathedrals with dates of foundation (F.) and of the major part of the present building (P.)

	F.	P.
Birmingham		1711–1719
Blackburn		1826
Bradford		14th cent.
Bristol	11th cent.	1306–1337
Canterbury	600	1174–1400
Carlisle	1092–1419	
Chelmsford		19th cent.
Chester	1053	1200–1315
		and 1485–1537
Chichester	1108	1187–1210
Coventry[1]	15th cent.	1956–1962
Durham	995	1104–1133
Ely	673	1100–1327
Exeter	1050	1260–1291
Gloucester	681	1089–1100
		and 1450–1500
Guildford	1936	1936–1961
Hereford	c. 680	1110–1220
Leicester		14th cent.
Lichfield	672	1200–1321
Lincoln	628	1140–1280
Liverpool	1904	1904–
London:		
(1) Westminster		13th–16th
Abbey	618	cent.
(2) St. Paul's	7th cent.	1674–1710
Manchester	1847	19th cent.
Newcastle		1400–1474
Norwich	1094	1274–1446
Oxford	727	1180–1480
Peterborough	667	1118–1237
Portsmouth	1190	1683–1695
Ripon	678	1330–1450
Rochester	601	1080–1137
St. Albans	793	c. 1360
St. Edmundsbury		15th cent.
Salisbury		1220–1258
Sheffield		15th cent.
Southwark	c. 7th cent.	12th cent.
		and 1470–1500
Southwell		1110–1250
Truro	1880	1887–1903
Wakefield		15th cent.
Wells	704	1306–1333

	F.	P.
Winchester	c. 7th cent.	12th cent. and 1367–1404
Worcester	964	1224–1374
York	627	1227–1361

[1] Original fabric, except for the spire, destroyed by bombing, 14 Nov. 1940.

Cathedrals, Roman Catholic, in England and Wales (O = Opened; C = Consecrated):

Birmingham (of St. Chad) (O) 1808, (C) 1841; Brentwood (of the Sacred Heart and St. Helen) (O) 1836, (C) 1869; Cardiff (of St. David). Destroyed by enemy action, 1941. Since rebuilt. (O) 1836, (C) 1887; Clifton (of the Apostles) (O) 1848, (C) 1848; Hexham and Newcastle (of St. Mary) (O) 1844, (C) 1860; Lancaster (of St. Peter) (O) 1799, (C) 1859; Leeds (of St. Anne) (O) 1838, (C) 1904; Liverpool ((old) of St. Nicholas) (O) 1807, (C) 1815; ((new) of Christ the King), (O) 1933, (C) 1967; Menevia (Wrexham) (of Our Lady of Dolours) (O) 1857, (C) 1907; Middlesbrough (of St. Mary) (O) 1868, (C) 1911; Northampton (of St. Mary and St. Thomas) (O) 1825, (C) 1864; Nottingham (of St. Barnabas) (O) 1842, (C) 1844; Plymouth (of St. Mary and St. Boniface) (O) 1858, (C) 1880; Portsmouth (of St. John, Evangelist) (O) 1882, (C) 1887; Salford (of St. John (O) 1848, (C) 1890; Shrewsbury (of Our Lady Help of Christians and St. Peter of Alcantara) (O) 1856, (C) 1891; Southwark (of St. George). Seriously damaged during World War II. Restored since. (O) 1841, (C) 1894; Westminster (of the Most Precious Blood) (O) 1903, (C) 1910. *

Cathedrals, (Church of Wales).
Prior to the disestablishment of 1920 there were only four dioceses in Wales—Bangor, Llandaff, St. David's, and St. Asaph's. On the formation of a disestablished Anglican Church in Wales, 1920, two new dioceses were created, and existing churches in Brecon and Newport became Cs.
The following are the principal Welsh cathedrals with dates of foundation (F.) and of the major part of the present building (P.).

* St. John the Baptist, Norwich, became cathedral of diocese of E. Anglia, 1976

	F.	P.
Bangor	before 545	1496–1532
Brecon	1923	13th–14th cent.
Llandaff	before 612?	12th cent.
Newport	1921	c. 1150
St. Asaph's	6th cent.	15th cent.
St. David's	before 601?	1180

Catholic Apostolic Church (Irvingites).
Founded by Edward Irving (1792–1834), who seceded from the Presbyterian Church having been deposed from the ministry. The sect assumed the name C.A.C., 1832.

Catholic Association, Irish.
Organized, 1824; Act for its suppression, 1825, but it continued until 12 Feb. 1829, when it was voluntarily dissolved.

Catholic Emancipation
from sundry disabilities under the Penal Laws (1665, etc.) was begun in Britain by an Act introduced by Sir George Saville, 1778. This provoked the Gordon Riots (q.v.) and other disturbances in Scotland, and remained a dead letter. In 1791 a further Act was passed for England, and extended to Scotland, 1792. Some disabilities removed from Irish Catholics by Acts of 1774, 1778, 1782, and 1790. More comprehensive was the C.E. Bill which became law in 1829, and also applied to Ireland. The offices of sovereign, regent, and lord high commissioner (to the Church of Scotland) remain closed to Catholics, the office of lord chancellor being effectively opened to Catholics by the Lord Chancellor (Tenure of Office and Discharge of Ecclesiastical Functions) Act, 1974. See CLARENDON CODE.

Catholic League in France.
Organized against Huguenots (q.v.) by the Duke of Guise. See HOLY LEAGUE (4).

Catholics, Old.
See OLD CATHOLICS.

Catholic Truth Society.
Established, 1872, revised and enlarged, 1884.

Cato Street Conspiracy.
Formed by Arthur Thistlewood, 23 Feb. 1820, to murder Lord Castlereagh and other ministers. Thistlewood executed with four accomplices, 1 May 1820.

Cattaro.
See KOTOR.

Cavell Memorial.
London, 1920; inscription added, 1924; commemorates

British nurse, Edith Cavell, executed by German military authorities, 12 Oct. 1915.

Caves of a Thousand Buddhas. Rock-cut shrines of Kansu, China, date from the mid fourth century A.D., but mostly dug out and embellished between 618 and 1276.

Cawnpore. *See* KANPUR.

Caxton, William (c. 1422–91), set up the first printing press in England at Westminster Abbey, 1476.

Cayman Islands. A dependency of Jamaica (q.v.), described by Columbus, 1503, then by William Jackson, 1643. Victualling point for the Commonwealth Navy, 1655. Separate dependent ter. of U.K. since 1959. New constitution, 1972.

Celebes was a Portuguese possession, 1545–1660, and finally came into Dutch hands, 1669. Became part of Indonesia, 1950.

Celibacy of the Clergy. Spanish synod of Elvira first council to enjoin it on clergy, A.D. 305; condemned by Vigilantius, a presbyter of Barcelona, A.D. 406; strictly enjoined by council of 649; strictly enforced by Gregory VII, 1073. Reaffirmed by Vatican Council. II, 1962–5: but increasing questioning of C. within the Catholic Church from the mid-1960s. Successive popes have subsequently reaffirmed belief in its continuance.

Celluloid. Patented in Britain by Parkes, 1855; improvements made in America by Hyatt, 1870.

Celsius. *See* CENTIGRADE.

C.E.M.A. (Council for the Encouragement of Music and the Arts). Set up 1 Jan. 1940. Became the Arts Council of Great Britain (q.v.), 9 Aug. 1946.

Cenotaph (Whitehall, London). Temporary structure, July 1919; permanent, 1920.

Censorship of Drama in Britain was formerly exercised by the Lord Chamberlain, whose activities in this sphere began before 1509, at first through a functionary of his department called the Master of the Revels. The powers of the Lord Chamberlain became statutory by an Act of 1737 under the terms

of which the Examiner of Plays was appointed. He was allowed complete discretion until 1843, when the Theatres Act laid down principles on which plays were to be licensed or refused licence, and also permitted the licensing of playhouses, hitherto the prerogative of the crown alone, by other authorities. The Theatres Act, 1968, abolished theatre censorship and amended the laws relating to theatres and theatrical performances.

Censorship of Films (Britain). British Board of Film Censors established, 1912.

Census. A C. Bill was introduced into Parliament, 1753, but rejected on the plea that a C. was dangerous to the liberties of free-born Englishmen. The first C. taken in Great Britain, 1801. C. extended to cover British Empire, 1871. First C. in Australia, 1871. In U.S.A. the first C., 1790.

Centigrade, temperature scale invented by the Swedish astronomer Anders Celsius (1701–44), 1742. It, then **Celsius,** used increasingly in Britain from 1965 onwards.

CENTO (Central Treaty Organization). Formerly the Bagdad Pact (q.v.). Name of organization changed to CENTO on 21 Aug. 1959. Ineffectual after Iranian revolution, Jan. 1979.

Central African Federation. *See* RHODESIA AND NYASALAND, FEDERATION OF.

Central African Republic. Formerly one of the four territories of French Equatorial Africa (Ubangi Shari), became independent, Aug. 1960. From 1976–9 known as the Central African Empire under Bokassa I (formerly president). Bokassa overthrown, 1979: new constitution, 1981, was subsequently suspended.

Central American Common Market (C.A.C.M), estab. by treaty signed in Managua, 15 Dec. 1960, ratified 1963. Members are Costa Rica, Guatemala, El Salvador, Honduras and Nicaragua, but political events in Central America since 1980 have reduced its effectiveness.

Central Criminal Court. *See* OLD BAILEY.

Central Electricity Generating Board. In 1948 the British Electricity Authority was estab. and took over the functions, plant, and other assets of private and municipal electrical undertakings, as well as those of the Central Electricity Board (estab. 1927). In 1954 the title of the British Electricity Authority was changed to the Central Electricity Authority, now (1985), the **Central Electricity Generating Board.**

Central Intelligence Agency (C.I.A.). *See* NATIONAL SECURITY COUNCIL (U.S.A.).

Central Provinces and Berar. *See* MADHYA PRADESH.

Central Treaty Organization. *See* CENTO

Cetatea Alba. *See* BELGOROD-DNES-TROVSKIY.

Cetinje, Yugoslavia. Ancient capital of Montenegro (*q.v.*), founded, 1485. Captured but not held by the Turks, 1683, 1714, 1785. Captured by Austrians, 13 Jan. 1916, and by Serbs, 4 Nov. 1918.

Ceylon. *See* SRI LANKA.

Chaco or **Gran Chaco.** For wars in *see* BOLIVIA *and* PARAGUAY.

Chad. Fr. protectorate 1900, part of Fr. Equatorial Africa from 1908. Ceased to be a dependency of Ubangi-Shari Colony, 1920. French penetration of the region had begun in 1885. Under its African governor, Felix Eboué (*d.* 1944), C. was the first French colony to declare for Fighting France, 26 Aug. 1940. Forces based on C. began to raid Axis outposts in the Fezzan, Jan. 1941. In the winter of 1942–3 they completed the conquest of the Fezzan, and the Colonne du Chad or Colonne Leclerc effected a junction with the Eighth Army between Tripoli and Sfax. Member state of the French Community, 28 Nov. 1958. Became an independent republic, 11 Aug. 1960. Civil war between gov. and secessionist groups in N.C. lasted 1965–79, and restarted after Libyan intervention, 1980, on rebel side. Fr. troops sent to C., Aug. 1983, as 'advisers'; agreed Franco-Libyan withdrawal 1984–5.

Chalcedon (Turk. **Kadikeui**). Founded as a colony by the Megarians, 685 B.C., but was absorbed by Pergamum (*q.v.*),

whose king bequeathed it to Rome, 133 B.C. Ravaged by the Goths, notably in A.D. 256, and the Persians (616–26). The Council of C., 451, determined the bounds of the sees of Rome and Byzantium, C. being by then virtually a suburb of the latter, though separated from it by the Bosphorus. It was destroyed by the Turks after 1075.

Chaldea. *See* BABYLONIA, where the Chaldeans formed the ruling class from the eighth century B.C. until the death of Labashi Marduk, 556. *See also* UR OF THE CHALDEES.

'Challenger' Expedition. British scientific expedition under Capt. (later Sir) George Nares left England in the ship *Challenger*, 7 Dec. 1872, and returned, 24 May 1876.

Châlons, Battle of. Name of a battle now believed to have been fought near Troyes, in which Attila, King of the Huns, was defeated by Aetius and Theodoric, A.D. 451.

Chamberlain, Lord. In Britain, one of the chief officers of state from the thirteenth century. Parliament declared he must be a member of the Council *ex officio*, 1406. Remains today an officer of very high standing in the royal household.

Chambers of Commerce. First Chamber of Commerce founded in France, 1599. The oldest in Great Britain is at Glasgow, incorporated 1 Jan. 1783; Manchester Chamber of Commerce instituted, 1794; London, 1881. New York Chamber instituted, 1768; incorporated, 1770.

'Chambers of Reunion.' Established by Louis XIV of France for the purpose of asserting claims, through old feudal titles, to territories on German frontier, 1679.

'Chambres Ardentes.' French courts originally for trial of nobles. Notably those instituted under Francis I in 1535 for trial of heretics, and revived by Henry II, Oct. 1547. Under Louis XIV a *chambre ardente* tried poisoners, and condemned the Marquise de Brinvilliers in 1676; this court was abolished in 1682; but C.A. for the trial of embezzling farmers of the public revenues operated during the minority of Louis XV.

Champagne, France. Annexed to crown of Navarre by Theobald, 1234; passed to French crown by marriage of Philip IV to Joanna of Navarre, 1284; invaded by Emperor Charles V, 1523; entered by Prussians under Duke of Brunswick, 1792.

Champ de Mars, Paris. First Grand Federation of the, 14 July 1790; the second, 14 July 1791, at which a petition was signed praying for the abdication of Louis XVI.

Champlain, Lake, U.S.A. Discovered by Samuel de C., 1609. Scene of British naval defeat by the Americans, 1814.

Chanak. *See* TURKISH REPUBLIC. Occupied by British as a check to Kemalist advance, Sept. 1922; evacuated, Oct. 1923.

Chancellor, Lord High (Lat. *Cancellarius* = Usher or Chief Clerk). Originally an official responsible for preparation of writs and who acted as clerk of the council. Name C. said to have been used first in England during reign of Edward the Elder, 920. Was nearly always a cleric in the Middle Ages, and rose into prominence by administering equity and by presiding for the king over the House of Lords. First recorded as sitting in the chancery as a judge, 1377. Independent jurisdiction existed by 1474. The following are the most notable since Henry VII:

Cardinal Wolsey, 1515.

Sir Thomas More, 1529.

Stephen Gardiner, Bishop of Winchester, 1553.

Sir Francis Bacon, 1617.

Edward Hyde, Earl of Clarendon, 1660.

Anthony Ashley Cooper, Earl of Shaftesbury, 1672.

George, Lord Jeffreys, 1685.

Philip Yorke, Lord Hardwicke, 1737.

Edward, Lord Thurlow, 1778, 1783.

John Scott, Lord Eldon, 1801, 1807.

Thomas, Lord Erskine, 1806.

John Singleton Copley, Lord Lyndhurst, 1827, 1834, 1841.

Henry, Lord Brougham and Vaux, 1830.

Robert Monsey Rolfe, Lord Cranworth, 1852, 1865.

Frederic Thesiger, Lord Chelmsford, 1858, 1866.

John, Lord Campbell, 1859.

Richard Bethell, Lord Westbury, 1861.

Hugh McCalmont Cairns, Lord Cairns, 1868, 1874.

William Page Wood, Lord Hatherley, 1868.

Roundell Palmer, Lord Selborne, 1872, 1880.

Sir Hardinge Stanley Gifford, Lord Halsbury, 1885, 1886, 1895, 1902.

Sir Farrer Herschel, Lord Herschel, 1886, 1892.

Robert Threshie Reid, Lord Loreburn, 1905.

Richard Burdon Haldane, Lord Haldane, 1912, 1924.

Sir Stanley Owen Buckmaster, Lord Buckmaster, 1915.

Sir Robert Bannatyne Finlay, Lord Finlay, 1916.

Frederick Edwin Smith, Lord Birkenhead, 1919.

George, Lord Cave, 1922.

Sir Douglas McGarel Hogg, Lord Hailsham, 1924, 1935.

Sir John Sankey, Lord Sankey, 1929, 1931.

Sir Frederic Herbert Maugham, Lord Maugham, 1938.

Sir Thomas Inskip, Lord Caldecote, 1939.

Sir John Simon, Lord Simon, 1940.

William Allen, Visc. Jowitt, 1945.

Gavin Turnbull Simonds, Lord Simonds, 1951.

David Patrick Maxwell Fyfe, Visc. Kilmuir, 1954.

Reginald Manningham-Buller, Lord Dilhorne, 1962.

Gerald Gardiner, Lord Gardiner, 1964.

Quintin Hogg, Lord Hailsham, 1970.

Lord Elwyn-Jones, 1974.

Lord Hailsham, 1979.

Chancellor of the Exchequer. *See* EXCHEQUER.

Chancellor of Ireland, Lord High. Earliest nomination that of Stephen Ridel during Richard I's reign, 1189. Office abolished, 1922.

Chancellor of Scotland, Lord High. Office abolished in 1707.

Chandernagore, India. Former French settlement in Bengal, founded 1673. Transferred to India, 1952.

Channel Islands. Formed part of the duchy of Normandy when William I conquered England, 1066, and remained English after all other French territories were lost by the English crown. Part of the diocese of Coutances until 1568; then in the diocese of Winchester. Occupied by Germans, July 1940–May 1945. Hague Court confirms British, not French, title, to Minquiers and Ecrehous reefs, 17 Nov. 1953. *See* ABBEVILLE Treaties (1).

Channel Tunnel. First suggested (to Napoleon I) by the French engineer Mathieu, and again after 1825 by English and French railway engineers. A horse roadway was planned by W. Low in 1867, and a model exhibited at the Paris Exhibition of that year. An English C.T. Co., formed in 1872, actually began digging, but work was stopped by the representations of the War Office. The company continued in being, first as the Submarine Continental Railway, 1881, until after 1940. A British parliamentary committee also reported favourably, 1930, but on 30 June 1930 the House of Commons rejected the project. Renewed interest in scheme after World War II. Since 1960 schemes for both a C.T. and a Channel Bridge have been put forward; Anglo-French committee was established to consider the feasibility of a Channel tunnel or bridge, 1961, and recommended a rail tunnel, Feb. 1964. Project cancelled, 1975. Revived, 1984.

Chantrey Bequest. A fund left by Sir Francis Chantrey (1781–1841) to the Royal Academy for the encouragement of British painting and sculpture. First purchases made, 1877.

Chapel Royal of England existed, as a body of clergy and musicians, in the reign of Edward IV (1461–83), possibly earlier.

Chapel Royal of Scotland, founded by Alexander I (1107–24) at Stirling Castle, and moved by Mary Stuart (1542–87) to Holyrood Abbey Church.

Charing Cross, London. The original C.C. was erected by Edward I in memory of his wife Eleanor, 1291, on the site of a former village called C., immediately S. of Trafalgar Square. This cross was condemned and removed by order of Parliament, 1647. The present reproduction in the courtyard of C.C. Station was erected, 1865.

Charities. In England and Wales the Charitable Trusts Acts, 1853–1939, form the basis of modern charity administration. Charity Commission instituted under the Act of 1853 and reconstituted under the C. Act of 1960.

Charlemagne or **Charles I.** King of the Franks, the son of Pepin and Bertha; *b.* probably A.D. 2 Apr. 742, *d.* 28 Jan. 814. Crowned Emperor of the West by Pope Leo III, 800.

Charleston, S. Carolina. founded by William Sayle *c.* 1670. (*See* FORT SUMTER.) There was a severe earthquake here in 1886.

Charlotte Amalie, capital of the Virgin Islands, was known between 1921 and 1937 as St. Thomas.

Charlottenburg. Former town of Brandenburg, Germany, incorporated into Berlin, 1920. Grew up round the palace built there in 1696 by Frederick I of Prussia.

Charter, The Great. *See* MAGNA CARTA.

Charterhouse. Corruption of *Chartreuse.* Carthusian (*see* CARTHUSIAN ORDER) monastery founded in Clerkenwell, London, 1371, but when monasteries were dissolved by Henry VIII it was made a depository for the king's tents and pavilions, until granted to the Duke of Norfolk, 1539. Purchased by Thomas Sutton, who founded a school and hospital, 1611. School transferred to Godalming, Surrey, 1872.

Charters of Corporate Towns, granted by Henry I, gave security to industry and promoted manufactures, 1132; remodelled by Charles II, 1682; the new charter resisted at Nottingham, accepted by Plymouth and other corporations, 1684. Ancient C. restored, 1698; revised by Royal Commission, 1833; altered by Municipal Reform Act, 1835; whole system transformed by Local Government Act, 1972.

Chartism. A movement in Great Britain for extension of political power to the working classes, caused by economic distress. It began in 1836. In 1838 was drawn up by certain 'representatives of the people' the 'People's Charter', and riots known as Chartist riots were enacted all over the country. By 1848 extremists dominated the movement, which petered out by 1858.

Chartres, France. Besieged by Normans, 845 and 911. Henry I of England interviewed Pope Innocent II at, 1131; English from 1417 to 1431; taken by Count of Dunois, 1432; besieged by Duke of Condé, 1568. A fire is recorded in the cathedral as early as A.D. 753; extensive rebuilding, 1020–8. Towers built, 1145–65; main part of present structure finished by 1260.

Chatham, England. Dockyard and arsenal built by Queen Elizabeth, 1588; removed to its present position, 1662. Surprised by Dutch under De Ruyter, 1667. New docks opened, 21 June 1871; naval dockyard closed, 1983.

Chatham Chest. Charitable fund established by Sir Francis Drake and Sir John Hawkins in 1588. It was removed to Greenwich, 1802, and the fund incorporated with Greenwich Hospital.

Chatham House, St. James's Square, London, has been since 1923 the headquarters of the Royal Institute of International Affairs, which originated in 1919.

Chatham Islands, now under New Zealand administration, were discovered, 1791, by Lieut. W. R. Broughton. Conquered, 1831, by a Maori expedition; the aboriginals virtually exterminated by 1849.

Cheapside, originally Chepe = The Market, was the commercial centre of medieval London. Laws regulating this market were codified under Edward I (1272–1307). Chaucer about 1380 and Lydgate in the early fifteenth century often refer to Chepe.

Cheb (Ger. **Eger**). Acquired by the Holy Roman Empire, 1000. Colonized by Germans under leadership of Bavarian Cistercian abbots, from 1100. Reichstag (*q.v.*) met at C., 1213, and Imperial Chamber of Princes, 1239. Became part of the kingdom of Bohemia for the first

time in 1279, and finally in 1322. Wallenstein murdered in C. castle, 1634. From 1621 to 1918 the district had its own provincial Diet. Thereafter became a headquarters of the Sudeten German movement. *See* SUDETENLAND.

Cheka. Name applied to Russian Soviet Secret Police, 1917–22.

Chelsea Hospital or **College** (London), for old and disabled soldiers of British Army. Foundation stone laid, 1682; building by Christopher Wren opened, 1694.

Cheltenham, England. Priory of Benedictines founded about 790. Edward the Confessor lord of the manor and granted a charter in 1041. The grammar school and almshouses founded, 1578, by Richard Pate. The C. waters were first discovered, 1716. The C. College was established in 1840, followed by the Ladies' College, 1854. Govt. Communications Centre since World War II.

Chemistry. In earlier times known as alchemy, inaugurated in Egypt. Diocletian ordered the destruction of all the works of the alchemists, A.D. 297. A licence for practising alchemy was granted to Richard Carter in London, 1476. C. not a science until the seventeenth century. In 1772 Joseph Priestley published his discoveries, which commenced a new era in the science.

Chemnitz, *see* KARL-MARX-STADT.

Chequers (Court). Bequeathed to the nation, with a trust fund for its upkeep for the use of successive Prime Ministers, by Lord Lee of Fareham (then Sir Arthur Lee), 1917. First occupied by David Lloyd George, 8 Jan. 1921.

Cheques. Lawrence Childs, a banker, first printed C. *c.* 1761. Rules with regard to bills of exchange, defined in the Bill of Exchange Act, 1882, also apply to C. By the Cheques Act of 1947 an unendorsed C. which appears to have been paid by the drawer's banker is evidence of receipt by the payee of the sum payable by cheque. Payment by cheque permissible to any employee from 1 Mar. 1963, subject to the employee's agreement.

Cherasco.
1. Armistice of, between Napoleon I and the King of Sardinia, 28 Apr. 1796.
2. Treaty of, between Louis XIII of France and Victor Amadeus of Savoy, 6 Apr. 1631.

Cherbourg, France. Captured by Henry V of England, Aug. 1418; retaken by French, 12 Aug. 1450; harbour-works planned by Vauban, 1686, but not finally completed until 1856; fortifications destroyed by English, Oct. 1758; further harbour-works constructed, 1886; occupied by Germans, 18 June 1940; captured from them by Americans, 25 June 1944.

Cherkassy, Ukraine. Belonged to Kiev in the Middle Ages; Lithuanian in 1362; Polish, 1569, Russian, 1793.

Chernigov, Ukraine. From 1024 to 1239 capital of a Grand Principality. Finally became Russian in 1654.

Cherokees. Tribe of N. American Indians. Have a written alphabet of eighty-five letters invented by a Cherokee, George Guess, in 1821. Disbanded as a tribe to become U.S. citizens, 1906.

Chesapeake Bay, U.S.A. Explored by Capt. John Smith, 1607, who arrived there with colonists. British incursions in, 1779. Comte de Grasse with French fleet arrived at, 30 Aug. 1781, and battle took place between French and English fleets, 5 Sept. 1781. Blockaded by English, 5 Feb. 1812.

Chess. Learnt by the Persians from India, where it was known in the seventh century. Persians' name for it was *shatranj*. In A.D. 950 an Arabic author, Masudi, spoke of the game as having existed before his time. *The Game and Playe of the Chesse*, second book printed by Caxton, probably appeared, 1475. The first important writer on modern C. was the Spaniard, Ruy López de Segura, 1561.

Chester, England. Called by the Britons *Caerleon*. The *Deva* of the Romans, whose XXth Legion was stationed there until the end of the fourth century. Taken by Ethelfrid, King of Northumbria, 607. Occupied by a Danish army in 894, which retained it till rebuilt by Ethelfleda, Countess of Mercia, *c.* 908. Britons once more masters *c.* 918, but soon driven out by Edward the Elder (*d.* 924). Taken by parliamentary forces, 1645. Castle attacked by Fenians, 1867. C. cathedral (originally a Benedictine abbey) dated from 1053.

Chicago, U.S.A. Site visited by Joliet and Marquette, 1673; Fort Dearborn built, 1803; Indians massacred the settlers, 1812; fort rebuilt, 1816; C. received first city charter, 1837; almost entirely destroyed by fire, 7–11 Oct. 1871; rebuilt, 1872–3; serious stockyard fire, May 1934.

Chichester, Sussex, England. Site of Roman town, Noviomagus. Cathedral completed *c.* 1108; rebuilt, 1187. City captured by Parliamentarians, 1643; fortifications destroyed, 1648. New theatre opened, 1962.

Children Acts. That of 1908 was introduced into the House of Commons by Visc. (then Sir Herbert) Samuel, and much amended by the Children and Young Persons Act, 1933, and the Children Acts of 1948 and 1952, the Children and Young Persons Act of 1969, and the Children Act of 1975.

Children, National Society for Prevention of Cruelty to, established by Benjamin Waugh (1839–1908) in 1884, and incorporated under royal charter, 1895.

Chile. Peruvians acquired territory from Indians inhabiting C., 1450. Discovered by Magellan, 1520. Peruvian dominion ceased, 1533. Spanish invasion, 1435–6, driven back. Detached from Peru, 1568. Treaty of Spain and C. fixing boundary, 1722. Chileans declared independence of Spain, 18 Sept. 1810. Constitution established, 25 May 1833. War declared against Spain, 29 Sept. 1865. Treaty with Peru against Spain, 14 Jan. 1866. War with Bolivia and Peru, 1 Mar. 1879. Peace treaty with Spain confirmed, Sept. 1881. Peace treaty with Bolivia, 25 Jan. 1882; war resumed, July 1882. Peace with Peru, 20 Oct. 1883, by which Peru ceded southernmost province of Tarapaca. Treaty ending territorial dispute between C. and Bolivia signed, 17 Oct.

1905. Tacna ceded to Peru, 1929. Roman Catholic Church disestablished, 1925. Marxist rule 1970–3 followed by a right-wing coup, 1973. New constitution, 1981, provided for return to democracy within eight years.

The following are the presidents of C.:

O'Higgins 1818–1823
Freire 1823–1830
Prieto 1830–1841
Bulnes 1841–1851
Montt (Manuel) 1851–1861
Perez 1861–1871
Zanartu 1871–1876
Pinto 1876–1881
Santa Maria 1881–1886
Balmaceda 1886–1891
Montt (Jorge) 1891–1896
Errazuriz 1896–1901
Riesco 1901–1906
Montt (Pedro) 1906–1910
Albano 1910
Figueroa Larrain 1910
Luco 1910–1915
Sanfuentes 1915–1920
Alessandri 1920–1924
Altamirano 1924–1925
Bello 1925
Alessandri (restored) 1925
Barros 1925
Figueroa Larrain 1925–1927
Ibañez 1927–1931
Opazo 1931 (1 day only)
Montero 1931
Trucco 1931
Montero (again) 1931–1932
Socialist Junta 1932
Davila 1932
Blanche 1932
Oyanedel 1932
Alessandri 1932–1938
Aguirre 1938–1941
Mendez 1941–1942
Rios 1942–1946
Duhalde 1946
Merino 1946
Gonzalez 1946–1952
Ibañez (again) 1952–1958
Alessandri 1958–1964
Frei 1964–1970
Allende 1970–1973
Pinochet 1973–

Chiltern Hundreds. An ancient statute was amended in 1707 to provide that a member of Parliament might resign only provided he held an office of profit under the crown. By the Place Act, 1742, the stewardship of the C.H. and of the manor of Northstead in Yorkshire were accounted offices of profit for this purpose. A steward of the C.H. was first appointed as a pretext for resignation, 1750.

Chimborazo. Volcanic mountain (height 20,660 ft.) in Ecuador. First ascent by Edward Whymper, 1880.

Chimneys. First introduced into England about 1200. Tax on C. called 'hearth-money' levied, 1662; abolished, 1689.

China. Hsia Dynasty founded, 2205 B.C., and overthrown 1766 B.C. by T'ang, who founded the Shang Dynasty, which lasted until 1122 B.C., and had its capitals at Po, Nao, and Yin. In 1122 Wu Wang founded the Chou Dynasty. In 771 B.C. capital estab. at Loyang. 479 B.C. is the beginning of the period of the seven 'Warring States'. China conquered by Ch'in, one of the seven states, and the Chou Dynasty overthrown, 256 B.C. The first emperor of the Ch'in Dynasty, Shih Huang Ti, is said to have ordered the building of the Great Wall *c.* 220–210 B.C. Ch'in Dynasty overthrown by revolution led by Lio Pang, who as the Emperor Kao Ti established the Han Dynasty, 206 B.C. Beginning of the wars against the Huns, 133 B.C. Conquest of Sinkiang, 130–120 B.C. Conquest of S.C. and Canton, 111 B.C. Conquest of Laklang in Korea, 108 B.C. (Japan). Submission of the Hun *c.* 54 B.C. Usurpation of Wang Mang, A.D. 9, and civil war ending in re-establishment of the Han Dynasty, A.D. 25. Diplomatic contacts with the Roman Empire, 166. Civil war, end of the Han Dynasty, 220, and the period of the Three Kingdoms, 220–65, followed by the Tsin Dynasty. Hun invasions begin again *c.* 304, leading to the establishment of a Hun kingdom at Loyang, 311, and the Tsin emperors established a new capital at Nanking, 316, and repel Hun attempt to conquer the S. at the battle of Fei Shui, 387. C. reunited under Wen Ti, founder of the Sui Dynasty, 581. This dynasty was overthrown in 618, and authority was re-established by Kao Tsu, who founded the T'ang Dynasty, and consolidated by his son, the emperor T'ai Tsung. Rebellion of the unpaid army in Annam led by Huang Ch'ao, 875, leads to capture of Chang An, 881, and overthrow of the T'angs, 907. C. reunited once more by Chao K'uang-yin, who as T'ai Tsu founded the Sung Dynasty, 960. N.C. conquered by the Kin ('Golden') Horde, 1126, and established the Southern Sung Dynasty at Hang Chou, 1127. Mongols under Ogotai capture Kai Feng and destroy the Kin state in N. China, 1233. Under Bayan they capture Hang Chou, 1276, extinguish the Sung Dynasty, 1279, and with the accession of Kublai Khan establish the Yüan Dynasty at Peking, 1260. The weakness of the Mongols after Kublai's death, 1294, leads to a Chinese revolt, 1348, which results in the Mongols being driven out of Nanking, 1356, and from Peking, 1368. Chu Yüan-chang (Tai Tsu) establishes Ming Dynasty 1368, at Nanking. Yen seizes the throne, 1402, and reigns as Ch'eng Tsu. Capital moved to Peking, 1404, which was completed in its present form, 1422. Great Wall rebuilt, 1406–25. Christianity introduced by Jesuit missionaries, sixteenth and seventeenth centuries, and made considerable progress in court circles. Portuguese ship under Perestrello reaches Canton, 1516. Portuguese allowed to settle at Macao, 1557. Rebellion led by Li Tzu-cheng overthrows Ming Dynasty, 1644. Manchus found the Manchu Dynasty, 1644. Accession of Kang Tsi (1662–1722) marked period of intellectual progress and great Christian influence at court. His successor, Yung Cheng, began the policy of 'exclusion'. The 'Opium War' between Britain and C., 1840–2, ends with Treaty of Nanking, 29 Aug. 1842, under which Hong Kong was ceded to Britain. Tai-ping (Christian) rebellion in Kwangsi begins

under leadership of Hung Hsiu-chuan, 1850. Kung-Elgin Peace convention, 1860, by which in return for the management of the Chinese Customs the English and French were to assist in the suppression of the Tai-ping revolt. Korea becomes independent, 1876. Japan attacks C., 25 July 1894, and declares war, 2 Aug. Naval defeat at battle of the Yalu, 17 Sept. Massacre of Chinese at Port Arthur by Japanese, 21 Nov. 1894. Peace Treaty ratified with Japan, 8 May 1895. Boxer riots, 1900. War between Russia and Japan in Manchuria, Korea, and the Chinese seas, 1904; by the Treaty of Portsmouth, U.S.A., Aug. 1905, Port Arthur and Dalny were leased to Japan; Korea annexed to Japan, 23 Aug. 1910; revolution, 1911–12, abdication of the last Manchu Emperor P'u-yi, 12 Feb. 1912, and the establishment of a republic with Yuan Shih-k'ai as provisional president, 15 Feb. 1912. Civil war breaks out, Dec. 1925 and by 1930 Chiang Kai-Shek was effective ruler of C. Japanese attack Manchuria, Sept. 1931 and set up puppet republic. Goes on to attack C. proper. Armistice with Japan, 1933: by this time Communists a strong force in C. and independent of the official govt. 1937: The Peking 'Incident' 7 July. War breaks out again between Japan and C. Japanese take Peking, 8 Aug: Shanghai, 9 Nov.: Nanking, 12–13 Dec. Chungking made capital of Nationalist China: Burma Road completed, Dec. 1938. C. breaks off relations with Axis, July 1941; Japanese surrender in C., 12 Sept. 1945. War between Communists and Nationalists 1946–9 ends in establishment of People's Republic, 1949. Nationalists flee to Taiwan. Communist Chinese intervened in Korean War, 1950; invaded Tibet, 1950 which accepted Chinese suzerainty, 23 May 1951. By 1961, serious disagreements with Soviet Russia; in 1962, border dispute with India flared into open war. C. exploded first atomic bomb, Oct. 1964. In 1966 'Cultural Revolution' launched: purge of intellectuals. Increased Chinese aid to N. Vietnam. In

Oct. 1968 Liu Shao-ch'i, Chairman of the Republic since 1959, was expelled from the Communist party and deprived of office. C. admitted to the U.N. in 1971 in place of Nationalist Taiwan govt. 'Cultural Revolution' over by 1972: President Nixon visited China. Chiang Kai-Shek *d.*, 1975. Mao Tse- Tung *d.*, 10 Sept. 1976. Hua Kuo-feng headed govt. and party radicals, the 'gang of four' (including Mao's widow) arrested and found guilty of treason, 1981. U.S. recognized Peking govt., 1979. Growing contacts with W. after 1976 and steady liberalization of govt. Agreement with Brit. over future of Hong Kong, 19 Dec. 1984.

Dynasties, 2697 B.C.–A.D. 1126. Dynasties and Emperors, 1127–1911:
The Five Sovereigns (Legendary Epoch) 2697–2205 B.C.
The Hsia Dynasty 2205–1766 B.C.
The Shang or Yin Dynasty 1766–1122 B.C.
The Chou Dynasty 1122–255 B.C.
The Ch'in Dynasty 255–206 B.C.
The Han Dynasty 206 B.C.–A.D. 220
San Kuo (The Epoch of the Three Kingdoms) 220–265
The Tsin Dynasty 265–420
The Southern Dynasties 420–589
The Northern Dynasties 386–581
The Sui Dynasty 581–618
The T'ang Dynasty 618–907
Wu Tai (The Epoch of the Five Dynasties) 907–960
The Sung Dynasty 960–1279
(From 1127 the Sung Dynasty controlle diminishing area of S.C. only.)

The Sung Dynasty (Southern Line), 1127–1279:
Kao Tsung (S. Sung) 1127–1162
Hsiao Tsung 1162–1189
Kuang Tsung 1189–1194
Ning Tsung 1194–1224
Li Tsung 1224–1264
Tu Tsung 1264–1274
Kung Ti 1274–1276
Tuan Tsung 1276–1278
Ti Ping 1278–1279

The Mongol (Yüan) Dynasty, 1206–1368 (Imperial title from 1279):
T'ai Tsu (Jenghiz Khan) 1206–1229

T'ai Tsung (Ogotai Khan) 1229–1246
Ting Tsung (Kuyak Khan) 1246–1251
Hsien Tsung (Mangu Khan) 1251–1260
Shih Tsu (Kublai Khan) 1260–1294
Ch'eng Tsung 1294–1307
Wu Tsung 1307–1311
Jen Tsung 1311–1320
Ying Tsung 1320–1323
T'ai Ting Ti 1323–1328
Yu Chu 1328
Ming Tsung 1328–1329
Wen Tsung 1329–1332
Ning Tsung 1332–1333
Shun Ti 1333–1368

The Ming Dynasty, 1368–1644:
T'ai Tsu (Chu Yuan-chang) 1368–1398
Hui Ti 1398–1402
Ch'eng Tsu 1402–1424
Jen Tsung 1424–1425
Hsuan Tsung 1425–1435
Ying Tsung 1435–1449
Tai Tsung 1449–1457
Ying Tsung (restored) 1457–1464
Hsien Tsung 1464–1487
Hsiao Tsung 1487–1505
Wu Tsung 1505–1521
Shih Tsung 1521–1566
Mu Tsung 1566–1572
Shen Tsung 1572–1620
Kuang Tsung 1620
Hsi Tsung 1620–1627
Ssu Tsung 1627–1644

The Manchu (Ch'ing) Dynasty, 1644–1911:
Shih Tsu 1644–1661
Kang Tsi 1662–1722
Yung Cheng 1723–1735
Kao Tsung 1735–1795
Jen Tsung 1795–1820
Hsuan Tsung 1820–1850
Wen Tsung 1850–1861
Mu Tsung 1861–1875
Teh Tsung 1875–1908
P'u-yi 1908–1911

Effective Heads of Administration from 1911 to the Present Day:
Yuan Shih-k'ai: President of the Republic of C., 1911–16.
Sun Yat-sen: President of the Republic of C., 1921–5.
Chiang Kai-shek: C.-in-C., Northern Armies, 1926; Generalissimo of the National Republic of C., 1928;

Director-General of the Kuomintang, 1938; President of the National Republic of C., 1943; *effective ruler of the National Republic of C. 1925–49, then rule confined to Taiwan, 1949–75.*

Mao Tse-tung: Chairman of the Council of People's Commissars in Communist S.C., 1931; Chairman of the Central People's Council of the People's Republic of C., Sept. 1949; Chairman of the Central Committee of the Chinese Communist Party only since Dec. 1958; *but effective ruler of all C., excluding Taiwan, 1949–76.*

Hua Kuo-feng: Prime Minister of the People's Republic of C. and Chairman of the Central Committee of the Chinese Communist Party, 1976–81. Subsequently Hu Yaobang was effective ruler, followed by Teng Hsiao-Peng. In June 1983 Li Hsien-nien was appointed first president since disgrace of Liu in 1969. *See also* TAIWAN; KOREA.

Chinese Eastern Railway, a Russian-built extension of the Trans-Siberian Railway, was sold to the Government of Manchukuo in 1935. 1945–75 part of the Chinese system, jointly owned and operated by China and the U.S.S.R.; reverted to China in 1975.

Chinese Literature. *(All poets unless otherwise indicated.)*

Chang Chao, sixteenth century A.D.
Chang Fang-sheng, fourth century A.D.
Chang Tsai, third century A.D.
Ch'en Tzu-lung, A.D. 1607–47.
Ch'en Tzu-ang, A.D. 656–98.
Cheng Hsiao, *c.* A.D. 250.
Cheng-kung Sui, third century A.D.
Chien Wen-ti, sixth century A.D.
Chi Kang, A.D. 223–62.
Chin Chia, first century A.D.
Chü Yuan, 332–295 B.C.
Fu Hsüan, third century A.D.
Hsi Chün (Princess), second century B.C.
Hsieh T'iao, fifth century A.D.
Hsü Ling, A.D. 507–83.
Kung Fu-tze (Confucius the philosopher), 551–478 B.C.
Lao-tze, sixth century B.C., philosopher.
Li Po, A.D. 701–62.

Lu Yu, A.D. 1125–1209.
Lu Yün, fourth century A.D.
Miu Hsi, third century A.D.
Pao Chao, fifth century A.D.
Po Chü-i, A.D. 772–846.
Su Tung-po, A.D. 1036–1101.
Su Wu, *c.* 100 B.C.
Sung Tsu-Lou, second century A.D.
Sung Yü, fourth century B.C.
T'ao Ch'ien, A.D. 365–427.
T'ao Yün, *c.* A.D. 400.
Tsang Chih, sixth century A.D.
Tsao Chic (Prince), A.D. 192–233.
Tsao Sung, *c.* A.D. 900.
Tso Ssu, third century A.D.
Tu Fu, A.D. 712–70.
Wang Chi, *c.* A.D. 700.
Wei Wen-ti (Emperor), A.D. 188–227.
Wu Cheng-en, sixteenth century A.D., novelist.
Wu-ti (Emperor), 157–87 B.C.
Wu-ti (Emperor), A.D. 464–549.
Yang-ti (Emperor), seventh century A.D.
Yüan Chi, A.D. 210–63.
Yuan Chieh, eighth century A.D.
Yuan-ti A.D. 508–54.

Chinon, France. Geoffrey of Anjou imprisoned in castle of C., 1068–96. Henry II of England *d.* at, 6 July 1189. Arrival of Joan of Arc at, to meet Charles VII, 24 Feb. 1429.

Chios. Anciently one of the more powerful Ionian maritime states, submitted to the Persians, 546 B.C., but liberated by the battle of Mykale, 479, when C. joined the Delian League. Revolted against Athenian domination, 413 B.C.; renewed alliance with Athens, *c.* 403, but finally left the League, 357 B.C. Became part of the Roman Empire, 133. Under Genoese influence from A.D. 1346; conquered by Turks, but given considerable local autonomy, 1566; massacre by the Turks, 1822. C. became Greek territory after the First Balkan War in 1812. Devastated by earthquake, 1881. Used by British and French forces as a base for the Dardanelles operation, 1915. Revolt which led to fall of King Constantine began in C., 1922.

Chitral, NW. Frontier Province, Pakistan, virtually independent until 1895, when the British political agent and an Indian Army garrison were besieged in the fort of C., 4 Mar.–20 Apr., after which C. became a dependency of Kashmir.

Chivalry, Court of. Species of court-martial for officers, established in Edward III's reign (1327–77), was regulated by Richard II, 1390. Between 1737 and 1955 tried no cases. In 1955 upheld Manchester Corporation's claim that a certain theatre should not display the civic coat of arms.

Chivalry, Orders of. *See* KNIGHTHOOD, ORDERS OF.

Chlorine. Discovered by Scheele, 1774; experiments of Gay-Lussac and Thénard, 1809; Davy proved it to be an element, and gave it its present name, 1810; apparatus for making C. invented by Smith, 1847; used in warfare by the Germans, Apr. 1915, the British, Sept. 1915, and the Iraquis, 1983–4.

Chloroform. Discovered by Liebig, 1831. First used in 1847 by Bell and Simpson.

Cholera, bacillus isolated by Koch, 1883; last epidemic in Britain, 1866.

Chouans were Breton smugglers, at first under the leadership of Jean Cottereau (1767–94), who rose in revolt against the republican government, 1793. Their activities were mainly confined to the departments of Morbihan and Eure. The Vendéans proper, together with peasants of Anjou, Poitou, Maine, and Mayenne, rose in protest against the Convention's conscription decree of Feb. 1793; their Christian Army (later called Royal and Catholic Army) had possession of most of Brittany and Poitou by Sept. 1793, though they could not capture Nantes. Defeated at Châtillon in Oct., and at Savenay in Dec., guerrilla warfare continued, until the failure of the Quiberon expedition, 20 July 1795. State of siege declared at an end, 30 July 1796. In 1815 there was a Vendéan rising, and another in 1832 against the Orléans monarchy, led by Mme de Berry.

Christ, Disciples of. *See* CAMPBELLITES.

Christadelphians. Sect founded in the U.S.A., 1848, by an Englishman, John Thomas (1805–71).

Christchurch, New Zealand. Founded, 1851, by the Canterbury Association.

Christiania. *See* OSLO.

Christian Knowledge, Society for Promoting. Founded, 1698.

Christian Science. Theory of C.S. discovered by Mrs. Mary Baker Eddy, 1866. Church of Christ, Scientist established in Boston, Massachusetts, 1879.

Christmas Island, or **Kiritimati.** In the W. Pacific, discovered by Cook, 1777. Annexed by Britain, 1898. Part of the Gilbert and Ellice Islands colony 1919–79: since then part of Republic of Kiribati (*q.v.*). Chosen as the site for British H.-bomb tests, 1957, and subsequently used also for American tests.

Christ's Hospital (The Bluecoat School). Founded, 1552, on site of the monastery of the Grey Friars, Newgate Street, London. Charter dated 26 June 1553. School moved to W. Horsham, 29 May 1902. New buildings for the girls' school at Hertford (since 1798) opened 1906.

Chromium. First isolated by Vauquelin, 1797.

Chromosomes. Study begun *c.* 1883 by Ger. biologists Weismann (1834–1914) and Boveri (1862–1915).

Chronicles, Anglo-Saxon. *See* ANGLO-SAXON CHRONICLES.

Chronometers. Invented by John Harrison, 1726.

Chungking, China, capital of China, 1941–5. *See* BURMA ROAD.

Church Army. Mission of the Church of England, established, 1882.

Church Assembly. Set up in 1920 under the Church of England Assembly Powers Act, 1919.

Church Commissioners. Set up, 1947, to unite Queen Anne's Bounty and the Ecclesiastical Commissioners, and to exercise the functions of both bodies.

Church of England. *See* ENGLAND, CHURCH OF.

Church Missionary Society, founded 1799.

Church Union. Formed, 1859.

Cid Campeador (real name Rodrigo Diaz de Vivar), *c.* 1035–99. As the almost legendary champion of Spanish Christendom against the Moors he was the subject of a ballad-cycle, *Poema de mio Cid*, composed about 1140; of a drama, *Los Mocedades del Cid*, by Guillen de Castro, 1618, which was the basis of Corneille's tragedy, 1636; and of Southey's *Chronicles of the Cid*, 1808.

Cigarettes. Popularized in England by soldiers returning from the Crimean War. First factory established at Walworth, 1856. Royal College of Physicians report, 'Smoking and Health', alleged a casual relationship between cigarette-smoking and lung cancer, Mar. 1962. Ban on television advertising of cigarettes, 1965.

Cigars. Introduced into Britain *c.* 1812, by soldiers returning from the Peninsular War.

Cimbri. Germanic tribes from the SW. Baltic area, and the Jutland Peninsula. They advanced into Illyricum and defeated the consul Papirius Carbo, 113 B.C.; repulsed by Drusus in Thrace, 112 B.C., defeated the consul Junius Silanus, in Gaul, 109; ravaged the country till checked in Thrace by Minucius Rufus, 109; victorious over the consul Aurelius Scaurus, 108; forced their way into Roman Gaul, where they defeated the consul Cn. Mallius and the proconsul Caepio, 105; invaded Spain, 104; driven out by the natives, 103; defeated the proconsul Lutatius Catulus, 102; forced a passage into Italy, were totally crushed by Marius at Vercellae, their league dissolved, 101.

Cincinnati, Ohio, U.S.A. Maj. Doughty, in 1789, built Fort Washington, around which grew the present town.

Cincinnati, Order of. A republican society formed by Americans, 1783; first general meeting, May 1784.

Cinematography. Principle on which C. is based—the persistence of vision —described as early as the second century A.D. and demonstrated by Dr. Peter Mark Roget, 1824. Thaumatrope, 1826. J. A. Plateau's Phenakistiscope, 1833. The principle crudely embodied in the Zoetrope patented by W. G. Horner, 1833. Marey of Paris and Heyl of Philadelphia, by 1870, had both devised cameras for recording consecu-

tive photographs of glass discs. Goodwin (American) invented the celluloid film, 1887. Augustin le Prince granted a British patent for employment of perforated gelatine film, to reproduce a sequence of images taken through a single objective, 1888. William Friese-Greene (1855–1921) of Bristol filed English patent for camera and projector with intermittent movement and a single lens, using ribbon of sensitized celluloid, 21 June 1889. Edison's kinetoscope, on a different principle (no projection), was in use same year. A French patent for a 'cinématographe' taken out by brothers Auguste (1862–1954) and Louis (1864–1948) Lumière, 1895. A film passion-play produced in New York, 1897. First colour films ('Kinemacolor' of Smith and Urban), 1906; followed by 'Technicolor' *c.* 1929; by 'Kodachrome', 1935. 'Talking' film developed in America, 1928. 'Cinerama', 1952. 'Cinemascope', 1953.

Cinque Ports, England. Originally five in number: Dover, Hastings, Hythe, Romney, and Sandwich; Rye and Winchelsea were added by Richard I. Fortified by William I, 1067; Henry III granted privileges to, 1216. Charter surrendered to the crown, 1688.

Cintra, Portugal. Convention of, concluded between Sir Hew Dalrymple and Marshal Junot, 30 Aug. 1808.

Circassia, ceded to Russia by Turkey, 1829, but did not finally submit to Russian rule until 1859.

Circulation of the Blood, first demonstrated by Harvey, 1628.

Cirta. *See* CONSTANTINE.

Cisalpine Gaul. *See* GAUL.

Cisalpine Republic. N. Italian republic set up by Napoleon, 1797. Later known as the Italian republic, and converted into the Napoleonic kingdom of Italy, 1805.

Cistercian Order, founded at Cîteaux by St. Robert, Abbot of Molêsme, 1098.

City Companies. *See* LIVERY COMPANIES.

City University, London E.C.1., estab. 1966.

Ciudad Trujillo. *See* SANTO DOMINGO.

Civic Trust, founded 1957.

Civil Defence Bill. Passed, June 1939.

Civil List. The revenue awarded to the sovereigns of England in return for the crown lands. From 1697 C.L. fixed by Parliament.

Civil Rights Bill. Introduced into U.S. Senate, 29 Jan. 1866; passed 13 Mar. 1866; amended, 1875. New C.R.B. became law, 1964.

Civil Wars in Great Britain:
King Stephen and Matilda, 1139–53.
King John and Barons, 1215–16.
Henry III and Barons, 1263–5.
Edward II and Barons, 1321–7.
Henry IV and Owen Glendower, 1403–5.
Wars of the Roses (*q.v.*), 1455–71, also 1485.
Covenanters and Scottish Episcopalians, 1638–43, 1666, 1679, and intermittently until 1688.
Charles I and Parliament, 1642–6.
Charles II and Parliament, 1650–1.
James II and Duke of Monmouth, 1685.
See also JACOBITES.

Civil Wars. Major C. Ws., other than in Great Britain include:
Civil War, American, 1861–5.
Civil War, Russian, 1917–22.
Civil War, Spanish, 1936–9.
Civil War, Vietnamese, 1959–75.
Civil War, Yemeni, 1962–8.
Civil War, Nigerian, 1967–70.
Civil War, Jordanian, 1970.
Civil War, Zimbabwe-Rhodesia, 1970–9.
Civil War, Uganda, 1979.
Civil War, Lebanon, 1975–.
Civil War, Afghanistan, 1979–.
Civil War, Kampuchea, 1977–.
Civil War, Ethiopia, 1978–.
Civil War, El Salvador, 1980–.
Civil War, Nicaragua, 1982–.

Clan-na-Gael. Irish terrorist organization, with headquarters in Chicago, founded *c.* 1883.

Clarendon Code. A series of English statutes designed to establish the political supremacy of the Anglican Church and to destroy the power of the Presbyterians. The principal Acts were: Corporation Act, Dec. 1661. Act of Uniformity, May 1662. Conventicle Act, July 1664; Five-Mile Act, Oct. 1665.
The C.C. was called after Edward Hyde, Earl of Clarendon, who was Lord Chancellor, 1661, until banished, 1667.

Clarendon, Constitution of. Drawn up chiefly by Richard de Lucy at Council of C., near Salisbury, to limit the power of the clergy, 25 Jan. 1164. Abandoned by Henry II at Avranches, Sept. 1172.

Clarendon Press. The original name of the press of the University of Oxford, founded, fifteenth century; printing house erected by Sir John Vanbrugh, 1711–13 (with profits of Clarendon's *History of the Rebellion*, Oct. 1713).

Clayton-Bulwer Treaty. Negotiated in Apr. 1850 by John Middleton Clayton of the U.S.A. and Sir Henry Bulwer of Great Britain, superseded by new treaty, Feb. 1902.

Clearing-House. Bankers' C.-H. for exchange of drafts and bills set up in Lombard Street, 1770; joined by Bank of England, May 1804. Railway C.-H. established, 2 Jan. 1842.

Cleopatra's Needles. Two granite obelisks erected by Thothmes III at Heliopolis (*c.* 1475 B.C.) and re-erected by Augustus at Alexandria. (1) Transferred to London and placed on the Victoria Embankment, 1878. (2) Presented by the khedive to the U.S.A. and erected in Central Park, New York, 1881.

Clerkenwell (London). Grew up round St. John's Church, founded, 1140. C. Bridewell (house of correction) built, 1615; burnt down, 1669, but rebuilt. Succeeded by a House of Detention, 1775. Scene of a Fenian outrage, 1867; closed, 1877.

Cleveland, Eng. administrative co. estab. 1974 under the Local Government Act of 1972.

Cleves (Kleve). County, afterwards duchy, Germany. War of succession, 1609; concluded, 1614. C. given to Elector of Brandenburg; settlement confirmed, 1666. Seized by French, 1757; restored to Germany, 1763. In 1795 Prussia ceded the part on left bank of Rhine to France. Exchanges took place, 1803–15; outcome: France gave up all to Prussia and Holland.

Clocks. Chinese claim invention *c.* 2000 B.C. Water-C. (Clepsydrae) used in ancient Greece, fourth century B.C. Introduced into Rome *c.* 160 B.C.. Earliest C. of mechanical type in Europe, twelfth century A.D. First reliable C. set up in palace of Charles V of France by de Vick, 1379. Law of pendulum first applied to C. by Huygens *c.* 1657. First successful electric clocks invented by Hope-Jones and Bowell, 1894: quartz-crystal C. 1929: atomic C. 1952.

Closure. First authorized in the House of Commons by the Urgency Rules of 1881. Power first vested in Speaker, but transferred to House, 19 Mar. 1887.

Cloth of Gold, Field of the. Abortive conference between Henry VIII of England and Francis I·of France, held near Guisnes, 6 June 1520.

Clubs. First heard of in England during Elizabeth I's reign. Shakespeare and his friends met at the Mermaid Tavern. Ben Jonson set up a club at the Devil Tavern. The Rota instituted, 1659; the Kit-Kat, 1700; Beef-steak, 1735; Johnson's, 1764; Almack's 1765; Athenaeum, 1823; Reform, 1836; Savage, 1857.

Cluny, France. Benedictine abbey, founded 910. By 1150, 314 European monasteries had embraced Cluniac regime and were completely subject to C. In 1528 the monastery fell into 'commendam'; order abolished, 1790.

Clwyd. Welsh administative co. estab. 1974 under the Local Government Act of 1972.

Cnossos. *See* KNOSSOS.

Coach. First used in England in mid sixteenth century. Bill to prevent men from riding in coaches as too effeminate, 1601.

Stage-coaches used for public conveyance in England from the mid seventeenth to nineteenth centuries.

Coal seems to have been used for fuel in pre-Rom. times in Britain: written evidence that it was being mined in Newcastle, 1233; forbidden to be burnt in England, 1273. Nobility and gentry of London petition against use of, 1306. Not in general use in England until 1625. C. Commission established by C. Act, 1938, in which the ownership of all C. vested as from 1 July 1942. Mines nationalized as from 1 Jan. 1947.

Coalition of European States against France, generally brought about by British influence:

1. Great Britain, Austria, and Prussia, 1793.
2. Great Britain, Germany, Russia, Naples, Portugal, and Turkey, 1799.
3. Great Britain, Austria, Naples, and Russia, 1805.
4. Great Britain, Prussia, Russia, and Saxony, 1806.
5. Great Britain and Austria, 1809.
6. Prussia and Russia, 1813.

Coalition Governments in Britain, 1757, 1782, 1783, 1852, 1915, 1931, 1940.

Cobalt. Isolated in 1735 by Brandt.

Cobden Club. Founded London, 1866, to spread principles of Richard Cobden.

Coburg, in Franconia (*q.v.*), is first mentioned in documents, 1056, and became a city in 1331. It became the capital of the duchy of Saxe-Saalfeld-C., 1735, and of Saxe-C.-Gotha, 1926. During the nineteenth century members of its royal house succeeded to the thrones of Belgium, Bulgaria, Great Britain, and Portugal. *See* all of these.

Cocaine. First used as an anaesthetic by Koller, 1884. Recognized as an addictive drug after First World War: major illegal world traffic in, from 1980s.

Cochin, Kerala state, India, was once part of the kingdom of Kerala, where Jews and Christians of St. Thomas settled in the first century A.D.; these communities still exist. Vasco da Gama sighted the coast 1498, and Portuguese settled in C. city, 1502, with the permission of the local kings, independent since the ninth century, to build á fort. The Dutch expelled the Portuguese, 1663. C. became subject to Hyder Ali of Mysore, 1776, but was ceded to the British by Tippu Sahib, 1791.

Cochin China. See INDO-CHINA.

Cock-fighting. Prohibited by Edward III, 1365; by Cromwell, 1653; and finally in 1849.

Cock Lane Ghost. Sensation caused by fraudulent representations of William Parsons, his wife, and daughter in 1760–1 at Cock Lane, London. Parsons and wife convicted and imprisoned, 10 July 1762.

Cocoa and Chocolate. Cocoa beans first brought to Europe by Columbus, 1494. Cortez found Aztecs using chocolate as a beverage, 1519, and introduced it to Spain. First 'chocolate house' opened in London, 1657. Eating chocolate first produced in Britain, 1847.

Cocos (or **Keeling**) **Islands**, discovered by Capt. Wm. Keeling, 1609. British protectorate, 1856. Territory under the Commonwealth of Australia, 22 Nov. 1955. A referendum in 1984 voted for integration with Australia.

Code Napoléon. Codification of French civil law was promised by the constitutions of 1791 and 1793, but commissions did not begin work until 1800. The task lasted until 1802, and the necessary measures passed by the Assemblies, 1803–4. The name C.N. was suppressed between 1814 and 1852, but the third and final revision appeared in 1816.

Codex Alexandrinus. *See* ALEXANDRINUS, CODEX.

Codex Sinaiticus. *See* SINAITICUS, CODEX.

Coelacanths. Group of specialized crossopterygian fishes. Originally thought to have become extinct 50,000,000 years ago. But one caught off E. London, Cape Province, 1938; second specimen caught near Madagascar, 1952.

Coffee. Introduced to Europe in the seventeenth century. First English coffee-house opened in Oxford, 1650.

Cognac, Treaty of, between the parties to the Holy League of 1526 (*q.v.*).

Coimbra. Capital of Portugal, 1139–1260. Inez de Castro murdered, 1355.

Colchester, England (Lat. **Camulodunum**). Oldest recorded town in Britain. Cunobelinus reigned in C., 5 B.C.–A.D. 43. Became Roman headquarters in Britain, 43. Burnt by Boudicca, 61. End of Roman occupation *c.* 367. First charter, 1189. Castle surrendered to Fairfax in civil war, 1648. Univ. of Essex opened at, 1964.

Coleraine, Ulster. New Univ. of Ulster estab. at, 1965.

Cologne (Ger. **Köln**; Lat. **Colonia Agrippina**). Founded *c.* 37 B.C. by the Ubii. Colony of Roman veterans established there by Agrippina the Younger, A.D. 51. Diet held at by Charlemagne, 782, and made an archbishopric, 785. Joined Hanseatic League, 1201. Cathedral founded by Archbishop Conrad von Hochstaden, 1248. Town established its independence of the archbishop at the battle of Worringen, 1299. C. incorporated with France at the peace of Campo Formio, 1797, but annexed by Prussia, 1815. Cathedral completed, 1880. Garrisoned by British Rhine Army, 1918–25. City heavily bombed, 1942–5. Captured by American troops, 7 Mar. 1945; centre almost completely rebuilt since then.

Colombia. South American republic. Coast traditionally said to have been visited by Columbus, 1502. Area revolted against Spain, 1811, and achieved independence, 1819. Part of Greater Colombia, 1819–30; when Venezuela and Ecuador seceded, C. called itself the Republic of New Granada, 1831–50. Confederacion Granadina, 1858; United States of Colombia, 1863; Republic of Colombia, 1886.

Colombo, capital of Sri Lanka (*q.v.*). First mentioned by European sources, 1346, was taken by the Portuguese, 1517; from them by the Dutch, 1656; surrendered to the British, 1796.

Colombo Plan for Co-operative Economic Development in S. and SE. Asia, published 28 Nov. 1950, in force 1 July 1951, originally with seven Commonwealth members. Subsequently joined by U.S.A. and Japan and sev. countries in the Pacific area.

Colonial Office. Founded as the Council 'for the Plantations', 1660. Secretary of state for the colonies first appointed, 1854. Merged with the Commonwealth Relations Office (*q.v.*), 1966.

Colonies (British), many of which have since had a change of name and status, were declared as such on the dates given below:

Aden, 1839.
African Forts, 1618.
Anguilla, 1666.
Antigua, 1632.
Ascension, 1815.
Australia, S., 1834.
Australia, W., 1829.
Bahama Islands, 1629. Restored, 1783.
Barbados, 1605.
Bengal, 1652.
Berbice, 1803.
Bermudas, 1609.
Bombay, 1662.
British Burma, 1862.
British Columbia, 1858.
British Guiana, 1814.
British Honduras, 1862.
British Indian Ocean Territory, 1965.
British N. Borneo, 1946.
British Somaliland, 1884.
Canada, 1760.
Cape Breton, 1763.
Cape Coast Castle, 1667.
Cape of Good Hope, 1806.
Ceylon, 1815.
Cyprus, 1878.
Demerara and Essequibo, 1803.
Dominica, 1763.
Elmina and Dutch Guinea, 1871.
Falkland Islands, 1833.
Fiji, 1874.
Gambia, 1843.
Gibraltar, 1704.
Gilbert and Ellice Islands, 1915.
Gold Coast, 1874.
Grenada, 1763.
Hong Kong, 1841.
Jamaica, 1655.
Keeling Islands, 1857.
Kenya, 1920.
Kermadec Islands, 1886.
Labuan, 1846.
Lagos, 1861.
Leeward Isles, 1763.
Madras, 1640.
Malacca, 1795(–1818), 1824, 1946.
Malta and Gozo, 1800.
Mashonaland, 1890.
Matabeleland, 1890.
Mauritius, 1814.

Montserrat, 1632.
Natal, 1843.
Nevis, 1628.
New Brunswick, 1713.
Newfoundland, 1583.
New Guinea, 1884.
New Hebrides (Condominium), 1906.
New S. Wales, 1787.
New Zealand, 1840.
Niger districts, 1886.
Norfolk Island, 1787.
Nova Scotia, 1622.
Orange Free State, 1902.
Pegu, 1852.
Penang, 1786, 1946.
Pitcairn Island, 1898.
Port Phillip, 1840.
Prince Edward Island, 1745.
Prince of Wales Island, 1786.
Queensland, 1860.
Rhodesia, Northern, 1924.
Rhodesia, Southern, 1923.
St. Helena, 1673.
St. Kitts, 1623.
St. Lucia, 1803.
St. Vincent, 1763.
Sarawak, 1946.
Seychelles, 1810.
Sierra Leone, 1787.
Singapore, 1819.
Socotra, 1886.
Straits Settlements, 1826.
Tasmania, 1803.
Tobago, 1763.
Tortola, 1666.
Transvaal, 1901.
Trinidad, 1797.
Tristan da Cunha, 1816.
Vancouver Island, 1781.
Victoria. *See* Port Phillip.
Virgin Isles, 1666.
Windward Isles, 1803.

See also PROTECTORATES, BRITISH.

Colorado was partly acquired by the U.S.A. from France under the Louisiana Purchase, 1803, and partly from Mexico, 1848. Gold was found in 1858, and until 1910 C. was the leading U.S. state for the production of this metal. Indian wars, 1860–5. Admitted to the union, 1876.

Colorado Beetle. Potato pest which reached Europe from the U.S.A., 1922. There have been sporadic outbreaks of the pest in Britain since 1933.

Colosseum, Rome. Begun, A.D. 72, by Vespasian. Finished, 80, by Titus.

Colossus of Rhodes, *See* APOLLO OF RHODES.

Colour Bar. C.B. legislation in S. Africa dates from 1912, but there have been frequent amendments and extensions particularly since 1961. C.B. in S. Africa based on Nationalist Government's policy of 'apartheid', which Nationalists translate as 'separate development'. C.B. in the U.S.A. has no basis in legislation and has declined since the 1950s, due in great measure to the 'desegregationist' rulings of the Supreme Court under the Eisenhower Administrations (1952–60), and to the 'Civil Rights' legislation under Johnson (1963–8). In Britain, C.B. is outlawed by the Race Relations Acts, 1965, 1968, and 1976. Some amelioration in S. Africa since 1984.

Columbia, District of, originally an area of 100 sq. m., was ceded by Virginia and Maryland, 1790–1, divided by the Potomac; but in 1846 Virginia recovered her portion. Congress first met in the district, 1800. By its Act of 1895 the city of Washington (*q.v.*) became co-extensive with the district. Citizens of C. were given the right to vote in national elections by the 23rd Amendment to the U.S. Constitution, 30 Mar. 1962. See WHITE HOUSE.

Columbia University (New York, U.S.A.). Founded, 1754, as King's College; re-incorporated as C. College, 1784; the title of university adopted, 1896.

Columbus, Christopher (Cristobal Colón), *b. c.* 1446, *d.* 20 May 1506. Voyages:
1. 3 Aug. 1492–15 Mar. 1493 to San Salvador, Cuba, Haiti.
2. 24 Sept. 1493–11 June 1496 to W. Indies.
3. 30 May 1498–Summer 1499. Possibly American mainland.
4. 9 May 1502–7 Nov. 1504. Gulf of Mexico.

Combat, Trial by, or **Wager of Battle** does not appear to have been customary in England before 1066, except perhaps in the Danelaw. The custom was brought to Normandy from Scandinavia and thence to England, where it was condemned by the Church, 1215, and thus fell into desuetude though still legal. An accused murderer challenged his accuser—who shirked the challenge—and was acquitted, 1817; this led to the immediate abolition of Trial by Combat.

Combination Laws. Various measures, repealed 1824, which had the effect of rendering trade unions or manufacturers' associations illegal.

Comecon. *See* COUNCIL FOR MUTUAL ECONOMIC AID.

Comédie Française. In 1658 the touring company of Molière (*see* FRENCH LITERATURE) settled in the Rue Guénégaud, Paris, under the name of the Illustrious Theatre, where it had only one serious rival, the Hôtel de Bourgogne players. The two troupes were ordered by Louis XIV to amalgamate in 1680, and moved to the Rue de l'Ancienne-Comédie, 1687, and to the Tuileries, 1771. The company split in 1790 into two rival political groups—Théâtre de la Nation and Théâtre de la République, both of which perished before the Comédie was revived in 1802 by Napoleon, who in 1812 laid down regulations which are still largely binding on the company.

Cominform ('Communist Information Bureau'). A body formed at Russian dictation to direct the activities of the Communist parties of Europe, 1947. Yugoslav Communist Party expelled from, 28 June 1948.

Comintern ('Communist International'). Founded, 1919. Formally dissolved, 10 June 1943.

Commando, an Afrikaans word for a military unit, mobile column of varying size under a *Commandant* (roughly, lieutenant-colonel); became familiar to the British when the Second S. African War entered its guerrilla phase (1900 onwards), but had been in use since the early nineteenth century. British Cs. were formed from special service battalions, which themselves were made up of companies, once independent, of volunteers from the Army and Royal Marines, first raised in June 1940, and controlled and trained by Combined Operations Command under Sir Roger Keyes, who was succeeded, 27 Oct. 1941, by Lord Louis Mountbatten. Dates of some C. operations are: 6 Mar. 1941, Lofoten; Nov., Beda Littoria and Cyrene; 27 Dec., Vaagsö; 27 Feb. 1942, Bruneval; 28 Mar., St. Nazaire; May, Diego Suarez, Madagascar; 19 Aug., Dieppe; June 1944, Normandy; Oct., Walcheren. Cs. reverted to Marine command in Oct. 1945.

Committee of Imperial Defence, organized, 1890. Abolished on creation of Ministry of Defence, 1946.

Committee of Public Safety.
1. U.S.A. In Massachusetts, 1774.
2. France. In Paris, 6 Apr. 1793.

Committee of Safety. Formed by officers of the army after retirement of Richard Cromwell from the protectorship, 29 Oct. 1659.

Common Carrier, liabilities of, governed by Carriers' Act, 1830; Railway and Canal Traffic Act, 1854; Road and Rail Traffic Act, 1933; and Transport Act, 1947.

Common Council of London has existed since the fourteenth century; the constitution of its court is virtually unchanged from that period (except that members formerly elected by trades are now elected by ratepayers of wards). Elections take place annually, 21 Dec.

Common Market. *See* EUROPEAN ECONOMIC COMMUNITY.

Common Penny, The (Ger. **Das gemeine Pfennig**). Tax first levied in the Holy Roman Empire to raise money for the Turkish Wars, 1471; renewed, 1496; renewed again for the Venetian War, 1512.

Common Pleas, Court of. One of the old common law courts existing as a superior court of record. Merged in the C.P. division of the high court, 1873, and finally transferred to the Queen's Bench Division by an Order in Council, 1881.

Common Prayer, Book of. *See* PRAYER, BOOK OF COMMON.

Commons, House of. Originated in thirteenth-century practice of calling up knights and burgesses to give information to the government at Westminster. In embryonic form at Simon de Montfort's Parliament, 1265. 'Model' Parliament, 1295. Claimed right to take part in legislation, 1322. Claimed right to originate direct taxation, 1407. Committee of the whole House instituted *c.* 1600. Privileges confirmed by Petition of Right, 1628, and Bill of Rights, 1689. Franchise and basis of representation altered by Reform Act, 1832. Franchise further extended, 1867, 1884. Power to overrule the House of Lords (*q.v.*) given by Parliament Act, 1911, and extended by further legislation under the Labour Government, 1949. Franchise extended to women, 1918 and 1928. Further alterations in system of representation, 1945, 1969. *See* PARLIAMENT.

Commonwealth Day, inaugurated, 1902, as **Empire Day**, on 24 May. Queen Victoria's birthday. Name changed to C.D., 1958. From 1966 celebrated on the day chosen as the sovereign's official birthday.

Commonwealth, English. Lasted from 1649 until 1653.

Commonwealth Immigrants Act, 1962. Provided for restrictions on the number of Commonwealth citizens entering the U.K., and enabled undesirables to be deported to their place of origin. Provisions became law during 1962 (May–July). Further Acts, 1968 and 1971.

Commonwealth Institute (London). Built to commemorate Queen Victoria's Jubilee, 1887, and named the Imperial Institute; opened 1893. Changed its name to the C.I. under the Commonwealth Institute Act, 1958. Queen Elizabeth II opened the Institute's new buildings in Kensington, Nov. 1962.

Commonwealth Relations Office was separated from the Colonial Office, 1925 (under name of Dominions Office), and called C.R.O. from July 1947. The Colonial Office (*q.v.*) merged with the C.R.O., 1966; it was itself merged with the Foreign Office, 1968.

Commune of Paris.
1. The name of the City Council of Paris, set up 21 May 1791, and suppressed, 17 July 1794.
2. The revolutionary socialist government set up in Paris, 18 Mar., and suppressed, 28 May 1871. *See* FRENCH REVOLUTION, THE.

Communism. Karl Marx (1818–83) issued Communist manifesto, 1848. First volume *Das Kapital* issued, 1867. Communist Party of Great Britain founded, 1920. *See* INTERNATIONAL; RUSSIA; BOLSHEVIKS.

Community Relations Commission, estab. 1968 under the Race Relations Act and replaced 1977 by the Commission for Racial Equality (*see* RACIAL EQUALITY, COMMISSION FOR.)

Comoro Islands. French protectorate from 1886 to 1912 (Mayotte from 1841); then a French colony. Attached to Madagascar 1914–47: Fr. Overseas Ter. 1947–75: independent republic since 1975: Federal Islamic Republic since 1978.

Compass. Chinese claim to have invented it, 2634 B.C. Once thought that Marco Polo introduced it to Europe, but now considered that Europeans invented it independently during the twelfth century.

Compromise League of certain Dutch and Flemish nobles petitioned Philip II of Spain to cease religious persecution in Netherlands, 1566. Petition rejected.

Comptometer. Invented by Felt, 1884.

Computer. Babbage (1792–1871) investigated the first mechanical C., but first complete electronic one built in America, 1939–44.

Comrades of the Great War (U.K.). Founded, Aug. 1917, and absorbed in the British Legion (*q.v.*), 1921.

Concentration Camps. Existed in Nazi Germany, 1933–45. *See* separate articles on BUCHENWALD, DACHAU, OSWIECIM.

Concepción, Chile. Founded by Pedro de Valdivia, 1550, on a site seven miles NNE. of the present city. Destroyed by earthquakes in 1730 and 1751 but rebuilt.

Conclave, Papal. Papal election by two-thirds majority of cardinals (*q.v.*), instituted 1179 by Alexander III. Council of Lyons, 1274 (Gregory X), decreed that cardinals should be locked up until the election was completed.

Concord, Book of, a synthesis, together with the Nicene and Athanasian and Apostles' Creeds, of the following Lutheran theoretical works: Luther's Smaller Catechism, 1529; Luther's Larger Catechism, 1529; Augsburg Confession, 1530; Apology for Melanchthon's Confession, 1530; Luther's Articles of Schmalkald, 1537; Formula of Concord, 1577, made 25 June 1580 by order of Elector Augustus of Saxony.

Concordats. Treaties regarding ecclesiastical affairs between the pope and a temporal power. The following is a selection: Worms between Emperor Henry V and Calixtus II, 1122. Nürnberg between German Electors and Eugenius IV, 1447. Vienna between Emperor Frederick IV and Nicolas V, 1448. Against the Pragmatic Sanction of Bourges between Emperor Charles V and Clement VII, 1526, and again between Ferdinand VI of Spain and Benedict XIV, 1753. 'The Concordat' between Napoleon I and Pius VII, July 1801. Annulled, 1905. Between Frederick William III of Prussia and Pius VII, 16 July 1821. Between Mussolini and Pius XI, 11 Feb. 1929; revised C. between Italy and Papacy, Feb. 1984, whereby Vatican City lost territorial rights. Between General Franco and Pius XII, 27 Aug. 1953 (to replace that abrogated in 1931); abrogated Dec. 1978, since when there has been no established religion in Spain. *See also* VATICAN.

'Concorde', *see* AVIATION.

Confederate States of America. The following states seceded from the U.S.A.: S. Carolina, 20 Dec. 1860; Mississippi, 8 Jan. 1861; Florida and Alabama, 11 Jan.; Georgia, 19 Jan.; Louisiana, 26 Jan.; Texas, 1 Feb.; Virginia, Apr.; N. Carolina and Arkansas, May.

Jefferson Davis elected president of the Confederation at Montgomery, Alabama, 18 Feb. 1861. Constitution adopted, 11 Mar. 1861. *See* U.S.A.

Confederation, Articles of (U.S.A.). Signed, 9 July 1778.

Confederation of British Industry, formed Aug. 1965 from an amalgamation of the F.B.I. (*q.v.*), the Brit. Employers' Federation, and the National Association of Brit. Manufacturers.

Confederation of the Rhine. Formed by Napoleon I, 1806, after abolition of the Holy Roman Empire. Dissolved, 1813.

Confucianism. Ethical and philosophical system evolved during the Han era in China (206 B.C.–A.D. 220), but based on the teachings of Confucius (Chin. *Kung Fu-tze*), 551–479 B.C. System in its original form abandoned after 1912.

Congo (Brazzaville), formerly **Middle Congo,** one of the four territories of French Equatorial Africa. It became an independent republic on 15 Aug. 1960.

Congo, *see* ZAÏRE.

Congo Free State was set up under the auspices of the Association Internationale Africaine after the expeditions of Cameron, 1875, and Stanley, 1877, and internationally recognized by the Treaty of Berlin, 1885. Formally annexed to Belgium, 1908. *See* further under ZAÏRE.

Congo, River. Discovered by Diego Cão, the Portuguese explorer, in 1482. Known as **Zaïre River** since 1971.

Congregationalists (Independents, Brownists), under their first leader, Robert Browne (1550–1630), emigrated to Holland, 1581, and to Scotland, 1584. Their greatest period of power and expansion was 1645–60. Congregationalist Union of Scotland formed, 1811; of England and Wales, 1831. Combined with Evangelical Union, 1896. C. established in America, 1620; revival, 1730–40. United with the American Christian Church, 1931. Merger agreed with the Evangelical and Reformed Church, 1956. Congregational Church in England and Wales formed, 1966; united with Presbyterian Church in England to join the United Reformed Church (*q.v.*), 1972.

Congress of Industrial Organizations formed (U.S.A.), as Committee for Industrial Organization, 9 Nov. 1935.

Congress of the United States. The first C. met in 1789, in succession to the Continental C. (*q.v.*).

Congresses, Diplomatic. Principal occasions when sovereigns or their representatives have met to settle diplomatic affairs:

Aix-la Chapelle, 29 Sept.–22 Nov. 1818.

Berlin, 13 June–13 July 1878.

Cambrai, 1722–5.

Carlsbad (*q.v.*), Aug. 1819.

Châtillon, 4 Feb.–18 Mar. 1814.

Constantinople, 23 Dec. 1876–20 Jan. 1877.

Ferentino, 1223.

Frankfort, 16–31 Aug. 1863.

Laibach, 1821.

Paris, Jan.–Apr. 1856.

Prague, 5 July–9 Aug. 1813.

Rastadt, 9 Dec. 1797–8 Apr. 1799.

Reichenbach, 27 June 1790.

Soissons, 1 June 1728; moved to Fontainebleau, 18 Dec. 1729; ended by Treaty of Seville, 28 Sept, 1729.

Troppau, Oct. 1820.

Verona, Aug. 1822.

Vienna, 1 Nov. 1814–9 June 1815.

Connecticut. State of the U.S.A., one of the original thirteen. First settled, 1635; written constitution, 1639, confirmed by Charles II, 1662. Replaced by a state constitution, 1818.

Conscientious Objectors. Term came into prominence during World War I. Special measures taken to deal with C.O. in the Military Service Act, 1916; provision also made for them in the Military Training Act, 1939. C.O. after World War II released from further obligations by the National Service (Release of Conscientious Objectors) Act, 1946.

Conscription. Introduced by Jourdan into France, 5 Sept. 1798. Modern system of call up by age groups introduced in Prussia, 1806. C. introduced in Austria, 1868; Russia, 1870; Germany, 1871; Italy, 1873. Militia service compulsory in Canada, 1868. Introduced in U.K., Jan. 1916–Dec. 1920, and from 3

June 1939 (*but see* MILITIA). C. of women, 1941–6. C. in U.K. ended in 1962. Germany, Austria, and Bulgaria forbidden C. by peace treaties after World War I, but Germany resumed it in 1935. C. re-established in E. Germany, 1956, and W. Germany, 1957. U.S.A. adopted selective C., 19 Oct. 1940, and revived it temporarily during the Vietnam War in the 1970s.

Conservative. Word said to have been invented by J. W. Croker, in the *Quarterly Review*, Jan. 1833, as a more appropriate word than Tory (*q.v.*).

Conservative Party. History goes back to Restoration, but only towards end of 18th cent. begins to assume form like that of present. Disraeli founder of mod. Conservatism. Created Conservative Central Office in 1870. 1895, Liberal Unionists (dissenters from Gladstone's Home Rule Bill) coalesced with Cs. in Lord Salisbury's 3rd government. Between 2 World Wars, except 1924 and 1929–31, C.P. either in power or dominating group in 'National' governments. 1940, Coalition government took office with Churchill, a C., as Prime Minister. 1945 general election: defeated by Labour. Returned to power 1951 and remained until 1964 under Churchill, Eden, Macmillan and Douglas-Home. After losing general election of 1964, C.P. leader to be elected by parliamentary party, instead of 'emerging' as formerly. Douglas-Home resigned July 1964; Edward Heath succeeded him. Defeated by Labour, 1966. Returned, 1970. Defeated by Labour, 1974. Returned, under Margaret Thatcher, 1979: returned again with increased majority, 1983.

Consolidated Fund, first so-called, 1786.

Consols (Consolidated Annuities). An Act of 1731 consolidated certain perpetual and lottery annuities bearing interest at 3 per cent, and these consolidated annuities form the basis of Cs. Rate altered to 2¾ per cent, 1888, and 2½ per cent, 1905.

Constance. *See* KONSTANZ.

Constantine, Algeria, the Rom. **Cirta.** Town destroyed, 311, but rebuilt by Constantine the Great, 312; taken by the Arabs, 710, and the French, 1837.

Constantinople (Turk. **Istanbul).** The ancient Byzantium (founded from Megara, 667 B.C.) rebuilt as capital of the Roman Empire by Constantine the Great, A.D. 330. Seized by Venetians and Crusaders, Apr. 1204, when it became capital of the Latin Empire of the East. Recaptured by Byzantine emperor, Michael Palaeologus, 1261. Captured by Turks, who made it their capital, 29 May 1453. Ceased to be capital of Turkey, 1923. *See* OTTOMAN EMPIRE; TURKISH REPUBLIC; COUNCILS OF THE CHURCH; ROMAN EMPIRE, EASTERN.

Consulate, The. French regime, lasted from 1799 to 1804.

Consuls (mercantile) were first appointed by Italian republics about 1100. Except for a revival in the sixteenth century the custom died out, only to become universal in the nineteenth century. In 1943 the British Consular Service amalgamated with the Diplomatic Service to form the Consular Service.

Consuls (highest ordinary magistrates in republican Rome). Two elected annually and took office on 15 Mar. until 153 B.C.; thereafter on 1 Jan. Office open to patricians alone until *Lex Licinia* (367 B.C.) required one Consul to be a plebeian. C. still appointed in the W. until A.D. 534, and in the E. until 541.

Consumer Law in England and Wales, regulated by the Trades Description Act, 1968; the Hire Purchase Act, 1965; the Consumer Credit Act, 1974; the Unfair Contract Terms Act, 1977; the Fair Trading Act, 1973; and the Sale of Goods Act, 1979. There are parallel Acts applying to Scotland.

Consumer Credit Act, 1974, forms the basis of modern credit law in the U.K.

Contempt of Court Act, 1981, restricts court reporting in certain cases.

Continental Congress first met at Philadelphia, 1774, where all states, except Georgia, sent unofficial delegates to discuss ways and means of resisting the Stamp Act of 1765, and thereafter annually down to 1783.

Continental Drift. Concept put forward in detail by Wegener (1880–1930) in 1910 to explain movements within the earth.

Continental System. The name given to Napoleon I's embargo on trade between Britain and Europe. Begun by the Berlin Decrees, 21 Nov. 1806. Britain retorted by establishing a counter blockade by the Orders in Council of 7 Jan. 1807. The Russian tsar's refusal to co-operate with the C.S. led directly to Napoleon's invasion of Russia, 1812, whilst the English system was partly the cause of the American war of 1812.

Contraception. First clinic opened in Amsterdam, 1881; first in Britain (in London), 1921. Under National Health (Reorganization) Act, 1973, C. administered under the National Health Service.

Contributory Pensions (U.K.). Introduced, 1925. Scope enlarged, 1937. National Insurance Act, 1946.

Conventicle Acts. First passed, 1593. Revised, 17 May 1664. Repeal by Act of Toleration, 1689.

Convention. *See* FRENCH REVOLUTION, THE.

Convention Parliaments. The two English Parliaments convened without royal authority: (1) 25 Apr. 1660, to restore Charles II. (2) 22 Jan. 1689, to offer the crown to William III and Mary II.
Also the Scottish Parliament convened by William III, 1689, for the same purpose as (2).

Convocation.
1. Of Canterbury, first summoned by Archbishop Peckham, 1283. Practically suspended, 1717–1852.
2. Of York, first summoned *c.* 1300. Met only formally between 1717 and 1852. *See* ENGLAND, CHURCH OF.

Conway Castle. Built by Edward I, 1284.

Cook Islands or **Hervey Islands.** Discovered by James Cook, 1773; annexed by Great Britain, 1888; by New Zealand, 1901.

Co-operative Movement. Producers' C. started by Robert Owen at New Lanark, 1799, but declined from about 1828. Consumers' C. opened in Toad Lane, Rochdale, Lancashire, 1844–5. Federation of English Cs., founded 1863 as English Wholesale Society. Central C. Union founded, 1869. First C. bank opened, 1872, in England, though such banks had existed in Germany since 1849. C. Party in Britain established 1917; first M.P. elected, 1919.

Copenhagen, Denmark. Grew up round Axelhuus, a fortress built by Bishop Absalon, twelfth century. Became capital of Denmark, 1443. University founded, 1479. Surrendered to Christian I, 1479; to Christian III, 1536. Captured by Charles X of Sweden, 1658. Danish fleet attacked at, by Nelson and Parker, 2 Apr. 1801. Besieged and taken by British, 5 Sept. 1807. Seized by Germans, 9 Apr. 1940; liberated, May 1945.

Coptic Church. Monophysite Christian Church to which the Ethiopians also belong. It separated from the Orthodox, A.D. 451.

Copyhold Tenure. Abolished in England, 1922.

Copyright (Great Britain). First known grant to Richard Pynson, King's Printer, 1518. In 1642 it was ordered that no book be printed without the author's permission. First C. Act came into operation, 10 Apr. 1710, and gave protection to booksellers for 21 years. Authors protected for a life or 28 years, 1814. For a life plus 7 years, or 42 years at least, 1842. Act of 1911 (life plus 50 years) came into force, 1 July 1912. Modern law (Copyright Act, 1956) came into force, 1 June 1957.

Copyright, International. International C. laws passed in Britain, 1838 and 1852. In U.S.A., 1891. International C. Convention at Berne, Sept. 1886. Revised at Paris, 1896; Berlin, 1908; Rome, 1928; Brussels, 1948; Geneva, 1952.

Copyright (U.S.A.). Petition of Dr. D. Ramsay for C., 5 Apr. 1789. Bill passed, 1790. C. Act, 1831, gave sole rights for 28 years, with power to renew for a further 14. Further legislation, 1870,

1874. Act of 1909 granted 28 years after publication, and after expiration another 29 years to author and his heir. Further legislation in 1928 and 1956.

Cordeliers.

1. *See* FRANCISCANS, MONASTIC ORDER OF.
2. Since early fifteenth century applied to the Récollets or Observant Franciscans.
3. One of the earliest political clubs during the French Revolution, named after the convent in which they met. Many members executed, 24 Mar. 1794. Ordered to be discontinued, 1795.

Cordoba, Spain. Occupied by Romans under the Consul Marcellus, 152 B.C. Taken by Visigoths, A.D. 572. Capital of Moorish Spain, 756. Mosque, built eighth to tenth centuries, is now the cathedral. Reconquered by Spanish, 1236. Captured by French, 1808. Plundered by Carlists, 1836.

Corfe Castle, Dorset, England. Dates from the eleventh century. King Edward the Martyr murdered on its site, 978. Captured and sacked by Parliamentarians, 1645.

Corfu (anct. **Corcyra**), Greece. First colonized from Corinth, *c.* 700 B.C. Allied with Athens, 443 B.C., and so caused the Peloponnesian War. Taken by Romans, 229 B.C. Held by Robert Guiscard, A.D. 1081–5. By Roger, King of Sicily (*q.v.*), 1147–54. Semi-independent till annexed by Venice (*q.v.*), 1386. Attacked by Turks, 1536, 1716–18. Ceded to France, 1797. British protectorate, 1815, till united with Greece, 1863. Bombarded by Mussolini, 31 Aug. 1923 ('The C. Incident'). British destroyers mined by Albanians in C. Channel, 1946.

Corinth, Greece. Legendary foundation by Sisyphus *c.* 1350 B.C. Reached highest prosperity under tyranny of Cypselus and Periander, 655–582 B.C. Oligarchy restored 581 B.C. War with Athens, 459 B.C. Starts Peloponnesian War, 431 B.C. Destroyed by Romans, 146 B.C. Rebuilt by Julius Caesar, 46 B.C. One of earliest Christian churches established at, *c.* A.D. 40. Attacked by Alaric, 395.

Captured by Franks, 1205; by Turks, 1458. Held by Venetians, 1687–1715; by Turks, 1715–1822. Destroyed by earthquake, Feb. 1858. C. Canal opened, 1893. New town destroyed by earthquake, 1928.

Cork, Ireland. Occupies site of a seventh-century monastery. Perkin Warbeck landed at, 1649. Taken from Jacobites, 21 Sept. 1690. Queen's (now University) College founded, 1849.

Corn Laws (English). Passed to raise price of C. Robinson's Act, 1815, only allowed importation when price reached 80*s.* a quarter. Principle regulated by sliding scale under Act of 1828. Agitation against begun, 1836. New sliding scale introduced, 1842. Repealed by C. Importation Act, which came into force, 1 Jan. 1847, but was suspended 1847–8 temporarily.

Cornish Language, a Celtic tongue, was virtually identical with Breton until the sixteenth century. The last C. speaker died in the early nineteenth century, but the last recorded use of the language took place about 1780, though it has been revived in language societies since the 1970s.

Cornwall, England. The Celtic inhabitants of Dyvnaint (Dumnonia) who had once occupied Devon, C., Somerset, and Dorset, were driven W. of the Parret, and thus cut off from S. Wales, by King Coenwalh of Wessex, 658. Egbert, King of Wessex, began campaign against Cornishmen, 815, until they acknowledged his supremacy, 823. The last war of the Cornish against the W. Saxons was undertaken in alliance with the Danes, 836–7. The allies defeated and slew Æthelhelm, Alderman of Dorset, at Portland, but were finally beaten at Hingston Down by Egbert. Made a duchy vested in the heir to the throne by charter, 1337.

Coronation Oath settled in new form for William and Mary, 1689. Modified, 1706, 1821, 1910, 1937, 1953.

Coronation Stone. *See* SCONE, STONE OF.

Corporation Acts (U.K.). *See* CLARENDON CODE and BOROUGH.

Corsica. Successively a Phocaean, Etruscan, Carthaginian, and Roman settlement. Seized by Saracens, tenth century. Given to Pisa by papal bull, 1090. Ceded to Genoa, 1367. Rebellion, 1735, reduced by France for Genoa, 1739. Sold by Genoa to France, 1768. Occupied by British, 8 June 1794. Insurrection, 8 June 1796, led by P. Paoli (1725–1807). Abandoned by British, 22 Aug. 1796. Reoccupied by French, 22 Oct. 1796. Last bandit sentenced to death, 1935. Italian occupation, Nov. 1942–4 Oct. 1943. Anti-Fr. nationalist movement in, since 1970s.

Cortes, parliaments or 'estates' (of gentry, clergy, and burghers), once the legislative body in each Christian kingdom of the Iberian peninsula. They began to assume some importance at the beginning of the eleventh century, that of Leon being quite powerful in 1020. Their decline set in in the fifteenth century. A revived C. in Spain (1812) and Portugal (1822) was simply a name for a constitutional assembly on the French model, and had no real historical continuity. *See* SPAIN and PORTUGAL.

Corunna, Spain. Armada anchored here on the way to England, 1588. Part of town burnt by Drake and Norris, 1589. Sir John Moore killed at C., 1809.

Corvée. Forced labour. Unsuccessful attempt by Holy Roman Emperor, Joseph II, to abolish, 1775. Abolished in France, 1792. In Egypt, 1888–91.

Cosmic Rays. Experiments indicating existence of C.R. carried out by Rutherford and McLennan from 1903 onwards. Actual discovery attributed to Millikan, 1925.

Cossacks. Took Azov from Turks, 1637. Rising against Poles, led by Hetman Chmielnicki, 1648. Defeated at Khotin by John Sobieski, King of Poland, 1673. Treaty with Charles XII of Sweden, 1707. Mostly hostile to Soviet Government during civil war, 1917–22.

Costa Rica, Central America. First settled, 1502. Revolted from Spain and joined Mexican Empire, 1821. Independent, 1823. Part of Central American Confederation, 1824–39. Boundary dispute with Nicaragua settled, 1888; with Colombia, 1921; with Panama, 1921. Army abolished, 1948. Constitution last modified, 1949.

Cotopaxi. Volcano in the Andes, in Ecuador, S. America. Height 19,613 ft. Most violent eruption, 1768. First ascent made by Reid and Escobar, 1872.

Cotton. Introduced by Mohammedans into Europe. Manufactured in Spain, thirteenth century. Italy, fourteenth. England, seventeenth. Bombay, nineteenth. First machines, eighteenth cent: cotton 'gin', 1794. Cotton industry in England in decline since 1955.

Cottonian Library (England). Founded by Sir R. Bruce Cotton (1571–1631). Placed in Ashburnham House, Westminster, 1731, and partly burned. Formed part of original nucleus of the British Museum, 1753.

Council or **Curia Regis.** *See also* WITAN. From Norman feudal King's C. sprang (1) *c.* 1100–*c.* 1250 The Common Law Courts (*see under* COURTS). (2) *c.* 1250–1300 The House of Lords (*q.v.*). (3) *c.* 1350 The High Courts of Chancery and Admiralty. (4) *c.* 1460 The Star Chamber. (5) Early Tudor period other conciliar courts. (6) *c.* 1700–30 The Cabinet. (7) 1833 The Judicial Committee of the Privy Council. *See* COURTS and PRIVY COUNCIL.

Council for Mutual Economic Aid. E. European counterpart to the Common Market (*q.v.*) popularly known as 'Comecon'. Formed 1949. Its members in 1983 were the Soviet Union, the German Democratic Republic, Poland, Czechoslovakia, Hungary, Rumania, Bulgaria, Mongolia, Cuba and Vietnam. Albania ceased to be a member in 1962.

Council of Europe. Established 1949 by agreement of the consultative council of the Brussels Treaty Organization.

Council of Industrial Design. Established by the President of the Board of Trade, Dec. 1944. The Design Centre, Haymarket, London, opened Apr. 1956. Scottish Design Centre opened in Glasgow, 1957.

Council of the Marches. Instituted by Henry VII at Ludlow. Abolished, 1641.

Council of the North. Instituted, 1537, by Henry VIII after the Pilgrimage of Grace (*q.v.*) at York. Abolished, 1641.

Council of the West. Instituted, 1540. Abolished, 1550.

Councils of the Church. All churches recognize the general councils of Nicaea, 325; Constantinople, 381; Ephesus, 431; Chalcedon, 451. The Greek Church recognizes three others in addition: Constantinople II, 553. Constantinople III, 680–1. Nicaea II, 787. The Roman Church another thirteen: Constantinople IV, 869–70. Lateran I, 1123; II, 1139; III, 1179; IV, 1215. Lyons I, 1245; II, 1274. Vienne, 1311–12. Florence, 1438. Lateran V, 1512–17. Trent, 1545–63. Vatican I, 1869–70. Vatican II, 1962–5. Some French authorities substitute for Lyons, Florence, and Lateran V those of Pisa, 1409; Constance, 1414–18; and Basel, 1431–43.

Counter-Reformation. The Roman Catholic reaction to the Reformation (q.v.). First definite move organization of the Oratory of Divine Love, 1517. Franciscans (q.v.) reformed, 1526. Jesuits (q.v.) formally founded, 27 Sept. 1540. Roman Inquisition set up, 21 July 1542. Doctrinal codification carried out by Council of Trent, 1545–63. Establishment of the Congregation *de propaganda fide,* 1622.

Countess of Huntingdon's Connexion, sect of Calvinistic Methodists, founded, 1748, by Selina, Countess of Huntingdon (1707–91), widow of the ninth earl. Most of the chapels now (1985) served by ministers of the United Reformed Church (q.v.).

Countryside Act 1968, by which the National Parks Commission became the Countryside Commission with extended powers.

County Councils created by Local Government Act, 1888 and amended by Act of 1972.

County Courts established by Act of Parliament, 1846; amended 1924, 1934, and 1955.

County Hall, Lambeth, headquarters first of the L.C.C.; and since 1964 of the G.L.C.; foundations laid, 1913; formally opened, 1922.

'Coupon Election.' British General Election of Dec. 1918, which returned Lloyd George's Coalition Government.

Court of Session, supreme civil tribunal of Scotland established, 1532. Sits Oct. 15–Mar. 20 and May 12–July 20.

Courts (English). The following are the dates of the institution and abolition of the principal English C.:
N.B.—C. still in existence in *italics.*
1. Palatine C.: Chester, eleventh century–1830. Lancaster, 1351–1972. Durham, thirteenth century–1972.
2. Common Law C.: Common Pleas, twelfth century–1875. King's Bench, thirteenth century–1875. Exchequer, Henry I–1875. Exchequer Chamber, 1357–1875.
3. Travelling Commissions: Trailbaston, 1290–1380. Of Assize c. twelfth century–1972. Of Oyer and Terminer, twelfth century–1972. Of Gaol Delivery, twelfth century–1972. General Eyre, c. 1150–c. 1360.
4. Statutory Civil C.: Wards and Liveries, 1541–1660. Requests, eighteenth century–1846. *County Courts,* 1846. High Commission, 1558–1641. Probate, 1857–1875. Divorce, 1857–75.
5. Statutory Criminal C.: *Central Criminal Court,* 1834. *Justices of the Peace,* 1590. Quarter Sessions, 1362–1972. Crown Cases Reserved, 1848–1907. Criminal Appeal, 1908–1966. *Crown Courts,* 1972 (replacing the Assize and Quarter Sessions).
6. Conciliar C.: *House of Lords* (q.v.), c. 1250. Chancery, c. fourteenth century–1875. Requests, 1493–1642. Appeal in Chancery, 1851–75. Admiralty, c. 1340–1875. Star Chamber, fifteenth century–1641. *Judicial Committee,* 1833.

In 1875 the Common Law C., and the Cs. of Chancery, Probate, Divorce, and Admiralty were amalgamated into a single High Court of Judicature, from which there was to be appeal to a new Court of Appeal, which took the place of the Exchequer Chamber. In 1880 the Exchequer and Common Pleas Divisions were amalgamated with the King's Bench Division. Court of Criminal Appeal transferred to the

Criminal Division of the Court of Appeal, 1966. *See* COUNCIL or CURIA REGIS.

Courts Martial, instituted in England, 1625–49; up to 1640, officers were tried under royal ordinance by Courts of Chivalry (*q.v.*). Military law, largely influenced by continental custom, did not receive parliamentary sanction up to 1689 (*see* MUTINY ACTS), but from that date until the Army Discipline Act, 1879, C.M. administered discipline according to articles of war. The Army Act of 1881 was in force until amended in 1951 and 1955 by legislation prompted by the Lewis Committee, which reported as a result of the trial for mutiny of some two hundred British parachutists in Malaya, Oct. 1946. Naval C.M., also affected by the Lewis report, were hitherto regulated by the Naval Discipline Acts, 1866, 1884.

Covenant, Day of the. *See* DINGAAN'S DAY.

Covenanters. Supporters of the Solemn League and Covenant (*q.v.*), financed by Richelieu, raised an army, 1639. Negotiated with Charles I, 1640. Beaten at Rullion Green, 1666, and subsequently persecuted, but rose in revolt and defeated Graham of Claverhouse at Drumclog, 1 June 1679. Defeated by Monmouth at Bothwell Brig, 22 June 1679.

Covent Garden Market. The 'Covent' was, in fact, the Abbey of Westminster, and its garden included Long Acre. The whole parcel was granted to John Russell, first Earl of Bedford (1486?–1555) in 1552. The square, with St. Paul's Church (by Inigo Jones), was laid out by the fourth earl, 1631. Piazzas built on N. and E. sides, 1633–4. Market opened, 1634, but present buildings date from 1831. The Market was moved to Nine Elms, Battersea, in 1974. E. piazza burnt down, 1769. St. Paul's Church burnt down, 1795, and restored according to the original plans; rebuilt, 1872. Theatre dates from 1732; present building opened, 1858. Known as Royal Opera House since Oct. 1968. Theatre museum to be opened at by 1987.

Coventry, England, is first mentioned in a document dated 1043, referring to the foundation of a monastery by King Knut Sveinsson, 1016. The first charter to the town was issued by Earl Ranulf of Chester, 1155, and a corporation established, 1345, under Edward III. The legend of Lady Godiva was a tradition, first written down in Roger of Wendover's *Flores Historiarum c.* 1235, and has been fixed on to the historical Godgifu (*c.* 1040–80), a pious lady who was the consort of the almost equally pious Earl Leofric of Mercia (*d.* 1057), the mother of Hereward the Wake and grandmother of the earls Edwin and Morcar. The expression 'send to Coventry' is said by Clarendon, in his *History of the Revolution*, 1701, to have originated in the concentration of Royalist prisoners here by the Parliamentarian garrison of Birmingham, 1647. A German air-raid, 14 Nov. 1940, destroyed the fifteenth-century cathedral church. Cathedral rebuilding began, 1956. Consecrated in the presence of Queen Elizabeth II, 25 May 1962. Univ. of Warwick estab. at, 1965.

Cracow, Poland. Founded *c.* 700. University established, 1364. Capital of Poland, 1320–1609. Taken by Charles XII of Sweden, 1702. By Russians, 1768. Annexed by Austria, 1795. Independent republic, 1815. Again annexed by Austria, 1846. Restored to Poland, 1919. Taken by Germans, 6 Sept. 1939, and became centre of German administration in Poland until stormed by Russians, Jan. 1945.

'Cradle of American Liberty.' Faneuil Hall, Boston, erected, 1742. Burned and rebuilt, 1761. Meeting-place of American patriots during revolution.

Crédit Foncier. Created under official patronage in France, 1852, as a real-estate mortgage agency.

Crédit Mobilier. Set up at the same time as Crédit Foncier (*q.v.*) as a chattel mortgage agency. Taken over by the Banque de l'Union Parisienne, 1932.

Creeds, formulations of Christian faith. Apostles': Earliest mention by Rufinus, 410.
Athanasian: Ascribed to Hilary, Bishop

of Arles, 429–49. No direct connection with Athanasius (*c.* 326–73).

Nicene: Based on C. of Eusebius, 325. Reaffirmed at Council of Constantinople, 381, rest of the present creed except word *filioque* being then added.

Cremation was customary practice for disposal of the dead in Britain until the reintroduction of Christianity, or until *c.* A.D. 600. C. was not practised thereafter until 1884, by the Society for Promotion of C., founded 1874. The C. Acts, 1902 and 1952 control C., which is now (1985) extremely common in the U.K.

Cremona, Italy. Founded by Romans, 218 B.C. Destroyed by Vespasian, A.D. 70; by Goths, 540, and by the Lombards, 605. Passed to the Viscontis in the fifteenth century. Under Spanish control from 1535; Austrian from 1814, and Italian, 1859. The cathedral was begun in the twelfth century.

Crespy or **Crespi,** France, **Treaty of.** Between Francis I of France and Emperor Charles V, 17 Sept. 1544.

Crete or **Candia,** Mediterranean Island. Seat of Minoan civilization *c.* 3500–1000 B.C. (*see* KNOSSOS). Roman province from 66 B.C. Greeks expelled from Carthage by Hassan retire to C., A.D. 698; Saracens seize and make pirate centre, 823; recovered by Greeks 960; sold to Venetians, 1205; besieged and finally taken by Turks, 1645–69; Turkey accepted the major powers' ultimatum in 1898 and withdrew its army; palace of Minos and 'Labyrinth' discovered at Knossos, 1899. At the outbreak of the Balkan War Cretan deputies were admitted to the Greek chamber, and the island annexed by Greece, 14 Oct. 1912; formally handed over to Greece by the Treaty of Peace between Greece and Turkey, 1 Nov. 1913; the annexation of C. by Greece acknowledged by the powers, Dec. 1913; attacked by German airborne troops, 20 May 1941; flight of Greek Government and evacuation of allied forces, 2 June 1941. Germans withdrew, autumn 1944.

Cricket. Said to be a development of medieval 'club ball'. Word first used,

1598. First club formed (Hambledon Club), 1750. M.C.C. founded, 1787. First Test match played by Australia against England, Mar. 1877. 'Bodyline' bowling controversy, 1932–3 Test series in Australia.

Crimea, Black Sea. South C. colonized by Greeks in the seventh century B.C. Later belonged to Rome and Byzantium, and from the thirteenth century to Venice and Genoa. Conquered by the Turks, 1475. Annexed by Russia from Turks, 1783; war declared against Russia by England and France, 28 Mar. 1854; allied armies landed, 1854; war concluded, Apr. 1856. Crimean Autonomous Republic formed, 1921. Occupied by Germans, 1941–3. Crimean Autonomous Republic abolished, 1945, after deportation of the Tatar population for alleged collaboration with the Germans. *See* ALMA, BALAKLAVA, INKERMAN, SEBASTOPOL, *under* BATTLES, SIEGES, and WORLD WAR II.

Criminal Investigation Department, (C.I.D.), the detective branch of the Metropolitan Police, was set up, 1878. Its Special Branch, for the protection of state personages and the suppression of terrorism, was established in 1883 to guard against Fenian outrages.

Criminal Laws of England. Committee formed to inquire into their severity, 2 Mar. 1819; two Acts restricting capital punishment, 1820; eight further mitigating Acts passed soon afterwards, chiefly at the instance of Sir Robert Peel, notably five in 1823; Habitual Criminals Act, 1869; Criminal Law Amendment Act (relating to females), 1885; Aliens Act, 1905; Criminal Appeal, 1907; the Prevention of Crime Act, 1908; the Children Act, 1908; the Criminal Law Amendment Act, 1912. Criminal Justice Act, 1948, transferred responsibility for persons 'detained during His Majesty's pleasure' from Home Office to Ministry of Health. Further modifications as a result of Criminal Justice Acts, 1961 and 1967, by the Criminal Appeals Act, 1968 and by the Criminal Justice Act, 1983.

Cripplegate (London). Rebuilt, 1244 and 1491. Demolished, 1760–1. Institute opened, 1896.

Croatia (Hrvatska). Independent Croat kingdom, tenth–twelfth centuries. Linked with Hungary until the middle of the fifteenth century; then under Turkish domination until the beginning of the eighteenth century. Part of Illyria, 1809–13; subsequently part of Austria-Hungary. At the dissolution of the Austro-Hungarian monarchy, the National Assembly of C. and Slovenia proclaimed their independence of Hungary, 30 Oct. 1918. A composite ministry for the Serb, Croat, and Slovene kingdom (Yugoslavia, *q.v.*) was formed, 29 Dec. 1918. After conquest of Yugoslavia by Germans C. was declared an independent kingdom, 18 May 1941. In 1948 the province became a federal republic. *See* SERBO-CROAT LITERATURE.

Crofters. Small landholders in Scotland. Royal Commission appointed to inquire into condition of, 22 Mar. 1883–28 Apr. 1884; Act for their benefit passed, 25 June 1886; amended, 1888. Further safeguards for C. in the Crofters (Scotland) Act, 1955.

Croix de Guerre. French military decoration, instituted 8 Apr. 1915.

Crossword Puzzles first became a common newspaper feature in the U.S.A., 1923. *The Times* crossword first appeared, 1930.

Crown Courts, estab. 1972 as part of Supreme Court under the Court Act of 1971. *See* COURTS.

Crown Pieces. Gold crown first struck by Henry VIII (1509–47). The first silver crown struck by Edward VI (1547–53). The half-crown originated with Edward VI: and was demonetized, 31 Dec. 1969. Since that reign whole crowns have usually been minted only for commemorative purposes, e.g. Queen Victoria's two jubilees, 1887 and 1897, the Festival of Britain, 1951, the coronation of 1953, in commemoration of Sir Winston Churchill, 1965, and for the silver jubilee, 1977.

Crown, Suit against the, made possible by Act of Parliament in 1947. The crown of Great Britain, in the person of the responsible minister, not of the sovereign, can now be sued, as a result of appeals which went to the House of Lords, 1946.

Cruise, nuclear missile, sited in Britain from 1983.

Crusades. Jerusalem was captured by the Seljuk Turks, 1071, but it was not until 1095 that Pope Urban II was roused by the preachings of Peter the Hermit and appeals from Constantinople to consider a crusade. In Nov. 1095 the Council of Clermont invoked Western Europe to defend the Holy Land. The following are the eight great C.:

First: 1096. Led by (*a*) Walter the Penniless, a Burgundian, (*b*) Peter the Hermit, (*c*) Gottschalk, a German monk. These were disorganized bands and met with failure. The military crusade of 1096 divides itself into four sections: (*a*) Godfrey de Bouillon from the Rhine and N. Germany; (*b*) Hugh, Comte de Vermandois, and others from Central France, Normandy, and Britain; (*c*) Bohemond of Taranto from Italy; (*d*) Raymond, Comte de Toulouse, from Provence, Spain, and Lombardy. Nicaea captured, June 1097, and on 1 July of the same year the Sultan Solyman was defeated at Dorylaeum. Antioch taken, 3 June 1098. Jerusalem, 15 July 1099; and Godfrey de Bouillon elected king, 22 July 1099. Battle of Ascalon, 12 Aug. 1099. St. Jean d'Acre (*q.v.*) reduced, 1104.

Second: Louis VII of France and Emperor Conrad III, 1146. Damascus attacked, July 1148.

Third: Commenced by siege of St. Jean d'Acre (*q.v.*), 1189. Emperor Frederick Barbarossa led an army to Cilicia, 1190. Arrival of Richard I of England and Philip Augustus, 1191. Richard won battle of Azotus, captured Jaffa and Caesarea, 1191. Jerusalem reached, 1192.

Fourth: Set in motion by Pope Innocent III in 1200. Started from Venice, 1202. Led by Boniface of Montserrat and the Counts of Flanders and Blois.

Diverted by Venetians to attack Constantinople, which was stormed, Apr. 1204, and a Latin empire established there.

Fifth: To assist John of Brienne, titular King of Jerusalem, against the Sultan Saphadin, the successor of Saladin, 1217. Led by Andrew of Hungary, the Duke of Austria, the Earl of Salisbury, etc. Damietta captured by the English, 1219. The Emperor Frederick II obtained a ten years' treaty, including free access to the Holy City, 1228.

Sixth: Christians driven out of Jerusalem, 1238, caused two distinct C. together known as the Sixth. (a) French knights led by Thibaud of Champagne and the Comte de Bretagne; (b) arranged at Council of Northampton, led by Richard, Earl of Cornwall, which in 1240 arranged a treaty similar to that of Frederick II.

Seventh: Proclaimed by the Council of Lyons, 1245. Led by Louis IX (St. Louis) of France who, with William Longsword of Salisbury and others, set out from Cyprus in spring, 1249. Louis taken prisoner at the battle of Mansurah, 1250.

Eighth: Led by Louis IX of France and Charles of Anjou. Louis IX *d.* at Carthage, 2 Aug. 1270.

Children's C., 1212 was not a C. in the usual military sense of term.

Crystal Palace. Originally the building of the International Exhibition of 1851. Its re-erection begun at Sydenham, 5 Aug. 1852; opened by Queen Victoria, 10 June 1854; purchased by the Earl of Plymouth to hold in trust for the nation, 1911; destroyed by fire, 30 Nov. 1936; remaining tower removed, May 1941. Sports stadium opened, 1965.

Ctesiphon, Iraq. Capital of Parthian Empire *c.* 150 B.C. Captured by Romans, A.D. 116 and 196. Became capital of Persia under Sassanids, fourth century. Persians defeated at, by Julian the Apostate, 363. Destroyed by Arabs, 637. Scene of a battle between British and Turks, 22 Nov. 1915.

Cuba. Discovered by Columbus, 27 Oct. 1492; colonized by Spaniards, 1511; Havana fortified, 1584; insurrections of slaves, 1844 and 1848; López's expedition against, 1851; revolt for expulsion of Spaniards, 1868–71; frequent other revolts, notably that starting 1895; occupied by U.S.A. after Spanish-American War, 1898–1901, when it became a republic; Gómez insurrection, 1906; Taft of U.S.A. proclaimed provisional governor, Sept. 1906; evacuation of U.S. troops, 1908; further revolutions, interspersed by relatively settled government, 1917, 1924, 1931, and 1933. Batista became president for the second time, 1952, and instituted a dictatorship. Revolutionary movement against him initiated July 1953 by Fidel Castro, who overthrew the government, 1958, and instituted a left-wing regime, with drastic land reform, expropriation, and nationalization of foreign assets, and close ties with the Soviet bloc. Many middle-class Cubans fled to the U.S.A. U.S.A. broke off diplomatic relations with C., 3 Jan. 1961. C. invaded from Florida by anti-Castro forces, 18–20 Apr. 1961 ('Bay of Pigs' incident); the invasion was crushed. Soviet arms build-up in C. apparent in 1962. On Oct. 22 President Kennedy alleged that Soviet offensive-missile sites were being erected in C. and announced a U.S. naval blockade of the island, to start on 24 Oct. Russia retaliated by putting her army on the alert. Khruschev suggested a 'Summit Meeting', 24 Oct., to which Kennedy agreed, but stated that the blockade would continue until the Russian bases in C. were dismantled. On 28 Oct. Khruschev announced that Russia would dismantle the rocket bases in C. and ship them home. On 8 Nov. Russia stated she would allow U.S. Navy to inspect the ships removing the missiles from C. and on 20 Nov. the U.S. blockade was lifted. From mid. 1960s C. actively encouraged left-wing agitation in S. and Central America. Che Guevara killed in Bolivia, leading left-wing guerrillas there, 1967. Cubans involved in left-wing regimes and revolutionary movements in Africa (e.g. Mozambique: Namibia: Zimbabwe) from 1970s.

Heads of Administration since the end of Spanish Rule (1898).

United States Military Governors:
    Brooke 1899
    Wood 1899–1902
President of the Republic:
    Estrada Palma 1902–1906
United States Provisional Governors:
    Taft 1906
    Magoon 1906–1909
Presidents of the Republic:
    Gomez 1909–1913
    Menocal 1913–1921
    Zayas y Alfonso 1921–1925
    Machado y Morales 1925–1933
    Provisional Junta 1933
    San Martin 1933–1934
    Mendieta 1934–1935
    Barnet 1935–1936
    Gómez y Arias 1936
    Bru 1936–1940
    Batista 1940–1944
    San Martin 1944–1948
    Socarras 1948–1952
    Batista (again) 1952–1959
    Urrutia (Jan.–July) 1959
    Torrado 1959–1976
    Castro 1976–

(Castro has been the effective ruler of C. since 1 Jan. 1959; in 1985 was President of Council of State: President of the Council of Ministers and First Secretary of the Cuban Communist Party.)

Cubism. Term first used by artist Henri Matisse, 1908. Exhibitions at Paris and Brussels, 1911.

Culdees (Irish = Companions of God). Religious community, drawing their inspiration from the rule of St. Chrodigang, Archbishop of Metz from 742 to 766, which they introduced into Ireland and into Scotland before 800; converted into canons regular in the reign of David I, King of Scotland (1107–53) on the recommendation of his mother, St. Margaret (d. 1902). As a separate body, had disappeared by 1300.

Cullinan Diamond, found, Jan. 1905, at Premier Mine, Transvaal. Presented to Edward VII, 1907.

Cumbria, administrative county of England estab. 1974 under the Local Government Act of 1972, and based on Carlisle (q.v.).

Curaçao. Principal island of the Netherlands Antilles. Discovered by Spanish explorers, 1527, and acquired by the Dutch, 1634.

Curfew. Said to have been introduced in England by William I, 1068, but probably existed earlier. Still resorted to in various areas during periods of civil unrest, e.g. in Cyprus, 1956, and in the principal cities in Algeria, 1954–62.

Curzon Line. Proposed E. frontier of Poland recognized by the Allies in Dec. 1919 on suggestions by Lord C. but not adopted because of Poland's victory over Russia in 1920. The E. frontier awarded Poland in 1945 (agreed by the Allies at Teheran in 1943) is in fact based on the C.L., with some minor modifications in Poland's favour.

Customs. Granted to the crown in 1275. Commissioners appointed, 1671; consolidation of C., 26 Feb. 1787. C. Consolidation Act, 1876, may be regarded as the principal statute relating to C. Custom House, London, founded, 1559; rebuilt, 1718; new (the present) building, 12 May 1817.

Cyclamates. Use as a food additive banned in Britain, Oct. 1969, with effect from 1 Jan. 1970.

Cycle. Four-wheeled velocipede invented in France by Blanchard and Magurier in 1779; pedals applied to a tricycle by a Dumfriesshire blacksmith, McMillan, 1834; rubber tyres, 1868; bicycles made in England by Coventry Sewing Machine Co., 1869; improved by J. K. Starley, 1874; Starley's 'Rover', with nearly equal wheels, 1885. First C. club, Pickwick Bicycle Club, founded, London, 1870; National Cyclists' Union and Cyclists' Touring Club, 1878. First manufactured in America by A. A. Pope, 1878.

Cyprus. Greeks began to colonize C. before 1200 B.C.; Phoenicians followed, 1000–800 B.C. Subject in turn to Egypt, Assyria, Persia, Greece, and Rome. Arab raids in seventh century. Seized by Richard I of England, 1192, and sold by him to Guy de Lusignan, whose successors ruled C. as independent kings. Made tributary to the Mamelukes, 1426. Catherine Cornaro, widow of James II, ceded C. to Venice,

1489. C. was conquered by Turks, 1570–1; ceded to Britain by Anglo-Turkish Convention, 4 June 1878; annexed by Britain, 5 Nov. 1914. Crown colony, 1925. Church plebiscite showed overwhelming support for *enosis* (i.e. union with Greece), 1950. E.O.K.A. terrorist campaign to promote *enosis* began, Apr. 1955. Archbishop Makarios exiled to the Seychelles, 1956–7. Agreement signed in London by British, Greek, and Turkish premiers, and ratified by Greek and Turkish Cypriots, which provided for C. to become an independent republic within the Commonwealth, 19 Feb. 1959. Makarios became President of C., 14 Dec. 1959. Independence day, 16 Aug. 1960. Turkish resentment of Gk. majority rule led to Turkish invasion, 1974; since then C. divided. Makarios *d.*, 1977. Kyprianou president, 1977. Turkish C. declared itself independent, Nov. 1983, but only recognized by Turkey.

Cyrenaica. *See* LIBYA.

Cyrene. A colony founded from Thera, *c.* 630 B.C., became a republic about 431. *See* LIBYA.

Czechoslovakia. Czechoslovakian Republic proclaimed, with Thomas Masaryk as first president, 15 Nov. 1918. Masaryk re-elected president, 1927; resigned, 1935; succeeded by Beneš. Masaryk *d.*, 14 Sept. 1937. Germans incorporated Sudeten territories, 1 Oct. 1938. Poland took possession of zone beyond the Olza, 2 Oct.; Beneš resigned presidency, 5 Oct.; Father Tiso appointed minister for Slovakia (autonomous), 10 Oct.; Brody first premier of autonomous Ruthenia, 12 Oct.; Germany and Italy fixed new frontiers, 2 Nov.; Poles invaded Ruthenia, 24 Nov.; Emil Hacha elected president.

Slovakia seceded from the Czechoslovak State and proclaimed itself an independent republic, 14 Mar. 1939. Germany invaded and annexed the whole country and proclaimed protectorates of Bohemia, Moravia, and Slovakia, 15 and 16 Mar.; Hungary occupied Ruthenia, and granted it autonomy, 16

Mar.; Czechoslovak National Committee under Beneš formed in Paris, 17 Nov. Provisional Government recognized by Britain, 21 July 1940.

Ruthenia annexed by Russia, but rest of country recovered independence at surrender of Germany, May 1945, and President Beneš returned to Prague. Communist *coup d'état*, Feb. 1948. Jan Masaryk, Minister for Foreign Affairs, committed suicide. Beneš resigned, June, and *d.*, Aug.

Archbishop Beran imprisoned, 1951. Some liberalization, 1963 onwards, and Beran allowed to leave C. and reside in the Vatican, Feb. 1965. In Jan. 1968 Dubcek succeeded Novotny as Party Secretary and a rapid programme of liberalization followed. On 20 Aug. Russian troops invaded C., claiming that action was necessary to prevent a counter-revolution. The end of the new freedoms of press, travel, etc. soon followed. In April 1969 Dubcek forced to resign: replaced by 'hard-liner' Husak. Since 1970 C. has been a compliant member of the E. bloc, all resistance being rapidly stifled as it arises.

Presidents of C. since 1918:
Masaryk 1918–1935
Beneš 1935–1938
Hacha 1938–1939
   (*and President of Bohemia-Moravia,*
   under German 'protection',
   1939–1945)
Beneš 1940–1948
   (*administration in London,*
   1940–1945)
Gottwald 1948–1953
Zápotocky 1953–1957
Novotny 1957–1968
Svoboda 1968–1975
Husak 1975–

Czechoslovak Language and Literature. The sixth-century Byzantine mission of Cyril and Methodius to the Bohemians and other Slavs N. of the Middle Danube gave rise to a certain amount of vernacular church literature. The Caroline University founded by the patronage of the Emperor Charles IV, whose reign (1346–78) coincided with the first flowering of Czech culture, gave Bohemia predominance in arts and letters over the whole W. Slav area. The first printed book in C. was produced at Pilsen in 1468—a *Troan Chronicle*—just six years before Caxton's first English book, *Recuyell of the Historyes of Troye*, came out. *Lexicon Symphonicum*, the first scientific dictionary of the C.L., 1537, the *Elucidation of Grammar* by Jan Blahoslav, 1571, the Kralice Bible, 1579–93, and V. B. Nudozerský's complete Czech grammar, 1603, served to stabilize the language which had finally evolved from its medieval to its modern form before the battle of the White Mountain (1620) began a period of cultural as well as political stagnation, during which German instead of Latin became the official language of the Czech lands (1774) and similarly Magyar replaced Latin in Slovakia. The Prague National Theatre was founded in 1883. The Slovak dialects in the later Middle Ages did not undergo the vowel mutation characteristic of Czech, nor did the Slovak people enjoy any degree of political independence, so that Czech early became the literary language of Slovakia, though there exist Slovak glosses to medieval Latin texts. By the middle of the nineteenth century written Slovak was stabilized largely through the efforts of Ludovit Štúr (1815–56), Mihal Miloslav Hadz (1811–70), and Jozef Miloslav Hurban (1817–88), round the dialects of central Slovakia; Štúr published in 1846 a *Treatise on Slovak Speech*, which was reinforced by M. Hattala's Slovak grammar of 1852–65. Slovak an official language of the republic from 1918.

The following is a short list of authors writing in Czech, including some of Slovak birth mentioned above.

Březina, Otokar (Václav Jebavý), 1868–1929, poet.

Čapek, Josef, 1887–1945, dramatist.

Čapek, Karel, 1890–1938, dramatist and journalist.

Čapek-Chod, 1860–1927, novelist.

Čech, Svatopluk, 1846–1908, poet.

Comenius (Komensky), Jan Amos, 1592–1670, educationist.

Dobrovský, Josef, 1753–1829, philologian and historian.

Hálek, Vitězslav, 1835–74, poet and novelist.

Hašek, Jaroslav, 1884–1923, satirist.

Jirasek, Alois, 1851–1930, poet, novelist, and dramatist.

Jungmann, Josef, 1773–1847, lexicographer and historian.

Kollar, Jan, 1793–1852, poet.

Lützow, Count Francis, 1849–1916, historian.

Mácha, Karel Hynek, 1810–36, poet.

Masaryk, Tómaš Garrigue, 1850–1937, logician and sociologist.

Neruda, Jan, 1834–91, poet and critic.

Palacký, František, 1798–1876, historian.

Šafařik, Pavel J., 1795–1861, critic.

Sládek, Josef Václav, 1845–1912, poet and translator.

Vrchlicky, Jaroslav, 1853–1912, poet.

Zeyer, Julius, 1841–1901, poet.

Czestochowa, Poland. Prominent Polish Marian shrine. Monastery plundered by Hussites, 1430. Defended against Swedes, 1655. Bombed, 1939, but since restored.

Addenda

D

Dachau, near Munich, Upper Bavaria, was the site of a notorious concentration camp, 1933–45.

Dacia. Roman province, partly corresponding to modern Romania. Conquered by Trajan, A.D. 101–6; Aurelian withdrew Roman forces and left D. to the Goths, forming a new province of same name S. of Danube *c.* 275; added to Eastern Empire by Gratian, A.D. 379. *See* VLACHS.

Dadaism, art style, current 1915–22.

Dagestan or **Daghistan,** Asia. Conquered by Peter the Great, 1723; restored to Persia under Tsarina Anne, 1735; re-annexed to Russia, 1813. D. autonomous republic formed, 1921.

Daguerreotype. Invented by Louis Daguerre (1789–1851), a French painter, with the help of J. N. Niepce (*d.* 1833), between 1825 and 1839.

Dahomey, *see* BENIN.

Dail Eireann.
1. Name of a Sinn Fein Assembly, which sat in the Mansion House at Dublin, 1919.
2. Since 1922 the name of the Lower House of the Parliament of the Irish Republic.

'Daily Express', etc. *See under* NEWS-PAPERS.

Dairen, Dalny, or **Talienwan,** Manchuria. Leased by China to Russia as terminus for the Chinese Eastern Railway, 1898. Ceded to Japan, 1905. Restored to China, 1945. *See also* PORT ARTHUR.

Dakar, capital of Senegal. Formal possession taken by French, 1857: became capital of independent Senegal, 1960.

Dalai Lama. *See* TIBET.

Dalmatia. Balkan area subdued by Statilius Taurus, 23 B.C., and by Tiberius, A.D. 9. Diocletian *b.* at Salona (Solin) 245, *d.* at Split, 313. Occupied by Marcellinus, 461. Conquered by Coloman, King of Hungary, 1102–5. Under Venice, 997–1358. Venetian power largely shaken off as a result of the Wars of Chioggia and Negropont (*see under* EUBOEA), 1358–1573. Ceded to Austria by Treaty of Campo Formio (*q.v.*), 1797. Made part of kingdom of Illyria by Napoleon, 1805. Ceded to Austria, 1814. N. D. and D. Islands promised to Italy by Pact of London, 1915, but given to Yugoslavia, 1920. Italy seized Fiume and Zara, 1920. Annexed whole of D., 21 May 1941. Whole of D. returned to Yugoslavia at German surrender, May 1945. *See* DUBROVNIK; SPLIT; ZADAR.

Dalriada, ancient name of the northern half of County Antrim, home of a Scottish tribe whose eponymous ancestor was called Riada; they migrated across the N. Channel to Kintyre, and founded a new kingdom of D. *c.* A.D. 500, of which the nucleus was Argyllshire. The D. Scots were defeated in Ireland at Magh Rath, County Down, 637. By their union with the Picts under Kenneth MacAlpin, 843, the kingdom of Alban was founded. *See* SCOTLAND.

Damascus, Syria. Taken by Assyrians after battle of Karkar, 853, B.C. Finally conquered by Assyrians under Tiglath-Pileser III, 733. Captured by Alexander the Great, 333. Taken by Romans, 63 B.C. Captured by Arabs, A.D. 635. Capital of the Caliphate, 661–750. Attacked by Crusaders, 1126 and 1148. Sacked by Mongols, 1260 and 1399. Conquered by Turks under Selim, 1516. Captured by T. E. Lawrence and the Arabs, 1918. Occupied by French, 1920. Taken by combined Free French and British troops, 21 June 1941. Syrian independence proclaimed at D., 27 Sept. 1941, and D. became the Syrian capital. Coup which ended Syria's first union with Egypt (1958–61) originated in D., Nov. 1961, and that which heralded Syria's second abortive union with Egypt (1963) also started in D.

Danegeld. Tax to buy off attacks by foreign pirates first levied, 991, by Ethelred II. From 991 to 1012, 158,000 silver pounds was so spent. After the murder of Archbishop Aelfheah in 1012 a special tax, called *heregeld*, was levied to pay a standing army. This tax was still collected by the Danish kings Knut, Harald, Hardaknut (1016–42), and by Edward the Confessor, who abolished it in 1051. There is no recorded use of the actual *term* D. before 1066. William I reimposed the *heregeld* tax, under the name D., and his successors continued to collect it until 1163.

Danelaw. Territory covering most of E. England ceded to Guthrum by Alfred the Great in 878, after the battle of Edington. It was largely reconquered by Edward the Elder, but in 940 Edmund I was forced to cede part of the D. to Olaf Guthfrithson, the Viking king of Dublin. Edred campaigned to reassert his authority in the region, and at his death (955) it was acknowledged throughout the D.

Danes, a Scandinavian tribe unknown to Roman authors, even by name. Their kings play a large part in the English epic *Beowulf*, which is now thought to have an historical basis in various events of the late fifth century A.D. They were then settled in what is now southern Sweden (Scania). The D. probably did not move into Jutland and the islands E. of it until these had been vacated by the Angles and allied tribes when they migrated to Britain in the fifth and sixth centuries. The Skjoldung ('Children of Scyld') Dynasty began to dominate the whole Danish group in the eighth century, under Ivar Widefathom, whose uncle Gudröd's (Godred's) reign in Scania can be tentatively dated 720–40. *See* DENMARK, KINGDOM OF, for later history.

Danish Literature. The following is a list of prominent writers in D., both inhabitants of Denmark and authors of Norwegian, Faroese, or Icelandic origin. Some medieval D. writers not mentioned here will be found under LATIN LITERATURE, POST-CLASSICAL, because they produced no vernacular work which has survived. The order is that of date of birth.

Christian Pedersen, *d.* 1554, Bible translator.

Hans Tausen, 1494–1561, Protestant apologist.

Anders Sørensen Vedel, 1542–1616, translator of Saxo Grammaticus.

Arild Huitfeldt, 1546–1609, historian.

Anders Arreboe, 1587–1637, religious epic poet.

Anders Bording, 1619–77, poet and editor of the first D. newspaper, *Dansk Merkur*, which appeared in 1666.

Ludvig Holberg, 1684–1754, historian, poet, playwright.

Hans Adolf Brorson, 1694–1764, lyric poet.

Johan Herman Wessel, 1742–85, poet, playwright.

Johannes Ewald, 1743–81, poet, playwright.

Peder Andreas Heiberg, 1758–1841, poet.

Steen Steensen Blicher, 1782–1848, novelist, poet.

Nikolai Fredrik Severin Grundtvig, 1783–1872, poet, especially song-writer.

Bernhard Severin Ingemann, 1789–1862, novelist, poet.

Johan Ludvig Heiberg, 1791–1860, critic, playwright.

Poul Møller, 1794–1838, novelist, essayist.

Emil Aarestrup, 1800–56, poet.

Hans Christian Andersen, 1805–75, story-teller.

Frederik Paludan-Müller, 1809–76, novelist, poet.

Søren Kierkegaard, 1813–55, philosopher.

Holger Drachmann, 1846–1908, poet, novelist.

Herman Bang, 1857–1912, novelist.

Karl Gjellerup, 1857–1919, novelist.
Jakob Knudsen, 1858–1917, novelist.
Gustav Wied, 1858–1914, novelist,
playwright.
Ludvig Holstein, 1864–1943, poet.
Jeppe Aakjer, 1866–1930, poet.
Gyrithe Lemche, 1866–1945, novelist.
Helge Rode, 1870–1937, poet,
playwright.
Karin Michaelis, 1872–1949, novelist.
Johannes Vilhelm Jensen, 1873–1950,
novelist.
Harry Søiberg, 1880–1954, novelist.
Nils Petersen, 1897–1943, novelist.
Kaj Munk, 1898–1944, playwright.
Jorgen Franz Jacobsen, 1900–38,
novelist.
Mogens Klitgaard, 1906–45, novelist.

Dannebrog, Danish royal standard, first flown at the siege of Reval, 1219 (*see under* TALLIN).

Dannevirke, fortified boundary dike laid out by King Godred of Denmark (*d.* 810) along his frontier with the empire, 808; extended by Thyra, consort of King Gorm the Old (reigned 900–40). Repaired in the nineteenth century, but pulled down by the Prussians after their victory over Denmark in 1864.

Danube, River. Navigation set free by Treaty of Paris, 1856; regulated by Berlin Treaty, 1878; treaty restoring rights to Russia, 1883; Iron Gates Canal opened, 1898; International Commission for regulating navigation, 1904. Danubian Convention Aug. 1948, at Belgrade, resulted in the Danube Commission, 1949, with headquarters at Budapest since 1954, which monitors all rulings of the Convention.

Danubian Principalities, The. Moldavia and Wallachia formed into independent states by Convention of Paris, 19 Aug. 1858; united under title of Rumania (*q.v.*), 23 Dec. 1861.

Danzig, *see* GDAŃSK.

Dardanelles, Turkey, or **Strait of Gallipoli** (the anct. **Hellespont**). Here Xerxes crossed into Europe, 480 B.C. and Alexander the Great crossed into Asia, 334 B.C. Swum by Lord Byron, 1810; Treaty of, signed in London after conclusion of Syrian War, 1841; British and French fleets entered at the Sul-

tan's invitation, 8 Oct. 1853. British and French naval expedition at, 19 Feb.–18 Mar. 1915, was a failure. Land attack, 25 Apr. 1915–8 Jan. 1916; internationalized by the Treaty of Lausanne, 1923; League of Nations agreed to its refortification by Turkey, 1936. *See under* TURKISH REPUBLIC and WORLD WAR I.

Darien Scheme, The. A Scottish attempt to colonize the isthmus of D. (Central America), organized by Paterson, the founder of the Bank of England, 1695. Parliament voted supplies, and the expedition sailed on 26 July 1698; arrived after many difficulties, 30 Oct. 1698; left, 18 June 1699. In 1715 the sufferers from the scheme received compensation.

Dartford, England. Wat Tyler's insurrection began here, 1381. First paper mill in England said to have been erected here, 1590. Road tunnel under Thames completed, Nov. 1963.

Dartmoor Prison (S. Devon). Founded, Mar. 1806, for the reception of French prisoners of war. It fell into disuse after 1815; reorganized as a convict prison, 1855.

Dartmouth, England, was the rendezvous of the fleet destined for the Holy Land, 1190 (*see* CRUSADES). French pirates repulsed at D. after burning Plymouth, 1404; taken after four weeks' siege by Prince Maurice, 1643; retaken by Gen. Fairfax, 1646. Naval college founded at, 1905.

Dartmouth College (New Hampshire, U.S.A.). Chartered, 1769.

Darwinism. Charles Darwin's (1809–1882) works, *On the Origin of Species by Means of Natural Selection,* published in 1859, and *The Descent of Man,* 1871, new edition, 1874.

Dauphin. A southern French title, which from 1364 was always borne by the eldest son of the French king. The first royal D. was Charles (afterwards Charles VI of France), on his birth, 1368. The last D. was Louis Antoine, Duke of Angoulême, son of Charles X, who assumed the title on 16 Sept. 1824. It was abolished after the revolution of 1830.

Dauphiné, having belonged successively to the Burgundian and Frankish dominions, passed to the empire in 1032, and was immediately ruled by the counts of Vienne, one of whom, called Dolphin, gave his name to the province *c.* 1130. The Emperor Charles IV granted it as a fief to the King of France, 1356, and from 1364 to 1830 it was the customary apanage of the heir to the French throne. In 1794 the province was split up into the departments of Isère, Hautes-Alpes, and Drôme.

Davis Cup. International tennis trophy presented by Dwight F. Davis of St. Louis, U.S.A., in 1900 and competed for annually by teams from different countries. S. Africa barred from 1970.

Davis Strait. Separating N. America from Greenland, discovered by John Davis, 1585.

Davy Safety Lamp (for miners). Invented by Sir Humphry Davy (1778–1829) in 1816.

Dawes Plan to provide payments by Germany and to stabilize German currency; settled by a committee of which the U.S. general Charles G. Dawes (1865–1951) was leading member; submitted to Reparations Commission, 9 Apr., and accepted, 17 Apr. 1924. Superseded by Young Plan (*q.v.*) in 1930.

Day of Dupes. 11 Nov. 1630, when Marie de' Medici and Anne of Austria were outwitted by Cardinal Richelieu.

Daylight Saving, the Summertime Act, 17 May 1916, was due partly to the example of Germany which had adopted D.S. earlier in the year, and partly to the efforts of W. Willett (1856–1915), who first proposed such a measure, 1907. British summertime lasted continuously from 25 Feb. 1940 to 31 Dec. 1944, and for all but three months of 1945. During these years, and again in 1947, double summertime was in force from Apr. to Oct. With the British Standard Time Act, 1968, 'summer time' was extended throughout the whole year for a trial period. Under the Summer Time Act, 1972, 'summer time' was re-instated to run from March to October.

D-Day, 6 June 1944, when allied troops landed in Normandy to begin the invasion of Nazi-occupied Europe.

D.D.T., or Dichlorodiphenyltrichloroethane. First prepared by Zeidler, 1874, but not used as an insecticide until 1939. Use restricted in Britain, 1970.

Deal, England. Attempted landing by Perkin Warbeck, 3 July 1495. Outpost of Sandwich until 1699, when it was incorporated.

Dean, Forest of (Glos.). Royal demesne before the Norman Conquest. The Charter of the Swainmote, or Verderers Court, was granted by Knut in 1016. The deer, limited to 800 head by an Act of 1668, had dwindled to ten by 1810, and the last were killed by order of the crown in 1850. An Act to reafforest D. was passed, 1680. Free miners born in the Hundred of St. Briavels, under a charter of Edward I or Edward II, are entitled to mine in the forest on payment to the crown of $1d.$ per ton royalty. This right is not affected by the Coal Nationalization Act, 1947. Last perambulation by Justices in Eyre, 1833. Iron, first worked in prehistoric times, was last worked, 1941.

Debt, National. *See* NATIONAL DEBT.

'Decameron.' Written by Giovanni Boccaccio (1313–75) between 1348 and 1358.

Deccan, India. *See* INDIA.

Deceased Wife's Sister, Marriage with. Bill to legalize first introduced, 1841. Became law in 1908.

Decembrists (Dekabrists). Conspirators involved in the Russian mutiny of officers at St. Petersburg, 26 Dec. 1825 (14 Dec., Orthodox style). The survivors of those who were neither hanged nor shot were pardoned by Alexander II in 1856, after banishment to Siberia.

Decemviri. Magistrates appointed at Rome in 451 B.C. to draw up a code of laws that would secure the plebeians against magisterial caprice (*see* TWELVE TABLES). New commission appointed for 450–449, but they were forced to resign before the year was ended. In 367 B.C. a permanent board of D. was created to look after the Sibylline Books and to celebrate the Apolline and Secular Games.

Decimal Coinage. First used in modern times in U.S.A., 1792: in France, 1799. Under Decimal Currency Act, 1967, Britain changed to D.C., 15 Feb. 1971. ½ penny withdrawn, 31 Dec. 1984. £1 coin in circulation from 1983. S. Africa adopted D.C. in 1960; Australia in 1966, New Zealand in 1967.

Declaration of Arbroath. Letter to Pope John XXII from nobles and clergy, supporters of Robert Bruce, declaring Scottish Independence, 6 April 1320.

Declaration or **Bill of Rights** (English). The foundation of the Bill of Rights declared amongst other things William and Mary King and Queen of England; passed, 1689.

Declaration of Human Rights. Drafting begun, 1946, and subscribed, 10 Dec. 1948, by all member states of the United Nations except the U.S.S.R., Czechoslovakia, Poland, Yugoslavia, Ukraine, White Russia, S. Africa, and Saudi Arabia.

Declaration of Independence, 4 July 1776. *See* UNITED STATES OF AMERICA.

Declaration of London. Concerning contraband and blockade, provisionally ratified by European powers and by U.S.A., 1909. Promulgated by Order in Council, subject to vital modifications, 29 Oct. 1914. Withdrawn by Order in Council, 7 July 1916.

Declaration of Paris, signed by powers attending the Congress of Paris, 1856, and since then by all states except Venezuela, Spain, Mexico, and the U.S.A., renounces privateering and defines contraband of war.

Declaration of Rights (American). Passed by first American Congress at Carpenter's Hall, Philadelphia, Sept. 1774.

Declaration of Rights (Irish). Drawn up by Grattan, demanding legislative independence for Ireland; accepted by Irish Parliament, Apr. 1782, and practically confirmed by the English Parliament in the same year. *See* IRELAND.

Declarations of Indulgence.

1. By Charles II in 1672, by which all Acts against the Nonconformists and Roman Catholics were suspended; this was withdrawn and the Test Act (*q.v.*) passed, 1673.

2. By James II in 1687, similar to the above.

3. By James II in 1688, which was commanded to be read in the churches (*see* SEVEN BISHOPS, TRIAL OF THE). *See also* NONCONFORMISTS.

Decretals. Collection of papal decrees or decretal letters; part of canon law. First collection made by Dionysius Exiguus about A.D. 550; word generally applied to the compilation of Gratian in twelfth century; first official collection, 1210. What are known as the False D. were supposed to have been written between 425 and 450, but had no existence as a whole until about 850.

Defence, Ministry of. Created 5 Oct. 1946; formally instituted, 1 Jan. 1947. Much expanded since 1964.

Defence of the Realm Act.　　　*See* D.O.R.A.

Defender of the Faith (*Fidei Defensor*). Title conferred on Henry VIII of England by Pope Leo X, Oct. 1521, in recognition of his tract against Luther entitled, 'On the Seven Sacraments, against Martin Luther, the Heresiarch, by the Illustrious Prince Henry VIII.' Continued by Parliament, 1544, and since then borne by all British sovereigns.

De Haeretico Comburendo.　　　*See* HERESY, LAWS CONCERNING.

Deira, a kingdom of the Angles, founded by Aelle (reigned 560–88). Ethelfrid had united D. with Bernicia (*q.v.*) by 605, and from then onwards, apart from the period 633–55, the two kingdoms were merged into one as Northumbria (*q.v.*).

Delaware, U.S.A. First explored by Hendrik Hudson, 1609. Takes its name from Thomas West, third Baron de la Warr (1577–1618), who entered D. Bay, 1610. Settled by Swedes and Finns, 1638. Dutch from 1655 to 1664, when it was surrendered to the English. In 1682 the territory was leased to William Penn, and was part of Pennsylvania until 1776. D.–Maryland border stabilized and delineated, 1767. Declared itself independent, 1776. Was the first state to ratify the U.S. Constitution in 1787.

Delegates, Court of. Established, 1534. Abolished, 1832, and its powers transferred to the Privy Council.

Delft, Holland. Founded by Godfrey le Bossu, 1075. The famous earthenware first manufactured here late in the sixteenth century. Diet of D. agreed to throw off allegiance to King of Spain, 1575. Estates of Holland and Zeeland assembled in congress at D. and signed a new Act of Union, 25 Apr. 1576. Assembly of United Provinces arranged constitution, 13 Jan. 1581. William the Silent assassinated at, 10 July 1584.

Delhi, India. The present city of Old D. dates from the mid seventeenth century A.D. (The Red Fort was built in 1652.) Previously taken by Tamerlane, 1398; by Nadir Shah, 1739; by Mahratta, 1759; possessed by Great Britain, 1804. During Indian Mutiny seized by Sepoys, who massacred the British there, 1857; recaptured, 20 Sept. 1857. D. became the official capital of India (*see* CALCUTTA) at the Coronation Durbar of 12 Dec. 1911, when the foundation stone of New D., S. of the old city, was laid. New D. was inaugurated as capital of India, 1931 and remained so after independence, 1947. Delhi Conference, 1940.

Delian League. Organization of Gk. states formed 477 B.C. under Athens to prosecute war against Persia.

Delos. Smallest of the Cyclades Islands, Aegean Sea. Now known as **Mikra Dili**. Became a great trading centre after the fall of Corinth in 146 B.C. Devastated, 87 B.C., during the Mithridatic War.

Delphi (modern **Kastri**). The oracle of Apollo at D. in Phocis was a holy spot before the Hellenic invasion. The fame of the oracle declined after the fifth century B.C., and the treasure-houses in the walled precincts were sacked by the Phocians between 356 and 346 B.C. The Pythian Games (*q.v.*) were held under the protection of the shrine. The last oracle was uttered at the request of the Emperor Julian (reigned A.D. 361–3).

Delphin Classics. Collection of Latin authors prepared by thirty-nine scholars in the reigns of Louis XIV and Louis XV, *Ad usum Delfini* (for the use of the Dauphin, *q.v.*). At first under the editorship of Bossuet, and of the Dauphin's tutor, Pierre Huet, later Bishop of Avranches; published, 1674–1730.

Demarcation, Bull of, 1493. Issued by Pope Alexander VI, dividing New World discoveries between the Spanish and Portuguese.

Demerara, Guyana. Surrendered to British, 1781; again taken by Gen. White, 1796; restored to Dutch, Mar. 1802; recaptured by British, 25 Sept. 1803; ceded to Great Britain, 1814.

Democratic Party, in the U.S.A. 'Democrats' became the only familiar title for the party of Jefferson (anti-Federalist), in 1828; it has controlled the government for the following periods: 1801–41; 1845–9; 1853–61; 1885–9; 1893–7; 1913–21; 1932–52; 1960–8; 1976–80.

Dendermonde or **Termonde,** Belgium. Famous interview between William the Silent and Counts Horn, Egmont and Hoogstraaten, regarding Flanders's relationship with Spain held, 1566. Sluices opened against Louis XIV. 1667. Captured by Marlborough, 1706.

Denmark, Kingdom of. Danes began to achieve European prominence as searovers during the ninth century. Kingdom consolidated by Gorm the Old, 900–935. Jutland ecclesiastical see established, 948. Harald Bluetooth (936–86) baptized, 965. Defeated by Emperor Otto II, 974. Independence established, 983. Svein (986–1014) besieges London, 994. Conquers Norway and kills King Olaf at battle of Svold, 1000. Knut the Great (1018–35) loses Norway, 1015. Becomes King of England, 1016. Defeats Swedes and Norwegians at battle of Helge-aa, 1025. Reconquers Norway, 1028. Break-up of Danish Empire, 1035–42. Valdemar I (the Great, 1157–82) conquers Rügen, 1168. Valdemar II (1202–41) conquers Estonia, 1219. Is defeated by Germans at Bornhöved, 1227. Christopher II concedes royal prerogative to the estates, 1320. Valdemar III cedes Schleswig to Duke of Holstein, 1326. Defeated by Holsteiners at battle of the Dannevirke (*see under* BATTLES), 1331.

Margaret (1387–1412) becomes Regent of Norway and Denmark, and 'Sovereign Lady' of Sweden, 1388. Defeat and conquest of Sweden at battle of Falköping, 1389. Union of Kalmar (*q.v.*), 1397. Kings of D. become Dukes of Schleswig-Holstein, 1460. Defeated by Swedes under Sten Sture the Elder at battle of Brunkeberg, 1471. Revival of union, 1497. Swedish rebellion, 1521; ends union, 1523. Decisive defeat of Hanseatic League, 1535. Reformation, 1537. Wars with Sweden, 1563–70, 1611–13 (Peace of Knaeroed). Christian IV defeated by Tilly at battle of Lutter, 1626. Jutland overrun, 1627. Peace of Lübeck, 1629. War with Sweden, 1644–5. Loss of Scania, Blekinge, and Halland by Treaty of Brömsebro, 1645. Treaty of Roskilde, 1658. Peace of Copenhagen, 1660. War with Sweden, 1676–9 (Peace of Fontainebleau). Cession of Oldenburg to Prussia, 1773. Joins the Northern Confederacy against Britain, 1800. Nelson attacks Copenhagen, 1801. British seize Danish fleet, 2–5 Sept. 1807. D. allied with Napoleon, Oct. 1807. Norway ceded to Sweden at Treaty of Kiel, 1814. Cession of Schleswig-Holstein to Prussia by Peace of Vienna, 30 Oct. 1864. Self-government given to Iceland (*q.v.*), 1874. Prince Charles elected King of Norway as Haakon VII, 1905. Plebiscite in N. Schleswig, which is returned to D., 1920. German invasion, 9 Apr. 1940. German forces surrender, 5 May 1945. D. signed the North Atlantic Pact, 1949. New Succession. Law, 1953, admitted sovereign's daughter to the line of succession: Princess Margarethe succeeded father, 1972. Joined E.E.C., 1973.

Denmark, Sovereigns of:
Gorm the Old   *d. c.* 940
Harald Bluetooth   936–986
Svein Forkbeard   *c.* 986–1014
Harald II   1014–1018
Knut the Great   1018–1035
Hardicanute   1035–1042
Magnus the Good (of Norway) 1042–1047
Svein II Astridsson   1047–1074
Harald III (Hein)   1074–1080
Knut IV the Good (Saint)   1080–1086

Olaf Hunger   1086–1095
Eric the Evergood   1095–1103
Nils   1103–1134
Eric Emune   1134–1137
Eric Lam   1137–1147
Svein III   1147–1157
Knut V (for three days)   1157
Valdemar I the Great   1157–1182
Knut VI   1182–1202
Valdemar II the Victorious   1202–1241
Eric Plough-penny   1241–1250
Abel   1250–1252
Christopher I   1252–1259
Eric Klipping   1259–1286
Eric VI Maendved   1286–1319
Christopher II   1319–1326
Valdemar III   1326–1330
Christopher II (again)   1330–1332
Period of civil war   1332–1340
Valdemar IV Atterdag   1340–1375
Olaf   1375–1387
Margaret, Queen   1387–1397
         Regent   1397–1412
Eric of Pomerania (of Sweden, D., and Norway)   1397–1439
Christopher III of Bavaria   1440–1448
Christian I (Oldenburg)   1448–1481
John   1481–1513
Christian II   1513–1523
Frederick I (not of Sweden)   1523–1533
Period of civil war   1533–1534
Christian III   1535–1559
Frederick II   1559–1588
Christian IV   1588–1648
Frederick III   1648–1670
Christian V   1670–1699
Frederick IV   1699–1730
Christian VI   1730–1746
Frederick V   1746–1766
Christian VII   1766–1808
Frederick (Crown Prince Regent) 1784–1808
Frederick VI (not of Norway after 1814)   1808–1839
Christian VIII   1839–1848
Frederick VII   1848–1863
Christian IX   1863–1906
Frederick VIII   1906–1912
Christian X   1912–1947
Frederick IX   1947–1972
Margarethe   1972–

Deodand. Objects which had caused human death were forfeited to the crown as Ds. till 1846.

Department of Economic Affairs
(**D.E.A.**), estab. 1964; abolished 1970.

Départements. France divided into eighty-three, 1790. Napoleon divided France into 130 D., but the number of metropolitan D. is now (1985) 96.

Deposition, Bull of.
1. 1535, issued by Pope Paul III, excommunicating Henry VIII.
2. 1570, issued by Pius V ex-communicating Elizabeth I.

Deptford. Henry VIII's dock (established 1512) here used until 1869; Peter the Great (*see* RUSSIA) came here to study shipbuilding, 1689. Royal victualling yard of the Navy established at, 1745.

Deputies, Chamber of.
1. Lower house of French legislature so named under Louis XVIII, 1814. Dissolved by Charles X, 1827, and 16 May 1830. Superseded by National Assembly, 4 May 1848. Restored by Louis Napoleon, 2 Dec. 1851. During the Second Empire (1852–70) replaced by a 'Corps législatif'. Restored under Third Republic (1871–1940). Replaced by National Assembly, 1946.
2. Lower house of Belgian Parliament so named, 1831. Known as the Chamber of Representatives since 1921.

Derby. The original Anglian settlement was called Northworthige; this was captured *c.* 870 by the Danes, who renamed it D. It was retaken by the English, 917. First sent burgesses to Parliament, 1295. Grammar school built, 1554. Silk mills first set up, 1717: porcelain manufactured from 1770. Canal opened, 1836. Bishopric created, 1907.

Derby Day, second day of the summer meeting at Epsom, in late May or early June, when the D. Stakes, instituted 4 May 1780, are run for. Until 1891 Parliament adjourned specially on this day. The Kentucky D. is a celebrated annual horse race in the U.S.A.

Derry. *See* LONDONDERRY.

Despard's Plot, to assassinate George III, 1802. Col. D. and plotters executed, 21 Feb. 1803.

Detroit, U.S.A. First settled by Antoine Cadillac, 24 July 1701. Originally called *La Ville d'Étroit.* Centre of car industry since the beginning of the twentieth century.

Deventer, Holland. Taken by Maurice of Saxony from Spaniards, 10 June 1591.

Devil's Island. In the Îles du Salut group, N.W. of Cayenne, French Guiana. Was notorious for its penal settlement, 1854–1938.

Devil's Parliament. Met at Coventry, 1459.

Devonport. *See* PLYMOUTH.

Diamond. Manilius spoke of it, A.D. 16; Pliny said it was known only to kings, A.D. 100, and described six varieties. Mined in India from earliest times till the close of the nineteenth century; S. America from the middle of eighteenth century; S. Africa (discovered accidentally), 1870. Phosphorescence produced by friction discovered by Robert Boyle, 1663; combustibility established by Florentine academicians, 1694. Smithson Tennant demonstrated carbon composition of Ds., 1796. *See also* KOH-I-NOOR and CULLINAN DIAMOND.

Diamond Necklace Affair   (France). Queen Marie Antoinette, the Comtesse de Lamotte, the impostor Cagliostro, and the Cardinal de Rohan were implicated, 1785; Rohan's trial, 14 Apr. 1786. The countess was condemned, but escaped; Rohan was acquitted.

Diamond Sculls. Race for amateur single rowers instituted at Henley, 1844.

Dictionary. A Chinese D. by Hū Shin, containing 10,000 characters, published, 150 B.C.; Italian D. of the Accademia della Crusca published, 1612; Samuel Johnson's D., 1755; Noah Webster's, 1828 (now expanded into *Webster's New International Dictionary*, 1936); Sir William Smith's *Dictionary of Greek and Roman Antiquities*, 1842, *Biography*, 1849, *Geography*, 1857; Liddell and Scott's, 1843; Littré's French D., 1863–72; *Dictionary of National Biography*, edited by Leslie Stephen and Sidney Lee, 1885–1900; Funk's, 1893–5; Murray's *New English Dictionary* initiated,

1857; preparation for publishing began, 1879; first fascicule published, 1884; completed 1928; re-issued with supplement, as *Oxford English Dictionary*, 1933.

Dien-Bien-Phu, Vietnam. Scene of the final battle between French and Viet Minh forces in the 1945–54 Indo-China War. The Viet Minh captured the French positions, May 1954, with heavy losses to both sides.

Dieppe, Normandy. Occupied by the English, 1420–35. Bombarded by British, July 1694; 1794; 14 Sept. 1803. Occupied by Germans, Dec. 1870–July 1871, and again 10 June 1940. Anglo-Canadian landing at, 18–19 Aug. 1942. Liberated, 1 Sept. 1944, by same Canadian unit as had landed in 1942.

Diesel Engine. First model built, 1893–7, by Rudolf Diesel (1858–1913).

Diet. The following are the principal Ds. of the Empire, with their dates:
Augsburg, (*a*) 1530; (*b*) 1555.
Maglione, 1502.
Roncaglia, 12 Nov. 1158.
Speyer, (*a*) 1526); (*b*) 1529.
Worms, (*a*) 1495; (*b*) 1521 (associated with Martin Luther); (*c*) 1547; (*d*) 1578.
See also REICHSTAG.

'Dieu et mon Droit' ('God and my Right'). The parole of the day at the battle of Gisors, 20 Sept. 1198, at which Richard I was present. It first appeared on the Great Seal of Henry VI; discontinued by Queen Anne, but restored by George I.

Diggers' Conference, in Victoria, Australia, was a 'shadow' parliament, which demanded representation on the Legislative Council, 1854.

Dijon, France. Roman *Divonense Castrum*. Capital of Burgundy, 1180. Joined to French crown, 1477. Capitulated to Germans, Oct. 1870.

Dingaan's Day, anniversary of the victory of Pretorius's commando over D. at Blood River, 16 Dec. 1838. Now officially known as the **Day of the Covenant.** *See* VOORTREKKERS; ZULUS; TRANSVAAL.

Directors' Liability Act (Great Britain). Passed, 18 Aug. 1890, now contained in amended form in the Companies Act, 1948.

Directory, French. The Government established in France after the Convention, 27 Oct. 1795; abolished, 9 Nov. 1799.

Directory of Public Worship drawn up by Westminster Assembly of Divines, 1644; accepted by Scottish General Assembly, Feb. 1945.

Disestablishment. For D. of Anglican Church in Ireland, *see* IRELAND; in Wales, *see* WALES, CHURCH OF. The Church of Scotland virtually disestablished itself at the time of its union with the United Free Church in 1929. In France the Roman Catholic Church was disestablished in 1793–1801, and again in 1906.

Dissenters. *See* NONCONFORMISTS and PURITANS.

Dissolution of Monasteries. *See* MONASTERIES.

District Councils (England and Wales) first established by Local Government Act, 1894: a new form of D.C. resulted from the Local Government Act of 1972.

'Divine Comedy.' Begun probably in 1300 by Dante Alighieri (1265–1321). First printed, 1472.

Divine Right of Kings. The doctrine emphasized in opposition to the temporal claims of the Papacy and used as theoretical justification of secular interference in ecclesiastical affairs during and after the Reformation (*q.v.*), and of royal supremacy in secular affairs especially in England by James I (1603–25) and Charles I (1625–49).

Diving Bell. First used in Europe *c.* 1538.

Divorce (Britain). D. Court established, 1857; D. Amendment Act passed, 21 July 1868. Lord Buckmaster's Bill received royal assent, 1923. A. P. Herbert's Matrimonial Causes Act gave new grounds for decrees both of nullity and of D. – notably, incurable insanity, 1937; operating, Jan. 1938. Matrimonial Causes Act, 1973, radically liberalized divorce laws in Britain, making sole ground for D. irretrievable breakdown of marriage. Further amendments, 1984.

Djibouti, republic in Gulf of Aden, formerly Fr. Somaliland. Acquired by France 1856–83. Independent 1977, with cap. at D.

Dobruja. Bulgaria and Rumania. Ceded to Rumania, 1878 and 1913. To Bulgaria by Treaty of Bucharest, 1918. To Rumania again, 1919. Southern part to Bulgaria, 1940; confirmed by peace treaty of 1947.

Docking and Nicking of Horses Act, 1947. Makes docking of horses illegal (except on veterinary advice).

Doctors' Commons. College for doctors of civil and canon law established by Dr. Harvey, 1567. Charter, 1768. Dissolved, 1857.

Doctors of the Church. These were, traditionally, SS. Gregory the Great; Ambrose; Augustine of Hippo; Jerome; John Chrysostom; Basil; Gregory Nazianzen; Athanasius.

The foregoing were acknowledged as D. of the C. by the early Middle Ages. The following were so declared, in the years shown, by papal decree: SS. Thomas Aquinas, 1568; Bonaventure, 1588; Anselm, 1720; Isidore, 1722; Peter Chrysologus, 1729; Leo I, 1754; Peter Damian, 1828; Bernard of Clairvaux, 1830; Cyril of Alexandria, 1833; Cyril of Jerusalem, 1833; John of Damascus, 1833; Hilary of Poitiers, 1851; Alphonsus Lignori, 1871; Francis de Sales, 1877; The Venerable Bede, 1899; Ephrem, 1920; Peter Canisius, 1925; John of the Cross, 1926; Albert the Great, 1931; Robert Bellarmine, 1931. In 1970 the first two women to be declared Doctors of the Church were SS. Catherine of Siena and Teresa of Avila.

Dodecanese Islands. Seized by Italy from Turkey, 1912. Greece gave up claim in favour of Italy, 1920. Formally incorporated in Greece, 1948.

Dodo. Last living specimen seen, 1681.

Dog Licence, fixed at 7s. 6d. per annum (now 35p.) 1878, by Act of Parliament.

Doge. *See* VENICE.

Doggett's Coat and Badge. Thomas Doggett the actor (d. 1721) awarded prize of coat and badge to winner of annual race on Thames by six watermen, instituted 1 Aug. 1715, in honour of George I's accession.

Dole. Popular name for unemployment benefit, first became current, 1919–20.

Dollar, Thaler, Taler, originally **Joachimsthaler.** Coins, the currency of the Hapsburg dominions, were so called from the place in Bohemia (Cz. Jachymov), where they were first coined in 1519. Brought into common use in the U.S.A. *c.* 1794, having been officially introduced in 1787. Australia adopted a D. in its decimal coinage system, 1966.

Dollar Diplomacy. Associated with the Taft administration in the U.S.A., 1908–13, and repudiated by its Democratic successor.

Dolly's Brae, near Newcastle, County Down, was scene of riot, 12 July 1849, between Orange and Catholic factions, involving fatal casualties.

Domesday or **Doomsday Book.** Compiled as a survey for taxing and administrative purposes and also to obtain general information about his new territories by order of William the Conqueror, 1085–6.

Dominica, largest of the Windward Islands. Discovered by Columbus, 1493; settled by French, 1632; ceded to Great Britain by Treaty of Paris, 1763; French possession, 1778–83; to Great Britain by Treaty of Versailles, 1783; attacked by French, 2 Feb. 1805; finally restored to Great Britain, 1814. Independent republic, 3 Nov. 1978.

Dominican Order. Founded by St. Dominic (1170–1221) in 1216, who obtained a bull from Pope Honorius III. First chapter held at Bologna, 1220. In England they were known as Black Friars, and in 1221 set up a house in Oxford by permission of Stephen Langton.

Dominican Republic or **Santo Domingo.** E. portion of Hispaniola (q.v.). Discovered by Columbus, 1492; colony founded by his brother, Bartholomew, 1496. Ceded by Spain to France, 1795. Part of independent state of Haiti (q.v.), 1798–1801, French, 1801–3. Part of Haiti again, 1804–8.

British helped Spaniards to drive out French, 1809. Assured to Spain by Treaty of Paris, 1814. Declared its independence, as 'Columbia', 1821. Part of Haiti again, 1822–43. Became the independent D.R., 1844. Once more Spanish, 1861–3. Republic reconstituted, 1865. Occupied by U.S. forces, 1916–23. Rafael Trujillo carried out *coup d'état* and became dictator of the D.R., 1930–61. In 1965 the U.S.A. sent a force of Marines to D., fearing a Communist take-over. Constitutional gov. restored, 1966.

Dominions of the Commonwealth. Canada, (*q.v.*) became the first D. in the Commonwealth in 1867. Subsequently the majority of former Brit. colonies have become Ds. (see under separate entries). Ds. which subsequently left the Commonwealth were the Republic of Ireland (1949), South Africa (1961) and Pakistan (1971).

Dominions Office. *See* COMMONWEALTH RELATIONS OFFICE.

Doncaster, England. First charter granted by Richard I, 1194. Conference held here at which Henry VIII granted pardons (later dishonoured) to partakers in the Pilgrimage of Grace (*q.v.*), 6 Dec. 1536. Famous horse race instituted by Col. St. Leger, 1776.

Dongan Charter, granted to New York City (*q.v.*) by Thomas Dongan, governor of the city, 1686.

Donnybrook Fair, outside Dublin, was licensed 1204; abolished, 1855.

D.O.R.A. (Defence of the Realm Acts). First of the series was passed 27 Nov. 1914; extended to supply and sale of liquor, May 1915. Ceased to operate, 31 Aug. 1921; but the D.O.R. (Acquisition of Land) Acts, 1916 and 1920, operated for five years after end of war.

Dorchester (Dorset). Rom. foundation. Besieged and burnt by the Danes, 1003; fortified by Parliamentarians, 1642–3. The famous Bloody Assizes (*q.v.*) held here, 1685.

Dorchester (Oxon). Rom. foundation. Cynegils, King of the W. Saxons, baptized here by St. Birinus, A.D. 634.

Dordrecht or **Dort,** Netherlands. The meeting-place of the States of Holland after their revolt from Spain, 1572. The famous Synod of D., the first general synod of the Protestants, assembled 13 Nov. 1618, and finished 25 May 1619.

Dortmund-Weser-Ems Canal. Stretch of the Ems canalized, 1892–9. The banks breached by the R.A.F., causing complete draining of the canal, 4 and 21 Nov. 1944; 1 Jan. and 3 Mar. 1945.

Douai, France. Taken from Flemings by Philip the Fair, 1297; restored, 1368. Acquired by Spain, 1529. Attempted seizure by Admiral Coligny failed, 6 Jan. 1557; taken by Louis XIV, 1667; surrendered to Marlborough, 26 June, 1710; retaken 8 Sept. 1712; Roman Catholic English College founded at, 1568; refounded in England at Ushaw and Ware after the French Revolution. There was a Catholic school for English boys at D. from 1818 to 1903, when it moved to Woolhampton, Berks. The D. version of the Old Testament, published here by command of the pope, 1609–10.

Douglas Rebellion. Headed by William, Earl of Douglas, 1451, as a result of the appointment of Sir William Crichton by James II of Scotland. Douglas murdered by James II in Feb. 1452. Rebellion carried on by relatives, but finally suppressed in 1484.

Dover, England. Originally *Dwyr*, latinized as *Dubris*. One of the Cinque Ports (*q.v.*). King John resigned his kingdom to the papal legate at, 13 May 1213. The Emperor Charles V met by Henry VII at, 1520. Charles II landed here after his exile, 26 May 1660. Treaty of D. between Charles II and Louis XIV, 1670. New naval harbour opened, 1909. Repeatedly bombarded, 1941–4.

Dover Patrol. Established during World War I to maintain cross-Channel communications (1914–18). Monitors added, 1915. Frequent small raids by enemy, 1915–17. *Broke* and *Swift* defeated six destroyers, Apr. 1917. War memorial to D.P. erected on French coast after World War I destroyed by the Germans during World War II. Rebuilt memorial unveiled, 7 July 1962.

Downing Street (London). Named after

Sir George Downing (c. 1623–84). No. 10 has been the official residence of the Prime Minister since the time of Sir Robert Walpole. Renovated 1960–3.

D'Oyly Carte Opera Company. Richard D'Oyly Carte (1844–1901) in 1875 produced *Trial by Jury*, the first of the works of W. S. Gilbert (1836–1911) and Arthur Sullivan (1842–1900) to be publicly performed; he built the Savoy Theatre, 1881, and the English Opera House (now Palace Theatre, Cambridge Circus), 1891. The company controlled the copyright in words and music of Gilbert and Sullivan until 1961, after which other companies could perform the operas. It was disbanded, 1982.

Draft Riots (New York), to resist drafting of citizens into the Union Army, 1863.

Drama. Comedy said to have been introduced from Megara into Attica c. 580 B.C. Theatrical exhibitions first seen in Rome, 364 B.C. Mystery plays, the origin of D. in England, were performed as early as 1136 at Dunstable. The first original secular play extant is Udall's *Ralph Roister Doister*, written about 1531. The servants of the Earl of Leicester obtained in 1574 a patent for performing plays in any part of England, and in 1576 they built a theatre at Shoreditch, which was the first public building of its kind in England. Shakespeare, with others, received a similar patent, 19 May 1603. The theatres were all closed by a Parliamentary Act on 2 Sept. 1642. In 1737 plays were ordered to be revised and licensed by the Lord Chamberlain. *See also* CENSORSHIP OF THE THEATRE.

Drama (American). In 1733 there appears a mention of a theatrical performance in New York. A performance of Otway's *Orphans* was enacted in 1750. *The Beaux' Stratagem* was performed by a company of London actors at Annapolis, 1752.

'Drapier's Letters.' In 1722 the English Government gave contract for making Irish copper coinage to a Mr. William Wood, of Wolverhampton. This aroused the resentment of the Irish, resulting in the pub. of *Drapier's Letters*, by Dean Swift, 1724 and the withdrawal of the coinage.

Dreadnought, name of a battleship launched in 1906, the prototype of a class of Royal Naval battleships known as Ds., which continued to be built up to 1914.

Dred Scott Case, a test case in the slavery question, arose in 1848, and was finally decided on appeal to the Supreme Court, 1857.

Dresden, Germany. Capital of the Margravate of Meissen, 1270; seat of the Albertine line from 1485. Destroyed by fire and rebuilt in 1685; celebrated congress held by Napoleon, 1812; besieged by the allied armies on 26 Aug. 1813; capitulated after Napoleon had left on 11 Nov. 1813; occupied by Prussians, 1866. Bombed and severely damaged by British and American air forces, 13–14 Feb. 1945. Entered by the Russians, 8 May 1945. 'Dresden china' has been made at Meissen (q.v.) since 1710.

Dresden, Treaty of, between Frederick the Great and Maria Theresa of Austria, 25 Dec. 1745.

Dreyfus Case (France). Capt. Alfred Dreyfus (1859–1935) sentenced for high treason, Dec. 1894. New trial ordered through Émile Zola's exertions. Dreyfus again found guilty, 1899, but pardoned. Case reopened and Dreyfus declared innocent, July 1906. Dreyfus awarded the Legion of Honour, 1919.

Driving Licences. Procedure governed by the Road Traffic Acts of 1930, 1934, 1956, 1960, 1972 and 1974, and the Vehicle and Driving Licences Act, 1969.

Drogheda, Republic of Ireland. Here the chiefs of Ulster did homage to Richard II, 1395, and Poyning's Law (q.v.) was enacted, 1494. Stormed by Oliver Cromwell and garrison massacred, 11 Sept. 1649. Surrendered to William III, 1690.

Drug Addiction first became a social problem in Britain in the 1960s, notably among a section of the young. The Misuse of Drugs Act 1971, was intended to consolidate existing anti-drug legislation, i.e. the Pharmacy and Poisons Act, 1933, the Drugs (Prevention of Misuse) Act, 1964, and the Dangerous Drugs Acts, 1965 and 1967 and to distinguish between unlawful possession and trafficking, substantially increasing the penalties for the latter.

Drunken Parliament (Scotland), 1661.

Drury Lane was known as Aldwych Way until the reign of Elizabeth I, when it was an aristocratic quarter taking its present name from Drury Place, a fifteenth-century house owned by the Drury family. The street became increasingly disreputable from about 1690 onwards, until the clearance of the whole neighbourhood when Aldwych and Kingsway were built, 1899–1905. D.L. Theatre Royal is the fourth to be built on this site; the first opened, 1663, and was burnt down, 1672. The second, designed by Wren, opened, 1674. Sheridan and his partners acquired it from David Garrick, 1776; they pulled it down in 1791, and opened the third theatre, 1794, but this was destroyed by fire, 1809. The fourth theatre, opened 1812, is now (1985) the oldest theatre open in London for regular performances.

Druses. Reformed Moslem sect in Syria and the Lebanon, whose separate existence dates from the early eleventh century. They led an unsuccessful rebellion against the French, 1925–6, and have supported the Palestinian Arabs in Lebanon since the 1970s.

Dual Alliance between France and Russia. Began with contacts established 1887; agreement to co-operate in the Far E., 1891; understanding maintained at accession of Nicholas II, 1894; alliance proclaimed, 26 Aug. 1897; pact of mutual assistance between France and U.S.S.R. signed, 2 May 1935.

Dual Monarchy. Name given to the Austrian Empire, formed by the union of Austria and Hungary from 1867 until 1917.

Dublin (Baile-atha-Cliath), Ireland. St. Patrick is said to have visited D. in 448, but the Norsemen are regarded as the real founders of the city (eighth century). D. was sacked by the Danish leader Ragnar, 831, and captured by Olaf the White, 852. Battle of Clontarf fought near, 1014. Christ Church founded by Sihtric, 1038. Possessed by Crovan, King of Man, 1066. The Earl of Pembroke (Strongbow) captured it, 1170. Many citizens murdered by Irish of surrounding hills, Easter Monday, 1209—the day known as 'Black Monday'. Castle completed, 1220. Besieged by Edward Bruce, 1315. Visited by Richard II, 1394. Bull for the foundation of a university published, 1475. Trinity College founded, 1591. Oliver Cromwell arrived at, Aug. 1649. Visit of James II, who held a Parliament, 1688. Catholic pro-cathedral completed, 1825. National University of Ireland founded, 1909. Sinn Fein rebels, in rising that began 24 Apr. 1916, held G.P.O., City Hall, Four Courts, and Stephen's Green. G.P.O. burned in last days of Apr. Since the treaty of 1921 the capital of the Irish Free State, now the Republic of Ireland. Insurgents opposed to treaty took possession of Four Courts, 14 Apr. 1922, and maintained their hold until 30 June, when, after three days' siege (by Free State troops), they wrecked the building by explosion, destroying the records.

Dubrovnik, formerly **Ragusa,** founded in the seventh century by fugitives from the neighbouring town of Epidaurum. In the Middle Ages was a rival of Venice, but its importance declined after 1497, and still further during sixteenth and seventeenth centuries. The republic preserved its independence, though under Turkish suzerainty until 1808, when it was incorporated in Dalmatia (*q.v.*)

Duelling. Forbidden in England by an Act of Oliver Cromwell, 1654. Charles II also issued a proclamation against D., 1679. Anti-D. Association formed in England, May 1843; and three articles of war were issued in 1844 to prevent the practice in the Army. Last recorded duel in England was fought at Egham Hill, Surrey, in 1852.

Famous Duels:

Duke of Hamilton and Lord Mohun, both died. 15 Nov. 1712.

S. Martin wounded John Wilkes, M.P. 16 Nov. 1763.

Lord Byron killed Mr. Chaworth. 26 Jan. 1765.

Charles James Fox wounded by Mr. Adam. 30 Nov. 1779.

William Pitt and George Tierney. 27 May 1796.

Henry Grattan wounded Isaac Corry. 15 Jan. 1800.

Lord Castlereagh wounded George Canning, 21 Sept. 1809.

Duke of Wellington and Earl of Winchelsea. 21 Mar. 1829.

Duc de Grammont-Caderousse killed Mr. Dillon, Paris. Oct. 1862.

Don Enrique de Bourbon killed by Duc de Montpensier, near Madrid. 12 Mar. 1870.

Léon Gambetta and De Fortou, neither hit. 21 Nov. 1878.

Gen. Boulanger, seriously, and M. Floquet, slightly wounded, 13 July 1888.

Dukhobors. Russian heretic sect, sprang up during the eighteenth century. From 1755 to 1864 their leaders claimed to be reincarnations of Christ. Migrated to Canada, 1898–9.

Dulwich College. Founded and endowed by Edward Alleyn, 1619. In 1857 the college was reconstituted by special Act of Parliament and formed into D.C. and Alleyn's School (also in Dulwich).

Duma (Russian). Council of State created, 6 Aug. 1905. Abolished at Oct. Revolution, Nov. 1917.

Dumbarton Oaks, D.C., U.S.A., was the scene of a conference between the U.S.S.R., Great Britain, and the U.S.A., 21 Aug.–27 Sept., and between Great Britain, the U.S.A., and China, 29 Sept.–7 Oct, 1944, the outcome of which was the United Nations Organization (*q.v.*).

Dumfries, Scotland, derived its early importance from a bridge over the Nith, built 1280. John Comyn the Red was here assassinated by Bruce's followers for compounding with the English, 1306. Robert Burns (*d.* 1796)

lived in D. for the last five years of his life, and is buried here.

Dunces, Parliament of. Met at Coventry, 1404; also known as Unlearned Parliament, so called because no lawyer had a place in the assembly.

Dundee, Scotland. Taken by English under John of Gaunt, 1385. Sacked by Montrose, 1645. Besieged by Gen. Monk after battle of Worcester, 1651. Tay Bridge disaster, 28 Dec. 1879. Univ. estab., 1967.

Dunedin, New Zealand. Founded, 1848. University opened, 1871.

Dungannon Convention. Meeting of Irish Volunteers under Grattan, passed resolution for parliamentary reform for Ireland, 8 Sept. 1785.

Dunkirk or **Dunkerque,** France. Traditionally sprang up round a church built by St. Eloi in the seventh century. Sacked by the English, 1388. Taken by French, 1646; recovered by Archduke Leopold, 1652; given up to the English, 1658; sold to Louis XIV by Charles II, 17 Oct. 1662; bombarded by English, 26 July 1694. Works ordered to be demolished by Treaty of Utrecht, 1713. Duke of York forced to raise siege of, Sept. 1793. Allied troops evacuated from, May–June 1940. Fifty-year Anglo-French Treaty of Alliance signed at D., 4 Mar. 1947. War memorial at D. unveiled by Queen Elizabeth the Queen Mother, July 1957.

Dunkirk, Treaty of, between Britain and France, signed 4 Mar. 1947 (*see* preceding article).

Dunmow Flitch, first competed for, 1244; names of successful competitors first recorded, 1445.

Dunwich. The residence of the kings of E. Anglia (*q.v.*), and the seat of their bishops, then of the more northerly of the two E. Anglian sees, 673–870. The first E. Anglian church was built here in 627 by order of King Sigeberht (*d.* 637 ?) for St. Felix (*d.* 648). It began to be swallowed up by the sea in the fourteenth century. As a rotten borough its parliamentary representation was abolished, 1832; it had sent two burgesses to Parliament since 1296. Corporation abolished, 1886.

Duquesne, Fort (Pa., U.S.A.). Erected by French, 1754. Captured by Gen. Forbes and renamed Fort Pitt after the English statesman, 1758.

Durazzo, now known as **Durres** (anct. **Epidamnus** and **Dyrrachium**). Founded seventh century B.C. by settlers from Corinth and Corcyra. Captured by the Romans, fourth century B.C. Destroyed by earthquake, A.D. 345. Besieged, 481, 1082, and 1115. Venetian, 1392–1501, and subsequently Turkish (until 1913). Now Yugoslav.

Durban, Natal, S. Africa. Founded, 1824, received its present name, 1835. Salisbury Island naval base built, 1939–45.

Durham, England. Called by the Normans *Duresme.* Episcopal see, originally at Lindisfarne, then (from 883) at Chester-le-Street, transferred, A.D. 995. Besieged by Duncan of Scotland, 1040; entered by William the Conqueror, 1067. The present cathedral begun, 1092. Headquarters of Edward III and his army, 1327. Battle of Neville's Cross near, 1346. Henry VI visits shrine of St. Cuthbert, 1448. University founded, 1832.

Durham Report by the Earl of Durham on the state of Canada (*q.v.*) after Papineau's rebellion, 1838. Published, 1839.

Düsseldorf, Germany. Made a city, 1288; capital of the duchy of Berg. 1385, passed to the Palatinate, 1609. Taken by Ferdinand of Brunswick, 1758; by French, 6 Sept. 1795; incorporated in Prussia, 1815.

Dutch Guiana. *See* SURINAM.

Dutch and Flemish Literature. The following is a list of prominent writers in the Dutch and Flemish languages, now identical (in their literary form). Except where 'Belgian' is specified the nationality of the writers is Dutch (Netherlands).

Bijns, Anna (poet), *c.* 1494–1575.
Bilderdijk, Willem (poet), 1756–1831.
Bredero, Gerbrand (poet, playwright), 1585–1618.

Cats, Sir Jakob (poet), 1577–1660.
Cauwelaert, August van (Belgian poet and novelist), 1885–1945.
Coornhert, Dirk Volckertszoon (humanist), 1522–90.
Gezelle, Guido Pierre Théodore Joseph (Belgian poet), 1830–99.
Heijermans, Herman (novelist and playwright), 1864–1924.
Holst, Henriette Roland (poet), 1869–1953.
Hooft, Pieter (poet, playwright, historian), 1581–1647.
Huygens, Sir Constantine (poet), 1596–1687.
Mont, Charles Polydore (Pol) de (Belgian poet, novelist, and essayist), 1857–1931.
Potgieter, Everhard Johannes (publicist), 1808–75.
Querido, Israel (novelist, critic), 1873–1932.
Van den Vondel, Joost (poet, playwright), 1587–1679.
Van Eeden, Frederik Willem (poet, novelist), 1860–1932.
Van Lennep, Jakob (poet, novelist), 1802–68).
Vermeylen, August (Belgian novelist and essayist), 1872–1945.

Dutch Republic. *See* HOLLAND.

Dvinsk (Rus.), **Daugavpils** (Let.). Founded by Livonian knights in 1278. Polish till 1773. Russian, 1773–1919. In Latvian Republic until its annexation by U.S.S.R., 1940. Known as **Dünaburg** until 1893.

Dyarchy. A system of semi-popular government introduced into British India, 1919, as a result of the Montagu-Chelmsford report. Superseded, 1937.

Dyfed, administrative co. of Wales, created 1974 under Local Government Act of 1972. Headquarters are at Carmarthen.

Dynamite. Patented by Nobel (*see* NOBEL PRIZE), 1867. Manufactured in Ayrshire, 1872.

E

E.A.M. (Ellenikon Apelevtherotikon Metopon). Gk. political (predominantly Communist) committee controlling E.L.A.S. (*q.v.*).

Earl Marshal of England. This office has been hereditary in the family of Howard, Dukes of Norfolk, since 1672.

Earl Marshal (Mariscal) of Scotland. This office in the fourteenth century became hereditary in the family of Keith, who retained it until its suppression in 1716.

Early Bird, world's first commercial communications satellite, launched from the Kennedy Center, Cape Canaveral, U.S.A., 6 Apr. 1965. First television programme using it was shown to 24 countries on 2 May 1965.

Early Closing. Movement to reduce shop assistants' working hours inaugurated, 1842. Act for E.C. of shops passed 1919. Amended by Shops Acts, 1928, 1937, and 1950. Moves to amend, 1980 onwards.

Early English Text Society. Founded by F. J. Furnivall (1825–1910). First publications, 1864.

Earthquakes. Many recorded in Greek and Japanese history. An earthquake accompanied the famous eruption of Vesuvius in A.D. 79. An earthquake affecting all the known world occurred 6 Sept. 543. The following is a list of the most notable subsequent E. Figures in brackets denote the approximate number of fatal casualties.

Constantinople, 553 or 555
Thrace and Asia Minor, 26 Oct. 740
Syria and Palestine, 746
Glastonbury destroyed, 11 Sept. 1275
Lisbon, 26 Jan. 1531 (30,000)
Shensi, China, 24 Jan. 1556 (830,000)
London (damaged St. Paul's), 6 Apr. 1580

Japan, Aug. and Sept. 1596
Naples, July–Dec. 1631
Jamaica, 7 July 1692
Japan, 30 Dec. 1703 (200,000)
China, Oct.–Nov. 1731
Calcutta, 11 Oct. 1737 (300,000)
Peru, 28 Oct. 1746
Cairo, 2 Sept. 1754
Lisbon, 1 Nov. 1755 (very violent; 60,000)
Messina, 5 Feb. 1783 (60,000)
Aleppo, 1822 (20,000)
Salerno, 16 Dec. 1857 (12,000)
Quito, 22 Mar. 1859
Peru, 13–15 Aug. 1868
Ischia, July–Aug. 1883
Charleston (S.C.). 1886
Japan, 28 Oct. 1891
Assam, 12 June 1897
Mont Pelée, W. Indies, 1902 (20,000)
Kangra (India), 1905 (20,000)
San Francisco, 18 Apr. 1906
Valparaiso, 17 Aug. 1906
Kingston (Jamaica), 14–15 Jan. 1907
Messina, 28 Dec. 1908 (120,000)
Luristan (Persia), 1909
S. Mexico, 1911
Avezzano, Italy, 1915 (30,000)
Kansu, 1920 (180,000)
Tokyo and Yokohama destroyed, 1 Sept. 1923 (180,000); same area, 15 Jan. 1924
Horta (Azores), destroyed, 1926
Herzegovina and Dalmatia, 1927
N. Japan and Kamchatka, 16 Feb. 1927
Tajima (Japan), 7 Mar. 1927
Palestine, 11 July 1927
Chile (Talca), Dec. 1928
S. Italy, 23 July 1930
New Zealand, 3 Feb. 1931
Nicaragua, 31 Mar. 1931
Mexico, 3 June 1932
China, 1932 (70,000)
Quetta destroyed, 31 May 1935 (60,000)

Rabaul (New Britain), 2 June 1937
Alaska, 22 July 1937
Anatolia (Turkey), 19–20 Apr. 1938
S. Chile, over 20,000 dead, 26 Jan. 1939
Anatolia, over 23,000 dead, 26–9 Dec.
　1939 (also July 1940 and Dec. 1942)
Karachi, Nov. 1945
Dominican Republic, Aug. 1946
N. Peru, Nov. 1946
S. Japan, Dec. 1946
Fukui, Japan, June 1948
Central Ecuador, 5 Aug. 1949
N. Assam, Aug. 1950
El Salvador, 6 May 1951
Turkey, 18 Mar. 1953
Ionian Islands, 12 Aug. 1953
Cyprus, 10 Sept. 1953
Orléansville, Algeria, 9 Sept. 1954
Afghanistan, 10–17 June 1956
Iran, 4 Nov. 1956
Jangchal, Persia, 2–11 July 1957
Iran, 13 Dec. 1957
Agadir, Morocco, 29 Feb. 1960 (14,000)
Persia, 25 Apr. 1960
Chile, 21–5 May 1960 (5,000)
S. Italy, 21–2 Aug. 1962
S. Italy and Greece, 28 Aug. 1962
W. Iran, 1 Sept. 1962 (14,000)
Barce, Libya, 21 Feb. 1963 (over 250).
Skopje, Yugoslavia, 26 July 1963 (over
　1,000)
Alaska, 27 Mar. 1964 (180)
Chile, 28 Mar. 1965 (400)
E. Turkey, 20 Aug. 1966 (3,000)
Gediz, W. Turkey, 28 Mar. 1970 (over
　1,000)
Huaraz and N. Peru, followed by
　resultant avalanche and flood, 31
　May 1970 (over 66,000)
Managua, Nicaragua, 23 Dec. 1972
　(5,000)
Pakistan, 26 Dec. 1974 (5,200)
Guatemala, 4 Feb. 1976 (22,800)
Tangshan, China, 28 July 1976
　(650,000)
Rumania, 4 Mar. 1977 (1,540)
Severe earthquakes, Iran, 1977 and
　1979
N.W. Algeria, 10 Oct. 1980 (4,500)
S. Italy, 23 Nov. 1980 (4,800)
Popayán, Colombia, 31 Mar. 1983 (over
　500)
Erzurum, Turkey, 30 Oct. 1983 (over
　1,500)

East Anglia. Founded by Uffa on basis of existing Anglian settlements, 575. Submitted to Wessex, 826. The last three E. Anglian kings, Ethelweard, Oswald, and the martyred Edmund, were sub-kings or viceroys under W. Saxon protection, but belonged to the old royal house of Uffa. On the re-conquest of the Danelaw about 920 it was administered directly by Ealdormen under the W. Saxon crown. Knut made it one of the four principal earldoms or administrative regions of England (c. 1017), and so it remained until 1066.

Kings of E. Anglia: Uffing Dynasty:
Redwald 593–617
Eorpwald 617–628
State of anarchy 628–631
Sigeberht 631–634
Egric 634–635
Anna 635–654
Ethelhere 654–655
Ethelwald 655–664
Ealdwulf 664–713
Elfwald 713–749
Beorna 749–?
Ethelberht ?–794
Kings of Mercia (*q.v.*) 794–823
Athelstan of Wessex ? 829–? 839
Ethelweard ? 839–? 854
Oswald ? 854–? 856
Edmund (Saint) ? 856–870

Danish Kings:
Guthrum I (Guttorm) 878–890
Eohric (Eric) 890–902
Guthrum II 902–917

East Anglia, University of. Opened at Norwich, 1963.

East, Empire of the. See ROMAN EMPIRE, EASTERN.

Eastern Question, Near. See TURKISH REPUBLIC; SYRIA; PALESTINE; EGYPT; CYPRUS; GREECE, MODERN; IRAQ; ARABIA.

East India Company, The Honourable. Incorporated by Queen Elizabeth, 31 Dec. 1600. Charter renewed, 1609. Settlement established at Surat, 1613. Conflict with Dutch E.I.C., 1621–3. Factories established at Canton, 1637, Madras, 1639. St. Helena occupied, 1651. Fort William (Calcutta) founded and Bombay given to H.E.I.C., 1668. Factory at Calcutta established, 1690.

A rival New E.I.C. chartered, 1691. New E.I.C. charter extended, 1698. Bengal reorganized by Sir Charles Eyre, 1700. New E.I.C. merged with H.E.I.C., 1708 (see SEVEN YEARS WAR). Defeat of Oudh at battle of Buxar, 1764. Clive reforms Indian administration, 1765–7. Annexation of N. Circars, 1766. International complications arising out of the vast economic and political activities of the company led to the Regulating Act, 1773. H.E.I.C.'s trading monopoly abolished, 1822. As a result of the Indian Mutiny (q.v.) its political and administrative powers were abolished, 1858. Company finally wound up, 1873, its army having been absorbed into the forces of the crown by 1861.

East India Companies, Foreign.
1. Dutch. Founded, 1602.
2. French. Founded, 1604. Refounded, 1664. Dissolved, 1770.
3. Danish. Founded, 1614.
4. Austrian. Founded, 1720. Dissolved, 1727.

In 1621, having together eliminated the Portuguese, the English and Dutch quarrelled, and the Dutch massacred the English at Amboina in 1623. After the virtual blockade of Holland in the Anglo-Dutch wars of 1652–4, 1665–7, the French company was able to take its place and the struggle between it and the English company reached its climax in the Seven Years War (q.v.), 1756–63, and the total defeat of the French company. The Danish company never became a political organization, and the Austrians were persuaded by Walpole to dissolve their company.

East London, Cape Province, S. Africa. Site discovered, 1836, by John Baillie; city founded, 1847, and originally known as Fort Glamorgan.

East Prussia. See PRUSSIA.

Easter. Method of calculating date of E. settled by Council of Nicaea, 325.

Easter Island (Sp. **Isia de Pascua;** Polynesian **Rapa-nui**), Chile (since 1888). Discovered by Dutch in 1722. All traditions concerning the colossal E.I. statues, their origin and purpose, perished

c. 1850–90 when 'blackbirders' carried off most of the male population to work in the guano islands of Peru. After 1888 survivors were repatriated, but the population was decimated by disease, the ruling class of Polynesians became extinct, and there was a cultural breakdown. Sheep-farming introduced from Tahiti in the 1870s. Considerable archaeological research since 1950s.

Eboracum. See YORK.

Ecbatana, Asia Minor. Founded on site of the modern Hamadan, 700 B.C. Captured, 550 B.C. by Cyrus, who made it the capital and summer residence of the Persian kings, and by Alexander, 330 B.C.

Ecclesiastical Commission. Appointed, 1835. Amalgamated with Queen Anne's Bounty (q.v.), 1947, after which the two bodies together were known as the Church Commission. See CHURCH COMMISSIONERS.

Ecclesiastical Courts. See HIGH COMMISSION and ARCHES, COURT OF.

Economics and Political Science, London School of. Founded, 1895.

'Economist, The.' See under NEWSPAPERS.

Ecuador. After battle of Cajamarca, 1532, Spanish presidency of Quito established. Then became part of the new Gran Colombia republic by declaration of 17 Dec. 1819. Effective Spanish rule ended at battle of Pichincha, 24 May 1822. Constituted separate republic on break-up of the original state of Gran Colombia (q.v.), 1830. A new constitution, 1945, was followed by a series of coups and dictatorial regimes. New constitution, 1979.

Ecumenical or Oecumenical Councils. See COUNCILS OF THE CHURCH.

Eddas. Compilations of Scandinavian mythology and legend made in Iceland. The 'Elder' or 'Poetic Edda' compiled c. 1200 by an unknown editor. The 'Younger' or 'Prose Edda' c. 1230 by Snorri Sturluson.

Eddystone Lighthouse. Built, 1696. Destroyed, 1703. Rebuilt, 1706. Burnt, 1755. Rebuilt, 1759. Burnt, 1770.

Rebuilt, 1774. Present edifice opened, 18 May 1882.

Edessa (now **Urfa**), Turkey. Ancient city, originally Urhai. Rebuilt by Antiochus IV *c.* 170 B.C. Became capital of an independent kingdom of E. *c.* 132 B.C. Hadrian (A.D. 117–38) made it a Roman dependency. In 216 it became a Roman military colony and the chief frontier fortress of the Near E. Besieged by Persian King Kavad, 503. Withstood a determined siege by Persian King Chosroes, 544–5. Seized by Baldwin of Flanders and became Crusader principality, 1097. Captured by Zenghi Emir of Damascus, 1151. Lapsed into obscurity thereafter.

Edict, Perpetual. Arose out of the custom by which Roman judicial officials announced, by an edict at the beginning of their year of office, the manner in which they intended to administer justice. The form of this E. began to be standarized, *c.* 200 B.C., and was finally fixed into an unalterable code by Salvius Julianus at the order of the Emperor Hadrian, A.D. 132.

Edict of Châteaubriant. By Henry II of France against Calvinists, 27 June 1551.

Edict of Nantes. By Henry IV of France, giving toleration and a number of cities of refuge to the Huguenots (*q.v.*), 15 Apr. 1598. Revoked by Louis XIV, 24 Oct. 1685.

Edict of Restitution. By the Emperor Ferdinand II of Germany, ordaining surrender of certain Church lands, 1629.

Edinburgh, Scotland. Founded by and named after Edwin, of Northumbria, *c.* A.D. 617. Part of Northumbria till 936. Robert Bruce held Parliament at E., 1327 and 1328. Replaced Perth (*q.v.*) as Scottish capital, 1437. Pillaged by Henry VIII, 1544 and 1547. John Knox *d.* at, 1572. University established, 1582. Assembly of Convention of States, 10 Dec. 1599. Charles I crowned King of Scotland at, 16 May 1633. Castle surrendered to Cromwell, Dec. 1650. Porteous Riots (*q.v.*), 1736. Young Pretender occupies, 15–17 Sept. 1745. Building of New Town begun,

1767. Anti-Catholic riots, 1779. Royal visit of George IV, 17–28 Aug. 1822. Scottish National Gallery opened, 21 Mar. 1859. Forth Bridge opened, 4 Mar. 1890. Scottish National War Memorial opened, 1927. Annual international music and dramatic festival inaugurated, 1947. Heriot-Watt Univ. estab., 1966.

'Edinburgh Review.' Founded, Oct. 1802. Last issue, Oct. 1929.

Edinburgh University. Founded, 1582, by charter of James VI.

Edirne. *See* ADRIANOPLE.

Edmunds Law against polygamy passed by U.S. Congress, 1882.

Education (U.K.).

1. England and Wales. First grant of public money for E., 1833. Privy Council committee on E. formed, 1839. E. department established in two divisions: (*a*) Popular E. (*b*) Development of science and art, 25 Feb. 1856. Royal Commission appointed, 1858. Regulations published, 1860. Royal Commission reported, 1861. New regulations, 1862. Elementary E. Act passed, 9 Aug. 1870. Made compulsory, 1876. Free, 1891. Board of E. established, 1899. E. Act passed, 18 Dec. 1902. Royal Commission on university E. in London, 1909. New E. Act, 1918. R. A. Butler's Act, 1944. Board of E. replaced by a Ministry of E. Known as Ministry of E. and Science since 1964.

2. Scotland. Act to compel all barons and freeholders to send their sons to school, 1494. Act taxing agricultural land for maintenance of schools, 1633. Act for providing schools, 1696. Elementary E. compulsory, 1872. E. (Scotland) Act, 1945.

3. Ireland. Kildare Place Society for Promoting E. of the poor founded Dublin, 1811. Gladstone's University Bill thrown out by Commons, 1873. Intermediate E. Act passed, 1878. Compulsory E. Act, 1892. National University of Ireland founded, 1909. Compulsory instruction in Irish language introduced 1922.

4. N. Ireland. N. Ireland became a self-governing unit, 1920. First E. Act, 1923. Second Act, 1947, follows the pattern of the English Act of 1944.

Education (U.S.A.). E. Act, 1884. Blair E. Bill, Mar. 1886. Compulsory E. Act, 4 Apr. 1892.

See also UNIVERSITIES, and various colleges and academies.

Edward, Lake, Africa. Discovered by Stanley, 1889.

Edward VI Prayer Book. *See* PRAYER, BOOK OF COMMON.

E.E.C. *See* EUROPEAN ECONOMIC COMMUNITY.

Eger. *See* CHEB.

Egypt, Ancient. The following dates are approximate down to 945; all are B.C. *Earliest Dynasties:* I, 3200–3000; II, 3,000–2780. *Old Kingdom:* III, 2780–2720; IV, 2720–2560; V, 2560–2420; VI, 2420–2270. *First Intermediate Period:* VII and VIII, 2270–2240; IX and X, 2240–2100. *Middle Kingdom:* XI, 2100–2000; XII, 2000–1788. *Second Intermediate Period:* XIII–XVI, 1788–1600; XVII, 1600–1555. *The Empire:* XVIII, 1555–1350; XIX, 1350–1200; XX, 1200–1090; XXI, 1090–945; XXII, 945–c. 745; XXIII, c. 745–718, XXIV, 718–712. *Late Period:* XXV 712–663; XXVI, 663–525 (from 663 to 610 Egypt was subject to the suzerainty of Assyria); XXVII (Persian), 525–332: meanwhile Egyptian rebellion, which gradually ousted the Persians, established XXVIII, 405–399; XXIX, 399–379; XXX, 379–341. In 332 Egypt was conquered by Alexander the Great, at whose death (323) Ptolemy established the Greek dynasty. This lasted, with varying fortune, until 30, when Egypt was made a Roman province.

Egypt, Modern. Christianity existed in E., second century A.D. Roman E. conquered by Arabs, 640. Conquered for Moawlya the Ommayad, 658. Conquered by Abbasids c. 750. Coptic revolt crushed, 832. Ruled by Tulunid dynasty, 808–903. Returned to allegiance of Bagdad, 906. Conquered, 969, by the Fatimids, who ruled till 1171, when the country was conquered by Saladin. From 1261 country ruled by Mamelukes (*q.v.*) under nominal caliphs (*q.v.*), until conquered by the Ottoman Empire (*q.v.*) under the Sultan Selim, 1517. Invaded by French, under Napoleon, 1798. Expelled by British and Turks. Virtually independent after revolts of Mehemet Ali Pasha, 1831 and 1839. Mehemet Ali made hereditary khedive, 15 July 1841. De Lesseps obtained concession for the construction of the Suez Canal, 1856. Suez Canal opened for navigation, 1869. Britain purchased Suez Canal shares. Government defaulted on loans, 1876, and instigated anti-foreign rioting which led to British bombardment of Alexandria, July 1882, and Arabi's religious war, 24 July 1882. Arabi defeated at Tel-el-Kebir, 13 Sept. 1882. British interests in E. recognized by France (*see* ENTENTE CORDIALE), 1904. Khedive Abbas II deposed as pro-Turkish by British, 1914. British protectorate established, with Hussein Kamil as sultan, 20 Dec. 1914. Hussein *d.*, 9 Oct. 1917. Succeeded by Fuad. E. declared kingdom, 16 Mar. 1922. Makwar dam opened, Jan. 1926. Anglo-Egyptian agreement on rights in the waters of the Nile, May 1928. King Fuad *d.*, Apr. 1936; succeeded by Farouk 1 (*b.* 11 Feb. 1920). E.'s sovereignty and independence recognized by treaty with Britain, 26 Aug. 1936. British troops evacuated from Cairo and Alexandria, 1947. Palestine invaded, 15 May, 1948. Israeli troops entered Egyptian territory, Dec. 1948. A truce, 7 Jan. 1949, followed by a general armistice, 24 Feb. 1949.

Coup d'état by Gen. Mohammed Neguib after flight abroad of most of Wafd leaders, 22 July 1952. King abdicated and Prince Ahmed Fuad (*b.* 16 Jan. 1952) proclaimed, 28 July. Republic proclaimed with Neguib as first president, 18 June. Neguib resigned, April 1954. Government carried on by a council of ministers until 1956, when Nasser became premier, and subsequently president and virtual dictator of E. E. took over defence of the Suez

Canal from Britain, Nov. 1955. Last British troops left E., 31 Mar. 1956, and Nasser nationalized the Suez Canal Co. Hostilities broke out between E. and Israel again, Oct.; Israel invaded E. and an Anglo-French force occupied Port Said. E. blocked the Suez Canal with sunken ships. E. accepted a cease-fire on U.N. conditions, 7 Nov.; Britain and France called on by U.N. to withdraw forces from E. This they agreed to do on 3 Dec. Withdrawal of Anglo-French forces complete by 22 Dec. Suez Canal re-opened to traffic, 30 Apr. 1957. Union of Egypt and Syria proclaimed by Presidents of both countries, 1 Feb. 1958; two countries to be known henceforth as the United Arab Republic (*q.v.*) though name subsequently applied to E. only. Syria left the U.A.R. in 1961, Yemen shortly after, and E. reverted to old name, 2 Sept. 1971. In June 1967 war broke out between E. and Israel, E. being utterly defeated, losing the Sinai peninsula, the Gaza strip and the Gulf of Aquaba. Suez Canal blocked by E.; Nasser *d.* 1970; succeeded by Sadat. Unsuccessful war against Israel, 1973; Suez Canal re-opened 1975; peace treaty with Israel, 1979 and Sadat visited Israel. Sadat assassinated, 6 Oct. 1981; succeeded by Mubarak. Subsequently took a less sympathetic line to Israel. *See also* SUDAN; SUEZ CANAL; ISRAEL; ARAB LEAGUE; SYRIA.

Eidsvold, Norway. Norwegian constitution drawn up at and signed, 17 Mar 1814.

Eiffel Tower, Paris. Built, 1887–9.

Eight Articles. Drawn up by Cranmer, Ridley, and Latimer, 1555.

Eighty Club. Established, 1880.

'Eikon Basilike.' Published, 1649.

Einsiedeln, Switzerland. St. Meinrad, the hermit, was murdered here, 861, and an abbey founded on the site of his cell *c.* 934. Paracelsus *b.* in E., 1493, and Zwingli a parish priest here, 1516–18.

Eire. For previous history *See* IRISH FREE STATE. New constitution passed, 14 June 1937. British sold all naval bases in E. to E. Government for

£50,000,000, and a trade agreement, 25 Apr. 1938. Douglas Hyde first president, 4 May 1938. Neutrality in World War II announced, 28 Sept. 1939. General Election of 4–10 Feb. 1948 won by Fine Gael and Clann na Poblachta combination, and John A. Costello appointed prime minister. Thereafter *see under* IRELAND: *Republic of Ireland.*

Eisteddfod. Welsh festival of the arts, with origins at least as early as the sixth century A.D. but not called Es. before 1450. Modern conception of the E. dates back to the Corwen E. of 1789. National E. of Wales established 1880, and now held annually.

Ekaterinburg (now **Sverdlovsk**). The Tsar Nicholas II was murdered at, July 1918.

Ekaterinoslav. See DNIEPROPETROVSK.

El Alamein. Eighth Army offensive in the W. Desert, N. Africa, marking decisive turning-point of World War II, begun there, 23 Oct. 1942.

E.L.A.S. (Ellenikos Laiko Apelevtherotikos Stratos), the armed forces of E.A.M. (*q.v.*), became active against the Germans after June 1941; engaged in civil war, Dec. 1944, 12 Feb. 1945, and again, 1947–9.

Elba, Isle of, Italy. Taken by Nelson, 9 Aug. 1796. Given, 1814, to Napoleon, who escaped from it, 26 Feb. 1815.

Elders of Zion. Their alleged 'Protocols' published in Russia, 1903, 1905, 1907, were said to have been drawn up, 1897. Exposed as a forgery in *The Times,* 16, 17, 18 Aug. 1921.

Elections (U.K.) *See* FRANCHISE.

Electors of the Holy Roman Empire. The highest ranking princes of the H.R.E., to whom was accorded exclusively the right to elect the Holy Roman Emperor. Their position and rights were settled by the Golden Bull (*q.v.*) of Charles IV, 1356, and their number restricted to seven, viz.: the Archbishops of Cologne, Mainz, and Trier, the King of Bohemia, the Count Palatine of the Rhine, the Margrave of Brandenburg, and the Duke of Saxony. To this number were added Bavaria 1623, Hanover, 1692. Electoral rights ceased at abolition of H.R.E., 1806, though the title 'Elector' was used by the Duke of Hesse till 1859.

Electricity. Thales of Miletus said to have noticed the magnetic qualities of rubbed amber, 600 B.C. William Gilbert of Colchester (1540–1603) experimented with magnetic needle. Robert Boyle (1627–91) conducted experiments. Experiments of Royal Society, 1676, following observations of Sir Isaac Newton (1642–1727). Francis Hawksbee experimented with mercury, 1705, and published results, 1709. Dufay (1699–1739) distinguished experimentally two kinds of E. Leyden jar invented by Cunaeus, 1745, improved by Sir W. Watson (1715–1787). Royal Society experiments on velocity of E., 1747. Benjamin Franklin (1706–90) presented theory of positive and negative E. and identified lightning with electric spark. John Canton (1715–72) demonstrated induction. Experiments in atmospheric E. by Beccaria (1716–81), with silk by Robert Symmers, 1759. With metals and salts by Sir D. Brewster (1781–1868). With gases by Henry Cavendish (1731–1810). By Galvani, 1790, and Volta, 1800, which led to invention of galvanic battery and voltaic pile. Magnetic action of E. discovered by Oersted of Copenhagen, 1819. Ampère's theory, 1820. Faraday discovered electro-magnetic rotation, 1821. Seebeck discovered thermo-electricity, 1822. Ohm's law, 1827. Weber invented electro-dynamometer, 1832. Induction and transformer elaborated by Faraday, 1831. Lenz's Law, 1835. Daniell battery, 1836. Grove's battery, 1836. Bunsen battery, 1842. Sir William Thomson (Lord Kelvin)'s inventions, 1851 *et seq*. Siemens dynamo, 1867. Fauré accumulator, 1881. First electric power station in England opened at Godalming, 1881. D.C. and A.C. converter by Salomons and Pyke, 1892. Electric theory of matter by Niels Bohr, 1913. First power station producing E. from nuclear power opened at Calder Hall (*q.v.*), 1956.

Electricity Act, 1957, forms basis of present legislation regarding electricity in the U.K.

Electric Light. Carbon arc first produced by Sir H. Davy, 1810. Staite's patented lamp, 1847. Sérrins ditto, 1857. S. Foreland lighthouse lighted by E. L., 1857. Edison and Swan's incandescent lamp, 1878–80. Tungsten filament, 1904. Neon tubes for street advertisements, 1931. Mercury and sodium vapour lamps for street and floodlighting, 1937.

Electric Railway. First experiments by Robert Davidson, 1837. Siemens exhibited dynamo traction at Berlin, 1879. Permanent E. R. opened near Berlin, 1882. E. trams at Leytonstone, 4 Mar. 1882. The same Portrush to Bushmills, early 1882. Liverpool overhead E. R., 1893. City and S. London, 1890. Chicago, 1895 (first in U.S.A.). Underground Waterloo to Mansion House electrified, 11 July 1898. Central London line, 27 June 1900. Mersey railway, 1903. Subsequently considerable electrification of English railways; all underground railways electrified, most suburban services, and, since World War II, many main line routes. New underground line from Victoria to Brixton started, 1962.

Electric Telegraph. *See* TELEGRAPHY.

Electrons. Discovered by Sir Joseph John Thomson (1856–1940), 1897.

Elgin Marbles brought to England *c*. 1812 by Thomas Bruce, Lord E. (1766–1841) and bought for the British Museum (*q.v.*), 1816. Gk. gov. sought return to Greece, 1983.

El Salvador. *See* SALVADOR, EL.

Ely, England. Abbey founded by St. Etheldreda, 673. Burnt by Danes, 870. Re-founded by Ethelwold, Bishop of Winchester, 970. Present building begun, 1083. Resistance of Hereward the Wake, 1068–71. Barons' stronghold taken by Prince Edward, 1267. Cathedral octagon finished, 1328. King's school founded, 1543.

Elysée (Paris). Built, 1718. Became the presidential residence, 1870.

Élzevir or **Elsevier Press.** Founded at Leyden, 1580, by Louis E. (1540–1617): ceased to exist, 1712.

Emergency Powers Acts, include those of 1920, 1939 and 1964.

Emmet's Insurrection. Headed by

Robert E. (1778–1803) in Ireland, 23 July 1803. E. arrested 25 Aug. and executed 20 Sept. 1803. *See* UNITED IRISH-MEN.

Emperor of India. Title proclaimed for British sovereigns, 1 Jan. 1877 Abolished 15 Aug. 1947.

Empire Day. *See* COMMONWEALTH DAY.

Empire Settlement Act passed, 1922.

Empire State Building, New York. Built, 1930–1, at that time tallest building in city (1,250 ft. high).

Employment Act, 1980, made secondary picketing unlawful.

Employment, Department of, superseded the former Ministry of Labour (*q.v.*), April 1968.

Employers' Liability Acts, the first passed in 1880. In 1946 the E.L.A. was repealed by the Law Reform (Personal Injuries Act) which, together with the National Insurance (Industrial Injuries) Act (1946), effected far-reaching reforms in the field of workmen's compensation. Further amended by the E.L.A. of 1969 and subsequent industrial legislation.

Employment Exchanges. Instituted 1905 in U.K. under management of local authorities. Transferred to control of Board of Trade, 1909 (when they were known as Labour Exchanges, now Job Centres). To Ministry of Labour, 1917.

Ems Telegram from King William of Prussia to Bismarck, July 1870, which, when published by Bismarck, with parts deliberately suppressed, helped to provoke the 1870 war against France.

Encyclopaedia. Speusippus (*d.* 339 B.C.) is alleged to have compiled an E. which has not survived; neither has the work of Varro (*d. c.* 27 B.C.) entitled *Nine Books of Instruction.* The *Natural History* of Pliny the Elder (A.D. 23–79) is virtually an E. The most important medieval Es. in Latin were those of Martianus Capella the African (fifth century), Isidore of Seville (570–636), and the *Speculum Triplex* of Vincent de Beauvais (*d. c.* 1264). At the same time the Arabs both translated Greek Es. and compiled their own, of which

the geographical E. by Yaqut ibn 'Abdullah er-Rumi (1179–1229), a bookseller of Greek extraction, is the best known; it quotes the only surviving passages of Ibn Fadhlan's description of Scandinavians (*Rus*) in S. Russia, written in 921. The greatest Chinese E. was compiled in the reign of Yung Lao (*d.* 1425). Pierre Bayles's *Dictionnaire Historique et Critique* (1697) was the first E. of modern European type, of which the first English example was the *Cyclopaedia* of Ephraim Chambers (*d.* 1740). Diderot and D'Alembert's *Encyclopédie* (1751–72) was based on a translation of it. The *Encyclopaedia Britannica* was first printed, 1768–71; all editions from the 11th (1910–11) onwards produced under American proprietorship. *Chambers's Encyclopaedia* was first edited 1850–68 by Dr. Andrew Findlater. *Everyman's Encyclopaedia*, where conciseness and relatively low cost were combined with scholarship, was first published by J. M. Dent & Sons Ltd. in 1911; 6th edition, 1978.

Enderby Land, Antarctica. Visited by John Biscoe, 1831, and named after his employers. Now part of Australian Antarctic Territory.

Enforcing Act (U.S.A.). Passed by Congress, 9 Jan. 1809, for preserving strict neutrality in Napoleonic War. *See* BAYONNE DECREE.

Engagement, The. Agreement between Charles I and the Scots Commissioners in the Isle of Wight, 1647.

England, Church of. Christianity was brought to England by Roman soldiers in first century A.D., but Romano-Celtic Church overwhelmed by Anglo-Saxon invasions, although it survived in the W. and in Wales. St. Augustine sent from Rome, 596, and first church founded at Canterbury, 597 (traditionally on the site of a former Romano-Christian basilica). Metropolitan province of Canterbury set up, and that of York planned, by Pope Gregory, 601. Irish Celtic monks had settled at Iona, 563, and begun the evangelization of the N. Church of Northumbria founded by Paulinus,

627; of E. Anglia by Felix, 631; of Wessex by Birinus, 634. Real evangelization of Northumbria work of St. Aidan, an Iona monk, from 635 onwards. Dispute with Celtic Church settled at Synod of Whitby, 664. *Ecclesiastical History* written by Venerable Bede, who *d.* 735. Third province, with archiepiscopal seat at Lichfield, set up by King Offa in Mercia, but it lasted only from 787 to 802. Separation of church and lay courts, 1086. Murder of Becket, 1170. Legatine Council at London, 1237. Convocations organized *c.* 1283. Wycliffe condemned, 1382. Lollard Act, 1414. Papal authority repudiated and Henry VIII declared head of the church, 1534. Suppression of monasteries, 1536 and 1539. Ten Articles, 1536. Great Bible authorized, 1538. Act of Six Articles, 1539. English Litany, 1544. First Book of Common Prayer, 1549. Clerical marriage permitted, 1549. Second Book of Common Prayer, 1552. Forty-two Articles, 1553. Reconciliation with Papacy by Mary I, 1554. Independence re-established, 1559, by Queen Elizabeth I. Act of Uniformity restored the 1552 Prayer Book but with certain Catholic amendments. Thirty-nine Articles, 1563. Hampton Court Conference (*q.v.*), 1604. Authorized Version of Bible, 1611. Solemn League and Covenant (*q.v.*), 1643. Establishment of Presbyterianism, 1646. Savoy Conference, 1667. Trial of Seven Bishops, 1688. Establishment of Queen Anne's Bounty (*q.v.*), 1704. Ecclesiastical Commission (*q.v.*) incorporated, 1836. Church Discipline Act, 1840. Oxford Movement begun, 1833; its first phase ended with Newman's conversion to Rome, 1845. Welsh Church disestablishment came into operation, 1920. Lambeth Conferences (held periodically since 1867) increasingly concerned with Christian reunion. Church Assembly proposed a new Prayer Book, 1927, but this was rejected by Parliament, 1928. Archbishop of Canterbury visited Pope John XXIII, Dec. 1960. Many Prayer Book revisions put into practice 1964 onwards. Pope John Paul II visited

Canterbury Cathedral, 1982. General Synod voted for ordination of women, 15 Nov 1984.

See Bishoprics; Great Britain; Bible, Translations of; Prayer, Book of Common, etc.

English History. *See* Britain. English mercenaries hired by King Vortigern of Kent mutiny, and make their leader Hengest king, *c.* 450. His descendant, Ethelbert of Kent, marries Christian Frankish wife, 550. Arrival of St. Augustine (*see* England, Church of), 597. From 617 the leading English power was Northumbria, but in 730 supremacy of Mercia was established till battle of Ellendun, 821. Egbert, King of Wessex, becomes first king of the English, 829. He defeats first Danish invasion at battle of Hingston Down, *c.* 835. Arrival of the Danish Here (*q.v.*) in England, 864. It storms York, 865. Defeats Alfred the Great at battle of Ashdown, 870. Alfred driven into Athelney, 877. His great victory at Edington and Truce of Chippenham, 878. English Danes conquered by Edward the Elder, 901–25. Athelstan's great victory over Irish, Danes, Norwegians, Welsh, and Scots at Brunanburh, 937. Danegeld (*q.v.*) instituted, 991. At death of Ethelred the Unready and Edmund Ironside, 1016, Knut of Denmark (*q.v.*) becomes king of the English. He visits Rome, 1027; conquers Norway, 1028, and Scotland, 1031. Wessex dynasty restored by Edward the Confessor, 1042. Death of Earl Godwin, 1053. Battle of Fulford, 21 Sept. 1066. Battle of Stamford Bridge, 25 Sept. Harold II killed at battle of Hastings, 14 Oct. 1066. Domesday Book (*q.v.*), 1085–6. Henry II reconquers Normandy, 1106. Investiture (*q.v.*) compromise, 1105. Civil war and French attacks in Normandy, 1111–25. Civil war throughout reign of Stephen, 1135–54. Constitutions of Clarendon (*q.v.*), 1164. Murder of Becket, 1170. Invasion of Ireland by Strongbow, 1171.

Richard I leaves England for Palestine, 1190. Arrives Acre, 8 June 1191. Returns to England, 13 Mar. 1194. French War, 1194–9.

John loses Normandy, 1204–5. Excommunicated, 1209. Reconciled with Papacy, 1213. Battle of Bouvines, 1214, Grants Magna Carta, 1215 (*q.v.*).
Simon de Montfort killed at battle of Evesham, 1265. Model Parliament, 1295. Edward of Caernarvon proclaimed Prince of Wales, 1301. Robert Bruce's rebellion, 1305–7. Battle of Bannockburn, 1314. Hundred Years War begins, 1338. Naval victory at Sluys, 1340. Edward III claims French throne, 1340. Battle of Crécy, 1346. Capture of Calais, 1347. Battle of Neville's Cross, 1346. Black Death, 1346–7. Battle of Poitiers, 1356. Death of Black Prince, 1376. Peasants' revolt under Wat Tyler, 1381. Death of Wiclif, 1384. Death of John of Gaunt, 1399. Lancaster's revolt and deposition of Richard II, 1399. Glendower's rebellion, 1400. Persecution of Lollards (*q.v.*), 1401. Rebellion of Percys, 1403. Hundred Years War resumed, 1415. Battle of Agincourt, 25 Oct. 1415. Rouen captured, 1419. Treaty of Troyes, 1420. Orléans relieved by Joan of Arc, 29 Apr. 1429. Cade's rebellion, 1450. All France, except Calais, lost, 1454. Wars of Roses (*q.v.*) begin at battle of St. Albans, 22 May 1455. Henry VI deposed after battle of Towton, 1461.
Death of Warwick the Kingmaker at battle of Barnet, 1471. Caxton sets up printing press at Westminster, 1476. Edward V murdered ('The Princes in the Tower'), 1483. Wars of Roses end in death of Richard III (killed at battle of Bosworth, 1485): succession of Henry VII (Tudor).
Wolsey becomes Chancellor, 1515. Field of the Cloth of Gold, 1520. Fall of Wolsey, 1529. Henry VIII's church reforms, 1531–40 (*see* ENGLAND, CHURCH OF). Somerset Lord Protector, 1547. First Prayer Book of Edward VI used, 1549. Northumberland Protector, 1550. Second Prayer Book, 1552. Northumberland's attempt to put Jane Grey on throne foiled by Mary I, 1553. She marries Philip II of Spain, 1554. Lady Jane Grey executed, 1554. Reconciliation with Rome, 1554.

Persecution of Protestants and burning of Cranmer, Latimer, and Ridley, 1555–6. War with France, 1557. Calais lost, 1558. Acts of Uniformity and Supremacy, 1559. Papal Bull of Deposition issued against Elizabeth, 1570. Drake sails round the world, 1576–9. Throgmorton's plot, 1584. Babington's plot, 1587. Execution of Mary Queen of Scots, 1587. Drake attacks Cadiz, 1587. Defeat of the Armada (*q.v.*), July –Aug. 1588. Essex storms Cadiz, 1596. Foundation of E. Indian Co. (*q.v.*), 1600. Spanish expedition to Ireland, 1601. *D.* of Elizabeth I and succession to throne as James I of James VI of Scotland, 1603. (*For later history see* GREAT BRITAIN, HISTORY OF.)

English Literature.

The following is a list of prominent writers in the English language (excepting American, for whom *see* AMERICAN LITERATURE IN ENGLISH):

Abercrombie, Lascelles, 1881–1938, poet.

Acton, John E. E. Dalberg-Acton, Lord, 1834–1902, historian.

Addison, Joseph, 1672–1719, poet and essayist.

Aelfric, 955–*c.* 1022, theologian and educationist.

Agate, James Evershed, 1877–1947, dramatic critic.

Ainsworth, William Harrison, 1805–82, novelist.

Aldington, Richard, 1892–1962, poet, novelist, and biographer.

Alfred the Great, King, *c.* 849–99, translator.

Amis, Kingsley, 1922– , novelist.

Arbuthnot, John, 1667–1735, Scottish satirist (originator of the term 'John Bull').

Arnold, Matthew, 1822–88, poet and critic.

Arnold, Thomas, 1795–1842, historian.

Ascham, Roger, 1515–68, didactic writer.

Ashmole, Elias, 1617–92, antiquarian.

Aubrey, John, 1626–97, antiquarian.

Auden, Wystan Hugh, 1907–73, poet.

Austen, Jane, 1775–1817, novelist.

Austin, Alfred, 1835–1913, poet laureate.

Ayckbourn, Alan, 1939– , playwright.

Bacon, Francis, 1561–1628, philosopher.

Bacon, Roger, *c.* 1214–92, scientist and philosopher.

Bagehot, Walter, 1826–77, writer on economics, politics, and L.

Baillie, Joanna, 1762–1851, Scottish poet.

Balfour, Arthur J., Earl of, 1848–1930, statesman and essayist.

Baring, Maurice, 1874–1945, poet and novelist.

Baring-Gould, Sabine, 1834–1924, novelist and hymn-writer.

Barker, Harley Granville-, 1877–1947, dramatist and critic.

Barrie, Sir James Matthew, 1860–1937, novelist and dramatist.

Bates, Herbert Ernest, 1905–74, novelist.

Baxter, Richard, 1615–91, theologian and hymn writer.

Beaconsfield, Earl of (Benjamin Disraeli, 1804–81, novelist.

Beaumont, Francis, 1584–1616, dramatist.

Beckett, Samuel, 1906– , Irish author and playwright.

Bede, the Venerable, *c.* 673–735, historian.

Beeching, Henry Charles, 1859–1919, poet and essayist.

Beerbohm, Sir Max, 1872–1956, critic and miscellaneous writer.

Beeton, Mrs. Isabella, 1836–65, cookery writer.

Behn, Aphra, 1640–89, dramatist.

Beith, Maj.-Gen. J. H. *See* HAY.

Bell, Gertrude Margaret, 1868–1926, oriental traveller.

Belloc, Hilaire, 1870–1953, poet, essayist, and historian.

Bennett, Enoch Arnold, 1867–1931, novelist.

Benson, Arthur Christopher, 1862–1925, novelist and essayist.

Benson, Stella, 1892–1933, novelist.

Bentham, Jeremy, 1748–1832, political writer.

Bentley, Edmund Clerihew, 1875–1956, journalist and novelist.

Berkeley, George, 1685–1753, philosopher.

Betjeman, Sir John, 1906–84, poet.

Binyon, Laurence, 1869–1943, poet and dramatist.

Birkenhead, Lord, 1872–1930, jurist.

Birmingham, George (Canon J. O. Hannay), 1865–1952, novelist.

Birrell, Augustine, 1850–1933, essayist.

Blackie, John Stuart, 1809–95, scholar and man of letters.

Blackmore, Richard Doddridge, 1825–1900, novelist.

Blackstone, Sir William, 1723–80, jurist.

Blackwood, Algernon, 1869–1951, novelist.

Blake, William, 1757–1827, poet and painter.

Bland, Edith ('E. Nesbit'), 1858–1924, children's writer.

Blunden, Edmund, 1896–1974, poet.

Blunt, Wilfrid Scawen, 1840–1922, poet.

Blyton, Enid (Mrs. Kenneth Waters), *d.* 1968, children's writer.

Boece or Boethius, Hector, 1465? –1536, Scottish historian.

Booth, Rt. Hon. Charles, 1840–1916, sociologist.

Borrow, George, 1803–81, miscellaneous writer.

Boswell, James, 1740–95, biographer.

Bowdler, Thomas, 1754–1825, editor of Shakespeare.

Bowen, Elizabeth (Dorothea Cole), *d.* 1973, novelist.

Bridges, Robert Seymour, 1844–1930, poet.

Bridie, James (pseudonym of A. H. Mavor), 1888–1951, Scottish dramatist.

Brontë, Anne, 1820–49, novelist.

Brontë, Charlotte, 1816–55, novelist.

Brontë, Emily, 1818–48, poet and novelist.

Brooke, Rupert, 1887–1915, poet.

Brophy, John, 1899–1965, novelist.

Brougham and Vaux, Henry Lord, 1778–1868, essayist, founder of *Edinburgh Review.*

Browne, Sir Thomas, 1605–82, physician and miscellaneous writer.

Browning, Elizabeth Barrett, 1806–61, poet.

Browning, Robert, 1812–89, poet.
Buchan, John (Lord Tweedsmuir),
  1875–1940, novelist and historian.
Buchanan, George, 1506–82, Scottish
  historian.
Bullett, Gerald William, 1893–1958,
  novelist and poet.
Bunyan, John, 1628–88, allegorist.
Burke, Edmund, 1729–97, statesman
  and political philosopher.
Burnet, Gilbert, 1643–1715, historian.
Burnett, Frances Hodgson (Mrs.
  Stephen Townsend), 1849–1924,
  novelist.
Burney, Fanny. *See* D'ARBLAY.
Burns, Robert, 1759–96, Scottish poet.
Burton, Sir Richard Francis, 1821–90,
  anthropologist.
Burton, Robert, 1577–1640, humorist.
Butler, Samuel, 1612–80, satirist.
Butler, Samuel, 1835–1902, philo-
  sophical writer and novelist.
Byron, George Gordon, Lord,
  1788–1824, poet.
Cædmon, *d. c.* 680, Northumbrian
  poet.
Caine, Sir Thomas Henry Hall,
  1853–1931, novelist.
Camden, William, 1551–1623,
  antiquary.
Campbell, Thomas, 1777–1844,
  Scottish poet.
Carew, Thomas, 1595–1640, poet.
Carey, Henry, *c.* 1687–1743, dramatist
  and song writer.
Carlyle, Thomas, 1795–1881, historian
  and essayist.
Carman, William Bliss, 1861–1929,
  Canadian poet.
'Carroll, Lewis.' *See* DODGSON.
Chambers, Ephraim, *c.* 1680–1740,
  published first English encyclopaedia.
Chapman, George, 1559–1634,
  dramatist and translator.
Chatterton, Thomas, 1752–70, poet.
Chaucer, Geoffrey, 1340?–1400, poet.
Chesterfield, Philip Dormer Stanhope,
  Earl of, 1694–1773, letter-writer.
Chesterton, Gilbert Keith, 1874–1936,
  poet and critic.
Christie, Dame Agatha, 1890–1976,
  detective novelist.
Churchill, Sir Winston S., 1874–1965,
  statesman and historian.

Cibber, Colley, 1671–1757, poet, actor,
  and dramatist.
Clare, John, 1793–1864, poet.
Clarendon, Edward Hyde, Earl of,
  1609–74, historian. *See* CLAR-
  ENDON PRESS.
Clough, Arthur Hugh, 1819–61, poet.
Cobbett, William, 1763–1835,
  publicist.
Coke, Sir Edward, 1552–1634, jurist.
Cole, George Douglas Howard,
  1889–1959, political writer.
Coleridge, Hartley, 1796–1849, poet.
Coleridge, Samuel Taylor, 1772–1834,
  poet, philosopher, and critic.
'Collins, Tom.' *See* FURPHY.
Collins, William Wilkie, 1824–89,
  novelist.
Colman, George, 1732–94, dramatist.
Compton-Burnett, Dame Ivy,
  1892–1969, novelist.
Congreve, William, 1670–1729,
  dramatist.
Conrad (Korzeniowski), Joseph,
  1857–1924, novelist.
Coppard, Alfred Edward, 1878–1957,
  short-story writer and poet.
Corelli, Marie, 1855–1924, novelist.
Coverdale, Miles, 1488–1568,
  translator. *See* BIBLE.
Coward, Sir Noël, 1899–1973,
  playwright and composer.
Cowley, Abraham, 1618–67, poet.
Cowper, William, 1731–1800, poet.
Crabbe, George, 1754–1832, poet.
Craik, Dinah Marie, 1826–87, novelist.
Cranmer, Thomas, 1489–1556,
  liturgist.
Crashaw, Richard, 1612?–49, poet.
Crompton, Richmal, 1890–1969,
  children's writer.
Cynewulf, *fl.* 750, Northumbrian poet.
D'Arblay, Frances (Burney), 1752–
  1840, novelist.
Darwin, Charles Robert, 1809–82,
  naturalist. *See* DARWINISM.
Darwin, Erasmus, 1731–1802, botanist
  and poet.
D'Avenant, Sir William, 1606–68, poet
  and dramatist.
Davidson, John, 1857–1909, poet.
Davies, William Henry, 1871–1940,
  poet.
Day Lewis, Cecil, 1904–72, poet.

Defoe, Daniel, 1660–1731, journalist and novelist.

Dekker, Thomas, *c.* 1570–*c.* 1632, dramatist and pamphleteer.

Delafield, E. M. (Edmée de la Pasture), 1890–1943, novelist.

De la Mare, Walter John, 1873–1956, poet and novelist.

De la Ramée, Marie Louise ('Ouida'), 1839–1908, novelist.

De la Roche, Mazo, 1885–1961, Canadian novelist.

De Quincey, Thomas, 1785–1859, essayist and miscellaneous writer.

Dicey, Albert Venn, 1835–1922, jurist.

Dickens, Charles, 1812–70, novelist.

Dilke, Charles Wentworth, 1789–1864, journalist.

Disraeli, Benjamin. *See* BEACONSFIELD.

Dobson, Austin, 1840–1921, poet and essayist.

Dodgson, Charles Lutwidge ('Lewis Carroll'), 1832–98, writer of nonsense and mathematician.

Donne, John, 1573–1631, poet and divine.

Douglas, Gavin, 1474–1522, Scottish poet.

Douglas, Norman, 1868–1952, Scottish novelist and miscellaneous writer.

Doyle, Sir Arthur Conan, 1859–1930, novelist.

Drayton, Michael, 1563–1631, poet.

Drinkwater, John, 1882–1937, poet and dramatist.

Drummond, William (of Hawthornden), 1585–1649, poet.

Dryden, John, 1631–1700, poet, dramatist, and satirist.

Dugdale, Sir William, 1605–86, antiquarian.

Du Maurier, Dame Daphne (Lady Browning), 1907–   , novelist.

Dunbar, William, 1460?–1520?, Scots poet.

Edgeworth, Maria, 1767–1849, Irish novelist.

Eliot, George. *See* EVANS.

Eliot, Thomas Stearns, 1888–1965, Amer.-born poet and dramatist.

Ellis, Henry Havelock, 1859–1939, psychologist.

Elyot, Sir Thomas, 1490?–1546, miscellaneous writer.

Evans, Mary Ann ('George Eliot'), 1819–1880, novelist.

Evelyn, John, 1620–1706, diarist.

Farjeon, Eleanor, 1881–1965, poet and children's writer.

Farjeon, Herbert, 1887–1945, critic and playwright.

Farnol, John Jeffrey, 1878–1952, novelist.

Fielding, Henry, 1707–54, novelist.

Firth, Sir Charles Harding, 1857–1936, historian and critic.

Fisher, Herbert A. L., 1865–1940, politician and historian.

Fisher, St. John, 1459–1535, theologian.

FitzGerald, Edward, 1809–83, translator.

Flecker, James Elroy, 1884–1915, poet and dramatist.

Fleming, Ian. 1908–65, thriller writer.

Fletcher, John, 1579–1625, poet and dramatist.

Ford, Ford Madox (Hueffer), 1873–1939, poet and novelist.

Forester, Cecil Scott, 1899–1966, novelist.

Forster, Edward Morgan, 1879–1970, novelist.

Fortescue, Sir John, 1394–1476, jurist.

Fortescue, Sir John, 1859–1933, military historian.

Fox, George, 1624–91, Quaker diarist.

Foxe, John, 1516–87, martyrologist.

Francis, Sir Philip, 1740–1818, reputed author of *The Letters of Junius* (*q.v.*).

Frankau, Gilbert, 1884–1952, novelist.

Frazer, Sir James George, 1854–1941, anthropology and comparative religion.

Froude, James Anthony, 1818–94, historian.

Fry, Christopher, 1906–, dramatist.

Fry, Roger E., 1866–1934, art critic.

Fuller, Thomas, 1608–61, antiquary and biographer.

Furnivall, Frederick James, 1825–1910, lexicographer, editor *Oxford English Dictionary*.

Furphy, Joseph ('Tom Collins'), 1843–1912, Australian novelist.

Galsworthy, John, 1867–1933, novelist and dramatist.

Gardiner, Samuel Rawson, 1829–1902, historian.

Garnett, Edward, 1868–1937, critic.

Garvin, James Louis, 1868–1947, journalist.

Gaskell, Elizabeth Cleghorn (Stevenson), 1810–65, novelist.

Gay, John, 1685–1732, poet and dramatist.

Gibbon, Edward, 1737–94, historian.

Gibbs, Sir Philip Hamilton, 1877–1962, journalist and novelist.

Gilbert, Sir William Schwenck, 1836–1911, humorist and dramatist.

Gissing, George, 1857–1903, novelist.

Gladstone, William Ewart, 1809–98, statesman and man of letters.

Glyn, Mrs. Elinor, 1864–1943, Canadian novelist.

Godwin, Mrs. Mary Wollstonecraft, 1759–97, miscellaneous writer.

Godwin, William, 1756–1836, philosopher and novelist.

Golding, Louis, 1895–1958, novelist.

Golding, William Gerald, 1911–, novelist.

Goldsmith, Oliver, 1728–74, poet, dramatist, and essayist.

Gordon, Adam Lindsay, 1833–70, Australian poet.

Gosse, Sir Edmund William, 1849–1928, poet, critic, and essayist.

Gower, John, 1325?–1408, poet.

Grahame, Kenneth, 1859–1932, writer on child life.

Graves, Robert Ranke, 1895–, poet.

Gray, Thomas, 1716–71, poet.

Green, John Richard, 1837–83, historian.

Green, Thomas Hill, 1836–82, philosopher.

Greene, Graham, 1904–, novelist and playwright.

Greene, Robert, 1558–92, poet and dramatist.

Gregory, Augusta, Lady, 1852–1932, Irish dramatist.

Grenfell, Julian Henry Francis, 1888–1915, poet.

Greville, Charles Cavendish Fulke, 1794–1865, diarist.

Greville, Sir Fulke, Lord Brooke, 1554–1628, poet.

Grossmith, George, 1847–1912, miscellaneous writer (*Diary of a Nobody*).

Guthrie, Thomas Anstey ('F. Anstey'), 1856–1934, humorist.

Haggard, Sir Henry Rider, 1856–1925, novelist.

Hakluyt, Richard, 1552?–1616, collector of voyages.

Haldane, Richard Burdon, 1856–1928, critical philosopher.

Haliburton, Thomas Chandler ('Sam Slick'), 1765–1865, Nova Scotian humorist.

Hall, Edward, *c.* 1499–1547, chronicler.

Hall, Margaret Radclyffe, 1886–1943, novelist.

Hammerton, Sir John Alexander, 1871–1949, editor and critic.

Hammond, Barbara, *d.* 1961, economist.

Hannay, J. O. *See* BIRMINGHAM.

Hardy, Thomas, 1840–1928, poet and novelist.

Harington, Sir John, 1561–1612, miscellaneous writer.

Harrison, Mary St. Leger ('Lucas Malet'), 1852–1931, novelist.

Harrison, William, 1534–93, chronologist and topographer.

Hartley, Leslie Poles, 1895–1972, novelist.

Hawkins, Sir Anthony Hope, 1863–1933, novelist.

Hazlitt, William, 1778–1830, essayist and critic.

'Hay, Ian' (John Hay Beith), 1876–1952, novelist.

Heber, Reginald, 1783–1826, poet.

Hemans, Felicia Dorothea, 1793–1835, poetess.

Henley, William Ernest, 1849–1903, poet and critic.

Henryson, Robert, 1425 ?–1506 Scots poet.

Henty, George Alfred, 1832–1902, writer for boys.

Herbert of Cherbury, Edward, Lord, 1583–1648, philosopher and historian.

Herbert, George, 1593–1633, poet.

Herrick, Robert, 1591–1674, poet.

Hervey, John, Lord, 1696–1743, memorialist.

Hilton, James, 1900–54, novelist.

Hobbes, Thomas, 1588–1679, philosopher.

Hoccleve or Occleve, Thomas, 1368?–1450?, poet.

Hodgson,Ralph, 1871–1962, poet.

Hogg, James ('the Ettrick Shepherd'), 1770–1835, poet.

Holdsworth, Sir William, 1871–1943, jurist.

Holinshed or Hollingshead, Raphael, ?–1580?, historian.

Holtby, Winifred, 1898–1935, novelist.

Hood, Thomas, 1799–1845, poet and comic writer.

Hooker, Richard, 1554?–1600, theologian.

Hope, Anthony. See HAWKINS.

Hopkins, Gerard Manley, 1844–89, poet.

Housman, Alfred Edward, 1859–1936, poet.

Housman, Laurence, 1865–1959, dramatist and poet.

Howard, Henry. See SURREY.

Hudson, William Henry, 1841–1922, essayist and novelist.

Hughes, Ted, 1930–   , poet.

Hughes, Thomas, 1822–96, novelist.

Hume, David, 1711–76, philosopher and historian.

Hunt, James Henry Leigh, 1784–1859, essayist and poet.

Huxley, Aldous Leonard, 1894–1963, novelist and poet.

Hyde, Douglas, 1860–1949, poet in Irish and English and authority on Irish folklore.

Jacobs, William Wymark, 1863–1943, short-story writer.

Jefferies, Richard, 1848–87, naturalist and novelist.

Jennings, Elizabeth, 1926–, poet.

Jerome, Jerome Klapka, 1859–1927, novelist and dramatist.

Jerrold, Douglas William, 1803–57, dramatist, etc.

Johnson, Samuel, 1709–84, essayist and lexicographer.

Jonson, Benjamin, c. 1573–1637, poet and dramatist.

Jowett, Benjamin, 1817–93, scholar.

Joyce, James, 1882–1941, Irish novelist.

Kaye-Smith, Sheila, 1887–1956, novelist.

Keats, John, 1795–1821, poet.

Keble, John, 1792–1866, poet and divine.

Ken, Thomas, 1637–1711, hymn-writer.

Kendall, Henry Clarence, 1841–82, Australian poet.

Keynes, John Maynard, Lord, 1883–1946, economist.

Kilvert, Robert Francis, 1840–72, diarist.

Kingsley, Charles, 1819–75, novelist.

Kipling, Rudyard, 1865–1936, poet, novelist, and short-story writer.

Knox, John, c. 1513–72, Scottish reformer and historian.

Knox, Ronald (Monsignor), 1888–1957, theologian, translator, and miscellaneous writer.

Koestler, Arthur, 1905–83, Hungarian-b. novelist.

Kyd, Thomas, 1558–94, dramatist.

Lamb, Charles, 1775–1834, essayist and poet.

Lamb, Mary, 1764–1847, miscellaneous writer.

Landor, Walter Savage, 1775–1864, poet, etc.

Lanfranc, Archbishop, c. 1005–89, theologian.

Lang, Andrew, 1844–1912, poet and mythologist.

Langland, William, 1330?–1400?, poet.

Latimer, Hugh, 1485–1555, reformer and divine.

Lawrence, David Herbert, 1885–1930, novelist.

Lawrence, Thomas Edward, 1888–1935, historian and translator.

Layamon, fl. 1200, poet.

Leacock, Stephen, 1869–1944, Canadian essayist, etc.

Lear, Edward, 1812–88, writer of nonsense verse.

Lecky, William Edward Hartpole, 1838–1903, historian.

Le Fanu, Joseph Sheridan, 1814–73, novelist.

Leland, John, c. 1506–52, antiquary.

Lemon, Mark, 1809–70, journalist and humorist.

Lessing, Doris, 1919–   , novelist.

Lewis, Alun, 1915–44, poet.

Lewis, Clive Staples, 1898–1963, novelist.

Lewis, Dominic Bevan Wyndham, 1894–1969, biographer and journalist.

Linacre, Thomas, *c.* 1460–1524,
    physician and scholar.
Lindsay or Lyndsay, Sir David,
    1490–1555, Scots poet.
Lingard, John, 1771–1851, historian.
Locke, John, 1632–1704, philosopher.
Lodge, Thomas, 1558?–1625, poet and
    dramatist.
Lovelace, Richard, 1618–58, poet.
Low, Sir Sidney James Mark,
    1857–1932, historical writer.
Lucas, Edward Verrall, 1868–1938,
    story-writer and essayist.
Lydgate, John, 1370?–1450?, poet.
Lynd, Robert, 1879–1949, Irish essayist
    and critic.
Lytton, Edward Bulwer-Lytton, Lord,
    1803–73, novelist and statesman.
Lytton, Edward Robert Bulwer-Lytton,
    Earl of ('Owen Meredith'), 1831–91,
    statesman and poet.
Macaulay, Rose, 1887–1958, novelist
    and poet.
Macaulay, Thomas Babington, Lord,
    1800–59, historian and essayist.
MacCarthy, Sir Desmond, 1878–1952,
    critic.
MacDonald, George ('Phantastes'),
    1824–1905, poet and novelist.
MacNeice, Louis, 1907–63, poet.
Maitland, Sir Frederic William,
    1850–1906, historian.
Maitland, Sir Richard, Lord Leth-
    ington, 1496–1586, Scottish poet.
'Malet, Lucas.' *See* HARRISON, MARY
ST. LEGER.
Malory, Sir Thomas, *fl.* 1470,
    romancer.
Malthus, Thomas Robert, 1766–1834,
    economist.
Mansfield, Katherine, 1890–1923, New
    Zealand novelist.
Marlowe, Christopher, 1564–93,
    dramatist.
Marryat, Frederick, 1792–1848,
    novelist.
Martin, (Basil) Kingsley, 1897–1969,
    journalist.
Martineau, Harriet, 1802–76, novelist
    and economist.
Martineau, James, 1805–1900,
    Unitarian theologian.
Marvell, Andrew, 1621–78, poet and
    satirist.

Masefield, John Edward, 1878–1967,
    poet, playwright and novelist.
Massinger, Philip, 1583–1640,
    dramatist.
Massingham, Henry William,
    1860–1924, journalist and editor.
Maugham, William Somerset,
    1874–1965, novelist and dramatist.
May, Sir Thomas Erskine, Lord
    Farnborough, 1815–86, consti-
    tutional jurist and historian.
Meredith, George, 1828–1909, novelist
    and poet.
Meynell, Alice Christiana, 1847–1922,
    poet and essayist.
Meynell, Wilfrid, 1852–1948,
    journalist, poet, and essayist.
Middleton, Thomas, 1580–1627,
    dramatist.
Mill, James, 1773–1836, philosopher
    and historian.
Mill, John Stuart, 1806–73, philo-
    sopher.
Milne, Alan Alexander, 1882–1956,
    journalist, novelist, and playwright.
Milton, John, 1608–74, poet.
Mitford, Mary Russell, 1787–1855,
    novelist and dramatist.
Mitford, Nancy, 1904–73, novelist and
    biographer.
Moffat, Dr. James, 1870–1944,
    theologian and translator of Bible.
Monro, Harold, 1879–1932, poet.
Montagu, Lady Mary Wortley,
    1689–1762, letter-writer.
Montague, Charles Edward, 1867–
    1928, journalist and novelist.
Montgomery, James, 1771–1854, poet.
Montgomery, Lucy Maude, 1874–
    1942, Canadian novelist.
Moore, George Augustus, 1852–1933,
    dramatist and novelist.
Moore, Thomas, 1779–1852, poet.
More, Hannah, 1745–1833, miscel-
    laneous and religious writer.
More, St. Thomas, 1475–1535,
    historical and political writer.
Morgan, Charles, 1894–1958, novelist
    and playwright.
Morley of Blackburn, John, Visc.,
    1838–1923, statesman and man of
    letters.
Morris, William, 1834–96, poet and
    artist.

Mulock, Dinah Maria (Mrs. Craik),
  1826–1887, novelist.
Murdoch, (Jean) Iris, (Mrs. J. O. Bayley),
  b. 1919, novelist.
Murray, George Gilbert, 1866–1957,
  classicist.
Murry, John Middleton, 1889–1957,
  critic.
Nairne, Carolina Oliphant, Baroness,
  1766–1845, Scots poet.
Namier, Sir Lewis Bernstein,
  1888–1960, historian.
Nashe, Thomas, 1567–1601, dramatist
  and novelist.
Neale, John Mason, 1818–66,
  hymn-writer.
Nesbit, *see* Bland.
Newbolt, Sir Henry, 1862–1938, poet.
Newman, John Henry (Cardinal),
  1801–90, theologian and poet.
Newton, John, 1725–1807, divine and
  hymn-writer.
Nicolson, Sir Harold George,
  1886–1968, biographer and
  novelist.
Nichols, Robert Malise Bowyer,
  1893–1944, poet.
Northcliffe, Alfred Harmsworth, 1st
  Viscount, 1865–1922, journalist and
  newspaper proprietor.
Noyes, Alfred, 1880–1958, poet.
O'Brien, Edna, 1936–, Irish novelist.
O'Casey, Sean, 1884–1964, Irish
  dramatist.
Oman, Sir Charles William Chadwick,
  1860–1946, historian.
Onions, Charles Talbut, 1873–1965,
  philologist.
Oppenheim, Edward Phillips,
  1866–1946, novelist.
Orczy, Emmuska, Baroness, 1865–
  1947, novelist.
Orwell, George (Eric Blair), 1903–50,
  novelist and essayist.
Osborne, Dorothy (*Lady Temple*),
  1627–95, letter-writer.
Osborne, John, 1929–, dramatist.
O'Shaughnessy, Arthur William Edgar,
  1844–81, poet.
Otway, Thomas, 1652–85, dramatist.
Ouida. *See* DE LA RAMÉE.
Owen, Wilfrid, 1893–1918, poet.
Page, Dr. William, 1861–1934, editor
  of *The Victoria County Histories.*

Paine, Thomas, 1737–1809,
  pamphleteer.
Palgrave, Francis Turner, 1824–97,
  poet and anthologist.
Pares, Sir Bernard, 1867–1949,
  historian and Slavonic philologist.
Paris, Matthew, *c.* 1195–1259,
  chronicler.
Park, Mungo, 1771–1806, traveller.
Parker, Sir Gilbert, 1862–1932,
  Canadian novelist.
Parnell, Thomas, 1679–1718, poet.
Parry, Sir Edward Abbot, 1863–1943,
  miscellaneous author.
Passfield, Sidney James Webb, Baron,
  1859–1947, historian and economist.
Pater, Walter Horatio, 1839–94,
  essayist and critic.
Patmore, Coventry Kersey Dighton,
  1823–96, poet.
Pattison, Mark, 1813–84, scholar and
  biographer.
Peacock, Thomas Love, 1785–1866,
  novelist, critic, and poet.
Pearse, Padraic, 1879–1916, Irish poet.
Pepys, Samuel, 1633–1703, diarist.
Phillpotts, Eden, 1862–1960, novelist
  and dramatist.
Pickthall, Marjorie, 1883–1922,
  Canadian poet.
Pinero, Sir Arthur Wing, 1855–1934,
  dramatist.
Pinter, Harold, 1930–, dramatist.
Piozzi, Hester Lynch (Salusbury) (Mrs.
  Thrale), 1741–1821, miscellaneous
  writer.
Pope, Alexander, 1688–1744, poet.
Porson, Richard, 1759–1808, scholar
  and critic.
Porter, Jane, 1776–1850, novelist.
Powys, John Cowper, 1872–1963,
  novelist.
Powys, Llewellyn, 1884–1939, novelist.
Powys, Theodore Francis, 1875–1953,
  novelist.
Priestley, John Boynton, 1894–1984,
  novelist and dramatist.
Priestley, Joseph, 1733–1804, chemist
  and theologian.
Pringle, Thomas, 1789–1834, S.
  African poet.
Prior, Matthew, 1664–1721, poet.
Prynne, William, 1600–69, antiquarian
  and pamphleteer.

Pusey, Edward Bouverie, 1800–82, theologian.

Quiller-Couch, Sir Arthur Thomas, 1863–1944, novelist and critic.

Radcliffe, Mrs. Ann, 1764–1823, novelist.

Raleigh, Sir Walter, 1552?–1618, explorer, historian, etc.

Raleigh, Sir Walter Alexander, 1861–1922, critic.

Ramsay, Allan, 1686–1758, poet.

Randolph, Thomas, 1605–35, poet and dramatist.

Ransome, Arthur, 1884–1967, children's novelist and miscellaneous writer.

Rattigan, Sir Terence, 1911–83, dramatist.

Rawlinson, Sir Henry, 1810–95, orientalist.

Ray, John, 1627–1705, naturalist.

Read, Sir Herbert Edward, 1893–1968, poet and critic.

Reade, Charles, 1814–84, novelist.

Rhys, Ernest, 1859–1946, poet, critic, and editor of *Everyman's Library*.

Ricardo, David, 1772–1823, economist.

Richard of Cirencester, *d. c.* 1401, historian.

Richardson, Dorothy Miller, 1873–1957, novelist.

Richardson, Henry Handel (Ethyl Florence), 1870–1946, Australian novelist.

Richardson, Samuel, 1689–1761, novelist.

Ridley, Bishop Nicholas, 1500–55, theologian.

Rigg, James McMullen, 1855–1926, biographer and translator of the *Decameron*.

Robert of Gloucester, *c.* 1260–1300, metrical chronicler.

Roberts, Sir Charles George Douglas, 1860–1943, Canadian poet.

Robertson, John Mackinnon, 1856–1933, Shakespearian scholar.

Robinson, Henry Crabb, 1775–1867, journalist and diarist.

Rochester, John Wilmot, Earl of, 1647–80, poet.

Roger of Wendover, *d. c.* 1236, historian.

Rolle, Richard, *c.* 1300–49, mystic.

Roscoe, William, 1753–1831, historian.

Rose, John Holland, 1855–1942, historian.

'Ross, Martin' (Violet Florence), 1862–1915, novelist.

Rossetti, Christina Georgina, 1830–94, poet.

Rossetti, Dante Gabriel, 1828–82, poet.

Rowley, William, *c.* 1585–*c.* 1642, dramatist.

Ruskin, John, 1819–1900, writer on art, economics, etc.

Russell, Bertrand Arthur William, 3rd earl, 1872–1970, philosopher.

Russell, George William ('A. E.'), 1867–1935, Irish poet.

Russell, Sir William Howard, 1820–1911, journalist.

Rutherford, Mark. *See* WHITE, W. H.

Rymer, Thomas, 1641–1713, poet and critic.

Sackville, Thomas, 1536–1608, poet.

Sackville-West, Hon. Victoria, 1892–1962, poet, novelist, and biographer.

Sadleir, Michael T. H., 1888–1957, biographer and novelist.

Saintsbury, George, 1845–1933, critic.

Sala, George Augustus, 1828–95, novelist and journalist.

Sandys, George, 1578–1644, traveller and translator.

Sassoon, Siegfried Lorraine, 1886–1967, poet and novelist.

Savage, Richard, *c.* 1697–1742, poet.

Sayers, Dorothy Leigh, 1893–1957, novelist, essayist, and playwright.

Schreiber. *See* GUEST.

Scott, Charles Prestwich, 1846–1932, 57 years editor *Manchester Guardian*.

Scott, Michael, 1789–1835, novelist.

Scott, Sir Walter, 1771–1832, novelist and poet.

Seaman, Sir Owen, 1861–1936, poet, sometime editor of *Punch*.

Sedley, Sir Charles, 1639?–1701, poet and dramatist.

Seeley, Sir John Robert. 1834–95, historian and essayist.

Selden, John, 1584–1654, jurist and scholar.

Sewell, Anna, 1820–78, novelist.

Shadwell, Thomas, 1642?–92, dramatist and poet.

Shaftesbury, Anthony Ashley Cooper, Earl of, 1671–1713, philosopher.

Shakespeare, William (*q.v.*), 1564–1616, dramatist and poet.

Sharp, William (Fiona Macleod), 1856–1905, novelist and poet.

Shaw, George Bernard, 1856–1950, Irish dramatist.

Shelley, Mary Wollstonecraft, 1797–1851, novelist.

Shelley, Percy Bysshe, 1792–1822, poet.

Sheridan, Richard Brinsley, 1751–1816, dramatist.

Shirley, James, 1596–1666, dramatist.

Shirley, John, 1366–1456, translator.

Shute, Nevil, 1899–1960, novelist.

Sidney or Sydney, Algernon, 1622–83, political writer.

Sidney, Sir Philip, 1554–86, poet.

Sigerson, Dr. George, *d.* 1925, Gaelic scholar.

Simpson, Helen de Guerry, 1897–1940, Australian novelist.

Sinclair, May, 1870–1946, novelist.

Sitwell, Dame Edith Louise, 1887–1964, poet.

Sitwell, Sir Osbert, 1892–1969, poet and novelist.

Skeat, Walter William, 1835–1912, Anglo-Saxon scholar.

Skelton, John, 1460?–1529, poet.

Smart, Christopher, 1722–71, poet.

Smiles, Samuel, 1812–1904, biographer and miscellaneous writer.

Smith, Adam, 1723–90, philosopher and economist.

Smith, Sydney, 1771–1845, miscellaneous writer.

Smollett, Tobias George, 1721–71, novelist.

Snow, Baron Charles Percy, 1905–80, novelist.

Somerville, Edith Oenone, 1858–1949, Irish novelist.

Somerville, Mary, 1780–1872, mathematician.

Southerne, Thomas, 1660–1746, dramatist.

Southey, Robert, 1774–1843, poet and biographer.

Southwell, Robert, 1561?–95, poet.

Spark, Muriel, *fl.* 1960, novelist.

Speke, John, 1827–64, explorer.

Spelman, Sir Henry, 1564?–1641, historian.

Spencer, Herbert, 1820–1903, philosopher.

Spender, Sir Stephen, 1909–, poet.

Spenser, Edmund, 1552?–99, poet.

Stanley, Arthur Penrhyn (Dean of Westminster), 1815–81, historian, biographer, and theologian.

Stanley, Sir Henry, 1841–1904, traveller.

Stead, William Thomas, 1849–1912, journalist.

Steed, Henry Wickham, 1871–1956, journalist.

Steele, Sir Richard, 1672–1729, essayist and dramatist.

Stephen, Sir Leslie, 1832–1904, biographer and critic.

Stephens, James, 1882–1950, Irish story-writer and poet.

Stephens, James Brunton, 1835–1902, Australian poet.

Sterne, Laurence, 1713–68, novelist.

Stevenson, Robert Louis, 1850–94, novelist and essayist.

Stoppard, Tom, 1937–, playwright.

Stow, John, 1525?–1605, historian and antiquary.

Strachey, Giles Lytton, 1880–1932, biographer.

Strachey, John St. Loe, 1860–1927, critic and biographer.

Strickland, Agnes, 1796–1874, historical writer.

Strong, Leonard Alfred George, 1896–1958, poet and novelist.

Stubbs, William (Bishop), 1825–1901, historian.

Sturt, George ('George Bourne'), *d.* 1927, writer on English peasant life.

Suckling, Sir John, 1609–42, poet.

Surrey, Henry Howard, Earl of, 1517?–47, poet.

Swift, Jonathan (Dean), 1667–1745, satirist.

Swinburne, Algernon Charles, 1837–1909, poet.

Symonds, John Addington, 1840–93, historian, etc.

Symons, Arthur, 1865–1945, poet and symbolist writer.

Synge, John Millington, 1871–1909, Irish dramatist.

Tagore, Sir Rabindranath, 1861–1941, Indian poet.

Tate, Nahum, 1652–1715, poet.
Taylor, Jeremy, 1613–67, essayist.
Taylor, John, 1580–1653, the 'water-poet'.
Temple, Sir William, 1628–99, essayist.
Temple, William (Archbishop), 1881–1944, theologian and philosopher.
Tennyson, Alfred, Lord, 1809–92, poet.
Thackeray, William Makepeace, 1811–63, novelist.
Thomas, Dylan Marlais, 1914–53, poet.
Thomas, (Philip) Edward, 1878–1917, essayist and poet.
Thompson, Francis Joseph, 1860–1907, poet.
Thomson, James, 1700–48, poet.
Thomson, James, ('B.V.'), 1834–82, poet.
Thrale, *See* PIOZZI.
Tolkien, John Ronald, 1892–1973, novelist.
Tomlinson, Henry Major, 1873–1958, novelist.
Toynbee, Arnold, 1852–83, economist.
Traherne, Thomas, 1638–74, poet and theological writer.
Trevelyan, George Macaulay, 1876–1962, historian.
Trevelyan, Sir George Otto, 1838–1928, historian.
Trollope, Anthony, 1815–82, novelist.
Tupper, Martin Farquhar, 1810–89, versifier.
Tynan, Katherine (Mrs. Hinkson), 1861–1931, Irish novelist and poet.
Tyndale, William, *c.* 1490–1536, translator of the Bible.
Udall, Nicholas, 1505–56, dramatist and scholar.
Urquhart, Sir Thomas, 1611–60, Scottish translator of Rabelais.
Usk, Thomas, *d.* 1388, poet.
Ussher, James, 1581–1656, divine and scholar.
Vachell, Horace Annesley, 1861–1955, novelist.
Vanbrugh, Sir John, 1664–1726, dramatist.
Vaughan, Henry, 1622–95, poet.
Vaux, Thomas, Lord, 1510–56, poet.
Waddell, Helen Jane, 1899–1965, scholar.
Wallace, Edgar, 1875–1932, dramatist and novelist.

Waller, Edmund, 1606–87, poet.
Walpole, Horace, 1717–97, miscellaneous writer.
Walpole, Sir Hugh Seymour, 1884–1941, novelist.
Walsingham, Thomas, *d. c.* 1422, historian.
Walton, Izaak, 1593–1683, essayist.
Ward, Mrs. Humphry (Mary Arnold), 1851–1920, novelist.
Warton, Joseph, 1722–1800, critic.
Warton, Thomas, 1728–90, historian of English poetry.
Watts, Isaac, 1674–1748, poet and theologian.
Waugh, Evelyn Arthur St. John, 1903–66, novelist.
Webb, Beatrice, 1858–1943, economist and political philosopher.
Webb, Mary, 1881–1927, novelist.
Webster, John, 1580?–1625?, dramatist.
Wells, Herbert George, 1866–1946, novelist and writer on sociology.
Wesley, Charles, 1707–88, hymn writer.
Wesley, John, 1703–91, theological writer.
West, Dame Rebecca, 1892–1983, novelist and dramatist.
Whiting, John, *d.* 1963, dramatist.
White, Gilbert, 1720–93, naturalist.
White, Patrick Victor Martindale, 1912–, Australian novelist.
White, William Hale (Mark Rutherford), 1831–1913, novelist.
Wiclif, or Wycliffe, John *c.* 1324–84, translator.
Wilde, Oscar O'Flahertie, 1854–1900, poet and dramatist.
Wilkes, John, 1727–97, journalist, M.P.
William of Malmesbury, *b. c.* 1092, *d. c.* 1143, historian.
Williamson, Charles Norris, 1857–1920, novelist.
Williamson, Henry, 1895–1979, novelist.
Winchilsea, Anne Finch, Countess of, 1661–1720, poet.
Wither, George, 1588–1667, poet.
Wodehouse, Sir Pelham (Grenville), 1881–1975, humorist.
Wolfe, Humbert, 1885–1940, poet, critic, and biographer.

Wood, Anthony à, 1632–95, antiquarian, etc.

Wood, Ellen (Mrs. Henry), 1814–87, novelist.

Woodforde, James, 1740–1803, diarist.

Woolf, Leonard Sidney, d. 1969, publisher.

Woolf, Virginia, 1882–1941, novelist.

Wordsworth, Dorothy, 1771–1855, diarist.

Wordsworth, William, 1770–1850, poet.

Wotton, Sir Henry, 1568–1639, poet.

Wyatt, Sir Thomas, 1503–42, poet.

Wycherley, William, 1640?–1716, dramatist.

Wyndham, George, 1863–1914, critic.

Yates, Edmund, 1831–94, novelist and dramatist.

Yeats, William Butler, 1865–1939, Irish dramatist, poet, and critic.

Yonge, Charlotte Mary, 1823–1901, novelist.

Young, Arthur, 1741–1820, writer on agriculture and travel.

Young, Edward, 1683–1765, poet.

Young, Emily Hilda, 1880–1949, novelist.

Young, Francis Brett, 1884–1954, novelist.

Zangwill, Israel, 1864–1926, novelist and dramatist.

English National Opera Company, *See* SADLER'S WELLS OPERA COMPANY.

English Sovereigns and their Consorts. The names of some kings of the English tribes (notably Offa I) are known when they were still in S. Jutland, fourth century. Cerdic led the tribe which formed the nucleus of the W. Saxon kingdom to England, *c.* 500, and the sixteenth King of Wessex (*q.v.*) was Egbert, first king of all the English, from whom all subsequent English sovereigns are descended, except those in *italics* in the following list:

House of Cerdic

Egbert	802–839	Edmund I	939–946 assassinated
Ethelwulf	839–858	Edred	946–955
Ethelbald	858–860	Edwy	955–959
Ethelbert	860–865	Edgar	959–975
Ethelred I	865–870	Edward the Younger	975–978 assassinated
Alfred the Great	871–899	Ethelred II (the	
Edward the Elder	899–924	Unready)	979–1016
Athelstan	924–939	Edmund II (Ironside)	1016

House of the Skjöldungs or of Denmark

Canute the Great	1016–1035	*Harold I* (alone)	1035–1040
Harthacanute }	1035	*Harthacanute* (again)	1040–1042
Harold I			

House of Cerdic (again)
Edward the Confessor 1042–1066

House of Godwin
Harold II 1066 (killed at Hastings)

House of Normandy

SOVEREIGN		CONSORT
William I (the Conqueror)	1066–1078	Matilda of Flanders, *m.* 1053, *d.* 1084
William II (Rufus)	1087–1100	
Henry I	1100–1135	1. Matilda of Scotland (grand-daughter of Edmund Ironside), *m.* 1100, *d.* 1119
		2. Adela of Louvain, *m.* 1121, *d.* 1151
Stephen	1135–1154	Matilda of Boulogne, *m.* 1124, *d.* 1151

House of Anjou or Plantagenet

Henry II	1154–1189	Eleanor of Aquitaine, *m.* 1152, *d.* 1204
Richard I	1189–1199	Berengaria of Navarre, *m.* 1191, *d. c.* 1230

John	1199–1216	1. Hadwisa or Avis of Gloucester, *m.* 1189, divorced 1200
		2. Isabel of Angoulême, *m.* 1200, *d.* 1246
Henry III	1216–1272	Eleanor of Provence, *m.* 1236, *d.* 1291
Edward I	1272–1307	1. Eleanor of Castile, *m.* 1254, *d.* 1296
		2. Margaret of France, *m.* 1299, *d.* 1308
Edward II (deposed and murdered)	1307–1327	Isabella of France, *m.* 1308, *d.* 1358
Edward III	1327–1377	Philippa of Hainault *m.* 1328, *d.* 1369
Richard II (deposed and murdered)	1377–1399	1. Anne of Bohemia, *m.* 1382, *d.* 1394
		2. Isabella of France, *m.* 1396, *d.* 1409

House of Lancaster

Henry IV	1399–1413	1. Mary de Bohun, *m.* 1380, *d.* 1394
		2. Joan of Navarre, *m.* 1402, *d.* 1437
Henry V	1413–1422	Catherine of France, *m.* 1420, *d.* 1437
Henry VI (deposed)	1422–1461	Margaret of Anjou, *m.* 1445, *d.* 1482

House of York

Edward IV	1461–1470	Elizabeth Woodville, *m.* 1464, *d.* 1492
Henry VI (again)	1470–1471)	
Edward IV	1471–1483	
Edward V (murdered in the Tower)	Apr.–June 1483	
Richard III (killed at battle of Bosworth)	1483–1485	Anne Neville, *m.* 1474, *d.* 1485

House of Tudor

Henry VII	1485–1509	Elizabeth of York, *m.* 1486, *d.* 1503
Henry VIII	1509–1547	1. Catherine of Aragon, *m.* 1509, divorced 1533, *d.* 1536
		2. Anne Boleyn, *m.* 1533, executed 1536
		3. Jane Seymour, *m.* 1536, *d.* 1537
		4. Anne of Cleves, *m.* Jan. 1540, divorced June 1540, *d.* 1557
		5. Catherine Howard, *m.* 1540, executed 1542
		6. Catherine Parr, *m.* 1543, *d.* 1548
Edward VI	1547–1553*	
Mary I and Philip (1554)	1553–1558	Philip II of Spain, *m.* 1554, *d.* 1598
Elizabeth I	1558–1603	

House of Stuart

| James I | 1603–1625 | Anne of Denmark, *m.* 1589, *d.* 1619 |
| Charles I (beheaded) | 1625–1649 | Henrietta Maria of France, *m.* 1625, *d.* 1669 |

* Lady Jane Grey was proclaimed queen and 'ruled' for 10 days in 1553, but was never crowned, and was subsequently beheaded.

Commonwealth and Protectorate   1649–1660

Charles II	1660–1685	Catherine of Braganza, *m.* 1662, *d.* 1705
James II (fled)	1685–1688	1. Anne Hyde, *m.* 1660, *d.* 1671
		2. Mary of Modena, *m.* 1673, *d.* 1718
William III* and Mary II	1689–1694	*m.* 1677
William III alone	1694–1702	
Anne	1702–1744	George of Denmark, *m.* 1683, *d. 1708*

House of Hanover

George I	1714–1727	Sophia of Brunswick, *m.* 1682, *d.* 1726
George II	1727–1760	Caroline of Ansbach, *m.* 1705, *d.* 1737
George III	1760–1820	Charlotte of Mecklenburg-Strelitz, *m.* 1761, *d.* 1818
George IV	1820–1830	Caroline of Brunswick, *m.* 1795, *d.* 1821
William IV	1830–1837	Adelaide of Saxe-Meiningen, *m.* 1818, *d.* 1849
Victoria	1837–1901	Albert of Saxe-Coburg, *m.* 1840, *d.* 1861

House of Saxe-Coburg-Gotha

Edward VII	1901–1910	Alexandra of Denmark, *m.* 1863, *d.* 1925

House of Windsor†

George V	1910–1936	Mary of Teck, *m.* 1893, *d.* 1953
Edward VIII (abdicated)	1936	Mrs Ernest Simpson (Duchess of Windsor) m. 1936.
George VI	1936–1952	Lady Elizabeth Bowes–Lyon, *m.* 1923.
Elizabeth II**	1952–	Philip Mountbatten, Duke of Edinburgh, *m.* 1947

See also the separate kingdoms for the period before 802, viz. BERNICIA, DEIRA, EAST ANGLIA, ESSEX, KENT, MERCIA, SUSSEX, WESSEX.

*William III, whose mother was a Stuart, was himself a member of the House of Orange.
†George V renounced the surname of Saxe-Coburg-Gotha and adopted that of Windsor for himself and his descendants in 1917.
**Heir to the throne (1984) is the Prince of Wales, Charles Philip Arthur George, *b.* 1948, *m.* Lady Diana Frances Spencer, 1981, and has issue William Arthur Philip Louis, *b.* 21 June, 1982 and Henry (Harry) Charles Albert David, *b.* 15 Sept. 1984.

Engraving on Metal and Stone.   First metal plate from which impressions on paper were taken apparently executed, 1452. Early books with metal engravings, the *Kalender*, 1465, and the *Monte Santo di Dio*, 1477. First specialist in engraving, Marcantonio Raimondi (1475–1530). In England the earliest line engravings are in *The Birth of Mankind*, 1540. Earliest English engraver known by name, William Rogers (*fl.* 1580–1610). Mezzotint process invented by Ludwig von Siegen *c.* 1642. Introduced into England, 1660, by Prince Rupert, who had seen Siegen at work. Aquatints said to have been invented by Saint-Non (1730–1804) and first used in England, 1780. Lithography invented by Aloys Senefelder, 1796. *See* ARTS, THE PLASTICS.

Engraving on Wood.   Practised by Chinese some centuries B.C. Modern process, however, dates from fifteenth century, earliest dated example (1423) being at Memminingen (Germany). Caxton's second edition of *The Game and Playe of the Chesse*, 1476, contains earliest English woodcuts. The art was revolutionized by Albrecht Dürer (1471–1528) of Nürnberg. In England George, Edward, John, and Thomas Dalziel were very active from 1839 till process blocks began to supersede engraving *c.* 1879.

Enosis.   Campaign for the union of Cyprus with Greece, originated, 1912, and continued until the establishment of the Republic of Cyprus (*q.v.*) in 1960.

Ensign, military rank in British infantry units, was superseded by the term second lieutenant, 1871.

Ensign, national flag flown by shipping, is worn according to a convention adopted in 1864.

Entente Cordiale between England and France (partly brought about by the exertions of King Edward VII) and Anglo-French Agreement signed, 8 Apr. 1904.

Entertainments Tax (Britain). First levied, 1916.

Environment, Department of, estab. 1970, combining former ministries dealing with housing, planning and ancient monuments.

E.O.K.A. Cypriot guerrilla force organized 1954, to fight for *Enosis* (*q.v.*). Disbanded, 1960.

Ephesus, Asia Minor. Founded *c.* 1000 B.C. Fell under Lydian domination, sixth century. The Artemisium or Temple of Artemis, founded *c.* 750 B.C.; sacked by Cimmerii *c.* 650; rebuilt *c.* 545–425 in the form which was one of the Seven Wonders of the World (*q.v.*). Destroyed by Herostratus, 356 B.C., but restored shortly after. E. became the administrative capital of the Roman province of Asia *c.* 140 B.C., was visited by St. Paul (*see* Acts) *c.* A.D. 56. Temple destroyed by the Goths in A.D. 263. Church councils held at E., 197, 245, 431, 446, 447, 449.

Epirus, Greece. Rose to prominence for a short period during the wars of its King Pyrrhus against the Romans, which ended 275 B.C.

Episcopal Ordination Act (Scotland). Passed, 1662.

Epping Forest. Ancient royal forest bought and opened to the public by the City of London, 1882.

Epsom (Surrey). Sulphate of magnesia springs discovered, 1618. Races run at E. from about 1620. Derby Day (*q.v.*) takes place there.

Equal Opportunities Commission, estab. 1975. Baroness Lockwood being its first chairman.

Equatorial Guinea, as **Spanish Guinea** acquired by Spain at end of eighteenth century. Became independent, 1968. Marxist 1968–79 but subsequent military coup restored Catholic Church in E.G. and re-estab. economic links with Spain.

Erastians. A religious sect following the teachings of Erastus (1524–83). Their ideas much advocated at Westminster Assembly, 1643–9.

Erfurt, Germany. Bishopric, 741; ceded to the Elector of Mainz, 1648. Luther lived in the monastery of St. Augustine, 1508–11. Incorporated into Prussia, 1802. Brandt, Chancellor of the F.D.R. and Stoph, premier of the G.D.R., met for historic talks at E., March 1970.

Erie Canal (U.S.A.). Opened, 1825. Deepened, 1907.

Eritrea. Italians purchased Assab, 1870. Occupied Massawa, 1885. Province of E. organized, 1890. Amalgamated with Ethiopia in Italian E. Africa, 9 May 1936. British invasion begins, Dec. 1940. Under British Military administration, 1941–8. Scheme for federation with Ethiopia approved by United Nations, Dec. 1950. E. pronounced integral part of Ethiopia, 1962, but Eritrean agitation against this, 1966 onwards. *See* ETHIOPIA.

Erzurum, Turkey. Citadel founded *c.* 415 by Theodosius the Younger. Taken by Turks, 1517. By Russians, 1829 and 1878. Armenians massacred at, 1895 and 1915. Captured by Russians, Mar. 1916. Abandoned on Communist orders, Jan. 1918. Reoccupied by Turks, Mar. 1918.

Escheat. Abolished in England, 1925.

Escorial or **Escurial,** royal establishment outside Madrid consisting of palace, church, monastery, and college within a single precinct, founded by Philip II of Spain, 23 Apr. 1563. Charles V's remains conveyed there, 1574. Building completed, 1584. Philip II *d.* there, 1598.

Esperanto. International language, invented, 1887, by Dr. L. Zamenhof, a Warsaw oculist (1859–1917).

Essex, Kingdom of. Established by the E. Saxons *c.* sixth century. There was not always one ruler, power and territory being sometimes divided, though the kings were of a common dynasty. Between *c.* 600 and 824 the names of fifteen kings are known. As an independent kingdom it came to an end *c.* 830, and was ceded by Wessex to the Danish kings of E. Anglia under the Treaty of Wedmore (*q.v.*), 878.

Estate Duty (U.K.). First levied, 1894, on real property.

Estates, Committee of the. Appointed by Scots Parliament, 1640–8.

Este, Italy. Dukes of became dukes of Reggio and Modena (*q.v.*), 1452 and of Ferrara, 1471. Family of the Estensi died out in Italy, 1803.

Estonia. Two branches of the Finnish group of tribes originating on the Upper Volga—the Ests and the Livs—were settled respectively N. and W. of the Gulf of Riga by the beginning of the Christian era. The Russians from Novgorod built a fort at Tartu, in E., 1036. Danes under Bishop Albert of Riga, who founded Reval, conquered E., 1219. They sold their gains to the Teutonic Knights (*q.v.*), 1346, who amalgamated E. with Livonia. After dissolution of the Teutonic Order, 1560, northern E. passed to Sweden while southern E. went first to Poland until 1629, thence to Sweden, which ceded the whole country to Russia, 1720. Independence proclaimed, 24 Feb. 1918. Russian forces marched into E., 18 June 1940, and E. joined the U.S.S.R., as a constituent republic, 6 Aug. The Germans invaded E., Aug. 1941, and remained in occupation of the country, which became part of 'Ostland', 17 Nov. 1941, until ejected by Soviet troops, Feb. 1945.

Étaples, Treaty of, between Henry VII of England and Charles VIII of France, 3 Nov. 1492.

Etching. First E., on iron by Albrecht Dürer *c.* 1500. *See* ENGRAVING.

Ether. Faraday (1791–1867) discovered its soporific qualities, 1818. First used as an anaesthetic, 1846.

Ethiopia or **Abyssinia.** Former royal house claimed descent from Solomon and the Queen of Sheba. Kingdom of Axum *fl.* first–seventh centuries. Christianity introduced by St.

Frumentius *c.* A.D. 330. El-Esbaha conquered Yemen, 525–75. Revolution and country divided between Axum and Shoa, 1000. Reunited under the Solomonean dynasty by Tekuno Amtak, 1268. Arrival of the Portuguese Pedro de Covilha, 1490. Jesuit attempt at conversion of Copts to Roman Catholicism ends in expulsion of Portuguese by King Fasilidas, 1633. Victory of Kassai of Amhara at Gorgora, 1853. He proclaims himself Emperor as Theodore III, 1853. Defeat by British and suicide of Theodore at Magdala, 1868. Kassai of Tigré proclaimed Emperor as John I, 1872–89. Emperor Menelek (1889–1913) defeats Italians at Adowa, 1896. Regency of Empress Zauditu and Ras Tafari, 1916–30. Tafari becomes Emperor as Haile Selassie, 1930. Italian conquest of E., Oct. 1935–May 1936. Reconquest by British and Haile Selassie begun, Jan. 1941. Completed, Nov. 1941. Federation with Eritrea became effective, Sept. 1952; Eritrea fully integrated, 1962. Haile Selassie granted a more liberal Constitution on his Silver Jubilee, 1955. Haile Selassie deposed, 1974, and a left-wing republic established. Haile Selassie *d.*, 1975. Civil war in the Ogaden since 1978. Severe famine in E., since 1982.

Etna, Sicily. 10,758 ft. Several serious eruptions since 476 B.C. These include eruptions in 125 and 43 B.C., and in A.D. 1169 (when Catania was overwhelmed), 1444, 1537, 1553, 1669 (when a twelve-foot abyss was opened up in the mountainside), 1830, 1852, 1879, 1892, 1899, 1910, 1923, 1928, 1971, 1981 and 1983.

Eton College (England). Founded, 1440, by Henry VI and William of Waynflete. Supplementary charter, 1441, when buildings were commenced. Mutinies took place, 1743, 1768, 1783, 1810, and 1832.

Etruria, Italy. Inhabited by a people speaking a non-Indo-European language, who may have come from Asia some time before 800 B.C. and who probably supplied the Tarquin kings to Rome in seventh century B.C. Finally conquered by Cornelius Dolabella, 283 B.C. Received Roman franchise, 91 B.C.

Euboea or **Negropont,** Greece. Struggle between Chalcis and Eretria for leadership of, eighth century. Euboean colonies founded in Chalcidice eighth and seventh centuries B.C. In Sicily and Italy, 760–648. Eretria assists Ionian revolt against Persia, 499. Eretria sacked by Persians, 490. Athenian colony at Histiaea, 445. Athenian influence shaken off, 404. Joins Athenian confederation again, 357. Submits to Macedon, 336; to Rome, 146. Seized by Venetians, A.D. 1204. Conquered by Turks, 1470. Becomes Greek, 1832.

Euratom. *See* EUROPEAN ATOMIC ENERGY COMMUNITY.

Eureka Stockade. *See* BALLARAT.

European Association. Founded in London by Mazzini and others to promote republicanism in Europe, 1855.

European Atomic Energy Community (Euratom). Constituted, 1 Jan. 1958, to promote a powerful nuclear industry for peaceful purposes among members of the European Economic Community.

European Coal and Steel Community. Established, 10 Aug. 1952, to pool the Common Market countries' resources of coal, iron, and steel in a single market.

European Defence Community (E.D.C.). Proposed defensive federation of France, Belgium, Italy, Luxembourg, the Netherlands, and the German Federal Republic. Treaty establishing E.D.C. signed, May 1952, but the French National Assembly rejected it, 30 Aug. 1954, and it was subsequently superseded by the defence arrangements made under the London and Paris agreements (*q.v.*).

European Economic Community (E.E.C.), popularly known as the **Common Market**. Came into being 1 Jan. 1958, following ratification of the Treaty of Rome (signed 25 Mar. 1957). Original members ('The Six') were: Belgium, France, Federal Germany, Italy, Luxembourg and the Netherlands. Aim: to eliminate the tradi-

tional economic frontiers between member states by gradual abolition of customs barriers and adoption of common policies on agriculture, transport and commerce. Some kind of eventual political unity vaguely envisaged. The Six were also members of the European Coal and Steel Community (E.C.S.C.) estab. 1952 and the European Atomic Energy Community (Euratom) estab. 1958. Britain formally applied for membership, 10 Aug. 1961 but on 29 Jan. 1963 talks on Britain's entry finally broke down, due to Fr. pressure. Negotiations for Britain's entry restarted, 1970. In 1973 Britain, Ireland and Denmark joined the E.E.C., public referenda declaring in favour; but Norway remained outside, after a referendum against entry. European Parliament estab. 1975. Greece joined E.E.C., 1981. Britain reaches agreement on Budget deficit, 1984. Spain and Portugal to join E.E.C., 1 Jan 1986. Industrial tariffs between E.E.C. and E.F.T.A. to be abolished, 1984.

European Free Trade Association (E.F.T.A.). Founded 1960, when membership consisted of Austria, Denmark, Norway, Portugal, Sweden, Switzerland, and the U.K. Finland associated with E.F.T.A., 27 Mar. 1961: Iceland from 1970. U.K. and Denmark left E.F.T.A., 1973, on joining the European Common Market (*q.v.*), and membership 1985 consisted of Austria, Iceland, Norway, Portugal, Sweden and Switzerland, with Finland an associate member.

Eurovision. Direct television link-up between various European countries. Developed after 1953, when the B.B.C. coverage of Elizabeth II's coronation was relayed successfully to W. Europe. *See* TELEVISION.

Evacuation (U.K.) of mothers and children from danger areas before World War II began, 1 Sept. 1939.

Evacuation Day (New York, U.S.A.). Anniversary of the British evacuation of New York, 25 Nov. 1783.

Evangelical Alliance of German protestant states, 1608, opposed by Holy Alliance (founded 1609).

Evangelical Alliance, World's. Founded in London, 1846.

Evangelic League. Founded by certain Lutherans and Calvinists against the Emperor Mathias, 1613.

Evans Case. Timothy Evans was hanged for the murder of his baby daughter at 10 Rillington Place, London, in 1950. Subsequently John Christie, of the same address, was executed (1953) after confessing to the murder of several women, including Mrs. Evans. First inquiry into Evans's case, 1953, found that Evans killed both his wife and child. Second inquiry, 1965–6, reported that Evans probably did not kill his child, but more probably than not killed his wife. Evans's body reinterred in consecrated ground, 1965, and Evans granted a posthumous free pardon, Oct. 1966. Case and its aftermath influenced the campaign for the abolition of capital punishment in Britain (1965, and, permanently, 1969).

'Evening News.' *See* NEWSPAPERS.

'Evening Standard.' *See* NEWSPAPERS.

Everest, Mount, Expeditions to. Gen. C. G. Bruce (1), 1922; (2) 1924 (with Col. Norton). Marquess of Douglas and D. F. McIntyre flew over E., 1933. H. Rutledge, 1933. H. W. Tilman, 1938. Reconnaisance of western approaches by party under E. Shipton, 1951–2. Swiss expedition in autumn of 1952 abandoned, Dec. Climbed by Hillary and Tensing, 29 May 1953.

Everyman's Library. Comprehensive library of the representative works of all time, first published by J. M. Dent & Sons Ltd in 1906. Thousandth title issued 1976.

Evian Conference on refugees, 6–15 July 1938.

Evian Agreement, between France and the Algerian nationalists to end the civil war in Algeria and acknowledge Algeria's independence, signed 18 Mar. 1962.

Evil May Day. 1 May 1517. A riot of London apprentices which arose out of complaints against foreigners and the consequent conspiracy of 30 Apr. 1517.

Evora, Convention of, ended Portuguese civil war, 1834.

Exarch.
1. (of Ravenna). Title of the Byzantine governor of Italy, 584–782.
2. Title of the Patriarch of the Bulgarian orthodox church instituted, 1876.

Excess Profits Duty. Imposed Sept. 1915 to Mar. 1921.

Excess Profits Tax. Imposed as from 3 Sept. 1939. Abolished as from 1 Jan. 1954.

Exchange, Royal (London). Founded by Sir Thomas Gresham 7 June 1566. Queen Elizabeth I visited it, Jan. 1571, since when it has been called 'Royal'. Burnt, 1666. Rebuilt by Edward German, 1668. Burnt again, 1838. Present building, 1840–4.

Exchequer. Originally part of the Council (*q.v.*), it was already a separate department by reign of Henry II (1154–89), and also distinct from the court of the same name (*see* COURTS). Chancellor of E. office founded, 1221. E. Office founded, 1399. Chancellor of the E.'s judicial functions ceased to exist after 1735. E. and Audit Department instituted, 1866.

Chancellors of the Exchequer since 1924:

P. Snowden 1924
W. S. Churchill 1924–1929
P. Snowden 1929–1931
N. Chamberlain 1931–1937
Sir John Simon 1937–1940
Sir Kingsley Wood 1940–1943
Sir John Anderson 1943–1945
H. Dalton 1945–1947
Sir Stafford Cripps 1947–1950
H. Gaitskell 1950–1951
R. A. Butler 1951–1955
H. Macmillan 1955–1957
P. Thorneycroft 1957–1958
D. Heathcoat-Amory 1958–1960
Selwyn Lloyd 1960–1962
Reginald Maudling 1962–1964
James Callaghan 1964–1967
Roy Jenkins 1967–1970
Iain Macleod 1970
Anthony Barber 1970–1974
Denis Healey 1974–1979
Sir Geoffrey Howe 1979–1983
Nigel Lawson 1983–

Exchequer, Court of the. *See* COURTS.

Excise (U.K.). Introduced by Long Parliament, 1643. Sir R. Walpole fails to pass a new E. scheme owing to strong opposition, 1733. Board of Inland Revenue founded, 1849. Transferred to control of the Board of Customs and E., 1909.

Excise (U.S.A.). E. bill on liquor introduced into Congress, 1791. Caused rioting, 1794.

Exclusion Bill to disable the Duke of York (later James II) as a Roman Catholic from succeeding to the throne, introduced, 1679. It was passed three times by the House of Commons, but on each occasion Charles II dissolved Parliament.

Exeter, England. Originally *Isca Dumnoniorum* and a Roman military station. Known to the W. Welsh as *Caer Wisc*. Sacked by Sweyn, King of Denmark, 1003. Made a bishopric, 1050. Retaken by William the Conqueror after a rising in the W., 1068. Cathedral begun, 1112. E. school established, 1629. Captured by Prince Maurice, 1643. Retaken by Fairfax, 1646. The University College of the S.W. (incorporated 1922) was created University of E. by royal charter in 1955.

Exeter Book. Leofric, Bishop of E. from 1050 to 1071, gave this book to the cathedral library. Written before 1050, first transcribed, 1831, first printed, 1842.

Exeter Hall (Strand, London). Built, 1830–1; used for concerts, meetings, etc., till 1880. Demolished, 1907.

Exhibition of 1851, The Great (London). Royal Commission appointed and building begun in Hyde Park, 3 Jan. 1850. Opened by Queen Victoria, 1 May 1851. *See* CRYSTAL PALACE.

Exile, known in British law as Transportation (*q.v.*).

Existentialism, as a philosophy, was expressed in *Sein und Zeit* by Martin Heidegger, 1926; *Gegenwart: eine Kritische Ethik* by E. Grisebach, 1928; *Philosophie*, by Karl Jaspers, 1932; and from *c.* 1940, but especially since 1944, by the plays of Jean-Paul Sartre (1905–80). E. was condemned by the Pope, 1948.

Extradition Laws. Court of Exchequer declared a form of E.L., 1749. Ashburton Treaty with U.S.A., 1842; extended, 1890. With treaty with France, 1843. New Convention with France when exceptions regarding political offences were made, 1852. Present procedure in Great Britain based on the E. Acts of 1870–3 and the amendments of 1906 and 1932. Modified in practice by other legislation e.g. Misuse of Drugs Act, 1971; Hijacking Act, 1971; and British Nationality Act, 1982.

Eyre, Lake, Australia. Discovered by Edward E. (1815–1901) in 1840.

Eyre, Commissions of General. (Lat. '*Iter*.') Bodies of commissioners were sent round the kingdom at intervals to investigate the working of the Government and redress grievances, etc. Instituted by Henry II (1154–89). Henry III (1216–72) compelled to promise that they would not be held more often than once in seven years. Famous E. of Cornwall, 1221. E. of Kent, 1313, lasted a year. Declined in reign of Edward III (1327–77), disappeared under Richard II (1377–99).

F

Fabian Society. An intellectual society of non-revolutionary Socialists, founded in London, 1884, profoundly influenced by G. B. Shaw and the Webbs.

Factory Acts. First F. Act introduced by Sir Robert Peel the Elder passed, 1802, providing for F. inspectors. Second F. Act, 1819, relating to cotton mills. Sir Robert Peel's F. Act, 1844, provided a 10-hour limit for women and children. Mining Act, 1842, forbade female and child labour in mines. F. Act extension and Workshop Regulation Acts, 1867, included all Fs. in the previous Acts. Later important F.A. included those of 1901, 1911 and 1937. Present law based on F.A. of 1961, and subsequent amendments. *See* MINING ACTS; SHOP HOURS ACT; WORKMEN'S COMPENSATION.

Faenza, Italy. 'Faïence' pottery manufactured at since the end of thirteenth century.

Faeroe. *See* FAROE.

Fahrenheit Scale. Temperature divisions invented *c.* 1712 by G. D. Fahrenheit (1686–1736) of Danzig. Popularly used in Britain, but began to be superseded by Centigrade and Celsius, 1961 onwards.

Fair Isle, the most probable identification of the island known to the ancients as Thule; mentioned by Pytheas (300 B.C.), whose description would fit the F. I., and by Ptolemy, A.D. 150. For the rest of its history, *see* SHETLAND ISLANDS.

Falaise, France. Treaty of, between Henry II of England, his son Henry, and Louis VII of France, 1174. Besieged by Henry V of England, 1417. Captured from English, 1450. Scene of the celebrated 'gap' in the Normandy battle through which the German troops escaped, 7–22 Aug. 1944.

Falangists, member of the Falange Espa-

ñol, founded by José Antonio Primo de Rivera (*b.* 1903), 29 Oct. 1933, were Fascists of the radical type. On the outbreak of the civil war the F. were at a disadvantage as their leader was in Government hands, having been arrested, 15 Mar. 1936. He was executed at Alicante, 20 Nov. 1936. Franco took over the leadership officially, 1938. At the end of the civil war they were the only political party tolerated in Spain; dissolved, 1966.

Falciu, Rumania. Peace between Russia and Turkey, 1711.

Falkland Islands (Sp., Islas Malvinas), Brit. Crown colony. Discovered by John Davis, 1592. French settlement existed, 1764. Part taken by British, 1765. Ceded by France to Spain, 1767. Spain yielded by convention, 1771. Argentine settlement, 1829. New British settlement, 1833, and Argentinians expelled. Naval battle between British and Germans, 8 Dec. 1914. Argentine claims to became increasingly vocal 1946 onwards. In 1964 the U.N. recommended Britain and Argentina to seek a peaceful solution to the problem. Inconclusive Anglo-Argentine talks followed in 1970s, foundering on islanders' desire to remain Brit.

Falkland Islands War, 1982:
  19 Mar.—Over 50 Argentine troops landed on S. Georgia.
  2 Apr.—Argentine invasion of F.I. Brit. marines outnumbered and surrendered.
  5 Apr.—Brit. task force sails from U.K.; Brit. Foreign Secretary, Lord Carrington, resigns.
  25 Apr.—British recapture S. Georgia.
  30 Apr.—U.S. orders sanctions against Argentina following peace talks breakdown.

2 May—Argentine cruiser *Belgrano* sunk by Navy; 4 May, HMS *Sheffield* sunk by Argentine Exocets.

21 May—Brit. invade main F.I. and estab. beachhead at San Carlos.

28 May—Darwin and Goose Green recaptured.

14 June—Ceasefire; Argentine general Menendez surrenders nearly 10,000 troops.

25 June— Rex Hunt (former Governor, renamed Civil Commissioner) returns to F.I.

Subsequently measures taken to increase financial aid to F.I.: to grant all islanders Brit. citizenship: and to build international airfield.

1983: Britain reiterated that sovereignty of the F.I. not negotiable with Argentina.

1985: international airport in F.I. opened.

See also ARGENTINA.

Family Allowances, first provided in Manitoba, Canada, 1915. In France, 1932. Family Allowances Act in Great Britain became law, 15 June 1945.

Family Compact. Name given to three agreements between the French and Spanish branches of the House of Bourbon (*q.v.*). (1) 1733, between Louis XV and Philip V against English commerce. (2) Treaty of perpetual alliance signed at Fontainebleau, 25 Oct. 1743; (3) 15 Aug. 1761.

Family Law Reform Act, 1969. *See* AGE.

Faneuil Hall. *See* 'CRADLE OF AMERICAN LIBERTY.'

Fanning Island, or **Tabuaeran.** Annexed by Great Britain, 1888; part of Gilbert and Ellice colony 1915–75: of Kiribati (*q.v.*) since 1976.

Fan Vaulting. Earliest example of F.V. is in timber. F.V. in the chapel of Winchester College *c.* 1390. Earliest stone F.V. at Gloucester *c.* 1420.

Far Eastern Republic. Declared its independence of Moscow, 1921. Annexed to Soviet Russia, 1922.

'Farmer's Letters, The.' A series of letters by John Dickinson against English official measures. First appeared in *Pennsylvania Chronicle,* 2 Dec. 1767.

Farne Islands. Inner F. was the hermit-age of St. Cuthbert between 664 and 687. On its site a Benedictine priory was founded, 1082, of which one tower, called St. Cuthbert's, still stands. The famous rescue by Grace Darling took place here, 1838. F.I. acquired by the National Trust (*q.v.*), 1925, as a bird sanctuary.

Farnese Family. Following are the most distinguished members: 1. Alessandro Farnese, who became Pope Paul III (1534–49). 2. Pierluigi, his natural son. 1st Duke of Parma, 1503–47. 3. Alessandro (1520–89), who completed the famous F. palace at Rome. 4. Alessandro, 3rd Duke, 1545–92, famous Spanish general. 5. Elizabeth, 1692–1766, who married, 1714, Philip V of Spain.

Farnley Wood Plot against Charles II, 1663. Leaders executed, 19 Jan. 1664.

Faroe or **Faeroe Islands,** N. Atlantic. Irish hermits driven out by Norse pirates *c.* 795. More heavily settled by Norse immigrants up to *c.* 900. Annexed to Norway, 1035. Became Danish, 1380. Occupied by British troops, Apr. 1940–May 1945. Self-governing, 1948. Fishing limits around the F.I. extended to six miles, 1959. To 12 miles from Apr. 1963. In E.F.T.A. 1968–72.

Farringdon Market (London). Act for establishing of, 1824. Opened, 20 Nov. 1826. Discontinued, June 1892.

Farthing. First coined by Edward I (1272–1307) instead of quartering pennies. Ceased to be legal tender, 31 Dec. 1960.

Fascism.

1. Founded as a politically organized creed by Benito Mussolini, at Bologna, 1919. In Oct. 1922 the Fascists took over the Italian Government by force in the 'March on Rome'. *See* ITALY.)

2. In Britain Sir Oswald Mosley's British Union of Fascists (founded 1932) got notoriety by the use of violence at meetings in London and Oxford, 1936, which led to passing of the Public Order Act, 1936. Revived after World War II under name of Brit. Union Movement, later, National Front; subsequently fragmented.

Fashoda Question. French Major Marchand occupied F. on the Upper Nile, 10 July 1898. As Britain was in process of reconquering the Sudan from the Mahdi's followers, this interference was bitterly resented. After the Dervish defeat at Omdurman (2 Sept. 1898), and further diplomatic exchanges nearly leading to war, Marchand was withdrawn, 11 Dec. 1898.

Fathers of the Church (*Patres Ecclesiastici*).

The Apostolic F. (believed to have been disciples of the Apostles):

Clement of Rome *fl.* 93–101
Ignatius *fl. c.* 101
Polycarp *d. c.* 155
Barnabas *fl. c.* 120
Hermas *fl. c.* 150

The principal ante-Nicene F. are:
Justin Martyr *c.* 100–165
Irenaeus *c.* 130–202
Clement of Alexandria *c.* 150–*c.* 216
Tertullian *c.* 155–*c.* 222
Origen 185–254
Cyprian *c.* 200–258
Gregory Thaumaturgus *c.* 213–*c.* 270

The principal post-Nicene F. are:
Eusebius of Caesarea *c.* 260–340
Hilary of Poitiers *c.* 403–449
Athanasius *c.* 296–373
Basil *c.* 329–379
Cyril of Jerusalem *c.* 315–386
Gregory Nazianzus *c.* 328–390
Gregory of Nyssa *c.* 301–*c.* 394
Ambrose *c.* 340–*c.* 397
Epiphanius *c.* 330–403
John Chrysostom *c.* 334–407
Jerome 331–420
Augustine of Hippo 354–430
Cyril of Alexandria 376–444
Leo the Great *c.* 540–604
Bede *c.* 673–735
John of Damascus *d. c.* 752

Fatima, in Portugal, was the scene of a vision in which the Virgin is said to have appeared to three country children, and the sun stood still, 13 Oct. 1917.

Fatimites. Family claiming descent from Fatima, daughter of Mohammed, who ousted the Aghlabid dynasty from Tunis, and founded an anti-Caliphate at Al-Mehdiya, near Tunis, 909. After repeated attempts Egypt and Syria conquered from Abbasids, 969, and capital moved to Cairo, where the dynasty remained until extinguished at Saladin's conquest of Egypt (*q.v.*), 1171.

Faversham, England. Abbey founded, 1147–9.

Fawkes, Guy. *See* GUNPOWDER PLOT.

F.B.I. (Federal Bureau of Investigation), set up, 1908, as a branch of the U.S. Department of Justice, independent of State police forces. J. Edgar Hoover (1895–1972) became Director of F.B.I., 1924. Since 1945 the F.B.I. has been most prominent in anti-Communist activities, though its prestige has been diminished in counter-espionage activities by the rise of the Central Intelligence Agency (C.I.A.) since the 1960s.

F.B.I. (Federation of British Industries). Established, 1916; granted royal charter of incorporation, 1924. Absorbed in **Confederation of British Industry** (*q.v.*), Aug. 1965.

Federal Convention (U.S.A.). Representatives of twelve states assembled at Philadelphia, 1787, to prepare a constitution for U.S.A.

Federal German Republic. *See* GERMANY, FEDERAL REPUBLIC OF.

Federal Reserve System, reform of American finance and banking methods, introduced by Congress, 1913, and modified by the Banking Act, 1935, which led to the creation of the F.R. Board, 1936.

Federal Trade Commision. Set up by the U.S. Government in 1914 to check trusts and monopolies.

Federalist Party (U.S.A.). Advocates of national constitution, 1788. Defeated, 1800, by the election of Jefferson as president. Disbanded, 1820.

Federation of Rhodesia and Nyasaland. *See* RHODESIA AND NYASALAND, FEDERATION OF.

Fehmic Courts (Femgerichte), ancient native courts of Westphalia, corresponding to the English *Folkmoot* or Scandinavian *Thing*, as opposed to feudal courts of the common European type, first came into prominence, 1180; by the Emperor Charles IV's Westphalian statute of Nov. 1371 they were empowered to try crimes of violence instead of those involving real estate, as hitherto. The Fs. attained the summit of their power, 1430–40. spreading southwards to Switzerland. Reforms took place, 1437 and 1442. Jerome Bonaparte's edict of 1811 abolished F.C. Assassination by right-wing terrorists, 1922–4 (e.g. of Walter Rathenau, 24 June 1922), vulgarly called F. murders, had nothing in common with the original F. court.

Fenian Association. Name (derived from Irish legend) adopted by John F. O'Mahony (1816–77) for the American section founded by him of the Irish Republican Brotherhood, 1858. The main section in Ireland was led by James Stephens (1825–1901) and the name Fs. came to be applied to the whole membership. Attempted raid into Canada, 1866. Abortive attempt at rebellion in Ireland, and outrages in England, 1867. Attempt to blow up Clerkenwell jail, 13 Dec. 1867. Further raids into Canada, 1870. Plot of the 'Irish Invincibles', 1882.

Fens (U.K.). *See also* BEDFORD LEVEL. Romans made attempts to drain the F. Unsuccessful attempt to drain Deeping Fen during reign of William I (1066–87). Vermuyden's efforts *c.* 1640. As a whole the major drainage operations in the F. were completed in 1807. Measures to strengthen flood defences announced, Nov. 1947. Extensive flooding, 1 Feb. 1953. Flood-protection scheme begun, 1954; complete by 1964.

Fernando Po, W. coast of Africa. Discovered by Portuguese Fernão do Po, 1472. Spanish from 1778, repossessed 1844 and then part of Sp. Guinea, now Equatorial Guinea (*q.v.*).

Ferrara, Italy. Ancient city in the Exarchate of Ravenna *c.* A.D. 753–4. Este family (*q.v.*) became rulers, 1208. University founded, 1391. A council which unsuccessfully tried to reconcile Roman and Greek churches held, 1438. Taken by French, 1796. Given to Papacy, 1814. Held by Austrian garrison, 1849–59. Annexed by Sardinia, Mar. 1860.

Ferrers Arrest. George F., M.P. for Plymouth, was arrested by the sheriffs of the City of London for debt, Mar. 1542. The Commons had them imprisoned for contempt, 28 Mar. 1542, but released on 30th.

Festival of Britain, 3 May–30 Sept. 1951.

Fettmilch Insurrection led by Vincenz F. and others at Frankfurt-am-Main against municipal mismanagement, 1612–16. Leaders executed, 1616.

Feudalism. A medieval system of society based on land in which a division of labour is achieved by committing governmental functions to those prepared to render military protection in return for agricultural and other services. Arose out of the anarchy of western Europe in the eighth and ninth centuries, and introduced into Britain in modified form after 1066. The decline of F. began almost immediately after it was introduced here, the principal dates being: Introduction of Judicial Circuits (*temp.* Henry II, 1154–89). Statute *Quïa Emptores* (*q.v.*), 1290. Introduction of the Use, fourteenth century. Statute of Uses, 1535. Statute of Wills, 1540. Act for the Abolition of Military Tenure, 1660. The last traces of F. were swept away by the Law of Property Acts, 1922–5.

Feuillants. Religious order in France, founded 1577, as a reformed branch of the Cistercians by Jean de la Barrière.

Feuillants Club. Founded 1791 by the moderate section of the 'Amis de la Constitution' (organized at Versailles, 1789). So called from their meeting-place, a disused Feuillant monastery. Disbanded, 10 Aug. 1792.

Fez, Morocco. Founded by Idris II, 808. Mosque of Mulai Idris built, 810. Occupied by French, Mar. 1911. Treaty of F. established French protectorate over Morocco, 1912, which terminated 2 Mar. 1956.

F.F.I. (Forces Françaises de l'Intérieur). Designation adopted by all French resistance forces when placed under unified command once the invasion of June 1944 had started.

Fianna Fail (Irish, meaning Soldiers of Destiny), followers of Eamon de Valera (*b.* 1882), organized as a party in 1926; formed government, 1932–48; again, 1951–4, 1957–81 and 1982.

Fidei Defensor. *See* DEFENDER OF THE FAITH.

F.I.D.O. (Fog, Intensive Dispersal Operation). Device for clearing airfield fog, invented by A. C. Hartley, 1942.

Field-Marshal (U.K.). Rank first conferred by George II on the Duke of Argyll, 1736.

Field of the Cloth of Gold. *See* CLOTH OF GOLD, FIELD OF THE.

Fiery Chamber. See CHAMBRE ARDENTES.

Fieschi's Plot to kill Louis Philippe of France, 28 July 1835. F. and accomplices executed, 19 Feb. 1836.

Fifth Column. Expression originating in 1936 at the outset of the Spanish Civil War, attributed to the Nationalist Gen. Mola. Used by the Germans in their invasions of Scandinavia and France and the Low Countries, 1940.

Fifth Monarchy Men. Religious anarchical sect founded in England, 1645. Admonished by Cromwell's council, Dec. 1653, and leaders imprisoned, Jan. 1654. Revolted against Charles II, 1661, and leaders executed.

Fifth Republic, France. Constitution came into force, 4 Oct. 1958.

Fifty-one, Committee of. Formed New York, 1774. Favoured a general congress.

Fighter Command, British, set up July 1936. Played crucial role under Dowding during Battle of Britain, 1940.

Figueras, Spain. Fortress built by Ferdinand VI, 1746–57. Taken by French, 24 Nov. 1794, 2 Mar. 1808, and 19 Aug. 1811. Restored to Spain by Treaty of Paris, 1814.

Fiji Islands, Polynesia. Discovered by Tasman, 1643. Visited by Capt. Cook, 1773. British protectorate, 1874. Independent, 10 Oct. 1970.

Film Institute, British. Founded 1933 and reconstituted, 1948.

'Financial Times.' *See* NEWSPAPERS.

Fingerprints. First used in England and Wales, 1901. Recording of F. of certain accused persons authorized by Criminal Justice Act, 1948.

Finland (in Finnish **Suomi**). Finns said to have settled in F. during eighth century. Swedish colonies in from eighth century onwards. Swedes under Jarl Birger Magnusson conquer South F. and Tavestehus, 1230–49, and the Finns adopted Christianity. Swedish influence extending to White Sea, 1293. Treaty of Göteborg (Russo-Swedish), 1323. Karl Knutsson sets out from F. to claim Swedish crown, 1448. Overrun by Russian troops, 1710–11. Province of Viborg (Viipuri) ceded to Russia by Treaty of Nystad, 1721. Swedish troops driven out by Russians, 1808. Emperor Alexander recognized as Grand Duke of F. by Finnish estates, 1809. Finnish estates suppressed and national leaders exiled, 1898. Exiles recalled and Diet reopened, 1904. Independence proclaimed, 6 Dec. 1917. Republican constitution adopted, 17 July 1919. Russian invasion, 30 Nov. 1939. Peace with Russia (Viipuri ceded), 12 Mar. 1940. F. joins Axis, June 1941. Britain declares war on F., 7 Dec. 1941. Allied armistice with F., 4 Sept. 1944. Treaties of peace with Allies, by which Petsamo was ceded and Porkkala leased to Russia (returned to F., 1956) as well as territory ceded and leased under the 1940 treaty, came into force, 15 Sept. 1947. Treaty of friendship with Russia, Apr. 1948, and extended in 1955 and 1970. F. associated with E.F.T.A., Mar. 1961.

Presidents of Finland:
J. K. Ståhlberg 1919–1925
L. Relander 1925–1931
P. E. Svinhufvud 1931–1937
K. Kallio 1937–1940
R. Ryiti 1940–1944
G. C. Mannerheim 1944–1946
J. K. Paasikivi 1946–1956
U. Kekkonen 1956–1982
M. Koivisto 1982–

Finnish Literature. The following is a list of prominent F. authors:

Aho, Juhani, 1861–1921, novelist.
Brofeldt (real name of Aho above).
Cajander, P. E., 1846–1913, poet.
Canth, Minna, 1844–97, playwright.
Haarla, Lauri, 1890–1944, novelist.
Ivalo, S., 1866–1937, historical novelist.

Järneveldt, Arvid, 1861–1932, novelist.
Jötuni, Marja, 1880–1943, playwright.
Kallas, A., 1878–1947, novelist.
Kivi, Alexis, 1834–72, playwright.
Leino, Einol, 1879–1926, poet.
Lehtonen, J., 1881–1946, novelist.
Linnankosi, Johannes, 1876–1913, poet.
Lönnbohm, A. E. M. (real name of Leino above).
Lönnrot, Elias, 1802–84, folklorist.
Oksanen, A., 1826–99, poet.
Paivärinta, P., 1827–1913, novelist.
Pakkala, T., 1862–1925, novelist.
Peltonen (real name of Linnankosi above).
Sarkia, Kaarlo, 1902–45, novelist.
Stenval, Alexis (real name of Kivi above).
Von Numers, G., 1848–1913, playwright (also in Swedish).

Finns and **Finnish Language.** The designation F. was not a native one, but bestowed on them by their western neighbours, perhaps by the Balts. Tacitus in the first century A.D. mentions Fenni and Ptolemy mentions Phennoi about a hundred years later: this could be a rendering of a W. Germanic name, cognate with *fen* and meaning 'people from the marshes', which adequately translates the western F.'s own name for themselves—Suomalaiset. Credit for reducing Finnish to writing is usually given to Bishop Michael Agricola (*d.* 1557). *See also* ESTONIA; KARELO-, etc.; LIVONIA.

Fire Brigades and Appliances. First reference to a fire brigade relates to China *c.* 4000 B.C. Egyptian F.B., 2000 B.C. Romans formed F.B. under a *praefectum vigilum c.* 150 B.C. Machine built by Hautsch of Nürnberg, 1657. Flexible hose introduced by Jan Vanderheide, 1672. First fire insurance office founded in London, 1680, and first English fire brigade then organized. Newsham's engine patented, 1700. In eighteenth century all insurance companies had their own fire brigade, and first fire engine acquired by a London insurance company, 1722. London parishes obliged to keep a fire engine by Act of Parliament, 1774. Several private insurance F.B. united, 1825. First steam fire engine invented by Braithwaite, 1829. All London private brigades united 1833. Metropolitan fire brigade set up, 1865, by which time steam engines had come into general use. Motor fire engines introduced, 1905. National Fire Service started, 1940. Repartitioned into local F. services, 1948.

Fire of London, The Great, broke out, 2 Sept. 1666, and burned until 6 Sept. Previous to this the term 'Great F. of L.' had meant the catastrophe of 1136.

Firearms. Crude cannon in use in Europe by 1300. Edward III used them against the Scots, 1327. First handguns made at Perugia, 1364, and at Augsburg by 1380. Wheel lock in use by 1575; flint-locks *c.* 1640. Percussion detonator patented by Forsyth, 1810. Automatic pistols *c.* 1900.

First Empire, in France, the reign of Napoleon I, 1804–14.

First Offenders Act, 1887, repealed by Probation of Offenders Act, 1907, which was amended by the Criminal Justice Acts, 1925, 1948, 1961, 1967 and 1983.

First Republic, in France, 27 Sept. 1792 until 1804.

Fishing Limits. Brit. F.L. were extended to 12 m. by Fisheries Limits Act, 1964, the inner 6 m. being exclusive of foreign fishing. E.E.C. regulations since 1972 have in practice affected these limits to the disadvantage of Brit. fishing.

Fitzwilliam Museum, Cambridge. A collection of engravings and books was bequeathed to the university by Richard, Visc. F. of Meryon (1745–1816). The building was begun, 1837; Marlay Galleries added, 1924; McClean MSS. Room, 1925; Courtauld Galleries, 1931; Henderson Galleries and Charrington Print Room, 1936; Graham Robertson Room, 1955.

Fiume (It.) or **Rijeka** (Serb.-Cr.), Yugoslavia. Part of the Empire, 1471. Joined to Hungary, 1870. Granted to Italy by secret Pact of London, 1915. Seized by Gabriele d'Annunzio, who proclaimed provisional government, 12 Sept. 1919.

Recognized by Italy and Yugoslavia as a free city by Treaty of Rapallo, 12 Nov. 1920. Italy annexed F., 9 March 1924. Permanently ceded to Yugoslavia, 1947.

Five Boroughs. Lincoln, Nottingham, Derby, Stamford, and Leicester established as Danish colonies *c.* 850. They retained certain Danish customs ('bylaws') till well into the thirteeenth century. *See* VIKING AGE.

Five Hundred, Council of. The lower house of the French legislature under the constitution of the year III (1795), the upper house being called the Council of Ancients. Lucien Bonaparte elected president of, 22 Oct. 1799. Dissolved by Napoleon, 10 Nov. 1799. *See* BRUMAIRE.

Five Members of the Long Parliament, Pym, Hampden, Hazelrigg, Strode, and Holles, whom Charles I attempted unsuccessfully to arrest, 4 Jan. 1642.

Five Mile Act. *See* CLARENDON CODE.

Five Power Naval Treaty signed at London, 22 Apr. 1930, between Britain, U.S.A., Japan, France, and Italy restricting the size of their respective navies.

Five-Year Plan (U.S.S.R.). To industrialize Russia. First F.-Y.P., 1928–33. Second, 1933–8 (completed by 1937). Third, 1938–42, but interrupted by war. Fourth, 1946–50. Fifth, 1951–5. Sixth, 1956–60. Succeeded by a 7-year plan, 1959–65, which in turn was superseded by a 20-year plan, 1961–81.

Flagellants. Most famous outbreaks of this ascetic sect, 1348–9 and 1417. Condemned by bull of Clement VI, 20 Oct. 1349.

Flamboyant Architecture. *See* GOTHIC.

Flaminian Way (Lat. **Via Flaminia**) from Rome to Rimini was built during the consulship of Flaminius, 220 B.C.

Flanders, Belgium and N. France. Colonized by Franks, 800–2. Annexed to France, 843. Famous for woollen manufactures, 962. Counts of F. refuse to recognize Hugues Capet as King of France, 987. Flemings take part in William I's conquest of England and in Earl Tostig's unsuccessful invasion, 1066. St. Omer first Flemish city to receive a charter, 1127. Zeeland Islands transferred from F. to Holland, 1256. French influence in F. becomes considerable after 1210. Flemings defeat French at Courtrai, 1302. Rebellion of Jacob van Artevelde of Ghent, 1337. He calls for English assistance, which being given signals the start of the Hundred Years War, 1338. Anglo-Flemish victory over French at Sluys, 1340. Flemings crushed at Ghent, 1349. Victory over the French at Roosebeke, 1382. Acquired by dukes of Burgundy, 1384. Collapse of Burgundians after death of Charles the Bold at Nancy, 1477. Great Privilege (*q.v.*), 1477. Artois annexed by France, 1483. Margaret of Burgundy, Regent of F., supports Lambert Simnel, 1487, and Perkin Warbeck, 1492–6. Abandons Warbeck in return for trading privileges called 'The Great Intercourse' (*q.v.*), 1497. The 'Bad Intercourse', 1506. French feudal rights in F. surrendered to Emperor Charles V at Treaty of Cambrai, 1529, and remained loyal to Spain when N. half of Spanish Netherlands broke away, 1579. For history after this date, *see* BELGIUM.

Fleet Air Arm. The Royal Naval Air Service fused with Royal Flying Corps, 1918, to form the Royal Air Force, which controlled *all* aviation, even that attached to the fleet. In 1922, an element of the naval air component, thenceforth called the F.A.A., was placed under complete operational and partial administrative and disciplinary command of the Admiralty. In 1937 complete command passed to the Admiralty, but F.A.A. as a distinct unit dissolved in reorganization after World War II.

Fleet Ditch (London). Covered in, 1733.

Fleet Market (London). Instituted, 30 Sept. 1737. Superseded by Farringdon Market (*q.v.*). Swept away, 1829.

Fleet Marriages (London) occurred in the Liberties of the Fleet and in the Liberty of the Savoy (notably in the Fleet Chapel) from 1614 until abolished by Lord Hardwick's Act, 1753.

Fleet Prison (London), for debtors, existed as early as 1197, possibly earlier.

Burnt by Wat Tyler, 1381. Star Chamber prisoners incarcerated in till 1641. Burnt in Great Fire of London (*q.v.*), 1666. Burnt by Gordon rioters (*q.v.*), 1780. Abolished, 1842. Demolished, 1844.

Fleet Street was part of the quarter burnt down in 982. In 1228 it was called F. Bridge Street, and F.S. first in 1311. Its connection with printing begins with Wynkyn de Worde (*d*. 1534), who set up his press at No. 32 in 1500.

Flemings in Britain. *See* WEAVING.

Fleur-de-lis. Emblem of the French monarchy. Origin traditionally ascribed to Clovis, A.D. 496. Definitely connected with the monarchy under Louis VII *c.* 1147. Number in the French royal arms reduced to three, 1376.

Flogging and Whipping. Powers of the British courts to pass a sentence of corporal punishment were abolished by the Criminal Justice Act, 1948, both for adults and juvenile offenders.

Florence (Lat: **Florentia**), Italy. The ancient Roman colony was rebuilt by Julius Caesar, 59 B.C. Baptistery built *c.* A.D. 1100. Independent republic, 1198. Defeated by Siena, 1260. Cathedral built, 1294–8. City partly burnt in rioting, 1304. University founded, 1321. Ponte Vecchio built, 1345. Papal attack repelled, 1375. Revolution of the Ciompi, 1378. Rule of the Albizzi, 1382–1434. Medici come to power, 1434. Library founded, 1444. Rule of Lorenzo de' Medici (the Magnificent), 1470–92. Founds Platonic Academy, 1476. The Pazzi Conspiracy against the Medici, Giuliano killed, Lorenzo escapes, Apr. 1478. Medici expelled, 1494. Death of Savonarola, 1498. Medici restored, 1512; again expelled, 1527. Again restored, 1530. Giovanni de' Medici becomes pope as Leo X, 1513–21. Medici become Grand Dukes of Tuscany, 1569. Accademia della Crusca founded, 1582. End of Medici family, 1737. F. presented by Napoleon to his sister Élise, 1808. Provisional capital of Italy, 1864–71. Heavily damaged during allied capture, 4–11 Aug. 1944. Further severe damage during unprecedented floods, Nov. 1966.

Florida, U.S.A. Discovered by Ponce de Leon on Easter Day, 1512. Conquered for Spain by Narvaez, 1528, and de Soto, 1539. Santo Augustino sacked by Sir Francis Drake, 1586. Ceded by Spain to Britain in exchange for Cuba at Treaty of Paris, 1763. Again ceded to Spain, 1783. Taken by U.S.A., 1811. Returned to Spain, 1812. Purchased from Spain, 1819. Admitted to union as a state, 8 Mar. 1845.

Florin. First struck in gold at Florence, eleventh century. Silver F. first struck, 1181. Gold F., value 6*s.*, first struck in England, 1343, by Edward III. Silver F., value 2*s.*, struck, 1849, and called 'Godless and Graceless', because *Dei Gratia* omitted from the superscription. Omission rectified, 1852. Name 'Florin' disappeared from superscription at accession of George VI. Decimal equivalent since 1971, 10 pence.

Flower Shows in England were started by the Royal Horticultural Society of London, 1804.

Fluorine. Isolated by Moisson, 1886. Theory that F. in drinking water could prevent tooth decay demonstrated in the U.S.A. by McKay (1874–1959). Results from three test areas in England, 1962, backed his theory and Ministry of Health then encouraged local authorities to add fluoride to their water supplies.

Flushing, Holland (Dutch **Vlissingen**). Jakobskerk founded, 1328. Fort dismantled, 1867. Harbour opened, 1873.

Flying Bombs (Vergeltungswaffe I, pilotless aircraft, jet propelled) were used against London, June–Aug. 1944, and against Antwerp and Liège, 13 Oct. 1944–31 Mar. 1945.

Flying Squadron. Scots political party led by Lord Tweeddale founded *c.* 1705, and secured settlement of the union question, 1706.

Fog Signals first regularized by the International Maritime Code, 1862.

Foix, France. County in the Pyrenees independent from *c.* 1000 until Count Francis Phoebus became King of Navarre, 1479. His sister married Jean d'Albret and F. passed with Navarre (*q.v.*) eventually to the Bourbons, and then to the French crown on the accession of Henry IV, 1589. Its counts were co-princes of Andorra (*q.v.*), and through this marriage Andorra is under the joint suzerainty of France and Spain. At the revolution it became the department of Ariège.

Fokker. Invention by Anton Fokker (1890–1940) of a wireless-directed bombing plane announced, Sept. 1919: responsible for design of planes in World War I and after.

Folk High Schools, Danish rural colleges, inaugurated, 1844, by Nicholas Frederick Grundtvig (1783–1872).

Fommonah, Treaty of. Between Britain and the King of Ashanti, 1874.

Fontainebleau, France. Treaty of F. between Napoleon and Godoy, the minister of Charles IV and the *de facto* King of Spain, 1807. Decree against British commerce, 1810. Napoleon signed abdication at, 6 Apr. 1814. The palace of F. was traditionally founded in the twelfth century, but, as it exists today, was begun by Francis I in the sixteenth century. S.H.A.P.E. (*q.v.*) functioned from F., 1950–66.

Foochow, China. Bridge of Ten Thousand Ages built *c.* 1000. Visited by Marco Polo *c.* 1290. Opened to British trade, 1842.

Food and Agriculture Organization. Agency of the U.N., established, 16 Oct. 1945, with headquarters in Rome.

Food Control (U.K.). Food Ministry under Lord Devonport formed, 1917. Maximum prices and rationing introduced, Sept. 1917. F. Ministry abolished, 1921. In World War II W. S. Morrison appointed F. Minister, 6 Apr. 1939. Price-fixing orders, 3 and 11 Sept. 1939. F. rationing in Britain began, 1939, and ended, 1954, and in 1955 the Ministry of F. was amalgamated with the Ministry of Agriculture and Fisheries.

Football Association (U.K.). Founded, 1863.

Football League (U.K.). Founded, 1888.

Foraker Act. Passed by U.S. Congress, 1900, establishing self-government in Puerto Rico.

Force Act. Passed by U.S. Congress, 1870, authorizing Federal agencies to interfere in individual states for the maintenance of order in certain cases.

Foreign Enlistment Act (U.K.). 1. 1819. Forbade British subjects to enlist in a foreign service at war with any state friendly to Great Britain. 2. 1870. Forbade, in addition, the export of arms, equipment, etc., to such service.

Foreign Legions. The French 'Foreign Legion' is a group of *Régiments Étrangers,* of which the first was raised by Louis Philippe, 9 Mar. 1831; its nucleus was the recently discharged soldiers of the two Guard and four Line regiments of Swiss, disbanded after the revolution of July 1830: between 1871 and 1914 it consisted largely of Alsatians and Lorrainers. In 1854 Napoleon III raised an *ad hoc* legion, mainly Swiss, for the Crimea, and in 1855 Great Britain raised two, one German-Swiss and one Italian, for the same purpose. F.L., including English, Scots, and Irish in some numbers, fought in Spanish interests in the war of French intervention, 1823; the First, 1834–8, and Second, 1872–6, Carlist Wars; and the Civil War of 1936–9 (International Brigade on Republican side and the professional *Tercio,* together with O'Duffy's volunteers, for Franco); also in the Graeco-Turkish wars of 1821–33 and 1897, on the Greek side. The French *Régiments Étrangers* were disbanded, 1940, but reconstituted, 1945. They fought with distinction in Indo-China, 1946–54, and Algeria, 1954–62. On 28 Apr. 1961, the First Foreign Legion Parachute Regiment was disbanded for its part in the abortive army mutiny in Algeria earlier that month. Sent to Chad (*q.v.*), 1983.

Foreign Office. Dates as such from 1872, when the redistribution of functions among Secretaries of State resulted in all foreign affairs being concentrated in the hands of one. The combined Foreign Service resulted from the merger of the F.O. and Diplomatic Service, the Commercial Diplomatic Service, and the Consular Service in 1943. Merged with the Commonwealth Relations Office, 1968.

British Secretaries of State for Foreign Affairs since 1924:

J. R. MacDonald 1924
Sir Austen Chamberlain 1924–1929
A. Henderson 1929–1931
Lord Reading 1931
Sir J. Simon 1931–1935
Sir S. Hoare 1935
A. Eden 1935–1938
Lord Halifax 1938–1940
A. Eden 1940–1945
E. Bevin 1945–1951
H. Morrison 1951
Sir A. Eden 1951–1955
H. Macmillan 1955
Selwyn Lloyd 1955–1960
Lord Home 1960–1963
R. A. Butler 1963–1964
P. Gordon Walker 1964–1965
M. Stewart 1965–1966
G. Brown 1966–1968
M. Stewart 1968–1970
Sir Alec Douglas-Home 1970–1974
Anthony Crosland 1974–1977
David Owen 1977–1979
Lord Carrington 1979–1982
Francis Pym 1982–1983
Sir Geoffrey Howe 1983–

Forest Laws. Introduced into England by William I, who destroyed several villages to make the New Forest, 1079–1085. Their severity was much mitigated by the F. Charter of Henry III, 1217, and the F. courts fell into disuse by the middle of sixteenth century. In 1631–2 they were revived by Charles I as a means of raising revenue, but the outcry which resulted prevented their penal jurisdiction ever being exercised again.

Formigny, Battle of, 1450. English defeated by French, who for the first time had artillery which could outrange the English long-bow.

Formosa, *see* TAIWAN.

Fort Augustus, built at Kilchumin, Inverness-shire, after the 1715 rebellion (*see* JACOBITES), and taken by the Highland Army, 1745. Reoccupied by Hanoverian troops, 1746, and named after the Duke of Cumberland.

Forth and Clyde Canal (Scotland). Begun 1768. Opened, 1790.

Forth Bridge (rail). Act passed, 1882.

Begun, Jan. 1883. Finished, 1889. Opened, 4 Mar. 1890.

Forth Road Bridge. Begun, 1958. Opened, 4 Sept. 1964.

Forties Oil Field, first major Brit. oilfield, discovered 1970: first oil brought ashore Nov. 1975.

Fort Sumter (U.S.A.), on an island in Charleston harbour, bombarded by Confederates, 12 Apr. 1861. This action is regarded as the beginning of the American Civil War. Captured by the Federal fleet, 1865. Became a national monument, 1948.

Fortune-telling. First specifically mentioned in English law as a form of witchcraft, and therefore a capital offence, in a statute of 1563. Now punishable under the Vagrancy Act of 1924.

Fotheringhay Castle (Northants, England). Founded, 1066. Richard III *b.*, Oct. 1452. Mary Queen of Scots executed, 8 Feb. 1587. Demolished by James I, 1604.

Foundling Hospitals.

1. London (St. Pancras), projected by Thomas Coram. Royal charter, Oct. 1739. Closed, 1926, and hospital transferred to Berkhamsted, Herts.
2. Dublin, instituted, 1704.

Fountains Abbey. Founded, 1132, by a body of Benedictine monks who seceded from the Abbey of St. Mary's, York, on land granted them by Archbishop Thurstan, and joined the Cistercians. Abbey dissolved, 1539, and much of the stone used to build F. Hall.

Four Cantons (Switzerland). Schwyz, Uri, Unterwalden, original members of the Swiss confederation, 1315, were joined by Lucerne, 1332. *See* SWITZERLAND.

Four Freedoms, peace aims for the Allies, enunciated while the U.S.A. was still neutral, by Franklin D. Roosevelt, 6 Jan. 1941.

Four Power Pact for peace of Europe between Britain, France, Germany, and Italy initialled at Rome, 1933.

Fourteen Points propounded by President Wilson in an address to U.S. Congress, 8 Jan. 1918, as a basis for a peace settlement with Germany. Considered at Allied Supreme War Council, 3 Nov. 1918, when Britain objected to freedom of the seas, Belgium to removal of economic barriers, and Italy to the readjustment of her frontiers on lines of nationality. Reply sent to Wilson same day.

Fourth Party. Independent group of Conservative politicians formed 1880 and led by Lord Randolph Churchill and A. J. Balfour.

Fourth Republic of France. Existed from 24 Dec. 1946 until 4 Oct. 1958.

France (Lat. **Gallia, Gaul**). Conquered by Romans, 121–51 B.C. Frankish incursions began *c.* A.D. 250. Settlement of Visigoths in F., 415–23. Defence of F. by Aëtius against Salian Franks, 425–30. With Frankish and Gothic help he repulses Attila at battle of Châlons (*q.v.*), 451. Collapse of Roman direct authority, 470–6. Clovis, king of Salian Franks, 481, defeats Syagrius at Soissons, 486; the Alemanni, 496; and embraces Christianity, 496. Defeats Alaric, king of the Visigoths, at Vouillé, 507; *d.* 511. Merovingian era, 481–716. Collapse of Merovingian power at death of Dagobert, 638.

Charles Martel, Mayor of the Kingdoms, 716. He defeats the Moors at Tours, 732. Pepin becomes king of the Franks, 751. Charlemagne sole king of the Franks, 771. Count Roland killed at Roncesvalles, 778. Charlemagne crowned Roman Emperor at Rome, 25 Dec. 800: *d.* 814. At Treaty of Verdun Carolingian Empire divided into three, 843. Invasions of Northmen begin *c.* 850. They besiege Paris, 885–6. End of the Carolingian House, 987.

Hugh Capet elected king of France, 987. French defeat by William (Conqueror) at Varaville, 1058. Norman invasion of England, 1066. First Crusade (*q.v.*), 1095. Statutes of the Templars (*q.v.*) drawn up by St. Bernard, 1128. With accession of Henry II of England Aquitaine and Anjou pass to the English kings, 1154. Conquest of Normandy by Philip Augustus, 1200–4. Philip's great

victory over the emperor and the Flemings at Bouvines, 1214. Albigensian Crusades, 1208–29. Death of Philip Augustus, 1223. Under Louis IX (St. Louis) F. reached the height of its medieval greatness, 1226–70. Alliance with Scotland and quarrel between Philip IV and Pope Boniface VIII, 1295. Boniface seized at Anagni, 1302. Clement V crowned pope at Lyons, 1305, and fixed his residence at Avignon, 1309 ('Babylonish captivity'). Templars suppressed, 1312.

Hundred Years War (*q.v.*) begins, 1338; interrupted by Treaty of Brétigny, 1360. Resumed, 1369. Truce of Bruges, 1375. Duke of Orléans murdered in Paris, 1407. English resume the war, 1415. Duke of Burgundy murdered, 1419. Treaty of Troyes, 1420. Joan of Arc drives the English from Orléans, 1429, and crowns Charles VII at Rheims, 1430. Treaty of Arras, 21 Sept. 1435. Paris goes over to the French king, 1436. The *Ordonnance sur la Gendarmerie*, 1439. The *Praguerie*, 1440. Battle of Formigny (*q.v.*), 1450. English driven out of all F. except Calais, 1453.

Charles VIII invades Italy, 1494–6. He marries Anne of Brittany, 1491. Captures Naples, 1504. League of Cambrai, 1508. Holy League (*q.v.*), Oct. 1511. Louis XII assumes title of *Pater Patriae*, 1513. Peace and alliance with England, 1514. Concordat of Bologna, 1516, between Francis I and Leo X.

Franco-Hapsburg Wars, 1521–59:
1. 1521–6 ending with Treaty of Madrid
   (battle of Pavia, 1525)
2. 1527–9 ending with Treaty of Cambrai
3. 1535–8 ending with Treaty of Nice
4. 1542–4 ending with Treaty of Crespy
5. 1552–9 ending with Treaty of Câteau Cambrésis

The Wars of Religion (between Huguenots and Catholics):

The First. 1562–3:
   ending with the Peace of Ambroise

The Second. 1567–8:
  ending with the Peace of Long-
  jumeau
The Third. 1569–70:
  ending with the Peace of Saint-Germain
  Massacre of St. Bartholomew, 1572,
  leading to:
The Fourth. 1572–3:
  ending with the Peace of La Rochelle
The Fifth. 1574–6:
  ending with the Peace of 'Monsieur'
The Sixth. 1577:
  ending with the Peace of Bergerac
The Seventh. 1579–80:
  ending with the Peace of Fleix
The Eighth. 1585–98:
  ending with the Treaty of Vervins,
  1598.

Henry of Guise murdered, 1588. Henry of Navarre acceded as Henry IV, 1589, becoming a Catholic in 1593. Treaty of Vervins, 1598. Edict of Nantes, 15 Apr. 1598. Henry IV assassinated by Ravaillac, 1610. Rebellion of Condé, 1614. Richelieu, first minister, 1624. Huguenot power broken by capture of La Rochelle, 1628. War with Spain, 1635. Death of Richelieu, 1642. Mazarin, first minister, 1643. Treaty of Westphalia (q.v.), 1648, whereby F. obtained Metz, Toul and Verdun, and Lorraine.

The first or Parliamentary Fronde, 1648–9. Second or Aristocratic Fronde, 1650–3. English Alliance (Treaty of Westminster), 1654. Peace with Spain at the Treaty of the Pyrenees, 1659. Death of Mazarin, 1661. Louis XIV takes over the government and appoints Colbert finance minister, 1661. French E. India Co. founded, 1664. War of Devolution against Spanish Netherlands, 1667–8. Dutch War, 1672. Revocation of the Edict of Nantes and the Dragonades, 1685. War of the League of Augsburg, 1688–97. Peace of Ryswick, 1697. War of the Spanish Succession (q.v.), 1701–13, ends by Treaty of Utrecht (q.v.), 1713. Death of Louis XIV, 1 Sept. 1715.

Triple Alliance (England, F., and Holland), Jan. 1717. Quadruple Alliance (England, F., Austria, Holland), 2 Aug. 1718. F. joins in War of the Austrian Succession (q.v.) against Austria, 1740. Britain joins in an alliance with Austria ('The War of Jenkins's Ear'), 1742. Battle of Fontenoy, 1745. Peace of Aix-la-Chapelle, 1748. The Seven Years War (q.v.), 1756–63. Loss of major part of French colonial possessions in America and India, 1759–60. Intervention in the War of American Independence, 1778. Treaty of Versailles, 1783. Meeting of the States-General, 5 May 1789.

The Great French Revolution (q.v.), 1789–92. Monarchy overthrown, 10 Aug. 1792. The First Republic proclaimed, 22 Sept. 1792. Louis XVI executed, Jan. 1793. The Directory comes into force, 1795. Napoleon conquers Italy and makes peace with Austria at Campo-Formio, 17 Oct. 1797. Napoleon in the Middle E., July 1798–Aug. 1799, when he returned to France. He overthrows the Directory (Brumaire, q.v.), 10 Nov. 1799. The Consulate. Napoleon First Consul of F., 15 Dec. 1799. Battle of Marengo, 14 June 1800. Treaty of Lunéville, 9 Feb. 1801. The Concordat, 1802. Treaty of Amiens, 1802. *Code Civile* published, 1804.

The First Empire: Napoleon crowns himself emperor, 2 Dec. 1804. Battle of Ulm, 20 Oct. 1805. Battle of Trafalgar, 21 Oct. 1805. Battle of Austerlitz, 2 Dec. 1805. Holy Roman Empire abolished and Confederation of the Rhine formed, 1806. Battle of Jena, 1806. Treaty of Tilsit, 1807. Battle of Baylen, 1808. Pope Pius VII deported to F., 1809. Russia deserts the Continental System (q.v.), 1810. Retreat from Moscow, 1812. Battle of Leipzig, Oct. 1813. Napoleon abdicated, 11 Apr. 1814. First Treaty of Paris, 1814. Napoleon returns to Paris, 20 Mar. 1815. Battle of Waterloo, 18 June 1815. Second Treaty of Paris, 15 Nov. 1815.

The Restoration: War with Spain, 1822–1827. Capture of Algiers, 1830. Polignac issues the July Ordinances, 1830. Revolution in Paris. Charles X abdicates, 2 Aug. 1830. The July Monarchy: Louis Philippe of Orléans proclaimed king of the French, 7 Aug. 1830. Conquest of Algeria, 1830–2. Revolution breaks out in Paris, 23 Feb. 1848. Louis Philippe abdicates, 24 Feb. 1848.

The Second Republic proclaimed, 26 Feb. 1848. Louis Napoleon Bonaparte (q.v.) elected president by universal suffrage, 11 Dec. 1848. Republic overthrown by Bonaparte, 2 Dec. 1851.

The Second Empire: Napoleon III proclaimed emperor, 2 Dec. 1852. Joins with Britain against Russia in Crimean War, 1854–6. Treaty of Paris, Mar. 1856. War with Austria, 1859. Battle of Solferino, July 1859. Truce of Villafranca, 11 July 1859.

Franco-Prussian War, 1870–1. Battle of Sédan, 2 Sept. 1870. Revolution in Paris, 3 Sept. 1870.

The Third Republic proclaimed, 4 Sept. 1870. Paris surrenders, 28 Jan. 1871. Proclamation of the Commune at Paris, Feb. 1871. Peace of Frankfort, 10 May. Commune suppressed, 21–8 May 1871. Republican constitution promulgated, 1875. The Panama scandal, 1888–92. Franco-Russian alliances, 1891, 1896, 1900. Gen. Boulanger flees the country, 1891. The Dreyfus case, 1894–1906.

Anglo-French Alliance (Entente Cordiale), 8 Apr. 1904. Rupture with Vatican, 1904. Separation Law (Church and State), 1906; Devolution of Church Property Bill passed, 1908. 1914–18: *see* WORLD WAR I. French troops occupied Ruhr, 1922. Bayonne municipal bank failed, involving Stavisky scandal, 30 Dec. 1933. 1934: Stavisky shot himself, 8 Jan.; King of Yugoslavia and French Foreign Minister (Barthou) murdered at Marseilles, 9 Oct.

1936: Triumph of Popular Front, May. Subsequent frequent changes of gov.

1938: Daladier, Premier and Bonnet visited London to confer about Czechoslovakia, 17 Sept.; Ribbentrop, in Paris, signed declaration that no territorial question existed between Germany and F., 6 Dec.

1939: F. declared war on Germany 3 Sept.

1940: Reynaud became Premier, 21 Mar.; German troops entered Paris, 14 June; F. capitulated and accepted armistice terms of Germany and Italy, 22 June. De Gaulle carried on the fight from London. Government set up at Vichy, 1 July; diplomatic relations with Britain broken off, 5 July; Pétain becomes head of state, with Laval as successor, 12 July; German-occupied zone announced, 28 July.

1942: Germans occupy Vichy F., 11–12 Nov. French fleet scuttled at Toulon, 27 Nov. Assassination of Darlan, 24 Dec.

1944: Invasion of France by Allies, 6 June. Most of France liberated by Sept. De Gaulle's Committee recognized as Provisional Government, 23 Oct.

1946: De Gaulle resigned, Jan. Fourth Republic came into being, 24 Dec. Beginning of Indo-China war.

1949: France signed North Atlantic Treaty (q.v.), 4 Apr.

1954: Fall of Dien Bien Phu (q.v.), May. Geneva conference of foreign ministers, May–July; as a result an armistice ending the Indo-China war signed there on 21 July. Civil war broke out in Algiers, Nov.

1956: Moroccan independence announced in Mar. Egypt nationalized the Suez Canal. Outbreak of the Israeli-Egyptian war; an Anglo-French force landed at Port Said, 5 Nov., agreed to withdraw without delay at the U.N.'s request, 3 Dec., and the withdrawal was completed by 22 Dec.

1957: F. a signatory to the Treaty of Rome, establishing the European Economic Community (q.v.), 25 Mar. Algerian situation becoming critical, and it was largely responsible for the fall of successive governments during the year.

1958: Growing impatience in the French Army coupled with serious rioting in Algeria led to the collapse of the Fourth Republic, 13 May. De Gaulle accepted an invitation to form a 'Government of National Safety', 29 May. De Gaulle elected President of the Fifth Republic, 21 Dec.

1961: Referendum in F. and Algeria approved de Gaulle's Algerian policy, 8

Jan. Army revolt in Algeria, 19–26 Apr. This was suppressed, and European resistance there to de Gaulle went underground (see O.A.S.).

1962: Franco-Algerian peace talks held in secret near Franco-Swiss border, 11–18 Feb., ended with agreement made at Evian (q.v.) ending the Algerian war and providing for an independent Algeria. In July Adenauer paid an official visit to F. A public show of Franco-German reconciliation reached its climax with a Mass in Rheims Cathedral attended by de Gaulle and Adenauer. De Gaulle pays first state visit ever made to Germany by a French President, Sept. De Gaulle threatened to resign if a referendum on the proposed new way of electing a president went against him, on 28 Oct. 5 Oct.: De Gaulle dissolved National Assembly. In the referendum, 28 Oct., de Gaulle got 61.75 per cent of the votes cast, and in the General Election, in Nov., his supporters won an overall majority over all other parties.

1963: De Gaulle made it clear that he neither expected nor wanted Britain in the E.E.C., 14 Jan. On 24 Jan. de Gaulle and Adenauer signed the Franco-German 'reconciliation treaty' in Paris. After the initialling of the nuclear Test Ban Treaty in Moscow, de Gaulle announced (29 July) that France would not be a signatory to it.

1966: Virtual French withdrawal from N.A.T.O.

1967: In Nov. de Gaulle vetoed Britain's new application for entry to the E.E.C.

1968: While de Gaulle was on a state visit to Rumania students joined striking workers in marches and sit-ins in Paris and other Fr. cities; but in June de Gaulle had an overwhelming electoral victory. France again vetoed British entry to E.E.C., Sept.

1969: Worsening economic situation brought disenchantment with de Gaulle's regime. De Gaulle resigned (30 April).

1970–80: F. notable for economic growth and pro-Arab stance; agreed to Britain's entry into E.E.C., 1973.

1981–: Disenchantment with gov. policies led to Socialist victory, 1981, and Mitterand elected president. F. suffered economic recession as in rest of W.

France, Heads of State.

1. Monarchy:

Merovingian Dynasty 481–716
Carolingian Dynasty 771–987
      Capetian Kings
Hugh Capet 987–996
Robert 996–1031
Henry I 1031–1060
Philip I 1060–1108
Louis VI 1108–1137
Louis VII 1137–1180
Philip II, Augustus 1180–1223
Louis VIII 1223–1226
Louis IX, the Saint 1226–1270
Philip III 1270–1285
Philip IV 1285–1314
Louis X 1314–1316
John I 1316
Philip V 1316–1322
Charles IV 1322–1328
      House of Valois
Philip VI 1328–1350
John 1350–1364
Charles V 1364–1380
Charles VI 1380–1422
Charles VII 1422–1461
Louis XI 1461–1483
Charles VIII 1483–1498
Louis XII 1498–1515
Francis I 1515–1547
Henry II 1547–1559
Francis II 1559–1560
Charles IX 1560–1574
Henry III 1574–1589
      House of Bourbon
Henry IV 1589–1610
Louis XIII 1610–1643
Louis XIV 1643–1715
Louis XV 1715–1774
Louis XVI 1774–1793

2. First Republic
Robespierre 1792–1794

3. The Directory
Barras 1795–1799
Rewbell 1795–1799
La Révellière-Lépeaux 1795–1799
Carnot 1795–1797
Letourneur 1795–1797
Barthélemy 1797

Merlin 1797–1799
François 1797
Siéyès 1799
Gohier 1799
Roger Ducos 1799
Moulin 1799

4. *The Consulate*

First Consul. Napoleon	1799–1804
Second Consul. Siéyès	1799–1800
Cambacérès	1800–1804
Third Consul. Ducos	1799–1800
Le Brun	1800–1804

5. *Empire*
 House of Bonaparte
Napoleon I (abdicated) 1804–1814

6. *Monarchy*
 House of Bourbon (restored)
Louis XVIII 1814–1824
Charles X (abdicated) 1824–1830
 House of Bourbon-Orléans
Louis Philippe (abdicated) 1830–1848

7. *Second Republic*
President: Louis Napoleon
 Bonaparte 1848–1852

8. *Empire*
 House of Bonaparte (restored)
Napolean III (abdicated) 1852–1870

9. *Presidents of the Third Republic*
Adolphe Thiers 1871
Marshal MacMahon 1873
Jules Grévy 1879
Sadi Carnot 1887 (assassinated, 1894)
Jean Casimir-Périer 1894
François Félix Faure 1895
Émile Loubet 1899
Armand Fallières 1906
Raymond Poincaré 1913
Paul Deschanel 1920
Alexandre Millerand 1920
Gaston Doumergue 1924
Paul Doumer 1913 (assassinated, 1932)
Albert Lebrun 1932
 Re-elected, 1939. Deposed, 1940

10. *Chief of the French State*
Marshal Pétain 1940–1944

11. *Head of the French Resistance*
Charles de Gaulle 23 June 1940
(Recognized as head of the Provisional Government of France, 23 Oct. 1944)

12. *Presidents of the Fourth Republic*
Vincent Auriol 1947
René Coty 1953

13. *Presidents of the Fifth Republic*
Charles de Gaulle 1958–1969
Georges Pompidou 1969–1974
Giscard d'Estaing 1974–1981
François Mitterand 1981–

Franche-Comté (the *County* of Burgundy, *q.v.*). Acquired by the *dukes* of Burgundy, 1384. Occupied by French, 1482–3. Seized by Louis XIV, 1678, and ceded to France by Treaty of Nijmegen, 1679.

Franchise, Elective (Britain).

1. *Counties:* Under Edward I county M.P.s were elected by freeholders. Conduct of county elections first regulated by statute, 1406. F. restricted to forty-shilling freeholders, 1430 till 1832.

2. *Boroughs.* There was no general statute on borough F. till 1832, voting qualifications depending exclusively on the terms of the borough charter.

3. *From* 1832. The local government F. in respect of both counties and boroughs was, until the passing of the Representation of the People Act, 1945, based on the occupation of rateable property, but that Act assimilated the local government F. with the parliamentary F. by making the normal basis that of residence. Successive classes of the population admitted to the F. by Acts of 1832, 1867, 1884; all males over 21 and females over 30 admitted, 1918; females between 21 and 30, 1929. Business F. of spouses abolished, 1945. University and business F. abolished, 1948. Universal suffrage for all over 18 years of age, effective, 1970.

Franciscans, Monastic Order of. Called also Minorites. Founded by St. Francis of Assisi (1182–1226) in 1212. First came to England, 1220, where they first founded monasteries at Canterbury (1224) and Northampton.

Franco-Prussian War. Lasted from 15 July 1870 until signing of peace on 10 May 1871, although the Paris Commune continued fighting for a few days longer.

Franconia (Franken). Since the Treaty of

Verdun, 843, it has meant a duchy comprising the land of the E. Franks, on both sides of the valley of the Main, from which the Franks first set out to conquer Gaul (*see* FRANCE) and the Low countries in the fourth century. Since *c.* 1500 it has been restricted to three counties (Upper, Middle, and Lower F.) centring upon Bamberg, Nürnberg, and Würzburg respectively, in north-western Bavaria. These counties were organized in 1837 by the Bavarian crown, which acquired the whole of F., 1803.

Francs were first struck for John of France, 1360, then again in 1576. In 1793 the franc became the monetary unit of France and maintained the same value until 1914, since when it has been devalued several times. Introduced by the Helvetic Republic, 1799. By the kingdom of the Belgians, 1831. De Gaulle 'New' or 'Heavy' F., 1960.

Frankfurt-am-Main, Hesse, was first mentioned by Einhard, A.D. 793. Diets held at, 822, 823, 951, 1015, 1069, 1109, etc. Became place for election of German emperors, 1152. Placed under an interdict during dispute between Louis the Bavarian and Papacy, 1329–49. By the Golden Bull (*q.v.*) declared the principal seat of imperial elections, 1356. Free city, 1372. Joined League of Schmalkalden, 1536. Garrisoned by Gustavus Adolphus, 1631; bombarded by French, 1796; made capital of Grand Duchy of Frankfort, 1810; entered by Prussians, 16 July 1866. Frankfort Peace signed, 1871. Heavily bombed, 1943–5. *See also* FETTMILCH INSURRECTION.

Frankfurt-an-der-Oder, Brandenburg. Incorporated, 1253. Joined Hanseatic League, 1368; taken by Sweden, 1631; Russians, 1759; French, 1806; Russians, 1945.

Franking of Letters (Great Britain). Members of Parliament had the right from A.D. 1660; abolished on institution of penny postage, 10 Jan. 1840. *See* POST OFFICE.

Fredrickshald (now called **Halden**), Norway. Charles XII of Sweden killed at siege of, 11 Dec. 1718.

Free Church Federal Council. Formed in 1940 by the union of the Free Church Council (established 1892) and the Federal Council (established 1919).

Free Church of Scotland. Formed by opponents of private patronage, 1843. Amalgamated with the Cameronians, 1876. Amalgamated, 31 Oct. 1900, with the United Presbyterian Church, the union assuming the name United F.C.; but a dissentient fraction, popularly called the Wee Frees, substantiated, before the House of Lords, 1904, a claim to the F.C. property. An Act of 1905 appointed a commission to allocate that property. The United F.C. united with the Church of Scotland on 2 Oct. 1929. The F.C., strongest in the Highlands, and stemming from the Wee Frees, is (1985) a relatively small body.

Freemasonry (Britain and general). The first grand lodge in England was established, 1717; in Ireland, 1725; in Scotland, 1736. Freemasons' Hall, London, built, 1775. Pope Clement XII issued a bull of excommunication against freemasons in 1738. Banned in Germany, 1934–45.

Freemasonry (U.S.A.). F. was introduced into America in 1730. In 1733 a lodge was established at Boston by Henry Price. First masonic hall built at Philadelphia, 1754.

Free Soil Party (U.S.A.). Founded on 9 Aug. 1848, against extension of slavery in various territories; disbanded, 1854.

Freiburg (Fr. **Fribourg**). Swiss canton, first belonged to the dukes of Zaehringen, one of whom, Bernard IV, founded the city in 1157. On the extinction of this dynasty, 1218, F. passed to the dukes of Kyburg; to the Hapsburgs, 1277–1452; to Savoy until 1477; joined the Swiss Confederation, 1481.

Freiburg-im-Breisgau. Founded, 1120, by dukes of Zaehringen; became separate county, 1218, until it passed to the Hapsburgs, 1369, who retained it until the dissolution of the empire in 1806; ceded to the Grand Duchy of Baden.

French Equatorial Africa. First settled 1839. Its four territories became independent republics in Aug. 1960 under the names of Central African Republic, Congo, Chad, and Gabon, (*qq.v.*).

French Fury, The. Francis, Duke of Anjou, in Jan. 1583, occupied Antwerp. The citizens resisted and massacred 2,000 of his troops, besides many officers and nobles.

French Guiana (Cayenne). F. settlement began in 1604, and involved a long struggle with the Dutch, which was only finally decided by the transplantation of dispossessed *habitants* from Acadia (*q.v.*) *c.* 1760. Occupied by the Portuguese during the Napoleonic Wars. Convicts were first sent out in 1854, but the attempt to form regular colonies of convicts, as opposed to mere penal settlements, was abandoned, 1864. Became Overseas Department of France, 19 Mar. 1946. Transportation ceased in Apr. 1946.

French Guinea. *See* GUINEA, REPUBLIC OF.

French Literature. The following is a list of prominent authors in the F. language, whether of F., Belgian, Swiss, Canadian, etc., nationality. Among medieval authors writers in the N.F. dialect, the *langue d'œil*, including Anglo-Normans, are in this list. But writers in the S.F. dialect (*langue d'oc*) of this period will be found in the list of PROVENÇAL AND CATALAN authors.

Abbo of Fleury, 945–1004, theologian.
Abélard, Pierre, 1079–1142, philosopher, famous for letters to Héloïse.
Adam de la Halle ('the Hunchback of Arras'), ?–1286, dramatist.
Adam, Paul Auguste Marie, 1862–1920, novelist.
Aicard, Jean François Victor, 1848–1921, poet and dramatist.
Amiel, Henri Frederic, 1821–81, Swiss philosopher.
Amyot, Jacques, 1513–93, translator.
Aragon, Louis, 1897–1983, poet.
Arnauld, Antoine, 1612–94, Jansenist theologian.
Arnault, Antoine Vincent, 1767–1834, dramatist, etc.
Arouet, François Marie. *See* VOLTAIRE.
Assoucy, Charles Cuypeau d', 1604–*c.* 1679, poet.

Aubigné, Jean Henri Merle d', 1794–1872, Swiss historian.
Aubigné, Théodore Agrippa d', 1552–1630, historian, poet, etc.
Augier, Guillaume Victor Émile, 1820–1889, dramatist.
Aymeric of Peyrac, ?–1400, chronicler.
Baillon, André, 1875–1932, Belgian novelist.
Balzac, Honoré de, 1799–1850, novelist.
Balzac, Jean Guez, Baron de, 1594–1654, miscellaneous.
Barbusse, Henri, 1873–1935, novelist.
Baron, Michel Boyron, 1653–1729, dramatist.
Barrès, Auguste Maurice, 1862–1923, novelist and political writer.
Bartas, du. *See* DU BARTAS.
Barthélemy, Abbé Jean Jacques, 1716–95, miscellaneous writer.
Baudelaire, Charles Pierre, 1821–67, poet and critic.
Bazin, René François, 1853–1932, novelist.
Beaumarchais, Pierre Augustin Caron de, 1732–99, dramatist.
Beauvoir, Simone de, 1908–, novelist.
Bellay, Joachim du. *See* DU BELLAY.
Belleau, Remi, *c.* 1528–77, poet.
Belloy, Pierre Laurent Beyrette de, 1727–75, dramatist.
Benoît de Sainte-Maure, twelfth century, poet.
Benserade, Isaac de, 1613–91, poet.
Béranger, Pierre Jean de, 1780–1857, ballad-writer.
Bergson, Henri Louis, 1859–1941, philosopher.
Bernanos, Georges, 1888–1948, novelist.
Bernard, Charles de, 1805–50, novelist.
Bernard, Paul (Tristan), 1866–1947, novelist and dramatist.
Bernard, St., of Clairvaux, 1090–1153, theologian.
Bertaut, Jean, 1552–1611, satirical and religious poet.
Beyle, Marie Henri (Stendhal), 1783–1842, novelist.
Bèze, Théodore de, 1519–1605, historian and theologian.
Blanc, Louis, 1811–82, historian.
Blondel de Nesle, living in 1193, ballad-writer.

Bloy, Léon, 1846–1917, essayist.

Bodin, Jean, 1530–96, sociologist.

Boëtie, Étienne de la, 1530–63, poet and political writer.

Boileau-Despréaux, Nicolas, 1636–1711, historian and satirist.

Bossuet, Jacques Bénigne (Bishop), 1627–1704, historian and theologian.

Bourget, Paul Charles Joseph, 1852–1935, poet, novelist, and essayist.

Boursault, Edmé, 1638–1701, dramatist.

Brantôme, Pierre de Bourdeille, Seigneur de, 1540–1614, memoir-writer.

Brébeuf, Guillaume de, 1618–61, poet.

Brémond, Henri, 1865–1939, essayist.

Brieux, Eugène, 1858–1932, dramatist.

Brillat Savarin, Anthelme, 1755–1826, writer on gastronomy.

Broglie, Achille Victor, Duc de, 1785–1870, political writer.

Broglie, Albert, Duc de, 1821–1901, political and historical writer.

Brueys, David Augustin de, 1640–1723, dramatist.

Calvin (Cauvin), Jean, 1509–64, theologian and philosopher.

Cammaerts, Émile, 1878–1955, Belgian poet, theologian, and essayist.

Camus, Albert, 1913–61, novelist, essayist, and dramatist.

Carton de Wiart, Henry, 1869–1951, Belgian sociologist and novelist.

Casaubon, Isaac, 1559–1614, theologian.

Chamfort, Nicolas Sébastien Roch, 1741–94, dramatist and miscellaneous writer.

Chapelain, Jean, 1595–1674, poet.

Chardin, Pierre Teilhard de, 1881–1955, philosopher and palaeontologist.

Charles, Duke of Orléans, 1391–1445, poet.

Charron, Pierre, 1541–1603, philosopher.

Chartier, Alain, c. 1385–1433, poet, historian, etc.

Chastellain, Georges, c. 1404–75, poet and chronicler.

Chateaubriand, François René, Vicomte de, 1768–1848, miscellaneous writer.

Chénier, André Marie de, 1762–94, poet.

Chrétien de Troyes, ?–1195, poet.

Christine de Pisan, 1363–1430, poet, historian, etc.

Cocteau, Jean, 1891–1963, poet and dramatist.

Colette (Madame Henri de Jouvenel), 1873–1954, novelist.

Collé, Charles, 1709–83, poet and dramatist.

Collin d'Harleville, Jean François, 1755–1806, dramatist.

Commines or Commynes, Philippe de, 1455–1509, diplomatist and historian.

Comte, Auguste, 1798–1857, philosopher.

Constant de Rebecque, Henri Benjamin, 1767–1830, novelist and philosopher.

Coppée, François Édouard Joachim, 1842–1908, poet.

Coquillart, Guillaume, 1450–1510, satirist.

Corneille, Pierre, 1606–84, dramatist.

Corneille, Thomas, 1625–1709, dramatist.

Coster, Charles de, 1827–79, Belgian story-writer.

Courteline, Georges, 1860–1929, novelist.

Crébillon, Claude-Prosper Jolyot de, 1707–77, novelist.

Crébillon, Prosper Jolyot de, 1674–1762, dramatist.

Crétin, Guillaume, ?–1525, poet.

Crousez, Jean Pierre de, 1663–1750, philosopher.

Cyrano de Bergerac, Savinien, 1619–55, novelist and dramatist.

D'Alembert or Dalembert, Jean le Rond, 1717–83, encyclopaedist.

Dancourt, Florent Carton, 1661–1725, dramatist.

Daudet, Alphonse, 1840–97, poet and novelist.

Daudet, Léon, 1867–1942, critic, novelist, and journalist.

Deffand, Mme du, 1697–1780, letter-writer.

Delavigne, Casimir, 1793–1843, dramatist.

Déroulède, Paul, 1846–1914, poet and dramatist.

Descartes, René, 1596–1650, scientific and philosophical writer.

Deschamps, Eustache (called Morel), 1338–1415, poet.

Destouches, Philippe (Néricault), 1680–1754, dramatist.

Diderot, Denis, 1713–84, miscellaneous writer.

Dierx, Léon, 1838–1912, poet.

Du Bellay, Joachim, c. 1524–60, poet and antiquarian.

Dudevant, Amandine Lucile Aurore (Dupin), Baronne ('George Sand'), 1804–76, novelist.

Dufresny, Charles Rivière, 1648–1724, dramatist.

Duhamel, Georges, 1884–1966, novelist.

Dumas, Alexandre Davy de la Pelleterie (père), 1803–70, novelist and dramatist.

Dumas, Alexandre (fils), 1824–95, novelist and dramatist.

Du Perron, Jacques Davy (Bishop), 1556–1618, essayist and poet.

Du Ryer, Pierre, 1606–68, dramatic poet and translator.

Eekhoud, Georges, 1854–1927, Belgian novelist and critic.

Elskamp, Max, 1862–1931, Belgian poet.

Eluard, Paul, 1895–1952, poet.

Erckmann Chatrian. The compound name of Émile Erckmann (1822–99) and Alexandre Chatrian (1826–90), who collaborated in fiction and drama.

Estienne. The name of a family of printers and scholars who lived in the sixteenth century.

Fénelon, François de Salignac de la Mothe (Archbishop), 1651–1715, miscellaneous writer.

Feuillet, Octave, 1821–90, novelist.

Feydeau, Georges, 1862–1921, farcical dramatist.

Flaubert, Gustave, 1821–80, novelist.

Fléchier, Esprit, 1632–1710, preacher.

Florian, Jean Pierre Claris de, 1755–94, novelist and poet.

Fontenelle, Bernard le Bovier de, 1657–1757, philosopher, etc.

Fournier, Alain, 1886–1914, novelist.

France, Anatole, See THIBAULT.

François de Sales (St.), 1567–1622, theologian.

Froissart, Jean, c. 1338–1406, chronicler.

Fustel de Coulanges, Numa Denis, 1830–89, historian.

Gaguin, Robert, 1433–1501, poet and historian.

Garnier, Robert, c. 1545–90, dramatist.

Gautier, Théophile, 1811–72, poet, novelist, and dramatist.

Genlis, Stéphanie Félicité Ducrest, Comtesse de, 1746–1830, romantic writer.

Gerlache, Étienne Constantin de, Baron, 1785–1871, Belgian historian.

Gerson, Jean Charlier de, 1363–1428, theologian and philosopher.

Gide, André Paul Guillaume, 1869–1951, novelist and dramatist.

Gilbert, Nicolas Joseph Laurent, 1751–80, poet.

Gilkin, Iwan, 1858–1924, Belgian poet, critic, and historian.

Giraud, Albert (A. Kayenbergh), 1860–1929, Belgian poet.

Giraudoux, Jean, 1882–1944, dramatist and essayist.

Gobineau, Arthur de, 1816–82, novelist, historian, etc.

Goncourt, Edmond de, 1822–96 } joint
Goncourt, Jules de, 1830–70, } novelists.

Gourmont, Rémy de, 1858–1915, journalist and critic.

Gras, Félix, 1844–1901, Provençal poet and novelist.

Gregory of Tours (St.), 538?–93, historian.

Grévin, Jacques, 1538–70, poet.

Guérin, Charles, 1873–1902, poet.

Guérin, Georges Maurice de, 1810–39, poet.

Guillaume de Nangis, ?–c. 1300, historian.

Guimond de la Touche, Claude, 1729–60, dramatist.

Guizot, François Pierre Guillaume, 1787–1874, historian.

Gyp. See MARTEL DE JANVILLE.

Halévy, Élie, 1870–1937, historian.

Halévy, Ludovic, 1834–1908, dramatist.

Héloïse, 1101–71. *See* ABÉLARD.

Helvétius, Claude Adrien, 1715–71, philosopher.

Heredia, José Maria de, 1842–1905, poet.

Herzog, Émile. *See* MAUROIS.

Hugo, Victor-Marie, Vicomte, 1802–85, novelist and poet.

Hugues de la Bachelerie, twelfth century, poet.

Huysmans, Joris Karl, 1848–1907, novelist.

Jacques de Guise, ?–1399, chronicler.

Jacques de Vitry (Bishop), ?–1240, chronicler.

Jaurès, Jean, 1859–1914, publicist.

Jean de Meung (Jean Clopinel), *c.* 1280–?, translator.

Jean de Troyes, living in 1480, chronicler.

Jean le Bel, ?–1370, chronicler.

Jodelle, Étienne, 1532–73, dramatist.

Joinville, Jean, Sire de, *c.* 1224–1317, historian.

Jouy, Victor Joseph Étienne, *c.* 1764–1846, novelist and dramatist.

Juvénal des Ursins (Archbishop), 1380–1422, historian.

Kervyn de Lettenhove, Joseph, Baron, 1817–91, Belgian historian.

Labaud, Valéry, 1881–1957, poet and essayist.

Labé, Louise ('La Belle Cordière'), 1526–1566, biographer and poet.

La Bruyère, Jean de, 1645–96, philosopher and moralist.

La Calprenède, Gautier de Costes de, 1614–63, novelist and dramatist.

La Chaussée, Pierre Claude Nivelle de, 1692–1754, dramatist.

Lacroix, Paul, 1806–54, novelist and historian.

La Fayette, Marie, Madeleine Pioche de la Vergne, Comtesse de, 1634–93, novelist.

La Fontaine, Jean de, 1621–95, fable-writer and poet.

Laforgue, Jules, 1860–87, poet and story-writer.

La Harpe, Jean François de, 1739–1803, dramatist.

Lamartine, Alphonse Prat de, 1790–1869, historian and poet.

Lamennais, Hugues Félicité Robert de, 1782–1854, theologian and journalist.

La Motte, Antoine Houdart, 1672–1731, dramatist and critic.

La Rochefoucauld, François, Duc de, 1613–80, writer on morals.

Larousse, Pierre, 1817–75, lexicographer.

La Salle, Antoine de, 1398–1462, romantic writer.

Leconte de Lisle, Charles Marie René, 1818–94, poet.

Lefreuc, Abel, 1862–1952, critic.

Legouis, Émile, 1861–1937, writer on English literature.

Le Maire de Belges, Jean, 1473–1524?, historian and poet, etc.

Lemonnier, Antoine Camille, 1845–1913, Belgian novelist and critic.

Lerberghe, Charles van, 1861–1907, Belgain poet and dramatist.

Lesage, Alain René, 1668–1747, novelist, author of *Gil Blas*.

Lorens or Laurent (Frère), thirteenth century, writer on morals.

Loti, Pierre. *See* VIAUD.

Maeterlinck, Maurice, Count, 1862–1949, Belgian poet, dramatist, and philosopher.

Maintenon, Françoise d'Aubigné, Marquise de, 1635–1719, letter-writer.

Maistre, Joseph, Comte de, 1754–1821, publicist and philosopher.

Maistre, Xavier de, 1763–1852, novelist.

Malebranche, Nicolas, 1638–1715, philosopher.

Malherbe, François de, 1555–1628, poet and critic.

Mallarmé, Stéphane, 1842–98, poet.

Malraux, André, 1901–76, miscellaneous writer.

Marguerite de Valois-Angoulême (Queen of Navarre), 1492–1549, poestess and tale-teller.

Marie de France, twelfth century, poetess.

Maritain, Jacques, 1882–1973, philosophical writer.

Marmontel, Jean François, 1723–99, dramatist, poet, and novelist.

Marot, Clément, 1497–1544, poet.

Martel de Janville, Sibylle Gabrielle Marie Antoinette, Comtesse de ('Gyp'), 1849–1932, novelist.

Masson, Pierre Maurice Alexandre, 1879–1916, critic.

Maupassant, Guy de, 1850–93, novelist and short-story writer.

Mauriac, François, 1885–1970, novelist.

Maurois, André (pseudonym of Émile Herzog), 1885–1967, writer and biographer.

Maurras, Charles Marie, 1868–1952, poet, critic, and miscellaneous writer.

Ménage, Gilles de, 1613–92, scholar.

Mendès, Catulle, 1841–1909, poet, novelist and dramatist.

Mérimée, Prosper, 1803–70, novelist.

Merrill, Stuart, 1863–1915, poet of American birth.

Meschinot, Jean, c. 1415–91, poet.

Michelet, Jules, 1798–1874, historian.

Mirabeau, Victor Riqueti, Marquis de, 1715–89, economist.

Mistral, Frédéric Joseph Étienne, 1830–1914, Provençal poet.

Mockel, Albert, 1866–1945, Belgian poet and critic.

Moliére, Jean Baptiste Poquelin de, 1622–1673, dramatist.

Montaigne, Michel Eyquem, Seigneur de, 1533–92, essayist.

Montalembert, Charles Forbes René de, 1810–70, historian and political writer.

Montesquieu, Charles Louis de Secondat, Baron de, 1689–1755, sociologist.

Musset, Alfred de, 1810–57, poet and dramatist.

Necker, Jacques, 1732–1804, statesman and miscellaneous writer.

Nerval, Gérard de, 1805–55, poet and novelist.

Noailles, Anna, Comtesse de, 1876–1933, poet.

Pascal, Blaise, 1623–62, philosopher and poet.

Pasquier, Étienne, 1529–1615, historian.

Péguy, Charles, 1873–1914, poet.

Perrault, Charles, 1628–1703, writer of fairy-tales.

Picard, Edmond, 1836–1924, Belgian essayist, dramatist, and poet.

Pigault-Lebrun, Charles Antoine Guillaume Pigault de l'Épinoy, 1753–1835, novelist.

Pirenne, Henri, 1862–1935, Belgian historian.

Poincaré, Jules Henri, 1854–1912, mathematician and philosopher.

Prévost d'Exiles, Antoine François, Abbé, 1697–1763, novelist.

Prévost, Eugène Marcel, 1862–1941, novelist and dramatist.

Prévost, Jean, 1901–44, miscellaneous writer.

Proudhon, Pierre Joseph, 1809–65, socialist writer.

Proust, Marcel, 1871–1922, novelist.

Prudhomme, Sully. *See* SULLY-PRUD-HOMME.

Quinault, Philippe, 1635–88, dramatist.

Rabelais, François, c. 1490–1553, satirist.

Racan, Honorat de Bueil, Marquis de, 1589–1670, poet, dramatist, and biographer.

Racine, Jean, 1639–99, poet and dramatist.

Regnard, Jean François, 1655–1709, poet and dramatist.

Régnier, Henri François Joseph de, 1864–1936, poet and novelist.

Régnier, Mathurin, 1573–1613, poet.

Renan, Ernest, 1823–92, historian and philosopher, etc.

Restif de la Bretonne, Nicolas Edmé, 1734–1806, novelist.

Retz, Jean François Paul de Gondi, Cardinal de, 1614–78, writer of memoirs and *pensées*.

Richepin, Jean, 1849–1926, poet and dramatist.

Rimbaud, Jean Nicolas Arthur, 1854–91, poet.

Rivarol, Antoine de, 1753–1801, scholar.

Robert de Sorbon, 1201–74, philosopher, founded the Sorbonne.

Roland, Marie Jeanne Phlipon, Mme, 1754–93, writer of memoirs and letters.

Rolland, Romain, 1866–1944, novelist, dramatist, and essayist.

Rollin, Charles, 1661–1741, historian.

Ronsard, Pierre de, 1524–85, poet.

Rostand, Edmond Eugène Alexis, 1868–1918, dramatist and poet.

Roumanille, Joseph, 1818–91, Provençal poet and story-writer.

Rousseau, Jean-Jacques, 1712–78, novelist, philosopher, etc.

Rutebeuf, *c.* 1230–80, poet.

Sagan, Françoise, 1935–, novelist.

Saint-Amant, Marc Antoine, Seigneur de, 1594–1661, poet.

Sainte-Beuve, Charles Augustin, 1804–69, critic, poet, moralist, historian, etc.

Saint-Évremond, Charles de Marguetel de Saint-Denis, Seigneur de, 1613–1703, miscellaneous writer.

Saint-Exupéry, Antoine de, 1900–44, novelist.

Saint-Gelais, Mellin de, 1491–1558, translator and epigrammist.

Saint-Gelais, Octavien de (Bishop), 1466–1502, poet.

Saint-Pierre, Charles Castel, Abbé de, 1658–1743, sociologist.

Saint-Pierre, Jacques Henri Bernardin de, 1737–1814, novelist and traveller.

Saint-Simon, Claude Henri de Rouvroy, Comte de, 1760–1825, philosopher.

Saint-Simon, Louis de Rouvroy, Duc de, 1675–1755, historian.

Sales. *See* FRANÇOIS DE SALES.

Samain, Albert, 1858–1900, poet.

Sand, George. *See* DUDEVANT.

Sartre, Jean-Paul, 1905–80, dramatist and existentialist philosopher.

Scarron, Paul, 1610–60, novelist, and satiriest.

Scève, Maurice, *c.* 1510–60, poet.

Scribe, Augustin Eugène, 1791–1861, dramatist.

Scudéry, Georges de, 1601–67, dramatist.

Scudéry, Madeleine de (sister of the above), 1607–81, novelist.

Segrais, Jean Regnauld de, 1624–1701, poet, memoir-, and story-writer.

Séverin, Fernand, 1867–1934, Belgian poet.

Sévigné, Marie de Rabutin-Chantal, Marquise de, 1626–96, letter-writer, etc.

Simenon, Georges, 1903–. Belgian detective novelist.

Sorel, Albert, 1842–1906, historian.

Sorel, Charles, 1602–74, novelist.

Sorel, Georges, 1847–1922, philosopher.

Staël-Holstein, Anne Louise Germaine (Necker), Baronne de, 1766–1817, novelist.

Stendhal. *See* BEYLE.

Sue, Eugène (Joseph Marie Sue), 1804–57, novelist.

Sully, Maximilien de Béthune, Duc de, 1560–1641, memoir-writer.

Sully-Prudhomme, René François Armand, 1839–1907, poet.

Taine, Hippolyte Adolphe, 1828–93, critic and historian.

Thibault, Jacques Antoine Anatole ('Anatole France'), 1844–1924, novelist and satirist.

Thierry, Amédée S. D., 1787–1873, historian.

Thierry, Jacques Nicolas Augustin, 1795–1856, historian.

Thiers, Louis Adolphe, 1797–1877, historian, critic, and statesman.

Thou, Jacques Auguste de, 1553–1617, historian.

Tocqueville, Alexis Clerel de, 1805–59, historian.

Tristan L'Hermite, François, 1601–55, poet.

Turgot, Anne Robert Jacques, Baron de l'Aulne, 1727–81, philosopher and political economist.

Tyard, Pontus de (Bishop), 1521–1605, poet.

Urfé, Honoré d', 1568–1625, novelist.

Valéry, Paul, 1871–1945, poet and dramatist.

Vauquelin de la Fresnaye, Jean, 1536–1608, poet.

Verhaeren, Émile, 1855–1916, Belgian poet.

Verlaine, Paul, 1844–96, poet.

Verne, Jules, 1828–1905, novelist.

Viau, Théophile, de (called Théophile), 1590–1626, poet.

Viaud, Julien ('Pierre Loti'), 1850–1923, novelist.

Vigny, Alfred, Comte de, 1797–1863, poet and novelist.

Villehardouin, Geoffroi de, 1155?–1213?, historian.

Villiers de l'Isle Adam, Philippe Auguste Mathias, Comte de, 1840–89, poet, story-writer, and dramatist.

Villon, François de Montcorbier (called), 1431–85?, poet.

Voltaire (François Marie Arouet de), 1694–1778, poet, dramatist, philosopher, novelist, etc.

Wace, Robert, of Jersey, *fl.* 1170, chronicler.

Weil, Simone, 1909–43, mystical writer.

Zola, Émile, 1840–1902, novelist.

French Revolution, The. Jean-Jacques Rousseau (1712–78) did much to prepare France for the revolution by his *Social Contract*. Meeting of the States-General, 5 May 1789, when the Third Estate demanded that the assembly should be composed of one order instead of three. The Third Estate met and took title of National Assembly, 17 June 1789. Louis XVI ordered Three Estates to separate. Led by Mirabeau, they refused, 23 June 1789. Royal troops sent to Paris, July 1789. Necker dismissed by Louis XVI, 11 July 1789. The Bastille (*q.v.*) captured by the mob, 14 July, 1789. Mob marched to Versailles and forced royal family to go to Paris, 5 Oct. 1789. Death of Mirabeau, 2 Apr. 1791. Massacre of the Champ de Mars, 17 July 1791. New constitution formed called the Legislative Assembly, 30 Sept. 1791, and the National Assembly dissolved. Mob invaded the Tuileries, 20 June 1792. The monarchy overthrown, 10 Aug. 1792. Dumouriez defeated the Prussians, who issued a manifesto against the French people, at the battle of Valmy, 20 Sept. 1792. National Convention took place of Legislative Assembly, and declared France a republic, 22 Sept. 1792. Louis XVI executed, 21 Jan. 1793. Committee of Public Safety formed, Jan. 1793. England, Holland, Spain, Portugal, Tuscany, Naples, and the Holy Roman Empire joined against France, 1 Feb. 1793.

Girondists overthrown, 2 June, 1793. Robespierre triumphant, Mar. 1794, but executed, 28 July 1794. Paris mob demands bread, Apr. 1795. Napoleon fires on mob, 5 Oct. 1795. *See* FRANCE.

French Somaliland. *See* DJIBOUTI.

Friedewald, Treaty of, 1552, between Henry II of France and the German Protestant princes, led by Maurice of Saxony.

Friendly Isles. Explored by Capt. Cook, 1773. *See* TONGA.

Friendly Societies (U.K.). First legalized by Act of Parliament, 1793. Registration made compulsory, 1923. Part of F.S. in National Insurance and social security came to an end under the terms of the National Insurance Act, 1946.

Friends, Society of. *See* QUAKERS.

Friends of the People.' Society formed 1792, to obtain parliamentary reform by constitutional means.

Friesland. From 1579 to 1795 one of the constituent parts of the republic of the United Provinces. William IV became hereditary stadtholder of F. (and all the other provinces) in 1747. Since 1815 a province of the Kingdom of the Netherlands.

Friesland, East. Region in N.W. Germany. A county in the fifteenth century, and later an independent duchy. Passed to Prussia, 1744, and annexed by Napoleon to Holland, 1806. Passed to Hanover, 1815.

Frigate.

1. Single-decked three-masted warship. First was the *Constant Warwick*, launched, 1646, and purchased for the Navy, 1649. Term abolished in the Royal Navy, 1883.

2. A type of all-purpose small warship introduced by Royal Navy in World War II, 1941.

Friuli, Province of, Italy and Yugoslavia. A county founded by the Carolingian emperors *c.* 780. Divided 1500 between Venice and Austria. Rest of it went to Austria at the fall of the Venetian Republic, 1797, and was ceded to Italy in 1866. Small portion ceded to Yugoslavia, 1947. *See* VENETIA.

Frobisher Bay, Arctic Ocean. Discovered by Sir Martin F., 1576.

Froebel System. Educational system founded by F. W. A. Froebel (1782–1852) as expounded in his book, *Die Menschenerziehung*, 1826. Froebel's first kindergarten opened in Switzerland, 1837.

Fronde, The. The First or Parliamentary F. originated in the Paris Parliament, June, 1648, against abuses in the Government. Closed with the Treaty of Rueil, 1 Apr. 1649. The Second or Aristocratic F. led by certain nobles under Condé, principally against Cardinal Mazarin, 1650; suppressed, 1653.

Fucino, Lake (anct. **Lacus Fucinus**). Overflow tunnel from, to Liri River, built at orders of Emperor Claudius, A.D. 37. Attempts to reopen it from 1240 onwards failed. Completely drained, 1876.

Fugitive Offenders Act, 1881, was replaced by the **Fugitive Offenders Act, 1967.**

Fugitive Slave Laws, passed by Congress, 1850; repealed, 1864.

Fulda. Abbey founded, 744, by Winfrith (Boniface) of Crediton, Apostle of Germany (680–755), who is buried there.

Fulham (London). Manor given to bishopric of London c. 691. First rector appointed, 1242. Bishops of London have resided at F. Palace since 1141, but present building not started until c. 1510–20.

Futurism. Movement founded by Marinetti, 1909. First Italian futurist exhibition held in Paris, 1911. Transferred to London, 1912. Movement collapsed c. 1915.

G

Gabelle. Certain taxes levied in France, especially on salt; first levied, 1286, finally abolished, 1790.

Gabon. Discovered by Portuguese, 1485. First French settlement, 1839. Libreville, founded 1848, made capital, 1849. Territory of French Equatorial Africa, 1946; member of the French Community, 1958; independent republic, 17 Aug. 1960.

Gadsden Purchase. In 1853 the U.S. Government bought certain lands from Mexico. The negotiations were managed by Gen. James G. (1788–1858), hence the name.

Gads Hill, Kent. Dickens bought a house here, 1856, and lived in it, 1860–70.

Gaeta, Italy. Besieged by Alfonso V of Aragon, 1435; by Austrians, 1707; by Charles of Naples, 1734; by French, 1806; by Austrians, 1815; by Italian National Party, 1860–1. Pope Pius IX took refuge here, 1848–9.

Gainsborough, England. Marriage of Alfred the Great at, A.D. 868. Destroyed by the Danes, 1013. Church founded by Templars, 1209. Captured from Parliamentarians, 1643.

Galapagos Islands. Discovered 1535, by Fra Tomas de Balanga, 3rd Bishop of Panama. Annexed by Ecuador, 1832.

Galatia. Ancient district of Asia Minor. The Gaulish or Galatian immigrants who settled there about the third century B.C. were defeated by Attalos I of Pergamum, 230 B.C. Came under Roman rule, 133 B.C.

Galicia, Spain. Settled at some time B.C. by the Gauls (q.v.), after whom it is named. G. became a Roman province, A.D. 137. The Suevi founded a kingdom of G., 411, which was overthrown by the Visigoths, 528. In the eighth century after a short spell of Saracen rule G. was absorbed into the kingdom of the Asturias, and in 1072 was incorporated with Leon and Castile.

Galicia (former Austrian crown-land), named after the principality of Halicz, was settled towards the E. by Ruthenians (q.v.) and towards the W. by Lechs (Poles) in the sixth century A.D. Western G., finally passed to Poland in the tenth century. Eastern G. was converted to Orthodox Christianity and Russian hegemony in the reign of Vladimir the Great of Kiev (d. 1015). G. formed, together with Volhynia, a short-lived independent principality (1199) which was absorbed by Lithuania, 1321, but fell to Poland under Casimir the Great, 1349. In 1371 a Galician Patriarchate, independent of Kiev, was set up, which at the Union of Brest-Litovsk, 1596, transferred its obedience to Rome (see RUTHENIAN CHURCH). The entire Galician territory passed to Austria in the Partitions of 1772 and 1795, and the Polish (less so the Ukrainian) element managed to retain considerable autonomy down to 1918. Polish, 1919–39. Occupied by the Russians from Sept. 1939 to July 1941. By treaty of 17 Aug. 1945 all G. E. of the San River passed to the Soviet Republic of Ukraine.

Galilee became part of the Assyrian Empire, 734 B.C., but was given up to the Israelites after their return from the captivity. Under the rule of the Idumean princes Herod the Great (37–4 B.C.) and his son Herod Antipas (4 B.C.–A.D. 39), the former being also King of Judea, but the latter only Tetrarch of G. Under Roman procurators from A.D. 44, G. became the chief refuge of the Jews after their expulsion from Jerusalem, 135. See SAFAD.

After the war of 1948 much of the Arab population fled to Jordan

Gallia Cisalpina or **G. Citerior**, practically identical with the modern regions of Piedmont, Lombardy, and Venetia, was divided into G. Cispadana on the right bank and G. Transpadana on the left bank of the Po respectively. The Gauls penetrated into the Po valley from the N. in the fifth century B.C. A Roman colony was established at Sena Gallica (Senegaglia), 282 B.C., and the whole country reduced, 203–191, the last Gallic tribe to resist being the Boii.

Gallia Transalpina or **G. Ulterior,** consisting of G. Narbonensis (Provence), Aquitania (basin of the Garonne), G. Lugdunensis (central plateau), and G. Belgica, which extended up the Rhine, is dealt with under FRANCE.

Gallican Church. Owing to its independent attitude towards the Roman See, the Church in France was often called the G.C. The Pragmatic Sanction of 1269 provided that the laws of the Church should conform with the common law. Philip IV in 1302 opposed Pope Boniface VIII and imprisoned him; and again in 1438, the Pragmatic Sanction of Bourges aimed at the encroachments of Rome. This last was superseded by the Concordat of Bologna, between Pope Leo X and Francis I. The declaration of the French clergy in 1682 (the Four Propositions) declared the Pope incompetent to interfere in civil affairs. Condemned by Pope Alexander VIII, 1690; by Clement XI, 1706; and by Pius VI, 1794. Declaration of 1682 was again put into force by Napoleon, 1810. In 1826 the French bishops confirmed this. However, at the Vatican Council, 1869–70, they declared the Pope competent to intervene.

Gallican Confession. Profession of faith of the French Reformed Church adopted at the Synod of La Rochelle, 1571.

Gallipoli, Turkey. Captured by Turks, 1357. British and French armies landed at, Apr. 1854, and proceeded against the Russians. For G. campaign, 1915–16, *see* Dardanelles, *under* WORLD WAR I.

Gallon, standardized for the U.K., 1824, as the volume of 10 lb. of distilled water at 62° F. and 30 in. barometric pressure. Being superseded by the litre 1960 onwards. The present standard G. in U.S.A. is the archaic wine G. of Queen Anne, standardized in 1707 at 231 c. in.

Gallup Poll invention, of George Horace G. (1901–85), who founded the G. Institute, 1935, which correctly forecast the results of sev. U.S. presidential elections. His methods form the basis of modern public opinion polling.

Galveston, Texas. Settled 1837. Captured by the Federals, 1862, and retaken by the Confederates, 1863. Seriously damaged by fire, 1885, and by the sea, 1900. Centre of oil industry since 1920s.

Galway, Ireland. Fortified *c.* 1244; surrendered to parliamentary forces, 10 July 1641. Gavazzi riots at, Mar. 1859.

Galway Election. In May 1872 a petition was presented to unseat Capt. Nolan, M.P. for G., owing to alleged intimidation of certain Irish Roman Catholics. The petition was successful, and the Bishop of Clonfert and others were tried but acquitted.

Gambia, W. Africa. Settlement founded by English on initiative of Portuguese in London, 1588. English factory established at, 1620. English right to G. confirmed by Treaty of Paris, 1815; separated from Sierra Leone, 1843; included in W. African Settlements, 1866; again made a separate crown colony, 1888. On 18 Feb. 1965 became an independent state within the Commonwealth. G. became a republic within the Commonwealth in April 1970: joined with Senegal to form Confederation of Senegambia, 1982.

Gaming and Gambling, Laws regulating (Great Britain). Act of Charles II, 1665, by which persons losing more than £100 at one time were not compelled to pay. An Act of 1710 provided that bonds and other securities won at play were not recoverable, and any person losing more than £10 might sue and recover this amount from the winner. Acts to amend previous laws, 1845, 1854, 1860, 1892, and 1922. Betting and Gaming Act, 1960, radically modified Brit. gambling laws. Amended, 1968. Gaming Board estab. Oct. 1968. Betting and Gaming Duties Act, 1972. *See* BETTING.

Gamma Rays. Discovered by Villard, 1900.

Gandamak, Treaty of, between Britain and Afghanistan, 1879.

Garde Nationale. First raised, 1789, under La Fayette, in Paris; they helped to crush the Parisian mob in 1795 (13th Vendémiaire), but in 1830 and 1848 declared for the revolutionaries. Disbanded after the suppression of the Commune at Paris, May 1871.

Garden City idea first mooted by Ebenezer Howard (1850–1928) in his book *To-morrow* (1898). First (Letchworth) G. C. founded, 1903, and second (Welwyn), 1920. *See* NEW TOWNS.

Garhwal, ravaged by Gurkhas, 1803 (*see* NEPAL, *also* SIKKIM), came under British protection, 1814, and was included in United Provinces. Now part of Uttar Pradesh.

Gas. Illuminating power demonstrated experimentally by Dr. John Clayton, Dean of Kildare, *c.* 1691. Illumination by, first attempted in Cornwall to replace candles and lamps at a factory, 1792. In London it was introduced, 1807, and generally used, 1816. G. flame used for cooking in J. Sharp's ovens, 1835. First practical internal combustion G. engine made by Lenoir, 1860. Used in conjunction with refrigerating plants, 1908. First used for illumination in U.S.A. at Boston, 1823. Natural gas discovered under N. Sea in Dutch waters, after World War II; British N. Sea gas finds, 1965 and 1966. Conversion of British gas supplies to N. Sea gas begun, 1968.

Gas Authority, British. Under the G. Act of 1948 took over all G. installations from private or municipal ownership, 1 May 1949, and reorganized them under twelve Area G. Boards. G. Compensation Stock is redeemable, 1990–5.

Gas, Poison, first used by Germans against Russians, Apr. 1915, and against Brit., Sept. 1915. Geneva Protocol 1925 banned its use in warfare. Allegedly used by Iraq against Iran, 1983–4.

Gascony, France. *See* AQUITAINE.

Gastein, Convention of, between Austria and Prussia at close of the Schleswig-Holstein War, 14 Aug. 1865.

G.A.T.T. (General Agreement on Tariffs and Trade), signed at Geneva, 1947. Came into force, 1 Jan. 1948.

Gaul. *See* FRANCE.

Gauls. A branch of the Celts, whose language does not survive. Their main body spread outwards from the Alps and settled widely in Gallia, Cisalpina, and Transalpina (*qq.v.*) in the fifth century B.C. The La Tène culture of the early Iron Age (500–1 B.C.) represents the peak of Gallic art. In the fourth century they invaded central Italy, taking Rome, 390, unopposed. At the same time elements migrating south-westwards from France reached Galicia (*q.v.*); another section pressed eastwards and settled in the interior of Asia Minor, 275 (*see* GALATIA). In the second century German tribes drove the Gallic Helvetii and allied tribes out of what is now Baden and Württemberg westwards over the Rhine and S. into the Jura. For the history of the western and southern branches, *see* FRANCE and GALLIA CISALPINA. For that of the eastern, *see* GALATIA.

Gavelkind. An ancient English form of land tenure, under which the inheritance was divided equally among all the sons. It existed only in Kent and was abolished by the Law of Property Act, 1925.

Gaza, Palestine. An ancient town mentioned in Genesis (x. 19) and other biblical books. Captured by Alexander the Great, 332 B.C.; ravaged by Saladin, 1170; citadel captured by him, 1187. Captured by Khwarizmians, 1244, and held by Moslems until taken by the French under Kléber, 1799. Taken by the Egyptians under Ibrahim Pasha, 1831; by the British under Allenby, Nov. 1917.

Gaza Strip came into existence as result of the armistice agreement between Israel and Egypt, 1949. It represented the area of Palestine left in Egyptian hands afer the 1948 fighting. Israel expelled Egyptian forces from the G.S., Nov. 1956, but in Mar. 1957 Israel troops withdrew and a U.N. force took their place. Egypt resumed the civil administration of the G.S. At Egypt's request, the U.N. force withdrew, 19 May 1967. 8 June 1967, Israel won control of the G.S. in the 'June war'; after the ceasefire Israel maintained control of it, and despite Arab and international opposition has since 1970 proceeded to turn the G.S. into a permanent Jewish settlement.

Gdansk, Ger., **Danzig**, by which name it was known until 1945. Capital of Dukes of Pomerania, 1230. Occupied by Teutonic Knights, 1308; reconquered by Poland, 1455; place of refuge of Charles VIII when driven from Sweden, 1457; an autonomous free city, 1466–1793; seized by Russians and Saxons, 29 June 1734; ceded to Prussia, 1793; surrendered to Napoleon, who declared it a free city again, 26 May 1807; restored to Prussia, 1814. Declared a free city by the Treaty of Versailles, 1919. Germany annexed G., 1 Sept. 1939. Heavily bombed by Anglo-U.S. and Russian air forces in World War II. Ceded to Poland by Yalta agreement. German population driven out, 1945–6.

Gdynia (Pol.), **Gdingen** or **Gotenhafen** (Ger.). Built by Poles as a Baltic port, 1921–30. Occupied by Germans, 14 Sept. 1939. Returned to Poland, 1945.

Geiger Counter. Invented by Rutherford and Geiger, 1908, and developed by Geiger and Müller, 1928.

Gelderland, Holland. Formed part of the Burgundian possessions, 1472–92. Formed part of the Burgundian Circle of the Holy Roman Empire, 1512. Passed to the Emperor Charles V, 1543. Province of the United Netherlands, 1578. Part of the kingdom of the Netherlands, 1815.

Gelnhausn, Compact or **Agreement of,** by the Electors of the Empire to resist the reforms of the Emperor Maximilian, June 1502.

General Agreement on Tariffs and Trade. *See* G.A.T.T.

General Assembly. *See* CHURCH OF SCOTLAND.

General Strike (Britain), 3–13 May 1926.

Geneva (Ger. **Genf**), Switzerland. Republic founded, 1512; allied with Freiburg, 1519, and Berne, 1526; adopted Protestant doctrines, 1535. Calvin (*see* CALVINISTS) went there, 1536, and exiled from, 1538; recalled, Sept. 1541; *d.* at, 1564. G. annexed to France, 1798. Joined Swiss Confederation, 1815. *see* LEAGUE OF NATIONS.

Geneva Conferences.

1. Held by foreign ministers of nineteen countries at Geneva, Apr.–July 1954, to discuss (*a*) unification of Korea, (*b*) a settlement in Indo-China. No settlement was reached over Korea; but an armistice ending the Indo-China war was signed, 21 July.

2. Heads of governments of Britain, France, Russia, and the U.S.A. met at Geneva, 18–23 July 1955, first such meeting since Potsdam (1945).

Geneva Conferences (Disarmament).

1. 1927: Sequel of the Washington Conference of 1922, on naval disarmament. Its sequel was the London Conference of 1930.

2. 1932: Came to an abrupt end in Oct. 1933 when Hitler announced Germany's withdrawal from the conference and from the League of Nations.

3. 1962: Between U.N. members, began 14 Mar.; little progress made subsequently, though these discussions probably indirectly influenced the events leading to the Test Ban Treaty initialled in Moscow between the U.S.S.R., U.S.A. and Britain in July 1963. Further inconclusive meetings 1965–83. Arms limitation talks started, Nov. 1981 were suspended, Nov. 1983, when Russians walked out. Restarted, 1985.

Geneva Convention. Signed by the representatives of twelve countries, 22 Aug. 1864, and dealt with the treatment of wounded during war. Revised 1906, to which fifty-seven nations became parties in 1929, when paragraphs relating to the civil population were raised. A new convention was signed in 1949.

Genoa, Italy (Lat. **Genua**, It. **Genova**). Submitted to Romans *c.* 200 B.C.; a free republic, A.D. 1000. Joins the First Crusade, 1095–9; and Third Crusade, 1191–6. Alliance with Venice, 1238; with the Pope, 1239; with Florence and Lucca, 1251. Quarrel with Venice at Acre, 1256. Defeat at naval battle of Acre, 1258. Assists the Greek Emperor Michael Palaeologus to retake Constantinople from the Latins, 1261. Treaty of Cremona, 1270. Naval battle of Curzola, 1298. War of Chioggia (*q.v.*), 1350–81. Annexes Corsica from Pisa, 1367. Commercial treaty with the Turks, 1452. Refuses help to the Knights of St. John, 1520. Sacked by Spanish and Italians under Colonna, 1522. Battle of Prevesa, 1540. Sends nominal contingent to fight at Lepanto, 1571. Walls built, 1626–32. Bombarded by French, 1684; by British, 1745. Sells Corsica to France, 1768. Converted into the Ligurian republic under French domination by Napoleon, July 1797. Annexed by France, 1806. Incorporated with Piedmont-Sardinia, 1815. Bombarded by the British fleet, Feb. 1942.

Gentlemen-at-Arms, Honourable Corps of. English royal bodyguard, founded 1509. First went into action as Henry VIII's bodyguard at Guingatte, 1513, then at the siege of Boulogne, 1544. It also took up action stations at St. James's Palace, 1848, in face of an alleged Chartist march on Westminster. Since the nineteenth century a custom has arisen where by the Government Chief Whip in the House of Lords is also Captain of the Corps.

Geographical Society, American. Established 1852.

Geographical Society, Royal, was founded, 1830. Caused the establishment of a school of geography, the first in an English university, at Oxford, 1899.

Geological Society, Great Britain. Founded, 1807, and incorporated, 1826.

Geophysical Year, International. July 1957–Dec. 1958, during which period observations of the action of natural physical forces on the earth were made by scientists from approximately forty countries at many places throughout the world.

George Cross. Honour instituted, 1940, to reward the performance of deeds of valour by civilians, both men and women. It ranks immediately after the Victoria Cross (*q.v.*). The G.C. was awarded to the island of Malta (*q.v.*) on 17 Apr. 1942, in recognition of its gallantry under enemy bombardment.

George Washington Bridge over the Hudson River opened, Nov. 1931.

Georgia, Caucasus (Rus. **Gruzia**; Georgian **Karthveli**). The 'Iberia' of the ancients. Converted to Christianity, 318. Invaded by Tatars, 1236; laid waste, 1386 and 1393–4, by Timur, who was driven out in 1403; invaded by Persians, 1618. The last king was George XIII, who resigned the crown in favour of Paul, Emperor of Russia, 1800; formally annexed to Russia, 1801. Soviet Socialist Republic proclaimed, 25 Feb. 1921. Became constituent Republic of the U.S.S.R., 1936.

Georgia, U.S.A. Founded by royal charter, granted 9 June 1732; named after George II; State constitution adopted, 5 Feb. 1777. State university at Athens chartered, 1785. One of original thirteen states of the Union. Seceded, 1861; readmitted to union, 1870. New constitution adopted, 1976.

German Baptists. A sect founded, 1708; settled in America early in the eighteenth century. The first congregation there was organized at Germantown, Pa., 25 Dec. 1723; their press in 1743 printed the first Bible to appear in a European language in America. J. C. Beissel (1690–1768) seceded with his followers, who are now known as the Seventh Day Baptists. Another faction, the Old Order Brethren, who abhorred higher education, seceded, 1880–90, and a Radical or progressive group, 1882. Since 1928 the G.B. have been known as the Church of the Brethren.

German Catholics. A sect in Saxony and Silesia, which seceded from the

Church of Rome, 1844, and may be regarded as the forerunners of the Old Catholics (q.v.).

German Literature. The following is a list of principal authors in the G., whether Germans, Austrians, or Swiss:

Arnim, Bettina von, 1785–1859, poetess.

Arnim, Ludwig Achim von, 1781–1831, miscellaneous writer.

Auerbach, Berthold, 1812–82, novelist.

Auersperg, Graf Anton Alexander von, 1806–76, poet.

Bernhard, Thomas (Austrian), 1931–, novelist.

Bodenstedt, Friedrich Martin von, 1819–92, poet.

Böhme, Jakob, 1575–1624, philosopher.

Böll, Heinrich, 1917–85, novelist.

Bonhoeffer, Dietrich, 1906–45, theologian.

Brant, Sebastian, 1458–1521, satirist.

Brecht, Bertolt, 1898–1956, dramatist.

Breitinger, Johann Jakob, 1701–76, miscellaneous writer.

Brentano, Clemens, 1788–1842, romantic writer.

Brockes, Barthold Heinrich, 1680–1747, poet.

Büchner, Georg, 1813–37, dramatist.

Bunsen, Christian Karl Josias, Baron von, 1791–1860, antiquarian.

Burckhardt, Jakob, 1818–97, Swiss art historian.

Canitz, Friedrich Rudolf Ludwig, Freiherr von, 1654–99, poet.

Carossa, Hans, 1878–1956, story-writer.

Dach, Simon, 1605–59, poet.

Döblin, Alfred, 1878–1957, novelist.

Droste-Hülshoff, Annette von, 1797–1848, poet.

Ebeling, Christoph Daniel, 1741–1817, historian.

Ebers, Georg, 1837–98, romance writer.

Eck, Johann Maier von, 1486–1543, theologian.

Eckhart, Johannes (Meister), 1260–1327, mystic.

Egestorff, Georg, pseudonym. *See* OMPTEDA.

Ekkehard of St. Gall, *fl. c.* 930, poet.

Fallada, Hans, 1893–1947, novelist.

Feuchtwanger, Leon, 1884–1958, novelist, dramatist, and critic.

Fichte, Immanuel Hermann von, 1797–1879, philosopher.

Fichte, Johann Gottlieb, 1762–1814, philosopher.

Fischart, Johann, *c.* 1546–90, satirist.

Fischer, Ernst Kuno Berthold, 1824–1907, philosopher.

Fischer, Johann Georg von, 1816–97, poet and dramatist.

Fleming, Paul, 1609–40, poet.

Fontane, Theodor, 1819–98, novelist and poet.

Fouqué, Friedrich Heinrich Karl de la Motte, 1777–1843, novelist.

Freiligrath, Hermann Ferdinand, 1810–76, poet.

Freud, Sigmund, 1856–1939, psychologist.

Freytag, Gustav, 1816–95, novelist.

Geiler von Kaysersberg, Johannes, 1445–1510, mystic.

George, Stefan, 1868–1933, poet.

Gessner, Salomon, 1730–88, poet.

Goethe, Johann Wolfgang von, 1749–1832, poet.

Gottfried von Strassburg, *c.* 1210, poet.

Gottschalk, Rudolf von, 1823–1909, dramatist, novelist, poet, and critic.

Gottsched, Johann Christoph, 1700–66, poet and dramatist.

Grass, Günter, 1927–, novelist and poet.

Grillparzer, Franz, 1791–1872, Austrian poet and dramatist.

Grimm, Jakob, 1785–1863, | philologists and folklorists;
Grimm, Wilhelm, 1786–1859, | brothers who collaborated.

Grimmelshausen, Hans Jakob Christoffel von, *c.* 1624–76, picaresque novelist.

Gryphius, Andreas, 1616–49, poet and dramatist.

Gunther, Johann Christian, 1695–1723, poet.

Hagedorn, Friedrich von, 1708–54, poet.

Haller, Albrecht von (Swiss), 1708–77, poet.

Hardenberg, Friedrich von, 1772–1801, poet.

Hartmann von Aue, c. 1170–c. 1210, poet.
Hauptmann, Gerhard, 1862–1946, dramatist.
Hebbel, Christian Friedrich, 1813–63, poet.
Hegel, Georg Friedrich, 1770–1831, philosopher.
Heine, Heinrich, 1797–1856, poet and dramatist.
Heinrich von Meissen ('Frauenlob'), c. 1250–1318, poet.
Heinrich von Morungen, end of twelfth century, poet.
Heinrich von Veldeke, c. 1170, poet.
Herder, Johann Gottfried von, 1744–1803, poet and philosopher.
Hesse, Hermann, 1877–1962, Swiss-domiciled novelist and poet.
Heyse, Paul Johann, 1830–1914, poet and story-writer.
Hoffmann, Ernst Theodor Wilhelm, 1776–1822, romanticist.
Hoffmann, Heinrich, 1809–94, children's writer.
Hofmannsthal, Hugo von, 1874–1929, poet and dramatist.
Hölderlin, Johann Christian Friedrich, 1770–1843, poet.
Hölty, Ludwig, 1748–76, poet.
Humboldt, Friedrich Heinrich Alexander von, 1769–1859, traveller and scientist.
Humboldt, Karl Wilhelm von, 1767–1835, critic and philologist.
Hutten, Ulrich von, 1488–1523, poet and controversialist.
Johnson, Uwe, 1934–, writer.
Kafka, Franz, 1883–1924, novelist.
Kant, Immanuel, 1724–1804, philosopher.
Kästner, Erich, 1899–1974, children's writer.
Kautsky, Karl, 1854–1938, historian of Socialism.
Keller, Gottfried, 1819–90, novelist and poet.
Keyserling, Count (Hermann Alexander), 1880–1946, philosopher and essayist.
Kirst, Hans Helmut, 1914–, novelist.
Kleist, Ewald Christian von, 1715–59, poet.
Kleist, Heinrich von, 1777–1811, dramatist.

Klopstock, Friedrich Gottlieb, 1724–1803, poet.
Knapp, Georg Friedrich, 1842–1926, economic historian.
Konrad von Würzburg, 1230?–87, poet.
Körner, Karl Theodor, 1791–1813, dramatist and poet.
Kotzebue, August Friedrich Ferdinand von, 1761–1819, dramatist.
Lassalle, Ferdinand Johann Gottlieb, 1825–64, economic writer.
Lavater, Johann Kasper, 1741–1801, Swiss poet.
Leibnitz, Gottfried Wilhelm, Freiherr von, 1646–1716, philosopher.
Lessing, Gotthold Ephraim, 1729–81, dramatist and critic.
Logau, Friedrich, Freiherr von, 1604–55, epigrammist.
Ludwig, Emil, 1881–1948, biographer.
Ludwig, Otto, 1813–65, poet and dramatist.
Luther, Martin, 1483–1546, hymn-writer and theologian.
Mann, Heinrich, 1871–1950, novelist.
Mann, Thomas, 1875–1955, novelist and critic.
Marx, Heinrich Karl, 1818–83, economist and philosopher.
Melanchthon, Philipp, 1497–1560, theologian.
Meyer, Konrad Ferdinand, 1825–98, Swiss novelist.
Mommsen, Theodor, 1817–1903, historian.
Mörike, Eduard Friedrich, 1804–75, poet.
Müller, Wilhelm, 1794–1827, poet.
Musil, Robert, 1880–1942, novelist and playwright.
Neidhart von Reuenthal, c. 1180–1250, poet.
Nestroy, Johann, 1801–62, dramatist.
Nietzsche, Friedrich Wilhelm, 1844–1900, philosopher.
Ompteda, Baron Georg von, 1863–1931, novelist.
Opitz von Boberfeld, Martin, 1597–1639, poet.
Oswald von Wolkenstein, 1367–1445, poet.
Ranke, Leopold von, 1795–1886, historian.

Remarque, Erich Maria, 1898–1970, novelist.

Reuter, Heinrich Ludwig Christian Friedrich ('Fritz'), 1810–74, story-writer.

Richter, Johann Paul Friedrich, 1763–1825, novelist, etc.

Rilke, Rainer Maria, 1875–1926, lyric poet.

Rosegger, Petri Kettenfeier, 1843–1918, novelist and poet.

Sachs, Hans, 1494–1576, poet and dramatist.

Schiller, Johann Christoph Friedrich von, 1759–1805, poet and dramatist.

Schlegel, August Wilhelm von, 1767–1845, poet, essayist, and translator.

Schlegel, Friedrich von, 1772–1829, novelist, dramatist, and critic.

Schleiermacher, Friedrich Ernst Daniel, 1768–1834, theologian and philosopher.

Schnitzler, Arthur, 1862–1931, dramatist and novelist.

Schopenhauer, Arthur, 1788–1860, philosopher.

Schubart, Christian Friedrich Daniel, 1739–91, poet and musician.

Spengler, Oswald, 1880–1936, philosopher.

Spitteler, Carl Friedrich, 1845–1924, poet.

Spyri, Johanna, 1829–1901, children's novelist.

Storm, Theodor Woldsen, 1817–88, poet and novelist.

Strauss, David Friedrich, 1808–74, theologian and biographer.

Sudermann, Hermann, 1857–1928, dramatist and novelist.

Sylva, Carmen (Elisabeth, Queen of Rumania), 1843–1916, miscellaneous writer.

Tauler, Johannes, c. 1300–61, mystic.

Tieck, Johann Ludwig, 1773–1853, dramatist.

Toller, Ernst, 1893–1939, dramatist and poet.

Treitschke, Heinrich von, 1834–96, historian.

Uhland, Johann Ludwig, 1787–1862, poet.

Wagner, Wilhelm Richard, 1813–83, dramatist and musician.

Walther von der Vogelweide, c. 1168–c. 1228, poet.

Wedekind, Frank, 1864–1918, dramatist.

Werfel, Franz, 1890–1945, Austrian novelist.

Wieland, Christoph Martin, 1733–1813, novelist, poet, and translator.

Wildenbruch, Ernst von, 1845–1909, dramatist.

Winckelmann, Johann Joachim, 1717–68, art historian.

Wolfram von Eschenbach, c. 1170–1220, poet.

Wyss, Johann Rudolf, 1781–1830, children's novelist.

Zweig, Stefan, 1881–1942, novelist and poet.

German Volga Republic. The region on both sides of the Lower Volga was settled by Germans at the invitation of Catherine the Great, 1760. In 1918 they set up an autonomous workers' commune, which in 1924 was transformed into an autonomous republic forming part of the R.S.F.S.R. After 1941, the republic forfeited its autonomy, and its German inhabitants were deported. It became part of the Saratov region, 1947.

Germanium. Chemical element discovered by Winkler in 1886.

Germany. For history previous to 12 July 1806, *see* HOLY ROMAN EMPIRE, also PRUSSIA. Confederation of the Rhine formed under Napoleon's mediation, 12 July 1806. German Confederation formed under Austrian presidency, 1815. N. German Zollverein (*q.v.*) founded, 1819. S. German Zollverein, 1828–31. Central German Zollverein, 1828. Revolutions, 1848–50. Resumption of the German Diet, 1851. German-Danish War, 1864. Austro- Prussian War leads to the exclusion of Austria from Confederation and the formation of the N. German Confederation under Prussia, 1866. Franco-German War, 1870–1.

German Empire proclaimed at Versailles, 1871. Peace of Frankfort-on-Main, 10 May 1871. First German Imperial Parliament, Mar. 1871. Triple Alliance constituted between Austria, Italy, and G., 1883. Togo, Cameroons, and S.W. Africa acquired, 1884; E. Africa, 1885; William II came to the throne, 1888. Bismarck resigned, 1890. Kiaochow seized, 1897. Steady rise of Socialism with strong Marxist tendencies, from 1900 onwards. Expansion of navy by Navy Bill, 1900; G. refused at Hague Conference of 1907 to abate naval building. Morocco crisis between G. and France, 1905, and Agadir incident (*q.v.*), 1911. War declared on Russia, 1 Aug.; on France, 3 Aug.; on Belgium, 4 Aug. 1914.

World War I (*q.v.*). Revolution breaks out, Nov. 1918. Kaiser William II flees, 9 Nov. The Weimar Republic established, 31 July 1919. G. declared herself unable to meet reparations, July 1922, and French troops occupied Ruhr, 10 Jan. 1923. Partial evacuation of Ruhr, Nov. 1924. Death of Ebert, 28 Feb.; election of President Hindenburg, 26 Apr. 1925. Locarno Treaty signed, Oct. 1925. Treaty with Soviet, Apr. 1926. Admission to League of Nations, 8 Sept. 1926. Hindenburg re-elected, 10 Apr. 1932.

1933: Adolf Hitler became Chancellor, 30 Jan.; legal Government of Prussia deposed, 6 Feb.; Reichstag fire, 27 Feb.; freedom of speech and press abolished, 28 Feb.; Hitler triumphant at polls, 5 Mar.; persecution of Jews began, 8 Mar.; Social-Democratic Party suppressed, 23 June; Centre Party wound up, 29 June; notice of withdrawal from League of Nations given, 14 Oct.; Hitler's policy approved by plebiscite, 12 Nov.

1934: 90 dissentient Nazis shot, including Schleicher, former Chancellor, and Röhm, chief of the S.A., 30 June; Hindenburg d., and office of president was abolished, Hitler becoming supreme as Führer, 2 Aug.

1935: Saar plebiscite, 13 Jan., returned to G., 1 Mar.; Hitler denounced Treaty of Versailles, 16 Mar.

1936: Troops reoccupied Rhineland, 8

Mar.; Edgar André, Communist leader, beheaded at Hamburg, 5 Nov.; Anti-Comintern Pact with Japan, 25 Nov.

1938: German troops entered Austria, 11 Mar.; union of Austria with the Reich ('Anschluss') proclaimed, 13 Mar.; Chamberlain flew, 29 Sept., to Munich, where four-power agreement regarding Czechoslovakia (between Britain, France, Italy, and Germany) signed, 30 Sept.; German occupation of the claimed portions of Czechoslovakia completed, 10 Oct.

1939: Czechoslovak (*q.v.*) republic destroyed by G., 15 Mar.; Slovakia a German protectorate; Memel transferred from Lithuania to the Reich by forced agreement, 22 Mar.; Poland rejected G.'s demands as to Danzig, etc. 5 May; 'Axis' announced to have become a military pact, 6–7 May; military alliance with Italy embodied in treaty, 22 May; Russo-German non-aggression pact signed at Moscow, 23 Aug.; Poland invaded at 5.30 a.m. and many of its towns bombed, Danzig's return to Reich proclaimed, 1 Sept. (*See* WORLD WAR II.) Refusal of Britain's demand for withdrawal from Poland; Britain and France declared war on G., 3 Sept.; Gdynia surrendered to G., 14 Sept. Warsaw surrendered to G., 28 Sept.; Western Poland annexed, Germans in Latvia invited to return to Reich, 8 Oct.; first shipload of Baltic Germans left Riga for Gdynia, 14 Oct.; repatriation of Germans from Estonia announced, 16 Oct.; government of occupied Polish territories established at Cracow, Hitler nearly killed in Bürgerbräukeller at Munich by a time-bomb, 8 Nov.

1940: Invasion of Denmark and Norway, 9 Apr.; and of Belgium and Holland, 10 May; France accepted armistice terms of G. and Italy, 22 June; Tripartite Pact (*q.v.*) with Italy and Japan signed in Berlin, 27 Sept.; German troops began occupation of Rumania, 13 Oct.; Hungary signs pact in Vienna, 20 Nov.; Rumania and Slovakia sign pact, 23 Nov.

1941: German troops occupy Bulgaria, which joins Axis (Tripartite) Pact, 1

Mar.; invasion of Yugoslavia and Greece, 6 Apr.; both countries occupied by end of Apr.: flight to Britain of Rudolf Hess, deputy Führer, 10 May; attack on Russia began, 22 June.

Hitler presumed dead in Berlin, 30 Apr. 1945. Final surrender, 8 May 1945. Four allied commanders-in-chief assumed supreme power and established zones of occupation, 5 June 1945. Potsdam Conference, July 1945. Formation of State governments begun in U.S. zone, Jan. 1946. Fusion of British and American zones begun, Dec. 1946. Four-power negotiations in the Council of Foreign Ministers in London broke down on the future of a politically and economically united G., Dec. 1947. Britain, France, and the U.S.A. therefore (1948) integrated their zones politically and economically. Currency reform in Western zones, June 1948, followed by Russian blockade of Berlin (*q.v.*), 28 June 1948–12 May 1949. Parliamentary Council met in Bonn to begin the task of drafting a constitution for W.G., Sept. 1948. For subsequent history of G. *see* the next two articles.

Germany, Democratic Republic of (Eastern). German Democratic People's Republic set up in Russian zone, 7 Oct. 1949. Pieck (1876–1960) became first President, but real power resided in Ulbricht's hands. After Stalin's death a more 'liberal' policy begun, June 1953, but after rioting in Berlin and several other cities had had to be crushed by Russian tanks, 16–17 June, a harsher policy was readopted. 'National people's army' created, 18 Jan. 1956. Due to defections to the West, the population of the republic fell by nearly 2,000,000 between 1948 and 1959. After Pieck's death (7 Sept. 1960) the presidency was abolished. Instead a council of state was established whose first chairman (Ulbricht, *d.* 1973) had dictatorial powers. Friction between the republic and the West increased during 1960–1, due to steady flow of refugees to the West through Berlin, and on 13 Aug. 1961 the republic closed the Berlin border and subse-

quently built a wall along it (20 Aug.). Some liberalization since 1960s and meetings between G.D.R. and F.G.R. leaders since 1970.

Germany, Federal Republic of (Western). A constitution for a Federal Republic in W.G. was approved by the Western Occupying Powers, 12 May 1949, and the republic came into being, with its capital at Bonn, 23 May. First elections to Federal Diet (Bundestag), 15 Aug. First chancellor, Konrad Adenauer, elected, 16 Sept. State of war between Western Powers and G. ended, 1951. Member of the Council of Europe, 1951. Reparations agreement concluded with Israel, 1952. Member of the European Coal and Steel Community, 1952. Diplomatic relations were established between Russia and the federal republic, and several thousand German prisoners repatriated from Russia. The republic joined Western Union and N.A.T.O., May 1955. Saar reunited to Germany at midnight on 31 Dec. 1956. Member of the European Economic Community, 1958. A foreign ministers' conference at Geneva, attended by representatives of both German republics, failed to reach agreement on reunification of Germany, 1959. Franco-German friendship demonstrated by Adenauer's official visit to France, July 1962, when there was a ceremony of reconciliation between the two countries. 1963: Franco-German 'reconciliation treaty' signed in Paris, 24 Jan. In the elections Sept. 1969 the Social Democrats made big gains: on 21 Oct., Brandt was elected chancellor of a Coalition of Socialists and Free Democrats. Schmidt succeeded as Chancellor, 1974: closer relations with the G.D.R. from 1970 onwards. Christian Democrats regained power under Helmut Kohl, 1983.

Gertruydenberg. Conference to end War of Spanish Succession (*q.v.*) frustrated, 1710.

Gestapo (GEheimeSTAatsPOlizei) was first set up in Prussia by Goering, 1933. Other federal states of Germany followed and the separate forces amalgamated into one for the whole Reich under Himmler, 1934. Pronounced a criminal organization, membership of which made one automatically liable to imprisonment, at the Nürnberg trials, 1946.

Gettysburg, Pa., U.S.A. The Federal Army of the Potomac defeated the confederates under Lee and thereby saved the union from defeat in the civil war, 1–3 July 1863. Lincoln's celebrated speech was made in Nov. 1863, at dedication of the cemetery.

Ghana. Came into being, 6 Mar. 1957, on attainment of Dominion status by the former colony of the Gold Coast (*q.v.*) and the trusteeship territory of Togoland (*q.v.*). Name is that also held by a powerful medieval W. African monarchy. Became a republic, 1 July 1960, with Nkrumah as President. While Nkrumah was visiting China a 'National Liberation Council' under Gen. Ankrah took over the gov., 18 Feb. 1966, and declared Nkrumah deposed. March 1969 Ankrah resigned; replaced by Afrifa. Free elections, August 1969, and Dr. Kofi Busia became prime minister. Army coup, 1972. Further Army coups, 1978 and 1979. Civilian gov., 1979–81, then further military coup under Flt. Lt. Rawlings, 31 Dec. which estab. a Provisional National Defence Council.

Ghent, Belgium. Said to have been founded in the fifth century. Given to Count Baldwin IV, 1007; capital of Flanders (*q.v.*), twelfth century; John of Gaunt *b.* at, 1340. Insurrection of Jakob van Artevelde at, 1379; rebelled against the Emperor Charles V, 1539; surrendered to Spaniards, 1584; taken by Louis XIV of France, 1698; by Duke of Marlborough, 1706; seized by French, 1793; incorporated with Netherlands, 1814; became part of Belgium, 1830 (*see* FLANDERS).

Ghent, Convention of, granted the Great Privilege (*q.v.*), 1477.

Ghent, Pacification of, agreed to expulsion of the Spaniards and the establishment of Protestantism, 8 Nov. 1576.

Ghent, Treaty of, between U.S.A. and Great Britain ratified, 17 Feb. 1815.

Ghetto. Jewish quarter of any city, named after the G. of Rome, instituted, 1556, and demolished, 1885, though Gs. had existed at Valencia, 1239; Frankfort-on-Main, 1462; Venice, 1516. Its counterpart in London was the Old Jewry, a Jewish quarter from 1066 to 1291, where pogroms took place in 1261 and 1264. After the conquest of Poland in 1939 a quarter of Warsaw was walled off by the Germans and designated G. (*Judengasse*); its inmates rose against the Germans, 18 Apr. 1943, the quarter was burnt out and razed to the ground, as was the G. of Bialystok after a similar rising in Sept. 1943, which lasted a fortnight, and involved 40,000 Jewish casualties. Since the 1950s the term G. has been loosely applied to city areas housing a particular ethnic group which for economic or other reasons is not able to move out of it, e.g. Harlem, New York, has become known as a Negro-Puerto Rican G.

Ghibellines. *See* GUELPHS.

Gibraltar. Taken by Moors, 711; captured by Spaniards, 1462; formally annexed to Spain, 1502; surrendered to combined English and Dutch fleet under Sir George Rooke, 1704; finally ceded to Great Britain by Treaty of Utrecht, 1713; frequently besieged by Spaniards, most famous attempt, 1779–83. Spain renewed her claim to G. after World War II. In Sept. 1967 the Gibraltarians voted to remain British by 12,438 to 44: but Spain refused to accept this vote. Spain closed land frontier with G., May 1968; and the ferry service from Algeçiras suspended by Spain, 26 June. New constitution, 1969. Further Anglo-Sp. talks, resulting in reopening of frontier, Jan. 1985.

Gilbert and Ellice Islands, Pacific. British protectorates (1892) annexed to the Crown as colonies, Nov. 1915. Ellice Island severed connection on 1 Oct. 1975 and became **Tuvalu** (*q.v.*) and Gilbert Island became independent, 1976, and a republic, 1979, as **Kiribati** (*q.v.*).

Gilbertine Order, founded in England

by St. Gilbert of Sempringham, 1135. Suppressed at the Reformation.

Gin Act, 1736. Imposed duty on G. sold by retail. Repealed, 1743.

Gipsies, Acts against (U.K.). Banished from England, 1531. From Scotland, 1541. Act forbidding intercourse with G., 1562. Acts repealed, 1783.

Girl Guides. Movement founded in 1910 by Lord Baden-Powell as a parallel organization to the Boy Scouts (*q.v.*).

Girls' Public Day School Trust. Founded, 1872; one of the pioneers of girls' public day schools in England and Wales.

Girondists or **Girondins.** A party of moderate republicans led by Danton during the French Revolution, 1791. The earliest members of the party were returned by the Gironde district of France. Louis XVI formed a Girondist ministry, 1792. On 1 Oct. 1793 many of them were tried before the National Convention, and several executed. The party had disappeared by 1794.

Gladiators (Lat. *Swordsmen*) were originally either performers in funeral games or the victims of funeral sacrifices. Professional G. were said to have been first employed by Marcus and Decimus Brutus at their father's obsequies, 264 B.C. The revolt of G. under Spartacus took place 73–71. Gladiatorial displays were unsuccessfully prohibited by Constantine, A.D. 325, and they were finally abolished by Theodoric, 500.

Glasgow, Scotland. St. Mungo (Kentigern) founded a bishopric here *c.* 560. See restored by David, prince of Cumbria, 1115. Present cathedral structure begun, 1175. G. made a burgh of barony *c.* 1176; made a burgh of regality by James II, 1450. University founded by Bishop Turnbull, 1450–1; endowed by James, Lord Hamilton, 1460, and a new deed of erection granted by James VI, 1577. University of Strathclyde estab. at, 1964. Headquarters of co. of Strathclyde (*q.v.*) since 1974.

Glastonbury (Somerset). Abbey traditionally said to have been founded by Joseph of Arimathea about A.D. 63. It is historically certain that a British monastery was founded here *c.* 610, and was replaced *c.* 708 by a Saxon abbey built by Ina. The Chapel of St. Joseph built, 1101–20; destroyed by fire, 1184. The last abbot, Richard Whiting, was hanged on G. Tor for his adherence to the Roman Catholic faith, 15 Nov. 1539. A Celtic lake- village was discovered at G. in 1892.

Glencoe, The Massacre of. The Government issued a proclamation in Scotland promising pardon to all who before 31 Dec. 1691 would lay down their arms and promise to live peaceably. One of the heads of clans, Alexander MacIan Macdonald of G., was late in doing so, and he and others of his clan were ruthlessly killed by a company of Argyll's Regiment quartered upon them, 13 Feb. 1692.

Gleneagles Agreement, 1977, whereby the Brit. Government bound itself to sever sporting links with S. Africa.

Globe Theatre (London). Erected by Richard and Cuthbert Burbage, 1599; associated with William Shakespeare; burnt, 1621; rebuilt shortly afterwards; destroyed by Puritans, 1649.

Glorious First of June. Usual name of a naval victory over the French, won by Howe in the open sea off Ushant, 1794. Known in France as the battle of Prairial of the year II.

Gloucester, England. The Roman **Glevum** (later **Claudia Castra**). Founded by Nerva, A.D. 96–8; Abbey of St. Peter founded, 681; fabric of present cathedral erected by Abbot Serlo (1072–1104); first charter granted by Henry II, 1155; incorporated by Richard III, 1483; made a bishopric, 1541.

Glyndebourne Festival. An operatic season held annually at Glynde, Sussex, in a private opera house erected by John Christie (1882–1962). First year, 1934.

Goa, India. Discovered, 1498, by Vasco da Gama. Seized, 1510, by Portuguese under Alfonso de Albuquerque, and made capital of their Indian Ocean trading empire, 1511. St. Francis Xavier visited G. 1542–52. By 1570 it had become one of the wealthiest cities in India, but after 1580 it declined commercially. In 1946 it was given the status of a metropolitan province. On 18 Dec. 1961 Indian troops invaded G., which surrendered the following day, and was subsequently incorporated in India proper.

Gobelin Tapestry. Called after a family of dyers, who set up dye works in Paris in the fifteenth century, and added tapestry-making in the sixteenth. The business was acquired by Colbert in 1662 for Louis XIV as royal upholstery works. Tapestry-making only, since 1697. Closed during revolutionary and Napoleonic periods, then reopened.

Godesberg was the scene of a conference between Hitler and Neville Chamberlain 22–24 Sept. 1938.

Godiva Legend. *See* COVENTRY.

Godolphin Administration. After Lord G., First Lord. 1. Formed, 1684; 2. 1690.

God Save the King (or **Queen**), Brit. national anthem, said to have been the first authentic national anthem. Authorship disputed, but it was first performed in London in 1745 to celebrate the victory over the Jacobites at Prestonpans, and since used on ceremonial and royal occasions.

God's Truce. An instrument for suspending hostilities on holy days and seasons used during the Middle Ages. Originated in S. France at the synod of Tuluges, in Rousillon, 1027; confirmed by Council of Clermont, 1095, and other councils. Fell into disuse in the thirteenth century.

'Goeben' and 'Breslau'. German warships which in 1914 escaped from Messina, 6 Aug., into Dardanelles, 10 Aug. Nominally sold to Turkey, 13 Aug. Sank monitor *Raglan*, 20 Jan. 1918. *Breslau* sunk, 20 Jan. 1918. *Goeben* surrendered, Oct. 1918.

Gog and Magog, figures in the Guildhall of London, were perhaps first placed there in the reign of Henry V, but were destroyed in the fire of 1666. Replaced by new figures, 1708, which were seriously damaged in the fire of 29 Dec.

1940. New figures were erected in 1951.

Golconda, India. City and kingdom which *fl.* independently from 1512 until conquered by the Mogul emperor Aurungzebe, 1687, and placed under the viceroyalty of Hyderabad (*q.v.*).

Gold Coast, W. Africa. Possessed by Portuguese, 1481–2; by Dutch, 1642; war between English and Dutch over settlements, 1664–5; Dutch forts and territory purchased by Great Britain, 1871; created a separate crown colony, 1874. Northern Territory added, 1897. Became the dominion of Ghana, 6 Mar. 1957. For subsequent history *see* GHANA.

Golden Bull, The, of Charles IV. Issued in its first form at the Diet of Nürnberg, 10 Jan. 1356, and in its final form at Diet of Metz, 25 Dec. 1356. It laid down the major principles of the constitution of the Holy Roman Empire (*q.v.*), confirmed the powers of the Diets, and of the Electors (*q.v.*). It remained in force till 1806.

Gold Rushes. California, 1848; Australia, 1851; S. Africa, 1886; Klondike, 1897.

Gold Standard. First introduced into Britain, 1821. Internationally established when adopted by India, 1893. Abandoned during World War I, 1914–19. Slowly re-established, 1919–28. Finally abandoned by Britain, 1931.

Golf. Game of Scottish origin, dating back at least to the middle of the fifteenth century.

Goncourt. Academy and Prize were founded under the will of Edmond de G., who *d.* 1896 (*see* FRENCH LITERATURE). Academy constituted, 1903.

Good Parliament, 1376. The only medieval parliament in which the Commons made sufficient show of independence to secure reforms in their favour.

Gordon Riots. After an Act, passed in 1778, had repealed certain laws against Roman Catholics. On 2 June 1780 Lord George G. headed a mob, which almost succeeded in forcing its way into the House of Commons. During the next few days much property was attacked, including Newgate Prison. The army dispersed the mob, and many of the ringleaders were executed. Lord George G. was acquitted of high treason; but was imprisoned, 28 Jan. 1788, on another account, and *d.* insane in Newgate, 1 Nov. 1793.

Gorizia (Slovene **Gorica**; Ger. **Goerz**). Seat of an important county under the Carolingian Empire, which was divided, 1001, between the county of Friuli (*q.v.*) and the bishopric of Aquileia. Inherited by the Hapsburgs, 1500. The city was founded, 1307. Demanded by Italy as part of the price of her defection from the Triple Alliance, 1915, and entered by King Victor Emmanuel at the head of Italian troops, 9 Aug. 1916. Recaptured by Austrians, 28 Oct. 1917, but awarded in 1919 to Italy, which retained it against Yugoslav claims after 1945.

Gorki, formerly **Nijni Novgorod,** under protection of Suzdal, 1221. Ceased to elect its prince, 1390. Annexed to Moscow, 1392. Fair estab. at Makaryev, 1641. Repels attack by Stenka Razin, 1667. Fair moves to Nijni Novgorod city, 1817. Revived after revolution, but abolished finally, 1930. Name changed to G. 1932.

Goshen, Land of. Boer republic, set up in southern Bechuanaland, 1882, and dissolved, 1884.

Gothenburg or **Göteborg,** Sweden. Founded, 1609–11, by Charles IX of Sweden. Destroyed by the Danes, 1611. Under the Treaty of Knäred Danes occupied Alvsborg, 1613, until indemnified. Dutch financiers raised indemnity and after the departure of the Danes G. was refounded, 1615–20. Successful defence against Danes, 1789.

Gothic Architecture. The transition stages leading from Roman to pure G. are given in the following chronological table. After the middle of the sixteenth century the practice of G.A. died out gradually, but its influence extended to the end of the seventeenth century, and was partially revived in the nineteenth.

Norman, or Romanesque, 1066–1154.

Transitional from Norman to Pointed, 1154–89.

Early English, First Pointed, or Lancet, 1189–1272.

Transitional from Early to Complete Pointed, 1272–1307.

Geometrical Pointed, 1307–27.

Flowing, or Curvilinear, 1327–77.

Transitional from Geometrical and Flowing (sometimes classed together as Decorated, or Middle Pointed) to stiff and hard lines, 1377–99.

Third Pointed, Rectilinear, or Perpendicular, 1399–1546.

Flamboyant, 1450–1600 (mainly on Continent).

Gothic Language, said by Procopius (*d.* *.c.* 560) in his book, *The Vandal War,* dealing with events of 530–40, to be identical with the Vandal and Gepidic languages, is preserved in the Ostrogothic dialect of Moesia, the Arian bishop Ulfilas (*d.* 383) having translated considerable passages of the scriptures into Moeso-Gothic. Ostrogothic survivors, tributary to the Tatars in the Crimea, are mentioned, and recognizable Gothic words cited, by the Imperial ambassador to Constantinople, Ghislain de Busbecq, *c.* 1550.

Goths. First known to history as settlers on the middle Vistula in first century A.D. According to their own tradition they had arrived there from Sweden (probably the Island of Gotland), via Pomerania. About A.D. 150 they migrated again south-eastward to the N. shore of the Black Sea and the Crimea. In the third century they invaded the Roman province of Moesia on the lower Danube; they conquered Dacia and raided Thrace, 321, but were beaten off by the Emperor Constantine. Their king, Hermanaric, *d.* *.c.* 370, after conquering numerous other German tribes as well as Slav and Estonia neighbours. Thereafter, *see* OSTROGOTHS and VISIGOTHS.

Gotland (island in Baltic). Not improbably, as the name implies, the former home of the Goths (*q.v.*), but they must have left the island about or just before the birth of Christ. St. Olaf introduced Christianity there, 1030.Island acknowledged Swedish suzerainty after battle of Roma, 1288. King Birger Magnusson repulsed, 1313. Island conquered by Danish king Waldemar, 1361. Reconquered by King Karl Knutsson of Sweden, except Visborg, 1449. Ravaged by constant wars between Sweden and Denmark till 1526. Finally passed to Sweden, 1644–5.

Göttingen, Germany. Joined Hanseatic League (*q.v.*) *c.* 1360. Captured by Tilly, 1626. By Saxons, 1632. University founded, 1734, by George II of England. Opened, 1737.

Gowrie Conspiracy, 5 Aug. 1600. The Earl of G. and his brother, Alexander Ruthven, attempted to murder James VI of Scotland at G. House. An alarm was raised, however, and the two brothers were killed.

G.P.U., O.G.P.U.(Rus. State Political Department), new designation for the Cheka, adopted 1922–34, after which the name was changed to N.K.V.D. (*q.v.*).

Graeco-Turkish Wars.

1. 1897, broke out 18 Apr., the result of anti-Christian excesses and anti-Turkish risings in Crete (*q.v.*), then part of the Ottoman Empire, but claimed by Greece. Turks entered Larissa, 23 Apr. Greeks defeated in Epirus, but won battle in Thessaly, 29 Apr. Turkish mountain position of Imaret-Grimbovo stormed, 12–15 May. Greek volunteers who had been landed in Crete before the outbreak of war (Feb.) were withdrawn, 9 May, under pressure from the Concert of Europe, and the terms finally settled at Constantinople, 6 Dec., included only slight frontier adjustments and the payment by Greece of £4,000,000 indemnity. Turks evacuated Thessaly, June 1898.

2. 1921–2. Greek offensive in Asia Minor, 23 Mar. 1921. Greeks defeated near Eskishehr, Apr. 1921;

resumed offensive from Ushak and Brusa, July 1921; entered Eskishehr, 20 July. Turks fell back on Sakaria River; Greeks heavily defeated, Sept. 1921; retired on Eskishehr and repulsed Turkish attacks at Afion Karahissar, Oct. 1921. Main Turkish offensive opened, 26 July 1922; Greeks in headlong flight, Aug.–Sept. 1922; Mudania Armistice, Oct. 1922, terminated the war.

'Graf Spee, Admiral.' German 'pocket' battleship engaged and crippled by three British cruisers off River Plate, took refuge in Montevideo, 14 Dec. 1939; scuttled by order of Hitler, 17 Dec.; captain committed suicide, 20 Dec.

Gramophone (American 'phonograph': its modern successor currently known as a 'recordplayer'), which was invented by Edison, 1877, was perfected by E. Berliner, 1888. Electrical recording first practised, 1920. Superseded by the recordplayer after World War II.

Granada, Spain. Invaded by the Moors, A.D. 745. Wall of the Alhambra built *c.* 1019. Part of the Arab kingdom of Murcia, 1229–38. Fell into hands of Abu Abdullah Mohammed Ibn al Ahmar, who formed the kingdom of G., 1238. Alhambra Palace begun, 1213. Captured by Christians, 1492.

Grand Alliance.

1. Against France, began with the Treaty of Vienna, May 1689, between the emperor and the Dutch. It came to include Spain, Holland, Sweden, Savoy, and Great Britain. Renewed at The Hague, 1696; ended, 1697.

2. Concluded at The Hague, 7 Sept. 1701, between England, Holland, and the empire; joined by Prussia, 20 Jan. 1702; by Portugal, 16 May 1703; by Savoy, 25 Oct. 1703. It dealt mainly with the conquest of Spain. *See* SPANISH SUCCESSION, WAR OF.

Grand Juries (England). Abolished, except for a few minor exceptions, 1933: finally abolished, 1948.

Grand National horse race at Liverpool instituted at, Aintree, 1839.

Grand Remonstrance. *See* REMON-
STRANCE, THE GRAND.

Grantham, England. Mentioned as a
Royal Demesne in Domesday Book,
1085. Incorporated by Edward IV, 1463.
Captured by royalists, 1642–3.

Grattan's Parliament. The Irish parliament, whose legislative independence
was granted, May 1782, through the
exertions of Henry G. (1746–1820). It
came to an end, 2 July 1800.

Gravelines, France. Founded by Henry
Count of Flanders, 1160. Defeat of
French by Spanish Army, 1558. Defeat
of Spanish Armada (*q.v.*) by the English
at, 1588. Taken by French, 1658, and
ceded to them, 7 Nov. 1659.

Gravesend, England. Mentioned in
Domesday Book, 1085. Burned by the
French, 1380. Incorporated, 22 July
1562. Princess Pocahontas *d.* at G.,
1617.

Great Britain, History of (for previous
history *see* ENGLISH HISTORY; SCOT-
LAND; ENGLISH SOVEREIGNS). G.B.
formed by union of the crowns of England and Scotland, 10 Apr. 1603. Hampton Court Conference and peace
with Spain, 1604. Gunpowder plot discovered, 5 Nov. 1605. Plantation of
Ulster, 1607. War with France, 1624–9.
Petition of Right, 1628. Dissolution of
Parliament and beginning of the personal rule of Charles I, 1629. Charles
attempts to introduce C. of E. Prayer
Book into Scotland, 1637. The Ship
Money trial (R. *v.* Hampden), 1637.
Scots sign the National Covenant,
1638. First Bishops' War begins, May
1639. The Long Parliament meets, 3
Nov. 1640. Root-and-Branch Petition,
Dec. 1640. Strafford beheaded, Star
Chamber and High Commission abol-
ished, May 1641. Irish Rebellion, Oct.
1641. Grand Remonstrance, Nov.
1641. Charles I attempts to arrest the
Five Members, Jan. 1642. Civil war be-
gins, Aug. 1642. Charles I surrenders to
Scots, May 1646. Scots begin Second
Civil War, Apr. 1648. Pride's Purge,
Dec. 1648. Charles I beheaded, 30 Jan.
1649. England declared a Common-
wealth, 29 May 1649. Scots defeated at
Dunbar, Sept. 1650. Charles II defeated

at Worcester, Sept. 1651. War with
Holland, 1652–4. Cromwell becomes
Protector, 1653. War with Spain,
1656–9. Oliver Cromwell *d.*, 3 Sept.
1658. Long Parliament restored, 7 May
1659. Richard Cromwell resigns the
Protectorship, 25 May 1659. Convention Parliament called by Monck, 15
Apr. 1660. The Restoration, 25 May
1660. Charles II sells Dunkirk to
France. Act of Settlement, 1662. Second Naval War with Holland, 1665–7.
Great Plague, 1665. Fire of London,
1666. Secret Treaty with Louis XIV,
1667. Secret Treaty of Dover, 1670.
The 'Popish Plot', 1678. Habeas Corpus Act, 1679. Monmouth's rebellion
defeated at Sedgemoor, July 1685.
James II's Declaration of Indulgence, 2
Apr. 1687. Trial of the Seven Bishops,
29–30 June 1688. William III lands at
Torbay, 15 Nov. 1688. Bill of Rights,
Oct. 1689. James II defeated at battle of
the Boyne, July 1690. War with France,
1690–7. Massacre of Glencoe, 1692.
French naval defeat at La Hogue, 1692.
National Debt established, 1693. Bank
of England, 1694. Treaty of Ryswick,
1697. Partition Treaties (*q.v.*),
1698–1700. War of the Spanish Succes-
sion, 1701–13. Parliamentary Union of
England and Scotland, 1 May, 1707.
Treaty of Utrecht, 1713. Jacobite rising,
1715; Septennial Act, 1716. S. Sea
Bubble, 1720. War of Jenkins's Ear,
1739–48. Jacobite Rebellion in Scotland, 1745. Defeated at Culloden, 16
Apr. 1746. Treaty of Aix-la-Chapelle,
1748. Seven Years War (*q.v.*), 1756–63.
American Stamp Act, 1765. Royal
Marriage Act, 1772. Boston Assembly
threatens secession, 1772. The Boston
Tea-party, 1773. First congress of
American colonies, 1774. Quebec Act,
1774. War of American Independence
begins with battle of Lexington, 19
Apr. 1775. American Declaration of
Independence, 1776. British defeat at
battle of Saratoga, Oct. 1777. France
declares war on Britain, 1778. Spain,
1779. British capitulation at Yorktown, 1781. Independence of U.S.A.
recognized at Peace of Versailles, 1783.
War with France (*q.v.*), 1793–1802.

Treaty of Amiens, 1802. War with France (*q.v.*), 1803–14, 1815. 'Battle of Peterloo', 1819. Six Acts, 1819. First Burma War, 1824. Trade unions legalized, 1825. First steam locomotive railway opened, 1825. Catholic emancipation and Metropolitan police established, 1829. Reform Act passed, 1832. Municipal Corporations Act, 1835. Chartist agitation, 1838–9. Penny postage introduced by Rowland Hill, 1840. Chartist riots, 1842. Factory Act, 1844. Repeal of Corn Laws 1846. Oregon Treaty with U.S.A., 1846. Great Exhibition, 1851. Crimean War, 1854–6. Peace of Paris, 1856. Divorce legalized, 1857. First Atlantic cable laid, 1857. Ionian Islands ceded to Greece, 1863. Second Reform Act, 1867. Queen Victoria proclaimed Empress of India, 1877. Gladstone defeated on Home Rule Bill, 1886. S. African War, 1899–1902. *Entente Cordiale* between Britain and France, 8 Apr. 1904. Anglo-Japanese alliance, 1905. Lords reject Lloyd George's finance bill, Nov. 1909. Parliament Act, 1911. National Insurance Act, 1912. World War I (*q.v.*), 1914–18. Welsh Church disestablished, 1920. General Strike, 3–13 May 1926. Two million unemployed by Dec. 1929. 'Landslide' election for a 'National' government, Oct. 1931. George V *d.*, 20 Jan. 1936. Edward VIII abdicated, 10 Dec. 1936. Coronation of King George VI, 12 May 1937. Eden resigned Foreign Secretaryship, 20 Feb. 1938. Chamberlain sees Hitler at Munich, 17 Sept, Godesberg, 22 Sept. Munich agreement, 29 Sept. 1938. British guarantee to Poland, 31 Mar. 1939; to Greece and Rumania, 13 Apr.; Military Training Act, 27 May. British ultimatum to Germany, 1 Sept. followed by World War II (*q.v.*), 3 Sept. 1939–12 Sept. 1945. Churchill forms coalition government, 10 May 1940. Roosevelt and Churchill issue Atlantic Charter, 11 Aug. 1941. Education Act, 1944. Labour party leaves government, 26 May 1945. General Election, 5 July 1945; Labour government returned and sweeping programme of nationalization (*q.v.*) and social reform follows.

'Austerity' government. India and Pakistan independent, 1947. Princess Elizabeth marries Lt. Philip Mountbatten, 20 Nov. 1947. Britain signs N. Atlantic treaty, 4 Apr. 1949: Korean War breaks out, June 1950 and Brit. troops in action there by Sept. 1951: Festival of Britain opened 3 May: General Election in October returns Conservative government under Churchill. King George VI *d.* 6 Feb. 1952, succeeded by Elizabeth II, who is crowned, 2 June 1953. Some denationalization: food rationing ended, 1954. Eden helps to obtain Indo-China setlement at Geneva: agreements with Egypt over Suez and Iran over oil. Eden succeeds Churchill as premier, 1955: Suez crisis Oct.–Nov. 1956 and Eden is succeeded by Macmillan, 1957. Britain joins E.F.T.A., 1959. S. Africa leaves Commonwealth, 1961 and President Kennedy visits London, June: Britain applies unsuccessfully for membership of the E.E.C. Macmillan signs Nassau Agreement with Kennedy, 1962, under which Britain agrees to accept Polaris missiles. 1963 is worst winter since 1947; Profumo affair, June, undermines confidence in Government. Philby granted asylum in Moscow, July; Ward trial, July–Aug.; Great Train Robbery, Aug.; Macmillan resigns and succeeded by Douglas-Home, Oct. 1964: Labour wins control of Greater London Council and majority in General Election in Oct.; Wilson Prime Minister. Churchill *d.* 1965 and given state funeral. Rhodesia declared unilateral independence, Nov. Labour increases its majority in 1966 General Election. Economic crisis and sterling devalued, 1967. Growing unrest in N. Ireland from 1968; Prince of Wales invested at Caernarvon, 1 July. Conservatives returned to power under Heath, 1970: Decimalization of coinage, Feb. 1971. Britain joins E.E.C. (*q.v.*), 1973, a referendum endorsing this. Serious economic difficulties leading to 'winter of discontent', 1973–4 and Labour returned to power, 1974. Margaret Thatcher Conservative leader, 1975; Callaghan succeeds

Wilson as premier, 1976. Growing inflation and unemployment in late 1970s. Conservatives returned under Margaret Thatcher, 1979; U.D.I. in Rhodesia ends, Dec. 1979, resulting in independent republic of Zimbabwe (*q.v.*), April 1980. Prince Charles marries Lady Diana Spencer, July 1981. Falklands War, 1982 (*see* FALKLAND ISLANDS). Rise of Social Democrats (*q.v.*) from 1982. Conservatives returned with increased majority, June 1983, and Kinnock as Labour leader, Oct. Unemployment highest since 1930s. Coal strike, Mar. 1984–5. I.R.A. attempt to assassinate Cabinet at Brighton fails, Sept. 1984.

Great Council of Peers. *See* MAGNUM CONCILIUM.

Great Intercourse, 1495. Commercial treaty between Henry VII of England and Philip of Burgundy relating to trade with Flanders.

Great Plague. In London and Derbyshire, 1665.

Great Privilege (*Groote Privilegie*). On 3 Feb. 1477 a congress of the Netherlands met at Ghent. The Duchess Mary, then regent, granted to this assembly a charter known as the G.P. on 11 Feb. 1477. It has been called the 'Magna Carta of Holland'.

Great Schism. After the return of the Papal Court from Avignon, 1378. Urban VI was elected pope, but the French Party elected Clement VII as a rival. The two parties continued to elect rival popes until 1409, when Gregory XII at Rome was deposed and Alexander V and John XXIII successively elected in his place. As Gregory XII refused to recognize his successors there were therefore three rival popes until 1415, when at the Council of Constance John XXIII was deposed and Gregory XII resigned. Martin V was then elected pope at Rome in their stead in 1417. This is generally called the end of the G.S., though a French anti-papacy continued (as successors to Clement VII) till 1429. *See* PAPACY.

'Great Train Robbery.' The Scotland to London Post Office express was ambushed near Cheddington, Bucking-

hamshire on 8 Aug. 1963 and over £2½ million stolen. A number of men were subsequently sentenced to heavy terms of imprisonment but two of these subsequently escaped from prison. Only a small proportion of the money was ever recovered.

Greater London Council, estab. under the London Government Act of 1963. It superseded the London County Council (*q.v.*), and embraced a much larger area and pop. G.L.C. took over running of London Transport, 1969. Abolition of G.L.C. envisaged by 1986.

Greece, Ancient. Earliest settlements known at Tiryns and Mycenae, *c.* 3000 B.C. Minoan supremacy in the Aegean, *c.* 2300–1400. Achaeans' invasion of G., *c.* 1270–1250. They attack Egypt, 1223, and sack Troy (The Iliad), *c.* 1180. Dorians overrun G., *c.* 1100–1000. Ionian settlements of Asia Minor, *c.* 1040. Athenian monarchy made elective, 683. Sparta threatened by the First, 736–716, and the Second, 650–630, Messenian wars; introduces the Reforms of Lycurgus *c.* 610. Ionia falls under the power of Croesus of Lydia, 560–546, when Lydia was conquered by the Persians under Cyrus. Persian Darius invades Thrace, 516. Ionian revolt, 499. Helped by Athens, 498; defeated at naval battle of Lade, 494. Persian invasion of G., 491; battle of Marathon, 490. Second Persian invasion, 480. Battle of Thermopylae and Salamis, 480. Battles of Plataea and Mycale, 479.

Delian confederacy formed under Athens, 478. Battle of the Eurymedon, 466. Athenians attack Egypt, 459. Delian Treasury moved to Athens, 454. Thirty years' peace between Athens and Sparta signed, 445. Peloponnesian War begins, 431. Battle of Pylos (Sphacteria), 425. Battle of Amphipolis, 422. Peace of Nicias, 421. Athenian expedition to Syracuse, 415, and final defeat at, 18 Sept. 413. Decelean War, 413. Resumption of Peloponnesian War, 412. Battle of Aegospotami, 405. Surrender of Athens, 404. Sparta supreme in G., 404; till overthrown by Thebes at battle of Leuctra, 371. Thebes collapses after death of Epaminondas at battle of Mantinea, 362. Philip becomes king of Macedonia, 359. Checked by Athenians at Thermopylae, 352. Demosthenes delivers First Philippic, 351. Battle of Chaeronea, 338. Philip forms Pan-Hellenic League at Corinth, 338. Murdered, 336. Alexander the Great puts down Theban revolt, 335. Alexander conquers Persian Empire and dies, 323. Aetolian League founded, 323. Achaean League revived, 281. Romans defeat Macedon at Cynoscephalae, 197. Macedon conquered and made a Roman province, 146. Rest of G. conquered the same year. Remained a Roman province until the Turkish Conquest, A.D. 1440–60. *See* ROMAN EMPIRE; OTTOMAN EMPIRE; GREECE, MODERN.

Greece, Modern. For previous history *see* GREECE, ANCIENT; ROMAN EMPIRE; OTTOMAN EMPIRE; ROMAN EMPIRE, EASTERN. War of independence began, 25 Mar. 1821, and practically ended in the battle of Navarino, 20 Oct. 1827, when the Egyptian fleet was destroyed by Britain, France, and Russia. On 7 May 1832, G. declared independent kingdom under British, French, and Russian protection. War with Turkey (*see* GRAECO-TURKISH WARS (1)). Otto I expelled, 1862. Ionian Islands (*q.v.*) incorporated, 1863. The powers compelled Turkey to withdraw her forces from Crete, 1898, and Crete was granted autonomy under a Greek prince; Balkan Wars (*q.v.*), Oct. 1912–Aug. 1913; Salonika captured by the Greeks, 9 Nov. 1912; King George of G. murdered, 18 Mar. 1913; Crete ceded to G., Nov. 1913; Venizelos (pro-Ally), Premier, 1914–15, invited allied troops to Salonika, Oct. 1915. Constantine repudiated invitation and Venizelos resigned, Oct. 1915. Bulgarian invasion, Aug. 1916. Cretan revolution under Venizelos, Sept. 1916. Allies bombarded Athens, 1 Dec. 1916. Constantine abdicated, June 1917, and succeeded by Alexander, who *d.* 1920. Constantine king again, 1920–2. Graeco-Turkish War (*q.v.* (2)), 1921–2. Republic proclaimed, 25 Mar. 1924. Royalist revolt

in Athens, 9 Sept. 1935; end of the republic, 10 Oct. 1935; plebiscite, and restoration of King George II, 3 Nov. 1935. Parliamentary government suspended after *coup d'état* by Gen. Metaxas, 4 Aug. 1936. Italian invasion of G., 28 Oct. 1940; Greek forces thrust back Italians into Albania, 1940. British troops landed in G., Mar. 1941; German invasion, 6 Apr. 1941; removal of Government to Crete, 23 April. 1941; occupation of Greek mainland by Germans completed, 2 May 1941. Withdrawal of German troops, Sept. 1944. Communists start civil war, 12 Oct. 1944. Truce negotiated, Dec., and peace agreement signed, 12 Feb. 1945. Monarchy restored by plebiscite, 1946; and Communist rising. King George II *d.*, Apr. 1947; succeeded by Paul I. Annexation of Dodecanese, 7 Mar. 1948; total defeat of Communists as a result of Papagos's military campaign against them, Aug. 1948. G. joined N.A.T.O., 1951. Papagos formed new party, the Greek Rally, which came to power in the election of Nov. 1952. He dominated Greek politics until his death in 1955. From 1953 Greek politics increasingly influenced by Cyprus (*q.v.*) question. Problem resolved by the Zürich and London Agreements of 1959 to which G. was a party. King Paul *d.*, Mar. 1964 and was succeeded by his son as King Constantine. In April 1967 a group of army officers took over gov. In Dec. 1967 Constantine went into exile. Military regime ousted, 1973. Monarchy abolished, 1973: formally voted out, 1974. New constitution, 1975. G. joined E.E.C., 1981. Socialist govt. returned, 1981, with anti-American bias. Campaign to restore Elgin Marbles (*q.v.*) to G. intensified after 1981.

Kings of Modern Greece:

Otto (Prince Otto of Bavaria) 1833–1862

George I (Prince William of Denmark) 1863–1913

Constantine I 1913–1917

Alexander 1917–1920

Constantine I (again) 1920–1922

George II 1922–1923

Republic 1924–1935
George II (again) 1935–1944
Regency 1944–1946
George II (again) 1946–1947
Paul I 1947–1964
Constantine II 1964–1974

Greek Authors, Classical, of whom complete works or fragments survive:

Aeschines, 389–314 B.C., orator.

Aeschylus, 525–456 B.C., tragedian.

Agathon, *c.* 448–400 B.C., tragedian.

Alcaeus, *fl.* 606 B.C., lyric poet.

Anacreon, 570–*c.* 485 B.C., lyric poet.

Apollonius Rhodius, *c.* 222–180 B.C., poet and grammarian.

Appian (Roman of Alexandria who wrote in Greek), second century A.D., historian.

Archilochus, *fl. c.* 700 B.C., lyric poet.

Archimedes, 287–212 B.C., mathematician.

Aristarchus of Samos, *c.* 280 B.C., mathematician and astronomer.

Aristophanes, *c.* 445–*c.* 385 B.C., comic poet and playwright.

Aristotle, 384–322 B.C., philosopher.

Arrian, *c.* A.D. 95–*c.* 170, historian and philosopher.

Asclepiades of Samos, third century B.C., lyric poet.

Aurelius, Marcus, A.D.121–80, philosopher.

Bacchylides, *fl. c.* 460 B.C., lyric poet.

Bion, *c.* 280 B.C., bucolic poet.

Callimachus, *c.* 305–*c.* 250 B.C., poet and grammarian.

Corinna, *fl. c.* 500 B.C., lyric poet.

Critias of Athens, *d.* 403 B.C., orator.

Democritus, *c.* 460–361 B.C., natural philosopher.

Demosthenes, *c.* 384–322 B.C., orator.

Dio Cassius, *c.* A.D. 150–235, historian.

Diodorus Siculus, late first century B.C., historian.

Diogenes Laertius, second or third century A.D., biographer.

Dionysius of Halicarnassus, *fl. c.* 30 B.C., historian and rhetorician.

Epictetus, *fl. c.* A.D. 55–138, philosopher.

Epicurus, 341–270 B.C., philosopher.

Epimenides, sixth century B.C., poet.

Euclid, *c.* 330–283 B.C., geometrician.

Euripides, *c.* 484–407 B.C., tragedian.

Galen, A.D. 130–200, physician.

Heliodorus of Emesa, third century A.D., romantic writer.

Heraclitus of Ephesus, *c.* 540–*c.* 475 B.C., philosopher.

Herodas, third century B.C., dramatist.

Herodotus, *c.* 484–424 B.C., historian.

Hesiod, ? *c.* 700 B.C., didactic poet.

Hippocrates, *c.* 460–377 B.C., physician.

Homer, *fl.* ? between 810 and 730 B.C., epic poet.

Isaeus, *c.* 420–*c.* 350 B.C., orator.

Isocrates, 436–338 B.C., rhetorician.

Lucian, *c.* A.D. 125–90, satirist.

Lycophron, *fl.* 285–247 B.C., grammarian and poet.

Lysias, 458–380 B.C., orator.

Menander, 342–292 B.C., comedian.

Mimnermus, *fl. c.* 634–600 B.C., elegiac poet.

Moschus, *fl. c.* 150 B.C., bucolic poet.

Pausanias, second century A.D., geographer.

Pindar, 518–442 B.C., poet.

Plato, *c.* 428–357 B.C., philosopher.

Plutarch, *c.* A.D. 46–after 120, biographer and philosopher.

Polybius, *c.* 204–122 B.C., historian.

Sappho, *b. c.* 612 B.C., poet.

Simonides of Amorgos, *fl. c.* 664 B.C., iambic poet.

Simonides of Ceos, *c.* 556–467 B.C., lyric poet.

Sophocles, 496–406 B.C., tragedian.

Stesichorus, *c.* 640–*c.* 555 B.C., lyric poet.

Strabo, *c.* 63 B.C.–*c.* A.D. 24, geographer.

Theocritus, *c.* 310–*c.* 267 B.C., bucolic poet.

Theognis, *b. c.* 540 B.C., elegiac poet.

Theophrastus, *c.* 370–286 B.C., philosopher.

Thucydides, *c.* 464–*c.* 402 B.C., historian.

Tyrtaeus, *fl. c.* 685–668 B.C., poet.

Xenophon, *c.* 430–*c.* 356 B.C., historian.

See also BYZANTINE AUTHORS.

Greek Fire, pre-eminently a naval weapon, but also used in sieges, was invented by Callinicus of Heliopolis, a Syrian in the employ of the Emperor

Constantine Pogonatus (648–85); this so-called 'wet fire' (because the liquid when it came in contact with water was self-igniting) is the true G.F. as used during the Crusades.

Greek Orthodox Church. First signs of disunion between the Greek and Roman Churches in A.D. 385, when celibacy of priests was enforced, and a demand that the Pope should be recognized as supreme, and doctrinal differences were raised. In A.D. 484 the two Churches separated for a period of 40 years. In 734 the Greeks condemned image worship (Iconoclastic Controversy). The final separation was the Great Schism of 1054, when Pope Leo IX excommunicated the patriarchs of Constantinople. The 'Orthodox Confession' was drawn up in 1643. On 7 Dec. 1965 Orthodox Church annulled its 1054 excommunication of the Church of Rome.

Greenback Party, advocating that treasury notes, as opposed to bank-notes, should be the sole legal tender of U.S.A., *fl.* 1874–84.

Greenham Common, Berks. Women's anti-nuclear 'peace-camp' there from 1981.

Greenland. Original Scandinavian settlement, begun in 982, died out *c.* 1480. Visited by Frobisher, 1577. Danish settlements re-founded, 1721. On 5 June 1953 G. became an integral part of the Danish kingdom (had been a colony since 1261), with same rights and measure of self-government as the rest of Denmark.

Greenville, Treaty of. Between U.S.A. and the NW. Indian tribes, 3 Aug. 1795.

Greenwich, London, celebrated for its hospital and observatory (*see* succeeding articles). A palace was built here by Humphrey, Duke of Gloucester, in 1428, and later came into Henry VI's possession. It was a favourite residence of the Tudors; Mary I and Elizabeth I were *b.* there, and Edward VI *d.* there. Charles II started to rebuild it, but in 1694 William and Mary gave up residence and decided on its conversion to a sailors' hospital.

Greenwich Hospital (England). Founded, 1694, on the site of G. Palace. Opened, 1705. Ceased to be a pensioners' hospital, 1869. Became Royal Naval College, 1873.

Greenwich Observatory (London). Built, 1675, by Wren. Opened, 1675–6. Removed to Herstmonceux, 1947–58.

Gregorian Chants. Named after Pope Gregory I (540–604), who is traditionally said to have added extra tones to the Ambrosian Chants then in use.

Grenada, W. Indies. Discovered by Columbus, 1498; colonized by French, 1651; ceded to England by Treaty of Paris, 1763; recaptured by French, 1779; restored to England by Treaty of Versailles, 1783. 'Brigands' War', 1795. Massacre of governor and loyal subjects, 1796. Crown colony, 1876; member of W. Indies Federation, 1958–62; associated state, 1967; independent within the Commonwealth, 1974. Left-wing coup, 13 Mar. 1979, and constitution suspended. Extremist left-wing coup, Oct. 1983, in which premier and 3 ministers murdered. U.S.A. and sev. Caribbean states invaded G., 23 Oct., to 'restore order'. U.S. troops left, Dec. 1983.

Grenadiers. A few G. were first attached to the French *Régiment du Roi* in 1667. Formed into companies in 1668–70. The British Grenadier Guards (First Foot Guards) were organized in 1660. They received their present name in 1815 after Waterloo, as a result of the conspicuous part taken by them in defeating the G. of the French Imperial Guard. G. in the German Army derived prestige from the traditions of the Prussian G., the élite infantry units of the Seven Years War and other mid eighteenth century campaigns, most of which had been raised by King Frederick William I (reigned 1713–40).

Gresham's Law, or the proposition 'Bad money drives out good', was formulated in 1560 by Sir Thomas G. (1519–79), founder of the Stock Exchange (*q.v.*), and of the school at Holt which bears his name.

Gretna Green, Scotland. After the abolition of Fleet marriages (*q.v.*) in 1754, those in England wishing to marry clandestinely, crossed the border to G.G. to take advantage of the Scottish marriage laws. By a law passed in 1856, these marriages were invalid unless one of the parties had resided in Scotland for three weeks: completely illegal after 1940.

Grey Friars. Franciscan monastery established in London, 1224. Afterwards Christ's Hospital (*q.v.*).

Greyhound Racing. The National Greyhound Racing Club was set up in Britain in 1927, exercising a rigid control over the standards of G.R.

Grisons (Ger. **Graubünden**; It. **Grigioni**; Romansch **Grischun**). Largest of the Swiss cantons. The Raetians living about the sources of the Rhine and Inn were conquered by Rome, 15 B.C., and the district formed the nucleus of Rhaetia Prima. Christianity was introduced, A.D. 400. Conquered by the Franks, 536, who entrusted civil government to the Bishop of Chur. In 806 Charlemagne separated the civil power and placed it under a count. The 'Grey League' from which the canton takes its name was founded, 1395, as a defensive union of rural communities; this *Graubund* joined in federation with the League of God's House (founded, 1367), and the League of Ten Laws (founded, 1436) to form the Free State of Ten Leagues, which became more and more closely associated with the original Swiss Confederation from 1497 to 1524. In 1794 Veltlin (Valtellina) seceded, and was attached by Napoleon to the Cisalpine Republic, 1797, since when it has been Italian with a short interval of Austrian hegemony. The rest of G. joined the Helvetic Republic, 1797, but regained its independence in 1803. Finally adhered to the Swiss Confederation, 1854.

Groats. First coined, 1351. Discontinued, 1662. Revived, 1838. In Scotland first issued, 1358. In Ireland, 1460. Last coined in Great Britain, 1856, except for a special issue coined for Maundy money. *See* MAUNDY THURSDAY.

Groningen, Holland. Joined Hanseatic League (*q.v.*) *c.* 1282. Part of United Netherlands, 1594.

Ground-nuts Scheme, Tanganyika, launched early in 1947; reorganized under the Overseas Food Corporation, 1950; Overseas Food Corporation wound up, 1955.

Guadalcanal. One of the largest and most important of the Solomon Islands (*q.v.*). It is remembered as the scene of a protracted campaign against the Japanese, who landed powerful forces there in summer, 1942. American and Australian forces were landed shortly afterwards and drove the Japanese out by 9 Feb. 1943.

Guadalupe-Hidalgo, Treaty of. Between U.S.A. and Mexico, signed, 2 Feb. 1848.

Guadeloupe, W. Indies. Discovered by Columbus, 1493, colonized by France, 1635; captured by Britain, 1759; restored to France, 1763; ceded to Sweden, 1813; restored to France, 1814. Overseas Department of France, 19 Mar. 1946; administrative region, 1973. Its dependency, St. Martin, was simultaneously occupied by the French and Dutch, but amicably partitioned 1648.

Guam, Pacific island, discovered by Magellan, *c.* 1521; ceded to U.S.A. by Spain, 1898; occupied by Japanese, 10 Dec. 1941, and scene of heavy fighting, July–Aug. 1944, when Americans recaptured it. Since 1950 administered by the U.S.A. Interior Dept. and inhabitants hold full U.S. citizenship.

Guardians of the Poor. Abolished, 1929, by Local Government Act. *See* POOR LAWS.

Guatemala, Central America. Declared independent of Spain, 1821. Boundary treaty with Britain, 1859. Common boundary with Salvador and Honduras agreed, Mar. 1936. From Feb. 1948 to May 1951 the frontier with British Honduras (now Belize, *q.v.*) was closed as part of the recurrent claim, dating from Spanish colonial days, that this is Guatemalan territory. This claim still maintained. Arbenz's regime, 1951, instituted a left-wing policy and became increasingly pro-Communist till overthrown, 1954. Series of unstable regimes resulting in a bloodless coup,

1982, by military junta which followed extreme right-wing policies: this overthrown by a rival right-wing coup, 1983.

Guatemala City, capital of the preceding and before that of a Spanish colonial province, was founded, 1776, on the destruction of the previous capital, Antigua, in the earthquake of 1773.

Guelph, Welf. Surname of the dukes of Saxony since the eleventh century, and thence surname of the Hanoverian royal family of Great Britain. Proclamation changing name to Windsor, July 1917.

Guelphs and Ghibellines. Two factions caused by the rivalry between emperor and pope, after the death of Henry V in 1125. The Ghibellines, or emperor's party, took their name from Waiblingen, a castle in Württemberg, Italianized into Ghibellino. The G. or papal party had their name from Welf, the name of many princes of the House of Bavaria. The first outbreak of hostilities between the two parties occurred in 1154, when the Emperor Frederick Barbarossa made an expedition into Italy. After the Hohenstaufen defeat at Tagliacozzo, 1268, the struggle began to lose its real force. The names were temporarily revived during the French campaigns in Italy at the beginning of the sixteenth century.

Guernica, Spain. Famous because on 27 Apr. 1937, during the Spanish Civil War, it was heavily bombed by German planes supporting the Falangists.

Guernsey, Channel Islands. Probably granted to abbot of Dol by Childebert the Merovingian, A.D. 550. Became part of Normandy on its formation in tenth century. Its fortress, Castle Cornet, held out against the parliamentary forces, 1643–51. French made ineffectual attempts to land, 1779 and 1780. Occupied by Germans, 1 July 1940–9 May 1945. Constitution modified by Reform Law of 1948, which took effect from 1 Jan. 1949.

Gueux ('Beggars'). During the revolt of the Netherlands against Spain a confederacy of nobles drew up, in 1565, a 'Compromise' (*see* COMPROMISE LEAGUE) which in Apr. 1566 they presented to the regent, Margaret of Parma. The demonstration caused some alarm, but she was reassured by a councillor: 'Madam, is your Highness afraid of these beggars?' The 'Beggars of the Sea', under de la Marck, did much damage to the Spanish fleet, and captured Brill in 1572.

Guiana, S. America. *See* FRENCH GUIANA; GUYANA; SURINAM.

Guides, Girl. *See* GIRL GUIDES.

Guildford, England. Abbots Hospital founded, 1619. Diocese, 1927. Cathedral founded, 1936; consecrated, 1961. Assizes transferred to Kingston, 1930. University of Surrey established at, 1966.

Guildhall, London. An important hall has stood on this site since the eleventh century. A new building was erected, 1411–26, but much of this was destroyed in an air raid on 29 Dec. 1940. A new Great Hall was completed in 1954 to the designs of Sir Giles Gilbert Scott.

Guillotine. Supposed to have been invented by Joseph Ignace Guillotin (1738–1814), but in fact he merely recommended the use of the instrument, long known to the Scots and in certain parts of the N. of England. It was first used to execute a highwayman in Paris, 25 Apr. 1792. Discarded when capital punishment abolished in France, 1981.

Guinea. Gold coin first used in England, 1664. Last issued, 1813.

Guinea, Republic of, formerly French Guinea. Britain recognized France's rights in the area, 1882. Made a separate colony from Senegal, 1891. Boundaries finally settled, 1899. The territory voted to leave the French Community in the referendum of 28 Sept. 1958, and became an independent republic on 2 Oct. 1958. Agreement of unity with Ghana (Nov. 1958) and Ghana-Mali (Dec. 1960) never had practical effect.

Guinea Bissau, formerly **Portuguese Guinea**, discovered by Nuno Tristao, 1446, and made a separate colony of Portugal, 1879. Independent, 1974.

Ruled by a Revolutionary Council since 1980.

Guinea, Spanish. *See* EQUATORIAL GUINEA.

Guines, Treaty of. *See* CLOTH OF GOLD, FIELD OF THE.

Gun-cotton. Invented by Braconnot, 1832. Put to practical use by Schönbein (German), 1845. First manufactured in England, 1847.

Gundulph Bible, a Vulgate MS. copied in Amsterdam, was brought to England by G., a monk of Bec. In 1077 he became Bishop of Rochester, and his Bible was kept in the cathedral until 1540, when it disappeared. In Mar. 1952 it was rediscovered in a library at San Marino, California.

Gunpowder. The precise era of the invention and application of G. in Europe is doubtful but it was clearly known before the middle of the fourteenth century, and, before the end of the same, the use of artillery was familiar to the states of Germany, Italy, Spain, France, and England. G. is said to have been made by Berthold Schwartz of Brunswick *c.* A.D. 1320, although Roger Bacon mentions its composition in a work published, 1216.

Gunpowder Plot. Originated by Robert Catesby early in 1604, to blow up the Houses of Parliament. In July 1605, Guy Fawkes was commissioned to commit the deed, and 5 Nov. 1605, the day on which Parliament was to meet, was the day chosen. Catesby was killed during the course of his flight from the Government officers. Fawkes and other leaders executed, Jan and Feb. 1606.

Gupta. A famous dynasty under which India reached great prosperity, A.D. 320–480.

Gurkhas. Predominant ethnic group of Nepal (*q.v.*), from which were recruited ten regiments of Gurkha Rifles of the army of British India. By an agreement of Aug. 1947, eight of the nineteen Gurkha battalions then in being took service under the British crown, the rest entering the Indian service.

Guyana, formerly **British Guiana**, independent state within the Commonwealth. First partially settled by Dutch W. India Co. *c.* 1630. Captured by British, 1796, and ceded to Britain, 1814. G. independent under the name of Guyana, 26 May 1966. Republic, 22 Feb. 1970. Mass-suicide of 911 mostly American followers of religious leader Jim Jones in G., Nov. 1979. New constitution, 1980.

Guy's Hospital (London). Founded by Thomas Guy, 1721.

Gwalior, India. City and state founded by Mahadji Sindhia, 1769. Under British influence, 1782. British intervention, 1843. It became the nucleus of the Union of Minor States, known as Madhya Bharat, formed 15 June 1948, with G. city as its capital.

Gwent, Welsh co. authority estab. 1974 under terms of Local Government Act of 1972. Headquarters are at Cwmbran.

H

Haarlem, Holland. Besieged by Duke of Alva and the Spaniards, Dec. 1572–July 1573.

Habeas Corpus Act (Great Britain). Passed, 1679, to prevent illegal imprisonment; extended to cases other than criminal, 1816. In Scotland the Wrongous Imprisonment Act, passed 1701, is equivalent to the English Act; Irish Act passed, 1781–2.

Hackney Coaches. First used in London, 1625. Laws regarding hire of, 1831, 1853, 1869, 1896, and 1907. The London Cab Order, 1934, and the London Cab Acts of 1968 and 1973, regulate the London taxi service, the modern equivalent of H.C.

Hadfield's (James) attempt to assassinate George III at Drury Lane Theatre, 15 May 1800. Tried and acquitted, 26 June 1800.

Hadrian's Wall (England). Designed by the Emperor Hadrian during his visit to Britain in A.D. 122, but the work was executed largely by the legate Aulus Platorius Nepos, 122–6. Extended from the Tyne to the Solway Firth; repaired by Severus about 208. Wall abandoned, A.D. 383. Major excavations in 20th cent.: a major tourist attraction since World War II.

Hague, The, or **'s Gravenhage,** Holland. Founded, 1248. Spanish supremacy abjured at, 1580; the de Witts killed, 1672; captured by French, 19 Jan. 1795; evacuated by the French, Nov. 1813; the Permanent Court of Arbitration at The H. established in 1899; the Palace of Peace at The H., instituted by the Carnegie Foundation for the Permanent Court of Arbitration, inaugurated Aug. 1913. Academy of International Law founded, Jan. 1914. Permanent Court of International Justice founded, 1920.

Hague, The, Peace Conferences at.
1. Met, 18 May 1899; Arbitration Court instituted, Apr. 1899;
2. met 15 June–18 Oct. 1907.

Hague, The, Treaties of.
1. between England, France and Holland to enforce Peace of Roskilde (q.v.), 21 May 1659;
2. between England and Holland, July 1659;
3. between England, France and Holland, Aug. 1659;
4. between Great Britain and Holland, 23 Jan. 1668; receives name of Triple Alliance after Sweden joins, 25 Apr. 1668;
5. between Portugal and Holland, 7 May 1669;
6. between the Emperor, Holland, and Spain against France, 25 July 1672;
7. Grand Alliance (q.v.) renewed, 1696;
8. second Triple Alliance (q.v.), 4 Jan. 1717;
9. between Spain, Savoy, and Austria, 17 Feb. 1717;
10. convention between Great Britain, Austria, Holland, and Sardinia against France and Spain, 26 Jan. 1748;
11. between France and Holland, 16 May 1795.

Haifa, Israel. Developed commercially since c. 1890. Harbour completed, 1933. Town severely damaged by terrorist sabotage of Shell refinery, 30 Mar. 1947. After Israel's independence (1948) the oil pipe-line from Kirkuk was cut, and the refining of oil curtailed.

Haileybury and Imperial Service College (Herts., England). Founded 1806 by the E. India Co., originally occupied Hertford Castle, but removed to its present site, 1809. In 1862 it was reopened as a public school, and incorporated, 1864. The Imperial Service College was amalgamated with it in 1942.

Hainaut (Hainault, Henegouwen) acquired as part of a dowry by Baldwin, Count of Flanders, 1051; passed to Bavaria, 1345; Burgundy, 1433; Austria, 1477; Spanish Netherlands, 1555; France, 1659; Austrian Netherlands, 1714. Became French province, 1794; was ceded to the United Netherlands, 1814; became Belgian province, 1830.

Hair-powder Tax. In Great Britain, 1795. Repealed, 1869.

Haiti. Once signified the W. Indian island of Hispaniola (*q.v.* for early history). Now the name of the western portion of the island. Jean Jacques Dessalines, an ex-slave, proclaimed himself Emperor of H., 1804; assassinated, 1806. Henri Christophe, in the N., proclaimed life-president, 1807. Rival Government, headed by Alexandre Pétion, formed at Port-au-Prince, 1807–18. Christophe proclaimed king, 1811; crowned, 1812; committed suicide, 1820. Pétion's successor, Jean Pierre Boyer, seized Christophe's dominion, drove Spaniards from eastern portion, and ruled the whole island, 1822–43. For subsequent history of eastern portion, *see* DOMINICAN REPUBLIC. H. proper proclaimed an empire by Faustin Soulouque, 1849; republic restored, 1859. Many revolutions since. U.S.A. intervened, 1915. Treaty with U.S.A., 1916, brought H. under U.S. protection. U.S. marines left, 15 Aug. 1934. *Coup d'état*, 10 May 1950, led by Col. Paul Eugène Magloire, who was the first president (Oct. 1950) to be elected by universal *direct* suffrage. A period of political upheaval and army rule ended with François Duvalier's election as President, Sept. 1957: became president for life, 1964: Succeeded as president for life by his son, Jean-Claude Duvalier, 1971.

Halicarnassus. City of Asia Minor on S.W. coast of Caria, founded by Dorians from Troezane and Argos. Became subject to Persia, sixth century

B.C. The satrap Lygdamis obtained power as tyrant; his daughter and successor, Artemisia I, present with Xerxes at Salamis, 480 B.C. H. was a member of the Delian League until the Peace of Antalcidas restored it to Persian suzerainty, 387 B.C. The satrap Mausolus (377–353 B.C.) made himself independent. His wife and successor, Artemisia II, built the Mausoleum *c.* 352 B.C. H. was destroyed by Alexander, 334 B.C.

Halifax, Nova Scotia. Founded, 1749: garrisoned by British troops until 1906; explosion in harbour caused 5,800 casualties, 16 Dec. 1917.

Halifax Fisheries Award. One of the articles of the Treaty of Washington (*q.v.*), 1871, provided for a commission to inquire into the value of the fishery privileges allowed to the U.S.A. by the treaty; met at Halifax, Nova Scotia, 5 June 1877. Great Britain awarded $5,500,000 for fishing privileges for twelve years.

Halifax Law (summary trial and execution by guillotine for certain types of larceny) arose in Halifax, Yorkshire, in the fifteenth century and was last enforced in 1650.

Hall Marks (Britain).

1. The London assay office established by statute, 1300. The earliest marks of this office now known date from 1390. The date letter series begins, 1478. Its marks were: 1478–1697: A crowned leopard's head. 1697–1719: Britannia. 1719–1820: A crowned leopard's head. 1820 to now: Leopard's head uncrowned.

2. The Chester office probably existed before 1300. Date letter series begins, 1701. Its marks were: 1300–1701: A shield with three sheaves and a dagger. 1701–19: As before, halved with three English leopards. 1719: The London leopard's head was added. In 1779 the old shield was readopted. In 1839 the London mark was dropped. Office closed, 1962.

3. The Birmingham office opened, 1773. Its mark is an anchor.

4. The Sheffield office opened, 1773. Its mark is a crown.
5. The Edinburgh office was in existence, 1485, from which its earliest marks date. The date letter series begins, 1681. Its mark is a three-towered castle on a rock.
6. The Glasgow office instituted, 1819. Its mark is the fish, tree, bell, and bird of the Glasgow arms.
7. The Dublin office was in existence by 1500. Date letter series begins, 1638. Its mark is a crowned harp. From 1730 a figure of Hibernia was added to denote payment of a tax. The tax was abolished, 1890, but the figure is still in use.
8. The following offices have also existed:
(a) Exeter date letter series begins, 1544. Mark, a three-towered castle. Office closed, 1883.
(b) Newcastle founded, 1423. Date letter series begins, 1658. Mark is three towers on a shield. Office closed, 1864.
(c) Norwich founded, 1423. Date letter series begins, 1565. Marks are a crowned rose, and a shield with a gate tower over an English leopard. Office closed, 1697.
(d) York founded, 1423. Date letter series begins, 1562. Marks are a fleur-de-lys and a crowned leopard's head halved with each other, and a cross charged with five leopards. Office closed, 1857.

The Excise Duty Mark (the sovereign's head in profile) was used between 1784 and 1890. The heads of both sovereigns were used in the year 1935 only.

Halle, Saxony. Part of Archbishopric of Magdeburg from 968. Member of Hanseatic League, 1281–1478; passed to Brandenburg, 1648. Cathedral built, 1520–36. Martin Luther University founded, 1694; incorporated with University of Wittenberg, 1817.

Hallé Orchestra. Established in 1857 in Manchester by Sir Charles Hallé (1819–95).

Halley's Comet observed, 1682, by Edmund Halley (1635–1742), who correctly predicted its reappearance in 1758. Again appeared 1835 and 1910; next expected appearance, Nov. 1985. The comet which appeared in 1066, 1456, 1531, and 1607 was almost certainly H.C.

Hambledon, Hampshire, England. Traditional birth-place of cricket (*q.v.*), 1757.

Hamburg, Germany. Founded by Charlemagne, A.D. 808; bishopric, 831; archbishopric, 834; made a free imperial city, 1189; allied with Lübeck, 1241; Bank of, founded, 1619; peace of, 1762; occupied by French, 1806; annexed to France, 1810; evacuated by French on approach of Russians, 1813; freed from French, 1814; joined German Confederation, 1815; one-third of the town destroyed by fire, 1842; new constitution granted by the senate, July 1860; joined the N. German Confederation (*q.v.*), Aug. 1866; joined the Zollverein in, Oct. 1888; cholera epidemic, 1892; university founded, 1919. Lost privileges, 1933. Dock area mostly destroyed by allied bombing, 1942–3. Captured by British, 3 May 1945. Severe flooding, 16–17 Feb. 1962. *See* HANSEATIC LEAGUE.

'Hampshire,' The. British armoured cruiser on the way to Russia mined and sunk off Marwick Head in the Orkneys, Lord Kitchener and staff perishing, 6 June 1916.

Hampton Court Conference. Held at H.C.,12–18 Jan. 1604, between the Church party and the Puritans.

Hampton Court Palace (Middlesex, England). Built by Cardinal Wolsey, and presented by him to King Henry VIII, 1526; Edward VI *b*. there, 12 Oct. 1537; enlarged by Christopher Wren for William III, 1694, when the famous chestnut avenue was planted; vine planted, 1768; state apartments opened to public, 1837; excavation of ancient moat completed and restoration, 14 Oct. 1910.

Hampton Roads Conference between Lincoln and Seward for the Federal Government and Confederate vice-president Stephens, 3 Feb. 1865.

Hanaper Office of the Court of Chancery founded *c*. 1670. Abolished, 1842.

Hangchowfu. Described (as Kinsai) by Marco Polo, who visited it *c.* 1280. Capital of Sung dynasty, 1127–1278. Held by Taiping rebels, 1851–4. Nationalist stronghold in civil war, 1926.

Hankow, China. Founded during Ming dynasty (1300–1644). Sacked and largely destroyed in the Taiping rebellion, 1851–1854. Opened to European trade, 1862.

Hanover, Germany. Made an electorate, 1692. Elector George acquired Celle by marriage, 1705. Became King of Britain, 1714. Acquired Bremen and Verden from Sweden, 1715. Made a kingdom, 1814. Acquired E. Friesland, 1815. At accession of Victoria crown of H. went to Ernest Augustus, hitherto deputy-elector of H. and Duke of Cumberland, 1837, because Salic Law obtained in H. Joined Austria in the Austro-Prussian War of 1866, and annexed by Prussia, 26 Sept. 1866. Monarchy abolished after World War I.

Hanover, House of. *See* ENGLISH SOVEREIGNS AND THEIR CONSORTS.

Hanover, Treaties of.
1. Between England, France, and Prussia, signed, 3 Sept. 1725, to oppose the secret Treaty of Vienna (20 Apr. 1725) between Spain and Austria, who pledged themselves to assist in the restoration of the Stuarts, joined by Holland, 9 Aug. 1726; by Sweden, 26 Mar. 1727; by Denmark, 18 Apr. 1727.
2. Between George II and Maria Theresa, 24 June 1741.
3. Between H. and England, 1834.

Hanoverian Succession. Established by law, 12 June 1701; arranged that the Princess Sophia of Hanover and her heirs should succeed to the British throne after the death of Queen Anne, provided the latter *d.* without issue.

Hansard. Record of parliamentary debates, begun by Luke Hansard (1752–1828), a printer. The name 'Hansard' was dropped from the *Parliamentary Debates* between 1889 and 1943, but restored in the latter year as the result of a House of Commons Select Committee's recommendation.

Hanseatic League, or **Hansa.** Hamburg and Lübeck in alliance, 1241. First meeting of Hanse towns (The Wendish Group), 1256. Gothland association existed in 1229 when it negotiated a treaty with the Russians, but was subsequently absorbed by the H.L. Was given privileges in England, 1237. The Free Counter at Bruges established, 1309. At Bergen, 1343. Wars with Denmark, 1361–70. Lübeck recognized as head of the H.L., 1418. Baltic trading monopoly broken by Peace of Copenhagen, 1441. Novgorod counter closed, 1494. Bruges counter closed, 1540. Last general assembly held, 1669. Counters at Bergen closed, 1775; London, 1852; Antwerp, 1863.

Hapsburg or **Habsburg, House of.** Family called after H., in Switzerland, to which they came in 1028. Rudolf of H. elected Holy Roman Emperor, 1273. Austria and Styria acquired soon after. Carinthia and Carniola, 1335. Tirol, 1363–4. Franche-Comté, 1493 (lost, 1555). Württemberg and Breisgau, 1520 (lost, 1534). Bohemia, Moravia, Croatia, Silesia, and Christian Hungary, 1526. Rest of Hungary reconquered from the Turks, 1650–99. Netherlands, 1712 (lost, 1797). Milan, 1714 (lost, 1797). Banat of Temesvar, 1718. Craiova and Serbia, 1718 (lost, 1739). Parma, 1735 (lost, 1748). Tuscany, 1737 (lost, 1801). Silesia lost, 1742. Galicia, 1772. Lublin, 1795 (lost, 1809). Venetia, 1797 (lost, 1805). At Vienna Congress (1814–15) Hs. obtained Tuscany, Modena, Parma, Milan, Venetia, which were all lost, 1859–66, and permanently acquired Trento and Salzburg. Through marriages with the houses of Burgundy and Spain the Emperor Charles V was also King of Spain, but at his death the Spanish and the Germanic lands descended in different branches of the family until the extinction of the Spanish Hs., 1700 (*see* SPANISH SUCCESSION). The death of the Emperor Charles VI, 1740, extinguished the true Austrian branch, but through the marriage of his daughter Maria-Theresa with Prince Charles of Lorraine the family was known as H.-Lorraine. At abolition of the Holy Roman Empire (*q.v.*), 1806, the Hs. took the title of Emperor of Austria. They ceased to reign in Austria and Hungary, 1918. The head of the H. house was allowed to return to Austria, 1966.

Hara-Kiri. Japanese form of honourable suicide required on certain occasions, customary during the Middle Ages. Abolished officially, 1868, but practised by sev. Japanese officers during World War II.

Harar or **Harrar,** Ethiopia. Became seat of Arab government of Zelia, 1521. Occupied by Egyptians, 1875–85. Conquered by Ethiopian Emperor Menelek II, 1887. Captured by British forces, Mar. 1941, and this signalled the beginning of the collapse of Mussolini's colonial empire.

Harare, cap. of Zimbabwe (*q.v.*). Founded, as Fort Salisbury, 1890. Cap. of S. Rhodesia, 1923. Cap. of Zimbabwe, under name of H., since 1980.

Harfleur, Normandy. Captured by Henry V of England, 1415. English expelled, 1433. Recaptured by English, 1440. Driven out by Dunois, 1450. Sacked by Huguenots, 1562.

Harleian Collection. Valuable MSS., books, and pamphlets, whose collection was started by Robert Harley (1661–1724), 1st Earl of Oxford, and continued by his son. Much of it was acquired in 1753 by the British Museum.

Harper's Ferry, W. Va., U.S.A. The scene of John Brown's celebrated raid before the American Civil War, 16 Oct. 1859.

Harrow School. Founded by John Lyon, a Harrow butcher, 1571. Originally intended for education of poor boys of the parish. Original red-brick school house built, 1608–15. Mutinies at, 1771 and 1815.

Hartford, Conn., U.S.A. Settled by the Dutch, 1633, by the English, 1635.

Hartford Conventions.
1. 20 Oct. 1779, to inquire into the depreciation of continental paper money.
2. 15 Dec. 1814, to deliberate upon security and defence.

Harvard University (U.S.A.). Founded by the general court of Massachusetts Bay Colony, 10 Oct. 1638, and subsequently named H. College after Rev. John Harvard (*b.* 1607), who went to America in 1637, and bequeathed in 1638 his library and a sum of money towards the foundation of the college at Cambridge (*q.v.*), Mass. Charter granted, 1650. Transformed into a university, 1780. Under control of state until 1865, since when it has been self-governing.

Harwich, Essex, England. Danes defeated off, A.D. 885; incorporated, 1318, and charter further extended, 1604; Isabel, queen of Edward II, landed at, 1326; Dutch fleet defeated by Duke of York near, 3 June 1665.

Hastings, Sussex. One of the Cinque Ports, founded *c.* 893. King Athelstan established a mint here. H. was a borough before 1086. The battle of H. was fought six miles inland; William's army halted at H. on the night of 13–14 Oct. 1066, preceding the battle. Importance as a port declined after English loss of Normandy in 1204. Burned by French, 1377 and 1380.

Hastings, Warren, Trial of. Commenced before the House of Lords, 12 Feb. 1788; lasted until 23 Apr. 1795.

Hatfield, Council of (England). Held to declare the orthodoxy of the English Church regarding Monothelite heresy; also accepted the decrees of the five first general councils, 17 Sept. 680.

Hatfield House (Herts., England). Old Palace built *c.* 1496 by Archbishop Morton, Henry VII's minister. Later it passed to the crown. Elizabeth I succeeded to crown here. James I gave it to Robert Cecil, Earl of Salisbury, in exchange for Theobalds. Substantial rebuilding undertaken between 1607 and 1611.

Hatteras Expedition. The Confederate forts at H. Inlet (U.S.A.), attacked by Federal army, under Gen. Butler, and a small fleet, 28 Aug. 1861; Confederates, under Maj. W. S. G. Andrewes, surrendered on following day.

Havana. See CUBA.

Havana, Declaration of, published by Pan-American Conference, 30 July 1940.

Havre, France. Originally *Havre de Notre-Dame de Grâce.* Founded by Louis XII, 1509; given to Queen Elizabeth by Huguenots, 1562; besieged and captured by Montmorency, 1563; bombarded unsuccessfully by English, 1678, 1694, 1759, 1794, 1795.

Hawaian or **Sandwich Islands.** Shipwrecked Spaniards settled here, 1527. Juan Gaetano made landfall, 1555. Rediscovered by Capt. Cook, 1778. Cook murdered by the natives here, 1779. Constitution granted by reigning king, 1840; independence guaranteed by Great Britain and France, 1844; revolution at, 1893, when reigning Queen Liliuokalani (*d.* 11 Nov. 1917) was deposed. Republic proclaimed, 1894; annexed to U.S.A., 1898. Became a state of the Union, 1959.

Hawkers or **Pedlars,** Acts respecting, in Great Britain. Pedlars Act, 1871, by which they were placed under surveillance of the police; extended, 1881. H. Act, 1888, repealed by Local Government Act, 1966.

Haymarket Square Riot by anarchists in Chicago, 1886.

Hay-Pauncefote Treaty. Between Britain and U.S.A., 1901, to amend Clayton-Bulwer Treaty regarding canal scheme between Atlantic and Pacific.

Head Act (Ireland), 1465, permitting wholesale slaughter of the Irish.

Health Centre. The first H.C. to be set up under the National Health Service Act, 1946, was opened at Stoke Newington, 14 Oct. 1952.

Health, Ministry of. Established by Act of 1919. First minister appointed, 1920. Part of the **Department of Health and Social Security** (*q.v.*) since 1968.

Health and Social Security, Department of, major department of state, formed from the former ministries of Health and Social Security, 1968.

Hearth or Chimney Money. A tax on every hearth introduced in England, 1663. Abolished, 1689.

Hearts of Steel (Ireland). Protestant tenants of Tyrone and Antrim formed this society, 1772.

Heavy Hydrogen (Deuterium). Discovered by Urey in 1931.

Heavy Water. Discovered by Urey in 1931; first prepared by Lewis, 1933.

Hebdomadal Board (Oxford). Instituted, 1631.

Hebdomadal Council, supplanted preceding, 1854.

Hebrides. Settled and Christianized by the Scots of Dalriada, sixth century. Immigration from Norway begun *c.* 800. H. subjugated by Harald Fairhair, King of Norway, *c.* 875, and granted to the Jarls of Sudreyar (Lords of the Isles, *q.v.*), who remained Norwegian vassals until 1266. Thereafter *see under* SCOTLAND.

Heidelberg, W. Germany. University founded by Elector Rupert I, 1385; reconstituted by Charles Frederick, Grand-Duke of Baden, 1803. H. plundered by Tilly, 1622, by the Swedes, 1633, and by the Imperialists, 1635; sacked by the French, 1688 and 1693.

Hejaz, Arabia. Sherif Hussein of Mecca proclaimed independent of Turkey, June 1916. Recognized as King of the H., 29 Oct., and enthroned, 4 Nov. After unsuccessful war with Ibn Sa'ud, King Hussein abdicated, 1924. After the Saudi capture of Mecca, 1925, Hejazi independence was extinguished.

Hejira. The name given to Mohammed's flight from Mecca to Medina, A.D. 622.

Helicopter. First constructed, 1872; first successful model (built by Crocker and Hewitt) flown, 1918. Used extensively for air-sea rescue during and since World War II. First heliport opened in London, 1959. Used extensively in Vietnam War, 1959–75; in Falklands' campaign, 1982, and since 1950s in N. Sea oil industry.

Heligoland (Frisian island off mouth of Elbe) was a place of pilgrimage for the Angles and Frisians in heathen times, containing sacred groves in which were temples of Forseti and the mother goddess Herta. The former building was destroyed by St. Ludger, first Bishop of Münster (*d.* 809). Ceded to Britain, 1814. Exchanged for certain German E. African possessions, 1890. Fortress blown up by British, 1945–7. Formally returned to Federal German Republic, 1 Mar. 1952.

Helium. Discovered in the sun by Sir Joseph Lockyer (1836–1920), 1868. Onnes (1853–1926) of Leyden succeeded in liquefying it, 1908.

Helsinki or **Helsingfors,** Finland. Founded by Gustavus I of Sweden in sixteenth century; made capital of Finland instead of Abo, 1812; bombarded by allied fleets, Aug. 1855; bombed by Russians during Russo-Finnish wars, 1939–40 and 1941–4. *See* FINLAND.

Helsinki Agreement, 1975, signed by the U.S.A., Great Britain, and U.S.S.R. to safeguard human rights. Never implemented by Communist countries.

Helvetic Confession. First H.C. drawn up, 1536, by the Swiss theologians assembled at Basel. H.C. at Zürich, 1566, formed basis of union between Calvin's party and the Zürich reformers.

Henley-on-Thames Regatta, first held, 1839.

Heralds' College of Arms. Founded by Richard III of England, 1483.

Herculaneum (It. **Ercolano**). Damaged by a severe earthquake, A.D. 63. H. was destroyed by the eruption of Vesuvius, 79, as described by Pliny the Younger (62–c. 120). Excavations on a small scale began, 1719, and were continued more ambitiously, 1927–30 and since 1960.

Hereford was a Mercian outpost in A.D. 600, but was retaken by the Welsh, who in 1055 destroyed a castle built by Ralph, the Norman earl installed by Edward the Confessor. Chartered as a city by Richard I, 1189. The cathedral, founded 680, was also destroyed, 1055, but a new Norman building was finished in 1140. Other portions built between 1220 and 1500. The Mappa Mundi in the cathedral library is the oldest extant example of its kind, executed c. 1300. *See also* THREE CHOIRS' FESTIVAL.

Heregeld ('Army Tax'), levied after the murder of Archbishop Alfheah in 1012, to pay Danish mercenaries who had deserted from Knut's army. Abolished, 1051.

Heresy, Laws concerning (England). In 1382 provided that sheriffs should arrest 'persons certified by the bishops to be heretics'. By the *De Haeretico comburendo* Act, 1401, the bishops themselves were empowered to punish H. This Act was enlarged, 1414. In 1533 an Act declared that offences against the See of Rome were not H. The Bill of the Six Articles, 1559, defined various heretical acts. Punishment of death for H. abolished, 1677.

Heretics. The following are some of the better known sects regarded as heretical by the Roman Catholic Church.

Gnostics. Appeared in first century A.D., but had pre-Christian origins. Among the principal exponents were Simon Magus (first century); Marcion, Basilides, and Valentinus (second century), Mani (third century).

Montanists. c. 156 Montanus proclaimed himself prophet of the Spirit. Tertullian joined the sect c. 202, and it lingered on in Africa and the E. until c. 400.

Monarchians. (a) Dynamists (or Adoptionists) founded by Theodotus of Byzantium c. 190–200; died out in the middle of the third century; (b) Sabellians (or Patripassians or Medalists) arose c. 215 with the arrival of Sabellius in Rome. Condemned at Council of Nicaea, 325.

Donatists. Followers of Donatus, Bishop of Carthage, in opposition to Majorinus, 311; opposed by Pope Melchiades, 313, the Council of Arles, 314, and finally condemned by the Council of Carthage, 411. The sect disappeared after the Saracenic invasion of Africa.

Arians. Commenced at Alexandria in 313, when Arius (c. 250–336) quarrelled with the Bishop Peter. Condemned at Nicaea, 325, and lost its hold after the Second Council of Constantinople, 381. Its continuation among the barbarian kingdoms was of political rather than doctrinal significance.

Pelagians. Pelagius began to preach, c. 405, at Rome. Doctrine condemned at Councils of Carthage, 418, and Orange, 529. The Semi-Pelagians, founded by Cassian (c. 360–c. 435),

Abbot of St. Victor; condemned at Orange, 529.

Nestorians. Nestorius (*d. c.* 451), a disciple of Theodore of Mopsuestia (*c.* 350–428) was condemned at the Councils of Ephesus, 431, and Chalcedon, 451. His doctrines already preached by Diodorus of Tarsus (*d. c.* 392). The sect survives in the E.

Monophysites. Principal teachers were: Eutyches (*c.* 378–*c.* 454). Dioscurus (*d.* 454) who was condemned at Chalcedon, 451, and Timothy Aelurus (*d.* 477). The teaching survives among the Copts and Syrian Jacobites.

Monothelites. The doctrine first appears *c.* 622 in an address delivered before the Emperor Heraclius by Paul, head of the Acephali; but the principal exponent was Sergius (*d.* 638), patriarch of Constantinople. Monothelitism was finally condemned at Constantinople, 680–1.

Modernism. Condemned by papal decree *Lamentabili*, 3–4 July 1907, and by the encyclical *Pascendi*, 8 Sept. 1907. Chief exponents: A. Loisy (1857–1940) in France and G. Tyrrell (1861–1909) in England.

Heritable Jurisdictions Act abolished hereditary jurisdictions in Scotland, 1746, as a result of the 'Forty-Five'.

Hermandad (Sp. brotherhood), a defensive alliance of Castilian and Aragonese cities, formed *c.* 1250, and reinforced, 1295. Ceased to exist *c.* 1550.

Hertogenbosch (Fr. **Bois-le-Duc**), Netherlands. Became a fortified town, 1184. Taken by the Duchy of Brabant, 1629. In French hands, 1794–1814.

Herzegovina. United with Bosnia (*q.v.*), 1326; formally ceded to Turkey, 1699, by Peace of Carlowitz; rebelled against Turkish rule, 1875; occupied by Austrians, Aug. 1878; formally annexed to Austria-Hungary, 7 Oct. 1908; became part of Yugoslavia, 1918. Formed, with Bosnia, one of the federal republics of Yugoslavia, 1945.

Hesse, Germany. Became a principality, 1292. Divided into four, 1567. By 1622 there were three H.s, viz. H.-Darmstadt, H.-Homburg, H.-Cassel. The

two latter annexed by Prussia, 1866. H.-Darmstadt became a republic, 1919. The province, reunited, became a federal unit of the Federal German Republic after 1945.

Hexham (Northumberland). The early English abbey church is on the site of the church of St. Andrew, which St. Wilfrid founded 673. It was the seat of a Northumbrian bishopric associated with the sub-kingdom of Bernicia (*q.v.*). The see finally merged into that of Lindisfarne, 821, and was absorbed by that of Durham. A district called Hexhamshire surrounding H. was under the jurisdiction of the Archbishop of York, as County Durham was of the Earl Bishop, until 1545.

Hibbert Lectures on theology founded, 1878.

High Church Party. Term first used in England *c.* 1703, and referred to the party who opposed the Dissenters (*see* NONCONFORMISTS), and enforced the laws made against them.

High Commission, The Court of. Established by Queen Elizabeth I, 1559, to investigate ecclesiastical cases; abolished by the Long Parliament, July 1641. James II in 1686 revived it, but it was finally abolished by the Bill of Rights in Dec. 1689. A similar court existed in Scotland, 1608–38.

Highland Garb Act forbade the wearing of H. dress, 1746. Repealed, 1782.

High School, term denoting, in U.S.A., school maintained by the states from *c.* 1850.

Hindenburg Line. *See* WORLD WAR I.

Hire Purchase Act (Britain) came into force, 1 Jan. 1939, since superseded by the Consumer Credit Act of 1974.

Hiroshima, Japan. Atom bomb dropped at H., 6 Aug. 1945.

Hispaniola. Name given to the island that now contains Haiti and the Dominican Republic, by Columbus, on his discovery thereof, 1492. Santo Domingo, first European town in western hemisphere, founded by Bartholomew Columbus, 1496. Negroes, introduced 1505, soon displaced native population. Western portion, invaded by French buccaneers, ceded to France by

Treaty of Ryswick, 1697; negroes of western portion rose against whites, 1791. Eastern portion ceded by Spain to France, 1795. Toussaint l'Ouverture quelled British invaders, 1798; crushed mulatto revolt, 1799; completed conquest of whole island, but was deported by the French, 1801. French had to leave, 1803. Eastern portion reoccupied by Spain, 1816–21; for later history, *see* HAITI and DOMINICAN REPUBLIC.

Hitler Youth (Hitlerjugend), official National Socialist (*see* NATIONAL SOCIALISM) youth movement initiated in 1926 and made virtually compulsory for all 'Aryan' children in Germany, 1936.

Hittites. Settled in Asia Minor by 2000 B.C. Rose to greatest power under Shuppiluliuma (*c.* 1375–1340 B.C.). Fell *c.* 1200 B.C.

Hoare-Laval Pact, proposing for Ethiopia unacceptable terms as the price of peace with Italy, signed Dec. 1935. *See* ETHIOPIA.

Hohenstaufen, a famous German family who, as Holy Roman Emperors (*q.v.*), 1138–1254, conducted a controversy with the Papacy until the male line was extinguished by the murder of Conradin in 1268.

Hohenzollern. Name of the Swabian family which became successively Electors of Brandenburg (*q.v.*), kings of Prussia (*q.v.*), and German emperors. The regime of the senior branch ended in Germany, Nov. 1918, and the last H. to have ruled Prussia *d.* 4 June 1941, but the Sigmaringen branch continued on the throne of Rumania (*q.v.*) till abdication of King Michael, 30 Dec. 1947.

Holland, *see* NETHERLANDS, KINGDOM OF THE.

Holland House, Kensington, built 1608–10, by Sir Walter Cope. Henry Richard Vassall Fox, third Baron H. (1773–1840), nephew of Charles James Fox, made H.H. a headquarters of the Whig Party from 1800 until his death. Demolished after World War II and grounds now a public park.

Holloway. Prison for women built, 1849–51.

Holy Alliance. Signed at Paris, 26 Sept. 1815, between the rulers of Russia, Prussia, and Austria. It was offered for signature to the other powers, and all except Great Britain signed.

Holy Island (Lindisfarne). St. Aidan (*d.* 651) founded a priory, 635, which was destroyed, 793 (*see* VIKING AGE). Lindisfarne with Hexham (*q.v.*) was one of the two episcopal sees associated with Bernicia (*q.v.*) under the house of Bamburgh, and the Lindisfarne Gospels traditionally produced here. After about ninety years of actual harassing, or the threat of it, by Scandinavian pirates (*see* VIKING AGE), the first monastery was abandoned in 883 (*see* DURHAM). Benedictines from Durham re-established a cell on H.I., 1082.

Holy Leagues, The.
1. Formed in 1511 between Pope Julius II, the Emperor Maximilian I, Henry VIII of England, and Ferdinand, King of Aragon, to crush France; dissolved, 1513.
2. Formed by Pope Clement VII in 1526 against the Emperor Charles V; France, Venice, and Milan were also in the league.
3. Formed by Pope Pius V, Spain, and Venice against the Turks, 1570.
4. Formed by the Catholic party against the Huguenots in 1576, also known as the Catholic League.
5. Formed by Catholic princes of Germany under Maximilian of Bavaria in 1609 as a counterblast to Protestant Union of 1608.
6. Formed by Pope Innocent XI, the Emperor, Poland, Venice, and Russia, against the Turks in 1684.

'Holy Maid of Kent.' Elizabeth Barton, during Henry VIII's reign. She prophesied the violent death of the king if he married Anne Boleyn. She and her confederates executed, 1534.

Holy Places. *See* CRUSADES. Dispute over their custody ultimately caused war in Crimea (*q.v.*), 1854.

Holy Roman Emperors. (Rivals and Anti-Caesars in *italics*)
Charles I (Charlemagne) 800–814
Louis I (the Pious) 814–840
Lothar I 840–855

Louis II (in Italy) 855–875
Charles II (the Bald) 875–881
Charles III (the Fat) 882–887
Guido (in Italy) 887–894
Lambert (in Italy) 894–896
Arnulf 896–899
Louis the Child 899–901
Louis III of Provence (in Italy) 901–911
Conrad I 911–915
Berengar (in Italy) 915–918
Saxons
Henry I (the Fowler) 918–936
Otto I. King of the E. Franks 936–962
    H. R. Emperor 963–973
Otto II 973–983
Otto III 983–1002
Henry II (the Saint) 1002–1024
Salians
Conrad II (the Salic) 1024–1037
Henry III (the Black) 1037–1056
Henry IV 1056–1106
Rudolf of Swabia 1077–1081
Hermann of Luxemburg 1081–1093
Conrad of Franconia 1093–1106
Henry V 1106–1125
Lothar II 1125–1138
Hohenstaufen
Conrad III 1138–1152
Frederick I (Barbarossa) 1152–1190
Henry VI 1190–1197
Philip ⎫
Otto IV ⎭ as rivals 1197–1208
Otto IV, alone 1208–1212
Frederick II 1212–1250
Henry Raspe 1246–1247
William of Holland 1247–1256
Conrad IV 1250–1254
Interregnum 1254–1257
Richard of Cornwall ⎫ 1257–1272
Alfonso of Castile ⎭
Rudolf I of Hapsburg 1273–1291
Adolf of Nassau 1292–1298
Albert I of Hapsburg 1298–1308
Henry VII of Luxemburg 1308–1313
Louis IV of Bavaria 1314–1347
Frederick of Austria 1314
Charles IV of Luxemburg 1347–1378
Günther of Schwartzburg 1347
Wenzel of Luxemburg 1378–1400
Rupert of the Palatinate 1400–1410
Sigismund of Luxemburg 1410–1437
Jobst of Moravia 1410
Hapsburgs
Albert II 1438–1440

Frederick III 1440–1493
Maximilian I 1439–1519
Charles V 1519–1558
    (Abdicated 25 Oct.)
Ferdinand I 1558–1564
Maximilian II 1564–1576
Rudolf II 1576–1612
Matthias 1612–1619
Ferdinand II 1619–1637
Ferdinand III 1637–1657
Leopold I 1658–1705
Joseph I 1705–1711
Charles VI 1711–1740
Charles VII of Bavaria 1742–1745
Francis I of Lorraine 1745–1765
Joseph II 1765–1790
Leopold II 1790–1792
Francis II 1792–1806
    (Abdicated)
NOTE. Francis I was elected as husband of Maria Theresa of Austria because no woman had ever held the throne. Charles VII is therefore the only true exception to the permanent Hapsburg tenure beginning in 1438.
Ferdinand I and his successors were never crowned by the Pope.

Holy Roman Empire. Leo III crowns Charlemagne Roman Emperor at Rome, 25 Dec. 800. Civil war, 840, leads to Partition of Verdun, 843. Deposition of Charles the Fat, 887. Henry the Fowler defeats the Magyars at battle of the Unstrut, 933. Magyars finally defeated by Otto I on the Lech, 955. Otto I crowned emperor of the H.R.E. of the German nation by John XII, 963. Henry III reforms Papacy at Synod of Sutri, 1046. Choice of popes transferred from H.R. Emperor to the cardinals, 1059. Hildebrand (Gregory VII) denounces Lay Investiture (*q.v.*), 1075. Henry IV submits to Gregory VII at Canossa, 1077. War of Investiture, 1077–1122. Concordat of Worms (Investiture Compromise), 1122. Elective principle asserted at election of Lothar, 1125. Frederick Barbarossa begins war with Lombard cities, 1158. Defeated at battle of Legnano, 1176. Peace of Constance, 1183. Frederick II leaves Sicily for his Peaceful Crusade, 1228. Papal deposition of Frederick II at Council of Lyons, 1245. Hohenstaufen defeat and destruction at battle of Tagliacozzo, 1268. Election of Rudolf of Hapsburg, 1273. He conquers Austria from Bohemia, battle of the Marchfeld, 1278. First Union of Swiss Cantons, 1307. Battle of Morgarten, 1315. Charles IV establishes Electoral Constitution of the H.R.E. by the Golden Bull, 1356. John Hus burned by Council of Constance, 1415. Bohemian (Hussite) War, 1419–36, ends with Compact of Iglau, 1436. Turkish raids begin after battle of Kossovo, 1448. Maximilian fails to introduce effective reforms at Diets of Worms, 1495. Augsburg, 1500. After battle of Mohacs (1526) Turks besiege Vienna, 1529. Charles V rejects confession of Augsburg, 1530. Formation of League of Schmalkalden (Protestant), 1530. Truce of Frankfort, 1539. Protestant defeat at battle of Mühlberg, 1547. Interim of Augsburg, 1548. Peace of Augsburg, 1555. War of Dutch Liberation begins, 1572. Union of Utrecht, 1579. Counter Reformation, 1551–1620. Defenestration of Prague, 1618. Thirty Years War, 1618–48. Wallenstein becomes Imperial C.-in-C., 1625. Dismissed, 1630. Tilly sacks Magdeburg, 1631. Defeated by Swedes at battle of the Breitenfeld, 1631. Wallenstein defeated and Gustavus Adolphus of Sweden killed at battle of Lützen, 1632. Wallenstein murdered, 1634. Peace of Westphalia (*q.v.*), 1648. Repulse of the Turks from Vienna, 1683. War of Spanish Succession (*q.v.*), 1701–14. Treaty of Utrecht, 1713. Treaty of Rastatt, 1714. Pragmatic Sanction guaranteed by Prussia, 1728. War of Austrian Succession, 1740–2. Second Silesian War, 1744–5. Peace of Aix-la-Chapelle (*q.v.*), 1748. Seven Years War (*q.v.*), 1756–63. Napoleon forms Rhenish Confederation, 12 July 1806. Francis II renounces crown of H.R.E., 6 Aug. 1806. *See* AUSTRIA.

Holyrood Abbey and Palace (Edinburgh). Abbey founded, 1128, by David I of Scotland. The palace was built in 1501 by James IV of Scotland; destroyed by English, 1544, but immediately rebuilt; Rizzio murdered at, 1566; burned by Cromwell's troops, 1650; rebuilt by Charles II, 1670–9. The monastery was dissolved at the Reformation, and the chapel became the parish church until James II made it a chapel royal (1687).

Home Guard came into being as a voluntary force, May 1940. Members reached their peak—about two million men in a thousand battalions and A.A. batteries —about June 1943. The force stood down, 1 Nov. 1944, and was disbanded, 31 Dec. 1945. Re-formed, Jan. 1952. Placed on a reserve basis, 1956. All activities suspended, 1957. *See also* VOLKSSTURM.

Home Office. Dept. of state, dates in present form from 1792, but powers much increased after 1914 and again since 1939. Home Secretaries since 1914:

Sir John Simon 1915
Herbert Samuel 1916
Sir George Cave 1916
Edward Shortt 1919
William Bridgeman 1922
Arthur Henderson 1924
Sir William Joynson-Hicks 1924
John Clynes 1929
Sir Herbert Samuel 1931
Sir John Gilmour 1932
Sir John Simon 1935
Sir Samuel Hoare 1937
Sir John Anderson 1939
Herbert Morrison 1940
Sir Donald Somervell 1945
James Chuter Ede 1945
Sir David Maxwell-Fyfe 1951
Gwilym Lloyd-George 1954
R. A. Butler 1957
Henry Brooke 1962
Sir Frank Soskice 1964
Roy Jenkins 1965
James Callaghan 1967
Reginald Maudling 1970
Robert Carr 1972
Roy Jenkins 1974
Merlyn Rees 1976
William Whitelaw 1979
Leon Brittan 1983

Home Rule. *See* IRELAND.

Homestead Act.

1. New Zealand, passed 1885, providing land for emigrants free of charge.

2. Western Australia, similar Act, 1893.

Homestead Act (U.S.A.). Passed by Congress, 1862, by which every U.S. citizen of the age of 21 years was entitled to claim a certain portion of unappropriated land.

Homicide Act. *See* CAPITAL PUNISHMENT.

'Homilies, Book of.' The Convocation of 1542 decided to publish it for the guidance of preachers. First published, 1547; reprinted, 1560. Second book published, 1563.

Homs (Hims), Syria, the Roman city of Emesa, was taken by the Saracens, A.D. 636, and by the Crusaders, 1098. Ibrahim Pasha defeated the Turks at, 1832. *See* FIRST CRUSADE.

Honduras, republic of Central America. Discovered by Columbus, 1502. First settlements, 1524 (Spanish). Independent of Spain, 1821. Independent of the Federation of Central America, 1838. Frequent wars with other states till 1876, and several civil wars, notably in 1883 and 1903. Pan-American Highway completed, 1943. Dispute with El Salvador led to the 'football war', July 1969; settled, 1980. New constitution, 1982. H. providing bases for anti-govt. Nicaraguans from 1982.

Honduras, British. *See* BELIZE.

Hong Kong, China. Occupied by British, 1841. Ceded to Britain at Treaty of Nanking, 1842. Kowloon added, 1860. Chinese Government grant 99-year lease of other mainland areas, 1898. University opened, 1912. Bombed by Japanese, 21 Feb. 1939. Captured by Japanese, 7–25 Dec. 1941. Liberated, 30 Aug. 1945. Considerable influx of refugees from China, from 1950 onwards. Agreement signed in Peking, 19 Dec. 1984, that H. should return to China in 1997.

Honourable Artillery Company (H.A.C.). Founded 1537 in London as a guild for Trained Band instructors. In 1638 some members of it migrated to America and founded the Ancient and H.A.C. of Boston (Mass.).

Hops. First introduced from Netherlands into England *c.* 1525. Prohibited temporarily, 1528, because certain physicians thought them harmful.

Horse Guards, Royal. Present regiment raised by Earl of Oxford in 1661, out of the remains of Cromwell's New Model. Their headquarters, in Whitehall, London, erected, 1758.

Hospitallers, Knights. *See* MALTA, KNIGHTS OF.

Housing and Local Government, Ministry of. Estab. 1951. Absorbed in Ministry of Local Government and Planning, 1969: subsequently in Department of the Environment (*q.v.*).

Hovercraft. First public service began between Rhyl and Wallasey, 20 July 1962. Cross-Channel service, 1966. SRN4, then world's biggest H., launched at Cowes, 4 Feb. 1968.

Hubertusburg, Treaty of, 1763, between Prussia and Austria at end of Seven Years War. By it the Empress Maria Theresa finally ceded Silesia to Frederick the Great.

Hudson Bay Territory or **Prince Rupert's Land,** NW. America. Discovered by Cabot, 1498; revisited and explored by Hudson, 1610; Hudson's Bay Co. formed, 1670; English factories at captured by French, 1685; restored by Peace of Utrecht, 1713; part of territory became British Columbia (*q.v.*), remainder was purchased by Canada, 1858; formal transfer to the Dominion, 19 Nov. 1869. Most of the H.B.T. has formed part of the North-West Territories (*q.v.*) since 1918.

Huguenots. The name originated between 1510 and 1535 at Geneva, when those in favour of an alliance with Freiburg were called *Eidgenossen* ('partakers of an oath'), a popular French adaptation having introduced association with the personal name Hugues. They joined themselves with the Bernese, who had declared for the reformed religion. The name gradually came to be attached to the French Protestants. *See* BARTHOLOMEW, MASSACRE OF ST., and FRANCE.

Hull (Kingston-upon-), England. Chartered by Edward I, 1299. Defences built, 1541. Manor granted, 1552. University college founded, 1927; reconstituted as the University of Hull, 1954.

Human Rights. *See* DECLARATION OF HUMAN RIGHTS.

Humane Society, Royal, founded, 1774.

Humber Bridge, 1981, has (1985) largest single central span (4626 ft) of any suspension bridge in the world.

Humberside, England, administrative co. estab. 1974 under Local Government Act of 1972. Headquarters are at Beverley. H. embraces areas formerly in Lincolnshire and Yorkshire.

Humble Petition and Advice. The second paper constitution of the English Protectorate, 1657. It arranged for future government in the event of the death of Cromwell. The petition collapsed on the dissolution of Parliament by Cromwell in 1658.

Hundred Associates, The. Cardinal Richelieu, in 1627, annulled a charter of the Trading Co. of New France in America belonging to a family of Huguenots, and organized a company known as the H.A., to drive out the Huguenots and colonize the district.

Hundred Years War, 1338–1453. France assists Scotland against England, 1334. All Englishmen in Flanders arrested, 1336. Rebellion of Jacob van Artevelde of Ghent, 1338. Edward III renews claim to the French crown, 1340. Naval battle of Sluys, 1340. English sack Poitiers, win battle of Crécy and Neville's Cross, 1346; capture Calais, 1347. Black Death, 1347–50. Battle of Poitiers, 1356. The *Jacquerie*, 1358. Peace of Brétigny, 8 May 1360. War resumed, 1369. English driven out of most of France by Bertrand de Guesclin, 1369–75. Peasants revolt in England, 1381. Duke of Orléans murdered by Burgundy, 1407. England resumes war again, 1415. Harfleur captured and battle of Agincourt, 1415. Burgundy murdered, 1419. Treaty of Troyes, 1420. Joan of Arc relieves Orléans, May 1429. Dauphin crowned at Rheims, 1430. Joan of Arc burnt, 28 May 1431. Burgundy changes sides at Treaty of Arras, 1435. *Ordonnance sur la Gendarmerie*, 1439. *La Praguerie*, 1439–43. Battle of Formigny, 1450. English driven out except at Calais by 1453.

Hungarian Literature. The following is a list of prominent Hungarian authors:

Ady, Endve, 1871–1915, poet.
Arany, Janos, 1817–82, poet.
Babits, Mihaly, 1883–1941, poet.
Balassi, Balint, 1554–94, poet.
Bessenyei, György, 1747–1811, dramatist.
Csiky, Gregor, 1842–91, dramatist.
Döbrentei, Gabor, 1786–1851, philologist.
Eötvös, Baron József, 1813–71, poet.
Fejer, György, 1766–1852, historian.
Jókai, Maurus, 1825–1904, novelist.
Jozsef, Attila, 1906–37, poet.
Kazinczy, Ferenc, 1759–1831, literary reformer and critic.
Kemény, Baron Zsigmund, 1816–75, novelist.
Kisfaludy, Károly, 1788–1830, poet and dramatist.
Kosztolanyi, Dezsö, 1885–1939, poet.
Miksáth, Kálmán, 1847–1910, novelist.
Molnar, Ferenc, 1878–1952, dramatist.
Petöfi, Sandor, 1823–49, poet.
Szigligeti, Ede (József Szatmáry), 1814–78, dramatist.
Vörösmarty, Mihály, 1800–55, poet and dramatist.

Hungary. The Hungarians or Magyars crossed the Carpathians, A.D. 889. Were driven out of Germany after battle of Unstrut, 933, by Henry the Fowler. Last invasion of Germany defeated by Otto I at the Lech, 955. Converted by King Stephen to Christianity, 1000. Stephen II abdicates, 1131. Invaded by Mongols, 1226. Turkish slave raids begin after their capture of Adrianople, 1361. Defeat of Christian confederacy by Turks at the first battle of Kossovo, 1389, and of crusades at Nicopolis, 1396. Rise of John Hunyadi, 1437. His victory at the Haemus, 1444. Defeated at Varna, 1444. Decisive defeat by Turks at second battle of Kossovo, 1448. Election of Matthias Corvinus to the throne, 1458. Invades Bohemia, 1468. Seizes Vienna, 1485. Conquest of H. at battle of Mohacz, 1526. Treaty of Torok, 1606. Turks repulsed at second siege of Vienna, 1683. Prince Eugene reconquers H., 1683–99. Peace of Carlowitz, 1699. Maria Theresa appeals to the Hungarians against Prussia, 1741. Rebellion against Hapsburg rule, 1848. Defeated by Jellaçic at battle of Schwechat, 30 Oct. 1848. Capitulation of Villagos, 14 Aug. 1849. The *Ausgleich*, Feb. 1867. (For events during the war of 1914–18 *see* WORLD WAR I.) Declared a republic, 1918; succeeded by Bela Kun's Communist dictatorship, Mar. 1919. Rightwing Regency under Horthy, 1920–45. Claimed part of Czechoslovakia and occupied it, Oct. 1938. Joined Anti-Comintern Pact, 2 Feb. 1939. Gained half of Transylvania from Rumania by Vienna Award, 30 Aug. 1940; signed Axis Pact, Nov. 1941: invaded Yugoslavia, Apr.: declared war on Russia, 27 June (*see* WORLD WAR II). Occupied by Russia, 1945: republic, Feb. 1946; People's Republic, 18 Aug. 1949. Cardinal Mindzenty sentenced to life imprisonment for treason: persecution of Catholic Church. In Oct. 1956 an anti-Soviet rising in Budapest; Nagy became premier, 24 Oct. and Mindzenty released. Russian troops crushed uprising, Nov.: Mindzenty took refuge in U.S. embassy and died in Rome, 1975; Nagy took refuge in Yugoslav embassy but subsequently abducted and shot. Thousands of refugees fled to W. Europe and policy of repression followed. From early 1960s there was liberalization and economic progress. Crown of St. Stephen, in U.S. custody since 1945, returned to H., 1978.

Huns. A Turanian group of tribes which invaded Europe in fourth and fifth centuries, and were defeated at battle of Châlons, 451.

Hussars, light cavalry of Hungarian origin, first raised by Matthias I (Corvinus), 1458. For the dates of conversion of British Light Dragoon regiments to H., *see under* REGIMENTS OF THE BRITISH ARMY.

Hussites. The followers of John Hus (*b.c.* 1373) who was burned as a heretic by the Council of Constance, July 1415. Led by Ziska they carried out the 'Defenestration of Neustadt', 1419, and took up arms to prevent Catholic reconquest. Establishment of Tabor, 1420, and the split between the Taborites and the Calixtines. Death of Ziska, 1424. Rise of Procopius the Great, 1425. Victory over Cesarini at battle of Tauss, Aug. 1431. Annihilation of Taborites by Calixtines at battle of Lipan, 1434. Maintained a position of semi-independence until battle of the White Mountain, 1620.

Hyde Park (London). Originally belonging to Westminster Abbey it became crown property, 1536. Opened to public, 1670. Serpentine formed, 1730–3. Underground car park opened, 15 Oct. 1962.

Hyderabad, India. At the conquest of the Deccan by Aurungzebe, 1687, H. became the residence of the governor of the Deccan. By 1748 this official under the title of the Nizam of H. had made himself virtually independent of the Moguls. He ceded the Circars to the French, 1755. Defeated by Marathas at battle of Kurdla, 1795. Accepted permanent British alliance, 1799. Acquired Berar from the Marathas, 1804. Loyal to Britain, 1857; new treaty, 1860. At division of India, 15 Aug. 1947, delayed accession. Indian troops entered the State and set up military government, Sept. On 1 Dec. 1949 the State acceded to the Indian Union. Redrawing of state boundaries in 1956 meant that H. was partitioned between various units, and the Nizam became a private Indian citizen.

Hydro-electric Power. First hydro-electric station in the British Isles begun in 1883, in N. Ireland.

Hydrogen. Discovered by Paracelsus *c.* 1500; experiments by Boyle, 1672; proved to be an element by Cavendish, 1766; presence in water was discovered by Watt and Cavendish, 1781.

Hydrogen Bomb. U.S. Atomic Energy Commission announced on 16 Nov. 1952 that tests involving 'thermonuclear weapons' had taken place on Eniwetok Atoll, Marshall Islands. This was generally taken to mean that explosions felt in the Pacific area 1–4 Nov. had been caused by the detonation of a H.B. Marshal Voroshilov claimed Russia had H.B., Nov. 1953. H.B. first officially detonated by U.S.A. in the Marshall Islands on 1 Mar. 1954. Russia detonated her first H.B. in Sept. 1954. First Chinese H.B. exploded, Oct. 1964. French exploded a H.B., 24 Aug. 1968.

Hypnotism, first investigated in modern times by Paracelsus (1493–1541). Used therapeutically by Mesmer, 1774 (whence *mesmerize*). Brought into disrepute by Cagliostro (1743–95). The word H. was coined by Dr. Braid of Manchester, 1841.

Hythe, one of the original *Cinque Ports* (*q.v.*) under Edward the Confessor (1042–66), lost its maritime importance with the silting up of the River Leman. Its ancient liberties were conferred by King John, 1205. The infantry of Picton's Light Division, which gained distinction in the Peninsular War, was largely trained here *c.* 1809, at which time the Royal Military Canal from H. to Rye was cut. The Small Arms School, as it was first called in 1919, was founded at H. as the School of Musketry, 1853.

I

Ice Hockey. Canada's national sport. Has developed rapidly since the formulation of rules in 1879. Played increasingly in Britain since 1927 and in sev. other European countries since World War II.

Iceland. Discovered by Irishmen at the beginning of ninth century. Colonized by Norwegians *c.* 870–90. (*See* VIKING AGE.) First Parliament (*Althing*), 930. Christianity officially adopted, 1000. Inhabitants acknowledged sovereignty of Norway, 1262–4. United to Denmark with Norway, 1380; at separation of Norway and Denmark in 1814 became part of Denmark. Danish-Icelandic Federal Constitution, making both I. and Denmark independent states under the same sovereign, 1 Dec. 1918. Occupied by British troops, 10 May 1940. As a result of separation from Denmark crown prerogatives assumed by the *Althing*, 16 May 1941. American troops landed, July 1941. Declared a republic and Sveinn Björnsson elected first president, 17 June 1944. Signed North Atlantic Treaty (*q.v.*) 1949, and agreed to U.S. forces being stationed in I., 30 June 1958. Fishing dispute with Britain, 1953–61. I. joined E.F.T.A., Mar. 1970. First woman president, Vigdis Finnbogadottin, elected 1980.

Icelandic Language and Literature. Great period of Old Icelandic literature *c.* 1000–1200. Old I. authors include:

Arnor Jarlaskald, *d.* 1067?, poet.

Egil Skallagrimsson, 900–83, poet.

Einar Jinglescale (Skalaglamm), *fl.* 1130–60, poet.

Eysteinn Asgrimsson, *fl.* 1350.

Halldor Skvaldri, *fl.* 1110.

Hallfred Vandradaskald, *fl.* 995–1000, poet.

Jon Arason, 1484–1551, poet and historian.

Sighvat Thordarson, *fl.* 1015–30, poet.

Snorri Sturluson, 1179–1242, historian.

Sturla Thordarson, 1214–84, poet.

Thorarin Stuttfeldr, *fl.* 1110.

Thord Sigvaldi's Skald, *fl.* 1000–30, poet.

Modern I. letters begin with the Reformation and the introduction of the printing-press, as in the rest of Northern Europe. The last of the Catholic bishops of Holar, Jon Arason (*see above*), may be regarded as also the last of the older poets in the skaldic tradition, and it was he who in 1525 brought the first printing-press to Iceland. It was not used to produce the first vernacular version of the New Testament (which was printed at Copenhagen 1540), but in 1584 this press at Holar printed the first I. edition of the entire Bible.

Iceni revolted under Boudicca, A.D. 61.

'Ich Dien.' Motto of John of Luxemburg, King of Bohemia, found on his helmet after the battle of Crécy, 26 Aug. 1346. Thereupon adopted as the motto of the Prince of Wales by the Black Prince.

Iconoclasts (Gk. 'Image Breakers'). Name given in the eighth century to those who opposed the use of images in the Church. The Emperor Leo the Isaurian issued edicts against images in A.D. 726 and 730. Images allowed in churches, 787. Images restored in the E., 843.

Idaho. State of the U.S.A. Territory formed, 1863; present limits defined, 1868; state admitted to Union, 1890.

Identity Cards (Britain). Issued 30 Sept. 1939 and following days. Abolished, Apr. 1952.

Ido, adapted from Esperanto, 1907.

Iglau, Treaty of, 1436, ended the war of the Emperor Sigismund against Hussites (*q.v.*).

Ijsselmeer. Remnant of Zuider Zee formed by irruption of N. Sea through W. Frisian coastline in thirteenth century. Bill for reclamation became law, 1918. Work begun, 1923. Wieringer Polder completed, 1930; wrecked, 1945; restored, 1946. NE. Polder completed, 1942; E. Flevoland, 1957; Zuidelijk Flevoland, 1967. Whole 'Delta project' completed by 1980.

Illinois, U.S.A. Explored by Jacques Marquette, Jesuit missionary, and Louis Joliet, representing the Government of New France, 1673. By treaty passed to English, 1763, ceded to U.S.A., 1783; admitted into the Union as a state, 3 Dec. 1818.

Illyria (more properly **Illyricum**). Greek colonies on coast, sixth century B.C. Country except Dalmatia annexed by Romans, 168 B.C. Dalmatia also annexed, A.D. 9. At partition of empire fell to Byzantium, 379. The Napoleonic 'Kingdom of I.' formed 1809 and attached to 'Kingdom of Italy'; ceded to Austria, 1814.

'Imitatio Christi' (*The Imitation of Christ*). Generally held to be the work of Thomas à Kempis (*c.* 1379–1471). First printed at Augsburg *c.* 1471. Translated into English at least as early as 1438 (MS. now in Magdalen College, Oxford).

Immaculate Conception. Established as an article of the Roman Catholic faith by the bull *Ineffabilis Deus*, 8 Dec. 1854.

Impeachment. The first recorded exercise of the power was in 1376, when an attack was made on Richard Lyons and Lord Latimer by the 'Good Parliament'. Fell into disuse owing to the more general employment of Acts of Attainder until the I. of Sir Giles Mompesson, 1620. By Act of Settlement, 1701, a royal pardon cannot be pleaded in bar of I. Last I., 1806.

Imperial College of Science and Technology, S. Kensington; part of University of London formed by the fusion in 1907 of the City and Guilds Technical College, Royal College of Science (founded 1881), and the Royal School of Mines (founded 1851).

Imperial Conference of Premiers of Great Britain and Self-Governing Dominions. Resolution of Colonial Conference of 1907 to hold such conferences every four years. First held, 1911. Since 1937 superseded by **Prime Ministers' Meetings** (*q.v.*).

Imperial Defence College. Formed in London, 1927.

Imperial Institute. *See* COMMONWEALTH INSTITUTE.

Imperial War Museum, London. Founded, 1917.

Inauguration Day, U.S.A. 20 Jan., the day on which (at four-year intervals) the newly elected President takes the oath of office.

Incas (Peru). The Inca dynasty was probably established in Peru in A.D. thirteenth century. Tupac Inca Yupanqui conquered Chile *c.* 1450. Huayna Capac conquered Quito *c.* 1490. Accession of Atahualpa, 1525. He massacred many I., 1532. Was seized and murdered by Pizarro, 1533.

Incitement to Disaffection Act, 1934, enables the police, on leave given by a High Court judge, to search the premises of persons suspected of endeavouring to seduce members of H.M. forces from their allegiance.

Income Tax first imposed in Great Britain, 1799, at rate of 2*s.* per £ on incomes over £200. Discontinued during Peace of Amiens, and again in 1815. Reintroduced by Peel in 1842 at 7*d.* in the £. 'Pay-as-you-earn' (P.A.Y.E.) system instituted, 1944.

Income Tax (U.S.A.). First enacted by Congress, 1 July 1862.

Incumbered Estates Act (Ireland). Passed 28 July 1849. First Court of Commissioners sat in Dublin, 24 Oct. 1849.

Indemnity Acts (Britain). Usually passed to relieve servants of the Crown of the consequences of any illegal act done by them in an emergency. Originated, 1715.

Independence Day, 4 July, public holiday in U.S.A. since 1776.

Independent Labour Party. Formed at

Bradford, 1893. Dominated Labour Party (*q.v.*) until 1914. Seceded, 1932, under James Maxton (1885–1946). Last I.L.P. M.P. joined Labour Party, 1948.

Independent Television Authority. Set up under the Television Act of 1954 to provide television services additional to those provided by the British Broadcasting Corporation (*q.v.*).

Independents. *See* CONGREGATIONALISTS; *also* NONCONFORMISTS.

'Index Expurgatorius.' Part of the Prohibitory Roman Index (*see* following entry); a list of books to be expurgated before being sanctioned to be read. First printed, 1601.

'Index Librorum Prohibitorum' (*List of Prohibited Books*). Drawn up by the Council of Trent, submitted for papal approval, and published, 1564; it was revised and brought up to date by the Congregation of the Index, and underwent modifications under Leo XIII. An early list had been previously drawn up by the university of Louvain, and the first Roman Index was issued in 1557 and 1559 under Paul IV. Abolished, 1966.

India. Punjab invaded by Alexander the Great, 327–325 B.C. Rise of Asoka and annexation of Baluchistan from Seleucus Nicator *c.* 250 B.C. Kushan invasions, A.D. 150. Kushan decline *c.* 330. Rise of Guptas under Samudragupta, 340. Conquest of Gujarat from Sassanids by Chandragupta, 400. First Mohammedan raid, 664. I. split into numbers of ·small states till the conquest of the Punjab by Mahmud of Ghazni, 1000–1. Afghans conquered most of the country, 1206–10, and founded the 'Slave Dynasty', which *fl.* till 1250, and declined on Tamerlane's invasion, 1398. Marco Polo visits I. *c.* 1290–3. Formation in S.I. of Vijayanagar, fourteenth century. Vasco da Gama reaches I., 1498. Defeat of Egyptians at Diu by Francisco d'Almeida, 1509. Albuquerque's viceroyalty and establishment of Portuguese trading empire, 1509–15. Baber's invasion, 1525, and establishment of Mogul Empire (1525–50), which reached its peak under Akbar, 1556–1605. Destruction of Vijayanagar at battle of Talikota, 1565. Accession of Jehangir, 1605. Dutch blockade of Goa, 1606. Death of Jehangir and accession of Shah Jehan, 1629. Reign of Aurungzebe, 1659–1707. Invasion of Nadir Shah from Persia, 1739. Rise of Marathas, 1720 onwards. Clive's defence of Arcot, 1751. Cession of Northern Circars to French, 1753. Suraj-ud-Dowlah's capture of Calcutta (*q.v.*), 1756. Seven Years War, 1756–63. Battle of Plassey, 1757. French defeat at battle of Wandewash and Marathas capture Delhi, 1760. First Mysore War, 1767–9. Warren Hastings governor of Bengal (*q.v.*), 1772. Second Mysore War, 1780. Arrival of French fleet under Suffren, 1782. Third Mysore War, 1790. Capture of Pondicherry, 1793. Fourth Mysore War, 1799. Storming of Seringapatam and death of Tipu Sahib, 1799. Treaty of Bassein (*q.v.*), 1802. Maratha Wars, 1802–5. E.I. Co.'s trading monopoly abolished, 1813. Nepal War, 1814. Pindari War, 1817–18. First Burma War, Dec. 1825–Feb. 1826. Measures against Thugs (*q.v.*) and Suttee (*q.v.*), 1829. Mysore rebellion, 1830. First Afghan War, 1837–42. Sind War, 1843. First Sikh War, 1845–6, Annexation of Sattara, 1848. Second Sikh War, 1848–9. Annexation of Punjab, 1849. Second Burma War, 1852. Railway built from Bombay to Thana, 1853. Treaty with Afghanistan, 1855. Persian War, 1856. Indian Mutiny (*q.v.*), 1857. Assumption of Government of I. by the crown, 1858. Queen Victoria proclaimed Empress of I., 1 Jan. 1877.

Frontier War, 1897–8. Mohmand incursions, joined by the Afghans, 1908. Government of I. Bill passed, June 1912, by which the seat of government was transferred from Calcutta to Delhi, and changes were made in the constitution of Bengal and Assam. World War I: Indian Expeditionary Force sent to France, Aug.–Sept. 1914; in action, 28 Oct. 1914, at Neuve-Chapelle; mixed division sent to E. Africa, Sept. 1914; two divisions infantry and one cavalry brigade sent to Egypt,

Oct.–Nov. 1914; Indians co-operate with Japanese at Tsingtau, Nov. 1914; Indians in Mesopotamia from 31 Oct. 1914. Indian National Congress demanded self-government for I., 1917. Delhi and Punjab disturbances and martial law in Punjab, Apr. 1919. Amritsar riots, in which Brig.-Gen. Dyer ordered troops to fire on the mob, 13 Apr. 1919; Indian Legislature established, 1919. Council of State and Legislative Assembly inaugurated, 8 Apr. 1921. Round Table Conference met in London, Oct. 1930; second conference 1931. Gandhi's third civil disobedience campaign began, 1932, and Gandhi twice arrested. He transferred charge of Congress to Nehru, 1935. In 1936 Government of India Bill became law, but was rejected by Congress. Burma and Aden separated from I., 1937. World War II, Sept. 1939: Congress continued opposition to Brit. rule but first Indian troops reached France, Dec. Some Indian troops joined dissident Indian National Liberation Army, 1942–4. Cripps's proposals rejected by Congress, 1942. By 1945 Moslem and Hindu Nationalists irreconcilably divided. 1947: I. given Dominion status and Pakistan (*q.v.*) separated from it; religious massacres and migrations followed. Gandhi assassinated, 30 Jan. 1948; Nehru prime minister, Oct. Revolt in Kashmir, 1948. In 1949 Hindi declared the official language but in practice has not superseded English. I. proclaimed a republic, 26 Jan. 1950. Between 1952 and 1954 all former Fr. settlements in I. transferred to I. At Afro-Asian Conference held at Bandoeng, 1955, I. estab. herself as spokesman for the 'uncommitted nations'. 1956: Acts dividing I. into fourteen states and six centrally administered territories came into force. 1959: Dalai Lama of Tibet (*q.v.*) given political asylum in I, 1961: Indian forces occupied Goa, Dec. In 1962 there was border fighting with China and I. received Brit. and U.S. arms. Attempts to settle Kashmir question led to inconclusive talks between India and Pakistan, 1964–5. Nehru *d.*, May 1964, succeeded by Shastri, who *d.* 1966. He was succeeded by Mrs Indira Gandhi, daughter of Nehru, who continued policy of nonalignment. From 1967 economic crises and government corruption led to discontent culminating in Mrs Gandhi's defeat by Janata coalition, 1977, but this later fell apart. Mrs Gandhi re-elected, 1980, but assassinated by Sikh extremists 31 Oct. 1984. Succeeded by son, Rajiv Gandhi, who won landslide election victory, Dec. 1984.

India, Governors-General (or **Viceroys**) **of**:

Warren Hastings, 1774.
Sir John Macpherson, 1785.
Marquess of Cornwallis, 1786.
Sir John Shore, 1793.
Marquess of Cornwallis, 1796.
Sir Alured Clarke, 1798.
Marquess of Wellesley, 1798.
Marquess of Cornwallis, 1805.
Sir George Barlow, 1805.
Earl of Minto, 1807.
Marquess of Hastings, 1813.
Hon. John Adam, 1 Jan.–1 Aug. 1823.
Lord Amherst, 1823.
Hon. W. Butterworth Bayley, 1828.
Lord William Bentinck, 1828.
Sir Charles Metcalfe, 1835.
Earl of Auckland, 1836.
Earl of Ellenborough, 1842.
Viscount Hardinge, 1844.
Marquess of Dalhousie, 1848.
Earl Canning, 1856.
Earl of Elgin, 1862.
Sir John Lawrence, 1864.
Earl of Mayo, 1869.
Lord Northbrook, 1872.
Earl Lytton, 1876.
Marquess of Ripon, 1880.
Earl of Dufferin, 1884.
Marquess of Lansdowne, 1888.
Earl of Elgin, 1894.
Lord Curzon, 1899.
Earl of Minto, 1905.
Lord Hardinge, 1910.
Lord Chelmsford, 1916.
Earl of Reading, 1921.
Lord Irwin, 1926.
Earl of Willingdon, 1931.
Marquess of Linlithgow, 1936.
Viscount Wavell, 1943.
Earl Mountbatten, 1947.

India, Dominion of, Governors-General of:
Earl Mountbatten, 15 Aug. 1947–21 June 1948.
Mr. Rajagopalachari, 21 June 1948–24 Jan. 1950.

Indian Mutiny. Began at Meerut, 10 May 1857; at Lucknow (*q.v.*), 30 May; Delhi taken, 20 Sept.; rebels defeated at Agra, 10 Oct.; Lucknow relieved, 17 Nov.; Gwalior captured, 19 June 1858.

Indian National Congress. First met, 1885. Combined with the Moslem League in a declaration for Indian Home Rule, 1917.

Indian Territory, former name of Oklahoma (*q.v.*).

Indian Union, Presidents of (Presidents of the Republic of India).
Dr. Rajendra Prasad 1950–1962
Dr. Sarvepalli Radhakrishnan 1962–1967
Dr. Zazir Husain 1967–1969
Varaha Giri 1969–1977
Sanjiva Reddy, 1977–1982
Zail Singh 1982–

Indiana. First settled by French, who had trading posts *c.* 1672. Made part of Canada by Quebec Act, 1774. Passed into American control, 1779. Indian Wars, 1785–95. Territory partitioned from North-Western Territory, 1800. Further partitioning, 1809. Admitted to the Union as state, 1816.

Indo-China. French influence in Tongking and Annam (*q.v.*) dates from the seventeenth century. Cochin-China was invaded by French and British forces, 1861. Annam and Tongking proclaimed a French protectorate, 1884, and finally united to Cambodia, 1887, at the instigation of Jules Ferry (1832–93). The local Vichy Government surrendered to the Japanese, 1941, who ejected them in favour of Viet Nam republican authority, Mar. 1945. Peace between re-established French authorities and Viet Minh lasted 6 Mar.–19 Dec. 1946. French military operation began in Tongking, Oct. 1947. A treaty between the Emperor Bao Dai and the French republic, signed 8 Mar. 1949, theoretically marked the end of the French colonies in I.-C.

and the beginning of Viet Nam 'independent within the French Union'. In Jan. 1950 China and the U.S.S.R. recognized the rival government of Ho Chi Minh. Viet Minh invaded kingdom of Laos, hitherto immune from war, 14 Apr. 1953. France suffered increasing reversals in her fight against the Communists in I.-C., culminating in the final defeat at Dien Bien Phu (*q.v.*) in May 1954. As a result of the Geneva Conference, an armistice ending the I.-C. war was signed there on 21 July 1954, and this marked the end of French authority in the area. *See also* CAMBODIA and VIET NAM.

Indonesia, formerly **Netherlands E. Indies.** Republic of I. proclaimed by Sukarno and Hatta on 17 Aug. 1945, but not recognized by the Dutch, who, except for a brief period during the Napoleonic wars, had controlled the territories concerned since *c.* 1620. Sporadic fighting, interspersed by negotiations, between Dutch and Indonesian nationalists, 1945–50. The United States of I. were officially inaugurated in Aug. 1950. Netherlands-Indonesian Union dissolved, 1954. Bandoeng Conference, Apr. 1955; this established I. as one of the principal 'uncommitted nations'. Under agreement signed between Holland and I., 15 Aug. 1962, W. New Guinea was transferred to Indonesian control on 1 May 1963. I. encouraged the nationalist revolt in Brunei, Dec. 1962, and in 1963 asserted ultimate claim to Australian New Guinea. I. protested against creation of Malaysia, 1963, and began a 'confrontation' against her which lasted until 1966. A coup in 1966 resulted in Sukarno's being deprived of all real power and more moderate policies followed. In Aug. 1966 I. signed a treaty with Malaysia, ending confrontation. Sukarno finally dismissed, 1967 and Suharto took over gov. (Feb.). *See* NEW GUINEA; NETHERLANDS.

Indulgence, Declaration of, allowing liberty of conscience, 1687. A second declaration was issued in 1688. *See* SEVEN BISHOPS.

Indulgences. Commenced in the Roman Catholic Church *c.* A.D. 800 by Pope Leo III. In the twelfth century they were given principally as rewards to the Crusaders. Clement V in 1313 instituted the public sale of I. Leo X's abuse of the issue of I. led amongst other things to the publication of Luther's theses at Wittenberg, 1517.

Industrial Design, Council of. *See* COUNCIL OF INDUSTRIAL DESIGN.

Industrial Revolution, British, took place *c.* 1740–1840. Arnold Toynbee first used the term, 1884.

Infallibility, Papal, defined by Vatican Council, 1870.

Information, Ministry of, formed, Sept. 1909, from publicity department of Foreign Office, largely reduced 1945, and succeeded by:

Information, Central Office of, in Apr. 1946.

Ingolstadt, Germany. Danube diverted to pass it, 1363. University was founded, 1472. City fortified, 1539.

Inland Revenue, Board of, originated in the Commissioners of Stamps, appointed, 1694. Commissioners of Taxes appointed, 1719. Consolidated Board of Stamps and Taxes established, 1834. Commissioners of Excise absorbed, 1849. Excise matters transferred to Customs Board, 1908.

Innsbruck, Tirol (*q.v.*). Became a city, 1232. Taken by Maurice of Saxony, 1552. By Bavarians, 1703. By French and Bavarians, 1805. University founded, 1669.

Inns of Court and Chancery.

Lincoln's Inn moved to present site, 1415, but existed 150 years earlier. To it were attached the following Inns of Chancery: Thavies', 1550–1769; Furnival's, 1406–1890.

Gray's Inn. Established *c.* 1295. Freehold of present site acquired, 1733. Inns of Chancery: Staple, end of fourteenth century; Barnards, *c.* 1440–1894.

Inner Temple. Established by 1326. Freehold of present site acquired, 1609. Inns of Chancery: Cliffords, 1345; Clements, *c.* 1460.

Middle Temple. See INNER TEMPLE. Separate by 1404. Inn of Chancery: New Inn, 1485.

Serjeants' Inn. Fleet Street, 1443–1758. Chancery Lane, 1416–1876.

Only Lincoln's Inn, Gray's, and the Inner and Middle Temple now exist as organizations.

Inquisition or **Holy Office of the Church of Rome.** Was constituted when the imperial rescripts of 1220 and 1224 were adopted into the ecclesiastical criminal law in 1231. The direction of the court was entrusted chiefly to the Dominican Order, 1233, when the bishops of S. France also were instructed by Pope Gregory IX. It operated principally in the Latin countries, and in the Spanish and Portuguese possessions. In Spain it became largely a political instrument wielded by the Spanish kings.

Institute of International Affairs, Royal. *See* CHATHAM HOUSE.

Instrument of Government. Passed by English Parliament, 16 Dec. 1653, constituting Oliver Cromwell Lord Protector of England. It also arranged that parliaments should be triennial.

Insulin for diabetes introduced 1921 by Dr. Banting (1891–1941) of Canada.

Insurance (Great Britain). The earliest record of any life policy being issued was on 15 June 1523, at the 'Office of Insurance within the Royal Exchange'. First fire insurance office opened in London, 1680. The first general I. company was established in 1696 under the name of the 'Amicable Contributionship for the I. of Houses'; it was using 'Hand-in-Hand' as subtitle in 1706, and under that name it lasted till absorbed by the Commercial Union Assurance Co. Ltd., 1905. The oldest *life* I. office was the 'Society of Assurance for Widows and Orphans', started in 1699.

Insurance (U.S.A.). The first I. company was established in Boston, Mass., by the Sun I. Co. (English), 1728. The first fire I. policy was issued in Hartford, Conn., 1794. First accident I. company established at Hartford, Conn., 1863.

Interdict. The most famous are those issued (1) against Poland by Gregory VII after the murder of Bishop Stanislaus, 1080; (2) against Scotland by Alexander III, 1181; (3) against France by Innocent III, 1200; (4) against England under King John by Innocent III, 1208; (5) against England under Henry VIII by Paul III, 1535.

Interim of Augsburg. A system of doctrine issued by the Emperor Charles V, May 1548, attempting to reconcile religious differences.

International.

　First: Developed from I. Working Men's Association formed by Marx and Engels, 1864.

　Second: Held its First World Congress at Paris, July 1889.

　Third: Identical with Comintern (*q.v.*).

　N.B. *The Socialist International* was formed in 1951, being a descendant of the Second International (*see above*).

International Bank for Reconstruction and Development, popularly known as the 'World Bank', established by the Bretton Woods Agreement (*q.v.*) in 1944.

International Justice, Permanent Court of. Established, 1920. Superseded after 1945 by the **International Court of Justice.**

International Labour Office. Established at Geneva in 1919 at same time as League of Nations. In 1946 the I.L.O. became a specialized agency associated with the U.N.

International Monetary Fund. One of the institutions established by the Bretton Woods Agreement (*q.v.*) of 1944. It came into existence in Dec. 1945.

Interpol (International Criminal Police Commission). Established, 1923, in Vienna.

Invalides, Hôtel des (Paris). Established by Louis XIV for wounded soldiers, 1670. Dome built, 1693. Endowed by Napoleon I, 1811. His remains deposited at, 1861.

Invasions of British Isles. From the Norman Conquest, the following are the principal invasions of the British Isles:

William the Conqueror, 1066.
The Scots, 1091.
Robert of Normandy, 1103.
The Scots, 1136.
Empress Maud, 1139.
Ireland, by Fitz-Stephen, 1169.
Ireland, by Edward Bruce, 1315.
Queen Isabel, 1326.
Duke of Lancaster, 1399.
Queen Margaret, 1462.
Earl of Warwick, 1470.
Edward IV, 1471.
Queen Margaret, 1471.
Earl of Richmond, 1485.
Lambert Simnel, 1487.
Perkin Warbeck, 1497.
Ireland, by Spaniards and Italians, 1580.
Ireland, by Spaniards, 1602.
Duke of Monmouth, 1685.
William of Orange, 1688.
Ireland, by James II, 1689.
James Stuart, the Old Pretender, 1708.
Second invasion of Pretender, 1715.
Glenshiel, by Spaniards and Jacobites, 1719.
Charles Edward Stuart, the Young Pretender, 1745.
Wales, by the French, 1797.
Ireland, by the French, 1798.
Channel Islands, by the Germans, 1940.

Inventions Board set up by Admiralty, July 1915, to encourage and co-ordinate scientific effort for naval uses.

Investiture, Lay. The power of a lay sovereign to control the appointment of ecclesiastical dignitaries. Condemned by Gregory VII (Hildebrand), 1075. Urban II forbade ecclesiastics to do homage to any layman even in respect merely of temporalities, 1095. Holy Roman Emperor surrendered his rights of I. at the Concordat of Worms, 1122. *See also* REFORMATION.

Iodine. Discovered by Courtois at Paris, 1811.

Iona, Hii, Y, Icolumcille. Monastery founded by St. Columba (Columcille, 521–97), a native of Donegal, A.D. 563. I. was an episcopal see from the ninth century until 1507, when the title and boundaries were changed to that of 'The Isles' (and later to 'Sodor and Man' the present designation: *see* LORD OF THE ISLES): the see depended on Trondhjem (*q.v.*) from *c.* 1000 to 1263. Since 1938 the I. Community has restored the ancient monastery buildings.

Ionia, narrow strip of land with adjacent is. on the W. coast of Asia Minor. Colonized by Gks. in prehistoric times. Historically, there were 12 Ionian cities, forming a league with its sanctuary on Mt. Mycale.

Ionian Islands, Mediterranean. In 1081 Corfu and Cephalonia were seized by Robert Guiscard. Corfu became Venetian property, 1386. Ceded to France, 1797. Seized by Russia and Turkey, 1799, when they were formed into the republic of the Seven United Islands. Restored to France by Treaty of Tilsit, 1807. After Napoleonic Wars, 5 Nov. 1815, formed into the United States of the I.I. under British protectorate. Incorporated with Greece by treaty, 14 Nov. 1863. *See* CORFU.

Iowa, U.S.A. Territory formed 1838 by partition of Wisconsin Territory and its boundaries reduced to present limits on formation of state, 1846.

Ipswich, England. First charter, 1200.

Iran, formerly **Persia.** Establishment of Achaemenid dynasty when Cyrus defeated Medes at battle of Pasargadae, 550 B.C. Reached their zenith under Darius I, 522–485. Xerxes I was defeated by Greeks at Salamis, 480. The dynasty fell with the conquest of P. by Alexander the Great, 331, and the assassination of Darius III. At Alexander's death, 323, P. was ruled by the Seleucids until conquered by the Arsacid (Parthian) dynasty, 129. Scythian invasions repelled by Mithridates the Great, 123–90. Defeat of Crassus at Carrhae, 53. Phraates IV enters into a treaty of dependency with Rome, 4 B.C. Arsacids overthrown by the Sassanids under Ardashir I, A.D. 226. Unsuccessful wars under Sapor I (240–73) with Rome. Sassanids reach their greatest power under Kavad I, 488–531. Chosroes I, 531–79. Defeat and destruction of Sassanids by Arabs at battles of Kadisiya, 637, and Nehavend, 641. Population converted to Islam, eighth century. P. divided and in confusion until conquered by the Mongols under Hulagu, 1256. Mongol rule continued till

death of Tamerlane, 1404. After civil wars Safavid dynasty seized power, 1499. Defeat of the Uzbegs, 1510. War with Turkey, 1514–55. Zenith of Safavids under Shah Abbas I, 1587–1628. Russian and Turkish invasions, 1722–7. Nadir Shah overthrows Safavids, 1736. Invades India, 1738. Bokhara and Khiva, 1740. Nadir assassinated, 1747. Zand dynasty, 1750–94. Kajar dynasty takes the throne, 1794. Treaty of Tehran with Britain, 1814. Defeated by Russia in war for Georgia, 1812–28. Invasion of Afghanistan, 1837–8. Anglo-Russian agreement fixes spheres of influence in P., 1907. Constitutional revolution, 1909. Last Kajar Shah deposed and succeeded by Reza Shah Pahlavi, 1925. Anglo-Russian action forces Reza to abdicate, 1941, in favour of his son, Mohammed Reza Pahlavi (1919–80). Government troops drive Soviet puppet government from Azerbaijan, 11–13 Dec. 1946; and from Kurdistan, 15 Dec. 1946. Anglo-Iranian Oil Co. nationalized under Mussadeq, 1952; Shah reasserted authority, Sept. 1953 and oil dispute with Britain settled, 1954. P. joined Bagdad Pact (later CENTO, *q.v.*), 1955. Earthquake in W.P. on 1 Sept. 1962 caused 10,000 deaths. Women voted for the first time, 1963. Increasingly grave economic situation and govt. corruption from 1970 led to overthrow of Shah, Jan. 1979, and estab. of hard-line Islamic republic under Ayatollah Khomeini. U.S. hostages held in I., 1979–80. Iraq (*q.v.*) invaded I., Sept. 1980: war still continuing inconclusively, 1985.

Iraq. Conquered from Turkey by British forces, 1914–18. Entrusted to Great Britain as a mandate, 1919, and name officially adopted, 1921, when Feisal became first king of I. British mandate ended, 1932. I.—Mediterranean pipeline inaugurated, Jan. 1935; Bagdad railway completed, July 1940. Pro-Ger. coup crushed by British, Apr. 1941; most British troops withdrawn from I. by 1947. Mass exodus of Iraqi Jews to Israel, 1950–1. In 1958 a left-wing coup, led by Kassem, overthrew the monarchy and the royal family was murdered and a left-wing republic established. In 1959 I. withdrew from the Bagdad Pact (signed in 1955). Anti-Communist coup, and Kassem shot, 1963: subsequent governments followed more moderate policies. Kurdish settlement announced, 1970. I. under Saddam Hussein invaded Iran (*q.v.*), 1980, and alleged to have used poison gas in war, 1983–4.

Ireland. Until the arrival of St. Patrick from Rome in A.D. 432 the history of I. is not at all well documented. The five chief kingdoms of I. in the fifth century were: Ulster, Leinster, Meath, Connaught, and Munster. According to Celtic tradition, Tara was the chief residence of the Irish kings in ancient times, a central monarchy being established here, and 150 monarchs reigned till it was destroyed in 563. In the tenth century the famous Brian Boru brought the country into subjection to his rule; he was killed at Clontarf, where the Scandinavian power in I. was finally destroyed, 1014 (*see* VIKING AGE). After his death various dynasties disputed the overlordship of I. Much-needed church reforms put in hand at Synod of Kells, 1152. When Strongbow invaded I. Roderick O'Connor, High King of I., did homage to Henry II, and at Synod of Cashel Henry enforced papal claims on Irish Church, 1172. I. divided into a series of virtually independent palatinates by the Anglo-Normans. Division of English pale into counties by King John, 1212. Statute of Kilkenny, forbidding inter-marriage of Anglo-Normans and Irish, 1367. Richard II landed with armed force, 1394. Poynings' Law, 1494. Insurrection of Tyrone, 1601. Maguire's rebellion (Ulster Civil War) to expel English, great massacres, 23 Oct. 1641. Oliver Cromwell subdued the whole land with great cruelty, 1649–50. Landing of the deposed James II, 1689. Landing of William III, 14 June 1690. Battle of Boyne, 1690. Treaty of Limerick (*q.v.*), 3 Oct. 1691. Irish Parliament declared independent (*see* GRATTAN'S PARLIAMENT), 1782. Act of

Union, which joined English and Irish Parliaments, 1 Jan. 1801; followed by Robert Emmet's insurrection, 23 July 1803. Act of Catholic Emancipation, 1829. Daniel O'Connell's great agitation for repeal of Act of Union commenced, 1842; trial of O'Connell, 15 Jan. 1844. Irish famine; subsequent decades saw large-scale Irish emigration to the U.S.A., 1846. Disestablishment of Anglican Church in I., 1869. Murder of Lord Frederick Cavendish, chief secretary for I., and T. H. Burke, permanent under-secretary, in Phoenix Park, 6 May 1882. Gladstone's first Home Rule Bill brought and defeated, Mar. 1886; Gladstone's second Home Rule Bill passed by Commons, but thrown out by Lords, 1893. Irish Land Act, Aug. 1907; Irish Universities Act, 1908; Irish Land Act, Dec. 1909. Home rule Bill introduced by Asquith, 11 Apr. 1912; second reading moved by Churchill, 30 Apr., carried by 372 votes to 271 on 9 May; committee stage begun, 11 June; in Ulster there was an anti-Home Rule movement led by Sir Edward Carson, and on 28 Sept. a covenant was signed by Ulster men at Belfast against the Bill; the Bill was twice passed by the Commons and twice rejected by the Lords between 1 Jan. and 14 Aug. 1913. A Home Rule Bill was placed on statute book in 1914, with suspensory clause for duration of World War I. A hopeless rebellion, 'organized' by Sinn Fein ('Ourselves Alone'), broke out, 24 Apr. 1916. Irish Convention met, 25 July 1917; report, Apr. 1918. After the war, Home Rule Act was superseded by Government of Ireland Act, 1920, the greater part of Ulster electing to remain united with Great Britain. The Republicans or Sinn Fein Party rejected the Act, and a state of war between I. and England existed until a peace treaty was signed, 6 Dec. 1921, by which the Irish Free State (*q.v.*), with Arthur Griffith as president, was set up in southern I. British evacuated 1921. Boundary (between Northern and Free State I.) Commission appointed, 1924; its report suppressed and superseded by consent, 1925. *See* IRELAND, NORTHERN; FENIAN ASSOCIATION; IRELAND, LORDS LIEUTENANT OF. For events between 1921 and 1948 *See* IRISH FREE STATE *and* EIRE.

Republic of Ireland, brought into existence by R.o.I. Act, 1948, which came into operation, 18 Apr. 1949. President Kennedy visited I., summer 1963. In Jan. 1965 the premiers of the republic of I. and of N.I. met in Belfast, the first such meeting for 40 years. Relations between the two governments again subject to strain, 1969 onwards, as a result of the disturbances in N. Ireland. Papal visit to I., 1980. Anti-abortion amendment to constitution approved by referendum, 1983. Unsuccessful joint efforts by I. and Britain to solve N.I. problem, 1970–85.

Presidents of Ireland:
Douglas Hyde 1938–45
Sean O'Kelly 1945–59
Eamonn de Valera 1959–73
Erskine Childers 1973–74
Cathal O'Daly 1974–76
Patrick Hillery 1976–

Ireland, Lords Lieutenant and Lords Deputy of:
1172. Hugh de Lacy
1173. Richard, Earl of Pembroke
1176. Raymond le Gros
1177. Prince John
1184. Lord Justices, no Lord Deputy
1189. Hugh de Lacy
1199. Meyler FitzHenry
1203. Hugh de Lacy
1204. Meyler FitzHenry
1205. Hugh de Lacy
1215. Geoffrey de Marisco
1308. Piers Gaveston
1312. Edmund le Botiller
1316. Roger de Mortimer
1320. Thomas Fitzgerald
1321. John de Bermingham
1327. Earl of Kildare
1328. Prior Roger Outlow
1332. Sir John d'Arcy
1337. Sir John de Cherlton
1340. Prior Roger Outlow
1344. Sir Raoul de Ufford
1346. { Sir Roger d'Arcy / Sir John Moriz
1348. Walter de Bermingham

1355. Maurice, Earl of Desmond
1356. Thomas de Rokeby
1357. Almaric de St. Amand
1359. James, Earl of Ormonde
1361. Lionel, Duke of Clarence
1367. Gerald, Earl of Desmond
1369. William de Windsor
1376. { Maurice, Earl of Desmond / James, Earl of Ormonde
1380. Edmund, Earl of March
1385. Robert, Earl of Oxford
1389. Sir John Stanley
1391. James, Earl of Ormonde
1393. Thomas, Duke of Gloucester
1395. Roger de Mortimer
1398. { Reginald Grey / Thomas de Holland } Lord Justices
1398. Sir John Stanley
1401. Thomas, Earl of Lancaster
1413. { Sir John Stanley / Sir John Talbot
1420. James, Earl of Ormonde
1423. Edmund, Earl of March
1425. Sir John Talbot
1427. Sir John Grey
1428. Sir John Sutton
1431. Sir Thomas Stanley
1438. Lionel, Lord de Wells
1446. John, Earl of Shrewsbury
1449. Richard, Duke of York
1461. George, Duke of Clarence
1470. Tiptoft, Earl of Worcester
1472. George, Duke of Clarence (again)
1478. John de la Pole, Earl of Suffolk
1483. Gerald, Earl of Kildare
1484. John de la Pole, Earl of Lincoln
1488. Jasper, Duke of Bedford
1494. Henry, Duke of York (afterwards Henry VIII)
1496. Gerald, Earl of Kildare
1521. Thomas, Earl of Surrey
1529. Henry, Duke of Richmond
1560. Thomas, Earl of Sussex
1599. Robert, Earl of Essex
1603. Charles, Lord Mountjoy
1622. Henry, Visc. Falkland
1629. Thomas, Earl of Strafford
1643. James, Marquess of Ormonde
1647. Philip, Lord Lisle
1649. Oliver Cromwell
1657. Henry Cromwell
1662. James, Duke of Ormonde
1669. John, Lord Robartes
1670. Lord Berkeley of Stratton

1672.	Arthur, Earl of Essex
1677.	James, Duke of Ormonde
1685.	Henry, Earl of Clarendon
1687.	Richard, Earl of Tyrconnel
1692.	Visc. Sydney of Shepey
1695.	Lord Capell of Tewkesbury
1700.	Laurence, Earl of Rochester
1703.	James, Duke of Ormonde
1707.	Thomas, Duke of Pembroke
1709.	Thomas, Earl of Wharton
1710.	Thomas, Duke of Ormonde
1713.	Charles, Duke of Shrewsbury
1717.	Charles, Duke of Bolton
1721.	Charles, Duke of Grafton
1724.	Lord Carteret
1731.	Lionel, Duke of Dorset
1737.	William, Duke of Devonshire
1745.	Earl of Chesterfield
1746.	William, Earl of Harrington
1751.	Lionel, Duke of Dorset
1755.	William, fourth Duke of Devonshire
1756.	John, Duke of Bedford
1761.	George, Earl of Halifax
1763.	Earl of Northumberland
1765.	Earl of Hertford
1767.	George, Visc. Townshend
1772.	Simon, Earl Harcourt
1777.	Earl of Buckinghamshire
1780.	Earl of Carlisle
1782.	{ Duke of Portland / Earl Temple
1783.	Earl of Northington
1784.	Duke of Rutland
1787.	Marquess of Buckingham (the Earl Temple, appointed 1782)
1790.	Earl of Westmorland
1795.	{ Earl Fitzwilliam / Earl Camden
1798.	Marquess Cornwallis
1801.	Earl of Hardwicke
1806.	Duke of Bedford
1807.	Duke of Richmond
1813.	Visc., afterwards Earl, Whitworth
1817.	Earl Talbot
1821.	Marquess of Wellesley
1828.	Marquess of Anglesey
1829.	Duke of Northumberland
1830.	Marquess of Anglesey (again)
1833.	Marquess of Wellesley
1834.	Earl of Haddington
1835.	Visc., afterwards Marquess of, Normanby

1839.	Lord, afterwards Earl, Fortescue
1841.	Earl de Grey
1844.	Lord Heytesbury
1846.	Earl of Bessborough
1847.	Earl of Clarendon
1852.	Earl of Eglinton
1853.	Earl of St. Germans
1855.	Earl of Carlisle
1858.	Earl of Eglinton (again)
1859.	Earl of Carlisle (again)
1864.	Lord Wodehouse (Earl of Kimberley)
1866.	Marquess of Abercorn
1868.	John, Earl Spencer
1874.	James, Duke (formerly Marquess) of Abercorn
1876.	Duke of Marlborough
1880.	Earl Cowper
1882.	John, Earl Spencer
1885.	Henry Herbert, Earl of Carnarvon
1886.	Earl of Aberdeen
1886.	Marquess of Londonderry
1889.	Earl of Zetland
1892.	Lord Houghton (afterwards Earl of Crewe)
1895.	Earl Cadogan
1902.	Earl of Dudley
1905.	Earl of Aberdeen (again)
1915.	Lord, afterwards Visc, Wimborne
1918.	Visc. French of Ypres
1921.	Visc. FitzAlan

Ireland, Northern (*see also* ULSTER).
King George V opened Parliament, 1921. Sir James Craig, later Visc. Craigavon, first Prime Minister of N.I. I.R.A. outrages 1937–9.

1949: Ireland Act (U.K. Parliament) further defined N.I.'s constitutional position: limited I.R.A. activity, 1954–62.

By 1965 relations between N.I. and the Irish republic much improved at government level.

1967–8: Growth of the 'civil rights' movements in N. Ireland and hardening by extremists on both Catholic and Protestant sides. There were disturbances in Londonderry, Oct. 1968.

1969–70: Civil rights agitation grew. Following serious rioting in Aug., 1969, Brit. troops took over responsibility for law and order in N.I. Under legislation of 1973 and 1974 N.I. directly governed from Westminster. Subsequent attempts, 1980 and 1982, to produce a representative N.I. Assembly failed. Since 1969 the I.R.A. and Protestant extremists have pursued a campaign of violence in N.I. and, sporadically by the I.R.A., in mainland Britain.

Irish Free State. (For early history *see* IRELAND.) Civil war, 1921–3. Griffith *d.*, 1922. Michael Collins murdered, 1922. Cosgrave president, 1922. I.F.S. Agreement Act, 1922, enforced Treaty of, 6 Dec. 1921, conferring Dominion status on Ireland. I.F.S. Constitution Act, 1922. First Governor-General, Timothy Healy, 1922. British soldiers attacked at Queenstown, 21 Mar. 1924. Protection adopted, 1924. Fianna Fail Party formed, 1926. Kevin O'Higgins (Minister of Justice) murdered, 10 July 1927. Republicans renounced abstention from Dail and took their seats, 12 Aug. 1927. General Election caused a stalemate, 20 Sept. 1927. Oaths of allegiance to king, and appeals to Privy Council abolished, 1933, by de Valera's administration; Somerville murdered, 24 Mar. 1936. University representation abolished, 12 Dec. 1936. Name changed to 'Eire' (*q.v.*), a 'sovereign independent and democratic state' with directly elected president, 30 Apr. 1937.

Irish National Liberation Army, formed as an extreme splinter group from the Irish Republican Army in the late 1970s. Marxist, and responsible for many murders in N.I. and the U.K.

Irish Republic. Sinn Feiners declared themselves 'the Provisional Government of the I.R.' in 1916. *See* IRELAND.

Irish Republican Army(I.R.A.). Formed in 1920 to fight for complete independence of the whole of Ireland. Active until the end of 1921; and in Northern Ireland and England in 1938 and 1939 in terrorist bombing. Declared illegal by the Government of Eire, 23 June 1939. After World War II the I.R.A. became active again in both N. Ireland and England. There was a minor campaign of violence, 1957–62: but a concentrated campaign of violence and murder has been waged since 1969 in both N. Ireland and the British mainland. I.R.A. (1985) constitutes a breakaway (Provisionals) from the original movement, which took place in the 1960s.

Irish Volunteers. Formed by Sinn Feiners, Sept. 1913, following a famous speech by John Redmond in that year. In Nov. 1915 they joined forces with the Citizen Army, and thereafter planned rebellion against British Government.

Iron Cross. Prussian Order instituted by Frederick William III in 1813 for service in the War of Liberation; revived (by William I), 19 July 1870; again in the war of 1914, and by Hitler in 1939.

Iron Crown of Lombardy, containing a circlet said to have been made from one of the nails of the Cross, *c.* 591. Used by all emperors who were kings of Lombardy, including Napoleon I, crowned at Milan, 26 May 1805.

Iron Curtain. Description, used in Mar. 1946 by Winston Churchill to denote the barrier separating Communist and non-Communist states in Europe, which has passed into popular usage.

Iron Mask, The Man in the. An unknown prisoner of the Bastille, supposed to have been imprisoned, 18 Sept. 1698, and who almost certainly *d.* 19 Nov. 1703.

Iroquois. Name given by the French to one of the great confederations of N. American Indians. The I. reached the height of their power *c.* 1720; they always sided with the English against the French and fought on the English side in the War of Independence.

Isfahan, Ispahan, capital of Persia, A.D. 1587–1800. Masjid-i-Shah (Royal Mosque) built *c.* 1600; Masjid-i-Juma (Friday Mosque) begun, 760; completed eleventh century; rebuilt, seventeenth century; Palace of Forty Pillars remodelled, 1700; Madrasseh-i-Shah Husain, 1710; Maidan-i-Shah (Royal Square) and Chahar Bagh (Four Gardens Avenue) laid out, 1600–23. Sacked by Afghans, 1722, and ceased to be royal residence, 1749.

Islam or **Mohammedanism,** religion founded by Mohammed (571–632). He started preaching between 600 and 610 and fled to Medina, 622. I.'s holiest shrine is at Mecca; between the seventh and sixteenth centuries I. spread across Asia Minor and N. Africa and into W. Europe, and penetrated S.E. Asia. Some revival of militant I. (e.g. in Iran) in 1970s and 1980s.

Ismailis. Moslem sect, founded in the mid eighth century.

Israel. (For history prior to 1948 *see* PALESTINE, ANCIENT *and* PALESTINE, MODERN.) State proclaimed, 14 May 1948. Transjordan Arab Legion reached Old Jerusalem, and Egyptian Army entered Beersheba, 20 May 1948. Armistice, June–Oct. 1948. United Nations mediator Count Folke Bernadotte murdered, 17 Sept. Jews overrun Negeb and destroy Palestinian Arab Army in Galilee, Nov. 1948. King Abdullah makes peace with Israelite Government, Dec. 1948. Truce with Egyptian forces, 7 Jan. 1949. General armistice with Arab League signed at Rhodes, 24 Feb. 1949. Large-scale exodus of Arabs from I., 1949 onwards; equally large influx of Jews from all over the world. Knesset (legislative assembly) first met, 8 Mar. 1949. Chaim Weizmann, first president (*b.* 1874), *d.,* 9 Nov. 1952. Treaty with W. German Federal Republic concluded, 1952. I. invaded Egypt (*q.v.*) and occupied Sinai peninsula and Gaza Strip, Oct. 1956. Anglo-French intervention and arrival of U.N. forces in area followed. Premier Ben Gurion announced capture of Adolf Eichmann, a leading Nazi war criminal, May 1960; he was tried in I., 1961, and executed there, 1962. War broke out between I. and Egypt (with Jordan, Lebanon, Iraq and Syria), 5 June 1967, ending in an overwhelming Israeli victory. Egypt accepted a cease-fire, 8 June, by which time I. had won control of the Sinai peninsula, Gulf of Aqaba, Gaza Strip and Old Jerusalem. The Arab states never accepted these terr. as permanently Israeli but I.'s attitude equivocal, though she insisted she would welcome peace talks. Arab guerrilla resistance to I. increased 1968 onwards. Eshkol *d.* 1969, and succeeded as premier by Mrs. Golda Meir. I. retaliated severely when Arabs attacked her: in Dec. 1968 an attack by Arabs on Israeli airliners at Athens was followed by an Israeli attack on Beirut airport. Egyptian attack repulsed, 1973: cease-fire, 1975: Mrs Meir *d.* 1978; Camp David (*q.v.*) conference, 1978: Peace Treaty signed with Egypt, 26 Mar. 1979: I. to withdraw from Sinai Desert by Apr. 1982. Israeli intervention in Lebanon (*q.v.*) since 1978: partial withdrawal, 1983. Begin resigned as premier, 1983, succeeded by Shamir. Govt. of national unity, 1984.

Presidents of Israel:
Weizmann 1949–52
Ben-Zvi 1952–63
Shazar 1963–8
Katzir 1968–78
Navron 1978–83
Herzog 1983–

Istanbul. *See* CONSTANTINOPLE.

Istria. Conquered from the Illyrians by Rome, 177 B.C.; from the Ostrogoths by Byzantium, A.D. 539. Incorporated in the kingdom of Lombardy by Charlemagne, 788. Under Dukes of Carinthia (*q.v.*), 1173, and Patriarchs of Aquileia, 1209. In the fourteenth century partitioned between Venice and the Hapsburgs. By Treaty of Campo Formio, 1797, the whole peninsula came to Austria, which retained it until 1918 except during Napoleon's 'Illyrian Kingdom' (1805–9), who developed Pola as a naval base. After 1918 the greater part of it was incorporated in Italy. After 1947 most of it went to Yugoslavia.

Italy. (For early history of I. *see* ROME.) Odoacer deposed the last W. emperor, 476. Invasion of I. by Theodoric, King of the Ostrogoths, A.D. 489. Reign of Theodoric, 493–526. Power of Goths overthrown, 553. Lombard invasion under Alboin, 568. Charlemagne's invasion, 774; he was crowned emperor at Rome, 800. Hildebrand (Gregory VII) becomes pope, and the great struggle between Guelph and Ghibelline (*q.v.*)

begins, 1073. During the fourteenth and fifteenth centuries I. was split up between five principal powers (*see under* titles of various duchies, Ferrara, Venice, etc.). Invasion of Charles VIII of France, 1494. Louis XII assumed titles of King of Naples and Duke of Milan, 1499. Treaty between him and Ferdinand of Spain, Ferdinand to have Calabria and Apulia, and Louis the remainder of Neapolitan kingdom, 1501. France and Spain at war in I., 1502. French driven out of I. by Holy League, 1513. Francis I conquered Milan, 1515; lost it, 1521; captured at battle of Pavia, 1525. Emperor Charles V sacked Rome and made Pope prisoner, 1527. After another campaign, Francis renounced Italian claims at the Peace of Cambrai, 1529. Charles took possession of Milan for Spain, 1535, and Naples came to be governed by Spanish viceroys for 200 years. Savoy again independent, 1574. Francis, with allies, warred against Spain in Northern I., 1635–59; Neapolitan revolt under Masaniello, 1647. Austrian predominance assured by end of reign of Louis XIV. Sicily, wrested from Spain, exchanged by Savoy for Sardinia; Duke of Savoy took title King of Sardinia, 1720. Bourbons established in the Two Sicilies (kingdom of Naples), 1734–5; obtained Parma and Piacenza, 1748. Forty-five years of peace ended, 1793. Napoleon Bonaparte entered I., 1796 (*see* BONAPARTE); crowned himself King of I., 1805. By Congress of Vienna, 1815, I. was reorganized, and French rule ended. States of central I. annexed to kingdom of Victor Emmanuel, Mar. 1860. First Italian Parliament met at Turin, Feb. 1861, and Victor Emmanuel proclaimed King of I. Emancipation of I. completed by Victor Emmanuel's triumphal entry into Rome, 2 July 1871. I. joined Germany and Austria in Triple Alliance, 1882; seized Massawah on Red Sea, 1885, and established colony of Eritrea. Set up a protectorate over Somaliland, 1889–92. War with Ethiopia, 1896, and (29 Feb.–1 Mar.) the disaster of Adowa. Assassination of King Umberto, 29 July

1900, by an anarchist. War with Turkey on the question of Tripoli, 29 Sept. 1911, ended by the Treaty of Lausanne, 18 Oct. 1912; Electoral Reform Bill passed, May 1912. Socialist rising in the N. suppressed, June 1914 (*see* WORLD WAR I). Protectorate over Albania (*q.v.*) proclaimed, 20 June 1917. D'Annunzio seized Fiume (*q.v.*), Sept. 1919 (*see* RAPALLO). Fascisti's first success, in suppressing Bologna riots, Nov. 1920. Venice Conference with Austria, 8 Oct. 1922. Fascisti 'march on Rome', 28 Oct. 1922; came into office, 31 Oct. Corfu occupied, 31 Aug. 1923 (*see* JANINA). Vatican established as a sovereign state, 7 June 1929. Fighting with Ethiopia (*q.v.*) began at end of 1934. Sanctions against I. by 50 countries began, 18 Nov. 1935. Chamber of Deputies replaced by National Assembly of Corporations, 23 Mar. 1936.
1937: Adherence to German-Japanese Anti-Comintern Pact (formed 1936), 6 Nov.
1938: D'Annunzio *d.*, 1 Mar.; Mussolini conferred at Munich with Chamberlain and Hitler concerning Czechoslovakia, 29 Sept.
1939: Mussolini spoke in Rome on twentieth anniversary of the Fascist March, reiterating demands on France as to Tunisia, Djibouti, and Suez Canal, 26 Mar.; I. invaded Albania, 7 Apr.; the King of I. accepted the Albanian crown, 13 Apr.; military alliance with Germany signed in Berlin, 22 May.
1940: I. declared war on Allies, 10 June (*see* WORLD WAR II); France accepted armistice terms of Germany and I., 22 June; mutual assistance pact with Germany and Japan (Tripartite Pact), 27 Sept.; ultimatum to and invasion of Greece, 28 Oct.
1941: War declared on Yugoslavia, 6 Apr.; crown of 'independent' Croatia (*q.v.*) offered to House of Savoy, 18 May; Dalmatia annexed, 21 May; war declared on Russia, 22 June.
1943: Mussolini overthrown and succeeded by Badoglio, 25 July; surrender to Allies, 9 Sept.; I. declared war on Germany, 13 Oct.
1945: Mussolini executed by partisans, 28 Apr.

1946: King Victor Emmanuel III abdicates in favour of Prince Umberto, 9 May; referendum, 2 June, led to proclamation of I. as a republic, 11 June, and departure of King Umberto, 13 June;

1947: Peace Treaty signed with Allies at Paris, 10 Feb.; Lateran treaties adopted as part of constitution, July; peace treaty finally ratified, 6 Sept.; Istria ceded to Yugoslavia. I. joined N.A.T.O. in 1949. In 1954 I. and Yugoslavia settled their 9-year dispute over Trieste (*q.v.*); death of de Gasperi, architect of post-war I. I. joined the E.E.C. in 1958. Christian Democrat monopoly of power eroded by economic problems and government corruption from 1960 onwards. Financial scandals involved the Vatican, 1982–3. A new concordat, 1984, resulted in the Catholic Church being no longer the state religion in I., and Vatican lost its territorial rights.

Presidents of Italy:

Einaudi 1948–55

Gronchi 1955–62

Segni 1962–4

Saragat 1964–71

Leone 1971–8

Pertini 1978–

Italian Literature. The following is a list of prominent I. writers:

Alberti, Leone Battista, 1404–72, humanist.

Alfieri, Vittorio, Count, 1749–1803, poet and dramatist.

Amicis. *See* DE AMICIS.

Ammirato, Scipione, 1531–1601, historian.

Angiolieri, Cecco, *c.* 1260–*c.* 1312, poet.

Aretino, Pietro, 1492–1556, dramatist.

Ariosto, Lodovico, 1474–1533, poet and dramatist.

Bandello, Matteo, *c.* 1485–1561, writer of tales.

Baretti, Giuseppe, 1719–89, miscellaneous writer.

Basile, Giovanni Battista (Count of Morone), seventeenth century, writer of tales.

Belli, Giuseppe Gioacchino, 1791–1863, poet.

Bello, Francesco, *c.* 1450–1505, poet.

Bembo, Pietro (Cardinal), 1470–1547, poet and historian.

Bentivoglio, Ercole, 1506–73, poet.

Berni, Francesco, *c.* 1497–1535, poet.

Betti, Ugo, 1892–1953, dramatist.

Boccaccio, Giovanni, 1313–75, writer of tales and poet.

Bruni, Leonardo, 1369–1444, biographer.

Bruno, Giordano, 1548–1600, poet.

Calvino, Italo, 1923–, novelist.

Campanella, Tommaso, 1568–1639, poet.

Carducci, Giosuè, 1836–1907, poet.

Caro, Annibale, 1507–66, poet and translator.

Casa, Giovanni della, 1503–56, poet.

Casanova de Seingault, Giovanni Jacopo, 1725–98, diarist and adventurer.

Castiglione, Baldassare, 1478–1529, author of *The Book of the Courtier.*

Cavalcanti, Guido, *c.* 1250–1300, poet and philosopher.

Cellini, Benvenuto, 1500–71, artist and autobiographer.

Cena, Giovanni, 1870–1917, novelist and poet.

Cinzio. *See* GIRALDI.

Colonna, Vittoria, 1490–1547, poet.

Compagni, Dino, ?–1324, chronicler.

Coppetta, Francesco, 1510–54, poet.

Costanzo, Angelo di, 1507–*c.* 1591, poet and historian.

Croce, Benedetto, 1866–1952, philosopher and critic.

D'Annunzio, Gabriele, 1863–1938, poet and novelist.

Dante Alighieri, 1265–1321, poet.

De Amicis, Edmondo, 1846–1908, novelist, writer of travel books, etc.

Deledda, Grazia, 1875–1936, novelist.

Ficino, Marsilio, 1433–99, humanist.

Filelfo, Francesco, 1398–1481, humanist.

Filicaja, Vincenzo da, 1642–1707, poet.

Folengo, Teofilo ('Merlino Coccaio'), 1491–1544, macaronic poet.

Foscolo, Ugo, 1778–1827, poet.

Ginzburg, Natalia, 1916–, novelist and playwright.

Giraldi, Giovanni Battista (Cinzio), 1504–73, writer of tales.

Goldoni, Carlo, 1707–93, dramatist.
Gregory I, Pope, 540–604, theologian.
Guarini, Giovanni Battista, 1537–
1612, poet and dramatist.
Guicciardini, Francesco, 1483–1540,
historian.
Guidiccioni, Giovanni, 1500–41, poet.
Guinizelli, Guido, *c.* 1230–1306, poet.
Jacopone da Todi, *c.* 1230–76, poet.
Lanzi, Luigi, 1732–1810, art historian.
Latini, Brunetto, 1230–94, poet.
Leopardi, Giacomo, 1798–1837, poet
and philosopher.
Lorenzo de' Medici, 1449–92, poet and
patron of letters.
Machiavelli, Niccolò, 1469–1527,
historian and political writer.
Manzoni, Alessandro, 1785–1873, poet
and novelist.
Marino, Giovanni Battista, 1569–1625,
poet.
Mazzini, Giuseppe, 1808–72, patriotic
writer.
Meli, Giovanni, 1740–1815, poet.
Metastasio (Trapassi), Pietro,
1698–1782, poet and dramatist.
Michelangelo, Buonarotti, 1475–1564,
poet.
Molza, Francesco Maria, 1489–1544,
poet.
Monti, Vincenzo, 1754–1828, poet.
Moravia, Alberto, 1907–, novelist.
Niccolini, Giovanni Battista,
1782–1861, dramatist.
Oriani, Alfredo, 1852–1909, novelist.
Parini, Giuseppe, 1729–99, poet.
Pascoli, Giovanni, 1855–1912, poet.
Pellico, Silvio, 1789–1854, poet and
dramatist.
Petrarca, Francesco (Petrarch),
1304–74, poet.
Pirandello, Luigi, 1867–1936,
dramatist.
Pius II, Pope (Aeneas Sylvius
Piccolomini), 1405–64, humanist.

Poliziano (Angelo Ambrogini),
1454–94, poet and dramatist.
Polo, Marco, 1254–1324, traveller.
Prati, Giovanni, 1815–84, poet.
Pulci, Luigi, 1432–84, poet.
Rossetti, Gabriele, 1783–1854,
translator.
Rucellai, Giovanni, 1475–1525, poet.
Sacchetti, Franco, *c.* 1330–99, writer of
tales.
Sannazaro, Jacopo, 1458–1530, poet.
Sarpi, Pietro (Fra Paolo), 1552–1623,
natural philosopher.
Serao, Matilde, 1856–1927, novelist.
Sforza, Count Carlo, 1873–1952, politi-
cal writer and philosopher.
Silone, Ignazio, 1900–78, novelist.
Stampa, Gaspara, 1523–54, poet.
Straparola, Giovanni Francesco, *d. c.*
1556, story-writer.
Tansillo, Luigi, 1510–68, poet.
Tasso, Bernardo, 1493–1569, poet.
Tasso, Torquato, 1544–95, poet.
Tassoni, Alessandro, 1565–1635, poet.
Testi, Count Fulvio, 1593–1646, poet.
Todi, Jacopone da. *See* JACOPONE DA
TODI.
Tozzi, Federigo, 1883–1920, novelist.
Troya, Carlo, 1784–1858, historian.
Uberti, Fazio degli, *c.* 1310–*c.* 1370,
poet.
Vanini, Lucillo (Giulio Cesare), *c.*
1585–1619, poet.
Vasari, Giorgio, 1511–74, biographer.
Verga, Giovanni, 1840–1922, novelist.
Villani, Giovanni, *c.* 1275–1348,
historian.
Villari, Pasquale, 1827–1917, historian.
Vinci, Leonardo da, 1452–1519, artist,
and writer on painting and natural
philosophy.
Ivory Coast, W. Africa. Territory of Fr.
W. Africa from 1904. Became an inde-
pendent republic. 7 Aug. 1960.

J

Jack the Ripper. Between 1887 and 1889 eight women were murdered and mutilated in the E. end of London by a criminal popularly nicknamed 'J. the R.', who was never caught. A series of murders in the N. of England prior to 1982, eventually leading to the conviction of Peter Sutcliffe, led to the murderer being popularly named 'The Yorkshire Ripper'.

Jacobins. Members of an extremist political club, formed during French Revolution, originally known as *Club Breton*, founded at Versailles, 1789, by members of States-General. Later called J. because of their meetings in a building in the Rue St. Honoré, Paris, which belonged to the Dominican Order. Practically dissolved at the death of Robespierre, 1794; formally closed, 9 Nov. 1794.

Jacobites. Followers of the exiled Stuarts. Name first adopted after revolution of 1688, especially in the Irish war of 1689–90 between Williamites and J.

Insurrection of 1715. An attempt to set James Edward Stuart, son of James II, on the throne after Queen Anne's death, 1714. Earl of Mar (John Erskine, 1675–1732) set up James's standard at Braemar, 6 Sept. 1715. Indecisive battle against the Duke of Argyll at Sheriffmuir, 13 Nov. James landed at Peterhead, 22 Dec., but re-embarked with Mar in Feb. 1716 (O.S. 1715) and left for Avignon, France.

1719: Highland rising began Apr. under George Keith (the last Earl Marshal of Scotland, 1603–1778), but only Mackenzies and Macraes 'came out'. Ended June in drawn battle at Glensheil. Some 300 Spanish troops sent to support the Highlanders laid down their arms.

Rebellion of 1745. Led by Charles Edward Stuart, son of James Edward, who gained victory at Prestonpans, 21 Sept. Reached Derby, 6 Dec. (*see* BLACK FRIDAY). Defeated at Culloden by ('Butcher') Cumberland, 16 Apr. 1746. It led to the abolition of heritable jurisdictions in Scotland, 1746.

Last Jacobite executed (Dr. Archibald Cameron), 7 June 1753.

The last Stuarts: James Francis Edward: 'James III'—*The Old Pretender,* 1688–1766. Charles Edward: 'Charles III'—*The Young Pretender,* 1720–80. Henry Benedict Maria: 'Henry IX'—*Cardinal York,* 1725–1807. James Fitzjames, Duke of Berwick: *Marshal of France and political adviser to the Old Pretender,* 1670–1734.

Jacquerie. A rebellion of French peasants in 1358. Word taken from 'Jacques Bonhomme', the name given by the nobles to the peasants; finally suppressed at battle of Meaux, 9 June 1358.

Jaffa, Israel (Arab., **Yafa**; Gr., **Joppa**). Within the Roman province of Syria from 64 B.C. Captured by Crusaders, 1099. Incorporated as a fief in the kingdom of Jerusalem, 1100. Captured by Saladin, 1187. Recaptured by Crusaders under Richard I, 1190. Sacked by Bibars, 1267. Captured by Napoleon, 1799; and by British, 1917. Centre of Arab nationalism until 1948. Administration united with that of Tel-Aviv in Oct. 1949.

Jaipur, India. The capital was transferred to J. city, newly founded in 1728. J. joined Rajasthan 30 Mar. 1949.

Jakarta, Indonesia. City of NW. Java

founded by the Dutch as **Batavia** in 1619. Headquarters of Dutch E. India Co. Name reverted to J. after 1945.

Jamaica. Discovered by Columbus, 1494; possessed by Spaniards, 1509; British expedition sent out by Cromwell conquered J., 1655; ceded to England by Treaty of Madrid, 1670; earthquake at Kingston, destroying practically whole town, 14 Jan. 1907. Various defence sites leased to U.S.A., Nov. 1940. Member of Caribbean Federation (*q.v.*), 1956; independent within the Commonwealth, 6 Aug. 1962.

Jameson Raid. An invasion of the Transvaal by the forces of the British S. Africa Co., 31 Dec. 1895–2 Jan. 1896. The leader was Dr. Jameson, who was tried in July 1896 under the Foreign Enlistment Act (*q.v.*) and sentenced to imprisonment.

Jamestown, Virginia. Named after James I by English settlers who landed, 13 May 1607.

Janina (Alb.), **Ioannina** (Gr.), or **Yannina** (Turk.), Epirus. Murder of Gen. Tellini and other Italian members of boundary commission in Albania, Aug. 1923. Result was the 'Corfu Incident', Sept. 1923. Siege of, by Greeks in Second Balkan War, 25 Nov. 1912–6 Mar. 1913.

Janissaries. Troops originally recruited exclusively from Christian children for the Ottoman Army. First raised by Sultan Orkhan *c.* 1330. Reorganized by Murad I *c.* 1360. Insurrection of, 14 June 1826, resulted in their destruction.

Jan Mayen Island, Arctic Ocean. Sighted by Hudson, 1607. Said to have been rediscovered by Jan Mayen, 1614. Annexed to Norway, 1929.

Jansenism. Religious movement based on ideas of Cornelius Jansen (1585–1638) in France. His work *Augustinus* (published, 1640) led to the foundation of the Port Royal (*q.v.*) community. It was condemned in 1642, and the controversy led to Pascal's *Provincial Letters,* 1656–7; continual persecution and the practical dissolution of the movement in 1713, though the ideas of the Jansenists con-

tinued to influence French Catholicism into the nineteenth century.

Japan. (Traditional date of the foundation of the Japanese Empire by the Emperor Jimmu, 11 Feb. 660 B.C. This date is, however, discredited.) Japanese missions visit Korea, A.D. 57, 107. War with Korea under the Empress Jingu early third century. Japanese naval defeat by Koreans, 516. Buddhism introduced, 552. Religious and political rivalry of the Soga and Nakatomi clans, 554–93. Issue of the Code of Shōtoku Taishi, 604. First embassy to China, 607. Death of Shōtoku Taishi, 621. Soga overthrown by Nakatomi-no- Kamatori, 645. The Taikwa or Great Reform Edict introduced a new system of Land Tenure, 646. The Taiho edict sets up administration on Chinese model 702. Nobility reorganized on Chinese model, 707.

Nara founded, 710. Fujiwara family in power, 710–59, and from 782 to 1068. Capital moved to Nagaoka, 784. To Heian (Kyoto), 794. Wars against the Ainu in N.J., 782. Ainu subdued, 812. Decline of the Fujiwara with the rise of the Cloistered Emperors, 1087–1156. Taira supremacy, 1156–85. Taira clan overthrown by Minamoto Yoritomo at naval battle of Dannoura, 1185.

Kamakura made capital of the Shogun (*q.v.*) Yoritomo, 1185. Hojo family became regents on behalf of the Minamoto Shoguns, 1205. Defeat of the Mongol invasions, and Mongol fleet destroyed in a storm ('Divine Wind'), 1281. End of the Hojo regency and the destruction of Kamakura, 1333.

Establishment of a Northern Court at Kyoto and a Southern Court at Yoshino and civil war between them, 1336–92. With the settlement of the dynastic dispute power passes to the Shoguns of the Ashikaga family, who move the capital to Muromachi, a suburb of Kyoto, 1392. The Onin Civil War, 1467–77. Total collapse of government and civil war, 1480. Portuguese reach J., *c.* 1542. Order restored by Hobunaga, 1568. Hideyoshi destroys power of western feudatories,

1577. First Christian persecution, 1587.

Yedo founded, 1590. Hideyoshi's unsuccessful invasion of Korea, 1592. Jyeyasu establishes himself by defeat of the Toyotomi clans at Sekigahara, 1600, and by storming Osaka, 1615. 'Law of the Military Houses', 1615. Spaniards expelled, 1624. Shimabara rebellion, 1637. Japanese forbidden to go abroad, 1638. Portuguese expelled, 1638. All other Europeans expelled, 1640, except Dutch, who were confined to Deshima, 1641. Beginning of the Nito School of Historians, 1660. The 'Genroku' period, 1688–1703. Relaxation of edicts against western learning, 1716. Famine and rioting, 1783–6. American Commodore Perry compels the Shogun to conclude commercial treaty, 1854. End of Shogunate, 1867, and rise in real power of the emperor. Feudal system abolished 1871, and westernization begun. By first Treaty of Shimonoseki China cedes Formosa (*see* TAIWAN) and Liaotung, 17 Apr. 1895. By Second Treaty Russia, France, and Germany take Japanese gains except Formosa, 8 May 1895. Anglo-Japanese alliance, 1902. Russo-Japanese War, 8 Feb. 1904. Russian defeat on land at battle of Mukden, 1–9 Mar. 1905. At sea in battle of Tsushima, 27–8 May 1905. Treaty of Portsmouth, 5 Sept. 1905. Annexation of Korea, 1910. On Allied side in World War I. Leaves League of Nations, 1933: Anti-Comintern Pact with Germany, 1936. The Peking Incident, 7 July 1937 (for war with China, see CHINA). J. joins the Axis, 27 Sept. 1940. 1941–5 see WORLD WAR ii. 1945: Atomic bombs dropped on Hiroshima and Nagasaki, Aug. 6 and 9; J. surrenders unconditionally, 14 Aug. New constitution in force, 1947 and elections held: 'democratized' on W. lines. Peace treaty signed between J. and representatives of 48 countries, 8 Sept. 1951; Security Treaty with U.S.A. ratified, 26 Oct. J. joins U.N., 1956. 1960: J.-U.S. Mutual Security Treaty; from 1960 increasing Japanese prosperity and penetration of traditional W. markets. 1971: Okinawa Reversion Treaty.

Jarrow, County Durham. The Venerable Bede was associated with the Benedictine abbey founded here, 682, by Benedict Biscop (628–90). March of unemployed from J. to London, 1936.

Jassy (Rum. **Iasi**) was a centre of Greek as well as Vlach culture, and capital of Moldavia, in the sixteenth century. Here Alexander Ypsilanti (1792–1828) proclaimed the independence of Greece, 1821, but his forces were defeated by the Turks, and he fled into exile.

Java, Indonesia. Dutch rule began, 1619. Occupied by British, 1811. Regained by Dutch, 1816. Conquered by Japan, Feb.–Mar. 1942. Became part of the republic of Indonesia, 1950. *See* INDONESIA.

Jedburgh, Scotland. Abbey founded by David, I, 1118–47. Burned by English, 1544–5.

Jena, Germany. First documentary mention of, A.D. 863. Granted municipal rights in thirteenth century. Came into hands of the Saxon Wettin dynasty, 1331, and was an independent dynasty known as Saxe-Jena, 1672–90. Came by inheritance to the principality of Saxe-Weimar, 1741, whose ruler, Karl August (-reigned 1775–1828), was a great patron of the arts and of J. University (founded 1558). Battle of J., between Napoleon I and the Prussians, 14 Oct. 1806.

Jenkins's Ear (War of). Robert Jenkins, master of the brig *Rebecca*, had his ship boarded off Havana, 9 Apr. 1731, by Spanish coastguards, who, Jenkins alleged, cut off the ear in question. He complained to his own Government with no result, but in 1738 was called to the bar of the House of Commons, where he repeated his story, which was used as a *casus belli* for the war of 1739–42. Jenkins *d.* 1745.

Jericho. The walls traditionally destroyed by Joshua were excavated *c.* 1900, and in 1920 and 1930, and would appear to have been continuously occupied from 2000 to 1600 B.C., the outer works dating from *c.* 1800 B.C. Further investigations since World

War II have shown that J. probably existed as early as 7000 B.C.

Jersey. United to the English crown, 1066. Occupied by Germans, June 1940–9 May 1945. British military government lasted, 12 May–25 June 1945. Legislative reforms, 1948. See CHANNEL ISLANDS.

Jerusalem (Arab. **al Qds**, colloquially 'Udes). Letters signed by the ruler of 'Urusalim', and written c. 1375 B.C., are extant. Taken by David c. 1050 B.C. Hezekiah repels Assyrian siege, 701. Destroyed by Nebuchadnezzar, 586. Rebuilt by Nehemiah, 445. Taken by Alexander the Great, 332. Temple destroyed by Antiochus Epiphanes, 168. Rebuilt by Maccabees c. 150. J. taken by Pompey, 65. Temple plundered by Crassus, 54. Rebuilt by Herod, 35–34. Sacked by Titus, A.D. 70. Captured by Arabs, 637. Occupied by Crusaders, 1099–1244 (see CRUSADES). Captured from Turks by Allenby, 1917. British evacuate, 1948. During the Israeli-Arab War of 1948–9, Jordan forces occupied the Old City and Israeli forces the New, which the Knesset proclaimed as the capital of Israel, 23 Jan. 1950. In the 'June War' of 1967, Israel conquered and occupied the Old City, which she has subsequently retained.

Jervaulx Abbey (Yorks). Founded 1156. Last Abbot hanged, 1537.

Jesuits (Society of Jesus). Founded, 1534, by Ignatius Loyola (1491–1556). Constitutions approved by papal bull, 1540. First colleges in Portugal, 1542; France (at Billom), 1545; Paris, 1550. Expelled from France, 1594. Restored, 1603. Again expelled, 1764; again restored, 1814. Again expelled, 1880. Expelled from England, 1579, 1581, 1586, 1602, 1829. Suppressed by Pope Clement XIV, 1773. Restored by Pius VII, first in Russia, 1801, then in the Two Sicilies, 1804; completely, 1814. Today permitted establishments in most non-Communist countries.

Jet Propulsion. Basic principles first stated by the French engineer, René Lorin, 1913. In 1930 Sir Frank Whittle, then a R.A.F. cadet, began work on gas turbines, which received official sup-

port from the Air Ministry, 1937. His first J.P. aircraft flew, 14 May 1941. Independent experiments started by the German, Heinkel, 1939, and the J.P. Heinkel 53B was flown on 27 Aug. that year.

Jew, the Wandering. First mentioned in the Chronicle of St. Alban's Abbey, 1228.

Jews in England. Mentioned in ecclesiastical documents as early as A.D. 740. Came to England in large numbers after the Norman Conquest (1066). Riots against them in 1189 at coronation of Richard I. Driven from England by Edward I, 1290; but from 1580 to 1640 Portugal was conquered by and annexed to Spain, and a great many Jewish refugees from Portugal, some of them marranos—i.e. descendants of persons who had pretended to embrace Christianity in face of persecution by the Spanish and Portuguese authorities, 1480–98—were engaged in clandestine trade with Portugal encouraged by the English Government. Many of them were settled in Bristol and London between 1590 and 1600. This *fait accompli* was acknowledged, and J. officially readmitted by Cromwell, 1656. Bill passed to naturalize J., 1753, repealed, 1754. Allowed to obtain freedom of City of London, 1832. Act to relieve J. elected to municipal offices from taking oaths, 1845; extended when they were admitted to Parliament, 1858. Universities Tests Act, 1871, enabled J. to graduate at the universities. First admitted to House of Lords, 1885. Considerable influx of J. to Britain from E. Europe, 1880–1910; from Nazi Germany, 1933–8.

Jibuti, See DJIBOUTI.

Johannesburg, Transvaal. Founded, 1886, and probably named after Johannes Meyer, the Mining Commissioner of that time. Jameson Raid (*q.v.*) organized at, 1895. Made into a city, 1928.

John Bull. Personification of the English nation. Name and character first popularized in 1712 by John Arbuthnot, an anti-Whig pamphleteer.

Johns Hopkins University. Founded by

a gift from Johns Hopkins, of Baltimore, made 1867. Opened, 1876. The present buildings are on a site outside Baltimore, Maryland, U.S.A., presented by the city in 1902.

Johore, former Unfederated Malay State, entered into treaty relations with Britain, 1885. Became a member state of the Malay Federation, 1948; of Malaysia, 1963.

Joinville, Treaty of, 1584, between Philip II of Spain and Henry of Guise.

Jordan (formerly **Transjordan**). Conquered by Moslem armies, 637. Hashimite Kingdom established when, after the expulsion of the Emir Feisal from Syria (1920), his brother, Sharif Abdullah, was dissuaded from invading Syria again (which he threatened to do, Apr. 1921) by being recognized as emir of the territory E. of J., between Es Salt and Ma'an. An independent, though mandated, state, proclaimed by the British, 1923. Boundary with Nejd province of Saudi Arabia fixed by Treaty of Hadda, 1925.
Britain recognized total independence by treaty of 22 Mar. 1946. Name changed to J. officially, 17 June 1946. In the war with Israel, 1948, J. conquered *c.* 2,000 square miles of Arab Palestine, and subsequently annexed this, Apr. 1950. King Abdullah murdered, 20 July 1951 grandson Hussein enthroned, 1953. All British military and air bases handed back to J. by May 1957. The kings of J. and Iraq (*q.v.*) united their kingdoms in the 'Arab Federation', 14 Feb. 1958; this lapsed after 14 July 1958, and was officially dissolved, 1 Aug. 1958. J. joined the 'June War', 1967, on side of Egypt but her forces were pushed back from the Old City of Jerusalem and the l.b. of the Jordan. Arab guerrillas made J. their base, 1968 onwards and constituted a 'state within a state'. Hussein's army launched an attack against them, 1970, and Arab guerrilla activity subsequently based in Lebanon (*q.v.*).

Juan Fernandez Island, Pacific. Discovered in sixteenth century by Juan Fernandez. The famous Alexander Selkirk lived here, 1704–9. Occupied by Spain, 1750, and passed to Chile in 1810.

Judicature Acts passed 1873, 1875, and 1925. The Act of 1925 consolidated Acts, 1873–1910, and has been considerably amended by the Administration of Justice Acts, 1928 and 1973. *See* COURTS, ENGLISH.

Judiciary of the U.S.A. Supreme Court organized, 1789; Court of Claims established, 1855; Circuit Court of Appeals established, 1891. Women admitted to practise in the Supreme Court, 15 Feb. 1879.

Jülich. Occupied in Roman times, the medieval city was chartered in the thirteenth century, ruled from 1336 by margraves, and from 1386 by dukes; captured by Maurice of Orange, 1610, during the J.-Cleves succession dispute (1609–14). Became part of Prussia, 1814, having been included in the French Empire since 1801. *See* CLEVES.

'June War' (1967). Fought between Israel, on the one hand, and Egypt, Lebanon, Jordan, Syria and Iraq on the other. Began, 5 June: Israel made immediate and sweeping military gains and Egypt and her allies agreed to a cease-fire, 8 June. Israel had gained control of Old Jerusalem, the Gulf of Aqaba, the Gaza Strip, and the Sinai peninsula.

'Junius, Letters of.' A series of seventy political letters signed 'Junius', which appeared in the *Public Advertiser* between 21 Jan. 1769 and 21 Jan. 1772. The printer and publisher, H. S. Woodfall, was prosecuted in Dec. 1769 for a certain letter which appeared against King George III, but acquitted. Sir Philip Francis (1740–1818) reputed to have been the author. Claims have also been made for the authorship of Burke, Wilkes, Horace Walpole, etc.

Jury, Trial by. Use of juries first appears in compilation of Domesday Book (*q.v.*), 1085–6. Established as a method of trial by Henry II, 1154–89, in civil cases. In criminal cases, *c.* 1215, as a result of abolition of trial by ordeal. Introduced by Act of Parliament for civil cases in Scotland, 1815. Grand Juries abolished for most purposes,

1933; totally, 1948. Majority verdicts permissible under Criminal Justice Act, 1967.

Justice of the Peace. Knights to keep the peace appointed by royal proclamation in England, 1195. *Custodes Pacis* appointed by Simon de Montfort, 1262–4. Regular provision for their appointment made by an Act of 1327. Known as J.P.s since 1362. Commissions of the Peace finally settled, 1590. Women have been eligible to become J.P.s since 1919. Justices of the Peace Act, 1949, imposed an age limit on J.P.s. Justices of the Peace Act, 1968, and Administration of Justice Act, 1973, imposed further conditions on J.P.s.

Justice, Royal Courts of. From the Norman Conquest to 1873, situated at Westminster Hall. Then reorganized and transferred to the present building in the Strand.

'Justification', The, of William of Orange. In 1567 the Council in Spain declared William (the Silent) of Orange an outlaw if he did not surrender himself for trial. William's reply was his 'J.', published in 1568, and sent to all the courts of Europe.

Justinian's Legislation. The following are the principal legal works issued at J.'s orders:
Codex Vetus, 529.
The Fifty Decisions, 529–31.
The Digest or Pandects, 533.
The Institutes, 533.
Codex Repetitae Praelectionis supersedes the Codex Vetus, 534.
The Novels, 534–65.

Jutland. N. Slesvig ceded to Prussia, 1864, but returned to Denmark after a plebiscite, 1920.

Juvenile Offenders Acts. Act for instituting a prison for the correction of J.O., 1838. Act for committal to reformatories, 1854. J.O. Act. 1901. By the Act of 1908, separate courts set apart for trial of children. Children and Young Persons Act of 1933 provided for less formal court procedure. Criminal Justice Acts of 1948, 1961, 1972 and 1983 made various changes in the procedures for dealing with delinquent juveniles.

K

K-2, Himalayas, otherwise known as Mount Godwin-Austen. First climbed, 31 July 1954, by an Italian expedition.

Ka'aba (Mecca). Present building erected, 1626, but so as to preserve the essential features of the original building and some part of the fabric of the mosque which the Caliph Mahdi left unfinished at his death (A.D. 785). The holy black stone 'cube' built into the wall of the pre-Islamic shrine was carried off by raiders, A.D. 930, but restored, A.D. 952.

Kabul, Afghanistan (q.v.). Captured by Tamerlane, 1394; by Nadir Shah, 1702. Made capital of Afghanistan, 1774.

Kaffir Wars with British: 1779–81, 1789–93, 1799–1802, 1811–12, 1817–19, 1834–5, 1846–8, 1850–3.

Kaffraria, S. Africa. British colony from 1847 till 1865, when it was joined to Cape Colony.

Kaleidoscope. Invented, 1817, by Sir David Brewster.

Kaliningrad, U.S.S.R. Founded as Koenigsberg by Teutonic Knights c. 1255. First came into possession of Brandenburg-Prussia, 1618 (see PRUSSIA). Annexed by U.S.S.R, and name changed to K., 1945.

Kalmar, Union of, June 1397. Norway, Sweden, and Denmark united dynastically by Queen Margaret of Denmark under a Danish dynasty. Sweden (q.v.) seceded from the Union when Gustavus Vasa was elected king of Sweden at the Diet of Strängnäs, 6 June 1523. See KIEL, TREATY OF.

Kamchatka. Discovered by Cossacks, A.D. 1690; in Russian possession, 1697; visited by Bering, 1728; unsuccessful attempt made on fort of Petropavlovsk by combined British and French fleets, 1854.

Kampala, Uganda. British flag hoisted at K. fort, 1 Apr. 1893. Capital of Uganda (q.v.) since 1962.

Kampuchea, formerly the **Khmer Republic,** originally **Cambodia** (q.v.) estab. 8 Jan. 1979 with Vietnamese backing after the defeat of the Khmer Rouge. Civil war has since continued between factions variously backed by Thailand and Vietnam (qq.v.).

Kandahar, Afghanistan. Capital of Afghanistan, 1747–74. Held by British from 1839 until 1842; finally evacuated by British, Apr. 1881. See AFGHANISTAN.

Kanpur, formerly **Cawnpore,** India, formally possessed by Britain, 1801. Besieged by Nana Sahib, 1857: massacre of women and children by mutineers, 6 June 1857.

Kansas, state of the U.S.A. The greater part of the territory was acquired by the Louisiana Purchase, 1803; more territory taken over from Mexico, 1850. The K.-Nebraska Act, 1854, regulated the boundaries of these two states, allowed local option in the slavery question. Admitted to the Union, 1861.

Kappel, Switzerland. First Peace of, between the Forest Cantons and the Zwinglian Party, June 1529; second Peace of, 11 Oct. 1531, after Zwingli had been killed in battle there.

Karachi, Pakistan. Founded, 1843. Became capital of Pakistan (q.v.), 1947.

Karelo-Finnish S.S.R. (Fenno-Carelia or Soviet Karelia) occupies the area of the White Sea, and is populated chiefly by Finns. Known under the tsars as Olonets Province it became the Karelian Autonomous Soviet Socialist Republic, July 1923. The present designation and constitutional status were assumed, 31 Mar. 1940, when all territory ceded by Finland (*q.v.*) to the U.S.S.R. was included. But in 1946 the areas containing Vyborg (*see under* VYBORG) and Käkisalmi were transferred to the Russian R.S.F.S.R.

Karen Rebellion, 1947. *See* BURMA.

Kariba Hydro-electric Scheme. Building of the dam begun, 6 Nov. 1956; opened by Queen Elizabeth the Queen Mother, 17 May 1960.

Karl-Marx-Stadt, town in Upper Saxony. Formerly called **Chemnitz**, it was renamed K.-M.-S., with effect from 1 May 1953.

Karlsbad Decrees, 1819. Issued against liberalism in Germany at Congress of K. at the instance of Metternich.

Kashmir, India. Part of Mogul Empire, 1587: became part of Sikh monarchy, 1819 and Jammu dynasty of Gulab Singh established by British influence, 1846. Hindu maharajah acceded to India, 1947, and Moslem uprising followed. In 1949 K. was partitioned between India and Pakistan, the Indian section forming state of K. and Jammu. Dispute concerning final disposition of K. between India and Pakistan still unresolved, 1985.

Kassel, Germany. *See* CASSEL.

Katanga, richest state in Zaïre (*q.v.*). It declared itself independent of the central government, 11 July 1960. U.N. stated that K.'s secession was at an end, and attempted to terminate it by force in Sept. and Dec. K. eventually reintegrated into Zaïre, Jan. 1963.

Katrine, Loch, Scotland, has supplied Glasgow with water since 1859.

Kazakhstan Republic, created 1920. Became a constituent republic of the U.S.S.R., 1936. Its territory formerly was included in Siberia and Russian Turkestan (*q.v.*). Kazaks not reconciled to this regime emigrated to Sinkiang (*q.v.*), Kansu, and Chinguin in western China. In 1950 they fled again into Tibet, ultimately reaching Kashmir. In 1952 those who did not wish to settle in Kashmir accepted the offer of the Turkish Government to let them settle permanently in Turkey.

Kazan, Russia. Captured by Russians,

1552, from Tatars who founded it, mid thirteenth century, and made it their capital, 1445. Destroyed during the Cossack mutiny of Pugachev, 1774, and rebuilt by Catherine II. Capital of Tatar Soviet Republic since 1920.

Kedah, former Unfederated Malay State. The ruling house converted to Islam *c.* 1500. Known since 1516 to the Portuguese, who attacked it, 1611. English traders dealt with K. merchants in the seventeenth century, but the Dutch obtained a concession, 1641, and drove out the English company, 1683. By Treaty of 1791 the government of K. was subsidized by the E. India Co. The country was partitioned by the Siamese, who conquered it, 1821. By treaty between Siam and Britain, 1909, the whole territory, except Setul, was transferred to British suzerainty. K. adhered to the Malay Union, 1946, the Malay Federation, 1948, and has been part of Malaysia (*q.v.*) since Sept. 1963.

Keele, University of. Formerly the University College of N. Staffordshire. Granted charter, 1962.

Keeling Islands. *See* COCOS ISLANDS.

Kelantan, former Unfederated Malay State. Conquered by Mahmud, last Sultan of Malacca, who reigned, 1488–1511. Became temporarily independent under a prince from Johore at end of sixteenth century. Adhered to Malay Union, 1946, Malay Federation, 1948, and part of Malaysia since 1963.

Kellogg Pact. For 'outlawry of war'. Signed by representatives of fifteen nations, 27 Aug. 1928; called after its negotiator, Frank B. Kellogg (1856–1937), U.S. ambassador in London, 1923–5. Eventually fifty-nine nations signed it; but it had little practical effect on international politics.

Kenilworth (England). Castle founded by Geoffrey de Clinton *c.* 1120. Given by Queen Elizabeth to the Earl of Leicester, 1563.

Kenilworth, Dictum or **Ban of,** 31 Oct. 1266, enacted that all who took up arms against the king should pay the value of their lands for five years.

Kensington. Holland House, built 1608–10. Serpentine formed, 1733. K.

Gardens generally opened to the public, early nineteenth century. Victoria and Albert Museum established, 1857. Natural History Museum, 1881. Science Museum organized, 1909. Commonwealth Institute's new buildings opened at, Nov. 1962.

Kensington Palace. Originally Nottingham House. Bought by William III from the second Earl of Nottingham, 1689. Queen Victoria b. at, 1819. London Museum opened at, 1951. Princess Margaret in residence there since 1960.

Kent, Kingdom of. The arrival of Hengest and Horsa in K. as *foederati* in the service of the British king Vortigern is said by the early chroniclers to have taken place during the reigns of Martian and Valentinian III, Roman emperors of the E. and W., and is thus dated between 449 and 455. The laws of Ethelberht, written down late in the sixth century, show a social organization and system of land tenure different from that of other Old English kingdoms. The kingdom of K. was co-terminous with the modern county. Christianity estab., 597. Between 673 and 685 a second code of law, which survives, was issued by King Hlothere, in whose reign there were two destructive invasions, one by the Mercians c. 675, and one by the W. Saxons under Caedwalla and his brother Mull, beginning in 685. After c. 780 K. ceased to have any real independence, and if native kings ruled they did so only as the clients first of Mercia, then (after 825) of Wessex.

Rulers of, c. 449–860:
Hengest *fl*. 449–*d*. 488
Oisc ?
Octa ?
Eormenric ?
Ethelberht I *c*. 560–616
Eadbald 616–640
Eorcenberht 640–664
Egbert I 664–673
Hlothere 673–685
Eadric 684–686
State of anarchy 686–694
Wihtred 694–725
Eadberht 725–748
Ethelberht II 748–762

Kent divided among several kings, subject to Mercia 762–798
Cuthred of Mercia 798–805
Baldred (*probably subject to Mercia*) 805–823
Ethelwulf of Wessex 825–839
Athelstan of Wessex 839–*c*. 840
Ethelwulf of Wessex (*again*) 856–858
Ethelberht of Wessex 858–860

Kent, University of. Established at Canterbury, 1965.

Kentish Petition, The. Drawn up by William Colepeper, chairman of the Quarter Sessions at Maidstone, 1701, against the peace policy of the Tory Party.

Kentucky, U.S.A., was originally part of Virginia, and its early history is closely connected with that of W. Virginia and Tennessee (*q.v.*). Settlement made by Daniel Boone, 1775. Admitted to the Union, 1792.

Kenya. Prospected in 1880 by the Imperial E. Africa Co., which was chartered, 1885. Protectorate over coastal area leased from Sultan of Zanzibar (*q.v.*) set up under name of British E. Africa, 1895. Came under Colonial Office administration, 1905. United with Zanzibar Protectorate, renamed K., and made a colony, 1920. Northern boundary agreement with Ethiopia, 1947. Mau-Mau (*q.v.*) disturbances among Kikuyu tribe lasted 1952–7. Internal self-government, June 1963; full independence, Dec. K. became a republic, Dec. 1964, with Kenyatta, former Mau-Mau leader, as first president.

Kerch (anct. **Panticapaeum**), town in the E. Crimea. Founded by Greeks, sixth century B.C. Capital of the Bospor Kingdom, from the fifth century B.C. to the fourth century A.D.; then Byzantine, Tatar, and Turkish. Russian since 1774. Destroyed during Crimean War and 1941–3.

Kerguelen Islands, Indian Ocean. Discovered by Kerguélen-Trémarée (1745–97), 1772; annexed by France, 1893, but occupation only effective since 1949.

Ket's Rebellion. Instigated by Robert Ket, a Norfolk tanner, in July 1549. The rioters met at Norwich, but were soon disbanded. Ket, defeated at Dussindale, 26 Aug., was executed, 7 Dec. 1549.

Kew, Surrey, England. Royal Botanic Gardens founded, 1759; open to the public since 1840.

Keys, House of. *See* TYNWALD.

K.G.B. (Russian abbreviation for **Committee of State Security**). Name of Soviet security service since 1953.

Khalifa. Title taken by Abd'allah at Taashi, the successor of the Mahdi. He was defeated by Kitchener at Omdurman, 1898, and killed at Om Debrikah, 1899.

Khartoum, Sudan. Founded *c.* 1822 by Mehemet Ali; defended against the Mahdi, 1884–5, by Gen. Gordon, who was killed there, 26 Jan. 1885; after the battle of Omdurman, 2 Sept. 1898, K. was recovered from the Khalifa (*q.v.*).

Khedive, Persian word meaning prince, conferred as an hereditary title by the Turkish sultan on the rulers of Egypt (*q.v.*), 1867, and borne by them till 1914.

Khyber Pass, Afghanistan. Twice crossed by British Army during first Afghan War, 1841, 1842, and again in the second Afghan War, Nov. 1878. The Treaty of Gandamak, 1879, stipulated that the pass should be fully controlled by the British authorities, and these rights were acquired by Pakistan, 1947.

Kiakhta, Treaty of. Between China, Russia, and Outer Mongolia, for settlement of boundaries, 1915.

Kiaochow, now usually known as **Tsingtao.** Seized by Germans, 1897; ceded to Japan, 1919; restored to China, 1922, and again in 1945.

Kiel, founded, 1240; chartered, 1242; joined Hansa, 1248. Naval base developed *c.* 1890–1914 and 1934–9. Heavily bombed by the British, 1941–4.

Kiel Canal. Completed in July 1914.

Kiel, Treaty of, ceding Norway to Sweden, between Great Britain, Sweden, and Denmark, 14 Jan. 1814.

Kiev, Ukraine. According to the *Chronicle of Nestor* was founded by the Slav brothers, Kiy, Shchek, and Khoriv, 864, but seized by the Rus (Swedes), Askold

and Dir, same year (*see* VIKING AGE.) Capital of Russian Varangian principality by A.D. 880. Became centre of Russian Christianity after baptism of Vladimir, 988. Said to have had four hundred churches and eight markets by Thietmar, Bishop of Merseburg (975–1018). Captured by Andrei Bogolyubski, 1169. Destroyed by Tatars under Batu, 1240. Passed to Lithuania, 1320. Sacked by Crimean Tatars, 1483. Obtained the 'Magdeburg Right' (Civil Liberties), 1499. Ceded to Poland, 1569. Poles driven out, 1654. Elective magistracy instituted, 1667. Annexed by Russia, 1686. Dubno Contract Fair moved to K., 1797. In 1869 a hoard of Roman and central Asiatic coins, the profits of trading caravans in Varangian times, was discovered. Rebellion at, 1905. Ukrainian Rada at, Feb. 1917. Stormed by Communists, Dec. 1919. Occupied by Poles, May–June 1920. Bitter fighting at, and serious damage, 1941–3. *See* WORLD WAR II.

Kilimanjaro, highest mountain in Africa. First climbed, 1889.

Kilkenny, Statute of. Forbade amongst other things (1) marriage between English and Irish; (2) Englishmen to use Irish names or wear Irish apparel; passed, 1367.

Kilmainham Treaty, Apr. 1882, between Gladstone and Parnell, by which the latter promised to assist in the restoration of order in Ireland. It was abortive because of the Phoenix Park murders (*q.v.*), which immediately followed.

Kimberley, S. Africa. Relieved, 15 Feb. 1900, after a three-month siege in S. African War.

King's Bench Prison (London). Burnt during Gordon Riots, 7 June 1780; rebuilt, 1781; demolished, 1880.

King's Champion, an office dating from the reign of William I, involves tenure by service of the manor of Scrivelsby in Lincolnshire, and has been discharged by the family of Dymoke since 1377. The earliest written claim to perform the service is dated 1327. The last Champion actually to challenge all comers at the coronation banquet to deny the sovereign's title was the Champion of George IV in 1820.

King's (or Queen's) Counsel. Title first. granted in England by James I in 1604 to Sir Francis Bacon.

King's Cup. Aeroplane race instituted, 1922.

King's Evil or **Scrofula.** Supposed to have been cured by the touch of the sovereign. The custom was maintained from the time of Edward III, but fell into disuse with the accession of George I in 1714.

Kings and Queens of England and Great Britain. *See* ENGLISH SOVEREIGNS AND THEIR CONSORTS.

King's Prize for rifle shooting instituted, as Queen's Prize, 1860. Name subsequently reverted.

Kingston, Jamaica (*q.v.*). Founded 1693 after earthquake (1692) had destroyed Port Royal; became commercial capital on destruction of Port Royal by fire, 1703. Almost totally destroyed by earthquake, 1907.

Kingston-upon-Thames, Surrey. Incorporated in the time of Henry II; but first extant charter dated 1200. Saxon kings crowned here. Castle captured by Henry III during Barons' War, 1264. Gen. Fairfax made it his headquarters during civil war, 1647.

Kinshasa, Zaïre, formerly **Leopoldville.** Founded by H. M. Stanley, 1882. Name changed to K., 1966.

Kirghizstan became an autonomous republic, 1926, and a constituent member of the U.S.S.R., 1936. Its inhabitants, the Kara-Kirghiz and Kirghiz Kazaks, recognized Russian suzerainty in 1864 and 1810 respectively.

Kiribati, Pacific, formerly the Gilbert Islands (*see* GILBERT AND ELLICE ISLANDS) took the name K. when it became a republic, 12 July 1979.

Kiritimati. *See* CHRISTMAS ISLAND.

Kit-Cat Club, founded *c.* 1703 in London as a literary society, grew into a club patronized by influential supporters of the Hanoverian succession. Dissolved, 1720.

Kleve. *See* CLEVES.

Klondike gold rush began, 1896.

Klosterzeven, Convention of, con-

cluded by the Duc de Richelieu (1696–1788) and the Duke of Cumberland (*d.* 1760), respectively for the French and Anglo-Hanoverians, 1757.

Knighthood, Orders of, The following are the principal historical orders (many not now extant), with the dates of their foundations:

Great Britain

Bannerets, said to have been in existence, 1282.

Bath, 1399; renewed, 1725.

British Empire, 1917.

Garter, *c.* 1346–8.

Indian Empire, 1877.

Royal Victorian Order, 1896.

St. Michael and St. George, 1818.

St. Patrick, Ireland, 1783.

Star of India, 1861.

Thistle, 1687.

Foreign

Albert (Saxony), 1850. Albert the Bear (Anhalt), 1382 traditionally; revived, 1807 and 1836. Alcantara (Spain), 1156. Alexander Nevsky (Russia), 1725. Amaranta (Sweden), 1645. Andrew, St. (Russia), 1698. Anna, St. (Bavaria), 1784. Anne, St. (Russia), 1735. Annunciation (Italy), 1362 traditionally. Anthony, St. (Bavaria), 1382. Apostolic Order of St. Stephen (Hungary), 1764. Aviz, St. Benedict of (Portugal), 1147; became a spiritual order, 1162.

Bavarian Crown (Bavaria), 1808. Bear (Austria), 1213. Black Eagle (Prussia), 1701. Blood of Our Saviour (Austria), 1608.

Calatrava (Spain), 1158. Catherine, St. (Russia), 1714. Charles III (Spain), 1771. Charles XIII (Sweden and Norway), 1811. Charles Frederick (Baden), 1807. Christ (Portugal), 1317. Crescent (Turkey), 1801. Crown (Rumania), 1881.

Dannebrog (Denmark), 1219 traditionally; revived, 1671. De la Scaura (Spain), 1320. Ducal House (Oldenburg), 1838.

Elephant (Denmark), 1693. Ernest (Saxe-Coburg), 1690.

Falcon (Iceland), 1921. Faustin, St. (Haiti), 1849. Ferdinand, St. (Spain), 1811. Fidelity (Denmark), 1732. Francis Joseph (Austria), 1849. Frederick (Württemberg), 1830.

George, St. (Austria), 1470. George, St. (Bavaria), 1729. George, St. (Russia), 1769. George of Alfaura, St. (Spain), 1201. Golden Fleece (Spain and Austria), 1429.
Henry the Lion (Brunswick), 1834. Hermingilde, St. (Spain), 1814. Hubert, St. (Bavaria), 1444.
Iron Cross (Prussia), 1813. Iron Crown (Austria), 1805. Iron Helmet (Hesse), 1814. Isabella, St. (Portugal), 1801. Isabella the Catholic (Spain), 1815.
James, St. (Portugal), 1310. James of Compostella, St. (Spain), 1175. John, St. (Prussia), 1812. John of Malta, St. (Austria), 1043.
Legion of Honour (France), 1802. Leopold (Austria), 1808. Leopold (Belgium), 1832. Lily of Aragon (Spain), 1410. Louis (Bavaria), 1827. Louisa, St. (Prussia), 1814.
Maria Louisa (Spain), 1792. Maria Theresa (Austria), 1757. Maurice, St. (Italy), 1434. Maximilian (Bavaria), 1853. Medjidie (Turkey), 1852. Mercy (Spain), 1261. Merit (Prussia), 1740. Michael, St. (Bavaria), 1693. Military Merit (Russia), 1792.
Netherlands Lion, 1815. Nicani-Iftihar (Turkey), 1831.
Olaf, St. (Norway), 1847. Our Lady of the Conception (Portugal), 1818. Our Lady of Mercy (Spain), 1218. Our Lady of Montesa (Spain), 1317.
Palatine Lion (Bavaria), 1768. Polar Star (Sweden), 1748.
Red Eagle (Prussia), 1734. Redeemer (Greece), 1833. Rosary of Toledo (Spain), 1212.
Saviour (Spain), 1118. Saviour of the World (Sweden), 1561. Savoy (Italy), 1815. Seraphim (Sweden and Norway), 1280. Sincerity (Prussia), 1705. Slaves to Virtue (Austria), 1662. Stanislaus (Russia), 1765. Star (Rumania), 1877. Starry Cross (Austria), 1668. Swan (Prussia), 1449. Sword (Sweden and Norway), 1525.
Teutonic Order (Austria), 1191. Theresa (Bavaria), 1827. Tower and Sword (Portugal), 1459.
Ulrica (Sweden), 1734.
Vasa (Sweden and Norway), 1772. Vladimir (Russia), 1782.

White Eagle (Russia), 1713. White Falcon (Saxe-Weimar), 1732. William (Netherlands), 1815. Wing of St. Michael (Portugal), 1172.

Knights of Labor. A labour association founded at Philadelphia, U.S.A., 1869.

Knights Hospitallers. *See* MALTA, KNIGHTS OF.

Knights Templars. *See* TEMPLARS.

Knights' War, The, 1522–3, waged by the knights of Germany under Franz von Sickingen and Ulrich von Hutten, who espoused the Lutheran cause against the empire.

Knossos. Ancient city of Crete, originating before 4000 B.C.; neolithic beds contain pottery, stone implements, and idols; copper utensils from *c.* 3000 B.C. Its great palace (*c.* 2000 B.C.), whose complicated structure may have given rise to the legend of the Labyrinth, was destroyed by fire *c.* 1800 B.C., but immediately rebuilt. This second Minoan civilization was somehow destroyed in fourteenth century B.C. In twelfth and eleventh centuries B.C. Achaean culture superseded Minoan and K. ceased to be the principal city. Excavations by Sir Arthur Evans, 1900–8, and his account of them published, 1921–36. His account questioned by experts, 1961 and subsequently.

Koenigsberg. *See* KALININGRAD.

Koh-i-Noor Diamond. Owned by Nadir Shah, 1739. Given to Queen Victoria by E. India Co., 1850.

Konstanz (Fr. **Constance**). Federal German Republic, on the Rhine on its exit from Lake K. Bishopric since the sixth century. Free Imperial city, 1192. Council of K. (Constance) 1414–18. John Hus burnt here, 1415. Occupied by Austrians, 1548: besieged by Swedes, 1633. Became part of Baden, 1805. Bishopric suppressed, 1821.

Kopparberg, range of mountains and province in Sweden; the capital is Falun, where the K. Mining Co., founded 1284, still has its headquarters, and operates a copper mine.

Koran. Mohammed wrote none of the *suras* (chapters) himself. Some portion of his teaching would appear to have been written down as early as 615, and revised by him later; the remainder was collected after his death in 632 by Zaid ibn Thabit, his last secretary. (*See* ISLAM.) Translated into Latin, 1143.

Korea (Tai-Han: in Japanese, **Chosen**). A Chinese possession from *c.* 200 B.C. Anti-Japanese riots, 1882. Treaties with Britain, 1883; Russia, 1888. Invaded by Japan, 1894. Independence proclaimed, 1895. Annexed by Japan, 1910. Abortive revolt suppressed with great cruelty, Mar.–July 1919. NW. coast swept by tidal wave, 1923. Divided into Russian and American occupation zones, divided by the 38th parallel of latitude, Sept. 1945. Russian-American talks about the unification of the country broke down, May 1946. Elections were held in May 1948 in the American zone, and in July Syngman Rhee was elected first President of the Republic of K., which was proclaimed on 15 Aug. N. of the 38th parallel a Korean People's Republic (K.P.R.), claiming authority over the whole country, was proclaimed in Pyongyang, 12 Sept. 1948. Northern troops crossed the 38th parallel and invaded the southern republic of K., 25 June 1950. The Security Council of the U.N. demanded a N. Korean withdrawal and asked member countries to help it enforce its demands, 27 June. First U.S. troops landed in K., 30 June; MacArthur made Supreme Commander of the U.N. forces in K., 7 July. 1st Battalions of the Middlesex and Argyll and Sutherland regiments from Hong Kong were the first non-American U.N. forces to reach the theatre of war (29 Aug. 1950), where existing forces had been driven into a small perimeter round Pusan, out of which they broke, 15 Sept., when the U.S. X Corps from Japanese bases landed at Inchon and captured Seoul, 28 Sept. 3rd Battalion Royal Australian Regiment joined British units in 27th Commonwealth Brigade, Oct. S. Korean units crossed the 38th parallel, 1 Oct., and U.S. troops, 9 Oct. By the end of Oct. U.N. troops had almost reached the Manchurian

border, but on 26 Nov. Chinese troops, which had apparently been in K. since about 25 Oct., counter-attacked at several points. U.N. retreat terminated at Imjin River, end Mar. 1951. Ridgway replaced MacArthur, 11 Apr. 1951. Truce talks started 10 July 1951; armistice eventually signed, 27 July 1953. Talks between N. and S. Korea aimed at eventual unification held, 1972–5, but were inconclusive. President Park assassinated, 1979. Korean Jumbo jet shot down by Russians, Sept. 1983. 4 Korean cabinet ministers assassinated in Rangoon, Oct. 1983.

Kotor (It. **Cattaro),** a small Adriatic republic in the Middle Ages, absorbed by Venice, 1420. Ceded to Austria, 1814. Occupied by Italians, Nov. 1918, but ceded to Yugoslavia, 1919. Became part of the Federal Republic of Montenegro, 1945. Had severe earthquakes, 1563 and 1667.

Kowloon. China. The peninsula ceded to Britain, 1861, by the terms of the Convention of Peking, 1860. Further adjacent area leased to Britain for ninety-nine years by China, 1898. K. forms part of the Crown Colony of Hong Kong (*q.v.*).

Krakatoa. Volcano in E. Indies, which had a celebrated eruption in 1883.

Kremlin (Rus. **Kreml'**). A citadel, especially that of Moscow, which once (in the early fifteenth century) comprised the whole area of the city. It contains within fortified walls the cathedral of Uspensky (1474) and other contemporary churches and palaces. Has been the seat of government for all Russia, except for the period 1703–1917. Closed to the public during Stalin's regime, but reopened, 1955.

Kriegspiel. Marshal Keith (1693–1788), a Scottish officer in the Prussian employ, invented a form of K., but its present form was evolved by von Reiss witz, 1824.

Kronstadt, Russia. Founded by Peter the Great, 1703; K. Canal, 1884.

Ku-Klux-Klan. A secret society said to have been founded in Tennessee in 1865. It gradually came to have far-reaching powers, but was disbanded,

Mar. 1869, and had entirely ceased to exist by 1871. The second organization of this name was started by W. J. Simmons in 1915, at a meeting near Atlanta, Georgia. Like its predecessor, it opposed negroes and stood for white Protestant domination in politics. It reached the height of its power in 1928, and was revived again after World War II by Dr. Samuel Green (1945). It had a temporary revival 1960–5 and was the subject of a Senate investigation, 1965–6.

'Kulturkampf.' Name given to the conflict between Bismarck and the Roman Catholic Church in Germany, 1871–87.

Kuomintang. Chinese radical republican party formed, Aug. 1912, to carry out political programme of Sun Yat-sen, who was its chairman till his death in 1925. By 1928 it was dominated by Chiang Kai-shek, who by defeating Chang Tso-lin at Peking made it the only party in China (q.v.), apart from the Communists, who originally formed part of the K., but were expelled in 1927. In 1985 still controlled the government in Taiwan (q.v.).

Kurds. Since 1920 divided between Turkey, Iraq, and Iran. Turkish K. rebelled following abolition of the caliphate, 1925. Iraqi K. have attempted (often with Soviet help) to assert their independence, 1922–3, 1944–5, and 1960–2, and after the overthrow of the Kassem regime in Feb. 1963 were offered considerable local autonomy, but continued to rebel. Iraq govt. claimed to have reached complete agreement with the K., Mar. 1970. K. in Iran in dispute with both royalist and Islamic govs. since 1945, and more particularly since 1979.

Kurile Islands, formerly Japanese territory, awarded to the U.S.S.R. in 1945 as the price of her participation in the war against Japan, under the terms of the Yalta agreement (q.v.).

Kutchuk-Kainardji, Treaty of, between Catherine II of Russia and the Sultan Abdul Hamid I, signed, 1774. By this treaty Turkey gave up the Crimea, Azov, and Taganrog.

Kuwait, Persian Gulf. Turkish attempt to occupy prevented by British, 1897. Under British protection, 1899. Britain recognized the amir of K. as an independent ruler, under British protection, 1914. Oil developed from 1934. Britain recognized complete independence of K., 19 June 1961. Iraq (q.v.) claimed K., 25 June 1961. British troops landed to protect her, 2 July, but had all been withdrawn by 10 Oct. A constitutional monarchy was instituted, Dec. 1961, which came fully into force in 1963.

Kyoto, founded A.D. 793, was the capital of the Japanese Empire until 1868.

L

Labour Day, in Europe, usually 1 May, perhaps because on that date in 1889 the Second International first proposed a workers' festival for all countries. In Great Britain the first Monday in May has been a Bank Holiday dedicated to labour since 1978. L.D. in the U.S.A. is the first Monday in September, and was federally adopted in 1894. Canada also celebrates L.D. on the first Monday in Sept; in New Zealand it is observed on the third Monday in Oct.

Labour Exchanges. Established by Robert Owen in England, 1832–4. Previously established at Cincinnati by Josiah Warren. New Act for L.E. 1909. Name subsequently changed to Employment Exchanges (*q.v.*), now Job Centres.

Labour Party of Australia, founded, 1891; first came to power, 1909; but lost power during World War I. Interwar years period of strong govts. under Lyons. Split by Communist issue during 1950s, ensuring long period out of office. Whitlam's L. govt. fell as a result of constitutional crisis, 1975. L.P. regained power under Hawke, 1983: party now pro-republican and anti-nuclear.

Labour Party of Great Britain. Arose out of the L. Representation Committee, appointed by representatives of the I.L.P. (*q.v.*), the Fabian Society, and the Trades Union Congress, 27 Feb. 1900. It took the name L.P. about the time of its successes at the polls, Jan. 1906. In office, 22 Jan.–4 Nov. 1924, and 8 June 1929–24 Aug. 1931. I.L.P. disaffiliated itself from, 30 July 1932. First obtained control of London County Council, 8 Mar. 1934. Leaders entered National Government, 10 May 1940. Victorious at General Election, 5 July 1945. Held office, 27 July 1945–Oct. 1951. Won narrow victory at General Election, Oct. 1964; overwhelming victory at General Election, Mar.1966; but defeated at General Election, June 1970. Returned to power, 1974, but defeated by the Conservatives in 1979, and, more overwhelmingly, in 1983.

Labour Party of New Zealand, first returned members to Parliament, 1890: first held office, 1935, retaining it until after World War II. Lost office, 1949: in power, 1954–60, and 1972–5. Regained office, 1984, under David Lange.

Labourers, Statutes of, were all passed in the reign of Edward III, and were the result of disturbed social conditions which followed on the Black Death of 1348. The most important were those of 1349 and 1351; all attempted to fix the agricultural wage at the level of 1347.

Labrador. Visited by Norsemen (who called it Helluland) in the tenth or eleventh centuries; explored by Frobisher, 1576; rediscovered by Hudson, 1610; the peninsula ceded to Britain by France in 1763. The part that drains into Hudson Bay belonged to the Hudson's Bay Co. Remainder given to the province of Quebec by Act of 1774. Newfoundland recovered its strip by Act of 1809. Part of this strip, from Ance Sablon to 52° N., restored to Quebec (Lower Canada), 1825. The Hudson's Bay Co.'s part surrendered to Canada, 1869. Newfoundland, under letters patent of 28 Mar. 1874, exercised jurisdiction along Atlantic coast. The remainder, under order in council of 18 Dec. 1897, was constituted Ungava, an unorganized territory of Canada, annexed to Quebec, 1912. In 1927 the Privy Council decided that Newfoundland was entitled to all that part that drained into the Atlantic. When Newfoundland acceded to the Dominion of Canada, 1949, all L. was brought into the confederation.

Labuan. Ceded to Britain by Sultan of Brunei, 1846: part of N. Borneo, 1946; part of Sabah (*q.v.*) since 1963.

Laccadive Islands. Discovered by Vasco da Gama, 1499; acquired by Britain, 1877; part of India since 1947.

Lado Enclave, surrounding the town of L. on the White Nile, was Egyptian territory from 1878, when Gen. Gordon founded it, to 1885, when it passed to the then Belgian Congo. In 1909 it became part of the Anglo-Egyptian Sudan (now the Sudanese Republic); part was transferred to N. Uganda in 1914.

Ladrones. *See* MARIANA ISLANDS.

Ladysmith, S. Africa. Founded, 1851. Relieved by Sir R. Buller after siege of 121 days during S. African War, 28 Feb. 1900.

Lagos, Nigeria (*q.v.*). District ceded from native king, 1861. Created a separate government, 1863; part of British W. African Settlements from 1866; made a colony, 1886; part of southern Nigeria, 1906. Capital of both colony and protectorate of all Nigeria, 1 Jan. 1914, and of the independent dominion 1960–82.

Lahore, Pakistan. British Council of Regency established at, 1846. Became capital of Punjab, 1849. Earthquake, 1905. Rioting at, Oct.–Nov. 1947.

Laissez-faire, laissez-aller, or, more correctly, *laisser-passer*, a phrase denoting a government policy of non-interference in economic matters. Its origin is usually attributed to Legendre, who, *c.* 1680, in an interview with Colbert regarding government interference with commerce, stated: 'Laissez-faire, laissez-aller.'

Lambeth Articles. Drawn up by Archbishop Whitgift, 1595. They embraced the doctrines of Calvinism and were disapproved by Parliament; again rejected at Hampton Court Conference, 1604.

Lambeth Bridge, built, 1862; demolished, 1929; new bridge opened, 1932.

Lambeth Conferences, of bishops of the Anglican communion from all over the world, originated in a letter from Bishop Hopkins of Vermont in 1851, followed by a request from the Church in Canada, 1865. The following conferences have been held, with their presidents: numbers of bishops attending have increased at each conference, from 76 in 1867 to some 500 in 1968.

1. 1867. Archbishop Longley
2. 1878. Archbishop Tait
3. 1888. Archbishop Benson
4. 1897. Archbishop Temple
5. 1908. Archbishop Davidson
6. 1920. Archbishop Davidson
7. 1930. Archbishop Lang
8. 1948. Archbishop Fisher
9. 1958. Archbishop Fisher
10. 1968. Archbishop Ramsey
11. 1978. Archbishop Coggan

Lambeth Palace (London), residence of the Archbishops of Canterbury since 1197, consists now largely of buildings erected, 1430–90, though the chapel, was built *c.* 1230. Sacked in Wat Tyler's rising, 1381.

Lambeth Walk, street in L. of no great antiquity celebrated in street songs current in the nineteenth century, printed versions of which appeared in 1899 and 1924. It inspired a song-and-dance number in the musical comedy 'Me and My Girl', 1937, and the dance invented for this purpose became popular, 1938.

Lambeth Ware. Pottery was first made in L. *c.* 1630, and figures of artificial stone were modelled at Goade's works from 1760. Doulton pottery was first produced in the Vauxhall Walk, L., by the firm of that name, in 1815.

Lampeter, Cardiganshire, the seat of St. David's College, establishment for training priests of the Episcopal Church in Wales before ordination, which was founded, 1822, and affiliated to Oxford and Cambridge.

Lancaster, England. Castle supposed to have been built by Agricola, A.D. 124; present structure begun by Roger de Poictou *c.* 1094; restored by John of Gaunt in the fourteenth century; burnt by Scots, 1322 and 1389. L. received its first charter, 1193. 'Lancashire witches' tried here, 1612. Given the title and dignity of a city, 1937. Univ. estab., 1964.

Lancaster, Duchy of. Settled on John of Gaunt and his heirs by royal charter, 1362. Annexed to the crown by Edward IV, 1461. The court of the county was abolished by the Judicature Act of 1873.

Lancers did not exist in Europe until the fourth century A.D., when the Roman Army adopted as part of its equipment the stirrup without the use of which no horseman can handle a lance. The lance continued to be the decisive cavalry weapon until about 1600, when the dragoon's pistol began to replace it. Thereafter only the Cossacks and Poles among European cavalry retained the lance, but such was the success of the latter in the French employ under Napoleon (1807–15) that first French (1811) and later other cavalry units readopted the lance (British in 1816) and often with it some characteristic features of Polish cavalry dress. The last British lancer unit to use the weapon in action was probably the 21 L. against the Mohmand rebels in World War I; in Sept. 1918 the 2nd Indian L. used it on the Turks at Lejjun, Palestine. Its use was abolished in the British Army in 1927.

Lancers, square dance of five figures, a form of quadrille (*q.v.*) invented in Paris, 1836; brought to London, 1850.

Land League. Founded in Ireland by Michael Davitt, 1879, for the purchase of land. Act of Parliament against, 1881.

Land Registry established by Act of 1862; re-formed by L. Transfer Act, 1875, L. Transfer Act, 1897, and L. Registration Act, 1925.

Landsknechte, term used for German dismounted mercenaries employed in France (Lansquenets), Italy, and occasionally England in the sixteenth century. Word first applied to units raised by Emperor Maximilian in (S.) Germany, 1492.

Land Taxes, payable in the U.K. under an Act of 1798: four new taxes, introduced in 1910, were abolished in 1920.

Lands Tribunal, set up under the Lands Tribunal Act, 1949.

Languedoc, France. Eastern L. annexed to French crown, 1229. Western L. (county of Toulouse), 1271. Estates first convoked, 1302. Civil war in L., 1561–98. Protestant rebellion, 1620–2. Replaced by the eight depts. of Haute-Loire, Lozère, Ardèche, Aude, Tarn, Hérault, Gard, and Haute-Garonne, 1791.

Laocoön, The. Famous ancient sculpture discovered at Rome, 1506, and placed in the Vatican by Julius II. Napoleon brought it to Paris, 1796. Restored, 1814. Fragments of a similar group found in a cave at Sperlonga, 1957.

Laos, independent state in SE. Asia. French protectorate, 1893; independent sovereign state within the French Union, 1949. Invaded by Vietminh forces, 1953, aided by Pathet-Lao (pro-Communist Laotian group). Agreement for cessation of hostilities reached at Geneva, 1954; but war between royalists and Pathet-Lao continued till 1973. A coalition govt. of both sides formed, 1974, but in 1975 King abdicated and People's Democratic Republic of L. proclaimed.

La Paz, Bolivia. Founded, 1548. Bishopric established, 1605. Rose against Spaniards, 1809. Became *de facto* capital of Bolivia, 1898.

La Plata, Argentine. Founded, 1882.

Lascaux Caves, the greatest gallery of palaeolithic art discovered hitherto, were first entered in modern times, 1940. Its paintings may have been executed some 100,000 B.C.

La Tène, an old Celtic settlement at the northern end of the lake of Neuchâtel, in Switzerland. It was inhabited from c. 250 to 100 B.C., first brought to the notice of archaeologists in 1858, and excavated after 1881. The period of prehistory named after it by archaeologists is that following the Hallstadt culture, and is alternatively called the Later Iron Age; it extends from 550 to 15 B.C.

Lateran, St. John (Rome). Palace and church rebuilt in twelfth century. Church entirely rebuilt by Sixtus V, 1586.

Lateran Treaty, 11 Feb. 1929. *See*
PAPACY.

Latin Literature, Classical; (principal
authors of whom works or fragments
survive):

Andronicus, Livius, *fl.* 240 B.C., epic
and dramatic poet.

Bassus, Caesius, *fl.* A.D. 60, lyric poet.

Caecilius Statius, *d. c.* 168 B.C., comic
poet.

Caesar, C. Julius, 102–44 B.C.,
historian.

Calpurnius Sienlus, T., first century
A.D., pastoral poet.

Cato, M. Porcius, 232–147 B.C.,
historian and writer on agriculture.

Cato, P. Valerius, first century B.C.,
poet and grammarian.

Catullus, C. Valerius, 84–*c.* 54 B.C.,
poet.

Catulus, Q. Lutatius, *d.* 87 B.C., orator
and poet.

Cicero, M. Tullius, 106–43 B.C., orator,
philosopher, etc.

Cinna, C. Helvius, *d.* 44 B.C., poet.

Commodianus, *fl. c.* A.D. 250, poet.

Cornificius, *fl. c.* 85 B.C., rhetorician.

Curtius Rufus, Q., *fl.* A.D. 41–54,
rhetorician.

Ennius, Q., 239–170 B.C., epic poet.

Eumenius, *c.* A.D. 260–*c.* 312,
panegyrist.

Fabius Pictor, Q., *b. c.* 254 B.C.,
historian.

Festus, S. Pompeius, second century
A.D., grammarian.

Flaccus, L. Valerius, *fl.* A.D. 70, epic
poet.

Florus, second century A.D., historian.

Fronto, M. Cornelius, *c.* A.D. 100–70,
grammarian and rhetorician.

Gellius, Aulus, *c.* A.D. 123–65,
miscellaneous writer and grammarian.

Graltius, first century A.D., didactic
poet.

Horace (Q. Horatius Flaccus), 65–8
B.C., poet.

Justinus, second century A.D., historian.

Juvenal (D. Junius Juvenalis), *c.* A.D.
50–*c.* 130, satirist.

Livy (T. Livius), 59 B.C.–A.D. 17,
historian.

Lucan (M. Annaeus Lucanus), A.D.
39–65, epic poet.

Lucilius, Gaius, *c.* 180–*c.* 102 B.C.,
satirist.

Lucretius Carus, *c.* 99–55 B.C.,
philosopher and poet.

Manilius, first century A.D.,
astronomer and poet.

Martial (M. Valerius Martialis), *c.* A.D.
40–*c.* 104, poet.

Mela, Pomponius, first century B.C.,
geographer.

Nepos, Cornelius, first century B.C.,
historian.

Ovid (P. Ovidius Naso), 43 B.C.–A.D.
17, poet.

Paterculus, C. Velleius, 19 B.C.–*c.* A.D.
40, historian.

Persius Flaccus, A., A.D. 34–62, satirist.

Petronius, *d.* A.D. 66, romance writer
and satirist.

Phaedrus, *b. c.* 30 B.C., fabulist.

Plautus, T. Maccius, *c.* 254–184 B.C.,
comic poet.

Pliny the Elder (C. Plinius Secundus),
A.D. 23–79, polymath.

Pliny the Younger (C. Plinius Caecilius
Secundus), A.D. 61–*c.* 113, panegyrist and letter-writer.

Propertius, S. Aurelius, *c.* 50–*c.* 16 B.C.,
elegiac poet.

Publilius Syrus, first century B.C.,
mimeographer.

Quadrigarius, *fl.* 100–78 B.C., historian.

Quintilian (M. Fabius Quintilianus), *b.
c.* A.D. 40, rhetorician and critic.

Sallust (C. Sallustius Crispus), 86–34
B.C. historian.

Seneca, L. Annaeus, *c.* 4 B.C.–A.D. 65,
Stoic philosopher.

Seneca, M. Annaeus, *c.* 55 B.C.–*c.* A.D.
41, rhetorician.

Silius Italicus, Tib. Catius Asconius, *c.*
A.D. 25–*c.* 101, epic poet.

Statius, P. Papinius, *c.* A.D. 61–96,
poet.

Suetonius Tranquillus, C., *fl.* A.D. 110,
historian.

Tacitus, P. Cornelius, *c.* A.D. 55–*c.* 120,
historian.

Terence (P. Terentius Afer), *c.* 195–159
B.C., comic poet.

Tibullus, Albius, *c.* 54–19 B.C., elegiac
poet.

Valerius Maximus, first century A.D., historian.

Varro, M. Terentius, 116–27 B.C., antiquary and writer on agriculture.

Virgil (P. Vergilius Maro), 70–19 B.C., poet.

Latin Literature: chief post-classical authors:

Abélard, Pierre (French), 1079–1142, philosopher, theologian, and poet.

Adam of Bremen (German), d. c. 1076, historian.

Adam of St. Victor (French), 1130–80, hymn-writer.

Adamnan, St. (Irish), 642–704, biographer and topographical writer.

Aeneas Sylvius. *See* PICCOLOMINI.

Albertus Magnus, Albert of Cologne, or Albrecht von Böllstadt (German), 1193–1280, scientific writer, philosopher, and theologian.

Alcuin (Northumbrian), 735–804, educational writer and theologian.

Aldhelm, St. (Wessex), c. 640–709, poet and ecclesiastical writer.

Anselm, St. (Italian), 1033–1109, philosopher and theologian.

Ascham, Roger (English), 1515–68, educational writer.

Asser (Welsh), d. c. 910, biographer.

Bacon, Roger (English), 1214–92, philosopher.

Bede, the Venerable (Northumbrian), c. 673–735, historian.

Bernard of Clairvaux, St. (French), 1090–1158, poet, theologian, and mystical writer.

Boccaccio, Giovanni (Italian), 1313–75, poet.

Bourne, Vincent (English), 1695–1747, poet.

Buchanan, George (Scottish), 1506–82, historian.

Calvin, John (French), 1509–64, religious reformer.

Cheke, Sir John (English), 1514–57, classical scholar.

Coffin, Charles (English), 1676–1749, poet.

Columba, St. (Irish), d. 597, poet.

Corippus, Flavius Cresconius (African), fl. 550–80, poet.

Dante Alighieri (Italian), 1265–1321, poet and political writer.

Duns Scotus, Johannes, or John the Scot (probably English), d. 1308, philosopher and theologian.

Einhard (German), c. 770–840, historian.

Ekkehard of Saint Gall (German), d. 973, poet.

Erasmus Desiderius (Dutch), 1466–1536, humanist and critic.

Estienne, Charles, or Stephanus Carolus (French), 1504–64, anatomist.

Florence of Worcester (English), d. 1118, chronicler.

Fortunatis, Verantius (Italian), fl. 569, poet.

Fulbert of Chartres (French), d. 1029, hymn and didactic writer.

Geoffrey (Norman Welsh) of Monmouth, or Geoffrey Arthur, c. 1100–54, chronicler.

Geoffrey of Vinsauf (Norman), fl. 1200, poet.

Gerard, John (English), 1564–1637, autobiographer.

Gerbert (Pope Sylvester II) (French), 999–1003, philosopher, theologian, and mathematician.

Gildas, St. (British), c. 516–70, moralist.

Giraldus Cambrensis, or Gerald de Barri (Norman-Welsh), c. 1147–1220, historian and topographical writer.

Godescalc of Orbais (Frankish), fl. 730, hagiographer.

Gregory I, Pope St. (Roman), d. 604, theologian and spiritual writer.

Gregory of Tours, St. (Frankish), d. 594, historian.

Grève, Philippe (French), d. 1236, hymn-writer.

Grossetête, Robert (English), c. 1175–1253, theologian and scholar.

Guido delle Colonne (Sicilian), thirteenth century, novelist.

Heiric of Auxerre (French), c. 834–c. 881, poet.

Henry of Huntingdon (English), 1080–c. 1150, historian.

Hildebert (French), d. 1134, poet.

Hrabanus Maurus (German), 784–856, theologian and pedagogic writer.

Hroswitha (German), d. c. 1000, poetess and playwright.

Isidore of Seville, St. (Spanish), c. 560–636, encyclopaedist.

John of Salisbury (English), *c.* 1115–80, philosopher and historian.

Johnson, later Cory, William (English), 1823–92, poet.

Jónsson, Arngrimr (Icelander), 1568–1648, historian.

Jónsson, Finnur (Icelander), 1704–89, ecclesiastical historian.

Jordanes (Romano-Gothic), *fl. c.* 550, historian.

Langton, Stephen (English), *d.* 1228, scriptural writer.

Liutprand (Lombard), *c.* 922–73, historian.

Luther, Martin (German), 1483–1546, religious reformer.

Magnusson, Arne (Icelander), 1633–1730, historian.

Map, Walter (English), *c.* 1140–*c.* 1210, poet and anecdotal writer.

Martin of Braga, St. (Spanish), *d.* 580, moralist.

Matthew of Vendôme (French), eleventh–twelfth century, poet.

Melanchthon (Philipp Schwarzerd) (German), 1497–1560, theologian and philologist.

Nennius (Welsh), *fl.* 840, chronicler.

Newton, Sir Isaac (English), philosopher and scientist, 1642–1727.

Notker Balbulus (German), 840–912, poet and historian.

Olaus Magnus or Olaf Stora (Swedish), 1490–1558, historian.

Owen, John (English), *d.* 1622, poet.

Paulus Diaconus (Lombard), *d. c.* 799, historian.

Pecham, John (English), *c.* 1240–92, poet, biographer, and letter-writer.

Peter Damian, St. (Italian), 1007–72, moralist.

Petrarca (Petrarch), Francesco (Italian), 1304–74, poet and moralist.

Piccolomini, Aeneas Sylvius (Italian), *d.* 1464, humanist and critic. He became Pope Pius II.

Poggio Bracciolini, Giovanni Francesco (Italian), 1380–1459, historian.

Poliziano, Angelo (Politian) (Italian), 1454–94, poet.

Pontano, Giovanni (Italian), 1426–1503, poet.

Prudentius, Aurelius Clemens (Spanish), 348–*c.* 405, poet.

Reuchlin, Johann (German), 1455–1522, critic and grammarian.

Richard of Bury (English), 1286–1345, bibliophile.

Sannazaro, Jacopo (Italian), 1458–1530, poet.

Santeul, Claude de (French), 1628–84, poet.

Santeul, Jean de (French), 1630–97, poet.

Saxo Grammaticus (Danish), *fl.* 1140–1206, historian.

Scaliger, Jules-César (French), 1484–1558, philologist, critic, and classical scholar.

Scaliger, Joseph Justus (French), 1540–1609, classical scholar.

Simeon of Durham (English), *fl.* 1130, historian.

Spagnoli, Giovanni Battista (Italian), 1448–1516, poet.

Theodulf (Spanish), *d.* 821, poet and theologian.

Thomas Aquinas, St. (Italian), 1226–74, philosopher, theologian, and poet.

Thomas of Celano (Italian), *d. c.* 1251, poet.

Torfaeus (Thormodur Torfason), (Icelander), 1636–1719, historiographer.

Verecundus (African), *d.* 552, ecclesiastical writer.

Vergil, Polydore (Italian), *c.* 1470–*c.* 1555, miscellaneous writer.

Vincent of Beauvais (French), *d.* 1264, encyclopaedist.

Walafrid 'Strabo' (German), 807–49, poet and theologian.

William of Malmesbury (English), *d.* 1143?, historian.

Wipo (French), eleventh–twelfth century, historian.

Wycliffe, John (English), 1324–84, religious writer.

Latitudinarians. A school of theologians in England which grew up after 1688. They were the forerunners of the nineteenth-century Broad Church Party.

Latvia. Consisted in the Middle Ages of three provinces: Courland or Kurland, Livonia or Livland, and Zemgale or Semigallia; came under the domination of the Teutonic Order and of

(German) prince-bishops, 1158. Under Polish rule from 1562 to 1795, except for Livonia, which was ruled by the Swedes from 1629 to 1721. From 1795 to 1918 L. was merely one of the Baltic provinces of Russia. Independent republic proclaimed, 18 Nov. 1918. After ultimatum presented, 16 June 1939, Russian troops entered L. without resistance, 17 June. Latvian S.S.R. admitted to Soviet Union, Aug. 1940. German occupation of L. complete, July 1941. Reconquered by the Soviet Union, 1944–5.

Presidents of L.:
Jānis Čabste 1922–1927
Gustaus Zenigals 1927–1930
Alberts Kviesis 1930–1936
Kārlis Ulmanis 1936–1940

Laureate, Poet. The first poet laureate proper was appointed by Queen Elizabeth in 1591. The following is a list of the poets laureate:

Edmund Spenser 1591–1599
Samuel Daniel 1599–1619
Ben Jonson 1619–1637
Vacant from 1637–1660
Sir William Davenant 1660–1668
John Dryden 1670–1689
Thomas Shadwell 1689–1692
Nahum Tate 1692–1715
Nicholas Rowe 1715–1718
Laurence Eusden 1718–1730
Colley Cibber 1730–1757
William Whitehead 1757–1785
Thomas Warton 1785–1790
Henry James Pye 1790–1813
Robert Southey 1813–1843
William Wordsworth 1843–1850
Alfred Tennyson 1850–1892
Alfred Austin 1896–1913
Robert Bridges 1913–1930
John Masefield 1930–1967
Cecil Day Lewis 1968–1972
Sir John Betjeman 1972–1984
Ted Hughes 1984–

Lausanne Conference, of Britain, France, Italy, Belgium, and Germany, 1932, ended war debts (with one exception as to Germany) as between those parties, but U.S.A. would not assent.

League of Nations. Covenant of the L. accepted by Allies, 28 Apr. 1919; subscribed by the signatories of the Treaty of Versailles, 28 June 1919; came into force, 1 Jan. 1920. President Wilson's action in committing U.S.A. to participation repudiated in the presidential election of 1920. L. Council's first meeting, Paris, 16 Jan. 1920. First meeting of Assembly, Geneva, 15 Nov.–18 Dec. 1920; Permanent Court of International Justice established, Sept. 1919. Council's ineffectiveness shown by events of Italo-Ethiopian war, 1935–6, and Sp. civil war 1936–9. Final meeting, 8 Apr. 1946. Existence formally terminated, 31 Aug. 1947.

League, The, in full the Holy Catholic L., was organized by the Duc de Guise (1550–88) in 1576 to prevent the accession of Henry of Navarre (Henri IV), the Protestant claimant to the throne of France.

Lease-Lend. Bill introduced into both Houses of U.S. Congress, 10 Jan. 1941. Passed by Senate, 9 Mar.; by Representatives, and signed by President, 11 Mar. 1941. L.-L. officially terminated, 20 Aug. 1945.

Lebanon. Under predominantly Maronite influence from *c.* 650 A.D.; Fr. influence 1860–1914. Made a state separate from Syria, under French mandate, 1920. Occupied by British and Free French forces, 1941. Independent republic proclaimed at Beirut, 26 Nov. 1941, and Fr. transferred administrative power to L. Government, with effect 1 Jan. 1944. Moslem revolt, May 1958, and L. asked for U.S. aid. U.S. troops in L., July–Oct. 1958: internal peace restored. L. aloof from Arab-Israeli dispute until early 1970s when she became the main P.L.O. base (*see* PALESTINE LIBERATION ORGANIZATION). L. sank rapidly into civil war. Israeli troops invaded L., 1978, with Lebanese Christian support. Further Israeli invasion, 1982, devastation of Beirut and massacre of Palestinians. Assassination of Christian President Gemayel, Sept. 1982. Partial Israeli withdrawal, 1983, led to increased Syrian domination of

Palestinian forces in L. despite presence of U.N. peacekeeping force 1983–4. P.L.O. pro-Arafat forces defeated by extremists, Nov. 1983 and left L. U.N. force withdrawn, 1984. L. abrogates 1983 treaty with Israel, Mar. 1984. Renewed serious fighting, 1985.

Leeds, Yorks, England. Captured by parliamentary forces under Gen. Fairfax, 1643; incorporated, 1626, and again in 1673, after the charter had been forfeited. University founded as a college, 1874; granted university status, 1904.

Leeward Islands Federation lasted 1871–1956, when its component members separated.

Legal Aid Act, 1974, consolidated rules governing free or assisted Legal Aid as embodied in the Legal Aid and Advice Acts, 1949–72.

Leghorn (It. **Livorno**), first mentioned, 891, was under the dominion of Pisa in the fourteenth century, but *c.* 1400 passed to France, and was sold to the Genoese, 1407. They sold it to the Florentines, 1421, whose Medici princes extended and fortified the port, 1550, and opened it to ships of all nations, 1606. It was a free port from 1691 to 1867. There was a severe earthquake in 1741. During the allied Fifth Army's offensive in July 1944 L. was heavily bombed and shelled.

Legion of Honour created by Napoleon I, 1802.

Legitimacy. The Legitimacy Act of 1926 provided for legitimation of children by subsequent marriage of parents. The Act of 1959 carried this process further by enacting that marriage legitimized a person even if the father or mother was married to a third party when the illegitimate person was born. Further amendments resultant on the Matrimonial Causes Act, 1973, and the Legitimacy Act, 1976.

Legitimists, word now applied to any partisans of monarchy, or of a particular branch of a royal house as against another branch (cadet) or republican regime, but only current since 1830, when it was coined to

describe those royalists who supported the senior Bourbon as opposed to the cadet Orléans branch of the French royal house.

Leicester, England. In Old English, *Legerceastre.* Site of Roman *Ratae* on the Fosse Way. Seized by the Danes, A.D. 874. Incorporated by King John, 1199. Cardinal Wolsey *d.* at the abbey, 1530. Captured by royalist forces, May 1645, when the castle was dismantled; retaken by parliamentary forces under Fairfax, June 1645. University College became the University of L., 1957.

Leipzig, Germany. First mentioned in 1015. L.'s fair first mentioned, 1268. University founded, 1409. L. Conference between Luther, Eck, and Carlstadt, 1519. L. Book Fair instituted, 1545. During the Thirty Years War (1618–48) it was five times besieged and taken; captured by Prussian Army, 1756; allied armies entered the city after defeat of Napoleon, 16–19 Oct. 1813. Centre of town largely destroyed by allied air attack, 4 Dec. 1943. Now part of the German Democratic Republic.

Lemnos (Modern Gk. **Limni**) was captured from the Venetians by the Turks, 1478. Mudros Bay on the S. coast of L. was used as an allied base from 1915, and here the Turks signed an armistice, 30 Oct. 1918.

Lend-Lease, *see* LEASE-LEND.

Leningrad. Formerly St. Petersburg and Petrograd (*qq.v.*) So renamed, 22 Apr. 1924. Kirov assassinated at, 1934. Besieged by Germans, 21 Aug. 1941–18 Jan. 1944.

Leon, Spain. Kingdom founded tenth century A.D. First united with Castile, 1037. Finally, 1230.

Kings of Leon. See under CASTILE.

Leopoldville. *See* KINSHASA.

Lesotho, formerly **Basutoland**, African kingdom within the Commonwealth. Annexed by Britain, 1868. Annexed to Cape Colony, 1871. Rebellion, 1879–80, resulted in its being made a protectorate directly under Britain, 1883. Swift constitutional progress 1959 onwards, and on 3 Oct. 1966 became an independent kingdom within the Commonwealth, changing its name from Basutoland to L.

Letters of Marque. Licences first granted, 1295, permitting seizure of an enemy's ships or property. Abolished by Treaty of Paris, 1856.

Lettres de Cachet. Warrants of imprisonment granted by the kings of France from about the fourteenth century. Abolished by National Assembly, 1 Nov. 1789.

Levant Company, The. Founded 1581. Chartered by Queen Elizabeth I for trade with Middle E., 1592. British Government took over consular representation from L.C. in Turkey, 1803. Company dissolved, 1825.

Levellers. Ultra-republican party in the parliamentary army during the civil war, 1647. In 1649 it brought about a mutiny, but was suppressed. The leader was Lieut.-Col. John Lilburne (1618–57).

Leyden or **Leiden,** Holland. University founded 1575 by William of Orange in commemoration of the citizens' defence of the town against the Spaniards from Oct. 1573 to Oct. 1574.

Lhasa, Tibet (*q.v.*). Became capital of Tibet in seventh century. Became seat of the Dalai Lama, 1641. The Potala built, 1641–1701. Occupied by the Chinese, Mar. 1959. The Dalai Lama fled to India.

Liampo. *See* NINGPO.

Liberals. Covenanters termed 'Whigamores', 1679; name Whig came to be fastened on all Scottish Presbyterian zealots, then on English politicians who opposed the court and treated Nonconformists leniently. Terms Whig and Tory came into use, 1679–80, and more advanced Whigs and reformers first named L. in a derogatory sense (meaning French revolutionary) *c.* 1820. Last held office, 1918; last represented in gov., 1940–5. In alliance with Social Democratic Party (*q.v.*) since 1982.

Liberia, W. Africa. A negro republic originally of liberated slaves. Founded by the American Colonizing Society, 1821; republic constituted, 1847. Boundaries determined by Anglo-Liberian (1885) and Franco-Liberian (1892, 1907, 1910) agreements. In 1911 a small exchange of territory with Sierra Leone took place. Govt. in hands of few select families till 1980, when President Tolbert assassinated and his govt. overthrown. Samuel Doe, a former master-sergeant, became head of state and commander-in-chief.

Liberum Veto was written into the Polish constitution in the first half of the seventeenth century. First exercised, 1652; and abolished, 1791.

Libraries, Ancient. Chaldean L. said to have existed as early as 1700 B.C. First public library founded at Athens by Pisistratus, 540. Founding of the great Alexandrian library by the first of the Ptolemies, 284; partially destroyed when Julius Caesar set fire to the city in 47. First library in Rome brought from Macedonia by Aemilius Paulus, 167. Library at Constantinople founded by Constantine *c.* A.D. 355.

Libraries, Modern. The following are the most famous L., with the dates of their foundation:

Austria. Vienna: Imperial Library, founded by Frederick III *c.* 1440.

France. Paris: Royal Library, now the Bibliothèque Nationale, founded by Francis I *c.* 1520.

Canada: Parliamentary Library, Ottawa, founded, 1849.

Denmark: Royal Library, Copenhagen, founded, 1661.

Germany. Berlin: Royal Library, founded, 1659. Dresden: Royal Library, founded, sixteenth century. Munich: Royal Library, founded by Duke Albert V of Bavaria, sixteenth century. Stuttgart: Royal Library, founded, 1765.

Great Britain and Ireland. Library Association of the U.K., founded, 1877. Aberystwyth: Welsh National Library, founded, 1911. Cambridge: University Library, founded, fifteenth century, enlarged by George I, 1715. Dublin: King's Inns' Library, founded, 1787; Trinity College Library, founded, 1601. Edinburgh: Advocates' Library founded, 1682; Scottish National

Library, 1925. University Library, founded, 1580. St. Andrews: University Library, founded, 1456; London: British Museum (*q.v.*), 1757 (since 1973 the British Library, *q.v.*); Royal Society Library, founded, 1660; Royal College of Physicians' Library, founded, 1518; London Library, founded, 1840; University of London Library, founded *c.* 1838. Oxford: Bodleian Library, founded, 1598; Radcliffe Library, founded under the will of Dr. Radcliffe, 1714, opened, 1749. Manchester: Chetham Library, founded, 1653, claims to be first free library in England.

Holland, Royal Library, The Hague, founded, 1798.

India. Imperial Library, Calcutta, founded, 1903.

Italy. Florence: library, founded by Niccolo Nicoli, 1436; Mediceo-Laurenziana, 1571; Marucelliana, 1703; Nazionale (amalgamation of Magliabechiana and Palatina), 1861. Rome: Biblioteca Casanatense, founded, 1701; Vatican Library, founded by Pope Nicholas V, 1446, enlarged by Sixtus V, 1588; Vittore Emanuele Library, 1875.

Portugal. Lisbon: Biblioteca Nacional, founded, 1796. Oporto; Municipal Library, founded, 1833.

South Africa. Cape Town Library, 1818 (holds copyright privilege for Cape Province).

Spain. The Escorial's library, founded soon after the building, which began, 1562. Salamanca: University Library, founded, 1254.

U.S.A. Baltimore: Enoch Pratt Free Library, 1857; Johns Hopkins University, 1876; Peabody Institute Library, 1857. Boston: Public Library, 1885–1905. California: Leland Stanford University Library, 1891. Chicago: John Crerar Library, 1894; Newberry Library, 1887; University Library, 1892. Harvard University Library, 1638. Massachusetts: Amherst College Library, 1821. Michigan: University Library, 1837. New Haven: Yale College Library, 1701. New Jersey: Princeton University,

1746. New York: Astor Library, opened, 1854; Columbia University, 1763; Lenox Library, 1870. Pennsylvania: Lehigh University Library, 1877; State Library, 1777; University of Pennsylvania, 1749. Washington: Bureau of Education, 1868; Geological Survey, 1882; House of Representatives Patent Office, 1836; Library of Congress, 1800.

Libya. Originally a Greek name signifying the N. African littoral, not including Egypt. After the Jugurthine War of 106 B.C. L. proper, known as the Regio Tripolitana, was annexed to the province of Africa, but under Diocletian (emperor, A.D. 284–305), the name L. was reintroduced and the western part named Marmarica. In 476 the Vandals (*q.v.*) conquered the whole of the diocese of Africa, including L. It was recovered by Count Belisarius in 534, and remained part of the *Praefectura Africae* until its conquest by the Arabs, 647. In the fifteenth century it was conquered by the Turks, who granted a measure of local independence, 1711, but proclaimed the country a vilayet, 1835. Seized from Turks by Italians, 1911. Italian conquest recognized at Treaty of Ouchy, 18 Oct. 1912. 'Pacification' by Italian forces under Marshal Balbo in 1925 necessitated a treaty with Egypt, signed 6 Dec. 1925, whereby the Bay of Sollum was ceded to Egypt in return for the Oasis of Jarabub, a Senussi stronghold, occupied by Italian forces, 7 Feb. 1927. Scene of much fighting in World War II, it was finally conquered by British, Feb. 1943. In June 1949 the British Government recognized Mohammed Idris es Senussi as King of L., and by his constitution, promulgated 18 Sept. 1949, a Federal State came into being with alternating capitals at Benghazi and Tripoli. Massive oil discoveries and exploitation revolutionized L's economy, 1960 onwards. Sept. 1969, a military coup deposed King Idris and a republic was proclaimed, under leadership of Gadaffi. L. subsequently adopted extreme leftist but Moslem line, interfering in politics of sev.

neighbouring countries. Police-woman shot, from London Libyan Embassy, 1984.

Licensing Laws (Britain). The present law founded on Consolidation Act of 1826. Wine and Beer House Act of 1869 regulated 'off-licence' houses. Act of 1902 increased penalties for drunkenness, convicted habitual drunkards, and compelled clubs to be registered. Children Act, 1908, prohibited presence in bars of children under 14; and it and L. (Consolidation) Act, 1910, restricted sale of liquor to such. 'Permitted Hours' system established, 1921. Sale to persons under 18 restricted by Act of 1923. Further provisions in Acts of 1933 and 1934. Licensing Act, 1949, made minor amendments; but Licensing Act, 1961, increased permitted hours of drinking in public houses, and selling hours in off-licences, and introduced principle of local option to Wales in respect of Sunday opening. Position in England and Wales now governed by Licensing Act of 1964. Flexible licensing hours in Scotland since 1976. *See also* LOCAL OPTION.

Lichfield (Staffs), England. The Mercian See founded here in the seventh century, by St. Chad, first Bishop of L. Cathedral dates from thirteenth century. Besieged by parliamentary army, 1643.

Lick Observatory (California). Founded by James L. (1796–1876), who left a sum of money for the purpose.

Lidice, Czechoslovakia. After assassination of Heydrich, the German Protector of Bohemia and Moravia, the Germans destroyed the village, 10 June 1942, killed all the adult males, shot the women or sent them to concentration camps, and sent the children to German foster-homes or concentration camps. Village rebuilt after 1945.

Liechtenstein, Principality of. Named after the L. family, who acquired the county of Vaduz, 1699, and the lordship of Schellenberg. 1713. Became a principality, 1719. Preserved its independence at extinction of the Holy Roman Empire, 1806.

Liège (Flem. **Luik**), Belgium. Cathedral founded, 712. Captured by Charles the Bold, 1467; by the French, 1691; by the English under Marlborough, 1702; by French, 1794; university founded, 1817.

Lifeboat. The first L. patented, 1785, by Lionel Lukin, an Essex coachbuilder. Henry Greathead, *c.* 1789, also patented one, and is generally regarded as the inventor of the L. First steam-propelled L. designed, 1890; first with motor power, 1904.

Lifeboat Institution, Royal National, Founded in 1824 through the exertions of Sir William Hillary and Thomas Wilson, M.P. for the City of London.

Life Guards. *See under* REGIMENTS.

Light, Velocity of, determined by Römer, 1675; more accurately by Michelson, 1926.

Lighthouses. One at Sigeum on the Hellespont preceded the Pharos at Alexandria which was erected *c.* 280 B.C. A Phoenician one at Corunna was re-established *c.* 1634, and modernized in 1847. The oldest extant is at Cordonan at the mouth of the Gironde, built, 1584–1611. The first Eddystone one, mainly of wood, erected, 1696, by Henry Winstanley, was destroyed, 1703, by a storm in which the architect lost his life. Rudyerd's, 1706, was destroyed by fire, 1755. Smeaton's, 1759, though burnt, 1770, was rebuilt and lasted till 1877; demolished then because of wear in rock foundation. Douglass's, farther out, completed, 1882. Northern Lighthouse Board instituted by Act of Parliament, 1786. In America an Act of Congress dated 1789 provided for the building of L. *See also* TRINITY HOUSE.

Ligurian Republic. Set up at Genoa by Napoleon on 6 June 1797. Annexed to France, 1805.

Lille, France. Founded in the eleventh century by counts of Flanders. Mortgaged to France, 1305; became part of Burgundy, 1369; captured by Louis XIV, 1667; by the Duke of Marlborough, 1708; restored, 1713; bombarded by Austrians, 1792.

Lillibullero or **Lilliburlero,** words

published in 1687, attributed to Lord Wharton (1648–1715), and set to Purcell's (1658–95) arrangement of an old Irish tune. British Commando units adopted the tune as a march during World War II.

Lima, Peru (*q.v.*). Founded, 1535, by Pizarro, who was murdered here in 1541. University founded, 1551. Severe earthquake, 1746.

Limburg. Dutch province, part of a county founded in Carolingian times, which became a duchy in the twelfth century, and passed to Brabant in 1228, then to Burgundy (*q.v.*), and thus to the Austrian Netherlands, 1713. Included in the kingdom of the United Netherlands, 1815, it was partitioned in 1839, when the western portion became **Limbourg** or **Limburg**, Belgian province, whose coal-mines were first exploited in 1920.

Limerick, Ireland. Incorporated, 1195. Taken by Ireton, 1651; invested by English and Dutch, Aug. 1690; again invested and surrendered, Oct. 1691. The cathedral founded, 1142; rebuilt, 1490.

'Limericks.' Earliest known, appeared in print *c.* 1820. Popularized through publication of Edward Lear's *Book of Nonsense*, 1846.

Limousin, anct. province of France centring on Limoges, came into English hands, 1152, as the dowry of Eleanor of Aquitaine, bride of Henry II. Restored to France, 1369. Partitioned into the départements of Corrèze, Haute-Vienne, Creuze, and (parts of) Charente, Dordogne, 1791.

Limousins, name given to a clerical party, a group of cardinals native to the above region, dominant at the papal court of Avignon, 1342–78.

Lincoln, England. Bishop of L. present at Council of Arles, 314. Castle commenced by William I, 1068. Cathedral built between 1068 and 1501. Fight known as 'Fair of Lincoln', 1217. Five Parliaments held here between 1301 and 1386. Besieged by parliamentary army under the Earl of Manchester, 1644.

Lincolnshire Insurrection, The. Was largely the outcome of the dissolution of the monasteries and of fiscal oppression. It originated in Oct. 1536 and had been largely suppressed by the end of that month.

Lindisfarne. *See* HOLY ISLAND.

Linnean Society (London). Founded, 1788, by Sir J. E. Smith; incorporated, 1802; named after Carl Linnaeus, the Swedish botanist (1707–78).

Lion League. Formed by the knights against the tax instead of personal service levied by Albert IV of Bavaria, 1488.

Lisbon. Conquered by Moors, A.D. 716. Retaken by the Portuguese with English assistance and cathedral built, 1147. Vasco da Gama embarked from Belem, 1497, and monastery of Belem commenced, 1500. Made capital of Portugal, 1506. Seized by Spaniards under Alva, 1580. Retaken by Braganza, 1640. Almost totally destroyed by earthquake, 1 Nov. 1755. Cathedral rebuilt, 1756–7. Held by French, 1807–8. University founded, 1911 (that founded in 1290 was transferred to Coimbra, 1537).

Lithography. Invented by Alois Senefelder (1771–1834) *c.* 1796. *See* ENGRAVING.

Lithuania (Lith. **Lietuva**). Lithuanians first politically united under Mindaugas, Grand Prince from 1236 to 1263. His most prominent successors were Gediminas (1316–41), Algirdas (1345–77), and Vestutis, the last heathen ruler, who was murdered after being taken prisoner by the Teutonic Knights, 1382. The latter's son, Vytautas the Great, allied with Poland to smash the Teutonic Knights at the first battle of Tannenberg (1410); the alliance became a union with the marriage (1386) of the Grand Prince Jogaila to the Polish princess Jadwiga (1369–99) by which he became King Jagiello (Wladislaw II) of Poland (*q.v.*), and converted the Lithuanians to Christianity. The joint power of L. and Poland now extended to the Black Sea and their legislatures were merged at the Union of Lublin, 1569, from which time L. shared the history of Poland, its partitions, and suppression. Except for Memel (Klaipeda) most of L. fell to Russia, and became known as the Government of Kovno, 1795. A Soviet republic, estab. 1918, was overthrown and an independent republic estab., 1919. L. was totally occupied by the Red Army, 15 June 1940. Occupied by Germany, 1941–4; then reconquered by Russia. Sporadic anti-Russian activity in L. since 1960s.

Little Entente (Czechoslovakia, Yugoslavia, and Rumania). Formed, Aug. 1920. Scope enlarged, 1922 and 1923.

Liverpool, England. Founded by King John, 1199. Attacked by Prince Rupert, 26 June 1644. Principal dock-building began, *c*. 1780. University College founded, 1880. Made a city and diocese, 1880. Mersey railway tunnel open, 1886. Chief magistrate made Lord Mayor, 1893. Independent university set up, 1903. Anglican cathedral founded, 1904. Roman Catholic cathedral founded, 1933: opened 1967. Mersey road tunnel opened, 1934, extensions begun, 1969. Severe bombing by the Germans, 1941. Considerable rebuilding of central L. since 1960. Labour council abolished office of Lord Mayor, 1983.

Livery Companies of London. So called: not all have livery. In order of precedence; with earliest date at which each is known to have existed (E.), and date of incorporation (I.). Names in square brackets are of extinct companies. Names marked 'NL' are of companies that have no livery:

	E.	I.
1. Mercers	1172	1393
2. Grocers	1345	1428
3. Drapers	1180	1365
4. Fishmongers	1321	1364
5. Goldsmiths	1180	1327
6. Skinners	1272	1327
7. Merchant Taylors	1267	1327
8. Haberdashers	1371	1448
9. Salters	—	{ Reign of Edward III
10. Ironmongers	1364	1463
11. Vintners	1321	1437
12. Clothworkers	1480	1528

The above are the 'Great Companies'.

	E.	I.
13. Dyers	1188	1471
14. Brewers	1345	1438
15. Leather-sellers	1372	1444
16. Pewterers	1348	1473
17. Barbers	1308	1462
18. Cutlers	1285	1416
19. Bakers	1155	1486
20. Waxchandlers	1358	1483
21. Tallowchandlers	1363	1462
22. Armourers and Braziers	{ Reign of Edward II }	1453
23. Girdlers	1180	1448
24. Butchers	1180	1605
25. Saddlers	1216	1395
26. Carpenters	1333	1477
27. Cordwainers	1272	1439
28. Painter-Stainers	1466	1581
29. Curriers	1272	1606
30. Masons	1356	1677

	E	I
31. Plumbers	1365	1611
32. Innholders	{ 1327 as Hostelers }	1515
33. Founders	1365	1614
34. Poulters	1345	1504
35. Cooks	1311	1482
36. Coopers	{ Reign of Edward II }	1501
37. Tylers and Bricklayers	?1502	1568
38. Bowyers	1488	1621
39. Fletchers	1371	None
40. Blacksmiths	1325	1571
41. Joiners	1309	1571
42. Weavers	{ Not later than reign of Edward I }	{ Reign of Henry I }
43. Woolmen	? 14th cent.	Unknown
44. Scriveners	1357	1617
45. Fruiterers	1416	1606
46. Plaisterers	—	1502
47. Stationers	?1403	1556
48. Broderers	—	1561
49. Upholders	14th cent.	1626
50. Musicians	{ 1350 as Minstrels }	1604
51. Turners	1310	1604
52. Basket-makers	1422	? None
53. Glaziers	1328	1638
54. Horners	1376	1638
55. Farriers	1272	1685
56. Paviours	{ Before 1479 }	{ 1673 (withdrawn) }
57. Loriners	1260	1711
58. Apothecaries	1511	1617
59. Shipwrights	1456	1605
60. Spectacle-makers	?1628	1629
61. Clockmakers	1627	1631
62. Glovers	14th cent.	1638
63. [Combmakers]	—	?1650
64. Feltmakers	1180	1667
65. Framework Knitters	—	1657
66. [Silk-throwers]	—	?1629
67. [Silkmen]	—	—
68. [Pinmakers]	—	?1636
69. Needle-makers	{ Reign of Henry VIII }	{ Commonwealth }
70. Gardeners	1345	1605
71. [Soap-makers]	—	?1638
72. Tinplate Workers	{ 1469 as Wire-drawers }	1670
73. Wheelwrights	—	1670

	E	I
74. Distillers	—	1638
75. [Hatband-makers]	—	?1638
76. Patten-makers	14th cent.	1670
77. Glass-sellers	—	1664
78. [Tobacco-pipe Makers]	—	?1663
79. Coach and Coach-Harness Makers	—	1677
80. Gunmakers	—	1638
81. Gold and Silver Wyre Drawers	1423	1623
82. [Longbow-string Makers]	—	—
83. Playing-card Makers	—	1628
84. Fan-makers	—	1709
85. [Woodmongers]	—	—
86. [Starchmakers]	—	?1632
87. [Fishermen]	—	?1687
88. Parish Clerks NL	1233	1442
89. Carmen	1516	1524
90. [Porters]	—	—
91. Watermen and Lightermen NL	Unknown	None
92. [Surgeons]	—	?1308

		E	I
{ Not num-bered	Solicitors NL	1908	None
	Master Mariners	1926	1930

Livingstonia Mission. Suggested by Dr. Livingstone, the explorer (1813–73), for the abolition of slavery on the E. coast of Africa; expedition first fitted out in 1875, and settled at Cape Clear. Moved to Bandawé, 1883.

Livonia (Let. **Vidzeme;** Est. **Libmaa**), territory since at least the beginning of the Christian era inhabited by and named after the Livs, a Finnish tribe related to the Estonians; subject to and converted to Christianity by the Teutonic Order (*q.v.*), after whose decline L. submitted to Polish suzerainty, 1561, until 1629, when it passed to · Sweden; Russian territory from 1721. In 1918 partitioned between Estonia and Latvia. *See* LATVIA and ESTONIA.

Llandaff. Cathedral begun 1120; restored 1844–69; bombed 1941; restored 1957.

Lloyd's Marine Intelligence Department. Originally in a coffee-house kept by Edward L. (*c.* 1648–1713) in seventeenth century; moved from Tower Street to Lombard Street, 1691; to Royal Exchange, 1774; parliamentary inquiry into management of, 1810; incorporated, 1871. Moved to Leadenhall Street, 1928; further new building opened by Queen Elizabeth the Queen Mother, 1957.

Lloyd's Register of Shipping had its origins in Lloyd's coffee-house (*see* previous article) *c.* 1760; became an independent organization, 1834.

Load Line. *See* PLIMSOLL.

Local Defence Volunteers (L.D.V.). *See* HOME GUARD.

Local Government (U.K.). Municipal corporations made elective by ratepayers in Scotland, 1832. In England, 1835. County Councils set up, 1888. Urban and Rural District Councils set up, 1894. Franchise extended to all parliamentary electors, 1945. To 18-year-olds, 1970. Pattern of L.G. in U.K. entirely transformed by Local Government Act of 1972.

Local Government and Planning, Department of, developed, 1969 from Ministry of Housing and Local Government (*q.v.*) which became subordinate to it.

Local Government Board (U.K.). Superseded the Poor Law Board, 1871. Replaced by Ministry of Health, 1919.

Local Option as to the granting of licences to sell liquor became law in Scotland under the Temperance Act, 1913, but was not introduced in practice until 1920. An attempt to introduce the system in England had failed, 1895. The principle of L.O. was applied in Wales, under the Licensing Act of 1961, to determine whether public houses should open or not on Sundays, the decision being determined by a majority vote in each county and county borough.

Locarno Treaties, 16 Oct. 1925. Three treaties:

1. Mutual guarantee by Germany, Belgium, France, Great Britain, and Italy. Denounced by Germany, 1936.
2. France and Poland, against Germany should she break the peace.
3. France and Czechoslovakia, similar to 2.

Lochaber Hydro-Electric Power Scheme begun, 1926.

Lofoten Islands, Norway, raided by British forces, 6 Mar. and 29 Dec. 1941.

Logarithms invented, 1614, by John Napier (1550–1617).

Lollards. Name applied, after his death, to the followers of Wyclif (1324–84). In 1395 they presented a petition to Parliament protesting against abuses in the Church. In 1401 the statute *De Haeretico Comburendo* was passed against them, and on 12 Feb. 1401 William Sawtrey, the first victim, was burnt at the stake for his views. Persecution continued spasmodically, Sir John Oldcastle being one of the most famous victims in 1417. After this date the sect lost its importance.

Lombardy, Italy. Occupied by the Lombards or Langobards, A.D. 568. Joined by Charlemagne to his empire, 774. From 843 ruled by its own kings until 1337, when it passed to the dukes of Milan. Became part of Spain under Charles V, 1529. Fell to Austria, 1714. After Napoleon's campaign and his downfall it was restored to Austria, 1815. Annexed by Savoy, 1859.

London and Paris Agreements (1954) evolved a formula to supersede the defensive arrangements which E.D.C., rejected by France, had been intended to cover.

London Airport, Heathrow, opened, 1946. Subsequent L.A.s are at Gatwick and Stansted.

London Bridge. Originally built of wood, the first bridge of which we have documentary evidence (963) was wrecked by Olaf the Saint, when a mercenary in the service of Ethelred II, 1014. Another was built, destroyed by a hurricane in 1091, not rebuilt till 1120, and burnt down, 1136. A temporary structure followed. A new (stone) one commenced, 1176, and completed, 1209. It suffered frequently from fire, and was restored. Toll discontinued, 27 Mar. 1782. New bridge commenced, 15 Mar. 1824, and opened by William IV, 1 Aug. 1831, when the old structure was demolished. This bridge in turn put up for sale, Oct. 1967, and bought by a U.S. company and re-erected in the U.S.A. Present L.B. begun, 1967; completed, 1973.

London, City of. Said to have been founded before A.D. 43. Burned by Boudicca 61. Fortified, 350–69. Destroyed by Danes, 839. Tower of L. commenced, 1078. First charter granted to city, 1079. First mayor appointed, 1089. Privileges granted by the regent, Prince John Lackland, 1191. Divided into wards, and aldermen appointed, 1242. Chief magistrate know as 'Lord Mayor' since 1354. Royal proclamations against further building, 1580 and 1611. Great Plague, 1665. Great Fire, 1666. Street lamps first used, 1677. Charter forfeited, 1682; restored, 1689. Great fires caused by German raids, Dec. 1940 and May 1941. Right to send two M.P.s to Parliament abolished, 1948.

London Conference on naval armaments opened, 22 Jan. 1930. Treaty concluded between five powers—Great Britain, U.S.A., France, Italy, and Japan—22 Apr. 1930.

London County Council. County of L. formed by Local Government Act, 1888, and L.C.C. set up to administer the same area as was served from 1855 onwards, by the Metropolitan Board of Works, whose powers the L.C.C. inherited. Labour Party gained control of L.C.C., 1934, retaining it until the L.C.C. was superseded by the Greater London Council (*q.v.*) under the London Government Act, 1963.

London, County of. Defined by Local Government Act of 1888, and a county council formed. Formed into 28 municipal boroughs by L. Government Act, 1899. Disappeared under the L. Government Act, 1963, which created Greater London.

Londonderry (Irish **Doire**), locally still called **Derry**, and so called by all English speakers until its colonization in the seventeenth century by the Irish Society of London. Grew up round a monastery founded in A.D. 546 by St. Columba. The twelfth-century cathedral church was demolished, 1600. Besieged, 19 Apr.–30 July 1689, by Jacobites. Civil rights disturbances in, 1968, and very serious rioting, Aug. 1969 (*see* IRELAND, NORTHERN). Subsequently scene of considerable I.R.A. violence. City council changed name to Derry, 1984.

Londonderry Air, traditional Irish tune, first printed, 1855.

London, Diocese of. Following is a list of bishops since 1044:
William, 1051
Hugh d'Orivalle, 1075
Maurice, 1086
Richard de Belmeis I, 1108
Gilbert Universalis, 1128
Robert de Sigillo, 1141
Richard de Belmeis II, 1152
Gilbert Foliot, 1163
Richard Fitzneal, 1189
William de Santa Maria, 1199
Eustace de Fauconberg, 1221
Roger Niger, 1229
Fulk Basset, 1242
Henry de Wengham, 1260
Henry de Sandwich, 1263
John de Chishull, 1274
Richard Gravesend, 1280
Ralph de Baldock, 1306
Gilbert Segrave, 1313
Richard de Newport, 1317
Stephen de Gravesend, 1319
Richard de Bintworth, 1338
Ralph de Stratford, 1340
Michael de Northburgh, 1355

Simon de Sudbury, 1362
William Courtenay, 1375
Robert de Braybroke, 1382
Roger Walden, 1405
Nicholas Bubwith, 1406
Richard Clifford, 1407
John Kemp, 1421
William Gray, 1426
Robert FitzHugh, 1431
Robert Gilbert, 1436
Thomas Kemp, 1450
Richard Hill, 1489
Thomas Savage, 1496
William Wareham, 1502
William Barons, 1504
Richard FitzJames, 1506
Cuthbert Tunstall, 1522
John Stokesley, 1530
Edmund Bonner, 1540
Nicholas Ridley, 1550
Edmund Bonner, 1553
Edmund Grindal, 1559
Edwin Sandys, 1570
John Aylmer, 1577
Richard Fletcher, 1595
Richard Bancroft, 1597
Richard Vaughan, 1604
Thomas Ravis, 1607
George Abbot, 1610
John King, 1611
George Mountain, 1621
William Laud, 1628
William Juxon, 1633
Gilbert Sheldon, 1660
Humfrey Henchman, 1663
Henry Compton, 1675
John Robinson, 1714
Edmund Gibson, 1723
Thomas Sherlock, 1748
Thomas Hayter, 1761
Richard Osbaldeston, 1762
Richard Terrick, 1764
Robert Lowth, 1777
Beilby Porteous, 1787
John Randolph, 1809
William Howley, 1813
Charles James Blomfield, 1828
Archibald Campbell Tait, 1856
John Jackson, 1869
Frederick Temple, 1885
Mandell Creighton, 1896
Arthur Foley Winnington-Ingram, 1901
Geoffrey Francis Fisher, 1939

John William Charles Wand, 1945
Henry Montgomery Campbell, 1956
Robert Wright Stopford, 1961
Gerald Alexander Ellison, 1973
Graham Douglas Leonard, 1981

'London Gazette.' *See* Newspapers.

London Library. Founded 1840, and opened, 3 May 1841. Reading-room opened, 15 May 1843. Removed from 40 Pall Mall to Beauchamp House, St. James's Square, 1845. Rebuilt, 1896.

London Museum. Founded, 1910, and opened at Kensington Palace, 1912. Transferred to Lancaster House, St. James's, 1913–14, but closed in 1939. Reopened at Kensington Palace, 1951. In 1976 Kensington Palace and Guildhall Museums amalgamated to form the Museum of London in a new building near London Wall in the City.

London, Pact of. Between Britain, France, and Russia, who mutually engaged not to conclude peace separately, Sept. 1914. A secret agreement, signed 26 Apr. 1915, by the Allies and Italy, comprising the terms on which Italy would enter the war on the side of the Allies. *See* Fiume.

London Transport Executive, superseded, 1948, the **London Passenger Transport Board**, which had been estab. in 1933. The Greater London Council was responsible for the L.T.E.'s overall policy 1969–84, when the govt. took over renaming the L.T.E. **London Regional Transport**.

London, Tower of. The present White Tower, the earliest part of the structure, was built by William the Conqueror *c.* 1078. In 1140 Stephen used the tower as a residence. In Henry III's reign (1216–72) the regalia were removed to the tower. The famous attempt to steal the crown jewels by Col. Blood from the tower, 9 May 1671.

London, Treaties of.

1. Between England and Holland, signed 1674, ending war of 1672.
2. Between England, France, and Russia, during Greek War of Independence; contracting parties bound themselves to take action for the purpose of securing the independence of Greece under Turkish suzerainty; signed, 1827.
3. Between Great Britain, France, and Holland, providing for the erection of the Flemish and Walloon provinces into an independent kingdom; signed 1833.
4. Between Austria, France, Great Britain, Prussia, and Russia, confirming the treaty of 1833.
5. Between England, France, Russia, Austria, and Turkey, after conclusion of Syrian War; it provided that the Bosphorus and Dardanelles should be closed to ships of war (also known as the Treaty of Dardanelles); signed, 1841.
6. Between Austria, France, Great Britain, Prussia, Russia, and Sweden, settling the succession to the Danish throne; signed, 1852.
7. Treaty of L., 30 May 1913, ending the First Balkan War.
8. Treaty of L. (Naval), defined relative strengths of fleets of the powers, 1936. *See also* London and Paris Agreements.

London University. Institution in Gower Street (now University College) founded, 1828. King's College founded as a rival institution, 1829. University chartered by William IV, 28 Nov. 1836: students from both existing colleges to sit for examinations conducted by the university. Amended charter, 1858. Degrees granted to women, 1878. University of London Acts, 1898 and 1926. New buildings in Bloomsbury begun, 1933; completed, 1936.

Long Island, first settled 1636. L.I. City created, 1870, and officially absorbed by New York City (borough of Queens), 1898.

Long Parliament. The fifth Parliament summoned by Charles I; met, 3 Nov. 1640 (*see* Pride's Purge); dissolved forcibly by Oliver Cromwell, 20 Apr. 1653; recalled twice, and finally declared itself dissolved, 16 Mar. 1660.

Lonsdale Belt for boxing first awarded, 1911, by Hugh Cecil Lowther (1857–1944), fifth Earl of L.

Lord of the Isles. Title of the rulers of

the Western Isles of Scotland. First conferred by David I of Scotland on Somerled of Argyll, 1135. Somerled's line supplanted by Iain MacDonald of Islay, 1346. The Ls. of the I. were intermittently vassals of Norway until the Treaty of Perth, 2 July 1266, when Haakon of Norway surrendered his claims. Title forfeited to Scottish crown, 1493, and became an apanage belonging to the heir male of the Scottish crown in 1540, which it has since remained.

Lord Privy Seal. Office first held by laymen in reign of Henry VIII (*q.v.*). Specific duties abolished, 1884, and position now generally held by a senior member of the Cabinet.

Lord's Day Observance Society. Founded, 1831.

Lords, House of. Earliest extant writ is dated 1265. Mitred abbots excluded, 1536. Abolished by Commons, 6 Feb. 1649. Cromwell recalled a selection of peers to be called House of Lords, 20 Jan. 1658. House of Lords constituted as before 1649 reassembled, 25 Apr. 1660. Sixteen Scottish peers elected by their order added under Act of Union, 1707. Crown's power to create peers used to secure a Tory majority, 31 Dec. 1711. Twenty-eight Irish peers, elected for life, added, 1801; no election of Irish peers has taken place, however, since the Irish Free State Act of 1922. Proxy voting waived since 1868. L. of Appeal added by Appellate Jurisdiction Act, 1876. Parliament Act restricting Lords' veto to a delaying power of two years became law, 18 Aug. 1911. New bill to restrict delaying power to one year became law in 1948. Life Peerages Act, 1958, empowered the sovereign to create men and women life peers and peeresses. Peerages Act, 1963, allows hereditary peers the option of remaining commoners (in which case they can stand for election to the Commons), though their heirs are free to revive the title. Wilson government proposed radical reforming legislation for H. of L. in a Bill introduced 19 Dec. 1968, but after opposition from their own supporters and the official Opposition the Bill was abandoned, 17 April 1969. H. of L. voted for televising of sessions, Dec. 1983.

Loreto or **Loretto,** Italy. Virgin Mary's house reputed to have been miraculously translated from Nazareth to L., 1295. The Holy Image was taken to France, 1796; but restored, 1803.

Loro Sae. *See* TIMOR.

Lorraine, founded as kingdom of Lotharingia, A.D. 843. Duchy of L. given to King of Poland, 1736. Incorporated in France, 1766. Thereafter changed hands in same manner as Alsace (*q.v.*).

Lorraine, Cross of. Carried by Joan of Arc in the fifteenth century, and adopted as an emblem of French resistance to the Germans by de Gaulle in 1940. From 1958 onwards he used it as his political emblem in France.

Los Angeles, California, settled in 1781, became the Mexican capital of California, and was seized by a U.S. naval force in 1846. U.S. city charter granted, 1850. Aqueduct 233 miles long from Sierra Nevada mountains built through Mojave desert to L.A., 1913.

Lost Ten Tribes of Israel, not accounted for after the deportation of the original twelve Israelite tribes to Media by the Assyrians, 722 B.C. Frequently 'rediscovered', e.g. by Antonio de Montezinos, 1644, in America, but first in England by John Sadler, 1649. The doctrine of the British Israelites was first developed by Richard Brothers (1757–1824).

Loughborough University of Technology, established 1966.

Louisbourg, Nova Scotia. Fortified by French, 1713. Taken by British, 1745. Restored to France, 1748. Again captured by British, 1758. Finally ceded to Britain, 1763.

Louis d'Or. Gold coin in use in France, 1641–1795.

Louisiana, U.S.A. Originally claimed for France by the explorer La Salle (1643–87), who named the territory after Louis XIV. Handed over to the Mississippi Co. (*see* MISSISSIPPI SCHEME), 1719. Ceded to Spain by England, 1762; to France, 1800. Sold to U.S.A. by Napoleon, 1803; admitted as a state, 1812. Present constitution, 1921. Huey Pierce Long's governorship, 1931–5.

Lourdes, France. Virgin Mary said to have appeared to a peasant girl, Bernadette Soubirous, 11 Feb. 1858. Church declared the facts to be authentic, 1862. The basilica erected, 1876. St. Bernadette canonized, 1933. Underground basilica consecrated, 1958.

Lourenço Marques. *See* MAPUTO.

Louvain (Flem. **Leeuwen**), Belgium. University founded, 1426; suppressed, 1797; refounded, 1817, and designated the Catholic University, 1835. Seriously damaged by Germans in 1914 and 1940. Language disputes at, 1964–6.

Louvre, The (Paris). Present building started in 1541 by Francis I. Formerly a royal palace, now a museum and picture gallery; enlarged during reign of Louis XIV (1643–1715).

Loyalists, United Empire, migrated to Canada, 1783, from United States. *See* ONTARIO.

Lübeck, Germany. Founded by Saxons, A.D. 1143; held by French, 1806–14; joined N. German Confederation, 1866. Relinquished status as free city, 1937. *See* HANSEATIC LEAGUE.

Lucca, Italy. Originally *Luca*. Since at least the eleventh century the cathedral of St. Martin has contained the *Volto Santo* (Holy Face), a woodcarving of Christ attributed to His contemporary, St. Nicodemus. Made a Roman colony. 177 B.C.; independent republic from 1369 to 1797; made a principality by Napoleon, 1805; passed to Spain, 1815; ceded to Tuscany, 1847.

Lucerne (Luzern), Switzerland. Joined Swiss Confederation, 1332.

Lucknow, India. Ancient city. Capital of Oudh, 1775; besieged during the Indian Mutiny, 1 July 1857; reinforced by Gen. Havelock, 25 Sept. 1857; relieved by Sir Colin Campbell, 17 Nov. 1857; final capture by him, 19–22 Mar. 1858. Now the capital of Uttar Pradesh.

Luddite Riots. Broke out first in Nottinghamshire, in reaction to increasing use of industrial and agricultural machinery, in Nov. 1811. The name L. originated with one Ned Ludd, a worker who is said to have broken some machinery some years before. Renewed, July 1816, when much damage was done.

Luftwaffe, German Air Force which had existed in fact since at least 1933, first officially mentioned in a proclamation by Goering, Mar. 1935. Post-war L. estab., 1956.

Lundy Island, presented to the National Trust, 1969.

Lunéville, Peace of. Signed between Germany and France, 9 Feb. 1801, confirming the Treaty of Campo Formio.

Lupercalia, ancient Roman festival, celebrated on 15 Feb., until its abolition, A.D. 494, when Pope Gelasius I decreed its replacement by the Christian Lady Day (2 Feb.).

Lusaka. Capital of Zambia (formerly N. Rhodesia) since 1935.

Lusatia (Wend. **Lužica**; Ger. **Lausitz**), principally inhabited by the Wends (*q.v.*), was one of the Bohemian crown lands for the period 1160–1360. It was acquired by the Electors of Saxony, 1620. All but a part of Upper L. was ceded to Prussia, 1815. Since 1949 has formed part of the German Democratic Republic, with the exception of a portion which lies E. of the R. Neisse, and which has belonged to Poland since 1946.

'Lusitania.' Unarmed Cunard liner sunk by German submarine off Old Head of Kinsale, 7 May 1915. 1198 passengers and crew, including 124 Americans, were drowned, and the sinking influenced the U.S.A.'s subsequent decision to enter the war on the allied side.

'Lutine,' H.M.S. A 32-gun ship wrecked in a storm off Vlieland, Netherlands, 9–10 Oct. 1799, with specie on board to the value of £1,175,000. Dutch claimed the wreck, and not until 1823 did the Dutch Government acknowledge that Lloyd's were entitled to half. Much had already been taken. Operations on Lloyd's behalf began 1857. By 1859 they had received £22,162 6s. 7d. Operations resumed, May–June 1938, when some bars of gold were recovered.

Lutterworth (Leics.), England. Wyclif was rector at the church here,

1374–84. The church, containing many relics of the reformer, was carefully restored, 1867–9.

Luttrell or **Louterell Psalter.** Illuminated MS. of *c.* 1340. Acquired for the nation, 1929.

Lützen, Germany. Wallenstein defeated by Gustavus Adolphus (who was killed), 1632; allies by Napoleon, 1813.

Luxemburg (in the local Franconian dialect **Letzeburg**). Settled by Franks, A.D. 459. Independent county, 963. Became Burgundian territory, 1443. Then Hapsburg, 1482; Spanish, 1555; French, 1684–97; Spanish until 1714; Austrian until 1795; then French again until allotted tothe United Netherlands at Congress of Vienna, 1815, and garrisoned by Prussia. Seceded from Belgium, 1839, losing thereby Belgian L. Constitution granted, 1848. In 1867, by Treaty of London, it was declared an independent grand duchy, and the Prussians withdrew. The fortifications were at the same time demolished. Occupied by the Germans, 1914–18. Invaded by Germany, 10 May 1940; liberated, 1944. Constitutional revision of 1948, abolished L.'s 'perpetually neutral' status. Joined N.A.T.O., 1949. Member of the E.E.C. since its inception on 1 Jan. 1958. Grand-duchess Charlotte abdicated, 1964, and succeeded by her son Jean.

Lvov. Founded *c.* 1250. Became Polish, 1340. From 1848 centre of the Ukrainian national movement. Part of Austria, 1772–1918, and then Polish until 1939, when it was annexed by the U.S.S.R.

Lydia, Asia Minor. Before 700 B.C. known as Maeonia. Conquered by Persians, 546. Independent, 334, but after a period of Syrian and Pergamite domination became part of the Roman province of Asia, 133.

Lynne River Flood Disaster. On the night of 15–16 Aug. 1952 the E. and W. L.Rs. burst their banks, and wrecked the town and harbour of Lynmouth, Devon, causing many deaths.

Lyons, France. Roman colony of Lugdunum founded, 43 B.C. Burnt A.D. 59; by Romans, 197. Made capital of Burgundy (*q.v.*), 478. United to French crown, 1312. The silk-weaving industry was introduced by Italian refugees about the second decade of the fourteenth century; it was fostered by Charles VII, Francis I, Henry II, and Henry IV. In 1793 refused to acknowledge National Convention, and was besieged for 70 days and destroyed. Its name was temporarily changed to Ville-Affranchie. Capitulated to Austrians, Mar. 1814 and July 1815. Important centre of French resistance movement, 1940–4; liberated from the Germans by French and American troops, 3 Sept. 1944.

M

M.1. First British motorway intended originally to link London and Birmingham. First section officially opened, Nov. 1959. Marked start of nationwide motorway development.

'Mabinogion, The.' Title of a collection of eleven medieval Welsh folk-tales found in *The White Book of Rhydderch* (*c.* 1300–25) and *The Red Book of Hergest* (*c.* 1375–1425) and other MSS.

Macadamization of Roads. Named after J. L. McAdam (1756–1836). First used in England between 1810 and 1816. Word 'Tarmac' registered, 1903.

Macao, China. Portuguese settled at, 1557. Declared a free port, 1845. Treaty with China, 1 Dec. 1887, confirmed Portuguese rights to the territory; under 1974 agreement M. is a Chinese ter. under Portuguese administration.

Macassar, Indonesia. First Dutch settlement, 1607. Massacre, 1618.

Macedonia, peopled by Grecian tribes, became united under one government *c.* 700 B.C. Capital: first, Aegae; then, Pella. Persians subdued it *c.* 490 B.C.; its king, Alexander I, compelled to help invasion of Greece by Xerxes. Recovered independence after battle of Plataea, 479 B.C. Prospered under Archelaus (*d.* 399 B.C.). Civil wars till accession, 359 B.C., of Philip II, who became leader of Greece. His son, Alexander the Great, ruled 336–323 and was succeeded by Antipater (*d.* 319 B.C.). Civil wars ensued; security regained under Antigonus Gonatos, 277–239 B.C. Conquered by Rome, 168 B.C.; became a Roman province, 143 B.C.; later, part of Eastern Roman Empire (*q.v.*). Overrun by Slavs at end of sixth century A.D. Dominated by Bulgarians, ninth–eleventh centuries. Mission of Cyril and Methodius, *c.* 860, led to Macedonian, first among Slavonic languages, being reduced to writing in the Cyrillic and Glagolithic scripts invented by the missionaries. Eleventh-century MSS. (Codex Zagrophenic, etc.) still extant. Thereafter the language was not written until *c.* 1764, when the first Macedonian dictionary was published. Byzantine rule re-established, early eleventh century. Included in Serbia in fourteenth, fell to Turks in fifteenth. Claimed by Greece, Serbia, and Bulgaria in nineteenth; and was in a continuous state of civil war till 1903, when the Bulgarians rose and the Turks were massacred. The Balkan League's victory over Turkey, 1912–13, and the defeat of Bulgaria, resulted in division of M. between Greece, Bulgaria, and Serbia, 1913. Macedonian recognized as a separate nationality and language at AVNOJ session of 29 Sept. 1943, and Macedonian Republic set up, as a constituent part of Yugoslavia, 2 Aug. 1944. Civil war started by Communists with Yugoslav and Bulgarian assistance in Greek M., 1945: ended 1948. *See* GREECE, MODERN and BULGARIA.

McGill University of Canada, founded by James McG. of Glasgow (*d.* 1813). Incorporated, 1821 and 1852. Women's college added, 1899.

Machu Pichu, ancient Peruvian city of the Andes, built *c.* A.D. 800, rebuilt in the sixteenth century after having been abandoned once. Site rediscovered, 1911, by Hiram Bingham who, in 1948, formally opened a new highway to the city, named after him.

M'Naughten Rules, the answers to a set of questions put to the judges as a body by the House of Lords following the acquittal on grounds of insanity of Daniel M'N., who in 1843 shot dead Sir R. Peel's private secretary. Now superseded.

Madagascar. Appears on Arab charts of twelfth century. Visited by Diego Diaz (Portugal), 1500. Granted, 1642, by Louis XIV to the Compagnie de l'Orient. French massacred by natives, 1672. British took possession, 1814; French returned after 1815. British ascendancy 1810–28. Under Queen Rànavàlona I missionaries were persecuted and trade hampered, 1829. Europeans returned to Antananarivo after 1853. Fr. protectorate estab. 1895, monarchy abolished. M. made a Fr. colony, 1896. Occupied by British, May–Sept. 1942. French resumed administration, 1944. M. became an independent republic, 26 June 1960; military rule, 1972–5. New constitution approving the Democratic Republic of M. approved by referendum, 21 Dec. 1975.

Madeira, Atlantic. Porto Santo discovered, 1418; Mitrelf, 1420, by João Gonçalves Zarco. Colonized by Portuguese, 1431. Occupied by British, 1801 and 1807–14, in trust for Portuguese crown. Unsuccessful rebellion against Portuguese rule, Apr.–May 1931.

Madhya Pradesh, India. Present state came into existence, 1 Nov. 1956, with the merger of the states of Madhya Bharat and Vindhya with most of the former Central Provinces (renamed M.P. from 1947 onwards), excluding the Mahratta-speaking districts of the latter.

Mad Parliament, 1258. It appointed the committee which drew up the Provisions of Oxford (*q.v.*).

Madras, India (*q.v.*). City and state. English established themselves in, 1644; city captured by French, 1746; restored to English, 1748; besieged by French, 12 Dec. 1758.

Madras Mutiny, among European officers of the E. India Co.'s army, broke out, 1809.

Madrid, Spain. Founded by Moors in tenth century as *Medina Majerit.*

Taken by Ramiro II, King of Leon, 939, but not permanently conquered until 1083. First charter, 1202. Cortes first held there, 1309. Treaty between Charles V and Francis I, 1526. Declared capital of Spain by Philip II, 1561. Captured from French by allied forces under Wellington, 1812. University of M. was established by the removal of that of Alcalá to the capital, 1836–7.

Madrigal Society of London. Founded by John Immyns, 1741.

Mafeking Night, 18 May 1900, when the news reached London that M. had been relieved after a seven-month siege by the Boers.

Mafia, Sicilian secret movement, founded at some time between 1800 and 1825. Its period of greatest activity and power was from 1860 to 1870, and in the 1890s its influence spread to the U.S.A., where a large number of immigrants to New York were of Sicilian origin. The Fascists claimed to have crushed the organization in 1928, but there was a recrudescence of violence and extortion in Sicily after World War II, admitted by the Sicilian authorities by 1960. Despite efforts by the It. central and provincial govs., the M. continued unchecked in Italy, especially in the S. in 1985, being prominent in kidnapping, vice and drug dealings in both Italy and the U.S.A.

Magdeburg, German Democratic Republic. Founded by Charlemagne, A.D. 805; destroyed by the Wends, 924, and refounded shortly afterwards by Editha; made seat of a bishopric, 968; joined Luther, 17 July 1524; joined League of Schmalkalden (*q.v.*), 1531; surrendered to Maurice of Saxony, Nov. 1551; besieged in vain by Wallenstein, 1629; sacked by Tilly, 1631; annexed to kingdom of Westphalia, 1803; restored to Prussia, 1814. Part of the German Democratic Republic since 1949.

Magellan, Straits of, discovered, 1520, by the Portuguese navigator, Ferdinand M. (1480–1521).

Maginot Line. Pre–1939 eastern fortifications of France, constructed 1928–34. Named after André Maginot (1877–1932), minister of war. 'Turned' during Ger. offensive, 1940.

Magna Carta or **The Great Charter** of England. The barons compelled King John to grant it at Runnymede, 15 June 1215.

Magnum Concilium or Great Council of Peers last met at York, 1640.

Mahdi. *See* SUDAN.

Mahrattas. First appear in Indian history in the middle of seventeenth century. Defeated by Afghans, Jan. 1761. From 1780 onwards they were continually at war with the British and their allies. Of their leaders the Peishwa of Poona was compelled to accept a British alliance in 1802, the Gaekwar of Baroda in 1803, the Scindiah and the Bhonsla of Nagpur in 1804, the latter being then forced to cede Berar to the Nizam of Hyderabad (*q.v.*). War nevertheless continued intermittently and culminated in the submission of the Holkar of Indore in 1817, the British annexation of Poona in 1818, and the abolition of the Peishwaship. The claimant to this office, Nana Sahib, later played a leading part in the Indian Mutiny (*q.v.*). Satara was annexed in 1848, Nagpur in 1853.

Maiden, beheading machine used in Scotland and in some northern English boroughs (*see* HALIFAX LAW) in the Middle Ages. That of Edinburgh was first used, 1561; last used, 1710.

Maiden Castle, earthwork in Dorset surrounding a site inhabited from *c.* 2000 B.C. until the inhabitants were forcibly evacuated by the Romans *c.* A.D. 70. It was excavated by Sir Mortimer Wheeler, 1934–7. Further excavations and repairs 1985.

Maine, French province up to 1789, with capital at Le Mans. From *c.* A.D. 800 was ruled by counts who were themselves vassals of the counts of Anjou (*q.v.*). United with Anjou under the Angevins, 1110. English territory, 1154–1204. It belonged to the Count of Provence, 1246–1328, then passed again to the French crown. It returned permanently to the French crown in 1481. M. became a province *c.* 1600.

Maine, U.S.A. First permanent settlement, at Pemaquid, 1623. Western territory, known as province of M., 1635, from 1651 to 1820 a detached part of Massachusetts. The present state of M. founded, 1820; boundary dispute with Great Britain settled, 1842.

Mainz or **Mayence,** Germany. Of Celtic origin; Roman military station called *Moguntiacum* dates from 13 B.C.; cathedral built, A.D. 975–1009; head of the confederacy of Rhenish cities, thirteenth century; in French possession, 1797–1814; by Congress of Vienna, 1814–15, ceded to Hesse-Darmstadt; declared a federal fortress, 1870. Heavily damaged during fighting in 1945.

Majorca (Sp. **Mallorca**), Mediterranean, conquered by the Romans, 123 B.C.; by the Vandals, A.D. 423; by the Moors, 790; became a Moorish kingdom, 1009; independent Christian kingdom, 1276–1349, when finally annexed by Aragon. M. favoured the cause of Charles in the War of the Spanish Succession, but submitted to Philip V of Spain, 1715; held by the insurgents during the civil war of 1936–9.

Major-General. Term first used in technical military sense (commander of infantry of an army), early seventeenth century. Rank was instituted in Britain with special sense by Oliver Cromwell in 1655, after he had quarrelled with his first Parliament. Each M.-G. was to govern a district. This scheme was dropped in 1657.

Malacca, Malaysia (*q.v.*). Settled by Portuguese, 1511, who held it until 1641, when the Dutch seized it and, in turn, held it until 1795, when the English took possession; restored to the Dutch by the Peace of Amiens, 1801; exchanged with Britain for Sumatra, 1825; made part of Straits Settlements, 1867. Incorporated in the Malayan Union, 1947, in the Malayan Federation, 1948, and in Malaysia, 1963.

Malaga, Spain. Captured from Moors by Ferdinand and Isabella, 1487. Sacked by French, 1810.

Malagasy. *See* MADAGASCAR.

Malawi, formerly **Nyasaland,** E. Africa. Visited by Bocarro, 1616. By Livingstone, 1859. African Lakes Co. established, 1878. Rhodes obtained charter for British S. Africa Co. to develop Nyasaland, 1884. Protectorate established, 1891. Suppression of slave trade, 1893–7. John Chelembwe's revolt, 1915. United with the Rhodesias in Central African Federation, 1953, but African population, led by Hastings Banda, continued to agitate strongly against federation. In 1963 became a self-governing colony, Banda being premier. Federation dissolved, Dec. 1963. On 6 July 1964 Nyasaland, under the new name of **Malawi,** became an independent state within the Commonwealth, subsequently becoming a republic, with Banda as president, July 1966 (life president since 1971). *See also* RHODESIA AND NYASALAND, FEDERATION OF.

Malaya. Main treaties establishing British predominance made with Perak, 1874; Selangor, 1874; Negri Sembilan, 1896; Pahang, 1888. These states were federated in 1896. By treaty with Siam, Siamese suzerainty over Kelantan, Trengganu, Kedah, and Perlis ceded to Britain, 1909. Johore came under British influence after 1815, and ceded Singapore to Britain, 1819. Penang was purchased from Kedah, 1786. Malacca ceded by the Dutch, 1825. Japanese invasion began, 8 Dec. 1941. *See* MA-LAYAN FEDERATION, MALAYAN UNION, MALAYSIA, and all the separate states and territories mentioned above.

Malayan Federation, including all former British colonies and protectorates in the Malay Peninsula and Islands, excluding the colony of Singapore, inaugurated its Legislative Council, 24 Feb. 1948. Communist rebellion broke out, May 1948; crushed by 1955. The M.F. became a self-governing Dominion within the Commonwealth, 31 Aug. 1957. Became part of Malaysia (*q.v.*), 16 Sept. 1963.

Malayan Union. Proposal for reorganization of M. states and colonies published 22 Jan. 1946. Union inaugurated, 1 Apr. 1946. Came to an end, 1 Feb. 1948.

Malaysia, union of the Malayan Federation, Singapore, N. Borneo, (renamed Sabah *q.v.*), and Sarawak. M. came

into being on 16 Sept. 1963. Indonesia began a policy of aggressive 'confrontation' which ended Aug. 1966. Singapore (*q.v.*) seceded from M. by mutual agreement, 9 Aug. 1965.

Maldive Islands, former British protectorate having treaty relations with Sri Lanka (*q.v.*). A new constitution established a sultanate, 1932, which was abolished in 1952 when the M.I. became a republic. Sultanate restored, 1954. Became independent, 26 July 1965; republic since 1968.

Mali, independent African republic since 22 Sept. 1960. Military regime since 1968. For previous history *see* SUDAN: *French Sudan.*

Malines or **Mechelen,** Belgium. Made a separate fief, 754. Passed to Philip the Bold of Burgundy, 1384. Became archbishopric, 1559. Sacked by Spaniards, 1572.

Mall, The, began to have houses built along the N. side, 1650–60.

Malta, G.C. Phoenicians colonized the island, sixteenth century B.C.; Greeks dispossessed them, 736 B.C.; driven out by Carthaginians *c.* 500 B.C. Became finally Roman, 201 B.C. St. Paul shipwrecked at, first century A.D. Fell to Vandals, then Goths, in the fifth century; liberated by Belisarius, 533, and nominally united with E. Empire. Arabs drove out the Greeks, 870, and made M. a centre of piracy. Count Roger of Sicily drove Arabs from, 1090; conquered by Spain, 1282; given by the Emperor Charles V to the Knights of the Order of St. John of Jerusalem, 1530, who owned the island until 1798, when the French took possession; the Maltese rebelled, and after much fighting the island was recognized as British by the Congress of Vienna, 1814–15. Constitutional progress, 1887–1939. Maltese superseded Italian as language of courts, 1934. Severely damaged by Italian and German bombing in the years 1940–3. Island awarded the George Cross by King George VI, 17 Apr. 1942. Agitation, first for 'integration,' with Britain, and then for independence, from 1945. M. independent state within Common wealth since 21 Sept. 1964. Labour party under Mintoff in power since 1972. M. became a republic within the Commonwealth, 1974. non-aligned policy pursued since 1972 and Brit. base closed, 1979.

Malta, Knights of. Known also as the Order of the Knights of St. John of Jerusalem, the Knights of Rhodes, and the Hospitallers; founded by one Gerald or Gerard in a hospital at Jerusalem c. 1070; sanctioned by Pope Paschal II, 1113; Frederick Barbarossa took the Order under his protection, 1185; captured Rhodes, 1310, which they held until 1523; Charles V presented them with the island of M. (q.v.), 1530, which they surrendered in 1798, when the Order became a charitable religious institution, establishing its headquarters at Rome in 1878. The modern English Order of St. John is a purely secular and philanthropic institution, incorporated by charter in 1888.

Malvern Festival. Founded, 1929, and partially revived in 1970s.

Mamelukes. The Turkish M. under Kutuz seized the government of Egypt, 1250. They were superseded by the Circassian M., 1390, and the latter ruled till the Ottoman conquest of 1517.

Man, Isle of. Ruled by Welsh kings from sixth to ninth centuries, when the Norwegians conquered the island; ceded to the kings of Scotland, 1266; inhabitants placed themselves under protection of Edward I of England, 1290; kingdom granted to Sir John Stanley, 1406; surrendered to parliamentary army, 1651; fell by inheritance to the Duke of Atholl, from whom it was purchased by the British Government after prolonged negotiations (1765–1829).

Manchester, England. There was a Roman fort, called *Mancunium* or *Mamucium*, in the Castleford district of M., founded c. A.D. 79 during Agricola's conquest. It was later called *Mamecestre*. Captured by Edwin, King of Northumbria, 620; King Edward the Elder sent forces to repair and man it, 923; first charter granted, 14 May

1301; grammar school founded, 1515; during civil war Fairfax captured it, 1643; walls and fortifications removed, 1652; Peterloo Massacre at, 1819; University founded (as Owens College), 1851: reorganized 1880 and 1903. M. Ship Canal built, 1887–94. Centre of cotton industry in Britain from eighteenth to mid-twentieth century.

Manchuria or (Japanese) **Manchukuo.** Conquered China (q.v.), 1644, and founded the Chinese dynasty that reigned there till 1911; the occupation of M. by Russia (q.v.) caused the Russo-Japanese War, 1904–5. Made into a state separate from China, 18 Feb. 1932, by Japan (q.v.), who installed the former emperor of China, Pu Yi, as emperor (under the name of Kang Teh) of Manchukuo, 1 Mar. 1934. Absorbed into Nationalist China, 1945: into Communist China, 1949.

Mandalay, built as the capital city of Burma by King Thebaw c.1860. Captured by British, 1885. Largely destroyed by fire, 1892. Held by Japanese, 8 May 1942–13 Mar. 1945.

Mandates, trusteeship system of gov. devised, after World War I, under League of Nations auspices, for former German and Turkish overseas ters. Sev. M. held by Britain and France: system defunct after 1945.

Manhattan Island, U.S.A. Purchased for Dutch W. India Co. by Peter Minuit, 1624. Basis of modern New York (q.v.).

Manichaeism. A dualistic religion ascribed to Mani (c. 215–77). Numerous Persians converted, 241 onwards. Spread to Roman Empire, 280–440. From it are descended the Bogomil, Paulician, Catharist, and Albigensian (q.v.) doctrines.

Manila, capital of the Philippine Islands. Founded by Legaspi, 1571. Attacked by British, 1762. Spanish squadron destroyed by U.S. Navy, May 1898. Occupied by the Japanese, 2 Jan. 1942. Retaken by the Americans in desperate fighting between 5 and 24 Feb. 1945.

Manila Conference.
1. Held 6–8 Sept. 1954, on S.E. Asia defence, and ended with the signing of

the South East Asian Collective Defence Treaty.

2. Held Oct. 1966, attended by Australia, New Zealand, the Philippines, the U.S.A., Thailand, S. Korea, and S. Vietnam in an (abortive) attempt to secure a settlement in Vietnam.

Manitoba. Known as Red River Colony from 1812 and administered by Hudson Bay Co. (*see under* HUDSON BAY TERRITORY) till 1869. Became a province of Canada, 1870.

Mansion House (London). The official residence of the Lord Mayor; building begun, 1739.

Mantua, Italy. Ruled by the Gonzagas, 1328–1708. Taken by French, 1797; by Austrians, 1814; surrendered to Italy, 1866.

Maori Wars.

1. Between the settlers of New Zealand and the Maoris, 1843–7; it resulted in the definition of boundaries.
2. Boundary disputes caused war, 1863–Aug. 1864.
3. In consequence of a massacre of Europeans by Maoris, July 1869–Jan. 1870.

Maputo. Mozambique, founded by the Portuguese, 1544, as **Lourenço Marques**.

Maquis (Corsican dialect for Italian **Macchia**). Mediterranean heath, hence hilly country covered by it; since the Napoleonic Wars synonym for outlawry, phrase popularized by romances of Prosper Mérimée (1803–70); applied to young Frenchmen who took to the hills to avoid forced labour after the occupation by the Germans of 'Vichy' France, Nov. 1942, and became a loose synonym for F.F.I. (*q.v.*).

Marathon, in Attica, scene of the defeat of the Persians by Athenians and Plataeans, 490 B.C. Of the several monuments, which were described by Pausanias, A.D. 110, only the burial mound of the 192 Athenians killed in the action is now known. In twentieth century, name of long-distance running race.

Marble Arch (London). Originally erected in front of Buckingham Palace by

Nash, 1828. Moved to present site, 1851.

Mariana Islands, formerly **Ladrones Islands**, Pacific Ocean. Discovered by Magellan *c.* 1521. Guam, the largest, ceded to U.S.A. by Spain, 1898; remainder sold to Germany, 1899; mandated to Japan, 1919. Scene of heavy fighting in World War II, particularly Guam. U.S.A. took over administration as a trusteeship for the U.N., 18 July 1947.

Marine Corps (U.S.A.). Established by Congress in Nov. 1775; became a permanent arm of the service by the Act of 11 July 1798.

Marketing Boards for agricultural products. Established under Act of 1933; sev. since wound up.

Marlborough House (Pall Mall), built by Wren, 1709, for John Churchill, first Duke of M., who died there, 1722. Occupied by Queen Mary, 1936–53, and given to the nation by Queen Elizabeth II, 17 Feb. 1959, for use as a Commonwealth Centre.

Marlborough, Parliament of, 1267, after the Barons' War (*q.v.*).

Maronites, Syrians who adopted Christianity in the fifth century, abandoned Monothelite heresy, 1182, when they adhered to the Church of Rome, though they left it again temporarily 1382–1445.

Maroon (from Spanish **Cimarron**, a runaway slave especially in the Caribbean). The Ms. of Jamaica, who lived in the interior mountains, were in a state of rebellion against the English from 1655 till the Maroon War of 1796, most of the survivors of which were transported to Nova Scotia and Sierra Leone.

Marprelate Controversy. Caused by certain writings against episcopacy by Elizabethan Puritans, 1587–9; supposed to have been written by John Penry, who was executed in 1593.

Marquesas Islands, the first European to sight which was the Spaniard Mendaña de Nera, 1594, were not all known to navigators until 1701. Became a French protectorate, 1842. Overseas territories of the French Community since 1958; form a part of French Polynesia.

Marriage Laws (Britain). Lord Hardwicke's Act of 1753 provided that Ms. must be performed in the parish church, with the exception of those of Jews or Quakers. This Act superseded by the Marriage Act of 1823. Dissenters' M. Act, 1836, permitted Dissenters to marry in their own chapels or churches or enter into a civil contract by giving notice to the registrar. This was followed by sev. M. Acts, the most important of which are: Deceased Wife's Sister's M. Acts, 28 Aug. 1907; Deceased Brother's Widow's M. Act, 28 July 1921; Age of M. Act (making void Ms. of persons under 16), 10 May 1929. Present statute M.L. contained in the M. Acts, 1949–70. Foreign Marriages Acts, 1892–47, provide for Brit. subjects marrying abroad: the Royal Marriages Act, 1772, legislated regarding royal marriages. M.L. affected by modern divorce laws (*see* DIVORCE) and by 1983 Nationality Act.

Married Women's Property Act, 18 Aug. 1882, abolished the rule whereby upon marriage a woman's property passed at law to her husband. Amended subsequently, notably in 1893, 1907, 1925, 1935 and 1949.

Marseillaise, The, national anthem of the French Republic, was partly written and composed in 1792 by Rouget de Lisle, an officer stationed at Strasbourg. Originally called *Chant de guerre pour l'Armée du Rhin*. It was forbidden under the Restoration and Second Empire, and again became the national song during the Franco-Prussian War of 1870. Official national anthem since 1879.

Marseilles, France. One of the oldest towns in France, originally known as *Massalia* or *Massilia*. Captured by Julius Caesar, 49 B.C.; became a republic, A.D. 1112; treacherously surrendered to Henry IV; shortly after it finally lost its independence. Old port district and port destroyed by Germans 1943–44: since rebuilt.

Marshall Islands came under German protection, 1885. Mandated to Japan, 1920. Overrun by U.S. forces, 1944. Put under U.N. trusteeship, 1946, the U.S.A. to administer. Negotiations for change of status proceeding since 1981.

Marshall Plan or **European Recovery Programme (E.R.P.).** Original proposal made by George M. (1880–1959), U.S. Secretary of State, in speech at Harvard University, 5 June 1947. Interim Aid Bill signed by President Truman, 17 Dec. 1947. Convention for European Economic Co-operation (16 nations) signed at Paris, 16 Apr. 1948. This was the foundation of O.E.E.C. (*q.v.*), although the M.P. itself came to an end in 1952.

Marshalsea Prison, in what is now the Borough High Street, Southwark, was built at some time between 1327 and 1377, and was first used to confine those who 'broke the King's peace' within a certain radius of Westminster Palace; then it housed those convicted of piracy and other maritime crimes. It became specifically a debtors' prison *c.* 1560, but at some time the site was changed because the M. prison where the father of the novelist Charles Dickens was imprisoned, 1824–5, was farther down the Borough High Street, was united with the King's Bench and Fleet prisons in 1842, and was demolished, 1887.

Martello Towers. Built as English coast defences at the end of the eighteenth century, after the model of a fort on Cape Mortella, bombarded unsuccessfully by British in 1794.

Martinique. Discovered by the Spaniards, 1493. Settled by French, 1635. Slavery abolished, 1860. An overseas dept. of France since 1946.

Maryland, U.S.A. Explored by John Smith, 1608. First settled by Capt. William Claiborne, 1634. Named after Henrietta Maria, queen of Charles I. One of the original 13 states of the U.S.A., 1776.

Marylebone Cricket Club, better known as M.C.C., first so called in 1787, when an already existing club began to play in Dorset Square, M.

'Mary Rose', warship of Henry VIII, sank 1545; salvaged, 1982.

Mashonaland, Zimbabwe. Placed under British protection, 1888; powers of administration granted to British S. Africa Co., 1889.

Mason and Dixon Line, drawn by two English surveyors, M. and D., who in settlement of a dispute between the proprietors of the various colonies demarcated the boundary between Maryland and Pennsylvania, 1763–7. This line and its westward continuation became from 1820 onwards the boundary between 'slave' and 'free' states and the phrase and its abbreviation 'Dixie' achieved greatest currency in the Civil War (1863) period.

Massachusetts, U.S.A. Explored by Gosnold, 1602; Champlain, 1604; John Smith, 1614. Settled by English Puritans, Nov. 1620, who sailed over in the *Mayflower.* First constitution framed, 1780; amended, 1820. Constitution of U.S.A. adopted, 1788.

Master of the King's (or **Queen's**) **Musick,** an office instituted, 1660, was conferred on Malcolm Williamson in 1975.

Masulipatam, India. English settlement founded, 1611. Held by Dutch, 1686–90. Given to French by Nizam of Hyderabad, 1750. Captured by British under Forde, Apr. 1758.

Matabeleland, Zimbabwe. Ceded to the British S. Africa Co., 1889. Matabele rebellion, 1896; ended by Rhodes' mediation, Aug. 1896.

Matterhorn (Switzerland). Summit first reached, 14 July 1865. First winter ascent of the N. face made by two Swiss climbers, 4 Feb. 1962.

Mau-Mau, a revolutionary movement among the Kikuyu tribe aiming to dominate first it and then all other Africans in Kenya (*q.v.*) with a view to seizing power in Kenya. Its existence became known to the authorities in 1950. Its first large-scale outbreak of cattle-maiming occurred 25 Sept. 1952 at Timau. First Europeans killed, 2 Oct. Trial of Jomo Kenyatta, Dec. 1952–Mar. 1953. Kenyatta found guilty of managing M.-M. and sentenced to life imprisonment. By 1957 M.-M. had been crushed. Kenyatta

was freed in Aug. 1961 and subsequently became leader of an independent Kenya (*q.v.*).

Maumbury Rings, late Neolithic or early Bronze Age (*c.* 1800 B.C.) fortification converted during the Roman occupation (after A.D. 200) to an amphitheatre which was excavated 1908 and 1913.

Maundy Thursday. The Thursday before Good Friday, also known as Holy Thursday, on which day alms are still given to the poor in the form of 'M. money' by the sovereign.

Mauritania, independent Islamic republic in W. Africa, made a French protectorate, 1903, and a colony, 4 Dec. 1920. From Nov. 1958 M. was a member of the French Community, and became an independent republic on 28 Nov. 1960. Under military rule since 1978.

Mauritius, Indian Ocean. Discovered by the Portuguese between 1505 and 1512; occupied by the Dutch, and named M. after Prince Maurice of Orange, 1598; abandoned by Dutch, 1710; occupied by French, 1715; captured by English, 1810; formally ceded to England by Treaty of Paris, 1814. Became an independent dominion, 1968.

Mausoleum. Named after the tomb erected for King Mausolus of Halicarnassus, in Caria (377–353 B.C.), by his widow, Queen Artemisia II, *c.* 352 B.C.

Mayas, a race based on Yucatan in Central America. The first M. Empire lasted from the second to the eighth centuries A.D. The second empire was founded A.D. 1000, and was still flourishing at the time of the Spanish conquest.

May Day, in pagan times was an almost universal feast in Europe, taking place at or soon after the vernal equinox, as the Roman Floralia did. Tolerated in England from the time of Augustine's mission until 1644, when it was banned, but revived in 1661. *See also* LABOUR DAY.

'Mayflower,' The. Sailed from Plymouth, England, 6 Sept. 1620. The M. compact was signed off Cape Cod, 2

Nov., and the Pilgrim Fathers (*q.v.*) landed in Massachusetts, 16 Dec. 1620. Society of M. Descendants founded, 1894. On 20 Apr. 1957 *Mayflower II*, a replica of the first ship, sailed from Plymouth to Cape Cod, in connection with the 350th anniversary of the first permanent English settlement in N. America (at Jamestown, Virginia).

Maynooth College (Ireland). Founded, 1795, by Irish Parliament for education of candidates for Irish Roman Catholic priesthood.

Mayor as a title for the chief dignitary of a city first appears in England *c*. A.D. 1100.

Meal Tub Plot, 1679. Pretended conspiracy against the Duke of York originated by Dangerfield.

Mecca (Arab. **Om al Kora**). Holiest of Moslem shrines. Known to Ptolemy in the second century A.D. Expelled Mohammed, 622, who returned and captured it, 630. Captured by Wahabis, 1803, but ceded to Mehemet Ali, pasha of Egypt, 1833. Captured again by Wahabis under Abdul Aziz ibn Sa'ud, 13 Oct. 1924, who was proclaimed king of the Hejaz here, 1926.

Mecklenburg. German Democratic Republic. Became duchy, 1348. Lutheranism became state religion, 1549. Partitioned, 1611. Repartitioned into M.-Schwerin and M.-Strelitz, but with joint diet, 1701. Serfdom abolished, 1819. Joined N. German Confederation, 1866. Part of Russian zone, 1945; subsequently part of G.D.R.

Media, in NW. Iran, became independent of Assyria *c*. 708 B.C., and overthrew the Assyrian Empire, 612. Amalgamated with Persia, 560. Became part of the Macedonian Empire, 331. After 624 the north-western portion became independent and remained so, under the name of Atropatene, until the first century A.D. The remainder thereafter was alternately in the possession of Persia, Syria, and Parthia.

Medici Family. Chiefs of the Florentine Republic from 1434. Contributed to the renaissance of literature and the arts in Italy. Cosimo de' M. (1389–1464)

was the first chief. Lorenzo de' M. ruled, 1469–92; he was the father of Pope Leo X. Caterina de' M. became Queen of France, 1547; Maria de' M., 1600. The family became extinct, 1737.

Medina (Arab. 'the city'), in full **Medinat Rasul Allah**, was the residence of Mohammed in A.D. 622. He *d*. and was buried here, 632.

Medina del Campo, Treaty of, 1489. By it Henry VII of England betrothed his infant son Arthur to Catherine of Aragon.

Meissen, Saxony, a castle founded here by Henry I, 929, as the nucleus of a margravate (border county) established, 966, which became part of the electorate of Saxony, 1423. The manufacture of porcelain began, 1710. Some leading designers were Hörold (1720–35), Kändler (1735–56), Count Marcolini (1774–1813). Most so-called 'Dresden' ware, 1710–1863, was made at M.

Melbourne, Australia. Site first occupied, 1835. Named M., 1837. Made an Anglican diocese, 1849. Became capital of Victoria, 1851. University founded, 1854.

Melfi, Apulia, founded, A.D. 304, became capital of the Norman duchy of Apulia, 1044. Its cathedral, built in 1155, was almost totally destroyed in the earthquake of 1851.

Mellifont (County Meath), first Cistercian abbey in Ireland, founded, 1142, by St. Malachy (1094–1148). Ruins excavated, 1884–5.

Melos (It. **Milo**), island in the Cyclades, taken by Athenians, 416 B.C.; by Turks, 1566. The statue of Venus called 'of Milo' found here, 1820.

Melrose Abbey (Scotland). Founded by David I in 1136; partly destroyed by English in 1322 and 1385; reduced to ruin by Lord Hertford, 1545.

Memel (Lith. **Klaipeda**). Founded, 1253. Detached from Germany by Treaty of Versailles, 1919. Given conditionally to Lithuania, 1923. Annexed by Germany, 22 Mar. 1939; by U.S.S.R., 1945.

Menai Straits. Telford's suspension bridge open, 1826 (reconstructed 1940).

Stephenson's tubular railway bridge, 1850, severely damaged by fire, 24 May 1970.

Mendelianism. Theory of heredity propounded between 1860 and 1884 by G. J. Mendel (1822–84) while abbot of the Augustinian monastery at Brno in Czechoslovakia.

Menin Gate (Ypres, Belgium). Unveiled by Lord Plumer, 24 July 1927.

Mennonites, pacifist Protestant sect, successors to the Anabaptists, formed *c.* 1537, taking their name from the preacher Menno Simons (1492–1559). Several colonies of M. formed in S. Russia, 1786, and the first Mennonite congregation established at Germantown, Pennsylvania, 1683. In 1871 considerable numbers settled in Kansas and Minnesota.

Mensheviks (Rus. **menshinstvo**, minority), a wing of the Russian Social Democratic Party, founded, 1903. Suppressed, 1922.

Mercator. Gerhard Kremer, *alias* Gerardus M., born at Rupelmonde, 5 Mar. 1512. His 'Projection' for maps was published, 1568. He *d.* 2 Dec. 1594.

Merchant Adventurers, The. A guild of traders established in Brabant, 1296. The branch in England received the title by patent of Henry VII, 1505; incorporated, 1553. Became known as the Hamburg Company, 1578; dissolved, 1808.

Merchants, Charter of. Granted in 1303 by Edward I to foreign merchants.

Merchants, Statute of. *See* ACTON BURNELL, STATUTE OF.

Merchant Shipping Acts. Consolidating Act, 1854; this superseded by the Act of 1894 which remains the principal Act on the subject, various amendments and additions having been made to it since it became law.

Merchant Taylors' School (London). Founded, 1561; school house destroyed during Great Fire of 1666; rebuilt, 1671–4; rebuilt on new site, 1873–4; rebuilt, Northwood, Middlesex, 1931–3.

Mercia. Anglian kingdom, founded 500–50 in central England. Rose to supremacy *c.* 730, which lasted through the reigns of Ethelbald and

Offa, and ended by the defeat of Coenwulf at Ellendun, 821, after a period in which it was tributary to Wessex. Completely absorbed in Wessex, 825–9. It was finally conquered by the Danes, 874, and split into English (SW.) and Danish (NE.) Mercian earldoms; reunited in 1016 under Knut, the territory ceased to be an administrative unit in 1066.

Mercia, rulers of, c. 593–874:
Creoda *d. c.* 593
Pybba *c.* 593–*c.* 606
Cearl *c.* 606–*c.* 626
Penda 626–655
Peada 655–656
Oswy (of Bernicia) 656–659
Wulfhere 659–675
Ethelred 675–704
Cenred 704–709
Ceolred 709–716
Ethelbald 716–757
Beornred 757
Offa 757–796
Ecgfrith 796
Coenwulf 796–821
Ceolwulf I 821–823
Beornwulf 823–825
Ludeca 825–827
Wiglaf 827–829
Egbert (of Wessex) 829–830
Wiglaf (restored) 830–839
Beorhtwulf 839–852
Burgred 852–874
Ceolwulf II 874

Merciless (or **Wonderful**) **Parliament.** Summoned in 1388 by the Lords Appellant after the defeat of Richard II. It condemned eight of Richard's supporters to death.

Merit, Order of, instituted, 1902.

Mermaid Tavern (Cheapside), first mentioned, 1464. M. Club founded, reputedly by Sir Walter Raleigh, 1603. Burnt down, 1666.

Merovingians, Frankish dynasty, reigning 448–751. *See* FRANCE.

Mersey Tunnel (railway) opened, 1886; first road tunnel opened, 1934; second, 1971, and third, 1974.

Mesopotamia. *See* IRAQ.

Messina, Italy. Founded by Greeks *c.* eighth century B.C. Taken by the

Saracens in the ninth century A.D. and in 1072 by the Normans. Ruled by Spain, 1282–1713. Devastated by plague, 1743; by earthquake, 1783 and 1908.

Metaphysics, Institute of International. Opened at Paris, 1919.

Meteorological Office set up, 1855. Transferred from Board of Trade control to that of the Royal Society, 1867. From 1919 administered by the Air Ministry; subsequently by the Ministry of Defence. Headquarters at Bracknell, Berks.

Methodists. Name first given to followers of John and Charles Wesley at Oxford, 1729; Wesleyan Methodist Society founded by John Wesley, 1739; first conference, 1744; conference constituted supreme authority, 1784; Dr. Coke constituted 'bishop' of the American M., 1784; death of Wesley, 1791, after which the sect split up; union of many divisions into the 'United Methodist Church', 1907; Enabling Bill for union of Wesleyan, Primitive, and United M. passed, 1929; final denominational vote, 1931. Reunion became effective, 1932. Proposals for a two-stage reunion with the Church of England published 25 Feb. 1963. In 1969 the M. Conference first voted in favour of unity plan with Church of England: but plan made defunct by subsequent Anglican rejections of it (most recently in 1981).

Methuen Treaty. Negotiated by Sir Paul M., English ambassador in Portugal, 1703. It reduced the duty on Portuguese wines to the detriment of French wines, thus helping to form the upper-class English habit of port drinking. Annulled, 1836.

Metric System. Became the legal system in France, 1795. Though not in commercial use the system was made legal in the U.K. by an Act of 1864. Britain began adopting the M.S. over a nominal 10-year period from 1965: still incomplete in 1985.

Metronome, invented *c.* 1814.

Mexico. Had a considerable Indian culture before 1519. In 1519 Hernando Cortes (1485–1547), the Spanish adventurer, landed at Vera Cruz, and conquered the land, 1521. In 1540 M. was united with other American territories and called New Spain. Declared itself independent of Spain, and Gen. Iturbide made emperor, May 1822. Proclaimed a republic, 1824. War with the U.S.A. regarding boundary dispute, May 1846–19 May 1848, when a peace treaty was signed. War with France, 1862–7. Emperor Maximilian shot, 1867. Period of revolution and social change 1910–21. Campaign against Catholic Church 1924–31. Trotsky murdered at Coycacán, 21 Aug. 1940. Rapid industrialization following exploitation of Mexican oil industry since 1950: but financial crises caused international repercussions in 1980s.

Heads of State, from 1821. (All presidents, except where otherwise indicated):

Iturbide (Regent) 1821–1822
       (Emperor) 1822–1823
Victoria 1824–1829
Pedraza 1829
Guerrero 1829
Bustamante 1829–1832
Pedraza 1832
Santa Anna 1833–1836
Bustamante 1836–1841
Santa Anna 1841–1842
Bravo 1842–1843
Santa Anna 1844
Herrera 1844–1846
Paredes 1846
Santa Anna 1846–1847
Herrera 1848–1851
Arista 1851–1853
Santa Anna (Dictator) 1853–1855
Alvarez 1855–1856
Comonfort 1856–1857
       (Dictator) 1857–1858
Juarez 1858–1863
Zuloaga 1858
Miramon 1859–1861
Maximilian (Emperor) 1864–1867
Juarez 1867–1872
Lerdo 1872–1876
Diaz 1877–1880
Gonzalez 1880–1884
Diaz 1884–1911
Madero 1911–1913

Huerta 1913–1914
Carranza 1914–1920
Obregon 1920–1924
Calles 1924–1928
Portes Gil 1928–1930
Ortiz Rubio 1930–1932
Rodriguez 1932–1934
Cardenas 1934–1940
Camacho 1940–1946
Alemán Valdes 1946–1952
Cortines 1952–1958
Lopez Mateos 1958–1964
Ordaz 1964–1970
Echevarria 1970–1976
Lopez 1976–1982
Hurtado 1982–

Mexico City. Founded as Tenochtitlan by Aztecs (*q.v.*) *c.* A.D. 1325. Captured by Spaniards, 1521. Cathedral begun, 1573. Olympic Games held at, 1968; World Football Cup finals held at, 1970.

Michelson-Morley Experiment. Albert Abraham Michelson (1852–1931) and Edward Williams Morley (1822–94) performed an experiment in 1887 to determine the velocity with which the earth moved through the ether. Its negative results led to the hypothesis on which the theory of relativity (*q.v.*) is based.

Michigan, U.S.A. Discovered by French, 1618, and settled by French missionaries, 1671. Detroit founded, 1701; possessed by British, 1763; by Americans, 1796; erected into an independent territory, 1805; fell into the hands of the British, Aug. 1812; reconquered by Gen. Harrison, 1813; admitted to the Union as a state, Jan. 1837.

Microphone, invented by E. Berliner (1851–1929), 1877.

Microscope. The first compound M. said to have been made by Janssen, a Dutchman, 1590. It was not, however, of much practical use until the achromatic lens was invented *c.* 1758.

Middelburg, Holland. St. Nicholas Abbey founded, 1106. Bell-tower rebuilt, 1718.

Midway Islands, discovered and annexed to the U.S.A., 1859. Made an American reservation, 1903. Japanese fleet defeated by U.S. Navy off M., June 1942.

Midwives Acts (Great Britain), since 1902, are consolidated by the Midwives Act of 1951. Men are now (1985) permitted to train as midwives.

Mikado, title of the emperors of Japan (*q.v.*), the first of whom is supposed to have begun his reign, 660 B.C.

Milan, Italy (Lat. **Mediolanum**). Taken from Gauls by Romans, 222 B.C.; Constantine's edict in favour of Christians, A.D. 313; sacked by Huns, 452; by Goths, 539; head of Lombard League from 1167; ruled by Visconti family, 1227–1447, by Sforza family, 1450–1535; from 1535 to 1713 under the rule of Spain, then of Austria; after Napoleonic wars restored to Austria, 1815; capital of Austro-Italian kingdom until 1859, when it became part of Italy; present cathedral founded, 1386; and completed, 1805–13.

Mildenhall Treasure, a hoard of Roman silver-ware found near M. in Suffolk, 1942–3, presumed to have been buried for safety by the occupants of a villa during pirate raids in the fourth century A.D.

Mile. English statute M. legalized, 1593.

Military Training Act, 1939, compelling every male subject between 20 and 21 to undergo 6 months' training and then to be 3½ years in auxiliary force. Superseded by National Service (Armed Forces) Act, 3 Sept. 1939, and National Service Act, 1947: but ended when conscription abolished in Britain, 1962.

Militia (Great Britain). M. statutes, 1661–3; general M. Act passed, 1802; M. Reserve Act, 1867; M. Enlistment Act, 1875; title of M. abolished on introduction of Territorial and Reserve Force Act, 1907; superseded by Special Reserve (1908); Special Reserve renamed M., 1921, but it remained a merely nominal force. The conscripts under the Military Training Act, 1939, were termed M. *See* FYRD.

Militia (U.S.A.). Bill for the organization of the M. passed House of Representatives, 27 Mar. 1792.

Millbank Prison (London). Erected

1813–16; closed 1890; demolished, 1903; on the site now stands the Tate Gallery (*q.v.*).

Milo, Venus of. *See* MELOS.

Minnesota, U.S.A. Explored by two Huguenots, Groseilliers and Radisson, 1658–9; formally possessed by French, 1671; divided between Spain and Great Britain, 1762–3; visited by Jonathan Carver, 1766; part of territory of Indiana, 1800; purchased by U.S.A., 1803; territory of M. created, 1849; admitted to the Union, 11 May 1858.

Minorca, Mediterranean. Captured by English, 1708, during War of Spanish Succession, ceded to England by Treaty of Utrecht, 1713; recaptured by French, 1756 (as a result of which the English executed Admiral Byng); restored to England by Treaty of Paris, 1763; recaptured by French and Spaniards, 1781; ceded to Spain, 1782; retaken, 1798, but restored to Spain by Treaty of Amiens, 1802. At the end of the Spanish Civil War the island surrendered bloodlessly to Nationalists, 9 Feb. 1939.

Mint (Great Britain). Regulations for the government of the M. made by King Athelstan *c.* A.D. 928; by Act of Parliament the present M. was founded on Tower Hill, 1811; new constitution, 1815; complete change in administration, and a master, deputy master, and comptroller appointed, 1850; office of Chancellor of the Exchequer amalgamated with that of master, and the office of deputy master and controller combined, 1870. Mint moved from London to Llantrisant, S. Wales, in 1972–74. Ms. established at Sydney, Australia, in 1855, and at Melbourne, Australia, 1872.

Mint (U.S.A.). The earliest M. was established at Boston, 27 May 1652. The power of coinage was exercised by several states from 1778 until the adoption of the National Constitution. Establishment of a M. by Act of Congress, 1795, at Philadelphia.

Minton porcelain, first made by Thomas and Herbert M. at Stoke-on-Trent, 1796.

Misericordia, Confraternity of the. Florentine volunteer ambulance service, raised, 1244, or, according to some, not until 1292. Records destroyed in floods of 1557. From 1425 to 1430 merged with the charitable Guild of Sta. Maria del Bigallo. Present constitution dates from the latter year. Primarily intended to function during plagues, the last of which (cholera) occurred in 1855.

Missal. Tridentine M. ordered to be used in all Roman Catholic churches by Council of Trent (*q.v.*), 1570; phased out after 1962–3.

Mississippi, U.S.A. The lower course of the river discovered by de Soto, 1541; visited by La Salle, 1682; territory of M. created, 7 Apr. 1798; admitted to the Union as a state, 1817.

Mississippi Scheme. A proposal to develop Louisiana (*q.v.*), the country on the borders of the M. The scheme was the idea of John Law (1671–1729), who floated a company in 1717. The scheme was not a success, and in July 1720 the bubble broke.

Missouri, U.S.A. Originally called Upper Louisiana. Ste. Genevieve said to have been founded, 1735; by Treaty of Paris, 1763, territory passed to the English; ceded to U.S.A., 1803; admitted into the Union as a state, 10 Aug. 1821.

Missouri Compromise, The. In 1818 the inhabitants of the M. territory petitioned for admission into the Union as a state; a bill was introduced into Congress, 13 Feb. 1819. A question of the abolition of slavery in the territory caused the bill to be delayed and it was not until 27 Feb. 1821 that a final compromise was adopted, and M. admitted to the Union as a state.

Mithraism, a branch of Zoroastrianism (*q.v.*). Introduced into Rome from Asia Minor, 68 B.C. It *fl.* in Britain, mainly as a cult in garrison stations, throughout the Roman occupation, and a temple to Mithras was excavated in London in 1953. M. ceased to exist in the W. with the victory of Theodosius in 394, when it was superseded by Christianity.

Moabite Stone, The. Probable date of inscription, *c.* 850 B.C. Now in the Louvre, Paris. Discovered by Rev. F. Klein at Dibon in 1868.

Modena, Italy. Ruled by the Estes, 1288–1860. Made a duchy, 1452; duke expelled by French, 1796; restored, 1814; finally expelled and duchy incorporated in Italy, 1860.

Mohammedanism. *See* ISLAM.

Mohawks or **Mohocks, The.** A club of wealthy young London men about town who committed such outrages that on 18 Mar. 1712 they were the subject of a royal proclamation.

Moldavian Republic. Constituted 2 Aug. 1940 as the thirteenth Soviet Socialist Republic. Occupied almost immediately on outbreak of war in June 1941 by German and Rumanian forces, until May 1944. The former M. Autonomous Soviet Republic was created within the Ukraine, 1921. *See* BESSARABIA.

Molly Maguires, in Ireland, an anti-landlord society which *fl.* 1835–55. In America, an Irish-led terrorist society which attempted to dominate the Pennsylvanian coal-mining area, 1862–77.

Mombasa, Kenya. Originally an Arab town in E. Africa, was first visited by the Portuguese, 1498. Sacked (1500) and occupied by them, 1505. Retaken by Arabs, 1698. Included in British E. African protectorate, 1896. Linked by rail to Uganda, 1895–1901.

Monaco. An independent principality on the Mediterranean, ruled by the Grimaldi family since 1297; made a French protectorate, 1644; Menton and Roquebrune annexed by Sardinia, 1846; became part of Italy, 1859; sold to Napoleon III, 1861. Until 1911 the Prince of Monaco was an absolute ruler; in that year constitution providing for universal manhood suffrage was adopted.

By a treaty of 1918, succession to the throne of M. must be approved by the French Government. Rainier III became Prince of M. in 1949; he married Grace Kelly (*d.* 1982), an American film actress, in 1956. A 'good neighbour' treaty was signed between France and M., 23 Dec. 1951. Dispute with France, 1959, settled, 1963.

Monasteries (England). M. on the Celtic pattern certainly existed in SW. and NW. Britain in the fifth century. The first monastery in England with Benedictine influence appears to have been erected about A.D. 597 by St. Augustine. A large number, belonging to many different orders, grew up in England. In 1535, during Henry VIII's reign, a commission was issued for the visitation of the M. In 1536 an Act was passed for the suppression of the religious houses with an income of less than £200. The large houses were suppressed in 1539.

Mongolia, Outer, People's Republic of. Chinese province, 1686–1911. Chinese officials expelled by the chiefs, 1911. Again a Chinese province, 1919–21. Communist revolution and proclamation of a People's Government, Mar. 1921. Treaty with U.S.S.R., Nov. 1921. Republic proclaimed, 1924, on death of Khan Bogdo Gezen. Dispute with and defeat of Japanese, Sept. 1939 (*see* NOMANHAN and CHANG-KUFENG incidents). Independent Outer M. recognized by China, 5 Jan. 1946, further guaranteeing it in Sino-Soviet Treaty of Feb. 1950. Modified Cyrillic alphabet introduced, 1946.

Monmouth's Rebellion. Originated by James, Duke of Monmouth (1649–85), who landed on 11 June 1685 at Lyme Regis. He was defeated at Sedgemoor, 6 July 1685, and executed, 15 July.

Monopolies. In 1597 Parliament protested to Elizabeth against grants of M. The Parliaments of Charles I protested still more strongly, and by an Act of 1624 most of these M. were abolished, and in 1639 the whole system was done away with. In more modern times, M. have been regulated by the Monopolies and Restrictive Practises Act, 1948, superseded subsquently by the Fair Trading Act, 1973, which estab. the Monopolies and Mergers Commission to deal with M.

Monroe Doctrine. Proclaimed by President James M. (1758–1831) of the U.S.A. in his message to Congress on 2 Dec. 1823. In the words of M. himself, the doctrine was that the U.S.A. 'should consider any attempt on their [the foreign Powers'] part to extend their system to any portion of this [the American] hemisphere as dangerous to our peace and safety'.

Montagnards or **Montagne,** extremist republican wing in the French National Convention *c.* 1792–5.

Montana, first settled, 1809. Organized as a territory, 1864. Admitted to the Union as a state, 1889.

Mont Blanc (France and Italy). In 1760 Saussure offered a reward for a practicable route to the summit. Two guides in June 1786 gained it. Saussure reached the top himself in 1787. Construction of the M.B. tunnel begun, 1959; opened by President de Gaulle, and President Saragat of Italy, 16 July 1965.

Mont de Piété or **Monte di Pietà.** Institutions founded for lending money to the poor at low interest, first established at Orvieto, 1463, and Perugia, 1467.

Montecassino, oldest monastic house in Europe, founded by St. Benedict, A.D. 529. Sacked by Lombards, 585; destroyed by Saracens, 884, and by Allied air forces and shell-fire, Feb.–May 1944; occupied by Polish forces, 18 May 1944. Restored after each event: during the restoration of 1950–6 an urn believed to contain remains of St. Benedict and his sister Scholastica (missing since *c.* 1550) rediscovered. Abbey formally reopened, 1956.

Montenegro (Serb.-Cr. **Crnagora**). The history of M. as an independent state begins with the battle of Kossovo, 1389; Cetinje made capital, 1484; captured by the Turks, 1623, 1687, and 1714; fresh war with Turkey, 1853; peace finally restored, Nov. 1858; Turkish supremacy recognized, Sept. 1862; declared independent of Turkey by Treaty of San Stefano, 3 Mar. 1878; first Montenegrin Parliament assembled at Cetinje, Oct. 1906; Prince Nicholas assumed title of king, 28 Aug. 1910. During the first Balkan War, Oct. 1912–May 1913, M. allied with Bulgaria, Serbia, and Greece against Turkey; during the second Balkan War, June–Aug. 1913, M. allied with Serbia and

Greece against Bulgaria, Rumania, and Turkey. King Nicholas fled the country in face of Austrian invasion, 1916. *See* YUGOSLAVIA, with which M. was united, 1918. Capital moved from Cetinje to Podgorica (renamed Titograd), 1945.

Montessori Method. Education system founded, 1906–9, by Maria Montessori (1870–1952).

Montevideo, Uruguay. First settlement made, 1726; taken by the English, 1807; in 1828 it was made the capital of Uruguay or Banda Oriental. German warship *Graf Spee* driven into M., Nov. 1939.

Montreal, Canada. Originally **Ville Marie.** Founded by French settlers, 1642; captured by British, 8 Sept. 1760; by Americans, 12 Nov. 1775; recaptured by British, 15 June 1776. McGill College founded, 1813; made a university by royal charter, 1821; new charter granted, 1852. Bishopric founded, 1850. Great fire destroyed the greater part of the town, 8–9 July 1852. Christ Church, the Anglican cathedral, destroyed by fire, 10 Dec. 1856. M. University founded, 1878. Underground railway opened, 1966.

Montserrat, discovered by Columbus, 1492: colonized by Irish and British, 1632.

Montyon Prizes. Awarded each year by the French Academy for examples of disinterested goodness. The fund for this purpose was bequeathed by the Baron de M. (1733–1820).

Moravia. Occupied in early period successively by Boii (Celts); Quadi (Teutons); Rugii and Heruli, fifth century; soon displaced by Slavs; they sided with Charlemagne in suppressing the Avars on the E., end of eighth century; received part of Avars' territory. Allied with Bulgars and Byzantine Empire *c.* 850. Converted to Christianity by Cyril and Methodius, 863. King Svatopluk extended dominions to the Oder and the Gran. Magyars entered at his death, 894. From 1029 usually incorporated with Bohemia. On death of Louis II at battle of Mohácz came under rule of Austria,

1526; made a separate crown land, 1849. Became part of Czechoslovakia, 1918. Some territory ceded to Germany and Poland, Oct. 1938; part of the German protectorate of Bohemia-Moravia, 15 Mar. 1939 until 1945.

Moravian Brethren or **Moravian Church.** A religious sect founded in the E. of Bohemia *c.* 1457; first synod held, 1467. It grew out of the Hussites. In 1749 the British Parliament passed Acts to encourage their settlement in the English-American colonies.

Moriscos. Moors who remained in Spain after their final conquest in 1492, and who were finally expelled by Philip III, 1609–14.

Morley-Minto Reforms introduced in India by Lord Morley (1838–1923). Secretary of State, and the fourth Earl of Minto (1847–1914), Viceroy, 1909.

Mormons, The, or **Latter-Day Saints.** A sect founded by Joseph Smith (1805–44). *The Book of Mormon* was first published at New York in 1830. The first church was founded on 6 Apr. 1830 at Fayette; moved to Kirtland, Ohio, Jan. 1831. Their headquarters at Salt Lake City founded, 1847, by Brigham Young.

Morocco (Arab. **Maghreb**, 'Far W.'). Occupied by Berbers since at least 1200 B.C. Conquered by Arabs, A.D. 682. Successful Berber revolt, 739. Idrissi dynasty (Arab) 788–988 founded Fez, 808. Almoravide (*q.v.*) (Berber) rule, 1061–1149. Marrakesh founded, 1062, by Yusuf Ben Tashfin. Almohade (*q.v.*) (Moorish) rule, 1149–1269. Marinid (Tribal Berber) dynasty established, 1269. Yakub II subdues Spain, 1269–86. Ali V takes Tlemcen, 1337. Fall of Marinids, 1360–1471. Wattassi dynasty (1471–1548) loses coastal towns to Spanish and Portuguese. Portuguese driven out by Saddi dynasty (Arab), 1550–1668. Conquest of Timbuktu end sixteenth century. Present Filali (Berber) dynasty seized Marrakesh, 1668. Unification under Moulay Ismail, 1672–1727. French conquest of Algeria, 1830, resulted in wars, 1844 and 1859. Spaniards take Tetuan, and Ifni ceded to them, 1860.

Britain relinquishes her interests to France, 8 Apr. 1904. Tangier crisis, 1905. Algeciras Conference, 1906, drafted Act of Algeciras, 7 Apr. French occupy Casablanca, 1907. Agadir crisis, 1911. Spanish and French protectorates established by treaty of Fez, 30 Mar. 1912. Anglo-Franco-Spanish Convention, 18 Dec. 1923, defined the status of Tangier (*q.v.*). Abd-el-Krim's rebellion against Spanish, 1923–6. Ifric occupied and effectively annexed by Spaniards, 1934. France and the Sultan terminated the treaty of Fez, 2 Mar. 1956; Spanish protectorate ended, 7 Apr.; and the international status of Tangier was abolished, 29 Oct., thus making M. a completely independent monarchy by the end of that year. Sultan took title of king as from Aug. 1957. Hassan II succeeded to the throne, 26 Feb. 1961. New constitution, 1972.

Mortmain, Statute of, 15 Nov. 1279. It forbade any person to buy or sell or, under cover of any gift, term, or other title, to receive any lands or tenements in such a way that such lands and tenements should come under the ownership of a corporation without royal licence. A second Statute of M. was passed in 1391.

Moscow, Russia. Founded *c.* 1147; captured by the Tatars (i.e. by Toktamish, Khan of the Golden Horde), 1382; burnt by the Khan of the Crimea, 1571; the city was burnt by the inhabitants in 1812, when Napoleon entered, and he was forced to leave it. Ceased to be Russian capital on founding of St. Petersburg, 1712. Again made capital, 1917.

Mosul. Finally included in Iraq by Treaty of Angora, 5 June 1926.

Mountains, First Ascents of:

Etna (Sicily), Emperor Trajan, approximately A.D. 100.
Titlis (Switzerland), four peasants, 1744.
Mont Blanc (France-Italy), M. G. Paccard and J. Balmat, 1786.
Gross Glockner (Austria), five local men, 1800.
Jungfrau (Switzerland), J. R. and H. Meyer, 1811.

Ararat (U.S.S.R.), Parrot, 1829.

Finsteraarhorn (Switzerland), J. Leuthold, 1829.

Piz Bernina (Switzerland-Italy), J. Coaz, 1850.

Monte Rosa, Dufourspitze (Switzerland), five British, 1855.

Dom (Switzerland), J. Ll.-Davies, 1858.

Aletschhorn (Switzerland), F. F. Tuckett, 1859.

Gran Paradiso (Italy), J. J. Cowell, 1860.

Monte Viso (Italy), W. Matthews, 1861.

Weisshorn (Switzerland), J. Tyndall, 1861.

Les Ecrins (France), E. Whymper, 1864.

Grandes Jorasses (France-Italy), E. Whymper, 1865.

Aig Verte (France), E. Whymper, 1865.

Matterhorn (Switzerland), E. Whymper, 1865.

Elbruz (Caucasus), D. W. Freshfield, A. W. Moore, C. C. Tucker, 1868.

Cimone della Pala (Italy), E. R. Whitwell, 1870.

Meije (France), E. B. de Castelnau, 1877.

Grand Teton (U.S.A.), N. P. Langford, J. Stevenson, 1872.

Grand Dru (France), C. T. Dent, 1878.

Chimborazo (Ecuador), E. Whymper, 1880.

Mt. Cook (New Zealand), W. S. Green, 1882.

Aig du Géant (France-Italy), four Signori Sella, 1882.

Kabru (Himalaya), W. W. Graham, 1883.

Kilimanjaro (Kenya), Hans Meyer, 1887.

Ushba (Caucasus), J. G. Cockin, 1888.

Aconcagua (Chile-Argentine), M. Zurbriggen, 1897.

Mt. St. Elias (Alaska), Duke of Abruzzi, 1897.

Mt. Kenya (Kenya), H. J. Mackinder, 1899.

Ruwenzori (Central Africa), Duke of Abruzzi, 1906.

Trisul (Himalaya), T. G. Longstaff, 1907.

Mt. McKinley (Alaska), Parker-Browne expedition, 1912.

Mt. Robson (Canada), W. Foster, A. H. McCarthy, C. Kain, 1913.

Mt. Logan (Alaska), A. H. McCarthy, 1925.

Illampu (Bolivia), German-Austrian expedition, 1929.

Kamet (Himalaya), Kamet expedition, 1931.

Nanda Devi (Himalaya), British-American expedition, 1936.

Annapurna (Himalaya), French expedition, 1950.

Everest, E. P. Hillary (New Zealand) and Tensing (Nepal), 29 May 1953.

Nanga Parbat (Himalaya), H. Buhl (Austria), 3 July 1953.

K-2 (Himalayas), Italian expedition, 31 July 1954.

Kangchenjunga, British expedition, 25 May 1955.

Manaslu (Nepal), Japanese expedition, 1956.

Lhotse (Himalaya), Swiss expedition, 1956.

Broad Peak, Austrian expedition, 1957.

Rakaposhi, British-Pakistani expedition, led by M. Banks, 1958.

Shisha Pangma, Tibet, Chinese expedition, 2 May, 1964.

Mozambique. Discovered by Vasco da Gama, 1498. Colonized by Portuguese from 1505. Large areas chartered to the M. Co., and the Nyasaland Co., 1891, and the Zambesi Co., 1892. Vatua rebellion and siege of Lourenço Marques Aug. 1894. Vatuas broken by battles of Marracuene. Coolela. and Chaimite, 1895. Gazaland reconquered, 1897. Overseas province of Portugal, 1951. Guerrilla activity from 1950s resulted in independence, 1975. M. became a one-party Marxist state in 1977. Peace agreement with S. Africa, 1984.

Mufti, Grand, office abolished in Turkey, 1924. The office of M. of Jerusalem was instituted, 1922.

Muggletonians. A religious sect which was founded in England *c.* 1651 by John Reeve and Lodowick Muggleton.

Mugwumps, faction of the Republican Party in the U.S.A., first so called, 1889. Obsolete.

Mukden (China **Shenyang**), Manchuria, largely burnt out in the Boxer rising of 1900. Russians defeated by Japanese, Mar. 1905.

Munich or **München,** Germany. Capital of Bavaria (*q.v.*). Supposed to have been founded, A.D. 962, by Henry of Saxony; taken by Gustavus Adolphus of Sweden, 1962; by Austrians, 1704, 1741, 1746; by French, 2 July 1800; university founded, 1826. Scene of first National Socialist *putsch*, 8 Nov. 1923. M. Conference on Czechoslovakia, 30 Sept. 1938.

Munitions, Ministry of. British Government set up a M. of M., June 1915. Abolished, 1920.

Münster, Westphalia, by 1186 had grown into a town; declared for the Protestant faith, 1532; famous during 1535 for the Anabaptist disturbances, when the Roman Catholic bishop was expelled, but returned after besieging the city the same year.

Münster, Treaty of. Also known as the Treaty of Westphalia (*q.v.*), 1648.

Murder (Abolition of Death Penalty) Act. *See* CAPITAL PUNISHMENT.

Murmansk, founded, 1915, as Romanovna-Murmane, allied base in the abortive Archangel expedition of 1918–19. Besieged by Finns and Germans, 1941–4. Capital of province of same name, whose area was increased by the cession of Petsamo (*q.v.*), 1945.

Muscat, Persian Gulf. Occupied by Portuguese, 1508. Driven out by the Sultan of Oman, 1650, who made it his capital, 1741.

Musical Composers. The following are among the most celebrated of the world's M.C. with their dates:

American:
Buck, Dudley, 1839–1909
Chadwick, George Whitefield, 1854–1931
Copland, Aaron, 1900–
De Koven, Henry Louis Reginald, 1859–1920
Foster, Stephen, 1826–64
Gershwin, George, 1898–1937
Griffes, Charles Tomlinson, 1884–1920
Herbert, Victor (*b.* Irish), 1859–1924
Loeffer, Charles Martin Tornov (*b.* French), 1861–1935
MacDowell, Edward Alexander, 1861–1908

Nevin, Ethelbert Woodbridge, 1862–1901
Paine, John Knowles, 1839–1906
Parker, Horatio William, 1863–1919
Schelling, Ernest, 1876–1939
Sousa, John Philip, 1854–1932

Austrian:
Berg, Alban, 1885–1935
Bruckner, Anton, 1824–96
Czerny, Karl, 1791–1857
Dittersdorf, Karl Ditters von, 1739–99
Fall, Leo, 1878–1925
Goldmark, Karl, 1830–1915
Haydn, Franz Josef, 1732–1809
Kreisler, Fritz, 1875–1962
Lanner, Josef Franz Karl, 1801–43
Mahler, Gustav, 1860–1911
Mozart, Wolfgang Amadeus, 1756–91
Pleyel, Ignaz Josef, 1757–1831
Schubert, Franz Peter, 1797–1828
Schönberg, Arnold, 1874–1951
Strauss I, Johann, 1804–49
Strauss II, Johann, 1825–99
Suppé, Franz von, 1819–95
Wolf, Hugo, 1860–1903

Belgian:
Benoît, Pierre Léopold Léonard, 1834–1901
Des Prés, Joaquin, *c.* 1450–1521
Dufay, Guillaume, *c.* 1400–74
Franck, César August, 1822–90
Gossec, François Joseph, 1734–1829
Grétry, André Ernest Modest, 1741–1813
Jannequin, Clément, *c.* 1475–1560
Lassus, Roland de (Orlando di Lasso) *c.* 1552–94)
Lekeu, Guillaume, 1870–94
Ockeghem, Jean de, *c.* 1430–*c.* 1495
Tinel, Edgar, 1854–1912
Verdelot, Philippe, *c.* 1530–*c.* 1567
Vieuxtemps, Henri, 1820–81
Willaert, Adrian, *c.* 1480–1562

Brazilian:
Villa-Lobos, Heitor, 1887–1959

British:
Arne, Thomas Augustine, 1710–78
Attwood, Thomas, 1765–1838
Balfe, Michael William, 1808–70
Bateson, Thomas, *c.* 1575–1630
Bax, Sir Arnold Edward, 1883–1953
Benedict, Sir Julius, 1804–85
Bennett, Sir William Sterndale, 1816–75

Bishop, Sir Henry Rowley, 1786–1855
Blow, John, 1649–1708
Boyce, William, 1710–79
Bridge, Frank, 1879–1941
Bridge, Sir John Frederick, 1844–1924
Britten, Benjamin, Baron 1913–76
Bull, John, c. 1562–1628
Burney, Charles, 1726–1814
Butterworth, George Sainton Kaye, 1885–1916
Byrd, or Byrde, William, 1543–1623
Campion, Thomas, 1567–1619
Carey, Henry, c. 1687–1743
Cellier, Alfred, 1844–91
Clarke, Jeremiah, 1673–1707
Coleridge–Taylor, Samuel, 1875–1912
Cowen, Sir Frederick Hymen, 1852–1935
D'Albert, Eugene Francis Charles, 1864–1932
Davies, Sir Henry Walford, 1869–1941
Delius, Frederick, 1862–1934
Dibdin, Charles, 1745–1814
Dowland, John, 1563–1626
Dunstable, John, d. 1453
Elgar, Sir Edward, 1857–1934
Farnaby, Giles, c. 1565–c. 1640
Field, John (Irish), 1782–1837
German, Sir Edward, 1862–1936
Gibbons, Orlando, 1583–1625
Greene, Maurice, 1695–1755
Gurney, Ivor, 1890–1937
Handel, George Frederick, 1685–1759 (b. Germany)
Harty, Sir Herbert Hamilton (Irish), 1879–1941
Henschel, Isidor Georg (Sir George) (b. German), 1850–1934
Heseltine, Philip ('Peter Warlock'), 1894–1930
Holst, Gustav Theodore, 1874–1934
Hullah, John Pyke, 1812–84
Humfrey, Pelham, 1647–74
Ireland, John, 1879–1962
Lehmann, Liza (Mrs. Herbert Bedford), 1862–1918
Locke, Matthew, c. 1630–77
MacCunn, Hamish (Scottish), 1868–1916
Macfarren, Sir George Alexander, 1813–1887
Mackenzie, Sir Alexander Campbell (Scottish), 1847–1935
Miles, Philip Napier, 1865–1935

Monckton, Lionel, 1862–1924
Morley, Thomas, 1557–1602
Nares, James, 1715–83
Novello, Ivor (Davies), 1893–1951 (Welsh)
O'Neill, Norman Houston, 1875–1934
Ouseley, Sir Frederick Arthur Gore, 1825–89
Parratt, Sir Walter, 1841–1924
Parry, Joseph, 1841–1903
Parry, Sir Charles Hubert Hastings, 1848–1918
Purcell, Henry, 1659–95
Ronald, Sir Landon, 1873–1938
Rubbra, Edmund, 1901–
Sharp, Cecil James, 1859–1924
Somervell, Sir Arthur, 1863–1937
Stainer, Sir John, 1840–1901
Stanford, Sir Charles Villiers, 1852–1924
Sir Arthur Seymour, 1842–1900
Tallis, Thomas, c. 1505–85
Taverner, John, c. 1495–1545
Tippett, Sir Michael, 1905–
Tomkins, Thomas, 1573–1656
Tosti, Sir Francesco Paolo (b. Italian), 1846–1916
Tovey, Sir Donald Francis, 1875–1940
Tye, Christopher, c. 1500–72 or '73
Vaughan Williams, Ralph, 1872–1958
Wallace, William Vincent, 1812–65
Walton, Sir William, 1902–83
Warlock, Peter. *See* HESELTINE, PHILIP
Weelkes, Thomas, c. 1575–1623
Wesley, Samuel, 1766–1837
Wesley, Samuel Sebastian, 1810–76
White, Robert, c. 1535–74
Willbye, John, 1574–1638
Williamson, Malcolm, 1931–
Wood, Charles, 1866–1926

Czech:
Dvořák, Anton, 1841–1904
Fibich, Zděnek, 1850–1900
Hammerschmidt, Andreas, 1611–75
Janáček, Leoš, 1854–1928
Kozeluch, Leopold Anton, 1754–1818
Nedbal, Oscar, 1874–1930
Smetana, Bedrich, 1824–84
Suk, Josef, 1874–1935

Danish:
Buxtehude, Diderik, 1637–1707
Gade, Niels Vilhelm, 1817–90
Hartmann, Johan Peter Emil, 1805–1900

Horneman, Christian Frederik Emil,
  1841–1906
Lassen, Eduard, 1830–1904
Nielsen, Carl August, 1865–1931
Dutch:
  Isaak, Hendrick, 1450–1517
  Obrecht, Jakob, 1430–1505
  Röntgen, Julius, 1855–1934
  Sweelinck, Jan Pieterszoon, 1562–1621
Finnish:
  Kajanus, Robert, 1856–1935
  Melartin, Errki Gustav, 1875–1937
  Sibelius, Jean, 1865–1957
French:
  Alkan (Morhange), Charles Henri
    Valentin, 1813–88
  Auber, Daniel François Esprit,
    1782–1871
  Audran, Edmond, 1840–1901
  Benoist, François, 1794–1878
  Berlioz, Hector, 1803–69
  Bizet, Georges, 1838–75
  Boëllmann, Léon, 1862–97
  Boïeldieu, François Adrien, 1775–1834
  Bourgault-Ducoudray, Louis Albert,
    1840–1910
  Bruneau, Louis Charles Bonaventure
    Alfred, 1857–1934
  Campra, André, 1660–1744
  Caplet, André, 1879–1925
  Chabrier, Alexis Emmanuel, 1841–94
  Chausson, Ernest, 1855–99
  Couperin, François, 1668–1733
  David, Félicien César, 1810–76
  Debussy, Claude, 1862–1918
  Delibes, Léo, 1836–91
  Dukas, Paul, 1865–1935
  Duparc, Henri, 1848–1933
  Erlanger, Camille, 1863–1919
  Fauré, Gabriel Urbain, 1845–1924
  Godard, Benjamin Louis Paul, 1849–95
  Goudimel, Claude, 1510–72
  Gounod, Charles François, 1813–93
  Guilmant, Félix Alexandre, 1837–1911
  Halévy, Jacques Fromental Élie,
    1799–1862
  Hérold, Louis Joseph Ferdinand,
    1791–1833
  Indy, Paul Marie Théodore Vincent d',
    1851–1931
  Lalo, Victor Antoine Édouard, 1823–92
  Lecocq, Alexandre Charles, 1832–1918
  Lesueur, Jean François, 1760–1837
  Lully, Jean Baptiste, 1632–87

Magnard, Albéric, 1866–1914
Massenet, Jules Émile Frédéric,
  1842–1912
Méhul, Étienne Nicolas, 1763–1817
Messager, André Charles Prosper,
  1853–1929
Messiaen, Olivier Eugéne Prosper
  Charles, 1908–
Monsigny, Pierre Alexandre,
  1729–1817
Offenbach, Jacques, 1819–80
Onslow, George (Anglo-French),
  1784–1853
Philidor, François André, 1726–95
Pierné, Henri Constant Gabriel,
  1863–1937
Poulenc, François, 1899–1963
Planquette, Robert, 1848–1903
Rameau, Jean Philippe, 1683–1764
Ravel, Maurice Joseph, 1875–1937
Reyer (Rey), Ernest, 1823–1909
Roussel, Albert, 1867–1937
Saint-Saëns, Charles Camille,
  1841–1921
Satie, Erik (Alfred Eric Leslie),
  1866–1925
Séverac, Joseph Marie Déodat de,
  1873–1921
Thomas, Charles Louis Ambroise,
  1811–1896
Widor, Charles Marie Jean Albert,
  1844–1937
German:
  Bach, Carl Philipp Emanuel, 1714–88
  Bach, Johann Christian, 1735–82
  Bach, Johann Sebastian, 1685–1750
  Beethoven, Ludwig van, 1770–1827
  Brahms, Johannes, 1833–97
  Bruch, Max, 1838–1920
  Cornelius, Peter, 1824–74
  Draeseke, Felix, 1835–1913
  Flotow, Friedrich, Freiherr von,
    1812–1883
  Franz, Robert, 1815–92
  Gluck, Christoph Willibald, 1714–87
  Goetz, Hermann, 1840–76
  Graupner, Christoph, 1683–1760
  Handl, Jakob, 1550–91
  Hasse, Johann Adolf, 1699–1783
  Hassler or Hasler, Hans Leo,
    1564–1612
  Henselt, Adolf von, 1814–99
  Hiller, Johann Adam, 1728–1804
  Hindemith, Paul, 1895–1963

Hoffman, Ernst Theodor Amadeus, 1776–1822
Hummel, Johann Nepomuk, 1778–1837
Humperdinck, Engelbert, 1854–1921
Jensen, Adolf, 1837–79
Karg-Elert, Sigfrid, 1877–1933
Keiser, Reinhard, 1674–1739
Kirchner, Theodor, 1824–1903
Kücken, Friedrich Wilhelm, 1810–82
Kuhnau, Johann, 1660–1722
Lachner, Franz, 1804–90
Lortzing, Gustav Albert, 1801–51
Löwe, Johann Karl Gottfried, 1796–1869
Marschner, Heinrich August, 1795–1861
Mendelssohn-Bartholdy, Jakob Ludwig Felix, 1809–47
Meyerbeer, Giacomo, 1791–1864
Moscheles, Ignaz, 1794–1870
Moszkowski, Moritz, 1854–1925
Mottl, Felix, 1856–1911
Naumann, Johann Gottlieb, 1741–1801
Neukomm, Sigismund von, 1778–1858
Nicodé, Jean Louis (*b*. Polish), 1853–1919
Nicolai, Karl Otto Ehrenfried, 1810–49
Pachelbel, Johann, 1653–1706
Raff, Joseph Joachim, 1822–82
Reger, Max, 1873–1916
Rheinberger, Josef Gabriel, 1839–1901
Scharwenka, Ludwig Philipp, 1847–1917
Scharwenka, Xaver, 1850–1924
Schreker, Franz, 1878–1934
Schumann, Robert, 1810–56
Schütz, Heinrich, 1585–1672
Spohr, Ludwig, 1784–1859
Steibelt, Daniel, 1765–1823
Strauss, Richard, 1864–1949
Telemann, Georg Philipp, 1681–1767
Vogler, Georg Josef, 1749–1814
Volkmann, Friedrich Robert, 1815–83
Wagner, Wilhelm Richard, 1813–83
Weber, Karl Maria Friedrich Ernst von, 1786–1826
Weill, Kurt, 1900–50,
Hungarian:
Bartók, Béla, 1881–1945
Dohnanyi, Ernö, 1887–1960
Erkel, Ferenc, 1810–92
Heller, Stephen, 1814–88

Joachim, Joseph, 1831–1907
Kodaly, Zoltan, 1882–1967
Lehár, Ferencz (Franz), 1870–1948
Liszt, Franz, 1811–86
Mosonyi, Michael Brandt, 1814–70
Italian:
Abbatini, Antonio Maria, *c*. 1595–1677
Albinoni, Tomaso, 1671–1750
Allegri, Gregorio, 1582–1652
Arditi, Luigi, 1822–1903
Bellini, Vincenzo, 1801–35
Boccherini, Luigi, 1743–1805
Boito, Arrigo, 1842–1918
Bononcini or Buononcini, Giovanni Maria, 1642–78
Bossi, Marco Enrico, 1861–1925
Busoni, Ferruccio Benvenuto, 1866–1924
Caccini, Giulio, 1545–1618
Carissimi, Giacomo, 1605–74
Catalani, Alfredo, 1854–93
Cavalieri, Emilio di, *c*. 1550–1602
Cavalli, Pietro Francesco, 1602–76
Cherubini, Maria Luigi Zenobio Carlo Salvatore, 1760–1842
Cimarosa, Domenico, 1749–1801
Clementi, Muzio, 1752–1832
Corelli, Arcangelo, 1653–1713
Donizetti, Gaetano, 1797–1848
Durante, Francesco, 1684–1755
Frescobaldi, Girolamo, 1583–1643
Gabrieli, Andrea, 1520–86
Gabrieli, Giovanni, 1557–1612
Gagliano, Marco da, *c*. 1575–1642
Geminiani, Francesco, 1687–1762
Gesualdo, Carlo, Prince of Venosa, 1560–1613
Jommelli, Niccolò, 1714–74
Legrenzi, Giovanni, 1625–90
Leo, Leonardo, 1694–1744
Leoncavallo, Ruggiero, 1858–1919
Locatelli, Pietro Antonio, 1693–1764
Lotti, Antonio, 1667–1740
Marcello, Benedetto, 1686–1739
Marenzio, Luca, 1553–99
Martucci, Giuseppe, 1856–1909
Mercadante, Giuseppe Saverio Raffaele, 1795–1870
Merulo, Claudio, 1533–1604
Monteverdi, Claudio, 1567–1643
Paer, Ferdinando, 1771–1839
Paesiello or Paisiello, Giovanni, 1741–1816
Paganini, Niccolò, 1782–1840

Palestrina, Giovanni Pierluigi da,
1525–1594
Pergolese, or Pergolesi, Giovanni
Battista, 1710–36
Piccinni, or Piccini, Niccolò,
1728–1800
Pinsuti, Ciro, 1829–88
Puccini, Giacomo, 1858–1924
Respighi, Ottorino, 1879–1936
Rossini, Gioacchino Antonio,
1792–1868
Sacchini, Antonio Maria Gaspare,
1734–1786
Salieri, Antonio, 1750–1825
Sarti, Giuseppe, 1729–1802
Scarlatti, Alessandro, 1660–1725
Scarlatti, Domenico, 1685–1757
Sgambati, Giovanni, 1841–1914
Spontini, Gasparo Luigi Pacifico,
1774–1851
Steffani, Agostino, 1654–1728
Stradella, Alessandro, 1642–82
Tartini, Giuseppe, 1692–1770
Traetta, Tommaso, 1727–79
Vecchi, Orazio, *c.* 1550–1605
Verdi, Giuseppe, 1813–1901
Viadana (Grossi), Ludovico, 1564–1645
Vicentino, Nicolà, 1511–*c.* 1576
Vivaldi, Antonio, *c.* 1675–1741
Zingarelli, Nicolà Antonio, 1752–1837
Mexican:
Ponce, Manuel, 1882–1948
Norwegian:
Grieg, Edvard Hagerup, 1843–1907
Selmer, Johan Peter, 1844–1910
Svendsen, Johan Severin, 1840–1911
Polish:
Chopin, Frédéric François, 1810–49
Godowsky, Leopold, 1870–1938
Moniuszko, Stanislaus, 1819–92
Noskowski, Zygmunt, 1846–1909
Paderewski, Ignacy Jan, 1860–1941
Szymanowski, Karol, 1882–1937
Russian:
Arensky, Antonin Stepanovitch,
1861–1906
Balakirev, Mily Alexeievitch,
1837–1910
Borodin, Alexander Porfirievitch,
1833–1887
Cui, César Antonovitch, 1835–1918
Dragomijsky, Alexander, 1813–69
Glazunov, Alexander Constantino-
vitch, 1865–1936

Glinka, Mikhail Ivanovitch, 1804–57
Kastalsky, Alexander Dmitrievitch,
1856–1926
Liadov, Anatol Constantinovitch,
1855–1914
Liapunov, Serge Mikhailovitch,
1859–1924
Mussorgsky, Modest Petrovitch,
1839–1881
Napravnik, Eduard (*b.* Czech),
1839–1916
Prokofiev, Sergei, 1891–1953
Rachmaninov, Serge, 1873–1943
Rebikov, Vladimir Ivanovitch,
1866–1920
Rimsky-Korsakov, Nicolas Andreie-
vitch, 1844–1908
Rubinstein, Anton, 1830–94
Scriabin, Alexander Nicolaievitch,
1871–1915
Taneiev, Alexander Sergeievitch,
1850–1915
Taneiev, Serge Ivanovitch, 1856–1915
Tchaikovsky, Peter Ilyitch, 1840–93
Spanish:
Albeniz, Isaac, 1860–1909
Bretón, Tomás, 1850–1923
Chapi, Ruperto, 1851–1909
Falla, Manuel de, 1876–1946
Granados Campina, Enrique,
1867–1916
Pedrell, Felipe, 1841–1922
Sarasate, Pablo de, 1844–1910
Victoria, Tomás Luis de, *c.* 1535–1611
Swedish:
Hallén, Johan Andréas, 1846–1925
Hallström, Ivar, 1826–1901
Sjögren, J. G. Emil, 1853–1918
Swiss:
Huber, Hans, 1852–1921

Musical Festivals. Festival of the Sons
of the Clergy in St. Paul's Cathedral,
annual since 1698. Three Choirs Festival held annually in cathedrals of
Gloucester, Hereford, and Worcester,
in succession, from 1715. Birmingham
Festival began, 1768; held at irregular
intervals till 1912. Norwich Festival
held at irregular intervals since 1770.
Crystal Palace Handel Festival began,
1857; irregular, and then triennial.
Leeds Festival instituted, 1858; held
again, 1874; since then, triennial.
Bayreuth Festival, 1876. Edinburgh

International Festival instituted, 1947. Aldeburgh, Suffolk, festival instituted, 1948. In U.S.A. festivals began at Boston and Worcester, 1858; Cincinnati, 1873. Bach Festival at Bethlehem, Pennsylvania, 1900. Berkshire Festivals, established at Pittsfield, Massachusetts, 1918, were in 1931 transferred to Library of Congress, Washington. The Boston Symphony Orchestra acquired Tanglewood, Berkshire, Massachussets, as permanent festival home in 1937. In Germany the Lower Rhine Festival, dating from 1817, was the most important. Salzburg Festival founded 1870; held annually since 1920.

Mutiny Acts, the legal basis of military law and hence of the existence of a standing army in the U.K., were passed annually from 1689 to 1881, when they were merged in the Army Acts, still passed annually.

M.V.D., executive forces of the Ministry of the Interior of the U.S.S.R., and including frontier and security troops of all arms, and warders and administrative personnel of forced-labour camps, as well as the secret police force, known until 1945 as the N.K.V.D. (*q.v.*), and after 1953 as the K.G.B. (*q.v.*).

Mysore, India. Continually at war with the British, 1760–99. In 1799 Tipu Sahib finally defeated; M. made to accept a subsidiary alliance and to cede Coimbatore to British, and Kurnool to Hyderabad, 1801. State completely annexed by British, 1834, but retroceded to a native rajah, 1881. Joined the Indian Union, Dec. 1947.

N

Nagaland, inaugurated as 16th state of India, 1 Dec. 1963. Unrest, 1960–75, terminated by the Shillong Agreement of 1975.

Nagasaki, Japan. From 1640 the Dutch were the only European nation permitted to trade with Japan, and they were allowed only one trading post on Deshima, near N. This continued till Japan was opened to trade, 1859. City mostly destroyed by atomic bomb, 9 Aug. 1945.

Nairobi, Kenya. Founded, 1898.

Namibia, formerly **South-West Africa**. This ter. (excluding certain is. and Walvis Bay) proclaimed a Ger. protectorate, 1884. Mandated to S. Africa by League of Nations, 17 Dec. 1920. In July 1949 S. Africa told the U.N. no further mandate reports would be submitted, and N. henceforth virtually incorporated in S. Africa despite U.N. objections. U.N. envisaged Namibian independence by 31 Dec. 1978, but elections held in Dec. 1978 without U.N. supervision returned a pro-S. African assembly, the left-wing Swapo party boycotting the elections. Guerrilla resistance to S. African rule, based on Mozambique (*q.v.*), has existed since the mid-1970s.

Namur, Belgium. Captured by Louis XIV in 1692; recaptured in 1695 by William III; in French possession, 1702–12; bombarded by allies, 1704; subsequently in possession of different powers, and assigned to Belgium, 1830.

Nancy, France. Captured by Charles the Bold, 29 Nov. 1475; lost by him, 5 Oct. 1476; captured by French, 1633 and 1670; restored to Duke Leopold, 1697; became French possession, 1766; put to ransom by the Prussians, 1870.

Nanking, China. Capital of China, 1368,

till abandoned by Yung-lo, 1405. Captured by British, 1842. By Taipings, 1853. Railways to Tientsin and Shanghai opened, 1909. Became capital again, 1928. Stormed and sacked by Japanese, Nov. 1937. Became capital of Wang Ching Wei's Japanese-sponsored government, 1940–5. Officially ceased to be Chinese capital after Communist victory in 1949.

Nantes, France. Of Roman origin. In possession of Clotaire I, A.D. 560; held by Normans, 843–936; communal constitution granted by Francis II, 1560; scene of Carrier's *noyades,* 1793.

Nantes, Edict of, by which the Huguenots were permitted to exercise their own religion, was published on 15 Apr. 1598 by Henry IV of France. Its revocation on 24 Oct. 1685, by Louis XIV, drove many of the Protestants into exile.

Naples, Italy. The Romans subdued the territory in 326 B.C.; it fell into the hands of the Goths, but they were driven out by Belisarius in A.D. 536; Charles of Anjou in possession, 1266; great massacre of the French at Palermo known as the Sicilian Vespers (*q.v.*), 1282; separated from Sicily (*q.v.*), 1303; reunited with Sicily, 1442; annexed to Spain, 1504; insurrection headed by Masaniello, 1647; possessed by Austria, 1713; recovered by Spain, 1734; invaded by French Republican Army, 1789; by Napoleon, 1806; restoration of the Bourbons, 1815; incorporated in the kingdom of Italy, 1860.

Narbonne, France. A considerable time before the Roman invasion of Gaul, N. was a famous city. In 118 B.C. the first Roman colony in Gaul was founded under the name of *Narbo Martius;* seized by the Visigoths, A.D. 413; by

Saracens after a two years' siege, 719; retaken by Pepin le Bref, 759; united to French crown, 1507; Cinq-Mars arrested at for conspiracy, 1642.

Narvik, formerly **Viktoriahavn,** was connected with the ironstone mines in northern Sweden (Kiruna, etc.), 1903. Four German destroyers sunk in N. fiord, 13 Apr. 1940; town captured by Allies, 28 May, but abandoned, 10 June.

Nassau, Germany. Early occupied by the Alamanni, who were defeated by Clovis towards the close of the fifth century; became part of German kingdom, 843; annexed to Prussia, 1866.

Natal, S. Africa. Discovered by Vasco da Gama on Christmas Day, 1497, hence the name; declared part of British dominions, 1843; formally annexed to Cape Colony, 31 May 1844; declared a separate colony, 15 July 1856; Zululand annexed to, 1897; Boers finally driven from, 1900. An original member of the Union of S: Africa, 1910.

National Anthem. First N.A. said to have been the English **God Save the King** (or **Queen**) first performed in London in 1745 to celebrate the victory over the Jacobites at Prestonpans, and since used on all royal ceremonial occasions.

National Art Collections Fund. Founded, 1903.

National Assembly, 1789–91. *See* FRENCH REVOLUTION.

National Assistance Act, 1948, was intended to replace by a new principle a system which hitherto had been based on successive modifications of the Elizabethan Poor Laws (*q.v.*). National Assistance Board replaced by the Supplementary Benefits Commission, Nov. 1966.

National Book League. Founded, 1944, as the successor to the National Book Council (founded, 1924).

National Debt (Great Britain). Originated in the reign of William III, and was introduced by Charles Montagu, Earl of Halifax (1661–1715) on 15 Dec. 1692. Became a permanent institution, 1694. Deadweight debt on 31 Mar. in years named: 1914, £649,770,091; 1939, £7,130,800,000; 1969, £33,963,000,000; 1980, over £96,000,000,000.

National Dental Service provided for under N. Health Service Act, 1946, which came into operation 5 July 1948.

National Front. *See under* BRITISH UNION OF FASCISTS.

National Gallery (London). Founded, 1824. Present building completed, 1838; enlarged, 1860, 1869, 1876, 1886, 1930 and 1975; and further extension planned, 1985; N. Portrait Gallery founded, 1856, established at S. Kensington, 1869; removed to Bethnal Green Museum, 1885; transferred to new buildings adjoining N.G., 1896.

National Gallery of British Art. *See* TATE GALLERY.

National Governments, coalitions in the U.K. which came to power in Aug. 1931 and Nov. 1935, and which continued in office during World War II, being, however, largely reconstituted in the spring of 1940. A Nat. Govt. continued in office until 1945.

National Guard (France). Introduced into Paris during French Revolution, July 1789; superseded by present military system, 1870.

National Guard (U.S.A.). Founded, 1903.

National Health Service Act was evolved from proposals made in the White Paper of Feb. 1944. It became law in 1946, but did not come into operation until 5 July 1948. Charges for medicine, etc., supplied under this Act first made, June 1952.

National Insurance. An insurance against ill health and unemployment, introduced in 1911, and came into force, 15 July 1912. Entire structure of N.I. in Britain changed by the Act of 1946 (*see* next article).

National Insurance Act, 1946, based on recommendations made in the report of the Beveridge Committee, 1942, and developed in a White Paper of Sept. 1944, repealed all previous legislation on the subject of unemployment, etc., insurance, and pensions, and became law, 1946. Many amending Acts since, including those of 1965, 1966, 1967, 1968, 1969, 1973 and 1975.

National Parks and Access to the Countryside Act, 1949, set up the National Parks Commission with powers to designate national parks and areas of outstanding beauty in England and Wales. Ten national parks had been established by 1969, when the N.P. Commission was succeeded by Countryside Commission.

National Portrait Gallery, London, founded 1856 and opened 1859.

Nationality Act, British, 1981, replaced a previous Act, 30 July 1948, which itself replaced the Act of 1914. It amended the Immigration Act of 1971 regarding rights of abode in the U.K. and estab. 3 categories of citizenship.

Nationalization. The following is a list of principal measures of N. taken since 1944.
Bank of England, 1946; cable and wireless, 1946; coal, 1946; civil aviation, 1946; electricity, 1948; gas, 1948; road transport, 1948; steel, 1949–51; shipbuilding, 1977; aircraft industry, 1977. Since 1979 denationalization a major feature of govt. policy; by 1985 road transport, steel, shipbuilding and telecommunications already denationalized.

National Physical Laboratory. As from 1 Apr. 1918, the Department of Scientific and Industrial Research, appointed by Order in Council, 28 July 1915, has been responsible for maintenance of N.P.L., which was founded in 1899.

National Playing Fields Association. Founded, 1925; chartered, 1933.

National Register.
1. Taken, 15 Aug. 1915.
2. Register taken and identity cards issued, 29 Sept. 1939. Closed, 1952.

National Research Development Corporation. Set up by the Development of Inventions Act, 30 July 1948.

National Savings Bank, name given, 1971, to the **Post Office Savings Bank,** established 1861.

National Savings Certificates first issued, Feb. 1916.

National Security Council, U.S.A., established by the N.S. Act, 1947 (since amended). The Central Intelligence Agency (C.I.A.) is under the Council's direction.

National Service, Ministry of. Set up as a temporary recruiting expedient,

1917, and dissolved after the war. Revived as part of Ministry of Labour and N.S., 19 Dec. 1938.

National Socialism (Germany). A pan-German party with the title N. Socialist Labour Party was founded in Bohemia in 1912, but had no direct traceable connection with that which Anton Drexler founded at Munich in 1919, and called simply German Labour Party (Deutsche Arbeiter Partei). This was used by Hitler as the nucleus of his N. Socialist German Labour Party (N.S.D.A.P. for short in German). It adopted a detailed pan-German nationalist programme, with some vague socialist tenets, 1920, and from 1933 to 1945 was the only permitted party in the country.

National Temperance League. *See* ANTI-SALOON LEAGUE.

National Theatre, Great Britain. Sir Laurence Olivier agreed to become its first director, Aug. 1962. First season at Old Vic, 1963: new building completed, 1976.

National Trust, founded by Octavia Hill and others, 1895. Status confirmed by N.T. Acts of 1907, 1919, 1937, and 1939. N.T. for Scotland founded in 1931.

Nativity, formally appointed to be observed on 25 Dec. by the Synod of Salzburg, 800, but this was only confirmation of practice general since *c.* 690.

Nativity, Church of the, at Bethlehem. St. Helena (*c.* 250–330), mother of the Emperor Constantine, built a church here in 325, over a cave first mentioned as the scene of the N. by Justin Martyr in 155, and which was shown to Origen in 215. St. Helena's building was burnt, probably in the Samaritan rising of 529; but by order of the Emperor Justinian (reigned 527–65) a church was built on the same site. On the Moslem conquest of Palestine the church was given special protection by command of the Caliph Omar (*c.* 640). From then until 1947, except for the period 1099–1187, the site was in Moslem hands; since 1947, in Israel.

N.A.T.O. (North Atlantic Treaty Organization). N. Atlantic Treaty (*q.v.*)

signatories set up permanent council of ministers' deputies, May 1950. Defence Committee decided on a permanent integrated force on a war footing on the European mainland, Sept. 1950. General Eisenhower appointed Supreme Commander, and Field-Marshal Montgomery appointed Deputy-Commander Land Forces, Dec. Their headquarters, S.H.A.P.E., became operational, Apr. 1951. Turkey and Greece joined N.A.T.O., 1952. Lord Ismay first Secretary-General, Oct. 1952. German Federal Republic joined N.A.T.O., Oct. 1954 (effective 9 May 1955), and German units thereafter included in N.A.T.O. forces. France withdrew her naval Atlantic force from N.A.T.O., June 1963, and by 1966 had virtually withdrawn from it altogether. HQ moved from Paris to Brussels, 1967. Spain joined N.A.T.O., 1982.

Secretaries-General of N.A.T.O.:
Lord Ismay 1952–1957
Paul-Henri Spaak 1957–1961
Dirk Stikker 1961–1964
Manlio Brosio 1964–1971
Joseph Luns 1971–1984
Lord Carrington 1984–

Supreme Commanders of N.A.T.O.:
General Eisenhower 1950–1952
General Ridgway 1952–1953
General Gruenther 1953–1956
General Norstad 1956–1962
General Lemnitzer 1962–1969
General Alexander Haig 1970–1979
General Bernard Rogers 1979–

Naturalization Act (Great Britain). Passed, 1870; a treaty with U.S.A. was entered into the same year, by which both countries pledged themselves to recognize claims of N. Brit. naturalization processes affected by the British Nationality Act, 1981.

Nauru, republic in the Pacific, discovered by Capt. Fearn, 1798; annexed by Germany, 1888, mandated to Britain, 1920. Administered jointly by Britain, Australia and New Zealand, 1947–68, when N. became independent.

Naval Discipline Acts begin in England with the N. Laws of Olèron, 1194. Henry VIII codified Sea Laws, 1530. Naval discipline now (1985) regulated by the Naval Discipline Act, 1957 (as amended).

Naval Limitation Conference (at Geneva)—Great Britain, U.S.A., and Japan—failed to come to any agreement, 4 Aug. 1927. *See* LONDON CONFERENCE.

Navarre. United all Basques tenth–eleventh centuries. United with Aragon, 1076–1134. Vizcaya and Guipúzcoa annexed by Castile *c.* 1200. French dynasty took throne, 1285. Spanish N. annexed by Castile, 1512. French N. united when Henry of N. ascended French throne as Henry IV, 1589. Spanish N. was a viceroyalty till 1833. *See* SPAIN.

Navigation Laws (Great Britain). Oliver Cromwell in 1650 excluded all foreign ships without a licence from trading with the plantations of America. The N. Act of Cromwell passed, 1651. Act providing that all colonial produce should be exported in English vessels, 1660. Colonies prohibited from receiving goods in foreign vessels, 1663. N. Acts of Charles II, 1672, extended Cromwell's Act and ruined the Dutch Navy. N. Act repealed, 1826, but a new code of regulations still prevented free trade. These laws abolished, 1842, 1846, and 1849. Coasting trade of Britain thrown open to foreign vessels, 1854.

Navy, Royal (British). Alfred the Great built a fleet to resist the Danes, 897; Richard I equipped a large fleet for the crusades, 1189; Edward III defeated the French at Sluys, 1340; Henry V increased the number and size of the ships, 1413–22; Henry VII built the *Great Harry*, 1488; the English N. defeated the Armada, 1588; the *Sovereign of the Seas* launched, 1637; the first British frigate built, 1649; first steamer built for the Royal N., 1814; screw propeller introduced, 1845; reserve volunteer force established, 1859; first ironclad of the N. built, 1860; Royal School of Naval Architecture established, 1864; first armour-clad turret ship built, 1868; breech-loading guns manufactured for the N., 1881; torpedo cruiser built,

1887; first British submarine launched, 1901; 13·5-in. guns replace 12-in. on *Orion* class, 1912; 15.-in. on *Queen Elizabeth*, 1915–16; 18-in. on monitors, 1917–18. All big ships equipped with seaplanes, 1919–20. See WORLD WARS I and II, and BATTLES. Number of Royal N. ships in commission first declared to be exceeded by total U.S.S.R. strength, Mar. 1953. Work completed on first nuclear-powered submarine, 1963.

Navy, U.S.A. On 13 Oct. 1775 Congress authorized the fitting out of a gun-carrying vessel. This was the beginning of the U.S. N. Board of Admiralty established, 1779. Other vessels fitted out, 1775. In 1794, the N. having fallen into neglect, Congress voted a sum of money 'for creating a small N'. See WORLD WARS I and II, and BATTLES. In 1985 the U.S. Navy was probably still the most powerful sea force in the world, though numerical comparison is impossible, as exact Russian naval figures are not known.

Nazi Party. See NATIONAL SOCIALISM.

Neanderthal, valley near Düsseldorf, Germany, giving its name to a primitive human, or near-human, race, a skull of one of its members having been found there, 1856.

Nebraska, territory ceded by France to Spain, 1762, returned to France, 1801, and forming part of the Louisiana (*q.v.,* 1803) Purchase. Territory organized, 1854; state admitted to Union, 1867.

Negri Sembilan, former Federated Malay State, is largely populated by the descendants of Sumatrans who immigrated in the sixteenth century. Dominated by Johore (*q.v.*), 1641–1773. British intervention in local politics first invited, 1874. A confederation of smaller states gave N.S. its present extent, 1895. Since 1963 part of Malaysia (*q.v.*).

Negropont. See EUBOEA.

Nejd. See SAUDI ARABIA.

N.E.P. (New Economic Policy). The revolution having led to economic breakdown in Russia, Lenin introduced the N.E.P. as a temporary capitalist dilution of Soviet socialism, 1921–8.

Nepal. Conquered by Harisinha-Deva, 1324. Jayastithi-Malla (1386–1429) introduced caste system. Divided into four states, 1429–1768. Conquered by Gurkhas, 1768–70. War with China, 1790–2. Treaties with British, 1792–1801. First Gurkha War, 1814–16, ended in cession of Kumaon province to British India. British residency established at Katmandu, 1817. Jung Bahadur Rana seizes power ('The Kot Massacre'), 18 May 1845. Rana family consolidated their power and established new system of government, 1845–56. Gurkhas assist British in Indian Mutiny, 1857. Treaty with Britain recognized independence of N., 1923. Rana family power ended, 1951, when king proclaimed a constitutional monarchy. Constitution last amended, 1975.

Netherlands, Kingdom of the, popularly known as **Holland**, became a separate entity after the Sp. victory at Gembloux, 1578, had driven the Catholic Netherlanders to make terms and instituted the Union of Arras, 1579 (see BELGIUM). The Northern Protestant provinces repudiated Sp. sovereignty in the Act of Abjuration, 26 July 1581, being led by Holland. William I of Orange assassinated, 1584. Jacob van Oldenbarneveldt in power, 1586–1618. Spanish naval defeat at Gibraltar, 1607. Truce of Antwerp, 1609. Wars with Britain, 1653–4, 1666–7. Joins Triple Alliance against France, 1668. Wars against France and Britain, 1672–8. William of Orange becomes King of Britain, 1689. Treaty of Ryswick, 1697. Joins in War of Spanish Succession against France, 1701–13. Office of Stadhouder declared hereditary in family of Orange, 1747. French Republican army invades N., 1794; William V expelled, 15 Jan. 1795; Louis Bonaparte declared king, 5 June 1806, abdicated, 1 July 1810. House of Orange restored under William Frederick, 1 Dec. 1813; N. and Belgium united by Treaty of London, 14 June 1814, and William made King of the united N., 15 Mar. 1815. Separated from Belgium (*q.v.*), 12 July 1831;

peace between N. and Belgium, 19 Apr. 1839 and William Frederick abdicated; William II succeeded, 1840; William III, 1849; Wilhelmina crowned (after queen-mother's regency), 1898. Ex-Kaiser sought refuge in N., Nov. 1918. German invasion, 10 May 1940. Dutch military surrender, 14 May, but Dutch royal family fled to Britain. Ex-Kaiser *d.* at Doorn, 4 June 1941. Brit. airborne forces land at Arnhem (*q.v.*), 17 Sept. 1944. British land at Walcheren, 1 Nov. 1944. Member of Benelux (*q.v.*), 1949. Wilhelmina abdicated, 4 Sept. 1948 (*d.* Nov. 1962); succeeded by daughter Juliana. N. member of N.A.T.O., 1949. Dutch E. Indies became republic of Indonesia (*q.v.*), 1950; Indonesia obtained W. Dutch New Guinea, 1963. Member of European Economic Community (*q.v.*), 1958. Juliana abdicated, 1980, and succeeded by daughter Beatrix (*b.* 1938). The following is a list of the sovereigns of the Netherlands:

William I* (*d.* 1843)	1815–40
William II	1840–9
William III	1849–90
Wilhelmina	1890–1948
Juliana (*b.* 1909)	1948–80
Beatrix (*b.* 1938)	1980–

* 'I' means first *king*. He would have been sixth Stadhouder of that name.

Neuchâtel, Switzerland. Originally *Novum Castellum*, whose original possessors took the name of count mid twelfth century; under Prussian rule from 1707 to 1857, excepting the years 1806–14, when Napoleon granted it to Marshal Berthier; became a full republican member of the Swiss Confederation, 1857.

Neuilly, Treaty of, by which Bulgaria, after World War I, gave up all claims to Macedonia and Thrace, signed 27 Nov. 1919.

Nevada, first settled, 1849. At first part of the territory of Utah which was set up, 1850 (*see* UTAH), but made a territory on its own, 1861, and became a state, 1864.

Nevis, Nievis, or **Mevis,** formed with St. Kitts and Anguilla into a presidency, 1882. Discovered by Colum-

bus, 1493. Granted to the Earl of Carlisle, 1627, and colonized from St. Kitts, 1628. Devastated by the French, 1706, and again captured by them, 1782, but restored by the Treaty of Versailles in the following year. Anguilla (*q.v.*) seceded, 1967. N., with St. Kitts (*q.v.*), became independent within the Commonwealth, 1983.

New Brunswick, Canada. Discovered by Cabot, 1497; colonized by French, 1630 and 1672; ceded to Britain, 1713, and in 1784 separated from Nova Scotia and made a separate colony; was incorporated into Dominion of Canada, 1867.

New Caledonia, Pacific, was discovered by Capt. Cook, 1774; closely explored by d'Entrecasteaux, 1793; claimed by France, 1843; British claim withdrawn, 1853. Became an Overseas Territory, 1958.

Newcastle upon Tyne, England. Named after castle erected 1080 by Robert Curthose; besieged by William Rufus, 1095; present castle built, 1172–7; besieged by Scots under Gen. Leslie, 1644; bishopric founded, 1882. Tyne Bridge opened, 1928. University reorganized 1963.

New Deal. Name given to policy of Franklin D. Roosevelt, President U.S.A., adumbrated during his first presidential campaign at Atlanta, 22 May 1932.

New Delhil. *See* DELHI.

New England, U.S.A. Visited by Sir Humphrey Gilbert, 1583, and by Bartholomew Gosnold, 1602; Puritans sailed in the *Mayflower*, and founded settlement, 1620. *See* MASSACHUSETTS and MAINE.

New Forest, England. Already a forest when Canute issued his Laws at Winchester, 1016. Wiliam I extended its area, 1079, and enforced the Forest Laws more harshly.

Newfoundland. Discovered by John Cabot, 24 June 1497. Visited by five Anglo-Portuguese expeditions, 1500–5. Formally annexed to England by Sir Humphrey Gilbert, Aug. 1583. Island divided between English and French at Treaty of Ryswick, 1697.

Wholly given to Britain by Treaty of Utrecht, 1713. Responsible govt., 1855. N. was one of the Dominions given independent status under the Statute of Westminster, 1931, but owing to bankruptcy the government was surrendered to a commission nominated by the British Treasury, 18 Dec. 1933. Became a province of Canada, 31 Mar. 1949.

Newgate Prison (London). In existence at least as early as 1190. Being rebuilt when burnt down in the Gordon Riots (*q.v.*), 1780, and building completed, 1783. Executions took place here in public, 1783–1868. Demolished, 1902–3.

New Guinea. Probably sighted by Antonio d'Abreu (Portuguese), 1512. First visit by Europeans: either Jorge de Menesis (Portuguese), 1526, or Alvaro de Saavedra (Spanish), 1528. E. India Co. made a settlement in Geelvink Bay, 1793; but in 1814 British Government admitted claims of the Netherlands. Dutch proclaimed sovereignty over western half of island, 1848. Remainder divided between Britain (S.) and Germany (N.), 1884. The British part, called Papua, was placed under the Commonwealth of Australia in 1906. In 1914 the German territory was occupied by Australian forces. Petroleum discovered, 1919. Civil administration of former German territory appointed by Commonwealth, 1921, under League of Nations mandate of 1920. Scene of much fighting in World War II (*q.v.*). Dutch New Guinea was handed over to Indonesia on 1 May 1963; the Australian trust ter. became the independent state of Papua New Guinea (*q.v.*) on 16 Sept. 1975.

New Hampshire, U.S.A., first settled, 1623, founder member of the Union, signatory of the Declaration of Independence (*q.v.*). Has a pre-revolutionary university in Dartmouth College, Hanover (founded, 1769).

New Haven, Conn., U.S.A. Originally *Quinnipiac*. First settled by English Puritans, 1637. Collegiate school of Connecticut removed to N.H., 1716. This later became Yale University.

New Hebrides. *See* VANUATU.

New Jersey, U.S.A., discovered by John Cabot, 1497; settlements made in early seventeenth century by Dutch taken by British, 1664. Founder member of Union.

New Jerusalem Church. *See* SWEDENBORGIANS.

New Mexico, U.S.A., organized as a territory, 1850, admitted to the Union, 1912, as state which, however, consisted only of the rump of the territory, which had ceded large areas to Texas, Utah, and Colorado (1861), and out of which the whole of Arizona was carved (1863). First Spanish settlement, 1598. For the Mexican War, ending Feb. 1848, after which Mexico ceded N. M., *see* TEXAS.

New Model Army. The name given to the new parliamentary force raised by Cromwell and Fairfax, 15 Feb. 1645.

New Orleans, Louisiana, U.S.A. Founded, 1718; possessed by Spain, 1763; fell to France, 1800, and purchased from her as part of the Louisiana Purchase, 1803; attacked by British, Dec. 1814, who were repulsed, 8 Jan. 1815; surrendered to the Federals, Apr. 1862.

New South Wales, Australia. Named, 1770, by Capt. Cook. Colony established by transported prisoners, 1788. Transportation ceased, 1840. Gold discovered at Bathurst, 1851. Responsible government, 1855, part of Australian Commonwealth since 1901. *See* AUSTRALIA.

Newspapers. In the fifteenth century in some German towns news-sheets were issued in the form of letters. The first official paper was issued in Venice in 1566, and was known as the *Notizie Scritte*, published by order of the Venetian Government. First English newspaper: H. G. Aldis (*Cambridge History of English Literature*) says of the printer, Nathaniel Batter: 'He is said to have issued a *Courant*, or *Weekly Newes from Foreign Parts* as early as Oct. 1621; but his first entry of *A Currant of Newes* in the [Stationers'] registers is dated 7 June 1622, and this publication must very shortly afterwards have assumed a regular periodical issue, for "Number 24" is entered on 26 Mar. 1623.' The *Publick Intelligencer* first issued by Nedham as a bi-weekly, 1659; after his flight abroad, Oliver Williams issued another with the same title. *Cambridge History* says of Sir Roger L'Estrange: 'His two periodicals, *The Intelligencer* and *The News* (31 Aug. 1663 to 29 Jan. 1666), were . . . in 1664 paged and numbered together as one periodical.' The *London Gazette* was started by Henry Muddiman, 7 Nov. 1665. In 1662 a press censorship was started and continued until 1695. First English daily newspaper, the *Daily Courant*, existed from 1702 until 1735. A tax of one halfpenny on N. introduced, 1712, increased by stages to fourpence in 1815; in 1836 reduced to one penny, and abolished altogether, 1855. The following famous London daily papers have ceased to exist:

Morning Chronicle, 28 June 1769–2 Mar. 1865.
Morning Post, Nov. 1772–30 Sept. 1937 (absorbed by *Daily Telegraph*).
Globe, 1803–5 Feb. 1921.
Standard, 21 May 1827–16 Mar. 1916.
Daily News (founded by Charles Dickens), 21 Jan. 1846–31 May 1930.
Pall Mall Gazette, 7 Feb. 1865–27 Oct. 1923.
Echo, 8 Dec. 1868–31 July 1905.
Daily Chronicle, 6 Mar. 1871–31 May 1930.
Westminster Gazette, 31 Jan. 1893–31 Jan. 1928 (absorbed by *Daily News*).
Daily Graphic, Jan. 1890–16 Oct. 1926.
News Chronicle, May 1930–17 Oct. 1960 (incorporated into the *Daily Mail*).
Star, 17 Jan. 1888–17 Oct. 1960 (absorbed by the *Evening News*).
Daily Herald, 15 Apr. 1912–14 Sept. 1964 (replaced by the *Sun*).
Daily Sketch (1909) merged with *Daily Mail*, 1971.
Evening News (1881) merged with *Evening Standard*, later renamed *Standard*, 1980.

London daily papers still existing, with dates of first issues:

The Times, 1 Jan. 1788 (had been running three years as the *Daily Universal Register*).
Morning Advertiser, 8 Feb. 1794.
Guardian, started in Manchester, 1821, as the *Manchester Guardian*; changed its name to *Guardian* in 1959 and began printing a London edition.
Daily Telegraph, 29 June 1855.
Standard, formerly *Evening Standard*, 11 June 1860.
Financial Times, 1888.
Daily Mail, 4 May 1896.
Daily Express, 24 Apr. 1900.
The Mirror, 2 Nov. 1903 (until April 1985, *Daily Mirror*)
Daily Star, 1978 (*The Star*, July 1985)
Morning Star, formerly the *Daily Worker* (name changed, 1966), 1930 (suppressed under Defence Regulations, Jan. 1941–Sept. 1942).
Sun, 15 Sept. 1964.

English weekly papers, with dates of first issues:

Observer, 4 Jan. 1801.
Sunday Times, 20 Oct. 1822.
Spectator, 5 July 1828 (original *Spectator*, 1 Mar. 1711–20 Dec. 1714).
Economist, 1843.
News of the World, 1 Oct. 1843.
People, 16 Oct. 1881.
Sunday Pictorial, 1915 (renamed *Sunday Mirror*, Apr. 1963).
Sunday Express, 29 Dec. 1918.
New Statesman, 21 Feb. 1931.
Sunday Telegraph, 5 Feb. 1961.
Mail on Sunday, 1981.

Newspapers (U.S.A.). The first newspaper issued in America was in 1690 at Boston. Its title was *Public Occurrences*. It, however, lasted only a day owing to its too outspoken nature. The first permanent paper was the *Boston News-Letter*, which was issued in Apr. 1704. The first daily paper was the *Pennsylvania Packet* or *General Advertiser* (afterwards as *Daily Advertiser*), first issued in 1784.

New Towns. First to be built was Welwyn Garden City (1920). Seven N. T. round London projected under New Towns Act, 1946. Work begun on the first of these (Stevenage), 1947. *See* GARDEN CITY.

New York City, New York. Settled by

the Dutch and named N. Amsterdam, 1624; captured by English and the name changed to N.Y., 27 Aug. 1664; surrendered to the English during War of Independence, 15 Sept. 1776; British evacuated, 25 Nov. 1783; temporary national capital, 1789.

New York State, U.S.A., coast first explored by Verrazano, 1524, and hinterland by Samuel de Champlain (from Canada), 1609. The British Colonel Nicolls took possession in name of the Duke of York, 1664. Founder state of the Union.

New Zealand. Discovered by Tasman, 1642; surveyed by Capt. Cook, 1769; ceded to Great Britain by Treaty of Waitangi, 1840, and colonized the same year; self-government granted, 1852; Wellington made capital, 1865; called Dominion of N. Z., 1907. Earthquake, Feb. 1931. Labour Party won majority for first time in General Election, 27 Nov. 1935. War on Germany declared, 3 Sept. 1939; and on Italy, 11 June 1940. Statute of Westminster adoption Bill passed, 28 Nov. 1947, and New Zealand Constitution (Amendment) Act, 1949, was then enacted. Anti-nuclear Labour govt. under Lange elected, 1984.

Prime Ministers since the Granting of Dominion Status, 1907:
Ward 1906–1911
Mackenzie 1911–1912
Massey 1912–1925
Coates 1925–1928
Ward (again) 1928–1930
Forbes 1930–1935
Savage 1935–1940
Fraser 1940–1949
Holland 1949–1957
Holyoake (2 months) 1957
Nash 1957–1960
Holyoake (again) 1960–1972
Marshall 1972
Kirk 1972–1974
Muldoon 1975–1984
Lange 1984–

Governor-Generals since 1917 (Date of Establishment of the Office):
Earl of Liverpool 1917–1920
Viscount Jellicoe 1920–1924
Sir Charles Fergusson 1924–1930
Lord Bledisloe 1930–1935

Viscount Galway 1935–1941
Sir Cyril Newall 1941–1946
Lord Freyberg 1946–1952
Lord Norrie 1952–1957
Vicount Cobham 1957–1962
Sir Bernard Fergusson 1962–1967
Sir Arthur Porritt 1967–1972
Sir Denis Blundell 1972–1977
Sir Keith Holyoake 1977–1980
Sir David Beattie 1980–1985
Paul Reeves 1985–

Niagara Falls. Discovered, 1678, by a French priest. Blondin was the first to cross them on a tight-rope, 1859. Rainbow bridge opened, 1941.

Nicaea (Turk. **Isnik**) in Bithynia (*q.v.*), built 316 B.C. under the name of Antigonea, name changed by order of the Macedonian Gen. Lysimachus (*d.* 281). Chosen as capital by the Sultan Soliman 1078; taken by the Franks in the First Crusade, 1096. After the capture of Constantinople by the Latins, 1204, was the temporary capital of the Eastern Empire. Scene of First Ecumenical Council, 325, when Nicene Creed formulated, and the Seventh, held in 787, which dealt with the Iconoclast controversy.

Nicaragua, Central America. Discovered by Columbus in 1502; explored by Gil Gonzalez De Avila, 1522; declared itself independent, 1821; joined Federal Union of the five Central States, 1823; separate republic, 1838; independence acknowledged by Spain, 1865; war with Honduras, Feb.–Apr. 1907. In 1916 U.S. Government purchased canal route and naval bases in Fonseca Bay and Corn Island by Bryan Chamarro Treaty, Feb.–June. President Somoza assassinated, Sept. 1956, succeeded by his son, Luis Somoza, who was re-elected for a six-year term, 1957. Bryan Chamarro Treaty abrogated, 1970. Somoza overthrown by leftist revolt, 1979, and constitution abrogated. N. since run by a left-wing junta, with close links with Cuba. State of emergency declared, 1982: country in state of civil war, rebels being backed by the U.S.A., since 1980.

Nice, France. Founded by the Phocaeans of Marseilles *c.* 600 B.C.; Saracens repulsed, A.D. 729; burnt by Saracens,

880; attached to Savoy from 1388; attacked by Francis I and Barbarossa, 1543; captured by Duke of Guise, 1600; by Catinat, 1691; restored to Savoy, 1696; besieged by French, 1705, and captured; by Treaty of Utrecht was again restored to Savoy, 1713; again captured by French, 1795, who owned it until 1814, when it reverted to Savoy. Finally ceded to France after a plebiscite, 1860.

Nice, Truce of. Between Charles V and Francis I for ten months from June 1538.

Nicobar Islands. See ANDAMAN AND NICOBAR ISLANDS.

Nicosia, Cyprus. Pillaged by the Mamelukes, 1426. Fortified by the Venetians, 1567. Taken by the Turks, 1570, and 20,000 Christians massacred in street fighting. Earthquake, 1741. British flag raised over N., 1878. Capital of the Republic of C. since 1960.

Nidaros. See TRONDHJEM.

Nigeria. Includes what was formerly the Niger Coast (or Oil Rivers) Protectorate, formed, 1844. Remainder of N. acquired by British United African Co., 1879–86. Constituted, 1 Jan. 1900; Lagos (*q.v.*) added, 1906. Governments of Southern and Northern N. amalgamated, 1 Jan. 1914. Legal status of slavery abolished by Slavery Ordinance, 1917. N. became a Dominion within the Commonwealth, 1 Oct. 1960. N. became a republic within the Commonwealth, Oct. 1963. A series of army coups followed.

On 30 May 1967, Ojukwu, military governor of the E. states, announced his state's secession from N. and proclaimed it the independent republic of Biafra (*q.v.*). A full-scale war followed, but Biafra did not finally capitulate till Jan. 1970. New constitution ratified 1977–8 confirmed re-estab. of civilian govt. Abuja (*q.v.*) replaced Lagos as capital, Sept. 1982. In 1983 2 million non-Nigerians expelled; military coup, Dec.

Nijmegen, Gelderland province of the Netherlands, was a residence of the Frankish emperors in the ninth century A.D. Devastated in the Allied attack by air and ground forces, Sept. 1944.

Nijni Novgorod. See GORKI.

Nîmes, France. Taken by Romans, 121 B.C. Made a military colony under Augustus. Amphitheatre built, first–second century A.D. Belonged to Toulouse, A.D. 1185–1207. Catholics massacred by Protestants, 1567. Trestaillons and his bandits massacred Bonapartists, 1815.

Nineveh, adjoining the modern Mosul, in Iraq, became the capital of Assyria under Sennacherib (704–681 B.C.). Destroyed, 612, by combined forces of Babylonians, Medes, and Scythians. The deserted site was first investigated by western archaeologists early in the nineteenth century.

Ningpo, formerly **Liampo,** was a Portuguese 'factory', 1522–45. Occupied by British, 1841–2.

Nitroglycerine first produced by Sobrero, 1846.

N.K.G.B., the Soviet security service, 1943–6. It had essentially the same functions as its predecessor, the N.K.V.D. (*q.v.*).

N.K.V.D. (Narodnij Kommissariat Vnutrennich Djel = People's Commissariat for Internal Affairs), designation of the Russian Interior Office and its internal security forces, but not of the ordinary urban police ('militia') from 1934 to 1943. In 1943 it was divided into two commissariats, the N.K.V.D. and the N.K.G.B. (*q.v.*), the latter being responsible for state security.

Nobel Prize. Founded by Alfred N. (1833–96), the inventor of dynamite, to be awarded annually for excellence in learning and the furtherance of universal peace. First awarded in 1901.

Nomanhan, on the borders of Inner and Outer Mongolia, was the scene of a six weeks' undeclared war between Mongolian, Japanese, and Russian troops in 1939. The Japanese and Inner Mongolian forces had to retire, and the incident led to the Russo-Japanese non-aggression pact of 1941.

Non-Compounders. The extremist section of the Jacobite Party formed *c.* 1692. Were prepared to restore James II unconditionally.

Nonconformists and **Nonconformity,** the religious attitude of Dissenters in England. Word first used in this sense *c.* 1563, but gaining wider currency at the Restoration, especially with the passing of the Act of Uniformity, 1662. Some disabilities were suspended by Charles II's Declaration of Indulgence, 1672, and by James II's Declaration of Indulgence of 1687. They were accorded freedom of worship by Toleration Act, 1689, but excluded from municipal office by the Occasional Conformity Act, 1711, which was itself repealed, 1718. The Schism Act, 1711, excluded N. from schools and was also repealed, 1718. Political disabilities of N. removed, 1828. Admitted to universities, 1871. During the sixteenth and seventeenth centuries the essence of Nonconformity was the particularism of numerous sects, but in 1730 a phase of amalgamation and consolidation set in which may be said to have culminated in the reunion of the Methodist Church in 1932, previously split into three factions. Formation of United Reformed Church (*q.v.*), 1972, signalled union of English Presbyterian and Congregationalist churches. *See also* FREE CHURCH FEDERATION.

Non-Intervention Committee of European powers to watch conduct of civil war in Spain, first met in London, 9 Sept. 1936.

Nonjurors. Clergy in Britain who refused the oath of allegiance to William and Mary. An Act of 1 Aug. 1689 required them to take the oath within six months or suffer deprivation. In Scotland all the bishops refused and episcopacy was abolished.

Nordic Council. Assembly of elected representatives from the Scandinavian parliaments (Denmark, Norway, Sweden, Finland, and Iceland), established, 1952, to foster closer co-operation between their countries. Passport regulations between the Scandinavian countries abolished, 1952.

Norham, Conference of. Between Edward I and the competitors for the crown of Scotland, June 1291. The question of the disposal of the Scottish crown was settled, Nov. 1292.

Normandy, France. Rollo appointed first duke, A.D. 912; united with the crown of England under William the Conqueror (Duke of N.), 1066; united to crown of France, 1204; English claim formally renounced, 1259; conquered by Edward III, 1346; by Henry V, 1418; English finally driven out, 1449. Invaded by Allies, 6 June 1944. *See* WORLD WAR II.

North Atlantic Treaty signed at Washington, 4 Apr. 1949, between Britain, Canada, the U.S.A., France, Belgium, Holland, Luxemburg, Norway, Denmark, Iceland, Italy, and Portugal. Greece and Turkey were admitted to the treaty, 1951 (effective, 1952), the German Federal Republic, 1954 and Spain, 1982. *See* N.A.T.O.

'North Briton' Newspaper. Instituted by John Wilkes. 'Number 45', the issue dated 23 Apr. 1763, was publicly burnt by the hangman, 3 Dec. 1763, as containing a libel against the king. *See* WILKES'S CASE.

North Carolina, U.S.A. Coasts said to have been discovered by Cabot, 1498; first settled, unsuccessfully, 1585–6; named after Charles II of England, who, in 1663, granted the region to certain of his courtiers; made a royal province, 1728; declared itself independent of Great Britain, May 1775; state constitution adopted, 1 Dec. 1776. Seceded, 20 May 1861; readmitted to the Union, 25 May 1868.

North Dakota, U.S.A., part of the old territory of Dakota, organized as such, 1861. Admitted to the Union, 1889. First settlements took place *c.* 1766. *See also* SOUTH DAKOTA.

Northern Fisheries. *See* FISHERIES, NORTHERN.

Northern Ireland. *See* IRELAND, NORTHERN.

Northern Territory, Australia, formerly **Alexandra Land**, originally part of New S. Wales (*q.v.*), but annexed to S. Australia, 1863. Placed under direct Commonwealth Gov. rule, 1911. Divided into N. Australia and Central Australia, 1926, but united under a single administration by an Act of 1931. Self-government granted, 1 July 1978.

Coast first explored by P. P. King, 1818, by J. C. Wickham, 1838, and J. L. Stokes, 1839. Interior explored by A. C. Gregory, 1855.

North German Confederation, league of German states established, 1867, under Prussian leadership. Dissolved in the German Empire, 1871.

North Pole. First reached, 6 Apr. 1909, by the American Robert E. Peary. *See* ARCTIC AND ANTARCTIC REGIONS.

North Sea Fisheries Convention. Entered into by Great Britain, Germany, Holland, Belgium, and France on 6 May 1882; supplementary convention signed, 16 Nov. 1887.

North Sea Outrage. On the night of 21 Oct. 1904 the Russian Baltic Fleet fired on some English fishing boats in the N.S. An international commission of inquiry was held on the affair from 22 Nov. 1904 to 25 Feb. 1905.

North Staffordshire, University College of. *See* KEELE, UNIVERSITY OF.

North, The Council of the. Instituted in 1536 by Henry VIII originally to try persons connected with the Pilgrimage of Grace (*q.v.*); abolished by Long Parliament, 1641.

Northstead, Manor of, in Yorkshire, has a stewardship in the gift of the crown, the holding of which by the Place Act, 1742, is not compatible with membership of the House of Commons, and is thus used as formal excuse for resignation of an M.P. *See* CHILTERN HUNDREDS.

Northumbria, Kingdom of. *See* BERNICIA and DEIRA.

Kings of c. *457*–c. *913*:

Bernicia:
    Ida 547–559
    His elder sons 559–586
    Ethelric 586–593
    Ethelfrith 593–617
    Edwin (of Deira) 617–632
    Eanfrith 632–633
    Oswald 633–642
    Oswy 642–670

Deira:
    Aelle 560–588
    Ethelric (of Bernicia) 588–? 593
    Ethelfrith (of Bernicia) ? 593–617
    Edwin 617–632

Osric 632–633
Oswald (of Bernicia) 633–642
Oswine 642–651
Ethelwald 651–-655
Oswy (of Bernicia) 655–670
Kings of all N.:
Ecgfrith 670–685
Alfrith 685–704
Eardwulf I 704–705
Osred I 705–716
Cenred 716–718
Osric 718–729
Ceolwulf 729–737
Eadberht 737–758
Oswulf 758
Ethelwald Moll 759–765
Alhred 765–774
Ethelred I 774–779
Elfwald I 779–788
Osred II 788–790
Ethelred I (restored) 790–796
Osbald 796
Eardwulf II 796–808
Elfwald II 808
Eardwulf II (restored) 808–810
Eanred 810–840
Ethelred II 840–844
Raedwulf 844
Ethelred II (restored) 844–848
Osberht 848–866
Elle 866–867
Egbert I 867–872
Ricsige 873–876
Egbert II *fl.* 876
Eadwulf ?–913

North-West Frontier Province. Created by the British administration in India, 25 Oct. 1901. Merged into West Pakistan Province, 1955.

North-West Mounted Police, raised, 1873; title changed to Royal Canadian Mounted Police, 1920. Mechanized, 1953.

North-West Passage. Sought since fifteenth century. First completed, 1850–4, by Robert McClure: first sailed by Amundsen, 1906.

North-West Territories of Canada, formed from the former Northern Territory and Rupert's Land, and divided into the districts of Keewatin, MacKenzie, and Franklin by Order in Council of 16 Mar. 1918. Under N.-W.T. Act, 1952, government is in the hands of a commissioner. Yellowknife made capital of N.-W.T., 1967.

Norway. Battle of Hafursfjord, 872, and N. united for the first time under Harald Fairhair. First Norwegian settlement in Iceland, 874. Rolf the Ganger's expedition against Normandy, 876. Erik Bloodaxe king, 930. Haakon the Good comes from England and is made king at Trondhjem, 935. Erik Bloodaxe goes to England, 939, and is killed there, 950. Battle of Rastarskalf, 955. Death of Haakon the Good after battle of Stord, 961. N. ruled by Jarl Haakon of Lade, 970–95. Christianity introduced, 998. Death of King Olaf Tryggvason at battle of Svold, 1000. N. under Swedish and Danish rule till battle of Nesjar and election of St. Olaf as king, 1015. He makes alliance with Sweden, 1019. Defeated by Knut (Canute) of Denmark at Helge-Aa, 1027. N. conquered by Denmark, 1027–8. Death of St. Olaf at battle of Stiklestad, 29 July 1030. Danes driven out by King Magnus the Good, 1035–6. Harald Hardrada king, 1047. Killed at Stamford Bridge, 1066. After Haakon IV, 1217–63, N. declined into chronic civil war (for history down to this point *see* VIKING AGE). It was finally united with Sweden under the Danish crown by the Union of Kalmar (*q.v.*), 1397. N. remained under Danish rule till virtually cut off from Denmark by the British blockade, 1794–1814. As a reward for Swedish participation in the war against Napoleon I it was proposed that Denmark should cede N. to Sweden (Treaty of Kiel, 14 Jan. 1814). The Norwegians called a national convention which drew up and signed a parliamentary constitution at Eidsvold, 17 May 1814, and then accepted the suzerainty of the Swedish crown. Separated from Sweden, Oct. 1905. Haakon VII elected to the throne, 18 Nov. 1905. Prohibition 1919–26. Christiania renamed Oslo, 1 Jan. 1925. Spitzbergen (Svalbarth) annexed, 14 Aug. 1925. Greenland awarded to Denmark by International Court of Justice, 5 Apr. 1933. Part of Antarctica annexed, 14 Jan. 1939. Declarations of neutrality, 2 Sept. and 26 Dec. 1939. *Altmark* incident, 17 Feb. 1940. Attacked by Germany, 9 Apr. Battles of Narvik, 10 and 13 Apr. Liberated, 8 May 1945. Signed North Atlantic Treaty (*q.v.*), 1949. Fishing dispute with Great Britain settled in favour of N. by Hague International Court, 1951. Member of Nordic Council, 1952. Death of Haakon VII and accession of Olaf VI (*b.* 1903), 1957. Member of European Free Trade Association (*q.v.*), 1959. Voted against joining European Economic Community (*q.v.*), 1973.

Rulers of c. *839–1349; 1905–51:*
Halfdan the Black *c.* 839–*c.* 860
Harald I Fairhair *c.* 860–933
Erik Bloodaxe 930–935
Haakon I the Good 935–961
Harald II Greyskin 961–970
(Jarl) Haakon of Lade 970–995
Olaf I Tryggvason 995–1000
(Jarls) Erik and Svein 1000–1015
Olaf II, Saint 1015–1030
Svein Knutsson 1030–1035
Magnus I, the Good 1035–1047
Harald III, the Stern 1048–1066
Olaf III, the Quiet 1067–1093
Magnus II 1067–1069
Magnus III, Barelegs 1093–1103
Haakon 1093–1095
Olaf IV 1103–1116
Eystein I 1103–1122
Sigurd I, the Pilgrim 1103–1130
Magnus IV, the Blind 1130–1135
Harald Gille 1130–1136
Sigurd II, Mund 1136–1155
Inge 1136–1161
Eystein II 1142–1157
Haakon, II, the Broad-shouldered 1161–1162
Magnus V 1162–1184
Sverre 1184–1202
Haakon III 1202–1204
Anarchy 1204–1217
Haakon IV, the Old 1217–1263
Magnus VI 1263–1280
Erik 1280–1299
Haakon V 1299–1319
Magnus VII 1319–1343
Haakon VI 1343–1380
Olaf V 1381–1387
Margaret (Lady of N.) 1387–1389
Eric of Pomerania 1387–1439

(*See further under* DENMARK, KINGS OF, 1439–1814; SWEDEN, KINGS OF, 1814–1905).

Modern Norway:
Haakon VII 1905–1957
Olaf VI 1957–

Norwegian Language and Literature. From the Union of Kalmar down to the end of the nineteenth century the written language of Norway, both for official and artistic purposes, was Danish; therefore some N. authors have been listed under Danish Literature *supra*. There are two modern idioms: the urban, or *riksmål*, developed from the Danish, which is the official idiom, and the rustic, or *landsmal*, now generally called *nynorsk*. The progress of the language was assisted by *Dølen*, the first newspaper to be printed in it (1858), under the editorship of Aasmund Olafsen Vinje (1818–70).
The following are mainly *riksmål* authors not now living (those marked * wrote *nynorsk*):
Johan Sebastian Welhaven, 1807–73, poet.
Henrik Wergeland, 1808–45, poet.
Peter Christen Asbjørnsen, 1812–85, folklorist.
Jørgen Moe, 1813–82, folklorist.
Henrik Ibsen, 1828–1906, playwright.
Bjørnstjerne Bjørnson, 1832–1910, playwright.
Amalie Skram, 1846–1905, novelist.
Camilla Collett, 1849–1906, novelist.
* Arne Garborg, 1851–1924, novelist.
Gunnar Heiberg, 1857–1929, playwright.
Knut Hamsun, 1859–1952, novelist.
Nils Collett Vogt, 1864–1937, poet.
Hans E. Kinck, 1865–1926, novelist and poet.
Tryggve Andersen, 1866–1920, novelist.
Sigbjørn Obstfelder, 1866–1900, poet.
Niels Kjaer, 1870–1924, essayist.
Vilhelm Krag, 1871–1933, poet.
* Olav Duun, 1876–1939, novelist.
Sigrid Undset, 1882–1949, novelist.
* Olaf Aukrust, 1883–1929, poet.
Olaf Bull, 1883–1933, poet.
Olav Nygard, 1884–1924, poet.
Sigurd Christiansen, 1891–1947, novelist.

Ronald Fangen, 1895–1946, novelist.
Rudolf Nilsen, 1901–29, poet.
Nordahl Grieg, 1902–43, poet.
Jonas Lie, 1833–1908, novelist.
A. L. Kielland, 1849–1906, novelist.
* Jens Tvedt, 1857–1935, novelist.

Norwich, England. First mentioned in *Saxon Chronicle*, 1004, when sacked by Svein. Cathedral founded, 1096. Charter, 1158; extended, 1194. Cathedral completed *c.* 1500. New city hall, 1938. University of E. Anglia opened at N., 1963.

Nottingham, England. One of the five Danish boroughs, 868. Fortified by Edward the Elder, 922–4. Parliaments held at N., 1334, 1337, 1357. Charles I set up standard at, 1642. Castle dismantled, 1644. Goose Fair instituted under Queen Anne, 1702–14. University College opened, 1881; made a university, 1948.

Nova Scotia. Discovered by John Cabot, 1497; partly colonized by the French, as 'Acadia', 1598; French settlements destroyed by English from Virginia, 1614; granted by James I to William Alexander, Earl of Stirling, 1621; ceded to France by Treaty of Breda, 1667; captured by English, 1689; restored to France by Treaty of Ryswick, 1697; Port Royal captured by English under Gen. Nicholson, 1710; formally ceded to England by Treaty of Utrecht, 1713; became part of the Dominion of Canada, 1867.

Novaya Zemlya, archipelago off the N. coast of Russia, explored by Stephen Borough, 1556, and Baron Nordenskjold, 1895–7. Also by H. J. Pearson, 1895–7, and O. Ekstam, 1900–3.

Novgorod, formerly **Veliki Novgorod** ('N. the Great'), founded by Scandinavians, traditionally, 862, but probably on the site of an existing Slav settlement. Though it acknowledged princes of the house of Rurik it was virtually an independent republic of merchants, and obtained a charter from Yaroslav the Wise, 997, which was regarded as the basis of its liberties, of which it was deprived by the Muscovite Ivan III, 1478. It was burnt to the ground by Ivan IV (the Terrible), 1570.

Noyon, Treaty of, Between Charles of Spain and Francis I, signed 1516; by it Francis gave up all claims to Naples, and France's right to Milan was acknowledged.

N.R.A. (U.S.A.). National Recovery Administration appointed under National Industrial Recovery Act, 1933, empowered to promulgate codes for industry. It imposed conditions as to child labour, minimum wages, and maximum hours. The U.S. Supreme Court held codes unconstitutional, 18 Feb. 1935.

Nubia. *See* SUDAN.

Nuclear Reactor. Harwell, Berks, built 1947, was the first British N.R.; the first American N.R. was built at the University of Chicago in 1942.

Nuclear Test Ban Treaty signed, Moscow, between the U.S.A., U.S.S.R, and Great Britain, 5 Aug. 1963.

Nürnberg (Ger.: anglicized as **Nuremberg,** which form is also current in other non-German countries), Germany. Made an Imperial Free City, 1219. Embraced Protestantism *c.* 1525. Annexed by Bavaria, 1806. First Nazi Party congress, 1933. Heavily bombed in World War II.

Nürnberg Laws, anti-Semitic code decreed by the Nazi Government, Sept. 1935.

Nürnberg Trials, international trials of war criminals, lasted from Nov. 1945 to Oct. 1946.

Nyasaland. *See* MALAWI.

Nylon. Discovered by Du Ponts, U.S.A., 1927.

Nyon Conference to end submarine piracy in Mediterranean: Britain, France, Greece, Yugoslavia, Turkey, Egypt, Albania, Russia, Rumania, and Bulgaria, 11–14 Sept. 1937.

O

Oak-apple Day anniversary of the restoration of Charles II to the English throne, 29 May 1660. The oak leaves formerly worn on this occasion commemorate his hiding in an oak-tree when a fugitive from Worcester, 6 Sept, 1651.

O.A.S. (Organisation de l'Armée Secrète). Clandestine, ultra-right-wing organization founded by General Raoul Salan, in Madrid, in May 1961, after the failure of the anti-Gaullist rising in Algiers. Its object initially was to keep Algeria French, and though weak in France itself it had strong support in Algeria. After Algerian independence, in July 1962, the O.A.S. transferred its activities entirely to France, concentrating on destroying the Gaullist regime by force and attempting to assassinate de Gaulle. General Salan was captured, Apr. 1962, and sentenced to life imprisonment for treason, May 1962. After this O.A.S. power declined, and after his resignation, 1969, its *raison d'être* ceased.

O.A.S. (Organization of American States). Charter adopted, 30 Apr. 1948. Cuba expelled from the O.A.S., 31 Jan. 1962; in Oct. 1962 the O.A.S. backed President Kennedy's blockade of Cuba (*q.v.*). Adopted peace-keeping role in the Dominican republic, 1965. Meeting at Uruguay in 1967 estab. the basis of a Latin-Amer. Common Market. Protocol of Buenos Aires, modifying the 1948 charter, effective, 27 Feb. 1970.

O.A.U. (Organization of African Unity), established in Addis Ababa, 25 May 1963, to further African political development, unity and solidarity.

Oaths, Parliamentary. Oath of supremacy, imposed on M.P.s, 1534; oath of allegiance, 1610. In 1678 no member could take his seat until the O. of allegiance, supremacy, and abjuration were taken. By Act of 1829 Roman Catholics could use special form of oath; provision made for Jews, 1858. In 1866 the three O. were combined in one, and in 1868 the form included all religious denominations. O. Act of 1888 allows an affirmation in lieu of the oath.

Oberammergau (Germany). Passion play commemorates a plague of 1633. The decision to produce a play every ten years was taken in 1634 in thanksgiving for the town's deliverance. The next production is in 1994.

Observer Corps, Royal. An O.C. composed of special constables, was raised in 1925 under War Office auspices, but operational command in 1927, and administration in 1939, passed to the Air Ministry. Operationally controlled by Fighter Command, the O.C. was given the title Royal in Apr. 1941. It stood down, 12 May 1945.

October Revolution. So called because it occurred in Oct., according to the Julian Calendar. Kerensky's government overthrown and the Communists established in power, 7 Nov. 1917 (25 Oct., Old Style).

Oddfellows. A friendly society bearing this name was formed at Manchester in 1810, and the movement spread to U.S.A. in 1819, where a Grand Lodge of O. was formed, 1821. This severed its connection with the parent organization at Manchester, 1842, but established a branch at Montreal, which became the first Oddfellow Lodge of Canada, 1843.

Oder-Neisse Line. Has formed the boundary between Germany and

Poland since 1946, and all Germans formerly living E. of it have been deported W. of it.

Odessa, Ukraine. Disputed between Lithuania and Tatars, fourteenth–sixteenth centuries. Captured by Turks, 1764. By Russians, 1789. Finally occupied by Russians, 1791. Inhabitants supported the 'Potekkin' rising, 1905. Occupied by the Rumanians, 1941–4, becoming the capital of Transnistria during that time.

O.E.E.C. (Organization for European Economic Co-operation) became effective in the passing by Congress of the Economic Co-operative Act, Apr. 1948, with the object of restoring the European economy by the end of 1951. Convention signed in Paris, setting up a permanent constitution for O.E.E.C., 16 Apr. 1948. After Marshall Aid ended, 1952, O.E.E.C. continued as a permanent instrument of European economic co-operation. Spain joined it, 1959. In Dec. 1960 the organization was reconstituted as the **O.E.C.D. (Organization for Economic Co-operation and Development.)**

Offa's Dyke, built *c.* 785 as a boundary between his dominion and the Welsh (whom he defeated, 779) by O., King of Mercia, who reigned *c.* 755–94, abdicated, and *d.* at Rome, 796.

Ohio, U.S.A. First explored by La Salle *c.* 1680; N. of the O. River was held by French until 1763, when it was surrendered to the English; unofficially admitted to the Union as a state, 1803; entrance made official retroactive to 1803, 8 Aug. 1953.

Ohm's Law, in electricity, 1827, by the Ger. physicist G. S. Ohm (1787–1854).

Oklahoma, U.S.A., then known as the Indian country, was extensively settled from 1866 onwards by government purchase of land from the Choctaw, Cherokee, Creek, Chickasaw, and Seminole Indians. Organized as a territory, 1890, and admitted as a state to the Union, 1907.

Old Age Pensions (Britain). First proposed in 1772 by Francis Maseres, and again in 1787 by Mark Rolle, M.P.; other schemes proposed, notably by W. E. Gladstone's royal commission in 1893, but nothing was done until passing of O.A.P. Act, 1908, which came into force on 1 Jan. 1909. Amended 1911, 1914, and 1924. Widows', Orphans', and Old Age Contributory Pensions (Voluntary Contributors) Act, 1 July 1937. Since 1946, covered by the provisions of the National Insurance Act (*q.v.*).

Old Bailey. A court held in a house on 'Balehill' is mentioned in Stow's *Survey of London*, 1603. Sixty persons attending the court, including two judges and the Lord Mayor, *d.* of jail fever from the adjacent Newgate Prison (*q.v.*), 1780. The present Central Criminal Court occupies the site of the old sessions and part of the former Newgate Prison, demolished to make way for it, 1902.

Old Catholics. Those Catholics who refused to accept the doctrine of papal infallibility proclaimed at the Vatican Council of 1870. Dogmatic base of all groups of O.C. contained in the Declaration of Utrecht (1889). The O.C. of Germany in communion with the Eastern Orthodox Church, 1930, and with the Church of England, 1931.

Old Contemptibles, name applied to the (predominantly Regular) British Expeditionary Force of Aug. 1914. In Sept. a B.E.F. Routine Order quoted the Kaiser Wilhelm II on 'Gen. French's contemptible little army', but without giving chapter and verse: no one has ever established when (or whether) this (or a similar) phrase was actually used, and in 1925 the ex-Kaiser denied that he had ever done so.

Oldenburg, Germany. Independent county, 1180. United with Denmark, 9 June 1667. Ceded to Russia, 16 Oct. 1776. Made an independent duchy under Frederick of Holstein-Gottorp, 22 Mar. 1777. Joined German Empire, 1871. Became a republic, 1918. Since World War II part of the *Land* of Lower Saxony.

Old Vic. A theatre called the Coburg was built on this site in the Waterloo Road, 1818. In the middle nineteenth century it became a music hall, but classical concerts were given there from 1880 onwards, and in 1914 regular performances of Shakespeare's plays were produced under Lilian Baylis (1874–1937). Association with Sadler's Wells (*q.v.*) began, 1929. Rendered unusable in the 1939–45 war; performances recommenced, 1950. Dramatic School closed, 1952.

The last performance by the O.V. company was given in the theatre, June 1963. The theatre then became, 1963–76, the temporary home of the new National Theatre (*q.v.*). In 1983 it was refurbished and reopened under Canadian ownership as a commercial theatre.

Olive Branch Petition, by moderate Americans to avert civil war. Presented, July 1775, to George III, who took no notice of it.

Olmütz, Convention of. Austro-Prussian agreement of 1850, reviving Austrian influence in Germany at the expense of Prussia, and regarded by the latter as 'the humiliation of Olmütz'.

Olympia, Greece. The site of the original Olympic games. The earliest building is the temple of Hera, *c.* 1000 B.C. The method of calculating time by Olympiads or quadrennial periods between celebrations of the games, reckoned from 776 B.C., was first adopted *c.* 264 B.C. After the year A.D. 394 the games were discontinued, and in 426 the temple was destroyed. The Olympic games were revived at a meeting of delegates from various nations, 16 June 1894. Games were held at Athens, 1896; Paris, 1900; St. Louis, 1904; London, 1908; Stockholm, 1912; Antwerp, 1920; Paris, 1924; Amsterdam, 1928; Los Angeles, 1932; Berlin, 1936; London, 1948; Helsinki, 1952; Melbourne, 1956; Rome, 1960; Tokyo, 1964; Mexico City, 1968; Munich, 1972; Montreal, 1976; Moscow, 1980; Los Angeles, 1984.

Olympiad. *See* OLYMPIA.

Omaha Beach. Code-name for the stretch of beach from the Vire R. to Port-en-Bessin, where the U.S. 5th Corps landed on D-Day, 6 June 1944, and from which they only narrowly averted being dislodged by the defending Germans.

Oman, known till 1970 as **Muscat and Oman** (*see* MUSCAT), independent Arabian state, with close ties with Britain since early nineteenth century, confirmed by Treaty, 1951, and Memorandum of Understanding, June 1982.

Ombudsman. For the parliamentary O., *see* PARLIAMENTARY COMMISSIONER FOR ADMINISTRATION. Subsequently Os. have been estab. to deal with maladministration in both local govt. and the Health Service.

Omnibus. The first O. to ply in London was run by Shillibeer, 1829. The London General O. Co. was founded, 1856. First double-decker appeared, 1904; last horse-bus, 1911. Electric trolley-buses from 1911 onwards; diesels took over after 1955.

Ontario, Canada. First settled by the French in the late seventeenth century; British territory from 1763; its prosperity founded by loyalist emigrants from the U.S.A. after the latter had declared its independence; made into a separate province in 1791, and known as Upper Canada, but in 1867 it again received its original name.

O.P.E.C. *See* ORGANIZATION OF PETROLEUM EXPORTING COUNTRIES.

Open University, estab. 1969 with headquarters at Milton Keynes, awarding degrees based on tuition by correspondence, in co-ordination with television programmes, summer schools, and a locally-based tutorial system. There were 90,000 students in 1981.

Opera. First O. proper was *Dafne*, 1597, by Peri and Rinuccini; first O. whose music survives complete was *Euridice*, 1600, by the same collaborators.

Opium War. Between China and Britain, 1840–2.

Oporto, Portugal. Originally *Portus Cale*, the origin of the name *Portugal*, to which in the fifth century a new northern quarter, the *Castrum Novum* of the Alani, was added. Captured by Visigoths, A.D. 540; by the Moors, 716; recaptured by Christians, 997; captured by the Duke of Wellington, 12 May 1809; besieged by Dom Miguel,

1832–3. The thirteenth-century cathedral occupies the site of a church built by Theodomir, king of the Visigoths, 589, to house the relics of St. Martin of Tours (316–97).

Oradour-sur-Glane, Haute-Vienne, France, scene of a notorious German atrocity, 10 June 1944, when the men of the town were all shot or hanged and the women and children driven into the church, which was then set on fire.

Oran, a Spanish settlement established in 1509, was finally abandoned, 1792, and occupied by the French, 1831. French fleet attacked after ultimatum by Admiral Somerville, 3 July 1940, in the harbour of Mers-el-Kebir at O. Scene of violent O.A.S. (*q.v.*) disturbances, Mar.–June 1962.

Orange Free State, S. Africa. Inhabited by the Dutch Boers, 1836; annexed to British crown, 1848; given up to the Boers, 1854; became part of British Empire after Boer War as the Orange River Colony, 1902; joined Union of 1910 as the O.F.S.

Orange, House of. Came to principality of O. (S. France), 1393. Philibert of O. given lands in Netherlands by Emperor Charles V, 1522. These lands passed to William of O.-Nassau (William the Silent), 1544. The family held the offices of Stadhouder and Captain- and Admiral-General of the Netherlands, 1577–1650 and 1672–1702. William III was King of England, 1688–1702. William VI became King William I of the Netherlands, 1815. *See* NETHERLANDS, KINGDOM OF.

Orangemen, The. A term applied to Protestants in Ireland in 1689; the first Orange lodge instituted, 21 Sept. 1796; all Orange societies suspended, 1813–28; of considerable significance in N. Ireland since 1921, and notably since civil violence erupted there in late 1960s.

Oratory of St. Philip Neri, Congregation of the (or Oratorians). A Roman Catholic order founded, 1556, by Philip Neri (1515–95); confirmed by papal bull, 1575, and again in 1612; first congregation in England established, 1847.

Ordeal, Trial by. O., together with compurgation, was the commoner form of assessing the value of evidence in pre-Conquest English law-courts; for instance, the weight of red-hot iron to be carried by an accused person pleading not guilty is laid down by the Laws of Athelstan (between 925 and 940) as 3 lb. Queen Emma Aelfgifu, widow of Ethelred, was so tried for adultery, and acquitted, 1043. Trial by O. was abolished in England, 1215–19 (except for Trial by Battle, which was not formally abolished till 1819). It survived longer on the Continent, and unofficially, in the form of witch-ducking, much longer in England. A case of Trial by O. was reported from Charleston, N. Carolina, 26 Feb. 1951.

Orders in Council (Britain). First issued in eighteenth century. 'The O. in C.' were issued in 1807 in reply to Napoleon's Berlin Decrees (*see under* CONTINENTAL SYSTEM).

Orders of Knighthood. *See* KNIGHTHOOD, ORDERS OF.

Ordnance Board existed before 1660, and was recognized as a civil department of state, 1683. The duties of the O.B. were transferred to the War Department, 1855.

Ordnance Survey was formed in 1791, to make a map on the scale of 1 inch to 1 mile of the whole of Great Britain. This task was completed for England, except the six northern counties, 1840. Its establishment was doubled, 1880, after being transferred from the War Department, 1870. Cultivated area of England completely mapped on scale of 1:2500 by 1890.

Oregon. Name first applied to whole area of modern O. and Washington. Columbia River discovered by Capt. Gray, 1792. Fur trading post established on river, 1811. Dispute between Britain and U.S.A. about boundary between Canada and U.S.A. from the Lake of the Woods to Pacific arose, 1816. Fixed along 49° N. by provisional treaty of Nov. 1818 between Lake of the Woods and the Rocky Mountains. Area comprising the modern states of Idaho, O., Washington, and the southern half of British Columbia in joint Anglo-American occupation till 49° N. boundary extended to Queen Charlotte Sound by treaty of 1846. Admitted as state of the Union, 1859. Vancouver Island given to Canada by arbitration 1872.

Organization of Petroleum Exporting Countries, estab. 1960 to represent oil exporting countries and constitutes a price control. O.P.E.C. ability to influence cartel declined after 1980.

Oriental and African Studies, School of, opened by King George V, 23 Feb. 1917. Charter issued, 5 June 1916. African branch added, 1938.

Orkney Islands, N. of Scotland. Possessed by Northmen in ninth century; formally subject to the Norwegian crown, 1098; pledged by Christian I of Denmark for the payment of the dowry of his daughter Margaret, betrothed to James III of Scotland in 1468; the money was never paid, so the islands passed to the Scottish crown. Denmark renounced all claims to the O.I., 1590.

Orléanists. A French political party who supported the royal claims of the house of Orléans, founded shortly after the French Revolution; after the revolution of 1848 it practically ceased to exist.

Orléans, France. Originally *Civitas Aureliani.* Vainly besieged by Attila, A.D. 451; captured by Clovis, 498; entered by Joan of Arc, 29 Apr. 1429; besieged by the Duke of Guise, 1563; held by Huguenots, 1567–8; surrendered to Henry IV of France, 1594.

Orsini Affair. Felix O. and accomplices attempted the life of Napoleon III, 14 Jan. 1858, and were subsequently executed. The plot had been arranged in London, and the French protested so strongly in London that the British Government introduced a propitiatory bill into Parliament, and so was forced to resign.

Orthodox Eastern Church. *See* GREEK ORTHODOX CHURCH and CALENDAR.

Orvieto, Italy. Captured by Belisarius, A.D. 539; Pope Hadrian IV resided at, 1157; cathedral commenced before 1285; town became part of kingdom of Italy, 1866.

Osborne House (Isle of Wight). Purchased by Queen Victoria, 1845; Queen Victoria *d.* there, 1901; presented to the nation by Edward VII as a convalescent home for officers, 1902; Royal Naval College at Osborne opened, 1903. State and private apartments now open to the public.

Osborne Judgment. Disallowing a forced political levy on trade union members, handed down by the House of Lords, 1909. Largely nullified by the Trades Union Act of 1913.

Oslo, Norway. Founded by Harald Hardrada, 1047. King Sigurd the Crusader buried here, 1130. Burnt down, 1624. Rebuilt by Christian IV of Denmark, who renamed it Christiania. Reverted to older name, 1925.

Oslo, Convention of, a free trade convention between the 'O. Powers'—Belgium, Luxemburg, the Netherlands, Sweden, Norway, and Denmark, signed, Dec. 1930. Finland adhered, Feb. 1933.

Ossewabrandwag. Extremist Afrikaner political party, deriving its political inspiration from the Voortrekkers (*q.v.*) of 1836. Supplanted the Broederbond Party *c.* 1935, and achieved its maximum influence and membership, 1941.

Osteopathy formulated by Andrew Taylor Still (1828–1917), an American doctor, 1874. British School of O. founded, 1917. London College of O. founded, 1946.

Ostrogoths. Soon after A.D. 370 the eastern portion of the hitherto united Gothic tribes came under the supremacy of the Huns (*q.v.*). A raid of O. under King Radagais penetrated into Italy as far as Florence, 406. Ostrogothic bands fought in the army of Attila at Châlons-sur-Marne, 451, but after the death of the Hunnish king regained their liberty of action. They sued the Empire for permission to settle in Pannonia (*q.v.*), which was granted in the second half of the fifth century. Their king, Theodoric (Dietrich, 454–526), became a figure of Germanic legend, and founded an Ostrogoth kingdom in Italy *c.* 500, having first, in the service of the eastern emperor Zeno, reconquered Dalmatia and the Danube lands from the mutinous western Gen. Odoacer, himself probably a Goth. He married his daughter to Alaric II, king of the Visigoths (*q.v.*), effecting a reunion of the E. and W. Goths, who again separated at his death. Under his grandson and successor Athalaric the Ostrogoth kingdom came to an end, 555.

Oswiecim, Poland (Ger. **Auschwitz**). The Germans began the construction of a camp here in 1941. By Mar. 1945 a million and a half persons, mostly Jews, had been killed in O. 'destruction camp' by various branches of the S.S. (*q.v.*). The commandant and other S.S. officers were tried and executed at Warsaw for crimes against humanity in 1947.

Otranto, anciently **Hydruntum**, taken from the Byzantines by the Norman, Robert Guiscard, 1068. The Romanesque cathedral was consecrated, 1088. Taken by the Turks, 1480. The castle of O., subject of Walpole's novel published in 1764, was built in 1450.

Ottawa, Canada. Discovered by Champlain, 1613; first permanent settlement, 1826; originally known as Bytown; name changed to O., 1854, when it was incorporated as a city; made capital of Canada, 1858; first Parliament opened at, 1865. *See* CANADA.

Ottawa Conference between Britain and the Dominions (except Irish Free State) agreed upon trade preferences, Britain to raise tariffs against other countries, 1932.

Ottoman Empire. *See* OTTOMAN RULERS and TURKISH REPUBLIC. Ertogrul (*d.* 1288) obtains lands near Ankara from Seljuks (*q.v.*), and later moves to Sugut. Osman conquers Karaja Hissar, 1295. Orkhan takes Brusa, 1326; Karasi, 1338; Gallipoli, 1355. Foundation of the Janissaries by Orkhan, 1326–59. Murad I takes Ankara and Adrianople, 1361. Adrianople becomes capital, 1367. Acquires Kutahiah, 1381. Overthrows the allied Balkan forces at battle of Kossovo, 27 Aug. 1389. Bayazid I besieges Constantinople; takes Salonika, 1395. Recognized as Sultan of Rum by caliph, 1396. Defeated and captured by Tamerlane at battle of Ankara, 1402. Revival of Os. under Mohammed I, 1413–21. Murad II defeats John Hunyadi at Kossovo, 1448. Mohammed II takes Constantinople, 29 May 1453. Naval victory over Venice, 1499. Selim I (the Grim) drives Bayazid II from throne, 1512. Persians defeated, 1515. Syria and Egypt annexed, 1516–17. Assumes caliphate, 1517. O.E. reaches its greatest extent under Soliman I (the Magnificent or the Lawgiver), 1520–66. He annexes Belgrade, 1521. Destroys Hungarian Army at battle of Mohacz; conquers most of Hungary, 1526–47. Bagdad captured from Persians, 1534. Kheir-ed-Din Barbarossa's naval victory over allied Christians at Prevesa, 1538. Peace with Persia, 1555. Unsuccessful attack on Malta, 1563–5. Naval defeat at battle of Lepanto, 1571. First capitulations granted to Britain, 1580. First serious Janissary revolt, 1591. They murder Osman II, 1622; Ibrahim, 1648. Siege of Vienna marks beginning of O. decline, 1683. Defeat of Russia, 1710. Phanariot Greeks given governorships of Moldavia and Wallachia, 1710–1821. Austrian reconquest of Hungary, 1680–1718. Belgrade passes to Austria by Treaty of Passarowitz, 1718. Popular rising of Patrona Khalil, 1730. Treaty of Belgrade, 1739. Persian war, 1743–6. Women's faces ordered to be veiled, 1755. Russians conquer the Crimea, 1771. Treaty of Kuchuk-Chainardji, 1774. War with Napoleon, 1798–1802. Treaty of Bucharest, 1812. Beginning of Serbian independence, 1817. Greek rising begins, 1821. Mahmud II destroys Janissaries, 1826. Turko-Egyptian fleet destroyed at Navarino, 1827. French occupy Algiers, 1830. Greece independent by Treaty of London, 1832. Governorship of Egypt (*q.v.*) made hereditary, 1840. First Straits Protocol, 1841. Crimean War, 1854–6.

The 'Bulgarian Atrocities', 1876. War with Russia, 24 Apr. 1877. Treaty of San Stefano, 3 Mar. 1878. Cession of Cyprus to Britain, 4 June 1878. Berlin Treaty, 13 July 1878. Decree of Muharram gives the Turkish debt administration to European delegates, 1881. Bulgaria autonomous, 1885. Armenian revolts and 'massacres'. 1894–6. War with Greece, 1897. Germans begin the 'Bagdad–Berlin' railway, 1899. Macedonian insurrections, 1901–3. Austria annexes Bosnia. Bulgaria declares independence, 1908. Young Turk Revolution and dethronement of Abdul Hamid II, 1909. Italian aggression, 1911; and annexation of Tripoli and Dodecanese, 1912. *See* BALKAN WARS and WORLD WAR I. Sultanate abolished, 1 Oct. 1922. Caliphate abolished, 3 Mar. 1924. For later history *see* TURKISH REPUBLIC.

Ottoman Rulers. Those marked 'A' abdicated. Those marked 'M' were murdered. Those whose reigns were ended by the Janissaries are marked 'J'.

Osman I ('Ottoman') 1288–1326
Orkhan 1326–1359
Murad I 1360–1389
Bayazid I 1389–1403
   Sultan 1396
   Interregnum 1402–1413
Mohammed I 1413–1421
Murad II 1421–1451
Mohammed II (the Conqueror) 1451–1481
Bayazid II (A) 1481–1512
Selim I (the Grim) 1512–1520
   Caliph 1517
Soliman I (the Magnificent or the Lawgiver) 1520–1566
Selim II (the Sot) 1566–1574
Murad III 1574–1595
Mohammed III 1595–1603
Ahmed I 1603–1617
Mustafa I ')imbecile) 1617
Osman II (J M) 1618–1622
Mustafa I (again) (J A) 1622–1623
Murad IV 1623–1640
Ibrahim (J M) 1640–1648
Mohammed IV (J A) 1648–1687
Soliman II 1687–1691

Ahmed II 1691–1695
Mustafa II (J A) 1695–1703
Ahmed III (J A) 1703–1730
Mahmud I 1730–1754
Osman III 1754–1757
Mustafa III 1757–1773
Abdul Hamid I 1773–1789
Selim III (J A) 1789–1807
Mustafa IV 1807–1808
Mahmud II 1808–1839
Abdul Mejid I 1839–1861
Abdul Aziz (A) 1861–1876
Murad V (insane) 1876
Abdul Hamid II (A) 1876–1909
Mohammed V 1909–1920
Mohammed VI (A) 1920–1922
Abdul Mejid II (as caliph only) (A) 1922–1924

Oudh, India. Became independent of Mogul *c.* 1732. War with the British, 1759–64, ended in defeat at battle of Buxar, 1763, and acceptance of subsidy at treaty of alliance, 1764. Half territory ceded to Britain, 1801. Completely annexed, 1856. Formed, with Agra, the United Provinces (*q.v.*), 1902. Part of Uttar Pradesh since 1949.

Outward Bound Schools. Sea school opened, 1941. O.B. Trust formed, 1946. Mountain school opened, Eskdale, 1950. Training courses started for girls, 1951.

Owens College (Manchester). Founded from a bequest by John Owens (*d.* 1846). Opened, 1851. Extended, 1873. *See* MANCHESTER.

Oxford City, England. Mentioned in the *Anglo-Saxon Chronicle*, 912. Empress Maud besieged in, 1142. Charter, 1199. Mad Parliament held at, 1258. Made a bishopric, 1542. Occupied by Charles I, 1644–6. Charles II holds Parliament at, 19–28 Mar. 1681. Growth of the motor industry transformed Oxford into an industrial city, 1925–38.

'Oxford Group.' A movement started by Frank Buchman (an American) (1878–1961). Having become a Lutheran pastor, 1902, he formed a First Century Christian Fellowship at Oxford, 1921, with which he toured S. Africa, 1929, where the S. Africans dubbed the party 'the O.G.'. Popularly known as 'Moral Rearmament' rather than the O.G. since World War II.

Oxford Movement. Founded, 1833, by Newman and others for reforming the Church of England along Catholic lines. When Newman was converted to Rome, 1845, the O.M. lost its initial impetus; nevertheless, its views on matters of liturgy and theology have had a penetrating and lasting effect upon Anglicanism everywhere.

Oxford, Provisions of. Drawn up by Simon de Montfort, 1258, and annulled, 1261, by Henry III.

Oxford University. Schools founded early twelfth century. Vacarius lectured on Roman law at O., 1149. University as a corporate body dates from late twelfth or early thirteenth centuries. A migration from O. to Cambridge traditionally started the latter university, 1209. Earliest known charter, 1214. Recognized as a *Studium Generale* by the Pope, 1296. Famous Town and Gown Riot, 1354. University reorganized, 1571. Given right to representation in the House of Commons, 1604. New statutes, 1636, 1854, 1877, 1926. Women admitted to degrees, 1920. Parliamentary representation abolished, 1948.

The following are the colleges, halls, and societies (most of which are now open to both sexes), with dates of foundation and the names of their founders:

All Souls, 1438. Henry VI and Archbishop Chichele.

Balliol c. 1263. John and Devorguilla Baliol.

Brasenose, 1509. William Smyth, Bishop of Lincoln and Sir R. Sutton.

Campion Hall, 1896. Richard Clarke.

Christ Church, 1546. Henry VIII.

Corpus Christi, 1517. Richard Foxe, Bishop of Winchester.

Exeter, 1314. Walter Stapeldon, Bishop of Exeter.

Green, 1970.

Greyfriars, 1953.

Hertford, 1740. Richard Newton. Dissolved, 1805.
　　　　1874. T. C. Baring, M.P.

Jesus, 1571. Queen Elizabeth I.

Keble, 1868. Erected by subscription as a memorial to John Keble.

Lady Margaret Hall, 1878.

Linacre, 1962.

Lincoln, 1427. Richard Fleming, Bishop of Lincoln.

Magdalen, 1458. William Waynflete, Bishop of Winchester.

Mansfield, 1886.

Merton, 1264. At Merton.
　　　　1274. At Oxford. Walter Merton, Bishop of Rochester.

New, 1379. William of Wykeham, Bishop of Winchester.

Nuffield, 1937. Lord Nuffield.

Oriel, 1326. Adam de Brome and Edward II.

Pembroke, 1624. Thomas Tesdale and Richard Wightwick.

Queen's, 1340. Robert Eglesfield.

Regent's Park, 1886.

Ruskin, 1899.

St. Anne's, 1952. (Originally Society of Oxford Home Students, 1879.)

St. Antony's, 1950. M. Antonin Besse.

St. Benet's, 1897.

St. Catherine's (as a society), 1868. Refounded as a college, 1962.

St. Cross, 1965.

St. Edmund Hall, 1270.

St. Hilda's, 1893.

St. Hugh's, 1886.

St. John's, 1555. Sir Thomas White.

St. Peter's, 1929.

Somerville, 1879.

Trinity, 1554. Sir Thomas Pope.

University, 1249. William of Durham.

Wadham, 1612. Dorothy and Nicholas Wadham.

Wolfson. Sir Isaac Wolfson, 1966.

Worcester, 1714. Sir Thomas Cooke.

Oxford University Press. Founded, 1585.

Oxygen. First obtained, 1727, by Stephen Hales. First described by J. Priestley, 1774. Word 'O.' first used by Lavoisier c. 1775.

P

Pacific Ocean. First sighted from Panama by Balboa in Sept, 1513. Magellan sailed, 1520, through the strait named after him, and gave the ocean its name.

Padua, Italy (Lat. **Patavium**), came under Roman supremacy, 215 B.C.; sacked by Attila, A.D. 452; under rule of the Franks, 774; university founded by the Emperor Frederick II in 1222, and the present buildings date from 1493 to 1552; the town was conquered by the Venetians in 1405, who ruled it until 1797, when it was taken by the French; ceded to Austria, 1814; incorporated with kingdom of Italy, 1866.

Paestum (now **Pesto**). Greek colony of Poseidonia, founded by Sybarites, c. 600 B.C. Became subject to Rome, 273 B.C. Sacked by Saracens, 871, and partially dismantled by Normans c. 1055. Eventually abandoned during sixteenth century. Temple 'of Peace', built second century B.C., excavated, 1830. Temple 'of Ceres' built c. 530 B.C. Temple of Poseidon built, sixth century B.C. Other remains accidentally uncovered, 1943; excavated since 1945 under auspices of the Neapolitan Museum.

Pagalu, formerly **Annobon Is.**, in the Gulf of Guinea, discovered by Portuguese, 1 Jan. 1471. Ceded to Spain 1778. Part of Republic of Equatorial Guinea (q.v.) since 1968.

Pagan, anct. ruined city of Upper Burma. Capital of the country from 849 to 1287, when it was sacked by Kublai Khan.

Pahang, former Federated Malay State. Became British protectorate, 1888. Invaded by Japanese, 1942. Part of Malaysia since 1963.

Painting. P. on canvas known at Rome A.D. 66, and to Bede, A.D. 735. The brothers Van Eyck founded Flemish school of P. in oil, 1415. Royal Academy founded, 1768. Modern movements are: Impressionism, 1831; Neo-Impressionism, 1886; Post-Impressionism, 1890; Fauvism, 1906; Cubism, c. 1908; Futurism, 1911; Expressionism, 1908; Dadaism, c. 1920; Surrealism, 1925. For list of eminent painters, see ARTS.

Pakistan. Name first coined, 1933. Agitation in favour of a separate Moslem state in India begun by All India Moslem League, 1938. P. became independent dominion with the Quaid-i-Azam Mohammed Ali Jinnah as first Governor-General, 14 Aug. 1947. Country made a federation of two units—E. and W. P.—Nov. 1954. Joined Bagdad Pact (later CENTO, q.v.), Sept. 1955. Proclaimed an Islamic Republic within the Commonwealth, 23 Mar. 1956. Internal situation unstable, increasingly so from 1956 onwards, and martial law regimes 1956–70. In Sept. 1965 there was serious fighting between P. and India on the Kashmir border. Elections, 1970, highlighted secessionist feelings in E.P. (see BANGLADESH). E.P., as Bangladesh, seceded from P., 1971, and P. then withdrew from the Commonwealth. Bhutto came to power, 1971, but was overthrown by a military coup under General Zia, 1977, and executed in 1979.

Pakistan, East. See BANGLADESH.

Palace Court instituted, 1631; abolished, 1849.

Palatinate (Ger. **Pfalz**). First Count Palatine, 945–96. P. given to Otto of Bavaria, 1215. Became independent at division of Wittelsbach possessions, 1255. Received electoral vote under

Golden Bull, 1356. Divided into four, 1410. Reunited 1559. Reunited with Bavaria, 1777. Again divided up after the Napoleonic Wars, 1815.

Palermo, Sicily (Lat. **Panormus**). Conquered by Pyrrhus, 276 B.C.; by Romans 254 B.C.; by Vandals, A.D; by Belisarius, 535; by Saracens, 832; by Normans, 1071; cathedral built by Archbishop Walter, an Englishman, 1169–85; university founded, 1777; revolts against the Bourbon kings, 1820 and 1848; incorporated with Italy, 1860.

Palestine, Ancient (Arab. **Falastin**). Herew monarchy established *c.* 1000 B.C. Rise of Jehu, 841. Assyrians take Samaria, 721. Under Persia from *c.* 539. Conquered by Alexander the Great 333–332. Maccabaean War of Independence, 168. Roman conquest, 65–63. Jewish rebellion and suppression of Jewish state by Titus, A.D. 70. Another rebellion, 132–5. Conquered by Persia, 616. By Arabs under Omar, 636. Invaded by Seljuk Turks, 1072 (*see* CRUSADES). Taken by Ottoman Turks, 1517.

Palestine, Modern. Conquered by Napoleon, 1799; by the Egyptians, 1831. Europeans and many Jews immigrated during nineteenth century; Jewish agricultural movement began, 1870. Country freed from Turks by British, 1917–18. The Balfour Declaration, 2 Nov. 1917. Britain became mandatory power, 1920. Jerusalem University opened, 1 Apr. 1925. Wailing Wall outrages, 1929. Jews and Arabs began conflict at Jaffa, 19 Apr. 1936. Royal commission proposed partition, 7 July 1937, but World Zionist Congress of Zürich declared partition unacceptable, 11 Aug. P. Conference opened in London, 7 Feb. 1939; P. Conference ended in rejection of British plan by Arabs and Jews, 17 Mar. and outbreaks of Arab and Jewish terrorism in P. Jewish terrorism in P. began again, June 1945. Partition between Jews and Arabs voted by the United Nations, 29 Nov. 1947. British mandate ended, 14 May 1948. *See further under* ISRAEL and JORDAN.

Palestine Liberation Organization (P.L.O.), Palestinian resistance movement, formed, 1964, from Al Fatah, which had existed since 1956. Its president was Yasser Arafat, one of the founders of Al Fatah. He addressed the U.N., 1974. The P.L.O. made its effective base in Lebanon (*q.v.*) from the early 1970s but after the official expulsion of the P.L.O. forces from Lebanon in 1982 its H.Q. was Tunisia. From 1982 Arafat's leadership increasingly challenged by Syrian-backed extremists and in Dec. 1983 his forces obliged to abandon their last Lebanese stronghold (Tripoli) and be evacuated from Lebanon under U.N. protection.

Panama Canal. International Congress for building of canal convened through influence of F. de Lesseps, builder of Suez Canal, 1879. Company formed and surveying begun, Feb. 1881. Company liquidated through financial embarrassment, 1 Jan. 1889. New company formed, 1894. Work resumed, 1899. Britain conceded her claims to U.S.A. by Hay-Pauncefote Treaty, 1891. Company agreed to sell its rights to U.S. Government, 16 Feb. 1903. Treaty between U.S.A. and Panama, defining use of canal and government of Panama zone, Nov. 1903. Canal formally opened, 15 Aug. 1914. U.S.A. increased its annuity to Panama for use of Panamanian territory, 1955. Canal Zone handed over to Panama by the U.S.A., 1979.

Panama, Republic of. Treaty between U.S.A. and Colombia concerning canal concession ratified by U.S. Senate, 18 Mar. 1903. Colombian Senate refused ratification, and P., hitherto a department of Colombia, revolted against Colombia (*q.v.*), 4 Nov. 1903. U.S.A. prevented Colombian Government from suppressing the revolt and Panamanian independence recognized by Colombia, 13 Nov. 1903. P. then ceded canal zone to U.S.A., 18 Nov. 1903. Independence recognized by Colombia, 1914, in Treaty of Bogotá with U.S.A., ratified, 1921. Diplomatic relations between Colombia and P. established, 3 May 1924. Canal Zone handed over to P., 1979. First elections for 12 years held in 1980.

Pan-American Conferences. Arranged for by Act passed by U.S. Congress, 1888. First conference: Washington, Oct. 1889–Apr. 1890; ten nations signed arbitration treaty. The Organization of American States (*q.v.*) grew out of the P.-A.C.

Pannonia. Natives conquered by Augustus, 35 B.C. Insurrections suppressed, 12 B.C. and A.D. 6–9, after which P. was included in the province of Illyricum; separate province, A.D. 10. Divided into Upper and Lower P. *c.* A.D. 105. Conquered by Ostrogoths, 453; then by Lombards, 527; finally by Magyars *c.* 900. *See* HUNGARY.

Panslavism began *c.* 1830. First Pan-Slav Congress held at Prague, 1848. Moscow Congress, 1867.

Papacy. Christianity lawful in Roman Empire by the Edict of Milan, 313. Primacy of the Roman See established by Innocent I, 402–17. P. had acquired considerable temporal power in the district around Rome (*q.v.*) by the time of Leo the Great, 440–61. First decree on papal elections issued by Synod of Rome, Mar. 499. Gregory I sends Augustine to England, 596. Gregory II sends Boniface to Germany, 715. Pepin cedes papal states to Stephen II, 753. Leo III crowns Charlemagne emperor at Rome, 25 Dec. 800. Leo IV fortifies Rome, 847. The False Decretals forged in France *c.* 850. John VIII murdered by Roman nobles, 882. Martin I the first bishop to become pope, 882. The pornocracy of the two Theodoras and Marozia, 904–63. End of the rule of the nobles, 980. Cluniac reform movement reaches its climax with election of Gerbert of Reims to the P. as Silvester II, 999. The counts of Tusculum hold the P., 1012–45. Synod of Rome pronounces against simony and regulates the P., 1047–8. Papal election by cardinals only established 1059. *Dictatus Papae* outlines papal temporal claims, 1075. The Investiture Dispute, eleventh–twelfth centuries. Emperor Henry IV humiliated at Canossa, 1077, by Gregory VII (Hildebrand). Only

Englishman to become pope, Nicholas Breakspear, reigned as Adrian IV, 1154–9. P. reached the summit of its temporal power under Innocent III (1198–1216) and began to decline after the death of Innocent IV, 1254. Political struggle against the Hohenstaufen emperors ended in the defeat of Conradin at Tagliacozzo, 1268, after which the P. passed under French influence and moved to Avignon, 1309. The return of Gregory XI to Rome, 1377, was followed by the French-provoked 'Great Schism', 1378–1417, when the antipopes resided at Avignon and elsewhere. The schism was ended at the election of Martin V, 1417, by the Council of Constance, 1414–18. Temporary union with the Greek and Armenian Churches, 1439. Owing to inability of the Renaissance popes to reform the abuses of the Church the Reformation began with the issue of Luther's 95 Theses, 31 Oct. 1517. Luther burns the papal bull of excommunication, 1520. Paul III starts internal reforms, 1537, and confirms the Jesuit Order, 1540. Council of Trent redefines Roman Catholic doctrine, 1545–63. Counter-reformation in Germany, 1550–1600. In France, 1623–44. Pius VI taken to France as a prisoner, 1799. During the Roman revolution of 1848 Pius IX fled to Gaeta, but was retored with French help. All the states of the Church, except Rome and the Patrimony of St. Peter, annexed to Italy, 1860. Remainder annexed, 1870. Papal infallibility proclaimed by the Vatican Council on 18 July 1870. Rupture of diplomatic relations with France, 1904. Encyclical on modernism, 1907. Temporal sovereignty within Vatican City restored by Lateran Treaty, 11 Feb. 1929, amended by Concordat of 1984. Pope John XXIII convened 4th Ecumenical Council of the Church, Oct. 1962. Council closed, 8 Dec. 1965. The following is a list of popes, with antipopes in *italics*.

1. St. Peter (*d.* between A.D. 64 and 67)
2. St. Linus, 67–76, or 67–79

3. St. Anacletus I, 76–88, or 79–91
4. St. Clement I, 88–97, or 92–101
5. St. Evaristus, 97–105, or 101–5
6. St. Alexander I, 105–15
7. St. Sixtus I (Xystus), 115–25
8. St. Telesphorus, 125–36
9. St. Hyginus, 136–40
10. St. Pius I, 140–55
11. St. Anicetus, 155–66
12. St. Soter, 166–75
13. St. Eleutherius, 175–89
14. St. Victor I, 189–99
15. St. Zephyrinus, *c.* 199–217
16. St. Calixtus I, 217/18–222
    St. Hippolytus, antipope,
    217/18–235
17. St. Urban I, 222–30
18. St. Pontianus, 230–5
19. St. Anteros, 235–6
20. St. Fabian, 236–50
21. St. Cornelius, 251–3
    Novatian, antipope, 251
22. St. Lucius I, 253–4
23. St. Stephen I, 254–7
24. St. Sixtus II, 257–8
25. St. Dionysius, 259–68
26. St. Felix I, 269–74
27. St. Eutychianus, 275–(?)283
28. St. Gaius, 283–(?)296
29. St. Marcellinus, 296–304
30. St. Marcellus I, *c.* 308–*c.* 309
31. St. Eusebius, 309 (? 310)
32. St. Miltiades, 311–14
33. St. Sylvester I, 314–35
34. St. Marcus, 336 (Jan.–Oct.)
35. St. Julius I, 337–52
36. St. Liberius, 352–66
    Felix II, antipope, 355–65
37. St. Damasus I, 366–84
    Ursinus, antipope, 366–7
38. St. Siricius, 384–99
39. St. Anastasius I, 399–401
40. St. Innocent I, 401–17
41. St. Zosimus, 417–18
42. St. Boniface I, 418–22
    Eulalius, antipope, 418–19
43. St. Celestine I, 422–32
44. St. Sixtus III, 432–40
45. St. Leo I, 440–61
46. St. Hilarius, 461–8
47. St. Simplicius, 468–83
48. St. Felix III, 483–92
49. St. Gelasius I, 492–6
50. Anastasius II, 496–8

51. St. Symmachus, 498–514
    Laurentius, antipope, 498–*c.* 505
52. St. Hormisdas, 514–23
53. St. John I, 523–6
54. St. Felix IV, 526–30
55. Boniface II, 530–2
    Dioscorus, antipope, autumn 530
56. John II, 533–5
57. St. Agapetus I, 535–6
58. St. Silverius, 536–7
59. Vigilius, 537–55
60. Pelagius I, 555–61
61. John III, 561–74
62. Benedict I, 574–9
63. Pelagius II, 579–90
64. St. Gregory I, 590–604
65. St. Sabinian, 604–6
66. Boniface III, 607 (Feb.–Nov.)
67. St. Boniface IV, 608–15
68. St. Deusdedit (or Adeodatus 615–18
69. Boniface V, 619–25
70. Honorius I, 625–38
71. Severinus, 638–40
72. John IV, 640–2
73. Theodore I, 642–9
74. St. Martin I, 649–55 (*d.* in exile)
75. St. Eugenius I, 654–7
76. St. Vitalian, 657–72
77. Adeodatus II, 672–6
78. Donus, 676–8
79. St. Agatho, 678–81
80. St. Leo II, 681–3
81. St. Benedict II, 683–5
82. John V, 685–6
83. Conon, 686–7
    Theodore and *Paschal, rival*
    antipopes, 687 (Sept.)
84. St. Sergius I, 687–701
85. John VI, 701–5
86. John VII, 705–7
87. Sisinnius, 708 (Jan.–Feb.)
88. Constantine, 708–15
89. St. Gregory II, 715–31
90. St. Gregory III, 731–41
91. St. Zacharias, 741–52
92. Stephen II, 752–7
93. St. Paul I, 737–67
    Constantine, antipope, 767–8
    Philip, antipope, 768 (July)
94. Stephen III, 768–72
95. Adrian I, 772–95
96. St. Leo III, 795–816
97. Stephen IV, 816–17
98. St. Paschal I, 817–24

99. Eugenius II, 824–7
100. Valentinus, 827 (Aug.–Sept.)
101. Gregory IV, 827–44
    John, antipope, 844 (Jan.)
102. Sergius II, 844–7
103. St. Leo IV, 847–55
104. Benedict III, 855–8
    Anastasius, antipope, 855
105. St. Nicholas I, 858–67
106. Adrian II, 867–72
107. John VIII, 872–82
    (wrongly called Martin II)
108. Marinus I, 882–4
109. St. Adrian III, 884–5
110. Stephen V, 885–91
111. Formosus, 891–6
112. Boniface VI, 896 (Apr.)
113. Stephen VI, 896–7
114. Romanus, 897 (Aug.–Nov.)
115. Theodore II, 897 (Nov.–Dec.)
116. John IX, 898–900
117. Benedict IV, 900–3
118. Leo V, 903 (July–Sept.)
    Christopher, antipope, 903–4
119. Sergius III, 904–11
120. Anastasius III, 911–13
121. Lando, 913–14
122. John X, 914–28
123. Leo VI, 928 (May–Dec)
124. Stephen VII, 928–31
125. John XI, 931–5
126. Leo VII, 936–9
127. Stephen VIII, 939–42
128. Marinus II (wrongly called
    Martin III), 942–6
129. Agapetus II, 946–55
130. John XII, 955–964 (deposed Dec.
    963)
131. Leo VIII, 963–965 ⎫ Rivals, one or
131. Benedict V, ⎬ other of
    964–5 or 966 ⎪ whom may
    ⎪ be regarded
    ⎭ as an antipope.
132. John XIII, 965–72
133. Benedict VI, 973–4
    Boniface VII, antipope, 974
    (June–July), expelled
134. Benedict VII, 974–83
135. John XIV, 983–4 (expelled)
    Boniface VII, antipope, returned,
    984–5
136. John XV, 985–96
137. Gregory V, 996–9
    John XVI, antipope, 997–8

138. Sylvester II, 999–1003
139. John XVII, 1003 (June–Dec.)
140. John XVIII, 1004–09
141. Sergius IV, 1009–12
142. Benedict VIII, 1012–24
    Gregory, antipope, 1012 (May–
    Dec.)
143. John XIX, 1024–32
144. Benedict IX, 1032–44
145. Sylvester III, 1045 (Jan.–Mar.)
146. Benedict IX, 1045 (Apr.–May)
    resigned
147. Gregory VI, 1045–6
148. Clement II, 1046–7
149. Benedict IX (restored), 1047–8
150. Damasus II, 1048 (July–Aug.)
151. St. Leo IX, 1049–54
152. Victor II, 1055–7
153. Stephen IX, 1057–8
    Benedict X, antipope, 1058–9
154. Nicholas II, 1059–61
155. Alexander II, 1061–73
    Honorius II, antipope, 1061–72
156. St. Gregory VII, 1073–85
    Clement III, antipope, 1080,
    1084–1100
157. Bl. Victor III, 1086–7
158. Bl. Urban II, 1088–99
159. Paschal II, 1099–1188
    Theodoric, antipope, 1100
    Albert, antipope, 1102 (Feb.–
    Mar.)
    Sylvester IV, antipope, 1105–11
160. Gelasius II, 1118–19
    Gregory VIII, antipope, 1118–21
161. Calixtus II, 1119–24
162. Honorius II, 1124–30
    Celestine II, antipope, 1124
    (Dec.)
163. Innocent II, 1130–43
    Anacletus II, antipope, 1130–8
    Victor IV, antipope, 1138
    (Mar.–May)
164. Celestine II, 1143–4
165. Lucius II, 1144–5
166. Bl. Eugenius III, 1145–53
167. Anastasius IV, 1153–4
168. Adrian IV, 1154–9
169. Alexander III, 1159–81
    Victor IV, antipope, 1159–64
    Paschal III, antipope, 1164–8
    Calixtus III, antipope, 1168–78
    Innocent III, antipope, 1179–80
170. Lucius III, 1181–5

171. Urban III, 1185–7
172. Gregory VIII, 1187 (Oct.–Dec.)
173. Clement III, 1187–91
174. Celestine III, 1191–8
175. Innocent III, 1198–1216
176. Honorius III, 1216–27
177. Gregory IX, 1227–41
178. Celestine IV, 1241 (Oct.–Nov.)
179. Innocent IV, 1243–54
180. Alexander IV, 1254–61
181. Urban IV, 1261–4
182. Clement IV, 1265–8
183. St. Gregory X, 1271–6
184. St. Innocent V, 1276 (Jan.–June)
185. Adrian V, 1276 (July–Aug.)
186. John XXI, 1276–7
187. Nicholas III, 1277–80
188. Martin IV, 1281–5
189. Honorius IV, 1285–7
190. Nicholas IV, 1288–92
191. St. Celestine V, 1294 (July–Dec.)
192. St. Boniface VIII, 1294–1303
193. St. Benedict XI, 1303–4
194. Clement V, 1305–14 (to Avignon in 1309)
195. John XXII, in Avignon, 1316–34
     Nicholas V, antipope in Italy,
     1328–30
196. Benedict XII, 1334–42 in Avignon
197. Clement VI, 1342–52 in Avignon
198. Innocent VI, 1352–62 in Avignon
199. Bl. Urban V, 1362–70 (in Rome from 1367)
200. Gregory XI, 1370–8 (to Rome 1377)
201. Urban VI, 1378–89
     Clement VII, antipope, 1378–94
202. Boniface IX, 1389–1404
     Benedict XIII, antipope, 1394–1423
203. Innocent VII, 1404–6
204. Gregory XII, 1406–15
     Alexander V, antipope, 1409–10
     John XXIII, antipope, 1410–15
205. Martin V, 1417–31
     Clement VIII, antipope, 1423–9
     Benedict XIV, antipope, 1425–30
206. Eugenius IV, 1431–47
     Felix V, antipope, 1439–49
207. Nicholas V, 1447–55
208. Calixtus III, 1455–8
209. Pius II, 1458–64
210. Paul II, 1464–71
211. Sixtus IV, 1471–84

212. Innocent VIII, 1484–92
213. Alexander VI, 1492–1503
214. Pius III, 1503 (Sept.–Oct.)
215. Julius II, 1503–13
216. Leo X, 1513–21
217. Adrian VI, 1522–3
218. Clement VII, 1523–34
219. Paul III, 1534–49
220. Julius III, 1550–5
221. Marcellus II, 1555 (Apr.)
222. Paul IV, 1555–9
223. Pius IV, 1559–65
224. St. Pius V, 1566–72
225. Gregory XIII, 1572–85
226. Sixtus V, 1585–90
227. Urban VII, 1590 (Sept.)
228. Gregory XIV, 1590–1
229. Innocent IX, 1591 (Oct.–Dec.)
230. Clement VIII, 1592–1605
231. Leo XI, 1605 (Apr.)
232. Paul V, 1605–21
233. Gregory XV, 1621–3
234. Urban VIII, 1623–44
235. Innocent X, 1644–55
236. Alexander VII, 1655–67
237. Clement IX, 1667–9
238. Clement X, 1670–6
239. Bl. Innocent XI, 1676–89
240. Alexander VIII, 1689–91
241. Innocent XII, 1691–1700
242. Clement XI, 1700–21
243. Innocent XIII, 1721–4
244. Benedict XIII, 1724–30
245. Clement XII, 1730–40
246. Benedict XIV, 1740–58
247. Clement XIII, 1758–69
248. Clement XIV, 1769–74
249. Pius VI, 1775–99
250. Pius VII, 1800–23
251. Leo XII, 1823–9
252. Pius VIII, 1829–30
253. Gregory XVI, 1831–46
254. Pius IX, 1846–78
255. Leo XIII, 1878–1903
256. St. Pius X, 1903–14
257. Benedict XV, 1914–22
258. Pius XI, 1922–39
259. Pius XII, 1939–58
260. John XXIII, 1958–63
261. Paul VI, 1963–1978
262. John Paul I, 1978
263. John Paul II, 1978–

Papal States. Temporal rule of the Papacy began with the bestowal of the

Exarchate of Ravenna, hitherto administered from Byzantium, on Pope Stephen II (752–7). Greatly reduced in extent, 1859, and suppressed, 1870. In 1929 a successor to this state, known as the Vatican (*q.v.*) City was recognized as a sovereign power by concordat with Italy; amended, 1984.

Paper. Said to have been invented in China, A.D. 105, by Tsai-Lun.

Papua New Guinea. The P.N.G. Act 1949–72 provided for the administrative union by Australia (as a U.N. nominee) of New Guinea (*q.v.*) and Papua. Self-gov. was granted on 1 Dec. 1973 and P.N.G. became fully independent on 16 Sept. 1975.

Parachute first used by a human being from an aircraft (balloon), Paris, 22 Oct. 1797.

Paraguay. Explored by Juan Diaz de Sotis, 1515. By Irala, Ayotas, and Garay, 1519–32. First settlement founded by Pedor de Mendoza, 1537. Further exploration by Cabeza de Vaca, 1541–2. First Jesuits arrive, 1557. Foundation by Father Diego de Torres of the Jesuit Missionary State in P. ('The Reductions'), 1608–11. Civil War between the Spanish planters and the Jesuits, 1723–5. Rebellion of the *Comuñeros* led by Mompox, 1726–35. Jesuit rule abolished, 1767. Declaration of P.'s independence from Spain, 1811, and Francia's dictatorship, 1814–40. War with Brazil, Argentina, and Uruguay, 1865–70. Brazilian occupation, 1870–6. War with Bolivia, 31 July 1932–12 July 1935. Frontier with Bolivia fixed by arbitration, 10 Oct. 1938. Civil war, Mar.–Aug. 1947, resulted in victory of Colorados. Stroessner became President, 1954, and established a right-wing dictatorship. Many ex-Nazis reputedly in P. after World War II.

Paratroops, first demonstrated by Russians, 1936. First used by Germans in Holland, May 1940. Development of British P. from 1942 onwards.

Paris, France. First mentioned by Caesar under title of *Lutetia Parisiorum*. In 52 B.C. it became a Roman town of some importance; Clovis made it his capital,

A.D. 508; between 1180 and 1223 the cathedral of Notre-Dame was commenced and the University of P. founded; revolution of P. headed by Étienne Marcel, 1358; reconstruction of the city under Napoleon III, 1851–70; fell to German Army, 1871 and 14 June 1940; liberated by Fighting French forces under Leclerc, Aug. 1944. Considerable growth of population and rebuilding since 1945. Market of Les Halles moved to Rungis, 1969. *See* FRANCE and BASTILLE.

Paris, Declaration of. Drawn up at the Congress of P. in 1856. It settled four important points of international law.

Paris, Treaties of. Name of sev. treaties, the most notable of which are:

1. Between France, Spain, and England, by which the Seven Years War was ended and Canada ceded to England, signed Feb. 1763.
2. Between Britain and the American Commissioners, recognizing American independence, 3 Sept. 1783.
3. Between the allies, after the abdication of Napoleon in May 1814.
4. After the close of Napoleon's final campaign in Flanders, 20 Nov. 1815.
5. Between Russia, Turkey, England, France, and Sardinia at the close of the Crimean War, signed 30 Mar. 1856.
6. Between England and Persia: amongst other things it abolished the slave trade in the Persian Gulf, signed 3 Mar. 1857;
7. Terminating the Spanish-American War, 10 Dec. 1898.

Parliament (*see also* LORDS, HOUSE OF; COMMONS, HOUSE OF; FRANCHISE). In Jan. 1265 there was a meeting (summoned by Simon de Montfort) of citizens and burgesses, together with knights of the shire; but until 1295 there appears, despite frequent summons to the burgesses to attend, to have been for the most part only one legislative chamber. Acts of P. were first printed in 1501. First P. of Great Britain met, 23 Oct. 1707. Septennial Act became law, 7 May 1716; first P. of the U.K. of Great Britain and Ireland, 1801; Roman Catholic Relief Act,

1829; Reform Act, 1832; Houses of P. destroyed by fire, 16 Oct. 1834; new buildings commenced, 1840; new House of Lords completed, 15 Apr. 1845; new House of Commons completed, 4 Nov. 1852; Act for enabling Jews to sit, 1858; Parliamentary Elections Act (as to corrupt practices), 1868; Ballot Act, 1872; closure adopted, 1882; P. Act, 1911, made five years instead of seven maximum length of a P., and curtailed powers of House of Lords, as did that of 1949. Act of 1948 abolished plural voting, by abolishing University and business franchises. Peerage Bill establishing Life Peerages became law, 31 July, 1963. House of Lords reform Bill dropped by gov. 1969. 18-year-olds to vote in parliamentary elections from Feb. 1970 under Representation of the People Act, 1969. *See* LORDS, HOUSE OF.

Parliamentary Commissioner for Administration (popularly, the **'Ombudsman'**), appointed under the Parliamentary Commissioner Act, 1967, to investigate administrative action taken on behalf of the Crown, i.e. alleged maladministration.

Parma, duchy of, created 1545, for Pierluigi Farnese, natural son of Pope Paul III. Conquered by the French, 1796. Assigned to Marie Louise, wife of Napoleon, after 1815. Became part of the kingdom of Italy, 1859.

Parnell Commission. Caused through facsimile reproduction, in *The Times* of 18 Apr. 1887, of a letter purporting to have been written by Charles S. Parnell (1846–1891): it excused the Phoenix Park murders (*q.v.*). Further letters having been produced (July 1888) by defendants in F. H. O'Donnell's libel action against *The Times*, the Government (Aug. 1888) appointed a special commission, which reported, 13 Feb. 1890. It acquitted P. on all charges.

Parthenon at Athens, building begun, 447 B.C.; dedicated, 438; sculptures completed, 432. Converted into a Christian church, fifth century, and into a mosque, A.D. 1456. Blown up, 1687. Sculptures removed by Lord Elgin, 1801 to British Museum; demanded back by Greek govt., 1983.

Parthia, anct. W. Asian kingdom. Controlled a considerable empire between 250 B.C. and A.D. 224 when the country was annexed to Persia.

Partition Treaties between William III, representing England and Holland, and Louis XIV, attempted to settle the devolution of the Spanish dominions at the death of the reigning King Charles II.

1. 2 Oct. 1698. By this treaty Spain, its colonies, and the Netherlands were to go to the Electoral Prince of Bavaria, Milan to the Archduke Charles of Austria, Naples, Sicily, and other Italian possessions to the Dauphin. This arrangement was frustrated when Charles II left all the Spanish dominions to the Electoral Prince by a will, published 14 Nov. 1698, and the Electoral Prince *d.,* 6 Feb. 1699.

2. 11 June 1699. The Archduke Charles to have the Electoral Prince's share. The Dauphin to have the same as before, plus Milan. This treaty was ratified, 13 Mar. 1700. It was frustrated because the Austrian emperor refused ratification, and Charles II, by a will signed 7 Oct. 1700, gave all the territories to the Duke of Anjou (grandson of Louis XIV). Charles II *d.* 1 Nov. 1700. Louis XIV accepted the Spanish offer, 12 Nov. Acceptance publicly announced 16 Nov. 1700. *See* SPANISH SUCCESSION, WAR OF.

Paston Letters, The. A series of letters written to or by the Ps., a Norfolk family, between 1422 and 1509; they give an invaluable insight into English life of the fifteenth century.

Patagonia. Since 1881 part of Argentina (*q.v.*).

Patent Laws (Britain). First granted for exclusive privilege of printing books, 1591; properties and rights of inventors first protected in 1623; this law was repealed and a new Act passed known as the P. Act in 1883; amended, 1885, 1886, 1888, 1901, 1902, 1907, 1919, 1928, 1932, and 1946. Important changes contained in new Act, which was passed 1949 and came into operation, 1 Jan. 1950. Bill to develop useful inventions introduced, 1948. Some amendments to P.L. under Patents Act, 1957, and since.

Pavia, Italy (anct. **Ticinum**; later **Papia**). Founded by the Ligurii. Taken from the Lombards by Charlemagne, 774. Taken by the Viscontis, 1359. Sacked by the French, 1500. Charles V captured Francis I of France here, 1525. Annexed by Austria, 1744. Became part of a united Italy, 1859. Church Councils held at P., 1081, 1160, 1423.

Pawnbrokers' Acts, 1872–60, repealed by the Consumer Credit Act of 1974 (*q.v.*), sections 114–122 of the latter act regulating matters traditionally covered by pawnbroking.

Pay As You Earn (P.A.Y.E.), part of modern British income tax system, was introduced in 1944.

Peace Ballot, conducted by the League of Nations Union, secured 11,640,066 British votes for adherence to the League, and 10,500,000 for all-round reduction of armaments, 27 June 1935.

Peace Conferences (International). *See also* HAGUE.

1. Met at The Hague, 1899; arbitration court formed at the conference, and founded 29 July 1899.
2. Met at The Hague, 15 June–18 Oct. 1907.
3. Inter-Allied and Associated Powers held first plenary session, in Paris, on 18 June 1919. Draft treaty handed to German delegates, 7 May 1919. After the treaty was ratified further conferences were held at San Remo, Apr. 1920, and at Hythe, May, and Spa, June 1920, to discuss reparations, disarmament, mandates, and the Adriatic question. For P.C. with Turkey *see* TURKISH REPUBLIC.
4. A Peace Conference held in Paris in 1946 resulted in peace treaties between the Allies and Italy, Hungary, Rumania, Bulgaria, and Finland being signed and ratified in 1947. The treaty with Austria, however, was not signed until 1955. For other

P.C. since World War II *see* GENEVA CONFERENCES.

Pearl Harbor, American naval base in the Hawaiian Islands. Dredging of P.H. completed, 1912; dry dock opened, 1919. Japanese attack on P.H., 7 Dec. 1941, brought the U.S.A. into World War II on the Allied side.

Peasants' Revolt. Accelerated by enforcement of poll-tax (1379). Rebels suppressed after breaking into Tower of London, 15 June 1381.

Peasants' War.

1. France. *See* JACQUERIE.
2. Germany: Decay of feudal protection, together with continuance of feudal tyranny, led to a P. League which rose in the Rhine countries in 1502, and to another rising in Württemberg in 1514. Great insurrection began in Swabia, 1524, and spread through S. Germany. Demands of P. set out in 12 Articles issued by insurgents of Swabia, Easter, 1525; Under the Anabaptist Münzer, they were overwhelmed by Philip of Hesse at Frankenhausen, 15 May 1525.

Peep-of-Day Boys. Irish Protestant secret society, founded *c.* 1785.

Peine Forte et Dure, form of torture to extort plea or evidence, authorized in England, 1406. Last recorded instance, 1741. Abolished, 1772.

Peking or **Peiping,** capital of China. Captured by Khitan Tatars, A.D. 986; recaptured by Chinese in twelfth century; again captured by Tatars, 1151; first settlement of foreigners in 1860; Boxer riots and the siege of the legations, 1900. Capital of China from 1421 until 1928, when Chiang Kai-Shek removed the government to Nanking and renamed Peking Peiping. Occupied by Japanese, 1937–45. Surrendered to the Communists, 1 Feb. 1949, and re-established under its original name of Peking as the capital of China, 1 Oct. 1949.

Pelagians. The followers of Pelagius (*c.* 360–420), a British theologian, who was summoned before a synod of bishops at Jerusalem, 415, where he successfully defended his views. Pope

Innocent, however, in 416 upheld the opponents of Pelagius, amongst whom was St. Augustine of Hippo. The doctrine of Pelagianism finally condemned, 418, by the Western Church, and in 431 by the Eastern Church.

Penal Servitude, as punishment for felony, substituted for transportation in English law, 1853–7. Abolished, 1948.

Penang. Ceded to E. India Co. by Rajah of Kedah, 1785. Incorporated with Singapore and Malacca, 1826. Capital of Straits Settlements, 1837–1936. Part of Malaysia since 1963.

P.E.N. Club founded, 1921.

Penicillin. Discovered, 1928, by Sir Alexander Fleming (1881–1955).

Peninsular War, The (1808–14). Between France and England, begun in consequence of the alliance between Spain and England, July 1808, when the Duke of Wellington, then Sir Arthur Wellesley, was dispatched to the peninsula with troops; there were two campaigns, and the British Army was forced to evacuate the country in Jan. 1809. A fresh force was landed in Apr. 1809; the war had commenced with the battle of Vimiero, 21 Aug. 1808, when Wellington defeated Junot, and ended with the battle of Toulouse, 10 Apr. 1814, when Wellington defeated Soult (*see* PORTUGAL and SPAIN).

Pennsylvania, U.S.A. Founded by William Penn, who in 1681 obtained a grant of land in America from Charles II. In Sept. 1682 Penn embarked on the *Welcome* for America, and landed on 28 Oct. of the same year; as one of the thirteen original colonies it became a state of the Union, 1787.

Penny. First mentioned in Laws of King Ine (*fl.* 689–726), King of Wessex. Halfpennies not coined before the late ninth century. Copper pence first struck, 1797; bronze substituted for copper, 1860. New P., one-hundredth part of Britain's decimal currency system from Feb. 1971, is worth 2.4 old Ps.

Pensions, Ministry of, created, 1916. Merged with the Ministry of National Insurance, to form the M. of P. and National Insurance, 1953; part of the Dept. of Health and Social Security (*q.v.*) since 1968.

Pentagon Building (Washington, D.C., U.S.A.), built 1941–3.

Perak, former Federated Malay State, made treaty (1765) with Dutch, who first established factories there, 1650. Ceded Dinding and Pangkor Island to Britain by treaty of 1826, but these were returned, 1934–5. Part of Malaysia since 1963.

Perceval Administration. Spencer P. (1762–1812) at the head. Formed, Oct. 1809; dissolved on assassination of P. in the lobby of the House of Commons, 11 May 1812.

Pergamum. Said to have been founded by Aeolian Greeks; a place of some importance by 420 B.C. Ruled by Philetaerus, 283–263; Eumenes I, 263–241; Attalus I, 241–197; Eumenes II, 197–159; Attalus II, 159–138; Attalus III, 138–133. The last three made alliances with Rome, who greatly enlarged their kingdom, and to whom it was bequeathed in 133 B.C.

Perlis, former Unfederated Malay State, became subject to Siam, 1821, and independent, 1841. By treaties of 1909 and 1930 the ruler of P. accepted British protection and the services of a British adviser. Part of Malaysia since 1963.

Persia. *See* IRAN.

Persian Authors, Classical.

Avicenna (Abu Ibn Sina), 980–1036, philosopher and physician.

Firdausi, Abulkasim Mansur, *c.* 950–1020, poet.

Hafiz, Shamseddin Muhammed, *d. c.* 1390, poet.

Jalaluddin Rumi, 1207–73, poet.

Khayyám, Omar, *d.* 1123, poet.

Saadi, *d.* 1291, poet.

Zoroaster, *c.* seventh century B.C., poet and prophet.

Perth, Australia Cap. of W. Australia, founded 1829. Grew rapidly after gold-rush of 1893.

Perth, Scotland. Said to have been founded by Agricola, A.D. 70. Made a royal burgh by William the Lion, 1210; besieged and captured by Robert Bruce,

1311; captured by Edward III, 1335; retaken by Scots, 1339; after 1437, the year of the murder of James I, P. was no longer capital of Scotland; captured by Montrose, 1644; by Cromwell, 1651; Old Pretender proclaimed at, 16 Sept, 1715.

Peru, Republic of. Independence proclaimed, 28 July 1821. Declared independent of Colombia, 26 Jan. 1827. Constitution proclaimed, 21 Mar. 1828. United with Bolivia, 1835–9. Joined with Bolivia against Chile in the 'Nitrate War', 1879. Defeated and forced to cede the province of Tarapaca to Chile, 1883. Series of alternating military juntas and elected presidents ended by new Constitution, 1980, and election of Belaúnde Terry.

Peru, Spanish Viceroyalty of. Conquered by Pizarro, 1531–4. Lima founded, 1534. Manco Inca's unsuccessful revolt, 1535. Pizarro killed, 1541. 'New Laws' according liberty to Indians, 1542. Execution of Inca Tupac Amaru, 1571. Viceroyalty of New Granada separated from P., 1739. Viceroyalty of the River Plate separated from P., 1776. Condorcanqui's rebellion, 1780.

Perugia, Italy. Originally *Perusia.* Captured by Pope Leo X from the Baglioni, 1520; occupied by French, 1797; by Austrians, 1849; united to kingdom of Italy, 1860.

Peter I Island, in the Antarctic Ocean, sighted by the Russian admiral Bellinghausen, and named by him in 1821; proclaimed Norwegian territory, 23 Apr. 1931.

Peterborough, England. Originally called *Medehamstede.* In 655 Saxulf, a monk, founded a monastery there, and the name was altered subsequently to *Burgus sancti Petri;* cathedral founded, 656; destroyed by Danes, 870; the present building founded, 1117. Catherine of Aragon buried at, 1536. See founded by Henry VIII, 1541. Cathedral despoiled by Cromwell, 1643.

Peterloo Massacre at St. Peter's Field, Manchester, 16 Aug. 1819.

Peter's Pence. A tax levied on the English by the popes, and probably dating fromentioned in a letter of Canute's dated 1031, from Rome to the English clergy; in 1534 the tax was abolished by Henry VIII; still exists (1985) in the Roman Catholic Church in England and Wales.

Petition of Right. Presented to Charles I by Parliament, 28 May 1628; it asked for a reform of various constitutional abuses. Until the Crown Proceedings Act, 1947, a P. of R. was the only way in which the subject could obtain legal relief against the crown.

Petrograd. St. Petersburg (*q.v.*) renamed Aug. 1914 to remove any suggestion of German influence. Name changed to Leningrad (*q.v.*), 1924.

Petsamo (Fin.), **Petchenga** (Rus.). A port in the Barents Sea, together with a small province named after it, E. of Lake Inari. It did not form part of the Grand Duchy of Finland (*q.v.*), but was ceded to the Finnish republic by the U.S.S.R. under the Treaty of Dorpat, 24 Oct. 1920. The treaty of 1940 secured the Russians access to the port and freedom of movement across the province, but that of 1944 ceded both to the U.S.S.R. outright.

Pharmaceutical Society. Founded, 1841; incorporated, 1843. Membership became automatic and compulsory for all qualified chemists and druggists, 1933. Constitution revised by granting of a supplementary charter, 1953, and the coming into operation of the Pharmacy Act, 1953.

Phi Beta Kappa. Oldest American college fraternity, formed at William and Mary College, Williamsburg, Virginia, 1776. Women eligible since 1876.

Philadelphia, Pa., U.S.A. Founded by William Penn, 1682. Was capital of Pennsylvania and of United (at first Federal) States until 1800.

Philippine Islands. Discovered by Magellan, who was killed there, 1521. Occupied by Spaniards, who built Manila, 1564–71. Admiral Montojo's fleet destroyed at battle of Manila, 1 May 1898. Ceded to U.S.A. by Treaty of Paris, 10 Dec. 1898. Granted local autonomy, 1916. Council of State created by executive orders, 1918 and

1928. U.S. Congress declares P.I. independent as from 1945 (but this in fact delayed by World War II), 24 Mar. 1934. Japanese attack and occupy Manila, 2 Jan. 1942. Siege of Bataan, 5 Jan.–1 May 1942. Surrender of Corregidor, 6 May 1942. Americans land in P.I. 20 Oct. 1944. Final liberation, 6 Aug. 1945. Republic of the Philippines came into being 4 July 1946. Manila Conference, 1966, held in the P.I. Under 1973 constitution Marcos confirmed indefinitely as president.

Phoenicia conquered by Egyptians *c.* 1600 B.C. Became independent again *c.* 928 B.C. Hegemony of Tyre lasted until 876 B.C., when Phoenician cities became tributary to Assyria and thereafter to other great powers; but the colony of Carthage (*q.v.*) was founded *c.* 700 B.C.

Phoenix Park Murders. Lord Frederick Cavendish, Chief Secretary for Ireland, and T. H. Burke murdered by terrorists in Dublin, 6 May 1882.

Phosphorus. Discovered, 1669, by Dr. Brandt, of Hamburg.

Photography. In the sixteenth century the action of light on chloride of silver was known, but it was not until *c.* 1802 that Thomas Wedgwood (1771–1805) published his *Account of a Method of copying Painting upon Glass, and of making Profiles by the Agency of Light upon Nitrate of Silver*; in 1819 Sir John Herschel improved Wedgwood's method, and in 1824 Louis J. M. Daguerre produced photographic plates, afterwards known as daguerreotypes; the first *negative* was produced by Talbot in 1839; celluloid roll films introduced by George Eastman, 1889; telephotography invented by T. R. Dallmeyer (1859–1906) in 1891; direct colour P. by the Lumière Autochrome Plate, patented, 1904.

Photogravure. Invented by Klietsch (1841–1926), 1895.

Physicians, Royal College of (London). Charter granted through exertions of Dr. Linacre, Henry VIII's physician, in 1518.

Pianoforte or **Hammerklavier** developed by modification of the harpsichord by Bartolomeo Cristofori (1655–1731).

Pietists began to hold meetings, 1670, of German Lutherans under Jakob Spener (1625–1705). Community at Herrnhut founded by Nikolaus Ludwig, Graf von Zinzendorf (1770–60).

Pilgrimage of Grace. The name given to the insurrection caused by the dissolution of the monasteries and the agrarian injustices resulting from enclosures; it originated in Yorkshire and Lincolnshire in 1536; the leaders were executed in Mar. 1537.

Pilgrim Fathers, *émigré* Puritans from Lincolnshire, left England, 1608, for Leyden, sailed from Delftshaven, July 1620; from Southampton, 5 Aug.; from Plymouth, Devon, 6 Sept.; landed at Plymouth, Massachusetts, 16 Dec. 1620.

Pilgrim Trust founded, 1930.

Pillory, offences punishable by defined, 1266, in 'Statute of the P'. Limited to cases of perjury and subornation, 1816; last used, 1830; and finally abolished in England, 1837. Abolished in France, 1832; in state of Delaware, 1905; in rest of U.S.A., 1839.

Piltdown Man's skull partially dug up, 1912, and further skull fragments found, 1915. It was decided that Piltdown Man must have lived some 50,000 years ago. Detailed technical examination by modern methods, 1953–4, resulted in the 'discovery' being exposed as a fraud, 1955.

'Pinkville', Massacre of, allegedly of Vietnamese civilians, by Amer. troops on 16 March, 1968.

Piraeus. *See* ATHENS.

Pisa, Italy (anct. **Julia Pisana** or **Julia Obsequeus**). Independent republic by the eleventh century; leaning tower built, 1173–1350; power crushed by Genoa in a naval battle off Melovia, 1284; university founded, 1343; subject to Florence, 1405; becomes independent under French protection, 1494; retaken by Florence, 1509.

Pitcairn Islands. Discovered by Carteret, 1767; occupied by mutineers from the *Bounty*, 1790, and not visited by anyone else from the outside world until 1808. Population removed to Tahiti, 1831, but returned to P.I., 1832. Removed to Norfolk Island, 1856, but several soon returned. Original P.I. Bible returned to P.I., 1949. Under Fijian jurisdiction from 1952–70, since when Brit. Commissioner in New Zealand has been Governor of P.I. *See* 'BOUNTY' MUTINY.

Pittsburgh, Pa., U.S.A., began to grow *c.* 1785 on the site of Fort Pitt (formerly Fort Duquesne, which was built, 1754).

Plastics. First plastic (celluloid) discovered by Alexander Parkes, 1865. Bakelite produced from 1908. Considerable developments since 1920, and especially since 1939.

Platinum. Discovered, 1538, in Spain; first found in 1741 in England by Brownrigg.

Player Piano invented, 1842.

Plebiscite, originally a law enacted by the Plebs (*see* ROME) in their own assembly, the *comitia tributa,* established 449 B.C., as opposed to the Senate. Such laws came to be valid for the whole nation by the *Lex Hortensia,* 286 B.C. For modern Ps. *see* CARINTHIA; GREECE, MODERN; ITALY; SAARLAND; SILESIA.

Plebs under King Servius Tullius (578–534 B.C.) acquired some constitutional rights and the obligation of military service. Office of Tribune of Plebs instituted, 493.

Plimsoll Line, compulsory load-line, obtained, 1876, by the efforts of Samuel P. (1824–98).

Plombières. The Pact of P. was signed by Napoleon III and Cavour, 1858. *See* FRANCE and ITALY.

Pluralism forbidden in England by Act of 1529 in certain cases. Also by the Acts of 1838, 1850 and 1885: but terms virtually abrogated by Pastoral Reorganization Measure, 1949 and Pastoral Measure, 1968.

Plural Voting in Great Britain completely abolished by Representation of the People Act, 1948.

Plymouth, England, was frequently attacked by the French during the fourteenth and fifteenth centuries. First English town to be incorporated by Act of Parliament, 12 Nov. 1439. Witnessed the departure of Drake on his expedition round the world, 1577; of the Elizabethan fleet in the encounter with the Spanish Armada, 1588; and of the *Mayflower,* 1620. Severely damaged by German bombing, 1941.

Plymouth Brethren. Religious sect founded *c.* 1830 at P.; John Nelson Darby (1800–82) is generally regarded as the founder.

Pola. *See* ISTRIA.

Poland, Kingdom of. First appears as independent state, tenth century. Mieszko I (962–92) converted to Christianity. Boleslaw III divides P. between his sons, 1138, but country reunited by Casimir II (1177–94). Teutonic Knights settle in Kulm, 1208. Mongol invasion, 1241; P. again divided. P. reunited under Wladislaw Lokietek, 1306. Kingdom revived, 1320. First Diet, 1331. Casimir the Great, 1333–70. Personal union with Lithuania, 1386. Witowt and Jagiello (Wladislaw II) defeat Teutonic Knights at Tannenberg, 1410. Union of Horodlo, 1413. Prussia acquired from the Knights by Treaty of Thorn, 1466. War with Turkey, 1485 onwards. Escheat of Masovia and Warsaw, 1526. Religious dissensions, 1550–64. Decrees against heretics, 1564. Political union with Lithuania (Union of Lublin), 1 July 1569. Interregnum, 1572–3, following which monarchy becomes elective. Election of Henry of Valois, 1573. Reign of Stephen Báthory, 1575–86. University of Vilna founded, 1579. Sigismund III tried for treason by a Court of Inquisition, 1592. Creation of the Uniate Church, 1596. War with Russia, 1608–18. Defeat of Turks at battle of Czoczim, 1621. Cossack rebellions, 1640–9. Bogdan Khmelnitzki recognized as Hetman of the Cossacks at Zborow, 1649. Khmelnitzki defeated at battle of Beresteczko, 1651. War with Russia, 1651–64. Loss of Ukraine and Smolensk to Russia at Truce of Andrussov, 1667. John Sobieski rescues Vienna from the Turks, 1683. Peace of Karlowitz, 1699. Confederation of Radom, 1767. Russian influence attacked by Confederation of Bar, 1768. First Partition of P., 1772. Second Partition, 1793. Kosciuszko proclaims national insurrection, Mar. 1794. Russians suppress Kosciuszko, 1794. Third Partition, 1795–6. King Stanislaw abdicates, 1795, and *d.* in Russia, 1798. Napoleon creates Grand Duchy of Warsaw, 1806–15. Congress of Vienna creates a kingdom of P. under the Russian crown, usually called 'Congress P.', 1815. Suppressed, 1831, following the rising of 1830. Rising in Russian provinces of P., 1863.

Kings of Poland, 962–1795:
Mieszko I 962–992
Boleslaw I the Brave 992–1025
Mieszko II 1025–1034
Casmir I the Restorer 1040–1058
Boleslaw II the Bold 1058–1079
Wladislaw Herman 1079–1102
Boleslaw III the Wry-Mouthed 1102–1138

Partitional Period of Rival Duchies, 1138–1305:
Wladislaw 1138–1159
Boleslaw the Curly 1146–1173
Mieszko the Old 1173–1177
Casimir II the Just 1177–1194
Mieszko the Old (again) 1194–1202
Wladislaw Longshanks 1202–1206
Leszek the White 1206–1227
Henry the Bearded 1231–1238
Henry the Pious 1238–1241
Boleslaw the Modest 1243–1279
Leszek the Black 1279–1288
Henry Probus 1289–1290
Przemyslaw 1295–1296
Waclaw 1300–1305
Wladislaw I the Dwarf (King of all Poland, 1319) 1306–1333
Casimir III the Great 1333–1370
Louis of Hungary 1370–1382
Wladislaw II Jagiello 1386–1434
Wladislaw III of Varna 1434–1444
Casimir IV 1447–1492
John Albert 1492–1501
Alexander 1501–1506
Sigismund I 1506–1548
Sigismund II 1548–1572
Henry of Valois Feb. to June 1574
Stephen Báthory 1576–1586

Sigismund III 1587–1632
Wladislaw IV 1632–1648
John Casimir 1648–1668
Michael Korybut 1669–1673
John Sobieski 1674–1696
Augustus II 1697–1704
Stanislaw Leszczynski 1704–1709
Augustus II (again) 1709–1733
Stanislaw Leszczynski (again) 1733–1734
Augustus III 1734–1763
Stanislaw Poniatowski (*d.* 1798) 1764–1795

Poland, Republic of. The risings of 1830 and 1863 (*see* preceding article) had really been in support of a republic, which was at last proclaimed, Nov. 1918. Independence guaranteed under Versailles Treaty, 1919. Wars of aggrandizement with Lithuania, western Ukraine and Soviet Russia, Apr. 1919–Mar. 1921 (*see* Russia). *Coup d'état*, with bloodshed, by Marshal Pilsudski, 12 May, 1926. Took possession of zone in Czechoslovakia beyond the Olza, 2 Oct. 1938. In 1939 P. rejected Ger. claims to Danzig (Gdansk) and the 'Polish Corridor'; Germans invaded P. at 5.30 a.m., 1 Sept.; Soviet Russian troops crossed into P. at 4 a.m., Brest-Litovsk fell, 17 Sept. and Polish Gov. fled to Rumania; Fourth Partition of P. between Germany and Russia announced from Moscow, 22 Sept.; all P. subjugated by Oct. 1, and new Polish Govt. in exile estab. in France.

1940: Russians massacre 12,000 Polish officers at Katyn *c.* May. Polish Government established in London, 21 June. 1943: Warsaw ghetto rising, 18 Apr.–1 June. 1944: Poles rise against Germans in Warsaw, 1 Aug. Russians refuse help, 20 Aug. Rising crushed, 2 Oct. Poles forced to concede Curzon Line to Russia at Moscow Conference, 9–19 Oct. 1945: Russians enter Warsaw, 11 Jan. Communist-dominated Government of National Unity established, 28 June, based on Soviet regime estab. at Lublin in 1944. Russo-Polish frontier treaty, 17 Aug. Large-scale deportations of Germans from new Polish territories in the W. By 1948 Communist control in P. complete and all other parties banned. By the revised constitution of July 1952 the presidency fell into desuetude, being replaced by a Council of State. Persecution of the Catholic Church; Wyszinski, primate of P., imprisoned, 1953–6. Workers and students rioted in Poznan, June 1956; 'liberal' elements gained control of the Communist regime in P.; Gomulka became the real ruler of Poland, Oct. 1956. Wyszinski released; increasing contacts with W. Europe and greater religious freedom. Gomulka replaced by more liberal Gierek, 1970, but following political and economic unrest Gierek resigned, 1980, and expelled from Communist party, 1981. Brief period of liberality followed by martial law, 1981–2, and banning of trade unions (*see* SOLIDARITY). Some liberalization after 1983.

Presidents of Poland from 1918:
Pilsudski ('Chief of the State')
    1918–1922
Narutowicz (assassinated after five
    days of office) 1922
Wojciechowski 1922–1926
Moscicki 1926–1939
Bierut 1947–1952

Heads of Administration in Poland from 1918:
Parliamentary government in P. proved unstable from the outset, and between 1922 and 1926 governments changed constantly. After the *coup d'état* by Pilsudski in 1926 parliamentary government in the sense known in Britain ceased to function. The following were the effective heads of administration in P:
Pilsudski 1918–1922
Paderewski 1919–1921
Pilsudski 1926–1935
Smigly-Rydz 1935–1939

From 1939 to 1945 the Polish Government was in exile. Heads of administration in London were:
Sikorski 1939–1943
Mikolajczyk 1943–1945
The real ruler of Poland, since 1947, has in fact been the individual holding the position of first secretary of the Communist party; a position held by General Jaruzelski since 1981.

Polish Literature. The following are among the most celebrated P. authors:

Fredro, Count Aleksander, 1793–1876, dramatist.
Krasicki, Ignatius, 1735–1801, poet and critic.
Kraszewski, Jósef Ignacy, 1812–87, novelist, historian, and critic.
Kraszinski, Zygmunt, 1812–49, dramatist.
Mickiewicz, Adam, 1798–1855, poet.
Niémcewicz, Julian Ursin, 1757–1841, poet, dramatist, and novelist.
Orzeszkowa, Eliza, 1842–1910, novelist.
Przybyszewski, Stanislas, 1868–1927, novelist.
Reymont, Ladislas Stanislas, 1867–1925, novelist.
Sienkiewicz, Henryk, 1846–1916, novelist.
Slowacki, Juljusz, 1809–49, poet and dramatist.
Tetmajer, K., 1865–1939, poet.
Wyspianski, S., 1869–1907, poet and playwright.
Zapolska, Gabriela, 1860–1921, dramatist.

Police. In Britain the modern police force derives from Sir Robert Peel's reorganization of the Metropolitan Police Force, 1829.

Political Uniforms. Prohibited in Britain by Public Order Act, 1936.

Poll-Tax. Levied in England, 1377, 1379, and 1380. The latter was a cause of Wat Tyler's rebellion in 1381; revived, 1513; finally abolished, 1689.

Polotsk, independent principality from the tenth century, absorbed by Lithuania, 1307. Retaken by Ivan the Terrible, 1563. Became Polish, 1582; and finally Russian, 1772.

Polygamy. *See* MORMONS and UTAH, where it was forbidden by the Edmunds-Tucker Act of 1887.

Pompeii, Italy. Entirely destroyed by eruption of Vesuvius, 24 Aug. A.D. 79; in 1763 systematic excavations were commenced. Further considerable excavations from 1861; especially in 1921, 1941, and since World War II.

Pondicherry, first settled by French, 1674. Transferred to India *de facto*, 1 Nov. 1954; cession formally recognized by treaty, 28 May 1956.

Pontefract Castle (Yorks). Built *c.* 1069; Richard II murdered at, 10 Feb. 1400. Castle dismantled, 1649.

Poor Laws (Britain). Overseers were appointed for parishes, 1601; the word 'guardian' first used in this connection in a bill introduced into the Commons, 11 May 1735, by William Hay (1695–1755); first systematization of unions of parishes accomplished by Gilbert's Act, 1782, by which the relief of the poor was entrusted to visitors and guardians appointed by the justices. Poor Law Commission, 1832–3; Poor Law Board appointed, 1834; dissolved, 1846; Poor Law Amendment Act passed, 1834; amended, 1836, 1838, 1846, 1868; New Poor Law Act passed, 1889; amended, 1890. Overseers abolished by Rating and Valuation Act, 1925, as from 1 Apr. 1927; boards of guardians by Local Government Act, 1929, as from 1 Apr. 1930: these Acts transferred care of poor to the local authorities. Whole system abolished, 1948, by the National Assistance Act.

Poor Persons' Legal Aid, provided by the Poor Prisoners' Defence Act, 1930, superseded by the Legal Aid and Advice Acts, 1949–72, consolidated by the Legal Aid Act, 1974.

Popish Plot. Imaginary Roman Catholic plot against Charles II, invented by Titus Oates. He deposed before Sir E. Berry Godfrey, 28 Sept. 1678. Godfrey was murdered, 14 Oct. 1678. Oates convicted of perjury, May 1685. Reinstated, 1688.

Popular Front, suggested by Comintern, 1935. (*See* FRANCE and SPAIN.) Sir Stafford Cripps suggested a similar combination in England, which led to his temporary expulsion from the Labour Party, Apr. 1939.

Port Arthur. Massacre of Chinese by Japanese, 21 Nov. 1894; surrendered by Russian garrison to Japan, 1 Jan. 1905. In 1945 China and Russia agreed to joint use of P.A. for next thirty years; but under the Sino-Russian treaty of 1950 P.A. was handed over to China in 1955.

Porteous Riots. Caused by the hanging of a smuggler in Edinburgh, 1736; Capt. P. ordered the military to fire on the rioters and killed many; he was sentenced to death, but respited; the mob, however, seized him afterwards and hanged him.

Portland, Me., U.S.A., first settled, 1632. Capital of Maine, 1820–31.

Portland Vase recovered from a tomb in the seventeenth century; bought by Sir William Hamilton from the Barbarini family, 1770, and sold by him to the Duchess of P., who lent it to the British Museum, 1810. Broken by a maniac, 1845, but repaired. Auctioned by the Duke of P., 1929, but withdrawn. Sold to the British Museum, 1946.

Port of London Authority set up under the P. of L. Act, 1908. Revised, 1975.

Porto Bello, Panama, built on site of earlier settlement called Nombre de Dios (1502), which was sacked by Drake, 1572. P.B. was built, 1584, and sacked by Henry Morgan, 1668, and John Spring, 1680. Captured by the English for the last time, 1739.

Port Royal des Champs (France). Convent founded, 1204, by Mahaut de Montmorency. It became a Bernardine house with the privilege of receiving laity desiring retirement. The nuns moved to Paris, leaving P.R. to the lay community, 1626. Schools founded, 1643. The house supported the Jansenists (*q.v.*). Some nuns returned, 1648. Schools suppressed by royal order, 1660. Society reconstituted under the 'Peace of Clement IX', 1669. Angélique Arnauld (1624–84) abbess, 1678. On Louis XIV's suppression of Jansenism the nuns were dispersed and the buildings demolished, 1709.

Portsmouth. Granted its first charter, 1194. Importance as a naval dockyard dates from *c.* 1545. Became seat of a diocese, 1924, and a city, 1926. Scene of the assassination of the Duke of Buckingham, 1628, and the marriage of Charles II to Catherine of Braganza, 1662.

Portugal. Conquered by Carthaginians under Hamilcar Barca, 241–230 B.C. By Romans, 193–178 B.C. Lusitanian revolt, 154–150 B.C. Rebellion of Viriatus, 146–139 B.C.; of Sertorius,

80–72 B.C. First mention of Christianity, A.D. 250. Invasion of Goths, Alans, and Vandals, 409–10. Swabian kingdom established in N.P., 410–29. Oporto sacked by Visigoths, 456. Swabian kingdom incorporated in Visigothic kingdom by Leovigild, 585. Visigoths converted to Christianity, 586–610. Collapse of Visigothic kingdom in the Moorish invasion, 710–12. Moors conquer P., 712–16. Ommayad rule established, 755. Christian reconquest begun *c.* 747. Rise of the Cordoban monarchy, 796–812. Viking raids, 844–60. Battle of Simancas, 939. P. overrun by Almanzor, 987–8. Viking raids under St. Olav, 1017. Christian conquest of Coimbra, 1064. Henry of Burgundy first Count of P., 1095. Portuguese independence from Leon established at, by Alfonso Henrique at battle of São Mamede, 1128. He wins great victory over Moors at Ovrique, and takes title of king, 1139. Anglo-Portuguese conquest of Lisbon, 1147. Almohade (*q.v.*) invasion, 1191. Quarrel with the Church and deposition of Sancho II, 1248. Moors finally driven out, 1249. Treaty of Badajoz with Castile, 1267. Treaty of Alcañices, 1297. Victory with Castilians over the Moors at the battle of the Salado, 1340. Ines de Castro, mistress of Pedro, the heir to the throne, murdered by Coelho, 7 Jan. 1355. Civil war ensues, 1355–7. Castilian War, 1369. Burgundian dynasty ends, 1383. John of Avis made regent, Nov. 1383. Proclaimed king, 6 Apr. 1385. Castilians decisively defeated at battle of Aljubarrota, 14 Aug. 1385. Anglo-Portuguese Alliance at Treaty of Windsor, 9 May 1386. Peace with Castile, Oct. 1411. Capture of Ceuta, 1415. Final peace with Castile at Treaty of Medina del Campo, 1431. Trading stations established on African coast, 1448–9. Tangier captured, 1471. Bartholomew Dias rounds the Cape of Good Hope, 1488. Treaty of Tordesilhas fixes Spanish and Portuguese spheres of discovery, 7 June, 1494. Legal reforms of Manoel I, 1498–21. Vasco da Gama reaches India, 1498. Cabral discovers Brazil, 22

Apr. 1500. Trading empire established in Indian Ocean, 1501–08. Goa made capital of Portuguese India by Albuquerque, 1510. Inquisition introduced, 1536. Loss of most of the N. African possessions at battle of Alcazar-Kebir, 1578. End of the house of Avis, 28 Jan. 1580. P. seized by Philip II of Spain, June 1580. Dutch and British reduce most of the Far Eastern possessions, 1595–1620. Independence re-established by John IV, 1 Dec. 1640. Anglo-Portuguese Treaty, 1654. Catherine of Braganza marries Charles II of England, and Bombay becomes British, 25 Apr. 1662. Castelo Melhors palace revolution, 1662. The Methuen Treaty (*q.v.*), 1703. P. enters the War of Spanish Succession (*q.v.*), 1703. Absolute government established, 1706. Lisbon earthquake, 1 Nov. 1755. War with Spain, Feb.–June 1801. French invasion, 1807; royal family fled to Brazil. Sir Arthur Wellesley arrived at Oporto, July 1808 (*see* PENINSULAR WAR). Masséna defeated by British and Portuguese, at Busaco, 27 Sept. 1810. Wellington at Torres Vedras, Oct. 1810. Retreat of Masséna, defeated at Fuentes de Oñoro, 5 May 1811. Popular rising began at Oporto, 29 Aug. 1820. Inquisition abolished. Brazil independent, 1822. Dom Miguel, absolutist regent, proclaimed king, 4 July 1828. Capitulation of Miguel at Evora, 26 May 1834. Constitution of 1822 revived after Sept. *coup d'état*, 1836. Further revolutions, 1846 and 1851. Assassination of Carlos I, 1 Feb. 1908; revolution, 1910; de Arriaga first president of republic, 1911. P. joins World War I on Allied side, 1916. Salazar becomes finance minister, 1928 and prime minister with dictatorial powers, 1932. P. neutral during World War II but in 1943 signed agreement with Allies for use of Azores against Germans. Joined N.A.T.O., 1949. Discontent with Salazar regime and colonial unrest increased from 1960s. In 1961 India absorbed Goa (*q.v.*). Gaetano replaced Salazar, 1968. Military coup, 1974, resulted in brief neo-Communist regime in P. and independence for P.'s former colonies. Leftwing policies largely reversed by 1979. P. to join the E.E.C. on 1 Jan. 1986. See also ANGOLA: MOZAMBIQUE: GOA.

The following is a list of prominent Portuguese authors:

Alcoforado, Marianna, 1640–1723, author of *Letters of a Portuguese Nun.*

Barros, João de, 1496 ?–1570, historian.

Bocage, Manuel Maria Barbosa de, 1765–1805, poet.

Braga, Joaquim Theophilo, 1843–1924, historian and poet.

Camoens, Luis de, 1524–80, poet.

Castello Branco, Camillo de, Viscount, 1825–90, novelist and dramatist.

Castilho, Antonio Feliciano de, Viscount, 1800–75, poet.

Castro, Eugenio de, 1869–1944, poet.

Deus, João de, 1830–96, poet.

Ferreira, Antonio, 1528–69, poet and dramatist.

Garrett, João Baptista da Silva Leitão de Almeida, Viscount, 1799–1854, poet, dramatist, and novelist.

Goes, Damião de, 1502–74, historian.

Herculano de Carvalho e Araujo, Alexandre, 1810–79, historian and poet.

Lopez, Fernão, 1380 ?–1460 ?, chronicler.

Macedo, José Agostinho de, 1761–1831, poet.

Nascimento, Francisco Manoel de, 1734–1819, poet.

Oliveira Martins, Joaquim Pedro de, 1845–94, historian.

Pascoais, Teixeira de, 1877–1952, poet.

Pinto, Fernão Mendes, 1509–83, adventurer.

Queiroz, José Maria Eça de, 1843–1900, novelist.

Resende, Garcia de, 1470–1536, poet.

Sá de Miranda, Francisco de, 1485?–1558, poet and dramatist.

Vicente, Gil, 1465 ?–1536 ?, dramatist.

Kings of Portugal, 1139–1910:
Burgundian Dynasty:
  Alfonso I 1139–1185
  Sancho I 1185–1211
  Alfonso II the Fat 1211–1223
  Sancho II 1223–1248
  Alfonso III 1248–1279
  Diniz 1279–1325

  Alfonso IV 1325–1357
  Pedro I the Cruel 1357–1367
  Ferdinand 1367–1383
Civil War
Aviz Dynasty:
  John I 1385–1433
  Edward 1433–1438
  Alfonso V the African 1438–1481
  John II 1481–1495
  Manoel I 1495–1521
  John III 1521–1557
  Sebastian 1557–1578
  Henry 1578–1580
Under Spanish Suzerainty *1581–1640
Braganza Dynasty:
  John IV 1640–1656
  Alfonso VI 1656–1683
  Pedro II 1683–1706
  John V 1706–1750
  Joseph 1750–1777
  Pedro III 1777–1786
  Maria I the Mad 1777–1816
  John VI 1816–1826
  Pedro IV 1826
  Maria II 1826–1828
  Miguel 1828–1834
  Maria II (again) 1834–1853
  Pedro V 1853–1861
  Luiz I 1861–1889
  Carlos I 1889–1908
  Manoel II (*d.* in exile in England, 1932) 1908–1910
Presidents of the Republic:
  Manoel de Arriaga 1911–1915
  Teofilo Braga May–Oct. 1915
  Bernardino Machado 1915–1917
  Sidonio Paez 1917–1918
  Admiral de Canto e Castro 1918–1919
  Antonio de Almeida 1919–1923
  Manuel Gomes 1923–1925
  Bernardino Machado 1925–1926
  Marshal Antonio Carmona 1926–1951
  Marshal Francisco Higino Craveiro Lopez 1951–1958
  Rear-Admiral Americo de Deus Rodrigues Tomas 1958–1974
  General Antonio de Spinola, 1974
  General Antonio Ramalho Eanes, 1974–

* *See* Spanish kings, Philip II, III, and IV.

Positive Rays discovered, 1886, by Goldstein.

Post Office (Britain). The first English postmaster of whom there is any account is Sir Brian Tuke, mentioned *c.* 1533; in 1619 Matthew de Quester was appointed 'Postmaster-General of England for foreign parts'; new postal system organized by the Common Council of London, 1649; rates of postage and rights and duties of postmasters settled by Parliament, 1657 Act for erecting and establishing a P.O. passed, 1660. *Penny Post* instituted in London and suburbs by William Dockwra, 1680; annexed to the crown revenues department, 1690; new Penny Postage Law introduced through exertions of Rowland Hill, 1839; adhesive stamps invented by James Chalmers, 1834, first issue, 6 May 1840; new general P.O. at St. Martin's-le-Grand opened, 1830; extensions, 1873, 1891; public office removed to King Edward Street, 1910. Pillar boxes first erected (at St. Helier, Jersey), 1852. The red cylindrical pattern generally adopted, 1876. Biggest robbery suffered by the P.O. took place in a hold-up of the Glasgow-London mail train in Buckinghamshire, Aug. 1963, when over £2,500,000 was stolen. P.O. reorganized as a public corporation, under the P.O. Act, 1969. Telecommunications Act, 1981, separated telecommunications from the P.O. and estab. British Telecom (*q.v.*).

Post Office Savings Bank. *See* NATIONAL SAVINGS BANK.

Potassium. First isolated by Davy in 1807.

Potato introduced into Britain from America by Sir Walter Raleigh in sixteenth century. Crop failure caused famine in Ireland, 1846–9.

Potsdam Agreement, result of conference between Churchill, Attlee, Truman, and Stalin at P., 16 July–1 Aug. 1945.

Poynings' Law. Called after Sir Edward P. (1459–1521), lord-deputy of Ireland; passed, 13 Sept. 1494; this law made the Irish legislature subordinate to and completely dependent on the English Privy Council. Repealed, Apr. 1782.

Poznan (Pol.) or **Posen** (Ger.). Town known as the seat of an episcopal see from 968, which became fused with that of Gniezno in the twelfth century. Ceded to Prussia in first and second partitions of 1772 and 1793 (*see* POLAND). Assigned to Poland by Treaty of Versailles, 1919. Annexed by Germany, Sept. 1939. Reassigned to Poland, 1945.

Praemunire, Statutes of, passed, 1353 and 1392, for the purpose of restricting papal authority in England.

Praetorian Guard, regular but extra-legionary cohorts, nine of which were raised by Augustus, 2 B.C. Their barracks NE. of the Palatine at Rome were laid out in the reign of Tiberius (A.D. 14–37). The corps was disbanded by Constantine, 312.

Pragmatic Sanctions.
1. 1385. Against papal interference in the French Church.
2. Of Bourges, 1438, imposed limits on papal authority in France; temporarily annulled, 1461.
3. 1713. Securing the succession of Maria Theresa to the Austrian lands. Ratified by Prussia, 1728. By majority of other German states, 1735. Prussia's disregard of the P.S. caused the War of the Austrian Succession (*q.v.*).
4. Of Naples, 1759, when Charles II of Spain made Naples over to his third son.

Prague, Czechoslovakia. Founded *c.* 600. Became a bishopric, 973. Rebuilt by Charles IV, 1348. Captured by Swedes, 1648. By French, 1741. By Prussians, 1744. Treaty of P. ended Austro-Prussian War, 23 Aug. 1866. Germans seized P., 15 Mar. 1939. Liberated, 10 May 1945.

Prayer, Book of Common. First P.B. of Edward VI, 1549; second P.B. of Edward VI, 1552. Revised, 1559; suppressed, 1645; restored, 1660; and revised, 1662. A further revision, completed 1927, was placed before Parliament, passed by the Lords, but rejected by the Commons. Sev. revisions (known as 'Series 2, 3,' etc.) since 1960s. *And see* PROTESTANT EPISCOPAL CHURCH.

Preference, Imperial. I.P. on articles produced in and consigned from the

British Empire instituted by Finance Act, 1919; extended by Finance Acts, 1925 and 1926. After World War II Commonwealth development and especially Brit. entry into the European Economic Community (*q.v.*), meant the eventual dismantling of I.P. *See also* TARIFFS.

Premium Bonds. Form of government savings lottery introduced by Harold Macmillan, then Chancellor of the Exchequer, in the Budget of 1956.

Premonstratensians. Order founded by St. Norbert *c.* 1120, and following the Augustinian Rule.

Pre-Raphaelite School of Painting. Founded *c.* 1850 by John Everett Millais (1829–96), William Hunt (1827–1910), Dante Gabriel Rossetti (1828–82).

President of the Council, Lord. Became a political office, 1680.

Press Association, The. Founded, 1868. *See also* REUTERS NEWS.

Press Council, estab. 1953 on the recommendation of the Royal Commission on the Press, 1947–9. Its constitution was radically amended, 1963.

Pretoria. Founded, 1855, by Marthinus Wessels Pretorius (1819–1901). Became capital of Transvaal (*q.v.*), 1860. Surrendered to Lord Roberts, 1900. Became administrative capital of S. Africa, 1909. University founded, 1930.

Prices and Incomes, National Board of, established, 1965, and merged with the Monopolies Commission, 1969.

Pride's Purge. The name given to the expulsion and arrest of certain members of Parliament who opposed the trial of Charles I. Col. Pride, at the head of two parliamentary regiments, on 6 Dec. 1648, effected the 'purge'.

Prime Minister. This office existed in England, *de facto*, from 1710, but its existence was first officially recognized and its holder given a definite precedence, 1905. A deputy P.M. was officially named for the first time, 13 June 1962.

Prime Ministers (British), (since the beginning of the modern cabinet system). Sir Robert Walpole, 1721.

George II:
Sir Robert Walpole, 1727.

John Carteret, Lord Carteret, Feb. 1742.
Hon. Henry Pelham, Nov. 1743.
William Pulteney, Earl of Bath, 10–12 Feb. 1746.
Hon. Henry Pelham, Feb. 1746.
Thomas Pelham Holles, Duke of Newcastle, Apr. 1754.
William Pitt, Nov. 1756.
Thomas Pelham Holles, Duke of Newcastle and William Pitt as Secretary of State, known as the Coalition Ministry, 19 June 1757.

George III:
Thomas Pelham Holles, Duke of Newcastle, 1760.
Earl of Bute, May 1762.
George Grenville, Apr. 1763.
Marquess of Rockingham, July 1765.
William Pitt, Earl of Chatham, Aug. 1766.
Duke of Grafton, Dec. 1767.
Frederick, Lord North, Jan. 1770.
Marquess of Rockingham, Mar. 1782.
Earl of Shelburne, July 1782.
Duke of Portland, Lord North, and Charles James Fox, known as Coalition Ministry, Apr. 1783.
William Pitt, the Younger, Dec. 1783.
Henry Addington, Mar. 1801.
William Pitt, May 1804.
Lord Grenville ('All the Talents' Ministry), Feb. 1806.
Duke of Portland, Mar. 1807.
Spencer Perceval, Oct. 1809.
Earl of Liverpool, June, 1812.

George IV:
Earl of Liverpool, Jan. 1820.
George Canning, Apr. 1827.
Visc. Goderich, Sept. 1827.
Duke of Wellington, Jan. 1828.

William IV:
Earl Grey, Nov. 1830.
Visc. Melbourne, July 1834.
Provisional government during absence of Sir Robert Peel, Nov. 1834.
Sir Robert Peel, Dec. 1834.
Visc. Melbourne, Apr. 1835.

Victoria:
Visc. Melbourne, June 1837.
Sir Robert Peel, Sept. 1841.
Lord John Russell, July 1846.

Earl of Derby, Feb. 1852.
Earl of Aberdeen, Dec. 1852.
Visc. Palmerston, Feb. 1855.
Earl of Derby, Feb. 1858.
Visc. Palmerston, June 1859.
Lord John Russell, Oct. 1865.
Earl of Derby, June 1866.
Benjamin Disraeli, Feb. 1868.
William Ewart Gladstone, Dec. 1868.
Benjamin Disraeli, Earl of Beacons-
field, Feb. 1874.
William Ewart Gladstone, Apr. 1880.
Marquess of Salisbury, June 1885.
William Ewart Gladstone, Feb. 1886.
Marquess of Salisbury, July 1886.
William Ewart Gladstone, Aug. 1892.
(Gladstone resigned Mar. 1894),
succeeded by Earl of Rosebery.
Marquess of Salisbury, June 1895.
Edward VII:
Arthur James Balfour, 12 July 1902.
Sir Henry Campbell-Bannerman, 5
Dec. 1905.
Herbert Henry Asquith, 16 Apr. 1908.
George V:
Herbert Henry Asquith, Dec. 1910.
David Lloyd George, 7 Dec. 1916.
Andrew Bonar Law, 23 Oct. 1922.
Stanley Baldwin, 22 May 1923.
James Ramsay MacDonald, 22 Jan.
1924.
Stanley Baldwin, 4 Nov. 1924.
James Ramsay MacDonald, 8 June
1929.
James Ramsay MacDonald, 24 Aug.
1931.
Stanley Baldwin, 6 June 1935.
Edward VIII:
Stanley Baldwin, 22 Jan. 1936.
George VI:
Stanley Baldwin, 4 Dec. 1936.
Arthur Neville Chamberlain, 28 May
1937.
Winston Spencer Churchill
(Coalition), 10 May 1940.
Winston Spencer Churchill (without
Labour Party), 26 May 1945.
Clement Richard Attlee, 27 July 1945.
Clement Richard Attlee, 23 Feb. 1950.
Winston Spencer Churchill, 25 Oct.
1951.
Elizabeth II;
Winston Spencer Churchill, 8 Feb.
1952.

Anthony Eden, 7 Apr. 1955.
Harold Macmillan, 13 Jan. 1957.
Sir Alec Douglas-Home (formerly 14th
Earl of Home), 19 Oct. 1963.
Harold Wilson, 16 Oct. 1964.
Harold Wilson, 31 March 1966.
Edward Heath, 19 June 1970.
Harold Wilson, 12 Mar. 1974.
James Callaghan, 5 April 1976.
Margaret Thatcher, 4 May 1979.
Margaret Thatcher, 9 June 1983.

Prime Ministers' Meetings have, since 1937, superseded the **Imperial Conference** (*q.v.*). Since 1944 these have taken place at irregular intervals, whenever the occasion demanded.

Primitive Methodism. *See* METHODISTS.

Primrose League. Conservative association founded, 1883, in memory of Disraeli.

Prince Edward Island, Canada. Discovered by Cabot, 1497; possessed by French, 1603; captured by Great Britain from French, 1758; admitted to Dominion of Canada, 1873.

Princeton. University founded, 1746. Moved from Elizabethtown to P., 1756.

Printing, Origins of. Practised by the Chinese in very early times (*see* ENGRAVING); the origin of the European system seems to be very doubtful, though recent evidence points not to Gutenberg (1397–1468), once accepted as the first printer from movable type, but to Laurens Coster of Haarlem, who printed from wood blocks in 1440. Gutenberg, however, appears to have been the first European to make a practical business of P. from movable types.

Privateering. *See* LETTERS OF MARQUE.

Privy Council (England). By an Act passed, May 1612, P. Councillors took precedence after Knights of the Garter; dissolved on the demise of the crown; in 1679 the council was remodelled and the P. Councillors by this Act held office for six months after the sovereign's death. (*See* COUNCIL.) The whole P.C. has not met except at an accession since 1839, when Queen Victoria's impending marriage was declared in Council.

Prize Money originated in England before 1243. Paid for the last time in the Royal Navy, 1945.

Probate Court established under the Court of Probate Act, 1857, and merged with the Supreme Court, 1875.

Probation for first offenders first introduced in Massachusetts, 1878. Became legally recognized in England under the Probation of Offenders Act, 1907.

Production, Ministry of, set up, 1942. Merged with Board of Trade (*q.v.*), 1945.

Profiteering. Act to check excessive profits passed, Aug. 1919. Attempts to stop P. during World War II by Prices of Goods Act, 1939, and the Goods and Services (Price Control) Act, 1941.

Profits Tax. First introduced as a temporary tax, and called the National Defence Contribution, by Neville Chamberlain, 1937.

Prohibition. Scottish Temperance Act, 1920, resulted in some local P. P. introduced in Sweden, 1922, and in modified form in Norway, 1922. Abolished in Finland, 1932, in Norway, 1946, in Sweden, 1955. P. in America lasted from 1920 until 1933. P. in theory virtually total in India from 1950 onwards but not in practice: but in force in such Moslem countries as Saudi Arabia, Libya, Pakistan and Iran. *See* U.S.A., CONSTITUTION OF.

Promenade Concerts, first given in Queen's Hall, 10 Aug. 1895, and continued there until the hall's destruction by bombing, 1941. Since then held in the Albert Hall.

Propaganda or **De Propaganda Fide.** An institution of the Roman Catholic Church at Rome, founded for the propagation of the Roman Catholic faith originally by Pope Gregory XIII (1572–84), but more fully developed by Gregory XV, 1622.

Propaganda, Ministry of. Established in Germany under Goebbels, 1936–45.

Propagation of the Gospel, Society for, founded by royal charter, 1701.

Protectorates, British (some of which have since had a change of name and all of status). Basutoland,* 1868; Bechuanaland,* 1895; Brunei, 1888; Johore, 1914; Malay States, Federated

* [Nominally not P., but High Commission Territories.]

(Perak, Selangor, Pahang, Negri Sembilan), 1874; Malay States, Unfederated (Kedan, Perlis, Kelantan, Trengganu), 1909; N. Borneo, 1881: Nyasaland, 1891 (called British Central Africa until 1907); Solomon Islands, 1893; Somaliland, 1884; Swaziland, 1890; Tonga Island, 1899; Uganda, 1894; Zanzibar, 1890.

Protestant Episcopal Church. American form of Anglicanism, introduced into Virginia, 1607. Movement for union of all its American branches began *c.* 1784. Its first bishop (of New York) consecrated *in London*, 1786.

Protestantism. *See* REFORMATION.

Provençal and Catalan Writers.

Aldobrandini of Florence, Provençal (Italian), thirteenth century.

Anellier, Guillaume, Provençal, *fl. c.* 1280.

Aribau, Carlos, Catalan, 1798–1862.

Bernard of Ventadour, Provençal, mid twelfth century.

Bertan de Born, Provençal, *c.* 1170–1200.

Brueys, Claude, Provençal, 1570–1650.

Brunetto Latini, Provençal (Italian), thirteenth century.

Carner, José, Catalan, *b.* 1554.

Cortete, Fançois de, Provençal, 1571–1655.

Costa y Llebera, Miguel, Catalan, 1854–1922.

Daniel, Arnaut, Provençal, late twelfth century.

Favre, Abbé, Provençal, 1729–83.

Folquet of Marseilles, Provençal, *c.* 1150–1231.

Gaillard, Augor, Provençal, 1530–95.

Ganas, Gaston Pey de, Provençal, *fl.* 1565.

Ganulin, Faidit, Provençal, late twelfth century.

Girant of Borneil, Provençal, twelfth century.

Goudelin, Pierre, Provençal, 1579–1649.

Guimerá, Angel, Catalan, 1849–1924.

Iglesias, Ignacio, Catalan, 1871–1928.

Lull, Ramon, Catalan, *c.* 1235–1315.

Maragall, Juan, Catalan, 1860–1911.

Marcubru, Provençal, *fl.* 1140.

March, Ausias, Catalan, 1379–1459.

Metge, Bernat, Catalan, ? 1350–after 1410.

Mila y Fontanals, Manuel, Catalan, 1818–84.

Mistral, Frédéric, Provençal, 1830–1914.

Mutaner, Ramon, Catalan, 1265–1336.

Peter of Auvergne, Provençal, twelfth century.

Rigaud, Auguste, Provençal, 1760–1835.

San Jordi, Jordi de, Catalan, end fourteenth century–before 1430.

Satoly, Nicholas, Provençal, 1614–75.

Verdagner, Mosén Jacinto, Catalan, 1845–1902.

Vidal de Besalù, Raimon, Provençal, mid twelfth-early thirteenth century.

Vidal of Toulouse, Peire, late twelfth century.

William IX, count of Poitiers, Provençal, eleventh century.

Provisors, Statute of, passed 1350, to prevent papal pretensions to the disposition of ecclesiastical benefices in England.

Prussia. *See* BRANDENBURG. Albert of Hohenzollern, Grand Master of the Teutonic Knights, converts P. into a secular duchy, 1525. Treaties of mutual succession with Silesia, 1537. Pomerania, 1571. Arrangement of Gera, 1599. P. comes under Brandenburg as a Polish fief, 1618. Poland renounces suzerainty at Treaty of Wehlau, 1657. Defeat of Swedes at Fehrbellin, 1675. Frederick of Brandenburg crowned king of P., 18 Jan. 1701. By Treaty of Stockholm with Sweden acquires W. Pomerania, 1720. P. guarantees Pragmatic Sanction (*q.v.*), 1728. Frederick the Great invades Silesia, 1740. Obtains Silesia by Treaty of Berlin, 1742. Second Silesian War, 1744–6. Treaty of Aix-la-Chapelle, 1748. Frederick invades Saxony and starts the Seven Years War, 1756–63. Austria finally recognizes Prussian acquisition of Silesia at Treaty of Hubertusburg, 1763. First Partition of Poland, 1772. Second Partition of Poland, 1793. Third Partition of Poland, 1795. Joins Northern Confederacy against Britain, 1800. Occupies Hanover, 1801. Defeated by Napoleon at Jena and Auerstädt, 1806. Congress of Vienna gave P. large additions in Rhineland and Saxony, 1815. Organizes the Zollverein (*q.v.*) 1818 onwards.

War with Denmark, 1848. Convention of Olmütz, 1850. Austro-Prussian attack on Denmark, 1864. Austro-Prussian War, 16 June–26 July 1866. Franco-Prussian War, 19 July 1870. King William I proclaimed German Emperor at Versailles, 18 Jan. 1871. (*See* GERMANY.) Proclaimed a republic, 9 Nov. 1918. Nazis take over by force, 20 July 1932. P. liquidated by Allied Control Council, Feb. 1946. Of the territory called P. at its greatest extent, E.P. was joined to Russia in 1945, W.P. (Pomerelia) to Poland at the same date.

Kings of Prussia:
Frederick I 1701–1713
Frederick William I 1713–1740
Frederick II 1740–1786
Frederick William II 1786–1797
Frederick William III 1797–1840
Frederick William IV 1840–1861
William I (became German Emperor, 1871) 1861–1888

Public Debt. *See* NATIONAL DEBT.

Public Health Acts in England and Wales passed 1848, 1875, 1936, and 1961.

Public Lending Right Act, giving authors revenue from the borrowing of their books in libraries, in operation from Sept. 1982.

Public Order Act, banning political uniforms, etc., passed, 1936. Fell into desuetude but revived against both right- and left-wing extremist groups since the 1960s.

Public Prosecutor. Office separated from that of Solicitor to the Treasury, 1908, and known as the **Director of Public Prosecutions**.

Public Schools (British). First P.S. said to have been St. Peter's, York, founded by Alcuin in 627. Sev. subsequently wealthy foundations, e.g. Eton and Harrow (*qq.v.*), began as charitable schools for poor scholars. For principal P.S. *see under* separate entries, e.g. CHARTERHOUSE, MERCHANT TAYLORS', etc.

Public Trustee office opened, 1908, under Official Trustee Act, 1906.

Public Works Loan Board created, 1817. Regulated by P.W.L. Acts since 1875.

Puerto Rico, formerly **Porto Rico**, discovered by Columbus, 1493; explored by Ponce de Léon, 1508. Ceded to U.S.A. by Spain, 1898. Constitution established by 'Jones Act', 1917; amended, 1947. Governor elected quadrennially, from 1948. Considerable emigration to U.S. mainland since 1930. 'Commonwealth status' since 1952.

Pullman Coaches. Invented by G. M. P. of New York (1831–97). First car built, 1849.

Punjab. Invaded by Alexander the Great, 326 B.C. Devastated by Genghiz Khan, A.D. 1221. Ruled by Mogul emperors, 1556–1707. Sikh kingdom under Ranjit Singh, 1799–1820. *See* SIKHS. War against the British, 1845 and 1848–9, who annexed P., 1849. Lieutenant-Governor appointed, 1859. Severe plagues between 1896 and 1910. Provincial autonomy introduced, 1937. Communal rioting began, Mar. 1947. Partitioned between India and Pakistan, 14 Aug. 1947, into E. and W.P.. Serious unrest among Punjabi separatists in 1980 s led to Indian gov. sending the army in to the Golden Temple at Amritsar, 1984, and subsequent assassination of Mrs Gandhi by Sikhs.

Purchase Tax imposed first by the Finance Act, 1940. Came into effect, 21 Oct. 1940. Replaced by **Value Added Tax** (*q.v.*), 1973.

Puritans. Name first derisively given to Anglicans who, between 1564 and 1569, wished to purge the established ecclesiastical system from so-called popish abuses. Earliest P. thus a party within the established Church. In the later seventeenth century the term came to be applied to dissenters outside the Church of England, e.g. Congregationalists, Baptists, Quakers, etc.

Pythian Games, originally held every nine, later every four, years. Regulated by Amphictyonic Council after 586 B.C. Coincided with the third year of each Olympiad (*see under* OLYMPIA). Laurel wreath first awarded to victor, 582.

Q

Qatar, state in the Persian Gulf; its relations with Britain governed by the treaty of 3 Nov. 1916, until it achieved full independence on 3 Sept. 1971.

Quadi, a tribe living to the E. of the Marcomanni, and classified by Latin writers as 'Suevi', i.e. nomadic Germans. They rebelled against Rome, A.D. 167, and again, 171, but were finally crushed, 173.

Quadrille.
1. Country dance of French origin, introduced into England, 1818.
2. Card game, became fashionable in England *c.* 1726, and remained so until the introduction of whist (*q.v.*) into upper-class families.

Quadruple Alliance.
1. England, France, Austria, Holland, 1718.
2. Britain, France, Portugal, and Spain, 1834.

Quakers or **Society of Friends.** Founded by George Fox between 1647 and 1666; the name 'Quaker' was given to the sect by Mr. Justice Bennet, 1650, who was admonished by Fox to tremble at the word of the Lord; first meeting- house was opened in London, 1650. Q. in America, 1656. Their 'affirmation of the truth' was declared by Act of Parliament to be sufficient in place of the usual oaths in courts of justice, 1696; and for municipal offices, 1828 and 1837. Nobel Peace Prize awarded jointly to the American Friends' Service Committee and the Friends' Service Council, in recognition of Quaker work for international reconciliation, 1947.

Quantum Theory. First expounded by Max Planck, 1900. Applied by Niels Bohr, 1913, to gases and the frequency of light emitted. New Q.T. evolved by de Broglie, 1924.

Quarter Sessions. Established, 1363. Regulated, 1831. Abolished 1972.

'Quarterly Review.' First published by John Murray to counteract the Whig *Edinburgh Review*, Feb. 1809. Ceased publication, 1967.

Quebec, Canada. Town and province. Town founded by Champlain, 1608; captured by Britain, 1629; restored to France, 1632; finally captured by British under Gen. Wolfe, 13 Sept. 1759; formally ceded to Britain by Treaty of Paris, 1763; the 'Quebec Act' of 1774 gave the French-Canadians the right to exercise their customs, laws, and religion. Province united with Ontario, 1841. Separated and made a province of the new dominion, 1867. Boundary extended, 1912. Separatism became a political force after 1945: a separatist provincial govt. ('*parti québecois*') was in power in 1985.

Queen Anne's Bounty. Instituted in 1703 for the relief of the poor clergy. Queen Anne devoted the funds arising from first-fruits and tithes which were at her disposal to this object. United with the Ecclesiastical Commissioners, 1947, since when functions of both bodies have been exercised by the Church Commissioners.

Queen Charlotte Island. *See* BRITISH COLUMBIA.

Queen Mary Land, in Antarctica, was discovered by the Australasian Antarctic Expedition of 1911–14. The Shackleton expedition took possession of Q. M. L. for the British crown, 1912.

Queen Mary's Army Auxiliary Corps. Formed, 1917. Disbanded, 1920.

Queen Maud Land, in Antarctica, is Norwegian territory, with effect from 14 Jan. 1939. The Anglo-Scandinavian Antarctic expedition was based there, 1949–51.

Queen Victoria Memorial (Buckingham Palace). Unveiled, 16 May 1911.

Queensberry Plot. In Mar. 1703 a pardon was granted to the Jacobites who would take the oath to Queen Anne; Lord Lovat took advantage of the pardon, but his name was forged to a letter which would have led to disgrace and perhaps death; the fraud was discovered, and the Duke of Q., who was a party, had to resign his office as High Commissioner.

Queensberry Rules of boxing drawn up by eighth Marquess of Q., 1867.

Queensferry was the site of the earliest bishopric in Scotland from 681 to 685.

Queensland, Australia. Visited by Captain Cook, 1770. Explored, 1823. Divided from New. S. Wales, 1859.

Queens of England.   *See*   ENGLISH SOVEREIGNS AND CONSORTS.

Quetta, Pakistan. British Residency established at, 1876. Disastrous earthquake, 31 May 1935.

Quia Emptores, a statute passed in 1290 to stop the practice of subinfeudation.

Quintuple Treaty, guaranteeing Belgian integrity, signed by Austria, France, Great Britain, Russia, and Prussia, 1839.

Quisling, term synonymous with traitor, derived from the Norwegian Nazi Vidkun Quisling, *b.* 1887; puppet-ruler 1940–5; executed 1945.

Quoits originated in the fifteenth century. Still played in Scotland and N. England.

R

R.101. *See* AIRSHIPS.

Race Relations Acts. The Acts of 1965 and 1968 have been repealed and replaced by the Act of 1976.

Racial Equality, Commission for, estab. 1977, under the Race Relations Act of 1976. It replaced the Community Relations Commission (*q.v.*).

Rack. This instrument of torture is thought to have been introduced into England by John Holland, Duke of Exeter (1352–1400). Its use was declared illegal in 1628.

Radar (for **Radio Detection and Ranging**). The principle—that of reflected short range wireless waves—became generally known shortly after 1920. The Appleton Layer from which waves are reflected was discovered in 1928. Sir Robert Watson-Watt projected aircraft detection apparatus, 1935, and first R. station in world set up in Britain. Belt of coastal systems almost complete in 1939. Germans captured intact Coastal Command anti-submarine R. set, 1942, enabling U-Boats to carry counter-device which was defeated, 1943, by new shorter-wave detection beam carried in aircraft.

Radcliffe College (Cambridge, Mass., U.S.A.). A college for women, founded 1878, and part of Harvard University; named after Annie R., the first woman who left money to Harvard University.

Radiation. Theory first developed by Max Planck (1858–1947), 1900.

Radical. The word applied to a political party was probably originated in a speech by Charles J. Fox in 1797, when he referred to the necessity for 'R. reform'.

Radioactivity discovered, 1896, by Henri Becquerel (1852–1908).

Radiometer invented, 1873–6, by Sir W. Crookes.

Radium. Marie Curie's investigations, on her taking the principle of radioactivity as subject for her doctorate degree, led her and her husband (1859–1906) to the discovery, in 1898, of R. Its burning effect on human tissue accidentally discovered by Becquerel, 1901; and a 'Laboratoire biologique du R.' was established in Paris in 1906; similar laboratory in London in 1909. Mme Curie (1867–1934) and André Debierne isolated metallic R. from its chloride in 1910.

Ragged Schools, first opened in Portsmouth, 1820. R.S. Union founded, 1844, by Earl of Shaftesbury (then Lord Ashley). Discontinued after the Eduction Act, 1870 (*q.v.*). *And see* SUNDAY SCHOOLS.

Railways (Britain). First line opened for passenger and general traffic was Stockton–Darlington, 1825. Except for metropolitan R., grouped in four main systems: London, Midland, and Scottish; London and N. Eastern Railway; Great Western Railway; and the Southern Railway by Act of 1921 as from 1 Jan. 1923. Metropolitan systems were united under the London Passenger Transport Board as from 1 July 1933 (replaced by London Transport Executive, 1948, now (1985) London Regional Transport. All R. were nationalized by Act of 1947 as from 1 Jan. 1948, as British R. under railway executive. Beeching Reports, 1963 and 1965. Many unprofitable branch lines closed, 1963–70. *See also* ELECTRIC RAILWAY.

Rajasthan, a union of Indian states approximately the same as the former Rajputana. First nine states united, Apr. 1948. Jaipur, Jodhpur, Bikaner, and Jaisalmer then joined union, and formal inauguration celebrated, 30 Mar. 1949. Redrawing of state boundaries, 1956.

Rand. *See* TRANSVAAL, SOUTH AFRICA.

Ranelagh pleasure garden at Chelsea laid out, and wooden rotunda built, 1742. Decline set in *c.* 1788. Closed down, 1804.

Ranelagh polo club, Barnes, founded, 1894.

Rangoon, made Burmese capital, 1752, on site first inhabited, A.D. 746, near Shwe Dagon Pagoda; this building last modified in sixteenth century A.D. E. India Co. factory established, 1790. Town rebuilt, 1841. Captured by British, 1852. Captured by Japanese, 8 Mar. 1942. Reoccupied by British and Indian troops, 3 May 1945. Instrument of surrender for all imperial Japanese forces in Burma signed here, 13 Sept. 1945.

Rapallo, Treaty of.
1. Between Italy and Yugoslavia. Settled Italo-Yugoslav frontiers, Nov. 1920.
2. Between Germany and the Soviet Union, for the mutual renunciation of reparations and the re-establishment of diplomatic and economic relations, 18 Apr. 1922.

Rationing. *See* FOOD CONTROL.

Ravenna. Became seat of W. Empire, 404; conquered by Belisarius, 540, and seat of the exarchs of the E. Empire from 553 until 752, when it was sacked by the Lombards. Pepin forced the Lombard king to bestow the exarchate on the Pope, 756. Subject to Venice, 1441; again part of the papal states, 1509.

Reading, England. Danish Army under Ivar and Ubbe quartered here, 871. Abbey founded, 1121; consecrated, 1164. University College became Univ. of R., 1926.

Receiver in Bankruptcy. The Official R.'s department was established in 1914, and its administration regulated by Acts of that year, of 1926, and of 1929.

Rechabites, Independent Order of, established, 25 Aug. 1835; inspired by a Jewish sect of pastoral ascetics of the same name who *fl.* tenth century B.C.

Recife, or **Pernambuco,** Brazil. Founded, 1537. Occupied by Dutch, 1624–54, when it was recaptured by the Portuguese.

Reconstruction, Ministry of. Established 21 Aug. 1917. Wound up, May 1919.

Record Office, Public. Established in London as result of the P.R.O. Act of 1838; the publication of the Calendars of State papers was commenced in 1856. Parallel offices opened at Kew in 1970s. The Scottish R.O., in Edinburgh, dates from 1774.

Red Cross. As a result of the efforts of the Swiss Henri Dunant (1829–1910), the Geneva Conference, 1863–4, by the Convention of 1864, set up the International R.C. with its headquarters at Geneva. The British R.C. Society was founded, 1870, and incorporated, 1908. The American National R.C. was founded, 1881, and reincorporated, 1893.

Red River Settlement in the present Manitoba province was made on land sold to Thomas Douglas, the fifth earl, of Selkirk (1771–1820) by the Hudson's Bay Co., 1811. Intermittent fighting between Indians and local inhabitants, who were led by the North-West Fur Co., continued up to its amalgamation with the Hudson's Bay Co., 1821.

Red Sea Expedition, sent by Wellesley from India to expel the French from Egypt, 1800.

Redundancy Payments Act, 1965.

Reform Acts.
1. The 'Great' R. Act introduced by Lord J. Russell, 1 Mar. 1831, but defeated on amendment. Reintroduced, June 1831, but rejected by the Lords. Introduced a third time, Dec. 1831, but amended out of recognition by the Lords. Government persuaded William IV to threaten wholesale creations of peers, 15 May 1832. Passed by Lords, 4 June, and received royal assent, 7 June 1832.
2. The Second R. Act passed by Disraeli's Government, 1867, conferred household and lodger franchise in boroughs.

3. The Third R. Act by Gladstone, 1884, made household and lodger franchise uniform in U.K. It was followed by a drastic Redistribution of Seats Act, 1885. *See* REPRESENTATION OF THE PEOPLE ACTS.

Reformation. Martin Luther (1483–1546) issues the 95 Theses at Wittenberg in protest against the sale of indulgences, 31 Oct. 1517. He refuses to recant before Cardinal Cajetan at Augsburg, 12 Oct. 1518. He disputes with Eck at Leipzig, 27 June–16 July 1519. He burns papal bull of excommunication, 10 Dec. 1520. Lutherans outlawed by Edict of Worms and Luther retires to the Wartburg, May 1521. Zwingli carries out a R. in Zürich, 1519–25; killed in battle, 1531. Luther's translation of the New Testament appears, Sept. 1522. Philip of Hesse joins the R., 1523. R. in Sweden, Denmark, and Lüneburg, 1527. Henry VIII of England proclaimed Supreme Head of the Church in England, Feb. 1531. Act of Supremacy in England, 1534. Dissolution of English monasteries, 1536–9. Calvin goes to Geneva, 1536, and his movement supersedes Zwinglianism as the main Protestant force in Switzerland. Cardinal Contarini's attempt at reconciliation, 1540. Calvin organizes the Geneva Church and Knox begins R. in Scotland, 1541. Cardinal Beaton murdered in Scotland, 1546. The *Interim* of Augsburg, 15 May 1548. First English Act of Uniformity and Prayer Book, 9 June 1549. Second English Act of Uniformity and Prayer Book, Jan. 1552. Treaty of Passau annuls *Interim*, 2 Aug. 1552. Queen Mary I's counter-R. in England, 1553–8. Religious peace of Augsburg, 25 Sept. 1555. First Covenant signed in Scotland, Dec. 1557. Elizabethan Act of Supremacy, 8 May 1559. Issue of the Gallican Confession by the French Calvinists, May 1559. Scots Parliament abolishes papal jurisdiction, Aug. 1560. Knox establishes Scottish Church, 1561. Netherlands Confession of Faith, 1562. Queen Elizabeth I excommunicated, 25 Feb. 1570. Thirty-nine Articles sanctioned, 1571.

Massacre of French Protestants (St. Bartholomew). 23–4 Aug. 1572. Presbyterian system established in Scotland, 1592. Edict of Nantes grants toleration to the Huguenots, 13 Apr. 1598. Authorized Version of the Bible appears, 1611. Calvinist Synod of Dort, 1618–19.

Regency Acts (Great Britain).

1. 1751, on death of Frederick, Prince of Wales, appointing Princess of Wales regent in the event of George II's death before the Prince of Wales (i.e. George III—to be) was 18.

2. 1765, on the recovery of George III from his first attack of mental disease.

3. 1788, during the second mental attack of George III.

4. 1810, when the mind of George III finally gave way.

5. 1830, Duchess of Kent appointed regent during minority of Victoria should the latter succeed to the throne before the age of 18.

6. 1837, provided for the carrying on of the Government by lords justices in the event of the Duke of Cumberland, the heir-presumptive, being abroad.

7. 1840, on the marriage of Queen Victoria with Prince Albert; it enacted that in the event of Victoria's demise, and any child of hers succeeding to the throne under the age of 18, Prince Albert should act as regent.

8. 1910, appointed Queen Mary regent in the event of a child of George V's succeeding to the throne before the age of 18.

9. Acts providing for a regency in the event of the Sovereign dying and leaving an heir who is a minor have subsequently been passed at the beginning of the reigns of George VI and Elizabeth II, the most recent being the Act of 1953, designating the Duke of Edinburgh as regent, should a regency have arisen during the minority of Queen Elizabeth II's children.

Regent's Park, London. Laid out by John Nash for the Prince Regent, 1812. Park opened to the public, 1838.

Regicides, The. Those who tried and

condemned Charles I in 1649; the Bill of Indemnity in 1660 ordered severe penalties against the R.

Regiments of the British Army (U.K. Establishments). The following is a list of British Cavalry and Infantry R. of the line and of the Household, with the dates when they were first raised, and the numbers they bore up to 1881.

	Horse			Dragoon Guards			Dragoons
1	1661 Tangier				1	1693	Royals
2	1678	1	1746	King's	2	1691	Scots Greys
3	1685	2	1746	Queen's Bays	3	1685	King's Own
4	1685	3	1746	Prince of Wales's (3/6)*	4	1685	Queen's Own
5	1685	4	1788	(4/7)	5	1685	Disbanded, 1799
6	1685	5	1788	Inniskilling (5/6 Dragoon Guards)	6	1689	Inniskilling (5/6 Dragoon Guards)
7	1685	6	1691	Carabiniers (3/6)	7	1690	Queen's Own
8	1688	7	1788	(4/7)	8	1693	
					12	1715	

	Light Dragoons		Hussars			Lancers
3	1715	3	1859			
4	1715	4	1859			
					5	1859 Re-raised (16/5)
7	1715	7	1805			
8	1715	8	1822			
9	1715				9	1806
10	1715	10	1806			
11	1715	11	1840			
12	1768 (Prince of Wales's)				12	1806
13	1715	13	1861			
14	1715	14	1861			
15	1759	15	1806			
16	1759				16	1806 (16/5)
17	1759				17	1806 (17/21)
18	1763	18	1807			
19	1759	19	1861 Ex-East India Company's 1st, 2nd,			
20	1759	20	1861 and 3rd European Cavalry			
21	1760	21	1861		21	1896 (17/21)
22	1760 Disbanded 1799					
23	1781				23	1816 Disbanded
					27	Raised 1941

* 3rd Carabiniers from 1929.

Household Cavalry:
First Life Guards, 1660, and Second Life Guards, 1661: Amalgamated, 1922. Each became a *regiment* (not troop as before), 1788.
Horse Guards, 1661 (Ex-Cromwellian Crook's Regiment).

Foot Guards:
Scots Guards (Third Foot Guards), 1641. Totally destroyed at Worcester, 1651. Re-raised, 1661, in Scotland. On British Establishment, 1707.
Grenadiers (First Foot Guards). *Émigré* regiment raised, 1656; re-formed, 1660.

Coldstream (Second Foot Guards). Monk's Regiment (1650) entered Charles II's service, 1660.
Irish Guards, 1902.
Welsh Guards, 1915.

Infantry:

No.	Date Raised	Title in 1881
1	1633	Royal Scots.
2	1661	Queen's Royal West Surrey.
3	1665	Buffs (East Kent).
4	1680	Lancaster.
5	1685	Northumberland Fusiliers.
6	1673	Warwickshire (now Royal Warwickshire Fusiliers).

No.	Date Raised	Title in 1881	No.	Date Raised	Title in 1881
7	1685	Royal (English) Fusiliers.	51	1755	1st King's Own Yorkshire Light Infantry (*see* 105).
8	1685	King's Liverpool.			
9	1685	Norfolk.	52	1741	2nd Oxford and Bucking- hamshire Light Infantry (*see* 43).
10	1685	Lincolnshire.			
11	1685	Devon.			
12	1685	Suffolk.	53	1755	1st Shropshire Light Infantry (King's) (*see* 85).
13	1685	Somerset Light Infantry.			
14	1685	West Yorkshire.	54	1755	2nd Dorset (*see* 39).
15	1685	East Yorkshire.	55	1755	2nd Border (*see* 34).
16	1688	Bedfordshire and Hert- fordshire.	56	1755	2nd Essex (*see* 44).
			57	1755	1st Middlesex (*see* 77).
17	1688	Leicestershire.	58	1750	2nd Northamptonshire (*see* 48).
18	1684	Royal Irish.			
19	1688	The Green Howards.	59	1755	2nd East Lancashire (*see* 30).
20	1688	Lancashire Fusiliers.			
21	1678	Royal Scots Fusiliers.	60	1755	King's Royal Rifle Corps (formerly Royal Americans).
22	1689	Cheshire.			
23	1689	Royal Welch Fusiliers.			
24	1689	South Wales Borderers.	61	1756	2nd Gloucestershire (*see* 28).
25	1689	King's Own Scottish Borderers.			
			62	1757	1st Wiltshire (*see* 99).
26	1689	1st Cameronians (Scottish Rifles) (*see* 90).	63	1756	1st Manchester (*see* 96).
			64	1756	1st North Staffordshire (was 2nd/11th till 1758) (*see* 98).
27	1690	1st Inniskilling Fusiliers (*see* 108).			
28	1694	1st Gloucestershire (*see* 61).	65	1756	1st York and Lancaster (*see* 84).
29	1694	1st Worcestershire (*see* 36).	66	1756	2nd Royal Berkshire (*see* 49).
30	1702	1st East Lancashire (*see* 59).			
31	1702	1st East Surrey (*see* 70).	67	1756	2nd Hampshire (*see* 37).
32	1702	1st Duke of Cornwall's Light Infantry (*see* 46).	68	1756	1st Durham Light Infantry (*see* 106).
33	1702	1st West Riding (*see* 76).	69	1756	2nd Welch (*see* 41).
34	1702	1st Border (*see* 55).	70	1758	2nd East Surrey (*see* 31).
35	1701	1st Royal Sussex (*see* 107).	71	1766	1st Highland Light Infantry (*see* 74).
36	1701	2nd Worcestershire (*see* 29).			
			72	1778	1st Seaforth Highlanders (*see* 78).
37	1702	1st Hampshire (*see* 67).			
38	1702	1st South Staffordshire (*see* 80).	73	1786	2nd Black Watch (*see* 42).
			74	1787	2nd Highland Light Infantry (*see* 71).
39	1702	1st Dorset (*see* 54).			
40	1712	1st South Lancashire (Prince of Wales's Volunteers) (*see* 82).	75	1787	1st Gordon Highlanders (*see* 92).
			76	1787	2nd West Riding (*see* 33).
41	1719	1st Welch (*see* 69).	77	1787	2nd Middlesex (*see* 57).
42	1743?	1st Black Watch (*see* 73).	78	1793	2nd Seaforth Highlanders (*see* 72).
43	1741	1st Oxford and Bucking- hamshire Light Infantry (*see* 52).			
			79	1793	Cameron Highlanders.
44	1741	1st Essex (*see* 56).	80	1793	2nd South Staffordshire (*see* 38).
45	1740	1st Sherwood Foresters (*see* 95).	81	1793	2nd North Lancashire (*see* 47).
46	1741	2nd Duke of Cornwall's Light Infantry (*see* 32).	82	1793	2nd South Lancashire (*see* 40).
47	1741	1st North Lancashire (*see* 81).	83	1793	1st Royal Irish Rifles (*see* 86).
48	1741	1st Northamptonshire (*see* 58).	84	1793	2nd York and Lancaster (*see* 65).
49	1741	1st Royal Berkshire (*see* 66).	85	1794	2nd Shropshire Light Infantry (King's) (*see* 53).
50	1755	1st Queen's Own Royal West Kent (*see* 97).	86	1799	2nd Royal Irish Rifles (*see* 83).

No.	Date Raised	Title in 1881
87	1793	1st Royal Irish Fusiliers (see 89).
88	1793	1st Connaught Rangers (see 94).
89	1794	2nd Royal Irish Fusiliers (see 87).
90	1794	2nd Cameronians (Scottish Rifles) (see 26).
91	1794	1st Argyll and Sutherland Highlanders (see 93).
92	1794	2nd Gordon Highlanders (see 75).
93	1800	2nd Argyll and Sutherland Highlanders (see 91).
94	1800	2nd Connaught Rangers (see 88).
95	1816	2nd Sherwood Foresters (see 45).
96	1800	2nd Manchester (see 63).
97	1798	2nd Queen's Own Royal West Kent (see 50)
98	1824	2nd North Staffordshire (see 64).
99	1824	2nd Wiltshire (see 62).
100	1858	1st Leinster (see 109).
101	1861	1st Munster Fusiliers (see 104).
102	1861	1st Dublin Fusiliers (see 103).
103	1861	2nd Dublin Fusiliers (see 102).
104	1861	2nd Munster Fusiliers (see 101).
105	1861	2nd King's Own Yorkshire Light Infantry (see 51).
106	1861	2nd Durham Light Infantry (see 68).
107	1861	2nd Royal Sussex (see 35).
108	1861	2nd Inniskilling Fusiliers (see 27).
109	1861	2nd Leinster (see 100).
	1800	1st Rifle Brigade; 1805, 2nd Rifle Brigade, up to 1816 known as 1st and 2nd Battalions, 95th regt. (q.v.); 1855, 3rd Rifle Brigade; 1857, 4th Rifle Brigade.

Nos. 101–109 were formerly the European element of the E. India Co.'s Army.

Between 1958 and 1980 considerable amalgamations of R. took place, and the total number is now much reduced.

Registers, Parish, were regularly kept in France from about 1308, but in England only since 1538, and then, erratically. From 1837 they record only baptisms, marriages, and deaths.

Registrar-General first appointed, 1836, to conduct census and carry on **Registration of Births, Marriages, and Deaths,** which was first generally enforced in England by the Registration Act, 1837, and extended to Scotland, 1855, and Ireland, 1864. Consolidating Act, 1874, gave rise to the General Registry, Somerset House. Optional shortened form of birth certificate issued, from 1947, which omitted details of parentage.

Regium Donum (royal gift). Originally an annual grant to Nonconformist bodies in Britain and Ireland by the king. In 1690 William III first made a grant of £1,200 a year to the Presbyterian ministers in Ireland; which continued, and increased till it ceased on passing of Irish Church Act, 1869. This grant was also paid to English Nonconformist clergy from 1721, but withdrawn by mutual consent in 1857.

Regius Professor. All these chairs endowed by Henry VIII, 1546, except that of Modern History at Oxford which George I founded, 1724.

Regulating Act. Introduced by Lord North in 1773 to cause the British Government to interfere in the administration of India.

Regulating Act. Passed by Parliament, 1774, for the subversion of the charter of Massachusetts.

Reichsrat, or Imperial Council, second chamber of several European legislatures, but especially the Upper House of the German legislature, set up under the Weimar Constitution, 1919, as a council of Federal republics; it survived, in theory at least, until 1945.

Reichstag, a modern form of the Imperial Diet (q.v.), revived under the regime of Bismarck as the legislature of the N. German Confederation (1867) and then of the German Empire (Reich: 1871). The name and the institution continued little altered under the Weimar Constitution of 1919; though the power of the Upper House (Reichsrat, q.v.) was curtailed, the R. never had the initiative that the English Commons in Parliament have had, and in

1933 it yielded to Hitler practically without a struggle. Following the R. elections of 5 Mar. 1933 the trial of certain persons, alleged agents of the Comintern, took place on charges of arson in that they caused the fire whereby the R. building was burnt out, 27 Feb. 1933.

Relativity, Theory of. Einstein's paper on the Special Theory of R. published, 1905. On the General Theory, 1915.

Remonstrance, The Grand. A petition drawn up by Parliament against the cruelty and injustice of Charles I; presented, 1 Dec. 1641.

Remonstrants. The Dutch Protestants who, in 1610, after the death of Arminius, presented to the Holland and Friesland states a remonstrance in which the doctrines of Calvinism were repudiated; their confession of faith was drawn up in 1621; they were bitterly persecuted, 1625–52, and received official recognition, 1795.

Renaissance. The great cultural movement in Europe after the Middle Ages, representing the emergence of the modern age. It was much more than a revival of old forms, as its name might imply, and its span is such that it is impossible to fix it with dates. The following, however, are relevant: Cimabue's *Madonna della Trinità* completed, 1260. Roger Bacon's *Opus Majus* completed, 1266. Dante completed *La Vita Nuova*, 1292, and *De Monarchia*, 1313, and *Divina Commedia*, 1321. Boccaccio finished the *Decameron*, 1353. Manuel Chrysoloras lectured on Greek at Florence, 1396. Lorenzo Valla, humanist, *b.* 1405, *d.* 1457. Printing reached Italy, 1456. St. Mark's, Venice, completed, 1484. St. Peter's, Rome, commenced, 1513.

Rennes, capital of Brittany from the ninth century, became an episcopal see in the fifth century. Burnt down and radically replanned, 1720. Second trial of Dreyfus (*q.v.*) took place here, 1899.

Rent Restriction Acts. Had their origins in the Act of Dec. 1915. Rent tribunals established under the Furnished Houses (Rent Control) Act, 1946. Rent Act of 1957 drastically cut the number of houses protected by R.R. It was much modified by the Rent Acts, 1965 and 1968, which reintroduced R.R. in many cases; present day R.R. governed by the Rent Act and the Protection from Eviction Act of 1977.

Reparations. Germany's reparation debt put at £6,600,000,000, 1920. Allied ultimatum, 1921. Germany applied for reductions, Dec. 1921. Moratorium granted, Jan. 1922. London Conference Aug. 1922. Abortive negotiations among Allies, 1922. French and Belgian forces advanced into the Ruhr, Jan.–Feb. 1923. German passive resistance in Ruhr, Feb.–Sept. 1923. (Lord Curzon's speech, Imperial Conference, 5 Oct, 1923.) Dawes Plan (*q.v.*), 1924. Young Plan (*q.v.*), 20 Jan. 1930. Obligations cancelled, 1932.

Representation of the People Acts. Women over 30 enfranchized, 1918. Extended to all women over 21, 1928. Extension of local franchise, 1945. Act of 1948 abolished plural voting. Act of 1969 gave votes to all those over 18, from 1970.

Republican Party U.S.A. was formed in 1828 when a faction seceded from the Democratic Party. Modern R.P. dates from 1854, beginning as a union of elements opposed to slavery. First National Convention held, 1856. First R. president—Abraham Lincoln—elected, 1860. Dwight D. Eisenhower, R. candidate, elected president, 1952; held office until 1960 after which the Democrats filled the presidency until 1969, when the Republican Richard Nixon was elected. He resigned, 1974. R.P. defeated, 1977, but regained presidency under Reagan, 1981.

Resale Price Maintenance. The Restrictive Trades Practices Act, 1956, outlawed collective price maintenance in Britain. Resale Prices Act, 1964, was intended to abolish R.P.M. except in specified cases.

Rescissory Act. Passed by Scottish Parliament, 1661; it was proposed by Sir Thomas Primrose with the object of annulling the Acts establishing Presbyterianism in Scotland.

Restoration, in English context, means the return of Charles II, his family, and court to England in 1660, and his coronation. In French history, means the R. of the Bourbons, and the reigns of Louis XVIII and Charles X (1814–30).

Resurrectionists, *c.* 1826–30, provided anatomical specimens for surgeons, especially in Scotland, by robbing graves; after Burke and Hare were hanged, 1829, for murdering people as an easier alternative to digging, public attention was directed to the R., and an Act of 1832 required licences to be procured for the dissection of human bodies.

Réunion or **Bourbon.** Indian Ocean. Discovered, 1513, by Portuguese navigator, Pedro Mascarenhas; formally possessed by French, 1643; attacked and captured by British, 1810; restored to France, Apr. 1815. Became an overseas department of France, 1946.

Reuters News (originally **Telegraph Agency**), founded by Baron Julius Reuter (1816–99), who in 1849 at Aachen began to transmit commercial intelligence by pigeon post, and transferred his agency, now working by electric telegraph, to London, 1851. Became a limited liability company, 1865, and a private trusteeship, 1918. In 1947 the company became the joint property, together with the Press Association, of British, Australian, and New Zealand newspaper concerns, joined in 1949 by the Press Trust of India. Stock Exchange flotation, 1984.

Reval. *See* Tallin.

Revolutionary Tribunal, The. Established in Paris, Oct. 1793, for the trial of criminal cases; it was suppressed, 31 May 1795.

Reykjavik, capital of Iceland. The first settler on the site of the town was Ingolf, who landed in 874. *See* ICELAND.

Rhaetia, Central Alpine region conquered by the Romans, 15 B.C., and organized, as a province. Enlarged by addition of Vindelicia, late first century A.D. Divided into R. Prima and R.

Secunda in the reign of Diocletian, A.D. 284–305. R. Prima corresponded to the present Swiss cantons of Grisons, St. Gall, Appenzell, Thurgau, Glarus, parts of Zürich and Schwyz, the Austrian provinces of Vorarlberg and Tirol, and the Italian province of Bolzano. R. Secunda, or Vindelicia, consisted of Swabia and Bavaria N. to the Danube and E. to the Inn. *See* articles on all of the above provinces.

Rheims or **Reims,** France. *Durocortorum* mentioned by Julius Caesar as the capital of the *Remi*; Clovis baptized at, 496; from 1179 to 1825 the sovereigns of France were crowned here. Cathedral built between 1211 and 1430; restored, 1877 *et seq.*; damaged by German bombardment, Sept. 1914; restored and consecrated, 18 Oct. 1937; reopened, 10 July 1938. Ceremony of Franco-German 'reconciliation' held at Rheims, in presence of Adenauer and de Gaulle, July 1962.

Rhine, Confederation of the. *See* CONFEDERATION OF THE RHINE.

Rhineland, or **Rheinland,** a German region corresponding to Rhenish Prussia (*see* PRUSSIA). Demilitarized under terms of Versailles Treaty; French efforts to form a separatist R. state finally failed in 1924. The demilitarized zone was reoccupied by the Wehrmacht, 7 Mar, 1936. Heavily bombed by the Allies, 1942–5.

Rhode Island, U.S.A. Explored by the Dutch, 1614; commonwealth of R.I. founded, 1636, by Roger Williams; patent for the government of the settlement granted, 1644; first General Assembly met, 1647; patent confirmed by Cromwell, 1655; charter granted by Charles II, 1663; ratified National Constitution of U.S.A., 29 May 1790.

Rhodes, Dodecanese, Islands. Early settlement by Dorians. Enrolled in Delian League, fifth century B.C. Revolted from Athens, 412. City of R. built, 408. Great prosperity from 330 onwards. Successful resistance to Demetrius Poliorcetes, 304. Colossus completed, 280; destroyed, 224. In alliance with Rome, 180–160. Sacked by C. Cassius, 43. Finally ruined by earthquakes, A.D.

155. Occupied by Saracens, 653–8 and 717–18. Conquered by Knights of St. John, 1309. Turkish siege, 1480. Turkish conquest, 1522. Occupied by Italians, 1912 (see DODECANESE ISLANDS). Given to Greece, 1947.

Rhodesia, Southern, name, until 1980, of **Zimbabwe** (q.v.).

Rhodesia and Nyasaland, Federation of, existed 1953–63, when after concentrated African opposition it was dissolved.

Rhodesia, Northern. See ZAMBIA.

Rhodesia, earlier, **Southern Rhodesia.** See ZIMBABWE.

Richborough, the Roman *Rutupiae*, was the beachhead of Claudius's invasion, A.D. 43. A monumental building in honour of the Emperor Domitian, final conqueror of Britain, was erected, 85. Signs of Roman occupation continue into the early fifth century. The port was heavily fortified c. 287–93 against Saxon pirates. In 1943–4 units of the Mulberry harbour and the cross-channel petrol supply pipe, 'PLUTO', were made at R.

Ridolfi Conspiracy. A Roman Catholic plot instigated by Roberto R., in which the Duke of Norfolk was involved, against Queen Elizabeth, 1571. It arose out of the papal bull *Regnans in Excelsis* against Queen Elizabeth, 25 Feb. 1570. Norfolk was executed with others, June 1572.

Rievaulx Abbey (Yorks). Founded by Cistercians, 1131.

Rifle. Invention of spiral groove attributed among others to J. Koller of Vienna, fifteenth century. Such a rifled weapon is recorded at Guastalla (Italy), 1476. Occasionally found, especially among French troops, in seventeenth century. Introduced by Swiss colonists into America, 1721. A R. factory existed in Pennsylvania, 1754. The British 95th Regiment armed with the Baker R., 1800. General introduction of breechloading Rs. into Prussian Army, 1841–8. Smooth bores abolished in British Army c. 1852. Magazine Rs. used in American Civil War, 1861. Lee- Enfield R. introduced to Britain, 1895; British Army changed to Belgian FN.30 Rs., 1954.

Riga, founded, 1201, by Bishop Albert of Livonia, seat of an archbishopric from 1225. Joined Hanseatic League, 1282, with the same privileges and laws as Hamburg. Came into possession of the Teutonic Knights, 1330, adopted Protestant faith (Lutheran), 1522. Free City of the Empire from the decay of the Teutonic Knights' dominions (1561) until 1582, when it became Polish. Passed to Sweden, 1621; to Russia, 1710; to Latvia, 1919. See TREATIES. Leased to U.S.S.R. as military base, 3 Oct, 1939; taken by Germans, 1 July 1941; by Russians, 13 Oct. 1944.

Rights, Bill of (Britain), Oct. 1689, confirmed the Declaration of R. made to William and Mary, Feb. 1689. It affirmed the liberties of the subject and settled the succession.

Rights, Bill of (U.S.A.). The collective name given to the first ten amendments to the U.S. Constitution passed together, 15 Dec. 1791.

Rights of Man, Declaration of. Proclaimed by the French National Assembly, 4 Aug. 1789.

Rio de Janeiro, Brazil. Discovered, 1502, by Coelho. City founded, 1566. Capital of Brazil, 1822–1960.

Rio de Janeiro, Treaty of, 2 Sept. 1947, for the mutual defence of the Americas.

Riot Act (Britain), **1714.**

Ripon, Treaty of, 1640; ended the war between England and Scotland; peace was finally concluded in London, Aug, 1641.

Road Safety Act, 1967, provided for breath-tests for drivers involved in traffic offences.

Robot (from Czech *robotnik*—worker), a term invented by Karel Čapek in his play *R.U.R.*, 1923. See CZECH LITERATURE.

Rochelle, La, France. Became part of English possessions by marriage of Henry II to Eleanor of Aquitaine; taken by Louis VIII of France, 1224; ceded to England, 1360; retaken by France, 1372; resisted siege as Huguenot stronghold, 1573; besieged (1627) and taken by Richelieu, 1628.

Rochester, England. Bishopric founded, 604, by St. Augustine; present cathedral founded, 1077–1107; earliest city charter, 1189; castle of very early construction, captured by King John, 1215; besieged in vain by Simon de Montfort, 1264; captured by Wat Tyler, 1381.

Rockefeller Foundation, endowed by John Davidson R. (1839–1937). Chartered, 1913.

'Rocket, The.' Steam locomotive built by Stephenson, which in Oct. 1829 won the Rainhill competition, and so inaugurated the use of locomotives on the Liverpool and Manchester Railway.

Rockets. As a firework and missile, invented by the Chinese, twelfth-thirteenth centuries A.D. A small rocket missile used by the British in India at the end of the eighteenth century. Modern interest in Rs. dates from *c.* 1920. First flight of a liquid-propelled R. made at Massachusetts, 1926. Germany did much work on Rs. after 1933 and Rs. were used against Britain in Second World War. Subsequent research carried out on space Rs. and military Rs. by America and Russia, and by an unknown number of other countries. First man in space was a Russian, 12 Apr. 1961; he orbited the earth; an American made a sub-orbital flight in May 1961. *See also* SPACE FLIGHTS.

Roman Catholics in England. Absolved from allegiance to Henry VIII by Pius III, 1535, to Queen Elizabeth I by Pius V, 1570. Excluded from the throne, 1689. Laws against repealed, 1780, 1791. Catholic Emancipation Act, 13 Apr. 1829. Episcopate re-established 1850.

Roman Emperors before the division of the Empire. Dates of accession only:
Augustus 27 B.C.
Tiberius A.D. 14
Caligula 37
Claudius 41
Nero 54
Galba ⎫
Otho ⎬ 68
Vitellius ⎭
Vespasian 68
Titus 79

Domitian 81
Nerva 96
Trajan 98
Hadrian 117
Antoninus Pius 138
Marcus
 Aurelius 161
Commodus 180
Pertinax ⎫
Didus Julianus ⎬ 193
Niger ⎭
Septimus Severus 193
Caracalla ⎫ 211
Geta ⎭
Macrinus 217
Elagabalus 218
Alexander Severus 222
Maximin 1 235
Gordian I and II ⎫
Balbinus ⎬ 238
Pupienus ⎭
Gordian III 238
Philip 244
Decius 249
Gallus 251
Aemilian ⎫
Valerian ⎬ 253
Gallienus ⎭
Gallienus alone 260
Claudius II 268
Aurelian 270
Tacitus 275
Florian 276
Probus 276
Carus 282
Carinus ⎫ 284
Numerian ⎭
Diocletian 284
 (abdicated 305)
Maximian associated with
Diocletian 286
Constantius ⎫ 305
Galerius ⎭
Severus 306
Constantine the Great ⎫
Licinius │
Maximin │
Galerius ⎬ Jointly 309
Maxentius │
Maximian ⎭
Constantine alone 323
Constantine II ⎫ 337
Constantius II ⎭
Constans

Constantius II (alone) 353
Julian 361
Jovian 363
Valens
Valentinian I   364
Valentinian I
Gratian   367
Gratian
Valentinian II   375
Theodosius the Great 379–95

See also ROMAN EMPERORS (LATER WESTERN) and ROMAN EMPIRE, EASTERN.

Roman Emperors (Later Western).

(Usurpers in italics.) (*See also* ROMAN EMPERORS.)

Honorius 393–423
Constantine III 407–411
Constantius III 421
John 423–425
Valentinian III 425–455
Maximus 455
Avitus 455–456
Majorian 457–461
Severus 461–465
Anthemius 467–472
Olybrius 472
Glycerius 473
Julius Nepos 473–480
Romulus 475–476

NOTE: Romulus surnamed Augustulus is wrongly known as the last R. Emperor in the W.; he was never recognized in the E., and Julius Nepos survived him.

Roman Empire.

Organization of by Augustus, 30 B.C.–A.D. 14. Defeat of Romans by Germans under Arminius, A.D. 9. Annexation of Mauritania, 41–2. Of Britain, 43–5. Boudicca's rebellion in Britain, 61. Batavian rising, 69–71. Fortification of the German frontier, 96. Empire reaches its widest extent under Trajan, 98–117. The *Perpetual Edict* of Julius Salvianus drawn up *c.* 130. Germanic invasion of Italy, 161. Beginning of serious praetorian interference in central government, 193. *Constitutio Antoniniana* extends Roman citizenship to all freeborn subjects, 212. Defeat of Emperor Valerian by Sapor I of Persia, 260. Defeat of the Goths at Nish, 269. Diocletian organizes the R.E. into two great circums-criptions (Eastern and Western), 285. Britain independent under Carausius, 286–93, and under Allectus, 293–6. Constantine legalizes Christianity by the *Edict of Milan*, 313. Defeat of Emperor Valens by Visigoths at Adrianople, 378. Definite partition of the Empire at death of Theodosius the Great, 395.

Roman Empire, Eastern, or Byzantine Empire.

The name given to that part of the R.E. whose capital was at Constantinople and which continued after the end of the Western Imperial line in A.D. 476. For previous history *see* ROME, ROMAN EMPIRE, etc. First schism between Eastern and Western Churches begins, 484. Justinian closes Athens University, 529. Belisarius reconquers N. Africa, 533–4. Invades Italy, 535–40. Narses makes Italy a Byzantine province, 552–5. Hagia Sophia Cathedral consecrated, 563. War with Persia, 572–91. Persians conquer Syria and Palestine, 614; Egypt, 618–19. Heraclius recovers Jerusalem, 629. Arabs under the Caliph Omar defeat Byzantines at battle of the Yarmuk, 634; take Damascus, 635; Jerusalem, 638; Egypt, 639–40; Tripoli, 647; Cyprus, 649. They begin conquest of N. Africa, 670. Arab siege of and defeat at Constantinople, 673–7. Arab raids on Constantinople, 717–19. Lombards take Ravenna from Byzantines, 751. The Iconoclastic controversy, 726–842. Arabs take Crete, 826; and invade Sicily, 827; and S. Italy, 838. Cyril and Methodius convert the Bulgars, 864, Basil I recovers S. Italy, 867–80. Arabs expel Byzantines from Sicily, 902. Saracens attack Salonika, 904. Romanus I (Lecapenus) extends Byzantine Empire to the Euphrates, 920–44. Crete reconquered, 961; and Cyprus, 964–6. Victorious wars under John Zimisces and Basil II (Bulgaroktonos—'Kill-Bulgars') against Bulgars, 971–1025. Conquest of Armenia, 1045. Disastrous defeat of Romanus IV (Diogenes) by Seljuk Turks at Manzikert and loss of central Anatolia, 1071. Norman invasion of the Balkans, 1081–5. Alexius Comnenus de-

feats Petchenegs at Leburnium, 1091; and
the Cumans at Adrianople, 1095. (*See*
CRUSADE (FIRST), 1096–9.) Commercial
agreements with Venice, 1126.
Venetian merchants excluded, 1171.
Seljuks defeat Manuel I at
Myriokephalon. 1176. Cyprus
becomes independent, 1184. (*See*
CRUSADE (THIRD), 1189–93, and
CRUSADE (FOURTH) which, led by
Venice, captures Constantinople and
establishes a Latin Empire, 1204.) (*See*
TREBIZOND.) Theodore Lascaris
established at Nicaea, 1208. Vatatzes
expels Latins from Anatolia, 1224;
and captures Salonika, 1246. Michael
VIII Palaeologus retakes Constantinople and overthrows Latin Empire,
1261. Osman I (Ottoman) defeats
Byzantines at battle of Baphaion,
1301. He takes Brusa, 1326. John VI
Cantacuzene, Turkish-supported
candidate for imperial throne,
1347–54. First Turkish settlement in
Europe, 1353. Turks take Adrianople,
1357. John V visits the W. to get aid
against the Turks, 1366. Final loss of
Anatolia, 1390. Defeat by Turks at
battle of Nicopolis, 1396. First
Turkish siege of Constantinople,
1422. Turks storm Constantinople
and bring the Eastern R.E. to an end,
29 May 1453. See OTTOMAN EMPIRE.

*Eastern Roman Emperors from the
Foundation of Constantinople,* A.D.
330.

(Usurpers in italics. The *Basileus Auto-
crator's* name is given always in capitals. Constantine II and Constans I are
not included, as they never exercised
effective power in the E.)

Constantinian Dynasty:
  Constantine I, the Great *d.* 337
  Constantius 337–361
  Julian, the Apostate 361–363
  Jovian 363–364
  Valens 364–378
Theodosian Dynasty:
  Theodosius I, the Great 379–395
  Arcadius 395–408
  Theodosius II 408–450
  Marcian 450–457
Leonine Dynasty:
  Leo I 457–474

  Leo II 474
  Zeno 474–491
  Basilicus 475–476
  Anastasius I 491–518
Justinian Dynasty:
  Justin I 518–527
  Justinian I 527–565
  Justin II 565–578
  Tiberius II 578–582
  Maurice 582–602
  Theodosius, co-Emperor 590–602
  Phocas 602–610
Heraclian Dynasty:
  Heraclius I 610–641
  Constantine III 613–641
  Heracleonas 638–641
  Constantine III 641
  Heracleonas 641
  Constans II 641–668
  Constantine IV 659–668
  Heraclius 659–681
  Tiberius 659–681
  Constantine IV, Pogonatus
    668–685
  Justinian II, Rhinotmetus 685–695
  Leontius 695–698
  Tiberius III, Apsimar 698–705
  Justinian II, Rhinotmetus 705–711
  Tiberius 706–711
  Philippicus, Bardanes 711–713
  Anastasius II, Artemius 713–716
  Theodosius iii 716–717
Isaurian Dynasty:
  Leo III, the Isaurian 717–740
  Constantine V, 720–740
  Constantine V, Copronymus
    740–775
  Leo IV 750–775
  Leo IV, the Chazar 775–780
  Constantine VI 776–780
  Constantine vi 780–797
  Irene 797–802
  Nicephorus I 802–811
  Stauracius 811
  Michael I, Rhangabe 811–813
  Leo V, the Armenian 813–820
Amorian Dynasty:
  Michael II, the Amorian 820–829
  Theophilus 821–829
  Theophilus 829–842
  Michael III, the Drunkard 842–867
  Basil I 866–867
Macedonian Dynasty:
  Basil I the Macedonian 867–886

Constantine 869–880
Leo VI 870–886
Alexander 871–912
Leo VI, the Wise 886–912
Constantine VII 911–913
Alexander 912–913
Constantine VII, Porphyro-
    genetus 913–919
Romanus I, Lecapenus 919–944
Constantine VII 919–944
Christopher Lecapenus 921–931
Stephen Lecapenus 924–945
Constantine Lecapenus 924–945
Constantine VII, Porphyro-
    genetus 944–959
Romanus II *c.* 950–959
Romanus II 959–963
Basil II 960–963
Constantine VIII 961–1025
Basil II, Bulgaroctonus 963
Nicephorus II, Phocas 963–969
Basil II 963–976
John I, Tzimisces 969–976
Basil II, Bulgaroctonus 976–1025
Constantine VIII 1025–1028
Romanus III, Argyrus 1028–1034
Michael IV, the Paphlagonian
    1034–1041
Michael V, the Caulker 1041–1042
Zoe and Theodora, Porphyro-
    genetae 1042
Constantine IX, Monomachus
    1042–1055
Theodora, Porphyrogeneta
    1055–1056
Michael VI, Stratioticus 1056–1057
Isaac I, Comnenus 1057–1059
Ducas Dynasty:
Constantine X, Ducas 1059–1067
Michael VII *c.* 1060–1067
Michael VII, Parapinaces
    1067–1068
Romanus IV, Diogenes 1068–1071
Michael VII 1068–1071
Michael VII, Parapinaces 1071–
    1078
Nicephorus III, Botaniates 1078–
    1081
Comnenian Dynasty:
Alexius I, Comnenus 1081–1118
Constantine, Ducas 1081–1090
John II 1092–1118
John II, Calojohannes 1118–1143
Alexius 1119–1142

Manuel I 1143–1180
Alexius II 1172–1180
Alexius II 1180–1183
Andronicus I 1182–1183
Andronicus I 1183–1185
Angelus Dynasty:
Isaac II, Angelus 1185–1195
Alexius III 1195–1203
Alexius IV 1203–1204
Isaac II 1203–1204
Alexius V, Murtuphlus 1204
Latin Emperors:
Baldwin I 1204–1205
Henry 1206–1216
Peter of Courtenay 1216–1217
Robert 1221–1228
Baldwin II 1228–1237
John of Brienne 1228–1237
Baldwin II (alone) 1237–1261
Lascarid Dynasty (Nicaean Empire,
1204–1261)
Theodore I, Lascaris 1204–1222
John III, Ducas Vatatzes 1222–1254
Theodore II, Lascaris Vatatzes
    1254–1258
John IV, Ducas Vatatzes 1258
Palaeologan Dynasty:
Michael VIII, Palaeologus 1258–
    1282
Andronicus II 1272–1282
Andronicus II 1282–1328
Michael 1295–1320
Andronicus III 1325–1328
Andronicus III 1328–1341
John V 1341–1347
John VI, Cantacuzene 1347–1355
John V 1347–1355
Matthew Cantacuzene 1348–1355
Andronicus IV 1376–1379
John VII 1376–1390
John V 1379–1390
Andronicus IV 1379–1385
Manuel II 1386–1391
John VII 1390
John V 1390–1391
Manuel II 1391–1425
John VII 1399–1412
John VIII 1423–1425
John VIII 1425–1448
Constantine XI, Palaeologus
    1448–1453

Roman Empire (Later Western). The
Vandal mercenary Stilicho seizes
power, A.D. 395. Alaric's first invasion

of Italy, 401–3. Capital moved to Ravenna, 401–3. Assassination of Stilicho, 408. Rome three times besieged by Alaric, 408–10. Visigoths (*q.v.*) settle in Gaul, the Vandals and Suevi in Spain, 415–23. Vandals (*q.v.*) invade and settle N. Africa, 429–42. Aetius defeats Huns at battle of 'Châlons' or the Catalaunian Fields (probably near Troyes), 451. Odoacer rules Italy, 473–89; Italy conquered by Theodoric the Ostrogoth, 489–93. Belisarius reconquers Italy, 536–49. Byzantine rule established, 552–5.

Roman Republic. Foundation of Rome, 753 B.C. Expulsion of the Tarquin dynasty, 510. First dictatorship, 501. Enactment of the XII Tables, 451–450. Rome sacked by the Gauls, 390. Final subjection of the Latin League, 338. Publication of the *Jus Flavianum*, 304. *Lex Hortensia* gives the plebs concurrent power of legislation by plebiscite, 267. First Punic War with Carthage is indecisive, 264–241. Conquest of Sardinia, Corcyra, and Lombardy, 241–218. Second Punic War, 218; ends with defeat of Hannibal at Zama, 202. Conquest of Syria, 190; Macedon, 168. In Third Punic War Carthage is destroyed, 149–146. Greece conquered, 146. Rise and fall of the Gracchi, 135–123. Marius defeats the Cimbri and Teutones, 106–101. The Social War, 91. Sulla crushes the Marians, 88. Defeats Mithradates of Pontus, 84. Institutes the proscriptions, 82. Resigns dictatorship, 79. *Lex Cornelia*, 67. First Triumvirate (Caesar, Pompey, Crassus), 63. Caesar conquers Gaul, 58–51. He crosses the Rubicon, Jan. 49. He defeats Pompey at Pharsalus, 48. Is murdered, 15 Mar. 44. Second Trumvirate (Octavius, Antony, Lepidus), 43. Defeat of Antony at Actium, 2 Sept. 31. Octavius changes his name to Augustus, 16 Jan. 27.

Romantic Movement, as a conscious literary school, had its first English manifesto in the preface to the *Lyrical Ballads* (the second edition, of 1800) by Wordsworth. The word *romantic* when given a literary connotation is of English origin, but was first introduced into the German language by Novalis *c.* 1795, and as used by him and Wieland and reintroduced into English by Coleridge, Southey, etc., came to have the anti-classical and medievalizing association of the R.M. which is largely the result of interaction between English, French, and German literature and philosophy; its influence on and derivation from the literature of the Mediterranean countries is negligible. France was drawn into the R. orbit last of the three, and Mme de Staël's *De l'Allemagne*, 1813, shows the origin of French R. ideas. R. traditions lasted longer in France than elsewhere, at least until the 1850s, perhaps because of the longevity and continued vigour of the chief French R. poet, novelist, and playwright, V. Hugo, who did not die until 1885. The R. heyday in Germany and England may be said to have come to an end *c.* 1832 with the deaths of Scott and Goethe.

Rome, City of. (*See also* ROMAN REPUBLIC; ROMAN EMPIRE, etc.; also PAPACY and ITALY.) Traditionally founded, 753 B.C. Capitol founded *c.* 614. Sacked by Gauls, 390. Aqua Appia built, 312. Aqua Julia, 33. Pantheon, 27. Colosseum begun, A.D. 72. Trajan's column, 114. Charlemagne crowned at, 25 Dec. 800. Sacked by Saracens, 846. By the Emperor Arnulf, 896. By the Normans under Guiscard, 1084. Taken by Barbarossa, 1167. University founded, 1245. Rienzi's republic at R., 1347. St. Peter's new cathedral begun, 1513. Completely sacked by the Spaniards, 1527. Consecration of St. Peter's, 1626. Walls restored, 1749. Proclaimed a republic by the French, 1798. Restored to Pope, retaken, and restored, 1799–1801. Annexed to Napoleon's kingdom of Italy, 1808. Restored to Pope, 1814. Garibaldi's Roman republic suppressed by French, 1848–9. Became capital of Italy, 1870. Papal temporal authority restored in Vatican City, 1929, modified, 1984.

Rome, Treaty of, signed, 25 Mar. 1957, between Belgium, France, Federal Germany, Italy, Luxemburg, and the Netherlands, which instituted the European Economic Community (*q.v.*)

Roses, Wars of the. Collective name for the English Civil Wars which broke out in 1455 and ended at battle of Bosworth, 1485. Red Rose = Lancaster; White Rose = York.

Rosetta Stone, inscribed *c.* 200 B.C.; dug up, 1779. True contents recognized, and demotic text partially translated, 1816, by Dr. Thomas Young (1773–1829). The whole deciphered, 1822, by Jean François Champollion (1790–1832). Ceded to Britain, 1801.

Rosicrucians. Rosicrucian tracts published soon after 1600 claim the existence of Rosicrucian societies in the fourteenth century. They first became widely publicized by Johann Valentin Andreae (1586–1654).

Roskilde, Roeskilde, was capital of Denmark until 1443. Most of the Danish kings from Harald Gormsson (*d.* 986) onwards are buried here in the cathedral which was consecrated, 1084, but the present building was erected, 1191–1200.

Rostock, founded, 1160, by the Polish Prince Pribislav, across the river from a Wendish castle, joined the Hanseatic League, 1218. Became part of Duchy of Schwerin, 1695. Fell to Russians, May 1945.

Rostov-on-Don. Founded by Slavs in 862, R. is first mentioned in a document of 988; was an independent principality from the tenth to the fourteenth century; assimilated by the Grand Duchy of Moscow, 1389. Fortified, 1761. Changed hands four times in World War II, the last time in Feb. 1943, when the retreating Germans destroyed most of the older buildings.

Rosyth was the residence of Margaret, sister of Edgar Atheling, wife of King Malcolm Canmore; she *d.* 1093. The naval base here was first laid down, 1903.

Rotary International, founded, 1905, in Chicago by P. P. Harris (*d.* 1947). New York R. Club founded, 1909. First non-American R. Club in Dublin, 1911. British Association of R. Clubs formed, 1914; known as the R.I. in Great Britain and Ireland since 1938.

Rotterdam, Holland. John I in 1299 granted various privileges to burghers of, and this date marks the origin of the present town; Erasmus *b.* at, 1467; plundered by Spaniards, 1572. Heavily bombed by the Germans, May 1940, and town centre destroyed; rebuilt since 1945.

Rouen, France. Originally *Ratuma*, latinized as *Rotomagus*. An archbishop's see in A.D. 260; became capital of Normandy, 912; death of William the Conqueror at, 1087; Joan of Arc burned at, 1431; sacked by Huguenots, 1562; occupied by Germans, Dec. 1870–July 1871 and June 1940–Aug. 1944.

Round Table Conferences (in London). Three were concerning government of India: first, Nov. 1930–Jan. 1931; second, Oct.–Dec. 1931; third, Nov.–Dec. 1932. Besides these, a Burma R.T. Conference was held, Nov. 1931–Jan. 1932, and there was a Malta R.T. Conference, 1955.

Royal Academy of Arts (London). Originally the Society of Incorporated Artists, founded by Hogarth *c.* 1739; first exhibition held, 21 Apr. 1760; the present institution founded, Dec. 1768, with Sir Joshua Reynolds as president; first exhibition held at Burlington House, 3 May 1869. The following are the presidents, with their dates of inauguration:

Sir Joshua Reynolds, 1768.
Benjamin West, 1792.
James Wyatt, 1805.
Benjamin West, 1806.
Sir Thomas Lawrence, 1820.
Sir Martin A. Shee, 1830.
Sir Charles Eastlake, 1850.
Sir Edwin Landseer, 1866.
Sir Francis Grant, 1866.
Sir Frederick Leighton, 1878.
Sir John Everett Millais, } 1896.
Sir Edward John Poynter, }
Sir Aston Webb, 1919.
Sir Frank Dicksee, 1924.
Sir William Llewellyn, 1928.

Sir Edwin Lutyens, 1938.
Sir Alfred Munnings, 1944.
Sir Gerald Kelly, 1949.
Sir Albert Richardson, 1954.
Sir Charles Wheeler, 1956.
Sir Thomas Monnington, 1966.
Sir Hugh Casson, 1976.
Roger de Grey 1984

Royal Air Force. Formed by Act of Parliament, 1 Apr. 1918, by amalgamation of the R. Naval Air Service and R. Flying Corps.

Royal Bounty, part of the Civil List, was fixed at £13,200 in 1837. Payment from R.B. to subjects whose wives are delivered of three or more children at one birth discontinued, 1957.

Royal Commissions. The first R.C. was estab. to enquire into Civil establishments and offices of State and reported in 1887.

Royal Exchange (London). *See* EXCHANGE, ROYAL.

Royal Flying Corps. *See* ROYAL AIR FORCE.

'Royal George', flagship of Admiral Kempenfelt, sank suddenly in Portsmouth harbour, 29 Aug. 1782.

Royal Hospital (Chelsea). *See* CHELSEA HOSPITAL.

Royal Institution of Great Britain. Founded, 1799. R. charter, 1800. Act of Parliament, 1810.

Royal Marriage Act arose out of the marriages of the Duke of Cumberland (1745–90) and the Duke of Gloucester (1743–1805) to Mrs. Horton and Lady Waldegrave respectively. By this Act, passed in 1772, all descendants of George II, other than the issue of princesses married into foreign R. families, must obtain the sovereign's consent before marriage, which is otherwise void. It would seem, however, that a descendant of George II over 25 years of age may marry without the royal consent on giving twelve months' notice to the Privy Council, provided Parliament in the interim makes no objection.

Royal Military Academy, founded at Woolwich, 1741. In 1946 it amalgamated with the R.M. College, which was established at Sandhurst in 1813;

the R.M. College buildings date mostly from 1911.

Royal Naval Air Service. *See* FLEET AIR ARM.

Royal Naval College. Opened at Osborne, 1903; closed, 1921. Another, at Greenwich, 1873. Another, at Dartmouth, 1905.

Royal Regiment of Artillery formed, 24 May 1716.

Royal Society. Originated 1660. Incorporated, 22 Apr. 1662.

Ruanda Urundi, annexed by Germany as part of German E. Africa, 1884, was awarded to Belgium, as mandatory of the League of Nations, 1919. United administratively to the then Belgian Congo, 1925. Trusteeship territory from 1946. Became independent on 1 July 1962 as the two states of Rwanda (*q.v.*) and Burundi (*q.v.*).

Rugby League. Seceded 1895 from Rugby Union (*q.v.*). First known as Northern Union, and took its present name in 1922.

Rugby School (England). Founded by Laurence Sheriff, 1567. Rebuilt, 1809. Thomas Arnold, headmaster, 1828–42. Rugby football originated here in 1823.

Rugby Union, founded, 1871, by adherents of a game played according to rules similar to those codified at R. School (*see* above) in 1846. The characteristic R.U. tactic of *carrying* the ball was first adopted by W. W. Ellis, in 1823. New rules, 1953.

Rumania. Came into existence by the union of Moldavia and Wallachia under Alexander Cuza, 23 Dec. 1861. Cuza succeeded by Charles of Hohenzollern, 22 Feb. 1866. Independent of Turkey, 13 July 1878. Proclaimed a kingdom, 26 Mar. 1881. Alliance with Austria, 30 Oct. 1883. Balkan Wars, 1912–13. Crushed by German-Austrian offensive, 1–9 Dec. 1916. Bessarabia proclaims union with R., 9 Apr. 1918. Treaty of Bucharest with Germany, 9 May 1918. Transylvania proclaims union with R., 30 Nov. 1918. Treaty of Bucharest annulled by treaties of St. Germain, 10 Sept. 1919 and Trianon, 4 June 1920. R. acquires N. Bukovina, 1920. Joins Little Entente, 17 Aug. 1920. First accession of King Michael, 20 July 1927. Ex- Crown-Prince Carol ordered to leave England, 1928. He is elected king instead of Michael (his son), 8 June 1930. Joins Balkan Pact, 9 Feb. 1934. Bessarabia and N. Bukovina ceded to U.S.S.R., 28 June 1940. S. Dobrudja to Bulgaria, 21 Aug. 1940. Vienna Award cedes half of Transylvania to Hungary, 30 Aug. 1940. Gen. Antonescu appointed leader (*Conducator*), 5 Sept. 1940. Second accession of King Michael, 6 Sept. German military occupation, Oct. 1940. Axis pact signed, 23 Nov. R. attacks U.S.S.R., 22 June 1941. Britain declares war on R., 7 Dec. 1941. Russians invade R., 2 Apr. 1944. King Michael overthrows Antonescu dictatorship, 23 Aug. 1944. Declares war on Germany, 25 Aug. 1944. Russians capture Bucharest, 31 Aug. 1944. King Michael abdicates and R. proclaimed a People's Republic, 30 Dec. 1947. Ex- King Carol *d.* Apr. 1953. Some liberalization of the regime 1963 onwards.

Kings of Rumania, 1881–1947:
Carol I 1881–1914
Ferdinand 1914–1927
Michael 1927–1930
Carol II 1930–1940
Michael (again) 1940–1947
See also Bessarabia; Vlachs; Moldavian Republic.

Rump. M.P.s remaining after Pride's Purge (*q.v.*).

Runes. The earliest decipherable runic inscriptions to which a date can be assigned are at Vimose, Fynen, Denmark, and date from *c.* A.D. 250. R. spread to Norway before 300, and thence to Sweden; they spread to the W. Germanic area (Germany, eastern France, and England) during the fifth century. Early R. found in the Rhineland all date from 450 to 550. The Franks casket (Anglian, probably Northumbrian work) was inscribed with R. before 650, and R. were extensively used in England until *c.* 860. The Old English *Rune Song*, a versified ABC of R., must have been composed before 900, though the only MS. known,

burnt in 1731, was of the eleventh century. The runic alphabet achieved its final form in Scandinavia *c.* 1100, and was in use in the N. generally for certain purposes, until the Reformation. As to the origin of R., according to Marstrander they were first adapted by Gothic traders or mercenaries on the Black Sea from the Greek alphabet: this would imply A.D. 150 at earliest. The theory of Von Freisen derives them from a N. Etruscan alphabet current in Noricum, and adapted by the Marcomanni of Bohemia: this could have happened *c.* A.D. 1.

Russia. Rurik comes from Sweden, and his successors found the principality of Kiev, 864. Vladimir of Kiev marries Anna, a Byzantine princess, 988. Is baptized, and sets about conversion of R., 990–1015. Conversion continued by Jaroslav, 1015–54. Sack of Kiev and foundation of Vladimir by Andrew Bogolinski of Suzdal, 1169. R. overwhelmed by Mongols at the battle of the Kalka, 1224, and of the Oka and the Sit, 1238. Batu established Empire of the Golden Horde, 1242. The reign of Alexander Nevski, 1252–63. Moscow becomes the leading feudatory under Ivan Kalita, 1328–41. Rise of Lithuania, 1315–77. Dimitri Donskoi defeats the Golden Horde of Kulikovo, 1380. The Horde is attacked by Tamerlane, 1390–4. Ivan the Great (1462–1505) proclaims himself tsar and overthrows the Golden Horde, 1480. He conquers Kazan, 1487. Russo-Polish War, 1512–22. Ivan the Terrible conquers Astrakhan, 1554. Boris Godunov regent, 1588. End of the dynasty of Rurik, 1598. The 'False Dimitriy', 1605–6. The Time of Troubles, 1606–13. Michael Romanov elected tsar, 1613. Serfdom of the peasantry legally established, 1649. Alexis takes Smolensk, 1654. Treaty of Vilna with Poland, 3 Nov. 1656. Truce of Andrussov with Poland secures Smolensk and Kiev, 1667. Peter the Great captures Azov from Turks, 1696. He destroys the Streltzi (Musketeers), 1698. Is defeated by Swedes at battle of Narva, 1700. He founds St. Petersburg, 1703.

He decisively defeats Charles XII of Sweden at Poltava, 8 July 1709. He obtains Baltic provinces from Sweden by the Peace of Nystad, 10 Sept. 1721. R. obtains S. Finland from Sweden by Treaty of Aabo, 1743. R. enters Seven Years War (*q.v.*) against Prussia, 1757. Peace with Prussia, 1762. First Partition of Poland, 1772. Treaty of Kuchuk Kainardji with Turkey, 1774. R. obtains N. Black Sea coast by Treaty of Jassy, 1792. Second Partition of Poland, 1793. R. suppresses Kosciuszko's rising in Warsaw, Mar. 1794. Third Partition of Poland, 1795. R. defeated at Zürich, 1799. Defeat at Austerlitz, 1805; at Eylau, 1807. Treaty of Tilsit, 9 July 1807. Napoleon's invasion of R., May–Dec. 1812. Congress of Troppau, 1820. Frontier treaty with U.S.A., 1824. Treaty of Adrianople with Turkey, 1829. Straits Convention, 1841. Poland made a Russian province, 1847. Assists Austrians to crush Hungarian nationalists at Vilagos, 13 Aug. 1849. Crimean War, 1853–6. Serfs emancipated, 3 Mar. 1861. Hereditary priesthood abolished, 1869. Russo-Turkish War, 1877–8. Murders of prominent ministers: Bogolepoff, 1901; Sipyagin, 1902; Plehve, 1904. Russo-Japanese War, 1904–5. Revolt in St. Petersburg, Jan. 1905. In Sebastopol, Oct. 1905. First Duma meets, 10 May 1906. *See* WORLD WARS I and II and U.S.S.R. for subsequent history.

Russian Literature. The following is a list of prominent Russian authors:

Aksakov, Ivan, 1823–86, poet and miscellaneous writer.

Aksakov, Serge Timofieievitch, 1791–1859, novelist.

Andreiev, Leonid Nicolaievitch, 1871–1919, novelist.

Artsibashev, Mikhail Petrovitch, 1878–1927, novelist.

Bakunin, Mikhail, 1814–76, anarchist writer.

Baratinksy, Evgen Abramovitch, 1800–1844, poet.

Bashkirtsev, Marie, 1860–84, diarist.

Batiushkov, Constantine, 1787–1855, poet and translator.

Bely, Andrey, 1880–1934, novelist and poet.

Belinsky, Vissarion, 1811–48, critic and philosopher.

Blok, Alexander Alexandrovitch, 1880–1921, poet.

Bunin, Ivan Alexeyevitch, 1870–1953, poet and novelist.

Chekhov. *See* TCHEKHOV.

Derzhavin, Gabriel Romanovitch, 1743–1816, poet.

Dmitriev, Ivan Ivanovitch, 1760–1837, poet.

Dolgorukaia, Princess Natalia, 1713–70, memoir writer.

Dostoevsky, Fedor Mikhailovitch, 1822–1881, novelist.

Ehrenburg, Ilya, 1891–1967, poet, novelist and journalist.

Fadeyev, Alexander Alexandrovitch, 1901–56, novelist.

Gogol, Nikolai Vasilievitch, 1809–52, novelist.

Gontcharov, Ivan Alexandrovitch, 1812–1891, novelist.

Gorky, Maxim (the pen name of Alexei Maximovitch Pyeshkov), 1868–1936, novelist.

Herzen (or Gertsen), Alexander Ivanovitch, 1812–70, novelist, etc.

Kantemir, Antiochus Dmitrievitch, 1708–1744, poet and satirist.

Karamzin, Nikolai Mikhailovitch, 1766–1826, historian.

Kheraskov, Mikhail Matvieievitch, 1733–1807, epic poet.

Khomiakov, Alexis, 1804–60, poet and theologian.

Kirieievsky, Ivan Vasilievitch, 1806–56, critic.

Koltzov, Alexis Vasilievitch, 1808–42, poet.

Korolenko, Vladimir Galaktionovitch, 1853–1921, novelist.

Kostomarov, Nikolai Ivanovitch, 1817–1885, historian.

Kovalevsky, Sonya, 1850–1901, novelist.

Krylov, Ivan Andreievitch, 1768–1844, fabulist.

Kuprin, Alexander Ivanovitch, 1870–1938, novelist.

Lermontov, Mikhail Yurevitch,
1814–41, poet.

Leskov, Nikolai Semenovitch,
1831–95, novelist.

Lomonosov, Mikhail, 1711–65, poet
and prose writer.

Lukin, Vladimir Ignatievitch,
1757–1824, dramatist.

Maïkov, Apollonius Nicolaievitch,
1821–1898, poet.

Merezh'ovsky, Dmitri Sergeievitch,
1866–1941, poet.

Nékrasov, Nikolai Alexeievitch,
1821–77, poet.

Nestor, *c.* 1050–*c.* 1100, historian.

Nikitin, Ivan Savitch, 1826–61, poet.

Novikov, Nikolai, 1744–1818, prose
writer and social reformer.

Ostrovsky, Alexander Nicolaievitch,
1823–1886, dramatist.

Pasternak, Boris, 1890–1960, poet and
novelist.

Polotsky, Simeon, *fl.* seventeenth
century, poet and dramatist.

Pososhkov, Ivan, *c.* 1673–1726,
reformer and miscellaneous writer.

Prokopovitch, Feofan, 1681–1736,
ecclesiastic reformer, controversialist,
author of prose works and poems.

Pushkin, Alexander Sergeievitch,
1799–1837, poet.

Pyeshkov, Alexei Maximovitch. *See*
GORKY.

Romanovna, Princess Dashkov,
1743–1810, prose writer and editor,
for some years president of the
Academy of Science.

Saltykov, Shtchedrin Mikhail
Evgrafovitch, 1826–89, novelist.

Sholokhov, Mikhail, 1905–84,
novelist.

Sologub, Fedor (pseudonym of Fedor
Kuzmitch Tchernikov), 1863–1927,
novelist and poet.

Soloviev, Sergei Mikhailovitch,
1820–79, historian.

Soloviev, Vladimir Sergeievitch,
1853–1900, philosopher.

Solzhenitsyn, Alexander, 1918–,
novelist.

Sumarokov, Alexis Petrovitch,
1718–77, dramatist.

Tchadaev, Peter Yakovlevitch,
1793–1855, writer and critic.

Tchekhov, Anton, 1860–1904,
dramatist and novelist.

Tchernishevsky, Nikolai, 1828–89,
critic, philosopher, and novelist.

Tiutchev, Fedor Ivanovitch, 1803–76,
poet.

Tolstoy, Alexei Nikolaievitch,
1883–1945, novelist.

Tolstoy, Alexis Constantinovitch,
1817–1875, novelist, etc.

Tolstoy, Leo Nikolaievitch, 1828–
1910, novelist, etc.

Trediakovsky, Vasili, 1703–69, poet
and prose writer.

Turgenev, Ivan Sergeievitch, 1818–83,
novelist.

Yesenin, Sergei, 1895–1925, poet.

Yevtushenko, Yevgeniy Alexandrovitch, 1933–, poet.

Zhukovsky, Vassili Andreievitch,
1783–1852, poet.

Russian Secret Police. Tsarist designation, Okhrana; since the revolution,
see CHEKA, M.V.D., N.K.G.B.,
N.K.V.D., etc.

Russian Tsars. The R. rulers from 864
till 1169 were Grand Princes of Kiev.
From 1169 to 1328 they were Great
Dukes of Vladimir, and from 1328 till
1480 Grand Dukes of Muscovy. Ivan
the Great proclaimed himself tsar,
1480. This list therefore begins with
him.

House of Rurik:
Ivan III (the Great) 1462–1505
Vassili III 1505–1533
Ivan IV (the Terrible) 1533–1584
Theodore I 1584–1598

House of Godunov:
Boris 1598–1605
Theodore II 1605
Interregnum 1605–1613

House of Romanov:
Michael 1613–1645
Alexis 1645–1676
Theodore III 1676–1682
Ivan V 1682–1689
Sophia (regent) 1682–1689
Peter I (the Great) 1682–1725
Catherine I 1725–1727
Peter II 1727–1730
Anne 1730–1740
Ivan VI 1740–1741
Elizabeth 1741–1762

Peter III 1762
Catherine II (the Great) 1762–1796
Paul 1796–1801
Alexander I 1801–1825
Nicholas I 1825–1855
Alexander II 1855–1881
Alexander III 1881–1894
Nicholas II (abdicated) 1894–1917

Ruthenia. Ruthenians, or Little Russians, or Ukrainians, are a linguistic division of the Slavs, the most south-westerly of the E. Slav group, whose language was identical with that of the other E. Slavs (Great Russians, White Russians) until *c.* 1240. All alike spoke Old Russian. From 1321 to 1772 the greater part of R. was under Lithuanian, then under Polish, dominion, while from 1772 to 1917 it was divided under Russian, Austrian, Hungarian, and occasionally Turkish suzerainty. In 1918 the easternmost province of the newly set up Czechoslovak Republic was named R., or Sub-Carpathian Russia. In 1938 it was isolated by the defection of the Slovaks from the republic, and was occupied by the Hungarian Army and annexed to Hungary. In 1945 the Ukrainian S.S.R., which had already acquired the territories of Galicia from Poland and N. Bukovina and Bessarabia from Rumania, obtained the cession of the province from Czechoslovakia. Now known as Transcarpathian Ukraine, it is politically united to the rest of the Little Russians for the first time in history. *See* UKRAINE.

Ruthenian Church is a name for the Uniate Catholic Church (Catholics of Slavonic rite but Roman allegiance), whose followers are spread over Polish, Russian (especially in Galicia),

Czechoslovak, and Rumanian territory. The Little Russians, for the most part, became Christian during the reign of Vladimir the Great of Kiev (980–1015), and at the time of the schism, 1054, sided with the Greek faction. But after numerous overtures they became attached to the Roman allegiance by the union of Brest-Litovsk, 1594. In 1946 about 3½ million members of the R.C. in Soviet territory withdrew their allegiance to Rome, under duress, and submitted to the Orthodox Patriarchate in Moscow.

Rutland. Former English county, dating from the thirteenth century, whose absorption into Leicester was recommended, 1961; proposal abandoned, 1963, but adopted under the Local Government Act of 1972.

Ruthven, Raid of. A *coup d'état* which involved kidnapping the boy James VI of Scotland from his guardians, the Duke of Lennox and the Earl of Arran; this was done by the Earls of Gowrie and Mar, Lord Lyndsay of the Byres, and the Master of Glamis, in 1582.

Rwanda, Africa. Independent republic created by the granting of independence to Ruanda-Urundi (*q.v.*) on 1 July 1962.

Ryder Cup, golfing trophy presented by Samuel Ryder and first competed for officially by Brit. and U.S. teams, 1927. Brit. team expanded to become a European team from 1983.

Rye House Plot. A conspiracy formed in 1683 to assassinate Charles II and the Duke of York; the plot was frustrated soon after its origin.

Ryswick, Treaty of, 1697. Ended the war between France and the coalition composed of England, Spain, Brandenburg, Holland, and the Empire.

Addenda

S

S.A. (Sturmabteilungen). National Socialist (*q.v.*) 'assault detachment' formed about 1922 for the purpose of breaking up meetings by rival parties, etc. Its chief of staff, Roehm, shot, 30 June 1934, when its influence ceased to predominate in Nazi politics.

Saarland (for earlier history *see* PALATINATE) was placed under control of League of Nations from 10 Jan. 1920 by Treaty of Versailles (*see end* of WORLD WAR I) for fifteen years, viz. until 1935, when plebsicite decided for return to Germany. From May 1945 occupied by French troops. New Landtag, elected Oct. 1947, passed constitution making S. an autonomous state, economcially united to France, Nov. 1947; ratified by French National Assembly, Feb. 1948. Agreement on future status of S. signed by France and Federal Germany, 23 Oct. 1954; this rejected by the Saarlanders in a referendum, Oct. 1955. Widespread agitation for unification with Federal Germany resulted in France and Federal Germany signing an agreement in Oct. 1956, whereby S. returned to Germany on 1 Jan. 1957. Completely reintegrated with Germany economically by 5 July 1959.

Sabah, formerly known as North Borneo (*see* BORNEO), ceded to a Brit. syndicate by local ruler 1877–78, which transferred to the British North Borneo Co., chartered 1881. Joined Malaysian Federation, 16 Sept. 1963, when name was changed to S.

Sacco and Vanzetti were accused of a double murder committed, 15 Apr. 1920, in U.S.A. Trial began, 31 May 1921, verdict of guilty given, 14 July. Celestino Madeiros confessed to the murder, 18 Nov. 1925. Judge Thayer refused re-trial and sentenced S. and V.

to death, 9 Apr. 1927. Sentence executed, 23 Aug. 1927.

Sadler's Wells Opera Company began playing in S.W. theatre, 1931, but was on tour permanently from 1940 to 1945 while the theatre was closed. Reopened after World War II but moved from Islington theatre to the Coliseum, 1968. Name changed to **English National Opera Company**, 1970.

Safad, Safed, N. Galilee, Israel. After 1492 became centre of Jewish learning and the residence of Isaac Luria ben Salomon (Ashkenazi) (1534–72) and other Cabbalistic scholars. First Palestinian printing-press installed, 1563. Severe earthquake, 1837.

Safty of Sports Grounds Act. 1975. Extended after Bradford football club disaster, May 1985.

Sahara crossed by Europeans: Hornemann, 1798–1800; Oudney, Denham, and Clapperton, 1822–4; Laing, 1826; Caille, 1828; Davidson, 1836; Richardson, 1845; Barth, 1850–5; Rohlfs, 1865–7; Nachtigal, 1869–70; Lenz, 1880; Flatters (perished), 1881; Buchanan, 1922, all with animal tansport. Laperrine lost his life attempting to fly across the desert, 1919. First motor-car crossing by de Prohuk, 1920.

Salford, University of, estab. 1967.

St. Albans, England. Present town, containing many ancient buildings, and near site of Roman *Verulamium*, is called after St. Alban, a Roman soldier martyred there, A.D. 303. Monastery erected *c.* 793; dissolved, 1539. Abbey (cathedral since 1877) consecrated, 1115. Battles at during Wars of the Roses: 1. 22 May 1455; 2. 17 Feb. 1461.

St. Andrews, Scotland. Royal burgh after 1140. Cathedral commenced in 1162;

consecrated, 1318; desecrated by Protestant mob, 1559. University founded, 1411. Robert Bruce held his first Parliament at, 1309. Golf club instituted, 1754.

St. Bartholomew, St. Barthélemy Island, was first settled by Frenchmen from St. Kitts in 1648. Taken by English, 1689, and restored to France, 1697. Retaken, 1746, restored, 1748. Ceded to Sweden, 1785, but bought back, 1878.

St. Bernard Pass. Great S.B.P. contained the hospice of St. Bernard of Mentone (923–1108), built 962, and served by Augustinian canons since thirteenth century. Hospice handed over to French, 1947; since closed. Crossed by Napoleon's army, 15 May 1800. Carriage road opened, 1895. Tunnel opened, 19 Mar. 1964. Little S.B.P. used by Hannibal's army, (?) 218 B.C.

St. Gothard Pass.· First opened to wheeled traffic, 1820–4. Railway (and tunnel) constructed, 1872–82.

St. Helena, Island of, S. Atlantic. Discovered by the Portuguese on St. Helena's Day, 21 May 1502; possessed by E. India Co. 1659; Napoleon *d.* at, 1821; became a British colony, 1834. Island of Ascension annexed to, 1922; Tristan da Cunha, 1938.

St. James's Palace, London. Built by Henry VIII, 1530–6. Extended by Charles II, 1668; by George IV, 1827. Official residence of the sovereign from 1698 until 1837.

St. John, Knights of. *See* MALTA, KNIGHTS OF.

St. Kilda. Sold by The Macleod, 1779; bought back, 1871; evacuated by remnant of population, 1930.

St. Kitts, W. Indies. Discovered by Columbus, 1493. Ceded to Britain, 1713; independent (with Nevis, *q.v.*) 19 Sept. 1983.

St. Lawrence Seaway. Complex of dredged channels, locks, and Great Lakes, linking centre of the American mainland to the Atlantic Ocean for sea-going vessels, started 1954, opened officially by Queen Elizabeth II, 26 June 1959.

St. Louis, U.S.A. Named after Louis IX of France, and founded in 1764 by Laclède. Possessed by Spain, 1768; by U.S.A., 1803.

St. Lucia. Discovered by Columbus, 1502. French, 1635. English settlement established, 1639; captured by English, 1664; English evacuated, 1667. Finally ceded to Britain, 1814. Independent, 22 Feb., 1979.

St. Paul's Cathedral (London). A church built in the early seventh century, traditionally on the site of a demolished Roman basilica, was burnt down in 1087. New cathedral, which was completed about 1287; in 1561 the spire was struck by lightning. About 60 years later Inigo Jones was entrusted with restoration, but in 1666, after its destruction by the Great Fire, Christopher Wren was commissioned to rebuild the cathedral; in 1675 the foundation-stone of the new building was laid, and the whole was completed, 1710. A 'dangerous structure' notice, in regard to the dome, served by the City of London, 6 Jan. 1925. Eastern part of cathedral thereupon cleared for five years while the building was made safe. Damaged by bombing, 1940–1; restored and renovated at the end of the war. Exterior cleaned, 1962–6.

St. Paul's School (London). Founded by Dean Colet in 1509; the school-house was destroyed by fire, 1666, and rebuilt by Wren; removed to Hammersmith, Apr. 1884: to Barnes, Sept. 1968.

St. Peter's (Rome). Church originally erected by the Emperor Constantine about A.D. 319 on the site of a chapel built over the tomb of St. Peter by Pope Anacletus at the beginning of the second century; the present church was designed by the architect Bramante, and in 1506 the first stone was laid by Pope Julius II; building began in earnest, 1513; the · church was consecrated, 18 Nov. 1626.

St. Petersburg, Russia. Founded by Peter the Great, 27 May 1703; became seat of government, 1712; Peace of, between Russian and Prussia, signed 5 May 1762; treaty of alliance signed at, between Bernadotte and the Emperor of Russia, Alexander, 24 Mar. 1812. *See* PETROGRAD and LENINGRAD.

St. Pierre and Miquelon Islands. First occupied by French, 1635; fortified, 1700. They have been in British hands for the following periods:1702–63; 1778–83; 1793–1802; 1803–14. Overseas dept. of France since 1976.

St. Sophia, Constantinople. Founded in the fourth century by Constantine; rebuilt by Theodosius (415) and Justinian (538–68); Moslem mosque, 1453–1927; museum since 1927.

St. Thomas, Virgin Islands. *See* CHARLOTTE AMALIE.

St. Vincent and the Grenadines. Became independent of Britain, 27 Oct. 1979.

Sakhalin. First settled by Russians, 1855, and Russian sovereignty extended over whole island, 1875; partitioned with Japan, 1905; penal settlement abolished, 1907; northern half occupied by Japanese, 1917–25; whole ceded to Russia, 1945.

Salamanca, Spain. Captured by Hannibal, 222 B.C.; Moors expelled from, 1055; university founded, 1243; library of the university founded, 1254; cathedral begun, 1513; defeat of French by Wellington, 1812.

Sale of Goods Act, 1893, repealed and replaced by **Sale of Goods Act**, 1979.

Salem, Mass., U.S.A. Founded, 1626; settlement under Endicott, who gave the place its present name, 1628; famous witchcraft trials, 1692.

Salerno, Italy. University, traditionally founded in the ninth century, and said to be the oldest in Europe; closed by order of Napoleon, 1811. S. beach was the scene of bitter fighting in Sept. 1943, when British and American forces fought to establish a beachhead there.

Salette-Fallavaux, La, France. Miracle at, 19 Sept. 1846. Missionaries of Our Lady of La Salette founded, 1852.

Salisbury, England. Founded, 1219, when the clergy were removed by Bishop Poore from Old Sarum (*q.v.*). Present cathedral built, 1220–58, except the spire. Spire built *c.* 1330–60. Walls of Old Sarum demolished, 1608. Cathedral destructively restored, 1782–1791. Spire repaired and summit rebuilt, 1950–1.

Salisbury, Zimbabwe, *See* HARARE.

Salisbury (England). **Councils held at**.

1. Summoned by William the Conqueror to take the oath of allegiance to himself, 1086.
2. Summoned by Henry I to swear to the succession of Prince William (1103–20), 1116.
3. National councils, 1296, 1328, 1384.

Salk Vaccine, against poliomyelitis, was developed by the American scientist Jonas Salk in 1954.

Salonika, Greece. Rebuilt by Cassander on the site of Therme and named Thessalonika, 315 B.C.; surrendered to the Romans, 168 B.C.; made a free city, 42 B.C.; St. Paul preached there, A.D. 52; taken by the Saracens, 904; by the Normans of Sicily, 1185; by the Turks, 1430; Young Turk revolution broke out here, 1908; captured by the Greeks, 8 Nov. 1912, during the First Balkan War. Assigned to Greece by Treaty of London, 30 May 1913. French and British troops entered, 5 Oct. 1915. Venizelist revolutionaries here declared war on Germany and Turkey, 23 Nov. 1916. Great fire, 18 Aug. 1917. French and British forces used S. as base for their operations against Bulgaria until end of World War I.

Salt Lake City, U.S.A. Founded by the Mormons (*q.v.*), 1847. Became a city, 1851.

SALT Treaties. First strategic arms limitation treaty (SALT I) signed between U.S.A. and U.S.S.R., May 1972. Second (SALT II) was signed in June 1979 but never ratified by the U.S. Senate.

Salvador, El. Conquered, 1526, by Spaniards under Pedro de Alvarado, who built capital San Salvador, 1528; formed part of Guatemala colony until 1821, of Mexico until 1823, and of Central American Federation, 1823–39; became independent, 1841. Dispute with Honduras erupted into the 'Football War', July 1969, followed by border-skirmishes. Left-wing coup, 1979, followed by right-wing military ascendancy. Archbishop Romero murdered by rightists, 1980, and open civil war since 1981. In 1984 elections Christian Democrats were largest single party.

Salvation Army, The. Founded by William Booth, 1865.

Salzburg, Austria. The S. music festival was founded in 1870; it became an annual event from 1920 onwards.

Samaria. City founded by King Omri (*c.* 887–876 B.C.), and extended by Ahab (*c.* 876–853 B.C.), kings of Israel. Destroyed by Assyrians, 721. Colonized by Alexander, 331. Burnt down, A.D. 66; but rebuilt, mostly by Herod the Great (39–34 B.C.), who renamed it Sebaste. Twentieth-century excavations have revealed the remains of Ahab's palace.

Sam Browne Belt. Named after its inventor Sir Samuel Browne (1824–1901). The British Army discarded it for field service after 1939.

Samoan Islands, Pacific. Visited by the Dutch, 1721–2; by Bougainville, 1768; Christianity introduced, 1830; independence recognized by European powers, 1889. Treaty of 1899 divided Pacific Islands between England, Germany, and the U.S.A.; W. Samoa ceded to Germany and Tutuila to U.S.A. W. Samoa was mandated to New Zealand, 1920 and became independent 1 Jan. 1962. Swain's Island ceded to the U.S.A., 1925, and considered an integral part of American Samoa.

Samos, Aegean island, colonized by Ionian Greeks, eleventh century B.C. Oligarchy overthrown, 535; tyranny of Polycrates, 535–522; then subject to Persia until 479, when it regained independence and joined the Delian League. Seceded in 440, but reduced by Athens and became tributary to her. Under Spartan domination, 404–394; again subject to Persia from 387 until its recovery by Athens, 366. Subsequent history uncertain until given by Rome to Eumenes II of Pergamum (*q.v.*) in 189 B.C. Genoese colony, A.D. 1346–1560; then Turkish until 1834, when it became a virtually independent principality. Annexed to Greece, 1912.

Sanctions. Use of term became current in present sense, 1919. S. were first applied, 1921: at, Düsseldorf by the French, and later, in 1935, against Italy. Used against Rhodesia, 1966–80.

Sanctuary, Right of. Abolished by law in 1624, so far as felons were concerned, although debtors were able to take refuge in London and elsewhere until the end of the seventeenth century.

Sandhurst. *See* ROYAL MILITARY ACADEMY.

Sandwich Islands. *See* HAWAIIAN ISLANDS.

Sandringham, Norfolk. Estate purchased by the Prince of Wales, 1862. House rebuilt, 1871. King George VI *d.* here, 6 Feb. 1952.

San Francisco, California. Formerly *Yerba Buena*. Spanish mission arrived at, 27 June 1776; American settlement, 1836; name changed to present one, 1847; discovery of gold, 1849; subject to U.S.A., 1850; disorder in and vigilance committee appointed, 1851; earthquake at, 1868, 1872, and 1906.

San Francisco Conference opened, 25 Apr. 1945. Broke up, July 1945.

San Marino City founded, A.D. 885. Republic reputedly dates from second half of fourth century A.D. Treaty relations with Italy established, 1862; treaties of friendship, 1897 and 1953.

Sans Souci (Potsdam), built and laid out by G. W. von Knabelsdorff for Frederick the Great, 1745–7.

Santa Cruz de Teneriffe. Spanish fleet destroyed by Blake, 1657; attacked by Nelson, who here lost his arm, 1797.

Santiago, Spain. Sacked by Moors, A.D. 995, who held it till taken by Ferdinand III, 1235; captured by French, 1809; restored, 1814.

Santo Domingo.
1. *See* DOMINICAN REPUBLIC.
2. The oldest European town in the Americas, founded, 1496, by Bartholomew Columbus. From 1936 until 1961 it was known as **Ciudad Trujillo.** It is the capital of the Dominican Republic (*q.v.*).

Sarajevo Crime. Archduke Franz Ferdinand, heir of Emperor Francis Joseph, and his consort Sophia, Duchess of Hohenberg, were assassinated in S., 28 June 1914.

Sarawak. By cession from the sultanate of Brunei (see BORNEO). James Brooke became Rajah of S., 24 Sept. 1841. Independence recognized by Britain, 1863. British protectorate, 1888. Japanese occupation 1941–45. Ceded by Rajah Sir Charles Brooke to Britain, Feb. 1946. Part of Malaysia (*q.v.*) since 1963.

Sardinia, Island of. Conquered by Vandals (*q.v.*), 435. Conquered by the Byzantines *c.* 540. Conquered by Saracens, tenth century. Successful revolt against Saracens, 1052, and acquired by Norman kingdom of Naples *c.* 1060. Came under Hohenstaufen rule, 1189. To Aragon, 1323. Placed under Spanish viceroys, 1478–1713. To Austria, 1713. To Duke of Savoy, 1720, who then took the title of King of S. *See* SARDINIA, KINGDOM OF and SAVOY.

Sardinia, Kingdom of. At the acquisition of S. by the dukes of Savoy (*q.v.*), the latter proclaimed themselves kings of S., 1720. Deprived of their mainland territories by Napoleon, 1796, but reinstated with Genoa added by Congress of Vienna, 1814. Merged in Italy when the kings of S. became kings of Italy, 1861.

Sardinian Convention, 1855, between Britain, France and Sardinia, by which the King of Sardinia agreed to furnish troops for the Crimea.

Sargasso Sea. First observed by Columbus, 1492.

Sark (Sercq) became fief of English crown, 1066. Demilitarized and occupied by Germans, 1 July 1940. Raided by British Commando, night 3–4 Oct. 1942. German garrison capitulated, 9 May 1945. New harbour opened, 23 June 1949.

Sarum, Old, became seat of bishopric formerly at Sherborne, in 1078. A cathedral, begun 1067, was burned down, 1092. See removed to New Sarum (i.e. Salisbury), 1219. Parliamentary borough abolished, 1832.

Saskatchewan, province of Canada (*q.v.*). Name means 'Rapid River' in the language of the Crees, who before 1869 were almost the sole inhabitants. In the 1870s a settlement began, partly by half-breeds who took part in Riel's second rebellion, 1885. Constituted a province, 1905. University of S., at Saskatoon, incorporated, 1907.

Satellites. First four man-made earth S. put into orbit were Sputnik I, 184 lb., 4 Oct. 1957; Sputnik II, 1118 lb. 3 Nov. 1957 (both Russian); Explorer I, 31 lb., 31 Jan. 1958, and Vanguard I, *c.* 3lb., 17 Mar. 1958 (both from the U.S.A.). Since then many S. launched by Britain, U.S.A., U.S.S.R., France etc., *see* ROCKETS and SPACE FLIGHTS.

Satellite Towns, since World War II known as **New Towns** (*q.v.*).

Satellite Towns. First to be built was Welwyn Garden City (1920). Seven S.T. round London projected under New Towns Act., 1946. Work begun on the first of these (Stevenage), 1947. *See* GARDEN CITY.

Saudi Arabia. Nominally a dependency of Turkish Empire from 1871. As Nejd, consisted of two emirates, Eastern and Western Nejd, until 1892, when Eastern defeated and absorbed Western. Ibn Saud, who seized the emirate in 1905, annexed province of Hasa, on the Persian Gulf, 1914. Inactive during World War I, by 1920 he had annexed parts of Asir; in 1921 Hail and other places. He subdued the new kingdom of Hejaz, 1925; proclaimed King of Hejaz, 1926, and Sultan of Nejd, 1927. The enlarged realm, in 1932, was named S.A. First oil concession agreement, 1933. Ibn Saud *d.* Nov. 1953; succeeded by his son, Saud ibn Abdul-Aziz. Treaty with Jordan, 1962. Prince Feisal, the new Prime Minister, announced the end of slavery in S.A., 6 Nov. 1962. King Saud deposed, 2 Nov. 1964, and his brother Prince Feisal became king. S.A. became leader of moderate Arab opinion from 1960s: and dominated OPEC (*q.v.*). By 1970s controlled virtually all own oil supplies. Feisal assassinated 1975; Khalid (ruled 1975–82) succeeded by Fahd, May 1982

Saurashtra, India. Confederation of former princely states of W. India set up, Mar. 1948. Merged into Bombay State in the reorganization of 1956.

Savannah, U.S.A. Taken by British, 1778. Americans and French repulsed,

1779. British evacuation, 1782. First steamship (the *Savannah*) to cross the Atlantic sailed from S. to Livepool, 1819.

Savings Banks. First suggested by Defoe, 1697, but first practical scheme started by Rev. J. Smith, who instituted a S. bank for his parish, 1799. Post Office S. bank established, 1861, (*see* NATIONAL SAVINGS BANK.) In U.S.A. first S.B. at Boston and Philadelphia, 1816. New York, 1819.

Savoy. Duchy founded by Umberto Biancamano, 1034. Piedmont acquired by marriage, 1056. The dukes of S. became kings of Sardinia (*q.v.*), 1720. The district of S. was annexed by France, 1792, but returned to Sardinia, 1814. In 1860 it was finally ceded to France.

Savoy Conference, The. For the purpose of discussing changes in the liturgy of the Church of England (*q.v.*); it was attended by Church and Puritan parties, and sat, 15 Apr.–24 July 1661.

Savoy Palace (London). Built by Peter of Savoy, 1245; burnt by Wat Tyler, 1381; restored by Henry VII; used as a hospital till eighteenth century; finally taken down, 1817. The chapel survives, having twice been considerably restored.

Saxony. Ancient tribal duchy in NW. Germany broken up, 1180. The name survived in districts of Lauenburg (annexed to Hanover, 1680) and Wittenberg, which with Thuringia and Meissen became under Frederick of Meissen the nucleus of the modern S. in E. Central Germany, 1423. Ravaged by Hussites, 1429–1430. S. divided between Ernestine and Albertine families at Partition of Leipzig, 1485. John Frederick (Ernestine) forced to transfer the electoral title to the Albertine branch (capitulation of Wittenberg), 1547. Treaty of Naumburg results in foundation of the five Thuringian duchies, 1554. Devastated in Thirty Years War, 1618–48. Augustus the Strong, Elector of S., elected King of Poland, 1697. Polish connection continues till 1762. S. joins the *Fürstenbund*, 1785, Frederick Augustus I assumes title of king, 1806, and becomes

Duke of Warsaw, 1807. Half S. annexed by Prussia, 1815. Revolutions, 1848–9. In alliance with Austria against Prussia, 1866. Last king abdicates 9 Nov. 1918. Since 1945 the name 'S.' has appeared in the names of three German *Länder*, two in the German Democratic Republic and one, Lower S., in the German Federal Republic.

Scala, La (Opera House, Milan), completed 1778; restored, 1878, 1922; severely damaged, 1943; reopened, 1947.

Scapa Flow. Admiral Reuter scuttled interned German fleet, 21 June 1919. German submarine penetrated the basin, 14 Oct. 1939, and sank the battleship *Royal Oak* with the loss of 810 lives.

Schism Act, The, 1714. Replaced by Occasional Conformity Act, 1719.

Schleswig-Holstein. Convention of Gastein, 1865, provided that H. should be under Austrian occupation and S. under Prussian; by the Treaty of Prague, 1866, Austria resigned her rights; it was stipulated that North S. should be reunited to Denmark if the people wished it; but the two countries were organized as a single Prussian province, 1867. After plebiscites of the inhabitants of North and South S., North S. was assigned to Denmark, and renamed South Jutland, 1919.

Schmalkalden, League of. Formed by the Protestants of Germany, who met at the town of S. on 22 Dec. 1530. It was finally organized in Dec. 1531.

Schneider Trophy. First race, 1913. Annual till 1927, when it became biennial; the trophy was won outright by Britain in 1931, and there have therefore been no contests since.

Schools, Brothers of the Christian. A Roman Catholic congregation for the education of the poor, founded, 1679, and organized by the Abbé de la Salle in France, 1683; Pope Benedict XIII acknowledged the order, 1725.

Scientific and Industrial Research, Department of, originally a committee of the Privy Council, appointed by Order in Council, 28 July 1915. Charters, 23 Nov. 1916 and 27 Apr. 1928. Department of Scientific and Industrial Research Act, 1956.

Scientists, Among the most prominent are:

Abbe, Enst, 1840–1905
Abel, Sir Frederick Augustus, 1827–1902
Adrian, Baron, 1889–1977
Agassiz, Alexander, 1835–1910
Ampère, André Marie, 1775–1836
Aquinas, St. Thomas, 1225–74
Archimedes, 287–212 B.C.
Aristotle, 384–222 B.C.
Arrhenius, Straute Augustus, 1859–1927
Avogadro, Amedeo, 1776–1856
Bacon, Roger, c. 1214–94
Baird, John L., 1889–1946
Banting, Frederick Grant, 1891–1941
Berthelot, Marcelin, 1827–1907
Black, Joseph, 1728–99
Bohr, Niels, 1885–1962
Boyle, Hon. Robert, 1627–91
Bragg, Sir William, 1862–1942
Braun, Wernher von, 1912–1977
Broglie, Louis de, 1892–
Bunsen, Robert, 1811–99
Cavendish, Henry, 1731–1810
Cockcroft, Sir John Douglas, 1897–1967
Copernicus, Nicolaus, 1473–1543
Crookes, William, 1832–1919
Curie, Marie, 1867–1934
Curie, Pierre, 1859–1906
Dalton, John, 1766–1844
Darwin, Erasmus, 1731–1802
Darwin, Charles, 1809–82
Davy, Sir Humphry, 1778–1829
Descartes,René, 1596–1650
Dewar, Sir James, 1842–1923
Dyson, Sir Frank, 1868–1939
Eddington, Sir Arthur, 1882–1944
Edison, Thomas, 1847–1931
Ehrlich, Paul, 1854–1915
Einstein, Albert, 1879–1955
Euclid, 330 ?–280 B.C.
Fabre, Jean Henri, 1823–1915
Faraday, Michael, 1791–1867
Fleming, Sir Alexander, 1881–1955
Florey, Lord, 1898–1968
Galileo, Galilei, 1564–1642
Gauss, Karl Friedrich, 1777–1855
Haeckel, Ernst, 1834–1919
Hahn, Otto, 1879–1968

Haldane, John B. S., 1892–1964
Haldane, John Scott, 1860–1936
Herschel, Sir William, 1738–1822
Hipparchus of Nicaea, 16–125 B.C.
Humboldt, Alexander von, 1769–1859
Huxley, Thomas Henry, 1825–95
Huxley, Sir Julian, 1887–1975
Jeans, Sir James, 1877–1946
Joliot-Curie, Pierre, 1900–58
Kepler, Johannes, 1571–1630
Lavoisier, Antoine, 1743–94
Leibnitz, Gottfried Wilhelm, 1646–1716
Lodge, Sir Oliver, 1851–1941
Low, Archibald Montgomery, 1888–1956
Marconi, Marchese Guglielmo, 1874–1937
Mayer, Julius Robert, 1814–78
Newton, Sir Isaac, 1643–1727
Nobel, Alfred Bernhard, 1833–96
Ohm, Georg Simon, 1789–1854
Oppenheimer, John Robert, 1904–67
Paracelsus, Theophrastus, 1493–1541
Pascal, Blaise, 1623–62
Pasteur, Louis, 1822–95
Penney, Lord, 1909–
Piccard, Auguste, 1884–1962
Poincaré, Jules Henri, 1854–1912
Priestley, Joseph, 1733–1804
Robinson, Sir Robert, 1886–
Röntgen, Wilhelm Konrad, 1845–1923
Ross, Sir Ronald, 1857–1932
Rutherford, Lord, 1871–1937
Salk, Jonas Edward, 1914–.
Saussure, Horace Bénédicte de (physicist), 1740–99.
Siemens, Werner S., 1816–92.
Thomson, Sir Joseph John, 1856–1940.
Vinci, Leonardo da, 1452–1519.
Volta, Count Alessandro, 1745–1827.
Wallace, Alfred Russell, 1823–1913.
Wallis, Sir Barnes, 1887–1979.
Watson-Watt, Sir Robert, 1892–1973.
Watt, James, 1736–1819.
Whittle, Sir Frank, 1907–.
Wilson, Charles Thomson Rees, 1869–1959.

Scilly Islands (Sillinae). Conquered by Athelstan, 938. Given to the abbey of Tavistock by Henry I. Became crown property on dissolution of monasteries, 1539; leased to Francis Godolphin, 1571; civil power granted him, 1593;

Godolphin leases ended, 1830; leases granted by Duchy of Cornwall to Augustus John Smith, 1834; his successors, the Dorrien-Smiths, in 1920 surrendered all except Tresco, Samson, and Tean. Exemption from income tax ended by Finance Act, 1953.

Scone, Stone of, taken to Westminster by Edward I, 1296. Taken away by Scottish Nationalists on Christmas Eve, 1950. Handed to the curator of Arbroath Abbey, Apr. 1951. Returned to Westminster Abbey, Feb. 1952.

Scotland. St. Columba founds Iona and begins the conversion of the Picts, 563. Rise of the Scots under Constantine I, 789–820. Kenneth McAlpine unifies south S. and founds kingdom of S. proper, 832–60. Malcolm I conquers Strathclyde (q.v.), 946. Malcolm II conquers Lothian, 1018. Duncan killed by Macbeth, 1040. Macbeth defeated by Siward and Malcolm Canmore at Dunsinane, 1054, and killed, 1057. Malcolm Canmore becomes king, 1058. He does homage to William I of England, 1070. David defeated by English at battle of the Standard, 1138. Malcolm IV subdues Galloway, 1160. Defeat of Haakon of Norway at battle of Largs, 1263. Acquisition from Norway of Hebrides and Isle of Man at Treaty of Perth, 1266. Margaret, the 'Maid of Norway', dies, 1290. Edward I awards throne of S. to John Baliol, 1292. Franco-Scots alliance, 1295. Wallace defeats English at Stirling Bridge, 1297. Wallace defeated at battle of Falkirk, 1298. Wallace captured, 1304. Robert Bruce crowned king, 25 Mar. 1306. Accepted by clergy, 1310. Defeats Edward II at Bannockburn, 1314. Edward Bruce invades Ireland, 1315–18. Anglo-Scots truce, 1323. Battle of Halidon Hill, 1333. David II captured at Neville's Cross, 1346. David released by Treaty of Berwick, 1357. Robert II, first of the Stuarts, succeeds to the throne, 1371. Battle of Chevy Chase (Otterburn), 1388. James I murdered at Perth, 1437. James II killed at Roxburgh, 1460. James III annexes Orkneys and Shetlands, 1471. James III murdered, 1488. James IV killed at battle of Flodden,

1513. Knox begins Reformation, 1541. Defeat at battle of Solway Moss, 1542. English sack Edinburgh, 1544. Henry VIII of England instigates the murder of Cardinal Beaton, 1546. Knox flees to France, 1547. The Covenant signed, 1557. Treaty of Berwick, 1560. Papal jurisdiction abolished, 1560. Mary Queen of Scots marries Darnley, 1565. Rizzio murdered, 1566. Darnley murdered, 1567. Mary flees to England, and is imprisoned by Elizabeth, 1568. James VI takes over government, 1578. He signs the second Confession of Faith, 1581. Mary beheaded at Fotheringhay, 1587. Presbyterianism established, 1592, but king reintroduces episcopacy, 1597. James VI becomes King of England as James I, 1603. Charles I authorizes new book of canons, 1635. First Bishops' War, 1637. National Covenant, 1638. Second Bishops' War, 1639–40. The Solemn League and Covenant, 1643. Covenanters' rebellion defeated by Monmouth at Bothwell Brig, 1679. Jacobites defeated at Killiecrankie, 1689. Massacre of Glencoe, 1692. Legislative Union with England, 1707. *See* ENGLISH HISTORY and GREAT BRITAIN, JACOBITES, etc.

Scotland, Sovereigns of:
Constantine I 789–820
Kenneth I (McAlpine) 832–860
Donald 860–863
Constantine II 863–877
Eocha 881–889
Donald I 889–900
Constantine III 900–942
Malcolm I 942–954
Indulf 954–962
Dubh 962–967
Cullean 967–971
Kenneth II 971–995
Cuilean 967–971
Kenneth II 971–995
Constantine IV 995–997
Kenneth III 997–1005
Malcolm II 1005–1034
Duncan 1034–1040
Macbeth 1040–1057
Lulach 1057–1058
Malcolm III (Canmore) 1058–1093
Donald Bane 1093

Duncan II 1094
(Donald Bane (again) 1094–1097
(Edmund 1094–1097
Edgar 1097–1107
Alexander I 1107–1124
David I 1124–1153
Malcolm IV 1153–1165
William the Lion 1165–1214
Alexander II 1214–1249
Alexander III 1249–1286
Margaret ('the Maid of Norway')
 1286–1290
Interregnum 1290–1292
John Baliol 1292–1296
Interregnum 1296–1306
Robert I (Bruce) 1306–1329
David II (Bruce) 1329–1372
Robert II (Stuart) 1372–1390
Robert III 1390–1406
James I 1406–1437
James II 1437–1460
James III 1460–1488
James IV 1488–1513
James V 1513–1542
Mary (Abdicated) 1542–1567
James VI 1567–1603
James VI became James I of England,
 1603. *See* ENGLISH SOVEREIGNS AND
 THEIR CONSORTS.

Scotland, Church of. Founded by John Knox (1505–72) and Andrew Melville (1545–1622). First Assembly ratified Confession of Faith, 20 Dec. 1560. Act of Scottish Parliament establishing the C. of S. passed, 1592. Episcopacy finally abandoned, 1690. Union with United Free Church of Scotland, 3 Oct. 1929.

Scotland Yard, the London palace of the Scottish kings, was demolished soon after 1603. Last Scottish sovereign to use it had been Queen Margaret (née Tudor) (*d.* 1541). Police office set up, 1829, which moved to New S.Y. and became H.Q. Metropolitan Police, 1891.

Seal of England, Keeper of the Great. First keeper, Richard, a chaplain, 1116; joined to Lord Chancellorship, 1563.

Seal of the United States, Great. Design adopted by Congress, 20 June, 1782.

S.E.A.T.O. *See* SOUTH-EAST ASIA TREATY ORGANIZATION.

Sebastopol. A town in the Crimea, built in 1784; famous for the eleven months'

siege by the English and French in 1854–1855, after which it was largely rebuilt, and the siege by the Germans, 1941–2, which also resulted in widespread destruction of the town.

Second Empire. Dec. 1852–4 Sept. 1871. *See* FRANCE.

Second Republic. 24 Feb. 1848–Dec. 1852. *See* FRANCE.

Secretary of State (U.S.A.). First appointment (that of Thomas Jefferson) made, 1789.

Secretary of State for Scotland appointed under terms of the Act of Union, 1707, but office abolished in 1746, when its duties devolved on the Home Secretary. In 1827 these were delegated to the Lord Advocate; Secretaryship created, 1885, and offices of S. of S. reestablished, 1926.

Sedan Chairs. First used in England, 1581; in general use, 1649.

Sederunt, Act of, 1532. James V of Scotland conferred on the Scottish Court of Session the power to regulate Courts of Law by means of A. of S. Power confirmed, 1540.

Seditious Meetings Act. Introduced by William Pitt in 1795. It prohibited the meeting of more than 50 persons (except county and borough meetings duly called) for the consideration of petitions or addresses for reform in Church or State. S.M. and Assemblies Bill, 1817.

Selangor, state of the Malaysian Federation, since 1963. Commercial treaty with E. India Co., 1818; accepted British resident and protection, 1874.

Selective Employment Tax (S.E.T.) type of 'pay-roll tax' instituted by the Labour Government, 1966. Abolished, 1972.

Self-Denying Ordinance. A measure introduced into the Long Parliament on 9 Dec. 1644. It was to enact 'that no member of either House of Parliament should during the war enjoy or execute any office or command, military or civil'. It was passed 3 Apr. 1645. Essex and other Presbyterians were removed and replaced by Cromwell's nominees, and since, under the Ordinance as finally passed, reappointment was allowed, Cromwell became cavalry commander.

Seljuk, Turkish dynasty, was descended from eponymous chieftain who *fl.* 950 as first Moslem Emir of Bokhara. His grandson, Toghrul Beg, became Shah of Persia, and established new capital at Merv, 1040; he captured Bagdad, 1055. Toghrul Beg's successor, Alp Arslan, defeated and captured the Emperor Romanus at Manzikert, 1071. On death of Malik Shah (1092) the S. domains were split among four branches of the dynasty the last of which was supplanted by the Ottomans *c.* 1300.

Selsey, original seat of the S. Saxon bishopric, founded by Wilfrid of Ripon *c.* 683, removed to Chichester, 1079.

Semaphore invented by Edgeworth, 1767; adapted by Chappe, 1794; by Sir G. Murray, 1795; Sir H. Popham's system adopted by Royal Navy for sea service, 1816, but replaced by Pasley's system, 1827. Present system not fully evolved until 1890.

Senate, Roman, first mentioned, 509 B.C., as having 300 members, all patricians; plebeians admitted shortly before 401 B.C. It existed, though largely deprived of effective power, as long as the Western Roman Empire (*q.v.*).

Senegal. First European explorer in modern times was Jean de Béthencourt (1406). French factories established, 1626, but displaced by English; returned, 1677; again displaced by British, 1720–63: this settlement confirmed, 1783; abandoned between 1789 and 1815, the colony was re-established and re-explored, 1824. Dakar (*q.v.*) founded by Gen. Faidherbe, who landed, 1852, and became governor, 1854. S. became an independent republic on 20 Aug. 1960, after having been a partner (with the Sudan) in the Federation of Mali from Jan. 1959 until Aug. 1960. On 1 Feb. 1982 joined with Gambia (*q.v.*) to form Confederation of Senegambia.

Seoul made capital of Korea (*q.v.*) by King Ni Taijo (*fl* A.D. 1392). Scene of heavy fighting during the Korean War, 1950–1.

Septennial Act, passed, 1716, in force until 1911.

Sepulchre, Church of the Holy, Jerusalem. The first building, commissioned by Constantine, 326, was combined with other small early churches in one building at the time of the Crusades (*q.v.*). Largely rebuilt, 1799 and 1810. East dome damaged in earthquake, 1927. Rockefeller Foundation undertook repairs as result of Harvey Report (1932). Damage caused in battle between Arab Legion (Jordan Army) and Israeli forces, 1947–8, and in the fire of 1949.

Sepulchre, Knights of the, received papal sanction, 1113.

Serbia. Serbs settled in present S. *c.* 610–40. Zhuponiya period, sixth to ninth centuries. Visheslav dynasty early ninth century to 890. Bulgarian supremacy, 890–924. Yovan Vladimir captured by Bulgars, 989. Michael Voislavich king, 1077. S. united and independent under Nemanyich dynasty, 1159–1331. Zenith under Tsar Stephen Dushan, 1331–55. After great Turkish victory at Kossovo Polje (The Field of Blackbirds) S. becomes tributary to Turks, 15 June 1389. Despotate of S., 1389–1459, suppressed by Sultan Mohammed II, 1459. S. a Turkish Pashalik, 1459–1805. Karageorge storms Belgrade, 1805. Limited international recognition of Treaty of Bucharest, 1812. Turkish reconquest, 1813–15. Miloš Obrenović frees S., 1815–17. Becomes hereditary prince, 1830. Milos abdicates 1839. Alexander Karageorgević elected prince, 1842. International guarantee by Treaty of Paris, 1856. Miloš Obrenović returns, 1858. Succeeded by Michael, 1860. Michael murdered, 1868. Milan elected prince, 1868. Regency till 1872. War with Turkey, 1876–8. Full independence recognized by Treaty of Berlin, 1878. Proclaimed a kingdom, 1882. War with Bulgaria, 1885–6. Milan abdicates, 1889. Alexander Obrenović deposes the regents, 1893. Assassination of Alexander and Queen Draga, 1903. Peter Karageorgević elected king, 15 June 1903. Austria annexes Bosnia, 1908. For later history *see* BALKAN WARS; WORLD WAR I; YUGOSLAVIA. Part of Yugoslavia since 1918.

Serbo-Croatian Language, spoken in the western half of the Balkan peninsula since its penetration by the Slavs in the seventh century A.D. Now the language of Yugoslavia (*q.v.*), except for its constituent republics of Macedonia and Slovenia.

Seringapatam. British defeated Tipu Sahib of Mysore, 15 May 1791. In a later war S. was stormed by Madras Army and Tipu killed, 4 May 1799. *See* MYSORE.

Serjeant at Law. This rank became obsolete in 1873.

Settlement, Act of, 1662. Relating to the forfeiture of estates by Irish rebels. Repealed, 1689. Restored, 1690.

Settlement, Act of, 1701. Secured the succession to the throne to the house of Hanover in default of Protestant heirs to the house of Stuart.

Seven Bishops. *See* BISHOPS, SEVEN.

Seven Years War, 1756–63.

1756: Anglo-Prussian alliance, 16 Jan. Franco-Austrian alliance, 1 May. Britain declares war on France, 15 May. Black Hole of Calcutta, 19 June. French take Minorca, 28 June. French take Oswego (Canada), 14 Aug. Prussia invades Saxony, 29 Aug. Saxon Army capitulates, 15 Oct.

1757: Clive takes Calcutta, 2 Jan. Russia, Poland, Sweden, and the Empire declare war on Prussia, 10 Jan. Austrians defeat Prussians at Kolin, 18 June. Clive wins victory at Plassey, 23 June. French defeat British at Hastenbeck, 26 July. Russians and Swedes invade Prussia, Aug.–Sept. British capitulate at Kloster Zeven, 8 Sept. Great Prussian victories at Rossbach over French and Imperialists, 5 Nov.; at Leuthen over Austrians, 5 Dec.

1758: British agree to finance Prussia, 13 Apr. French defeated at Krefeld, 23 June. British take Louisburg, 24 July. Prussians defeat Russians at Zorndorf, 25 Aug. Austrians defeat Prussians at Hochkirch, 14 Oct. British conquer Pittsburgh and French Senegal and Clive forces Dutch in India to surrender at Chinsura, Nov.

1759 (*Annus Mirabilis*): British take Masulipatam, 7 Apr. British defeat French at Minden, 1 Aug. Austro-Russians defeat Prussians at Künersdorf, 12 Aug. British capture Quebec, 18 Sept. British destroy French fleet at Quiberon, 20 Nov. Prussians defeated at Maxen, 21 Nov.

1760: Decisive French defeat in India at Wandewash, 22 Jan. Prussians defeated at Landshut, 23 June. Prussian victory at Liegnitz, 15 Aug. British capture Montreal, 8 Sept. Prussian victory at Torgau, 3 Nov.

1761: British victory at Patna, 15 Jan. British take Pondicherry, 16 Jan. Franco-Spanish alliance (Third Family Compact), 15 Aug. Austro-Russian invasion of Prussia, Oct.–Dec.

1762: Britain declares war on Spain, 4 Jan. British clear the W. Indies, Jan –Apr. British cease to subsidize Prussia, Apr. Sweden and Russia make peace with Prussia, May. Prussia defeats Austrians at Bürkersdorf, 21 July. French capitulation at Kassel, 1 Nov. Truce between Prussia, Austria, and Saxony, 24 Nov.

1763: Peace of Paris between Britain, France, Spain, and Portugal, 10 Feb. Peace of Hubertusburg between Prussia and Austria, 15 Feb.

Severn Road Bridge, opened by Queen Elizabeth II, Sept. 1966.

Seville (anct. **Hispalis**; Latin **Julia Romula**), taken by Julius Caesar, 45 B.C. became Roman colony. Taken A.D. 411, by Vandals, 441 by Visigoths, 712 by Moors. Reconquered 1248 by Castilians. Building of cathedral lasted 1402–1519, though some parts like the Sacristy (1532) were added later, and parts of the older Moorish mosque were incorporated, such as the Orangery and the quadrangular Giralda tower (1184). Other buildings include Alba Palace, 1483; University, 1502; Town Hall, 1527–64; and Exchange, 1583.

Sèvres porcelain first manufactured, 1756. Treaty of S. signed, 10 Aug. 1920.

Sewing-machine first built by Thomas Saint, 1790 (for shoemakers); for tailoring by Madersperger, 1814; B. Thimonier, 1830; Walter Hunt, 1834; Elias Howe, 1845; I. M. Singer, 1851; A. B. Wilson, 1852.

Seychelles, discovered by Portuguese, 1505. Explored by French, 1742 and 1744, and captured by the British, 1794. Ceded to Britain, 1814. Politically separated from Mauritius (*q.v.*), 1897. Leaders of Arab revolt in Palestine exiled here, 1937. Archbishop Makarios of Cyprus banished to S., 1956–7. Independent republic, 29 June 1976; left-wing coup, 5 June 1977.

Shakers (United Society of Believers in Christ's Second Appearing) founded *c.* 1747 in England. Moved to America, 1774. Community of Mt. Lebanon, New York State, founded 1787.

Shakespeare's Works. Shakespeare was *b.* in 1564 and *d.* in 1616. First collected edition of his works, 1623, in folio. The first plays produced about 1590, in which Shakespeare himself took part; the Globe Theatre, Southwark, was the scene of most of the early productions. Shakespeare's plays with conjectural dates of composition are: *Titus Andronicus* and *Love's Labour's Lost,* 1590; *The Two Gentlemen of Verona,* 1591; *Henry VI, The Comedy of Errors, Romeo and Juliet,* and *A Midsummer Night's Dream,* 1592; *Richard II* and *Richard III,* 1593; *King John,* 1594; *The Merchant of Venice* and *The Taming of the Shrew,* 1596; *Henry IV, Henry V,* and *The Merry Wives of Windsor,* 1598; *Julius Caesar,* 1598–9; *Much Ado about Nothing* and *As You Like It,* 1598–1600; *Twelfth Night,* 1600; *All's Well that Ends Well,* 1601; *Hamlet,* 1602; *Troilus and Cressida,* 1603; *Othello* and *Measure for Measure,* 1604; *Macbeth* and *King Lear,* 1606; *Timon of Athens,* 1607; *Pericles* and *Antony and Cleopatra,* 1608; *Coriolanus,* 1609; *Cymbeline,* 1610, *The Winter's Tale* and *The Tempest,* 1611; *Henry VIII,* 1612. Poems, with dates of publication:

Venus and Adonis, 1593; *The Rape of Lucrece,* 1594; *The Passionate Pilgrim* (partly Shakespeare's), 1599; *The Phoenix and the Turtle,* 1601; Sonnets, and *A Lover's Complaint,* 1609.

Shanghai first settled by Europeans under terms of Treaty of Nanking, 1842. Central Bank of China opened, 1928. Battles between Kuomintang and Japanese, 1932 and 1937. Occupied by Japanese, 1938, and International Settlement taken over by them, 1941. Treaty rights of European powers abandoned, 1947. S. captured by Communists, 1949.

Shan States annexed to Burma, 1885. Council of Chiefs instituted, 1922; combined with Wa States into single S. State, 1947.

Sharpeville, S. Africa. On 21 Mar. 1960, 67 Africans here were killed when police opened fire on a crowd agitating against the Pass Laws.

Sheerness. A royal dockyard in Kent, made by Charles II in 1663; taken by the Dutch under De Ruyter in 1667; Nore mutiny here, 1798; modern dockyard made in 1814.

Sheffield, England. First charter, 1297. Famous for knife-making in fourteenth century. Steelworks since nineteenth century. Borough, 1843; city, 1882. University founded, 1905.

Sheriffs became important in English provincial administration *c.* A.D. 1000, and more so after 1066. Yearly tenure of office introduced, 1100; confirmed, 1258. Ceased to command county militia, 1557. Modern practice regulated by Sheriffs' Act, 1887.

Sherman Act (U.S.A.), against trusts, passed 1890 at instance of John S. (1823–1900).

Shetland Islands. Written sources state Scandinavian settlement began *c.* A.D. 800, but contact with Scandinavia probably much earlier than this. Early Norse form of S. place-names indicates occupation before 700. Annexed to Norway, A.D. 875. Came under Scottish rule, 1466.

Ship. Roman '*corvus*' in use, 260 B.C. Light galleys became standard Mediterranean warships after battle of Actium, 31 B.C. Large warships built in England, 1413. Success of galleasses at battle of Lepanto, 1571. *Royal George* launched, 1756; *Victory* 1765. Earliest iron ship built at Foss (Yorkshire), 1777. Transatlantic packets began, 1816. First genuine clipper, 1832. First power boat, 1786. First paddle steamer,

Charlotte Dundas, 1801. First screw steamer, *Archimedes*, 1839. Twin-screw ship, *Flora*, 1862. Steam turbine, *Turbinia*, 1894. First Diesel and electric ship, *Wandal*, 1903. First gas-turbine driven ship, 1948. First nuclear-powered vessel, the U.S. submarine *Nautilus*, completed her trials, 1955.

Ship-money was first levied by Ethelred, 1007. Specifically forbidden by Petition of Right, 1628, but declared legal by a majority of judges of the Court of Exchequer, 1637. Abolished by statute, 1641.

Shipping, Ministry of, formed, 1916, wound up, 1919.

Shoguns of Japan. Originally a military C.-in-C. the first shogun was Otomo Otomaro, 794. When Yoritomo became shogun in 1192 the shogun was the political ruler of Japan. The shogunate was itself under a regency, 1205–1333. The office was held by the Ashillaga family, 1338–1500. Oda Nobunaga seizes shogunate, 1568. Succeeded by Hideyoshi, 1582. With the appointment of Iyeyasu in 1603 the office became hereditary in the Tokugawa family until its abolition, 1867. The following are the Tokugawa S.:

Iyeyasu	1603	Yoshimune 1716
Hidetada	1616	Iyeshige 1745
Iyemitsu	1622	Iyeharu 1760
Iyetsuna	1651	Iyenari 1786
Tsunayoshi	1680	Iyeyoshi 1838
Iyenobu	1709	Iyesada 1853
Iyetsugu	1713	Iyemochi 1858

Yoshinobu (Kei-Ki) 1866–7.

Shop Hours Acts (Britain), 1886, 1892, 1893, 1899, 1904.

Shops Acts, 1911, 1912, 1928, 1934, 1937, 1950 and 1965.

Shops and Offices Act, 1963, legislated to improve working conditions of white-collar workers.

Shoreditch (London). First public theatre in England built here, 1576.

Siam. *See* THAILAND.

Siberia. Explored by Russians in 1483. Tatar khanate, whose capital was Sibir on the Irtish, formed in sixteenth century. Russian conquest begun by Yermak, 1579. Tobolsk built on site of Sibir, 1587. Traders reached Sea of Okhotsk, 1639. Russians reached the Amur, 1651. Treaty of Nertchinsk established boundary between Russia and China, 1689. S. first used as place of banishment, 1710. Sakhalin (*q.v.*) occupied, 1853. Petropavlovsk abandoned, 1855. Convention of Aigun, making the Amur boundary between Russia and China, 1857. Country between Ussuri and the sea secured by Treaty of Pekin, and Vladivostok founded, 1860. Construction of Trans-Siberian Railway begun, 1891. Russia occupied Liaotung peninsula and established Port Arthur and Dalny, 1895. Trans-Siberian Railway was completed, partly through Chinese territory, in 1896. The Russo-Japanese War, 1904–5; Port Arthur fell, Jan. 1905, and Japan gained footing on mainland. Exile system abolished, 1914. A new line made the Trans-Siberian Railway complete on Russian territory, 1916. In the struggles that began in Nov. 1917, the Bolsheviks of S. were driven out by Czechs. Britain and France landed contingents at Vladivostok, Aug. 1918, and followed by Japanese, 12 Aug.; on the fall of Chita, 6 Sept., Bolshevik Government disappeared from S. The leader of the reaction, Admiral Koltchak, became dictator after a *coup d'état* at Omsk, 18 Nov. On the resurgence of Bolshevism, Koltchak lost Omsk in Nov. 1919; he was caught and shot, 7 Feb. 1920. Organization into Soviet Republics, 1922–3.

Sicilian Vespers. Massacre of the French began, 30 Mar. 1282.

Sicily. The Phoenicians founded colonies here in 735 B.C., and the Greeks 200 years later; made a Roman province, 241 B.C.; taken by Belisarius, A.D. 535; by Saracens, 832; in Norman possessions, 1072–1194; made one kingdom with Naples, 1130; Charles of Anjou King of the Two Sicilies, 1266; 'Sicilian Vespers', massacre of French at Palermo, 1282; became a Spanish dependency, 1501; revolution in, 1848; Garibaldi landed at Marsala, 1860; defeated Neapolitans at Milazzo,

1860; annexation with Sardinia and arrival of King Victor Emmanuel, 1860, annexation to kingdom of Italy, 1860; earthquake at Messina, 1908. In World War II Germans driven out by British, American, and Canadians, 10 July–17 Aug. 1943. Economic backwardness and Mafia extortion since 1945. *See also* NAPLES.

Sieges: Acre, 1189–12 July 1191; 16 Mar.–20 May 1799; Apr.–24 June 1832; 3–4 Nov. 1840.

Adrianople, Oct. 1912–26 Mar. 1913.

Alesia, 52 B.C.

Algeciras, 1324–4.

Algiers, 1682–3; 26–27 Aug. 1816; 14 June–5 July 1830.

Almeida, 17 Aug. 1810.

Amiens, 1597.

Ancona, Oct.–13 Nov. 1799.

Antwerp, 1584–5; Dec. 1832; 1914.

Arras, 1640.

Avignon, 10 June–13 Sept. 1226.

Badajoz, 1385; 1396; 1542; 1705; Mar. 1811; Apr. 1812.

Bagdad, 1258.

Barcelona, 1471; 1697; 1705; 1706; Sept. 1714.

Bataan, Jan.–Apr. 1942.

Belgrade, 1456; Aug. 1521; Aug. 1717; Oct. 1789.

Belle Isle, June 1761.

Bergen-op-Zoom, 1588; 1622; Sept. 1747; Mar. 1814.

Berlin (blockade), June 1948–May 1949.

Berwick, 1296; 1333; 1481.

Besançon, 1668; 1674.

Bethune, 1710.

Bilbao, 1835; 1874; 1937.

Bois-le-Duc, 1601; 1603; 1794.

Bologna, 1506; 1796; 1799.

Bomarsund, 1854.

Bonn, 1689; 1703.

Bordeaux, 1451; 1453.

Bouchain, Aug.–Sept. 1711.

Boulogne, Sept. 1544.

Breda, 1625; Feb. 1793.

Brescia, 1512; 1849.

Breslau, 1807.

Brisach, 1638.

Brussels, 1695; 1746.

Budapest, July 1541; Sept. 1686; Dec. 1944–13 Feb. 1945.

Burgos, Sept.–Oct. 1812; June 1813.

Cadiz, 1812.

Calais, Sept. 1346–Oct. 1347; 1558; 1596; 22–7 May 1940.

Calvi, 1794.

Candia, 1667–9.

Capua, 211 B.C.; 1501; 1799.

Cartagena, 1706; Nov. 1873–Jan. 1874.

Chalus, 1199.

Charleroi, 1672; 1690.

Charleston, U.S.A., 1780; Aug. 1863–Feb. 1865.

Chartres, 1568.

Cherbourg, 1418, 1758.

Chester, 1643–6.

Chillon, 1536.

Chitral, Mar.–Apr. 1895.

Ciudad Rodrigo, June–July 1810; 1812.

Colchester, June–Aug. 1648.

Como, 1127.

Compiègne, 1430.

Condé, 1676; 1793; 1794.

Coni, 1691; 1744.

Constantinople, 1453.

Copenhagen, 1658; 1801; 1807.

Cordova, 1012.

Corfu, 1536, 1716–18.

Corinth, 1205; 1209.

Cracow, 1702; 1794.

Cremona, 1702.

Cumae, 553.

Danzig, 1734; 1793; 1807; 1813–14.

Delhi, 1857.

Dien Bien Phu, Apr.–May 1954.

Douay, 1710.

Dresden, 1756; 1760; 1813.

Drogheda, 1649.

Dublin, 1170; 1500; 1649.

Dunkirk, 1646; 1793.

Edinburgh, 1093; 1296.

Edinburgh Castle, 1571.

Exeter, 1136.

Famagusta, 1571.

Flushing, Aug. 1809.

Fredrikshald, 1718.

Gaeta, 1707; 1734; Nov. 1860–Feb. 1861.

Genoa, 1684; 1747; 1800.

Gerona, 1808–9.

Ghent, 1706.

Gibraltar, 1704; 1779; 1782–3.

Glatz, 1622; 1742; 1807.

Gloucester, Aug.–Sept. 1643.

Göttingen, 1760.

Granada, 1491–2.
Groningen, 1594; 1678.
Haarlem, Dec. 1572–July 1573.
Harfleur, 1415.
Heidelberg, 1688.
Herat, 1837–8; 1856.
Humaitá (Paraguay), 1868.
Ismail, 1770; 1790.
Janina, 1913.
Jerusalem c. 1400 B.C.; 588 B.C.; A.D. 70; 637; 1099.
Kandahar, 1521; 1839–42.
Kars, 1855.
Kehl, 1796–7.
Khartoum, 1884–5.
Kimberley, Oct. 1899–Feb. 1900.
Komárom or Komorn, 1849.
Ladysmith, Nov. 1899–Feb. 1900.
La Motte, 1634.
Landau, 1702; 1703; 1793.
Landrecies, 1712; 1794.
Leipzig, 1547; 1642.
Leith, 1560.
Leningrad, 21 Aug. 1941–18 Jan. 1943.
Lerida, 1647; 1707; 1810.
Leyden, 1574.
Liège, 1468; 1702; 1914.
Lille, 1708; 1792.
Limerick, 1651; 1690–1.
Londonderry, 1689.
Lucknow, 1857.
Luxemburg, 1795.
Lyons, 1793.
Madrid, 1936–9.
Maastricht, 1579; 1673; 1703; 1748; 1793–4.
Mafeking, Oct. 1899–May 1900.
Magdeburg, 1631; 1806.
Mainz, 1689; 1793.
Malaga, 1487.
Malta, 1565; 1798; 1800; June 1940–Nov. 1942.
Mannheim, 1793.
Mantua, 1796–7.
Messina, 1282; 1719; 1848.
Metz, 1552–3; 1870.
Missolonghi, 1822; 1823; 1825–6.
Mons, 1691; 1709; 1746; 1792.
Montargis, 1427.
Montauban, 1621.
Montevideo, 1807; 1814.
Namur, 1692; 1695.
Naples, 1495; 1799; 1806.
Nice, 1705.

Numantia, 134–133 B.C.
Olivenza, 1811.
Olmütz, 1741; 1758.
Orleans, 1428–9; 1563.
Ostend, July 1601–Sept. 1604; 1706; 1745; 1798.
Oudenarde, 1708.
Padua, 1509.
Pampeluna or Pamplona, 1813.
Paris, 885–6; 1594; Sept. 1870–Jan. 1871.
Pavia, 1525; 1655.
Pekin legations, 1900.
Perpignan, 1542; 1642.
Phalsbourg, 1814; 1815; 1870.
Phillipsburg, 1644; 1676; 1688; 1734; 1799–1800.
Plevna, 1877.
Pondicherry, 1748.
Port Arthur, 1904.
Prague, 1741–4.
Quebec, 1759.
Quesnay, 1793–4.
Rheims, 1359.
Rhodes, 1306–9; 1480; 1522.
Richmond (Va.), 1864–5.
Riga, 1700; 1710.
Rochelle, 1573; 1628.
Rome, 1527; 1849.
Romorantin, 1356.
Rouen, 1419; 1449; 1591.
Roxburgh, 1460.
Saguntum, 219 B.C.
Saint-Quentin, 1557.
San Sebastian, 1813.
Saragossa, 1710; 1808; 1809.
Schweidnitz, 1762; 1807.
Scio, 1822.
Scutari, 1913.
Sebastopol, Oct. 1854–Sept. 1855; 1941–1942.
Seringapatam, 1792; 1799.
Seville, 1248.
Silistria, 1854.
Smolensk, 1611; 1812.
Stalingrad, Aug.–Nov, 1942.
Stralsund, 1715.
Strasbourg, 1870.
Tarragona, 1813.
Temesvar, 1716.
Thérouanne, 1303; 1479; 1513.
Thionville, 1792.
Thorn, 1703.
Tobruk, Apr.–10 Dec. 1941; 18–20 June 1942.

Toledo, 1936.
Tortosa, 1810–11.
Toulon, 1707; 1793.
Toulouse, 844; *c.* 848; 1229.
Tournai, 1340; 1513; 1581; 1667; 1709; 1792.
Tunis, 1270; 1535.
Turin, 1640; 1706.
Valencia, 1812.
Valenciennes, 1677; 1793; 1794.
Vannes, 1342.
Venice, 1849.
Verdun, 1792; 1916.
Vicksburg, 1863.
Vienna, 1529; 1683; 1848.
Warsaw, 1831; 1939; 1944.
Westerplatte, 1939.
Xativa, 1246; 1707.
Xeres, 1262.
York, 1644.
Ypres, 1648; 1794.
Zürich, 1544.
Zutphen, 1586.

Siegfried Line.
1. (Or **Hindenburg Line.**) German line of defence in France in Sept. 1918.
2. German fortifications, properly called the West Wall, stretching from the Dutch to the Swiss frontiers, partly on the E. bank of the Rhine, completed, 1939.

Sierra Leone. Discovered, 1462, by the Portuguese navigator. Pedro de Sintra. Became a settlement for freed slaves, 1786. British colony of S.L. originated in sale of land by native chiefs to some English settlers, 1788. Crown colony, 1808; protectorate, forming the hinterland of the colony, 1896. New constitution, 1958. Became an independent member of the British Commonwealth, 27 Apr. 1961; republic, 19 Apr. 1971.

Sikhs, religious order founded by Nanak (1469–1539). Became politically independent of the Moguls, 1764. Ranjit Singh became overlord of the confederation of Sikh states, 1805; in 1849 the Punjab, home of all S., came under British rule. Patalia and E. Punjab Union, a Sikh state forming part of the republic of India, was set up, 5 May 1948, but reorganized as the Punjab, 1956. Sikh agitation against alleged Indian discrimination, 1961–2, and again in 1980s. Sikhs assassinated Mrs Gandhi, 1984.

Sikkim suffered in eighteenth century from aggression by Nepal (*q.v.*), which was ended by alliance with Britain against Nepal (1814). Site of Darjeeling sold to British for 180,000 Rs., 1835. In Aug. 1947 India entered into the same treaty relations with S. as formerly had obtained between S. and Britain.

Silchester, Hants, formerly **Calleva Atrebatum**, was laid out as a Roman town in the first century A.D. Excavated 1890–1909, 1938–9, and 1954.

Silesia. Mutual succession pact between Hohenzollerns (of Prussia) and the Piasts (Rulers) of S., 1537. Last Piast dies and S. seized by the emperor as a Bohemian fief, 1675. Hohenzollern claims renounced in return for Schwiebus, 1686. Schwiebus returned to Austria, 1694. Seized by Frederick the Great of Prussia, 1740. Cession to Prussia finally recognized by Austria, 1763. After plebiscites Teschen ceded to Czechoslovakia and Upper S. partitioned between Germany and Poland, 1920. Teschen taken by Poland, 1938. S. east of the Neisse taken by Poland, 1945, and the German population expelled.

Silk. Silkworms introduced into Europe from China in 552 by two Persian monks; manufactured in Italy, Spain, and S. France, 1510; first S. mills in England, 1604; formerly all S. was brought from abroad.

Silver Coinage. Until Dec. 1920 contained 92.5 per cent silver. Coinage Act, 1920, authorized 50 per cent only. New Coinage Act of 1946 did not legally abolish S. as coinage, but for all practical purposes meant that S. coins were to be replaced by cupro-nickel.

Simplon Pass, Switzerland. Road built by Napoleon, 1800–7. Tunnel built, 1898–1906.

Sinaiticus, Codex, incomplete Greek MS. of Old and New Testaments and some other writings, on vellum. Probably copied in Egypt or Palestine *c.* 350. Tischendorf (1815–74) found the MS. in the monastery of St. Catherine, Mt. Sinai, 1844 and 1859; he published it in facsimile type, 1862. Photographic reproductions appeared, 1911 and 1922; about 340 leaves of MS. were bought for the British Museum from the Soviet Government, 1933.

Sind, Scinde, annexed to British India, 1843. Autonomous province of Pakistan, 1947–55, when it was integrated into Pakistan.

Singapore, the old Malay city, *fl.* in the fourteenth century A.D., but had been destroyed by 1391. Settlement founded by Sir Stamford Raffles, 1819; placed under Bengal Government, 1823; part of Straits Settlements, 1836–1946. British land forces in Malaya retired into S., 30 Jan. 1942. Japanese landed on S. Island, 8 Feb. 1942; garrison surrendered, 15 Feb. Reoccupied by British forces, 5 Sept. 1945. An agreement reached in London in Apr. 1957 provided for an internationally self-governing S. and the creation of a S. citizenship. A referendum on 1 Sept. 1962 produced a majority in favour of an autonomous S. within the projected Malaysia (*q.v.*), but the arrangement led to stresses and on 9 Aug. 1965 S. seceded from Malaysia by mutual agreement. S. became a republic within the Commonwealth, 16 Oct. 1965.

Sinkiang, formerly Chinese Turkestan, became a separate province at the territorial reorganization of the Manchu Empire, 1882. Russian influence increased steadily from 1911 until 1941, by which date S. was virtually another Soviet republic. In 1942 the Governor declared his allegiance to China, and Chinese control became more effective; authorities declared for Mao Tse-tung, 1949.

Sinking Fund first adopted, 1716, increased, 1727; exhausted, 1786, and new fund started. S.F. on new principle started, 1792; modified by Vansittart, 1813. Legislation on S.Fs. repealed, 1866; another new fund started, 1875; modified by Lloyd George, 1910. Other S.Fs. started by Baldwin, 1923, and Churchill, 1928.

Sinn Fein, Irish nationalist movement, formed about 1905, which, in the period before 1922, aimed at economic and political separation from England. Since 1960s regarded as the political wing of the Irish Republican Army (*q.v.*).

Sino-Japanese Agreement. Signed, 16 May 1918, to counteract common danger of German penetration towards Eastern Russia.

Sistine Chapel, built for Pope Sixtus IV, 1473–81; Michelangelo painted the ceiling 1508–12, and the E. wall, 1534–41.

Skoda steel works, Brno. Renamed Vladimir Ilyitch Lenin Works, Dec. 1951.

Slavery. Abolition of, in British colonies in 1833, and owners compensated; S. in British possessions terminated following year; the abolition in U.S.A. announced, 1861.

Slave Trade. In England began, 1562; abolished, 25 Mar. 1807.

Slovakia. Under Hungarian domination until 1918, when the Slovaks united with the Czechs of Bohemia, Moravia, and Silesia for form Czechoslovakia (*q.v.*). Nominally independent as a German satellite, 1938–45.

Slovene Literature. Following are some Slovene authors of the modern period:
Jurij Dalmatin, *fl.* 1584, translator (Old Testament).
Tomaz Hren, 1560–1630, theologian.
Matthias Kastelic, 1620–88, theologian.
Marko Pohlin, 1735–1801, grammarian.
Leopold Wolkmer, 1741–1815, fabulist.
Anton Linhart, 1757–95, dramatist.
Valentin Vodnik, 1758–1819, poet.
Jernej Kopitar, 1780–1844, philologist.
Matthias Cop, 1797–1835, critic.
France Preseren, 1800–49, poet.
Janez Blajvajs, 1808–81, essayist.
F. Levstik, 1851–87, popular lyricist.
S. Jenko, 1835–69, lyricist.
J. Stritar, 1836–1923, poet and critic.
J. Jurjic, 1844–81, novelist.
S. Gregorcic, 1844–1906, lyricist.
Stanislas Skrabec, 1844–1918, critic.
I. Tivcar, 1851–1923, novelist.
J. Kersnik, 1852–97, short stories.
A. Askerc, 1856–1912, novelist.
I. Cankar, 1856–1918, short stories.

Zofka Kveder, 1878–1926, novelist.
Prezhikov Voranc, 1893–1950, poet.

Slovenes migrated from the western Carpathians to the valley of the Drava (Drau) about A.D. 600. Threatened by the Avars they appealed for protection to the Franks, to whom they became subject about 790, first under the counts of Friuli and dukes of Carinthia, then, from 1056 onwards, under the counts, later dukes, of Styria. From 1260 to 1282 they formed part of the kingdom of Bohemia (Ottakar II); then passed under Hapsburg dominion, which was finally consolidated in 1335. No major political change took place until 1918 (*see* YUGOSLAVIA). Their language became separated from Croatian between A.D. 600 and 900, and its earliest written monument, the Freising Leaves, dates from the eleventh century. New Testament rendered into Slovene by Primoz Trubar (1508–86), 1582. First grammar, 1584, by Adam Bohoric, and quadrilingual dictionary, 1592, printed at Wittenberg.

Slovenia is historically speaking an ethnic, not a geographical, term, denoting the land of the Slovenes (*q.v.*). In 1918 S. was formed out of Lower Styria, Carniola, and a small part of Carinthia. The term went out of official use in the internal reorganization of Yugoslavia, 1922, the nearest geographical equivalent being the Banat of the Drava. In 1945 the Federal Republic of S. was constituted, including the same area as in 1918, but including parts of Istria and Venezia Giulia.

Smallpox. *See* VACCINATION.

Smithfield. A cattle market in 1150 till 11 June 1855; a meat market, 1 Dec. 1868. Famous as a place of Protestant martyrdom, notably during the reign of Mary Tudor, 1553–8.

Smithsonian Institute endowed by bequest of James Smithson (1765–1829) dated 1826. Formally organized, 1846, first buildings completed, 1854.

Smyrna (Turk. **Izmir**), founded by Greeks *c.* 1000 B.C.; passed into possession of Colophon and thence into the Ionian confederation, *c.* 690 B.C.; cap-tured by Lydians, 630 B.C.; besieged by Timur-i-leng, A.D. 1402; taken by Turks, 1424; occupied by Greek Army, 1919; awarded to Greece (for a trial period of five years) by Treaty of Sèvres, 1920; Greeks expelled, 1922; awarded to Turkey by Treaty of Lausanne, 1923.

Soane Museum (13 Lincoln's Inn Fields). Formed by Sir John Soane; opened, 1833.

Social Credit, the economic theory of C. H. Douglas (*b.* 1879), enunciated in his books *Credit Power and Democracy* and *Economic Democracy*, 1920, and *Social Credit*, 1933. S.C. parties in Canada owe their existence to this doctrine; they have held power in Alberta and British Columbia and held balance in national parliament 1962–3 but at present (1985) retain power only in British Columbia.

Social Democratic Party, (Great Britain), formed 26 Mar. 1981 initially mainly by disenchanted members of the Labour Party (Commons representation of S.D.P. initially 13 ex-Labour M.P.s and 1 ex-Conservative M.P.). Roy Jenkins first leader: succeeded 1983 by David Owen. Electoral Alliance with Liberals since 1981. Some notable by-election successes but did poorly in General Election of 1983.

Social Security, Ministry of, name given to the former **Ministry of Pensions and National Insurance** 1966–68 when it was merged in the Department of Health and Social Security (*q.v.*).

Society Islands, so named in honour of the Royal Society, his patrons, by James Cook, 1769.

Sofia, anciently **Serdica**, occupied by the Romans, A.D. 29; sacked by the Huns, 447; taken by Bulgars, 808; conquered by Turks, 1382; liberated, 1877; became Bulgarian capital, 1878.

Sokol movement (Panslav athletic youth clubs) founded, 1861, by Miroslav Tyrs (1832–84).

Soldiers and Sailors. The following is a selective list of outstanding military and naval commanders prior to 1900. Where not otherwise specified, their distinction is specifically military.

Alexander the Great, 356–323 B.C., Greek.

Attila the Hun, *c.* 400–53.

Belisarius, *c.* 505–65, served Byzantium, probably *b.* in Illyria.

Blake, Robert, 1598–1657, English soldier and sailor.

Blücher, Gebhard, Leberecht von, 1742–1819, Prussian.

Caesar, Gaius Julius, 102–44 B.C., Roman.

Charles XII of Sweden, 1682–1718.

Clive, Robert, 1725–74, English.

Condé, Louis II de Bourbon, 1621–86, French.

Cromwell, Oliver, 1599–1658, English.

Drake, Sir Francis, *c.* 1545–96, English sailor.

Prince Eugene of Savoy, 1663–1736, French *b.* but served the Empire.

Frederick II the Great of Prussia, 1712–1786.

Garibaldi, Guiseppe, 1807–82, Italian.

Genghiz Khan, 1162–1227, Mongol Emperor.

Gordon, Charles George, 1833–85, British.

Grant, Ulysses Simpson, 1822–85, American.

Grenville, Sir Richard, *c.* 1541–91, English sailor.

Gustavus VI Adolphus of Sweden, 1594–1632.

Hannibal, 247–*c.* 183 B.C., Carthaginian.

Henry V of England, 1387–1422.

Howard of Effingham, Baron Charles, 1536–1624, English sailor.

Howe, Earl Richard, 1726–99, English sailor.

Hunyadi, John Corvinus, *c.* 1387–1456, Hungarian.

Jackson, Thomas Jonathan, 1824–63, American.

Jones, John Paul, 1747–92, Scots-born American sailor.

Marlborough, John Churchill, Duke of, 1650–1722, English.

Napoleon I Bonaparte, 1769–1821, French.

Nelson, Horatio, Viscount, 1758–1805, English sailor.

Ney, Michel, 1769–1815, French.

Peter I the Great of Russia, 1672–1725.

Roberts, Frederick Sleigh, 1st Earl, 1832–1914, British.

Rupert of Bavaria, Prince, 1619–82 (served England).

Ruyter, Michael Adriaanszoon, 1607–1676, Dutch sailor.

Tamberlane (Timur Beg), 1335–1405, Mongolian.

Tilly, Johann, Count von, 1559–1632, Flemish born, served the Empire.

Turenne, Henri de la Tour d'Auvergne, Vicomte de, 1611–75, French.

Tromp, Martin Harpertszoon, 1597–1653, Dutch sailor.

Wallace, Sir William, *c.* 1272–1305, Scots.

Wallenstein, Albrecht von, 1583–1634, *b.* Bohemia, served the Empire.

Washington, George, 1732–99. American.

Wellington, Arthur Wellesley, Duke of, 1769–1852, British.

Wolfe, James, 1727–59, English.

Wolseley, Garnet, Viscount, 1833–1913, British.

Xerxes, *c.* 519–465 B.C., Persian.

Soldiers, Sailors, and Airmen of this Century. The following is a list of military, naval, and air commanders noted for their service since 1900.

American:

Clark, Mark W., 1896–1984, general.

Eisenhower, Dwight David, 1890–1969, general.

Fairchild, M. S., 1894–1950, general (air force).

Marshall, George, 1880–1959, general.

MacArthur, Douglas, 1880–1964, general.

Nimitz, Adam Chester, 1885–1966, admiral.

Patton, George Smith, 1885–1945, general.

Pershing, John Joseph, 1860–1948, general.

Stillwell, Joseph W., 1883–1946, general.

Australian:

Blamey, Sir Thomas, 1884–1951, field marshal.

Hobbs, Sir Talbot, 1864–1938, general.

Monash, Sir John, 1865–1931, general.

British:

Alanbrooke, Alan Francis Brooke, 1st Viscount, 1883–1963, field marshal.

Alexander, Rupert Leofric George, 1st Earl, 1891–1969, field marshal.

Allenby, Edmund Henry Hynman, Viscount, 1861–1936, field marshal.

Beatty, David, 1st Earl, 1871–1936, admiral.

Birdwood, William Riddell, 1st Baron, 1865–1951, field marshal.

Carton de Wiart, Sir Adrian, lieutenant-general, 1880–1963.

Cunningham, Sir Andrew, 1st Viscount, 1883–1963, admiral.

Cunningham, Sir John, 1885–1962, admiral.

Dempsey, Sir Miles Christopher, 1896–1969, general.

Dowding, Hugh, 1st Baron, 1882–1970, air chief marshal.

Freyberg, Sir Bernard Cyril, 1st Viscount, 1890–1963, general.

Gough, Sir Hubert de la Poer, 1870–1963, general.

Haig, Douglas, 1st Earl, 1861–1928, field marshal.

Hamilton, Sir Ian, 1853–1947, general.

Harris, Sir Arthur, 1892–1984, air marshal.

Ironside, Sir William Edmund, 1st Baron, 1880–1959, field marshal.

Ismay, Lord, 1887–1964, general.

Jellicoe, John Rushworth, 1st Earl, 1859–1935, admiral.

Keyes, Roger John Brownlow, 1st Baron, 1872–1945, admiral.

Kitchener, Horatio Herbert, Earl, 1850–1916, field marshal.

Lawrence, Thomas Edward, 1888–1935, lieutenant-colonel.

Methuen, Paul, 3rd Baron, 1845–1932, field marshal.

Milne, G. F., 1st Baron, 1866–1948, field marshal.

Montgomery, Viscount, 1887–1976, field marshal.

Mountbatten, Earl Louis, 1900–1979, admiral.

Mountevans, Sir Edward, 1st Baron, 1881–1957, admiral.

Plumer, Herbert, Viscount, 1857–1932, field marshal.

Tedder, Arthur William, 1st Baron, 1890–1967, marshal of the R.A.F.

Trenchard, Hugh Montague, first Viscount, 1873–1956, Marshal of the R.A.F.

Wavell, Archibald, 1st Baron, 1883–1950, field marshal.

Wingate, Francis Reginald, 1861–1953, general.

Wingate, Orde Charles, 1903–44, major-general.

Ypres, John French, 1st Earl of, 1852–1925, field marshal.

Cuban:

Castro, Fidel, 1927–, general.

Finnish:

Mannerheim, Baron, Carl Gustaf Emil von, 1867–1948, marshal.

French:

Darlan, Jean, L. X. F., 1881–1942, admiral.

Foch, Ferdinand, 1851–1929, marshal of France.

Gallieni, Joseph, 1849–1916, general.

Gamelin, Maurice Gustave, 1872–1958, general.

Gaulle, Charles de, 1890–1970, general.

Giraud, Henri, 1879–1949, general.

Joffre, Joseph C., 1852–1931, marshal of France.

Juin, Alphonse Pierre, 1888–1967, marshal of France.

Lattre de Tassigny, Jean-Joseph Marie de, 1889–1952, marshal of France.

Leclerc de Hautecloque, Philippe, 1902–1947, marshal of France.

Lyautey, Louis H. G., 1854–1934, marshal of France.

Marchand, J. B., 1863–1934, general.

Nivelle, Robert G., 1856–1924, general.

Pétain, Philippe, 1856–1951, marshal of France.

Sarrail, Maurice P. E., 1856–1929, general.

Weygand, Maurice, 1867–1965, general.

German:

Bock, Fedor von, 1880–1945, colonel-general.

Bülow, Karl von, 1846–1921, general.

Doenitz, Karl, 1891–1981, admiral.

Falkenhayn, Erich von, 1861–1922, general.

Fritsch, Werner von, 1880–1939, colonel-general.

Goering, Hermann, 1893–1946, field marshal.

Guderian, Heinz, 1889–1954, colonel-general.

Hindenburg und Beneckendorf, Paul von, 1847–1934, field marshal.

Hipper, Franz von, 1863–1932, admiral.

Kesselring, Albert, 1885–1960, field marshal.

Kluck, Alexander von, 1846–1934, general.

Kluge, Günther von, 1882–1944, field marshal.

P. von Lettow-Vorbeck, 1870–1964, general.

Liman von Sanders, Otto, 1855–1929, general.

Ludendorff, Erich, 1865–1937, general.

Mackensen, August von, 1849–1945, field marshal.

Paulus, F., *d.* 1957, field marshal.

Rommel, Erwin, 1891–1944, field marshal.

Raeder, Erich, 1876–1960, admiral.

Rundstedt, Gerd von, 1875–1953, field marshal.

Seeckt, Hans von, 1866–1936.

Tirpitz, Alfred von, 1849–1930, grand admiral.

Greek:

Metaxas, John, 1871–1941, general.

Papagos, Alexander, 1883–1955, marshal.

Italian:

Aosta, Amadeo Umberto Duca d', 1898–1942, general.

Badoglio, Pietro, 1871–1956, marshal.

Balbo, Italo, 1896–1940, marshal.

Cadorna, Luigi, Count, 1850–1928, general.

Diaz, Armando, marshal, 1861–1928.

Graziani, Rodolpho, Marchese de, 1882–1955, marshal.

Japanese:

Togo, Heihachiro, Count, 1847–1934, admiral.

Tojo, Hideki, 1884–1948, general.

Polish:

Anders, Wladyslaw, 1892–1970, general.

Bor-Komorowsky, *d.* 1966, general.

Pilsudski, Josef, 1867–1935, marshal.

Sikorski, Wladyslaw, 1881–1943, general.

Russian:

Alexeiev, Mikhail, 1857–1918, general.

Brussilov, Alexei, 1853–1926, general.

Budenny, Semyon Mikhailovitch, 1883–1919, marshal.

Krylenko, Nikolai Vasilievitch, 1885–1938, general.

Malinovski, Rodion Yakovlevich, 1898–1967, marshal.

Nikolai Nikolaievich, Grand Duke, 1856–1929, general.

Rennenkampf, Paul, 1854–1918, general.

Sokolovski, Vasilij Danilovich, 1897–1968, marshal.

Timoshenko, Semyon Konstantin-ovich, 1895–1970, marshal.

Tolbukhin, Fyodor, 1894–1949, marshal.

Tukhachevski, Mikhail Nikolaievitch, 1893–1937.

Voroshilov, Kliment E., 1881–1969, marshal.

Zhukov, Georgi Konstantinovich, 1896–1978, marshal.

South African:

Cronje, Piet, 1835–1911, general.

Botha, Louis, 1862–1919, general.

Smuts, Jan, 1870–1950, field marshal.

De la Rey, Jacobus, 1847–1914, commandant-general.

De Wet, Christian, 1854–1922, general.

Spanish:

Francisco Franco, 1892–1975, general.

Turkish:

Fevzi Chakmak, 1876–1950, marshal.

Mustapha Kemal Pasha (Kemal Atatürk), 1880–1938, marshal.

Yugoslav:

Mihailovich, Draza, 1893–1946, general.

Tito, Josip Broz, 1892–1980, marshal.

Solemn League and Covenant. Drawn up by Scots against Charles I's religious interferences, 1638. Agreed by English parliament, 1643. Declared illegal, 1661.

Solidarity, free Polish trade union movement estab. 1980, as a result of industrial and political unrest based on the Gdansk shipyards. Banned, 1982. Leader, Lech Walesa (*b.* 1943) awarded the Nobel Peace Prize, 1983.

Solomon Islands, first visited by Alvaro de Mendaña c. 1568, then by Carteret, 1767, and sighted by Bougainville, 1768. British protectorate recognized by treaties with Germany, 1886 and 1893, extended to more northerly islands, 1898–9: further islands transferred from German protectorate, 1900. Japanese invaded, Jan. 1942. American counter-attack began, Aug. 1942. Operations taken over by Australian forces, Dec. 1944; reconquest of islands completed, 1945. Independent, 7 July 1978.

Somalia (formerly British and Italian Somaliland). Conquered by Portuguese in the sixteenth century, and by the Sultan of Zanzibar, 1866, became an Italian protectorate by treaty, 1889. The former It. colony was incorporated in the government of Italian E. Africa, 1936; conquered by British, 1941 (Feb.–May); territory occupied by British troops from 1941 to 1 Apr. 1950 was handed over to Italians, United Nations trusteeship to expire in 1960. On 1 July 1960 S. became an independent republic, formed by the merger of S. with British Somaliland (see next article). One-party state since 1976.

Somaliland, British. Made a British protectorate, 1884. Conquered by Italians, Aug. 1940. Regained, Mar. 1941. Merged with Somalia (q.v.), 1 July 1960, to form an independent Somali republic.

Somaliland, French, see DJIBOUTI.

Somerset House. Founded, 1549, on the site of some old churches. Its founder, the Protector Somerset, was executed, and his house fell to the crown; demolished in 1775, and a new building erected. The E. wing forms King's College, and was built, 1833.

South Africa, Republic of, formerly the **Union of**. Union formed, 31 May 1910, with Botha as premier. Rebellion began Sept., ended Dec. 1914. S. African Military Command terminated, 1 Dec. 1921, when responsibility for defence devolved on the Union. Anti-Asiatic measure in Parliament; Colour Bar Bill passed, May 1926. Status of the Union Act, 1934. 1939: Hertzog moved declaration of neutrality, but Smuts's amendment declaring war on Germany carried, so the Hertzog ministry resigned, 4 Sept.; Smuts formed ministry, 5 Sept. 1948: Malan became prime minister as leader of the Nationalist Party. *Apartheid* the basis of government domestic policy. 1949: Merger of Afrikaner Party and Nationalists. Natives Representative Council abolished. Separate Representation of Voters Act passed. Nationalist majority now permanent. Virtual incorporation of SW. (former German) territory, July. Sharpeville (q.v.) incident, Mar. 1960. 1961: S. A. announced her intention of leaving the Commonwealth, 16 Mar.; she then became an independent republic. Gave independent white Rhodesia economic support, 1966–80. Verwoerd assassinated, 1966. S. A. increasingly barred from international sport because of her apartheid policies from 1970 onwards. Muldergate scandal, 1978–9. First 'black homeland' (Transkei) estab., 1976. Some liberalization of *apartheid* under Botha, Premier from 1978 and Executive President from 1984; Fifth Amendment of 1981 provided for some non-white participation in govt. State of emergency, 1985: internat. call for sanctions against S.A.

Governor-Generals of ten Union of South Africa, 1910–61:

Viscount Gladstone 1910–1914
Earl Buxton 1914–1920
H.R.H. Prince Arthur of Connaught 1920–1924
Earl of Athlone 1924–1931
Earl of Clarendon 1931–1937
Sir Patrick Duncan 1937–1943
N. J. de Wet (acting) 1943–1945
G. B. van Zyl 1946–1950
Dr. E. G. Jansen 1951–1959
C. R. Swart 1960–1961

State Presidents of the Republic of South Africa since 1961:

C. R. Swart 1961–1967
T. E. Donges 1967
J. F. T. Naudé (acting) 1967–1968
J. J. Fouché 1968–1975
B. J. Vorster, 1978–79

M. Viljoen, 1979–84
P.J. Botha, 1984–

See also CAPE PROVINCE; ORANGE FREE STATE; TRANSVAAL.

South African War. 1899: Ultimatum sent by Boers, 9 Oct. Lord Roberts appointed C.-in-C. after British reverses, 23 Dec.

1900: Relief of Kimberley, 15 Feb.; Cronje's surrender at Paardeberg, 27 Feb.; relief of Ladysmith, 28 Feb.; relief of Mafeking, 17–18 May; Transvaal Republic annexed to Great Britain, 1 Sept.; formally annexed, 25 Oct.

1902: Peace of Vereeniging, 31 May.

Southampton. A Roman town (*Clausentium*) and a Jutish port (*Hamwih*) existed in the suburbs of modern S., but the first town on the present centre was built shortly before 1066. Present system of wharves, begun 1927. The University College became S. University in 1952.

South Australia was surveyed by Tasman, 1644, and Flinders, 1802. Murray River explored, 1828. First settlement made, 1834. Province proclaimed, 28 Dec. 1836. Copper discovered, 1842 and 1845. Constitution adopted, 1856. Became a state of the Australian Commonwealth, 1901.

South Carolina, U.S.A., first permanently settled as proprietary government, 1670. Charleston founded, 1680. One of 'founder' states of U.S.A. Seceded from Union, 1861; readmitted, 1868.

South Dakota, U.S.A., first explored by brothers Verendrye, 1743. First permanent building by white men, 1794. Sold to U.S.A. by France, 1803, as part of Louisiana Purchase. Dakota Territory created, 1861. Gold struck in the Black Hills, 1874. Separated from N. Dakota and admitted to Union, 1889.

South-East Asia Treaty Organization (S.E.A.T.O.). Arose from the South-East Asia Collective Defence Treaty, S.E. Asian counterpart to the N. Atlantic Treaty (*q.v.*), signed in Manila, 8 Sept. 1954, between Britain, the U.S.A., Australia, New Zealand, Pakistan, France, Thailand, and the Philippines, for their 'continuous and effective self-help and mutual aid'. France took little part after 1964.

Southern Yemen, *see* YEMEN, PEOPLE'S DEMOCRATIC REPUBLIC OF.

South Pole. First reached, 16 Dec. 1911, by the Norwegian, Roald Amundsen. Scott reached it 17 Jan. 1912. *See* ARCTIC AND ANTARCTIC REGIONS.

South Sea Bubble. The financial scheme under which the S.S. Co. (incorporated 1710) offered in 1720 to pay off the national debt and to buy up the irredeemable annuities granted in the two previous reigns. Parliament accepted the offer, and a number of other bubble companies competed. Shares rose to fantastic prices and then slumped, the stock of the S.S. Co. which had risen to 1,000 falling to 135. Sir Robert Walpole tried to restore credit by arranging to assign £9,000,000 S. S. stock to the Bank of England, a like amount to the E. India Co., and to repay the bonus of £7,500,000 which the Government had received.

Southwark, though retaining its identity as a borough, was annexed to the city of London, 1327. Diocese of S. created, 1905.

South-West Africa *see* NAMIBIA.

Sovereigns when first minted (1503) were worth 22*s*. 6*d*., later 10*s*. and 11*s*. In 1817 the value was fixed at £1, which remained constant until 1917, when they were recalled by the bank. In 1949 some 100,000 S. were minted in order to preserve the art and craft of gold coining. Small nos. now made for commemorative occasions e.g. coronation of Queen Elizabeth, 1953.

Sovetsk. *See* TILSIT.

Soviet. *See* U.S.S.R.

Spa, in Belgium, where mineral springs were discovered in 1326, gave its name to an establishment for curative waters. Was German G.H.Q. in 1918, seat of the Armistice Commission, 1918–19, and venue of a conference, 1920, on German disarmament and reparations.

Space Flights (manned). Yuri Gagarin (U.S.S.R.) was the first man to orbit the earth (once: in 1 hr. 48 min.) on 12 April 1961. Alan Sheppard made the first Amer. space flight (sub-orbital) on 5 May 1961: John Glenn was the first

Amer. to orbit the earth (3 times) on 20 Feb. 1962. Valentina Tereshkova (U.S.S.R.) was the first woman to orbit the earth, 16 June 1963. On 12 Oct. 1964 Russia put the first 3-man space-ship into orbit. On 18 Mar. 1965 Leonov (U.S.S.R.) left a 2-man space craft and became the first man to 'walk' in space. On 23 Mar. a spaceship was pilot-manoeuvred for the first time by the Amers., Grissom and Young. In 1968 America's Apollo 8 made 10 orbits of the moon, transmitting the first live television pictures of the lunar orbit; in 1969 the Russian Soyuz 4 (1 man) and Soyuz 5 (3 men) linked up in space. The Amer. Apollo 11 (Armstrong, Collins, Aldrin) was launched, 16 July and on 21 July Armstrong became first man to walk on the moon. Soyuz-Apollo link-up, 17 July 1975 was a joint U.S.-Soviet project. In 1978 (11 Jan.) 2 Soviet space craft docked with an orbiting laboratory constituting the first triple space docking. In 1984 the American Bruce McCandless (from Challenger) became the first man to walk in space without being attached to his space craft (Feb. 7).

Unmanned S.F. by the U.S.A. and U.S.S.R. first concentrated on moon-probes (1960–70) and subsequently on probes to Mars and Venus. Defence and communications now (1985) play major part in unmanned S.F., in which Britain, France etc. also take part.

Spain (*Hispania*). Occupied (south of the Ebro) by Carthaginians, 238–210 B.C.; after which the country was slowly subjugated by Rome. S. was divided into two provinces after the second Punic War, and into three by Augustus. Overrun by the Vandals, Alans, and Suevi, A.D. 409. Visigoths overrun S. and establish kingdom, 416–18. Vandals migrate to Africa, 429. Visigothic state overthrown and S. conquered by Arabs, 711–18. Abdurrahman (I) founds the Ommayad caliphate of Cordoba, 755, which reaches its zenith in the reign of Abdurrahman III (912–61). Christian reconquest begins in earnest under Sancho I of Leon, 962.

Civil war destroys caliphate, 1031. Alfonso VI of Castile takes Toledo, 1085. Moslem revival under Almoravides (*q.v.*), 1086. Aragonese defeat at Fraga, 1134. Moslem revival under Almohades at battle of Alarcos, 1185. Great Christian victory at Navas de Tolosa, 1212. Cordoba captured 1236. Moors confined to Granada by 1257. Permanent union of Aragon and Valencia, 1309. Moslem defeat at battle of the Salado, 1340. French expel Pedro the Cruel from Castile and substitute Henry of Trastamara, 1366. English expel Henry and restore Pedro, 1367. Henry defeats Pedro at Montiel, 1369. John I of Portugal defeats Castilians at Aljubarotta, 1385. Union of Aragon and Castile under Ferdinand and Isabella, 1479. Granada conquered, 2 Jan. 1492. Treaty of Tordesillas, 1494. Cortez conquers Mexico, 1519–21. Victory over French at Pavia, 1525. Treaty of Câteau Cambrésis, 1559. Spanish sack of Antwerp, 1576. Annexation of Portugal, 1580. English defeat of the Armada, 1588. Portugal again independent, 1640 (see Partition Treaties). War of Spanish Succession, 1701–13. Treaty with France against Britain ('First Family Compact'), 1733. Second Family Compact, 1743. Third Family Compact, 1761 (see SEVEN YEARS WAR). S. at war with Britain, 1779–83. Alliance with France and war with Britain, 1796. Destruction of Franco-Spanish fleet at battle of Trafalgar, 21 Oct. 1805. French driven out by Wellington, 1812. Revolution, 1820, suppressed by French, 1823. First Carlist War, 1830–40. Second Carlist War, 1872–6. War with U.S.A., 1898. Primo de Rivera military dictator, 1923–30. Riff War in Morocco, 1924–5 (see MOROCCO). Revolution and flight of King Alfonso, Mar. 1931; republic declared. *Spanish Civil War 1936–39*—Popular front won elections, 16 Feb. 1936 and civil war, led by Army began in Morocco, 18 July; Gen. Mola set up Falangist Government at Burgos, 24 July; seaplanes brought Falangist reinforcements from Morocco, 26 July; Falangist captured Badajos, 14 Aug.; Republicans evacuated San Sebastian, 13 Sept.; the Alcazar of Toledo blown up by Republican forces, but Falangist defenders continued to resist, 18 Sept.; Republicans withdrew from Alcazar after two months' siege, 28 Sept.; Gen. Franco, head of Falangist Government, 30 Sept.; Republican Government granted autonomy to Basque provinces, 1 Oct.; Republican Government moved to Valencia, 7 Nov.; Franco recognized by Germany and Italy, 18 Nov. In 1937 the Falangist captured Malaga, 8 Feb.; Guernica, ancient Basque capital, destroyed by Falangist, who captured Durango, 27 Apr.; Bilbao captured by Falangist 19 June, and all Asturias surrendered by Nov. By April 1938 Catalonia was cut off from France; struggle for Ebro ceased, 18 Nov. Barcelona fell to Franco, 26 Jan. 1939, and there was a mass-exodus of refugees into France. President Azana resigned in Feb. and Madrid and Valencia fell to Franco in March: civil war ended in Franco's victory, 2 April.

Spain since the Civil War—S. neutral in World War II: ex-King Alfonso XIII *d.*, 1941. Cortes re-estab. on corporate lines, 1942. After referendum in 1947 in favour of a future monarchy, Franco told the Cortes, 1957 that the monarchy would be restored on his death or withdrawal from power. Concordat with Papacy, 1953; U.S. bases in S., 1953. From 1960 government liberalized; phenomenal growth in tourist trade. Franco *d.* 1975 and S. reverted, to constitutional monarchy under King Juan Carlos I. Unsuccessful military coup, 1981: Socialist government elected, 1982. Church in Spain disestablished, 1978. S. settled Gibraltar (q.v.) dispute with Britain, 1985; to join E.E.C., Jan 1. 1986.

Spain, Sovereigns of, from the Union of Castile and Aragon, 1479, under Ferdinand of Aragon and Isabella of Castile.
Isabella *d.* 1504
Ferdinand *d.*1516
House of Hapsburg:
Charles V (Emperor) I 1516–1556
(abdicated)
Philip II 1556–1598

Philip III 1598–1621
Philip IV 1621–1665
Charles II 1665–1700
House of Bourbon:
Philip V 1700-abdicated 1724
Luis Jan.–Aug. 1724
Philip V (again) 1724–1746
Ferdinand VI 1746–1759
Charles III 1759–1788
Charles IV 1788–1808 (abdicated)
Ferdinand VII 1808
Joseph Bonaparte 1808–1812 (abdicated)
Ferdinand VII (again) 1813–1833
Isabella II 1833-flees 1868
Interregnum 1868–1874
Alfonso XII 1874–1885
Alfonso XIII 1886-abdicated 1931
Juan Carlos I,* 1975–
*General Franco was Head of State 1936–75.

Spanish Literature. The following is a list of Spanish (and of Spanish-speaking S. American) authors:
Aguilera, Ventura Ruiz, 1820–81, poet.
Alarcón, Juan Ruiz de, *c.* 1581–1639, dramatist.
Alarcón, Pedro Antonio de, 1833–91, prose writer of tales, etc.
Alemán, Mateo, 1547–*c.* 1613, prose writer, author of the popular *Guzman de Alfarache.*
Alfonso X, the Learned, of Castile and Leon, 1226–84, poet and patron of letters.
Álvarez Quintero, Joaquin, 1873–1944, dramatist.
Álvarez Quintero, Serafin, 1871–1938, dramatist.
Argensola, Bartolomé Leonardo de, 1562–1631, historian and poet.
Argensola, Lupercio Leonardo de, 1559–1613, poet and dramatist.
Avilia, Juan de, 1500–69, mystic and prose writer.
Ayala, Adelardo López de, 1828–79 poet, and dramatist.
Ayala, Pero López de, 1332–1407, poet and prose writer.
Ayala, Ramón Pérez de, 1880–1962, poet, critic, and novelist.
Balmes y Uspia, Jaime, 1810–48, controversial writer.
Bazan, Emilia Pardo de, 1851–1921, novelist.

Becquer, Gustavo Adolfo, 1836–70, poet and tale writer.

Benavente y Martinez, Jacinto, 1866–1954, dramatist.

Berceo, Gonzalo de, 1198?–1264?, poet.

Boscan Almogavér, Juan, c. 1490–1542, poet and prose writer.

Bretón de los Herreros, Manuel, 1796–1873, dramatist.

Caballera, Fernán (pseudonym of Cecilia Böhl von Faber), 1797–1877, novelist.

Cadalso y Vázquez, José de, 1741–82, poet and dramatist.

Calderón de la Barca Henao de la Barreda y Riaño, Pedro, 1600–81, poet, dramatist, and prose writer.

Carrasquilla, Tomás, 1851–1941, Colombian novelist.

Castillejo, Cristobal de, d. 1556, poet.

Castro y Bellvis, Guillén de, 1569–1631, dramatist.

Cervantes Saavedra, Miguel de, 1547–1616, author of Don Quixote, poet, dramatist, and prose writer.

Cota de Maguaque, Rodrigo, fl. late fifteenth century, poet.

Cruz y Cano, Ramón de la, 1731–95, dramatist.

Darío, Rubén, 1867–1916, Hispano-American poet.

Diaz de Castillo, Bernal, fl. second half sixteenth century, historian of the conquest of Mexico.

Echegaray y Elizaguirre, José, 1832–1916, dramatist.

Espinel, Vicente Martinez, 1551–1624, poet and novelist.

Feijoo y Montenegro, Benito Jerónimo, 1677–1764, prose writer and critic.

Figueroa, Francisco de, d. 1620, poet.

Fuentes, Carlos, 1928–, Mexican novelist.

Galdos, Pérez, 1842–1920, novelist.

Gallego, Juan Nicasio, 1777–1853, poet.

Gana, Alberto Blest, 1830–1920, Chilean novelist.

García Gutiérrez, Antonio, 1812–84, dramatist.

Garcia Marquez, Gabriel, 1928–, Colombian novelist.

Garcilaso de la Vega. See VEGA, GARCILASO DE LA.

Garcilaso the Inca, 1539–1616, Inca b., historian.

Gómez de Avellaneda, Gertrudis, 1816–73, poet, dramatist, and novelist.

Góngora y Argote, Luis de, 1561–1627, poet.

Gracián, Baltasar, 1601–58, prose writer, Jesuit epigrammatic moralist.

Granada, Luis de, 1505–88, mystic and religious writer.

Guevara, Antonio de, c. 1480–1545, chronicler and moralist.

Guevara, Luis Velez, 1570–1644, dramatist.

Herrera, Fernando de, 1534–97, poet and critic.

Ibañez, Vicente Blasco, 1867–1928, novelist.

Iriarte y Oropesa, Tomás de, 1750–91, fabulist.

Isidore of Seville, St., c. 560–636, encyclopaedist and Doctor of the Church.

Isla y Roja, José Francisco de, 1703–81, humorous prose writer.

Jáuregui y Aguilar, Juan Martínez de, c. 1570–c. 1641, poet and translator.

Jimenez, Juan Ramón, 1881–1958, poet.

Jove-Llanos, Gaspar Melchior de, 1744–1811, poet, dramatist, and prose writer.

Juan de la Cruz, 1542–91, mystic, poet, and prose writer (St. John of the Cross).

Juan Manuel, Infante, 1282–1349, poet and miscellaneous writer; his chief prose work was El Conde Lucanor, a collection of tales.

López de Gómara, Francisco, 1519–60, historian of the conquest of Mexico.

Lorca, Federico García, 1899–1936, poet.

Loyola, St. Ignatius, 1491–1556, author of the Exercitia Spiritualia and the Constitutiones. See also JESUITS.

Lucena, Juan de, fl. fifteenth century, prose writer.

Lully, Raymond ('Ramon Lull'), 1235–1315.

Luzán Claramunt de Suelves y Gurrea, Ignacio, 1702–54, critic and poet.

Machado y Ruiz, Antonio, 1875–1939, poet and dramatist.

Machado y Ruiz, Manuel, 1874–1947, poet and dramatist.

Manrique, Gómez, 1412–91, poet.

Manrique, Jorge, 1440–79, poet.

Mariana, Juan de, *c.* 1535–1623, historian.

Martínez de la Rosa, Francisco, 1789–1862, poet, dramatist, and novelist.

Martínez de Toledo, Alfonso, 1398–1466 ?, prose writer and moralist.

Martínez Ruiz, José (Azorín), 1874–1967, novelist and critic.

Meléndez Valdés, Juan, 1754–1817, poet and dramatist.

Mendoza, Diego Hurtado de, 1503–75, poet and scholar.

Mistral, Gabriela (Lucila Godoy y Alcayaga), 1889–1957, Chilean poet and prose writer.

Molinos, Miguel de, *c.* 1640–96, author of the *Spiritual Guide*.

Montemayor, Jorge de, *c.* 1520–61, author of the prose pastoral, *Diana Enamorada*.

Morales, Ambrosio de, 1513–91, historian.

Moratin, Leandro Fernández, 1760–1828.

Moreto y Cabaña, Agustin, 1618–69, dramatist.

Naharro, Bartolomé Torres. *fl.* early sixteenth century, dramatist.

Nebrija, Elio Antonio de, 1444–1522, humanist.

Nuñez de Arce, Gaspar, 1833–1903, poet and dramatist.

Padilla, Juan de, 1468–1522?, poet.

Palacio Valdés, Armando, *c.* 1854–1938, novelist.

Paravicino y Arteaga, Hortensio Félix, 1580–1633, poet.

Pereda, José Maria de, 1833–1906, novelist.

Pérez Andrés ('Francisco Lopez de Ubeda'), *fl.* early seventeenth century, picaresque novel writer.

Pérez, Antonio, 1540–1611, miscellaneous writer.

Pérez de Guzmán, Fernán, 1378–1460, poet and historian.

Pérez de Montalban, Juan, 1602–38, dramatist.

Pérez Galdós, Benito, 1843–1920, novelist and dramatist.

Ponce de León, Luis, 1529–91, poet.

Pulgar, Hernando de, 1436–92?, historian.

Quevedo y Villegas, Francisco Gómez de, 1580–1645, poet and prose writer.

Quintana, Manuel José, 1772–1857, poet, dramatist, and prose writer.

Rivas, Duque de. *See* SAAVEDRA.

Rodo, José Enrique, 1872–1917, Uruguayan essayist.

Rojas, Fernando de, *fl.* late fifteenth century.

Rojas Zorrilla, Francisco de, 1607–48, poet and dramatist.

Rueda, Lope de, *c.* 1510–65, dramatist.

Ruiz de Alarcón, Juan. *See* ALARCON, JUAN RUIZ DE.

Ruiz, Juan *fl.* fourteenth century, poet.

Saavedra, Angel de (Duque de Rivas), 1791–1865, poet and dramatist.

Samaniego, Félix Maria de, 1745–1801, fabulist.

San Martin, Juan Zorrilla, 1855–1931, Uruguayan poet.

Sancho IV, *d.* 1295, author of *Castigos y Documentos*, and patron of letters.

Santillana, Iñigo Lopez de Mendoza, Marqués de, 1398–1458, poet and prose writer.

Sem Tob, *fl.* fourteenth century, author of a collection of proverbs and maxims in verse.

Silvestre, Gregorio, 1520–70, poet.

Solis y Rivadeneira, Antonio de, 1610–86, dramatist and historian.

Teresa, St., 1515–82, poet and prose writer.

Tirso de Molina, *c.* 1584–1648, poet, dramatist and prose writer.

Torre, Alfonso de la, *fl.* fifteenth century, didactic prose writer.

Torre, Francisco de la, 1534?–94, poet.

Unamuno, Miguel de, 1864–1936, novelist.

Urrea, Pedro Manuel de, 1486–1530?, poet.

Valdés, Armando P. *See* PALACIO VALDÉS.

Valdés, Juan de, *c.* 1500–44, mystic, scholar, and prose writer.

Valera, Juan de, 1824–1905, novelist and critic.

Vega Carpio, Lope Félix de, 1562–1635, poet, novelist, dramatist, and miscellaneous writer.

Vega, Garcilaso de la, 1503–36, poet.

Velez Guevara, Luis, *See* GUEVARA, LUIS VELEZ.

Villamediana, Conde de, 1582–1622, poet.

Villegas, Esteban Manuel de, 1596–1669, poet.

Villena, Enrique de, 1384–1434, poet, prose writer, and translator.

Yañez, Rodrigo, *fl.* fourteenth century, author of an epic work known as the 'Rhymed Chronicle', *Poema de Alfonso Onceno.*

Zorilla, José 1817–93, poet and dramatist.

Zurita, Jeronimo de, 1512–80, historian.

For certain other writers of Spanish nationality who did not write in Spanish, *see* PROVENCAL AND CATALAN WRITERS.

Spanish Succession, War of, 1701–13. Alliance of Britain, Holland, Austria, Prussia, and the Empire against Louis XIV, 1701.

Sparta or **Lacedaemon,** between 750 and 650 B.C. conquered the whole of Laconia, and by 550 the greater part of the Peloponnese. Defeated Athens in Peloponnesian War, 431–404, but after being beaten by the Thebans at Leuctra (371) the military decline of S. began, and became more rapid after about 335. It nominally retained its sovereignty after conquest by the Romans in 146. A village still exists on the site, which was the seat of a Frankish Count from A.D. 1212 to 1262.

Spartacists. Organized a revolutionary movement in Germany, 1918–19. Leaders, Karl Liebknecht and Rosa Luxemburg, killed, Jan. 1919. Movement crushed, Apr. 1919, by Ebert's provisional Government, but from it modern German Communism began.

Speaker of the House of Commons existed as an office, though perhaps not a title from about 1326. The first member known to have performed the functions of a S. was William Trussell, who *d.* 1346, though he is not yet referred to as *Parlour* or S., a title first definitely ascribed to Sir Thomas Hungerford in 1377. Sir Thomas More the last S. to die by violence (1535). The names of all Ss. since 1600 are known; since World War II Speakers have been:

D. Clifton-Brown 1943–51
W. S. Morrison 1951–59
Sir Harry Hylton-Foster 1959–65
Dr. Horace King 1965–70
Selwyn Lloyd 1971–76
George Thomas 1976–83
Bernard Wetherill 1983–

Spectrum (solar). Treated of by Newton in his *Optics,* 1704; chemical analysis by means of a S. invented by Bunsen and Kirchhoff, 1860.

Spitalfields (London), named after the hospital of St. Mary Spital (corruption of 'hospital'), founded 1197. Many silk-weaving Huguenots settled there after the revocation of the Edict of Nantes, 1685. Market received its original charter from Charles II in 1682.

Spitsbergen (Svalbard), so called by Dutch explorers, 1596. Placed under Norwegian sovereignty by Treaty of Sèvres, 9 Feb. 1920, to which Russia adhered, 1925. Canadian raid, Sept. 1941, destroyed mining installations and evacuated population. German naval landing, 1943. Russian mining camps reoccupied, 1947.

Split (It. **Spalato;** Scrb.-Cr. **Spljet**), Byzantine port opened *c.* A.D. 639 by refugees from Salona (*q.v.*). Municipal rights granted, 1239. Venetian territory from 1420 to 1797. Occupied by Italians, 1918. Yugoslav since 1920.

Spode Chinaware, first manufactured, 1770.

Sri Lanka. formerly **Ceylon**. Portuguese landed, 1505: first Portuguese settlement, 1517. Taken by Dutch 1656–8: by English, 1795–6. Ceded to Britain by Treaty of Amiens, 1802. H.Q. of Supreme Commander, Far East, in World War II. Became a Dominion, 4 Feb. 1948. Brit. naval and air bases phased out, 1954–7. Bandaranaike, prime minister, assassinated by Buddhist extremists, 1957. New constitution, making S.L. a republic, 1972, amended to allow for presidential system, 1978, with Jayawardene as first president. Serious anti-Tamil riots, 1983–5.

S.S. (Schutzstaffel = 'Protection Squads'), militant branch of German National Socialist (*q.v.*) Party, formed by separa.ion from S.A. (*q.v.*), 1928. Heinrich Himmler (1900–45) became commander, 1929. Subdivided into military and civil branches 1933–36.

Stage Carriage Act, 1832 required number of passengers carried to be painted on the vehicle. Revenue Act, 1869, defined S.C. as any public vehicle other than a railway carriage (*see also* HACKNEY COACHES). Under Road Traffic Act, 1960 a stage carriage is defined as a public service vehicle carrying passengers at separate fares, not being an express carriage.

Stalingrad, known until 1925 as **Tsaritsin** and since 1961 as **Volgograd.** Originally a military outpost, built in 1589 to protect farmers from predatory nomads, Tsaritsin was captured by the Cossack mutineer, Stenka Razin, 1670. During the civil war it was defended by Stalin and Voroshilov against the Whites, in the autumn of 1918. Between the end of the War of Intervention (1923) and 1939, its population increased about twenty-fold, and a huge industrial plant was constructed. The siege of S. began in Aug. and ended Nov. 1942, with the capitulation of von Paulus and his army.

Stamp Acts. That of 1765, which was a contributory cause of the American Revolution, was repealed in 1766. Present law relating to stamp duties is contained in the Stamp Act, 1891, and in various subsequent Finance and Revenue Acts.

Standard, Royal, bore only three leopards passant in 1200, which were quartered with the arms of France in 1340. The latter were removed and replaced by the arms of Ireland, then of Scotland, 1603. From 1714 to 1837 the Royal Standard also bore the arms of Hanover until the accession of Victoria (1837), when it assumed its present form.

Standards Institution, British. Had its origins in the Joint Engineering Standards Committee formed in 1901. This became the British Engineering Standards Association. Textile, chemical, and building industries joined it, 1923–9. Granted a royal charter, 1929, as the British Standards Institution.

Standard Time. Different countries began to adopt S.T., based on a variation of a whole number of hours from Greenwich mean time, in 1883.

Star Chamber. Prerogative court going back at least to the reign of Edward III (1327–77) and abolished by Parliament, 1641.

State Department. *See* SECRETARY OF STATE (U.S.A.).

States-General (France). Last meeting before French Revolution (*q.v.*) was in 1614. It met at Versailles on 5 May 1789. The *Tiers État* declared itself the National Assembly, 17 June 1789.

States-General (Holland). Began *c.* middle fifteenth century, established permanently at The Hague, 1593. Abolished with convocation of the National Assembly, 1 Mar. 1796. Name used since 1814 as the title of the Dutch Parliament.

Statesmen and Politicians of the Twentieth Century. The following list of political personalities, not now living, were all prominent in the present century, though not necessarily heads of state or of administrations:

Argentine:
Peron, Juan 1895–1974
Australian:
Curtin, John 1885–1945
Chifley, Joseph 1885–1951
Evatt, Herbert 1894–1965
Holt, Harold Edward 1908–1968
Hughes, William Morris 1864–1952
Lyons, Joseph Aloysius 1879–1939
Scullin, James Henry 1876–1953
Austrian:
Bauer, Otto 1881–1938
Dollfuss, Engelbert 1892–1934
Renner, Karl 1870–1951
Brazilian:

Vargas, Getulio 1882–1954
British:
Asquith, Violet 'Bonham-Carter,
Baroness 1887–1969
Astor, Nancy, Viscountess 1879–1964
Attlee, Clement Richard, 1st
Earl 1883–1967
Baldwin, Stanley, Earl of Bewdley
1867–1947
Beaverbrook, Lord 1879–1964
Bevan, Aneurin 1897–1960
Beveridge, William, 1st Baron 1879–
1963
Bevin, Ernest 1881–1951
Birkenhead, Earl of 1872–1930
Bondfield, Margaret 1873–1953
Brown, George, Lord George-Brown,
1914–1985
Burns, John 1858–1943
Butler, Lord 1902–82
Carson, Edward, Lord 1854–1935
Chamberlain, Sir Austen 1863–1937
Chamberlain, Joseph 1836–1914
Chamberlain, Neville 1869–1940
Churchill, Sir Winston 1874–1965
Cripps, Sir Stafford 1889–1952
Curzon of Kedleston, Marquess
1859–1925
Eden, Anthony, Earl of Avon 1897–
1977
Gaitskell, Hugh 1906–1963
Grey of Fallodon, Edward, Visc.
1862–1933
Haldane, Visc. 1856–1928
Halifax, Earl of 1881–1959
Henderson, Arthur 1863–1935
Law, Andrew Bonar 1858–1923
Lloyd George, David 1863–1945
MacDonald, James Ramsay 1866–
1937
Morrison of Lambeth, Lord 1888–1965
Mosley, Sir Oswald 1896–1980
Oxford and Asquith, Earl of 1852–
1928
Pankhurst, Dame Christabel 1880–
1958
Pankhurst, Emmeline 1858–1928
Reading, Rufus, Marquess of 1860–
1935
Salisbury, 5th Marquess of 1893–1972
Samuel, Herbert Louis, 1st Viscount
1870–1963
Snowden, Philip, Visc. 1864–1937
Stanley, Oliver 1896–1950

Wilkinson, Ellen 1891–1947
Woolton, 1st Earl 1883–1964
Bulgarian:
Dimitrov, Georgi 1882–1949
Liaptcheff, Andrea 1866–1933
Malinoff, Alexander 1867–1938
Stambolisky 1879–1923
Canadian:
Borden, Sir Robert L. 1854–1937
King, William Lyon Mackenzie
1878–1950
Laurier, Sir Wilfrid 1841–1919
Pearson, Lester Bowles, 1897–1972
Strathcona, Donald Alexander Smith,
Baron 1820–1914
Chinese:
Chiang Kai-Shek 1887–1975
Mao Tse-Tung 1893–1976
Sun Yat-Sen 1866–1925
Cypriot:
Archbishop Makarios, 1913–1977
Czechoslovak:
Beneš, Edward 1884–1948
Gottwald, Klement 1896–1953
Masaryk, Jan 1886–1948
Masaryk, Tomáš Garrigue 1850–1937
Dominican:
Trujillo, Rafael *d.* 1961
Egyptian:
Nasser, Gamal Abdel 1918–1970
Sadat, Anwar 1918–1981
Finnish:
Mannerheim, Carl 1867–1951
French:
Auriol, Vincent *d.* 1966
Barthou, Jean Louis 1862–1934
Blum, Léon 1872–1950
Briand, Aristide 1862–1932
Cambon, Jules 1845–1935
Clemenceau, George Benjamin
1841–1929
Darlan, J, L, X, F. 1881–1942
Delcassé Théophile 1852–1923
Doumer, Paul 1857–1932
Doumergue, Gaston 1863–1937
Gaulle, Charles de 1890–1970
Herriot, Édouard 1872–1957
Maginot André1877–1932
Monnet, Jean 1888–1979
Painlevé, Paul 1863–1933
Pétain, Philippe 1856–1951
Poincaré, Raymond 1860–1934
Pompidou, Georges 1911–1974
Reynaud, Paul 1878–1966

Schumann, Robert 1886–1963
Thomas, Albert 1878–1932
Thorez, Maurice 1900–1964
German:
Adenauer, Konrad 1876–1967
Bernstorff, Count Johann Heinrich
1852–1939
Ebert, Friedrich 1871–1925
Goebbels, Joseph 1897–1945
Goering, Hermann 1893–1946
Heuss, Professor Theodor 1884–1963
Hitler, Adolf 1889–1945
Pieck, Wilhelm 1876–1960
Rathenau,Walther 1967–1922
Schumacher, Kurt 1895–1952
Strésemann, Gustav 1878–1929
Ghana:
Nkrumah, Kwame 1909–72
Greek:
Konduriotis, Adam Paul 1855–1935
Metaxas, John 1871–1941
Papandreou,George *d.* 1968
Papagos, Alexander 1883–1955
Venizelos, Eleutherios 1864–1936
Hungarian:
Apponyi, Count Albert 1846–1933
Horthy, Nicholas 1868–1957
Karolyi, Count Michael 1875–1955
Nagy, Imre 1896–1958
Tisza, Count Istvan 1861–1918
Indian:
Gandhi, Indira, Mrs 1917–1984
Gandhi, Mahatma 1869–1948
Nehru, Jawaharial 1889–1964
Indonesian:
Sukarno, Achmed 1901–1970
Iraqi:
Nuri es-Said 1888–1958
Kassem, Abdul Karim *d.* 1963
Irish:
Collins, Michael 1890–1922
de Valera, Eamon 1882–1975
Hyde, Douglas 1860–1949
McBride, Maude (Gonne) 1866–1953
McNeill, James 1869–1938
Israeli:
Ben-Gurion, David, 1886–1973
Meir, Golda, 1898–1978
Weizmann, Chaim 1874–1952
Italian:
Badoglio, Pietro 1871–1956
Balbo, Italo 1896–1940
Ciano, Caleazzo 1903–1944
Gasperi, Alcide de 1881–1954

Giolitti, Giovanni 1842–1928
Mussolini, Benito 1883–1945
Orlando, Vittorio Emanuele 1860–
1952
Sforza, Carlo 1873–1952
Togliatti, Palmiro 1893–1964
Kenyan:
Kenyatta, Jomo *c.* 1889–1978
Korean:
Rhee, Syngman *d.* 1965
Japanese:
Tojo, Hideki 1884–1948
Yamamoto, Count 1852–1933
New Zealand:
Fraser, Peter 1884–1950
Holland, Sir Sidney 1893–1957
Holyoake, Sir Keith 1904–1983
Nash, Walter 1882–1968
Savage, Michael 1872–1940
Pakistani:
Jinnah, Mohammed Ali 1876–1948
Liaquat Ali Khan 1896–1951
Zulfilkar Ali Bhutto 1928–1979
Polish:
Beck, Josef 1894–1944
Sikorski, Wladislaw 1881–1943
Portuguese:
Salazar, Antonio de Oliveira 1889–
1970
Rumanian:
Antonescu, Ion 1882–1946
Averescu, Alexander 1859–1938
Bukharin, N. I. 1880–1938
Duca, Ion 1879–1933
Gheorgiu-Dej, Georgei *d.* 1965
Russian:
Andropov, Yuri, d. 1984
Beria, Lavrenti 1899–1953
Brezhnev, Leonid 1906–82
Chernenko, Konstantin 1911–85
Kamenev, Lev B. 1883–1936
Kerensky, Alexander 1881–1970
Khruschev, Nikita 1894–1971
Lenin, Vladimir Ilyitch Ulyanov
1870–1924
Litvinov, Maxim Maximovitch
1876–1951
Stalin, Josef Vissarionovitch
Dzhugashvili 1880–1953
Trotsky, Lev 1879–1940
Zinoviev, Grigori 1883–1936
S. African:
Botha, Louis 1862–1919
Hertzog, J. B. M. 1866–1942

Malan, Daniel 1874–1959
Smuts, Jan Christiaan 1870–1950
Strijdom, Johannes 1893–1958
Verwoerd, Hendrik 1901–1966
Spanish:
Franco, Francisco 1892–1975
Primo de Rivera, Miguel 1870–1930
Swedish:
Hammarskjöld, Dag 1905–1961
Turkish:
Atatürk, Mustafa Kemal 1881–1938
Menderes, Adnan 1899–1961
Gursel, Cemal 1896–1966
U.S.A.:
Bingham, Robert Worth 1871–1937
Bryan, William Jennings 1860–1925
Coolidge, Calvin 1872–1933
Dulles, John Foster 1888–1959
Eisenhower, Dwight David 1890–1969
Hoover, Herbert 1874–1964
House, Edward Mandell 1858–1938
Kellogg, Frank Billings 1856–1937
Kennedy, John Fitzgerald 1917–1963
Kennedy, Robert Francis 1925–1968
King, Martin Luther 1929–1968
La Follette, Robert M. 1855–1925
Long, Huey Pierce 1893–1935
MacCarthy, Joseph 1909–1957
Marshall, George 1880–1959
Morrow, Dwight Whitney 1873–1931
Roosevelt, Eleanor 1884–1962
Roosevelt, Franklin Delano 1882–1945
Roosevelt, Theodore 1858–1919
Root, Elihu 1845–1937
Stevenson, Adlai 1900–1965
Taft, Robert 1890–1953
Taft, William Howard 1857–1930
Truman, Harry S. 1884–1972
Vandenberg, Arthur 1884–1972
Welles, Sumner 1892–1961
Wilson, Thomas Woodrow 1856–1924
Vietnamese:
Ngo Dinh Diem *d.* 1964
Ho Chi-Minh 1892–1969
Yugoslav:
Kidrić, Boris 1912–1953
Mihailovich, Draza 1893–1946
Tito, Josip Broz 1892–1980
Stationers' Hall. Incorporated, 1556.
Stationery Office, Her Majesty's, established, 1786.
Steam Navigation. *See* SHIP.

Stellaland, short-lived Boer republic set up in Northern Cape Province, 1882. Declared British protectorate, 1884.
Stettin *see* SZCZECIN.
Stirling, University of, Estab. 1967.
Stock Exchange constitution regulated by Deed of Settlement of 27 Mar. 1802; modified by Deed of 31 Dec. 1875.
Stockholm Conference of European Social Democrats held, Aug. 1917. Arms limitation talks at, 1984.
Stoics. The disciples of Zeno (335–263 B.C.), whose school was held in a portico (Greek *stoa*).
Stonehenge, Wiltshire, built *c.* 1500 B.C.
Strand (London), first mentioned in Anglo-Saxon Chronicle, *sub anno* 1052.
Strasbourg or **Strassburg.** Capital of Alsace. Taken by France, 1681; captured by Germany, 1870; returned to France, 1918; Germany, 1940; France again, 1944. Contains a celebrated university, founded in 1538. H.Q. Council of Europe, 1949: subsequently meeting place of European Parliament.
Stratford-on-Avon, Shakespeare Memorial Theatre built, 1877–9; burnt down, 1926; rebuilt, 1932.
Strathclyde, Scottish administrative region since 1972, with H.Q. at Glasgow.
Strathclyde, Celtic kingdom of the Clyde Valley and parts of Galloway, at time linked to that of Cumbria, founded *c.* A.D. 560. Became subject to Northumbria about 650, but regained independence after the defeat of King Ecgfrith, by the Picts at Nectansmere, 685. Alcluith (Dumbarton), the capital, stormed by Picts, 736. King Eadberht of Northumbria conquered and annexed south-western S., 750, and temporarily subdued the whole kingdom, 756. Dumbarton sacked by the Danish king, Ivarr Ragnarsson, 870, and again invaded by him, 875 (*see* VIKING AGE). Thereafter more frequently invaded, and partly settled, by Norwegian Vikings, mainly via Dublin and Isle of Man. Submitted to Edward the Elder, King of England, about 921. Ceded by Edmund, King of England, to Malcolm I of Scotland, 946, but again became independent before 971. Last mention

of a king of S. (Owen), as ally of Malcolm Canmore, 1018. Independence finally lost before 1100.

Strathclyde University, Glasgow. Estab. 1864.

Street Offences Act. Came into force, 16 Aug. 1959.

Streptomycin. Isolated, 1943, by Waksman, a Russian-born scientist, who was awarded the Nobel Prize, 1952.

Stresa Conference, 11–14 Apr. 1935. Britain, France, and Italy agreed to maintain independence of Austria.

Strike, the General. *See* GENERAL STRIKE.

Stuttgart. Chartered in 1250. Became capital of the dukes of Württemberg in the fifteenth century.

Styria (Steiermark). Came under Frankish domination about 780, but only as part of Duchy of Carinthia (*q.v.*). Made a separate mark in 1056, and bestowed on Count Ottokar of Steyr, whence its name. Became a duchy in 1180, and was attached to the Duchy of Austria, 1192; belonged to Bohemia from 1260 to 1282, thereafer to the Hapsburg empire. Formed one province (*Land*) of the Austrian Federal Republics of 1918 and 1945. *See also* CARINTHIA and SLOVENES.

Submarines. First practicable submarine was demonstrated by the American Bushnell in 1775, the next by Robert Fulton in 1800; both capable of placing limpet charges. S. were first used in action in the American Civil War, 1863. First Brit. submarine launced, 1901. First nuclear-powered submarine was the U.S.S. *Nautilus*, 1955. First nuclear-powered British submarine, the *Dreadnought*, commissioned 1963.

Sudan, N. Africa, sovereign independent republic since 1 Jan. 1956, formerly Anglo-Egyptian territory. The area corresponds more or less to the territory anciently called Nubia (i.e. the Nile valley S. of the First Cataract— Aswan), which was penetrated by Egyptian influence as early as the Old Empire, almost 4000 B.C. Colonies and military posts were established regularly in the twelfth dynastic period (2700–2500 B.C.), and the conquest S.

to the Fourth Cataract consolidated under the eighteenth dynasty. (*c.* 1350 B.C.). About 200 years later fugitive priests of Amen from Thebes founded a new state, with sub-Egyptian culture, with its capital at Napata in S. An independent Nubian civilization arose *c.* 800 B.C., and for a time its kings dominated Egypt (from 749 to 667). The borrowed Egyptian culture declined after the withdrawal of Nubian rulers from Egypt, and the capital Napata was supplanted by Meroë *c.* 300. For three centuries thereafter Nubia was virtually independent of the Ptolemaic rulers of Egypt, but the Romans who succeeded them also conquered the S., and established their southern frontier to the S. of Wadi Halfa. Only at the end of the Romano-Nubian period (*c.* 550) was Christianity introduced. Moslem invasions began, 652, but strong Christian kingdoms persisted until *c.* 1350, and many Nubians professed Christianity until the sixteenth century. The triumph of Islam was due to direct migration from Arabia, led by the Beni Omayya tribe from the eighth century onwards. S. was conquered by Mehemet Ali, 1821. Gen. Gordon was appointed (Egyptian) governor-general, 1873–80; revolt of Sudanese under the Mahdi, 1882; annihilation of Hicks Pasha's forces, 1883; Gordon killed at Khartoum, 1885; battle of Omdurman, 1898. Anglo-Egyptian agreement on condominium, 19 Jan. 1899, determined the manner of S. administation for the first half of the twentieth century. Anglo-Eygyptian agreement, Feb. 1953, acknowledged the right of S. to self-determination, the population to choose, in 1955, between independence and union with Egypt. The Sudanese Parliament voted unanimously for complete independence immediately, 19 Dec. 1955, and an independent republic was proclaimed, 1 Jan. 1956. Increasing Islamization from 1960's led to civil war in S. between Christians and central govt. General discontent resulted in military coup, April 7 1985, when Numeiri, S's virtual dictator, ousted.

French S., the designation from 1920 until 1960 of Upper Senegal-Niger, a French colony formed in 1904. A partner (with Senegal) in the Federation of Mali, Jan. 1959–Sept. 1960. On 22 Sept. 1960 the territory became the independent republic of **Mali** (*q.v.*).

Sudetenland, district taking its name from the Sudetic Mountains in Bohemia and Moravia, and before 1945 largely inhabited by Germans from Saxony, Bavaria, and Franconia, whose immigration began shortly after A.D. 1100. Sudeten German *Heimatfront* (local Nazi and other Pan-German parties amalgamated) formed by Konrad Henlein (1898–1945), 1933. S. incorporated in German Reich, Oct. 1938. Some 3,700,000 S. Germans, out of an estimated 4,000,000, were expelled from Czechoslovakia, 1945.

Suevi. *See* SWABIA.

Suez Canal. Permission for its construction under de Lesseps, 1854; company formed, 1856; work begun, 1859; opened to traffic, 1869. Britain buys shares in, 1875. Under Article 8 of the Anglo-Egyptian Defence Treaty, 1938, Britain was responsible for defending the S.C. zone; but in Nov. 1955 Egypt took over. The last British troops left the zone, 31 Mar. 1956. Nasser nationalized the S.C., 26 July 1956 Anglo-French planes began bombing canal installations, Oct. 1956, and (Nov.) invaded the zone (*see* EGYPT). Egypt blocked the S.C. and it was not opened to traffic again until 30 Apr. 1957. Shareholders of the S.C. Company accepted compensation terms offered by Egypt, July 1958. S.C. was blocked by Egypt during the 'June War', 1967, and remained so till 1975. 2-stage development begun, 1976. Israeli ships again allowed to use S.C., 1979.

Sugar Beet Subsidy. Begun, 1925.

Suicide, ceased to be defined as a crime in Britain, under S. Act of 1961.

Sumatra was a Hindu kingdom from *c.* A.D. 600–1300. First European (Portuguese) settlement, 1509, was replaced by Dutch settlement *c.* 1600. Occupied by Japanese 1941–45, part of Indonesia since then.

'Summer Time.' *See* DAYLIGHT SAVING.

Sunday Observance Acts, 1625–1780, modified by the S. Entertainment Act, 1932, S. Trading Act, 1870, and Shops Act, 1950.

Sunday Schools. Originally in Milan under Borromeo, 1580, and in Engalnd under Robert Raikes and Rev. Stocks, 1780.

Sunspots were discovered by Galileo, 1610. Periodicity of eleven years deduced by Schwabe, 1843.

Supersonic speed, first attained by John Derry of de Havillands, 6 Sept. 1948.

Supertax first imposed by Lloyd George in Finance Act, 1909, and levied until 1929. *See* SURTAX.

Supply, Ministry of, set up in Apr. 1939. Duties transferred to Ministry of Aviation, 1959.

Supremacy, Act of, 1534, declared Henry VIII head of the English Church. Denial of this doctrine declared treasonable under Edward VI, 1457. Repealed by Philip and Mary, 1554. Restored in slightly modified form by Elizabeth I, 1559.

Supreme Council. British, French, and Italian Governments set up a S. War C. at Versailles, Nov. 1917. In 1919–20 it acted as the Executive Committee of the Peace Conference (*q.v.*).

Supreme Court of Judicature. The Judicture Act of 1873 formed one supreme court for England and Wales out of the courts of Chancery, Queen's Bench, Common Pleas, Exchequer, High Court of Admiralty, and Probate. The Bankruptcy Act, 1883, brought bankruptcy within the province of the S.C. effectively in 1884.

Surinam, formerly **Dutch Guiana**. First Eurpean settlement attempted by the English, 1630. Sugar planters (Dutch and Portuguese) entered the country, 1644. English settlement, 1650; capitulated to the Dutch, and exchanged for New Amsterdam (now New York) the following year. Again in English hands, 1799–1802 and 1804–16. Independent, 1975. Marxist coup, 1982.

Surrey, University of. Established at Guildford, 1966.

Surtax replaced supertax (*q.v.*) in 1929. Ceased to be a separate tax, 1971.

Sussex, Kingdom of. 477. Aelle and his sons Cymen, Wlencing, and Cissa landed at Cymenes ora.
485. Battle between Aelle and the Britons.
491. Aelle and Cissa besieged Andredesceaster (i.e. Anderida, now Pevensey), and killed the garrison.
514. Aelle died.
661–*c*. 685. Aethelwalh, King of Sussex, killed by Caedwalla of Wessex.
c. 685. References to two kings of Sussex, Berthun and Andhun, who resisted Caedwalla. About 687 Caedwalla seems to have become effective ruler of S. *See* SELSEY.
Later history suggests that S. was ruled by a number of sub-kings, probably subject to Wessex and then to Mercia.

Sussex University, estab. at Brighton, 1961.

Suttee. Suicide of an Indian widow on the husband's funeral pile. Forbidden by the British administration, 1829.

Swabia (Schwaben), originally an ethnic rather than geographical term denoting the land of the Suevi or Swabians. It is not clear that the term Suevi when used by Tacitus (A.D. 55–120) is anything more than a vague term for nomadic tribes at a rather lower cultural level than other Germans to the S. and W.; but by about A.D. 600 Swabians had come to mean tribes speaking the western or Alemmanic variant of the High German language, and their country the rough rectangle between the Main, the Rhine, Lake Constance, and the Lech. It was a 'tribal' duchy under the Carolingian Empire (751–987) and came into possession of the Stauffen dynasty, 1079, who retained it until 1268, when it was partitioned among the local nobility. The 'Swabian League', a confederation of Swabian cities formed in 1488, disintegrated, 1534. *See also* BADEN and WÜRTTEMBERG,

Swaziland. Independence recognized by Boer republics in Conventions of 1881 and 1884. Dual control by British and Boers set up, 1890; administration taken over by Transvaal, 1894; British protectorate declared, 1906. Independent dominion, 1968.

'Sweating'. A term applied in nineteenth century to underpaid and overworked labour. Cradley Heath chainmakers' sufferings disclosed, 1889; Anti-Sweating Leauge formed, 1889; Blue Book published, 1890.

Sweden. S. originated in the Sver Kingdom N. of Lake Mälar and the Gothic Kingdom in south S. which coalesced after the battle of Bråvalla (? *c*. 650) under the Uppsala Yngling dynasty. Swedes under Rurik found Novgorod *c*. 862. Ynglings die out and are succeeded by the Gothic Stenkil's dynasty, 1060. The Christian Sverker's dynasty follows, 1130–55, when civil war between Sverker's and Eric's dynasties follows till 1250. Folkung dynasty established by the jarl, Birger Magnusson, 1250 till 1387. By the Union of Kalmar (*q.v.*) S. comes under Danish rule, 1397. Engelbrekt Engelbrektsen raises revolt in Dalecarlia, 1434. He calls the first Riksdag (Parliament) at Arbog, 1435, and is murdered, 1436. Sten Sture the Elder defeats Danes at Brunkeberg, 1471. Papal charter granted to Uppsala University, 1477. Christian II of Denmark carries out massacre at Stockholm, 1520. Gustavus Vasa raises national revolt in Dalecarlia, Jan. 1521. Elected king by Riksdag at Stränghäs, 6 June 1523. *Reces* and *Ordinantia* of Västerås establish power of the Vasa monarchy and regulate church affairs, 24 June 1527. Pact of Succession, 1544. Eric XIV deposed, 1568. S. seize Novgorod, 1611. Peace of Stolbova, 1617. Gustavus Adolfus conquers Baltic provinces, 1621–2; Pomerania, 1630. Defeats Tilly at battle of Breitenfeld, 1631. Is killed at battle of Lützen, 6 Nov. 1632. New constitution, 1634. Abdication of Queen Christina, 1654. Defeat by Russians at Poltava, 1709, and collapse of Swedish Baltic Empire, 1709–18. Peace of Nystad with Russia, 1721. By *Riksdags ordningen* ('Parliamentary constituent'), Riksdag organized into Four Estates, 1723. Marshal Bernadotte elected Crown Prince, 1810. Norway transferred to Swedish crown, 1814. Bernadotte succeeded to throne as Charles XIV, 1818. Union with Norway dissolved, 1905. Prohibition introduced, 1922; abolished, 1955. Changed to driving on the right, Sept. 1967. S. neutral in both world wars. Under constitution of 1975 sovereign merely Head of State and inheritance passes to eldest child of either sex.

Sweden, Kings of, from c. 850–1951:
Olaf and Emund *c.* 850–*c.* 882
Eric Emundsson *c.* 882–*c.* 905
Bjorn Ericsson and Ring *c.* 905–*c.* 950
Eric the Victorious *c.* 950–*c.* 993
Period of confusion c. 993–999
Olaf Scatt-King 999–1022
Anund Jacob 1022–1050
Emund the Old 1050–1060
Stenkil 1060–1066
Period of confusion 1066–1080
Halstan *c.* 1080–*c.* 1093
Inge the Good *c.* 1090–*c.* 1118
Inge II Halstansson *c.* 1118–1130
Sverker *c.* 1132–1155
Eric IX (Saint) 1150–1160
Charles VII 1160–1167
Knut Ericsson 1167–1196
Sverker Carlsson 1196–1205 (?)
Period of confusion: rival kings
1205–1250
Valdemar 1250–1275
Magnus I Ladulas 1275–1290
Birger 1290–1318
Magnus II 1319–1365
Albert of Mecklenburg 1365–1388
Margaret (as 'Lady of Sweden') 1389–1397
Eric of Pomerania (XIII) 1397–1439
Christopher of Bavaria 1440–1448
Charles VIII Knutsson Bonde 1448–1457
Christian I 1457–1464
Charles VIII (again) 1464–1465
and 1467–1470
Regency under Sten Sture the Elder 1470–1497
John II 1497–1501
Regency under Sten Sture the Elder 1501–1503
Regency under Svante Sture 1504–1512
Regency under Sten Sture the Younger 1512–1520
Christian II 1520–1523

Gustavus I (Vasa) (of Sweden only) 1523–1560
Eric XIV 1560–1568
John III 1568–1592
Sigismund 1592–1599
Charles IX 1600–1611
Gustavus II, Adolphus 1611–1632
Christina 1632–1654
Charles X 1654–1660
Charles XI 1660–1697
Charles XII 1697–1718
Ulrica Eleonora 1718–1720
Frederick I 1720–1751
Adolphus, Frederick 1751–1771
Gustavus III 1771–1792
Gustavus IV, Adolphus 1792–1809
Charles XIII 1809–1818
and of Norway 1814–1818
Charles XIV, John (Bernadotte)
1818–1844
Oscar I 1844–1859
Charles XV 1859–1872
Oscar II (renounced throne of Norway, 1905) 1872–1907
Gustavus V 1907–1950
Gustavus VI, Adolphus 1950–1973
Charles XVI, Gustavus 1973–

Swedenborgians, followers of Emanual Swedenborg (1688–1772), more properly called the New (Jerusalem) Church, founded in England, 1788; their propaganda organ, the Swedenborg Society, instituted, 1810.

Swedish Literature. The following is a list of prominent Swedish authors:
Almqvist, Carl Jonas Ludvig, 1793–1866, novelist.
Atterbom, Per Daniel Amadeus, 1790–1855, poet.
Bellman, Carl Mikael, 1740–95, poet.
Benedictsson, Victoria ('Ernst Ahlgren'), 1850–99, novelist.
Bengtsson, Frans, 1894–1956, novelist and biographer.
Bergman, Hjalmar, 1883–1931, novelist.
Dahlgren, Karl Fredrik, 1791–1844, humorist and poet.
Dahlsjerna, Gunno (Eurelius), 1661–1709, poet.
Dalin, Olaf von, 1708–63, poet and historian.
Franzén, Frans Mikael, 1772–1847, poet.
Geijer, Erik Gustaf, 1783–1847, historian and poet.

Geijerstam, Gustaf af, 1858–1909, novelist and dramatist.

Gyalenborg, Gustaf Fredrik, 1731–1808, poet and dramatist.

Hansson, Ola, 1860–1925, poet.

Heidenstam, Verner von, 1859–1940, poet, novelist, and critic.

Kellgren, Johan Henrik, 1751–95, poet.

Konsenstjerna, Agnes von, 1894–1940, novelist.

Lagerlöf, Selma, 1858–1940, novelist.

Lundegård, Axel, 1861–1930, novelist.

Messenius, Johannes, 1579–1636, poet and dramatist.

Molander, Harald Johan, 1858–1900, dramatist.

Munthe, Axel Marten Fredrik, 1857–1949, miscellaneous writer.

Nordenflycht, Hedvig Charlotte, 1718–63, poetess.

Petri, Olaus, 1493–1552, historian.

Rosenhane, Gustaf, 1619–84, poet.

Runeberg, Johan Ludvig, 1804–77, poet.

Sjöberg, Erik ('Vitalis'), 1794–1828, poet.

Snoilsky, Count Carl Johan Gustaff, 1841–1903, poet.

Stagnelius, Erik Johan, 1793–1823, poet.

Stjernhjelm, Georg (Göran Lilja), 1598–1672, poet.

Strindberg, Johan August, 1849–1912, novelist and dramatist.

Swedenborg, Emanuel, 1688–1772, philosopher and scientist.

Tegner, Esaias, 1782–1846, poet.

Wägner, Elin, 1882–1949, novelist.

The following though writing in Swedish were born and lived in Finland, and regarded themselves as of Finnish nationality:

Hemmer, J., 1893–1944, poet.

Lybeck, M., 1864–1925, poet.

Numers, G. von, 1848–1913, playwright (also in Finnish).

Procope, H., 1868–1927, poet.

Runeberg, J. L., 1804–77, poet.

Schildt, R., 1888–1925, novelist and playwright.

Stenbäck, J., 1811–70, pot.

Tavastjerna, K. A. 1860–98, poet and novelist.

Topelius, Z., 1818–98, poet.

Wecksell, J. J., 1838–1907, playwright.

Swiss Guard (French). Raised, 1616; ceased to exist after 1792, when they suffered heavy losses in the defence of the Tuileries.

Swiss Guard (papal). Raised by Julius II, 1506. Had heavy casualties (two-thirds of total strength) at the sack of Rome, 1527. New establishment ordered by Paul III, 1548. Disbanded in 1794, reformed, 1825, by Leo XII. Now form part of Vatican security forces.

Switzerland. Struggle for independence against the Hapsburgs (*q.v.*), thirteenth-fourteenth centuries; victories at Morgarten, Sempach, and Näfels, 1315, 1386, and 1388; overthrow of Burgundians at Granson and Morat, 1476; defeated by French at Melegnano, 1515; religious wars during sixteenth century; Calvin at Geneva, 1536, till his death; declared independent at Peace of Westpahlia (*q.v.*), 1648; Peasants' Revolt, 1653; first Villemergen War, 1656; second Villemergen War, 1712; Helvetic Society founded, 1762; alliance with France, 1777; Helvetic Republic proclaimed, 29 Mar. 1798; independence secured by Treaty of Vienna, 1815; The Sonderbund Civil War, Oct.–Nov. 1847; Romansch declared an official language, 11 July 1937. Women's suffrage rejected by referendum, 1 Feb. 1959; but carried, 7 Feb. 1971. For early history, *see* articles on separate cantons and WALDSTÄTTE.

Sydney, New S. Wales, was founded by Capt. Arthur Philip, 1788. S. Harbour Bridge officially opened, 1932. Capt. Cook Dock completed, 1945. Opera House, 1961.

Synods. Convened formerly by the emperors, and afterwards by the Pope; rendered illegal in England except by royal permission, 1533. The Synod of Dort was held from Nov. 1618 to May 1619.

Syracuse, founded *c.* 734 B.C. as Corinthian colony. Beat off Carthaginians at Himera, 480 B.C.; defeated Athenian expedition, 414–413; allied to Carthage in second Punic War and taken by Romans, 212, despite brilliant defence by Archimedes (*b.* 287 B.C.), the chief engineer. Taken by Arabs, A.D. 878, and Normans, 1085.

Syria. Mandated to France in 1920. French commander in S., loyal to Vichy Government, announced cessation of hostilities with Germany, 28 June 1940. British and Free French forces carried through occupation of S. against Vichy opposition, 8 June–21 July 1941, and declared the independence of S., but in 1945 disagreements arose with the French which led to fighting. Independent republic, 12 Apr. 1946. With Egypt, formed the United Arab Republic (*q.v.*), 1958–61. S. joined in the 'June War', 1967, on the side of Egypt but lost important stragegic ter. thereby. Invaded Jordan, Sept. 1970, but troops repulsed and withdrew. Coup in 1970 brought Assad to power. Pro-Soviet policies folowed. Fought against Israel, 1973, but heavily defeated: in 1980s intervened decisively in Lebanon (*q.v.*) on side of the anti-gov. forces.

Szezecin (Ger.) grew up round a Wendish stronghold *c.* A.D. 1200; received muncipal charter, 1243, ceded to Sweden, 1648; to Prussia, 1720. In 1945 it was ceded to Poland.

T

Tabuearan , *see* FANNING ISLAND.

Tahiti, Pacific, discovered by Spaniard, de Quiros, 1607; French protectorate formally accepted by native ruler, 1847; French possession, 1880.

Tai-Pings. Followers of the Christian Hung Hsinchwan in the Chinese rebellion of 1851. Captured Nanking, Mar. 1853; Nanking retaken by the Imperialists under direction of Charles Gordon (later killed at Khartoum), 19 July 1864; and rebellion suppressed, 1865.

Taiwan, formerly **Formosa.** Colonized by Dutch, 1624. Spanish landed, 1626, and called the island Formosa, but expelled by Dutch. Dutch expelled by Chinese, 1662. Invaded by Japanese 1874: ceded to Japan 1895. Returned to Nationalist China, 1945. Since 1949 seat of the Kuomintang Government and the only ter. controlled by it. Mutual security pact between U.S.A. and Nationalist China pledged U.S. protection of T., 1954 but this abrogated when U.S.A. ceased diplomatic relations with T. on recognition of China, 1979, though close commercial links continued.

Tajikistan became an autonomous republic, 1924, and a Union republic of the U.S.S.R., 1929.

Taj Mahal, India, built by Shah Jehan, 1630–52, in memory of his favourite wife, who *d.* 1629.

Tallage, a characteristically Norman tax, was placed under the control of the Commons, 1297, which abolished it, 1340.

Tallies were used by the exchequer for accounting purposes until 1826, though an Act for their abolition was passed, 1782. An unsupervised bonfire of old T. was the cause whereby the greater part of the Palace of Westminster was burnt down, 1834.

Tallin (Reval), fortress founded by Danes in 1219, joined the Hanseatic League, 1248. Ceded to Sweden, 1561, by the Teutonic Knights, who had obtained possession of T. in 1346. Ceded, 1710, to Russians, who made it the capital of the Government of Estonia (*q.v.*), 1783. Capital of the independent republic of Estonia, 1919–40. Ceded to Russia as a naval base by the independent republic of Estonia, 28 Sept. 1939. Taken by Germans, Aug. 1941, and retained until the spring of 1945 when, with the rest of Estonia, it became part of the U.S.S.R.

Talmud. The civil and religious code of the Jews. The T. dating from the fifth century is the one in use, an earlier one having become unintelligible. It is divided into the Mishna and the Gemara. The first complete copy was published at Venice, 1520.

Tammany Society. A powerful Democratic association of New York, founded in 1789; chartered, 1805. Named after Tammany, a Delaware Indian chief of the seventeenth century; the name itself means 'affable'.

Tanganyika. Formerly German E. Africa; mandated to Britain under the peace treaty, 1919. Became an independent dominion within the Commonwealth, 9 Dec. 1961. On 9 Dec. 1962 became a republic, within the Commonwealth, with Nyerere as President. Brit. troops called in to put down an army mutiny, Jan. 1964; in Apr. 1964 T. united with Zanzibar to form what is now known as the republic of Tanzania (*q.v.*).

Tangier or **Tangiers,** Morocco (*q.v.*). The Roman **Tingis.** Captured by Portuguese, 1471; given to Charles II on his marriage to Catherine of Braganza,

1662; evacuated by English, 1684; bombarded by French, 1844; terrorized by Raisuli in early years of twentieth century; policed in 1906 as a result of Algeciras Convention. By treaty of Fez (Nov. 1912) T. was to become centre of an international zone, and it was finally formed into an internationally governed neutral port, 18 Dec. 1923, by France and Britain (Spain acceded to the agreement, 1924). Spanish troops occupied T., 14 June 1940, and in Sept. T. was incorporated into Spanish Morocco. Spanish troops withdrew and former status restored, 1945. France agreed to terminate treaty of Fez, 1956. Spanish protectorate abolished, and T.'s international status was terminated 1 Jan. 1957, when it became an integral part of Morocco.

Tanks. British War Office began experiments, 1915. First went into action on the Somme, 15 Sept. 1916.

Tanzania, formed by the union of Tanganyika and Zanzibar (*q.q.v.*), 27 Apr. 1964, though the name T. was not officially adopted until 29 Oct. 1964. Nyerere became president of the new state, which became a one-party one in 1977. Nyerere retired, 1985.

Taoism. One of the three religions of China. The system was founded by Lao-tsze in the sixth century B.C.

Tapestry. Introduced into Flanders during tenth century; Arras chief centre during fourteenth and fifteenth centuries; Gobelin (*q.v.*) factory founded in Paris, sixteenth century; famous T. factory founded at Mortlake by Sir Francis Crane, 1619; existed till 1703; another factory existed at Windsor, 1872–88. Revival of tapestry in twentieth century exemplified by one behind the high altar of the rebuilt Coventry Cathedral. It depicts 'Christ in Glory' and was designed by Graham Sutherland and woven, 1958–61, at the Aubusson factory in France.

Tara, Hill of, was the residence of the High Kings of Ireland until A.D. 560. The Danes were defeated there (*see* VIKING AGE), 980.

Taranto (Lat. **Tarentum;** Gr. **Taras**), Italy, founded 708 B.C. by Spartans. As-

sisted by Pyrrhus in war against Romans, 281 B.C.; captured by Romans, 272 B.C.; became ally of Rome, but went over to Hannibal, 213 B.C., and on being recaptured by Fabius, 209 B.C., was severely punished. Roman colony, 123 B.C. Taken by the Saracens, A.D. 830; by the Normans, 1083. British air raid on Italian fleet, 11 Nov. 1940.

Tariff Reform League. Inaugurated, July 1903.

Tariffs (Britain). Bill to promote Imperial Preference, protect 'key industries', and prevent dumping passed first reading, Nov. 1919, and was then dropped. Government proposals for Imperial Preference introduced at Imperial Conference, Oct. 1923. First protective measures passed by National Government, Nov. 1931. Import Duties Act, 1932. As a further 'weapon', Reprisal Quotas (for imports) were instituted, 1934. Drastic tariff modifications after World War II through G.A.T.T., the European Economic Community and the European Free Trade Association (*q.q.v.*).

Tarsus, Asia Minor. Founded by Ionian Greeks, *c.* 900 B.C. Occupied by Assyrians, 850. Birthplace of Saul (Paul the Apostle). Capital of the Roman province of Cilicia, A.D. 72. Captured by Arabs *c.* 660; taken by Tancred in First Crusade, 1099; under Turks since *c.* 1500.

Tartan. The word, which is not Gaelic and first appears in English usage in 1500, may be of French origin. The characteristic *setts* denoting clans and septs evolved probably during the seventeenth century. The wearing of T. was prohibited by law from 1746 to 1782, under the Highland Garb Act.

Tasmania. Discovered in 1642 by Abel J. Tasman. Penal settlement till 1853. Granted local government, 1856. Name then changed from Van Diemen's Land to T. United with the mainland states to form the Commonwealth of Australia, 1901.

Tatar or **Tartar Republic,** an autonomous republic of the U.S.S.R., formed in 1920 on the territory of the fifteenth-century T. kingdom of Kazan.

Tate Gallery. Opened, 1897; enlarged, 1899, 1910, 1926, 1937. Damaged by bombing during World War II, but reopened, 1946, and repairs completed, 1949. Further extensions, 1979.

Taunton. Castle first built by King Ine *c.* 710; rebuilt *c.* 1100; defended by Blake, 1644–5; 'Bloody Assize' opened by Judge Jeffreys, 1685.

Taxation (Britain). Income and property tax first levied by Parliament during the civil war, 1642. William Pitt the Younger introduced an income tax, 1798, which was repealed, 1815, and revived by Peel, 1842. Supertax introduced, 1914–18. Surtax replaced supertax, 1929; ceased to be separate tax, 1971.

Land tax first levied, 1690. Made perpetual but redeemable, 1798. Lloyd George introduced Land Value Tax, 1909. Abolished, 1920. Purchase tax introduced, 1940. A 'once-for-all' Special Contribution, similar to a capital levy, imposed, 1948. Capital Gains Tax, 1965. Selective Employment Tax, 1966. Value Added Tax, 1973.

Tay Bridge. Rail bridge first opened, 1877. Famous disaster, 28 Dec. 1879. New bridge opened, 1887. Road bridge opened, Aug. 1966.

Tea. Introduced in Europe, sixteenth century, but not into England until 1657.

Tehri-Garhwal, small tributary kingdom which in Mar. 1949 the Indian Government combined with Garhwal (*q.v.*) as part of the United Provinces (known as Uttar Pradesh since 1950).

Tel-Aviv, founded in 1909, originally as a garden city by Jewish residents of Jaffa, received its present name in 1910. T.-A. became the principal economic centre of Palestine (*q.v.*) in 1930, and the largest town in the country in 1936. It was the provisional capital of Israel (*q.v.*), 1948–50. Jaffa was absorbed into T.-A., 1950.

Telegraphy. Proposal to use electricity as means of communication made as early as 1753. First serviceable telegraphic device invented by Chappe (France), 1792. Ronald (England) produced his pith-ball telegraph, 1816.

Morse constructed an instrument in 1835, and Steinheil in 1837. Cooke and Wheatstone's, 1837. Earliest trial, 1837, on L.N.W. Railway. First public line from Paddington to Slough, 1843; London and Paris connected, 1851. Post Office took over telegraph systems on 5 Feb. 1870; acquired by British Telecom, 1981. First transatlantic stations, Poldhu, Cornwall, and St. John's, Newfoundland, Dec. 1901; first installed in ships, Feb. 1902. Internal telegrams in Britain abolished, 1 Oct. 1982; replaced by telemessages. *See* Wireless.

Telepathy. So named by F. W. H. Myers (1843–1901), 1882.

Telephone. Wheatstone's 'Magic Lyre' (for reproducing sounds by means of sound-boards connected by a rod), 1831. Philipp Reis's experiments to reproduce human speech, 1861. Alexander Graham Bell (1847–1922) invented electric T., 1876; patented, 1876. Edison patented an invention of his, July 1877. The T. Co. formed, 1878; Edison T. Co. formed, 1879. Action by British postmaster-general against Edison for infringement of monopoly, 1879. National T. Co. (amalgamation of various separate concerns) formed, 1889; trunk wires transferred to Post Office, 1896; Government, by agreement of 2 Feb. 1905, otained the whole undertaking of the National T. Co., 31 Dec. 1912. Automatic system developed in America from 1889 (Strowger's invention). Communication between London and Paris established, 1 Apr. 1891. First automatic exchange in U.K., Newport, 14 Aug. 1915. Service between New York and London opened, 7 Jan. 1927. Switch to subscriber trunk dialling in Britain, 1959 onwards. First public telephone call by Telstar (*q.v.*) London–New York, 19 July 1962. Telephone service transferred to British Telecom, 1981; telemessage service started, 1982.

Telescope. Traditionally invented by Roger Bacon, in the thirteenth century, but no definite evidence to prove this. Giambattista della Porta probably first to construct some form of instrument,

1558; Leonard Digges is also said, in a book published in 1571, to have arranged glasses so as to obtain 'miraculous effects'. First practical instruments constructed by Lippershey and Jansen in Middelburg, 1608; Galileo constructed his first T., 1609, and began astronomical observations at the beginning of 1610. Lord Rosse's at Birr, 1844; Greenwich T. erected, 1860; Lick Observatory, California, 1880; Pulkowa, Russia, 1885; Yorkes Observatory, Chicago, 1897; Mount Palomar, California, 1949; Jodrell Bank, Cheshire, 1958.

Television was first practically demonstrated by J. L. Baird (1888–1946) in 1926, though means of transmitting images electronically had been suggested by Boris Rosing (1905) and Campbell-Swinton (1911). Still pictures were experimentally diffused by the British Broadcasting Corporation (q.v.) in 1928. In Nov. 1936 a high-definition transmission station opened at Alexandra Palace. Baird system discontinued, 1937. T. ceased, Sept. 1939; transmissions resumed, 7 June 1946. Baird's contemporary in the same field in the U.S.A. was C. F. Jenkins. There were five stations transmitting in the U.S.A. in 1939, where T. was not, as in Europe, forced to close down during hostilities. In 1946 stations in New York State and Pennsylvania were linked by cable. Columbia Broadcasting System demonstrated coloured T., 1940, and colour T. used to a limited extent in the U.S.A. from 1949 onwards. Eurovision started, 1953. T. Act of 1954 established commercial T. in Britain, under the auspices of the Independent T. Authority (q.v.). T. first shown 'live' between Europe and the U.S.A. via Telstar (q.v.), June 1962. Britain began changing her line definitions from 405 to 625 lines gradually from 1964. First British colour T. on BBC 2, 1 July 1967: first live T. pictures from the lunar orbit transmitted by Apollo 8, Dec. 1968. Cable T. started in U.S.A. in 1970s. in Britain in 1980s. Videos became estab. in 1980s.

Telstar. American satellite launched from Cape Canaveral, Florida, 10 June 1962. A television picture from Andover, Maine, 'bounced off' T. and was picked up at Goonhilly, Cornwall, at 1 a.m. on 11 July 1962, and at Brittany (even more clearly) on 12 July. Pictures from France and England transmitted to the United States via T. First live television show from United States seen in Europe via. T., 23 July 1962.

Templars, Knights. Order of knighthood founded under Baldwin II of Jerusalem in A.D. 1118 by Hugues de Payen and Geoffroi de Saint-Adhémar for the protection of pilgrims to the Holy Land. Statutes drawn up at the Council of Troyes, 1128. Rendered independent of any bishop's authority by a bull dated 1172. Reached England c. 1185. By order of Philip the Fair, Oct. 1307, the Order was persecuted in France with great cruelties, and was abolished in 1312 by the Council of Vienne. See also TEMPLE CHURCH (London).

Temple Bar (London). Wren's gate built, 1670–2. Removed, 1878–9. Erected at Theobalds Park, Cheshunt, 1888. In 1985 the govt. announced that T.B. was to be re-sited in St Paul's Churchyard.

Temple Church (London). Built c. 1250.

Tennessee, originally a part of N. Carolina, was first explored by Spaniards in 1540. Though forming part of the grant made to Sir Walter Releigh in 1584, it was next explored by the French c. 1670–80. Settlement by British colonists began about 1750, and in 1776 the territory was annexed to N. Carolina under the name of Washington District, later Washington Co. T. partisans fought on the American side in the revolutionary war. Admitted to the Union as the sixteenth state, 1 June 1796. Seceded from the Union, June 1861; readmitted, 24 July 1866.

Tennessee Valley Authority (T.V.A.), created by an Act of Congress, May 1933.

Tennis. Played in France from the twelfth century onwards; popular in court circles in England from fifteenth century. Lawn T. evolved from real T., *c.* 1870. First Wimbledon championships, 1877. Lawn Tennis Association founded 1886. Lawn T. Association voted for open tournaments from 1968.

Ten Thousand, Expedition of the. Evacuation of Iraq by Greek mercenaries, formerly in the pay of the Persian King Cyrus, 401 B.C. The leader of the operation, Xenophon (427–355 B.C.), wrote an account of it (*Anabasis*).

Territorial. T. Force formed 1908 from Volunteers and Yeomanry (*q.v.*). Became T. Army, 1920. Re-formed, Jan. 1947, to include conscripts. Further reorganizations, 1956, 1958, 1966 and 1984.

Territorial Waters. An Act of 1878 gives British courts jurisdiction over offenders arrested in British T.W., viz. within three sea-miles of the coastline of the U.K. T.W. for fishery purposes extended to 12 miles by Acts of 1964 and 1968.

Temperance League of America. *See* ANTI-SALOON LEAGUE.

Tesin (Ger. **Teschen**; Pol. **Cieszyn**), town and environs in Silesia, was a principality of the Empire, since 1290 under Bohemian suzerainty. Became part of Bohemia, 1625. Passed to Austria, 1723. Divided, 1920, between Poland and Czechoslovakia, the whole territory was seized by Poland in 1938, but recovered by Czechoslovakia, 1945.

Teutonic Knights. Order of Military Knights, established 1189–91, for succouring the sick and wounded in the Holy Land; later they fought in parts of north-east Germany and the Baltic lands for the christianizing of the country; headquarters at Acre, 1191–1291, but transferred to Marienburg, 1308. Prestige hit by defeat at Tannenberg by Poles and Lithuanians, 1410. Grand Master of the Order, Albert of Brandenberg, became a Protestant, 1525, and the order was secularized; its last remaining possessions were taken by Napoleon in 1809.

Texas, first permanently settled by the French, 1685, was surrendered to Spain, 1713, and became part of Mexico when the latter declared its independence, 1821. Heavily settled by English-speaking cattle-ranchers, T. broke away from Mexican rule and declared itself independent in 1836. It joined the United States at the request of the Texans, Dec. 1845. The resultant war with Mexico over the Texan boundary lasted until 1848. T. seceded from the Union in 1861. The last battle of the civil war was fought at Palmito, T., 13 May 1865. Readmitted to the Union, Feb. 1870.

Thailand (Siam). Present kingdom founded when Ayuthia became capital, 1350. Burmese storm Ayuthia and conquer T. *c.* 1555. Independence re-established by Phra Naret, 1560–80. Siege and destruction of Ayuthia by Burmese, 1765–7. Phaya Tak Sin establishes new government at Bangkok, 1767–8. Succeeded by Phaya Chakri, 1782. Establishment of British interests in T. by John Burney, 1822–4. Eastern territories ceded to France, 1893. Anglo-French convention *re* T., 1895. Further cessions to France, 1902. Middle-class revolution establishes constitution, 1932. Name changed to T. from Siam, 1939. Japanese occupation, 8 Dec. 1941–45. King Ananda Mahidol murdered, 9 July 1946; succeeded by Bhumibol Adulyadej. New constitution, 1978.

Thaler. *See* DOLLAR. The official unit of currency of the German Monetary Union from 1857–1873.

Thalidomide. Proprietary name of tranquillizing drug developed in Germany and introduced into Britain, 1958. Withdrawn by the makers as the result of evidence that when taken in early pregnancy it was liable to cause deformalities in babies, Nov. 1961. Feb. 1968: in a High Court settlement, the British manufacturers of T. agreed to settle 'very substantial damages' on the British T. children affected.

Thames. Conservation of the 'stream' given to the mayors of the city of London, 1489; twelve conservators fixed by Act of Parliament, 1857; abolished, 1973. T. Tunnel opened, 1843; closed, 1866. T. Conservancy Act, 1894; further acts, 1910, 1911, 1921, 1924, 1932, and 1950. County Council steamboat service opened, 1905; discontinued, 1909. Port of London Authority instituted, 31 Mar. 1909. River bus service started, 1948. Thames Water Authority estab., 1973. Thames Barrier opened 8 May 1984.

Thames Embankment. N. side (Victoria) constructed, 1862–70; S. (Albert), 1866–70; Chelsea, 1871–4.

Theatres (London). Licence granted to Burbage, 1576: the 'Theatre' and the 'Curtain', 'Blackfriars', and 'Globe' were among the T. extant in the time of Elizabeth I, and were all used by Shakespeare. Prominent theatres, with dates of opening include:
Covent Garden, 1732
Old Vic (as Coburg) 1818
Coliseum 1904
Royal Court 1871
Aldwych 1905
Mermaid 1959
National Theatre 1976
Barbican 1982

Thebes, Egypt, *fl.* 1600–1100 B.C. as capital of Upper Egypt. Partly burnt by Persians, 525 B.C., captured and sacked by Greeks, 85 B.C.

Thebes, Greece, capital of Boeotia, arose about 1100 B.C., perhaps earlier. For a short time after 371 B.C. T. became the strongest city in Greece, but lost her supremacy after 362. Razed to the ground by Macedonians under Alexander, 335, restored 316. Captured by Demetrius Poliorcetes, 290 B.C. Repatriated Greeks from Asia settled in T., 1922.

Theosophists, a sect founded by Helena Petrovna Blavatsky (1831–91), whose principal disciple was Mrs. Annie Besant (1847–1933). The Theosophical Society was founded in America, 1875.

Thermometer. Invention of attributed to Galileo (1564–1642). General change from Fahrenheit to Centigrade in Britain during 1960s, to Celsius in 1980s.

'Thetis' Disaster. British submarine *Thetis* failed to resurface, 1 June 1939. Ninety-nine men died, and there were four survivors. Submarine was eventually beached, 3 Oct, 1939, recommissioned, and renamed the *Thunderbolt;*

lost during World War II off Sicily, 13 Mar. 1943, with all hands.

Thirty-nine Articles of Religion. (*See* ARTICLES OF RELIGION (ANGLICAN)). Were agreed by the Convocation held in London, 1562, and subsequently reduced to thirty-nine and confirmed, 1571 and 1604.

Thirty Years War, 1618–48. Waged between the Protestants and Catholic Imperialists of Germany; Frederick, Elector Palatine, the prince to whom the Bohemian Estates had offered the imperial succession which was the immediate *casus belli*, defeated at the White Mountain (*Bela Hora*), 8 Nov. 1620. English intervention against Spanish Netherlands, 1625. Protestant effort mainly directed by Denmark, 1625–30, thereafter by Gustavus Adolphus of Sweden, until his death in action at Lützen, 16 Nov. 1632. Wallenstein, recalled to command imperialist forces, 1632, murdered, 1634. From 1632 French intervention became the dominant factor, and the native Protestant leadership, such as it was, devolved on Bernard of Saxe-Weimar (*d.* 18 July 1639). *See* WESTPHALIA, PEACE OF.

Thomas's, St., Hospital. Founded in 1213 as an alms-house; enlarged by the Mayor of London in 1551; rebuilt, 1693; and 1868; extended after World War II.

Three Choirs Festival held annually at cathedrals of Gloucester, Worcester, and Hereford in rotation since 1724.

Thugs. Indian fanatics, a caste of professional thieves who strangled victims in honour of the goddess Bhowani (Mother Kali). Suppressed by British, 1830.

Thule. *See* FAIR ISLE.

Tibet. First king Lhato Nyan-tsen. Fourth Nam-ri Song-tsen, *d.* A.D. 630, and was succeeded by Song-tsen Gampo, who founded the secular monarchy of T. Nepalese rebellion, 703. Zenith of Tibetan power under Tisong Detsen, 743–89. War with China, 810–21. End of the dynasty of religious kings at assassination of Ral-pa-Chen, 838. Kingdom divided, 841 onwards. Dharmapala arrives from India, 1013.

Atisha also, 1026. Rule of the abbots of Sakya under Mongol protection, 1270–1340. Pakmodu founds dynasty *c.* 1350. Tsong Ka-pa founds Yellow Hat Order *c.* 1370–1380. System of priestly incarnation established, 1474. End of Pakmodu's dynasty, 1635. Fifth Dalai Lama established as ruler of T., 1641. Chinese resident established at Lhasa *c.* 1710. War with Gurkhas, 1788–92. Chinese resident insists on closure of T. to foreigners, 1792. Dogra invasion repelled, 1841. Gurkha invasion and treaty of friendship, 1855. Younghusband mission, after fighting, reaches Lhasa, 1906. Chinese occupation, 1910. Chinese expelled, 1911. New Dalai Lama enthroned, 1940; assumed full powers, 1950. Treaty of Peking signed by Panchen Lama, 23 May 1951. This gave the Tibetans the right of national regional autonomy within China. Dalai Lama and Panchen Lama visited Peking, 1954, and India, 1956. Tibetan revolt against China, Mar. 1959; T. declared herself independent. Chinese troops rapidly crushed the revolt and on 31 Mar. the Dalai Lama reached India, where he was granted political asylum.

Tichborne Case. Sir J. F. Doughty T., *d.* 1862. In 1872 a claimant to the estate, representing himself to be Sir Roger T., son of Sir Doughty, involved the T. family in litigation which cost them £70,000. In 1874 he was finally exposed as a butcher named Thomas Castro, and sentenced to fourteen years' penal servitude for perjury.

Ticino (Ger. **Tessin**). After the break-up of the Roman Empire the canton was part of the temporal domains of the Bishop of Como and the Chapter of Milan, taken over between 1100 and 1400 piecemeal by the secular communes of Milan and Como. The conquest of T. by the twelve 'old' cantons of Switzerland was gradual, and complete by 1512. In 1798 the Helvetic Confederation set up cantons of Lugano and Bellinzona, which fused, 1803 to form the canton of T.

Tides. Theory of T. first made clear by Kepler, 1598, but had been studied by

Posidonius of Apamea, 79 B.C.; completely explained by Sir Isaac Newton, 1683.

Tierra del Fuego, S. America, discovered by Magellan, 1520.

Tiflis, Tbilisi, capital of Georgia, founded in the fourth century A.D., and conquered by the Arabs in 645. Residence of the Christian kings of Armenia, 1121–6. From the sixteenth century until its seizure by Russia in 1801 it was disputed between Turkey and Persia. Became capital of the Georgian Republic (*q.v.*), 1922.

Tilbury Docks were opened, 1886.

Tilsit (U.S.S.R.) is noted for the peace treaty between the emperors, Alexander and Napoleon, 1807. It was founded by the Teutonic Knights in 1288 and was renamed **Sovetsk** in 1946.

'Times, The', Newspaper. First issued as *The Times*, 1788, but had been published as the *Daily Universal Register* since 1785. Founded by John Walter (1739–1812). Controlling interest bought by Lord Northcliffe, July 1907. On the death of Northcliffe, 1922, the paper was bought by John Walter the fourth and Maj. J. J. Astor. Acquired by Lord Thomson, 1966: by Rupert Murdoch, 1982.

Timor was divided between the Dutch and Portuguese colonial empires, 1859, by a boundary rearranged by arbitration, 1914. Both parts of the island were occupied and used by the Japanese as an air base, 1942–5. Dutch T. became part of Indonesia (*q.v.*), 1950; Portuguese T. became part of Indonesia 1976 and was renamed Loro Sae.

Tin. One of the earliest known metals, having been imported from England by the Phoenicians more than 1,000 years B.C.

Tirol (also **Tyrol**, but not locally). Trent becomes fief of Bishops of Trent, 1004. Bolzano (Bozen) and Vintschgau (Val Venosta) added, the rest of the area being given to the Bishops of Brixen, 1027. Bishops delegate authority to the Lords of T. Castle (near Merano) from which T. takes its name, *c.* 1100. They become counts in Trent, 1150. Acquire lands in Brixen, 1248. Finally displace the episcopal authorities, 1271. Family became extinct and T. passed to Austria, 1363. Held as an apanage of a junior line of the Hapsburgs till 1665. Ceded to Bavaria by Peace of Pressburg, 1805. Andreas Hofer's rising against French and Bavarians, 1809–10. Restored to Austria by Treaty of Paris, 1814. S.T. annexed to Italy, 1919. Agreement between Italy and Austria on local autonomy of S.T., 6 Sept. 1946, and this incorporated into the Italian Peace Treaty of 1957.

'Titanic'. White Star liner lost after striking iceberg near Cape Race, 14 Apr. 1912, with the loss of some 1,500 lives.

Tithes were commonly paid to monasteries up to 1215, but thereafter only to parish priests. The T. Act of 1936 (amended by the T. Act of 1951) was designed to replace T. by the payment of T. Redemption annuities which will cease to be payable, 1996.

Tobacco. First observed in Cuba, 1492; brought to England in 1565 or 1586 by Sir John Hawkins or Sir Walter Raleigh; cultivation in England was prohibited, 1684, and allowed in Ireland, 1779; Pure Tobacco Act, 1842; permission to cultivate T. in England under certain conditions was granted, 1886. Royal College of Physicians' Report, 'Smoking and Health', suggested a causal relationship between cigarette-smoking and lung cancer, Mar. 1962. Cigarette advertising banned on British television, Aug. 1965.

Toc H (for **Talbot House**) took its name from a military chapel and soldiers' club opened at Poperinghe, Flanders, Dec. 1915.

Togoland became a German protectorate, 1884. Became a League of Nations mandated territory, under British and French administration, 1920. British T. united with Ghana (*q.v.*) when the latter achieved independence in 1957. French T. became the independent republic of **Togo** on 27 Apr. 1960.

Tokyo. Capital of Japan (*q.v.*) since 1868. Formerly called Yedo; castle, built fif-

teenth century, grew, and was capital, 1603–1868. Practically destroyed by earthquake in Sept. 1923, when Yokohama was completely demolished. Heavily bombed by the Americans, 1945, and since reconstructed on American 'skyscraper' lines. *See also* EARTHQUAKES.

Toleration, Act of, 24 May 1689, for the relief of Dissenters. Roman Catholics included, 13 Apr. 1829. *See* NONCONFORMISTS.

Tolls. The first T. in England were collected in London, 1267; toll gates were instituted, 1663; from 1827 to 1893 toll gates were gradually abolished, and now very few remain in England. T. have, however, been applied to help finance certain new roadworks (e.g. the Severn and Humber bridges) since 1955. In the U.S.A. T. are levied to pay for several of the twentieth-century motorways.

Tolpuddle Martyrs. Six labourers living at the village of T., Dorset, convicted at Dorchester of 'administering unlawful oaths' (i.e. trade union activity), 19 Mar. 1834, and sentenced to seven years' transportation. Following nation-wide agitation, they were pardoned two years later.

Tomatoes were introduced into England, 1596, though not extensively consumed here before 1900.

Tonga or **Friendly Islands** were first explored by the Dutch under Cornelius Schouten and Jacob le Maire, 1616, then by Tasman, 1643. The first Englishman to land was Wallis (1767). Cook landed several times, 1773–7. In 1831 Tupou, the King of T., was baptized and took the name of George, his consort that of Salote (i.e. Charlotte). By 1845 he had extended his rule over the whole group; he *d.* 1893, aged 96. His successor, George Tupou II, signed a treaty of friendship and protection with Britain 1900. Salote, daughter of George Tupou II, came to the throne on his death, 1918; she *d.* 1965, and was succeeded by her son, Taufa'ahau Tupou IV, who was crowned 4 July 1967. From 1970 Britain ceased to control T's external affairs.

Tonnage and Poundage first levied, 1371, and abolished, 1787.

Tontines. Instituted by Tonti, a Neapolitan; first used in Paris, 1653. A tontine was a fund to which a group subscribed and out of which each member received an annuity, increasing as the group diminished through deaths, until the last survivor was left with the whole fund. The last English public tontine was in 1789.

Torgau, League of. Between the Elector of Saxony and the Landgrave of Hesse to uphold the opinions of Martin Luther, concluded at Gotha, Feb. 1526.

Toronto, site chosen as seat of government for Upper Canada, 1793. Occupied by U.S. forces, 1813, and legislative buildings burned. The mace carried away on that occasion was returned by Franklin D. Roosevelt, 1934. The city, first named York, adopted the present name, 1834.

Torpedoes. The word originally signified *mines*, and was so used till *c.* 1868. First T. devised by Whitehead, 1870.

Torres Vedras was captured by the Portuguese from the Moors, 1149, and was the seat of the Cortes in 1441. Wellington built a strong defensive position here, covering Lisbon, into which he retired at the end of the campaign of 1810. The French under Masséna closed up on the lines of T.V., but were unable to storm them, and having eaten the country bare were compelled to break contact in Mar. 1811.

Tory (Irish = a *persecutor, robber,* or *outlaw*). Nickname for any supporter of the Duke of York, 1679. From 1689 any opponent of the Whigs or Hanoverian party. Since about 1833 a Conservative.

Totalisator. First T. machine was set up at Christchurch, New Zealand, 1880, based on the *pari mutuel* system which was invented in France, 1872. The first machine in Europe operated at Longchamps, 1929, in Britain in the same year. In Maryland, U.S.A., T. machines were first used, 1930.

Toulon (anct. **Telo Martius**), France, docks and arsenal were begun by Vauban (1633–1707). The town was yielded to the British, Aug. 1793, who destroyed the military and naval installations before the Republicans retook them in Dec. Fire and explosion of battleship *Liberté* destroyed 200 ships in T. harbour, 1911. French fleet scuttled in the harbour, 27 Nov. 1942, before German occupation of the port.

Toulouse, in Roman times **Tolosa**, chief city of Gallia Narbonnensis, was colonized by the Romans in 106 B.C., became capital of a Visigothic kingdom, A.D. 419, and was captured by the Franks, 506. Became capital of Aquitaine, 630, then of a virtually independent county, one of whose rulers, Raymond IV (count from 1088 to 1105), was a principal commander in the First Crusade (*q.v.*), and refused the crown of Jerusalem. In 1271 the royal house of France inherited the county and its independence ceased.

Touraine, ancient province of France, roughly approximating to the department of Indre-et-Loire; became an independent county, 941, subject, 1040, to the counts of Anjou, and hence, 1154, to the English crown. From 1205 did homage to the French crown; won back by Joan of Arc; finally incorporated in France as a *gouvernement*, 1541.

Tours, ancient capital of Touraine (*q.v.*), was an episcopal see in the fourth century. It was captured by the Visigoths, 473, by the Franks in 507. Charles Martel defeated the Saracens near T., 732. Destroyed by Vikings, 853 and 903. From *c.* 1400 to 1685 centre of the silk industry in France. Seat of French Government, 13 Sept.–10 Dec. 1870, and June 1940.

Tower Bridge, built 1886–94. Proposal to demolish it in improvement scheme caused protests, 1961 and plan abandoned.

Tower of London. Begun in 1078 by William I: completed by William Rufus, 1098; additions made, 1680–5; a portion damaged by fire, 1841, and by bombing in World War II.

Town and Country Planning. An Act of 1943 provided for the appointment of a minister to perform plannings, functions formerly devolving on the Minister of Health and the Minister of Works (*q.q.v.*). Since 1970, these duties have devolved upon the Dept. of the Environment (*q.v.*).

Toynbee Hall opened, 1885. Named after Arnold T., 1852–93.

Tractarianism. Arose from *Tracts for the Times*, dealing with Church matters; published, 1833–41. All the tracts were condemned at Oxford, 1841.

Trade, Board of. *See* BOARD OF TRADE.

Trade Boards for settlement of wage disputes were authorized by the T.B. Acts of 1909 and 1918. Abolished, 1945.

Trade Marks in the U.K. are regulated principally by the T.M. Acts of 1905, 1910, 1937, and 1938, and the Merchandise Marks Act, 1926.

Trade Unions. Instituted, 1825, to withstand the influence of capital and competition. A commission of inquiry into the working of T.U. was held, 1867; an Act to protect the funds of T.U. was passed, 1869. To counteract T.U. a Federation of Employers was founded, 1873. First agricultural T.U. founded by Joseph Arch (1826–1919), 1874. T.U. instituted in France, 1834, and U.S.A., before 1833. In the U.S.A. the American Federation of Labour and the Congress of Industrial Organizations merged, 1955. Allowed to spend funds on parliamentary representation by T.U. Act, 1913. Act passed making illegal non-industrial strikes and lockouts, and the demanding of political contributions from the members that had not volunteered to make such, 29 July 1927. This Act was repealed, 1945. Trade Union and Labour Relations Act, 1974. Secondary picketing made illegal by Employment Act of 1980.

Trades Union Congress (T.U.C.) originated, 1868. A conference organized by the T.U.C., 1900, gave rise to the formation of the Parliamentary Labour Party (*q.v.*). The General Council of the T.U.C. formed, 1920. Withdrew from World Federation of Trade Unions, 1949.

Trafalgar Square. Construction was begun, 1829, completed, 1867. Board of Trade Linear Standards in bronze

placed on the N. side, 1876. Torsos of Admirals Jellicoe and Beatty erected, and N. side replanned, 1950.

Training Colleges. Established in Britain from 1840 onwards. Reorganized under Education Acts of 1902 and 1944. Two-year course extended to three years from 1960, and name subsequently changed to **Colleges of Further Education**.

Training Corps, Officers'. Founded, 1908. Merged in Army Cadet Force, 1940.

Trams. First street T. operated in New York, 1832; in Paris, 1853; in London, 1861. Electric T. inaugurated in Leeds, 1891. Last T. in London ran on 6 July 1952.

Transjordan. *See* JORDAN.

Transport, Ministry of. Established, Sept. 1919 to exercise the powers and duties of various existing government departments (including those of the Road Board) relating to public aspects of transport.

Transportation was first used as a punitive measure in England at time of Charles II (1600–85), seven years' T. being regarded as a suitable alternative to the death sentence. It was legalized under an Act of 1719. The first shipment of convicts to Botany Bay was in 1783, the last in 1840. Convicts continued to arrive in Tasmania until 1853. The practice finally ceased in 1864. The French Government sent no new shipments of convicts to Guiana after 1927. T. to Siberia existed in Czarist Russia; since 1917 it has continued to be practised by the various Soviet régimes.

Trans-Siberian Railway. Single track begun, 1891; completed, 1904. Railway finally finished, 1915.

Transvaal. Founded by Boers, 1836–1848; Britain recognized the independence of the territory, 1852; Volksraad elected M. W. Pretorius first president of the territory named the S. African Republic, 1857; under British protection, 1877; declared crown colony, 1879; Boers revolt and established republic, 1880; battle of Majuba Hill, 27 Feb. 1881; Orange Free State proclaimed neutrality, Feb. 1881; peace, 24 Mar. 1881; Paul Kruger president, 1883; Jameson Raid, 1 Jan. 1896; ultimatum from Boers, 9 Oct. 1899; war declared, 11 Oct. 1899; annexation of T., 25 Oct. 1900; Sir A. Milner appointed High Commissioner, 4 Mar. 1901; new constitution on representative lines, Dec. 1906; Botha Premier, 1907; became province of Union of S. Africa, 31 May 1910. *See* SOUTH AFRICAN WAR and SOUTH AFRICA, REPUBLIC OF.

Transylvania. Ceded to Rumania by Hungary, Dec. 1918. Returned to Hungary by Hitler's 'Vienna Award', 30 Aug. 1940. Occupied by Russians, Aug. 1944. Returned to Rumania, 10 Mar. 1945, and this decision confirmed in the peace treaties between the Allies and Hungary and Rumania, 1947.

Trappists, a branch of the Cistercian order, founded, 1664, by Armand Bouthillier de Rancé (1626–1700), at the abbey of La Trappe in Normandy.

Treadmill. First used as an instrument for irrigation by the Chinese. Introduction into English prisons by Sir William Cubitt, and first used in Buxton prison, 1818; in disuse by 1910.

Treason. Defined by Statute of Treasons, 1351. Other enactments relating to T., 1495, 1543, 1555, 1695, 1702, 1708, 1790, 1795, 1800, 1814, 1817: T. felony defined by Act of 1848. Treachery by Act of 1940.

Treasury. A Board of Commissioners, appointed for the first time in 1612, instead of a Lord High Treasurer as hitherto. Lords Commissioners of the T. have functioned continuously since 1714. The practice of combining the office of Prime Minister and First Lord of the T. arose, 1721. Reorganization of T. completed by end of 1962.

Treasury Bills first introduced, 1877.

Treaties. The following is a list of major historical treaties:

Abo, 1743. Aberdaron, 1406. Aix-la-Chapelle, 1668–1748. Algeciras, 1906. Altmark, 1629. Alton, 1101. Altranstädt, 1706. Amiens, 1527, 1802. Amsterdam, 1717. Anagri, 1176. Antananarivo, 1895. Aquisgran, 1749. Aranjuez, 1752. Ardes, 1546. Arras, 1482. Athis, 1305. Augsburg, 1686.

Badajoz, 1801. Baden, 1714. Bagdad, 1955. Bagnolo, 1484. Barcelona, 1493, 1529. Bärwalde, 1631. Basel, 1499. Belgrade, 1739. Berlin. 1728, 1850, 1878. Berwick, 1560. Björkö, 1905. Blois, 1504, 1505. Bologna, 1515, Boulogne, 1550. Breda, 1667. Brest, 1435. Bretigny, 1360. Bretton Woods, 1944. Brigham, 1290. Brömsebro, 1645. Bruges, 1521. Brussels, 1516, 1522, 1948. Bucharest, 1886. Beczacz, 1672.

Caen, 1091. Calais, 1416, 1520. Cambrai, 1529. Campo Formio, 1797. Câteau Cambrésis, 1559. Charlottenburg, 1723. Cherasco, 1631. Clayton-Bulwer, 1850. Cognac, 1526. Compiègne, 1624. Constantinople, 1479, 1573, 1724, 1889, 1897. Corbeil, 1258. Delft, 1428. Dordrecht, 1489. Dunkirk, 1947. Durham, 1136. Düsseldorf, 1624.

Edinburgh, 1560. Eisenburg, 1664. Escorial, 1733.

Ferrara, 1428. Fontainebleau, 1785. Fredericksborg, 1720. Frederickshamn, 1809. Fürstenberg, 1373.

Gandamak, 1879. Gastein, 1865, Gerstungen, 1074. Gisors, 1180. Grosswardein, 1538. Guérande, 1365. Guillon, 1360.

Hagenau, 1330. Hague, 1625, 1716, 1790. Hampton Court, 1562. Herrenhausen, 1725. Hubertusburg, 1763. Jassy, 1792.

Kalisz, 1343. Kardis, 1661. Kaschau, 1374. Khaeroed, 1613. Kuchuk Kainardji, 1774.

Labian, 1656. Lambeth, 1217. Lateran, 1929. Lauf, 1453. Lodi, 1454. London, 1518, 1839, 1954. Lorris, 1243. Lübeck, 1629. Lunéville, 1801. Lyons, 1504, 1601.

Madrid, 1618, 1630, 1715. Manila, 1954 (South-East Asia Collective Defence Treaty). Meaux, 1229. Mechlin, 1513. Melfi, 1059. Mersen, 870. Montebello, 1175. Moscow (nuclear Test Ban Treaty), 1963., Mürzsteg, 1903.

Nanking, 1842. Nettuno, 1925. Newcastle, 1334. Nicolsburg, 1886. Nijmegen, 1678–9. Northampton, 1328. Noyon, 1516. Nystad, 1721.

Oléron, 1287. Oliva, 1660. Olmütz, 1850. Ouchy, 1912.

Paris, 1259, 1303, 1320, 1657, 1763, 1898, 1947, 1954, 1963 ('Franco-German reconciliation'). Passarowitz, 1718. Passau, 1552. Peking, 1860, 1901. Perth, 1266. Picquigny, 1475. Prague, 1635. Pressburg, 1490, 1626, 1805. Pretoria, 1881. Pyrenees, 1659.

Rastatt, 1714. Redon, 1489. Reichenbach, 1790. Reval, 1488. Riga, 1920, 1921. Rome, 1957. Roskilde, 1658. Roxburgh, 1332. Ryswick, 1697.

St. Claire, 911. St. Germain, 1331, 1570, 1679. St. Omer, 1469. St. Petersburg, 1805. Salbai, 1782. Salisbury, 1289. San Germano, 1230. San Ildefonso, 1796. San Stefano, 1878. Saragossa, 1529. Schönbrunn, 1805. Senlis, 1493. Seville, 1729. Shimonoseki, 1895. Shrewsbury, 1267. Sistova, 1791. Stettin, 1570. Stockholm, 1720, 1724, 1959 (European Free Trade Association Convention). Stolbova, 1617. Sutri, 1111.

Tangier, 1844. Tarascon, 1291. Teschen, 1779. Thorn, 1466. Tientsin, 1858. Tilsit, 1807. Toledo, 1480, 1539. Tordesilhas, 1494. Trent, 1501. Troyes, 1420, 1562. Tyrnau, 1615.

Uccialli, 1889. Utrecht, 1474, 1712–13.

Valençay 1813. Vancelles, 1556. Venice, 1177. Verdun, 843. Vereeniging, 1902. Versailles, 1756, 1783, 1919–1920. Vervins, 1598. Vienna, 1731, 1738, 1814–15, 1864, 1955. Villafranca, 1859. Vincennes, 1330. Vossem, 1673.

Waitangi, 1840. Wallingford, 1153. Warsaw, 1955 (Eastern Security Treaty). Washington 1846, 1949 (North Atlantic Treaty). Wedmore, 878. Westminster, 1654, 1716, 1756. Westphalia (2), 1648. Windsor, 1899. Worms, 1743. Wusterhausen, 1726.

Xanten, 1614.

Zsitva-Torok, 1606. Zurawna, 1676. Zürich, 1859.

Trebizond, or **Trabzon,** the Greek city of **Trapezos,** originated, 600 B.C., in a colony from Sinope. Mentioned in connection with the retreat of the Ten Thousand (q.v.). At the time of the Fifth Crusade, when Constantinople was stormed by the Latins, the Byzantine refugee, Alexius Comnenus, founded an empire at T., which endured until the capture of the city by the Turks, 1462. Scene of the Armenian massacres, 1895.

Trelleborg, a unique archaeological site of the Viking Age (q.v.) in W. Zealand, Denmark. A large barracks or permanent camp occupied between 950 and 1050, presumably by the followers of Kings Svein Forkbeard and Knut (see under DENMARK), was excavated, 1932–42.

Trengganu, state of Malaysia since 1963, was a Mohammedan kingdom c. 1300. Did homage to the kingdom of Siam from 1776 to 1909. Entered into treaty relations with Britain, 1910.

Trent (in Alto Adige). The first Council of T, sat from 1545 to 1563; its decisions laid down the main lines of Roman Catholic development in post-Reformation times up to the changes of the 1960s and were confirmed by Pope Pius IV in 1564.

Trentino, another name for the region of Venetia Tridentina (q.v.).

Trials and Causes Célèbres: Sir Thomas More, 1 July 1535; beheaded 6 July.

Mary Queen of Scots: 14 Oct. 1586; executed, 8 Feb. 1587.

Sir Walter Raleigh: treason, 17 Nov. 1603; executed, 29 Oct. 1618.

Guy Fawkes and others: 27 Jan. 1606; Guy Fawkes executed, 31 Jan. 1606.

Charles I: 20–25 Jan.; executed, 30 Jan. 1649.

Dame Alice Lisle: treason, before Jeffreys; beheaded, 2 Sept. 1685.

Lords Kilmarnock and Balmerino: treason, 28 July 1746.

Lord Lovat: treason; executed, 9 Mar. 1747.

Mary Blandy: murdered father by arsenic, 3 Mar. 1752.

Elizabeth Canning: perjury, 29 Apr. 1784; transported.

Eugene Aram: murder, 3 Aug.; hanged, 6 Aug. 1759.

Earl Ferrers: murder of his steward; executed, 16 Apr. 1760.

John Wilkes: for obscene poem *Essay*

on Woman, 21 Feb. 1764 and 18 June 1768.

Elizabeth Brownrigg: murder of her apprentice; hanged, 12 Sept. 1767.

Duchess of Kingston: for marrying two husbands, 15 Apr. 1776.

Lord George Gordon: treason; acquitted, 5 Feb. 1781.

Warren Hastings: high crimes and misdemeanours, 13 Feb. 1788; acquitted, 23 Apr. 1795.

Thomas Paine: libel in *The Rights of Man*; guilty, 18 Dec. 1792.

Louis XVI in French Convention: 19 Jan.; beheaded, 21 Jan. 1793.

Marie Antoinette: 14 Oct.; executed, 16 Oct. 1793.

Wolfe Tone: 10 Nov.; committed suicide, 19 Nov. 1798.

Queen Caroline: for adultery, 16 Aug.–10 Nov. 1820.

Thurtell and Hunt: murder, 5 Jan.; Thurtell executed, 9 Jan. 1824.

Burke and Hare: body-snatchers, 24 Dec. 1828; Burke executed, 28 Jan. 1829.

William Palmer: poisoner, 14–27 May 1856.

Rev. S. Smith: murderous assault on John Leech, 6–7 Apr. 1858.

Jessie McLachlan: murder, 17–20 Sept.; respited, 27 Oct. 1862.

Dr. Pritchard: murder of wife and mother by poison; guilty, 2–7 July 1865.

Bank Forgery: Austin and George Bidwell, George Macdonnell, Edwin Noyes, Americans, forged bills for discounting at Bank of England and obtained £102,217; 18–26 Aug. 1873.

Tichborne Case: plaintiff claimed to be Sir Roger Tichborne, lost at sea, entitled to estates worth £24,000 a year. Trial began 11 May 1871, claimant nonsuited, 6 Mar. 1872. Trial of claimant for perjury began, 23 Apr. 1872; claimant sentenced, 28 Feb. 1874.

Penge Case: Louis Staunton, his brother Patrick, Elizabeth Ann, his wife, and her sister, Alice Rhodes, mistress of Louis, for murder by starvation of Louis's wife; 19–26

Sept, all convicted; respited, 13 Oct.; Alice Rhodes pardoned; others, penal servitude for life, 30 Oct. 1877.

Whistler *v.* Ruskin: for libellous criticism in *Fors Clavigera*; one farthing damages, 25–26 Nov. 1878.

City of Glasgow Bank Directors: for fraud; all convicted, 20 Jan.–1 Feb. 1879.

Charles Peace: murder; guilty, 4 Feb. 1879.

Florence Maybrick: murder of husband by arsenic; convicted, 21 July–7 Aug.; commuted to life imprisonment, 22 Aug. 1889.

Tranby Croft Case: Sir W. Gordon-Cumming *v.* Mr. and Mrs. Lycett Green and others. Gordon-Cumming charged them with cheating at baccarat at Tranby Croft, near Hull. Prince of Wales (Edward VII) gave evidence; verdict for defendants, 1–9 June 1891.

Dreyfus Case: Alfred Dreyfus, French soldier, for treason. Convicted, degraded, and sent to Devil's Island, 1894. Case reopened, 1898; again convicted, but sentence reduced and free pardon given almost at once. Proceedings against D. quashed, 1906.

Wilde Case: Oscar Wilde (1854–1900) *v*, Marquess of Queensbury, for libel, 1895; following the failure of this, he was convicted of immoral behaviour and sentenced to two years' imprisonment.

Oscar Slater: murdered of Miss Gilchrist, 3–6 May; found guilty, commuted to life sentence, 25 May 1909. Released 14 Nov. 1927; given government grant of £6,000. Conviction quashed, 20 July 1928.

H. H. Crippen: murder of wife; convicted, 18–22 Oct. 1910.

Brides in the Bath Case: George Joseph Smith, for murder of Misses Mundy, Burnham, and Lofty; guilty, 22–30 June 1915.

Sir Roger Casement: treason; convicted, 17 May; executed, 3 Aug. 1916.

Désiré Landru: for murder of ten women; convicted, 7–28 Nov. 1921; guillotined, 23 Feb. 1922.

Ronald True: murder; convicted 1–5 May. Sent to Broadmoor, 8 June 1922.

Edith Thompson and Frederick Bywaters: murder of Percy Thompson; guilty, 6 Dec. 1922; both hanged, 9 Jan. 1923.

Nicolo Sacco and Bartolomeo Vanzetti (U.S.A.): murder; first trial, 31 May–14 July 1921. Conviction affirmed, 12 May 1926. Sentence imposed, 9 Apr. 1927. Both executed, 23 Aug. 1927.

Clarence Hatry: fraud; 20–24 Jan. 1930; 14 years' penal servitude.

Blazing Car Murder: Arthur Alfred Rouse, murder of unknown man, 26–31 Jan. 1931. Guilty and hanged.

Kylsant Case: Lord Kylsant for issuing false prospectus of Royal Mail Steam Packet Co.; one year's imprisonment, 21–30 July 1931.

Metropolitan-Vickers Trial in Moscow: Thornton, Cushny, Gregory, Monkhouse, and Macdonald; for espionage and sabotage in U.S.S.R. Thornton three years, Gregory acquitted, Macdonald two years. Monkhouse and Cushny expelled from Russia, Apr. 1933.

Lindbergh Baby Case: Bruno Hauptmann, for kidnapping and murder of child of Charles Lindbergh; guilty, 14 Feb. 1935.

Alma Victoria Rattenbury and George Percy Stoner: murder of Mr. Rattenbury, 27–31 May; Mrs. Rattenbury discharged; Stoner convicted. Mrs. Rattenbury committed suicide, 3 June. Stoner reprieved, 25 June 1935.

Dr. Buck Ruxton: murder of wife and maid; guilty, 2–13 Mar. 1936. Hanged.

Ex-Marshal Pétain: for treason; found guilty, 1945, and sentenced to death, subsequently commuted to life imprisonment.

'Lord Haw-Haw' (William Joyce): for treason by broadcasting, 17–19 Sept. 1945. Hanged, 3 Jan. 1946.

Nürnberg Trials: Nov. 1945–Oct. 1946; of German war criminals.

Japanese War Criminals' Trials: 1946–8. The seven Japanese war-leaders condemned to death were hanged 23 Dec. 1948.

Timothy John Evans: tried for the murder of his baby daughter: guilty and hanged, 1950. Given a posthumous free pardon, 1966. *See* EVANS CASE.

John Reginald Halliday Christie: for murder of his wife, but also for murders of several other women on the file; guilty and hanged, 1953. *See* EVANS CASE.

Adolf Eichmann: in Israel, for crimes against the Jewish people; 11 Apr.–15 Dec. 1961; found guilty and hanged.

George Blake, former British vice-consul in Seoul, found guilty of espionage, 1961, and sentenced to 42 years' imprisonment, the longest sentence ever imposed in Britain. Escaped from Wormwood Scrubs Prison, Oct. 1966, and subsequently said to be in the Soviet Union.

Gordon Lonsdale, a Soviet citizen: tried in London for espionage; found guilty and sentenced to twenty-five years' imprisonment, 1961; subsequently exchanged for Greville Wynne. (*See* below.)

Ex-General Jouhaud, O.A.S. leader: for treason, in Paris, Apr. 1962; found guilty and sentenced to death, but sentence later commuted to life imprisonment.

Ex-General Salan, O.A.S. leader: for treason, in Paris, May 1962; found guilty but due to 'extenuating circumstances' sentenced to life imprisonment.

Greville Wynne, a British business man, and Oleg Penkovsky, a Russian scientist and civil servant, in Moscow for espionage, 7 May 1963; Wynne found guilty and sentenced to eight years' imprisonment; Penkovsky found guilty and sentenced to death. Wynne subsequently exchanged for Lonsdale. (*See* above).

Stephen Ward, a London osteopath, on charges of procuring and of living on immoral earnings, in London. July

1963; Ward found guilty on two charges of living on immoral earnings. Verdict was reached in his absence, as he was in hospital after taking an overdose of drugs. He died on 3 Aug., and was never sentenced.

'Great train robbery' trial: 12 men tried and found guilty of being involved in the £2½ million mail train robbery of 8 Aug. 1963. Apr. 1964: sentences totalling 307 years were imposed. Two of the convicted men subsequently escaped from prison and one had not been recaptured in March 1967.

'Moors Murder Case': Ian Brady and Moira Hindley tried for murders of Edward Evans, John Kilbride, etc., 1966; found guilty and sentenced to life imprisonment.

Peter Sutcliffe, 'The Yorkshire Ripper': convicted of the murder of 13 women, 1981. Sentenced to life imprisonment (to Broadmoor, 1984).

Geoffrey Prime, former officer at the Government Communications Headquarters in Cheltenham: convicted of spying for the Soviet Union, Nov. 1982 and sentenced to 35 years imprisonment.

Dennis Nilsen, found guilty of the murder of 6 young men and 2 attempted murders at Highgate: sentenced to life imprisonment, Nov. 1983.

Triennial Parliaments were established by Act, 1641. The Long Parliament of 1640–63 broke this Act, and it was repealed, 1664. A similar Act of 1694 was repealed, 1716, when the limit was increased to seven years (which in turn was reduced to five by the Parliament Act, 1911).

Trieste, the Roman colony of **Tergeste**, was settled by the Romans in 178 B.C. and was an established port some time between A.D. 69 and 79. Submitted to the Hapsburg Duke Leopold III, 1382. Free port, founded 1719. Held by French, 1797–1805, and by the puppet kingdom of Illyria, 1809–13. Returned to Austria, and became an imperial city, 1849. Ceded to Italy, 1918 (*see* VENETIA GIULIA). In Apr. 1945 the Ger-

man forces retreating from the Balkans passed through T.; their rearguard was driven out by two independent local guerrilla forces, Slovene and Italian, 30 Apr. Anglo-U.S. occupation followed. In Sept. 1947 a Free State consisting of T. and its environs was set up. On 25 Oct. 1954 T. city was handed over to Italy, less one small strip, which then passed under Yugoslav civil administration.

Trinidad was discovered and annexed to Spain by Columbus, 1498, but no settlement was made until the 1530s. Retained by the Spaniards, who by a new colonial policy, implemented in 1783, attracted large numbers of able foreigners to the cocoa industry, especially Frenchmen. The colony capitulated to Britain, 1797, and was formally ceded, 1802. T. and Tobago joined, 1889. U.S. leased defence bases there for ninety-nine years, 1941 (but given up except for one tracking station, 1960). After the dissolution of the Caribbean Federation (*q.v.*) T. became an independent dominion of the Commonwealth on 31 Aug. 1962. Republic, 1976.

Trinity House. An institution for regulating pilots; founded in its present form by Sir Thomas Spert, who was the first master, 1512, and given its first charter, 1514. The maintenance of lighthouses and buoys is also one of the duties of the brethren of T.H.

Tripartite Pact. Extension of German-Italian Axis Pact to include Japan signed in Berlin, 27 Sept. 1940; mutual cooperation in 'New World Order'. Hungary signed, 20 Nov. 1940; Rumania and Slovakia signed, 23 Nov. 1940; Bulgaria signed, 1 Mar. 1941; Yugoslavia signed, 25 Mar. 1941.

Triple Alliance, 1668. Was ratified for the protection of the Spanish Netherlands, the contracting parties being the States-General and England (Sweden joined later) against France. Other T. As. have been: 1717, England, France, and Holland against Spain; 1795, England, Russia, and Austria; 1882, Germany, Austria, and Italy. The last came to an end, as regards Italy, in May 1915. The Germano-Austro-Hungarian

Alliance was dissolved in 1918 at the end of World War I.

Tristan da Cunha. Discovered by Portuguese, 1506. Taken over by a British garrison, 1816, during Napoleon's residence at St. Helena. When the garrison was withdrawn, 1817, Corporal William Glass and his wife elected to remain; they were joined by two ex-naval men and some shipwrecked sailors, and formed the nucleus of the T. colony. Attached, 1938, to St. Helena Dependencies. An administrator appointed, 1948. Crawfishing company began operations there, 1949. In Oct. 1961 the volcano on the island erupted, destroying most of the settlement. All the inhabitants were evacuated and attempts made to settle them in Britain. Most had returned to T. by 1963, to live at the settlement of Edinburgh.

Trondhjem or **Trondheim.** The town of **Nidaros** (then sometimes called **Kaupangen**) was founded, 996, on an existing market site by Olaf Tryggvason, who was elected king here. Kings of Norway began to be crowned here again from 1814. Name T. adopted during the Middle Ages. Seat of archbishopric of Norway from 1152, but importance waned after the Reformation. German U-boat base, 1940–4.

Troubadours. Poets of Provence and Catalonia in eleventh to fourteenth centuries. *See* PROVENÇAL AND CATALAN WRITERS.

Troy. The earliest of the successive cities which *fl.* on the site at Hissarlik in Asia Minor has been dated about 3000–2560 B.C. The Homeric siege appears to have ended *c.* 1184 B.C. The site ceased to be inhabited at the end of the fifth century B.C. Excavations by Schliemann began, 1870, and lasted until 1890; Dörpfeld's from 1893 to 1894.

Truce of God (*Treuga Dei*). A device of the Church in the Middle Ages to check private warfare, by limiting the periods within which fighting would not be sacrilegious. Inaugurated at Tuluges in Roussillon by a synod, 1027. By 1041 the movement had spread all

over France; soon afterwards it reached England, and, by the end of the eleventh century, only about 80 days in the year remained unaffected. Confirmed by Urban II in 1095 at the Council of Clermont. Extended to the whole Church by oecumenical council of 1179. Fell into disuse during the thirteenth century.

Truck Acts, requiring payment of wages to be made in current coin of the realm only, and not in goods, were passed in 1831, 1887, and 1896; they also forbid fines, except under special conditions. The Truck Act, 1940, forbids the provision of canteen meals in lieu of wages. One effect of the T.A. in modern society was to prevent manual workers being paid by cheque; after 31 Mar. 1963 payment by cheque in such cases was permitted, but subject to the recipient's specific agreement only.

Trusts, commercial, first established by John D. Rockefeller (Standard Oil T.), 1882. Congress passed Sherman Anti-T. Act, 1890, and Supreme Court ordered dissolution of Standard Oil T., 1911.

Tuberculosis. The organism causing this disease isolated by Koch, 1882.

Tubular Bridge. The first T. bridge was built over the Menai Strait, 1846–60.

Tuileries Palace (Paris). Begun, 1564. Built by Catherine de' Medici, Henry IV, and Louis XIV. Stormed, 1792; and ransacked, 1830 and 1848. Destroyed by the Communards, 25 May 1871.

Tunis, N. Africa. Probably older than Carthage, and in 800–909 was a residence of the Agylabite dynasty. Repeatedly pillaged during tenth century. French occupation, 1881. Deep-water channel to harbour opened, 1893. Captured by Allies from Germans, 7 May 1943. Capital of independent Tunisia (*q.v.*) since 1956.

Tunisia corresponds in area with the Roman province of Africa, conquered by the Moslems in 698, and called by them Ifrikiya. Hussein ben Ali became Bey in 1705, acknowledging Turkish suzerainty, which was terminated by the Treaty of Bardo, 12 May 1881, and the Convention of La Marsa, 8 June

1883, which established the French protectorate. Important theatre of operations in World War II (*q.v.*). Nationalist agitation after the war resulted in France giving T. full independence 20 Mar. 1956. The monarchy was abolished, 1957, and Bourguiba became T.'s first president; made president for life, 1975.

Tunnels. *See* CHANNEL TUNNEL; also separate entries under BLACKWALL TUNNEL; DARTFORD etc.

Turbines. *See* SHIPS and AVIATION.

Turin. Capital of Italy, 1861–5. Besieged by the French, 1706; taken by French, 1798, but they were expelled by the Russians and Austrians in the following year; again surrendered to the French, 1800; restored to Sardinia, 1814.

Turkestan, Chinese. *See* SINKIANG.

Turkestan, Russian, was conquered by the Imperial Army, 1866–73. In 1920 the Emir of Bokhara and the Khan of Khiva were deposed and Soviet republics of Bokhara and Khiva set up. An autonomous Social Republic of Turkestan was constituted, 1921. These three states were reorganized in 1924, and their territory redistributed on an ethnical basis to form the republics of Turkmenistan, Uzbekistan, and Tadjikistan; the remaining areas of the old government of T. being attached to the Kazak, Kirgiz, and Kalpak republics.

Turkish Republic. (For previous history of the Turks *see* OTTOMAN EMPIRE.) Nationalist government set up under Mustafa Kemal Atatürk at Ankara, Oct. 1920. He refuses to accept the Treaty of Sèvres, Nov. 1920. Declares sovereign power to reside in National Assembly of the T. nation (*Kamutay*), Jan. 1921. Greek attempt to take over E. Anatolia resisted, June 1921. Greeks driven out, Sept. 1922. Mudania armistice, Oct. 1922. Sultanate abolished and Turkey becomes a republic, Oct. 1923. Moslem religion disestablished and caliphate (*q.v.*) abolished, 3 Mar. 1924. Treaty of Lausanne ratified with Allies, 1 Apr. 1924. Constitution passed, 21 Apr. 1924. Wearing of fez prohibited, 1925. Monogamy and civil marriage instituted, 1926. Latin alphabet supersedes Arabic, 1929–30. Refortifies Dardanelles, under League authority obtained 20 July 1936. Atatürk *d.*, 10 Nov. 1938. Declares war on Germany and Japan, 23 Feb. 1945. Genuine opposition parties allowed, 1945 onwards; growth of Democratic party under Menderes. T. joined N.A.T.O., 1952, and signed the Bagdad Pact (later CENTO) (*qq.v.*), 1955. Menderes became premier, 1950. In May 1960 the Menderes regime was overthrown by an army revolt, led by Gen. Gursel. Menderes was tried for plotting against the state and executed, 1961. Parliamentary government was re-established during 1961; T. invaded Cyprus (*q.v.*) 1974 and subsequently maintained troops in Turkish part of island; army took over power, 1980. In elections, Nov. 1983, Ozal, leader of Motherland party, elected. T. supported Turkish Cypriots' declaration of independence, Nov. 1983.

Turksib (i.e. Turkestan-Siberian) **Railway**, from Novosibirsk to Tashkent, begun 1927, was connected to the Transib, 1929, and opened to traffic, 1930.

Turner's Legacies. Pictures which J. M. W. Turner, the landscape painter, bequeathed to the nation, 1851.

Tuscany, in area corresponding roughly to the ancient Etruria (*q.v.*), was in the Middle Ages a margravate of the Frankish Empire established about 800, but dissolving into a loose league of city republics of which by the thirteenth century Florence (*q.v.*) was the leader. The family of Medici, who usurped power in the Florentine republic, became dukes of T., 1532, and grand dukes, 1557. On the death of the last Medici, 1737, T. fell to the Duke of Lorraine who, as consort of the Empress Maria Theresa, bequeathed it to the Austrian crown, which retained it until 1800, when Napoleon set up the puppet kingdom of Etruria. From 1808 to 1814 T. formed part of the French Empire. The Hapsburg-Lorraine restoration lasted peaceably until 1848, after which date it was only maintained by Austrian troops, who were driven out, 1859. T. was incorporated in the kingdom of Italy, 1861.

Tussaud's, Madame. Established in London, 1833. Destroyed by fire, 18 Mar. 1925. Reopened, 1928. Damaged by bombing, 1940, but subsequently restored. Now (1985) also owns Warwick Castle.

Tutankhamen's Tomb. Located near Luxor by Lord Carnarvon and Howard Carter, 1922, and opened Feb. 1923.

Tuvalu, formerly the **Ellice Islands,** became independent under name of T., 1 Oct. 1978.

Twelve Tables, The, a code of laws collected and formulated by a decemvirate of the Roman Republic, 451–449 B.C.

Tyburn (London). Here criminals were executed *c.* 1196–1783. Many Catholics died here for their faith during the sixteenth and seventeenth cen-turies. The gallows were near the present Marble Arch.

Tyler's Insurrection, 1381. *See* PEASANTS' REVOLT.

Tynwald, parliament and supreme court of Isle of Man, meets on T. Hill, consisting originally of three estates, now effectively only of the House of Keys. A characteristically Scandinavian legislative body dating from Norse occupation (800–1266). *See* MAN, ISLE OF and VIKING AGE.

Typewriters invented by Scholes, Gliden, and Soulé, 1868. First manufactured in commercial quantities, 1873.

Tyres, Pneumatic, were first fitted to horse-drawn vehicles by R. W. Thompson, 1845. Reinvented by J. B. Dunlop for bicycles, 1888. Pneumatic tyres for cars first made by Michelin, 1895, and for aeroplane undercarriages by Dunlop, 1910. Pneumatic tyres were first fitted to lorries, 1917, and to tractors, 1930.

U

'U-2' Incident. On 5 May 1960 Khrushchev told the Supreme Soviet that an American Lockheed U-2 aeroplane had been shot down over Soviet territory on 1 May and its pilot captured; on 7 May the U.S. Government admitted that the plane had been carrying out an intelligence mission. The incident was the excuse used by Khrushchev to humiliate the U.S. President and break up the Summit Conference in Paris on 17 May. Subsequently the pilot, Gary Powers, was tried and convicted of espionage at a 'show' trial in Moscow; in 1962 he was released in exchange for a Russian spy held by the U.S.A.

U-boats (Ger. *Unter-seebooten*), *see* SUBMARINES, which were so called when used by the Germany Navy from 1914.

Uganda, E. Africa, assigned to Britain by Anglo-German Treaty, 1890. Civil war, 1891. Protectorate declared, 1894. Rebellion, 1897. Treaty with dominant Buganda tribe, 1900. On 10 Oct. 1962 U. became a self-governing dominion within the Commonwealth. In 1966 the premier of U. Obote, deposed the president, Mutesa II of Buganda, and took over his functions. Republic, 1971. Obote deposed by Idi Amin, 1971 and reign of terror followed. Amin deposed, 1979: in Dec. 1980 the Uganda People's Congress under Obote gained power in elections. Unrest from 1980: Obote overthrown in military coup, 1985.

Ukraine. As the principality of Galicia-Volhynia, was independent *c.* 1300–20; part of Lithuania, 1321–1569; then Polish until 1772 (pro-Russian revolt under Hetman Khmielnitzky, 1648); until World War I U. was divided between Russia and Austria-Hungary. Encouraged by German Government U. declared itself independent, 20 Nov. 1917. Union of eastern and western U., Jan. 1919. Invasion by Bolsheviks, Feb. 1918. Fall of Kiev, Feb. 1918. Spoliation by German forces, 1917–18. Generals Petliura and Vinnichenko drove out the government established by Germany and set up dictatorship at Kiev, Nov.–Dec. 1918.

1919. Second Soviet Government set up, Mar.; Denikin's troops upset Soviet Government June; Soviet forces recaptured Kharkov and Kiev, Dec.

1920. Odessa taken by Soviet troops, and third Soviet Government set up, Feb.; by Treaty of Riga, Poland and Russia recognized independence of U., 12 Oct.

1923. U. joins U.S.S.R., 6 July: collectivization leads to mass starvation 1932–4.

1938. On being granted self-government, the Ruthenian province of Czechoslovakia called itself 'Carpatho-U.', Oct.

1939. Carpatho-U. annexed by Hungary, 14 Mar. The German-Soviet partition of Poland gave Polish (Western) U. to Russia, 28 Sept. Bessarabia ceded by Rumania, 1940, united to Soviet U. Carpatho-U. joined Soviet U., 1945. *See* U.S.S.R.; RUTHENIA; BESSARABIA.

Ukrainian or **Little Russian Language** became finally differentiated from Great Russian about the middle of the thirteenth century. The use of U. as a vehicle of instruction in Russian schools was forbidden by an imperial edict in 1863, and in 1876 it became a criminal offence to print or publish U. material in the tsar's dominions. The use of the written language again became legal in 1905. An official orthography was published by the U. Academy of Sciences, 1946.

Following are some better-known U. authors:

Ivan Kotlyarevsky, 1769–1838, satirist.

Pantaleimon Kulish, 1819–97, novelist, poet and translator.

Taras Shevchenko, 1814–69, poet.

Marko Vovchok, 1834–1907, novelist.

Leonid Hlibov, 1827–93, lyrical fabulist.

Oleksander Konysky, 1836–1900.

Mihailo Drahomaniv, 1841–95, philologist.

Ivan Franko, 1856–1916, poet.

Ulm, Germany. Peace signed, 1620. Cathedral built, 1377–1494. 550-ft. spire completed, 1894.

Ulster. Colonization of forfeited land, 1611. Rebellion, 1641. U. Convention against Home Rule, 17 June 1892. U. Convention League formed, Aug. 1892. Accepted under protest Government of Ireland Act, 1920, which set up two legislatures in Ireland. For later events *see* IRELAND, NORTHERN.

Ulster King of Arms. This office was joined to that of Norroy King of Arms in 1943.

Umbrella. Appears on Assyrian bas-reliefs eighth century B.C. First habitual user in London was Jonas Hanway (d. 1786).

Uncle Sam, nickname for the U.S. government, first used in the *Troy Post* for 7 Sept. 1813.

U.N.E.S.C.O. (United Nations Educational, Scientific and Cultural Organization) set up, 16 Nov. 1945. Became operative, Nov. 1946.

Ungava, interior territory of Labrador, round U. Bay, joined to province of Quebec, 1912.

U.N.I.C.E.F. (United Nations Childrens' Emergency Fund). set up, 1946.

Uniformity, Act of, 15 Jan. 1549, ordered use of the Common Prayer Book. Confirmed, 1552. Repealed by Queen Mary, 1553. Restored by Queen Elizabeth, 1559. Formed basis of the stringent Act of Charles II, which came into force, 24 Aug. 1662.

U.D.I. (Unilateral Declaration of Independence), made by Rhodesia (now Zimbabwe) on 11 Nov. 1965. Ian Smith, Rhodesian premier, declared Rhodesia

an independent dominion within the Commonwealth, but Britain refused to recognize the validity of this declaration. Ended, Dec. 1979. *See* GREAT BRITAIN; ZIMBABWE.

Union, Act of, with Scotland, 1707.

Union, Act of, with Ireland, 1801.

Union Jack. British flag, made up of: English flag, red cross on white ground (St. George); Scottish flag, diagonal white cross on blue (St. Andrew), incorporated, Apr. 1606; Irish flag, diagonal red cross on white (St. Patrick), incorporated, Jan. 1801.

Union Jack Club. Opened by King Edward VII, 1907, for British soldiers and sailors, as memorial to men killed in China and S. Africa.

Unit Trusts. First in Britain formed, 1931.

Unitarians. Sect founded by Socinus in Italy, 1546. English U. trace their descent from those mainly Presbyterian congregations whose ministers were ejected in 1662, many of whose chapels are now in Unitarian hands. The specifically Unitarian doctrines of these congregations became current *c.* 1700. International Unitarian Council, Geneva, 1905. General Assembly of Unitarian and Free Christian Churches formed, 1928.

United Arab Emirates, formed 2 Dec. 1971 from the Trucial States of Abu Dhabi, Dubai. Sharjah, Ajmaw, Umm al Qawain, Fujairah and Ras al Khaimah.

United Arab Republic. State formed on 1 Feb. 1958 by the union of Egypt and Syria (*qq.v.*). The Yemen (*q.v.*) federated temporarily with the U.A.R. on 8 Mar. 1958. Syria seceded from U.A.R. after anti-Egyptian revolt, 28 Sept. 1961. Yemen subsequently broke connection with U.A.R., but Egypt continued to be known as the U.A.R., finally reverting to name Egypt on 2 Sept. 1971.

United Free Church of Scotland, formed by union of the United Presbyterian Church and the Free Church of Scotland, 1900. Further united with the Church of Scotland (*q.v.*), 1929.

United Irishmen, formed, 1791, by Wolfe Tone (1763–98), organized risings in Northern Ireland, 1797 and 1798. Tone committed suicide when the latter rising failed.

United Kingdom, from 1801 to 1921, was styled 'United Kingdom of Great Britain and Ireland'.

United Nations Organization. Charter signed at San Francisco, 26 June 1945. Sufficiently ratified to begin existence, 24 Oct. 1945. First meeting of General Assembly: London, 10 Jan. 1946; New York, 23 Oct. 1946.

Secretaries-General of the U.N.:

Trygve Lie (Norway) 1946–1952

Dag Hammarskjöld (Sweden) 1953–1961

U Thant (Burma) 1962–1972

Kurt Waldheim (Austria) 1972–1982

Javier Perez de Cuellar (Peru) 1982–

United Presbyterian Church. Restoration, in 1712, of patronage in the Church of Scotland, led, in 1733, to formation of a Secession Church, which, in 1747, split over the scripturality of the burgess oath. The Burgher Auld Lichts were organized, 1799; the Anti-Burgher Auld Lichts, 1806. The two New Licht churches were united, 1820; the two Auld Lichts in 1842 as the Original Seceders. Meanwhile, in 1761, the Establishment had lost, by another anti-patronage secession, a group called the Relief Church. Secession Church and Relief Church amalgamated as U.P.C., 1847. This, in 1900, was amalgamated with Free Church, the result being the United Free Church.

United Provinces (of Agra and Oudh). Designation adopted, 1902. Now Uttar Pradesh (*q.v.*) (since 1950).

United Reformed Church, formed 1972, from a union of the Congregational Church in England and Wales and the Presbyterian Church in England and Wales.

United States of America. First American combined opposition to Stamp Act, Oct. 1765. Chests of tea destroyed at Boston and New York, 16 Dec. 1773. Declaration of Rights, Oct, 1774. First battle between British and Americans (Lexington), 19 Apr. 1775. Battle of Bunker Hill, 17 June 1775. Act of Per-

petual Union of States, 20 May 1775. Declaration of Independence, 4 July 1776. Articles of Confederation proposed by John Dickinson, 1776. Submitted to States, Nov. 1777. Battle of Saratoga, 17 Oct. 1777. Alliance with France, 6 Feb. 1778; ratified, Mar. 1781. Lord Cornwallis surrendered at Yorktown, 19 Oct. 1781. Peace signed at Paris, 3 Sept. 1783. Constitution proposed by Convention of Philadelphia, Sept. 1787; ratified, 21 June 1788. Death of Washington, 14 Dec. 1799. Louisiana Purchase, 30 Apr. 1803. Importation of slaves prohibited, 1 Jan. 1808. War with Britain, 18 June, 1812–24 Dec. 1814. Missouri Compromise, defining boundaries of slave area, 1820. Monroe Doctrine proclaimed, 1823. Texas annexed, 1845. Mexican War over the annexation of Texas, 1845–8. Mormons settled in Utah, 1847. Fugitive Slave Bill, 1850. Commercial treaty with Japan, 1854. Civil war in Kansas, 1856–7. Attack on Harper's Ferry by John Brown, 16 Oct. 1859. Execution of John Brown, 2 Dec. 1859. Republican convention at Chicago, 1860. S. Carolina, State Convention passed ordinance of secession, 20 Dec. 1860. Secession of Mississippi (9 Jan.), Florida (10 Jan.), Alabama (11 Jan.), Georgia (19 Jan.), Louisiana (26 Jan.), and Texas (1 Feb.), Jan.–Feb. 1861. 'Confederate' States' delegates met at Montgomery, Alabama; elected Jefferson Davis President, 9 Feb. 1861, and formed constitution, 11 Mar. 1861. Civil war began by an attack on Fort Sumter by the Confederates (S.), 12 Apr. 1861. Lincoln issued proclamation of blockade of southern ports, 19 Apr. 1861. N. Carolina and Arkansas seceded, May 1861. Battle of Bull Run, 21 July 1861. Battle of Ball's Bluff, 21 Oct. 1861. Jefferson Davis elected President of Southern Confederacy, Nov. 1861. Paper currency ('greenbacks') adopted, 25 Feb. 1862. Battle of Pea Ridge, 6–8 Mar. 1862. Battle of Winchester, 23 Mar. 1862. Battle of Pittsburg, 6–7 Apr. 1862. Battle of Fredericksburg, 10 Dec. 1862. Homestead Act passed, Dec. 1862. Abolition of slavery proclaimed, Jan. 1863. Battle of Chancellorsville, 2 May 1863. 'Stonewall' Jackson mortally wounded by his own troops in mistake at the battle of Chancellorsville; *d.*, 10 May 1863. Fugitive Slave Act repealed, 13 June 1864. Gen. Lee surrendered to Gen. Grant at Appomattox, 9 Apr. 1865. President Lincoln assassinated, 15 Apr. 1865. Gen. Johnston surrendered at Durham station, 26 Apr. 1865. Proclamation of amnesty, 29 May 1865. End of rebellion proclaimed by President Johnson, 3 Apr. 1866. Civil Rights (of negroes) Bill passed, 9 Apr. 1866. Impeachment of President Johnson carried in House of Representatives, 25 Feb.; acquitted by Senate, 26 May 1868. Engagement with Indians at Little Horn River, 25 June 1876. Edmunds's Anti-Polygamy Act, Mar. 1882. Chinese Exclusion Act passed, Apr. 1882. Nicaragua Canal Bill passed, Feb. 1889. McKinley Tariff Bill (protectionist) passed, Oct. 1890. Railway strikes at Chicago, much rioting, June–July 1894. Income tax declared by Supreme Court to be unconstitutional, 20 May 1895. Dingley Tariff Bill (highly protectionist) passed, July 1897. Hawaii annexed, 7 July 1898. *Maine* explosion, 15 Feb. 1898. Ultimatum sent to Spain, 19 Apr. 1898. War began, 21 Apr. 1898. Treaty of Paris between Spain and America, 10 Dec. 1898. McKinley assassinated, 1901. Panama Canal Bill passed, 26 June 1902. Alaska Boundary Treaty, 11 Feb. 1903. St. Louis Exhibition opened, 30 Apr. 1904. Riots in Chicago, May 1905. Asiatic Labourers Exclusion Act, Feb. 1907. Canadian Fisheries Treaty, Apr. 1908. Acts for reform of tariffs and for creating federal reserve of currency passed, 1913. War declared on Germany, 6 Apr. 1917. Wilson enunciated his 'fourteen points', Jan. 1918. Wilson announced League constitution, Feb. 1919. Wilson presented peace treaty in Congress, July 1919; eventually rejected by the Senate, which meant that the U.S.A. did not join the League of Nations. Women's suffrage,

1920. Prohibition came into effect, 1920; repealed, 1933. Immigration quota system started, 1921. 1927: Sacco and Vanzetti (Communists) convicted, on doubtful evidence, of a murder committed Apr. 1920; executed 23 Aug. at Charlestown, near Boston. 1929: New York Stock Exchange slump. 1930: London Naval Treaty signed by President Hoover, 22 July. 1932: Olympic Games (10th), Los Angeles, Aug. Franklin D. Roosevelt, Democrat, elected President, on the promise of a 'New Deal'. 1933: Gold standard suspended, 5 June; U.S.S.R. recognized, 17 Nov. Acts passed included the Economy Act; the National Industrial Recovery Act; the Agricultural Adjustment Act. 1935: Federal judge decided National Recovery Act invalid (confirmed by Supreme Court, 1936); dust bowl over Kansas, Mar.–Apr.; Huey Long of Louisiana shot 8 Sept. at Baton Rouge, *d.* 10 Sept; Roosevelt re-elected, 1936. In 1939 President delivered message to Congress warning of dangers from aggressor states, 4 Jan.; U.S.A. refused to recognize German annexation of Czechoslovakia, 21 Mar.; inauguration of regular transatlantic air service, 20 May; George VI and Elizabeth of England visit the U.S.A., 8 June; President appealed for peace to Italy, Germany and Poland, Aug.; signed three proclamations relating to U.S. neutrality, 5 Sept.; Neutrality Revision Bill law, 4 Nov. Arms production for Britain increased, 1940; Conscription Bill enacted, 16 Sept.; Roosevelt elected for a third term. Lease-Lend Act passed, 11 Mar. 1941; Atlantic Charter issued by Churchill and Roosevelt, 11 Aug; Japanese attacked Pearl Harbor, 7 Dec.; Germany and Italy declared war on U.S.A., 11 Dec. (*see further under* WORLD WAR II). 1942: Washington Pact, 1 Jan; Anglo-American Combined Chiefs of Staff appointed, Feb. 1943; Cairo meeting, 22–26 Nov.; Teheran meeting, 26 Nov.–2 Dec. 1944: Roosevelt elected for fourth term. 1945: Yalta Conference, Feb.; death of Roosevelt, 25 Apr. succeeded by Vice-President Harry S. Truman; San Francisco Conference, May–June; Potsdam Conference July–Aug.; Congress ratified U.N. Charter, 28 July, marking end of isolationism as a political force in the U.S.A. for next 30 years. Truman reelected, 1948. North Atlantic Treaty signed in Washington, 4 Apr. 1949. Korean War (*see* KOREA) began 25 June 1950. Constitutional amendment limiting president's tenure of office to two terms passed, Feb. 1951; Eisenhower elected Republican President, 1952; Korean ceasefire, 1953. Supreme Court ruled racial segregation in schools unconstitutional, 1954, and McCarthy's influence faded. Suez crisis of 1956 caused temporary rift in Anglo-U.S. relations. U.S. troops intervened temporarily in Lebanon, 1958. 1960: Summit Conference in Paris attended by Eisenhower broke up over U-2 Incident; Kennedy elected Democratic President, 9 Nov.

1961: Bay of Pigs' fiasco, Apr.; disarmament talks with Russia. Settlement of Cuban missile crisis (*see* CUBA) Oct. 1962 and in Feb. 1962 first American (Glenn) orbited the earth in space. Kennedy assassinated, Dallas, 22 Nov. 1963 and Vice-President Lyndon Johnson succeeds. He carries on Kennedy's civil rights policies, and Civil Rights Act becomes law, 2 July 1964. U.S. intervention in Vietnam escalates; bombing of N. Vietnam by U.S. planes, Feb. 1965 and anti-war student riots in U.S.A. Martin Luther King assassinated, Apr. 1968 and Robert Kennedy in June. Johnson orders halt to U.S. Vietnam bombing, 1 Nov. 1968; Nixon elected Republican president, 6 Nov. Decade 1970–80 great period of space progress in U.S.A.; consolidation of civil rights. But Vietnam dominated U.S. politics until 1974–5, when the war officially ended. Nixon forced to resign over the Watergate Scandal (*q.v.*) 1974; succeeded by Vice-President Ford. Jimmy Carter became Democrat President in 1976 and rapprochement with China, started by Nixon, continued: diplomatic relations estab. between Communist China and U.S.A. But Carter's term plagued by domestic problems of inflation and unemployment and hostage crisis in Iran, 1979–80. His major success the Camp David agreement of 1979 between Israel and Egypt. Carter defeated by rightwing Republican Reagan, 1979. Hardline foreign policy pursued; relations with U.S.S.R. worsened. U.S. troops intervened in Grenada (*q.v.*) 1983 and Lebanon (*q.v.*) 1983–4. Reagan re-elected 1984.

United States of America, Constitution of, passed, 17 Sept. 1787. Came into force, 21 June, 1788. The following amendments have been made: (1) Freedom of religion, expression, and assembly. (2) Freedom to keep arms. (3) Quartering of troops illegal. (4) General warrants illegal. (5) No deprivations or punishments without trial. (6) Trial by jury secured in criminal offences. (7) Trial by jury secured in most civil cases. (8) Fines and bail not to be excessive; punishments not to be cruel or unusual. (9) Rights enumerated in the Constitution not to deny other rights retained by the people. (10) Rights not specifically given to the Union to be retained by states or people. The above, collectively known as the Bill of Rights, were passed, 15 Dec. 1791. (11) Alteration of powers of the Supreme Court, 1798. (12) Alteration of method of election of President and Vice-President, 1804. (13) Slavery abolished, 1865. (14) Definition of citizenship. Apportionment of representation in House of Representatives. Former rebels excluded from office. Confederate debt repudiated, 1868. (15) Voting rights not to be denied on account of colour, 1870. (16) Income tax legalized, 1913. (17) Senators to be directly elected, 1913. (18) Prohibition instituted, 1918. (19) Female suffrage, 1920. (20) Alteration in election and terms of office of President, Vice-president, etc., 1933. (21) Prohibition to be left to state legislation, 1933; in effect, the repeal of the Eighteenth Amendment. (22) Limiting the President's tenure of office to two terms, or to two terms plus two years in respect of a Vice-President who has succeeded to presidential office, 26 Feb. 1951. (23) Giving citizens of the District of Columbia the right to vote in national elections, 30 Mar. 1961. (24) Banning the use of a poll-tax in federal elections, 4 Feb. 1964. (25) Dealing with Presidential disability and succession, 10 Feb. 1967. (26) giving citizens over the age of 18 the right to vote, 22 June 1970.

United States of America, Presidents of. Those marked V.-P. were Vice-Presidents and took office in the first instance by succession and not by election.

George Washington 1789–1797
John Adams 1797–1801
Thomas Jefferson 1801–1809
James Madison 1809–1817
James Monroe 1817–1825
John Quincy Adams 1825–1829
Andrew Jackson 1829–1837
Martin Van Buren 1837–1841
W. H. Harrison Mar.–Apr. 1841
John Tyler (V.-P.)· 1841–1845
J. Knox Polk 1845–1849
Zachary Taylor 1849–1850
Millard Fillmore (V.-P.) 1850–1853
Franklin Pierce 1853–1857
James Buchanan 1857–1861
Abraham Lincoln 1861–1865
Andrew Johnson (V.-P.) 1865–1869
Ulysses Grant 1869–1877
Rutherford Hayes 1877–1881
James Garfield 1881
Chester Arthur (V.-P.) 1881–1885
Grover Cleveland 1885–1889
Benjamin Harrison 1889–1893
Grover Cleveland (again) 1893–1897
William McKinley 1897–1901
Theodore Roosevelt (V.-P.) 1901–1909
William Howard Taft 1909–1913
Woodrow Wilson 1913–1921
Warren Harding 1921–1923
Calvin Coolidge (V.-P.) 1923–1929
Herbert Hoover 1929–1933
Franklin Delano Roosevelt 1933–1945
Harry S. Truman (V.-P.) 1945–1953
Dwight David Eisenhower 1953–1961
John Fitzgerald Kennedy 1961–1963
Lyndon Baines Johnson (V.-P.) 1963–1968
Richard Milhous Nixon 1968–1974
Gerald Ford (V.-P.) 1974–1976

James Earle Carter 1976–1980
Ronald Reagan 1980–

United States Marine Corps raised, 1775.

Universities. Salerno, reputed to have been found in ninth century, is the earliest of which there is record; Cordoba, 968; Bologna, 1116; Paris, 1200; Padua, 1222; Salamanca, 1243; Rome, 1245; Sorbonne, Paris, 1253; Cracow, 1364; Vienna, 1365; Prague, 1384; Heidelberg, 1386; Leipzig, 1409; Ingolstadt, 1472 (transferred to Landshut, 1800, to Munich, 1826); Uppsala, 1477; Wittenberg, 1502 (absorbed, 1694, by Halle); Strasbourg, 1538; Jena, 1558; Douai, 1563; Leyden, 1575; Harvard, 1638; Innsbruck, 1669; Besançon, 1676; Göttingen, 1734; Bonn, 1784. (*See* CAMBRIDGE UNIVERSITY and OXFORD UNIVERSITY.) The other U. of Great Britain and Ireland, with dates of foundation, are:

St. Andrews 1411
Glasgow 1450
Aberdeen 1494
Edinburgh 1582
Dublin (Trinity College) 1591
Durham 1832
London (*q.v.*) 1836
Manchester 1880
Wales (*q.v.*) 1893
Birmingham 1900
Liverpool 1903
Leeds 1904
Sheffield 1905
Ireland, National University of 1908
Queen's, Belfast 1908
Bristol 1909
Reading 1926
Nottingham 1948
Southampton 1952
Hull 1954
Exeter 1955
Leicester 1957
Sussex (at Brighton) 1961
Keele 1962
East Anglia (at Norwich) 1963
Newcastle upon Tyne 1963
York 1963
Essex (at Colchester) 1964
Lancaster 1964
Strathclyde (at Glasgow) 1964
Kent (at Canterbury) 1965

New University of Ulster (at Coleraine) 1965
Warwick 1965
Aston (at Birmingham) 1966
Bath 1966
Bradford 1966
Brunel (at Uxbridge) 1966
City (London E.C.1) 1966
Heriot-Watt (at Edinburgh) 1966
Loughborough University of Technology 1966
Surrey (at Guildford) 1966
Dundee 1967
Salford 1967
Stirling 1967
Open University 1969
Buckingham 1976
Under a royal charter, 1967, the Royal College of Art, London S. W. 7, also ranks as a U., able to confer its own degrees: the Cranfield Institute of Technology obtained similar status in 1969.

Universities, American. Privately endowed U. include: Harvard, 1633; William and Mary, 1693; Yale, 1701; Princeton, 1746; Washington and Lee, 1749; Columbia, 1754; Brown, 1764; Rutgers, 1766; Dartmouth, 1770; Miami and Ohio, 1809; Emory, 1837; Ohio Wesleyan, 1841; Notre Dame, 1842; Wilberforce, 1856; Atlanta, 1865; Cornell, 1865; Des Moines, 1865; Johns Hopkins, 1876; Drake, 1881; Stanford, 1885; Chicago, 1890; Duke, 1924.

The characteristic American U. for women founded are privately endowed; some of the better known are: Mount Holyoke, 1837; Elmira, 1853; Vassar, 1865; Wells, 1868; Humber, 1871; Smith, 1871; Wellesley, 1871; Radcliffe, 1875; Bryn Mawr, 1881; Barnard, 1889.

State U. are mostly of nineteenth century foundation, but a few date back to colonial times. In 1862 the federal government passed an Act setting aside public lands for the endowment of U. Owing to their being well provided with privately endowed establishments the following states have no state U.: Massachusetts, Rhode Island, Connecticut, Pennsylvania, New

York; and the New Jersey State university is merely Rutgers (*see* above), renamed in 1917. The following are some of the better known state U.: Pennsylvania, 1751; Georgia, 1785–1801; North Carolina, 1789; Virginia, 1819; Alabama, 1820; Indiana, 1838; Michigan, 1841; Missouri, 1841; Iowa, 1847; Mississippi, 1848; Wisconsin, 1848; Utah, 1850; Minnesota, 1851; Louisiana, 1860; Kansas, 1866; Illinois, 1867; West Virginia, 1867; California, 1869; Nebraska, 1871; Arkansas, 1872; Oregon, 1872; Nevada, 1873; Ohio, 1873; Colorado, 1877; South Dakota, 1882; Wyoming, 1886; Arizona, 1891; New Hampshire, 1891; New Mexico, 1892; Oklahoma, 1892; Montana, 1895; Florida, 1903; Kentucky, 1908; North Dakota, 1918; Maryland, 1920; Delaware, 1921.

U.N.R.R.A, (United Nations Relief and Rehabilitation Administration). Formed, 1943. Its major tasks were virtually complete early in 1947, the first shipload of its supplies having been dispatched, Mar. 1945.

U.N.S.C.O.B., a special committee, established 21 Oct. 1947, by resolution of the General Assembly of the U.N., on the Balkans, with headquarters at Salonika, charged with the solution of problems then involving Greece and neighbouring states.

Upper Volta, made a separate Fr. colony (from Upper Senegal and Niger), 1919. Abolished, 1932, but reconstructed, 1947. Independent, 1960. Marxist coup, 1983.

Uppsala, or **Upsala,** Sweden. University founded, 1477. New buildings, 1879–86. The cathedral was built, 1230–1435. Fourth Assembly of World Council of Churches at, 1968.

Ur of the Chaldees was founded shortly before 4000 B.C. Its recorded history begins not later than 2500 B.C. Its resplendent Third Dynasty came to an end, 1960 B.C. Excavated by Taylor, A.D. 1854; Campbell Thompson and Hall, 1918–19; and Sir Leonard Woolley, 1922–1934.

Uranus, planet discovered by Sir William Herschel, 13 Mar. 1781.

Uriconium Viroconium, near the site of the present village of Wroxeter at the crossing of Watling Street over the Severn. A Roman camp here appears to have been laid out *c.* A.D. 48 as the quarters of the XIV Legion. When the Legion was transferred to Chester in A.D. 70 the site continued in civil occupation and expanded to become the tribal capital of the Cornovii. A forum was completed by 130. Extensive damage caused by fire *c.* 300, but town continued in occupation until *c.* 350.

Ursuline Nuns. Founded by St. Angela Merici, 1535; approved as a religious order by Pope Paul V, 1612.

Uruguay. In 1603 Hernando Arias, the first American-born Spanish governor of La Plata, explored the eastern bank of the Plate River. Portuguese expedition, 1680. The Spaniards in 1726 erected a fort on the site of Montevideo. In 1810 the Creoles of Montevideo joined in the general rising against the Spanish royal garrisons, and besieged Montevideo with the help of republicans from the Argentine. It fell in 1814 to the Argentine General Alvear. The Portuguese invaded the territory from the N. in 1816, and from 1820 to 1825 U. was under Brazilian occupation. The war between Brazil and the Argentine republic was terminated at the instance of Britain and France by a treaty of 1828, making U. independent of either. Series of constitutional innovations since 1900, aimed at preventing dictatorship and resulting in periods of collegiate gov. e.g. 1917–33, and 1951–66 when presidential system re-established. First elections for 13 years, 1984.

U.S.S.R. (Union of Soviet Socialist Republics; Soviet Union)
1917: Riots at Petrograd, tsar abdicated, Provisional Government formed under Prince Lvoff, Mar.; Council of Workers and Soldiers formed at Petrograd, Baltic and Black Sea fleets mutinied, Apr.; autonomy granted to Finland and Ukraine, June; National ministry under Kerensky, 6 Aug.; a republic proclaimed, 15 Sept.; 'the October Revolution' (*q.v.*) 7 Nov; Kerensky overthrown by Lenin and Trotsky, rise of the Russian Socialist Federal Soviet Republic, Nov.–Dec. Treaty of Brest-Litovsk ends war with Germany, 3 Mar. 1918; tsar and family murdered at Ekaterinburg, 16 July.

Civil war, 1919–22 ends in Bolshevik victory; constitution of U.S.S.R. adopted, 6 July 1923, Lenin *d.,* 1924. Struggle for power followed: Trotsky expelled from Communist party, 1927 and exiled, 1929 (murdered on Soviet orders in Mexico, Aug. 1940) and Stalin in control. Enforced collectivization of land, 1932–4 leads to famine and mass starvation, especially in the Ukraine; programme of industrialization undertaken. Trials of foreign nationals, 1933, and purge of Communist officials and army officers, 1934–38. U.S.S.R. aids govt. forces in Spain (*q.v.*) 1936–39.

Clashes with Japan in Far E. settled, 1939; Russo–Ger. pact signed, 23 Aug. and U.S.S.R. invades Poland, 17 Sept. and occupies E. half of it, forces Baltic States to grant concessions. Invades Finland, 30 Nov. War with Finland ended, 13 Mar. 1940; U.S.S.R. occupies Rumanian provinces of Bessarabia and N. Bukovina, June and Baltic States annexed, Aug.

1941: Germany attacks U.S.S.R., 22 June (*see under* WORLD WAR II).

1942: Anglo-Russian 20 Year Treaty; 1943: Teheran meeting of Stalin, Roosevelt and Churchill, Yalta, 1945. World War II ends with U.S.S.R. in control of E. Europe including E. Germany.

1948: Berlin blockade; quarrel begins with Tito's Yugoslavia (*q.v.*). Increasingly repressive régime ended with Stalin's death, 5 Mar. 1953; Beria, Minister of the Interior, executed in July. Rise to power of Khruschev from 1955: German prisoners in Russia released and diplomatic relations estab. between U.S.S.R. and F.G.R. Khrushchev denounced Stalin in speech to congress of Communist party, 25 Feb. 1956 and dissolution of Cominform announced, 17 Apr. Some liberalization at home, but Russian troops savagely crushed Hungarian revolt (*see* HUNGARY), Nov.

U.S.S.R. making great progress in nuclear development and in space technology. Khruschev addressed U.N., 18 Sept. 1959 but Paris Summit of 1960 broke up over U–2 Incident. Berlin Wall built 1961. Worsening in Soviet-Chinese relations. Cuban crisis settled by Khruschev and Kennedy, Oct. 1962. Nuclear Test Ban Treaty signed by U.S.S.R., 1963. Khruschev fell from power, 1964: rise of Brezhnev. In 1968–9 Soviet troops crushed liberal movement in Czechoslovakia. There were subsequent attempts to improve agricultural and industrial production, with more concentration on consumer goods. Campaign against dissidents continued but some allowed to settle in West. Relations with U.S.A. worsened after Russia invaded Afghanistan (*q.v.*) 1979. From 1980 U.S.S.R. exerted pressure on Poland (*q.v.*) to prevent liberalization. Brezhnev *d.*, 1982, and power passed to Andropov. Increased propaganda campaign against N.A.T.O. use of nuclear missiles, 1980 onwards, led to breakdown of arms limitation talks in Geneva, 1983. Andropov *d.*, 1984: succeeded by Chernenko who was succeeded by Gorbachev, 1985. Geneva talkes to reopen, 1985.

Effective Soviet leaders since 1917:
Vladimir Ilyich Lenin 1917–24
Joseph Stalin 1924–53
Nikita Khruschev 1953–64
Leonid Brezhnev 1964–82
Yuri Andropov 1982–84
Konstantin Chernenko 1984–85
Mikhail Gorbachev 1985–

Uttar Pradesh, Indian State, the name, since 1950, of the former United Provinces (*q.v.*)

Usury Laws. Interest on loans limited to 8 per cent, 1623; 6 per cent, 1651; 5 per cent, 1713. Restraint removed, 1854.

Utah. Mormons under Brigham Young entered the Salt Lake Valley, 1847. Mexico ceded the territory to the U.S.A., 1848, and territorial government was organized in 1850. State admitted to Union, 4 Jan. 1896. *See* MORMONS.

'Utopia', by Sir Thomas More, published in Latin, 1516. In English, 1551.

Utrecht, Treaty of. Between Britain, the United Provinces, and France to end the War of the Spanish Succession, 11 Apr. 1713.

Uzbekistan admitted as an equal member of the U.S.S.R., 1925. *See* BOKHARA.

507

V

Vaccination (against smallpox). Conceived and developed by Sir E. Jenner, 1796. Made compulsory in U.K., 1853, but no longer so after 1948. Discontinued altogether after world eradication of smallpox in 1970s.

Vaccine Damage Payments Act, 1979, gives persons severely disabled as result of vaccination for diseases as prescribed under the Act (e.g. diptheria, tetanus, rubella, etc.) the right to £10,000 compensation.

Vagrancy Acts, constituted, with the Poor Laws (*q.v.*), the greater part of English social legislation down to the end of the eighteenth century, especially under the Tudors. The Act of 1459 authorized the imprisonment of vagrants, that of 1530 whipping, that of 1535 mutilation, to which by the Act of 1597 all entertainers unless employed by some nobleman were also subject. Transportation was authorized by Orders in Council, 1603 and 1662. In 1713 previous Acts were consolidated and rationalized, and branding ceased to be legal. Previous legislation repealed by Consolidation Act, 1740, amended by Vagrancy Acts, 1822, 1824, and 1838. Amendments under Sexual Offences Act, 1956, deal with males living on prostitutes' earnings; and Fraudulent Mediums Act, 1951, with persons claiming to foretell the future.

Valladolid, first mentioned, 1072, as having been recovered from the Moors a hundred years earlier. Residence of Castilian kings from *c.*1400. Cathedral begun, 1585.

Valparaiso, Chile. Founded 1536 by Juan de Saavedra; captured by Sir Francis Drake, 1578; sacked by the Dutch, 1600; severe earthquakes, 1730, 1822, 1839, 1873, and 1908.

Value Added Tax (V.A.T.) replaced Purchase Tax (*q.v.*) 1973.

Vancouver, British Columbia, began to be an important commercial city about 1885.

Vancouver, Washington, U.S.A., was founded 1825 as Hudson's Bay Co. trading post; taken over by U.S.A., 1846.

Vancouver Island, British Columbia, discovered and circumnavigated, 1792, by George Vancouver.

Vandals. Earliest references to V. in Roman authors do not denote any particular people but generally all E. Germanic tribes, such as Burgundians and Goths. About A.D. 330 they were defeated by the Goths, and moved into Pannonia (now Hungary), whence in 406 they migrated via Mainz across Gaul to Spain, where they gave their name to Andalusia ('Vandalitia'), 409. Another detachment settled in Galicia. In May 429 the V. under King Gaiseric, about 160,000 strong, crossed to Africa (Tunisia). They had captured nearly all the principal cities of Africa by 433. By treaty of 30 Jan. 435 the Emperor Valentinian ceded to Gaiseric the whole Roman territory of Africa except Carthage and its province. Gaiseric seized Carthage, 19 Oct. 439, and took and sacked Rome in 455. He built a large navy and conquered the Balearics. Carthage retaken by Count Belisarius, 533, to whom the last known Vandal king, Gelimer, surrendered, 534. No mention of V. made by historians after 536.

Vanuatu, formerly **New Hebrides**, visited by Spaniard de Quiros, 1606; by Bougainville, 1768; and Cook, 1774. Franco-British condominium, 1906; independent, 30 July 1980, as Republic of V.

Vanzetti. *See* SACCO.

Varangian Guard, marine infantry corps of the Byzantine Army performing the same functions as the praetorian cohorts of the old Roman Army. Originally recruited in Sweden by Vladimir the Great, Grand Duke of Kiev, about 977–84, they were transferred by him to the service of Byzantium under Constantine VIII, 999. From then till 1066 the preponderance of recruits from Sweden and the Baltic diminished in favour of Norwegians, Icelanders, and other western Scandinavians: after Oct. 1066 Englishmen in increasing numbers joined the V.G., and eventually they and other westerners completely displaced the Swedish and Russian element; they had heavy losses against the Normans at Durazzo, 1082; Edgar Ætheling, who renounced the throne of England, joined the V.G. in 1097. In 1453 the regiment still existed, but was exclusively English.

V.A.T., *See* VALUE ADDED TAX.

Vatican. A Roman hill, on which a palace, commenced in 1146, became the residence of the Pope in 1377; it is said to contain 7,000 rooms. The popes made the V. their voluntary prison, 1870–1929. Established as a sovereign state, 7 June 1929, as consequence of Mussolini's concordat with the papacy. This treaty was embodied in the constitution of the Italian Republic, 1947, amended Feb. 1984, whereby V. City lost its territorial rights and the Catholic Church in Italy many of its privileges.

Vatican Councils, *see* COUNCILS OF THE CHURCH.

Vaud (Ger. **Waadt**), canton of Switzerland. Burgundians settled there, A.D. 443. Acquired by Counts of Savoy about 1268. Alternated between Savoyard and Bernese rule, 1536–1617, then finally ceded to Berne. Republic of Leman declared, 1798. Entered the Confederation, 1803. Canton V. replaced designation Canton Leman, 1803.

Vauxhall Gardens. Laid out on the S. bank of the Thames, 1661. With George IV's permission called Royal, 1822. Closed, 1859.

Venetia, originally the land of the Veneti, an Illyrian tribe, who entered the area between 200 and 100 B.C.; then name applied to same area, as being the metropolitan territory of the republic of Venice (*q.v.*) It consists of three regions of Italy.

Venezia Tridentina (Alto Adige), ceded by Austria (provinces of Trento and Bolzano, formerly part of Tirol), 1918.

Venezia proper, or *Veneto*, Austrian only from 1815 to 1866, Italian since then.

Venezia Giulia, now known as *Friuli-Venezia Giulia*, acquired in 1918, then comprised the provinces of Fiume, Gorizia, Pola, Trieste, and Zara. It was partly occupied by Yugoslav troops in 1945, and by the settlement of 1947 Istria, the Forest of Ternova, and the upper Isonzo valley passed to Yugoslavia (*see* SLOVENIA), reducing the region more or less to the boundaries of medieval Friuli (provinces of Udine and Gorizia), while Trieste (*q.v.*) and its surroundings remain under neutral occupation. The agreement of 5 Oct. 1954, however, restored Trieste to Italy, while its surroundings were assigned to Yugoslavia.

Venezuela. Became independent of Spain as part of the Federal Republic of Gran Colombia, 1811. Separated from Colombia and set up a separate constitution, 1830. Petroleum production began, 1917. Exports of iron ore (by Bethlehem Steel Corporation) began, Mar. 1951. Venezuelan capital began to enter the country's oil industry, 1956. New constitution 1958.

Following is a list of heads of the Venezuelan State since 1945:

Romulo Betancourt 1945–1948
Romulo Gallegos (deposed) 1948
Carlos Delgado Chalbaud(assassinated) 1948–1950
G. Suarez Flamerich 1950–1952
Marcos Perez Jimenez 1952–1958
Wolfgang Larrazabal Ugueto 1958
Edgard Sanabira 1958–1959

Romulo Betancourt (again) 1959–1963
Raúl Leoni 1963–1969
Rafael Caldera 1969–74
C. A. Pérez Rodríguez 1974–79
Luis Herrera Campius 1979–

Venice, Italy. Founded *c.* A.D. 452. First Doge Paolo Zucio Anafesto, 697. Beginning naval power under D. Orso Ipato, 726. Venetian navy assists in overthrow of the Lombards, 787. At peace of Aix-le-Chapelle Charlemagne cedes suzerainty of V. to the Byzantines, 810. Seat of government moved from Malamocco to Rialto, 811. St. Mark's bones brought to V., 828. Defeat by Moslems in naval battle of Taranto, 839. Death of D. Pietro Candiano I at battle of Zara, 888. Venetian protectorate of Istria established under D. Pietro Candiano II, 932–9. D. Pietro Orseolo II conquers Dalmatia, 999–1000. 'Blessing of the Sea' first instituted, 1001. Commercial and political treaty with Byzantium concedes practical independence, 1081. Defeat of the Normans at Butrinto, 1085. Venetian fleet under D. Vitale Michiel I deserts the First Crusade, 1100. Capture and settlement of Tyre, 1124. Fourth Crusade diverted by D. Enrico Dandolo against Byzantium, 1204. Genoese defeated at Trapani, 1264. Sequins first coined, 1284. Defeat by Genoese at Curzola, 1297. The Great Council established, 1297. Council of Ten established, 1310. Ducal palace begun, 1310. The 'Closure' (*Serrata*) of the Great Council, 1315. Complete defeat of Genoa in the War of Chioggia under D. Andrea Contarini, 1378–81. Acquisition of Padua, 1406; Ravenna, 1441. Commercial treaty with Turks, 1453. Loss of Negropont to the Turks, 1470. Turkish victory at Prevésa, 1530. Loss of Cyprus, 1570. Victory over Turks at Lepanto, 1571. Siege and loss of Candia (Crete), 1648–69. Decline of the republic after death of D. Francesco Morosini, 1694. Republic extinguished by Napoleon and ceded to Austria, 1797. Annexed to Italy, 1805. To Austria, 1814. Finally to Italy, 1866. *See also* VENETIA.
The following is a list of doges:

Paolo Zucio Anafesto 697–717
Marcello Tegaliano 717–726
Orso Ipato 726–737
Six masters of soldiers 737–742
Orso Diodato 742–755
Galla Gaulo 755–756
Domenico Monegario 756–765
Maurizio Galbaio 765–787
Giovanni Galbaio 787–804
Obelerio de'Antenori 804–809
Angello Participazio 809–827
Giustiniano Participazio 827–829
Giovanni Participazio I 829–836
Pietro Tradonico 836–864
Orso Participazio I 864–881
Giovanni Participazio II 881–887
Pietro Candiano I 887–888
Pietro Tribuno 888–912
Orso Participazio II 912–932
Pietro Candiano II 932–939
Pietro Participazio 939–942
Pietro Candiano III 942–959
Pietro Candiano IV 959–976
Pietro Orseolo I 976–977
Vitale Candiano 977–978
Pietro Memmo 978–991
Pietro Orseolo II 991–1008
Otho Orseolo 1008–1025
Domenico Centranico 1026–1032
Domenico Flabianico 1032–1043
Domenico Contarini I 1043–1071
Domenico Selvo 1071–1084
Vitale Falier 1085–1096
Vitale Michiel I 1096–1102
Ordelafo Falier 1102–1117
Domenico Michiel 1117–1130
Pietro Polani 1130–1148
Domenico Morosini 1148–1156
Vitale Michiel II 1156–1172
Sebastiano Ziani 1173–1178
Orio Malipiero 1178–1192
Enrico Dandolo 1193–1205
Pietro Ziani 1205–1229
Giacomo Tiepolo 1229–1249
Marin Morosini 1249–1252
Renier Zeno 1253–1268
Lorenzo Tiepolo 1268–1275
Jacopo Contarini 1275–1280
Giovanni Dandolo 1280–1289
Pietro Gradenigo 1289–1311
Giorgio Marin 1311–1312
Giovanni Soranzo 1312–1328
Francesco Dandolo 1329–1339
Bartolomeo Gradenigo 1339–1342

Andrea Dandolo 1343–1354
Marino Falier 1354–1355
Giovanni Gradenigo 1355–1356
Giovanni Dolfin 1356–1361
Lorenzo Celsi 1361–1365
Marco Cornaro (Corner) 1365–1368
Andrea Contarini 1368–1382
Michele Morosini 1382
Antonio Venier 1382–1400
Michele Steno 1400–1413
Tomaso Mocenigo 1414–1423
Francesco Foscari 1423–1457
Pasquale Malipiero 1457–1462
Cristoforo Moro 1462–1471
Nicolo Tron 1471–1473
Nicolo Marcello 1473–1474
Pietro Mocenigo 1474–1476
Andrea Vendramin 1476–1478
Giovanni Mocenigo 1478–1485
Marco Barbarigo 1485–1486
Agostino Barbarigo 1486–1501
Leonardo Loredano 1501–1521
Antonio Grimani 1521–1523
Andrea Gritti 1523–1539
Pietro Lando 1539–1545
Francesco Donato 1545–1553
Marc'antonio Trevisano 1553–1554
Francesco Venier 1554–1556
Lorenzo Priuli 1556–1559
Girolamo Priuli 1559–1567
Pietro Loredano 1567–1570
Alvise Mocenigo I 1570–1577
Sebastiano Venier 1577–1578
Nicolo da Ponte 1578–1585
Pasquale Cicogna 1585–1595
Marin Grimani 1595–1606
Leonardo Donato 1606–1612
Marc'antonio Memmo 1612–1615
Giovanni Bembo 1615–1618
Nicolo Donato 1618
Antonio Priuli 1618–1623
Francesco Contarini 1623–1624
Giovanni Cornaro (Corner) I 1624–1630
Nicolo Contarini 1630–1631
Francesco Erizzo 1631–1646
Francesco Molin 1646–1655
Carlo Contarini 1655–1656
Francesco Cornaro 1656
Bertuccio Valier 1656–1658
Giovanni Pesaro 1658–1659
Domenico Contarini II 1659–1674
Nicolo Sagredo 1674–1676
Luigi Contarini 1676–1683

Marc'antonio Giustinian 1683–1688
Francesco Morosini 1688–1694
Silvestro Valier 1694–1700
Alvise Mocenigo II 1700–1709
Giovanni Cornaro II 1709–1722
Alvise (Sebestiano) Mocenigo III 1722–1732
Carlo Ruzzini 1732–1735
Luigi Pisani 1735–1741
Pietro Grimani 1741–1752
Francesco Loredano 1752–1762
Marco Foscarini 1762–1763
Alvise Mocenigo IV 1763–1779
Paolo Renier 1779–1789
Ludovico Manin 1789–1797

Verden. *See* BREMEN (3).

Vermont, first settled by French under Samuel Champlain, 1609. English and Dutch infiltration began with the eighteenth century, and a British fort was built at Battlebro in 1724. Intensive settlement began after the cession of Canada, 1760. Between then and the revolution the territory was disputed between the states of New York and New Hampshire. Independence declared, 1777; but state not admitted to Union (14th) until 1791.

Verner's Law. Phonetic law propounded, 1875, by the Danish philologist, Karl Adolf Verner (1846–96).

Verona became an independent republic, 1107. Mastino and Cangrande Scaliger, Lords of V., entertained the exiled Dante, 1291–1329. Added to Milanese territory under Galleazzo Visconti, 1387; but passed to Venice, 1405. Ceded to Austria, 1797; part of Italy since 1866. The last of the Scaligers, Brunoro della Scala, *d.* at Vienna, 1434. *See also* VENICE.

Versailles. A town in NW. France near Paris; here Louis XIII built a hunting-box on the site of which Louis XIV erected a palace, 1661–87; First Treaty of V., 1783; surrendered to Germans, 1870. *See end of* WORLD WAR I for Second Treaty.

Verulamium, near St. Albans, Herts., was the tribal capital of the Catuvellauni, established about A.D. 1. Roman *municipium* c. A.D. 45. Boudicca (Boadicea) sacked V. in the Icenian rising, 61, but it continued to develop until about 200. St. Alban martyred near, 303. St. Germanus found it still inhabited in 429. The theatre was excavated in 1847; parts of the forum in 1898. In 1930 a comprehensive excavation scheme was begun, which has made it possible to trace the complete plan of the Roman town. There have been further excavations since the end of the World War II.

Vesuvius. Volcano on the Bay of Naples. An eruption in A.D. 79 totally destroyed Pompeii and Herculaneum (*q.v.*). Last considerable eruption, 1944.

Vice-Chancellor. The first judicial V.-C., Sir Thomas Plumer (1753–1824), appointed, 1813; two additional V.-Cs. appointed, 1841; they became judges of the High Court of Justice, 1873. The last V.-C. was Sir James Bacon (1798–1895), appointed, 1870; retired, 1886.

Vichy, France, celebrated for its mineral waters. Known to the Romans, but did not become famous till the seventeenth century. French puppet Government established here after capitulation of France, 1 July 1940, and the word V. became synonymous with 'collaborator'.

Victoria, state of Australia, became a colony separate from New S. Wales, 1851. Following on the reports of Capt. Cook, who did not, however, land there, a party of convicts was sent out in 1785, to the site of Port Jackson. First permanent settlement by Edward Henty at Portland Bay, 19 Nov. 1834. Melbourne founded, 1835. Civil Government established, 1839. Responsible govt. conferred, 23 Nov. 1855.

Victoria, British Columbia, founded, 1843, by Hudson's Bay Co., and called Fort Camosun. Named Victoria, and made capital of Vancouver Island colony, 1849. Ceased to be capital when Vancouver Island was united with British Columbia, 1866; but capital status restored, 1868.

Victoria and Albert Museum. Originated as the Museum of Ornamental Art, 1852; merged in the S. Kensington Museum, 1857. Foundation stone of present building laid in 1899 by Queen Victoria; opened in 1909 by King Edward and Queen Alexandra.

Victoria Cross. For bravery in the forces, instituted 1856. The cross was manufactured out of the cannon taken from the Russians at Sevastopol, until the supply ran out in 1942. The colour of the ribbons, originally blue for the Navy and red for the Army, was changed to crimson for all services in 1918.

Victoria Falls (on the Zambesi, Africa). Discovered by Livingstone in 1855; spanned by a bridge of the Cape to Cairo railway, 1905. Hydro-electric station begun, 1938.

Victoria Falls Conference. 28 June–4 July 1963, held to wind up the Federation of Rhodesia and Nyasaland (*q.v.*)

Victoria, (now **Victoria-Nyanza) Lake,** Africa. Discovered by Speke, 1858; Wilson and Smith first voyaged across the lake, 1877; divided between England and Germany, 1890. Germans driven out, 1916.

Victory, H.M.S., was launched at Chatham, 7 May 1765; commissioned, 1778. Flagship of Howe, 1782; Hood, 1793; and Nelson, 1797–1805. Paid off from active service, 1812. Became flagship of C.-in-C., Portsmouth. 1825; permanently placed in dry dock, 1922, and restored throughout and re-rigged.

Vienna (Wien) capital of the Austrian republic, was already an inhabited site when the Romans laid out the permanent camp of Vindobona, A.D. 180. Name appears in something like its modern form in documents of 881. The Babenberg margraves of Austria chose V. for their seat, 1142, and granted charters, 1221. Became an imperial free city, 1237. Capital of Hapsburgs, 1278. University founded, 1365. After Austrian empire fell, V. counted as a province equal to the other Austrian provinces.

Vienna, Congress of. Opened, 1 Nov. 1814. Closed, 8 June 1815. Representatives of all the powers of Europe, led by Britain, Austria, Prussia, Russia, and France, met to settle the internal frontiers, etc., of Europe after the Napoleonic Wars. By it Poland was placed under Russian suzerainty. N. Italy was largely restored to Austria, Prussia received the Rhineland and part of Saxony, and Hanover, E. Frisia and Hildesheim. The German confederacy was organized under Austrian presidency, and Cracow made an independent republic.

Vienne, Council of, 1311–12. Decided the abolition of the Templars (*q.v.*)

Vietnam, at first under Japanese protection, intermittently at war with France (1945–9) when by unification of the provinces of Tongking, Annam, and Cochin China, V. became an integral part of the French Union. Convention signed between France and the Emperor Bao Dai, Dec. 1949. France transferred all sovereign rights to V., Dec. 1954, but retained military authority there until 1956. The civil war between Communists and anti-Communists split V. into N. and S. zones from 1946, the French influence extending only over the S. zone. During 1951–3 the Communists in the N. made gains at the expense of the S. The Geneva Agreement of 20 July 1954 brought about a cessation of official hostilities between N. and S. South V. became a republic in Oct. 1955, with Ngo Dinh Diem as president. He was assassinated, 1963, and a series of unstable régimes, with partial U.S. backing, followed. From 1959 a state of civil war existed between N.V., led by the veteran Communist Ho Chi Minh until his death in 1969, and S.V.N. American 'advisers' sent to help the S., 1960. In 1965 American troops committed to fighting in V. N.: by the end of the year there were nearly ¼ million U.S. troops there. American planes bombed N.V. War had debilitating effect on U.S. morale at home; agreement signed in Paris, 27 Jan. 1973, ending the war and U.S. troops withdrawn. But fighting between N. and S. continued until final defeat of the S. in 1975. President Thieu resigned 21 April and S.V. Army surrendered to the N., 30 Apr. Marxist régime for whole country adopted; new constitution, Dec. 1980. Poor relations with China

from 1979 and open hostilities, 1979–80. Expulsion of 'boat-people', 1979 onwards.

Viking Age proper extended from the eighth to the eleventh centuries. But excursions of Scandinavian pirates, though less frequent, did occur earlier. Thus a seaborne raid of the Gautar (Geatas) under their King Hugleikr (Chocilaicus or Hygelac) was made on Frisia about A.D. 530. Irish sources describe Scandinavian raids on the Hebrides and coast of Donegal in the seventh century. Danes began intermittent land warfare with the Franks after giving asylum to Wittekind of Saxony, 777. Three ships from Hordaland in Norway raided Dorset about 790; Lindisfarne sacked, 793; Jarrow sacked, 794; Norwegians in Skye, 795; Man, 798; Iona, 802; and Sligo, 807; Armagh sacked, 832. Turgeis (Thorgest) made himself King of Ulster, 841; but drowned by Irish, 844.

Danish attacks on England began, 833; on Ireland, 849; on Holland, 833; on Seine valley, 841; on Spain, Portugal, Morocco, 844; Paris besieged, and Hamburg sacked, 845. Danes under Björn and Hasteinn first entered Mediterranean from the W., 860, and ravaged Provence, the Balearics, Liguria, parts of Tuscany and Morocco until 862. Danish penetration of Frisia and Rhineland stopped by King Lothair II (855–69). Raids in Flanders, 882–5. Paris besieged again, 885–6, but Danes defeated at Verdun in June, and by Duke Alan in Brittany, 888. Evacuated to Kent, 892. Returned, 902, reinforced by Norwegians under Rollo (Hrolfr), who did homage for the fief of Normandy at Clair Sur-Epte, 911. Cork settled (by Danes) about 900.

Campaigns in England by the sons of Ragnar, 855–6 (mainly in Kent), by Guthrum (Guttorm), 866–78. King Edmund martyred, 870; truce in 876. Treaty of Wedmore, 878, gave most of Northumbria and Mercia to Danes. English recover London and W. Essex, 886. Campaign by Hasteinn's army (*see* above), 892–7; the army beaten by Alfred and disbanded. The Danelaw reconquered, 914–20. Svein Forkbeard, allied to Olaf Tryggvason (*see* NORWAY), attacks Ethelred, 994–1014; Svein's son Knut succeeds to English crown, 1016. *See* DANGEGELD and SHIP-MONEY.

Norwegian: the court of the Norse king of Dublin described by an embassy sent to Abd-er-Rahman II, Emir of Cordova (*d.* 852). Norse settlements in Ireland plundered by Danes, 851. Olaf the White arrived in Ireland, 853; became joint King of Dublin; went back to Norway, 873. Dublin captured by the Irish, 902, and Vs. expelled, but returned, 914, to capture Waterford and (916) Dublin. Norwegians kill the High King Niall Glundubh at Kilmashogue, 919. Norse-Welsh-Scottish confederacy beaten at Brunanburh (in Galloway?), 938. Irish resistance stiffens about 940 under King Muirchertach of Ailech, and in 980 the High King Maelsechlainn II defeated the Dublin and Hebridean Norsemen at Tara. Brian Boru beats Ivar of Limerick at Sulcoit (968) and becomes King of Munster, 976, and High King, 1002. He captured Dublin, 1000, but returned it to his son-in-law, Sigtrygg Silkbeard, whom he defeated again, together with a Norse coalition, including Earl Sigurd of Orkney, at Clontarf on Good Friday, 1014.

Punitive expedition by King Harald Fairhair of Norway, following on his victory at Stiklestad (872), established his suzerainty over the W. coast of Scotland, Man, the Hebrides, and all N. Atlantic islands except Iceland, 873. Earl Sigurd of Orkney and Thorsteinn the Red conquer Scotland as far S. as Strath Oykel, 874. Sigurd the Thick (*d.* 1014) conquered Scotland as far S. as Strath Spey—Moor of Rannoch—Strath Fillan—Loch Long. The last Norse earl of Orkney *d.* 1231, but Scottish earls continued to do homage to the King of Norway (*see* LORD OF THE ISLES).

Hebridean sovereignty renounced by King Magnus Hakonarson of Norway, 1266, as result of battle of Largs, 1263, which date is usually taken as end of V.A.

Swedish expansion, exclusively eastwards across the Baltic, is first recorded in 853 (attempt to reconquer Kurland from Danes, whose king, Gorm the Old, 900–40, made wide conquests in Pomerania). Danish base at Jomsborg set up by Harald Bluetooth (936–86) was destroyed, 1043, by the Norse King Magnus the Good. Russian chronicles first mention Swedish raiders in 859. Expelled in 862, they returned to Russia (to which they gave their name) at the invitation of certain Slav clans in the same year, when Rurik became prince of Novgorod. In 865 Rurik absorbed two other principalities, and Hoskuld and Dir founded Kiev, which was conquered by Oleg (Helgi) of Novgorod, 882. Commercial treaties with Byzantium, 911 and 944. Swedish-Russian habits described in detail by the Arab diplomat Ibn Fadhlan, 921. 'Varangians' mentioned for the last time in Russian chronicles, 1043, by which time (reign of Yaroslav of Kiev, 1036–54) the Scandinavian ruling class had become Slavonic in language and Greek Orthodox in religion. *See also* MAN, ISLE OF; HEBRIDES; ORKNEY ISLANDS; NORWAY; DENMARK; SWEDEN; IRELAND; NORMANDY; EAST ANGLIA; MERCIA; NORTHUMBRIA, KINGDOM OF; VARANGIAN GUARD.

Vilna or **Vilnius** (Pol. **Wilno**), probably founded in the tenth century, became capital of the Grand Duchy of Lithuania *c.* 1323. Partially destroyed by the Teutonic Knights, 1377. Became an episcopal see, 1387 (when the Catholic cathedral of St. Stanislaus was begun); after Lithuanian union with Poland, under Casimir IV, 1427–92, V. became a centre of Polish culture. In the Third Partition of Poland (1795) V. and its province fell to the Russian share. Occupied by German troops, 1915–Dec. 1918, during which time (Feb. 1918) the independence of Lithuania was proclaimed, with V. as capital. V. assigned to Poland by Entente council of ambassadors, 15 Mar. 1923. On collapse of Poland in 1939, the U.S.S.R. handed over V. to the republic of Lithuania. Russian since 1940, except for German occupation, 1941–5.

Vimy Ridge Memorial to Canadian soldiers killed storming the ridge, 9–10 Apr. 1917; unveiled by King Edward VIII, 1936.

'Vindictive'. British cruiser which figured in Sir Roger Keyes's attack on Zeebrugge mole, 23 Apr., and was sunk in the blocking attack on Ostend, 9–10 May 1918.

Virginia, U.S.A. The first permanent English settlement in N. America, 1607, by members of the London Co., led by John Smith. Negroes first imported, 1619. Indian raids, 1622, 1644, 1676. Became a crown colony, 1624. Though royalist in sympathy, V. surrendered to the Cromwellian fleet and accepted Cromwell's governor Bennett, 1652. Williamsburg became the state capital, 1699. Seceded from the Union, 1861, whereupon Federal sympathisers set up the separate state of W.V. (*q.v.*). From 1867 until its readmission to the Union in 1870, V., as 'military district No. 1', was governed by a Federal general.

Virgin Islands, W. Indies. Discovered by Columbus, 1493. Some probably included in Charles I's grant of the Caribean Islands to Earl of Carlisle, 2 July 1627. First settlement by Dutch buccaneers, in Tortola, 1648; ousted by British, 1672; Denmark made first permanent settlement (in St. Croix, St. Thomas, and St. John), 1672. Spain had Culebra, Culebrita, and Vieques. The Spanish islands passed to U.S.A., 1898. Danish islands bought by U.S.A., 1917.

Visigoths, the western group of the tribes collectively known as Goths (*q.v.*), separated from the eastern or Ostrogothic branch *c.* A.D. 376, when most of the V. followed their king Frithigern across the Danube into Moesia. By a treaty of 381 the V. entered the Roman service as *foederati*, and their king Athanaric was received with honour at Constantinople in that year. On the death of the Emperor Theodosius, 395, the V. elected Alaric (*d.* 410) king, and turned against the Empire: they besieged Rome itself in 408, 409, and 410; the last time they sacked the city. Alaric was succeeded by Ataulfus, who married the Emperor Honorius's sister, Placidia, and led the V. into S.W. Gaul and to Spain, where he was murdered in 415. His successor, Wallia, set up a Visigoth kingdom, centring upon Toulouse. At the battle of Chalons, 451 (*see* OSTROGOTHS), Theodoric I, king of the V., was killed leading them against the Huns and their Germanic vassal tribes. Under Euric (466–85) the centre of gravity of the Visigoth state shifted to Spain. Though now much romanized the V. adhered to the Arian heresy (*see* ARIANISM), and in 507, under Alaric II, were defeated by the more barbarous but Catholic Franks, but protected by the Ostrogothic (*q.v.*) King Theodoric; they did not become a separate kingdom again until he *d.* in 526. The most successful Visigoth kings in Spain were Leovogild (568–86) and his son Recared (586–601), the latter of whom by becoming Catholic reconciled the Roman interests with his own, though at the cost of abandoning the Gothic language (*q.v.*). A code of Visigoth laws, issued *c.* 654 under Recceswinth, survives. The Visigoth kingdom finally perished at the hands of the Moslem emirs, 711.

Vitoria. Capital of Alava, Spain. Founded, 581, by Leovogild, King of the Visigoths. A decisive victory, which freed Spain from France, was fought here during the Peninsular War, 1813.

Vlachs, name applied to the Latin-speaking Provincials of Dacia (*q.v.*); the bulk of them withdrew southwards over the Danube, A.D. 270, and in the sixth and seventh centuries inhabited Macedonia, Thrace, and parts of Epirus. Continually displaced by Avars, Magyars, and Slavs they became pastoral nomads, and are mentioned as such by Byzantine sources in 976. They set up an independent empire which reoccupied part of Dacia, and came to an end, 1257. Another branch inhabited Thessaly about 1050, and were conquered by the Turks, 1393. About 1150 there was a Vlach colony in Dalmatia, and another in Montenegro, elements of which wandered as far as Istria (where some survive) in the fifteenth century. *See* RUMANIA and BESSARABIA.

Vladivostok. Founded as a Russian port, 1860. Town since 1875.

Vlöne, Albania (It. **Valona**: Gr. **Avlona**; anciently **Aulon**). Occupied by Robert Guiscard the Norman, A.D. 1080. Retaken by Byzantines, 1085. Passed by marriage to kingdom of Sicily, 1295; thereafter alternately under Serbian rule or that of local despots, subject to Venice. Turkish, 1691–1912. Temporary capital of Albania, 1913. Occupied by Italians, 28 Dec. 1915 and 7 Apr. 1939. Reverted to Albania, 1945.

Volga German Republic, U.S.S.R. *See* GERMAN VOLGA REPUBLIC.

Volkssturm, German home defence force raised at the instance of Heinrich Himmler (1900–45) in his capacity as C.-in-C. Home Forces and Reinforcements, 18 Oct. 1944.

Volgograd. *See* STALINGRAD.

Volsci. The greatest enemies of Rome during the first century of the Roman Republic; they lived in S. Latium. They were subdued by Rome, 338 B.C., and enjoyed Roman citizenship by 304.

Volturno, Italy. The colony of Volturnum was founded here, 194 B.C., by the Romans. In 1860 the Neapolitans were defeated at the V. River by Garibaldi's army, and as a result Capua fell. German defensive position on V. forced by Anglo-American Fifth Army, Oct. 1943.

Volunteers (English). Honourable Artillery Co. granted charter by Henry VIII in 1537; V. organized on a larger scale, 1757; English and Scottish V. were disbanded, 1783, but raised again, 1794; National Volunteer force established, 1860; in 1900 V. supplied many service companies for the S. African War; converted into the Territorial force, 1908. For Local Defence V. *see* HOME GUARD.

Voortrekkers. The Great Trek of Afrikaners out of Cape Colony began in 1836. Columns under Pieter Uys and Hendrik Potgieter defeated the Matabele king, Moselekatze, 1837. Zulus decisively defeated by Andries Pretorius at Blood River, 16 Dec. 1838. Republic of Natal proclaimed, 1840; the whole country N. to the Limpopo open to European settlement by *c.* 1848. Monument to the V. at Voortrekkerhoogte, near Pretoria, dedicated, 1949.

Vorarlberg, province of Austria, acquired piecemeal by Hapsburgs, 1375–1765, finally consolidated by Maria Theresa. Josef II amalgamated it with Tirol (*q.v.*), 1782. Ceded to Bavaria, 1805, but retroceded, 1814.

Voronezh, U.S.S.R. Founded in 1586 to rebuff Tatars, but burned by them, 1590; here Peter the Great built boats for conquest of Azov; three times almost destroyed by fire: 1703, 1748, 1773.

Votes. *See* FRANCHISE.

Vryheid, town and county in Natal, were ceded to a group of Boers (Lukas Beyer and others) by the Zulus, 1884, and formed an independent republic until 1888.

Vulgate. Latin version of the Bible prepared by St. Jerome during the last quarter of the fourth century. First printed *c.* 1455; first dated edition, 1462; critical edition issued by order of Sixtus V, 1590; superseded by that of Clement VIII, 1592; translated by Wycliffe and his followers, 1356–84. Authorized Catholic translations into English: New Testament, Rheims, 1582; Old Testament, Douai, 1609–10; by R. A. Knox, New Testament, 1943; Old Testament, 1948–9. 'Jerusalem Bible', 1966.

Vyborg (Rus.), **Viborg** (Swed.), **Viipuri** (Fin.), grew up round a Swedish castle built by Torgils Knutsson, 1293. Became Russian, 1710, and Finnish, 1917. Ceded to Russia, 31 Mar. 1940;

recaptured by Finns in the autumn of 1941; retaken by Russians, 21 June 1944; became the capital of the Karelo-Finnish S.S.R. (*q.v.*) under the Russo-Finnish Armistice, 19 Sept. 1944. Transferred in 1946 to the Russian S.F.S.R.

W

Wadai. Once a powerful native state in the Sudan. Kingdom founded, 1635. Notorious as a slave-raiding state; came under French influence, 1899; annexed by France, 1909. Part of Chad Republic since 1960.

Wadi Halfa, Sudan. The British base in 1884 in the operations for the relief of General Gordon.

Wages. First fixed by Act of Parliament, 1350. Act prohibiting payment of miners' wages in public houses, 1872; extended to wages generally, 1883. Wages payable by cheque from 31 Mar. 1963. *See* TRUCK ACTS.

Wahabis. A Mohammedan Puritan sect founded by Mohammed ibn Abd al Wahhab (1703–87), son of a shepherd in Central Arabia. He converted Mohammed ibn Sa'ud, ruler of Derayeh, who married his daughter, and *d.* 1765: the Wahabi dynasty began with that daughter's son, Abd al Aziz, who with the sword spread Wahabi doctrines throughout Arabia. Wahabi rule established in eastern Arabia, with Riyāz as capital, by Faizul, 1830. Wahabi Army in India was crushed at Balakot, 1831. The remnants retired to Mahában on NW. Frontier, whither punitive expeditions were sent against them in 1853 and 1858; Indian W. finally defeated at Ambéla Pass, 15 Dec. 1863.

Wailing Wall, Jerusalem. Fighting between Jews and Moslems, Aug. 1929. In Old City, occupied by Jordan during and after Israelite-Arab War, 1948–9; after 'June War' of 1967 Israel recovered access to W.W.

Waits. A wait was a city watchman, who sounded his pipe or trumpet during the night. As early as thirteenth century a small band of wind-musicians maintained by a city was called W. By eighteenth century the name was applied to those that went round at Christmas time playing and singing carols.

Walcheren Island, Holland. British expedition under the second Earl of Chatham and Sir R. Strachan after capturing Flushing, 1809, came to a disastrous end and was withdrawn. Flooded and severely damaged in the course of allied reconquest, Nov. 1944. Monument to British Commandos unveiled, June 1952. Dykes burst again, Jan.–Feb. 1953.

Waldeck, a German county of the twelfth century, was united with Pyrmont, 1621, and became a principality, 1712; joined the Germanic League, 1815. From 1919 to 1928 W. was a separate province of the Weimar republic, but was absorbed by Prussia, 1929.

Waldenses or **Vaudois.** A sect once claiming to have been established in the reign of Constantine (306–37), but founded, 1176, at Lyons by Peter Waldo. Their doctrine prohibited by the Lateran Council, 1179; and W. included in an excommunicating Bull by Lucius III, 1184. Majority driven from France at time of the persecution of the Albigenses (*q.v.*), 1209, they took refuge in Piedmont, where their persecution began, 1220. Again ex-communicated, 1231. Many went to Calabria in fourteenth and fifteenth centuries. About 1532 they joined the Reformation. Those left in France again persecuted, 1545–55. Those in Piedmont attacked, 1655, when Cromwell obtained some respite for them. Persecutions recommenced, 1685, on revocation of Edict of Nantes. Many went to Switzerland from Piedmont. In 1689 they tried to recover their Piedmont valleys. Received permission to return,

1694; again exiled, 1698–?1740. They had liberty of conscience, 1799–1814. Civil and religious liberty accorded, 1848, in kingdom of Sardinia.

Waldstätte. 'Forest Cantons' Uri, Schwyz, and Unterwalden united in Perpetual League, 1291, to form the nucleus of Switzerland.

Wales. Occupied at the time of the Roman invasion, 55 B.C., by five tribes, the Gangani and Decangi, the Ordovices, the Demetae, and the Silures; Caractacus defeated by the Romans, A.D. 43, taken prisoner to Rome, 50; conquest of Silures and Ordovices by Julius Frontinus and Agricola, 78; Welsh became Christian *c.* 300, and maintained this faith when the rest of the island was repaganized; withdrawal of Romans, early fifth century; warfare with the Saxons: battle of Deorham, 577; with the Angles: battle of Chester *c.* 613; battle of Hatfield and death of Edwin, King of the Angles, 633; Cadwallon slain soon after in battle; continued dissension among the Welsh princes; the N. Welsh king Rhodri the Great (844–78) defeated the Danes; peaceful reign of Hywel the Good, who drew up a code of laws, tenth century; Gruffydd ap Llewelyn became king of Gwynedd, 1039, and killed (1044) Howel ap Edwin; defeated Gruffydd ap Rhydderch and became king of all W., 1055, and was finally crushed and slain by Harold and Tostig, 1063; gradual conquest of country by William the Conqueror and his sons; expedition into, under Henry I, 1121; general uprising under Ap Rhys, 1135, and victory over English at Cardigan, 1136; N. and S. divided between his sons and those of Ap Cynan; expedition into of Henry II, 1157, and peace concluded with princes of the N. and S.; later unsuccessful raid, 1169; peace made with Rhys ap Gruffydd, the ruling lord of S.W.; Llewelyn ap Iorwerth became powerful in the N. and married King John's bastard daughter Joan, 1206; joined the rebelling barons, became Prince of All W., *d.* 1240; disputes between various claimants to the kingship, among them Prince Edward, Henry III's son; victory of Llewelyn ap Gruffydd over English at Dynevor, 1255; peace concluded with Henry, 1267, and Llewelyn declared Prince of W.; Llewelyn refused homage to Edward I; invasion by the English king, and Llewelyn starved into submission, 1277; oppression of natives by English officers, and fresh rising under Llewelyn and Dafydd; English put to flight at the Menai Straits, and Llewelyn finally slain near Builth, 1282; completion of conquest by Edward I, 1283; Statute of Rhuddlan enacted, 1284; Owain Glyndwr's rebellion, 1400–15; Richmond (Henry VII) landed in Pembroke, 1485; Council of W. under Bishop Rowland Lee, 1534; W. incorporated into England, Act of 1535; Monmouthshire detached, 1536; great sessions established, 1542: Welsh Bible translated, 1567–88; Council abolished, 1689; circulating schools, 1730; Intermediate Education Act, 1889; Welsh Land Commission, 1893–4; investiture of Prince of W. at Caernarvon Castle, 1911; Welsh National Library begun, 1911; Cardiff made capital of W., Dec. 1955. Prince Charles invested as Prince of W. at Caernarvon, 1 July 1969. Office of Secretary of State for Wales created, 1964. *See* CAERNARVON and WELSH LITERATURE.

Wales, Calvinistic Methodist Church of, arose *c.* 1735. Its connection with English Methodism ceased before 1750.

Wales, Church in. There being no separate Welsh administration, either religious or secular, under the Tudors, its origin has the same date as the Church of England (*q.v.*). Bills for the Disestablishment of the (Anglican) Church in Wales were introduced in 1895 and 1909; a third Act, passed in 1914, did not become operative until 31 Mar. 1920. As a result of this the Welsh dioceses were increased to six by the creation of the sees of Monmouth and Swansea and Brecon in 1921 and 1923. *See also* CATHEDRALS, CHURCH IN WALES.

Wales, Princes of: *Welsh Princes only:*
  Maelgwn Gwynedd ?–550
  Rhun ap Maelgwn 547–584
  Cadvan 584–617
  Cadwaladr ap Cadwallon 617–634
  Idwal ap Cadwaladr 634–661
  Rhodri Molwynog 661–728
  Cynan and Hywel 728–755
  Mervyn Frych 825–844
  Rhodri the Great 844–877
  Anarawd, Cadell, and Mervyn 877–943
  Idwal Foel 915–943
  Hywel Dda, the Good 909–950
  Ieuan and Iago 948–979
  Hywel ap Ieuaf 979–984
  Cadwallon II 984–986
  Meredith ap Owen 986–999
  Idwal (II) ap Meyric ap Idwal Foel 992–997
  Aedan (usurper) 998
  Llewelyn ap Seisyll 1018–1023
  Gruffydd ap Llewelyn ap Seisull 1039–1063
  Bleddyn, Rhiwallon, Meredith ap Owain 1067–1073
  Trahaiarn ap Caradoc 1073–1079
  Meilir 1073–1079
  Caradoc 1073–1079
  Gruffydd ap Cynan 1079–1137
  Rhys ap Tewdwr 1079–1137
  Cadwgan ap Bleddyn 1079–1137
  Iorwerth ab Bleddyn 1079–1137
  Owain Gwynedd 1137–1169
  Howel ab Owain Gwynedd 1169–1194
  Daffydd ap Owain Gwynedd 1169–1194
  Llewelyn (II) ap Iorwerth, the Great 1194–1240
  Dafydd ap Llewelyn 1240–1246
  Llewelyn (III) ap Gruffydd ('Llewelyn y Llyw Olaf') 1246–1282
  From 1301 the Prince of Wales has always been the eldest son of the English sovereign.

Wales, University of. Received full charter, 1893; the university consisted of three colleges: Aberystwyth, 1872; Cardiff, 1883; and Bangor, 1884. To these have been added: Swansea, 1920; Welsh National School of Medicine (Cardiff), 1931.

Wallace Collection (London). Opened, 1900; consists of art treasures collected by the 3rd and 4th Marquesses of Hertford.

Wallachia. *See* RUMANIA and VLACHS.

Walsingham. The shrine of Our Lady of W., Norfolk, much resorted to by pilgrims in the Middle Ages, was built in 1061. Destroyed during sixteenth-century. Reformation; Catholic shrine (Slipper Chapel) officially reopened 1934; Anglican shrine, 1934. Catholic Chapel of Reconciliation, 1981.

Waltham Abbey, Waltham Cross. The Church of the Holy Cross, founded 1061 by Harold Godwinsson; an abbey in 1184.

Wampum. Shell money of N. American Indians, its value depending on colour; used by whites as well as Indians, and current in Connecticut in 1704.

War Crimes Commission, United Nations, established, Oct. 1943. International Military Tribunal established, Aug. 1945.

Warsaw (Pol. **Warszawa**). The date of its foundation is unknown, but a castle was erected there as early as the ninth century; not mentioned in writings before 1224; passed through many stirring periods, becoming capital of Poland, 1595; being taken by Sweden, 1655; retaken by Poles, 1656; taken again by Sweden, 1702; by Russians, 1764; and in 1806 was occupied by Napoleon's troops; taken finally by Russia, 1813; an insurrection in favour of independence took place, 1863; further insurrection, 1905–6. Surrendered, after siege, to Germany, 27 Sept. 1939. Polish rising against Germans, 1 Aug. 1944. Crushed after the Russians had refused assistance, 2 Oct. 1944. Russians entered Warsaw, 11 Jan. 1945. Largely rebuilt since 1945.

Warsaw Pact. Signed between U.S.S.R. and the E. bloc countries, as a twenty-year treaty of friendship and collaboration, on 14 May 1955. It represented the Soviet answer to the North Atlantic Treaty Organization (*q.v.*).

Wartburg. A castle in Thuringia, built by Landgrave Louis *c.* 1070. A poem written about 1280 describes the 'Tourney of Grief' which, however, did not really take place. W. was seat of landgraves until 1460. Luther was brought here for safety in 1521, and here he completed his translation of the New Testament.

Warwick, University of. Estab. at Coventry, 1965.

Washington, originally part of the Oregon territory (*q.v.* for earlier history), was ceded to the U.S.A. by Great Britain, 1846. Made a territory, 1853, and admitted to the Union, 1889.

Washington, D.C., U.S.A. Made capital of the U.S.A. by an Act of Congress, 1790; the American Government removed here in 1880. In 1814 the town was taken by the British, and the Capitol and President's house burned. A centre of operations during the civil war. Coextensive with the District of Columbia (*q.v.*), 1895.

Washington Conference, The, on naval armaments, opened Nov. 1921; on 1 Feb. 1922, treaties for limitation of naval armaments and for prohibiting submarine attacks on merchant vessels received the assent of U.S.A., Britain, France, Italy, and Japan.

Washington, Treaties of, 1846, settled the boundary question between U.S.A. and British America; 1854, a trade and fishery treaty with Canada; 1871, with Britain for the settlement of all causes of difference; 1922, *see* preceding article.

Watches. Invented in Germany *c.* fifteenth century, when they were known as 'Nürnberg Eggs'. The greatest advance was the invention of the deadbeat escapement by T. Tompion (1639–1713), an Englishman.

Waterford, Ireland, founded by Danes or 'Ostmen' (*see* VIKING AGE), was taken from them by the Norman, Strongbow, 1170. King John gave it a charter, 1205.

'Watergate Affair', name given to incident in June 1972 when Democratic Party Offices in the Watergate Building, Washington, were burgled. Several of President Nixon's staff subsequently implicated and convicted: W.A. eventually led to resignation of Nixon in Aug. 1974.

Waterloo Bridge (London). Originally built by Rennie, 1811–17. Subsidence of one pier, 1923. L.C.C. propose reconstruction, 1925. Rebuilding scheme rejected by Parliament, 1932. L.C.C. persist, begin demolition, 1934. Construction begun, 1937; half-width opened to traffic, 1942. Bridge formally opened for full use, 1945.

Wazzan, N. Morocco. Celebrated for manufacture of coarse woollen cloth and as burial-place of the Moorish saint, Idrisi Sharif, who lived there, 1727.

Weather Forecasts, first regularly issued by the Admiralty, 1860.

Weaving. First practised in China; during the tenth century the Flemings were important wool weavers, and during the fourteenth century England supplied them with most of the raw material; the first mention of W. in England is at York, 1331; early English centres of the industry were Canterbury, Colchester, and Norwich.

Wedgwood China. Josiah W. (1730–1795) first established own pottery, 1759. Brought out patent for porcelain, 1763.

Wedmore, Treaty of, between Alfred the Great of England and the Danes, by which England was divided between the English to the S. and the Danes to the N. of Watling Street, 878.

Weights and Measures. The shekel of Babylonia and Israel is traceable back to the eleventh century B.C.; it was about one-sixtieth of a pound avoirdupois. The cubit, or length of forearm, was a favourite measure in Egypt, Phoenicia, and Greece. A king of Argos, Pheidon, was renowned as having introduced a new system, the Aeginetan, into the Peloponnesus; but even his century is uncertain, probably eighth B.C. A standard of English measure was made in 972, and kept at Winchester; the first official examination of W. and M., 1795; an Act to enforce uniformity over the U.K. was passed, 1878, and is the basis of all subsequent amending legislation; a metric system Act was passed, 1897, but was not applied. Britain transferred to metric system, 1965 onwards.

Wei-hai-wei. Held by Japan pending payment of war indemnity by China, Jan. 1895, till leased to Britain, 1 July 1898, for so long as Port Arthur remained in occupation of Russia. Restored to China, 1 Oct. 1930.

Weimar, Germany. As capital of Saxe-W .-Eisenach from 1547 it *fl.* as a centre of German classical culture *c.* 1775–1828. The constitution of the German republic was drawn up here in 1919. Hence the name W. Republic.

Welland Ship Canal, between Lakes Ontario and Erie, built, 1824–9.

Wellington, capital of New Zealand, founded, 1840.

Wells. King Ine of Wessex is said to have founded first church here, 704. Work on the cathedral began before 1200, and the greater part of it was finished, 1242.

Welsh Laws. Code drawn up by Hywel Dda *c.* 943. For Statute of Rhuddlan, and later English statutes, *see* WALES.

Welsh Literature. The following is a list of Welsh authors, in chronological order, not now living:

Aneurin *c.* 560, poet.
Taliesin, *c.* 570 (*d.* 601), poet.
Myrddin, *c.* 570, poet.
Llywarch Hen, *c.* 580, poet.
Meilyr, *c.* 1137, poet.
Caradoc of Llancarvan *c.* 1150, historian.
Gwalchmai, *c.* 1157, poet.
Owain Cyveiliog, *c.* 1165, poet.
Hywel ab Owain Gwynedd, *c.* 1169, poet.
Einion, *c.* 1175, poet.
Dafydd Benvras, 1230 ?, poet.
Elidir Sais, 1230 ?, poet.
Cynddelw, 1250, poet.
Llywarch ap Llewelyn, 1250 ?, poet.
Einion Wann, 1200–50 ?, poet.
Phylip Brydydd, 1250, poet.
Einion ap Gwgan, 1260, poet.
Edeyrn Dafod Aur, *c.* 1270, grammarian.
Llygad Gwr, *c.* 1270, poet.
Einion ap Madoc, *c.* 1270, poet.
Y Prydydd Bychan, *c.* 1275, poet.
Howel Voel, *c.* 1280, poet.
Bleddyn Fardd, *c.* 1284, poet.
Gruffydd ab yr Ynad Coch, *c.* 1284, poet.

Gwilym Ddu o Arfon, *c.* 1300, poet.
Dafydd ap Gwilym, *c.* 1340–1400, poet.
Gruffudd ab Meredydd, *c.* 1380, poet.
Hywel ap Einion Llygliw, *c.* 1390, poet.
Iolo Goch, *c.* 1400, poet.
Llywelyn Goch ab Meurig Hen, *c.* 1400, poet.
Gruffudd Llwyd ab Dafydd ab Enion Llygliw, *c.* 1400, poet.
Rhys Goch Eryri, *c.* 1410, poet.
Sion Cent, *c.* 1410, poet.
Rhys Goch ap Rhiccert, *c.* 1420 ?, poet.
Gutto'r Glyn, wrote 1430–60, poet.
Lewis Glyn Cothi, 1440–90, poet.
Meredydd ap Rhys, *c.* 1450, poet.
Dafydd Nanmor, *c.* 1460, poet.
Howel Swrdwal, *c.* 1460, poet.
Ieuan Brydydd Hir Hynaf, *c.* 1460, poet.
Ieuan ap Howel Swrdwal, *c.* 1460, poet.
Llawdden, *c.* 1460, poet and prosodist.
Ieuan Deulwyn, 1460–90, poet.
Dr. Morris Clynnog, *d.* 1580–1, catechist.
Dr. Richard Davies, 1501–81, translator.
Sir John Prys, 1502–54, historian and miscellaneous writer.
Humphrey Llwyd, 1527–68, historian, etc.
Gruffud Hiraethog, 1530–66, poet.
Owain Gwynedd (or Owain Ifan), *d.* 1590, poet.
Dr. Thomas Huet, ?–1591, translator.
Maurice Kyffin, *d.* 1598, translator.
Dr. David Powel, *d.* 1598, historian, etc.
William Cynwal, 1530–1600, poet.
Dr. Sion Dafydd Rhys, 1534–161–?, poet, grammarian, etc.
William Llyn, 1535–80, poet.
Sion Tudur, 1535–1602, poet.
Edward Kyffin, ?–1603, translator.
Edmund Prys, 1541–1623, poet and translator.
Sion Phylip, 1543–1620, poet.
Rhys Cain, 1545–1614, poet and painter.
Simwnt Fychan, 1546–1606, poet and grammarian.
Dr. Roger Smyth, 1546–1625, translator.
Dr. William Morgan, 1547–1604, translator.
Sion Brwynog, 1550–67, poet.

Dr. Gruffydd Roberts, *fl.* 1555–95?, grammarian and philospher.

Dr. Richard Parry, 1560–1623, translator.

Henry Parry, 1561–1617, grammarian.

Henry Salesbury, *b.* 1561, grammarian.

Huw Lewys, 1562–1634, translator.

Edward James, 1570–1610, translator.

Dr. John Davies, 1570?–1644, grammarian.

John Salisbury, 1575–1625, translator.

Thomas Prys, ?–1634, poet.

William Salesbury, *c.* 1575, translator and lexicographer.

William Phylip, 1577–1669, poet.

Vicar Prichard, or Rhys Prichard, 1579–1644, religious poet.

William Myddelton, or Gwilyn Canoldref, *c.* 1590, poet, translator, etc.

Rowland Vaughan, ?–1667, miscellaneous writer.

Richard Jones, 1604–73, translator.

Thomas Gouge, 1605–81, educationist.

Morgan Llwyd o Wynedd, 1619–59, miscellaneous writer.

Stephen Hughes, 1622–88, translator, etc.

Edward Morus, *d.* 1689, poet.

Huw Morus, 1622–1709, poet.

Charles Edwards, 1628–?, religious writer.

Robert Llwyd, *c.* 1640, translator.

James Davies (Iago ab Dewi), 1648–1722, poet and translator.

Edward Lhuyd, 1660–1709, philologist.

Elis Wyn o Lasynys, 1671–1734, author of the *Barrd Cwsg*.

Edward Samuel, 1674–1748, miscellaneous writer.

Griffith Jones, Llanddowror, 1684–1761, educationist, etc.

Moses Williams, 1686–1742, translator.

Theophilus Evans, 1693–1767, historian.

Lewis Morris, 1700–79, poet and miscellaneous writer.

Daniel Rowland, 1713–90, religious writer and translator (?).

William Williams of Pantycelyn, 1717–91, hymn writer.

Joshua Thomas, 1719–97, historian.

David Lewis, *c.* 1720, philosopher.

Goronwy Owen, 1722–69, poet.

Simon Thomas, *c.* 1730, historian.

Evan Evans (Ieuan Brydydd Hir), 1731–1781, poet, etc.

Thomas Edwards (Twm o'r Nant), 1739–1810, interlude writer.

Owen Jones (Owain Myfyr), 1741–1814.

Edward Williams (Iolo Morganwg), 1746–1826.

David Richards (Dafydd Ionawr), 1751–1827.

Dr. Owen Pughe, 1759–1835, lexicographer.

David Thomas (Dafydd Ddu Eryri), 1760–1822.

Edward Jones, Maesyplwm, 1761–1836, religious poet.

John Jones (Sion Glanygors), 1767–1821.

Robert Williams (Robert ap Gwilym Ddu), 1767–1850.

Robert Davies (Bardd Nantglyn), 1769–1835.

David Saunders, Merthyr, 1769–1840, translator.

Griffith Williams (Gutyn Peris), 1769–1838.

John Jones, LL.D., 1772–1837, historian, etc.

John Howel (Ioan ab Hywel), 1774–1830.

David Owen (Dewi Wyn o Eifion), 1784–1841.

David Owen (Brutus), 1794–1866.

Evan Evans (Ieuan Glan Geirionydd), 1795–1855.

William Ellis Jones (Gwilym Cawrdaf), 1796–1848.

William Williams (Caledfryn), 1801–69.

Ebenezer Thomas (Eben Fardd), 1802–63.

William Rowlands (Gwilym Lleyn), 1802–1865.

Jane Williams (Ysgafell), 1806–85.

Robert John Pryse (Gweirydd ap Ryhs), 1807–89.

Reuben Davies (Prydydd y Coed), 1808–1833.

Robert Ellis (Cynddelw), 1810–75.

John Jones (Talhaiarn), 1810–69.

Rosser Beynon (Asaph Glan Taf), 1811–1876.

Roger Edwards, 1811–86, poet and miscellaneous writer.

Thomas Jones (Glan Alun), 1811–66.

John Williams (Ab Ithel), 1811–62.

Edward Williams (Iolo Fardd Glas), *fl.* 1839.

William Roberts, LL.D. (Nefydd), 1813–1872.

John Evans (I. D. Ffraid), 1814–75.

Edward Davies (Iolo Trefaldwyn), 1819–1887.

Edward Roberts (Iorwerth Glan Aled), 1819–67.

Thomas E. Davies (Dewi Wyn o Essyllt), 1820–91.

Evan Jones (Ieuan Gwynedd), 1820–52.

Ellin Evans (Elen Egryn), *fl.* 1850.

Evan Davies (Myfyr Morganwg), *fl.* 1855.

Thomas Stephens, Merthyr, 1821–75.

John Roberts (Ieuan Gwyllt), 1822–77.

Thomas Rowlands, 1824–84, grammarian.

Owen Wyn Jones (Glasynys), 1828–70.

John C. Hughes (Ceiriog), 1832–87.

W. Thomas (Islwyn), 1832–78.

Richard Davies (Mynyddog), 1833–77.

John Davies (Ossian Gwent), 1834–92.

Richard Foulkes Edwards (Rhisiart Ddu o Wynedd), 1836–70.

Daniel Owen, 1836–95, novelist.

John Robert Pryse (Golyddan), 1841–63.

David Griffiths (Dewi Eifion), *d.* 1871.

Emrys ap Iwan, 1851–96, critic.

Mary Olwen Jones, 1858–93, novelist.

Sir Owen Morgan Edwards, 1858–1920, critic.

Eivion Wyn, *d.* 1926, poet.

Sir John Morris-Jones, 1864–1929, poet.

Thomas Gwynne Jones, 1872–1949, poet.

H. Elvet Lewis (Elfed), 1860–1953, poet.

W. J. Gruffydd, 1881–1954, poet.

Dylan M. Thomas, 1914–53, poet.

Welwyn. See GARDEN CITY.

Wembley, British Empire Exhibitions at, 1924, 1925. Many events of 1948 Olympic Games held at W. stadium.

Wends or **Sorbs,** Slavonic tribes who are mentioned by the English missionary Winfrith (*alias* Boniface), who *d.* 754.

Under German rule from about A.D. 900, they formed part of the Polish kingdom, 1002–32, and were united under the Bohemian crown from the fifteenth century until 1621 when the region was partitioned between Saxony and Brandenburg.

Wesleyans. See METHODISTS.

Wessex, kingdom of the West Saxons, the political nucleus of which arose out of the Gewissae (i.e. Confederates); this confederacy, military and perhaps also religious, was led into Britain, 495, by Cerdic, and his son Cynric. In 519 Cerdic and Cynric 'undertook the government of the West Saxons ... from that day have reigned the children of the West Saxon kings.' Bede, mentioning the West Saxons for the first time, a century later, says they were 'formerly called Gewissae,' and were converted to Christianity in 635 by the Italian bishop Birinus (*d.* 690). Cerdic's grandson Ceawlin obtained possession of the country between the upper Thames and lower Severn, 571–578. The territory of the Hwicce (Worcestershire, Gloucestershire, S.W. Warwickshire) was lost to the militant pagan Penda, king of Mercia, 630. Somerset was conquered from the Britons of Cornwall about 660, and the Isle of Wight, 686. Ine, whose code of laws still survives, extended the W. dominions westward to include most of Devonshire. During the eighth century the kingdoms of Sussex and Kent were eliminated and annexed piecemeal by W., which then subdued its final internal enemy, Mercia, 825–9. Thereafter *see* ENGLAND.

Wessex, Kings of, c. 552–839:

Cynric *fl.* 552–*d.* 560

Ceawlin 560–592

Ceol 591–597

Coelwulf 597–611

Cyneglis 611–643

Cenwalh 643–645

Penda (of Mercia) 645–648

Cenwalh (restored) 648–672

(Queen) Seaxburg 672–674

Escwine 674–676

Centwine 676–685

Caedwalla 685–688

Ine 688–726
Ethelheard 726 740
Cuthred 740–756
Sigeberht 756–757
Cynewulf 757–786
Beorhtric 786–802
Egbert, KING OF ENGLAND 802–839
See further under ENGLISH SOVEREIGNS
AND THEIR CONSORTS.

Western Australia was first explored by the Dutch under Dirk Hartog, 1616. The first Englishman to land was William Dampier, 1688. Formal possession taken on behalf of the English crown by Vancouver, 1791. A settlement of convicts was sent from New S. Wales, 1826. Swan River Settlement founded, 1829. Responsible government granted, 1890.

Western Union had its beginnings in a 50-year treaty signed in Brussels on 17 Mar. 1948 by Britain, France, the Netherlands, Belgium, and Luxembourg. European Council established, May, 1949. In Dec. 1949 the W. U. defence organization was incorporated with the N. Atlantic Treaty command.

West Indies, Federation of. *See* CARIBBEAN FEDERATION.

Westminster. The abbey was founded *c.* seventh century, and refounded by Edward the Confessor *c.* 1050–65. The 'city' was governed by the abbots till 1547. St. Margaret's was founded *c.* 1100. The W. Hall was built, 1097–1100. Law Courts established in W. Hall *c.* 1200. Abbey rebuilt, 1245–69. Further additions *c.* 1350–1528, and *c.* 1722–40. The school attached to the abbey from early times was chartered by Henry VIII, but only properly endowed by Queen Elizabeth I. The abbey was converted into barracks for a time, 1643. First W. Bridge opened, 1750. W. Palace burned down, 1834. New palace completed, 1859. New bridge built, 1862. Law Courts removed from, 1883. Created a city and a metropolitan borough, 1899. Roman Catholic cathedral opened, 1903; consecrated, 1910.

Westminster Assembly. The Long Parliament, having in 1641 expelled the bishops, summoned an assembly of 121 divines, who, with 30 laymen from Parliament, formed the body that was to inaugurate a Presbyterian establishment for England and Wales. Meetings held in W. Abbey: the first, 1 July 1643; the last, 22 Feb. 1648; in all, 1,163 meetings. The assembly adopted the Solemn League and Covenant (*q.v.*), 25 Sept. 1643. It submitted to Parliament: a 'Directory of Public Worship' to supersede the Book of Common Prayer, 20 Apr. 1644; a 'Confession of Faith' and two Catechisms, both approved by Parliament, 15 Sept. 1648. The Commons ordered, 13 Oct. 1647, that Presbyterianism be tried for a year, bishops having been abolished, 9 Oct. 1643. Presbyterianism soon gave place to Independency in England. All the Assembly's work was swept away at the Restoration, so far as England and Wales were concerned; but the Confession and the Shorter Catechism remained binding in the Church of Scotland.

Westminster, Provisions of, drawn up, 1259. Re-enacted as the Statute of Marlborough, 1267.

Westminster Statutes of.
I. 1275. A miscellaneous code on revenue, etc., matters.
II. 1285. Part of this is called *De Donis Conditionalibus*, and legalized the creation of entailed interests.
III. 1290. Part of this is called *Quia Emptores*, and abolished further subinfeudation.
IV. 1931. This Act created the legally independent sovereign status under the crown of the British Dominions.

Westphalia, Kingdom of, created by Napoleon, 1807. Dissolved, 1814. *See* BUONAPARTE.

Westphalia, Peace of, 1648. This consisted of two treaties, which ended the Thirty Years War, negotiated at Münster and Osnabrück, and signed at Münster, 21 Oct. 1648.
1. A treaty of alliance between France, the Empire, and Sweden against Spain.
2. A treaty of peace by which Sweden received W. Pomerania, Bremen, and Verden, France received Metz,

Toul, Verdun, and Alsace, and the independence of Switzerland and the United Provinces of the Netherlands was guaranteed. Religious toleration was granted to Calvinists as well as Lutherans in Germany, but the principle was not extended to the Hapsburg territories. The peace marks the failure of the Austro-Spanish effort to restore Roman Catholicism in Central Europe, and the beginning of French hegemony in Europe.

West Point Military Academy, U.S.A. A resolution of Congress, Oct. 1776, proposed the establishment of a military academy, but no bill was passed until 1802. A further Act of 29 Apr. 1812 increased the establishment, and in 1817 a system of admitting a fixed proportion of cadets from each state was adopted. Women now admitted.

West Virginia was admitted to the Union in 1863 by fissure from Virginia (*q.v.*).

West Wall. Between 1936 and 1940 the Germans constructed a continuous fortified belt from Lörrach in the S. to a point opposite the junction of their frontier with those of Belgium and Luxemburg. From 1939 to 1945 it was extended to protect the southern flank from Lörrach to Lake Constance.

Wexford, Ireland. Founded by Vikings in the ninth century, was taken from their descendants by the Normans, 1169; received a charter, 1318; besieged by Cromwell, 1649; held by Williamites, 1690. During the second rising of the United Irishmen (*q.v.*), 1798, W. was the headquarters of the civil administration.

Wheel, Breaking on the. Continental form of torture first used in Germany, 1535, then abolished, 1827; used in Edinburgh, 1604.

Whig. A term of contempt under Charles II, probably of Scottish origin. It eventually became the honoured party name of those who took the lead in establishing William III and George I on the throne. *See* LIBERALS.

Whipsnade Park. *See* ZOOLOGICAL SOCIETY OF LONDON.

Whisky Insurrection, 1794, in western Pennsylvania against the enforcing of the excise law by the Federal Government.

Whist is first mentioned about 1621, but only became fashionable in the latter part of the eighteenth century, being displaced towards 1900 by bridge, which evolved from it.

Whitby, so called in the ninth century by Scandinavians, who used the harbour called by the English Streoneshalh, where a monastery, built by St. Hilda in 656, was the scene of a council, since called the Synod of W., in 664, attended by St. Wilfrid (634–709) and St. Colman (*d.* 676) in the Roman and Celtic interests respectively. The extant ruins of the abbey on the E. cliff date from 1220. James Cook, the navigator, sailed in a W. brig about 1745, and the *Endeavour*, in which he set out on his famous voyage to New Zealand in 1768, was a collier of local pattern built in a W. shipyard.

Whiteboys. Irish secret organization, founded *c.* 1860. It was of the type known as Ribbonism. The Westmeath Act (1871) declard Ribbonism illegal. The movement died down about 1885.

Whitehall (London). York House, the residence of the Archbishop of York, stood on this site, *c.* 1250. It was later acquired by Henry VIII, who made it a royal residence. A new hall was designed for James I, but only partially completed, 1622; through this hall Charles I passed to execution, 1649; and when the old palace was burned down in 1698 the hall was the only part to survive. The street now called W. was called King Street until the destruction of the palace.

White House (Washington, D.C.). Built between 1792 and 1799. Partly burnt out by British troops, 1814. Condemned as unsafe, 1949; repairs were completed in 1952 and much internal renovation was later done under the supervision of the wives of Presidents Eisenhower and Kennedy.

White Russia. *See* BELORUSSIA.

'Who's Who', biographical reference work first published, 1848, by Alfred

Baily. Acquired, 1896, by Adam and Charles Black.

Wilhelmshaven, the chief naval station of Germany on the N. Sea, was founded in 1853, at the time of the origin of the Prussian Navy; the harbour was opened in 1869; many important additions made to the naval station from 1900 onwards; the dry dock was destroyed by the R.N. in 1948; the naval installations in general having been already heavily damaged by R.A.F. bombing between 1942 and 1945.

Wilkes's Case. Trials of John Wilkes, alderman of London, for printing obscene poem, *Essay on Woman*, and publication of *North Briton*, 21 Feb. 1764 and 18 June 1768.

Winchester (Rom.: **Venta Belgarum**). A city in Hampshire. The first bishop was Hedda (*d.* 705), but no traces of the Saxon cathedral remain. Present cathedral begun in 1079; nave reconstructed, 1380–1400; major restoration, 1905. Public school at W. founded by William of Wykeham, 1394.

Window Tax, 1697. Brought in by William III to atone for the deficiency on damaged coin; repealed, 24 July 1851.

Windsor. Family name of the British royal house, adopted 1917, when George V renounced all German titles for himself and his family, together with the dynastic name of Saxe-Coburg-Gotha, acquired through Queen Victoria's marriage with Prince Albert.

Windsor Castle. The building was begun in wood by William I; stonework begun by Henry I *c.* 1110; in 1344 the Round Tower was built, and in 1356 practically the whole castle was rebuilt by Edward III, who was *b.* there, 1312; additions were made by (*inter alia*) Henry VIII, Elizabeth I, and Charles II. St. George's Chapel, was built 1473–1519 (begun by Edward IV); it was carefully restored by George III, 1787. Extensive improvements, 1824–30 and in the present century.

Winnipeg, Manitoba, first reached by white travellers, 1738. NW. Co.'s trading post, founded 1810, was replaced by a Hudson's Bay post, named Fort Garry, 1822. On the creation of the province of Manitoba in 1870 its capital was sited at W., which was chartered as a city in 1873.

Wireless. Broadcasting boom began in U.S.A., 1921. In Apr. 1922 British Postmaster-General announced a scheme for providing licences and for broadcasting from seven stations. Long-distance wireless tested, Aug. 1922. Music from America heard in England, 28–9 Dec. 1923. High-power station at Rugby opened, 1 Jan. 1926. Conversation, London and New York, 7 Mar. 1926; and regular telephone service begun, 7 Jan. 1927. First conversation London and San Francisco, 26 Feb. 1927; Anglo-S. African beam system opened, 3 July 1927; first broadcast from Australia to England, 4 Sept. 1927; beam service to India opened, 5 Sept. 1927. Regular foreign broadcasts begun, 1937. *See* BRITISH BROADCASTING CORPORATION.

Wisconsin, U.S.A., was first entered by a white man, Jean Nicolet, 1634. First permanent settlement, 1701. It was admitted to the Union, 1848.

Witchcraft. A Bull against W. was issued by Pope Innocent VIII in 1484, whilst in England Acts against it were passed in 1542, 1562, and 1601. Last person to be tried under these Acts was Jane Wenham of Walkern, Hertfordshire, 1712, but a woman was actually burned alive in Sunderland as late as 1722. An Act of 1736 penalizes '*pretending* to use W., etc.' The Vagrancy Act of 1824 was amended in 1950 to cover cases of reputed W. As late as 1895 (15 Mar.) a woman was burned as a witch in Ireland, at Cloneen, County Tipperary and a case of (illegal) witch burning was reported in Mexico, June 1963 and in a S. African tribal area, 1983.

Witenagemot or **Witan.** The Anglo-Saxon royal council; in seventh and eighth centuries separate Ws. were possessed by Wessex, Kent, Mercia, and Northumbria; there was no fixed meeting-place, but the king was always present; meetings were held three times a year: at Easter, Whitsun, and Christmas. The most celebrated meetings were at Luton, 931, and Winchester, 934.

Witney. A market town in Oxfordshire, seat of blanket-making industry, which was established in the reign of King Edgar, 909.

Wittenberg, Saxony. Mentioned, 1180; here, in the Augustinian monastery, Luther dwelt; in 1508 he was appointed professor of philosophy, and in 1517 he affixed his celebrated 95 Theses to the church door; bombarded by Austrians, 1760; taken by France, 1806; taken by Prussians, 1814.

Women's Auxiliary Air Force. *See* WOMEN'S ROYAL AIR FORCE.

Women's Colleges, English. Tennyson's *Princess*, written against women's higher education, 1847. Earliest W.C. were at London University (Queen's and Bedford), 1848 and 1849. For others *see under* CAMBRIDGE, LONDON, OXFORD UNIVERSITIES.

Women's Franchise. *See* FRANCHISE, ELECTIVE and U.S.A., CONSTITUTION OF.

Women's Institutes originated in Canada in 1897, and were introduced to the U.K. in 1915 by a Canadian, Mrs. Alfred Watt (1868–1948), who founded a branch at Llanfairpwllgwyngyll, Anglesey. The National Federation of W.I. was founded, 1917.

Women's Land Army raised 1917. the W.L.A. came into being again in Sept. 1939, organized by committees set up in May of that year. Disbanded, 1950.

Women's Royal Air Force.
1. An ancillary service of the R.A.F., raised in 1917 and disbanded in 1919.
2. A force formed round the nucleus of certain A.T.S. (*see* WOMEN'S ROYAL ARMY CORPS) companies which had been attached to the R.A.F. since 1938, and in July 1939 were permanently transferred. It was known as Women's Auxiliary Air Force until Feb. 1949, when the present designation was adopted.

Women's Royal Army Corps, designation adopted from 1 Feb. 1949, by the former Auxiliary Territorial Service,

the formation of which was proclaimed by royal warrant, 9 Sept. 1938. First Chief Controller, with equivalent rank of major-general, appointed, 3 July 1939. Officers received royal commissions, Apr. 1941. In this year the first mixed heavy A.A. batteries were formed.

Women's Royal Naval Service.
1. Raised, 1917; disbanded, Oct. 1919.
2. Re-formed, 1939; placed on permanent basis, Jan. 1949.

Women's Royal Voluntary Services, an association formed, 16 May 1938, by the Marchioness of Reading, and established on a permanent basis by the Home Office in May 1947. Originally the W.V.S., received addition of 'Royal' after World War II.

Wonders of the World. The seven W. of the W. were
1. the Egyptian pyramids, *c.* 4700 B.C.;
2. the tomb of Mausolus, 353 B.C.;
3. the Ephesian temple of Diana, *c.* 550 B.C.;
4. the walls and hanging gardens of Babylon, work of Nebuchadnezzar, *c.* 604–562 B.C.;
5. the Colossus of Rhodes, 280 B.C.;
6. the statue of Zeus at Olympia, *c.* 450 B.C.;
7. the pharos of Ptolemy Philadelphus, *c.* 282 B.C.

Woolsack. The seat of the Lord Chancellor in the House of Lords; placed there in the reign of Edward III as a reminder of the importance of the wool industry; the earliest authentic mention of the W., however, is in the reign of Henry VIII.

Woolwich, England, mentioned, 1064. Already an important royal dockyard in fifteenth century. The *Great Harry* launched at, 1515. Batteries erected against the Dutch, 1667. Royal Arsenal, 1805. Royal dockyard closed, 1869. Royal Military Academy, which was established 1741, was amalgamated with the Royal Military College at Sandhurst, 1946.

Woomera Rocket Range, Australia. Developed since 1946.

Worcester became an episcopal see, 680. Benedictine church built by St. Oswald

(d. 992), 964, extensively rebuilt by Wulfstan the bishop (1012?–95), 1084, as his cathedral church. He also founded the Hospital of St. Wulfstan, still standing now, but converted from its original purpose, 1541. King John is buried in the cathedral. Last material addition to cathedral was Prince Arthur's Chantry, built by Henry VII. The Royal W. Porcelain Works were opened, 1751.

Workmen's Compensation. W.C. Act, 1897, introduced principle of compulsory insurance by employers in a limited number of trades, against accidents arising in course of employment. Extending Act followed. All W.C. Acts were superseded by the National Insurance (Industrial Injuries) Act, 1946.

Works, Ministry of, H.M. Office of W. first so called, 1852. Ministry status, 1940; part of the Department of the Environment (*q.v.*) since 1970.

World Bank. *See* INTERNATIONAL BANK FOR RECONSTRUCTION AND DEVELOPMENT.

World Council of Churches, other than Roman Catholic, held its first assembly at Amsterdam, Aug. 1948.

World Health Organization. Constitution drawn up, 22 July 1946; came into effect, 1948. The W.H.O.'s status as a specialized agency of the United Nations Organization was recognized, 1950.

World War I. *Declaration of War*
1914: Austria-Hungary on Serbia, 28 July; Germany on Russia, 1 Aug.; Germany on France, 3 Aug.; Britain on Germany, 4 Aug.; Germany on Belgium, 4 Aug.; Montenegro on Austria-Hungary, 7 Aug.; France on Austria-Hungary, 10 Aug.; Britain on Austria-Hungary, 12 Aug.; Japan on Germany, 23 Aug.; Britain on Turkey, 6 Nov.
1915: Italy on Austria, 23 May; Italy on Turkey, 20 Aug.; Britain on Bulgaria, 15 Oct.; France on Bulgaria, 16 Oct.; Italy on Bulgaria, 19 Oct.
1916: Albania on Austria, 11 Jan.; Germany on Portugal, 9 Mar.; Rumania on Austria, 27 Aug.; Italy on Germany, 28 Aug.; Germany on Rumania, 28 Aug.; Turkey on Rumania, 30 Aug.; Bulgaria on Rumania, 1 Sept.
1917: U.S.A. on Germany, 6 Apr.; Cuba on Germany, 7 Apr.; Austria on U.S.A., 8 Apr.; Bulgaria on U.S.A., 9 Apr.; Panama on Germany, 10 Apr.; Siam on Central Empires, 22 July; China on Germany, 14 Aug.; China on Austria, 11 Sept.; Brazil on Germany, 26 Oct.

Military Events
France and Flanders:
1914: German invasion of Belgium begun, 4 Aug.; Brussels entered, 20 Aug.; Namur captured, 23 Aug.; Antwerp taken, 9 Oct. Battles: Mons, 23–24 Aug.; Le Cateau, 26 Aug.; Marne, 6–12 Sept.; Aisne, 12–15 Sept.; Ypres, 19 Oct.–22 Nov.
1915: Battles: Neuve-Chapelle, 10–13 Mar.; Ypres, 22 Apr.–25 May (first German attack with gas, 22 Apr.); Festubert, 15–25 May; Loos, 25 Sept.–8 Oct.
1916: Battles: Verdun, begun 21 Feb. (Douaumont, 25 Feb. and 24 Oct.); Somme, 1 July–18 Nov. (Beaumont-Hamel, 13 Nov.); Verdun, 15 Dec.; Ancre, 13–18 Nov.
1917: German retreat to Hindenburg Line, 14 Mar.–5 Apr. Battles: Arras, 9 Apr.–4 May (Vimy Ridge, 9–14 Apr.; Scarpe, 9–14, 23–24 Apr., 3–4 May); Chemin des Dames, 5 May; Bullecourt, 3–17 May; Messines, 7–14 June; Ypres, 31 July–10 Nov. (Passchendaele, 12 Oct., 26 Oct.–10 Nov.); Verdun, 20 Aug.; Cambrai, 20 Nov.–3 Dec.
1918: Battles: Somme, 21 Mar.–5 Apr.; Lys, 9–29 Apr. (Kemmel Ridge, 17–19 Apr.); Aisne, 27 May–6 June; Marne, 18 July; Ourcq, 23 July–2 Aug.; Amiens, 8–11 Aug.; Bapaume, 21–31 Aug.; Somme, 21 Aug.–3 Sept.; Arras, 26 Aug.–3 Sept. (Drocourt-Quéant, 2–3 Sept.); Saint-Mihiel, 12 Sept.; Hindenburg Line, 12 Sept.–9 Oct. (Épéhy, 18 Sept.; Cambrai, 8–9 Oct.); Argonne, 26 Sept.–2 Nov.; Ypres, 28 Sept.–2 Oct.; Selle River, 17–25 Oct.; Valenciennes, 1 Nov.; Sambre, 4 Nov.

Prussia—Poland—Russia—Austria-Hungary:
1914: Battles: Tannenberg, 26–30 Aug.; Lemberg, 1–3 Sept.; Augustovo, 1–4 Oct.; for Warsaw, 15–20 Oct., 18 Nov.–28 Dec.; Lodz, 1–5 Dec.
1915: Przemysl surrendered to Russians, 22 Mar.; recaptured, 3 June; Lemberg retaken, 22 June; third battle for Warsaw, 19 July; Warsaw evacuated by Russians, 5 Aug.; Kovno stormed, 7 Aug.; battle of Brest- Litovsk, 26 Aug.; battle of Tarnopol, 7–8 Sept.; Vilna taken by Germans, 17 Sept.
1916: Battle of Lake Narotch, Mar.–Apr.; Russian offensive in Ukraine, 4 June; in E. Galicia, 8 June; near Baronovitchi, 13 June; near Brody, 15 July.
1917: Russian offensive at Brzezany, 1 July; battle of Halicz, 10 July, 23 July; fall of Riga, 3 Sept.
1918: Odessa occupied by Germans, 13 Mar.

Rumania:
1916: Invasion of Transylvania, 28 Aug.; Silistria taken by Bulgarians, 12 Sept.; Constanza taken by Bulgarians, 22 Oct.; Bucharest occupied by Germans, 7 Dec.
1917: Evacuation of the Dobrudja, 8 Jan.; Galatz evacuated, 11 Jan.

Dardanelles:
1915: Landing at Cape Helles, 25–26 Apr.; battles for Krithia, 28 Apr., 6– 8 May, 4 June; Anzac battles, 25 Apr.–30 June; landing at Suvla, 6–15 Aug.; Suvla battles, 6–21 Aug. (Sari-Bair, 6–10 Aug.). Evacuation of Dardanelles declared, 8 Dec.
1916: Evacuation completed, 8 Jan.

Italy:
1915: First battle of the Isonzo, 2–29 July.
1916: Battle of Trentino, 14 May–16 June; battle of Gorizia, 6–14 Aug.
1917: Italian offensive on Isonzo, 14 May–10 June; Italian attack between Tolmino and sea, 19 Aug.; battle of Caporetto, 24 Oct.–18 Nov.
1918: Battle of Piave, 15–23 June, 26 Oct.; battle of Vittoria Veneto, 24 Oct.–4 Nov.

Balkans:
1915: Allied landing at Salonika, 5 Oct.; fall of Üsküb, 22 Oct.; battle of Kachanik, 4 Nov.; fall of Monastir, 2 Dec.
1916: Cettinje taken, 1–3 Jan.; Durazzo taken, 24 Feb.; Monastir retaken, 23 Nov.
1917: Battle of Doiran, 24–25 Apr., 8–9 May.
1918: Battle of the Vardar, 15–25 Sept.; battle of Doiran, 18–19 Sept.; Üsküb retaken, 30 Sept.

Egypt, Palestine, and Arabia:
Operations against the Senussi, Nov. 1915–Feb. 1917; battle of Romani, 3–4 Aug. 1916; battles of Gaza, 26 Mar.–7 Nov. 1917; capture of Jerusalem, 7–9 Dec. 1917; of Jericho, 19–21 Feb. 1918; Arab rising against Turks began, 7 June 1918; Mecca taken, 10 June 1918; battle of Megiddo, 19–25 Sept. 1918.

Mesopotamia—Persia:
1915: Battle of Kut, 28 Sept.; battle of Ctesiphon, 22–24 Nov.
1916: Kermanchah taken by Russians, 26 Feb.; Battle of Sanna-i-Yat, 6–22 Apr.
1917: British occupied Bagdad, 11 Mar.; Samaria, 19 Sept.; Ramadi taken, 28 Sept.; battle of Sherghat, 30 Oct.

Africa:
E. Africa: Tanga operations, Nov. 1914; surrender of Mafia Island, 12 Jan. 1915; Tanga occupied, 7 July 1916; Dar-es-Salaam surrendered, 4 Sept. 1916; final surrender, 25 Nov. 1918.
SW. Africa: Luderitzbucht occupied, 18 Sept. 1914; occupation of Windhoek, 12 May 1915; German capitulation, 9 July 1915.
Cameroons: Capture of Duala, 24 Sept. 1914; of Mora, 8 Sept. 1916.
Togoland: Lome captured, 8 Aug. 1914.
S. Africa: Rebellion began, 15 Sept. 1914; surrender at Reitz, 4 Dec. 1914.

Caucasus:
Erzerum taken, 12 Feb. 1916, retaken, Mar. 1918; Trebizond taken, 18 Mar. 1916, retaken, Mar. 1918;

Erzingan taken, July 1916, retaken, Mar. 1918; Batum occupied, Apr. 1918; Baku evacuated by British, 14 Sept. 1918.

N. Russia—Siberia:
Kem occupied, 7 June 1918; Irkutsk occupied by Czechslovaks, July 1918; Dukhovskaya, 23 Aug. 1918; Archangel occupied, 1 Aug. 1918; Troitsa, 10 Aug. 1919; British evacuation, 27 Sept. 1919.

Naval Events
1914: *Goeben* and *Breslau* reach Turkey, 11 Aug.; blockade of Kiaochow, 27 Aug.; battle of Heligoland Bight, 28 Aug.; siege of Tsingtao, 23 Sept.–5 Nov.; H.M.S. *Aboukir, Hogue,* and *Cressy* torpedoed, 22 Sept.; battle of Coronel (Admiral Cradock's squadron lost), 1 Nov.; Kiaochow surrenderd 7 Nov.; German cruiser *Emden* destroyed, 9 Nov.; battle of Falkland islands (Spee's squadron sunk), 8 Dec.; Germans bombard Yorkshire coastal towns, 16 Dec.; seaplane raid on Cuxhaven, 25 Dec.
1915: Battle of Dogger Bank, 24 Jan.; German submarine blockade of Britain opened, 18 Feb.; British attack on Dardanelles forts, 19 Feb.; again, 4–7 Mar.; German cruiser *Dresden* sunk, 14 Mar.; *Lusitania* torpedoed, 7 May; *Königsberg* destroyed in Rufiji River, 11 July.
1916: Germans bombard Lowestoft, 25 Apr.; battle of Jutland, 31 May; H.M.S. *Hampshire* with Kitchener aboard mined off Orkneys, 5 June; Allies bombard Athens, 1 Sept.; blockade of Greece, 19 Sept.
1917: Suffolk coast bombarded, 26 Jan.; Germans begin unrestricted submarine warfare, 1 Feb.; H.M.S. *Swift* and *Broke* figure in a destroyer action in the Channel, 23 Apr.; Ramsgate shelled, 27 Apr.; first U.S. destroyers arrive, 3 May; British naval success in Kattegat, 2 Nov.
1918: Germans bombard Yarmouth, 14 Jan.; British blocking attack on Zeebrugge and Ostend, 22–23 Apr.; another on Ostend, 9–10 May; German naval meeting at Kiel, 10 Nov.; Allied fleet passed through Dardanelles, 12 Nov.; German fleet surrenders, 21 Nov.

Armistices and Treaties
Armistices: Central Powers—Russia, 29 Nov. 1917; Rumania—Central Powers, 7 Dec. 1917; Central Powers —Ukraine, 9 Feb. 1918; Allies— Bulgaria, 29 Sept. 1918; Allies —Turkey, 30 Oct. 1918; Allies— Austria- Hungary, 3 Nov. 1918; Allies— Germany, 11 Nov. 1918.
Peace Treaties: Brest-Litovsk, between Russia and Germany, 2 Mar. 1918; preliminary peace between Rumania and Central Powers, Buftea, 5 Mar. 1918; ratified, 7 May 1918; annulled at Versailles, 1919. Versailles, signed by the Allies and Germany, 29 June 1919; ratified in Paris, 10 Jan. 1920. Saint-Germain, between Allies and Austria, signed, 10 Sept. 1919; ratified in Paris, 16 July 1920. Trianon, between Allies and Hungary, signed, 4 June 1920. Neuilly, between Allies and Bulgaria, signed, 27 Nov. 1919; ratified in Paris, 9 Aug. 1920. Sèvres, between Allies and Turkey, signed, 10 Aug. 1920 (never ratified). Lausanne, between Allies and Turkey, signed, 24 July 1923; ratified, autumn 1923.

World War II 1939: Germany invades Poland, 1 Sept.; Britain, New Zealand, Australia, and France declare war on Germany, 3 Sept.; Canada and S. Africa declare war: Russia invades Poland, 17 Sept.; Poland partitioned between Germany and Russia, 28 Sept.; *Royal Oak* sunk in Scapa Flow, 14 Oct.; Anglo-Turkish pact, 19 Oct.; U.S. 'Cash and Carry Act' repeals the arms embargo, 4 Nov.; Russia invades Finland, 30 Nov.; battle of the River Plate, 13 Dec.; *Admiral Graf Spee* scuttled, 17 Dec.
1940: *Altmark* incident, 17 Feb.; Russo-Finnish Peace, 13 Mar.; Reynaud French Premier, 20 Mar.; Germans attack Denmark and Norway, 9 Apr.; Germans invade the Low Countries, 10 May: Churchill forms coalition government, 10 May; Dutch Army surrenders and German victory at Sedan, 15 May; Belgian Army surrenders, 28 May; Dunkirk

evacuation, 26 May–3 June; British evacuate Norway and Italy declares war on Allies, 10 June; Spain seizes Tangier and Germans enter Paris, 14 June; French reject British offer of union and Pétain becomes Premier, 16 June; French surrender, 22 June; Russians seize Bessarabia from Rumania, 28 June; Rumania denounces Anglo-French guarantee, 1 July; British disable the French fleet in N. Africa at Oran, 3 July; Italians invade the Sudan, 4 July; Vichy breaks off relations with Britain, 5 July; British closes Burma road, 18 July; Lithuania annexed by U.S.S.R., 3 Aug.; Italians invade British Somaliland, 4 Aug.; U.S.S.R., annexes Estonia and Latvia, 5 Aug.; battle of Britain, 8 Aug.–6 Sept.; Vienna award dismembers Rumania, 30 Aug.; British obtain 50 destroyers from U.S.A. in return for bases in W. Indies, 2 Sept.; beginning of the London blitz, 7–8 Sept.; Italians invade Egypt, 13 Sept.; British attack on Dakar fails, 25 Sept.; the 'New Order' Pact (Germany, Italy, Japan), 27 Sept.; Germans occupy Rumania, 7 Oct.; Italy attacks Greece, 28 Oct.; Italian fleet severely damaged by British air attack at Taranto, 11 Nov.; blitz on Coventry, 14 Nov.; Wavell opens victorious offensive against Italians in N. Africa, 8 Dec. (till 8 Feb. 1941).

1941: Italian forces placed under German control, 20 Jan.; Germans occupy Bulgaria, 9 Feb.; Britain breaks off relations with Rumania, 10 Feb.; British capture Mogadishu, 26 Feb.; Bulgaria joins Axis, 1 Mar.; U.S. Lease-Lend Act becomes law, 11 Mar.; Rommel's counter-attack in Libya begins, 24 Mar.; General Simovic overthrows pro-Axis government in Yugoslavia, 27 Mar.; British naval victory over Italians at Cape Matapan, 28 Mar.; Rashid Ali's pro-Axis revolt in Iraq, 3 Apr.; British capture Addis Ababa, 5 Apr.; Germans invade Yugoslavia and Greece, 6 Apr.; Germans capture Sollum, 26 Apr.; Athens, 27 Apr.; Hess flies to Scotland, 10 May; Italians surrender at Amba Alagi, 19 May; German conquest of Crete, 19 May–1 June; H.M.S. *Hood* sunk, 24 May; *Bismarck* sunk, 27 May; British and French occupy Syria, 8 June–14 July; Germany invades U.S.S.R., 22 June; U.S.A. occupies Iceland, 7 July; British and Russians occupy Iran, Aug.–1 Sept.; Reza, Shah of Iran, forced to abdicate, 16 Sept.; Germans reach Leningrad, 4 Sept.; capture Kiev, 19 Sept.; second British offensive in Libya, 18 Nov.; final Italian surrender in Ethiopia at Gondar, 27 Nov.; Three- Power Conference at Moscow, 29 Nov.; Japanese attack Pearl Harbor, 7 Dec.; Japanese occupy Thailand and invade Malaya, 8 Dec.; H.M.S. *Prince of Wales* and *Repulse* sunk, 10 Dec.; Japanese take Guam and Axis declare war on U.S.A., 11 Dec.; Hitler takes immediate command of German Army, 19 Dec.; Japanese take Wake Island, 23 Dec.; Hong Kong, 25 Dec.

1942: United Nations Pact at Washington, 1 Jan.; Japanese take Manila, 2 Jan.; Japanese naval victory in Macassar Straits, 23–25 Jan.; Japanese invade Burma, 8 Feb.; capture Singapore, 15 Feb.; Rangoon, 8 Mar.; Java, 10 Mar.; American raid on Tokio, 18 Apr.; fall of Corregidor, 6 May; Japanese naval victory in the Coral Sea, 7–11 May; second German offensive in Libya opens, 12 May; first 1,000-bomber raid (on Cologne), 30 May; battle of Midway, 3–6 June; Japanese attack Aleutians, 3 June; Gen. Eisenhower C.-in-C. U.S. forces European theatre, 25 May; Germans reach El Alamein, 1 July; Germans take Sevastopol, 2 July; Americans attack Guadalcanal, 7 Aug.; British raid on Dieppe, 18–19 Aug.; first all-American air raid on Europe, 17 Aug.; Germans enter Stalingrad, 5 Sept.; British victory at Alamein, 23 Oct.–3 Nov.; allied landing in N. Africa, 8 Nov.; Germans occupy Vichy France, 11–12 Nov.; Russian counter-offensive at Stalingrad begins, 19 Nov.; French fleet scuttled at Toulon, 27 Nov.; Germans driven from Agheila, 13 Dec.; Russian victory at Kotelnikovo, 29 Dec.

1943: Casablanca Conference, 14–26 Jan.; British take Tripoli, 23 Jan.; Russians take Voronezh, 25 Jan.; final German surrender in Stalingrad, 2 Feb.; Gen. Eisenhower allied C.-in-C. N. Africa, 6 Feb; Russians take Kursk, 8 Feb.; Americans finally clear Guadalcanal, 9 Feb.; battle of the Bismarck Sea, 1–3 Mar.; battle of the Mareth, 21–29 Mar.; Allies take Tunis, 7 May; Axis surrender in N. Africa, 13 May; breaching of Möhne and Eder dams by R.A.F., 18 May; Allies take Pantelleria, 11 June; Allies conquer Sicily, 9 July–7 Aug.; Mussolini resigns, 25 July; Russians take Orel, 4 Aug.; Kharkov, 23 Aug.; Mountbatten becomes allied C.-in-C. SE. Asia, 25 Aug.; Allies land in Italy and Italy surrenders, 9 Sept.; allied landing at Salerno, 9 Sept.; Russians take Bryansk, 17 Sept.; Smolensk, 25 Sept.; Kiev, 6 Nov.; Allies allowed to use Portuguese Azores bases, Oct.; Americans capture Tarawa, 21–25 Nov.; Cairo Conference, 22–26 Nov.; Teheran Conference, 26 Nov.–2 Dec.; U.S.A. and Britain give aid to Tito, 20 Dec.

1944: Ciano executed, 11 Jan.; Russian offensive in Leningrad area begins, 15 Jan.; allied landings at Nettuno and Anzio, 22 Jan.; Americans capture Kwajalein, 1–6 Feb.; battle of Cassino, 1 Feb.–18 May; Japanese defeat in Manipur, 13 Mar.–30 June; Russians reach Polish and Rumanian frontiers, 2 Apr.; capture Sebastopol, 9 May; Allies enter Rome, 4 June; allied landings in Normandy, 6 June; flying bomb attacks on London begin, 15 June; break- through at St. Lô, 27 July; Polish rising in Warsaw begins, 1 Aug.; battle of the Falaise gap, 7–23 Aug.; allied landings in S. of France, 15 Aug.; Allies capture Paris, 24–25 Aug.; Brussels, 3 Sept.; Americans take Palau Island, 15 Sept.–13 Oct.; battle of Arnhem, 17–26 Sept.; Russians invade Hungary, 6 Oct.; Americans invade Philippines, 20 Oct.; decisive Japanese naval defeat in Philippine Sea, 23–25 Oct.; armistice with Bulgaria, 28 Oct.; British land on Walcheren, 1 Nov.; last German offensive in the Ardennes, 16–22 Dec.; Hungary changes sides, 30 Dec.

1945: Russians take Warsaw, 11 Jan.; Yalta Conference, 4–11 Feb.; Russians take Budapest, 13 Feb.; Turkey declares war on Germany and Japan, 23 Feb.; Americans cross the Rhine at Remagen, 7 Mar.; Russians denounce the neutrality pact with Japan, 5 Apr.; President Roosevelt dies, 12 Apr.; Russians occupy Vienna, 13 Apr., and reach Berlin, 21 Apr.; Russians and Americans meet near Torgau, 26 Apr.; Mussolini shot, and German plenipotentiaries in Italy sign terms of surrender, 29 Apr.; Hitler's death announced, 1 May; Berlin surrenders and armistice in Italy effective 2 May; German forces in NW. Europe surrender, 5 May; all German forces surrender, 7 May; Americans capture Okinawa, 21 June; atomic bomb on Hiroshima, 6 Aug.; Russia attacks Japan, 8 Aug.; atomic bomb on Nagasaki, 9 Aug.; Japan surrenders, 14 Aug.; Japanese forces in China surrender, 9 Sept.; in SE. Asia. 12 Sept.

Peace Treaties

1946: Between Britain and India on the one hand, and Thailand on the other. Between Australia and Thailand. Between France and Thailand.

1947: Between the Allies and the German satellites, signed and ratified, namely with Italy, Hungary, Rumania, Bulgaria, and Finland (the U.S.A. had not been at war with the last of these).

1951: Between Japan and forty-eight allied countries.

1955: Between Austria and the Allies.
* Up to 1985 there had been no all-German peace treaty. The Western powers terminated the state of war with Federal Germany in 1951; the U.S.S.R. did the same in 1955.

Worms, on the site of a Roman town Borbetomagus, was the capital of the Burgundian kingdom from A.D. 416 to 444. More than 100 Imperial Diets met in W., including those of 1122 and 1521 (*see* next two articles). Except for one cathedral (the oldest external parts of the present structure date from 1110, some internal parts of the structure built 1000–25) the whole town was destroyed by the French, 1689. Ceased to be an Imperial Free City, 1801, and became part of Hesse, 1815. An episcopal see, 614–1801.

Worms, Concordat of, 1122, abolished lay investiture of bishops and abbots in favour of election by cathedral chapter.

Worms, Edict of. Luther was summoned before the imperial Diet and was warned by Spalatin against entering W. His writings were recognized, but he had to remain in hiding. He was put under an imperial ban, 26 May 1521.

Writers to the Signet. Scottish law agents corresponding to English solicitors; by an Act of 1868 they prepare all crown writs.

Wroclaw, Poland, formerly **Breslau.** Bishopric, tenth century, and from 1163 capital of a duchy of Silesia. Destroyed by Mongols in the thirteenth century, but rebuilt by German settlers, and joined Hanseatic League. Acquired by the Hapsburgs, 1526. Jesuit College founded 1702. Captured by Frederick the Great, Jan. 1741, and became part of Prussian territory. University established, 1861. Extensively bombed in World War II and besieged by Russians for 9 weeks in 1945. Conceded to Poland for occupation by Yalta (*q.v.*) Conference. German inhabitants driven out 1945–6, and name Wroclaw superseded that of Breslau.

Wroxeter. *See* URICONIUM.

Württemberg, Germany. War between W. and the Swabian cities, 1377–88. Formation of Swabian League, 1488. W. raised to a dukedom, 1495. Ulrich Duke of W. expelled from W. by Swabian League, 1519. W. sold to the Emperor Charles V by Swabian League, 1520. Ulrich restored, with French support, 1534. Napoleon made W. into kingdom, 1806, which endured until 1918. Joined the S. German Zollverein, 1828–31. Joined the Prussian Zollverein, 1833. Fought Prussia in alliance with Austria, 1866. Fought against France, 1870. Joined German Empire, 1871. Combined with Baden in a south-western province of the German Federal Republic, 1950.

Wyatt's Insurrection, 1554. A futile revolt led by Sir Thomas W. the Younger (1521?–54), in opposition to the marriage of Queen Mary with Philip of Spain. He collected forces in Kent, marched to Blackheath, 29 Jan.; entered Southwark, 3 Feb.; then marched to Kingston, 6 Feb.; through Kensington to Hyde Park, 7 Feb.; by Charing Cross to Ludgate, turned back, and was arrested at Temple Bar, 8 Feb.; beheaded on Tower Hill, 11 Apr.

Wyoming, explored by Spaniards in the seventeenth, and French in the eighteenth centuries, was first entered by an American, John Colter, 1807. Part of it was acquired by the U.S.A. in the Louisiana Purchase, 1803, part from the British Oregon territory, 1846, part ceded by Mexico, 1848, and part annexed (with Texas), 1854. The first woman state governor in the U.S.A. took office in W., 1925. Admitted to the Union, 1890.

X

Xanthica. Named after Xanthicus, a month in Macedonian calendar, corresponding to Apr.; it was a military festival instituted 392 B.C.

Xanthus, Asia Minor. Twice sustained sieges which ended with the self-destruction of the inhabitants; first by the Persians under Harpagus (c. 546 B.C.), and secondly by the Romans under Brutus (43 B.C.).

Xenon. Discovered by Sir William Ramsay (1852–1916), 1898.

Xeres or **Jerez,** SW. Spain. The word sherry is the English corruption of X. Roderic, the last Visigothic king of Spain, was killed here by the Saracens in 711.

X-rays. Discovered by Professor Wilhelm Konrad von Röntgen (1845–1923) in 1895.

Y

Yacht. The word was used in England in the forms yeaghe, yoathe, etc., from 1557. Charles II had a Y. named *Mary*. The first Y. club was the Cork Harbour Water Club, 1720.

Yakutsk, Siberia. Celebrated for its great trade in furs; founded in 1632; now capital of Yakut Republic in U.S.S.R.

Yale University. The third oldest university in the U.S.A.; founded in 1701 by ministers selected by the churches of New Haven county. Took the name of Yale College, 1718, after Elihu Yale (1648–1721), its great benefactor, Charter, 1745. Known as Y.U. since 1887.

Yalta Agreement concluded allied conference, 4–11 Feb. 1945.

Yanaon. A former French settlement in India, founded, 1750; after many vicissitudes it was restored to France in 1815. Administration transferred to India, 1954; treaty of cession, May 1956.

'Yankee'. Used in Cambridge, Massachusetts, c. 1713, as a term of excellence. Derived by Thomas Anburey, 1789, from *eankee*, Cherokee for slave or coward; by J. G. E. Heckewelder, 1818, from Red Indian pronunciation of the word *English*. But possibly a Dutch diminutive of *Jan*: the personal name *Janke* is found in the Calender of State Papers, Colonial Series (1898), under date 1683. Derisively applied to the New Englander by British troops during the War of Independence; by the Confederates to the Union troops during the Civil War.

Yarkand. Chief town of Chinese Turkestan (Sinkiang); visited by Marco Polo, 1271, and by the Portuguese Goes, 1603; little known till Adolf Schlagintweit visited it in 1857.

Yellow Fever. First authentic account from Barbados, 1647. Cause discovered by Walter Reed, 1901. A preventive serum began to be used, 1919.

Yellowstone National Park, Wyo., U.S.A. Occupied by Sheepeater Indians when area was first visited by John Colter, 1807. First received publicity through account of Henry D. Washburn, surveyor-general of Montana, 1870. Made a public park and game preserve, 1872.

Yemen (*Arabia Felix*) settled before 1000 B.C. Conquered by Moslem tribes, A.D. 631; by Turks, 1517. Imam Yahya became independent of Turkish rule, 1918. Imam Yahya and the two emirs, his sons, murdered, Feb. 1948. Another son, the Emir Saif-el-Islam Ahmad ibn Yahya, succeeded, Mar. 1948. Imam Ahmad *d.*, 19 Sept. 1962, and a week later there was a republican revolt in Y. led by army officers: civil war between republicans and royalists followed. By 1968 the republican regime held effective control of the whole of the Y. Fighting between Y. and the Yemen People's Democratic Republic (*q.v.*) took place sporadically from 1979.

Yemen People's Democratic Republic, estab. 30 Nov. 1967 and comprises the former federation of S. Arabia and Aden (*q.v.*).

Yeomanry (British). Mounted volunteers. First units organized under Volunteer Act of 1794; served in the S. African War in Imperial Y. battalion, 1899–1901; merged in Territorial Force, 1980.

Yeoman of the Guard. A king's bodyguard instituted, 1485; the oldest professional military body in England; properly called Y. Warders of the

Tower, they were nicknamed 'Beef-eaters' *c.* 1669; their services, originally most comprehensive, are now largely ceremonial.

Yeti. *See* ABOMINABLE SNOWMAN.

Yezidis. A sect dwelling in Kurdistan, Armenia, N. Iraq, and the Caucasus; their sacred book is Al-Yalvah, interpreted by Sheikh Adi *c.* 1200.

Yokohama. A Japanese seaport on W. of Tokyo Bay. Opened to foreigners, 1859; it was then little more than a village. Silk and tea are the chief exports. Three-quarters of the town destroyed by the earthquake of 1 Sept. 1923. Heavily bombed by Americans, causing severe damage, 1945.

York Archbishopric of. Date of foundation of the see uncertain: probably *c.* 625. Independent till subordinated to Canterbury by papal decree, 1073. Scottish bishops asserted independence from 1176.

Following are the dates of investiture of the Archbishops of York:

Paulinus 625
Wilfrid I 664
Cead 664
Bosa 678
John of Beverley 705
Wilfrid II 718
Egbert 732
Ethelbert 766
Eanbald I 780
Eanbald II 796
Wulfsige ? 812
Wigmund 837
Wulfhere 854
Ethelbald 900
Redewald *c.* 928
Wulfstan *c.* 931
Osketyl 958
Oswald 972
Ealdulf 992
Wulfstan II 1003
Aelfric 1023
Kinesige 1051
Ealdred 1060
Thomas I 1070
Gerard 1101
Thomas II 1109
Thurstan 1119
William 1143
Henry Murdac 1147

Roger 1154
Geoffrey 1191
Walter Gray 1215
Sewal de Bovil 1256
Godfrey 1258
Walter Giffard 1266
Wm. Wickwain 1279
John le Roman 1286
Henry Newark 1298
Thos. Corbridge 1300
Wm. Greenfield 1306
Wm. Melton 1317
Wm. Zouche 1342
John Thoresby 1352
Alex. Neville 1374
Thos. Arundel 1388
Robt. Waldby 1397
Richd. Scrope 1398
Henry Bowett 1407
John Kemp 1426
Wm. Booth 1452
Lawrence Booth 1476
Thos. Rotherham 1480
Thos. Savage 1501
Christopher Bainbridge 1508
Thos. Wolsey 1514
Edward Lee 1531
Robt. Holgate 1545
Nicholas Heath 1555
Thos. Young 1561
Edmund Grindal 1570
Edwin Sandys 1576
John Piers 1589
Matt. Hutton 1595
Tobias Mathew 1606
George Monteigne 1628
Samuel Harsnett 1628
Richd. Neile 1632
John Williams 1641
Vacant 1650–60
Accepted Frewen 1660
Richd. Sterne 1664
John Dolben 1683
Thos. Lamplugh 1688
John Sharp 1691
George Neville 1464
Sir Wm. Dawes Bart. 1714
Lancelot Blackburne 1724
Thos. Herring 1743
Matt. Hutton 1747
John Gilbert 1757
Robt. Hay Drummond 1761
Wm. Markham 1777
Edward Harcourt 1807

Thos. Musgrave 1847
Chas. Thos. Longley 1860
Wm. Thomson 1862
Wm. Connor Magee 1891
Wm. Dalrymple Maclagan 1891
Cosmo Gordon Lang 1908
Wm. Temple 1929
Cyril Forster Garbett 1942
Arthur Michael Ramsey 1956
Fredk. Donald Coggan 1961
Stuart Blanche 1974
John Stapylton Habgood 1983

York, City of, England (Lat. **Eboracum**). In Roman times the headquarters of the IXth Legion till A.D. 120; thereafter of the VIth. Hadrian visited Y., 120. Severus *d.* at, 211. Constantine the Great proclaimed Emperor at, 306. Captured by the Deiran Angles, *c.* 520. Edwin of Northumbria baptized by St. Paulinus at, 627. First cathedral *c.* 625. Present structure built between 1070 and 1472. Stormed by Penda of Mercia and Cadwallon the Welshman, 653. Renowned as a seat of learning in the eighth century. Sigtrygg Ivarsson (*d.* 927), Danish King of Y., 921. Y. burnt by William I, 1068. Council of the North established at, 1537. Besieged by Parliamentarians, 1644. Renewed prosperity due to growth of railways after 1850. University of Y. opened, 1963. Major excavation of Viking Y., 1978–83.

Yosemite Valley, U.S.A. Discovered, 1851. Made a national park, 1866.

Young Men's Christian Association, founded 1844 by Sir George Williams (1821–1905). World Alliance of Y.M.C.As. established, 1855.

Young Plan. Despite the Dawes Plan (*q.v.*), Germany stopped paying reparations, etc. 1929. A committee of experts sat in Paris, 11 Feb. 1929, and one of their number, Owen D. Y. (*d.* 1962), of U.S.A., propounded a plan that they accepted, 7 June. With modifications made at The Hague, 31 Aug. 1929 and 20 Jan. 1930, it was signed there by fifteen nations, 20 Jan. 1930. The Y.P. was to have given place to the 'Lausanne Settlement' in June 1932; but reparation in payments had ceased for good by June 1931, and in 1932 all hope of them was abandoned.

Young Women's Christian Association, founded, 1855. Independent English branches amalgamated, 1887. World Y.W.C.A. established, 1894.

Youth Hostels Association of England and Wales formed, 1930. Scottish and N. Ireland Y.H.A. formed, 1931.

Ypres, medieval capital of W. Flanders. Cloth Hall built, 1201–1342. Belgian since 1830. Belonged to France between 1678 and 1715 and between 1794 and 1814; to Holland, 1814–30. Menin Gate memorial built, 1927. *See* BATTLES.

Yucatan, Mexico. Discovered, 1517.

Yugoslavia. (For previous history *see* SERBIA, MONTENEGRO, BOSNIA, CROATIA, SLOVENIA, MACEDONIA, etc.) King Nicholas of Montenegro deposed and Montenegro united with Serbia, 29 Nov. 1918. Yugoslav kingdom under the Serbian monarchy proclaimed, 1 Dec. 1918. D'Annunzio seizes Fiume for Italy, 12 Sept. 1919. Treaty of Rapallo with Italy gives Zara to Italy and makes Fiume independent, 12 Nov. 1920. Italy annexes Fiume, 9 Mar. 1924. King Alexander murdered at Marseilles, Oct. 1943; succeeded by Peter II and Regent Paul. Y. joins Axis, 25 Mar. 1941; Simovic coup, 26–27 Mar.; Paul flees and Peter assumes full powers; German invasion, 6 Apr. and official Yugoslav resistance ends, 17 Apr. 'Independent' Croatia formed and house of Savoy offered crown, 18 May; Dalmatia annexed to Italy, 21 May. *See* WORLD WAR II for events 1941–45. Underground resistance effective by end of 1941 but hampered by existence of two rival groups, under Mihailovic and Tito respectively. After 1944 the W. gave support exclusively to Communist Tito and country effectively under his control when war ended. Federal Republic proclaimed, 29 Nov. 1945; trial and execution of Mihailovic for alleged war crimes and treason, June–July 1946; internationalization of Trieste (*q.v.*) accepted, 3 Sept.; Archbishop of Zagreb imprisoned for war crimes, Oct. (but conditionally released 1951); ex-king and family deprived of nationality and property,

Mar. 1947; peace treaty with Italy. Bitter conflict begun between Y. and Soviet Russia, 1948; U.S. supplied massive credit as Y. isolated by Eastern bloc; harshness of régime relaxed. New constitution, 1950; Tito elected president and visits England; in 1954 Y. a party to the Trieste Agreement. Relations with Russia improved but Y. retained independent position after relations with Russia resumed, 1962. From 1960s onwards there was considerable liberalization of régime and a tourist boom from W. Europe. Tito *d.* 1980 and régime became more restrictive as economy faltered.

Yukon, Canada. Organized as a separate territory, 1898. Klondike gold rush, 1896–8.

Addenda

Z

Zadar (Serb.-Cr.) or **Zara** (It.), capital of Dalmatia, taken from Byzantine Empire by Venetians c. 990, from which time till 1409 Z. alternated between Venetian and Hungarian sovereignty; captured and then bought by Venetians, 1409. Became Austrian, 1797, then part of Illyrian kingdom (see ILLYRIA), 1809–13, then again Austrian. Ceded to Italy, 1918, and to Yugoslavia, June 1947.

Zagreb (Serb.-Cr.) or **Agram** (Ger.). Capital of Croatia from 1867, ceded to Yugoslavia by Hungary, 1918. Seat of (Hungarian) diocese, 1093, from which period the still extant Kaptol (fortified Old Town) dates.

Zaire, African republic, formerly known as the **Congo**, or **Belgian Congo**, became independent of Belgium, 30 June 1960. The colony originated with annexation of Congo Free State (q.v.) 1908. Katanga (q.v.) province declared itself independent of the government in Leopoldville (Kinshasa) and the central government appealed for U.N. help, 11 July 1960. U.N. troops arrived in Z.,·15 July. Army coup, 15 Sept. Premier Lumumba kidnapped by Katanga tribesmen and murdered, Feb. 1961. In Jan. 1963 President Tshombe of Katanga formally agreed to Katanga's reintegration into Z. From 1964–65 Tshombe was premier of Z. Dismissed by Kasavubu, Oct. 1965: in Nov. 1965 Kasavubu deported by Mobutu, who took over the govt. New constitutions, 1968, 1978, consolidated role of Mobutu as president.

Zambesi. The first European to explore the Z. was Livingstone in 1851–3.

Zambia, formerly **Northern Rhodesia**. Capital moved from Livingstone to Lusaka, 28 May 1935. Part of Federation of Rhodesia and Nyasaland (q.v.), 1953–63. Federation dissolved, Dec. 1963. Became republic within the Commonwealth under the name of Zambia, 24 Oct. 1964, with Kaunda as president. Trouble with the Lumpa Church, 1965. One-party rule estab., 1972.

Zante Island, Greece (ancient *Zacymthos*), traditionally belonged to Ulysses. Peopled by Achaeans c. 1390 B.C. Naval base for Athenians in Peloponnesian War. Attacked by Lacedaemonians, 430 B.C. Headquarters of Dion's Syracusan expedition, 357 B.C. Seized by Philip V of Macedon, 217 B.C. Taken by Romans, 211 B.C., but restored; annexed by Rome, 191 B.C. In A.D. eleventh century it passed to the Norman kings of Sicily. After the twelfth century it belonged at different times to despots of Epirus, emperors of Constantinople, and counts of Cephalonia. In hands of Tocco family, 1357–1482; then Venetian possession till ceded to France, 1797. Briefly occupied by a Russo-Turkish fleet, 1799; then British till ceded to Greece, 1820.

Zanzibar, E. Africa. Mentioned by Arab writers, 1328; fell into hands of the Portuguese in fifteenth century, and taken by Turks in seventeenth century; proclaimed a British protectorate, 1890. Slavery abolished, 1897. On 10 Dec. 1963 Z. became an independent state within the Commonwealth. A left-wing revolt in Jan. 1964 deposed the Sultan, and a republic was declared. In April 1964 Z. united with Tanganyika (q.v.) in a single state, subsequently named Tanzania (q.v.).

Zend-Avesta. The book of the religion of Zoroaster; mentioned by Hermippus in the third century B.C.

Zeppelin. *See* AIRSHIPS.

Zeta, or **Zero Energy Thermonuclear Assembly,** came into operation at Harwell, Berks., Aug. 1957.

Zimbabwe, formerly **Rhodesia**, earlier **Southern Rhodesia**. Named after Cecil Rhodes (1853–1902), who founded the British South Africa Co.; chartered 1889. The company administered both Northern and Southern Rhodesia until 1923 when Southern Rhodesia received responsible (white) self-government. After dissolution of Federation of Rhodesia and Nyasaland (*q.v.*), Rhodesian whites' demand for independence increased. Talks with Britain broke down and on 11 Nov. 1965 the Rhodesian premier, Smith, made a unilateral declaration (U.D.I., *q.v.*), of Rhodesia's independence. Britain did not recognise this and unsuccessfully imposed exchange and trade sanctions. A republic was declared in 1970. Economic difficulties, plus increasing black resistance to white rule, led by Nkomo and Mugabe, 1970–80, amounting to virtual civil war, led to the Lancaster House talks in London, 1979. U.D.I. was ended and Rhodesia became the Republic of Zimbabwe, under Mugabe, with black majority rule, on 18 Apr. 1980. Z. increasingly run on Marxist lines since then.

Zinc. Used in early times as a component of brass (referred to by Pliny); known to the ancients only in the carbonates and silicates called calamine. The word Z. first used by Paracelsus; and described by Libavius in 1597.

Zinoviev Letter, The. Allegedly sent by Zinoviev, head of the Comintern (*q.v.*) on 15 Sept. 1924, to Russian *chargé d'affaires* in London, advising agitation for a violent revolution in Britain. Published in London press, 25 Oct. 1924, just before General Election; possibly helped cause a Labour defeat.

Zionism. Congress of Basel, 1897, convended by Theodor Herzl (1860–1904), author of *The Jewish State*, 1896, who founded organization with headquarters first in Vienna, but from 1904 to 1911 in Cologne under David Wolfssohn (*d.* 1914). Practical work begun by actual purchase of land in Palestine, 1908, financed by Jewish National Fund, which was founded, 1901. Organization moved to Berlin for period, 1911–14. Balfour Declaration, 2 Nov. 1917, prompted by Chaim Weizmann (1874–1952) and Nahum Sokolow (1861–1936). The organization from 1917 to 1929 was identical with the Jewish Agency for Palestine, but thereafter other bodies participated in the agency. *See* ISRAEL and PALESTINE, MODERN.

Znaim, or **Znojmo,** Moravia. Founded, 1226, by Ottakar I of Bohemia. The armistice between Napoleon I and the Archduke Charles was concluded here after the battle of Wagram, 1809.

Zodiac, Signs of the. Names assigned by Anaximander *c.* 560 B.C.

Zollverein (*Customs Union*), term used especially of those economic alliances binding various German states between 1818 and 1871.

Zoological Nomenclature. First applied with any accuracy by Linnaeus in his *Systema Naturae*, the first sketch of which appeared in 1735.

Zoological Society of London. Founded, 1826. Gardens opened, 1828. Royal charter, 1829. Whipsnade Park opened, 1931.

Zoroastrianism. Founder Zoroaster lived *c.* 800 B.C. Z. became national religion of Persia *c.* 550 B.C. to *c.* A.D. 650.

Zouaves. French African infantry. First corps raised in Algeria, 1831; saw service outside Africa for first time in Crimean War (1855).

Zuider Zee, Holland. Formed by series of storms in the thirteenth and fourteenth centuries. Bill to reclaim passed, 1918. Work on dam begun, 1924. Completed and name of Z. Z. changed to Ijssel Meer, (*q.v.*) 1932. Reflooded by Germans, 1944, but largely reclaimed by the end of 1945. Flooding caused by high tides and storms, Jan.–Feb. 1953. Reclamation complete in 1980's.

Zululand. Annexed by Britain, 1887; annexed to Natal, 1897.

Zulus migrated southwards to the hinterland of Delagoa Bay during seventeenth century, and overran Natal, 1823, under King Chaka (*b.* 1783), who was murdered by his brother, Dingaan, who succeeded him, 1829. After Dingaan's defeat at Blood River (1838) by the Voortrekkers (*q.v.*) he was deposed by his brother Umhanda (Jan. 1840), and fled to Swaziland, where he was murdered. Civil war, 1856, won by Cetewayo, who succeeded his father Umhanda, 1873. Boundary dispute between Cetewayo and the Transvaal Republic (later Colony) led to Zulu War of 1879. Cetewayo captured and deposed, 27 Aug. 1879. Restored by British, 1882; *d.* of wounds, 1884. His son Dinizulu led a rebellion, June–Aug. 1888, and was exiled, but allowed to return by the Natal Government, 1898. His son, King Solomon, *d.* 1933, when the throne became vacant until the ap-pointment by the S. African Government of Cyrian Bhakuzulu (*b.* 1924) in Mar. 1952.

Zürich, Switzerland. Canton revised its constitution, 1336, and joined Swiss Everlasting League, 1351. Its subjects made free citizens of the Empire in 1262, granted complete autonomy within the Empire, 1400. Joined Helvetic Republic, 1798.

Zutphen, Holland. Sir Philip Sidney killed at battle of, 1586. Taken by Spaniards, 1587. Recovered by Dutch, 1591.

Zwinglianism. Followers of Swiss reformer Ulrich Zwingli (1484–1531). Now known as Swiss Evangelical Church. Since their defeat at the battle of Kappel, 1531, Zwinglian influence has been confined to Zürich and neighbouring cantons.

CHRONOLOGY OF EVENTS

30,000 BC *to the present day*

Date	History, Politics & People	Economics & Sociology
c.30000 BC	Last Ice Age: Old Stone Age Culture. First men reach N. America by land bridge then existing across Bering Sea.	
c.15000 BC	Men reach S. America.	
c.10000 BC	Middle Stone Age—nomadic societies.	Bows and arrows in S.W. Asia.
c.9000 BC	Beginning of New Stone Age (Neolithic) in S.W. Asia—start of more fixed agricultural society.	
c.8000 BC		
c.7000 BC	Evidence of first occupation of Jericho site.	Mud-brick building in Mesopotamia and grain being grown there.
c.4999–4500BC	Sumerians in Lower Mesopotamia (cf. carbon-dating of settlement remains).	Boomerang in Australia. Grain being grown in Mexico.
c.4449–4000BC	New Stone Age culture reaches Mediterranean. Foundation of Ur as permanent settlement.	
c.3999 BC– **3500** BC	Sumerians settle on historic site of Babylon.	

Religion, Education & Philosophy	Science, Exploration & Technology	Music & the Arts
		Earliest known surviving paintings, France/Spain.
	Copper being used.	
		Pottery in Japan.
	Boats with sails in Egypt.	Saharan rock paintings. Flutes & lyres in Egypt. Painted pottery in Mesopotamia.
	Start of Julian Calendar (4241 BC).	
	First map, on clay, showing R. Euphrates. Copper alloys used by Egyptians & Sumerians. Gold & silver smelted. Beginning of Jewish calendar (3760 BC). By 3500 BC, bronze alloys in Egypt & Sumeria.	

Date	History, Politics & People	Economics & Sociology
c.3499– 3000 BC	Sumerian civilisation at peak. 1st and 2nd Dynasties in Egypt (till 2780 BC). Historic Jericho being settled by 3000 BC.	Sumerian urban society, using the wheel, with a fixed agricultural base.
c.2999– 2500 BC	Phoenicians settle on Syrian coast. Semitic tribes in N. Assyria. Old Egyptian Kingdom, 3rd–6th Dynasties (2780–2270 BC). China: 'Sage King' period begins.	Lake dwellings in central Europe. Sumerians using coins, instead of grain, for trading.
2499– 2000 BC	Semitic tribes settle in Palestine: Abraham leaves Ur about 2000 BC. Sargon establishes empire in Mesopotamia 2350–2100 BC. Yao and Shun Dynasties in China (till 2205 BC). Hsia Dynasty (2205 till 1766 BC). Early Minoan civilisation in Crete. Indus civilisation in India. End of Old and beginning of Middle Kingdom in Egypt, 11th and 12th Dynasties (2100–1788 BC). Dynasty of Pharaohs, 2200–525 BC.	
1999– 1500 BC	Hittites unite in one kingdom. Rise of Persian Empire. Rise of Babylonian Empire. End of Egyptian Middle Kingdom. Shang Dynasty in China (1766–1122 BC). Bronze Age in Western Europe.	Legal Code in Babylon (under Hammurapi).
1499– 1000 BC	Mycenaen culture in Crete. Bronze Age in Scandinavia. Ganges culture in India. Building of Chiapa de Carzo, earliest known settlement in Mexico. Israelites leave Egypt for Canaan: Saul first king (1002–1000 BC). Demise of Babylonian Empire: foundation of Assyrian Empire under Tiglath-Pileser 1 (c.1120 BC). Trojan War: destruction of Troy (c.1184 BC).	Phoenicians principal trading power in Mediterranean: establishing chain of trading ports.

Religion, Education & Philosophy	Science, Exploration & Technology	Music & the Arts
	Potter's wheel in Sumeria. Mayan chronology: first date 3372 BC.	Cuneiform in Sumeria.
Fertility religions (based on mother-goddess dominate): in Egypt, Pharaoh regarded as a god-king.	Foundations of astronomy in Egypt, Assyria and China. Iron first manufactured.	Evidence of Sumerian poetry. In Egypt, building of the Great Sphynx of Gizeh and the Cheops Pyramid.
Resurrection doctrine propounded in Egypt (cult of Isis and Osiris).	Papyrus used in Egypt. Cotton being grown in Peru.	Libraries in Egypt. Script changes from Sumerian to Semitic style.
	Mercury used in Egypt. Irrigation to harness Nile floods. Geometry highly developed in Babylon.	Dancing used in Cretan religious ceremonies. Trumpets in Denmark. First palace at Mycenae: first at Knossos. Start of Stonehenge.
In Egypt Akhnaton establishes Monotheism, 1385: old gods re-established by successor, Tutankhamen. Ten Commandments brought down from Sinai by Moses: reassertion of Jewish Monotheism.		Harp developed in Egypt. Sculpting of head of Nefertiti: building of Abu-Simbel Temple. Erection of Cleopatra's Needle. Building of existing Stonehenge. Early Greek alphabet at Knossos. First Chinese dictionary

Date	History, Politics & People	Economics & Sociology
	19th Dynasty in Egypt (1350–1200 BC): Memphis made capital. 20th Dynasty in Egypt (1200–1090 BC): decline begins. 21st Dynasty: 1090–945 BC. Ethiopia independent of Egypt.	
999–900 BC	Under kings David and Solomon (1000–925 BC). Israel at height of power: Jerusalem capital. Decline follows.	Hut-culture in S. California.
899–800 BC	Teutonic tribes begin moving west across Europe.	
799–700 BC	Estruscans enter Italy. Rome founded (traditionally, 753 BC). Gk. settlements in S. Italy. Tiglath-Pileser III (745–727 BC) founds Nineveh: Assyria conquers Hittites, Israelites, Egypt and Judah. Celtic migration to Britain.	Olympic Games first dated at 776 BC: may have existed earlier. In Israel, prophets attack social and moral abuses.
699–600 BC	Assyrian tyranny: Babylon, Thebes & Memphis destroyed. Medes, Babylonians and Scythians destroy Nineveh: Assyrian Empire ends, 612 BC. Judah made tributary by Nebuchadnezzar II: 'The Babylonian Captivity'. Rise of Gk. city-states.	
599–500 BC	Rise of Persian Empire under Cyrus II 553–529 BC: conquest of Lydia, Medea, Babylonia (Israelites freed and repatriated) and Egypt. Rome a republic, 510 BC.	Sophisticated banking system in Babylon.

Religion, Education & Philosophy	Science, Exploration & Technology	Music & the Arts
		has 40,000 characters. Temple of the Sun, Teotihuacan, Mexico. 'Gilgamesh Epic' written down (c.1200 BC).
Pantheism in India. Classical paganism fully developed in Greece.	Sophisticated mathematics in China.	Temple of Hera, Olympia. Solomon builds Temple at Jerusalem: origins of Hebrew literature and religious music in present forms.
Early Jewish prophets: temporary reversion to paganism suppressed by Elijah.		*Iliad* and *Odyssey* written (Homer).
Jewish Messianic prophecies.	10 month calendar established in Rome. Hallstatt culture in Europe using horses and wheel.	'Book of Songs' contains earliest known Chinese poetry. Sumerian hymn found on cuneiform tablet. Gk. music permeating general as well as religious life.
Dracon's Code in Athens, 621 BC. Zoroastrianism in Persia. Brahminism in India.	Sophisticated irrigation schemes in Nineveh. Kaleus sails through Straits of Gibraltar.	Famous library at Nineveh. End of Indian Vedas. Age of Gk. classical literature begins: Sappho, Alcaeus etc. Building of Acropolis begun at Athens.
Confucianism in China. Buddhism in India. Peak of Delphic influence in Gk. religion. Solon's Laws promulgated in Athens, 594 BC.	Phoenicians, patronised by Egyptian Pharaoh, circumnavigate Africa. Babylonian astronomy starts applying modern calculation methods. Gk. mathematical progress—Pythagoras.	At Jerusalem, Temple rebuilt. Gk. art & literature flourish: Aesop, Aeschylus etc. Theatre built at Delphi: and at Ephesus. Gk. music influenced by Pythagoras and Pindar.

Date	History, Politics & People	Economics & Sociology
499–450 BC	Etruscans reach height of power in Italy: formation of Latin League, led by Rome, starts Etruscan decline. Ionian War 499–94 BC. Persian Wars with Greek states, 490–449 BC: Thermopylae, 480: Persian fleet destroyed at Salamis, 480: start of Persian decline. Athens becomes ascendant state. Rise of Pericles 462.	Paid civil service in Athens c.460 BC.
449–400 BC	Continued Roman expansion in Italy, except where Gk. colonies exist (in S.). Spartan challenge to Athens leads to Peloponnesian War (431–404) leading to Athenian defeat and Spartan supremacy.	
399–350 BC	Retreat of Ten Thousand under Xenophon 400 BC. Coalition of cities against Sparta leads to Spartan overthrow 371. Rise of Macedon under Philip (352–336). Rome sacked by Gauls, 390 BC. 30th (last native) Dynasty in Egypt, 380–341 BC. In Mexico, Indian dominance ends.	
349–300 BC	Philip of Macedon dominates Greece after Chaeronea, 338: his son Alexander crushes Persia, occupies Jerusalem, Babylon etc., invades India, 327, dies 323 when his Empire divided among his officers. In Italy, Samnite Wars 343–41 and 327–04 increase Rome's power. Egyptian dynasty founded by one of Alexander's generals, Ptolemy Soter, will last till Cleopatra.	
299–250 BC	Third Samnite War 298–290: Etruscans submit to Rome. Most of S. Italy subject to Rome by c.260. First Punic War 264–41 ends in stalemate between Rome and Carthage.	First public gladiatorial fights in Rome (264 BC).

Religion, Education & Philosophy	Science, Exploration & Technology	Music & the Arts
Continuing flowering of Gk. philosophy & learning under Sophocles, Pythagoras, Socrates. Twelve Tables of Roman Law, 451–450 BC.	Carthaginian exploration of W. African coast.	Temple of Castor and Pollux, Rome, 484 BC. Gk. literature flourishes: Aeschylus, Pindar, Herodotus, Euripides. Further musical development under Pindar. Gk. theatre flourishes.
The Torah, basis of Jewish morality, written.		Rebuilding of Acropolis in Athens, with sculptures, including 'Elgin Marbles' by Phidias.
Age of Plato and Aristotle in Greece.	Hippocrates revolutionises Gk. medicine.	Beginning of theatre in Rome.
Alexandria now a centre of Gk. learning.	Pytheas reaches Britain c.325. First Roman coins, c.340. Appian Way started, 312. Euclid's geometry, 323.	'Hellenic' period in art and letters. Aristotle defines musical theory.
Septuagint (Old Testament in Gk.) written.	Gk. medical theory and practice spreads to Rome.	Colossus at Rhodes completed, 280. 'New Comedy' literature in Greece. Sun Temple in Mexico (Teotihuacan) built.

Date	History, Politics & People	Economics & Sociology
249–200 BC	2nd Punic War 218 ends in defeat of Hannibal at Zama, 202. Gks. ally with Carthage.	Chinese rationalise weights and measures: build Great Wall of China, c.220–210. Romans build first prison, c.245.
199–150 BC	Rome conquers N. Italy: in wars against Greece, conquest of Macedon at Pydna, 168, marks start of Roman Empire. Revolt of the Maccabees, 167.	Foreign slaves become basic part of Roman economy after Gk. subjugation.
149–100 BC	Third Punic War 149–46 ends in total destruction of Carthage and Greece subjugated. By 133 BC, Roman Empire has 8 Provinces, including two Spains, Africa and Asia Minor. Decline of democracy in Rome.	Social and moral decadence in Rome exemplified in writings of Sallust etc.,
99–50 BC	Civil war in Roman Republic from 90: culminates in First Triumvirate under Caesar, Pompey and Crassus, 63. Wars in Spain and Gaul. Caesar invades Britain, 55 and 54. All Gaul subjugated by 50. Pompey conquers remainder of Syria and Palestine by 60.	Foreign and native slaves now a cornerstone of Roman economy, in Italy and elsewhere.
49 BC–0	Civil war in Rome: Caesar crosses Rubicon, 49: de facto dictator, 45: murdered, 44. 2nd Triumvirate, 43 ended by Octavian's Egyptian victories and suicide of Mark Anthony and Cleopatra, 31: Egypt absorbed in Empire and Octavian (Augustus) becomes Emperor (Caesar) 30. Herod king of Judaea, 40: Judaea annexed by Rome, 6.	Foreign troops used in increasing numbers in Roman armies.

Religion, Education & Philosophy	Science, Exploration & Technology	Music & the Arts
Chinese classical philosophy ends with death of Sun Tsi (233). Asoka's Laws in India.		Beginnings of classic Roman literature with Plautus and Ennius.
Jews persecuted by Antiochus IV: this leads to Revolt of Maccabees, 167.	Water wheel used in irrigation.	Roman theatre flourishes under Plautus and Terence.
		Venus de Milo dates from this period.
Caesar writing his Histories.		Great age of Roman oratory—Cicero.
Jesus probably born in Bethlehem, 4 BC.	Julian Calendar adopted.	Age of Virgil, Horace and Ovid. Roman Pantheon begun, 27.

Date	History, Politics & People	Economics & Sociology
1–50	Roman Army destroyed in Teutoburg Forest, German, by Arminius, 9. Roman annexation of Mauretania, 41–2: of Britain, 43–45: capture of Caractacus. Goths advance W. across Vistula.	
51–100	Emperor Claudius (poisoned 54) succeeded by Nero (suicide, 68). Boudicca's rebellion in Britain, 61. Under Trajan (98–117) Empire reaches greatest limits: German frontier fortified, 96, in attempt to stem Teutonic advance. Jewish revolt: Jerusalem destroyed, 70.	
101–50	Emperor Hadrian (117–38) visits Britain: Hadrian's Wall built 122–6.	
151–200	German invasion of Italy, 161: beginning of serious praetorian involvement in imperial choice, 193. Romans attempt subjugation of Scotland, but forced to retreat behind Hadrian's Wall, 180.	Plague sweeps Roman Empire 160–80
201–50	Goths invade Asia Minor and Balkans, 220. Roman citizenship extended to all freeborn subjects, 212. End of Han Dynasty in China 220: start of period of Three Kingdoms.	
251–300	Defeat of Valerian by Persia, 260. Goths reach Black Sea, 255, but defeated by Romans at Nish, 269. First partition of Empire into East and West by Diocletian, 285.	

Religion, Education & Philosophy	Science, Exploration & Technology	Music & the Arts
Jesus baptized by John the Bapt st, probably 27: crucified outside Jerusalem, probably 30. St Paul starts his mission, about 45, and Christianity begins to organise into a church.		
First Roman persecution of Christians starts, 64; executions in Rome of St. Peter (first Pope) and St. Paul. Four Gospels probably written down in this period. Ming Ti, Chinese Emperor, introduces Buddhism to China.		
Christianity, as an underground religion, spreads throughout Roman Empire.		Tacitus writes his *History*. Earliest known Sanskrit inscriptions in India.
Neo-Platonist philosophy dominates schools of learning. Pope (bishop of Rome) achieves predominant position in Christian church.	Ptolemy draws his maps of known world.	Cultural revival in Rome under Emperor Marcus Aurelius 161–80. Oldest Mayan monuments.
Increased persecution of Christians: martyrs now being named as saints: catacomb burials.	Diophantus of Alexandria writes algebra textbook.	
Mani, founder of Manichaenism, crucified, 277.		Diocletian's palace at Ragusa (modern Dubrovnik) built.

Date	History, Politics & People	Economics & Sociology
301–350	Constantine the Great becomes Emperor, 309: reunites Empire. Makes Constantinople capital, 330. Is baptized on deathbed 337 having tolerated Christians from 313. Empire again split, 340. First Gupta Emperor of N. India, 340.	Constantine forbids public gladiatorial combat.
351–400	Scottish invasion of Britain 360 defeated by Romans, 368. Theodosius the Great reunites Roman Empire, 392: permanently divided into East and West, 395. Visigoths under Alaric ravage Greece, 396: pressure growing on W. Empire from all sides and first evacuations from Britain c.390. Defence of W. Empire in hands of Germanic generals. Japanese historical records begin, 400.	Theodosius bans Olympic Games. Non-Romans control civil service and military commands.
401–50	Visigoths invade Italy, 401: Alaric sacks Rome, 410. Visigoths settle in Gaul, Vandals and Suevi in Spain, 415–23. Vandals in N. Africa, 429–42, establish a kingdom there. Romans abandon Britain c.429: renounce all responsibility for defence, 446. Raids by Germanic tribes: Romano-British withdrawal westwards, decay of Roman urban civilisation and abandonment of Christianity except in extreme west.	
451–500	End of Roman Empire in West, 476: Odoacer king of Italy till 489, then country ruled by Theodoric the Ostrogoth. Permanent Anglo-Saxon settlements in Britain: but advance westward temporarily halted by Romano-British victory at Mount Badon c.500. Clovis founds Frankish Merovingian dynasty, 481, becomes Christian, 496.	

Religion, Education & Philosophy	Science, Exploration & Technology	Music & the Arts
Edict of Milan: Christianity tolerated in Roman Empire, 313. Council of Nicaea, 325, condemns Arianism. First St Peter's, Rome, built.		
Attempt by Julian the Apostate to revive paganism in Empire fails, 361–3. Caves of Thousand Buddhas founded in Kansu, 360. Books replacing scrolls.		Hymns introduced into Christian worship by St Ambrose, 386.
St Augustine writes *City of God*, 411. St Patrick's mission to Ireland c.432. Goths and Vandals adopt Arian Christianity.	Alchemy begins: search for 'Philosopher's Stone'.	Mausoleum at Ravenna, 446.
First schism between East and West Christians begins, 484 (till 519). Armenian Church secedes, 491. First Shinto shrines in Japan, 478.		

Date	History, Politics & People.	Economics & Sociology
501–20	Death of Clovis the Great, 511: Frankish kingdom divided between his four sons. Wu Ti Emperor of China, 517.	
521–40	Death of Theodoric, Ostrogoth king of Italy 526. Accession of Justinian I as Byzantine Emperor 527: his general Belisarius quells internal revolts, conquers Vandals in N. Africa and Ostrogoths in Italy 533–40. Totila the Ostrogoth regains Italy, 540. Persia enjoys renaissance under Chosroes I (531–79). Arthur of Britain said to have been killed, c.538.	
541–60	Byzantines under Narses regain Italy 552–5. Frankish kingdom reunited under Clothair I, 558. Ethelbert becomes king of Kent c.560. Beginning of Turkish and Slav migration westwards.	Plague from Middle East reaches Constantinople and spreads west, 542. Silk made a state monopoly in Byzantium 553.
561–80	Byzantines driven from N. Italy by Lombards, 565–8. Frankish kingdom partitioned into 3, 567. War with Persia, 572 (till 591).	
581–600	Whole of Spain a Visigothic kingdom by 585. Ethelbert of Kent baptized by St Augustine, 597: Kent becomes Christian. Tibet emerges as a single state. End of century marks end of Teutonic invasions in West.	Plague in Europe dying out (estimated to have cut population by one third or over).

Religion, Education & Philosophy	Science, Exploration & Technology	Music & the Arts
End of 1st Schism between E. and W. churches. Buddhism reaches central China.		Century of Celtic literary and artistic achievement.
Justinian closes Athens University, 529: his first Law Code promulgated. Boethius executed for treason, Rome 524. Benedictine Order founded by St Benedict at Monte Cassino, 529.		St Sophia's, Constantinople, built. Tombs of Theodoric and Gallia Placida at Ravenna. Poetry flourishing in Wales. Earliest pagoda at Honan, China.
St David preaching in Wales, 550.		Zenith of Byzantine art and literature.
Buddhism introduced to Japan. Birth of Mohammed, 571. St Sophia consecrated, 563. St Columba establishes monastery at Iona, 563, begins converting Picts.		
First Buddhist monastery in Japan, 587. Visigoths and Lombards became Catholic. Pope Gregory sends Augustine to England, 596: he baptizes Ethelbert of Kent, 597. Irish missionaries in France.		

Date	History, Politics & People	Economics & Sociology
600–19	Revived Persian Empire spreads: overruns Palestine, Syria and Egypt 614–19.	
620–39	First Norse raids on Irish coast. Byzantine defeat Persians at Nineveh, 627: Persia in decline. Advance of Arabs, bringing with them Islam, from 632: they conquer Persia, Syria, Egypt and Armenia.	
640–59	End of Persian Empire, 641: Arabs impose Islam which replaces Zoroastrianism as Persian religion. Arabs spread to Mediterranean: capture Cyprus 649. In England, heathen Penda of Mercia killed by Oswiu, 655.	
660–79	Ommayads become caliphs, 660: Arabs begin conquest of N. Africa, 670. Bulgarian Empire on Danube c.668 recognised by Byzantium, now threatened from west and east.	
680–99	Franks united again under Pepin, 687: Clovis III king of Franks, 691. Growing power of Wessex in S. England. N. Africa conquered by Arabs, 697.	First Arab coinage, 695.

Religion, Education & Philosophy	Science, Exploration & Technology	Music & the Arts
Irish missions in N. England: Switzerland: Italy. Mohammed's vision on Mount Hira, 610.		Isidore of Seville compiling Roman and Greek classics. Height of Egyptian Coptic Art. Chinese artists settle in Japan.
The Hegira, 622: Mohammed's flight from Mecca to Medina. Start of spread of Islam over Asia Minor. In Byzantium, start of Monothelite controversy, 622. Spread of Christianity in Northumbria, East Anglia and Wessex.	622 is Year 1 in Moslem calendar.	Sutton Hoo ship burial, England, c.624–5, shows high quality of Anglo-Saxon art.
Arabs destroy School at Alexandria: library dispersed. Whitby Abbey founded, 656.		Dome of Rock in Jerusalem begun, 643.
Synod of Whitby, 664: Christian Britain adopts Roman, not Celtic, Christianity.	'Greek fire' first used against Arabs at siege of Constantinople 673–7: first weapon of modern warfare.	
Anglo-Saxon missionaries travel to Europe.		Great period of Anglo-Saxon Christian art and literature begins: poet Caedmon and historian Bede flourished.

Date	History, Politics & People	Economics & Sociology
700–19	Caliphate of Walid I: Arabs invade Spain across Straits of Gibraltar and kill last Visigothic king, 711, and by 718 control of all Spain except north-west corner. Leo III of Byzantium withstands Arab siege and defeats their fleet, 718. A Moslem state established in India (Sind).	Jews in Spain, previously persecuted, enjoy toleration and cultural revival under Islamic rule.
720–39	Arabs cross Pyrenees and capture Narbonne, 719; sweep north till blocked by defeat by Charles Martel at Tours, 732.	
740–59	Byzantium defeats Arabs, 745: Lombards take Ravenna from Byzantium, 751. Caliphate of Cordoba founded, 756. End of Merovingians in France: Franks recover Narbonne, 759. Abbasids overthrow Ommayads, 750. Arabs intervene in Chinese affairs, 751.	
760–79	Increased power of Tibet a threat to China. Charlemagne unites Franks, 771, subdues Saxony, conquers Lombardy, but defeated by Basques at Roncevalles, 778. Offa of Mercia leading English king, 780.	
780–99	Empress Irene defeat Iconclasts, 780: takes sole power, 797. Charlemagne extends power in Germany and Italy. Slav tribes cross Oder. 1st Viking raids on Britain about 790: Lindisfarne sacked, 793, Jarrow 794.	

Religion, Education & Philosophy	Science, Exploration & Technology	Music & the Arts
Christianity virtually eradicated in N. Africa (except Egypt).		Earliest Islamic art. Cultural revival in China: first Japanese history written.
Iconoclast controversy in Byzantium, 726–842), leads to excommunication of emperor, 730. Germany converted to Christianity by St Boniface (from England).		Chinese music develops 5-note scale.
Islam divides into 4 sects, 751.	Science and medicine flourish in Moslem Spain.	Gregorian Church Music in W. Europe: music school at Fulda, 746.
York the major seat of European learning under Alcuin. Islamic purge begins, 775. Christian Nestorian missions in China.		Book of Kells in Ireland: Chinese poetry flourishes. Arabs begin translation of Gk. classics.
Empress Irene defeats Iconoclasts, 780.	Arabs develop chemistry as distinct from alchemy.	Golden period of Arab culture under Haroun al Rashid: Building of the Great Mosque at Cordoba begins, 785. Charlemagne patronises arts: builds chapel at Aix la Chapelle.

Date	History, Politics & People	Economics & Sociology
800–19	Charlemagne crowned first Holy Roman Emperor by Pope Leo III at Rome, Dec 25, 800. Dies, 814. Emperor Nicephorus killed by Bulgars, 811. Iona sacked by Vikings, 802.	Growth of feudalism in W. Europe. W. European unity does not survive death of Charlemagne.
820–39	End of Mercian supremacy in England: king of Wessex 'overlord of the Heptarchy' 829. Danish raids on England increase. Arabs take Sicily, Sardinia, Crete and invade S. Italy.	
840–59	Slav confederation in central Europe c.840. Treaty of Verdun, 843, divides Frankish Empire. Arabs sack Rome, 846. Vikings found Dublin c.840: plunder Rouen and reach Paris, 841. Rurik, a Viking, from Sweden, invades Russia: his descendants found Kiev, 864. Other Vikings raid Mediterranean.	
860–79	Viking power extends: they sack Paris, Cologne and Aix: start settling permanently in England and found Viking kingdom at York c.865; Alfred of Wessex defeats them at Edington, 878 and Vikings accept Christianity in return for control of E. England, 'the Danelaw'. Vikings found Novgorod, 862. Decline of Tibetan power.	
880–99	Permanent separation of France and Germany, 887. Magyars settle in Hungary, c. 889. Under Alfred, united England becomes major power in Europe.	Alfred establishes a navy and a militia.
900–19	In England, Danelaw reconquered, 900–25. In Spain, beginning of Christian Reconquest under Alfonso III of Castile. Rise of Fatimids in Egypt.	Growth of castles in W. mainland Europe as power bases of kings and nobles.

Religion, Education & Philosophy	Science, Exploration & Technology	Music & the Arts
	School of Astronomy at Baghdad.	Doge's Palace in Venice started.
Harold of Denmark, baptized at Mainz, returns to propagate Christianity in Scandinavia.	Ptolemy's System translated into Arabic.	Founding of St Mark's, Venice, 828.
	Arabs perfect astrolabe.	First attempts at polyphonic music. 'Edda' poem cycle written down c.855.
SS Cyril and Methodius start conversion of Slavs, 864 and invent Cyrillic alphabet. English Vikings accept Christianity, 878. Much original Arabic philosophy.	Iceland discovered c.870. High period of Arabic medicine.	Angkor Thom, Cambodia, started c.865.
		Anglo-Saxon Chronicle traditionally started by Alfred the Great. Chinese and Japanese cultures separate about this time.
10th century a low-point in papal authority: many scandals 904–74. Abbey of Cluny founded, 910.		*Thousand and One Nights*—Arabian stories – begin to appear.

Date	History, Politics & People	Economics & Sociology
	Rome in almost permanent state of civil unrest during this century. Vikings settle in N. France: Rollo 1st duke of Normandy 912.	
920–39	Holy Roman Emperor Henry I makes gains in E. and N. Germany: subdues Bohemia. English defeat Danes and Scots at Brunanburh c.937. Civil war period starts in Japan, 937. Byzantine revival: Romanus I extends Empire to Euphrates 920–44.	
940–59	Otto I quells Bohemia and acquires Lombardy. Renewed Danish attacks on England.	
960–79	Byzantines recapture Crete and Cyprus from Arabs: victories against Bulgars from 971. Cordoba Caliphate at zenith: Sancho I of Leon pursues Christian Reconquest from 962. Renewed Viking attacks on Ireland.	
980–99	England under weak Ethelred tries to buy Danish peace by levying Danegeld (from 991). St Vladimir Prince of Kiev, 980: baptized, 988. First Viking colony in Greenland under Erik the Red, c.982.	Italy (ie cities of Venice and Genoa) doing extensive trade with Arabs.
1000–19	English massacre Danes, 1002: England overrun by Danes by 1013 and Canute King of England, 1016. At Clontarf, 1014, Norse rule in Ireland ended. Henry II (Holy Roman Emperor) campaigns in Italy, crowned in Rome, 1014. Cordoba Caliphate in decline.	Danegeld tax in England marks embryonic general taxation system.
1020–39	Henry II defeats Byzantium in Italy: Byzantine decline. Canute conquers Scotland and Norway and dominates N. Europe till death in 1035, when possessions divided between	

Religion, Education & Philosophy	Science, Exploration & Technology	Music & the Arts
Cluniac discipline, 927.	Cordoba becoming principal centre of Arab science and medicine.	
		Cluniac movement affects European architecture and art.
St Dunstan carries through monastic revival and church reform in England. Cordoba University, 968.		Great period of Icelandic literature.
Eastern Christianity introduced to Kiev area by St Vladimir, 988. Norway and Sweden become Christian. Canonisations become official.		Building of Cluny. Famous 400-pipe organ at Winchester.
Christianity spreads to Iceland and Greenland. Avicenna, Arabic philosopher, flourishes.	Leif Ericson said to have discovered N. America 'Vinland' c.1000.	English heroic poem *Beowulf* written. Art reviving in Italy but much influenced by Byzantine conventions. Music of Berno of Reichenau.

Date	History, Politics & People	Economics & Sociology
	3 sons. Poland becomes an imperial fief.	
1040–59	Rise of Seljuk Turks: Togrul Beg Shah of Persia, 1040, captures Baghdad, 1055. Edward the Confessor King of England 1042: power fluctuates between pro-Saxon and pro-Normans. Increasing power of Norman duchy vis-à-vis England and France: Normans under Guiscard found Norman kingdom, 1053, in S. Italy. Holy Roman Emperor no longer to choose Pope, 1059.	
1060–79	Seljuks conquer Armenia, Syria, Palestine and capture Emperor Romanus IV at Manzikert, 1071. Edward the Confessor dies, 1066: Harold Godwinson succeeds but William of Normandy invades and kills Harold at Hastings, Oct. 14, 1066: crowned king of England December 25th at Westminster Abbey. In Italy, struggle between Guelphs and Ghibellines begins, 1073. Emperor Henry IV does penance before Pope Gregory VII at Canossa, 1077.	Gradual imposition of Norman feudalism in England. After 1080 few great English nobles remain.
1080–99	Christians capture Toledo from Moors 1085 but Almoravids revive Arab kingdom in S. Spain, 1086. Henry IV renews quarrel with Pope: War of Investiture, 1077 (till 1122) and storms Rome.	Normans build castles in England. *Domesday Book*, 1086 (compiled for fiscal and administrative purposes).
1100–19	Baldwin I, Latin King of Jerusalem, 1100–18: Crusaders capture Acre, 1104. Beginning of colonization and forcible Christianization of E. Germany. Constant wars between England and France. Decline of Seljuk power.	
1120–39	Civil war in England from 1139, result of succession dispute of Matilda and Stephen.	Anarchy in England 1135–54: baronial excesses and

Religion, Education & Philosophy	Science, Exploration & Technology	Music & the Arts
Schism between E. and W. Churches permanent, 1054. Monasteries built around Kiev. From 1059, cardinals only to elect Popes.	Astrolabes reach Europe from E.	Building of Westminster Abbey begun. Writing of the *Mabinogion*—Welsh folk tales. Polyphonic singing replaces Gregorian chant.
Gregory VII (Hildebrand) Pope, 1073: reforms Papacy. Excommunication of married priests, 1074. Denounces Lay Investiture, 1075. Humiliates Emperor, 1077. Lanfranc and Anselm reform English Church. School of Moorish philosophy in S. Spain.	'Halley's Comet' seen.	Omar Khayam, Persian poet, flourished. Distinctive Romanesque architecture in England ('Norman').
Paris a centre of learning under Peter Abelard. First Cistercian monastery at Cîteaux, 1098.		
Era of Scholasticism in W. Europe begins.	Arabic science in decline.	*Chanson de Roland*, heroic French poem. First mystery plays performed in England. French and English languages start to emerge. Start of French Gothic architecture.
First Lateran Council, 1123, condemns simony.		Troubadours in France. Great period of English monastic chroniclers (till c.1400).

Date	History, Politics & People	Economics & Sociology
	Byzantines defeat Serbs and Hungarians: sign trade treaties with Venice. Attempts to solve differences between Emperor and Papacy inconclusive.	considerable social hardship.
1140–59	2nd Crusade begins, 1146: fails, 1147. Henry II, son of Matilda, king of England 1154: by marriage to Eleanor of Acquitaine, England controls more of France than the French king. Henry imposes strong rule, leading to clashes with Church under Becket, Archbishop of Canterbury. End of Toltec Empire, Mexico, c.1150.	
1160–79	Quarrel between Henry II of England and Becket begins, 1163, ends with Becket's murder, 1170: Henry does penance, 1174. Wars with Queen Eleanor and with France. Byzantium defeats Seljuks, 1176: Barbarossa allies with Venice against Byzantium. Saladin conquers Egypt and Syria.	Sophisticated exchequer system organised by Normans in England.
1180–99	Quarrel between Emperor and Papacy recommences. Florence an independent republic, 1198. Third Crusade, 1189–93: joined by Richard I of England who is imprisoned by the Emperor 1192–4. Saladin d.1193 at height of power. Second Mayan culture in S. America.	
1200–19	Rise of Genghiz Khan: he seizes Peking, 1214 and conquers Persia, 1218. Pope places England under Interdict, 1208 and excommunicates King John, 1209; baronial revolt leads to him signing Magna Carta at Runnymede, 1215. John d. and Fr. invade England 1216–7. Fr. defeat England and Empire at Bouvines, 1214: Eng. territory in France diminished. Fourth Crusade, 1202–4: Constantinople sacked by Crusaders at Venetian instigation and Latin Empire established. Fifth Crusade, 1217–28. Delhi Sultanate, 1206.	'Children's Crusade' phenomenon, 1212.

Religion, Education & Philosophy	Science, Exploration & Technology	Music & the Arts
Carmelites founded, 1155. Nicholas IV, only English Pope, 1154–9. Oxford University traditionally founded c.1149.		Courtly poetry in France and Germany.
Thomas Becket murdered at Canterbury, 1170: canonized, 1173. St Francis of Assisi born, 1182. Anti-semitism in England and France. Beginning of Waldensian movement in S. France.		First eisteddfod in Wales, 1176. Walter Map systemises Arthurian legends.
Pope Innocent III 1198–1216: a reformer, anxious to reassert papal authority.		Early English architectural style. Scandinavian *Edda*: German *Nibelungenlied*: French *fabliaux*.
First Franciscan rules, 1219. Albigensian heresy growth leads to Albigensian 'Crusade' in S. France and foundation of Dominican Order to combat heresy, 1215.		Golden age of German epic poetry: von Eschenbach's *Parsifal* and von Strassburg's *Isolde*. Century of finely illuminated books in W. Europe: *Books of Hours* etc.

Date	History, Politics & People	Economics & Sociology
1220–39	Mongols under Genghiz Khan invade Russia, 1223: overrun it, seizing Moscow, 1237. Cordoba falls to the Castilians, 1236. 1238: Sixth Crusade. Moorish kingdom of Granada founded, 1238.	Leprosy arrives in Europe (from Middle East).
1240–59	At Liegnitz, 1241, Mongols defeat Germans, invade Poland and Hungary. Then abandon Europe and 'Golden Horde' settles on Lower Volga, 1242. Kublai Khan governor of China, 1251, and Mongol ruler, 1259. Yuan dynasty estab. War starts between Venice and Genoa, 1256, resulting in eventual decline of Genoese power. Seventh Crusade, 1245: Louis IX of France captured by Saracens, 1250.	
1260–79	Eighth Crusade on which Louis IX d., 1270. Misgovernment in England leads to Barons War, 1262: leader, Simon de Montfort, killed at Evesham, 1265. English possessions in France further depleted. Michael VIII Palaelogus regains Byzantium from Latins, 1261. Death of Kublai Khan, 1294.	Florence becomes world banking centre.
1280–99	Edward I of England seizes Scottish throne, 1296; moves Stone of Scone to London. Attempts to conquer Wales and Scotland. 'Model Parliament', 1295. Sicilian Vespers: Fr. massacre in Sicily, 1282. End of Crusading era: Mamelukes take Acre, 1291. Teutonic Knights subdue Prussia. Osman I, founded of Ottoman Empire, succeeds, 1288.	

Religion, Education & Philosophy	Science, Exploration & Technology	Music & the Arts
Cambridge University founded (first charter, 1231). Franciscans reach England, 1224. Inquisition against Albigensians in Toulouse, 1229; Dominicans control Inquisition from 1233.	Porcelain manufacture begins in Japan. Arab geographic encyclopaedia compiled.	
Collegiate system taking shape at Oxford, Cambridge and Paris (there by nationality). Period of English mystical writing (till c.1400). Albigensians defeated and liquidated, 1245: Inquisition officially sanctions torture.	Roger Bacon, most notable scientist of his century flourished. Recorded existence of gunpowder substance.	Start of Alhambra, Granada, and modern Cologne Cathedral. Church of St Francis at Assisi finished.
Thomas Aquinas flourished. Scholasticism at height. Flagellant movement begins in Germany, spreads to France. Roger Bacon imprisoned for heresy (1277).	Marco Polo travels to China, 1271; enters service of Kublai Khan, 1275–92.	It. art flourishes with Cimabue and Giotto. First school of mastersingers (Mainz). Motet form evolves. Dante flourished. *Lohengrin* written.
	Marco Polo returns to Italy, 1292, starts writing account of travels from prison.	Much building and art activity in Florence, financed by banking wealth.

Date	History, Politics & People	Economics & Sociology
1300–19	Edward names his son Prince of Wales, 1301: Scots defeat Edward II at Bannockburn, 1314 and regain independence. Council of Ten established in Venice, 1310. Start of Swiss struggle for independence from the Empire, 1307. Osman I defeats Byzantines, 1301.	Salic Law adopted in France, 1317, excluding women from succession to crown.
1320–39	Edward II deposed and murdered, 1327: his son Edward III claims Fr. crown and Hundred Years War starts, 1338. First Valois king succeeds in France, 1328 (Philip VI). Height of Arabic civilization in Granada kingdom. Greater Serbia founded by Stephen Dushan, 1331. Aztecs build Mexico City.	First descriptions of bubonic plague (India).
1340–59	English win battles of Crecy, 1346 and Poitiers, 1356, when Fr. king taken prisoner. Treaty of London 1359. Hapsburgs sign Treaty with Swiss League, 1358. Ottoman Turks advance into Europe, 1353. Revolution in Rome under Rienzi, 1347: Rienzi murdered, 1354. Golden Bull, 1356, establishes electoral constitution of Holy Roman Empire.	Black Death reaches Europe, decimates England, 1349–51, then reappears sporadically. Exacerbates feudal decline and social changes. Edward III founds Order of Garter, 1348.
1360–79	England allies with Burgundy, 1360 against France: truce between England and France 1375–78. Stewarts accede to Scottish throne, 1371. Ming Dynasty replaces Yuan in China, 1368. Tamberlaine ascends throne of Samarkand, 1368.	Prolonged war with France leads to unrest and breakdown of social order in England.
1380–99	In England, Peasants' Revolt, 1381, suppressed: England losing war in France. Richard II deposed and murdered, 1399: accession of Henry IV, son of John of Gaunt. Norway, Denmark and Sweden unite in Union of Kalmar, 1397.	Poll taxes levied in England—early attempt at centralized personal taxation.

Religion, Education & Philosophy	Science, Exploration & Technology	Music & the Arts
Christianity tolerated in China. Clement V establishes Papacy at Avignon, 1309, beginning of the 'Babylonian Captivity'. Templars' Grand Master burnt for heresy in Paris, 1314.	Growth of medical studies in Germany.	Building of modern Doge's Palace in Venice.
Universities being founded all over Europe during next century. John Wyclif born, 1328.		Boccaccio and Petrarch flourished. Alhambra, Granada, extended. Counterpoint music developed.
	Hundred Years War leads to development of archery, resulting in crossbow: and development of heavy cannon.	Papal Palace at Avignon built.
Scholastic debates at Oxford alarm Church. Pope Gregory XI returns to Rome: beginning of Great Schism in Church, 1378. John Hus b. c.1370.	Crossbow first used in warfare.	Growth of vernacular literature. Chaucer, Langland in England, Froissart in France. Age of great Flemish Primitive painting.
Wyclif expelled from Oxford, 1382 and doctrines condemned. Hus lectures in Prague.	Gutenberg, traditional inventor of European printing, b.c. 1395.	Wyclif's Bible in English written.

Date	History, Politics & People	Economics & Sociology
	Turkish advance continues: capture Sofia, 1382. Byzantium loses last possessions in Asia Minor, 1390. Defeated at Nicopolis, 1396.	
1400–19	Growing power of Florence and Venice. Tamerlane's conquests in Middle East, 1405 temporarily halt Ottoman threat to Byzantium. Sigismund becomes Emperor 1410: war between Empire and Hussites starts 1419 (–36): Sigismund gains Bohemia. In France, civil war between Crown and Burgundy, 1406: Joan of Arc b., 1412. Henry V of England reasserts claim to Fr. throne, invades and defeats French at Agincourt, 1415. Collapse of French forces—country devastated.	Rise of Medici in Florence: they dominate European finance: Papal bankers from 1414.
1420–39	Henry V recognized as heir to Fr. throne by Treaty of Troyes, 1420, but d. and succeeded by infant Henry VI and Regency: Fr. rally under Joan of Arc, 1427, but she is captured by Burgundians (Eng. allies) and burned at Rouen, 1431. Fr.-Burgundian peace at Arras, 1435 and henceforth English steadily driven back. Hussites defeated by Emperor: Compact of Iglau, 1436: Bohemia subjugated. First Turkish siege of Constantinople, 1422. Growth of Aztec Empire in Mexico. Inca Empire founded c.1435.	Exotic Burgundian court influences courtly life all over Europe: Order of the Golden Fleece founded, 1429.
1440–59	Turks advance into Europe: rise of the Hunyadis in Hungary, who defeat them at Varna, 1444; Belgrade, 1456. Byzantium falls to Turks, 1453 and last E. Emperor, Constantine XI, killed: end of Eastern Empire. St Sophia's becomes a mosque. Athens captured and Acropolis sacked, 1458. Eng. lose all Fr. possessions except Calais and Hundred Years War ends, 1453: Wars of Roses start, 1455. Sforzas become dukes of Milan, 1450. In Empire, Turkish raids start after Kossovo, 1448. In Bohemia, temporary Hussite revival under Podebrad (1456–71).	African slave trade to Europe begun by Portuguese. Breakdown of law and order due to civil wars and aftermath all over W. Europe.

Religion, Education & Philosophy	Science, Exploration & Technology	Music & the Arts
Height of Lollard heresy in England: burnings, 1401–19. Hus burned for heresy at Constance, 1415. Council of Constance: Martin V elected Pope in Rome, 1417: end of Great Schism. Age of Flemish mysticism: Thomas à Kempis flourished.		'Early Renaissance' period. Golden Age of Burgundian court music and arts. Froissart flourished.
Empire persecutes Hussites in Bohemia and Germany.	Beginning of era of Portuguese exploration: Cabral discovers Azores, 1431–2. Heavy guns increasingly used in warfare by Byzantines.	Fr. poet François Villon flourished.
Virtual elimination of Christianity in Asian Byzantium after 1453: Islam spreads to Turkish-occupied E. Europe. St Sophia's becomes a mosque. Pope Pius II 1458–64: 'humanist' Pope. General decline of religious orders in West.	Tristao discovers Cape Verde, 1443. Coster printing from wooden blocks, Haarlem, 1440: Constance Mass Book printed by Gutenberg (movable type) 1450.	Eton and King's College Cambridge founded by Henry VI: King's chapel begun, 1446. Vatican Library begun, 1450.

Date	History, Politics & People	Economics & Sociology
1460–79	In England, Edward of York crowned Edward IV, 1461: defeats Lancastrians and has Henry VI murdered, 1471. Turks spread to Balkans: take Bosnia and Herzegovina. 1477 marriage contract ensures future union of Burgundy and Empire. 1479: union of Castile and Leon under Ferdinand and Isabella (married 1469). Age of condottieri in Italy.	Growth of German banking: Fuggers become Hapsburg bankers.
1480–99	In England, Tudors under Henry VII replace Plantagenets after defeat and death of Richard III at Bosworth, 1485: government centralized. Charles VIII of France invades Italy, 1494–5 and Italy becomes battlefield between France and Empire for next 50 years: Brittany joined to France, 1499. Spain conquers Granada, 1492: end of Moorish rule in Spain. Marriage between Joanna of Castile and Philip of Burgundy, 1496 foreshadows union of Spain and Empire. Swiss independence ensured by Treaty of Basel, 1499. Venice seizes Cyprus, 1489: but fleet defeated by Turks, 1499 and Venice in decline.	Syphilis ravages W. Europe: brought from Naples by invading French army, 1494.
1500–19	In England, Henry VIII succeeds, 1509 and marries Catherine of Aragon: with Wolsey, tries to make England a major world power: defeats Scots at 1513. Pope confirms that German king henceforth automatically Holy Roman Emperor, 1508: attempts to reform Imperial government founder. Pope Julius II tries to drive French from Italy but Francis I conquers Milan, 1515. Archduke Charles becomes King of Spain, 1516, and Emperor (as Charles V) 1519. Empire at height of territorial power. Turkish expansion continues in East, with conquest of Egypt and Arabia. Spanish Empire in S. America founded: Cortes received by Montezuma in Mexico, 1519.	Negro slavery introduced to S. America by Portuguese c.1510.

Religion, Education & Philosophy	Science, Exploration & Technology	Music & the Arts
Beginning of Humanism in W. Europe. Erasmus born, 1465; Thomas More, 1478; Machiavelli, 1469. Inquisition moves against Jews in Spain.	Gold Coast (Ghana) discovered by Portuguese. Caxton prints first book in English, Bruges, 1474: in England, 1477. Age of invention: Leonardo da Vinci etc.	Papacy becomes major art patron.
Italian campaigns, and papal involvement in them, detract from papal spirituality. Spanish Inquisition under joint control of Crown and Church from 1481: Jews expelled from Spain, 1492, from Portugal, 1496. Puritanical rule of Savonarola in Florence. Humanism begins to verge on religious dissent.	1492, Columbus, under Spanish patronage, discovers N. American continent. 1493: Pope Alexander III divides New World between Spain and Portugal. Cabots commissioned by Henry VII to find new trade route to Asia. Revised study of algebra astronomy etc.	Explosion of artistic activity in Italy and the Empire: Leonardo, Michaelangelo, Holbein, Dürer etc.
Luther nails theses on door of Wittenberg church, 1517, marking start of Reformation— touched off by Indulgence sales. Zwingli attacking papal doctrines in Zurich, 1519. 'New Learning' flourishes in England, especially at Cambridge: More, Colet and Fisher advocate reform within the Catholic Church. Erasmus publishes New Testament with Gk. and Latin text, 1516; More writes *Utopia*.	Portuguese explore Africa and Brazil: reach China, India and E. Indies. Magellan begins voyage to circumnavigate globe, 1519. Spanish explore W. Indies, S. and central America. Copernicus states earth revolves round sun, 1512. Printing flourishing in W. Europe.	Beginning of rebuilding of St. Peter's Rome, 1513 (leads to Indulgences' sales to finance it— hence Reformation). 'High Renaissance' in Italy.

Date	History, Politics & People	Economics & Sociology
	Fluctuating international treaties mark emergence of modern doctrine of 'balance of power'.	
1520–39	Henry VIII's failure to obtain papal consent to divorce from Catherine of Aragon results in Henry declaring himself Supreme Head of the Church in England, 1531; Cranmer archbishop of Canterbury, and Henry marries Anne Boleyn, 1533. English Reformation effective from 1536: monasteries dissolved, 1536–40. Luther excommunicated, 1520, but sheltered by Ger. princes dissatisfied with Imperial rule: Protestant Union against Charles V, 1524; Prussia secularized, 1525; German Peasants' Revolt savagely put down, 1524–5; Anabaptists in Munster, 1534; suppressed, 1535. Swiss Protestant and Catholic cantons at war, 1531; Zwingli killed. Calvin in Geneva, 1536; expelled, 1538. Protestantism spreads to France, Flanders and Scandinavia. Suleiman the Magnificent succeeds, 1520: defeats Hungarians at Mohacs, 1526; besieges Vienna, 1529. Imperialists sack Rome, 1527; imperial control of papacy results in denial of Henry VIII's divorce (from Emperor's aunt), hence English Reformation. 1533, Ivan IV, the Terrible, Tsar of Russia (aged 3). End of Aztec Empire in Mexico after Cortes's victory, 1521; in Peru, Pizarro crushes Incas, 1533.	Dissolution of monasteries in Protestant countries leads to deprivation and revolts (e.g. England and Germany). Severe inflation in W. Europe. Increased fluidity of social structures, especially in England and Low Countries. Beginnings of modern nationalism and capitalism.
1540–59	War in Germany between Protestant princes and Emperor ended by Peace of Augsburg, 1555; Lutheran states to have same rights as Catholic. Charles V abdicates, 1556; Empire goes to brother Ferdinand I and Spain to son Philip II. Henry VIII d., 1547. Succeeded by Edward VI, till 1553, and extreme Protestant regime. Catholic reaction under Mary Tudor, 1553–8, with many Protestants burned. Elizabeth succeeds, 1558 and Act of Settlement establishes Church of	

Religion, Education & Philosophy	Science, Exploration & Technology	Music & the Arts
Reformation in England, Scandinavia, parts of France, Germany, and Scandinavia: ideas spread to Italy and Poland. Luther translates Bible into German: Tyndale's translation of New Testament printed abroad, 1525. Growth of Anapbaptism in German. Universities in Protestant countries secularized. Beginnings of Counter-Reformation: Jesuit Order founded by Ignatius Loyola, 1534.	Cartier discovers St. Lawrence River, 1534. Name 'America' first used by Mercator, 1538.	In Protestant countries, destruction of monastic buildings, shrines etc. but expansion of church music among Catholics and Protestants. Luther a leading hymn-writer. Use of vernacular in Scriptures encourages learning down social scale in Protestant countries.
Calvin institutes Protestant theocracy in Geneva, 1541: John Knox leads Scottish Reformation. Roman Inquisition, 1542. Index established, 1543. Spanish Inquisition burns Protestants, 1543. Council of Trent 1545–63 establishes	Chancellor visits Russia via Archangel, 1553. Spaniards penetrate S.E. of N. America. Servetus discovers pulmonary circulation of the blood, 1540.	Literary and musical renaissance in France and England: Ronsard, du Bellay in France: Wyatt, Howard, in England.

Date	History, Politics & People	Economics & Sociology
	England in modern form, 1559, the 'Via Media'. England loses Calais, 1558. Reformation in Scotland from 1541; Catholic Mary Stuart becomes Queen of Scotland, 1542. In France, Protestants (Huguenots) increasingly powerful among nobility. Peace between Venice and Turkey, 1540; between Turkey and Empire, 1545. Calvin returns to Geneva, 1541 which becomes a Calvinist theocracy till his death (1564).	
1560– 79	Civil wars of religion in France: Henry of Navarre leader of Huguenots from 1577. Massacre of St Bartholomew, 1572. Mary Stuart returns to Scotland, 1562; civil war there results in her fleeing to England, where she is imprisoned, 1567 and becomes focus for Catholic unrest. Irish rebellions against English rule; Reformation resisted in Ireland after early compliance. Duke of Alba governor of the Spanish Netherlands, 1567 and active revolt against Spain follows: Spanish sack Antwerp, 1576; England supports rebels against Spain and Drake attacks Spanish ships and W. Indies' possessions. In Russia, Ivan IV attacks power of boyars. Turkey makes gains in Mediterranean; but fleet defeated by John of Austria at Lepanto, 1571 and forced to lift siege of Malta, 1565.	Slave trade introduced to W. Indies from W. Africa by English.
1580– 99	Spain absorbs Portugal: is defeated in Netherlands where William of Orange (d.1584) becomes effective ruler of N. Netherlands (Holland), 1583. Spain intervenes in Fr. civil wars but at Peace of Vervins, 1598 renounces claims to Fr. throne: suffers increasing Eng. harassment in Netherlands, Americas and Mediterranean (e.g. Drake attacks Vigo, 1585) and Armada, sent to invade England, destroyed, 1588. Philip II d.1598 and Spain now in decline. End of Valois dynasty in France, 1589 and	In Spain, economy falls into imbalance due to bullion imports from New World: outflow of younger sons to New World to colonize S. and Central America. Inquisition in Spain stifles enterprise in all fields. Colonial acquisitions make transportation a European punishment:

Religion, Education & Philosophy	Science, Exploration & Technology	Music & the Arts
principles of Counter-Reformation. Jesuit missions in Japan and S. America. Grammar Schools founded and refounded in England under Edward VI: secular colleges at Oxford and Cambridge.		
Influx of Protestant refugees to England from Low Countries: growth of Puritanism within English Church. Counter-Reformation in Poland. Congregation of the Oratory founded by Philip Neri in Rome, 1564. Pope excommunicates Elizabeth I, 1570: first Jesuits reach England and are executed. Jesuits make many converts in Japan. Period of Spanish mysticism: St. John of the Cross, Teresa of Avila.	Francis Drake starts on voyage round world, 1577. Medical advances by Pare in France. Map-making science improves as discoveries enhance knowledge: Mercator flourished.	Shakespeare b. 1564: growth of London theatre. Evolution of distinctive Elizabethan domestic architecture and gardens.
Execution of Jesuits in England, including Edmund Campion (1581). Growth of secularist-based philosophy in Europe. Elizabeth I founds Trinity College, Dublin, 1591. Catholic revival in Ireland, linked with nationalism.	England founds Newfoundland colony, 1583; Raleigh discovers Virginia, 1584. Dutch active in E. Indies. Exploration boom leads to revolution in navigational theory and instruments. Hakluyt writes his navigational works. Galileo professor of	Shakespeare's plays being performed: Marlowe, Sidney etc. flourished. In Spain, devotional art of El Greco. Byrd (England) and Palestrina (Italy) notable for church music.

Date	History, Politics & People	Economics & Sociology
	Protestant Henry of Navarre succeeds: war continues but in 1593 Henry becomes Catholic, crowned 1594. Huguenots tolerated and peace established. Empire fights off Turkish threats, but Turks reach Hungary. Empire resists claims of a revived Poland and Protestant threats in S. Germany. England gains international status by defeat of Armada: extends influence in New World. Executes Mary Stuart, 1587 and many Catholics over period. In Japan, dictatorship of Hideyoshi 1585–98: shogunate then revived (till 1867).	in England from 1597.
1600– 19	Elizabeth I d., 1603, succeeded by James of Scotland: England and Scotland united. Spanish army helping Irish rebels surrenders, 1602: rebellion collapses and N. Ireland resettled by Protestants from Scotland and England. Gunpowder Plot, 1605. Michael, first of Romanov Tsars, accedes 1613. Growth of Sweden as military power: becomes Protestant champion in Continental Europe. Empire attempts to assert authority and maintain Catholic dominance, especially in Hungary and Bohemia: 'Defenestration of Prague', 1618 leads to outbreak of Thirty Years War (till 1648) which devastates large parts of Germany. War between Turkey and Persia, 1602 (till 1627). Jesuit state in Paraguay, 1608–11.	England and Netherlands become dominant trading nations. First negro slaves arrive on N. American mainland (Virginia, 1619). Tobacco and potatoes reach Europe. Native societies of S. and Central America being destroyed by Spanish and Portuguese. English Poor Law System founded, 1601.
1620– 39	Empire defeats Bohemia at White Mountain, 1620: Thirty Years' War then moves to Germany proper. Gustavus Adolphus of Sweden, Protestant champion, defeats Empire at Lutzen, 1632, but is killed. After Peace of Prague, 1635, France intervenes on Protestant side against Hapsburgs: start of 150 years' conflict between France and Austria. In France, Richelieu crushes Protestant revolt at La Rochelle: centralises	Period marks consolidation of power of landed gentry and successful London tradesmen in England (as opposed to Crown and large landowners – the established hereditary nobility).

Religion, Education & Philosophy	Science, Exploration & Technology	Music & the Arts
Bodley starts rebuilding library at Oxford.	mathematics at Pisa, 1589. It. interest in antiquities: catacombs (part) and Pompeii rediscovered. Archery in warfare obsolete in Europe.	
Attempts at Counter-Reformation in Scandinavia (unsuccessful) and Poland (ultimately successful). Persecution of Bohemian Protestants by Empire. Growth of Protestant dissent in England. Authorized Version of the Bible, 'King James's', published London 1611. In Spain, expulsion of Moriscoes, 1609–14.	Astronomic cooperation of Brahe and Kepler at Prague, 1600 onwards. Galileo's telescope, 1608, but G. prohibited from working by the Church after 1616. John Speed's maps, 1610. Hudson Bay explored, 1610. Harvey's discovery of blood circulation, 1619.	In Spain, more secular art: Velasquez. In Netherlands, emergence of Protestant trading houses brings a new type of art patron.
Disputes in England between High and Low Church parties. Persecution of Dissenters, leading to emigration to New England. Religious intolerance in sev. Puritan New England colonies. Harvard founded, 1638.	Dutch colonies in America: Fr. colonial growth. Kepler's teachings censured by Catholic Church. Thirty Years' War produces advances in armaments.	Building of Taj Mahal by Shah Jehan c.1630–52. Century of literary brilliance in England and France: Charles I patron of art and invites Van Dyck to England. Golden age of painting in Italy, Netherlands and Spain.

Date	History, Politics & People	Economics & Sociology
	government. James I of England d., 1625 and Charles I attempts to govern without Parliament but unrest grows on fiscal, constitutional and religious issues. First Bishops' War (against Scots), 1639. Sev. crown colonies founded in America, e.g. Virginia and Maryland in reply to Puritan foundations, e.g. Pilgrim Fathers leave Plymouth in Mayflower, 1620, to found Plymouth Colony, New England. Shah Jehan becomes Great Mogul of India, 1627.	
1640–59	Outbreak of English Civil War, 1642: initial Royalist victories but eventual defeat by Parliament and Charles I executed, 1649. England proclaimed a Commonwealth, Cromwell Lord Protector, 1653; d., 1658. Trade wars with Dutch. Cromwell defeats Royalists in Ireland; savage repression there, 1649–50. Peace of Westphalia, 1648 ends Thirty Years War: religious toleration in Germany excluding Hapsburg territories. Independence of Netherlands and Switzerland guaranteed. Fr. gains mark beginning of French hegemony in Europe. In France, Mazarin crushes power of nobility in wars with Fronde 1648–53: Louis XIV accedes, 1643. Beginning of rise of Brandenburg in N. Germany. End of Ming dynasty in China: Manchus come to power, 1644 (till 1912). Japan closed to foreigners from c.1640.	Under Bourbons, state monopolies feature of Fr. economy. Tea appears in Europe. Colonization of N. America marks start of displacement of N. American Indians. Puritan laws on Sunday observance in England.
1660–79	Restoration of Charles II in England, 1660: he attempts tolerant rule but many Catholics die in Popish Plot, 1678; he obtains Fr. money secretly after Treaty of Dover, 1670, which gives him some independence of Parliament. Peace of Oliva, 1660, recognizes Brandenburg sovereignty over East Prussia. Rise of Sweden as major power.	Great Plague in England, especially London, 1665. Great Fire of London, 1666.

Religion, Education & Philosophy	Science, Exploration & Technology	Music & the Arts
Age of Donne, Bacon, in England: Descartes in France. Christianity obliterated from Japan, 1637–40: but missionaries welcomed in China.		
Limited religious toleration in non-Hapsburg Germany after 1648. Episcopacy in England abolished under Commonwealth but Dissent tolerated and Jews tolerated by Cromwell. Rise of Jansenism in France. Quakers founded by George Fox c.1647. Descartes, Pascal, Hobbes flourished. English replaces Latin in all legal documents, 1649. Civil war controversies encourage political writing at all levels: embryonic socialism of Levellers and Diggers.	Tasman discovers Tasmania and New Zealand, 1642: parts of Australia chartered, 1644. Aggressive colonizing brings conflicts between England and Holland, England and France: Dutch settle in S. Africa, English in S. India, 1639.	Milton flourished in England. Bernini working in Rome. Charles I's art collection sold by the Commonwealth and dispersed. Destruction of English stained glass and statuary in churches and cathedrals by Puritan extremists.
Restoration of episcopacy in England. Much religious writing: Bunyan, Watts, Burnet. 1662 Prayerbook issued. Charles II fails to get official toleration for Catholics. Fr. send missions to N. American Indians.	French explore Mississippi valley. Isaac Newton flourished: Greenwich Observatory built, by Wren, 1675.	Great period of Eng. Restoration theatre: actresses play female parts for first time. Rebuilding of St. Paul's after Great Fire, designed by Wren, and many City churches. Diarists Pepys and

Date	History, Politics & People	Economics & Sociology
	Louis XIV attempts to crush Dutch from 1667; Peace of Nijmegen, 1678. Turks invade Slovakia, 1663; truce with Empire, 1664. Capture Crete from Venice, 1669. Defeated by Poles 1673. Fr. build up colonial Empire in N. America.	
1680–99	Catholic James II succeeds Charles II, 1685: defeats Monmouth but deposed in 'Glorious Revolution', 1688 which establishes William III of Orange on Eng. throne. Beginning of 'Whig Supremacy'. England becomes involved in Dutch struggle against France. William III crushes Irish Jacobite rebellion at Battle of Boyne, 1691. Turks besiege Vienna unsuccessfully, 1683; Turkish decline begins. Emperor occupies Belgrade, 1688–90. Russia under Peter the Great attacks Turkey; captures Azov, 1696. Russia becomes champion of Balkan Christians occupied by Turkey. Louis XIV revokes Edict of Nantes, 1685 and Huguenots leave France: settle especially in Prussia and England. Peace of Ryswick 1697 concludes wars with Holland.	Bank of England founded, 1691. National Debt in England begins, 1692. 'Modernization' of Russian society forcibly carried out by Peter the Great.
1700–19	Great Northern War starts, 1700; Charles XII of Sweden builds an Empire extending into Poland and Russia but defeated by Peter the Great at Poltava, 1709, captured by Turks 1713–4, killed 1718. Thereafter Sweden declines. Elector Frederick III of Brandenburg crowns himself King of Prussia, 1703. In England Act of Settlement 1701 provides for Protestant Succession: Anne rules 1702–14. Union with Scotland, 1707. George I of Hanover succeeds, 1714: unsuccessful Jacobite Rising, 1715. Charles II of Spain d. 1700: Philip V, grandson of Louis XIV, heir to Spanish throne. War of Spanish Succession, 1702–13—France against England,	Last witchcraft execution in England, 1712. Centring of court life on Versailles by Louis XIV and XV finally destroys Fr. nobility's links with peasantry and Crown's links with Paris and intelligentsia. In England coffee houses play important part in political and business life.

Religion, Education & Philosophy	Science, Exploration & Technology	Music & the Arts
Trappist Order founded, 1664. Spinoza flourished. Royal Society founded, 1660.		Marvell in England. Purcell dominated Eng. music. Louis XIV great art patron: age of Molière and Corneille. Building of Versailles, 1661–87.
Edict of Nantes revoked by Louis XIV: Huguenots leave France, 1685. Pennsylvania founded as Quaker colony, 1682. New England Salem witch-trials, 1692. S.P.C.K. founded, 1698.	Newton's theory of gravity, 1683. Calcutta founded by British, 1687. Dampier explores N.W. Australia, 1698.	
Century of 'Rationalism' and 'Reason'. Christian teaching forbidden in China, 1716. Russia expels Jesuits, 1719. Age of Locke, Leibnitz etc. Growth of news-sheets.	Newton president of Royal Society, 1703. Fahrenheit's temperature scale, 1714. Edmund Halley flourished.	Bach, Handel flourished: modern opera and oratorio evolve. In France court and country life typified by Watteau and Chardin. In England, Clarendon's *History* published (1702): Professorship of Poetry, Oxford, founded 1708. Distinctive Georgian church and country house architecture evolves.

Date	History, Politics & People	Economics & Sociology
	Empire, Prussia, Holland. Military successes by Marlborough and Prince Eugène. English take Gibraltar, 1704. Peace of Utrecht, 1713, ends war: France and Sp. Bourbons separate: Fr. military power in Europe shattered. France bankrupted by wars and court extravagance: Camisard revolt 1702–6. Louis XIV d. 1715. 1713: Pragmatic Sanction, an attempt to ensure Maria Thérèsa's succession to Empire. Empire and Russia make progress against Turkey: Turks leave Hungary, 1716; Eugène defeats Turks at Belgrade, 1716. Russia acquires Finland, 1710–11.	
1720–39	Pragmatic Sanction receives assent of major powers. Maria Thérèsa marries Francis of Lorraine, 1736 and Empire gets Tuscany, 1737. Poland increasingly unstable and intrigued against. Frederick Wm. I of Prussia builds up army. France and England quarrel increasingly over American and Indian possessions. Russian expansion halted temporarily after Peter I's death, 1725; Turkish decline also halted, they drive Imperial army back to Belgrade, 1738. Persians sack Delhi, 1739. Tibet absorbed by China, 1720.	England establishes trade links with Russia. England becomes major financial centre: South Sea Bubble crisis, 1720–1. Lloyd's list issued, from 1726. Gin drinking in England a major social evil, especially in London. Evolution of a 'prime minister' in English government (from Sir Robert Walpole, 1721 ff).
1740–59	1740: death of Charles VI and accession of Maria Thérèsa leads to War of Austrian Succession 1741–48. Francis of Lorraine elected titular emperor, 1745 and Treaty of Aix recognizes Pragmatic Sanction but Prussia keeps Silesia, captured 1741. Frederick II succeeds in Prussia, 1740: attacks Austria and gains Silesia, 1741. England allies with Austria against France and Prussia. 1756: outbreak of Seven Years War: England allies with Prussia against France and Austria. England makes gains against France in New World and India. Clive arrives in India. 1744: Black Hole of Calcutta 1756. 1759: British take	Wearing of Scottish tartans prohibited in Britain, 1746–82. Anti-semitic pogroms in Russia. Cotton being imported to Britain from E. Smuggling a major industry in Britain for next 50 years. Hambledon cricket club, 1757.

Religion, Education & Philosophy	Science, Exploration & Technology	Music & the Arts
John and Charles Wesley found Methodist group at Oxford, 1730. Papal Bull against Freemasonry, 1738. Rationalism expounded by Hume, Butler, Pope, Voltaire.	Kay patents flying shuttle loom, 1733. Glassmaking starts at Murano, 1736. Linnaeus flourished. Revolutionary husbandry system begun in Norfolk by Townshend c.1730— beginning of the Agricultural Revolution.	10 Downing St. built, 1731. Covent Garden opened (as theatre) 1732. In Italy, Vivaldi flourished.
Encyclopaedists in France: Diderot, Rousseau flourished. Frederick the Great encourages Fr. philosophers to his court: Kant writing. In England, Burke putting forward progressive views; in America, Franklin.	1752: Britain adopts Gregorian calendar. Centigrade thermometer, 1742. Fr. explorers reach Rockies. Dutch explore S. Africa beyond Orange River. Halley's comet 1758.	Sans Souci, Berlin, begun, 1745. In England, school of portrait and landscape painting: Reynolds, Gainsborough etc. Johnson leading London literary figure. Emergence of the novel in England: Fielding, Richardson etc.

Date	History, Politics & People	Economics & Sociology
	Montreal and gain Quebec from France. In England, 2nd Jacobite Rising, 1745 under Charles Stuart ends in Jacobite defeat at Culloden, 1746. Catherine (Sophia of Anhalt) marries Peter II of Russia, 1744: Russia allies ineffectually with Austria against Prussia, 1757.	
1760– 79	1762 Catherine II becomes Empress of Russia: 1st Polish Partition, 1772, between Russia and Prussia, marks start of Poland's disappearance as an independent state. Russia conquers Crimea, 1771. Peace of Paris, 1763, confirms Britain's acquisitions in America, W. Indies and India. France militarily and economically weakened. George III succeeds, 1760: Britain now has vast overseas Empire. 1765 Stamp Act for taxing American colonies passed: opposed in Britain and America ('no taxation without representation') and repealed, 1766, but friction persists and American War of Independence breaks out, 1775 in New England. England uses Ger. troops to fight colonists: France (under Lafayette) and Holland intervene on American side. In S. America, Portuguese colonies organized in one unit, with Rio de Janeiro as capital, 1776.	Canal boom begins in England. Agricultural changes multiply—drift to towns and beginning of Industrial Revolution. (Similar processes start rather later in Europe.) American Congress stops importing of slaves, 1778. Papacy starts draining Rome marshes, 1779. Social awakening in England: John Howard writes on prison reform.
1780– 99	Britain defeated in N. America: 1783, war over with Peace of Versailles: Britain recognizes independence of USA. Loyalists emigrate to Canada (Ontario). First US Congress meets, 1789 and Washington first President. In Britain, Grattan demands Home Rule for Ireland, 1780; Pitt forms ministry, 1783 but progressive policy halted by threat from Fr. Revolution after 1789. At war with France 1793–1802. Nelson destroys Fr. fleet, 1798 at Aboukir Bay. In France, economic and political unrest forces Louis XVI to recall States General, 1789: outbreak of Fr. Revolution and	First building society in Birmingham c.1780. Fr. Revolution overturns society: estates broken up, church property seized. Metric system introduced, 1795. Income tax introduced in Britain (as temporary measure), 1799. Serfdom abolished in Austria, 1781: slavery abolished in Fr. colonies, 1794.

Religion, Education & Philosophy	Science, Exploration & Technology	Music & the Arts
Jesuits expelled from several countries and Order dissolved by Clement XIV, 1773. Spread of Methodism (not yet defined as such) in England and Wales. Rousseau's *Social Contract*, 1762: Smith's *Wealth of Nations*, 1776. Amer. problems encourage liberal political thought in England: Burke, Fox, Priestley etc. General spiritual decline in Europe.	New period of discovery in Pacific: Cook discovers Botany Bay, 1770, Hawaii, 1778. De Bougainville discovers Tahiti, Solomons, and New Guinea. Age of scientific enquiry in Britain: Priestley, Watts. Watts perfects steam engine, 1776.	Revival of historical interest in Britain with Hume, Gibbon etc. Royal Academy, London, founded 1768. Hogarth painting commentaries on English social scene. Vienna becomes world musical centre with Haydn and Mozart.
Religious freedom in Empire declared by Joseph II, 1781: religion banned in France, 1793 but toleration from 1795. Revolutionary philosphies of Thomas Paine, William Godwin. Ger. philosophic school led by Kant and Fichte. Gordon Riots (anti-Catholic) in England, 1780: Catholic Relief Act, 1781.	In Britain, inventions aid Industrial Revolution: Watt's engine in Nottingham cotton mill, 1785; iron being exported from 1790s. Threshing machine, 1784. First steam-driven mill, Manchester, 1789. Cotton gin, 1793. Montgolfiers build air balloon, 1782: Channel crossed by balloon, 1785.	Growth of romanticism in music and arts: in Germany, Goethe and Schiller, in Britain, Blake and Burns. Louvre becomes Fr. national art gallery: David paints the Fr. Revolution. Beethoven's first works published: modern piano and orchestra evolves. *Times* first published under this name, 1788.

Date	History, Politics & People	Economics & Sociology
	storming of Bastille. Feudalism abolished, Republic proclaimed, 1792. Jacobins seize power, Louis tried and executed. Fr. revolutionary army declares war on Austria, Prussia and Sardinia, 1792: first Coalition against France, 1793. Reign of Terror ends with Robespierre's execution 1794 and establishment of Directory, with Napoleon as C-in-C, 1795. Napoleon's Italian victories, 1796–8: in Middle East, 1799. Directory overthrown, 1799: Napoleon Consul. In Russia, Catherine the Great conquers the Crimea, 1783. 2nd Partition of Poland, 1793; 3rd 1795: Poland absorbed by Russia, Austria and Prussia.	Malthus' treatise on population growth, 1798. Transportation to Australia from 1788.
1800–19	Holy Roman Empire officially ended, 1806. Fr. wars halt with Peace of Amiens, 1802, but war with Britain renewed, 1803. Battle of Trafalgar, 1805. France defeats Prussia, 1806. Napoleon Emperor, 1804: crowned in Paris in Pope's presence. By 1810 Napoleon controls most of continental Europe but Russian campaign fails 1812–13 and Prussian victories 1813–14 lead to Napoleon's abdication and banishment to Elba, 1814. Congress of Vienna starts, 1814. 'Hundred Days': Napoleon escapes from Elba but defeated by Allies at Waterloo, 1815 and exiled to St Helena. Congress of Vienna settles Europe along conservative lines: Swedish throne to Bernadotte. Fr. Revolution leads to independence movements in S. and Central America. Britain acquires some Fr. colonies and India almost totally British. Anglo-US war, 1812–14: White House burned by British. In England, fears of Jacobinism lead to first anti-union laws: Luddites attempt to wreck new machines, 1811–15. Corn Laws instituted, 1815: depression follows end of war. Union of Ireland with England, 1801: rebellion 1803 fails.	In Britain, Wilberforce's Act abolishing slavery passed, 1801. Rapid growth of industry in Britain: slowly spreads to France, Germany etc. Growth of modern union concept: held down initially by establishment fears of Jacobin revolution. Large-scale European emigration to N. America begins. Potato now staple Irish diet.

Religion, Education & Philosophy	Science, Exploration & Technology	Music & the Arts
Compulsory education from age of 6 in France, 1793. Finding of Rosetta Stone in Egypt makes possible deciphering of hieroglyphics, 1799.	Steamboat on Delaware, 1787. Mont Blanc climbed, 1786. Jenner introduces smallpox vaccination, 1796.	M.C.C. founded 1787.
Irish Union of 1801 does not lead to promised Catholic Emancipation. Methodism spreads in Britain, and Evangelical revival in Church of England, with social implications. Baptist Union, 1812. Evangelical Union in Prussia, 1817. Code Napoleon, 1804. Philosophy tends to discount religion. Karl Marx b.1818.	First submarine built by Fulton, 1801. Stephenson builds first practical steam engine at Killingworth Colliery, 1814. Davy's safety lamp, 1815. Much research into electricity. Source of Ganges discovered, 1808.	Elgin Marbles brought to British Museum, 1816. In Eng. literature, period of Romantic poets: Byron, Shelley, Keats, Wordsworth; novels of Scott and Jane Austen. Realist paintings of Goya contrast with general romantic trend (Ingres, Turner etc.)

Date	History, Politics & People	Economics & Sociology
	Modern Egypt established when Mehemet Ali proclaimed Pasha, 1806, marking decline of Turkey's Middle East empire.	
1820–39	Period dominated by conservative reaction in Continental Europe (Metternich), but revolts against despotism in France, Spain, Portugal and Italian states, 1830. In France Charles X abdicates 1830 and more liberal rule of Louis Philippe follows: Belgian independence and neutrality guaranteed, 1830. In England, Great Reform Act of 1832 reforms electoral system. Accession of Victoria, 1837. Canning becomes champion of Greek independence: Greek independence assured, 1827: Serbia autonomous state by 1830. In Middle East Turks lose territory to Egypt. S. American states successfully gain independence. Britain first occupies Falkland Islands, 1822. In USA, push west and south continues. Texas independent of Spain, 1836: battle of Alamo, 1836. Dutch advance N. from Cape in S. Africa: 'The Great Trek', 1836. German unity being advanced de facto by the Zollverein from 1830 onwards. Colony established, S. Australia, 1834: colonization of Australia and New Zealand begins in earnest.	Chartists flourish in England: word 'socialism' current in Europe by 1830s. Population explosion in W. Europe: cholera scourge of many industrial cities from 1830s (arriving from India). Suttee abolished in British India, 1833. Poor Law in Britain amended, drastically, 1834. Registration of births, deaths and marriages in England and Wales from 1837 (Scotland 1855, Ireland 1864). 'Penny post' in England, 1839. Anti-slavery agitation growing in USA.
1840–59	In England, Victoria marries Albert, 1840: 'Victorian Age' proper begins. Britain acquires Hong Kong after Opium War with China, 1840–2. Indian Mutiny, 1857. Aim of Britain to protect Turkey from Russian expansion—'the Eastern Question', so sides with Turkey in Crimean War, 1854–6. In Europe, 1848 year of revolution: Louis Napoleon comes to power in France (emperor from 1852). Hungary fails to win independence. Nationalist movements growing all over Austrian Empire. In Germany, Prussian	In England Whigs and Tories now generally known as Liberals and Conservatives. Repeal of Corn Laws, 1846. In Ireland, disastrous potato famines from 1846 exacerbate nationalism: population declines through starvation and emigration (to Britain and USA).

Religion, Education & Philosophy	Science, Exploration & Technology	Music & the Arts
In England, Repeal of Test Acts, 1828: Catholic Emancipation Act, 1829. Growth of Oxford Movement in Church of England. Plymouth Brethren, 1827: Seventh Day Adventists, 1831: Mormons, 1830. Philosophic dominance of Germany and Britain: Carlyle, Hegel, Ranke, Bentham. Emerson in USA.	Advances in all fields of science and invention: great strides in mechanical engineering, electricity, photography. Stockton-Darlington railway carries first passengers, 1825. Brit. industrial products widely exported: industrial revolution taking place in Germany and France and USA. Darwin's survey and expedition in S. America and Australasia, 1831–6.	Period of Beethoven's greatest work. Building of West End of London (Nash).
Growth of modern British 'public school' (many based on old foundations). Newman becomes a Catholic, 1845: Bernadette's vision at Lourdes, 1858. Doctrine of the Immaculate Conception promulgated, 1854. Socialist writings of Marx, Engels and Lasalle.	Much medical advance: Lister, Pasteur flourished. Chloroform used, 1847. Darwin's *Origin of the Species*, published 1859, revolutionised views on natural science. Railways being constructed world-wide: steam taking over from sail in ships. Growth of the electric telegraph.	Great age of the English novel begins: Dickens, Brontes, Eliot, Trollope, Thackeray etc. In France, Napoleon III patron of arts, starts reconstruction of Paris. Pre-Raphaelite school of painting in Britain. Romanticism in music: Chopin, Mendelssohn, Schubert, Schumann etc. Great period of Italian

Date	History, Politics & People	Economics & Sociology
	influence growing: German National Association formed, 1859. US-Canadian boundaries—49th Parallel —defined, 1842: USA acquires Texas, New Mexico Slavery question dominates north-south state relations: 'Battle of Harper's Ferry' (John Brown), 1859. Opening of Japan started by Perry, 1854: leads to rapid superficial westernization of Japan. China weakened by internal decay and further conflict with Britain. Africa being carved up between major European powers, especially Britain and France. Austria declining: defeated by France (champion of Italian independence) at Magenta and Solferino, 1859.	End of transportation to New South Wales, 1840. Era of industrialisation in cities of US north. First popular newspaper, *Daily News* (Dickens the editor) started, 1846, in London. Great Exhibition, London, 1851. Hospital reforms as result of Crimean experiences of Florence Nightingale.
1860– 79	Progress towards Italian unity under Piedmont and Sardinia. Garibaldi takes Palermo and Naples, 1860 and proclaims Victor Emmanuel II King of Italy. Papal troops defeated: King of Naples surrenders to Garibaldi, 1861: Italy an independent kingdom, gains Venice from Austria after 1866 war, Rome capital from 1870. Lincoln elected US president, 1860: southern states secede, 1861, and Civil War begins: Emancipation Proclamation, 1863: Lincoln assassinated 1865, war ends in Union victory and 13th Amendment abolishes slavery. Decline of Austria: after defeat of 1866 loses territory to Prussia and Italy. Rise of Prussia under direction of Bismarck: gets Schleswig-Holstein, 1864, further German territory, 1866. Franco-Prussian War, 1870 ends in Prussian victory, annexation of Alsace-Lorraine and proclamation of German Reich. France's Mexican policy 1863–7 ends in Fr. humiliation and execution of Emperor Maximilian, France's nominee, Mexico again a republic. Fr. defeat in Franco-Prussian War, 1870, leads to abdication of Napoleon III and establishment of Third Republic. Paris	Russian serfs freed, 1861: American slaves, 1865. US industrial expansion in north: south declines. Industrial growth in Europe leads to modern unionism: first TUC Congress at Manchester, 1868. Red Cross founded, 1862: Krupp starts arms production, Essen, 1861. In sport, baseball popular in USA from c.1860: All-England Lawn Tennis Championship starts at Wimbledon, 1867. Football Association, 1863. First cricket Test Match between Australia and Britain, 1877. Elementary education in Britain compulsory from 1876: moves to ameliorate working-class poverty: Salvation Army founded, 1865,

Religion, Education & Philosophy	Science, Exploration & Technology	Music & the Arts
Anticlericalism in Europe: agnostic writings of Renan etc.		opera: Verdi.
Revival of Catholicism in Britain. Doctrine of Papal Infallability, 1871. Kulturkampf in Prussia, 1871. Salvation Army, 1865: Christian Science, 1866. In philosophy, Mill, Spencer, Marx: Newman a major Catholic apologist. Historians Bagehot, Lecky, Gardiner etc. Educational progress throughout Western world: first women's colleges at Oxford and Cambridge. Church of Ireland disestablished, 1869. Modern archaeology taking shape.	Exploration continuing in Africa, Arctic and Antarctica. Pasteurization, 1864: antiseptics (Lister), 1865. Mendel's Law on heredity, 1865. Bell invents telephone, 1876; Nobel invents dynamite, 1866. Start of London Underground, 1863. Bicycles popular from 1860s. Whymper climbs Matterhorn, 1865. Horsedrawn trams in London from 1861. Celluloid invented 1865.	Russian ballet now world-famous. Opera flourishing in France, Italy, Germany, (Wagner) and Britain (Gilbert and Sullivan). First Impressionist Exhibition, Paris, 1874. Russian novel flourishes with Tolstoy, Turgenev, Dostoievsky: Strindberg and Ibsen make Scandinavian theatre world-famous. Folklore expands with Grimms and Hans Andersen. US literature and art with James, Longfellow, Whistler etc., has world acclaim. Albert Hall and Memorial built in Britain. Japanese art introduced to Europe at Paris World Fair, 1867.

Date	History, Politics & People	Economics & Sociology
	Commune, 1871. Treaty of Berlin, 1878, intended to halt Russian expansion at Turkish expense: Turkish massacre of Bulgarians, 1876. In S. Africa, friction between British and Boers: Zulu wars, 1879. Prince Albert d.1861: parliamentary reform, 1867: Dominion of Canada established, 1867: Victoria Empress of India, 1877.	Barnardo's first home in Stepney, 1866. Bank Holidays established in England and Wales, 1871.
1880–99	In Britain, further parliamentary reforms: Dock Strike, 1889, first Labour MP, 1892. Increased Irish agitation for Home Rule. In S. Africa, outbreak of Boer War, 1899. In Sudan, Mahdi takes Khartoum and kills Gordon, 1885: Kitchener reconquers Sudan, 1898. Corruption in Fr. government: Dreyfus Case begins, 1894 Spain in decline: Cuba rebels 1895 and USA supports her, defeats Spain and acquires Cuba, Puerto Rico, Guam and Philippines, 1898. Brazil a republic, 1889. First Indian National Congress, 1886: start of modern Indian nationalism. Young Turk movement formed in Geneva, 1891: Crete proclaims union with Greece, 1897 and Greece defeats Turkey. Fall of Bismarck in Germany but German arms build-up continues: attempts at late colonial expansion. Korea and Japan attack China and defeat her, 1894.	Growth of leftwing and anarchist parties in Europe. Germany pioneers social insurance for workers, 1883. Discovery of gold leads to rise of Johannesburg, 1884. Klondike Gold Rush, 1896. Local government reform in Britain: London County Council established, 1889. Death duties introduced in Britain, 1894. First modern Olympic Games in Athens, 1896. Growth of women's suffrage movement especially in Britain.
1900–09	Queen Victoria d.1901. British military successes in S. Africa, 1900–01: Boer War ends with Brit. victory, 1902: Union of South Africa, 1908. Australia a Commonwealth Dominion, 1900: New Zealand, 1907. Boxer Rising against Europeans in China, 1900; Sun Yat-Sen begins campaign against Manchus, 1905. In France, Dreyfus rehabilitated, 1906; Entente Cordiale between Britain and	Rapid growth in popularity of motorcar: first British traffic laws, 1903; first Ford T-model, 1908. Oil drilling starts in Iran, 1909. Synthetics and mass production lead to cheaper clothing, furniture etc., in W. World.

Religion, Education & Philosophy	Science, Exploration & Technology	Music & the Arts
Persecution of Russian Jews leads to emigration to Britain and USA and growth of Zionism, 1897. Fabian Society, 1883: London School of Economics, 1895. Nobel Prizes founded, 1896. Secularist philosophy dominates, interest in anthropology and sexual behaviour—Havelock Ellis, Frazer etc. Christian missions in Africa, India and Asia at height of influence.	Medical advances include rabies vaccine, 1885; phenacetin, 1887; X-Rays, 1895; radium 1898. Electric lighting from 1880s. Start of modern motorcar: Diesel internal combustion engine, 1892; Henry Ford makes first car, 1893. Marconi invents radio-telegraphy, 1895; magnetic sound recording, 1899. First airship built, 1898. World communication much improved, journey-times shortened. Mass-travel possible. Paris Metro opens, 1898. First moving pictures, New York, 1890.	Realist school of literature (Hardy, Wells, Zola etc.) exists alongside Romantics (Tennyson, Kipling, Maeterlinck). English theatre flourishes with Wilde, Pinero, Shaw. Zenith of English music hall and Fr. cabaret. Romanticism dominates music: Richard Strauss, Dvorak, Smetana, Sibelius, Elgar etc. Art nouveau influential from 1890.
Modernism in Catholic Church condemned by Pope, 1907: Jesuit reforms, 1906. Church and State in France separated, 1906. Reunion of Brit. Methodists, 1907. Anthroposophy founded by Steiner, 1901. In Japan, Shintoism reinstated, 1900.	Quantum theory, 1900; Special Theory of Relativity, 1905. First motorcycles, 1901; Rolls Royce Company founded, 1904. Typewriters in common office use: women office workers become general. Wright brothers in USA fly powered aeroplane, 1903; Bleriot flys the	Picasso's 'Blue Period': sculptors Rodin and Epstein flourished. Steel increasingly used in industrial and commercial building. Light opera flourished especially in Vienna: rag-time develops into jazz, originating in the southern USA (from New Orleans.)

Date	History, Politics & People	Economics & Sociology
	France, 1904. Lords reject Lloyd George's Finance Bill, 1909. Japan defeats Russia in war, 1904; allies with Britain, 1905. Korea a Japanese protectorate, 1907. Norway separates from Sweden, 1905. Turkey surrenders Sinai to Egypt, 1906; Turkey and Serbia recognise Austrian annexation of Bosnia and Herzegovina, 1909. Treaty on US rights over Panama Canal, 1903; US occupies Cuba, 1906–8. Russian Socialists split into Mensheviks and Bolsheviks, 1903; Potemkin mutiny and localised revolts, 1905, followed by some reforms.	Arms race between Britain and Germany accelerates. San Francisco earthquake, 1906. Boy Scout Movement founded by Baden Powell, 1907.
1910–19	In Britain, Parliament Act, 1911; suffragette violence, 1913. After World War I, women get limited vote and Lady Astor first woman MP to take seat, 1919. Home Rule for Ireland, 1914, suspended for duration of war. Rebellion in Dublin, 1916; Home rule bill abandoned, 1918. Italy defeats Turkey and annexes Tripoli and Cyrenaica, 1911: Balkan Wars 1912–13 further weakens Turkey. Revolution in China, 1911, overthrows Empire. Sun Yat-Sen president: rapid modernization and industrialization in major cities. June 1914: assassination of Franz Ferdinand at Sarajevo causes start of World War I in August: major participants, France, Britain, Russia and Japan (later Italy and USA) against Germany, Austria and Turkey. (*See Dictionary article*: World War I). 1914: Germans occupy much of Belgium, invade France: first battle of Ypres. Russians defeat at Tannenberg, 1915: war further destabilises Russia. *Lusitania* sunk by U-boat, 1915. U-boat warfare a major factor in war: first air attacks on Britain. Gallipoli, 1915–16. 1916: battle of Somme. 1917: Bolshevik revolution leads to Russo-German armistice. USA enters war on Allied side. Middle East campaigns ending in Allied	Sinking of *Titanic*, 1912, on maiden voyage. Woolworths founded, 1912. Socio-economic upheaval in W. Europe and USA as a result of World War I: diminution of class distinctions in varying degrees everywhere, and enhancement of women's position. Population imbalances as result of heavy war casualties. Keynesian economics in embryo: Keynes's *Economic Consequences of the Peace*, 1919.

Religion, Education & Philosophy	Science, Exploration & Technology	Music & the Arts
Cult of violence in philosophy: Liebknecht, Lenin, Wallas. Psychoanalysis developed by Freud and Jung.	Channel, 1909. Invention of bakelite (1908: USA) heralds age of plastics. Decade of the silent film: development of cinemas—'picture-palaces'.	
Rapid spread of Marxism after Russian revolution of 1917: attempt to suppress religion in USSR. In Germany, separation of Church and State, 1919. In Britain, Church of Wales disestablished, 1920. Philosophic advocacy of sexual freedom in Europe and USA. World War sees growth of pacifism in all participating countries, given philosophic basis by such scholars as Bertrand Russell. Non-violence adopted as a political weapon by Gandhi in India.	Amundsen reaches S. Pole, 1911; Scott, 1912. World War I results in advances in production of arms, motor-vehicles, ships and aeroplanes: and communications' systems. First helicopter flown, 1918. Poison gas first used, 1915; tanks first used (by British, on the Somme), 1916. Medical advances in treatment of serious physical injuries and mental illness: shell-shock, neuroses etc. Alcock and Brown make first flight across the Atlantic, 1919. Atom first split by Rutherford, 1919.	Modernism in art and music: Picasso, Modigliani, Matisse, Spencer: Bartok, Prokoviev. Popular spread of jazz: major composers include Kern and Berlin. War causes reaction against literary romanticism: Owen, D.H. Lawrence, Sassoon, Remarque, Sinclair Lewis, Barbusse. Irish nationalism encourages literary revival: Yeats, Joyce. Abbey Theatre, Dublin becomes world famous.

Date	History, Politics & People	Economics & Sociology
	victories against Turks, aided by dissident Arabs. 1918: Allied victory, armistice November 11. Collapse and disintegration of German, Austrian and Turkish empires: emergence of such states as Czechoslovakia, Jugoslavia, Poland and Finland. Versailles Peace Treaty, 1918. Bolshevik regime in Russia has Russian royal family murdered, 1918.	
1920–29	League of Nations founded, 1920: confirmed, with HQ at Geneva, 1921, but USA did not join. Hague seat of International Court of Justice, 1921. In Britain, Zinoviev Letter influenced election results, 1924: first Labour government, 1929. Government of Ireland Act established two Irelands, 1920, but war existed between Britain and S. Ireland till 1922 when Irish Free State proclaimed. In Germany, reparations burden helped cause galloping inflation, 1921: political instability led to sporadic Communist uprisings and eventually to (at first insignificant) rise of Nazism. Hindenburg president, 1925. Mussolini marched on Rome, 1922 and formed Fascist government. Economic and political difficulties and fear of Bolshevism led to right-wing regimes in several European countries e.g. Poland, Greece, Rumania, Austria. In USA political corruption rife: era of isolationism began. Financial boom, followed by collapse of stock market. Oct. 28 1929, resulting in world depression. Kemal Ataturk made Turkey a republic, 1922: modernisation from 1926. In Middle East, stability of Arab emergent states affected by increased vociferousness of Zionism: and by impact of oil-based economy on those possessing vast oil-reserves. Civil war in USSR ended 1920 with Bolshevik victory: Lenin d.1924, and	Post-war inflationary boom period in W. followed by financial collapse, 1929, leading to world depression, deflation and mass unemployment. Tarriffs again being applied. Further growth in women's rights in W.: women gained vote in USA, 1920: forcibly emancipated in Turkey, 1926. USA adopted prohibition, 1920 (till 1933): organised crime flourished. Hoover made head of FBI, 1924. Great Exhibition, Wembley, 1923. Football increasingly popular. Motorcar availability widens: rail importance begins to decline. Expansion of air travel. BBC formed, 1922: radio soon generally available in average homes in W. 'Apartheid' term first used in S. Africa during this decade.

Religion, Education & Philosophy	Science, Exploration & Technology	Music & the Arts
Joan of Arc canonised, 1920. Presbyterian churches in Scotland reunited, 1929. Antisemitism in Germany, Poland, Austria: adds impetus to Zionist growth. In Mexico, systematic campaign to eradicate Catholicism eventually abandoned. In W., aftermath of war sees acceleration in decline of religious observance, especially in Protestant countries. New exposition of Protestantism by Barth. Logical positivism propounded, 1922. Socialist historical writing, begun by Wells, developed further by Tawney, Russell. Literacy continues to grow: colonial powers encourage foundation of higher education institutions in their overseas territories.	Medical advances swift, notably in neuro-surgery, tuberculosis, diabetes, tropical diseases, anaemia. Fleming discovers penicillin, 1928. Basic principle of autogyro developed, 1923: Lindbergh flies monoplane solo nonstop from New York to Paris, 1927. De Forest produces process for moving pictures with sound tracks, 1923: first colour movies, 1928. Baird transmits television pictures, 1926. Much astronomic research: embryonic work on space rockets. Further exploration in Tibet and at Poles. Gregorian Calendar established in USSR, 1923. Geneva Convention, 1925, banned poison gas in warfare.	Golden period of the 'Jazz Age'. Modernism dominates music and the arts: era of the skyscraper New York Empire State Building started, 1929. In Europe, Bauhaus concept influenced public building. Restless but productive literary period: Shaw, Galsworthy, Virginia Woolf, O'Neill, Maugham, Eliot, Pound. European ballet revival greatly influenced by influx of dancers leaving Bolshevik Russia.

Date	History, Politics & People	Economics & Sociology
	Stalin subsequently rose to power. Gandhi became leader of Indian nationalism: Round Table Conference on possible Dominion status for India convened, 1929. Beginnings of nationalism in several African and Asian colonies belonging to European powers, notably in Dutch East Indies and French Indo-China.	
1930–39	Period of high unemployment in W. world. Britain abandons gold standard, 1931; Edward VIII abdicates, 1936. Chamberlain flies to Munich—'peace in our time', 1938. Britain declares war on Germany, 3 September, 1939. Nazis gain most seats in Ger. elections, 1932; Hitler Chancellor, 1933, assumes dictatorial powers. Concentration camps established. Ger. rearms, begins building Siegfried Line, 1936. Occupies Austria, Sudetenland, 1938; rest of Czechoslovakia, 1939 and invades and occupies Poland, 1939. Alliance with USSR to partition Poland, 1939. Spanish Civil War 1936–9 ends with Franco's victory and formation of Fascist corporate state. Japan attacks China, 1937; rapid advances and Chungking becomes nationalist capital. Round Table Conference fails to solve Indian question: Gandhi's passive resistance campaign continues. Italy invades and conquers Ethiopia, 1936–36; international failure to act marks effective collapse of League of Nations. Italy occupies Albania, 1939. Roosevelt elected Democratic president in USA, 1933; 'New Deal' policy, with attempts at widespread social and economic reform. Prohibition abolished, 1933. Stalin purges his opponents, 1934 onwards; alliance with Hitler, 1939; invades Finland: forcible collectivisation 1932–4 leads to mass-starvation, notably in Ukraine.	Spread of radio and cinema leads to growing public awareness of international issues. Development of propaganda techniques in Germany. Mass-advertising in USA and Europe changes selling techniques. In W., revised divorce laws affect family structures. From mid-1930s rearmament leads to steady decline in unemployment in Britain: despite recession, improved mass-production processes lead to higher living standards for many. From 1934 German persecution of Jews results in mass-exodus to Britain and USA.

Religion, Education & Philosophy	Science, Exploration & Technology	Music & the Arts
Jehovah's Witnesses, 1931. Antisemitism in Germany; Protestant, Catholics and Socialists also imprisoned from 1933. Growth of Existentialism. Neo-Thomist school of Catholic philosophy founded by Gerson, Maritain etc.	Radar detection set up in Britain, 1935; aircraft development, especially in Germany. First jet engine built by Whittle, 1937. Much progress in fields of anaemia, kidney and liver therapy. Insulin used to control diabetes from 1937. RH factor in blood discovered, 1939. Boulder Dam, USA, completed, 1936, creating the then largest reservoir in world. Public television service in Britain, 1936.	Talking pictures supersede silent films; colour used increasingly. Cinema reaches standards of best theatre: Greta Garbo, Charlie Chaplin, Marlene Dietrich, Ingrid Bergman etc. 'Swing' music becomes popular. Novel continues to dominate literature: German art and literature decline under Nazi censorship and many artists emigrate. British music flourishes: Bax, Beecham, Henry Wood, Britten etc. Royal Academy holds major international exhibitions in London.

Date	History, Politics & People	Economics & Sociology
1940–49	World War II (*see Dictionary section article*: World War II). 1940: Finland signs armistice with USSR; Germany occupies Norway and Denmark; Churchill becomes premier of National Government in Britain. Germany invades and conquers Belgium, Holland and France and British army evacuated from Dunkirk. Battle of Britain in air, Aug—Sept. Italy joins war on German side. 1941: Yugoslavia, Greece and Crete invaded by Germans: they occupy rest of Balkans. June: Germans invade Russia; Japanese attack Pearl Harbor Dec. 7 and USA and Britain declare war on Japan who sweeps through Asia up to Indian frontier. 1942: Tide turns for Allies with battle of El Alamein, Oct—Nov. 1943: Allies reconquer N. Africa and invade Sicily and Italy, which surrenders. Heavy day and night bombing of Germany by Allies. Germans in retreat in Russia: surrender at Stalingrad. USA begins offensive against Japan in Pacific. 1944: Allied invasion of Europe, D-Day June 6; offensives on all fronts. Unsuccessful attempt to assassinate Hitler. 1945: British, Chinese and US offensives in Asia gather strength; Russians and Allies sweep forward in Europe. Germany surrenders May; atom bombs dropped on Japan August 6 and 9; Japan surrenders. War ends with Russia in control of E. Europe and China with civil war between Nationalists and Communists. Roosevelt d. After war, dismantlement of colonial empires. India independent 1947 and partitioned between India and Pakistan. Dutch E. Indies independent. Fr. Empire breaks up. Communists take control in China, 1949; Nationalists withdraw to Taiwan. Communist rebellion, Malaya, 1946. United Nations created, 1945. Civil	At end of World War II most countries institute some form of women's suffrage. Great diminution of class distinctions in W. countries: increased power of State almost everywhere. Decade of full employment. Vast increase in availability of higher education. Marshall Plan, 1947, aids recovery of W. Europe. By end of decade Germany and Japan becoming very prosperous. Keynesian economic theory dominates European economic strategies.

Religion, Education & Philosophy	Science, Exploration & Technology	Music & the Arts
Shintoism abolished in Japan, 1945. Persecution of Catholic Church by Communists after 1945; Hungarian primate imprisoned for treason, 1949. Protestant theologians e.g. Niehbuhr, Bonhoeffer, influential. Mass-extermination of Jews by Nazis, 1940–45. In former colonial territories, reaction against Christianity; Buddhist and Moslem revivals. Church of S. India formed from union of major Protestant churches after Indian independence. Dead Sea scrolls discovered, 1947. Existentialism popularized by Sartre.	War causes inventive and technological surge: aircraft vastly improved. Atomic bombs on Japan, Aug. 1945, followed by nuclear advances in military and civil fields. V I and V II German weapons forerunner of future space programmes. First electronic computer, 1947; transistor first developed, 1947. Major advances in antibiotics and plastic surgery. Aerial and underwater photography greatly developed.	Existentialist literature of Camus, Sartre etc. World War II sees popularity of radio and cinema at height. In Britain, vogue for 'social history': G.M. Trevelyan. Realist school of literature: Priestley, Steinbeck, Graham Greene: satirists like Waugh and Wodehouse. Mass rebuilding after war gives impetus to new forms: 'pre-fabs' and the 'tower block'. Much art religiously inspired: Spencer, Sutherland, Epstein. In contrast, mature work of Picasso. Age of mass-market publishing arrives.

Date	History, Politics & People	Economics & Sociology
	rights movement, USA. Yugoslavia independent of USSR after 1949; Germany divided into E. and W. Berlin airlift 1948–9. Israel created, 1948. In Britain Labour gain sweeping victory, 1945 and radical programme of nationalization and social reform instituted. In Europe war leads to growth of leftwing influences in most countries: but civil war in Greece, 1946, ends in Communist defeat. Italy a republic. NATO formed, 1949, to counter Russian threat. Apartheid dominates S. Africa after 1948.	
1950–59	Decade dominated by Communist threat: June 1950 N. Korean forces invade S. Korea; UN force (mainly US) opposes them; China intervenes; armistice July 1953 restores status quo. Communist uprising in Malaya crushed by 1955. Communist nationalists defeat French at Dien Bien Phu, 1954; N. Vietnam then Communist. Anti-Communist uprising, Hungary, 1957, crushed by Soviet intervention. In 1959 leftist revolutionary movement led by Fidel Castro gains power in Cuba. Fear of Communism leads to McCarthyism in USA 1953–4. Further growth of civil rights movement in USA; racial segregation in schools ruled unconstitutional, 1954. Britain reelects Conservatives, 1951; George VI d.1951, Elizabeth II succeeds. With France, intervenes in Egypt, 1956 and humiliated. Nationalist unrest in many Brit. colonies. Cyprus a republic, 1959. In France, nationalist war in Algeria leads to overthrow of republic and return to power of de Gaulle. Fifth Republic inaugurated. In USSR, d. of Stalin 1953 and rise of Khruschev. Warsaw Pact, counter to NATO, 1955. Egypt becomes a republic and nationalizes Suez Canal, 1956: war with	Period of rapid economic growth in West. In USA Civil Rights movement gains widespread white liberal support: in South Africa, machinery of apartheid tightened. Rapid growth of mass international air travel, leading to increases in tourism (new tourist areas e.g. Spain) and start of considerable 'New Commonwealth' immigration to Britain. World population explosion, with serious food and health problems in 'Third World'. Full employment in the West, but rapid inflation.

Religion, Education & Philosophy	Science, Exploration & Technology	Music & the Arts
Doctrine of the Assumption proclaimed, 1950. Pope John XXIII elected, 1959; convenes first Vatican Council since 1870. Protestant churches attempting closer ties. Christians playing increasing part in political issues: e.g. controversy over nuclear weapons and racial issues in USA and S. Africa. Evangelist movement in USA started by Billy Graham, 1954; spreads to Europe. Several modern Biblical translations.	Medical advances include antihistamines, tranquillizers and contraceptive pill. First allegation of connection between smoking and lung cancer, 1953. Nuclear advances: electric power first produced from atomic energy, 1951; first hydrogen bomb exploded by USA, 1953; USA launch first nuclear-powered submarine, 1955. Space programmes: USA and USSR establish space agencies: Van Allen discovers radiation belts round earth. US launches rocket to moon, 1959, which travels 79000 miles up; Russians launch rocket with two monkeys aboard, 1959. Russian rocket reaches moon, 1959. Vertical take-off invented: British 'flying bedstead', 1954.	Cheaper mass-produced records begin a western world boom in 'pop music'. Theatre, films and literature become more sexually explicit. US literature influential with Bellow, Vidal, Hersey, Wouk, Tennessee Williams. 'New' Coventry Cathedral begun, 1956. Painting and sculpture dominated by innovators like Hepworth, Moore, Chagall, Picasso. Television growth exerts increasing influence on all arts; cinema begins popular decline in west.

Date	History, Politics & People	Economics & Sociology
	Israel. Israeli-Arab conflict increasingly dominates Middle East politics. Under Nehru, India leads 'uncommitted nations'. In Europe, Treaty of Rome 1958 establishes the European Economic Community: non-EEC countries, led by Britain, form EFTA, 1959.	
1960–69	Kennedy President of USA, 1960; Bay of Pigs fiasco in Cuba, 1962 and Cuban missile crisis settled by Kennedy and Khruschev, 1963. Kennedy assassinated, Dallas, 22 Nov. 1963; Johnson president and carries on Kennedy's civil rights' programme but increasingly involved in Vietnam, where US advisers now replaced by US troops. Liberal and student oppostion to US involvement there becomes important; marches on the White House. In 1968 Nixon (Republican) elected president, promising end of Vietnam war and rapprochement with China. In S. Vietnam, government overthrown, 1963, and situation from then on increasingly unstable. Britain fails to join EEC: 'Profumo affair', 1963 and Labour under Wilson in power from 1964. Several former colonies gain independence but S. Rhodesia declares UDI, 1965. S. Africa leaves Commonwealth, 1961. Republican agitation in N. Ireland from mid-1960s and British troops sent to keep peace, 1969. Emigration from E. Germany through Berlin stopped by Berlin Wall, 1961; Czech revolt against hard-line Communism, 1968, ended by Russian intervention, 1969. Khruschev falls from power, 1964, rise of Brezhnev. In France student riots, 1968 lead ultimately to resignation of de Gaulle, 1969. In China, 'Cultural Revolution' begins, 1966. War between Israel and major Arab states, 1967, ends in Israeli victory and occupation by Israel of W. bank of Jordan	American involvement in Vietnam leads to moral crisis at home; youth reaction involves overthrow of traditional values, rapid spread of drug-abuse, which then spreads to Europe. Age of 'hippies' and 'flower-power'. 'Women's Liberation Movement', aggressively feminist, spreads from USA to Europe. Terrorism adopted by Irish and Arab extremists. Death penalty abolished in Britain, 1965.

Religion, Education & Philosophy	Science, Exploration & Technology	Music & the Arts
	International Geophysical Year, 1957. Hillary and Tensing climb Everest, 1953. Pollution begins to be a recognised threat: Carson's *The Sea Around Us*, 1959.	
Vatican Council 1962–3 results in radical changes in Catholic structure and practises. Vernacular replaces Latin in liturgy and theology more liberal, but Pope reaffirms Church opposition to artificial contraception, 1968. Frequent Papal visits overseas. Growing cooperation between Catholics and Protestants but sectarian violence in Ulster. Women's rights movement affects all churches: first woman priest ordained in Sweden, 1960. Pope Paul VI formally exonerates Jews from blame for death of Jesus, 1965. Growth of a 'philosophy of violence' propagated by Marcuse etc. Urban guerrilla movements in W. Europe often led by university graduates.	Space physics makes great advances: Gagarin (USSR) orbits the earth, 1961. Subsequently USA and USSR successfully launched many manned flights. In 1969 US astronauts land and walk on the moon. Progress also in fields of communication, meteorology and military surveillance. Development of supersonic aircraft: Concorde makes first flight, 1969. Britain starts gas and oil exploration in N. Sea, 1964. In medicine, thalidomide causes malformation of babies, from 1962; in 1962 Royal College of Surgeons report links cigarette smoking with lung cancer. In S. Africa Barnard performs first heart transplant, 1967, and transplant surgery subsequently becomes routine in USA, Britain and France. 'CS' gas used in riot control.	'The Swinging Sixties': growth of a 'pop culture' typified by the Beatles in Britain (1962 onwards) and Dylan and Baez in the USA. Abolition of theatre censorship in Britain, 1968. Cult of protest literature in literature and theatre in West. In USSR, growth of literary protest against regime as typified by Pasternak and Solzenitzhin. Thriller achieves classic status with Greene, Le Carré, Fleming. Aldeburgh becomes a leading musical centre. British opera revived by Britten, and British ballet leads internationally with Fonteyn, Markova and Helpmann.

Date	History, Politics & People	Economics & Sociology
	including all Jerusalem. Arab campaign against Israeli subsequently more violent; Jordan main Palestinian base. Nazi criminal Eichmann hanged in Israel, 1962. Some progress in quest for world peace: Nuclear Test Ban treaty signed by Britain, USA and USSR, 1963.	
1970– 85	Nixon, US president, withdraws US forces from Vietnam and effects rapprochement with China, but forced to resign over Watergate Scandal, 1974. Carter, president from 1976, effects Camp David Agreement between Egypt and Israel, 1979 (after further war, 1973). Overthrow of Shah in Iran, 1979 and failure of USA to get release of hostages, added to domestic recession, leads to Reagan (Republican) becoming president, 1979 and subsequent hardline policy in foreign affairs e.g. intervention in Grenada and Lebanon, 1983. All Vietnam effectively Communist from 1975. In China cultural revolution ends, 1972; Mao Tse-Tung dies, 1976. Some liberalization. Talks with Britain reach agreement over return of Hong Kong to China, 1984. Brezhnev d.1982, succeeded by Andropov who d.1984, succeeded by Chernenko, then by Gorbachev. Soviet expansionism continues in Afghanistan (from 1979) and Africa (Mozambique, Angola and Namibia, using Cuban mercenaries) but some liberalisation domestically and some dissidents allowed to leave Russia. Unrest in Poland: growth of 'Solidarity' movement. Britain joins EEC, 1973. Margaret Thatcher first woman (Conservative) Prime Minister, 1979. Successful campaign to expel Argentina from Falkland Islands, 1982. In India, Mrs Gandhi dominates politics; d.1984; Bangladesh becomes independent, 1971. Rhodesia problem settled, 1979 and Zimbabwe Republic	Economic recession in W. from late 1970s: high unemployment. Famines in Africa throughout period. In Britain, legislation relating to sexual and racial equality. Urban deprivation leads to riots in Brixton and Liverpool in early 1980s. Growth of Campaign for Nuclear Disarmament in Britain from early 1980s given impetus by arrival of Cruise missiles in Britain in 1983. 'Peace camps', feminist-dominated. Urban guerilla movements, notably in Germany and Italy. Kidnapping becomes a common European crime, especially in Italy. Large growth in heroin addiction in W. Europe; heroin then cocaine addiction in the USA.

Religion, Education & Philosophy	Science, Exploration & Technology	Music & the Arts
Revival of militant Islam in Libya and Iran (from 1979). Closer relations between Catholic and Protestant churches: Pope John Paul II visits Ireland, USA and Britain etc. Student unrest in West much diminished after end of Vietnam war and growth in unemployment. Christians divided on question of permissibility of nuclear warfare.	Further advances in space science. In medicine heart transplants achieving high success rate: kidney and liver transplants routine. Fertility drugs and 'test tube baby' techniques developed. Video becomes important, affecting television, cinema and record industries. Era of the 'silicon chip': increasing use of computers in offices and industry. Japan pioneers large-scale use of robots in industry. In Britain and Mexico, oil-boom alters economies. Energy conservation is of increasing concern in Europe and the USA and the use of nuclear power for energy purposes is questioned. Poison and nerve gas used in Iran-Iraq war, 1984.	Revival of 'entertainment' school in literature and theatre; cinema in popular decline due to television and video competition. State and large industries have by now largely replaced private individuals as principal patrons of the arts.

Date	History, Politics & People	Economics & Sociology
	declared, 1980. Following leftwing coup in Portugal, 1974, Angola and Mozambique establish independent leftwing regimes. Franco d.1975 and Spain reverts peacefully to constitutional monarchy. In N. Ireland, much sectarian fighting: bomb outrages in N. Ireland and mainland Britain from 1971. Jordan expels Palestinians, 1970, who then make Lebanon their base for attacks on Israel. Lebanon in state of civil war; Israelis invade, 1983. US, French, British and Italian peacekeeping force sent, 1983: withdrawn, 1984. Heavy fighting renewed, 1985.